Management 5e

CHUCK WILLIAMS
University of the Pacific

SOUTH-WESTERN
CENGAGE Learning

Australia • Brazil • Canada • Mexico • Singapore • Spain • United Kingdom • United States

SOUTH-WESTERN
CENGAGE Learning™

Management 5e
Chuck R. Williams,
Jim Jawahar,
Charles E. Bamford

VP/Editorial Director: Jack W. Calhoun

Editor-in-Chief: Melissa S. Acuña

Executive Editor: Joe Sabatino

Developmental Editor: Jamie Bryant, B-Books

Marketing Manager: Clint Kernen

Sr. Content Project Manager: Tamborah Moore

Manager, Editorial Media: John Barans

Technology Project Manager: Kristen Meere

Sr. Marketing Coordinator: Sarah Rose

Sr. Marketing Communications Manager: Jim Overly

Sr. Manufacturing Coordinator: Doug Wilke

Editorial Assistant: Ruth Belanger

Production House: Lachina Publishing Services

Sr. Art Director: Tippy McIntosh

Internal and Cover Designer: Trish and Ted Knapke

Cover Image: © Photonica, Jan Stromme

Sr. Image Permissions Manager: Deanna Ettinger

Photo Researcher: Susan Van Etten

For product information and technology assistance, contact us at
Cengage Learning Academic Resource Center, 1-800-423-0563

For permission to use material from this text or product, submit all requests online at **www.cengage.com/permissions**
Further permissions questions can be emailed to
permissionrequest@cengage.com

ExamView® and ExamView Pro® are registered trademarks of FSCreations, Inc. Windows is a registered trademark of the Microsoft Corporation used herein under license. Macintosh and Power Macintosh are registered trademarks of Apple Computer, Inc. used herein under license.

© 2009 Cengage Learning. All Rights Reserved.
Cengage Learning WebTutor™ is a trademark of Cengage Learning.

Library of Congress Control Number: 2007939235

Student Edition ISBN 13: 978-0-324-56840-0
Student Edition ISBN 10: 0-324-56840-1
Instructor's Edition ISBN 13: 978-0-324-57902-4
Instructor's Edition ISBN 10: 0-324-57902-0

South-Western Cengage Learning
5191 Natorp Boulevard
Mason, OH 45040
USA

Cengage Learning products are represented in Canada by Nelson Education, Ltd.

For your course and learning solutions, visit **academic.cengage.com**
Purchase any of our products at your local college store or at our preferred online store **www.ichapters.com**

Printed in Canada
1 2 3 4 5 6 7 11 10 09 08 07

BRIEF CONTENTS

CONTENTS

THE END OF EACH
CHAPTER CONTAINS
THE FOLLOWING
MATERIAL:

Key Terms
Self Assessment
Management Decision
Management Team Decision
Practice Being a Manager (an
experiential exercise)
Develop Your Career Potential
Reel to Real

2

PLANNING 152

WHAT'S NEW IN 5E?

ABOUT THIS EDITION

If you walk down the aisle of the business section in your local bookstore (or surf the "Business" page at Amazon.com), you'll find hundreds of books that explain precisely what companies need to do to be successful.

Unfortunately, these books tend to be faddish, changing every few years. Lately, the best-selling business books have emphasized technology, leadership, and dealing with change, whereas ten years ago the hot topics were reengineering, going global, mergers, and management buyouts.

One thing that hasn't changed, though, and never will, is the importance of good management. **Management** is getting work done through others. Organizations can't succeed for long without it. Well-managed companies are competitive because their work forces are smarter, better trained, more motivated, and more committed. Furthermore, good management leads to satisfied employees who, in turn, provide better service to customers. Because employees tend to treat customers the same way that their managers treat them, good management can improve customer satisfaction. Finally, companies that practice good management consistently have greater revenues and profits than companies that don't.

My goal in writing the first edition of *Management* was to write a textbook that students would enjoy, that students would refer to for practical, theory-driven advice, and that encouraged students to put theory-driven knowledge into practice for themselves. For the fifth edition, my goal was to update the content to reflect the changing face of management and to keep the text relevant, fresh, and interesting for students. In short, the ideas and concepts you'll learn about in this book can improve the performance of the organization and department where you work, help you solve job-related problems, and improve your own job performance, even if you're not a manager.

So welcome to *Management*, 5e! Please take a few minutes to read the preface and familiarize yourself with the approach (combining theory with specific stories and examples), features, pedagogy, and end-of-chapter assignments in *Management*. This is time well spent. After all, besides your instructor, this book will be your primary learning tool.

Combining Theory with Specific, Up-to-Date Stories and Examples

Say "theory" to college students and they assume that you're talking about complex, arcane ideas and terms that have nothing to do with the "real world," but which need to be memorized for a test and then forgotten (at least until the final exam). However, students needn't be wary of theoretical ideas and concepts. Theories are simply good ideas. And good theories are simply good ideas that have been tested through rigorous scientific study and analysis.

Where textbooks go wrong is that they stop at theory and read like dictionaries. Or, they focus on theoretical issues related to research rather than practice. However, good management theories (i.e., good ideas) needn't be complex, difficult to understand, or irrelevant. In fact, the late Rensis Likert, of the University of Michigan, once said that there is nothing as practical as a good theory.

So, to make sure that you're exposed to good ideas (i.e., good theories), that you can refer to for practical, theory-driven advice, and which encourage you to put theory-driven knowledge into practice for yourselves, each chapter in this book contains 50 to 60 specific stories and examples that illustrate how managers are using management ideas in their organizations. Let's use an example from Chapter 8 on Global Management to show you what I mean. One of the key issues in Global Management is successfully preparing employees for international assignments. In fact, the difficulty of adjusting to language, cultural, and social differences in another country is the primary reason that so many businesspersons fail in international assignments. Consequently, you'll read this passage in Chapter 8.

> *For example, although there have recently been disagreements among researchers about these numbers, it is probably safe to say that 5 to 20 percent of American expatriates sent abroad by their companies will return to the United States before they have successfully completed international assignments. Of those who do complete their international assignments, about one-third are judged by their companies to be no better than marginally effective.*

In other words, this is fairly standard, research-based information. You'll find it in most textbooks. Is it important for students to know this information? You bet! Is it likely that students will find this and the thousands of other pieces of theory and research-based facts throughout the book particularly compelling or interesting (and thus easier to learn)? Ah, there's the problem. However, what if we combined theory and research with specific, "real world" stories and examples that illustrated good or poor use of those theories? For instance, the passage shown below is also in Chapter 8, where it follows the research-based information about the difficulty of adjusting to foreign cultures.

> *In his book* Blunders in International Business, *David Ricks tells the story of an American manager working in the South Pacific who, by hiring too many local workers from one native group, unknowingly upset the balance of power in the island's traditional status system. The islanders met on their own and quickly worked out a solution to the problem. After concluding their meeting at 3 AM, they calmly went to his home to discuss their solution with him (time was not important in their culture). But since the American didn't speak their language, and couldn't understand why they would show*

up in mass outside his home at 3 AM, he called in the Marines, who were sta-
tioned nearby, to disburse what he thought was a riot.

After reading this passage, students have a vivid understanding about what can go wrong if people don't receive cultural and language training before traveling or moving to another country. Why does this help students learn? Because the first passage cites theory and research on the effectiveness of cross-cultural training and the second brings the theory and research alive by indicating what can go wrong if you don't get that cross-cultural training.

Moreover, the stories and examples you'll read in each chapter are relevant and up-to-date. You'll read how Wal-Mart has started using software to schedule shifts for its 1.3 million workers. What used to take a store manager an entire day now takes only an hour, freeing up Wal-Mart managers to, well, manage. You'll learn how surgeons and nurses at the Veterans Health Administration are using safety pauses in the operating room to overcome organizational silence and reduce mistakes. The surgical team pauses for a moment, is asked if anyone has concerns or comments, and then addresses them if need be. You'll also learn how companies incorporate flexibility into their planning process so they can react appropriately and quickly when disruptions occur. For example, Virgin Atlantic spent considerable time and effort developing a reclining seat for first-class passengers, but before the company was able to bring the new seat to market, British Airways unveiled its fully flat bed for business class. In an instant, Virgin Atlantic's original plan was all but useless, but the VA team regrouped, was allocated additional resources, and developed a suite (not just a seat) that helped it increase its market share amoung transatlantic passengers. You'll also read about how companies use outsourcing to increase productivity—even companies you might not associate with outsourcing, like McDonald's. Some franchises have all but eliminated the 10-second idle time a drive-thru employee experiences between orders waiting for the first car to pull away and the next one to pull up to the speaker. How? By outsourcing the order taking function to remote call centers. A call center employee can take an order from a hungry patron at one location and immediately after take an order from another hungry patron at a completely different location, perhaps a completely different state. As these stories show, each chapter has been updated with dozens of new real world business examples, straight from the latest pages of *BusinessWeek, Fortune, Forbes, Fast Company,* and *Inc.,* as well as the *Wall Street Journal,* the *New York Times,* and other leading newspapers, to help you understand how management concepts are being used.

In short, research *and* theory and stories and examples are important for effective learning. Therefore, this book contains over a thousand specific examples and stories to make management theories and ideas more interesting. So, to get more out of this book, read and understand the theories and theoretical ideas. Then read the stories or examples to learn how those ideas should or should not be used in practice. You'll find that both are current and up-to-date.

So What's New?

If you are already familiar with the previous editions' approach of reinforcing research and theory with stories and examples you may be asking yourself, "So what's new?" The answer is quite a bit.

To keep pace with the evolution of management, the Fourth Edition underwent a rigorous review process that identified areas where I could strengthen and refine the text. Reviewers gave wonderful feedback about which boxed features were not being used in class, so I have streamlined each chapter to focus on the main content, retaining only the most popular boxes from the Fourth Edition, "What Really Works?" and "Doing the Right Thing." To each chapter, I've also added a short box on current management issues or interesting management facts. Titled "Management Fact" and "Management Trend," these boxes provide short examples and issues that get students thinking beyond the book.

For this edition, all eighteen of the "What Would You Do?" chapter-opening cases are new, and feature companies like Sony, PETA, StubHub, Whirlpool, Walgreens, Louis Vuitton, Tommy Hilfiger, and Radio Shack, among others.

What *brand new* things will you find in **Management**, 5e? To start, you'll find:

Practice Being a Manager—Working through management issues before you even get to the workplace can be a beneficial way to practice being a manager. A new experiential exercise at the end of each chapter gives students a context in which to explore management issues and problems with other students. The guided exercises are supported by detailed teaching notes and role-playing instructions in the Instructor Manual.

Self Assessments—The Fourth Edition contained a self-assessment appendix, but for this edition, I wanted to better integrate the assessments into the chapters themselves. The chapter-ending cases and assignments now begin with a related assessment questionnaire to help students consider how their own perspectives influence their management skills. Basic scoring information follows each questionnaire, and the Instructor Manual contains directions for using the assessment tools in class.

Reel to Real Videos—When we asked professors how they used video in the classroom, we discovered two distinct preferences. Some like to use short video examples to reinforce certain points in the chapter; others like longer video cases that looked at various companies in-depth. In response to this feedback, each chapter of **Management**, 5e contains two video options. The first is a film clip from a popular Hollywood movie that relates to the chapter content. For example, students will see a "Biz Flix" clip from *In Good Company* for Chapter 2 on History of Management, from *The Bourne Identity* for Chapter 5 on Planning, from *October Sky* for Chapter 7 on Innovation, and from *Casino* for Chapter 18 on Managing Service and Manufacturing Operations, to name a few. The second video option is comprised of longer segments, called "Management Workplace," which are an average of 12 minutes and provide a deeper look at a single company, its operations, and how it addresses various management issues every day. In the Fifth Edition, we go inside Original Penguin (apparel), Lonely Planet (travel guides), Organic Valley (organic dairy products), Timbuk2 (backpacks and bags), PepsiCo, NEADS (training service animals), and Peapod (online grocer). Both the "Biz Flix" and the "Management Workplace" videos guide students on what to look for and think about as they watch the video. Detailed teaching notes for both videos are in each chapter of the Instructor Manual.

CengageNOW for Williams—**Management**, 5e has a dedicated CengageNOW study tool that tightly integrates the material in the text with a myriad of review opportunities. Students can test their understanding, concentrate their review on their weakest areas, and then verify their progress using the latest technology.

So what *is* new in *Management*, 5e? Quite a bit.

Book Features

A tremendous amount of time and thought went into planning this textbook. I reviewed over 25 top selling textbooks in Management, Marketing, Finance, Statistics, and Economics. I asked more than 200 students and dozens of professors what they specifically liked and disliked about their textbooks. And, I pulled some of my favorite books (many of which were not about business) from my bookshelf to figure out what made them great books. Only then did I create the plan and organization for *Management*. The Fifth Edition retains the popular features of previous editions and adds some new ones. So take a few minutes now to familiarize yourself with these features. Doing so will help you get more out of the book and your management class.

What Would You Do?—Each chapter opens with an engaging case outlining actual management problems facing a well-known company. After students read the case, they are presented several questions to help guide their thinking about the issues, and are ultimately asked "If you were the manager at this company, what would you do?" Putting students in the place of the manager personalizes the dilemma and forces students to solve common managerial problems. The solution to the case, or "What Really Happened?" is in the Instructor Manual. Allowing students to compare what they would have done to what the managers really did provides a great learning opportunity.

Doing the Right Thing—At the U.S. Military Academy, there is a strict code of conduct: "A cadet will not lie, cheat or steal, nor tolerate those who do." The code is concise and unmistakable. Regrettably, there is no equivalent code for managers because there's no doubt they need one. Numerous studies and well-known corporate scandals make clear the distressing state of managerial ethics in today's business world. Lying to stockholders about profits, cheating to win business, and stealing from companies have become all too common. And, because managers set the standard for others in the workplace, unethical behavior and practices quickly spread when they don't do the right thing. Therefore, in each chapter, you'll find practical, useful advice to help you become a more ethical manager or businessperson by "Doing the Right Thing." Topics include ethical competitive analysis, avoiding the slippery slope of cheating, dealing with gifts from suppliers, avoiding conflicts of interest, not cheating on travel expenses, enforcing fair and safe working conditions in foreign factories, giving credit rather than taking it, and many more.

What Really Works?—Some studies show that two drinks a day increases life expectancy by decreasing your chances of having a heart attack. Yet other studies show that two drinks a day will shorten your life expectancy. For years, we've "buttered" our morning toast with margarine instead of butter because it was supposed to be better for our health. However, new studies now show that the trans-fatty acids in margarine may be just as bad for our arteries as butter. Confusing scientific results like these frustrate ordinary people who want to "eat right" and "live right." It also makes many people question just how useful most scientific research really is.

Managers also have trouble figuring out what works, based on the scientific research published in journals like the *Academy of Management Journal*, the *Academy of Management Review*, the *Strategic Management Journal*, the *Journal of Applied Psychology*, and *Administrative Science Quarterly*. It's common for the *Wall Street Journal* to quote a management research article from one of these journals that says that total quality management is the best thing since sliced bread (without butter or margarine). Then, just six months later, the *Wall Street Journal* will quote a different article from the same journal that says that total quality management doesn't work. If management professors and researchers have trouble deciding what works and what doesn't, how can practicing managers know?

Thankfully, a research tool called *meta-analysis*, which is a study of studies, is helping management scholars understand how well their research supports management theories. Fortunately, meta-analysis is also useful for practicing managers, because it shows what works and the conditions under which management techniques may work better or worse in the "real world." Meta-analysis is based on the simple idea that if one study shows that a management technique doesn't work and another study shows that it does, an average of those results is probably the best estimate of how well that management practice works (or doesn't work). Fortunately, you don't need a Ph.D. to understand the statistics reported in a meta-analysis. In fact, one primary advantage of meta-analysis over traditional significance tests is that you can convert meta-analysis statistics into intuitive numbers that anyone can easily understand. Indeed, each meta-analysis reported in the "What Really Works?" sections of this textbook is accompanied by an easy-to-understand statistic called the *probability of success*. As its name suggests, the probability of success uses a bar graph and a percentage (0 percent to 100 percent) to indicate the likelihood that a management technique will actually work.

Of course, no idea or technique works every time and in every circumstance. However, in today's competitive, fast-changing, global marketplace, few managers can afford to overlook proven management strategies like those discussed in the "What Really Works?" feature of this book.

Pedagogy

Pedagogical features are meant to reinforce learning, but they don't have to be boring. Accordingly, the teaching tools used in **Management** will help students learn and hold their interest, too.

Chapter Outline and Numbering System, Learning Objectives, and Section Reviews—Because of their busy schedules, very few students have the opportunity to read a chapter from beginning to end in one sitting. Typically, it takes students anywhere from two to five study sessions to completely read a chapter. Accordingly, at the beginning of each chapter, you'll find a detailed chapter outline in which each major part in the chapter is broken out into numbered sections and subsections. For example, the outline for the first part of Chapter 4, on Ethics and Social Responsibility, looks like this:

What Is Ethical and Unethical Workplace Behavior?

1. Ethics and the Nature of Management Jobs
2. Workplace Deviance
3. U.S. Sentencing Commission Guidelines
    3.1   Who, What, and Why?
    3.2   Determining the Punishment

The numbered information contained in the chapter outline is then repeated in the chapter as learning objectives (at the beginning of major parts of the chapter) and as numbered headings and subheadings (throughout the chapter) to help students remember precisely where they are in terms of the chapter outline. Finally, instead of a big summary at the end of the chapter, students will find detailed reviews at the end of each section.

Together, the chapter outline, numbering system, learning objectives, section headings (which mark the beginning of a section), and section reviews (which mark the end of a section) allow students to break the chapter into smaller, self-contained sections that can be read in their entirety over multiple study sessions. Furthermore, the numbered headings and outline should make it easier for instructors and students to know what is being assigned or discussed in class ("In section 3.1 of chapter 3…").

Study Tip—Knowing how to study effectively is not an innate talent. So, to prepare students for studying the material, a detailed study tip appears in the chapter opener. Eighteen different tips give students many options for reviewing key concepts and mastering chapter content. Students are challenged to write their own tests and exchange them in a study group, explain the chapter concepts to a friend who is not in class, cut up the text glossary to make a quiz-bowl game, and much more.

Student Resources—The **Management** package has many resources to help reinforce the concepts in each chapter. For that reason, the opening of each chapter includes a list of various study tools and where they can be found. Each list contains information about CengageNOW and the student website.

Key Terms—Key terms appear in boldface in the text, with definitions in the margins to make it easy for students to check their understanding. A complete alphabetical list of key terms appears at the end of each chapter as a study checklist, with page citations for easy reference.

End-of-Chapter Assignments

In most textbooks, there are only two or three end-of-chapter assignments. By contrast, at the end of each chapter in **Management**, there are five assignments from which to choose. (But if you count the opening case, "What Would You Do?," and its answer, "What Really Happened?," it's really six assignments.) This gives instructors more choice in selecting just the right assignment for their classes. It also gives students a greater variety of activities, making it less likely that they'll repeat the same kind of assignment chapter after chapter.

Self Assessment—As described above, each chapter has a "Self Assessment" questionnaire that helps students explore their own management perspectives.

Management Decision—"Management Decision" assignments are focused on a particular decision. Students must decide what to do in the given situation and then answer several questions to explain their choices. For example, students must decide whether to give a new employee a raise before company policy allows, if the company should permit camera phones in the office, whether to use personality tests as part of hiring and promotion decisions, if creating a workplace blog is worth the effort, whether to mine employees' personal data to find out how to motivate them, and more. Some "Management Decision" features have optional extensions that turn the exercises into mini-projects. Information on how to do that is in the Instructor Manual.

Management Team Decision—"Management Team Decision" assignments are similar to "Management Decision" assignments in that students face a problem, must decide what to do, and then answer several questions to explain their choices. The difference, however, is that "Management Team Decision" assignments are designed to be completed by student teams or groups. Teams have the opportunity to practice the group decision-making techniques outlined in Chapter 5 (Planning and Decision Making). Student management teams will decide whether to implement a shopper card program at a chain of independent supermarkets, consider the pros and cons of becoming a Wal-Mart supplier, build a balanced scorecard for H&R Block, map a strategy for Paramount Pictures, determine the role of innovation at Colgate-Palmolive, and more.

Practice Being a Manager Experiential Exercises—The end of each chapter contains an experiential exercise to give students the opportunity to role play management scenarios, discuss management dilemmas, and resolve management problems. Some of the exercises have components that require individual, take-home preparation, but most are designed to be started and completed during the class session.

Develop Your Career Potential—"Develop Your Career Potential" assignments have one purpose: to help students develop their present and future capabilities as managers. What students learn through these assignments is not traditional "book-learning" based on memorization and regurgitation, but practical knowledge and skills that help managers perform their jobs better. Assignments include interviewing managers, dealing with the press, conducting a personal SWOT analysis, learning from failure, developing leadership skills, 360-degree feedback, and more.

Instructor Supplements

Comprehensive Instructor Manual—The instructor manual to accompany the Fifth Edition has been completely redone to help instructors in every type of class. In addition to the chapter outlines, additional activities, and solutions you expect, the new manual includes one pedagogy grid and three lesson plans per chapter.

Each chapter of the instructor manual opens with a pedagogy grid that details all of the pedagogy in the chapter and the companies and teaching points presented. By giving you all the options you have in the chapter and the chapter content addressed by each option, you will be able to decide what you want to emphasize in class and the work you want to assign your students. Following the pedagogy grid is a series of three lesson plans: a lecture lesson plan, including lists of PowerPoint slides; a group-work lesson plan for professors who have smaller sections and/or more time during the semester; and a complete video lesson plan, including pre-viewing, viewing, and post-viewing activities for both "BizFlix" and "Management Workplace." The purpose of the video-only lesson plan is to illustrate how to teach using video without "losing time."

Each type of lesson plan includes pre-class preparation for the professor and for students, how to organize the content for the chapter during the class period, a list of possible assignments, and more.

A detailed chapter outline (lecture notes) is still part of the instructor manual. The lecture notes include additional examples, teaching notes for key concepts and for feature boxes, prompts where relevant PowerPoint slides and transparencies correspond to chapter content, as well as prompts for where to show the video. Solutions for chapter features are included.

In addition to all of these teaching tools, an appendix titled "Teaching Your First Management Course" can be found at the end of the instructor manual. This appendix is designed specifically to meet the needs and concerns of the first-time instructor.

Certified Test Bank—The Test Bank for the Fifth Edition of *Management* builds on the solid foundation of previous editions. A team of professors reviewed the entire test bank to verify the quality of each question. Then an editorial professional verified that the question concepts and wording matched the presentation in the text, as well as corrected grammatical and typographical errors and page references.

Each test bank chapter contains at least 150 questions in a variety of types: true-false, multiple-choice, short-answer, and critical-thinking questions, and a scenario section that asks students to answer questions based on detailed management situations, including on the chapter-opening "What Would You Do?" case. Thorough solutions are provided for each question, including difficulty ratings, AACSB tags, and page references where solutions appear in the text.

A computerized version of the text bank is available on your Instructor Resource CD-ROM and by special request. ExamView allows to you create, edit, store, print, and otherwise customize your quizzes, tests, and exams. The system is menu-driven making it quick and easy to use.

Course Pre- and Post-Assessments—To help you better determine your students' baseline understanding of management principles, we have created an assessment test for your use at the beginning of the term. The 200-question pre-test covers the basic management concepts that students need to understand. As a conclusion to your course, you can administer the 200-question post-test. These tests are designed to help you track your students' proficiency levels semester to semester. Pre- and post-assessments are also broken down by chapter, so if you prefer, you can administer throughout the semester for each chapter of the text. Assessment tests are available in both Word and ExamView formats.

ExamView—A computerized version of the Test Bank (called ExamView) is available on your Instructor Resource CD-ROM and by special request. ExamView allows you to add or edit questions, instructions, and answers. You can create, edit, store, print, and otherwise customize all your quizzes, tests, and exams. The system is menu-driven, making it quick and easy to use.

Reel to Real Video—Nothing helps students master management concepts like seeing them put into practice in the real world. New "Management Workplace" videos give an extensive look into the workings of interesting and successful companies like Original Penguin, Lonely Planet, PepsiCo, Organic Valley, and Peapod. In addition to these longer segments, each chapter has a movie clip that ties into the management concepts presented in the chapter. Clips are short, so you can view and review them easily and quickly.

Both the "Biz Flix" and "Management Workplace" videos are available on DVD. The Instructor Manual includes detailed teaching notes so that you can incorporate video into your class in a meaningful way.

PowerPoint® Slides—A rich set of PowerPoint slides, with teaching notes, will make class preparations easy and interesting. The approximately 30 to 50 slides per chapter cover all key concepts, terms, features, cases, and even some exhibits from the text. Animations and transitions add movement to many of the slides, allowing instructors to show one point at a time and adding a dynamic feel that will hold student interest throughout the presentation. Ample teaching notes offer additional insights and examples plus important points to cover in lectures. For instructors wishing to integrate various media, we have also created a set of video PowerPoint slides in which the "BizFlix" movie clips are embedded in appropriate slides. And to support the Self Assessment questionnaires, we have created a separate set of PowerPoint files that enable professors to use the assessment inventories in the classroom setting. In each Self Assessment PowerPoint chapter, individual assessment items are placed on separate slides. Excel spreadsheets embedded on each slide allow instructors to use the data from a simple show of hands to create distributions for each assessment item. Students can see where they fit in the distribution, making the assessment tool more interesting and relevant.

Who Wants to Be a Manager?

—Games are an increasingly popular classroom review tool, so the Fifth Edition of *Management* includes a quiz game that uses JoinIn™ clicker technology. Each chapter has two rounds of 25 questions each, organized into 5 categories. Category names are fun, but the questions in each category are serious review of chapter concepts. A mixture of true-false and multiple choice questions keep students working through this enjoyable classroom review.

Instructor Resource CD-ROM (IRCD)

—For your convenience, the Instructor Manual, Test Bank, ExamView Software, PowerPoint presentations, and Who Wants to Be a Manager are available on a single CD-ROM, the IRCD.

The Business and Company Resource Center

—Put a complete business library at your fingertips with the Business & Company Resource Center (BCRC). The BCRC is a premier online business research tool that allows you to seamlessly search thousands of periodicals, journals, references, financial information, industry reports, company histories, and much more. The BCRC is a powerful and time-saving research tool for students—whether they are completing a case analysis, preparing for a presentation, creating a business plan, or writing a reaction paper. Instructors can use the BCRC like an online coursepack, quickly and easily assigning readings and research projects without the inconvenience of library reserves, permissions, and printed materials. BCRC filters out the "junk" information students often find when searching the Internet, providing only the high quality, safe, and reliable news and information sources. Visit **academic.cengage.com/bcrc** to learn more about how this powerful electronic tool integrates a diverse collection of resources to reflect the natural research process and contact your local representative for pricing and optional bundling information for the Business & Company Resource Center with your text.

Web Tutor™ (for both WebCT®, and Blackboard®)

—Online learning is growing at a rapid pace. Whether you are looking to offer courses at distance or to offer a Web-enhanced classroom, South-Western/Cengage Learning offers you a solution with WebTutor. WebTutor provides instructors with text-specific content that interacts with the two leading systems of higher education course management—WebCT and Blackboard.

WebTutor is a turnkey solution for instructors who want to begin using technology like Blackboard or WebCT but who do not have Web-ready content available, or who do not want to be burdened with developing their own content. WebTutor uses the Internet to turn everyone in your class into a front-row student. WebTutor offers interactive study guide features such as quizzes, concept reviews, flashcards, discussion forums, additional video clips, and more. Instructor tools are also provided to facilitate communication between students and faculty.

Williams Website (academic.cengage.com/management/williams)—
The Williams website contains a wealth of resources for both instructors and students. Here is what's available only for professors at the Instructor Resource page of the Williams website:

- The full PowerPoint presentations with teaching notes.
- Files for the full Test Bank.
- Files for the full Instructor Manual are also available online. If you don't have your materials on hand, you can download the chapters you need and customize them to suit your lesson plan.

Here is what's available for students at the Williams website:

- An abridged set of PowerPoint slides to help with review
- A quiz for each chapter
- Key terms with definitions

Student Supplements

CengageNOW for Management, 5e—CengageNOW for *Management, 5e* is an online assessment-driven and student-centered tutorial that provides students with a personalized learning plan. Based on a diagnostic Pre-Test, a customized learning path is generated for each student that targets their study needs and helps them to visualize, organize, practice, and master the material in the text. Media resources enhance problem-solving skills and improve conceptual understanding. An access code to CengageNOW for Williams can be bundled with new textbooks.

InfoTrac—Packaged free with every new copy of *Management, 5e* is a password for the InfoTrac database by Gale Research. InfoTrac enables students to connect with the real world of management through academic journals, business and popular magazines and newspapers, and a vast array of government publications. InfoTrac was used to create the end-of-chapter activities in each chapter; students can use InfoTrac for working through the "Management Decisions" at the end of each chapter.

Wall Street Journal Edition—This *Wall Street Journal* edition makes it easy to bring the real world into the classroom, providing numerous opportunities to relate economic concepts to daily news stories. New copies of *Management, 5e* can include an optional card entitling students to subscriptions to the *Wall Street Journal* and **WSJ.com**, giving students access to many articles used as examples in this textbook. Contact your local representative about pricing and optional bundling information.

Acknowledgments

Let's face it, writing a textbook is a long and lonely process. It's surely the most difficult (and rewarding) project I've ever tackled. And, as I sat in front of my computer with a rough outline on the left side of my desk, a two-foot stack of journal articles on the floor, and a blank screen in front of me, it was easy at times to feel isolated. But, as I found out, a book like this doesn't get done without the help of many other talented people.

First, I'd like to thank the outstanding team of supplement authors: Thomas K. and Betty Pritchett (Kennesaw State University), for the outstanding test bank; Eric Brengle (B-books, Ltd.), for the superb PowerPoint slide designs; and Teri Irvin (B-books, Ltd.) for her detailed video lesson plans.

I'd like to thank the world-class team at Cengage Learning for the outstanding support (and patience) they provided while I wrote this book; Joe Sabatino, who heads the Management group at Cengage Learning, was calm, collected, and continuously positive through the major ups and downs of this project; Clint Kernen, who was in charge of marketing the book, did an outstanding job of developing marketing themes and approaches; and Tamborah Moore, who managed the production process, was consistently upbeat and positive with me when I deserved otherwise. Authors are prone to complain about their publishers. But that hasn't been my experience at all. Pure and simple, everyone at Cengage Learning has been great to work with throughout the entire project. However, special thanks on this team goes to Jamie Gleich Bryant, of B-books, Ltd., who was my developmental editor and with whom I had the most contact while writing the book. Jamie and her team worked with reviewers, edited the manuscript, managed the development of supplements, provided superb feedback and guidance at every stage of the book, and nudged and prodded me to write faster, make improvements, and maintain the high quality standards that were set when I began writing. Jamie's enthusiasm, professionalism, commitment, and attention to detail made me a better writer, made this a better book, and made me appreciate my good fortune to work with such an outstanding talent. Thanks, Jamie, and here's to many more editions.

I'd like to thank an excellent set of reviewers whose diligent and thoughtful comments helped shape the earlier editions and whose rigorous feedback improved the Fifth Edition.

Ali Abu-Rahma
United States International University

William Acar
Kent State University

David C. Adams
Manhattanville College

Bruce R. Barringer
University of Central Florida

Gayle Baugh
University of West Florida

James Bell
University of Texas, Austin

Greg Blundel
Kent State University, Stark

Katharine A. Bohley
University of Indianapolis

Santanu Borah
University of North Alabama

Angela Boston
University of Texas, Arlington

Michael Boyd
Owensboro Community College

Jon L. Bryan
Bridgewater State College

Wayne Buchanan
Defiance College

Bruce Byars
University of North Dakota, Grand Forks

Diane P. Caggiano
Fitchburg State College

David Cassidy
College of Eastern Utah

Dan Cochran
Mississippi State University

C. Brad Cox
Midlands Technical College

Kathy Daruty
Pierce College

Nicolette DeVille Christensen
Guilford College

Michael DiVecchio
Central Pennsylvania College

Jennifer Dose
University of Minnesota-Morris

Jason Duan
Cameron University

Joyce A. Ezrow
Anne Arundel Community College

Kimborough Ferrell
Spring Hill College

Charles R. Franz
University of Missouri-Columbia

Paul R. Gagnon
Central Connecticut State University

Franco Gandolfi
Cedarville University

Janice Gates
Western Illinois University

Anu A. Gokhale
Illinois State University

Barry Allen Gold
Pace University

Martin Grossman
Bridgewater State College

Susan C. Hanlon
University of Akron

Russell F. Hardy
New Mexico State University

David Hennessey
Mount Mercy College

Dorothy Hetmer-Hinds
Trinity Valley Community College

Roger W. Hutt
Arizona State University at the Polytechnic Campus

Joseph Izzo
Alderson Broaddus College

Jim Jawahar
Illinois State University

Kathleen Jones
University of North Dakota

Paul N. Keaton
University of Wisconsin-La Crosse

Ellen Ernst Kossek
Michigan State University

Nancy E. Kucinski
Hardin-Simmons University

Lowell H. Lamberton
Central Oregon Community College
Linfield College

Donald R. Leavitt
Western Baptist College

Lee W. Lee
Central Connecticut State University

Jerrold Leong
Oklahoma State University

Randy Lewis
Texas Christian University

Bob Livingston
Cerritos College

Linda Livingstone
Baylor University

Thomas P. Loughman
Columbus State University

Larry Maes
Davenport University

George Marron
Arizona State University

Lynda Martin
Oklahoma State University

David McCalman
University of Central Arkansas

Robert McGowan
University of Denver

Don Mosley
University of South Alabama

Sherry Moss
Florida International University

Jaideep Motwani
Grand Valley State University

Victoria T. Mullennex
Davis & Elkins College

John J. Nader
Grand Valley State University

Charlie Nagelschmidt
Champlain College

Patrick J. Nedry
Monroe County Community College

Stephanie Newport
Austin Peay State University

Don A. Okhomina
Fayetteville State University

James S. O'Rourke, IV
University of Notre Dame

Rhonda S. Palladi
Georgia State University

Lynne Patten
Clark Atlanta University

Jane Pettinger
Minnesota State University, Moorhead

Clifton D. Petty
Drury University

John Poirier
Bryant University

David M. Porter, Jr.
UCLA

Michael Provitera
Barry University

Abe Qastin
Lakeland College

Robert Raspberry
Southern Methodist University

Levi Richard
Citrus Community College

Kim Rocha
Barton College

Linda Ross
Cleveland Community College

Penni F. Sikkila
Baker College

Amit Shah
Frostburg State University

Thomas Shaughnessy
Illinois Central College

Michelle Slagle
University of South Alabama

James Smas
Kent State University

James O. Smith
East Carolina University

Charlotte Nix Speegle
Cisco Junior College

Gregory K. Stephens
Texas Christian University

John Striebich
Monroe Community College

Joseph Tagliaferre
Pennsylvania State University

Jennie Carter Thomas
Belmont University

Neal F. Thomson
Columbus State University

James Thornton
Champlain College

Mary Jo Vaughan
Mercer University

Michael Wakefield
Colorado State University, Pueblo

James Whelan
Manhattan College

Joann White
Jackson State University

Xiang Yi
Western Illinois University

Finally, my family deserves the greatest thanks of all for their love, patience, and support. Writing a textbook is an enormous project with incredible stresses and pressures on authors as well as their loved ones. However, throughout this project, my wife, Jenny, was unwavering in her support of my writing. She listened patiently, encouraged me when I was discouraged, read and commented on most of what I wrote, gave me the time to write, and took wonderful care of me and our family during this long process. My children, two in college and one in a business career, also deserve special thanks for their patience and for understanding why Dad was locked away at the computer for all of this time.

Meet the Author:

Chuck Williams
University of the Pacific

Chuck Williams is Dean of the Eberhard School of Business at the University of the Pacific. Previously, Chuck was associate professor of Management at the M.J. Neeley School of Business at Texas Christian University, where he has also served as an associate dean and the chair of the Management Department. He received his B.A. in Psychology from Valparaiso University, and specialized in the areas of Organizational Behavior, Human Resources, and Strategic Management while earning his M.B.A and Ph.D. in Business Administration from Michigan State University. Previously, he taught at Michigan State University and was on the faculty of Oklahoma State University.

His research interests include employee recruitment and turnover, performance appraisal, and employee training and goal-setting. Chuck has published research in the *Journal of Applied Psychology*, the *Academy of Management Journal*, *Human Resource Management Review*, *Personnel Psychology*, and the *Organizational Research Methods Journal*. He was a member of the *Journal of Management*'s Editorial Board, and serves as a reviewer for numerous other academic journals. He was also the webmaster for the Research Methods Division of the Academy of Management (**http://www.aom.pace.edu/rmd**). Chuck is a co-recipient of the Society for Human Resource Management's Yoder-Heneman Research Award.

Chuck has consulted for a number of organizations, General Motors, IBM, JCPenney, Tandy Corporation, Trism Trucking, Central Bank and Trust, StuartBacon, the City of Fort Worth, the American Cancer Society, and others. He has taught in executive development programs at Oklahoma State University, the University of Oklahoma, and Texas Christian University.

Chuck teaches a number of different courses, but has been privileged to teach his favorite course, Introduction to Management, for nearly 20 years. His teaching philosophy is based on four principles: (1) courses should be engaging and interesting; (2) there's nothing as practical as a good theory; (3) students learn by doing; and (4) students learn when they are challenged. The undergraduate students at TCU's Neeley School of Business named him instructor of the year. He was also a recipient of TCU's Dean's Teaching Award.

Introduction to Management

  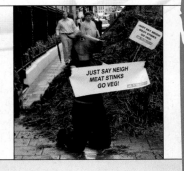

Chapter 1
Management

This chapter begins by defining management and discussing the functions of management. We look at what managers do, what it takes to be a manager, what companies look for in their managers, the most serious mistakes managers make, and what it is like to make the tough transition from being a worker to being a manager.

Chapter 2
The History of Management

This chapter reviews the historical origins of management ideas and practice and the historical changes that produced the need for managers. You'll learn about various schools of management thought and the key contributions made by important management theorists.

Chapter 3
Organizational Environments and Cultures

Chapter 3 examines the internal and external forces that affect business, including how those forces affect the decisions and performance of a company. We cover the general environment that affects all organizations and the specific environment unique to each company.

Chapter 4
Ethics and Social Responsibility

This chapter examines ethical behavior in the workplace and explains how unethical behavior can expose a business to legal penalties. You'll read about the influences on ethical decision making and learn the practical steps that managers can take to improve ethical decision making.

Management

© J. P. MOCZULSKI/REUTERS/LANDOV

Learning Outcomes:

1 Describe what management is.
2 Explain the four functions of management.
3 Describe different kinds of managers.
4 Explain the major roles and subroles that managers perform in their jobs.
5 Explain what companies look for in managers.
6 Discuss the top mistakes that managers make in their jobs.
7 Describe the transition that employees go through when they are promoted to management.
8 Explain how and why companies can create competitive advantage through people.

© VEER

In This Chapter:

WHAT WOULD YOU DO?

Nortel Headquarters, Toronto, Ontario, Canada.[1] When people use the Internet or make calls on their cell phones, the companies providing the Internet and cell phone service are probably using network or CDMA (code division multiple access) products made by Nortel Networks. And with its products used everywhere in the world, Nortel should be performing better. At least that's what you thought before deciding to become Nortel's new CEO and began working 100 hours a week to turn around this financially struggling company. You had hoped that your 25 years at GE, where you ran five of its key businesses, and your five years as the president and chief operating officer at Motorola would have prepared you to be Nortel's new CEO. But you underestimated the magnitude of the problems.

The most serious problem occurred six months after you started. After the previous management team overreported earnings to trigger corporate bonuses, Nortel had supposedly solved the company's financial-reporting problems. But now, for the third year in a row, Nortel incorrectly overestimated its profits and had to report, yet again, that it had earned substantially less than first reported. A financial analyst summed up the seriousness of the problem this way, " If you get three speeding tickets in a year, in many states you get your license pulled. . . . It's a big deal. It's a red flag." To no one's surprise, Wall Street hammered Nortel's stock price. Soon after, shareholders who had seen the value of Nortel stock lose $30 billion brought two class-action lawsuits against the company, seeking $9 billion in damages. The lawsuits, if successful, would put Nortel out of business. Restating earnings also had demoralizing effects within the company; the percentage of employees highly satisfied with their jobs dropped from 51 percent before to 40 percent after.

In addition, Nortel was running out of cash. Your job as CEO was to persuade skeptical financial companies to lend Nortel $2 billion to keep the company afloat. But before you could ask for more money, you had to cut costs by reducing retiree benefits and by laying off 1,900 employees and 350 managers. On top of that, Nortel's key cellular technology, CDMA, was aging, and losing out to newer, more powerful cell phone standards and equipment.

With problems mounting, you began losing sleep. Could you, in the end, fix the problems and return Nortel to profitability? With 35 percent of CEOs ultimately fired from their jobs, could you save yours? To do so, Nortel would have to get better, and fast. With billions in losses, and the need for an immediate $2 billion cash infusion, what steps must you take right now to ensure Nortel's short-term survival? Then, how should you deal with the $9 billion class-action suit that could put you out of business? Finally, if you solve those crises, what does Nortel need to do in the long run to become a more efficient company? **If you were the new CEO of Nortel Networks, what would you do?**

ACTIVITIES + VIDEOS

CengageNOW Audio study guide, electronic flashcards, author FAQ videos, On the Job and Biz Flix videos, concept tutorial, and concept exercise

Web (academic.cengage.com/management/williams) Quiz, PowerPoint slides, and glossary terms for this chapter

"WHAT'S NEW" COMPANIES

NORTEL NETWORKS
GENERAL MOTORS
UNITED PARCEL SERVICE
WAL-MART
AT&T
EXXONMOBIL
GOOGLE
YAHOO!
XEROX
CONTINENTAL AIRLINES
WHIRLPOOL
NORFOLK SOUTHERN
LLOYDS PHARMACY
HEWLETT-PACKARD
KIKKOMAN
CDW
J.M. SMUCKER
AND OTHERS . . .

Study Tip

Use your textbook more like a notebook and less like a reference book. The margins are a great place for writing questions, highlighting important concepts, and adding examples to help you remember the material. Writing in your book makes it a better study tool.

Each chapter opener contains an activities and videos list that alerts you to the materials outside your book that can help you better understand assignments, work on group projects, and study for tests and exams.

The management issues facing Nortel are fundamental to any organization: How do we plan to get things done, organize the company to be efficient and effective, lead and motivate employees, and put in place controls to make sure our plans are followed and our goals are met? Good management is basic to starting a business, growing a business, and maintaining a business once it has achieved some measure of success.

We begin this chapter by defining management and discussing the functions of management. Next, we look at what managers do by examining the four kinds of managers and reviewing the various roles that managers play. Then we investigate what it takes to be a manager by reviewing management skills, what companies look for in their managers, the most serious mistakes managers make, and what it is like to make the tough transition from being a worker to being a manager. We finish this chapter by examining the competitive advantage that companies gain from good management. In other words, we end the chapter by learning how to establish a competitive advantage through people.

WHAT IS MANAGEMENT?

Mistake #1. A high-level bank manager reduces a marketing manager to tears by angrily criticizing her in front of others for a mistake that wasn't hers.[2] Mistake #2. Six months after he attacked a female coworker but wasn't fired, a Dairy Queen employee sits next to a customer, bites her, and declares, "I am like Dracula."[3] Mistake #3. Guidant recalled 50,000 heart defibrillators after 45 failed and two people died. However, Guidant continued to sell these defective products for three years, knowing that they might short-circuit. Patients were told that if they heard a beeping noise, their defibrillator was malfunctioning and they should see their doctor or go to an emergency room.[4]

Ah, bad managers and bad management. Is it any wonder that companies pay management consultants nearly $150 billion a year for advice with basic management issues, such as how to lead people effectively, organize the company efficiently, and manage large-scale projects and processes?[5] This textbook will help you understand some of the basic issues that management consultants help companies resolve (and it won't cost you billions of dollars).

After reading the next two sections, you should be able to

> 1 describe what management is.
> 2 explain the four functions of management.

1 Management Is . . .

Many of today's managers got their start welding on the factory floor, clearing dishes off tables, helping customers fit a suit, or wiping up a spill in aisle 3. Similarly, lots of you will start at the bottom and work your way up. There's no better way to get to know your competition, your customers, and your business. But whether you begin your career at the entry level or as a supervisor, your job as a manager is not to do the work, but to help others do theirs. **Management** is getting work done through others. Pat Carrigan, a former elementary school principal who became a manager at a GENERAL MOTORS car parts plant, says, "I've never made a part in my life, and I don't really have any plans to make one. That's not my job. My job is to create an environment where people who do make them can make them right, can make them right the first time, can make them at a competitive cost, and can do so with some sense of responsibility and pride in what they're doing. I don't have to know how to make a part to do any of those things."[6]

Pat Carrigan's description of managerial responsibilities suggests that managers also have to be concerned with efficiency and effectiveness in the work process. **Efficiency** is getting work done with a minimum of effort, expense, or waste. For example, UNITED PARCEL SERVICE, which delivers over 3.5 billion packages a year, will save 14 million gallons of fuel annually when it fully implements its new PAL software. PAL, which stands for Pre-Load Assistance Label, is part of an overall computerized route and load planning system that shows truck loaders where to put packages on the delivery truck (to maximize the number of packages per truck), determines how many packages and stops a UPS driver has and what routes should be taken (to minimize travel time, distances, and fuel costs), and tells drivers exactly where your package is on the truck when they stop in front of your house (to minimize search time at each stop).[7]

By itself, efficiency is not enough to ensure success. Managers must also strive for **effectiveness,** which is accomplishing tasks that help fulfill organizational objectives, such as customer service and satisfaction. WAL-MART's new computerized scheduling system measures trends in store sales and customer traffic so it can have more employees on the job whenever its stores are busy. Tests in 39 stores indicated that 70 percent of customers reported improved checkout times and service using this scheduling system. Wal-Mart spokesperson Sarah Clark said, "The advantages are simple: We will benefit by improving the shopping experience by having the right number of associates to meet our customers' needs when they shop our stores."[8] The computerized system also frees managers to manage instead of calculating schedules. Normally, it takes a Wal-Mart manager a full day to schedule the weekly shift for a single store. By contrast, in that time the computerized scheduling system can calculate the schedules for all of Wal-Mart's 1.3 million workers.

management getting work done through others

efficiency getting work done with a minimum of effort, expense, or waste

effectiveness accomplishing tasks that help fulfill organizational objectives

UPS saves 14 million gallons of fuel each year, not to mention time, by planning its routes to minimize left-hand turns, which take longer to make than right-hand turns.

Review 1:
Management Is . . .

Good management is working through others to accomplish tasks that help fulfill organizational objectives as efficiently as possible.

© STEPHEN CHERNIN/GETTY IMAGES

2 Management Functions

mgmt: fact

History of Management
Management as a field of study may be just 125 years old, but management ideas and practices have actually been used from the earliest times of recorded history. Early on, the Greeks learned that they could improve the productivity of repetitive tasks by performing them to music. The basic idea was to use a flute, drum, or song lyrics to pace people to work in unison using the same efficient motion, stimulate them to work faster and longer, and make the boring work more fun.

© VEER

Henri Fayol, who was a managing director (CEO) of a large steel company in the early 1900s, was one of the founders of the field of management. You'll learn more about Fayol and management's other key contributors when you read about the history of management in Chapter 2. Based on his 20 years of experience as a CEO, Fayol argued that "the success of an enterprise generally depends much more on the administrative ability of its leaders than on their technical ability."[9] In other words, eBay, the world's largest online auction company, succeeds because of CEO Meg Whitman's capabilities as a manager and not because of her abilities to write computer code.

According to Fayol, to be successful, managers need to perform five managerial functions: planning, organizing, coordinating, commanding, and controlling.[10] Today, though, most management textbooks have dropped the coordinating function and refer to Fayol's commanding function as "leading." Consequently, Fayol's management functions are known today as planning, organizing, leading, and controlling. Studies indicate that managers who perform these management functions well are more successful. For example, the more time that CEOs spend planning, the more profitable their companies are.[11] Over a 25-year period, *AT&T* found that employees with better planning and decision-making skills were more likely to be promoted into management jobs, to be successful as managers, and to be promoted into upper levels of management.[12]

The evidence is clear. Managers serve their companies well when they plan, organize, lead, and control. Consequently, as shown in Exhibit 1.1, this textbook is organized based on the functions of management. Furthermore, throughout this text, the major sections within each chapter are numbered using a single digit: 1, 2, 3, and so on. The subsections are consecutively numbered, beginning with the major section number. For example, "2.1" indicates the first subsection under the second major section. This numbering system should help you easily see the relationships among topics and follow the topic sequence. It will also help your instructor refer to specific topics during class discussion.

*Now let's take a closer look at each of the management functions: **2.1 planning**, **2.2 organizing**, **2.3 leading**, and **2.4 controlling**.*

2.1 Planning

Planning is determining organizational goals and a means for achieving them. As you'll learn in Chapter 5, planning is one of the best ways to improve performance. It encourages people to work harder, to work hard for extended periods, to engage in behaviors directly related to goal accomplishment, and to think of better ways to do their jobs. But most importantly, companies that plan have larger profits and faster growth than companies that don't plan.

planning determining organizational goals and a means for achieving them

For example, the question, "What business are we in?" is at the heart of strategic planning, which you'll learn about in Chapter 6. If you can answer the question "What business are you in?" in two sentences or less, chances are you have a very clear plans for your business. *EXXONMOBIL* CEO Rex Tillerson states clearly and simply that "conventional oil and gas . . . is the business we are in." When asked why ExxonMobil is not heavily investing in ethanol, a crop-based renewable source of fuel, he replies, "We are not in those other businesses."[13] Likewise, *GOOGLE*, which makes its money from search-based Internet advertising, says that it is not in the advertising business. Its business is to "organize the world's information and make it universally accessible and useful."[14] So when Google spent $1.65 billion to buy YouTube, it was adhering to its business by helping users access and organize video content. You'll learn more about planning in Chapter 5 on planning and decision making, Chapter 6 on organizational strategy, Chapter 7 on innovation and change, and Chapter 8 on global management.

2.2 Organizing

Organizing is deciding where decisions will be made, who will do what jobs and tasks, and who will work for whom in the company.

Go to *YAHOO!*'s home page and take a look at the vast number of topics, news, mail, messenger, shopping (from autos and finance to Hot Jobs, music, and real estate), small business, and featured services (downloads, mobile, voice, and personal websites). How would you organize this vast array of topics and activities? Yahoo! does it with two customer groups, audience and advertiser/publisher, and one technology group. The audience group has responsibility for Yahoo!'s products in search, media, communities and communications. The advertising/publishing group helps large advertisers and agencies, small- and medium-sized businesses, local advertisers, resellers, and publishers connect with their target customers across the Internet. Finally, the technology group supports the entire organization by creating technological capabilities and platforms. Yahoo!'s CEO said, "We believe having a more customer-focused organization, supported by robust technology, will speed the development of leading-edge experiences for our most valuable audience segments."[15]

You'll learn more about organizing in Chapter 9 on designing organizations, Chapter 10 on managing teams, Chapter 11 on managing human resources, and Chapter 12 on managing individuals and a diverse work force.

Exhibit 1.1

Management Functions and Organization of the Textbook

organizing deciding where decisions will be made, who will do what jobs and tasks, and who will work for whom

META-ANALYSIS

what *really* works.

Some studies show that having two drinks a day increases life expectancy by decreasing the chances of having a heart attack. Yet other studies show that having two drinks a day shortens life expectancy. For years, we've "buttered" our morning toast with margarine instead of butter because margarine was supposed to be better for our health. Now, however, new studies show that the trans-fatty acids in margarine may be just as bad for our arteries as butter. Confusing scientific results like these frustrate ordinary people who want to "eat right" and "live right." They also make many people question just how useful most scientific research really is.

Managers also find themselves questioning the conflicting scientific research published in journals like the *Academy of Management Journal,* the *Academy of Management Review,* the *Strategic Management Journal,* the *Journal of Applied Psychology,* and *Administrative Science Quarterly.* The *Wall Street Journal* may quote a management research article from one of these journals that says that total quality management is the best thing since sliced bread (without butter or margarine). Then, just six months later, the *Wall Street Journal* will quote a different article from the same journal that says that total quality management doesn't work. If management professors and researchers have trouble deciding what works and what doesn't, how can practicing managers know?

Thankfully, a research tool called **meta-analysis**, which is a study of studies, is helping management scholars understand how well their research supports management theories. Meta-analysis is also useful for practicing managers because it shows what works and the conditions under which management techniques may work better or worse in the "real world." Meta-analysis is based on the simple idea that if one study shows that a management technique doesn't work and another study shows that it does, an average of those results is probably the best estimate of how well that management practice works (or doesn't work). For example, medical researchers Richard Peto and Rory Collins averaged all of the different results from several hundred studies investigating the relationship between aspirin and heart attacks. Their analysis, based on more than 120,000 patients from numerous studies, showed that aspirin lowered the incidence of heart attacks by an average of 4 percent. Prior to this study, doctors prescribed aspirin as a preventive measure for only 38 percent of heart-attack victims. Today, because of the meta-analysis results, doctors prescribe aspirin for 72 percent of heart-attack victims.

Fortunately, you don't need a Ph.D. to understand the statistics reported in a meta-analysis. In fact, one primary advantage of meta-analysis over traditional significance tests is that you can convert meta-analysis statistics into intuitive numbers that anyone can easily understand.

Each meta-analysis reported in the "What Really Works" sections of this textbook is accompanied by an easy-to-understand statistic called the *probability of success.* As its name suggests, the probability of success shows how often a management technique will work.

For example, meta-analyses suggest that the best predictor of a job applicant's on-the-job performance is a test of general mental ability. In other words, smarter people tend to be better workers. The average correlation (one of those often-misunderstood statistics) between scores on general mental ability tests and job performance is .60. However, very few people understand what a correlation of .60 means. What most managers want to know is how often they will hire the right person if they choose job applicants based on general mental ability test scores. Likewise, they want to know how much difference a cognitive ability test makes when hiring new workers. The probability of success may be high, but if the difference isn't really that large, is it worth a manager's time to have job applicants take a general mental ability test?

Well, our user-friendly statistics indicate that it's wise to have job applicants take a general mental ability test. In fact, the probability of success, shown in graphical form here, is 76 percent. This means that an employee hired on the basis of a good score on a general mental ability test stands a 76 percent chance of being a better performer than someone picked at random from the pool of all job applicants. So chances are you're going to be right much more often than wrong if you use a general mental ability test to make hiring decisions.[16]

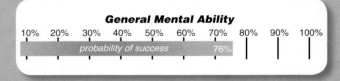

General Mental Ability

10% 20% 30% 40% 50% 60% 70% 80% 90% 100%

probability of success 76%

In summary, each "What Really Works" section in this textbook is based on meta-analysis research, which provides the best scientific evidence that management professors and researchers have about what works and what doesn't work in management. We will use the easy-to-understand index known as the *probability of success* to indicate how well a management idea or strategy is likely to work in the workplace. Of course, no idea or technique works every time and in every circumstance. Nevertheless, the management ideas and strategies discussed in the "What Really Works" sections can usually make a meaningful difference where you work. In today's competitive, fast-changing, global marketplace, few managers can afford to overlook proven management strategies like the ones discussed in "What Really Works."

2.3 Leading

Our third management function, **leading**, involves inspiring and motivating workers to work hard to achieve organizational goals.

When Anne Mulcahy became *XEROX*'s CEO, the company was on the brink of bankruptcy—it was $17.1 billion in debt and had only $154 million in cash. In addition, three years of steeply declining revenues and increasing losses had dropped the company's stock price from $64 a share to just $4.43. Mulcahy admits that the responsibility of turning the company around frightened her: "Nothing spooked me as much as waking up in the middle of the night and thinking about 96,000 people and retirees and what would happen if this thing went south."[17] Still, she took the job.

Mulcahy, who traveled to two and sometimes three cities a day to talk to Xerox managers and employees, implored them to "save each dollar as if it were your own." And at each stop, she reminded them, "Remember, by my calculations, there are [she fills in the number] selling days left in the quarter."[18] Mulcahy said, "One of the things I care most about at Xerox is the morale and motivation at the company. I think it is absolutely critical to being able to deliver results. People have to feel engaged, motivated and feel they are making a contribution to something that is important. I spend the vast majority of my time with customers and employees, and there is nothing more important for any of us to do as leaders than communicate and engage with our two most important constituencies."[19]

> *People have to feel engaged, motivated and feel they are making a contribution to something that is important.*

ANNE MULCAHY, CEO, XEROX

Today, as a result of Mulcahy's leadership and the hard work of dedicated Xerox employees, Xerox is back on its feet, having returned to profitability and financial stability.[20] You'll learn more about leading in Chapter 13 on motivation, Chapter 14 on leadership, and Chapter 15 on managing communication.

2.4 Controlling

The last function of management, **controlling**, is monitoring progress toward goal achievement and taking corrective action when progress isn't being made. The basic control process involves setting standards to achieve goals, comparing actual performance to those standards, and then making changes to return performance to those standards.

Needing to cut costs (the standard) to restore profitability (the goal), *CONTINENTAL AIRLINES* started giving passengers small cups of their soft drinks instead of an entire can (one corrective action among many). Company spokesperson Rahsaan Johnson defended the move, saying, "Flight attendants have been telling us that the trash bags they carry were so heavy because of all the [wasted] liquid. We were pouring almost half away."[21] Although Continental will still give entire soft drink cans to customers who request them, serving smaller drinks saves the company $100,000 a year in costs.

You'll learn more about the control function in Chapter 16 on control, Chapter 17 on managing information, and Chapter 18 on managing service and manufacturing operations.

meta-analysis a study of studies, a statistical approach that provides one of the best scientific estimates of how well management theories and practices work

leading inspiring and motivating workers to work hard to achieve organizational goals

controlling monitoring progress toward goal achievement and taking corrective action when needed

Review 2: **Management Functions**

Henri Fayol's classic management functions are known today as planning, organizing, leading, and controlling. Planning is determining organizational goals and a means for achieving them. Organizing is deciding where decisions will be made, who will do what jobs and tasks, and who will work for whom. Leading is inspiring and motivating workers to work hard to achieve organizational goals. Controlling is monitoring progress toward goal achievement and taking corrective action when needed. Studies show that performing these management functions well leads to better managerial performance.

WHAT DO MANAGERS DO?

Not all managerial jobs are the same. The demands and requirements placed on the CEO of Sony are significantly different from those placed on the manager of your local Wendy's restaurant.

> **After reading the next two sections, you should be able to**
>
> 3 describe different kinds of managers.
>
> 4 explain the major roles and subroles that managers perform in their jobs.

3 Kinds of Managers

As shown in Exhibit 1.2, there are four kinds of managers, each with different jobs and responsibilities: **3.1 top managers**, **3.2 middle managers**, **3.3 first-line managers**, and **3.4 team leaders**.

3.1 Top Managers

Top managers hold positions like chief executive officer (CEO), chief operating officer (COO), chief financial officer (CFO), and chief information officer (CIO), and are responsible for the overall direction of the organization. Top managers have the following responsibilities.[22] First, they are responsible for creating a context for change. In fact, the CEOs of Walt Disney, Fannie Mae, Boeing, Morgan Stanley, American International Group, Merck, and Pfizer were all fired within a year's time precisely because they had not moved fast enough to bring about significant changes in their companies. Indeed, in both Europe and the United States, 35 percent of all CEOs are eventually fired because of their inability to successfully change their companies.[23] Creating a context for change includes forming a long-range vision or mission for the company. As one CEO said, "The CEO has to think about the future more than anyone."

Second, much more than used to be the case, top managers are responsible for developing employees' commitment to and ownership of the company's performance. Trusting that his 61,000 employees could dramatically increase product innovation at **WHIRLPOOL** appliances, then-CEO David Whitwam put $135 million directly into their hands and told them to come up with new ideas. Furthermore, he encouraged them to go to their bosses with their ideas. And if

"WHAT'S NEW" COMPANY

top managers executives responsible for the overall direction of the organization their bosses wouldn't listen, they were to bring their new product ideas directly to him. Employees flocked to an in-house website with a course on innovation and a list of all the new suggestions and ideas, racking up 300,000 hits on the site each month. Of the commitment displayed by his workers, Whitwam says, "I had never seen a strategy that was so energizing to so many people." Today, revenue from innovative products has quadrupled. And instead of cutting prices to maintain sales, Whirlpool's prices are now rising 5 percent per year because customers are willing to pay more for its innovative products, such as the Duet washer and dryer, which were designed based on employees' ideas.[24]

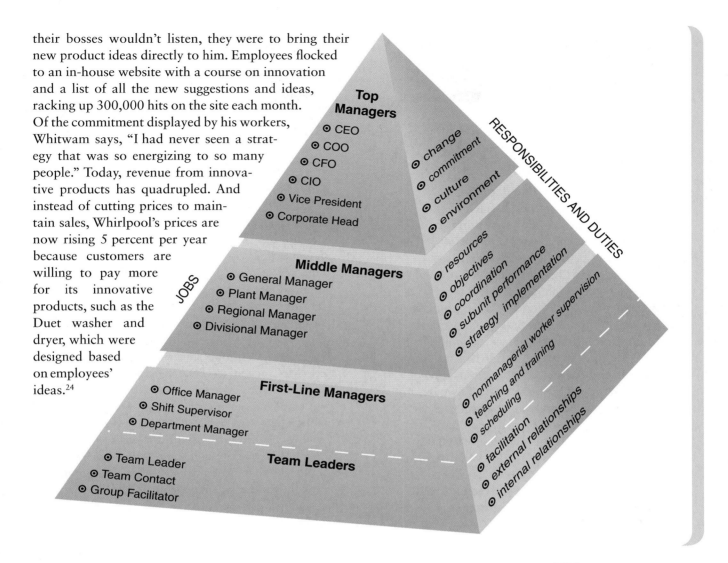

Third, top managers are responsible for creating a positive organizational culture through language and action. Top managers impart company values, strategies, and lessons through what they do and say to others, both inside and outside the company. One CEO said, "I write memos to the board and our operating committee. I'm sure they get the impression I dash them off, but usually they've been drafted 10 or 20 times. The bigger you get, the more your ability to communicate becomes important. So what I write, I write very carefully. I labor over it."[25] Above all, no matter what they communicate, it's critical for CEOs to send and reinforce clear, consistent messages.[26] A former *Fortune* 500 CEO said, "I tried to [use] exactly the same words every time so that I didn't produce a lot of, 'Last time you said this, this time you said that.' You've got to say the same thing over and over and over."[27]

Finally, top managers are responsible for monitoring their business environments. This means that top managers must closely monitor customer needs, competitors' moves, and long-term business, economic, and social trends. Rick Wagoner, CEO of General Motors, reads six daily newspapers, monitors his Internet connections and news sources all

Exhibit 1.2

Jobs and Responsibilities of Four Kinds of Managers

COURTESY, WHIRLPOOL CORPORATION

day, and skims a variety of magazines from all over the world. Says Wagoner, "You've gotta know what the hell is going on in your business. If you've got a problem in China, you've gotta get into it and make sure that it's getting fixed. You've got to be on top of your business enough to know where are the problems, where are the opportunities."[28]

3.2 Middle Managers

Middle managers hold positions like plant manager, regional manager, or divisional manager. They are responsible for setting objectives consistent with top management's goals and for planning and implementing subunit strategies for achieving those objectives.[29] One specific middle management responsibility is to plan and allocate resources to meet objectives. Another major responsibility is to coordinate and link groups, departments, and divisions within a company. After a hurricane destroyed five miles of railroad tracks outside New Orleans, Jeff McCracken, a chief engineer at **NORFOLK SOUTHERN**, consulted with three bridge companies, and managed a team of 100 employees and dozens of engineers who, by sleeping in campers and working around the clock, rebuilt the tracks in less than a week. McCracken said, "It was a colossal job that took more than 400 moves with heavy equipment." But McCracken was happiest about "working with people from all parts of the company—and getting the job done without anyone getting hurt."[31]

A third responsibility of middle management is to monitor and manage the performance of the subunits and individual managers who report to them. Graeme Betts is the manager of the Southwest region for **LLOYDS PHARMACY** in England. While Betts works with people at all levels, from health-care assistants to board directors, he spends most of his time with the nine area managers who report to him. In terms of monitoring and managing the performance of his area managers and, in turn, the store managers who report to them, Betts says, "We have 231 pharmacies, and as a [management] team our task is to ensure that our pharmacies are as good as they can be, and are offering a great service to our customers. To this end we are focused on providing an efficient [drug] dispensing service, and continually developing new professional services such as . . . smoking cessation and medicines-use reviews."[32]

Finally, middle managers are also responsible for implementing the changes or strategies generated by top managers. Wal-Mart's strategy reflects its advertising slogan, "Always Low Prices." When Wal-Mart began selling groceries in its new 200,000-square-foot supercenters, it made purchasing manager Brian Wilson responsible for buying perishable goods more cheaply than Wal-Mart's competitors. When small produce suppliers had trouble meeting Wal-Mart's needs, Wilson worked closely with them and connected them to RetailLink, Wal-Mart's computer network, "which allows our suppliers immediate access to all information needed

middle managers responsible for setting objectives consistent with top management's goals and for planning and implementing subunit strategies for achieving these objectives to help run the business." Over time, these steps helped the produce suppliers lower costs and deliver the enormous quantities of fresh fruits and vegetables that Wal-Mart's supercenters need.[33] They also helped Wal-Mart become the world's largest grocer.[34]

3.3 First-Line Managers

First-line managers hold positions like office manager, shift supervisor, or department manager. The primary responsibility of first-line managers is to manage the performance of entry-level employees, who are directly responsible for producing a company's goods and services. Thus, first-line managers are the only managers who don't supervise other managers. First-line managers have the following responsibilities.

First-line managers encourage, monitor, and reward the performance of their workers. For example, Jeff Dexheimer requires the waiters and waitresses he supervises at the upscale Melting Pot restaurant in St. Louis to memorize a complex menu and a 400-item wine list. Says Dexheimer, "They've got to know every liquor, every beer, every food item, as well as the sauces it comes with." To reduce turnover and keep his 65 employees motivated, Dexheimer gives out $25 nightly rewards for "best attitude" or for selling the most wine. Since his employees are young and mostly single, he makes sure they work only one night each weekend. And once a week, after the restaurant closes, he takes his entire staff out for drinks. Says Dexheimer, as a manager, "I don't make myself successful. My employees make me successful."[35]

First-line managers teach entry-level employees how to do their jobs. Damian Mogavero's company, Avero LLC, helps restaurants analyze sales data for each member of a restaurant's wait staff. Restaurant managers who use these data, says Mogavero, will often take their top-selling server to lunch each week as a reward. The best managers, however, will also take their poorest-selling servers out to lunch to talk about what they can do to improve their performance.[36] Likewise, Coca-Cola manager Tom Mattia says, "I try to make every interaction I have with someone on my team a teaching experience. There are always specific work issues that need to get addressed, but then I try to explain my thinking behind an approach so people can get more experience."[37]

First-line managers also make detailed schedules and operating plans based on middle management's intermediate-range plans. In fact, in contrast to the long-term plans of top managers (three to five years out) and the intermediate plans of middle managers (6 to 18 months out), first-line managers engage in plans and actions that typically produce results within two weeks.[38] For example, consider the typical convenience store manager (for example, 7-Eleven) who starts the day by driving by competitors' stores to inspect their gasoline prices and then checks the outside of his or her store for anything that might need maintenance, such as burned-out lights or signs, or restocking, like windshield washer fluid and paper towels. Then comes an inside check, where the manager determines what needs to be done for that day (Are there enough coffee and donuts for breakfast or enough sandwiches for lunch?). Once today is planned, the manager turns to weekend orders. After accounting for the weather (hot or cold) and the sales trends at the same time last year, the manager makes sure the store will have enough beer, soft drinks, and Sunday papers on hand. Finally, the manager looks 7 to 10 days ahead for hiring needs. Because of strict hiring procedures (basic math tests, drug tests, and background checks), it can take that long to hire new employees. Said one convenience-store manager, "I have to continually interview, even if I am fully staffed."[39]

first-line managers train and supervise the performance of nonmanagerial employees who are directly responsible for producing the company's products or services

3.4 Team Leaders

The fourth kind of manager is a team leader. This relatively new kind of management job developed as companies shifted to self-managing teams, which, by definition, have no formal supervisor. In traditional management hierarchies, first-line managers are responsible for the performance of nonmanagerial employees and have the authority to hire and fire workers, make job assignments, and control resources. Team leaders play a very different role because in this new structure, teams now perform nearly all of the functions performed by first-line managers under traditional hierarchies.[40] Instead of directing individuals' work, **team leaders** facilitate team activities toward goal accomplishment. For example, HEWLETT-PACKARD's ad for a team leader position says, "Job seeker must enjoy coaching, working with people, and bringing about improvement through hands-off guidance and leadership."[41] Team leaders who fail to understand this key difference often struggle in their roles. A team leader at Texas Instruments said, "I didn't buy into teams, partly because there was no clear plan on what I was supposed to do. . . . I never let the operators [team members] do any scheduling or any ordering of parts because that was mine. I figured as long as I had that, I had a job."[42]

Team leaders fulfill the following responsibilities.[43] First, team leaders are responsible for facilitating team performance. This doesn't mean team leaders are responsible for team performance. They aren't. The team is. Team leaders help their team members plan and schedule work, learn to solve problems, and work effectively with each other. Management consultant Franklin Jonath says, "The idea is for the team leader to be at the service of the group. It should be clear that the team members own the outcome. The leader is there to bring intellectual, emotional, and spiritual resources to the team. Through his or her actions, the leader should be able to show the others how to think about the work that they're doing in the context of their lives. It's a tall order, but the best teams have such leaders."[44]

Second, team leaders are responsible for managing external relationships. Team leaders act as the bridge or liaison between their teams and other teams, departments, and divisions in a company. For example, if a member of Team A complains about the quality of Team B's work, Team A's leader is responsible for solving the problem by initiating a meeting with Team B's leader. Together, these team leaders are responsible for getting members of both teams to work together to solve the problem. If it's done right, the problem is solved without involving company management or blaming members of the other team.[45]

Third, team leaders are responsible for internal team relationships. Getting along with others is much more important in team structures because team members can't get work done without the help of their teammates. For example, studies show that it's not the surgeon, but the interactions between the surgeon

team leaders managers responsible for facilitating team activities toward goal accomplishment

Even first-line managers perform the functions of management.

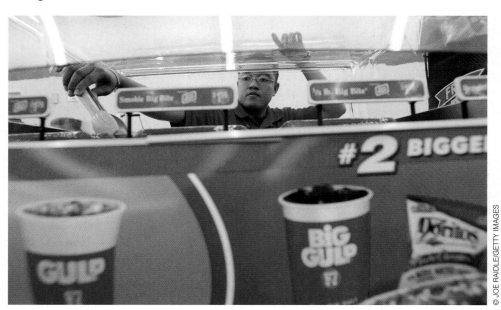

© JOE RAIDLE/GETTY IMAGES

and all operating room team members that determine surgical outcomes. However, at 20 hospitals, 60 percent of the operating room team members—nurses, technicians, and other doctors—agreed with the statement, "In the ORs here, it is difficult to speak up if I perceive a problem with patient care."[46] And when operating room team members don't speak up, serious mistakes can occur, no matter how talented the surgeon. Consequently, surgeons are using "safety pauses" to better involve members of their surgical teams. The surgeon will pause, ask if anyone has concerns or comments, and address them if need be. Studies show that safety pauses reduce mistakes, such as operating on the wrong leg or beginning surgery with key surgical instruments missing.[47] You will learn more about teams in Chapter 10.

Review 3: Kinds of Managers

There are four different kinds of managers. Top managers are responsible for creating a context for change, developing attitudes of commitment and ownership, creating a positive organizational culture through words and actions, and monitoring their company's business environments. Middle managers are responsible for planning and allocating resources, coordinating and linking groups and departments, monitoring and managing the performance of subunits and managers, and implementing the changes or strategies generated by top managers. First-line managers are responsible for managing the performance of nonmanagerial employees, teaching direct reports how to do their jobs, and making detailed schedules and operating plans based on middle management's intermediate-range plans. Team leaders are responsible for facilitating team performance, managing external relationships, and facilitating internal team relationships.

4 Managerial Roles

So far, we have described managerial work by focusing on the functions of management and by examining the four kinds of managerial jobs. Although those are valid and accurate ways of categorizing managerial work, if you followed managers around as they perform their jobs, you probably would not use the terms *planning*, *organizing*, *leading*, and *controlling* to describe what they do.

In fact, that's exactly the conclusion that management researcher Henry Mintzberg came to when he followed around five American CEOs. Mintzberg spent a week shadowing each of the CEOs. He analyzed their mail, whom they talked to, and what they did. Mintzberg concluded that managers fulfill three major roles while performing their jobs:[48]

- *interpersonal roles*
- *informational roles*
- *decisional roles*

*In other words, managers talk to people, gather and give information, and make decisions. Furthermore, as shown in Exhibit 1.3, these three major roles can be subdivided into 10 subroles. Let's examine each major role—**4.1 interpersonal**, **4.2 informational**, and **4.3 decisional roles**—and their 10 subroles.*

Interpersonal Roles
- Figurehead
- Leader
- Liaison

Informational Roles
- Monitor
- Disseminator
- Spokesperson

Decisional Roles
- Entrepreneur
- Disturbance Handler
- Resource Allocator
- Negotiator

Exhibit 1.3

Mintzberg's Managerial Roles and Subroles

figurehead role the interpersonal role managers play when they perform ceremonial duties

leader role the interpersonal role managers play when they motivate and encourage workers to accomplish organizational objectives

liaison role the interpersonal role managers play when they deal with people outside their units

4.1 Interpersonal Roles

More than anything else, management jobs are people-intensive. Estimates vary with the level of management, but most managers spend between two-thirds and four-fifths of their time in face-to-face communication with others.[49] If you're a loner, or if you consider dealing with people a pain, then you may not be cut out for management work. In fulfilling the interpersonal role of management, managers perform three subroles: figurehead, leader, and liaison.

In the **figurehead role**, managers perform ceremonial duties like greeting company visitors, speaking at the opening of a new facility, or representing the company at a community luncheon to support local charities. For example, when Japan-based KIKKOMAN Corporation, the world's largest soy sauce maker, opened its first soy sauce manufacturing plant in Europe (in Hoogezand Sappemeer, the Netherlands), its CEO, Yuzaburo Mogi, gave a speech pledging that Kikkoman would be a good corporate citizen by donating to a local environmental conservation and water quality project and to the Rembrandt House Art Gallery.[50]

In the **leader role**, managers motivate and encourage workers to accomplish organizational objectives. At CDW (Computer Discount Warehouse), new CEO John Edwardson promised CDW's 2,750 workers that he would shave his head if the company met its third-quarter goals. Despite the industry downturn in computer sales, company employees responded. After announcing at a company function that the third-quarter goals had been met, Edwardson, as promised, had his head shaved to the harmonic sounds of a barbershop quartet.[51] At J.M. SMUCKER, that's right, the jelly and jam company, managers regularly thank employees with celebratory lunches and gift certificates. Tonie Williams, director of marketing for peanut butter, says she's been thanked more in her two years at Smucker than she was in her nine years at Nestlé, Kraft, and Procter & Gamble combined.[52] *Fortune* magazine recently included both CDW and Smucker in its annual list of the top 100 places to work in the United States.[53]

In the **liaison role**, managers deal with people outside their units. Studies consistently indicate that managers spend as much time with "outsiders" as they do with their own subordinates and their own bosses. In addition to his normal duties, Rajesh Hukku, chairman of j-Flex Solutions, a maker of financial-services software, regularly goes on sales calls, helps close sales deals, and markets his product to potential customers at industry conventions and forums.[54] The same holds true for the convenience store managers discussed earlier. From dealing with vendors who make store deliveries and set up product displays, to working with computer technicians who help with computer glitches and satellite connections to headquarters, to ordering from sales representatives who supply the mops and deli aprons used in the store, to calling the sheriff about stolen credit cards, even first-line managers spend much of their time dealing with outsiders.[55]

4.2 Informational Roles

Not only do managers spend most of their time in face-to-face contact with others, but they spend time obtaining and sharing information. Indeed, Mintzberg found that the managers in his study spent 40 percent of their time giving and getting information from others. In this regard, management can be viewed as processing information, gathering information by scanning the business environment and listening to others in face-to-face conversations, and then sharing that information with people inside and outside the company. Mintzberg described three informational subroles: monitor, disseminator, and spokesperson.

In the **monitor role**, managers scan their environment for information, actively contact others for information, and, because of their personal contacts, receive a great deal of unsolicited information. Besides receiving firsthand information, managers monitor their environment by reading local newspapers and the *Wall Street Journal* to keep track of customers, competitors, and technological changes that may affect their businesses. Now, managers can also take advantage of electronic monitoring and distribution services that track the news wires (Associated Press, Reuters, and so on.) for stories related to their businesses. These services deliver customized electronic newspapers that include only stories on topics the managers specify. Business Wire (**http://www.businesswire.com**) offers services such as IndustryTrak, which monitors and distributes daily news headlines from major industries (for example, automotive, banking and financial, health, high tech).[56] CyberAlert (**http://www.cyberalert.com**) keeps round-the-clock track of new stories in categories chosen by each subscriber.[57] FNS NewsClips Online (**http://www.news-clips .com**) provides subscribers daily electronic news clips from more than 5,000 online news sites.[58]

Because of their numerous personal contacts and their access to subordinates, managers are often hubs for the distribution of critical information. In the **disseminator role**, managers share the information they have collected with their subordinates and others in the company. Although there will never be a complete substitute for face-to-face dissemination of information, the primary methods of communication in large companies like Continental Airlines and Cisco Systems are e-mail and voice mail. At Continental Airlines, the CEO broadcasts a voice mail message to all employees every Friday.[59] John Chambers, Cisco's CEO, says that 90 percent of his communication with employees is through e-mail and voice mail. Says Chambers, "If you don't have the ability to interface with customers, employees, and suppliers, you can't manage your business."[60]

In contrast to the disseminator role, in which managers distribute information to employees inside the company, in the **spokesperson role**, managers share information with people outside their departments and companies. One of the most common ways CEOs serve as spokespeople for their companies is at annual meetings with company shareholders or the board of directors. For example, at a Microsoft annual shareholder meeting, CEO Steve Ballmer told investors that Microsoft intended to offer its own Internet search service, **http://www.live.com**. Ballmer vowed that although Microsoft was late to the search engine business, "We will catch up, and we will surpass" Google and Yahoo in the Internet search and advertising business.[61]

4.3 Decisional Roles

According to Mintzberg, the time managers spend obtaining and sharing information is not an end in itself. The time spent talking to and obtaining and sharing information with people inside and outside the company is useful to managers because it helps them make good decisions. Mintzberg found that managers engage in four decisional subroles: entrepreneur, disturbance handler, resource allocator, and negotiator.

In the **entrepreneur role**, managers adapt themselves, their subordinates, and their units to change. VETERANS AFFAIRS (VA) HOSPITALS had long had a

"WHAT'S NEW" COMPANY

monitor role the informational role managers play when they scan their environment for information

disseminator role the informational role managers play when they share information with others in their departments or companies

spokesperson role the informational role managers play when they share information with people outside their departments or companies

entrepreneur role the decisional role managers play when they adapt themselves, their subordinates, and their units to change reputation for red tape, inefficiency, and second-class medical treatment. Today, though, independent groups rank VA hospitals as some of the best in the country. Improvements began 15 years ago when the VA's leadership instituted a culture of accountability and change aimed at improving its entire system. Procedures and outcomes were constantly evaluated. Doctors, nurses, staffers, and administrators met regularly to review possible improvements. For example, after a VA nurse in Topeka, Kansas, noticed that rental car companies used hand held bar-code scanners to check in returned cars, she suggested using bar codes on patients' ID bracelets and their bottled medicines. Today, the VA's bar-code scanners are tied to an electronic records system that prevents nurses from handing out the wrong medicines and automatically alerts the hospital pharmacy to possibly harmful drug interactions or dangerous patient allergies.[62]

In the **disturbance handler role**, managers respond to pressures and problems so severe that they demand immediate attention and action. Managers often play the role of disturbance handler when the board of a failing company hires a new CEO, who is charged with turning the company around. After FORD MOTOR COMPANY's market share shrank from 25 percent to 16 percent and the company lost $7 billion in nine months, Alan Mulally came from Boeing to become Ford's new CEO. Mulally quickly arranged $23.5 billion in financing to cover the losses. He plans to cut costs by reducing the number of cars Ford produces, standardizing the use of shared parts across Ford vehicles, and laying off half of Ford's 82,000 factory workers. Mulally said, "I've seen this movie before [at Boeing]. Some very good and loyal people are going to leave this company between now and next summer, and that's going to be tough on everyone. [But] As demoralizing as a slide down may be, the ride back up is infinitely more exhilarating."[63]

In the **resource allocator role**, managers decide who will get what resources and how many resources they will get. For instance, E-Trade Financial, which is known for its online stock trading accounts, increased its marketing budget by $46 million to make potential customers more aware of its additional banking, loan, and mortgage services.[64] Hoping to revive sales of its luxury cars, General Motors invested $4 billion in its Cadillac division, or nearly 10 percent of its total capital budget for a division that accounts for only 4 percent of GM sales.[65] In these instances, top managers acted as resource allocators by changing budgets (E-Trade) or redirecting long-term investment in the company (GM).

In the **negotiator role**, managers negotiate schedules, projects, goals, outcomes, resources, and employee raises. When Sprint bought Nextel (another cell phone company), the Federal Communications Commission required it to buy new radios for police and firefighters because its cell phone tower transmissions were interfering with emergency service communications in hundreds of locations. SPRINT NEXTEL, which will spend $2.8 billion to fix the problem, has, for instance, been negotiating with law-enforcement agencies in Maryland and Washington to replace 35,000 radios. Unfortunately, progress has been slow, as it took Sprint a year to negotiate a $609,000 deal with the city of Fairfax, Virginia, just to develop plans to replace its radios. Furthermore, some emergency service providers don't want new radios. Instead, they're requiring Sprint to replace the crystals in their ancient radios, which would retune them to a new communications band. Since no one makes radio crystals any more, Sprint has had to grow the crystals itself in its research and development labs.[66] Negotiating, as you can see from Sprint's dilemma, is a key to success and a basic part of managerial work.

disturbance handler role the decisional role managers play when they respond to severe problems that demand immediate action

resource allocator role the decisional role managers play when they decide who gets what resources

negotiator role the decisional role managers play when they negotiate schedules, projects, goals, outcomes, resources, and employee raises

Managers perform interpersonal, informational, and decisional roles in their jobs. In fulfilling the interpersonal role, managers act as figureheads by performing ceremonial duties, as leaders by motivating and encouraging workers, and as liaisons by dealing with people outside their units. In performing their informational role, managers act as monitors by scanning their environment for information, as disseminators by sharing information with others in the company, and as spokespeople by sharing information with people outside their departments or companies. In fulfilling decisional roles, managers act as entrepreneurs by adapting their units to incremental change, as disturbance handlers by responding to larger problems that demand immediate action, as resource allocators by deciding resource recipients and amounts, and as negotiators by bargaining with others about schedules, projects, goals, outcomes, and resources.

WHAT DOES IT TAKE TO BE A MANAGER?

I didn't have the slightest idea what my job was. I walked in giggling and laughing because I had been promoted and had no idea what principles or style to be guided by. After the first day, I felt like I had run into a brick wall. (Sales Representative #1)

Suddenly, I found myself saying, boy, I can't be responsible for getting all that revenue. I don't have the time. Suddenly you've got to go from [taking care of] yourself and say now I'm the manager, and what does a manager do? It takes a while thinking about it for it to really hit you . . . a manager gets things done through other people. That's a very, very hard transition to make.[67] (Sales Representative #2)

The above statements were made by two star sales representatives, who, on the basis of their superior performance, were promoted to the position of sales manager. As their comments indicate, at first they did not feel confident about their ability to do their jobs as managers. Like most new managers, these sales managers suddenly realized that the knowledge, skills, and abilities that led to success early in their careers (and were probably responsible for their promotion into the ranks of management) would not necessarily help them succeed as managers. As sales representatives, they were responsible only for managing their own performance. But as sales managers, they were now directly responsible for supervising all of the sales representatives in their sales territories. Furthermore, they were now directly accountable for whether those sales representatives achieved their sales goals.

If performance in nonmanagerial jobs doesn't necessarily prepare you for a managerial job, then what does it take to be a manager?

After reading the next three sections, you should be able to

> 5 explain what companies look for in managers.

> 6 discuss the top mistakes that managers make in their jobs.

> 7 describe the transition that employees go through when they are promoted to management.

5 What Companies Look for in Managers

Broadly speaking, when companies look for employees who would be good managers, they look for individuals who have technical skills, human skills, conceptual skills, and the motivation to manage.[68] Exhibit 1.4 shows the relative importance of these four skills to the jobs of team leaders, first-line managers, middle managers, and top managers.

Technical skills are the ability to apply the specialized procedures, techniques, and knowledge required to get the job done. For the sales managers described above, technical skills are the ability to find new sales prospects, develop accurate sales pitches based on customer needs, and close the sale. For a nurse supervisor, technical skills include being able to insert an IV or operate a crash cart if a patient goes into cardiac arrest.

Technical skills are most important for team leaders and lower-level managers because they supervise the workers who produce products or serve customers. Team leaders and first-line managers need technical knowledge and skills to train new employees and help employees solve problems. Technical knowledge and skills are also needed to troubleshoot problems that employees can't handle. Technical skills become less important as managers rise through the managerial ranks, but they are still important.

Human skills can be summarized as the ability to work well with others. Managers with human skills work effectively within groups, encourage others to express their thoughts and feelings, are sensitive to others' needs and viewpoints, and are good listeners and communicators. Human skills are equally important at all levels of management, from first-line supervisors to CEOs. However, because lower-level managers spend much of their time solving technical problems, upper-level managers may actually spend more time dealing directly with people. On average, first-line managers spend 57 percent of their time with people, but that percentage increases to 63 percent for middle managers and 78 percent for top managers.[69]

Conceptual skills are the ability to see the organization as a whole, to understand how the different parts of the company affect each other, and to recognize how the company fits into or is affected by its external environment, such as the local community, social and economic forces, customers, and the competition. Good managers have to be able to recognize, understand, and reconcile multiple complex problems and perspectives. In other words, managers have to be smart! In fact, intelligence makes so much difference for managerial performance that managers with above-average intelligence typically outperform managers of average intelligence by approximately 48 percent.[70] Clearly, companies need to be careful to promote smart workers into management. Conceptual skills increase in importance as managers rise through the management hierarchy.

Good management involves much more than intelligence, however. For example, making the department genius a manager can be disastrous if that

technical skills the ability to apply the specialized procedures, techniques, and knowledge required to get the job done

human skills the ability to work well with others

conceptual skills the ability to see the organization as a whole, understand how the different parts affect each other, and recognize how the company fits into or is affected by its external environment

Exhibit 1.4

Relative Importance of Managerial Skills to Different Managerial Jobs

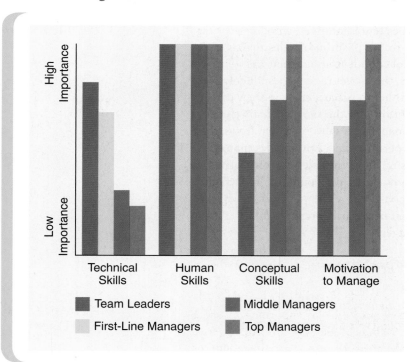

genius lacks technical skills, human skills, or one other factor known as the motivation to manage. **Motivation to manage** is an assessment of how motivated employees are to interact with superiors, participate in competitive situations, behave assertively toward others, tell others what to do, reward good behavior and punish poor behavior, perform actions that are highly visible to others, and handle and organize administrative tasks. Managers typically have a stronger motivation to manage than their subordinates, and managers at higher levels usually have a stronger motivation to manage than managers at lower levels. Furthermore, managers with a stronger motivation to manage are promoted faster, are rated as better managers by their employees, and earn more money than managers with a weak motivation to manage.[71]

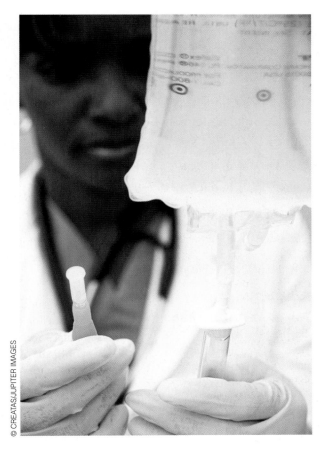

© CREATAS/JUPITER IMAGES

Technical skills are most important at the lower levels of management, but even top managers need technical skills

Review 5: *What Companies Look for in Managers*

Companies do not want one-dimensional managers. They want managers with a balance of skills. They want managers who know their stuff (technical skills), are equally comfortable working with blue-collar and white-collar employees (human skills), are able to assess the complexities of today's competitive marketplace and position their companies for success (conceptual skills), and want to assume positions of leadership and power (motivation to manage). Technical skills are most important for lower-level managers, human skills are equally important at all levels of management, and conceptual skills and motivation to manage increase in importance as managers rise through the managerial ranks.

6 Mistakes Managers Make

Another way to understand what it takes to be a manager is to look at the mistakes managers make. In other words, we can learn just as much from what managers shouldn't do as from what they should do. Exhibit 1.5 lists the top 10 mistakes managers make.

Several studies of U.S. and British managers have compared "arrivers," or managers who made it all the way to the top of their companies, with "derailers," managers who were successful early in their careers but were knocked off the fast track by the time they reached the middle to upper levels of management.[72] The researchers found that there were only a few differences between arrivers and derailers. For the most part, both groups were talented and both groups had weaknesses. But what distinguished derailers from arrivers was that derailers possessed two or more "fatal flaws" with respect to the way that they managed people! Although arrivers were by no means perfect, they usually had no more than one fatal flaw or had found ways to minimize the effects of their flaws on the people with whom they worked.

The number one mistake made by derailers was that they were insensitive to others by virtue of their abrasive, intimidating, and bullying management style. The authors of one study described a manager who walked into his subordinate's office and interrupted a meeting by saying, "I need to see you." When the subordinate tried to explain that he was not available because he was in the middle of a meeting, the

motivation to manage an assessment of how enthusiastic employees are about managing the work of others

1. Insensitive to others: abrasive, intimidating, bullying style.
2. Cold, aloof, arrogant.
3. Betrayal of trust.
4. Overly ambitious: thinking of next job, playing politics.
5. Specific performance problems with the business.
6. Overmanaging: unable to delegate or build a team.
7. Unable to staff effectively.
8. Unable to think strategically.
9. Unable to adapt to boss with different style.
10. Overdependent on advocate or mentor.

Source: M. W. McCall, Jr. & M. M. Lombardo, "What Makes a Top Executive?" *Psychology Today,* February 1983, 26–31.

Exhibit 1.5

Top 10 Mistakes That Managers Make

manager barked, "I don't give a damn. I said I wanted to see you now."[73] Not surprisingly, only 25 percent of derailers were rated by others as being good with people, compared with 75 percent of arrivers.

The second mistake was that derailers were often cold, aloof, or arrogant. Although this sounds like insensitivity to others, it has more to do with derailed managers being so smart, so expert in their areas of knowledge, that they treated others with contempt because they weren't experts, too. For example, *AT&T* called in an industrial psychologist to counsel its vice president of human resources because she had been blamed for "ruffling too many feathers" at the company.[74] Interviews with the vice president's coworkers and subordinates revealed that they thought she was brilliant, was "smarter and faster than other people," "generates a lot of ideas," and "loves to deal with complex issues." Unfortunately, these smarts were accompanied by a cold, aloof, and arrogant management style. The people she worked with complained that she does "too much too fast," treats coworkers with "disdain," "impairs teamwork," "doesn't always show her warm side," and has "burned too many bridges."[75]

The third and fourth mistakes made by the derailers, betraying a trust and being overly ambitious, reflect a lack of concern for coworkers and subordinates. Betraying a trust doesn't mean being dishonest. Instead, it means making others look bad by not doing what you said you would do when you said you would do it. That mistake, in itself, is not fatal because managers and their workers aren't machines. Tasks go undone in every company every single business day. There's always too much to do and not enough time, people, money, or resources to do it. The fatal betrayal of trust is failing to inform others when things will not be done on time. This failure to admit mistakes, quickly inform others of the mistakes, take responsibility for the mistakes, and then fix them without blaming others clearly distinguished the behavior of derailers from arrivers.

The fourth mistake, as mentioned above, was being overly political and ambitious. Managers who always have their eye on their next job rarely establish more than superficial relationships with peers and coworkers. In their haste to gain credit for successes that would be noticed by upper management, they make the fatal mistake of treating people as though they don't matter. An employee with an overly ambitious boss described him this way, "He treats employees coldly, even cruelly. He assigns blame without regard to responsibility, and takes all the credit for himself. I once had such a boss, and he gave me a new definition of shared risk: If something I did was successful, he took the credit. If it wasn't, I got the blame."[76]

The fatal mistakes of being unable to delegate, build a team, and staff effectively indicate that many derailed managers were unable to make the most basic transition to managerial work: to quit being hands-on doers and get work done through others. Two things go wrong when managers make these mistakes. First, when managers meddle in decisions that their subordinates should be making—when they can't stop being doers—they alienate the people who work for them. Rich Dowd, founder of Dowd Associates, an executive search firm, admits to constantly monitoring and interrupting employees because they weren't doing the job "in the way I saw fit, even when their work was outstanding." According to Richard Kilburg of Johns Hopkins University, when managers interfere with workers decisions, "You . . . have a tendency to lose your most creative people. They're able to say, 'Screw this. I'm not staying here.'"[77] Indeed, one employee told Dowd that if he was going to do her job for her, she would quit. Second, because they are trying to do their subordinates' jobs in addition to their own, managers who fail to delegate will not have enough time to do much of anything well.

Review 6: Mistakes Managers Make

Another way to understand what it takes to be a manager is to look at the top mistakes managers make. Five of the most important mistakes made by managers are being abrasive and intimidating; being cold, aloof, or arrogant; betraying trust; being overly ambitious; and failing to build a team and then delegate to that team.

7 The Transition to Management: The First Year

In her book *Becoming a Manager: Mastery of a New Identity*, Harvard Business School professor Linda Hill followed the development of 19 people in their first year as managers. Her study found that becoming a manager produced a profound psychological transition that changed the way these managers viewed themselves and others. As shown in Exhibit 1.6, the evolution of the managers' thoughts, expectations, and realities over the course of their first year in management reveals the magnitude of the changes they experienced.

Initially, the managers in Hill's study believed that their job was to exercise formal authority and to manage tasks—basically being the boss, telling others what to do, making decisions, and getting things done. One manager said, "Being the manager means running my own office, using my ideas and thoughts." Another said, "[The office is] my baby. It's my job to make sure it works." In fact, most of the new managers were attracted to management positions because they wanted to be "in charge." Surprisingly, the new managers did not believe that their job was to manage people. The only aspects of people management mentioned by the new managers were hiring and firing.

After six months, most of the new managers had concluded that their initial expectations about managerial work were wrong. Management wasn't being "the boss." It wasn't just about making decisions and telling others what to do. The first surprise was the fast pace and heavy workload involved in being a manager. Said one manager, "This job is much harder than you think. It is 40 to 50 percent more work than being a producer! Who would have ever guessed?" The pace of managerial work was startling, too. Another manager said, "You have eight or nine people looking for your time . . . coming into and

Managers who fail to delegate will not have enough time to do much of anything well.

MANAGERS' INITIAL EXPECTATIONS			AFTER SIX MONTHS AS A MANAGER			AFTER A YEAR AS A MANAGER					
JAN	FEB	MAR	APR	MAY	JUN	JUL	AUG	SEP	OCT	NOV	DEC

MANAGERS' INITIAL EXPECTATIONS	AFTER SIX MONTHS AS A MANAGER	AFTER A YEAR AS A MANAGER
⊙ Be the boss	⊙ Initial expectations were wrong	⊙ No longer "doer"
⊙ Have formal authority	⊙ Fast pace	⊙ Communicating, listening, and giving positive reinforcement
⊙ Manage tasks	⊙ Heavy workload	⊙ Learning to adapt to and control stress
⊙ Job is not managing people	⊙ Job is to be problem-solver and troubleshooter for subordinates	⊙ Job is people development

Source: L. A. Hill, *Becoming a Manager: Mastery of a New Identity* (Boston: Harvard Business School Press, 1992).

Exhibit 1.6

The Transition to Management: Initial Expectations, after Six Months, and after a Year

out of your office all day long." A somewhat frustrated manager declared that management was "a job that never ended . . . a job you couldn't get your hands around."

Informal descriptions like this are consistent with studies indicating that the average first-line manager spends no more than two minutes on a task before being interrupted by a request from a subordinate, a phone call, or an e-mail. The pace is somewhat less hurried for top managers, who spend an average of approximately nine minutes on a task before having to switch to another. In practice, this means that supervisors may perform 30 different tasks per hour, while top managers perform seven different tasks per hour, with each task typically different from the one that preceded it. A manager described this frenetic level of activity by saying, "The only time you are in control is when you shut your door, and then I feel I am not doing the job I'm supposed to be doing, which is being with the people."

The other major surprise after six months on the job was that the managers' expectations about what they should do as managers were very different from their subordinates' expectations. Initially, the managers defined their jobs as helping their subordinates perform their jobs well. For the managers, who still defined themselves as doers rather than managers, assisting their subordinates meant going out on sales calls or handling customer complaints. One manager said, "I like going out with the rep, who may need me to lend him my credibility as manager. I like the challenge, the joy in closing. I go out with the reps and we make the call and talk about the customer; it's fun." But when the managers "assisted" in this way, their subordinates were resentful and viewed their help as interference. The subordinates wanted their managers to help them by solving problems that they couldn't solve. Once the managers realized this contradiction, they embraced their role as problem-solver and troubleshooter. Thus, they could help without interfering with their subordinates' jobs.

After a year on the job, most of the managers thought of themselves as managers and no longer as doers. In making the transition, they finally realized that people management was the most important part of their jobs. One manager summarized the lesson that had taken him a year to learn by saying, "As many demands as managers have on their time, I think their primary responsibility is people development. Not production, but people development." Another indication of how much their views had changed was that most of the managers now regretted the rather heavy-handed approach they had used in their early attempts to manage their subordinates. "I wasn't good at managing . . . , so I was bossy like a first-grade teacher." "Now I see that I started out as a drill sergeant. I was inflexible, just a lot of how-to's." By the end of the year, most of the managers had abandoned their authoritarian approach for one based on communication, listening, and positive reinforcement. One manager explained, "Last night at five I handed out an award in the boardroom just to the individual.

It was the first time in his career that he had [earned] $100,000, and I gave him a piece of glass [a small award] and said I'd heard a rumor that somebody here just crossed over $100,000 and I said congratulations, shook his hand, and walked away. It was not public in the sense that I gathered everybody around. But I knew and he did too."

Finally, after beginning their year as managers in frustration, the managers came to feel comfortable with their subordinates, with the demands of their jobs, and with their emerging managerial styles. While being managers had made them acutely aware of their limitations and their need to develop as people, it also provided them with an unexpected reward of coaching and developing the people who worked for them. One manager said, "It gives me the best feeling to see somebody do something well after I have helped them. I get excited." Another stated, "I realize now that when I accepted the position of branch manager that it is truly an exciting vocation. It is truly awesome, even at this level; it can be terribly challenging and terribly exciting."

Review 7: The Transition to Management: The First Year

Managers often begin their jobs by using more formal authority and less people management. However, most managers find that being a manager has little to do with "bossing" their subordinates. After six months on the job, the managers were surprised at the fast pace and heavy workload and that "helping" their subordinates was viewed as interference. After a year on the job, most of the managers had come to think of themselves not as doers, but as managers who get things done through others. And because they finally realized that people management was the most important part of their job, most of them had abandoned their authoritarian approach for one based on communication, listening, and positive reinforcement.

WHY MANAGEMENT MATTERS

If you walk down the aisle of the business section in your local bookstore, you'll find hundreds of books that explain precisely what companies need to do to be successful. Unfortunately, the best-selling business books tend to be faddish, changing dramatically every few years. One thing that hasn't changed, though, is the importance of good people and good management: Companies can't succeed for long without them.

After reading this section, you should be able to

8 explain how and why companies can create competitive advantage through people.

8 Competitive Advantage through People

In his books, *Competitive Advantage through People* and *The Human Equation: Building Profits by Putting People First*, Stanford University business professor Jeffrey Pfeffer contends that what separates top-performing companies from their competitors is the way they treat their work forces—in other words, their management.[78]

Pfeffer found that managers in top-performing companies used ideas like employment security, selective hiring, self-managed teams and decentralization, high pay contingent on company performance, extensive training, reduced status distinctions (between managers and employees), and extensive sharing of financial information to achieve financial performance that, on average, was 40 percent higher than that of other companies. These ideas, which are explained in detail in Exhibit 1.7, help organizations develop work forces that are smarter, better trained, more motivated, and more committed than their competitors' work forces. And, as indicated by the phenomenal growth and return on investment earned by these companies, smarter, better trained, and more committed work forces provide superior products and service to customers, who keep buying and, by telling others about their positive experiences, bring in new customers.

Pfeffer also argues that companies that invest in their people will create long-lasting competitive advantages that are difficult for other companies to duplicate. Indeed, other studies clearly demonstrate that sound management practices can produce substantial advantages in four critical areas of organizational performance: sales revenues, profits, stock market returns, and customer satisfaction.

In terms of sales revenues and profits, a study of nearly 1,000 U.S. firms found that companies that use *just some* of the ideas shown in Exhibit 1.7 had $27,044 more sales per employee and $3,814 more profit per employee than companies that didn't. For a 100-person company, these differences amount to $2.7 million more in sales and nearly $400,000 more in annual profit! For a 1,000-person company, the difference grows to $27 million more in sales and $4 million more in annual profit!

Another study investigating the effect of investing in people on company sales found that poorly performing companies that adopted management techniques as

Exhibit 1.7

Competitive Advantage through People: Management Practices

1. Employment Security—Employment security is the ultimate form of commitment that companies can make to their workers. Employees can innovate and increase company productivity without fearing the loss of their jobs.

2. Selective Hiring—If employees are the basis for a company's competitive advantage, and those employees have employment security, then the company needs to aggressively recruit and selectively screen applicants in order to hire the most talented employees available.

3. Self-Managed Teams and Decentralization—Self-managed teams are responsible for their own hiring, purchasing, job assignments, and production. Self-managed teams can often produce enormous increases in productivity through increased employee commitment and creativity. Decentralization allows employees who are closest to (and most knowledgeable about) problems, production, and customers to make timely decisions. Decentralization increases employee satisfaction and commitment.

4. High Wages Contingent on Organizational Performance—High wages are needed to attract and retain talented workers and to indicate that the organization values its workers. Employees, like company founders, shareholders, and managers, need to share in the financial rewards when the company is successful. Why? Because employees who have a financial stake in their companies are more likely to take a long-run view of the business and think like business owners.

5. Training and Skill Development—Like a high-tech company that spends millions of dollars to upgrade computers or research and development labs, a company whose competitive advantage is based on its people must invest in the training and skill development of its people.

6. Reduction of Status Differences—These are fancy words that indicate that the company treats everyone, no matter what the job, as equal. There are no reserved parking spaces. Everyone eats in the same cafeteria and has similar benefits. The result: much improved communication as employees focus on problems and solutions rather than on how they are less valued than managers.

7. Sharing Information—If employees are to make decisions that are good for the long-run health and success of the company, they need to be given information about costs, finances, productivity, development times, and strategies that was previously known only by company managers.

Source: J. Pfeffer, *The Human Equation: Building Profits by Putting People First* (Boston: Harvard Business School Press, 1996).

simple as setting expectations (establishing goals, results, and schedules), coaching (informal, ongoing discussions between managers and subordinates about what is being done well and what could be done better), reviewing (annual, formal discussion about results), and rewarding (adjusting salaries and bonuses based on employee performance and results) were able to improve their average return on investment from 5.1 percent to 19.7 percent and increase sales by $94,000 per employee![79] So, in addition to significantly improving the profitability of healthy companies, sound management practices can turn around failing companies.

In 2007, Fortune ranked Google as America's Best Company to Work for. One of the perks at the Googleplex: Free—and good—food at the cafeteria. And that includes a company sushi chef.

To determine the effect of investing in people on stock market performance, researchers matched companies on *Fortune* magazine's list of "100 Best Companies to Work for in America" with companies that were similar in industry, size, and—this is key—operating performance. In other words, both sets of companies were equally good performers; the key difference was how well they treated their employees. For both sets of companies, the researchers found that employee attitudes such as job satisfaction changed little from year to year. The people who worked for the "100 Best" companies were consistently much more satisfied with their jobs and employers year after year than were employees in the matched companies. More importantly, those stable differences in employee attitudes were strongly related to differences in stock market performance. Over a three-year period, an investment in the "100 Best Companies to Work for" would have resulted in an 82 percent cumulative stock return compared with just 37 percent for the matched companies.[80] This difference is remarkable given that both sets of companies were equally good performers at the beginning of the period.

Finally, research also indicates that managers have an important effect on customer satisfaction. Many people find this surprising. They don't understand how managers, who are largely responsible for what goes on inside the company, can affect what goes on outside the company. They wonder how managers, who often interact with customers under negative conditions (when customers are angry or dissatisfied), can actually improve customer satisfaction. It turns out that managers influence customer satisfaction through employee satisfaction. When employees are satisfied with their jobs, their bosses, and the companies they work for, they provide much better service to customers.[81] In turn, customers are more satisfied, too. You will learn more about the service-profit chain in Chapter 18 on managing service and manufacturing operation.

Review 8: *Competitive Advantage through People*

Why does management matter? Well-managed companies are competitive because their work forces are smarter, better trained, more motivated, and more committed. Furthermore, companies that practice good management consistently have greater sales revenues, profits, and stock market performance than companies that don't. Finally, good management matters because good management leads to satisfied employees who, in turn, provide better service to customers. Because employees tend to treat customers the same way that their managers treat them, good management can improve customer satisfaction.

© VEER

Each chapter has a related self-assessment to help you consider how your own perspectives influence your management skills. Each assessment tool starts with a short description and ends with basic scoring information. (Your instructor will have interpretations of your scores.) As you advance through the book, take time to review your assessment scores together. Doing so will help you see patterns in your own perceptions and behaviors and give you insights into how those perceptions may affect your performance as a manager.

Is Management for You?

As you learned in Section 7 of this chapter, many managers begin their careers in management with specific ideas about what it means to be the boss. Although you may want to be a manager because of excitement, status, power, or rewards, knowing how to manage is not automatic; it requires specific skills and competencies, as well as a desire to manage. This assessment is meant to establish your baseline ability in the skills covered in the chapter. It will not tell you whether you should or should not be a manager, or whether you have "what it takes" to be a manager. It will, however, give you feedback on general skills that influence your overall managerial style.

Be candid as you complete the assessment by circling the appropriate responses.[82]

ML = Most like me
SL = Somewhat like me
NS = Not sure
SU = Somewhat unlike me
MU = Most unlike me

1. I can get others to do what I want them to do.
    ML   SL   NS   SU   MU

2. I frequently evaluate my job performance.
    ML   SL   NS   SU   MU

3. I prefer not to get involved in office politics.
    ML   SL   NS   SU   MU

4. I like the freedom that open-ended goals provide me.
    ML   SL   NS   SU   MU

5. I work best when things are orderly and calm.
    ML   SL   NS   SU   MU

6. I enjoy making oral presentations to groups of people.
    ML   SL   NS   SU   MU

7. I am confident in my abilities to accomplish difficult tasks.
    ML   SL   NS   SU   MU

8. I do not like to write.
    ML   SL   NS   SU   MU

9. I like solving difficult puzzles.
    ML   SL   NS   SU   MU

10. I am an organized person.
    ML   SL   NS   SU   MU

11. I have difficulty telling others they made a mistake.
    ML   SL   NS   SU   MU

12. I like to work set hours each day.
    ML   SL   NS   SU   MU

13. I view paperwork as a trivial task.
    ML   SL   NS   SU   MU

14. I like to help others learn new things.
    ML   SL   NS   SU   MU

15. I prefer to work alone.
    ML   SL   NS   SU   MU

16. I believe it is who you know, not what you know, that counts.
    ML   SL   NS   SU   MU

17. I enjoy doing several things at once.
    ML   SL   NS   SU   MU

18. I am good at managing money.
    ML   SL   NS   SU   MU

19. I would rather back down from an argument than let it get out of hand.
    ML   SL   NS   SU   MU

20. I am computer literate.
    ML   SL   NS   SU   MU

Scoring

Start by reversing your scores for items 5, 8, 11, 15, and 16. For example, if you used ML, change it to MU, and vice versa; if you used SL, change it to SU, and vice versa. Now assign each answer a point value.

KEY TERMS

conceptual skills 22
controlling 11
disseminator role 19
disturbance handler role 20
effectiveness 7
efficiency 7
entrepreneur role 19
figurehead role 18
first-line managers 15
leader role 18
leading 11
liaison role 18
management 7
meta-analysis 10
middle managers 14
monitor role 19
motivation to manage 23
negotiator role 20
organizing 9
people skills 22
planning 8
resource allocator role 20
spokesperson role 19
team leaders 16
technical skills 22
top managers 12

Number of ML answers ____ times 5 points each = ____   Number of MU answers ____ times 1 point each = ____

Number of SL answers ____ times 4 points each = ____   TOTAL = ____

Number of NS answers ____ times 3 points each = ____   You can find the interpretation for your score at:

Number of SU answers ____ times 2 points each = ____   **academic.cengage.com/management/williams.**

MANAGEMENT DECISION

Making decisions is part of every manager's job. To give you practice at managerial decision making, each chapter contains a "Management Decision" assignment focused on a particular decision. You'll need to decide what to do in the given situation and then answer several questions to explain your choices.

Betting on an Employee

Although you've been in your new executive management position for barely a year, you have had abundant opportunities for decision making.[83] You have had the final say on a new advertising campaign, an employee washroom remodel, and the selection of the company's uniform vendor. You've met with community leaders to discuss your company's participation in a fundraiser for the local food pantry and with the press to announce your company's plan to bring 50 new jobs to the area. Surprisingly, however, you've had little experience with human resources issues.

But that changed this morning, when a colleague mentioned that a relatively new executive assistant named Andrew had taken a second job with another company in the evenings. Andrew has been at your company for only three months, but in that time has proved to be reliable, resourceful, and intelligent.

"He's doing well, though. Doesn't he like his job here?" you asked your colleague.

"He does, but he can earn an extra $250 a week at the second job. He says he's saving to go back to school," she responded.

"Oh," you replied. "Well, I'll talk to him."

Andrew is fast becoming a valuable employee, but the company has a policy against moonlighting. You expect your employees to give their best each day on the job. If they spend what would otherwise be leisure time working for someone else, they won't be fresh, alert, and productive when they come to work for you. At the same time, you remember how you worked several jobs to save money for graduate school. If you had been able to make enough money at one job, you wouldn't have pushed yourself to work three. You think briefly about giving Andrew a raise, but then recall that the company's policy is not to review new employees for raises or promotions until they've spent at least six months on the job. Andrew is only halfway there. Still, it would be a shame to see such a promising employee lose his spark from overwork and fatigue.

Questions

1. How is this decision emblematic of your job as a manager and your transition into that position?

2. What are the advantages and disadvantages to giving Andrew a raise before the customary period?

3. Do you break the company policy and give Andrew a raise three months early, or not? If not, how do you handle the moonlighting situation? Explain your decision.

4. Regardless of Andrew's situation, would it be better in the long run for your company to continue or end its "no moonlighting" policy?

MANAGEMENT TEAM DECISION

From sports to school to work to civic involvement, working in teams is increasingly part of our experience. But although working in teams is more and more common, making decisions as teams is not necessarily any

easier. You will learn more about managing teams in Chapter 10, but to give you more experience with teamwork, a "Management Team Decision" exercise designed for a group of three to five students is included in each chapter. As a group, you must come to a mutually agreeable decision on the scenario presented. Each "Management Team Decision" will focus on a management topic presented in the chapter. For Chapter 1, you'll work with the management function of planning and organizing, as you decide whether to let a team member have a night off.

Baggage Claims—Is RFID the Ticket?

What a trip![84] You're exhausted from changing planes (three times because of cancellations) and trying to corral your colleagues as well as their luggage. And after all the cramped seats, complaining travelers, long lines, and marginal food, your team still hasn't come to a decision about what do to—at your own airport.

Last month, you and your management team from Hartsfield-Jackson Atlanta International Airport began discussing using radio-frequency identification (RFID) tags in the airport's baggage-handling operations. Recent reports on lost luggage have caused more than a ripple of concern, with roughly one in every 150 U.S. passengers losing a bag in any given year. U.S. airlines spent an estimated $400 million to replace mishandled luggage in a recent year, yet passengers are regularly incensed that the airlines give only partial reimbursements for lost bags and belongings. The cost of lost luggage, however, is not just the $400 million in reimbursements. There's the time and expense of staffing large customer-service departments to take complaints, process claims, track down and identify missing baggage, and deliver found bags to either the owner's travel destination or home. Multiple deliveries are often made, as the bag arrives at the passenger's destination after he or she has left for another destination or returned home. The International Air Transport Association estimates that airlines worldwide could save $760 million a year by reducing lost luggage.

Your team would love to reduce the costs associated with lost luggage at Hartsfield-Jackson (ATL), which consistently wins the title of world's busiest passenger airport. Nearly 6.5 million travelers pass through the airport in a given month and bring about 75 metric tons of luggage with them. That's more than the either the monthly amount of mail or commercial freight (think FedEx and UPS) that passes through the airport's facilities!

Thirty-one airlines take off and land at ATL, but Delta accounts for over 58 percent of passenger volume. As (bad) luck would have it, Delta has a dismal ranking for lost luggage, reporting 6.8 mishandled bags per 1,000, second only to US Airways' 7.7 losses per 1,000. Company-wide, Delta handles 1.3 bags per passenger, and there's no reason to think this number is any lower in Atlanta, its biggest hub. That means Delta alone puts over 160,000 bags into the ATL system each day!

To manage this tremendous flow of personal belongings, ATL uses the bar-coding system in use at the majority of U.S. airports. Adhesive paper tags are very economical at 4 cents each, but they also rip, smudge, get misread, or get torn off completely. Scanners even have trouble with twisted tags. Baggage sorting with bar-coded tags is only 80 to 90 percent accurate. And once they're printed, that's it. If a passenger's destination changes due to, say, inclement weather, flight cancellations, or being rerouted, the bar-code label can't change to reflect the new itinerary.

Armed with all this, well, baggage, your team went on a trip to Las Vegas's McCarran International Airport, which has been using radio-frequency identification tags to manage its bag handling. McCarran is the fifth-busiest airport in the United States, and it handles more than 70,000 outbound bags per day. Using bar-code readers, as many as 7,000 bags per day were not read properly and tossed into an "unknown" pile to be hand sorted. There was also the headache of lost luggage for passengers on quick three- and four-day excursions to consider. In the end, the airport decided to invest in a system based on RFID tags. Tags costs 21 cents apiece, or five times the cost of a bar-code tag, but the accuracy of the RFID system has cut the number of hand-sorted bags by 90 percent, and the tags can be rewritten electronically mid-travel if itineraries change. The RFID system has enabled the airport to let inbound passengers on long flights check their bags all the way to their casino or hotel, so that their luggage is waiting for them when they arrive.

What to do? ATL is already in the middle of a $5.4 billion campaign to improve facilities. Management does a great job managing the finances of the airport, and Hartsfield Jackson is considered a good risk (meaning a safe bet) for lenders. The hardware required to start using RFID is cheaper than maintaining the hardware that manages the system of traditional bar-code tags, but the difference in the cost of the tags is substantial if decreasing. And who's going to foot the bill? Should the airlines, which are nearly all suffering financially, be expected to pay for the program that will ultimately benefit them as well? Delta already stopped paying its $3.4 million annual rent to the airport as part of its bankruptcy restructuring. If they don't pay for the hardware required to read the tags, should airlines at least pay for the tags themselves?

Maybe you need to take another trip, this time to Furth, Germany, where Siemens, a provider of industrial software, has built a mock airport to demonstrate how automated technology can help airports improve efficiencies in nearly every aspect of their organization.

Siemens's automated luggage belts equipped with RFID readers can move at up to 30 feet per second, which means that passengers wouldn't have to wait hours for their bags to show up at the carousel, as they often do now. Even though the people at McCarran were helpful, their airport has less than half the traffic of Hartsfield-Jackson. Perhaps consulting with the folks at Siemens will help you better frame the issues for your massive operations. Or maybe you'd be better off visiting Denver International Airport, which is known for its notoriously flawed—and inefficient—automated baggage handling system.

Form a team of four or five students to act as the management team of Hartsfield-Jackson International Airport to determine if the tradeoffs of implementing RFID are worth the costs.

Questions

1. Implementing RFID is a complex situation that draws on many managerial roles. Describe the ways that the management team from Hartsfield-Jackson will fulfill Mintzberg's managerial roles and subroles (see Exhibit 1.3) as it thinks through the decision.

2. Additional information gathering at Siemens's mock airport is a good idea, but who to send? Identify how many and which type of managers to recommend for a fact-finding team and to tour the facility at Furth, Germany. Estimate how much money will be required to fund such a trip.

3. Do you implement RFID at Hartsfield-Jackson immediately, or do you schedule a trip to Furth, Germany, before deciding? Or do you decide not to implement RFID at all?

PRACTICE BEING A MANAGER

Finding a Management Job

Management is a wide ranging and exciting area of work. One way to gain a sense of the possibilities is to study the advertisements for management job openings. Companies advertise their management openings in a variety of ways, including print advertisements in such newspapers as the *Wall Street Journal* (especially its Friday career section) and online ads at job sites like Monster.com and CareerBuilder.com.

Step 1: Find a job you'd like to have. Search through the newspaper and online ads and locate several detailed job descriptions for management positions. Select the one that you find most appealing—a job that you could picture yourself interviewing for either in the near future or later in your career. Do not be too concerned about your current qualifications in making your selection, but you should see realistic prospects of meeting the qualifications over time (if a job requires an MBA, for example, you should see yourself completing this degree sometime in the future). Print your selected detailed job description and bring it to your next class session.

Step 2: Share your job description. In class, your professor will assign you to a pair or group of three. Write your name on your selected management job description, and exchange your job description with your partner(s). Each member of the pair or triad should now have a job description other than their own.

Step 3: Think like a hiring manager. Read the job description you received from your partner. Imagine that you are the manager responsible for hiring someone to fill this position. A human resources specialist in your company has already screened the applicants' resume and background. Thus, you may assume that your partner has met all the basic qualifications for the job. Your job as a senior manager is to ask questions that might get beyond the resume to the person—what might you ask to learn if someone is well-suited to thrive in this management job, and in your company?

Step 4: Take turns interviewing. Each member of the group should be briefly interviewed (5–10 minutes) for the job they selected.

Step 5: Debrief. Discuss your experiences with your partner(s). What was it like to be interviewed for your selected position? What was it like to role-play interviewing someone for a management position? Now imagine the real thing. Brainstorm about how you might prepare yourself over time to be the top candidate for an attractive management position, and to be a senior manager responsible for hiring the best qualified managers for your company.

Step 6: Discuss with the class. Share your interview experiences and brainstorming ideas with the class. Do you hear any similarities across the pairs/triads? What ideas or questions are most significant to you as you consider management job interviews?

DEVELOP YOUR CAREER POTENTIAL

Interview Two Managers

Welcome to the first "Develop Your Career Potential" activity! These assignments have one purpose: to help you develop your present and future capabilities as a manager. What you will learn through these assignments is not traditional "book learning" based on memorization and regurgitation, but practical knowledge and skills that help managers perform their jobs better. Lessons from some of the assignments—for example, goal setting—can be used for immediate benefit. Other lessons will obviously take time to accomplish, but you can still benefit now by making specific plans for future improvement.

Step 1: Interview two practicing managers. In her book *Becoming a Manager: Mastery of a New Identity*, Harvard Business School professor Linda Hill conducted extensive interviews with 19 people in their first year as managers.[85] To learn firsthand what it's like to be a manager, interview two managers that you know, asking them some of the same questions, listed below, that Hill asked her managers. Be sure to interview managers with different levels of experience. Interview one person with at least five years' experience as a manager and then interview another person with no more than two years' experience as a manager. Ask the managers these questions:

1. Briefly describe your current position and responsibilities.
2. What do your subordinates expect from you on the job?
3. What are the major stresses and challenges you face on the job?
4. What, if anything, do you dislike about the job?
5. What do you like best about your job?
6. What are the critical differences between average managers and top-performing managers?
7. Think about the skills and knowledge that you need to be effective in your job. What are they, and how did you acquire them?
8. What have been your biggest mistakes thus far? Could you have avoided them? If so, how?

Step 2: Prepare to discuss your findings. Prepare to discuss your findings in class or write a report (if assigned by your instructor). What conclusions can you draw from your interview data?

REEL TO REAL

BIZ FLIX
8 Mile

Jimmy "B-Rabbit" Smith, Jr. (Eminem), wants to be a successful rapper and to prove that a white man can create moving sounds. He works days at a plant run by the North Detroit Stamping Company and pursues his music at night, sometimes on the plant's grounds. The film's title refers to Detroit's northern boundary, which divides the city's white and African American populations. This film gives a gritty look at Detroit's hip-hop culture in 1995 and Jimmy's desire to be accepted by it. Eminem's original songs "Lose Yourself" and "8 Mile" received Golden Globe and Academy Award nominations. This scene is an edited composite of two brief sequences that show Jimmy interacting with his manager, Manny, at the stamping plant.

What to Watch for and Ask Yourself

1. What kind of manager is Manny?
2. What management function is Manny fulfilling when he considers giving Jimmy extra shifts?
3. What managerial roles do you see in the clip?

MANAGEMENT WORKPLACE
Original Penguin

Penguins have always been cool. But golf shirts with a little flapping bird printed on them experienced a lull in coolness. In fact, their popularity remained frozen for two decades, largely because they were worn by aging golfers. Now the penguins are back, flapping furiously—and, many would argue, coolly—not just on golf shirts but also on a wide array of men's and women's clothing and accessories, including shirts, shoes, hats, belts, neckties, handbags, and even bathing suits. These items represent the extreme makeover of a 50-year-old brand of clothing called Original Penguin. Now owned by Perry Ellis International, the Original Penguin brand of clothing is experiencing rejuvenation—thanks largely to Penguin's vice president, Chris Kolbe. This video allows you to follow Kolbe around the management workplace to see what his job entails.

What to Watch for and Ask Yourself

1. Describe the conceptual skills you think Chris Kolbe needs for his job as vice president of Original Penguin.
2. Which management roles does Kolbe fulfill in the course of the video segment?
3. What do you think is the most difficult part of Kolbe's job? Why?

CHAPTER 2

The History of Management

Learning Outcomes:

1 Explain the origins of management.

2 Explain the history of scientific management.

3 Discuss the history of bureaucratic and administrative management.

4 Explain the history of human relations management.

5 Discuss the history of operations, information, systems, and contingency management.

In This Chapter:

WHAT WOULD YOU DO?

ISG Steelton–International Steel Group, Steelton, Pennsylvania.[1] As the day-shift supervisor at the steel plant, you summon the six college students who are working for you this summer doing whatever you need done (sweeping up, sandblasting the inside of boilers that are down for maintenance, running errands, and so forth). You walk them across the plant to a field where the company stores scrap-metal "leftovers." The area, about the size of a football field, is stacked with organized piles of metal. You explain that everything they see has just been sold. Metal prices, which have been depressed, have finally risen enough that the company can earn a small profit by selling its scrap.

You point out that railroad tracks divide the field into parallel sectors, like the lines on a football field, so that each stack of metal is no more than 15 feet from a track. Each stack contains 390 pieces of metal. Each piece weighs 92 pounds and is about a yard long and just over 4 inches high and 4 inches wide. You tell the students that working as a team, they are to pick up each piece, walk up a ramp to a railroad car that will be positioned next to each stack, and then neatly position and stack the metal for shipment. That's right, you repeat, *92 pounds, walk* up the ramp, and *carry* the metal onto the rail car. Anticipating their questions, you explain that a forklift could be used only if the metal was stored on wooden pallets (it isn't), if the pallets could withstand the weight of the metal (they would be crushed), and if you, as their supervisor, had forklifts and people trained to run them (you don't). In other words, the only way to get the metal into the rail cars is for the students to carry it.

Based on an old report from the last time the company sold some of the metal, you know that over an eight-hour shift, workers typically loaded about 30 pieces of metal parts per hour. At that pace, though, it will take your six students six weeks to load all of the metal, and the purchasing manager who sold it says it must be shipped in two weeks. That means that without more workers (there's a hiring freeze) and without forklifts, all of the metal has to be loaded by hand by these six workers in two weeks. But how do you do that? What would motivate the students to work much, much harder than they have all summer? They've gotten used to a leisurely pace and easy job assignments. Motivation might help, but motivation will only get so much done.

After all, short of illegal steroids, nothing is going to work once muscle fatigue kicks in from carrying those 92-pound pieces of metal up a ramp all day long. What can you change about the way the work is done to deal with the unavoidable physical fatigue? **If you were the supervisor in charge, what would you do?**

ACTIVITIES + VIDEOS

CengageNOW Audio study guide, electronic flashcards, author FAQ videos, On the Job and Biz Flix videos, concept tutorial, and concept exercise

Web (academic.cengage.com/management/williams) Quiz, PowerPoint slides, and glossary terms for this chapter

"WHAT'S NEW" COMPANIES

ISG Steelton
Ford Motor Company
Chicago Harvester
Pullman Company
Midvale Steel Company
Comambault
Western Electric Company
AT&T
New Jersey Bell Telephone
Beretta
Oldsmobile Motor Works

Study Tip

Build a management time line. On a blank sheet of paper, construct a time line that shows the evolution of management theory. Draw a line that divides the paper down the middle. Then, place management theories on one side and overall historical events on the other. This will help you see what was happening in management as a part of what was happening in the world in general. Examining theories in context can help you identify trends that are likely to emerge in the future.

Certainly, the problems that the ISG steel plant supervisor is facing in the *What Would You Do?* case are difficult, but they aren't unique. Each day, managers are asked to solve challenging problems and are given only a limited amount of time, people, or resources. Yet it's still their responsibility to get things done on time and within budget. Furthermore, most of the management practices and ideas that today's managers use to solve their daily problems have their roots in the people and ideas you'll read about in this chapter on the history of management. Indeed, by reading the theories in this chapter, you will be able to figure out a solution to the ISG supervisor's problems.

We begin this chapter by reviewing the origins of management ideas and practice throughout history and the historical changes that produced the need for managers. Next, you'll learn about various schools of management thought. Beginning with scientific management, you'll learn about the key contributions made by Frederick Taylor, Frank and Lillian Gilbreth, and Henry Gantt. Next, you'll read about Max Weber and bureaucratic management and then about Henri Fayol and administrative management. Following that, you'll learn about human relations management and the ideas of Mary Parker Follett (constructive conflict and coordination), Elton Mayo (Hawthorne Studies), and Chester Barnard (cooperation and acceptance of authority). Finally, you'll learn about the history of operations management, information management, systems management, and contingency management.

IN THE BEGINNING

In this textbook, you learn that *management* is getting work done through others, that *strategic* plans are overall plans that clarify how a company will serve customers and position itself against competitors over the next two to five years, and that *just-in-time inventory* is a system in which the parts needed to make something arrive from suppliers just as they are needed at each stage of production. Today's managers would undoubtedly view those ideas and many of the others presented in the book as self-evident. For example, tell today's managers to "reward workers for improved production or performance," "set specific goals to increase motivation," or "innovate to create and sustain a competitive advantage," and they'll respond, "Duh! Who doesn't know that?" A mere 125 years ago, however, business ideas and practices were so different that today's widely accepted management ideas would have been as "self-evident" as space travel, cell phones, and the Internet. In fact, 125 years ago, management wasn't yet a field of study, and there were no management jobs and no management careers. Now, of course, managers and management are such an integral part of the business world that it's hard to imagine organizations without them. So if there were no managers 125 years ago, but you can't walk down the hall today without bumping into one, where did management come from?

After reading the next section, you should be able to

1 explain the origins of management.

1 The Origins of Management

Management as a field of study may be just 125 years old, but management ideas and practices have actually been used from the earliest times of recorded history. For example, 2,500 years before management researchers called it *job enrichment,* the Greeks learned that they could improve the productivity of boring repetitive tasks by performing them to music. The basic idea was to use a flute, drum, or song lyrics to pace people to work in unison using the same efficient motions, stimulate them to work faster and longer, and make the boring work more fun.[2] Although we can find the seeds of many of today's management ideas throughout history, not until the last two centuries did systematic changes in the nature of work and organizations create a compelling need for managers.

Let's begin our discussion of the origins of management by learning about **1.1 management ideas and practice throughout history** *and* **1.2 why we need managers today**.

1.1 Management Ideas and Practice throughout History

Examples of management thought and practice can be found throughout history.[3] For example, as shown in Exhibit 2.1, in 5000 BC in an early instance of managing information, which is part of the control function, Sumerian priests developed a formal system of writing (scripts) that allowed them to record and keep track of the goods, flocks and herds of animals, coins, land, and buildings that were contributed to their temples. Furthermore, to encourage honesty in such dealings, the Sumerians instituted managerial controls that required all priests to submit written accounts of the transactions, donations, and payments they handled to the chief priest. And just like clay or stone tablets and animal-skin documents, these scripts were first used to manage the business of Sumerian temples.[4] Only later were the scripts used for religious purposes.

A thousand years after the Sumerians, the Egyptians recognized the need for planning, organizing, and controlling; for submitting written requests; and for consulting staff for advice before making decisions. The practical problems they encountered while building the great pyramids no doubt led to the development of these management ideas. The enormity of the task they faced is evident in the pyramid of King Cheops, which contains 2.3 million blocks of stone. Each block had to be quarried, cut to precise size and shape, cured (hardened in the sun), transported by boat for two to three days, moved onto the construction site, numbered to identify where it would be placed, and then shaped and smoothed so that it would fit perfectly into place. It took 20,000 workers 23 years to complete this pyramid; more than 8,000 were needed just to quarry the stones and transport them. A typical "quarry expedition" might include 100 army officers, 50 government and religious officials, and 200 members of the king's court to lead the expedition; 130 stonemasons to cut the stones; and 5,000 soldiers, 800 barbarians, and 2,000 bond servants to transport the stones on and off the ships.[5]

The remainder of Exhibit 2.1 shows how other management ideas and practices throughout history are clearly related to the management functions in the textbook. Besides the achievements of the Sumerians and Egyptians, we might note King Hammurabi, who established controls by using witnesses and written documents; King Nebuchadnezzar, who pioneered techniques for producing goods and using wages to motivate workers; Sun Tzu, author of *The Art of War,* who emphasized the importance of strategy and identifying and attacking an opponent's weaknesses;

Exhibit 2.1

Management Ideas and Practice throughout History

Time	Individual or Group	Planning	Organizing	Leading	Controlling	Contributions to Management Thought and Practice
5000 BC	Sumerians				√	Record keeping.
4000 BC to 2000 BC	Egyptians	√	√		√	Recognized the need for planning, organizing, and controlling when building the pyramids. Submitted requests in writing. Made decisions after consulting staff for advice.
1800 BC	Hammurabi				√	Established controls by using witnesses (to vouch for what was said or done) and writing to document transactions.
600 BC	Nebuchadnezzar		√	√		Wage incentives and production control.
500 BC	Sun Tzu	√		√		Strategy; identifying and attacking opponent's weaknesses.
400 BC	Xenophon	√	√	√	√	Recognized management as a separate art.
400 BC	Cyrus		√	√	√	Human relations and motion study.
175 BC	Cato the Elder		√			Job descriptions.
284	Diocletian		√			Delegation of authority.
900	Alfarabi			√		Listed leadership traits.
1100	Ghazali			√		Listed managerial traits.
1418	Barbarigo		√			Different organizational forms/structures.
1436	Venetians				√	Numbering, standardization, and interchangeability of parts.
1500	Sir Thomas More			√		Critical of poor management and leadership.
1525	Machiavelli		√	√		Cohesiveness, power, and leadership in organizations.

Source: C. S. George, Jr., *The History of Management Thought* (Englewood Cliffs, NJ: Prentice-Hall, 1972).

Xenophon, who recognized management as a distinct and separate art; King Cyrus, who recognized the importance of human relations and used motion study to eliminate wasteful steps and improve productivity; Cato the Elder, who espoused the importance of job descriptions; Diocletian, a Roman emperor, who mastered the art of delegation by dividing the widespread Roman Empire into 101 provinces, which were then grouped into 13 dioceses, which were in turn grouped into four geographic divisions; Alfarabi and Ghazali, who began defining what it takes to be a good leader or manager; Barbarigo, who discussed the different ways in which organizations could be structured; the Venetians, who used numbering and standardization to make parts interchangeable; Sir Thomas More, who, in his book *Utopia*, emphasized the negative societal consequences associated with poor leadership; and Machiavelli, who wrote about the importance of cohesion, power, and leadership in organizations.

Management ideas have been in use from well before the Romans, but only recently has management become a profession and a topic of study.

1.2 Why We Need Managers Today

Working from 8 AM to 5 PM, coffee breaks, lunch hours, crushing rush hour traffic, and punching a time clock are things we associate with today's working world. Work hasn't always been this way, however. In fact, the design of jobs and organizations has changed dramatically over the last 500 years.

For most of humankind's history, people didn't commute to work. In fact, travel of any kind was arduous and extremely rare.[6] Work usually occurred in homes or on farms. For example, in 1720, almost 80 percent of the 5.5 million people in England lived and worked in the country. Indeed, as recently as 1870, two-thirds of Americans earned their living from agriculture. Even most of those who didn't earn their living from agriculture didn't commute to work. Blacksmiths, furniture makers, leather-goods makers, and other skilled tradesmen or craftsmen, who formed trade guilds (the historical predecessors of labor unions) in England as early as 1093, typically worked out of shops in or next to their homes.[7] Likewise, cottage workers worked with each other out of small homes that were often built in a semicircle. A family in each cottage would complete a different production step with work passed from one cottage to the next until production was complete. For example, textile work was a common "cottage industry": Families in different cottages would shear the sheep; clean the wool; comb, bleach, and dye it; spin it into yarn; and weave the yarn into cloth. Yet with no commute, no bosses (workers determined the amount and pace of their work), and no common building (from the time of the ancient Egyptians, Greeks, and Romans through the middle of the 19th century, it was rare for more than 12 people to work together under one roof), cottage work was very different from today's jobs and companies.[8] And because these work groups were small and typically self-organized, there wasn't a strong need for management.

During the Industrial Revolution (1750–1900), however, jobs and organizations changed dramatically.[9] First, thanks to the availability of power (steam engines and later electricity) and numerous inventions, such as Darby's coke-smelting process and Cort's puddling and rolling process (both for making iron) and Hargreave's spinning jenny and Arkwright's water frame (both for spinning cotton), low-paid, unskilled laborers running machines began to replace high-paid, skilled artisans. Whereas artisans made entire goods by themselves by hand, this new production system was based on a division of labor: Each worker, interacting with machines, performed separate, highly specialized tasks that were but a small part of all the steps required to make manufactured goods. Mass production was born as rope- and chain-driven assembly lines moved work to stationary workers who concentrated on performing one small task over and over again. While workers focused on their singular tasks, managers were needed to effectively coordinate the different parts of the production system and optimize its overall performance. Productivity skyrocketed at companies that understood this. For example, at FORD MOTOR COMPANY, the time required to assemble a car dropped from 12.5 man-hours to just 93 minutes after switching to mass production.[10]

Second, instead of being performed in fields, homes, or small shops, jobs occurred in large, formal organizations where hundreds, if not thousands, of people worked under one roof.[11] In 1849, for example, with just 123 workers, CHICAGO HARVESTER (the predecessor of International Harvester) ran the largest factory in the United States. In 1870, the PULLMAN COMPANY, a manufacturer of railroad sleeping cars, was the largest factory, with only 200 employees. Yet by 1913, Henry Ford employed 12,000 employees in his Highland Park, Michigan, factory alone. With the number of people working in manufacturing having quintupled from 1860 to 1890, and with individual factories employing so many workers under one roof, companies now had a strong need for disciplinary rules (to impose order and structure). For the first time, they needed managers who knew how to organize large groups, work with employees, and make good decisions.

The number of people working in manufacturing quintupled from 1860 to 1890.

Review 1: **The Origins of Management**

Management as a field of study may be just 125 years old, but management ideas and practices have actually been used since the beginning of recorded history. From the Sumerians in 5000 BC to 16th-century Europe, there are historical antecedents for each of the functions of management discussed in this textbook: planning, organizing, leading, and controlling. Despite these early examples of management ideas, there was no compelling need for managers until systematic changes in the nature of work and organizations occurred during the last two centuries. As work shifted from families to factories, from skilled laborers to specialized, unskilled laborers, from small, self-organized groups to large factories employing thousands under one roof, and from unique, small batches of production to large standardized mass production, managers were needed to impose order and structure, to motivate and direct large groups of workers, and to plan and make decisions that optimized overall company performance by effectively coordinating the different parts of organizational systems.

THE EVOLUTION OF MANAGEMENT

Before 1880, business educators taught only basic bookkeeping and secretarial skills, and no one published books or articles about management.[12] Over the next 25 years, however, things changed dramatically. In 1881, Joseph Wharton gave the University of Pennsylvania $100,000 to establish a department to educate students for careers in management. By 1911, 30 business schools, including those at Harvard, the University of Chicago, and the University of California, had been established to teach managers how to run businesses.[13] In 1886, Henry Towne, president of the Yale and Towne Manufacturing Company, presented his ideas about management to the American Society of Engineers. In his talk, entitled "The Engineer as Economist," he emphasized that managing people and work processes was just as important as engineering work, which focused on machines.[14] Towne also argued that management should be recognized as a separate field of study with its own professional associations, journals, and literature where management ideas could be exchanged and developed. Today, because of the forethought and efforts of Joseph Wharton and Henry Towne, if you have a question about management you can turn to dozens of academic journals (such as the Academy of Management's *Journal* or *Review*, *Administrative Science Quarterly*, the *Strategic Management Journal*, and the *Journal of Applied Psychology*), hundreds of business school and practitioner journals (such as *Harvard Business Review*, *Sloan Management Review*, and the *Academy of Management Perspectives*), and thousands of books and articles. In the next four sections, you will learn about other important contributors to the field of management and how their ideas shaped our current understanding of management theory and practice.

After reading the next four sections, which review the different schools of management thought, you should be able to

> 2 explain the history of scientific management.
>
> 3 discuss the history of bureaucratic and administrative management.
>
> 4 explain the history of human relations management.
>
> 5 discuss the history of operations, information, systems, and contingency management.

2 Scientific Management

Before scientific management, organizational decision making could best be described as "seat of the pants." Decisions were made haphazardly without any systematic study, thought, or collection of information. Customer orders were transmitted verbally from sales representatives to shop floor supervisors. They were not written down. If the "managers" hired by the company founder or owner decided that workers should work twice as fast, little or no thought was given to worker motivation. If workers resisted, "managers" often resorted to physical beatings to get workers to work faster, harder, or longer. In general, with no incentives for "managers" to cooperate with workers and vice versa, managers and workers gamed the system trying to systematically take advantage of each other. Likewise, nothing was standardized. Each worker did the same job in his or her own way with different methods and different tools. In short, there were no procedures to standardize operations, no standards by which to judge whether performance was good or bad, and no follow-up to determine if productivity or quality actually improved when changes were made.[15]

This all changed, however, with the advent of **scientific management**, which, in contrast to the unsystematic "seat-of-the-pants" approach, thoroughly studied and tested different work methods to identify the best, most efficient ways to complete a job.

*Let's find out more about scientific management by learning about **2.1 Frederick W. Taylor, the father of scientific management; 2.2 Frank and Lillian Gilbreth and motion studies;** and **2.3 Henry Gantt and his Gantt charts**.*

scientific management thoroughly studying and testing different work methods to identify the best, most efficient way to complete a job

Frederick Taylor is known today as the "father of scientific management." One of his many contributions to modern management is the common practice of giving employees rest breaks throughout the day.

soldiering when workers deliberately slow their pace or restrict their work outputs

rate buster a group member whose work pace is significantly faster than the normal pace in his or her group

2.1 Father of Scientific Management: Frederick W. Taylor

Frederick W. Taylor (1856–1915), the "father of scientific management," began his career as a worker at MIDVALE STEEL COMPANY. He was later promoted to patternmaker, supervisor, and then chief engineer.

At Midvale, Taylor was deeply affected by his three-year struggle to get the men who worked for him to do, as he called it, "a fair day's work." Taylor, who had worked alongside the men as a coworker before becoming their boss, said, "We who were the workmen of that shop had the quantity output carefully agreed upon for everything that was turned out in the shop. We limited the output to about, I should think, one-third of what we could very well have done." Taylor explained that as soon as he became the boss, "the men who were working under me … knew that I was onto the whole game of **soldiering**, or deliberately restricting output."[16] When Taylor told his workers, "I have accepted a job under the management of this company and I am on the other side of the fence … I am going to try to get a bigger output," the workers responded, "We warn you, Fred, if you try to bust any of these rates [a **rate buster** was someone who worked faster than the group] we will have you over the fence in six weeks."[17]

Over the next three years, Taylor tried everything he could think of to improve output. By doing the job himself, he showed workers that it was possible to produce more output. He hired new "intelligent" workers and trained them himself, hoping they would produce more. But they would not because of "very heavy social pressure" from the other workers. Pushed by Taylor, the workers began breaking their machines so that they couldn't produce. Taylor responded by fining them every time they broke a machine and for any violation of the rules, no matter how small, such as being late to work. Tensions became so severe that some of the workers threatened to shoot him. Looking back at the situation, Taylor reflected, "It is a horrid life for any man to live, not to be able to look any workman in the face all day long without seeing hostility there and feeling that every man around one is his virtual enemy." He said, "I made up my mind either to get out of the business entirely and go into some other line of work, or to find some remedy for this unbearable condition."[18] The remedy that Taylor eventually developed was scientific management.

Taylor, who once described scientific management as "seventy-five percent science and twenty-five percent common sense," emphasized that the goal of scientific management was to use systematic study to find the "one best way" of doing each task. To do that, managers must follow the four principles shown in Exhibit 2.2.[19] First, "develop a science" for each element of work. Study it. Analyze it. Determine the "one best way" to do the work. For example, one of Taylor's controversial proposals at the time was to give rest breaks to factory workers doing physical labor. We take morning, lunch, and

Exhibit 2.2

Taylor's Four Principles of Scientific Management

First	Develop a science for each element of a man's work, which replaces the old rule-of-thumb method.
Second	Scientifically select and then train, teach, and develop the workman, whereas in the past he chose his own work and trained himself as best he could.
Third	Heartily cooperate with the men so as to ensure all of the work being done is in accordance with the principles of the science which has been developed.
Fourth	There is an almost equal division of the work and the responsibility between the management and the workmen. The management take over all the work for which they are better fitted than the workmen, while in the past almost all of the work and the greater part of the responsibility were thrown upon the men.

Source: F. W. Taylor, *The Principles of Scientific Management* (New York: Harper, 1911).

afternoon breaks for granted, but in Taylor's day, factory workers were expected to work without stopping.[20] When Taylor said that breaks would increase worker productivity, no one believed him. Nonetheless, through systematic experiments, he showed that workers receiving frequent rest breaks were able to greatly increase their daily output.

Second, scientifically select, train, teach, and develop workers to help them reach their full potential. Before Taylor, supervisors often hired on the basis of favoritism and nepotism. Who you knew was often more important than what you could do. By contrast, Taylor instructed supervisors to hire "first class" workers on the basis of their aptitude to do a job well. In one of the first applications of this principle, physical reaction times were used to select bicycle ball-bearing inspectors who had to be able to examine and reject poor-quality ball bearings as fast as they were produced on a production line. For similar reasons, Taylor also recommended that companies train and develop their workers—a rare practice at the time.

Third, cooperate with employees to ensure implementation of the scientific principles. Labor unrest was widespread at the time; the number of labor strikes against companies doubled between 1893 and 1904. As Taylor knew from personal experience, more often than not workers and management viewed each other as the enemy. Taylor's advice ran contrary to the common wisdom of the day. He said, "The majority of these men believe that the fundamental interests of employees and employers are necessarily antagonistic. Scientific management, on the contrary, has for its very foundation the firm conviction that the true interests of the two are one and the same; that prosperity for the employer cannot exist through a long term of years unless it is accompanied by prosperity for the employee and vice versa; and that it is possible to give the workman what he most wants—high wages—and the employer what he wants—a low labor cost—for his manufactures."[21]

The fourth principle of scientific management was to divide the work and the responsibility equally between management and workers. Prior to Taylor, workers alone were held responsible for productivity and performance. But, said Taylor, "Almost every act of the workman should be preceded by one or more preparatory acts of the management which enable him to do his work better and quicker than he otherwise could. And each man should daily be taught by and receive the most friendly help from those who are over him, instead of being, at the one extreme, driven or coerced by his bosses, and at the other left to his own unaided devices."[22]

Above all, Taylor felt these principles could be used to determine a "fair day's work," that is, what an average worker could produce at a reasonable pace, day in and day out. Once that was determined, it was management's responsibility to pay workers fairly for that fair day's work. In essence, Taylor was trying to align management and employees so that what was good for employees was also good for management. In this way, he felt, workers and managers could avoid the conflicts that he had experienced at Midvale Steel. And one of the best ways, according to Taylor, to align management and employees was to use incentives to motivate workers. As Taylor wrote:

> *In order to have any hope of obtaining the initiative of his workmen the manager must give some special incentive to his men beyond that which is given to the average of the trade. This incentive can be given in several different ways, as, for example, the hope of rapid promotion or advancement; higher wages, either in the form of generous piecework prices or of a premium or bonus of some kind for good and rapid work; shorter hours of labor; better surroundings and working conditions than are ordinarily given, etc., and, above all, this special incentive should be accompanied by that personal consideration for, and friendly contact with, his workmen which comes only from a genuine and kindly interest in the welfare of those under him. It is only by giving a special inducement or "incentive" of this kind that the employer can hope even approximately to get the "initiative" of his workmen.*[23]

Almost every act of the workman should be preceded by one or more preparatory acts of the management.

FREDERICK W. TAYLOR,
MIDVALE STEEL COMPANY

Although Taylor remains a controversial figure among some academics who believe that his ideas were bad for workers, nearly a century later it is inarguable that his key ideas have stood the test of time.[24] These include using systematic analysis to identify the best methods; scientifically selecting, training, and developing workers; promoting cooperation between management and labor; developing standardized approaches and tools; setting specific tasks or goals and then rewarding workers with financial incentives; and giving workers shorter work hours and frequent breaks. In fact, his ideas are so well accepted and widely used that we take most of them for granted. As eminent management scholar Edwin Locke says, "The point is not, as is often claimed, that he was 'right in the context of his time,' but is now outdated, but that *most of his insights are still valid today.*"[25]

2.2 Motion Studies: Frank and Lillian Gilbreth

The husband and wife team Frank and Lillian Gilbreth are best known for their use of motion studies to simplify work, but they also made significant contributions to the employment of disabled workers and industrial psychology. Like Frederick Taylor, their early experiences significantly shaped their interests and contributions to management.

Though admitted to MIT, Frank Gilbreth (1868–1924) began his career as an apprentice bricklayer. While learning the trade, he noticed the bricklayers using three different sets of motions—one to teach others how to lay bricks, a second to work at a slow pace, and a third to work at a fast pace.[26] Wondering which was best, he studied the various approaches and began eliminating unnecessary motions. For example, by designing a stand that could be raised to waist height, he eliminated the need to bend over to pick up each brick. Turning to grab a brick was faster and easier than bending down. By having lower-paid workers place all the bricks with their most attractive side up, bricklayers didn't waste time turning a brick over to find it. By mixing a more consistent mortar, bricklayers no longer had to tap each brick numerous times to put it in the right position. Together, Gilbreth's improvements raised productivity from 120 to 350 bricks per hour and from 1,000 bricks to 2,700 bricks per day.

As a result of his experience with bricklaying, Gilbreth and his wife Lillian developed a long-term interest in using motion study to simplify work, improve productivity, and reduce the level of effort required to safely perform a job. Indeed, Frank Gilbreth said, "The greatest waste in the world comes from needless, ill-directed, and ineffective motions."[27] The Gilbreths' motion study, however, is different from Frederick W. Taylor's time study.[28] Taylor developed time study to put an end to soldiering and to determine what could be considered a fair day's work. **Time study** worked by timing how long it took a "first-class man" to complete each part of his job. After allowing for rest periods, a standard time was established, and a worker's pay would increase or decrease depending on whether the worker exceeded or fell below that standard. By contrast, **motion study**, as we saw in Frank Gilbreth's analysis of bricklaying, broke each task or job into separate motions and then eliminated those that were unnecessary or repetitive. Because many motions were completed very quickly, the Gilbreths used motion-picture films, then a relatively new technology, to analyze jobs. Most film cameras, however, were hand-cranked and thus variable in their film speed, so Frank Gilbreth invented the microchronometer, a large clock that could record time to 1/2,000th of a second. By placing the microchronometer next to the worker in the camera's field of vision and attaching a flashing strobe light to the worker's hands to better identify the direction and sequence of key movements, the Gilbreths could use film to detect and precisely time even the slightest, fastest movements. Motion study typically yielded

time study timing how long it takes good workers to complete each part of their jobs

motion study breaking each task or job into its separate motions and then eliminating those that are unnecessary or repetitive production increases of 25 to 300 percent.[29] It is even used in hospitals to clearly identify the large amount of time that surgeons wasted looking for the next surgical instrument they needed. Frank Gilbreth improved this process by making a nurse responsible for organizing, retrieving, and handing surgical instruments to surgeons, a process still in use today.[30]

One of the Gilbreths' most overlooked accomplishments was the critical role they played in rehabilitating and employing disabled workers.[31] After World War I, there were 13 million wounded and disabled soldiers in the United States and Europe. Frank Gilbreth worried, "What is to be done with the millions of cripples, when their injuries have been remedied as far as possible, and when they are obliged to become again a part of the working community?"[32] Sensitive to this issue because of Frank's recovery from a rheumatism attack that had left him temporarily paralyzed from the neck down, the Gilbreths applied motion study to identify the kinds of tasks that disabled workers could effectively perform. Nearly 75 years before the Americans with Disabilities Act became law (see Chapter 12 for more information), the Gilbreths argued that the government, employers, and engineers had an important role to play in employing disabled workers. The government's job, they said, was to provide vocational training. Indeed, in 1918, the U.S. Congress passed the Vocational Rehabilitation Act, adopting most of the Gilbreths' key recommendations. Employers, they said, should identify jobs that disabled people could perform. To help employers do this, the Gilbreths created a large slide show of pictures documenting the hundreds of ways in which disabled people could effectively perform jobs. Also, according to the Gilbreths, engineers had a responsibility to adapt and design machines so that disabled workers could use them.

Lillian Gilbreth (1878–1972) was an important contributor to management as well. She was the first woman to receive a Ph.D. in Industrial Psychology, as well as the first woman to become a member of the Society of Industrial Engineers and the American Society of Mechanical Engineers. When Frank died in 1924, she continued the work of their management consulting company (which they had shared for over a dozen years) on her own. Lillian, who was concerned with the human side of work, was one of the first contributors to industrial psychology, originating ways to improve office communication, incentive programs, job satisfaction, and management training. Her work also convinced the government to enact laws regarding workplace safety, ergonomics, and child labor.

2.3 Charts: Henry Gantt

Henry Gantt (1861–1919) was first a protégé and then an associate of Frederick Taylor. Gantt is best known for the Gantt chart, but he also made significant contributions to management with respect to pay-for-performance plans and the training and development of workers. As shown in Exhibit 2.3, a **Gantt chart**, which shows time in various units on the *x*-axis and tasks on the *y*-axis, visually indicates what tasks must be completed at which times in order to complete a project. For example, Exhibit 2.3 shows that to start construction on a new company headquarters by the week of November 18, the following tasks must be completed by the following dates: architectural firm selected by October 7, architectural planning done by November 4, permits obtained from the city by November 11, site preparation finished by November 18, and loans and financing finalized by November 18. Though simple and straightforward, Gantt charts were revolutionary in the era of "seat of the pants" management because of the detailed planning information they provided to managers. As Gantt wrote, "By using the graphical forms [the Gantt chart] its value is very much increased, for the general appearance of the sheet is sufficient to tell how closely the schedule is being lived up to; in other words, whether the plant is being run efficiently or not." Gantt said, "Such sheets show at a glance where the delays occur, and indicate what must have our attention in order to keep up the proper output." Today, the use of Gantt charts is so widespread that nearly all project management software and computer spreadsheets have the capability to create charts that track and visually display the progress being made on a project.

Gantt chart a graphical chart that shows which tasks must be completed at which times in order to complete a project or task

Exhibit 2.3

Gantt Chart for Starting Construction on a New Headquarters

	Current Week									
Weeks		23 Sep to 30 Sep	30 Sep to 7 Oct	7 Oct to 14 Oct	14 Oct to 21 Oct	21 Oct to 28 Oct	28 Oct to 4 Nov	4 Nov to 11 Nov	11 Nov to 18 Nov	18 Nov to 25 Nov
Tasks										
Interview and select architectural firm		Architect by October 7								
Hold weekly planning meetings with architects				Weekly planning with architects by November 4						
Obtain permits and approval from city						Permits & approval by November 11				
Begin preparing site for construction							Site construction done by November 18			
Finalize loans and financing								Financing finalized by November 18		
Begin construction										Start building
Tasks										
Weeks		23 Sep to 30 Sep	30 Sep to 7 Oct	7 Oct to 14 Oct	14 Oct to 21 Oct	21 Oct to 28 Oct	28 Oct to 4 Nov	4 Nov to 11 Nov	11 Nov to 18 Nov	18 Nov to 25 Nov
	Current Week									

Gantt, who was much more sympathetic toward workers than Frederick Taylor was, introduced a significant change to Taylor's well-known piece-rate reward system. Unlike Taylor's system, in which payment was completely dependent on production—if you produced at substandard levels, you got substandard pay—Gantt's task and bonus system did not punish workers for not achieving higher levels of production. Workers who produced more received a daily bonus, but those who didn't simply received their standard daily pay. The key, according to Gantt, was that his task and bonus system didn't punish workers for lower production as they took time to learn how to increase their production efficiency. Production usually doubled under Gantt's system.[33]

Finally, Gantt, along with Taylor, was one of the first to strongly recommend that companies train and develop their workers.[34] In his work with companies, he found that workers achieved their best performance levels if they were trained first. At the time, however, supervisors, fearing that they could lose their jobs to more knowledgeable workers, were reluctant to teach workers what they knew. Gantt overcame the supervisors' resistance by rewarding them with bonuses for properly training all of their workers. Said Gantt, "This is the first recorded attempt to make it in the financial interest of the foreman to teach the individual worker, and the importance of it cannot be overestimated, for it changes the foreman from a driver of men to their friend and helper."[35] Thus, Gantt's approach to training was straightforward: "(1) a scientific investigation in detail of each piece of work, and the determination of the best method and the shortest time in which the work can be done. (2) A teacher capable of teaching the best method and the shortest time. (3) Reward for both teacher and pupil when the latter is successful."[36]

Review 2: *Scientific Management*

In contrast to "seat of the pants" management, scientific management recommended studying and testing different work methods to identify the best, most efficient ways to complete a job. According to Frederick W. Taylor, the "father of scientific management," managers should follow four scientific management principles. First, study each element of work to determine the "one best way" to do it. Second, scientifically select, train, teach, and develop workers to reach their full potential. Third, cooperate with employees to ensure implementation of the scientific principles. Fourth, divide the work and the responsibility equally between management and workers. Above all, Taylor felt these principles could be used to align managers and employees by determining a "fair day's work," what an average worker could produce at a reasonable pace, and "a fair day's pay," what management should pay workers for that effort. Taylor felt that incentives were one of the best ways to align management and employees.

The husband and wife team of Frank and Lillian Gilbreth are best known for their use of motion studies to simplify work. Whereas Taylor used time study to determine "a fair day's work," based on how long it took a "first-class man" to complete each part of his job, Frank Gilbreth used film cameras and microchronometers to conduct motion study to improve efficiency by categorizing and eliminating unnecessary or repetitive motions. The Gilbreths also made significant contributions to the employment of disabled workers, encouraging the government to rehabilitate them, employers to identify jobs that they could perform, and engineers to adapt and design machines they could use. Lillian Gilbreth, one of the first contributors to industrial psychology, originated ways to improve office communication, incentive programs, job satisfaction, and management training. She also convinced the government to enact laws regarding workplace safety, ergonomics, and child labor. Henry Gantt is best known for the Gantt chart, which graphically indicates when a series of tasks must be completed to perform a job or project, but he also developed ideas regarding pay-for-performance plans (where workers were rewarded for producing more, but were not punished if they didn't) and worker training (all workers should be trained and their managers should be rewarded for training them).

3 Bureaucratic and Administrative Management

The field of scientific management, which quickly developed in the United States between 1895 and 1920, focused on improving the efficiency of manufacturing facilities and their workers. At about the same time, equally important ideas were developing in Europe. German sociologist Max Weber's ideas about bureaucratic management, which presented a new way to run entire organizations, were published in *The Theory of Economic and Social Organization* in 1922. Henri Fayol, an experienced French CEO, published his ideas about administrative management, including how and what managers should do in their jobs, in *General and Industrial Management* in 1916. Though developed at the same time as scientific management, the ideas of Weber and Fayol would not begin to influence American ideas about management until after World War II, when their books were translated into English and published in the United States in 1947 and 1949, respectively.

*Let's find out more about Weber's and Fayol's contributions to management by learning about **3.1 bureaucratic management** and **3.2 administrative management**.*

3.1 Bureaucratic Management: Max Weber

Today, when we hear the term *bureaucracy*, we think of inefficiency and red tape, incompetence and ineffectiveness, and rigid administrators blindly enforcing nonsensical rules. When German sociologist Max Weber (1864–1920) first proposed the idea of bureaucratic organizations, however, monarchies and patriarchies, not bureaucracies, were associated with these problems. In monarchies, where kings, queens, sultans, and emperors ruled, and patriarchies, where a council of elders, wise men, or male heads of extended families ruled, the top leaders typically achieved their positions by virtue of birthright. For example, when the queen died, her oldest son became king, regardless of his intelligence, experience, education, or desire. Likewise, promotion to prominent positions of authority in monarchies and patriarchies was based on who you knew, who you were (heredity), or ancient rules and traditions. In short, for much of humankind's history, people often rose to positions of wealth and power because of family, political connections, or personal loyalty.

It was against this historical background of monarchical and patriarchic rule that Weber proposed the then new idea of bureaucracy. *Bureaucracy* comes from the French word *bureaucratie*. Since *bureau* means desk or office and *cratie* or *cracy* means to rule, *bureaucracy* literally means to rule from a desk or office. According to Weber, however, **bureaucracy** is "the exercise of control on the basis of knowledge."[37] So, in a bureaucracy, rather than ruling by virtue of favoritism, or personal or family connections, people would lead by virtue of their rational-legal authority—in other words, their knowledge, expertise, or experience. Furthermore,

bureaucracy the exercise of control on the basis of knowledge, expertise, or experience the aim of bureaucracy is to achieve an organization's goals in the most efficient way possible.

Exhibit 2.4 shows the seven elements that, according to Weber, characterize bureaucracies. First, instead of hiring people because of their family or political connections, or personal loyalty, they should be hired because their technical training or education qualifies them to do their jobs well. Second, along the same lines, promotion within the company would no longer be based on who you knew or who you were (heredity), but on your experience or achievements. And to further limit the influence of personal connections in the promotion process, managers, rather than organizational owners, should decide who gets promoted. Third, each position or job is part of a chain of command that clarifies who reports to whom throughout the organization. Those higher in the chain of command have the right, if they so choose, to give commands, take action, and make decisions concerning activities occurring anywhere below them in the chain. Unlike many monarchies or patriarchies, however, those lower in the chain of command are protected by a grievance procedure that gives them the right to appeal the decisions of those in higher positions. Fourth, to increase efficiency and effectiveness, tasks and responsibilities are separated and assigned to those best qualified to complete them. Furthermore, authority is vested in positions, not people. If you move to a different job, your authority increases or decreases commensurate with the responsibilities of that job. And, to reduce confusion and conflict, the authority of each position or job is also clearly divided and defined. Fifth, because of his strong distaste for favoritism, Weber felt that an organization's rules and procedures should apply to all members, regardless of their position or status. Sixth, to ensure consistency and fairness over time and across different leaders and supervisors, all rules, procedures, and decisions should be recorded in writing. Finally, to reduce favoritism, "professional" managers rather than company owners should manage or supervise the organization.

When viewed in historical context, Weber's ideas about bureaucracy represent a tremendous improvement in how organizations should be run. Fairness supplanted favoritism, the goal of efficiency replaced the goal of personal gain, and logical rules and procedures took the place of traditions or arbitrary decision making. Today, however, after more than a century of experience we recognize that bureaucracy has limitations as well. In bureaucracies, managers are supposed to influence employee behavior by fairly rewarding or punishing employees for compliance or noncompliance with organizational policies, rules, and procedures. In reality, however, most employees would

Exhibit 2.4

Elements of Bureaucratic Organizations

Qualification-based hiring	Employees are hired on the basis of their technical training or educational background.
Merit-based promotion	Promotion is based on experience or achievement. Managers, not organizational owners, decide who is promoted.
Chain of commands	Each job occurs within a hierarchy, the chain of command, in which each position reports and is accountable to a higher position. A grievance procedure and a right to appeal protect people in lower positions.
Division of labor	Tasks, responsibilities, and authority are clearly divided and defined.
Impartial application of rules and procedures	Rules and procedures apply to all members of the organization and will be applied in an impartial manner, regardless of one's position or status
Recorded in writing	All administrative decisions, acts, rules, or procedure will be recorded in writing.
Managers separate from owners	The owners of an organization should not manage or supervise the organization.

Source: M. Weber, *The Theory of Economic and Social Organization*, trans. A. Henderson & T. Parsons (New York: Free Press, 1947), 329–334.

argue that bureaucratic managers emphasize punishment for noncompliance much more than rewards for compliance. Ironically, bureaucratic management was created to prevent just this type of managerial behavior. By encouraging managers to apply well-thought-out rules, policies, and procedures impartially and consistently to everyone in the organization, bureaucratic control is supposed to make companies more efficient, effective, and fair. Perversely, as you'll read in Chapter 16 on control, it can sometimes have just the opposite effect. Managers who use bureaucratic control often put following the rules above all else. Another limitation of bureaucratically controlled companies is that due to their rule- and policy-driven decision making, they can be highly resistant to change and slow to respond to customers and competitors. Despite its advantages over monarchical and patriarchic organizational forms, even Weber recognized bureaucracy's limitations. He called it the "iron cage" and said, "Once fully established, bureaucracy is among those social structures which are the hardest to destroy."[38]

" Once fully established, bureaucracy is among those social structures which are the hardest to destroy. **"**

MAX WEBER, SOCIOLOGIST

3.2 Administrative Management: Henri Fayol

Though his work was not translated and widely recognized in the United States until 1949, Frenchman Henri Fayol (1841–1925) was as important a contributor to the field of management as Frederick Taylor. Like Taylor and Frank and Lillian Gilbreth, Fayol's work experience significantly shaped his thoughts and ideas about management. But whereas Taylor's ideas changed companies from the shop floor up, Fayol's ideas, which were shaped by his experience as a managing director (CEO), generally changed companies from the board of directors down.[39] Fayol is best known for developing five functions of managers and 14 principles of management, as well as for his belief that management could and should be taught to others.

Henri Fayol conceived of the principles which today have been distilled into the four functions of management.

Like his father, Henri Fayol enrolled in France's National School of Mines, graduating with an engineering degree at the age of 19.[40] His first job as a mining engineer was spent learning how to contain and put out underground fires. In this job, he began the valuable habit of recording notes about actions or happenings that either improved or decreased the productivity of the mine and its workers.[41] For instance, he wrote this note to himself about the cause of a work stoppage that occurred when his boss, the managing director, was gone: "May 1861. The horse on the sixth level of the St. Edmund pits broke its leg this morning. I made out an order for its replacement. The stableman refused to accept the order because it did not bear the Director's signature. The Director was absent. No one was designated to replace him. Despite my entreaties, the stableman persisted in his refusal. He had express orders, he said [not to provide a replacement horse unless the managing director ordered]. The injured horse was not replaced and production at the sixth level was lost."[42] It's very possible that this experience helped him form the now widely accepted management principle that a manager's authority should equal his or her responsibility.[43] In other words, because he was responsible for the productivity and production of coal at the St. Edmund's pit, his boss, the managing director, should have given him the authority to take actions, such as signing for a replacement horse, commensurate with that responsibility (see Chapter 9 for more on delegation, authority, and responsibility).

© ROGER VIOLLET/THE IMAGE WORKS

It's likely, however, that the most formative events in Fayol's business career came during his 20 plus years as the managing director (CEO) of Compagnie de Commentry-Fourchambault-Decazeville, commonly known as C O M A M B A U L T, a vertically integrated steel company that owned several coal and iron ore mines and employed 10,000 to 13,000 workers. Fayol was initially hired by the board of directors to shut the "hopeless" steel company down. The company was facing increased competition from English and German steel companies, which had lower costs, and from new steel mills in northern and eastern France, which were closer to major markets and thus could avoid the large shipping costs incurred by Fayol's company, which was located in central France.[44] In the five years before Fayol became CEO, production had dropped more than 60 percent, from 38,000 to 15,000 annual metric tons. The company had exhausted a key supply of coal needed for steel production, had already shut one steel mill down, and was losing money at another.[45] The company had quit paying dividends to shareholders and had no cash to invest in new technology, such as blast furnaces, that could lower its costs and increase productivity. Therefore, the board hired Fayol as CEO to quickly dissolve and liquidate the business. But after "four months of reflection and study," he presented the board with a plan, backed by detailed facts and figures, to save the company.[46] With little to lose, the board agreed. Fayol then began the process of turning the company around by obtaining supplies of key resources, such as coal and iron ore; using research to develop new steel alloy products; carefully selecting key subordinates in research, purchasing, manufacturing, and sales and then delegating responsibility to them; and cutting costs by moving the company to a better location closer to key markets.[47] Looking back 10 years later, Fayol attributed his and the company's success to changes in management practices. He wrote, "When I assumed the responsibility for the restoration of Decazeville, I did not rely on my technical superiority.... I relied on my ability as an organizer [and my] skill in handling men (*manoeuvrier des hommes*)."[48] Fayol concluded, "With the same [coal] mines, the same [steel] mills, the same financial resources, the same markets, the same Board of Directors and the same personnel, solely *with the application of a new way of running the company* [italics added], the firm experienced a rise [in its performance] comparable to its earlier decline."[49]

Based on his experience as a CEO, Fayol argued that "the success of an enterprise generally depends much more on the administrative ability of its leaders than on their technical ability."[50] And, as you learned in Chapter 1, Fayol argued that this means that if managers are to be successful, they need to perform five managerial functions or elements: planning, organizing, coordinating, commanding, and controlling.[51] Today, though, most management textbooks have dropped the coordinating function and now refer to Fayol's commanding function as "leading." Consequently, Fayol's management functions are widely known as planning (determining organizational goals and a means for achieving them), organizing (deciding where decisions will be made, who will do what jobs and tasks, and who will work for whom), leading (inspiring and motivating workers to work hard to achieve organizational goals), and controlling (monitoring progress toward goal achievement and taking corrective action when needed). In addition, according to Fayol, effective management is based on the 14 principles in Exhibit 2.5.

Finally, along with Joseph Wharton, Fayol was one of the first to argue that management could and should be taught to others. In short, Fayol believed that the principles of management could be taught in colleges and universities and that managers are not born but can be made through a combination of education and experience.

1.	**Division of work**	Increase production by dividing work so that each worker completes smaller tasks or job elements.
2.	**Authority and responsibility**	A manager's authority, which is the "right to give orders," should be commensurate with the manager's responsibility. However, organizations should enact controls to prevent managers from abusing their authority.
3.	**Discipline**	Clearly defined rules and procedures are needed at all organizational levels to ensure order and proper behavior.
4.	**Unity of command**	To avoid confusion and conflict, each employee should report to and receive orders from just one boss.
5.	**Unity of direction**	One person and one plan should be used in deciding the activities to be used to accomplish each organizational objective.
6.	**Subordination of individual interests to the general interest**	Employees must put the organization's interests and goals before their own.
7.	**Remuneration**	Compensation should be fair and satisfactory to both the employees and the organization; that is, don't overpay or underpay employees.
8.	**Centralization**	Avoid too much centralization or decentralization. Strike a balance depending on the circumstances and employees involved.
9.	**Scalar chain**	From the top to the bottom of an organization, each position is part of a vertical chain of authority in which each worker reports to just one boss. For the sake of simplicity, communication outside normal work groups or departments should follow the vertical chain of authority.
10.	**Order**	To avoid conflicts and confusion, order can be obtained by having a place for everyone and having everyone in their place; in other words, there should be no overlapping responsibilities.
11.	**Equity**	Kind, fair, and just treatment for all will develop devotion and loyalty. This does not exclude discipline, if warranted, and consideration of the broader general interest of the organization.
12.	**Stability of tenure of personnel**	Low turnover, meaning a stable work force with high tenure, benefits an organization by improving performance, lowering costs, and giving employees, especially managers, time to learn their jobs.
13.	**Initiative**	Because it is a "great source of strength for business," managers should encourage the development of initiative, the ability to develop and implement a plan, in others.
14.	**Esprit de corps**	Develop a strong sense of morale and unity among workers that encourages coordination of efforts.

Sources: H. Fayol, *General and Industrial Management* (London: Pittman & Sons, 1949); M. Fells, "Fayol Stands the Test of Time," *Journal of Management History* 6 (2000): 345–360; C. Rodrigues, "Fayol's 14 Principles of Management Then and Now: A Framework for Managing Today's Organizations Effectively," *Management Decision* 39 (2001): 880–889.

Exhibit 2.5

Fayol's 14 Principles of Management

Review 3: **Bureaucratic and Administrative Management**

Today, when we hear *bureaucracy*, we think of inefficiency and red tape. Yet according to German sociologist Max Weber, bureaucracy, that is, running organizations on the basis of knowledge, fairness, and logical rules and procedures, would accomplish organizational goals much more efficiently than monarchies and patriarchies, where decisions were made on the basis of personal or family connections, personal gain, and arbitrary decision making. Bureaucracies are characterized by seven elements: qualification-based hiring;

merit-based promotion; chain of command; division of labor; impartial application of rules and procedures; recording rules, procedures, and decisions in writing; and separating managers from owners. Nonetheless, bureaucracies are often inefficient and can be highly resistant to change.

The Frenchman Henri Fayol, whose ideas were shaped by his 20-plus years of experience as a CEO, is best known for developing five management functions (planning, organizing, coordinating, commanding, and controlling) and 14 principles of management (division of work, authority and responsibility, discipline, unity of command, unity of direction, subordination of individual interests to the general interest, remuneration, centralization, scalar chain, order, equity, stability of tenure of personnel, initiative, and esprit de corps). He is also known for his belief that management could and should be taught to others.

4 Human Relations Management

As we have seen, scientific management focused on improving the efficiency of manufacturing facilities and their workers; bureaucratic management focused on using knowledge, fairness, and logical rules and procedures to increase the efficiency of the entire organization; and administrative management focused on how and what managers should do in their jobs. In contrast, the human relations approach to management focused on the psychological and social aspects of work. Under the human relations management approach, people were more than just extensions of machines; they were valuable organizational resources whose needs were important and whose efforts, motivation, and performance were affected by the work they did and their relationships with their bosses, coworkers, and work groups. In other words, according to human relations management, efficiency alone is not enough to produce organizational success. Success also depends on treating workers well.

Let's find out more about human relations management by learning about **4.1 Mary Parker Follett's theories of constructive conflict and coordination; 4.2 Elton Mayo's Hawthorne Studies;** *and* **4.3 Chester Barnard's theories of cooperation and acceptance of authority.**

4.1 Constructive Conflict and Coordination: Mary Parker Follett

Mary Parker Follett (1868–1933) was a social worker with a degree in political science who, in her 50s, after 25 years of working with schools and nonprofit organizations, began lecturing and writing about management and working extensively as a consultant for business and government leaders in the United States and Europe. Although her contributions were overlooked for decades, perhaps because she was a woman or perhaps because they were so different, many of today's "new" management ideas can clearly be traced to her work.

Follett is known for developing ideas regarding constructive conflict and coordination. Constructive conflict, also called cognitive conflict, which is discussed in Chapter 5 on decision making and Chapter 10 on teams, is one of Follett's most important contributions. Unlike most people, then and now, who view conflict as bad, Follett believed that conflict could be beneficial. She said that conflict is "the appearance of difference, difference of opinions, of interests. For that is what conflict means—difference." She went on to say, "As conflict—difference—is here in this world, as we cannot avoid it, we should, I think, use it to work for us. Instead of condemning it, we should set it to work for us. Thus we shall not be afraid of conflict, but shall recognize that there is a destructive way of dealing with such moments and a constructive way."[52]

Follett believed that managers could deal with conflict in three ways: domination, compromise, and integration. She said, "**Domination**, obviously, is a victory of one side over the other. This is the easiest way of dealing with conflict, the easiest for the moment but not usually successful in the long run.... As for the second way of dealing with conflict, that of **compromise**, we understand [it] well, for it is the way we settle most of our controversies; each side gives up a little in order to have peace, or, to speak more accurately, in order that the activity which has been interrupted by the conflict may go on." Follett continued, "Yet no one really wants to compromise, because that means a giving up of something. Is there then any other method of ending conflict? There is a way beginning now to be recognized at least, and even occasionally followed: when two desires are *integrated*, that means that a solution has been found in which both desires have found a place that neither side has had to sacrifice anything." So, rather than one side dominating the other or both sides compromising, the point of **integrative conflict resolution** is to have both parties indicate their preferences and then work together to find an alternative that meets the needs of both. According to Follett, "Integration involves invention, and the clever thing is to recognize this, and not to let one's thinking stay within the boundaries of two alternatives which are mutually exclusive." Indeed, Follett's ideas about the positive use of conflict and an integrative approach to conflict resolution predate accepted thinking in the negotiation and conflict resolution literature by six decades (see the best-selling book *Getting to Yes: Negotiating Agreement without Giving In* by Roger Fisher, William Ury, and Bruce Patton).

Follett's writing on the role of coordination in organizations is another of her important contributions. According to Follett, there are four fundamental principles of organizations:

1. *Coordination as reciprocal relating all the factors in a situation.*
2. *Coordination by direct contact of the responsible people concerned.*
3. *Coordination in the early stages.*
4. *Coordination as a continuing process.*

Follett's first principle recognizes that most things that occur in organizations are interrelated. Make just one change in an organization, and other changes, some expected but some not, will occur. Cut costs, and quality may be affected. Change the raw ingredients used to make a product, and manufacturing procedures may no longer work. Marketing offers customers special incentives to buy more products, and operations has to work overtime to keep up with the increased demand. Accordingly, because of these interrelations, leaders at different levels and in different parts of the organization must coordinate their efforts to solve problems and produce the best overall outcomes in an integrative way. In short, managers cannot manage their part of the organization while ignoring its other parts. What each manager does affects other parts of the organization and vice versa.

Follett explains her second principle, coordination by direct contact of the people concerned, and her third principle, coordination in the early stages, this way: "Direct contact must begin in the earliest stages of the process.... If the heads of departments confront each other with finished policies, agreement will be found difficult.... But if these heads meet while they are forming their policies, meet and discuss the questions

domination an approach to dealing with conflict in which one party satisfies its desires and objectives at the expense of the other party's desires and objectives

compromise an approach to dealing with conflict in which both parties give up some of what they want in order to reach agreement on a plan to reduce or settle the conflict

integrative conflict resolution an approach to dealing with conflict in which both parties indicate their preferences and then work together to find an alternative the meets the needs of both involved, a successful co-relation is far more likely to be reached. Their thinking has not become crystallized. They can still modify one another."[53] In other words, better outcomes will be achieved if the people affected by organizational issues and problems meet early and directly to address them. Working with those involved or affected will produce more effective solutions than will isolating or ignoring them.

With respect to her fourth principle, coordination as a continuing process, Follett said: "It is a fallacy to think that we can solve problems—in any final sense. The belief that we can do so is a drag upon our thinking. What we need is a process for meeting problems. When we think we have solved one, well, by the very process of solving, new elements or forces come into the situation and you have a new problem on your hands to be solved." Consequently, there is always a need for early, integrative coordination of the people affected by organizational situations, problems, or issues. The need for coordination never goes away.

Exhibit 2.6 summarizes, in Follett's own words, her contributions to management regarding power ("with" not "over" others), the giving of orders (discussing instructions and resentment), authority (flowing from job knowledge and experience, not position), leadership (that leaders make the team and that aggressive, dominating leaders may be harmful), coordination, and control (should be based on facts, information, and coordination). In the end, Follett's contributions added significantly to our understanding of the human, social, and psychological sides of management. Peter Parker, the former chairman of the London School of Economics, said about Follett: "People often puzzle about who is the father of management. I don't know who the father was, but I have no doubt about who was the mother."[54]

4.2 Hawthorne Studies: Elton Mayo

Australian-born Elton Mayo (1880–1948) is best known for his role in the famous Hawthorne Studies at the WESTERN ELECTRIC COMPANY. His ideas became popular during the early 20th century when labor unrest, dissatisfaction, and protests (some of them violent) were widespread in the United States, Europe, and Asia. In 1919 alone, for example, more than four million American workers went on strike.[55] Working conditions contributed to the unrest. Millions of workers in large factories toiled at boring, repetitive, unsafe jobs for low pay. Employee turnover was high and absenteeism was rampant. With employee turnover approaching 380 percent in his automobile factories, Henry Ford had to double the daily wage of his manufacturing workers from $2.50, the going wage at the time, to $5.00 to keep enough workers at their jobs. Workers joined labor unions to force companies to improve their pay and working conditions. In 1913, the federal government created the U.S. Department of Labor "to foster, promote and develop the welfare of working people, to improve their working conditions and to enhance their opportunities for profitable employment." In 1935, Congress passed the National Labor Relations Act (also known as the Wagner Act), which gave workers the legal right to form unions and collectively bargain with their employers, but prevented companies from engaging in unfair labor practices to "bust" unions. In this historical context, Mayo's work on the Hawthorne Studies proved highly relevant as managers looked for ways to increase productivity and also to improve worker satisfaction and working conditions.[56]

The Hawthorne Studies were conducted in several stages between 1924 and 1932 at a Western Electric plant in Chicago. Although Mayo didn't join the studies until 1928, he played a significant role thereafter, writing about the results in his book, *The Human Problems of an Industrial Civilization*.[57] The first stage of the Hawthorne Studies investigated the effects of lighting levels and incentives on employee productivity in the Relay Test Assembly Room, where workers took approximately a minute to

"WHAT'S NEW"
COMPANY

Exhibit 2.6

Some of Mary Parker Follett's Key Contributions to Management

Constructive conflict	• "As conflict—difference—is here in this world, as we cannot avoid it, we should, I think, use it to work for us. Instead of condemning it, we should set it to work for us."
Power	• "Power might be defined as simply the ability to make things happen, to be a causal agent, to initiate change."
	• "It seems to me that whereas power usually means *power-over*, the power of some person or group over some other person or group, it is possible to develop the conception of *power-with,* a jointly developed power, a co-active, not a coercive power."
The giving of orders	• "Probably more industrial trouble has been caused by the manner in which orders have been given than in any other way."
	• "But even if instructions are properly framed, are not given in an overbearing manner, there are many people who react violently against anything that they feel is a command. It is often the command that is resented, not the thing commanded."
	• "An advantage of not exacting blind obedience, of discussing your instructions with your subordinates, is that if there is any resentment, any come-back, you get it out into the open, and when it is in the open you can deal with it."
Authority	• "Indeed there are many indications in the present reorganization of industry that we are beginning to rid ourselves of the over and under idea, that we are coming to a different conception of authority, many indications that there is an increasing tendency to let the job itself, rather than the position occupied in a hierarchy, dictate the kind and amount of authority."
	• "Authority should go with knowledge and experience, that is where obedience is due, no matter whether it is up the line or down."
Leadership	• "Of the greatest importance is the ability to grasp a total situation.... Out of a welter of facts, experience, desires, aims, the leader must find the unifying thread. He must see a whole, not a mere kaleidoscope of pieces.... The higher up you go, the more ability you have to have of this kind."
	• "The leader makes the team. This is pre-eminently the leadership quality—the ability to organize all the forces there are in an enterprise and make them serve a common purpose."
	• "[It is wrong to assume] that you cannot be a good leader unless you are aggressive, masterful, dominating. But I think not only that these characteristics are not the qualities essential to leadership but, on the contrary, that they often militate directly against leadership."
Coordination	• "One which I consider a very important trend in business management is a system of cross-functioning between the different departments.... Each department is expected to get in touch with certain others."
	• "Many businesses are now organized in such a way that you do not have an ascending and descending ladder of authority. You have a degree of cross-functioning, of inter-relation of departments, which means a horizontal rather than a vertical authority."
	• "The most important thing to remember about unity is—that there is no such thing. There is only unifying. You cannot get unity and expect it to last a day—or five minutes. Every man in a business should be taking part in a certain process and that process is unifying."
Control	• "Control is coming more and more to mean fact-control rather than man-control."
	• "Central control is coming more and more to mean the co-relation of many controls rather than a superimposed control."

Source: M. P. Follett, *Mary Parker Follett—Prophet of Management: A Celebration of Writings from the 1920s,* ed. P. Graham (Boston: Harvard Business School Press, 1995).

put "together a coil, armature, contact springs, and insulators in a fixture and secure the parts by means of four machine screws."[58] Two groups of six experienced female workers, five to do the work and one to supply needed parts, were separated from the main part of the factory by a 10-foot partition and placed at a standard work bench with the necessary parts and tools. Over the next five years, the experimenters introduced various levels and combinations of lighting, financial incentives, and rest pauses (work breaks) to study the effect on productivity. Curiously, however, whether they increased or decreased the lighting, paid workers based on individual production or group production, or increased or decreased the number and length of rest pauses, production levels increased. In fact, Mayo and his fellow researchers were surprised that production steadily increased from 2,400 relays per day at the beginning of the study to 3,000 relays per day five years later. The question, however, was why?

© BETTMANN/CORBIS

Although Mayo's studies used several variables, like lighting and incentives to increase productivity, it turned out that productivity increased no matter what changes were made. Mayo concluded that paying more attention to the workers and the development of the workers into a cohesive group produced higher levels of productivity and job satisfaction.

Mayo and his colleagues eventually concluded that two things accounted for the results. First, substantially more attention was paid to these workers than to workers in the rest of the plant. Mayo wrote, "Before every change of program [in the study], the group is consulted. Their comments are listened to and discussed; sometimes their objections are allowed to negate a suggestion. The group unquestionably develops a sense of participation in the critical determinations and becomes something of a social unit."[59]

The "Hawthorne Effect" cannot be understood, however, without giving equal importance to the "social units," which became intensely cohesive groups. (For years, the "Hawthorne Effect" has been *incorrectly* defined as increasing productivity by paying more attention to workers.[60]) Mayo said, "What actually happened was that six individuals became a team and the team gave itself wholeheartedly and spontaneously to cooperation in the experiment. The consequence was that they felt themselves to be participating freely and without afterthought, and were happy in the knowledge that they were working without coercion from above or limits from below."[61] Together, the increased attention from management and the development of a cohesive work group led to significantly higher levels of job satisfaction *and* productivity. Mayo and his research colleagues concluded:

- *"There has been an important increase in contentment among the girls working in the test-room conditions."*
- *"There has been a decrease in absences of about 80 percent among the girls since entering the test-room group."*
- *"The changed working conditions have resulted in creating an eagerness on the part of the operators to come to work in the morning."*
- *"The operators have no clear idea as to why they are able to produce more in the test room; but as shown in the replies to the questionnaires … there is the feeling that better output is in some way related to the distinctly pleasanter, freer, and happier work conditions."*[62]

For the first time, human factors related to work were found to be more important than the physical conditions or design of the work. In short, workers' feelings and attitudes affected their work.

Workers' feelings and attitudes affected their work.

The next stage of the Hawthorne Studies was conducted in the Bank Wiring Room, where "the group consisted of nine wiremen, three solderers, and two inspectors. Each of these groups performed a specific task and collaborated with the other two in completion of each unit of equipment. The task consisted of setting up the banks of terminals side-by-side on frames, wiring the corresponding terminals from bank to bank, soldering the connections, and inspecting with a test set for short circuits or breaks in the wire. One solderman serviced the work of the three wireman."[63] In contrast to the results from the Relay Test Assembly Room, where productivity increased no matter what the researchers did, productivity dropped in the Bank Wiring Room. Again, the question was why?

Interestingly, Mayo and his colleagues found that group effects were just as responsible for the decline in performance in the Bank Wiring Room as they were for the increased performance in the Relay Test Assembly Room. The difference was that the workers in the Bank Wiring Room had been an existing work group for some time and had already developed strong negative norms that governed their behavior. For instance, despite a group financial incentive for production, the group members decided that they would wire only 6,000 to 6,600 connections a day (depending on the kind of equipment they were wiring), well below the production goal of 7,300 connections that management had set for them. Individual workers who worked at a faster pace were socially ostracized from the group, or "binged," hit on the arm, until they slowed their work pace. Thus, the group's behavior was reminiscent of the soldiering that Frederick Taylor had observed. Mayo concluded, "Work [was] done in accord with the group's conception of a day's work; this was exceeded by only one individual who was cordially disliked."[64]

In the end, the Hawthorne Studies demonstrated that the workplace was more complex than previously thought, that workers were not just extensions of machines, and that financial incentives weren't necessarily the most important motivator for workers. By highlighting the crucial role, positive or negative, that groups, group norms, and group behavior play at work, Mayo strengthened Mary Parker Follett's point about reciprocal relating—make just one change in an organization and others, some expected and some unexpected, will occur. Thanks to Mayo and his colleagues and their work on the Hawthorne Studies, managers better understood the effect that group social interactions and employee satisfaction and attitudes had on individual and group performance.

4.3 Cooperation and Acceptance of Authority: Chester Barnard

Like Henri Fayol, Chester Barnard (1886–1961) had experiences as a top executive that shaped his views of management. Barnard began his career in 1909 as an engineer and translator for *AT&T*, becoming a general manager at Pennsylvania Bell Telephone in 1922 and then president of *NEW JERSEY BELL TELEPHONE* in 1927.[65] Furthermore, like Fayol's views, Barnard's ideas, published in his classic book, *The Functions of the Executive*, influenced companies from the board of directors down. Barnard is best known for his ideas about cooperation, the executive functions that promote it, and the acceptance of authority.

In *The Functions of the Executive*, Barnard proposed a comprehensive theory of cooperation in formal organizations. In fact, he defines an **organization** as a "system of consciously coordinated activities or forces of two or more persons."[66] In other words, "organization" occurs whenever two people work together for some purpose. Thus, organization occurs when classmates work together to complete a class project, when Habitat for Humanity volunteers donate their time to build a house, and when managers work with subordinates to reduce costs, improve quality, or increase sales. Why did Barnard place so much emphasis on cooperation? Because, he said, it is the

organization a system of consciously coordinated activities or forces created by two or more people "abnormal, not the normal, condition." "Failure to cooperate, failure of cooperation, failure of organization, disorganization, disintegration, destruction of organization—and reorganization—are characteristic facts of human history."[67]

Barnard argued that managers can gain others' cooperation by completing three executive functions: securing essential services from individuals, formulating an organization's purpose and objectives, and providing a system of communication. By "securing essential services from individuals," Barnard meant that managers must find ways to encourage workers to *willingly* cooperate with each other and management to achieve organizational goals. According to Barnard, managers can gain workers' willing cooperation by offering them *material incentives*, such as money or tangible rewards; *nonmaterial incentives*, such as recognition, prestige, personal power, improved working conditions, or satisfaction of personal ideals or needs; and *associational incentives*, such as the chance to work with people they like or to be more directly involved or associated with key events or processes in the organization.[68]

By "formulating an organization's purpose and objectives," top executives unify people in the company by making clear what needs to be accomplished. If the organization's purpose is clear, then each person in each job at each level of the company should understand how his or her daily activities, behaviors, and choices contribute to the accomplishment of that purpose. This is the ultimate form of cooperation in an organization. If, however, the organization's purpose is not clear, then departmental or personal objectives may become more important than organizational objectives. The result is a less cohesive organization in which workers are less likely to cooperate to accomplish the organization's goals.

By "providing a system of communication," Barnard meant that managers must create an organizational structure with a clear hierarchy (one that delineates responsibilities, tasks, and jobs) and hire and promote the right people into management, that is, talented people with the right skills and education who will put the organization's needs before their own. Those managers, in turn, are responsible for promoting cooperation by effectively communicating the organization's purpose and objectives and by minimizing organizational politics.

Finally, the extent to which people willingly cooperate in an organization depends on how workers perceive executive authority and whether they're willing to accept it. According to Barnard, for many managerial requests or directives, there

doing the right thing

A Dangerous Mix: Power, Authority, and Autonomy

Because of their authority to hire, fire, and reward employees, nearly all managers have the power to influence those who work for them. With jobs, promotions, or pay raises on the line, few will challenge what the boss wants, unless, as Chester Barnard suggested, they're asked to do something wrong. Even then, the boss's power and authority can be enough to get some subordinates to comply. Most dangerous of all, though, are managers who have power, authority, *and* autonomy. Adding the freedom and independence of autonomy to power and authority is like dropping a tank of gasoline on an already burning fire. An explosion is sure to result. Why? The reason is that managers with autonomy may begin to believe that the "rules" don't apply to them. When that happens, they're much more likely to engage in questionable, unethical, or illegal behavior. According to Wake Forest University professors John Dunkelberg and Debra Ragin Jessup, who studied six managers who engaged in spectacular cases of unethical and illegal behavior, "The desire to commit unethical acts is nothing without the autonomy to do so. Autonomy is the factor in the equation that sends intelligent successful people over the ethical edge. They believe they are invincible because no one is looking over their shoulder." The solution, say Dunkelberg and Jessup, is to make sure that even the most powerful people in the company haves checks, balances, and controls on their autonomy.[69]

is a *zone of indifference*, in which acceptance of managerial authority is automatic. For example, if your boss asks you for a copy of the monthly inventory report, and compiling and writing that report is part of your job, you think nothing of the request and automatically send it. In general, people will be indifferent to managerial directives or orders if they (1) are understood, (2) are consistent with the purpose of the organization, (3) are compatible with the people's personal interests, and (4) can actually be carried out by those people. Acceptance of managerial authority (that is, cooperation) is not automatic, however. Ask people to do things contrary to the organization's purpose or to their own benefit and they'll put up a fight. So, while many people assume that managers have the authority to do whatever they want, Barnard, referring to the "fiction of superior authority," believed that workers ultimately grant managers their authority. Consequently, rather than threatening workers to force cooperation, Barnard maintained that it is more effective to induce their willing cooperation through incentives, clearly formulated organizational objectives, and effective communication throughout the organization.

Review 4: Human Relations Management

Unlike most people who view conflict as bad, Mary Parker Follett, the "mother of modern management," believed that conflict could be a good thing, that it should be embraced and not avoided, and that of the three ways of dealing with conflict—domination, compromise, and integration—the latter was the best because it focuses on developing creative methods for meeting conflicting parties' needs. Follett also used four principles to emphasize the importance of coordination in organizations. She believed that the best overall outcomes are achieved when leaders and workers at different levels and in different parts of the organization directly coordinate their efforts to solve problems in an integrative way.

Elton Mayo is best known for his role in the Hawthorne Studies at the Western Electric Company. In the first stage of the Hawthorne Studies, production went up because the increased attention paid to the workers in the study and their development into a cohesive work group led to significantly higher levels of job satisfaction and productivity. In the second stage, productivity dropped because the workers had already developed strong negative norms, in which individual "rate busters" who worked faster than the rest of the team or cooperated with management were ostracized or "binged." The Hawthorne Studies demonstrated that workers' feelings and attitudes affected their work, that financial incentives weren't necessarily the most important motivator for workers, and that group norms and behavior play a critical role in behavior at work.

Chester Barnard, president of New Jersey Bell Telephone, emphasized the critical importance of willing cooperation in organizations and said that managers could gain workers' willing cooperation through three executive functions: securing essential services from individuals (through material, nonmaterial, and associational incentives), unifying the people in the organization by clearly formulating the organization's purpose and objectives, and providing a system of communication. Finally, although most managerial requests or directives will be accepted because they fall within the zone of indifference, Barnard maintains that it is more effective to induce cooperation through incentives, clearly formulating organizational objectives, and effective communication throughout the organization. Ultimately, he says, workers grant managers their authority, not the other way around.

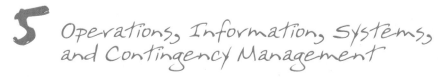

5 Operations, Information, Systems, and Contingency Management

In this last section, we review four other significant historical approaches to management that have influenced how today's managers produce goods and services on a daily basis, gather and manage the information they need to understand their businesses and make good decisions, understand how the different parts of the company work together as a whole, and recognize when and where particular management practices are likely to work.

*To better understand these ideas, let's learn about **5.1 operations management**, **5.2 information management**, **5.3 systems management**, and **5.4 contingency management**.*

5.1 Operations Management

In Chapter 18, you will learn about *operations management*, which involves managing the daily production of goods and services. In general, operations management uses a quantitative or mathematical approach to find ways to increase productivity, improve quality, and manage or reduce costly inventories. The most commonly used operations management tools and methods are quality control, forecasting techniques, capacity planning, productivity measurement and improvement, linear programming, scheduling systems, inventory systems, work measurement techniques (similar to the Gilbreths' motion studies), project management (similar to Gantt's charts), and cost-benefit analysis.[70]

Today, with those tools and techniques, we take it for granted that manufactured goods will be made with standardized, interchangeable parts; that the design of those parts will be based on specific, detailed plans; and that manufacturing companies will aggressively manage inventories to keep costs low and increase productivity. Surprisingly, these key elements of operations management have some rather strange origins: guns, geometry, and fire.

Since 1526, in Gardone, Italy, the descendants of Bartolomeo Beretta have been making world-renowned **BERETTA** firearms and gun barrels. Throughout most of the company's history, skilled craftsmen made the lock, stock, and barrel of a Beretta gun by hand. After each part was made, a skilled gun finisher assembled the parts into a complete gun. The gun finisher did not simply screw the different parts of a gun together, as is done today, however. Instead, each handmade part required extensive finishing and adjusting so that it would fit together with the other handmade gun parts. This was necessary because, even when made by the same skilled craftsman, no two parts were alike. In fact, gun finishers played a role similar to that of fine watchmakers, who meticulously assembled expensive watches—without them, the product simply wouldn't work. Today, we would say that these parts were low quality because they varied so much from part to part. You'll learn more about variation and quality in Chapter 18 on managing service and manufacturing operations.

"WHAT'S NEW" COMPANY

All this changed in 1791, however, when the U.S. government, worried about a possible war with France, ordered 40,000 muskets from private gun contractors. Like Beretta, all but one contractor built handmade muskets assembled by skilled gun finishers who made sure that all the parts fit together. Thus, each musket was unique. If a part broke, a replacement part had to be handcrafted. But one contractor, Eli Whitney of New Haven, Connecticut, who is better known for his invention of the cotton gin, determined that if gun parts were made accurately enough, guns could be made with standardized, interchangeable parts. So he designed machine tools that allowed unskilled workers to make each gun part the same as the next. Said Whitney, "The tools which I contemplate to make are similar to an engraving on copper plate from which may be taken a great number of impressions perceptibly alike." Years passed before Whitney delivered his 10,000 muskets to the U.S. government. In 1801, however, he demonstrated the superiority of interchangeable parts to President-elect Thomas Jefferson by quickly and easily assembling complete muskets from randomly picked piles of musket parts.

Today, because of Whitney's ideas, most products, from cars to toasters to space shuttles, are manufactured using standardized, interchangeable parts. But even with this advance, manufacturers still faced the significant limitation that they could not produce a part unless they had seen or examined it firsthand. Thanks to Gaspard Monge, a Frenchman of modest beginnings, this soon changed.

In Monge's time, maps were crude, often inaccurate, and almost never up-to-date. In 1762, however, as a 16-year-old, Monge drew a large-scale map of the town of Beaune, France. He developed new surveying tools and systematic methods of observation so that every feature on the map was in proportion and correctly placed. Monge's advanced skills as a draftsman led to his appointment to the prestigious Ècole Militaire de Mézières, a military institute, where one of his first assignments was to determine the proper placement of cannons for a military fortress. This task normally involved long, complicated mathematical computations, but using the geometrical principles he had developed as a draftsman, Monge calculated his estimates so quickly that, at first, commanders refused to believe they were accurate. Soon, however, they realized the importance of his breakthrough and protected it as a military secret for more than a decade.[71]

Monge's greatest achievement, however, was his book *Descriptive Geometry*. In it, he explained techniques for drawing three-dimensional objects on paper. For the first time, precise drawings permitted manufacturers to make standardized, interchangeable parts without first examining a prototype. Today, thanks to Monge, manufacturers rely on CAD (computer-aided design) and CAM (computer-aided manufacturing) to take three-dimensional designs straight from the computer to the factory floor.

Once standardized, interchangeable parts became the norm, and parts could be made from design drawings alone, manufacturers ran into a costly problem that they had never faced before: too much inventory.

Once standardized, interchangeable parts became the norm, and parts could be made from design drawings alone, manufacturers ran into a costly problem that they had never faced before: too much inventory. *Inventory* is the amount and number of raw materials, parts, and finished products that a company has in its possession. In fact, large factories were accumulating parts inventories sufficient for two to three months, much more than they needed on a daily basis to run their manufacturing operations. A solution to this problem was found in 1905 when the OLDSMOBILE MOTOR WORKS in Detroit burned down. At a time when cars were far too expensive for most Americans, Oldsmobile had become the leading automobile manufacturer in the United States by being the first to produce an affordable car. When the Oldsmobile factory burned down, management rented a new production facility to get production up and running as quickly as possible. But because the new facility was much smaller, there was no room to store large stockpiles of inventory

"WHAT'S NEW" COMPANY

(which the company couldn't afford anyway as it was short on funds). Therefore, the company made do with what it called "hand-to-mouth inventories," in which each production station had only enough parts on hand to do a short production run. Fortunately, since all of its parts suppliers were close by, Oldsmobile could place orders in the morning and receive them in the afternoon (even without telephones), just like today's computerized, just-in-time inventory systems. So, contrary to common belief, just-in-time inventory systems were not invented by Japanese manufacturers. Instead, they were invented out of necessity a century ago because of a fire. You can learn more about just-in-time inventory management in Chapter 18.

5.2 Information Management

The earliest recorded use of written information occurred nearly 60,000 years ago when Cro-Magnons, from whom modern humans descended, created and recorded a lunar calendar. The calendar consisted of 28 symbols carved into a reindeer antler and indicated when the waters would be high. The calendar was used to track and kill deer, bison, and elk that would gather at river crossings. For most of recorded history, information has been costly, difficult to obtain, and slow to spread. Because of the immense labor and time it took to hand-copy information, books, manuscripts, and written documents of any kind were rare and extremely expensive. Word of Joan of Arc's death in 1431 took 18 months to travel from France across Europe to Constantinople (now Istanbul, Turkey). Most people literally heard news and information from the town crier (Hear ye! Hear ye!) or from minstrel and acting groups who relayed information as they traveled from town to town.

Moreover, as you will learn in Chapter 17, accurate, timely, relevant, and complete information has been important to businesses throughout history. Indeed, 99 percent of the clay tablets and animal-skin documents unearthed in our earliest cities are business and economic texts. Traders, craftspeople, and local businesspeople used them to keep track of trades, orders, and how much money (or gold, pigs, or chickens) was owed to whom.

Consequently, throughout history, organizations have pushed for and quickly adopted new information technologies that reduce the cost or increase the speed with which they can acquire, store, retrieve, or communicate information. The first "technologies" to truly revolutionize the business use of information were paper and the printing press. In the 14th century, water-powered machines were created to pulverize rags into pulp to make paper. Paper prices, which were already lower than those of animal-skin parchments, dropped dramatically. Less than a half-century later, Johannes Gutenberg invented the printing press, which greatly reduced the cost and time needed to copy written information. For instance, in 1483 in Florence, Italy, a scribe would charge one florin (an Italian unit of money) to hand-copy one document page. By contrast, a printer would set up and print 1,025 copies of the same document for just three florins. Within 50 years of its invention, Gutenberg's printing press cut the cost of information by 99.8 percent!

What Gutenberg's printing press did for publishing, the manual typewriter did for daily communication. Before 1850, most business correspondence was written by hand and copied using the "letter press." With the ink still wet, the letter would be placed into a tissue-paper "book." A hand press would then be used to squeeze the "book" and copy the still-wet ink onto the tissue paper. By the 1870s, manual typewriters made it cheaper, easier, and faster to produce and copy business correspondence. Of course, in the 1980s, slightly more than a century later, typewriters were replaced by personal computers and word processing software for identical reasons.

During the Renaissance, the Medici were at the forefront of managing information and ensuring that information was delivered speedily.

As the volume of printed information increased, businesses needed new ways to organize and make sense of it. Vertical file cabinets and the Woodruff file, invented in 1868, represented major advances in information storage and retrieval. Once sales orders or business correspondence were put in the proper file drawer, they could be found easily and quickly by anyone familiar with the system. The cash register, invented in 1879, kept sales clerks honest by recording all sales transactions on a roll of paper securely locked inside the machine. But managers soon realized that its most important contribution was better management and control of their business. For example, department stores could track performance and sales by installing separate cash registers in the food, clothing, and hardware departments. Time clocks, introduced in the 1890s, helped businesses keep track of worker hours and costs.

Finally, businesses have always looked for information technologies that would speed access to timely information. For instance, the Medici family, which opened banks throughout Europe in the early 1400s, used posting messengers to keep in contact with their more than 40 "branch" managers. The post messengers, who predated the U.S. Postal Service Pony Express by 400 years, could travel 90 miles per day, twice what average riders could cover, because the Medicis were willing to pay for the expense of providing them with fresh horses. This need for timely information also led companies to quickly adopt the telegraph in the 1860s, the telephone in the 1880s, and, of course, Internet technologies in the last decade. See Chapter 17 for more on how companies are using today's technologies to lower the cost and increase the speed with which accurate, timely, relevant, and complete information is acquired.

5.3 Systems Management

Today's companies are much more complex than they used to be. They are larger and employ more people. They most likely manufacture, service, *and* finance what they sell, not only in their home markets but in foreign markets throughout the world, too. They also operate in complex, fast-changing, competitive, global environments that can quickly turn competitive advantages into competitive disadvantages.

How, then, can managers make sense of this complexity, both within and outside their organizations? One way to deal with organizational and environmental complexity is to take a systems view of organizations, which derived from theoretical models in biology and social psychology in the 1950s and 1960s.[72] A **system** is a set of interrelated elements or parts that function as a whole. So rather than viewing one part of an organization as separate from the other parts, a systems approach encourages managers to complicate their thinking by looking for connections between the different parts of the organization. Indeed, one of the more important ideas in the systems approach to management is that organizational systems are composed of parts or **subsystems,** which are simply smaller systems within larger systems. Subsystems and their connections matter in systems theory because of the possibility for managers to create synergy. **Synergy** occurs when two or more subsystems working together can produce more than they can working apart. In other words, synergy occurs when $1 + 1 = 3$.

system a set of interrelated elements or parts that function as a whole

subsystems smaller systems that operate within the context of a larger system

synergy when two or more subsystems working together can produce more than they can working apart

Whereas **closed systems** can function without interacting with their environments, nearly all organizations should be viewed as **open systems** that interact with their environments and depend on them for survival. Therefore, rather than viewing what goes on within the organization as separate from what goes on outside it, the systems approach also encourages managers to look for connections between the different parts of the organization and the different parts of its environment. Successful interaction with organizational environments is critical because open systems tend toward **entropy**, which is the inevitable and steady deterioration of a system.

As shown in Exhibit 2.7, organizations operate in two kinds of complex environments. The *general environment* consists of the economy and the technological, sociocultural, and political/legal trends that indirectly affect all organizations. Changes in any sector of the general environment eventually affect most organizations. In addition, each organization has a specific environment that is unique to that firm's industry and directly affects the way it conducts day-to-day business. The *specific environment* includes customers, competitors, suppliers, industry regulation, and advocacy groups. Both the general and specific environments are discussed in detail in Chapter 3. As Exhibit 2.7 shows, organizational systems obtain inputs from the general and specific environments. Managers and workers then use their management knowledge and manufacturing techniques to transform those inputs into outputs, such as products and services, which are then consumed by persons or organizations in the environment, which, in turn, provide feedback to the organization, allowing managers and workers to modify and improve their products or services.

A systems view of organizations offers several advantages. First, it forces managers to view their organizations as part of and subject to the competitive, economic, social, technological, and legal/regulatory forces in their environments.[73] Second, it also forces managers to be aware of how the environment affects specific parts of the organization. Third, because of the complexity and difficulty of trying to achieve synergies between different parts of the organization, the systems view encourages managers to focus on better communication and cooperation within the organization. Finally, it makes managers acutely aware that good internal management of the organization may not be enough to ensure survival. Survival also depends on making sure that the organization continues to satisfy critical environmental stakeholders, such as shareholders, employees, customers, suppliers, governments, and local communities. For more on ideas related to the systems view of management, see Chapter 3 on environments and cultures, Chapter 4 on ethics and social responsibility, Chapter 6 on organizational strategy, and Chapter 8 on global management.

5.4 Contingency Management

Earlier you learned that the goal of scientific management was to use systematic study to find the "one best way" of doing each task and then use that "one best way" everywhere. The problem, as you may have gathered from reading about the various approaches to management, is that

closed systems systems that can sustain themselves without interacting with their environments

open systems systems that can sustain themselves only by interacting with their environments, on which they depend for their survival

entropy the inevitable and steady deterioration of a system

mgmt: fact

Fad Jumping
Management consultants are seemingly everywhere, and many make a living trying to convince companies that the latest management idea holds the key to previously unattainable success. Managers may be tempted to adopt these ideas and implement them across their organizations without considering their company's industry, business model, financials, workforce, or culture. But embracing one-stop, quick-fix management programs can be detrimental to a business and its employees. That's not to say all of the latest management ideas are bunk. Instead of jumping from fad to fad to fad, however, try cherry-picking the best ideas that are the most appropriate for your business. And really, just learn to manage.

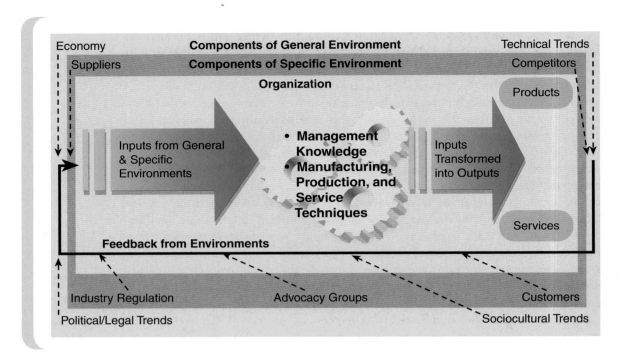

Exhibit 2.7

Systems View of Organizations

no one in management seems to agree on what that "one best way" is. Furthermore, more than 100 years of management research has shown that there are clear boundaries or limitations to most management theories and practices. No management ideas or practices are universal. Though they may work much of the time, none works all the time. But then how is a manager to decide what theory to use? Well, it depends on the situation. The **contingency approach** to management precisely states that there are no universal management theories and that the most effective management theory or idea depends on the kinds of problems or situations that managers or organizations are facing at a particular time.[74] In short, the "best way" depends on the situation.

One of the practical implications of the contingency approach to management is that management is much harder than it looks. In fact, because of the clarity and obviousness of management theories (OK, most of them), students and workers often wrongly assume that if management would take just a few simple steps, then a company's problems would be quickly and easily solved. If this were true, few companies would have problems. A second implication of the contingency approach is that managers need to look for key contingencies that differentiate today's situation or problems from yesterday's situation or problems. Moreover, it means that managers need to spend more time analyzing problems, situations, and employees before taking action to fix them. Finally, it means that as you read this text and learn about management ideas and practices, you need to pay particular attention to qualifying phrases such as "usually," "in these situations," "for this to work," and "under these circumstances." Doing so will help you identify the key contingencies that will help you become a better manager.

Review 5: **Operations, Information, Systems, and Contingency Management**

contingency approach holds that there are no universal management theories and that the most effective management theory or idea depends on the kinds of problems or situations that managers are facing at a particular time and place

Operations management uses a quantitative or mathematical approach to find ways to increase productivity, improve quality, and manage or reduce costly inventories. The manufacture of standardized, interchangeable parts, the graphical and computerized design of parts, and the accidental discovery of just-in-time management were some of the most important historical events in operations management.

For most of recorded history, information has been costly, difficult to obtain, and slow to spread. Consequently, throughout history, organizations have pushed for and quickly adopted new information technologies that reduce the cost or increase the speed with which they can acquire, store, retrieve, or communicate information. Historically, some of the most important technologies that have revolutionized information management were the use of horses in Italy in the 1400s, the creation of paper and the printing press in the 14th and 15th centuries, the manual typewriter in 1850, vertical file cabinets for storage of information and the telegraph in the 1860s, cash registers in 1879, the telephone in the 1880s, time clocks in the 1890s, the personal computer in the 1980s, and the Internet in the 1990s.

A system is a set of interrelated elements or parts that function as a whole. Organizational systems obtain inputs from the general and specific environments. Managers and workers then use their management knowledge and manufacturing techniques to transform those inputs into outputs, such as products and services, which are then consumed by persons or organizations in the environment, which, in turn, provide feedback to the organization, allowing managers and workers to modify and improve their products or services. Organizational systems must also address the issues of synergy, open versus closed systems, and entropy.

Finally, the contingency approach to management precisely states that there are no universal management theories. The most effective management theory or idea depends on the kinds of problems or situations that managers or organizations are facing at a particular time. This means that management is much harder than it looks and that managers need to look for key contingencies by spending more time analyzing problems and situations before they take action to fix them.

Dealing with Conflict

Conflict is an inevitable part of work life (and life in general), and the success of individual employees, teams, and entire organizations depends on how they manage interpersonal conflict. How do you deal with conflict? Do you look for it, avoid it, or something in between? This 20-question assessment is designed to provide insight into how you manage conflict.[75] This information will provide you with a baseline for future development of conflict-management skills.

You can also use this self-assessment as a precursor to doing the Management Team Decision below. At a minimum it will raise your awareness of how you handle differences of opinion before you begin working in a team. It may even inspire you to make conscious changes in your conflict-management style, helping you—and your team—be more effective.

Rate each statement using the following scale:

1   Strongly disagree
2   Disagree
3   Not sure
4   Agree
5   Strongly agree

When I have a conflict at work, I do the following:

1. I give in to the wishes of the other party.
    1   2   3   4   5
2. I try to realize a middle-of-the-road solution.
    1   2   3   4   5
3. I push my own point of view.
    1   2   3   4   5
4. I examine issues until I find a solution that really satisfies me and the other party.
    1   2   3   4   5
5. I avoid a confrontation about our differences.
    1   2   3   4   5
6. I concur with the other party.
    1   2   3   4   5
7. I emphasize that we have to find a compromise solution.
    1   2   3   4   5
8. I search for gains.
    1   2   3   4   5
9. I stand for my own and other's goals and interests.
    1   2   3   4   5
10. I avoid differences of opinion as much as possible.
    1   2   3   4   5
11. I try to accommodate the other party.
    1   2   3   4   5
12. I insist we both give in a little.
    1   2   3   4   5
13. I fight for a good outcome for myself.
    1   2   3   4   5
14. I examine ideas from both sides to find a mutually optimal solution.
    1   2   3   4   5
15. I try to make differences loom less severe.
    1   2   3   4   5
16. I adapt to the other parties' goals and interests.
    1   2   3   4   5
17. I strive whenever possible toward a 50–50 compromise.
    1   2   3   4   5
18. I do everything to win.
    1   2   3   4   5
19. I work out a solution that serves my own as well as other's interests as much as possible.
    1   2   3   4   5
20. I try to avoid a confrontation with the other person.
    1   2   3   4   5

KEY TERMS

bureaucracy 50
closed systems 67
compromise 56
contingency approach 68
domination 56
entropy 67
Gantt chart 48
integrative conflict
   resolution 56
motion study 46
open systems 67
organization 60
rate buster 44
scientific management 43
soldiering 44
subsystem 66
synergy 66
system 66
time study 46

This inventory can be broken down into five sections:

(A) Add together your scores for items 1, 6, 11, and 16: _____

(B) Add together your scores for items 2, 7, 12, and 17: _____

(C) Add together your scores for items 3, 8, 13, and 18: _____

(D) Add together your scores for items 4, 9, 14, and 19: _____

(E) Add together your scores for items 5, 10, 15, and 20: _____

You can find the interpretation for your score at: **academic.cengage.com/management/williams.**

MANAGEMENT DECISION

Scripted Service

It has been two years since you took over your family's chain of specialty neighborhood bakeries located in areas with high foot traffic.[76] Throughout the city, your stores are *the* choice for birthday cakes, Christmas cookies, Valentine's Day cupcakes, and the daily doughnut. Even though sales are steady, you want to grow and are having a difficult time figuring out exactly how to increase revenues. For the past three weeks, you have spent each day in a different store, stocking cases, slicing bread, and generally pitching in where needed, but mostly you have been observing.

As luck would have it, about 80 percent of your stores are located near or next to a Starbucks. On your way to the stores each morning, you have stopped to get your morning coffee, and at each Starbucks, you have been greeted quickly, chatted with the clerk, ordered, heard your order repeated across the bar, used a loaded Starbucks card to pay, been asked if you want your balance, and been told to have a nice day. Today is the same. As you wait for your coffee, you think about the contrast between this prescribed sequence and what you have been seeing in your own stores. Even though your clerks serve customers efficiently, they do so in various ways. Some clerks are outgoing, talking and laughing with the customer while assembling the order. Other clerks are more reserved, filling the order quickly but with little conversation and barely a smile.

Now that you have noticed these differences, everywhere you shop you've been paying attention to sales speech patterns, which appear scripted and repetitive but pleasantly predictable. From the grocery ("Do you have any coupons?" and "Paper or plastic?") to the fast-food restaurant ("Do you want fries with that?" and "For here

or to go?"), the patterns are most noticeable during busy periods. Clerks follow the same speech sequence with every customer.

A little research reveals that numerous companies require employees to follow a script. At McDonald's, the script is concerned with speech: for example, workers must say "May I help you, ma'am?" instead of "Can I help someone?" At Olive Garden, the script adds actions to the words: greet the table within 30 seconds of sitdown; take the drink order within three minutes; during ordering, suggest five items (drink, side dish, dessert, specials, and special offers); after food arrives, check back within three minutes. At Starbucks, things are more relaxed, but there is still a script to guide employee interactions with customers looking for a latte.

After a week of observing these scripted encounters, you begin to wonder if you should write a sales script for your bakery staff. If interactions were standardized, you might be able to increase efficiency and sales revenue. A script might be a great help during the morning and the after-school rush, as well as a useful training tool for new hires; it might help them feel more confident behind the counter. Since you want to grow, a script could also help you get up and running faster in new locations. But how would your current employees feel about it? They all have different ways of working with customers. About half of them have been with you for many years and know the ropes already. And how would your customers respond? The bakery could lose some of its neighborly appeal when customers recognize the canned speech.

You hear the barista call out, "Triple-shot venti extra-hot latte," so you go collect your coffee. She looks you right in the eye, smiles, and says, "Have a nice day!"

Questions

1. Which historical management technique best describes scripted service speech and scripted employee behavior? Explain your choice.

2. Do you implement a customer-encounter script at your bakeries? Why or why not?

3. Imagine that you have decided to implement a script for your frontline employees. Write the service script for bakery clerks.

MANAGEMENT TEAM DECISION

Peer Review for Conflict Resolution

Your troubles began when the teenage clerk at one of your convenience stores wrestled a gun away from a would-be robber. On hearing the story, your friends said, "How brave!" and "Did you give him an award?" but you and the other managers in the company all had a very different reaction. You know you will have to fire the employee for violating a long-standing and well-known company policy against heroism. Convenience store robberies are a common occurrence, and if your (mostly young) workers, manning dozens of stores, begin to attempt behind-the-counter vigilantism, you will have a serious problem on your hands.

Despite the unanimous mind-set of your management team, you realize that firing the employee outright may create negative fallout among the other employees. At least one employee in particular is likely to vocally protest the firing. As you sit with your team trying to decide how to resolve this issue, one of your managers proposes implementing a peer review process at the company. A panel of employees would be responsible for arbitrating disputes and resolving any disagreements between how managers enforce the rules and how employees experience those rules being enforced.

Advocates trumpet the benefits of peer review systems. Peer reviews are practical and cost-effective, particularly compared with formal legal arbitration, and they allow disputes to be resolved internally. Because peer reviews give employees some say in the outcome of disputes, the employees are more likely to find the decisions credible and acceptable. Many managers also like peer reviews because they help to avert the backlash that a manager may experience for unilaterally disciplining an employee who has violated company rules.

Detractors, however, say that peer reviews may give employees too much control over the management decision process. Review panels effectively diffuse the decision-making function throughout the organization in a way that is counter to the centralized decision making of traditionally structured companies. In addition, creating and maintaining peer review systems requires a commitment of time and resources. Employees lose work hours (and thus productivity) when they participate on panels. And management should consult with a knowledgeable attorney to make sure that review panel procedures conform to National Labor Relations Board (NLRB) dictates about work teams. The process must be shared with all employees, who also must be trained in the process. And what will you do if employees reverse a management decision?

Nonetheless, the number of companies using peer review systems is increasing as their popularity grows. One consultant alone has over 500 companies, including Kodak, Hooters, Marriott, and Red Lobster, using his peer review process.

For this exercise, assemble a team of five students to act as the management team for the convenience store chain in this scenario.

Questions

1. Which historical management theory gives the best justification for implementing peer review systems? Which theory would not support peer reviews?

2. Do you implement a peer review process in the convenience store scenario? Explain your decision.

3. Regardless of your answer in question 2, as a team draw up guidelines for a peer review process. What would you need to consider if you were to create a review panel? For example, do you need to set restrictions on the ratio of employees to managers on the panel (will there even be managers on the panel?). How many years of service should an employee have to participate? Should the panel include a mix of employees from different departments?

4. Now, following the guidelines you established in question 3, imagine that your team is the review panel for the convenience store clerk who foiled a robbery. Discuss the situation and come to a decision regarding the outcome. Do you fire the employee, warn the employee, or commend his actions?

Observing History Today

The topic of management history may sound like old news, but many of the issues and problems addressed by Max Weber, Chester Barnard, and other management theorists still challenge managers today. *How can we structure an organization for maximum efficiency and just treatment of individuals? What is the basis for, and limits to, authority in organizations?* It is rather amazing that these thinkers of the late 19th and early 20th centuries generated such a wealth of theory that still influences our discussion of management and leadership challenges in the 21st century. This exercise will give you the opportunity to draw upon some ideas that trace their roots back to the pioneers of management thinking.

Preparing in Advance for Class Discussion

Step 1: Find an observation point. Identify a place where you can unobtrusively observe a group of people as they go about their work. You might select a coffee shop, bookstore, or restaurant.

Step 2: Settle in and observe. Go to your selected workplace and observe the people working there for at least 20 minutes. You should take along something like a notebook or PDA so that you can jot down a few notes. It is a good idea to go during a busy time, so long as it is not so crowded that you will be unable to easily observe the workers.

Step 3: Observe employees at work. Observe the process of work, and the interaction among the employees. Consider some of the following issues:

- Identify the steps that employees follow in completing a work cycle (for example, from taking an order to delivering a product). Can you see improvements that might be made, particularly steps that might be eliminated or streamlined?

- Observe the interaction and mood of the workers. Are they stressed? Or are they more relaxed? Does it seem to you that these workers like working with each other?

- Listen for signs of conflict. If you see signs of conflict, is the conflict resolved? If so, how did the workers resolve their conflict? If not, do you think that these workers suppress (bottle up) conflict?

- Can you tell who is in charge here? If so, how do the other workers respond to this person's directions? If not, how does the work group sort out who should be doing each task, and in what order?

Step 4: Consider what you saw. Immediately after your observation session, look through this chapter on management history for connections to your observations. For example, do you see any signs of the "Hawthorne effect"? Would Fredrick Taylor approve of the work process you observed, or might he have suggested improvements? What might Chester Barnard's theory have to say about how the workers you observed responded to instructions from their "boss"? Write a one-page paper of bullet-point notes describing possible connections between your observations and the thinking of management pioneers such as Mary Parker Follett.

Class Discussion:

Step 5: Share your findings as a class. Discuss the various points of connection that you found pioneering management thinkers and your own observations of people at work. Are some of the issues of management "timeless"? If so, what do you see as timeless issues of management? What are some ways in which work and management *have changed* since the days of the management pioneers?

Know Where Management Is Going

As you read in the chapter, management theories are dynamic. In other words, they change over time, sometimes very rapidly. In addition, management theories have often been cumulative, meaning that later theorists tend to build on theories previously advanced by other scholars. Thus, a new theory becomes the starting point for yet another theory that can either refine or refute the management thinking of the day.

One way to prepare for your career as a manager is by becoming aware of management trends today. The best (and easiest) way to do that is by regularly combing through business newspapers and periodicals. You will always find at least one article that relates to management concepts, and as you scan the business press over time, you will see which theories are influencing current management thinking the most. By understanding management history and management today, you will be better able to anticipate changes to management ideas in the future. This exercise is designed to introduce you to the business press and to help you make the connection between the concepts you learn in the classroom and real-world management activities. Done regularly, it will provide you with invaluable insights into business activities at all types of organizations around the world.

Activities

1. Find a current article of substance in the business press (for example, the *Wall Street Journal*, the *Financial Times, Fortune, BusinessWeek, Inc.*) that discusses topics covered in this course. Although this is only Chapter 2, you will be surprised by the amount of terminology you have already learned. If you are having trouble finding an article, read through the table of contents on pages iv–viii to familiarize yourself with the names of concepts that will be presented later in the term. Read your article carefully, making notes about relevant content.

2. Write a one-paragraph summary of the key points in your article. List the terms or concepts critical to understanding the article, and provide definitions of those terms. If you are unfamiliar with a term or concept that is central to the article, do some research in your textbook or see your professor during office hours. Relate these key points to the concepts in your text by citing page numbers.

3. How does your article relate to the management theories covered in this chapter? Explain the situation detailed in your article in terms of the history of management.

REEL TO REAL

In Good Company

In Good Company is a 2004 film featuring Dennis Quaid in the role of Dan Foreman, an advertising sales executive at a top publication. After a corporate takeover, Dan is placed under a supervisor half his age named Carter Duryea (Topher Grace). Matters are made worse when Carter becomes romantically involved with Dan's daughter Alex (Scarlett Johansson), a college student. The film's working title was *Synergy*, and in this clip you will see Carter Duryea explaining how that concept works to the benefit of the company and its clients.

What to Watch for and Ask Yourself

1. Does Carter Duryea's explanation of synergy reflect the discussion of synergy in Section 5.3?
2. What potential downside with Carter's plan does Dan identify during the meeting? Do you agree with Dan or Carter?
3. What kind of system is Carter Duryea describing in the clip? Explain.

Original Penguin

Ideas about managing people and their work have changed over the past 125 years. At Original Penguin, Chris Kolbe has used a nontraditional, hands-on management style to transform a clothing icon that had its heyday over 30 years ago into a popular brand for today. Instead of ordering his employees around, Chris works with them to achieve a shared vision. His personal style motivates others to take pride in their work and to see themselves as part of an exciting project.

What to Watch for and Ask Yourself

1. Where does Chris Kolbe's authority come from? How do his ideas about authority compare to those of Mary Parker Follett?
2. Kolbe likes to use one-on-one communication with his employees. Is this a good idea? Why or why not?
3. Chester Barnard claimed that managers need to encourage workers' willing cooperation through incentives. How does Kolbe do this?

DESTINATION XM

Organizational Environments and Cultures

Learning Outcomes:

1 Discuss how changing environments affect organizations.
2 Describe the four components of the general environment.
3 Explain the five components of the specific environment.
4 Describe the process that companies use to make sense of their changing environments.
5 Explain how organizational cultures are created and how they can help companies be successful.

In This Chapter:

External Environments

1. Changing Environments
   1.1 Environmental Change
   1.2 Environmental Complexity
   1.3 Resource Scarcity
   1.4 Uncertainty
2. General Environment
   2.1 Economy
   2.2 Technological Component
   2.3 Sociocultural Component
   2.4 Political/Legal Component
3. Specific Environment
   3.1 Customer Component
   3.2 Competitor Component
   3.3 Supplier Component
   3.4 Industry Regulation Component
   3.5 Advocacy Groups

4. Making Sense of Changing Environments
   4.1 Environmental Scanning
   4.2 Interpreting Environmental Factors
   4.3 Acting on Threats and Opportunities

Internal Environments

5. Organizational Cultures: Creation, Success, and Change
   5.1 Creation and Maintenance of Organizational Cultures
   5.2 Successful Organizational Cultures
   5.3 Changing Organizational Cultures

Key Terms
Self Assessment
Management Decision
Management Team Decision
Practice Being a Manager
Develop Your Career Potential
Reel to Real

WHAT WOULD YOU DO?

XM Satellite Radio Holdings, Inc, **Washington, D.C.**[1] As the new director of marketing for XM Satellite Radio, you're starting to wonder if you've joined the crew of a sinking ship. Despite years of hopeful forecasts, XM and its main competitor in the satellite radio industry, Sirius, recently reported a combined annual loss in excess of $1.5 billion. XM's shares are now trading for less than 30 percent of their initial offering price, and the company's net subscriber increase (the number of new subscribers minus defecting ones) has slowed considerably.

When the company was formed in the late 1980s, there were no iPods or MP3s, so a music lover away from home had no choice but to tote around cassette tapes or compact discs. In March 1997, American Mobile received the first Satellite digital audio radio license and contracted with Hughes Space (now Boeing Space Systems) to build and launch two satellites. Over the next four years, the company sold shares of stock to the public, signed licensing agreements with media providers to provide content for each channel, and prepared for the launch of its first satellite (Rock) followed in May by its second satellite (Roll). XM started with almost 200 channels of mostly commercial-free content. Its competitor Sirius Satellite Radio was founded in as CD Radio. Sirius launched their service, which was very similar to XM, and the two have competed fiercely for customers ever since. In the original charter agreements granting each the satellite frequencies, congress specifically forbade any merger between the two companies.

The stakes were raised to almost astronomical levels when shock jock Howard Stern moved from CBS Radio to Sirius under a contract that paid him $500 million over five years. XM countered by announcing deals for Major League Baseball ($650 million over 11 years), the National Hockey League, and Oprah Winfrey; Sirius announced deals with the National Basketball Association, the National Football League ($220 million over seven years) and the English Premier League. These deals have coincided with almost ritualistic restatements lowering subscriber forecasts. These forecasts (their prediction about how many subscribers they will retain and attain each quarter) are crucial to their stockholders because that information provides insights into the potential success of the company.

According to the *Wall Street Journal*, "many people are simply having iPod adapters installed in their cars and skipping satellite altogether." Indeed, XM and Sirius compete with established ground-based stations and personal music devices as well as each other in a bid for listeners' attention. Both companies have offered free trial subscriptions, reduced rate radios that can be installed in your car, pre-installed radios on new vehicles, and cut-rate programs that provide up to a year of free service.

To separate itself from Sirius and standard AM/FM radio, XM introduced NavTraffic, a system that compiles ground-based traffic information into recommended travel routes for cars equipped with navigation systems. The new XM2go devices that allow the customer to take their radio with them when they leave the car have received rave market feedback. Unfortunately, the record industry is not pleased with a new system that can capture digital songs and sued XM *(Atlantic Recordings Corp. v. XM Satellite Radio, Inc.)*. On another front, the Federal Communications Commission began investigating these new receivers as their powerful signal interferes with radios in nearby automobiles.

XM is facing competition from areas they never anticipated when they spend hundreds of millions to launch a satellite service. They have a large physical and contractual commitment to provide continuous satellite radio and yet they must find a way to evaluate the new environment in which they are working. How would you evaluate their current situation? XM needs to find a way to be unique relative to their new competitors (including the iPod). What should XM do if they want to be successful? **If you were the director of marketing, what would you do?**

ACTIVITIES + VIDEOS

CengageNOW Audio study guide, electronic flashcards, author FAQ videos, On the Job and Biz Flix videos, concept tutorial, and concept exercise

Web (academic.cengage.com/management/williams) Quiz, PowerPoint slides, and glossary terms for this chapter

"WHAT'S NEW" COMPANIES

XM SATELLITE RADIO

NATURAL OVENS

EA SPORTS

NAPSTER

APPLE COMPUTER

NOVARTIS

DINNER BY DESIGN

GOODYEAR

HOOVER

DYSON

AND OTHERS . . .

Wherever XM's top managers look, they see changes and forces outside the company that threaten their ability to continue to make XM a successful business. Their direct competitor spent hundreds of millions of dollars to acquire the type of content that listeners would prefer and previously unknown technologies have threatened to make their business obsolete.

This chapter examines the internal and external forces that affect business. We begin by explaining how the changes in external organizational environments affect the decisions and performance of a company. Next, we examine the two types of external organizational environments: the general environment that affects all organizations and the specific environment unique to each company. Then, we learn how managers make sense of their changing general and specific environments. The chapter finishes with a discussion of internal organizational environments by focusing on organizational culture.

EXTERNAL ENVIRONMENTS

External environments are the forces and events outside a company that have the potential to influence or affect it. Ask adults what their favorite after-school snack was, and they're likely to tell you "milk and cookies." But that's not true today, as overall cookie sales, including those of Oreos and Chips Ahoy, have dropped over 8 percent in the past five years.[2] Several trends in cookie companies' external environments are behind this decline. As part of the fight against obesity, parents and school systems are replacing cookies with healthier alternatives, such as fruits and vegetables. Consequently, the Vista, California, school district stopped buying 28,000 chocolate-chip cookies *per month* for its students. Also, thanks to microwaves, nobody bakes any more. Fifteen minutes to bake a batch of cookies seems an eternity. Quaker Oats' annual baking contest attracts only half the entries it did a decade ago. Trying to reverse the decline, Kraft Foods has developed the Vanilla Oreo, which has no unhealthy trans fats, and small, prewrapped 100-calorie packages of Oreos and Chips Ahoy "thin crisps." Can the "cookie" be saved? Mike Senackerib of Kraft says, "I absolutely think we can revive the category." It's not a positive sign, however, that for the last nine years, Elmo, and not the Cookie Monster, has been the most popular character on the children's show *Sesame Street*.[3]

> *After reading the next four sections, you should be able to*
>
> *1 discuss how changing environments affect organizations.*
> *2 describe the four components of the general environment.*
> *3 explain the five components of the specific environment.*
> *4 describe the process that companies use to make sense of their changing environments.*

1 Changing Environments

Let's examine the three basic characteristics of changing external environments: 1.1 environmental change, 1.2 environmental complexity, 1.3 resource scarcity, and 1.4 the uncertainty that environmental change, complexity, and resource scarcity can create for organizational managers.

external environments all events outside a company that have the potential to influence or affect it

1.1 Environmental Change

Environmental change is the rate at which a company's general and specific environments change. In **stable environments**, the rate of environmental change is slow. For instance, except for more efficient ovens, bread is baked, wrapped, and delivered fresh to stores each day much as it was decades ago. And although some new breads have become popular, the white and wheat breads that customers bought 20 years ago are still today's best sellers. So after two decades of consistent double-digit growth, NATURAL OVENS, which makes preservative-free breads, spent $10 million to build a second baking facility. Soon after it was built, however, sales unexpectedly dropped. According to owner Paul Stitt, "We couldn't figure out what was going on because we have been accustomed, on average, to having a 15 percent sales growth in each of the last 25 years." What happened? The Atkins plan. The popularity of the diet, which advocates restricting carbohydrates, caused nationwide bread sales to drop for the first time in decades. Fortunately, the company adjusted to the first major change in its business in years by developing a very-difficult-to-bake low-carb bread, whose sales have increased from 1,200 to 60,000 loaves a week. Ironically, says Stitt, "We have a higher profit margin on our low-carb breads than on most of our other breads."[4]

"WHAT'S NEW" COMPANY

> Although you might think that a company's external environment would be *either* stable *or* dynamic, research suggests that companies often experience both.

"WHAT'S NEW" COMPANY

In contrast to Natural Ovens, which is in a stable environment, EA SPORTS competes in an extremely dynamic external environment—video games. In **dynamic environments**, the rate of environmental change is fast. EA Sports' best-selling products are sports games like *Madden NFL* (football), *NBA Live* (basketball), *NHL* (hockey), *Tiger Woods PGA Tour* (golf), and *FIFA* (soccer). EA Sports' business environment is dynamic primarily because gaming technology changes so quickly. The company's first product was designed for the Atari 800, one of the earliest computers designed to play computer games. The Atari 800 was soon replaced by the more powerful Commodore 64, which was then replaced by the Commodore Amiga, followed by the 8-bit Nintendo, the 16-bit Sega Genesis, the 32-bit and 64-bit Segas, Nintendos, Sony PlayStations, desktop computers, and now the Sony PlayStation3, Nintendo's Gamecube and Wii, and Microsoft's Xbox 360. With development costs exceeding $10 million per game and marketing costs running as high as $15 million for some games, if EA Sports guesses wrong and develops games that prove to be unpopular or quickly become obsolete, it could join the dozens of game companies that have already closed their doors.[5]

Although you might think that a company's external environment would be *either* stable *or* dynamic, research suggests that companies often experience both. According to **punctuated equilibrium theory**, companies go through long periods of stability (equilibrium) during which incremental changes occur, followed by short, complex periods of dynamic, fundamental change (revolutionary periods), finishing with a return to stability (new equilibrium).[6]

Exhibit 3.1 shows one example of punctuated equilibrium—the U.S. airline industry. Three times in the last 30 years, the U.S. airline industry has experienced revolutionary periods. The first, from mid-1979 to mid-1982, occurred immediately after airline deregulation in 1978. Prior to deregulation, the federal government

environmental change the rate at which a company's general and specific environments change

stable environment an environment in which the rate of change is slow

dynamic environment an environment in which the rate of change is fast

punctuated equilibrium theory the theory that companies go through long periods of stability (equilibrium), followed by short periods of dynamic, fundamental change (revolution), and finishing with a return to stability (new equilibrium)

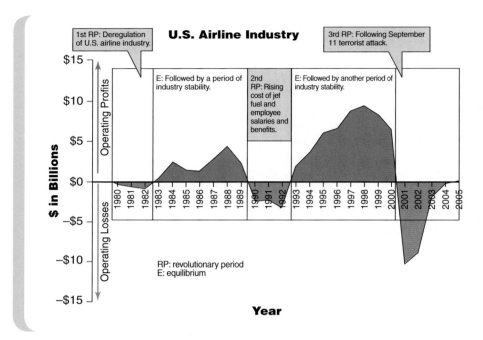

U.S. Airline Industry

1st RP: Deregulation of U.S. airline industry.

3rd RP: Following September 11 terrorist attack.

E: Followed by a period of industry stability.

2nd RP: Rising cost of jet fuel and employee salaries and benefits.

E: Followed by another period of industry stability.

RP: revolutionary period
E: equilibrium

Operating Profits

Operating Losses

$ in Billions

Year

Exhibit 3.1

Punctuated Equilibrium: U.S. Airline Profits since 1979

Source: "Annual Revenues and Earnings: U.S. Airlines—All Services," Air Transport Association, available at http://www.airlines.org, January 2007.

environmental complexity the number and the intensity of external factors in the environment that affect organizations

simple environment an environment with few environmental factors

complex environment an environment with many environmental factors

controlled where airlines could fly, how much could be charged, when they could fly, and the number of flights they could have on a particular route. After deregulation, these choices were left to the airlines. The large financial losses during this period clearly indicate that the airlines had trouble adjusting to the intense competition that occurred after deregulation. By mid-1982, however, profits returned to the industry and held steady until mid-1989.

Then, after experiencing record growth and profits, U.S. airlines lost billions of dollars between 1989 and 1993 as the industry went through dramatic changes. Key expenses, including jet fuel and employee salaries, which had held steady for years, suddenly increased. Furthermore, revenues, which had grown steadily year after year, suddenly dropped because of dramatic changes in the airlines' customer base. Business travelers, who had typically paid full-price fares, comprised more than half of all passengers during the 1980s. However, by the late 1980s, the largest customer base had changed to leisure travelers, who wanted the cheapest flights they could get.[7] With expenses suddenly up and revenues suddenly down, the airlines responded to these changes in their business environment by laying off 5 to 10 percent of their workers, canceling orders for new planes, and eliminating unprofitable routes. Starting in 1993 and lasting till 1998, these changes helped the airline industry to achieve profits far in excess of their historical levels. The industry began to stabilize, if not flourish, just as punctuated equilibrium theory predicts.[8]

The third revolutionary period for the U.S. airline industry began with the terrorist attacks of September 11, 2001, in which planes were used as missiles to bring down the World Trade Center towers and damage the Pentagon. The immediate effect was a 20 percent drop in scheduled flights, a 40 percent drop in passengers, and losses so large that the U.S. government approved a $15 billion bailout to keep the airlines in business. Heightened airport security also affected airports, the airlines themselves, and airline customers. Five years after the 9/11 attacks, United Airlines, U.S. Airways, Delta, and American Airlines had reduced staffing by 169,000 full-time jobs to cut costs after losing a combined $42 billion.[9] Due to their financially weaker position, the airlines have now restructured operations to take advantage of the combined effect of increased passenger travel, a sharply reduced cost structure, and a 23 percent reduction in the fleet to move their businesses back to profitability.[10] As a result, the airlines may be moving back to a more stable period of equilibrium.

1.2 Environmental Complexity

Environmental complexity is the number and the intensity of external factors in the environment that affect organizations. **Simple environments** have few environmental factors, whereas **complex environments** have many environmental factors. The dairy industry is an excellent example of a relatively simple external environment.

Even accounting for decades-old advances in processing and automatic milking machines, milk is produced the same way today as it was 100 years ago. And while food manufacturers introduce dozens of new dairy-based products each year, U.S. milk production has grown a meager 1.25 percent per year over the last decade. In short, producing milk is a highly competitive but simple business that has experienced few changes.[11]

At the other end of the spectrum, few industries have dealt with more change in their environment than the recording industry. The first 12-inch-diameter records were released in the early 1900s and were virtually the only format for music delivery until the 1960s. In the next few decades came new formats including eight-track tapes, cassette tapes, and, in the early 1980s, the compact disc. The record labels balanced their shipments to handle the changing desires of their customers, and in 1988 CDs outsold the vinyl-record album format for the first time. The MP3 format was patented in Germany in 1989 and over the next 10 years became a standard format for compressing high-quality digital sound to CDs or other storage devices.

In 1999 a company called *NAPSTER* created a peer-to-peer network that allowed (albeit illegally) users to share digital files with each other. Within a year, 30 percent of all PCs were running this software program, and the recording industry blamed illegal file sharing for the sharp declines in CD sales. In an effort to create a legal downloading mechanism that would support the rights of the recording industry, *APPLE COMPUTER* developed iTunes.com, where individual songs could be legally purchased and downloaded for 99 cents per song. Apple followed this up with the October 2001 release of the iPod, the now-ubiquitous MP3 player that uses an internal hard drive to hold up to thousands of songs. More than one billion songs have been downloaded from iTunes since the inception of the iTunes/iPod model, clearly changing the way the recording industry distributes and profits from music. In fact, previous nondigital formats have either all but disappeared or are in serious decline. Interestingly, sales from the digital media (which is dramatically cheaper for the producers) have more than made up for any decline in other formats.[12]

1.3 Resource Scarcity

The third characteristic of external environments is resource scarcity. **Resource scarcity** is the abundance or shortage of critical organizational resources in an organization's external environment.

For example, the primary reason that flat-screen LCD (liquid crystal display) televisions with lifelike pictures are six times more expensive per inch than regular TVs, two times more expensive than rear-projection TVs, and 25 percent more expensive than plasma TVs is that there aren't enough LCD screen factories to meet demand. As long as this condition persists, LCD TV prices will remain high. At $2 billion to $4 billion each, LCD factories are the scarce resource in this industry. LCD factories are expensive to build because, like computer chips, LCD flat screens must be made in superclean environments. Furthermore, the manufacturing process is complex and difficult to manage because the liquid crystal, which can be ruined by just one speck of dust, must be poured onto glass in a layer thinner than a sheet of paper. Each generation of factory has been focused on increasing the size of the glass panels from which the screens are cut. A seventh-generation factory (the latest) can produce a panel big enough to cut as many as twenty-four 23-inch LCD screens or as few as six 46-inch screens. The market is still growing at a torrid pace; despite recent predictions of manufacturing gluts, the demand for increasingly larger LCD panels has continued

resource scarcity the abundance or shortage of critical organizational resources in an organization's external environment to outpace production. The industry has also continued to advance its technical capability and can now successfully produce 100-inch LCD panels.[13]

1.4 Uncertainty

As Exhibit 3.2 shows, environmental change, environmental complexity, and resource scarcity affect environmental **uncertainty**, which is how well managers can understand or predict the external changes and trends affecting their businesses. Starting at the left side of the figure, environmental uncertainty is lowest when environmental change and environmental complexity are at low levels and resource scarcity is small (that is, resources are plentiful). In these environments, managers feel confident that they can understand, predict, and react to the external forces that affect their businesses. Because the AM/FM radio market had remained relatively unchanged from its founding (meaning that it was predictable), the founders of XM Radio saw an opportunity to change the industry. By contrast, the right side of the figure shows that environmental uncertainty is highest when environmental change and complexity are extensive and resource scarcity is a problem. In these environments, managers may not be confident that they can understand, predict, and handle the external forces affecting their businesses.

Review 1: **Changing Environments**

Environmental change, complexity, and resource scarcity are the basic components of external environments. Environmental change is the rate at which conditions or events affecting a business change. Environmental complexity is the number and intensity of external factors in an external environment. Resource scarcity is the scarcity or abundance of resources available in the external environment. The greater the degree of environmental change, environmental complexity, and resource scarcity, the less confident managers are that they can understand, predict, and effectively react to the trends affecting their businesses. According to punctuated equilibrium theory, companies experience periods of stability followed by short periods of dynamic, fundamental change, followed by a return to periods of stability.

uncertainty extent to which managers can understand or predict which environmental changes and trends will affect their businesses

Exhibit 3.2

Environmental Change, Environmental Complexity, and Resource Scarcity

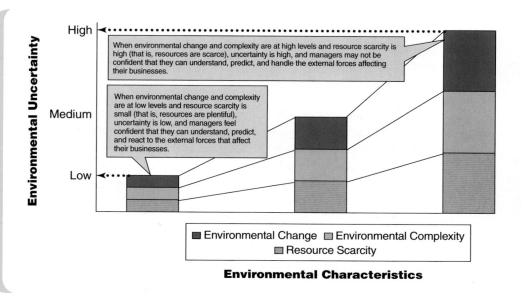

2 General Environment

As Exhibit 3.3 shows, two kinds of external environments influence organizations: the general environment and the specific environment. The **general environment** consists of the economy and the technological, sociocultural, and political/legal trends that indirectly affect *all* organizations. Changes in any sector of the general environment eventually affect most organizations. For example, when the Federal Reserve lowers its prime lending rate, most businesses benefit because banks and credit card companies often lower the interest rates they charge for loans. Consumers, who can then borrow money more cheaply, might borrow more to buy homes, cars, refrigerators, and plasma or LCD large-screen TVs. By contrast, each organization also has a **specific environment** that is unique to that firm's industry and directly affects the way it conducts day-to-day business. For example, when the cost of coffee beans increased dramatically, Starbucks increased its prices, as did Kraft Foods, the maker of Maxwell House coffee.[14] But because that change came from the specific environment for this industry and not the general environment (which influences all businesses), only coffee-related businesses were affected. The specific environment, which will be discussed in detail in Section 3 of this chapter, includes customers, competitors, suppliers, industry regulation, and advocacy groups.

general environment the economic, technological, sociocultural, and political trends that indirectly affect all organizations

specific environment the customers, competitors, suppliers, industry regulations, and advocacy groups that are unique to an industry and directly affect how a company does business

Exhibit 3.3
General and Specific Environments

Let's take a closer look at the four components of the general environment: *2.1 the economy*, *and 2.2 the technological*, *2.3 sociocultural*, *and 2.4 political/ legal trends that indirectly affect all organizations*.

2.1 Economy

The current state of a country's economy affects virtually every organization doing business there. In general, in a growing economy, more people are working and wages are growing, and therefore consumers have relatively more money to spend. More products are bought and sold in a growing economy than in a static or shrinking economy. Though an individual firm's sales will not necessarily increase, a growing economy does provide an environment favorable to business growth. In contrast, in a shrinking economy, consumers have less money to spend and relatively fewer products are bought and sold. Thus, a shrinking economy makes growth for individual businesses more difficult.

Because the economy influences basic business decisions, such as whether to hire more employees, expand production, or take out loans to purchase equipment, managers scan their economic environments for signs of significant change. Unfortunately, the economic statistics that managers rely on when making these decisions are notoriously poor predictors of *future* economic activity. A manager who decides to hire 10 more employees because economic data suggest future growth could very well have to lay off those newly hired workers when the economic growth does not occur. In fact, a famous economic study found that at the beginning of a business quarter (a period of only three months), even the best economic forecasters could not accurately predict whether economic activity would grow or shrink in that same quarter![15]

Because economic statistics can be poor predictors, some managers try to predict future economic activity by keeping track of business confidence. **Business confidence indices** show how confident actual managers are about future business growth. For example, the *Fortune* Business Confidence Index is a monthly survey of chief financial officers at large *Fortune* 1000 firms.[16] Another widely cited measure is the U.S. Chamber of Commerce Business Confidence Index, which asks 7,000 small business owners to express their optimism (or pessimism) about future business sales and prospects. Managers often prefer business confidence indices to economic statistics because they know that other managers make business decisions that are in line with their expectations concerning the economy's future. So if the *Fortune* or U.S. Chamber of Commerce business confidence indices are dropping, a manager might decide against hiring new employees, increasing production, or taking out additional loans to expand the business.

2.2 Technological Component

Technology is the knowledge, tools, and techniques used to transform inputs (raw materials, information, and so on) into outputs (products and services). For example, the inputs of authors, editors, and artists (knowledge) and the use of equipment like computers and printing presses (technology) transformed paper, ink, and glue (raw materials) into this book (the finished product). In the case of a service company such as an airline, the technology consists of equipment, including airplanes, repair tools, computers, as well as the knowledge of mechanics, ticketers, and flight crews. The output is the service of transporting people from one place to another.

Changes in technology can help companies provide better products or produce their products more efficiently. For example, advances in surgical techniques and imaging equipment have made open-heart surgery much faster and safer in recent years. While technological changes can benefit a business, they can also threaten

business confidence indices indices that show managers' level of confidence about future business growth

technology the knowledge, tools, and techniques used to transform input into output it. Companies must embrace new technology and find effective ways to use it to improve their products and services or decrease costs. If they don't, they will lose out to those companies that do. For example, over-the-counter medications have traditionally been available in either pill or liquid form; now the new technology is edible film. Like those little, thin strips of breath freshener, medicinal edible film dissolves instantly on the tongue, allowing the medicine to enter the bloodstream more quickly. This new technology has applications in areas where administering oral medication can be challenging, such as to children and pets. *Novartis* has added edible film to many of its product lines, and its Triaminic line of cold medicines now sells multiple flavors of film in children's strength. The Triaminic franchise has grown from nothing to claim a 20 percent share of the pediatric cough and cold market. "Most of the growth has been driven by the Thin Strip [edible film]," says Brian McNamara, a vice-president at Novartis Consumer Health in Parsippany, New Jersey. Pet-care company Hartz Mountain Corp., which already produces breath-freshening strips for dogs, is investigating using edible film for delivering pet medication, an annual market valued at over $1 billion. Imagine: Instead of wrestling your pet to force pills down its throat, you'll simply place the edible medicine film on its tongue. Sales of edible film are estimated to increase from under $1 million to $350 million in the next few years.[17] Chapter 7, on organizational change and innovation, provides a more in-depth discussion of how technology affects a company's competitive advantage.

> "Companies must embrace new technology and find effective ways to use it to improve their products and services or decrease costs."

"WHAT'S NEW" COMPANY

2.3 Sociocultural Component

The sociocultural component of the general environment refers to the demographic characteristics, general behavior, attitudes, and beliefs of people in a particular society. Sociocultural changes and trends influence organizations in two important ways.

First, changes in demographic characteristics—such as the number of people with particular skills or the growth/decline in particular population segments (marital status, age, gender, ethnicity)—affect how companies staff their businesses. Exhibit 3.4 shows

% of Married Women (with Children) Who Work

Married women with children are much more likely to work today than four decades ago. In 1960, only 18.6 percent of women with children under 6 years old and 39 percent of women with children between the ages of 6 and 17 worked. In 2004, those percentages had risen to 59.3 percent and 75.6 percent, respectively. Sociocultural changes like this affect the demand for products and services. Consequently, today's harried worker/parents can hire baby-proofing agencies (to baby-proof their homes), emergency babysitting services, bill payers, birthday party planners, kiddie taxi services, personal assistants, and personal chefs.

Year	Children under 6	Children 6 to 17
1960	18.6	39.0
1970	30.3	49.2
1980	45.1	62.0
1985	53.4	68.0
1990	58.9	73.6
1995	63.5	76.2
2000	62.8	77.2
2004	59.3	75.6

Exhibit 3.4

Demographics: Percentage of Married Women (with Children) Who Work

Sources: U.S. Census Bureau, Statistical Abstract of the United States, 1999, 2001, and 2004–2005. (Washington, D.C.: U.S. Government Printing Office, 1999, 2001, and 2004), "Employment Status of Women by Marital Status and Presence and Age of Children: 1960 to 1998," Table No. 631; "Employment Status of Women by Marital Status and Presence and Age of Children: 1970 to 2004," Table No. 586.

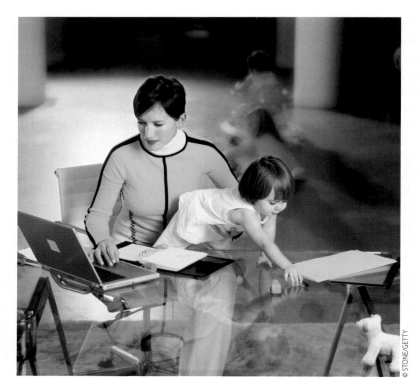

© STONE/GETTY

that married women with children are much more likely to work today than four decades ago. In 1960, only 18.6 percent of women with children under 6 years old and 39 percent of women with children between the ages of 6 and 17 worked. By 2004, those percentages had risen to 59.3 percent and 75.6 percent, respectively. Today, with traffic congestion creating longer commutes and both parents working longer hours, employees are much more likely to value products and services that allow them to recapture free time with their families. Priscilla La Barbera, a marketing professor at New York University, believes that there's been a "societal shift" in the way people view their free time. She says, "People are beginning to realize that their time has real value."[18] Companies such as CDW (Computer Discount Warehouse) in Vernon Hills, Illinois, help their employees by providing a service that picks up their dry cleaning at their desks.[19] At First Command Financial Planning in Fort Worth, Texas, employees can borrow movies for two nights of home viewing and drop off shoes for free shining as well as their cars for free washing.[20] Circles, an organization that provides employee concierge services, has more than 300 employees helping over 250,000 client employees find more free time by planning their vacations, finding pet sitters, or running their errands.[21]

Second, sociocultural changes in behavior, attitudes, and beliefs also affect the demand for a business's products and services. Because more women with children are in the workforce, families are deliberately selective about how they spend their free time. With free time at a premium, working mothers in particular use numerous services to help reduce the amount of time they spend doing chores and household-management tasks. Julie Duffy, the founder of *DINNER BY DESIGN*, a meal-assembly service, knows this. Duffy creates menus that are easy to prepare and reconstitute at home. She does all the shopping and clean-up for her clients, who spend two hours every two weeks assembling meals in the Dinner by Design kitchens. One session of meal assembly takes about the same amount of time as creating a grocery list, shopping for all the items, and putting everything away, but Dinner by Design customers don't do any of that. And they have full, healthy meals to feed their families for up to two weeks.[22] Duffy's company is one of many take-and-bake meal-assembly services that have started up recently in response to the working-mother sociocultural change.

"WHAT'S NEW" COMPANY

2.4 Political/Legal Component

The political/legal component of the general environment includes the legislation, regulations, and court decisions that govern and regulate business behavior. New laws and regulations continue to impose additional responsibilities on companies. Unfortunately, many managers are unaware of these new responsibilities. For example, under the 1991 Civil Rights Act (**http://www.eeoc.gov/policy/cra91.html**), if an employee is sexually harassed by anyone at work (a supervisor, a coworker, or even a customer), the company—not just the harasser—is potentially liable for damages, attorneys' fees, and back pay.[23] Under the Family and Medical Leave Act (**http://www.dol.gov/esa/whd/fmla**), employees who have been on the job one year are guaranteed 12 weeks of unpaid leave per year to tend to their own illnesses or to their elderly parents, a newborn baby, or a newly adopted child. Employees are guaranteed the same job, pay, and benefits when they return to work.[24]

Many managers are also unaware of the potential legal risks associated with traditional managerial decisions like recruiting, hiring, and firing employees. Increasingly, businesses and managers are being sued for negligent hiring and supervision, defamation, invasion of privacy, emotional distress, fraud, and misrepresentation during employee recruitment.[25] More than 24,000 suits for wrongful termination (unfairly firing employees) are filed each year.[26] In fact, wrongful termination lawsuits increased by 77 percent in the last decade and now account for 13 percent of all lawsuits against companies.[27] One in four employers will at some point be sued for wrongful termination. Employers lose 70 percent of these cases, and on average, the former employee is awarded $500,000 or more.[28]

Companies also face a variety of potential legal risks from customer-initiated lawsuits. For example, under product-liability law, manufacturers are liable for products made decades ago. Also, the law, as it is now written, does not consider whether manufactured products have been properly maintained and used by the customer. For instance, a Texas jury awarded $37 million in damages against GOODYEAR TIRE AND RUBBER COMPANY after concluding that one of its tires caused a traffic death. The tire in question was nine years old, twice the normal four- to five-year life span of most tires, and had been patched four times (once incorrectly).[29] Still, the jury required Goodyear to pay $37 million in damages. Why? Under product-liability law, plaintiffs only have to demonstrate that they were injured by the manufacturer's product. Under the concept of "strict liability," the burden of proof is shifted to the company, which must prove that the product was safe.[30] Thus, once injuries have been shown, the company is assumed guilty until it proves its innocence. Today, jury verdicts in product-liability cases cost companies an average of $6.8 million per case.[31]

Not everyone agrees that companies' legal risks are too severe. Indeed, many believe that the government should do more to regulate and restrict business behavior and that it should be easier for average citizens to sue dishonest or negligent corporations. From a managerial perspective, the best medicine against legal risk is prevention. As a manager, it is your responsibility to educate yourself about the laws, regulations, and potential lawsuits that could affect your business. Failure to do so may put you and your company at risk of sizable penalties, fines, or legal charges.

Review 2: **General Environment**

The general environment consists of economic, technological, sociocultural, and political/legal events and trends that affect all organizations. Because the economy influences basic business decisions, managers often use economic statistics and business confidence indices to predict future economic activity. Changes in technology, which transforms inputs into outputs, can be a benefit or a threat to a business. Sociocultural trends, like changing demographic characteristics, affect how companies run their businesses. Similarly, sociocultural changes in behavior, attitudes, and beliefs affect the demand for a business's products and services. Court decisions and new federal and state laws have imposed much greater political/legal responsibilities on companies. The best way to manage legal responsibilities is to educate managers and employees about laws and regulations and potential lawsuits that could affect a business.

3 Specific Environment

As you just learned, changes in any sector of the general environment (economic, technological, sociocultural, and political/legal) eventually affect most organizations. By contrast, each organization also has a specific environment that is unique to that firm's industry and directly affects the way it conducts day-to-day business. For instance, if your customers decide to use another product, your main competitor cuts prices 10 percent, your best supplier can't deliver raw materials, federal regulators mandate reductions in pollutants in your industry, or environmental groups accuse your company of selling unsafe products, the impact from the specific environment on your business is immediate.

Let's examine how the **3.1 customer**, **3.2 competitor**, **3.3 supplier**, **3.4 industry regulation**, and **3.5 advocacy group components** of the specific environment affect businesses.

3.1 Customer Component

Customers purchase products and services. Companies cannot exist without customer support. Therefore, monitoring customers' changing wants and needs is critical to business success. There are two basic strategies for monitoring customers: reactive and proactive.

Reactive customer monitoring is identifying and addressing customer trends and problems after they occur. One reactive strategy is to identify customer concerns by listening closely to customer complaints. This strategy involves not only listening to complaints but also responding to customer concerns. For example, companies that respond quickly to customer letters of complaint are viewed much more favorably than companies that are slow to respond or never respond.[32] In particular, studies have shown that when a company's follow-up letter thanks the customer for writing, offers a sincere, specific response to the complaint (not a form letter, but an explanation of how the problem will be handled), and contains a small gift, coupons, or a refund to make up for the problem, customers are much more likely to purchase products or services again from that company.[33] By contrast, companies that don't respond promptly to customer complaints are likely to find customer rants and tirades posted publicly on places like **http://www.planetfeedback.com**. Customers hope that posting complaints on these sites will force someone to address their problems. It worked for Lena West. The day after she posted a complaint against Budget Rent-a-Car, she received an e-mail containing an apology and a promise to resolve her problem.[34]

Proactive monitoring of customers means identifying and addressing customer needs, trends, and issues *before* they occur. For example, over the past few years more stores that sell toys have switched from selling gift certificates to selling electronic gift cards that are preprogrammed with a dollar amount and are swiped like credit cards. With kids' bedrooms stuffed with toys, savvy retailers accurately predicted that parents and grandparents might rather give gift cards than worry about getting a wrong or duplicate item leading to a boon in the sales of these cards.[35] Another example of proactive monitoring is the fast-food industry's use of multibranding, in which two or more food chains share space under the same roof. Multibranding brings in more customers by giving them more choice. Customer research suggested that people dining together might like to eat at different places at the same time. Families were a particular target of Yum! Brands, which often pairs its subsidiaries Taco Bell and KFC in one building, finds that sales are one-third higher in multi-brand restaurants than in traditional single-brand restaurants.[36]

3.2 Competitor Component

Competitors are companies in the same industry that sell similar products or services to customers. General Motors, Ford, Toyota, Honda, Nissan, Hyundai, Kia, and DaimlerChrysler all compete for automobile customers. NBC, ABC, CBS, and Fox (along with hundreds of cable channels) compete for TV viewers' attention. McDonald's, Burger King, Wendy's, Hardee's, Chick-fil-A, and a host of others compete for fast-food customers' dollars. Often the difference between business success and failure comes down to whether your company is doing a better job of satisfying customer wants and needs than the competition. Consequently, companies need to keep close track of what their competitors are doing. To do this, managers perform a **competitive analysis**, which involves deciding who your competitors are, anticipating competitors' moves, and determining competitors' strengths and weaknesses.

competitors companies in the same industry that sell similar products or services to customers

competitive analysis a process for monitoring the competition that involves identifying competition, anticipating their moves, and determining their strengths and weaknesses

Surprisingly, managers often do a poor job of identifying potential competitors because they tend to focus on only two or three well-known competitors with similar goals and resources.[37] Historically Coke and Pepsi spent more time keeping track of each other than they spent on other competitors, but when they each started losing ground to start up energy drinks, bottled water, and fruit juices, both giants began to buy businesses to help them compete in these growing markets.[38] Likewise, *HOOVER*, Dirt Devil, and, more recently, Oreck competed fiercely in the market for vacuum cleaners. Because these companies produced relatively similar vacuum cleaners, they mostly competed on price. When *DYSON* entered the market with its radically different vacuum that developed and maintained significantly more suction power, the company garnered 20 percent market share within its first 12 months on the shelves.[39]

Another mistake managers may make when analyzing the competition is to underestimate potential competitors' capabilities. When this happens, managers don't take the steps they should to continue to improve their products or services. The result can be significant decreases in both market share and profits. For nearly a decade, traditional phone companies ignored the threat to their business from VoIP (Voice over Internet Protocol). Early on, software products like Cool Talk, Internet Phone, and

Web Phone made it possible to make inexpensive long-distance phone calls using VoIP; aside from the software, the only requirements were an Internet service provider and a computer that had a sound card, speakers, and a microphone. The sound quality was only as good as AM radio, but people who were used to poor-quality sound on their cell phones didn't care because the calls were so much cheaper.[40]

Primarily because phone companies were slow to adopt VoIP capabilities themselves, today they're facing a rash of new, unexpected VoIP competitors, all of which have slashed prices and taken market share using high-speed Internet service connections to people's homes. For example, COMCAST, a cable-TV provider that also offers high-speed Internet service, plans to roll out Internet phone service to 40 million U.S. homes over the next two years.[41] In Hong Kong, City Telecom, which has built a fiber-optic network throughout the province, charges only $38 a month for phone service, high-speed Internet, *and* cable TV (delivered over fiber-optic cables).[42] Most U.S. consumers pay four to five times that much per month for the same services. Vonage, **http://www.vonage.com**, an Internet phone company, charges just $24.95 per month (maybe less by the time you read this) for unlimited calls in the United States, Canada, Puerto Rico, and Europe. Its non-European international long-distance charges start at six cents per minute. How much of a threat is Internet phone service to traditional phone companies today? Jeff Pulver, CEO of Pulver.com, which owns the Internet phone company Free World Dialup, says, "Within the next 10 years, it's quite possible that 50 percent or more of voice traffic will take the place of the traditional public telephone network and run on the Internet, wireless, or other systems."[43]

3.3 Supplier Component

Suppliers are companies that provide material, human, financial, and informational resources to other companies. U.S. Steel buys iron ore from suppliers to make steel products. When IBM sells a mainframe computer, it also provides support staff, engineers, and other technical consultants to the company that bought the computer. If you're shopping for desks, chairs, and office supplies, chances are Office Depot will be glad to help your business open a revolving charge account to pay for your purchases. When a clothing manufacturer has spent $100,000 to purchase new high-pressure "water drills" to cut shirt and pants patterns to precise sizes, the water drill manufacturer, as part of the purchase, will usually train the workers on the machinery.

A key factor influencing the impact and quality of the relationship between companies and their suppliers is how dependent they are on each other.[44] **Supplier dependence** is the degree to which a company relies on that supplier because of the importance of the supplier's product to the company and the difficulty of finding other sources for that product. Supplier dependence is very strong in the diamond business, given that DE BEERS CONSOLIDATED MINES provides 66 percent of the wholesale diamonds in the world. De Beers has dominated the diamond industry for more than a century, controlling the supply, price, and quality of the best diamonds on the market. The company's 125 customers, or "sightholders," as they're known in the industry, are summoned to De Beers's London office 10 times a year and given a shoebox of diamonds that they are required to buy. If they refuse, they lose the opportunity to purchase any more diamonds. De Beers initiated a Supplier of Choice (SoC) program that requires sightholders to pay more of the marketing, advertising, and branding costs for De Beers diamonds. SoC sightholders sign two-year contracts that spell out their responsibilities to develop marketing plans and advertising initiatives and to adhere to ethical guidelines. Just two-thirds of De Beers sightholders, however, qualified as SoCs. The one-third who didn't qualify as SoCs are no longer permitted to sell De Beers dia-

suppliers companies that provide material, human, financial, and informational resources to other companies

supplier dependence the degree to which a company relies on a supplier because of the importance of the supplier's product to the company and the difficulty of finding other sources of that product monds and must now get their diamonds from less prestigious diamond suppliers.[45] Sightholders agree to all this because they are dependent on their supplier De Beers.

Buyer dependence is the degree to which a supplier relies on a buyer because of the importance of that buyer to the supplier's sales and the difficulty of finding other buyers of its products. For example, SUPERIOR INDUSTRIES, which makes car wheels, gets 85 percent of its $840 million in annual sales from Ford and General Motors. When the two automakers demanded that Superior match the low prices that Chinese wheel suppliers were offering, it had little choice. Superior's president, Steve Borick, says the ultimatum was presented very simply: "They said, 'This is the price we are getting [from Chinese suppliers] for this product. You either match that, or we'll take our business to them.'" He adds, "It's that black and white. Close the [cost] gap [of 20 to 40 percent] no matter how" you do it.[46]

As the De Beers and Superior Industries examples show, a high degree of buyer or seller dependence can lead to **opportunistic behavior**, in which one party benefits at the expense of the other. Though opportunistic behavior between buyers and suppliers will never be completely eliminated, many companies believe that both buyers and suppliers can benefit by improving the buyer-supplier relationship.[47] In contrast to opportunistic behavior, **relationship behavior** focuses on establishing a mutually beneficial, long-term relationship between buyers and suppliers.[48] TOYOTA is well known for developing positive long-term relationships with its key suppliers. Donald Esmond, who runs Toyota's U.S. division, says, "I think what they [suppliers] appreciate . . . is we don't go in and say, 'Reduce the costs by 6 percent; if you don't, somebody else is going to get the business.' We go in and say we want to come in and help you [figure out] where you can save costs so we can reduce our overall price. So it's a different approach."[49]

3.4 Industry Regulation Component

Whereas the political/legal component of the general environment affects all businesses, the **industry regulation** component consists of regulations and rules that govern the practices and procedures of specific industries, businesses, and professions. For example, if your neighbor decides to make a little extra money selling homemade baked goods and sells you two apple pies, your neighbor could be fined. In most states, it is illegal to sell food from your home. State regulations typically require a food business to obtain a license and a state certificate of inspection that indicates that the food is stored properly; insects have not infested the premises; ovens are state approved; electrical wiring, lighting, and smoke detectors are up to code; and so on.[50] Likewise, the auto industry is subject to CAFE (Corporate Average Fuel Economy) regulations that require cars and sport utility vehicles to average 27.5 and 22.5 miles, respectively, per gallon.[51]

Regulatory agencies affect businesses by creating and enforcing rules and regulations to protect consumers, workers, or society as a whole. For example, the U.S. Department of Agriculture and the Food and Drug Administration regulate the safety of seafood (as well as meat and poultry) through the science-based Hazard Analysis and Critical Control Points program. Seafood processors are required to identify hazards (toxins, chemicals, pesticides, and decomposition) that could cause the fish they process to be unsafe. They must also establish critical control points to control hazards both inside and outside their fish-processing plants and then establish monitoring, corrective action, and verification procedures to certify that the fish they process is safe to consume.[52]

The nearly 100 federal agencies and regulatory commissions can affect almost any kind of business. Exhibit 3.5 lists some of the most influential federal agencies

buyer dependence the degree to which a supplier relies on a buyer because of the importance of that buyer to the supplier and the difficulty of finding other buyers for its products

opportunistic behavior a transaction in which one party in the relationship benefits at the expense of the other

relationship behavior the establishment of mutually beneficial, long-term exchanges between buyers and suppliers

industry regulation regulations and rules that govern the business practices and procedures of specific industries, businesses, and professions

Federal Agency	Regulatory Responsibilities
Consumer Product Safety Commission http://www.cpsc.gov	Reduces risk of injuries and deaths associated with consumer products, sets product safety standards, enforces product recalls, and provides consumer education
Department of Labor http://www.dol.gov	Collects employment statistics and administers labor laws concerning safe working conditions, minimum hourly wages and overtime pay, employment discrimination, and unemployment insurance
Environmental Protection Agency http://www.epa.gov	Reduces and controls pollution through research, monitoring, standard setting, and enforcement activities
Equal Employment Opportunity Commission http://www.eeoc.gov	Promotes fair hiring and promotion practices
Federal Communications Commission http://www.fcc.gov	Regulates interstate and international communications by radio, television, wire, satellite, and cable
Federal Reserve System http://www.federalreserve.gov	As nation's central bank, controls interest rates and money supply, and monitors the U.S. banking system to produce a growing economy with stable prices
Federal Trade Commission http://www.ftc.gov	Restricts unfair methods of business competition and misleading advertising, and enforces consumer protection laws
Food and Drug Administration http://www.fda.gov	Protects nation's health by making sure food, drugs, and cosmetics are safe
National Labor Relations Board http://www.nlrb.gov	Monitors union elections and stops companies from engaging in unfair labor practices
Occupational Safety & Health Administration http://www.osha.gov	Issues and enforces standards to protect the lives and health of workers
Securities and Exchange Commission http://www.sec.gov	Protects investors in the bond and stock markets, guarantees access to information on publicly traded securities, and regulates firms that sell securities or give investment advice

Exhibit 3.5

Federal Regulatory Agencies and Commissions

and commissions, as well as their responsibilities and their websites. Overall, the number and cost of federal regulations has nearly tripled in the last 25 years. Today, for every $1 the federal government spends creating regulations, businesses spend $45 to comply with them.[53] In addition to federal regulations, businesses are also subject to state, county, and city regulations. Complying with all of these regulations costs businesses an estimated $189 billion per year or $1,700 per employee.[54] Surveys indicate that managers rank dealing with government regulation as one of the most demanding and frustrating parts of their jobs.[55]

3.5 Advocacy Groups

advocacy groups concerned citizens who band together to try to influence the business practices of specific industries, businesses, and professions

public communications an advocacy group tactic that relies on voluntary participation by the news media and the advertising industry to get the advocacy group's message out

Advocacy groups are groups of concerned citizens who band together to try to influence the business practices of specific industries, businesses, and professions. The members of a group generally share the same point of view on a particular issue. For example, environmental advocacy groups might try to get manufacturers to reduce smokestack pollution emissions. Unlike the industry regulation component of the specific environment, advocacy groups cannot force organizations to change their practices. Nevertheless, they can use a number of techniques to try to influence companies, such as public communications, media advocacy, web pages, blogs, and product boycotts.

The **public communications** approach relies on *voluntary* participation by the news media and the advertising industry to send out an advocacy group's message. For example, a public service campaign to encourage people to quit smoking ran the following ads in newspapers and magazines throughout Europe: a photo showing the foot of a young person with a toe tag (indicating the person was dead), with the caption "Smokers die younger"; a picture showing clean lungs next to brown- and black-stained lungs, with the caption "Smoking causes fatal lung cancer"; and, a photo of a baby in an intensive care unit hooked up to a respirator, with the caption "Smoking when pregnant harms your baby."[56]

Media advocacy is much more aggressive than the public communications approach. A **media advocacy** approach typically involves framing the group's concerns as public issues (affecting everyone); exposing questionable, exploitative, or unethical practices; and creating controversy that is likely to receive extensive news coverage. *PETA* (People for the Ethical Treatment of Animals), which has offices in the United States, England, Italy, and Germany, uses controversial publicity stunts and advertisements to try to change the behavior of large organizations, fashion designers, medical researchers, and anyone else it believes is hurting or mistreating animals. PETA cofounder and president Ingrid Newkirk says, "People now know that if they do something ghastly to an animal, they can't necessarily get away with it. When we started, nobody knew what animal rights meant. . . . Now, it's an issue." PETA protesters have stripped naked in front of the White House in front of a banner reading "I'd rather go naked than wear fur." From PETA's perspective, any animal-based product is bad. In one of its latest protests, PETA distributed 2,000 blood-covered, knife-holding, "evil Colonel Sanders" bobblehead dolls to news organizations and KFC restaurants. PETA spokesperson Joe Hinkle says, "We'd like them to stop breeding and drugging chickens so that they grow so big that they actually cripple under their own bulk." KFC issued this response: "PETA has disparaged our brand and misrepresented the truth about our responsible industry-leading animal welfare standards. KFC is committed to the humane treatment of chickens."[58]

doing the right thing

Dealing with Gifts and Suppliers

In hopes of getting a buyer's business or getting more business, suppliers sometimes offer buyers trips to exotic locations, dinners at expensive restaurants, or luxurious gifts. Excessive gift giving and receiving creates a conflict of interest between what's best for the company (purchasing items of the optimal quality and cost) and what's personally best for the buyer who receives the gifts. Follow these general guidelines to avoid conflicts of interest:

- **Remember that there is no such thing as a free lunch.**
- **Make sure that business meals and entertainment (parties, outings, sporting events) have a valid business purpose and that the buyer and the supplier take turns paying for or hosting them.**
- **Don't accept gifts worth more than $25. If you are offered a gift worth more than $25, ask your manager if the gift is appropriate.**
- **Never accept cash or cash equivalents, such as gift certificates.**
- **Don't accept discounts on goods and services, unless the discounts are generally available to others.**
- **Don't accept offers of stock in suppliers' companies.**
- **Don't allow personal friendships with suppliers to influence buying decisions.** [57]

media advocacy an advocacy group tactic that involves framing issues as public issues; exposing questionable, exploitative, or unethical practices; and forcing media coverage by buying media time or creating controversy that is likely to receive extensive news coverage

A **product boycott** is a tactic in which an advocacy group actively tries to persuade consumers not to purchase a company's product or service. One example of this is the RAINFOREST ACTION NETWORK (RAN), whose members have chained themselves to wood piles at select Home Depot stores to get the company to stop selling old-growth lumber. Members also shadowed Citigroup's then-CEO Sandy Weill until he agreed to implement environmentally friendly lending policies. In 2006, the group targeted Ford Motor Company as the automobile manufacturer with the worst record of fuel efficiency. When Ford stated that RAN would have no impact upon the company, RAN's executive director Michael Brune responded, "Every company says we are not having an effect—straight up to the time they make their policy change."[59]

Review 3: Specific Environment

The specific environment is made up of five components: customers, competitors, suppliers, industry regulation, and advocacy groups. Companies can monitor customers' needs by identifying customer problems after they occur or by anticipating problems before they occur. Because they tend to focus on well-known competitors, managers often underestimate their competition or do a poor job of identifying future competitors. Suppliers and buyers are dependent on each other, and that dependence sometimes leads to opportunistic behavior, in which one benefits at the expense of the other. Regulatory agencies affect businesses by creating rules and then enforcing them. Overall, the level of industry regulation has nearly tripled in the last 25 years. Advocacy groups cannot regulate organizations' practices. Nevertheless, through public communications, media advocacy, and product boycotts, they try to convince companies to change their practices.

4 Making Sense of Changing Environments

In Chapter 1, you learned that managers are responsible for making sense of their business environments. As our discussions of the general and specific environments have indicated, however, making sense of business environments is not an easy task. Because external environments can be dynamic, confusing, and complex, managers use a three-step process to make sense of the changes in their external environments:

> **4.1 environmental scanning, 4.2 interpreting environmental factors, and 4.3 acting on threats and opportunities.**

4.1 Environmental Scanning

product boycott an advocacy group tactic that involves protesting a company's actions by persuading consumers not to purchase its product or service

environmental scanning searching the environment for important events or issues that might affect an organization

Environmental scanning is searching the environment for important events or issues that might affect an organization. Managers scan the environment to stay up-to-date on important factors in their industry. For example, with one out of every four new car buyers purchasing highly profitable sport utility vehicles (SUVs), auto executives hadn't paid much attention to environmental groups' complaints about SUVs' extremely poor gas mileage. Now, however, market research is showing that current SUV owners are unhappy with their vehicles' poor gas mileage. In addition, the rapid rise in retail gas prices and increasingly strong disapproval of SUVs by younger car buyers have resulted in large unsold inventories of SUVs. After gas prices rose, GENERAL MOTORS dealers had 125 days of inventory for the Chevrolet Tahoe, a full-size SUV. The optimal inventory for such a car is about half that.[60] James Schroer, DaimlerChrysler's executive vice president for sales and marketing, says that the increasingly negative view of SUVs is "a big deal, and it's real."[61]

Managers also scan their environments to reduce uncertainty. Faced with the responsibility of developing the marketing campaigns that sell their companies' most important products, the chief marketing officers (CMOs) of the world's best organizations willingly pay $50,000 a year to join the "Marketing 50," an exclusive group of CMOs who meet several times a year to exchange ideas and pick each others' brains. Richard Smith, founder of the group, says, "It's a noncompetitive group with just one executive from a particular industry, so they have a chance to get ideas they can use that their competitors may not know about and also try to figure out some of their common problems." Michael Linton, Best Buy's CMO, believes the "Marketing 50" is fantastic for finding out what other companies and CMOs are doing which helps him reduce uncertainty. He says, "It's impossible for any one company to know about every new tool, so hearing what is working for others helps."[62]

Organizational strategies also affect environmental scanning. In other words, managers pay close attention to trends and events that are directly related to their company's ability to compete in the marketplace.[63] MICROSOFT used to take software hackers to court to prosecute them for the damage caused by their efforts. However, since Chairman Bill Gates declared that security is Microsoft's top priority, the company is actively trying to engage the services of friendly hackers. Though companies like Microsoft long considered computer hackers to be the enemy, they are now a source of competitive advantage. One hacker who has seen his fortunes with respect to Microsoft improve is H.D. Moore, the director of security for BreakingPoint Systems in Austin, Texas, who was wined and dined by Microsoft employees during a hacker convention in Las Vegas. He says that Microsoft has "been on a hacker buying spree" as the company tries to convince so-called security researchers to work with it rather than against it. From Microsoft's perspective, teaming up with the hacker community to solve software problems prior to release simply makes good business sense. Microsoft security-program manager Steven Toulouse stated that with the "researchers" assistance, "we have discovered things during the development of these products that we might not have discovered otherwise."[64]

"WHAT'S NEW" COMPANY

Finally, environmental scanning is important because it contributes to organizational performance. Environmental scanning helps managers detect environmental changes and problems before they become organizational crises.[65] Furthermore, companies whose CEOs do more environmental scanning have higher profits.[66] CEOs in better-performing firms scan their firm's environments more frequently and scan more key factors in their environments in more depth and detail than do CEOs in poorer-performing firms.[67]

> "Environmental scanning helps managers detect environmental changes and problems before they become organizational crises."

4.2 Interpreting Environmental Factors

After scanning, managers determine what environmental events and issues mean to the organization. Typically, managers view environmental events and issues as either threats or opportunities. When managers interpret environmental events as threats, they take steps to protect the company from further harm. For example, now that Internet phone service (VoIP) has emerged as a threat, traditional phone companies have responded by announcing billion-dollar plans to expand their fiber-optic networks so that they can offer phone (using VoIP), Internet service, and TV packages, just like those the cable and satellite companies offer. However, the phone companies, such as Southwestern Bell, are finding that they are far behind the cable companies, which have already spent $65 billion over the last five years upgrading their digital networks. Industry analyst Glenn Greenberg says, "The telephone companies are way behind the curve."[68]

By contrast, when managers interpret environmental events as opportunities, they consider strategic alternatives for taking advantage of those events to improve company performance. Apple is known for recognizing opportunities and capitalizing on them. The market for high-end "smart" phones, full-featured mobile phones that also function as a handheld personal computer, is growing roughly 2 percent per year. These phones retail for between $500 and $20,000, generate high profit margins, and as luxury goods are insulated from fluctuations in consumer buying. To enter this attractive market (and so capitalize on an opportunity), Apple developed its own smart phone—the iPhone. CEO Steve Jobs announced the release more than six months in advance to generate hype, stimulate demand, and dampen sales of their competitors. The iPhone features a wider screen and a camera, the capability to use the new faster Wi-Fi networks so that users can use their e-mail, surf the Web, and communicate with Bluetooth-enabled devices—plus, of course, download and play iTunes music. Apple hopes to sell 10 million iPhones within the first 18 months on the market, which will account for only a modest 1 percent of global handset sales but roughly half the U.S. demand for smart phones.[69]

cognitive maps graphic depictions of how managers believe environmental factors relate to possible organizational actions

4.3 Acting on Threats and Opportunities

After scanning for information on environmental events and issues, and interpreting them as threats or opportunities, managers have to decide how to respond to these environmental factors. Deciding what to do under conditions of uncertainty is always difficult. Managers can never be completely confident that they have all the information they need or that they correctly understand the information they have.

Because it is impossible to comprehend all the factors and changes, managers often rely on simplified models of external environments called "cognitive maps." **Cognitive maps** summarize the perceived relationships between environmental factors and possible organizational actions. For example, the cognitive map shown in Exhibit 3.6 represents a small clothing-store owner's interpretation of her business environment. The map shows three kinds of variables. The first variables, shown as rectangles, are environmental factors, such as a Wal-Mart or a large mall 20 minutes away. The second variables, shown in ovals, are potential actions that the store owner might take, such as a low-cost strategy; a good-value, good-service strategy; or a "large selection of the latest fashions" strategy. The third variables, shown as trapezoids, are company strengths, such as low employee turnover, and weaknesses, such as small size.

The plus and minus signs on the map indicate whether the manager believes there is a positive or negative relationship between variables. For example, the manager believes that a low-cost strategy won't work because Wal-Mart and Target are nearby. Offering a large selection of the latest fashions would not work either—not with the small size of the store and that large nearby mall. However, the manager believes that a good-value, good-service strategy would lead to success and profits because of the store's low employee turnover, good knowledge of customers, reasonable selection of clothes at reasonable prices, and good location.

In the end, managers must complete all three steps—environmental scanning, interpreting environmental factors, and acting on threats and opportunities—to make sense of changing external environments. Environmental scanning helps managers more accurately interpret their environments and take actions that improve company performance. Through scanning, managers keep tabs on what competitors are doing, identify market trends, and stay alert to current events that affect their company's operations. Armed with the environmental information they have gathered, managers can then minimize the impact of threats and turn opportunities into increased profits.

Review 4: Making Sense of Changing Environments

Managers use a three-step process to make sense of external environments: environmental scanning, interpreting information, and acting on threats and opportunities. Managers scan their environments based on their organizational strategies, their need for up-to-date information, and their need to reduce uncertainty. When managers identify environmental events as threats, they take steps to protect the company from harm. When managers identify environmental events as opportunities, they formulate alternatives for taking advantage of them to improve company performance. Using cognitive maps can help managers visually summarize the relationships between environmental factors and the actions they might take to deal with them.

Exhibit 3.6
Cognitive Maps

INTERNAL ENVIRONMENTS

"WHAT'S NEW" COMPANY

External environments are *external* trends and events that have the potential to affect companies. By contrast, the **internal environment** consists of the trends and events *within* an organization that affect the management, employees, and organizational culture. The internal environment at **SAS**, the leading provider of statistical software, is unlike most software companies. Instead of expecting its employees to work 12- to 14-hour days, SAS has a seven-hour workday and closes its offices at 6 PM every evening. Employees receive unlimited sick days each year. To encourage employees to spend time with their families, there's an on-site day-care facility and the company cafeteria has plenty of highchairs and baby seats. Plus, every Wednesday, the company passes out M&M chocolate candies, plain and peanut, to all employees—a total of more than 22.5 tons of M&Ms per year. SAS senior vice president Jim Davis says, "We are firm believers that happy employees equal happy customers."[70]

Internal environments are important because they affect what people think, feel, and do at work. Given SAS's internal environment, it shouldn't surprise you to learn that almost no one quits. In a typical software company, 25 percent of the work force quits each year to take another job. At SAS, only 4 percent leave.[71] Jeff Chambers, SAS's vice president of human resources, says, "We have always had a commitment to investing in and cultivating meaningful, long-term relationships with our employees and clients. This has led to unusually low turnover in both populations and is at the core of our 28 years of sustained profitability and success."[72]

Comments such as these reflect the key component in internal environments, organizational culture. More specifically, **organizational culture** is the set of key values, beliefs, and attitudes shared by organizational members.

After reading the next section, you should be able to

> 5 explain how organizational cultures are created and how they can help companies be successful.

5 Organizational Cultures: Creation, Success, and Change

*Let's take a closer look at **5.1 how organizational cultures are created and maintained, 5.2 the characteristics of successful organizational cultures**, and **5.3 how companies can accomplish the difficult task of changing organizational cultures**.*

5.1 Creation and Maintenance of Organizational Cultures

A primary source of organizational culture is the company founder. Founders like Thomas J. Watson, Sr. (IBM), Sam Walton (Wal-Mart), and Bill Gates (Microsoft) create organizations in their own images and imprint them with their beliefs, attitudes, and values. For example, Thomas J. Watson proclaimed that IBM's three basic

internal environment the events and trends inside an organization that affect management, employees, and organizational culture

organizational culture the values, beliefs, and attitudes shared by organizational members beliefs were the pursuit of excellence, customer service, and showing "respect for the individual," meaning company employees. Microsoft employees share founder Bill Gates's determination to stay ahead of software competitors. Says a Microsoft vice president, "No matter how good your product, you are only 18 months away from failure."[73]

Though company founders are instrumental in the creation of organizational cultures, eventually founders retire, die, or choose to leave their companies. When the founders are gone, how are their values, attitudes, and beliefs sustained in the organizational culture? Answer: stories and heroes.

> **When the founders are gone, how are their values, attitudes, and beliefs sustained in the organizational culture?**

Organizational members tell **organizational stories** to make sense of organizational events and changes and to emphasize culturally consistent assumptions, decisions, and actions.[74] At *WAL-MART*, stories abound about founder Sam Walton's thriftiness as he strove to make Wal-Mart the low-cost retailer that it is today.

In those days, we would go on buying trips with Sam, and we'd all stay, as much as we could, in one room or two. I remember one time in Chicago when we stayed eight of us to a room. And the room wasn't very big to begin with. You might say we were on a pretty restricted budget. (Gary Reinboth, one of Wal-Mart's first store managers)[75]

Today, Sam Walton's thriftiness still permeates Wal-Mart. Everyone, including top executives and the CEO, flies coach rather than business or first class. When employees travel on business, it's still the norm to share rooms (though two to a room, not eight!) at inexpensive motels like Motel 6 and Super 8 instead of Holiday Inns. Likewise, for business travel, Wal-Mart will reimburse only up to $15 per meal, which is half to one-third the reimbursement rate at similar-sized companies (remember, Wal-Mart is one of the largest companies in the world). At one of its annual meetings, CEO Lee Scott reinforced Sam Walton's beliefs by exhorting Wal-Mart employees to bring back and use the free pencils and pens from their travels. Most people in the audience didn't think he was kidding, and he probably wasn't.[76]

A second way in which organizational culture is sustained is by recognizing and celebrating heroes. By definition, **organizational heroes** are organizational people admired for their qualities and achievements within the organization. *BOWA BUILDERS* is a full-service construction company in Virginia. When it was renovating a large auto dealership, its carpet subcontractor mistakenly scheduled the new carpet to be delivered two weeks *after* it was to be installed. Rather than allow construction to be delayed, a Bowa employee kept the project on schedule by immediately reordering the carpet, flying to the carpet manufacturer's factory, renting a truck, and then driving the carpet back to the auto dealership, all within 48 hours of learning about the problem. CEO and company cofounder Larry Weinberg says this story is told and retold within Bowa Builders as an example of heroic customer service. Moreover, the car dealership was so delighted with this extraordinary service that it has referred $10 million to $12 million in new business to Bowa Builders.[77]

organizational stories stories told by organizational members to make sense of organizational events and changes and to emphasize culturally consistent assumptions, decisions, and actions

organizational heroes people celebrated for their qualities and achievements within an organization

© JAY L. CLENDENIN

5.2 Successful Organizational Cultures

Preliminary research shows that organizational culture is related to organizational success. As shown in Exhibit 3.7, cultures based on adaptability, involvement, a clear vision, and consistency can help companies achieve higher sales growth, return on assets, profits, quality, and employee satisfaction.[78]

Adaptability is the ability to notice and respond to changes in the organization's environment. Cultures need to reinforce important values and behaviors, but a culture becomes dysfunctional if it prevents change, and one of the surest ways to do that is to discourage open discussion and disagreement. Organizational psychologist Kathleen Miller began working with a company that recognized the need to change its nonadaptive culture. However, she didn't realize how dysfunctional the culture was until she tried to start an honest discussion about the company's problems at one of her first meetings. The top managers simply would not speak up. They were so afraid to disagree with each other that they wrote their comments and questions anonymously on note cards and had them read aloud to the rest of the group.[79]

Bowa Builders has no shortage of organizational heroes, in part because management supports employees' efforts to go to extraordinary lengths to please customers. Every Friday, managers bring lunch to workers on the job site.

In cultures that promote higher levels of *employee involvement* in decision making, employees feel a greater sense of ownership and responsibility. Employee involvement has been a hallmark of **GENENCOR** since its creation as a joint venture between Genentech and Corning in 1982. Genencor designs its human resources programs by regularly polling employees about which benefits they enjoy and which they would like the company to offer. Most dramatically, when Genencor built its headquarters, it gave its employees a say in the design. Scientists requested that the labs be placed along the building's exterior so they could receive natural light. "I've worked in labs without windows," says staff scientist Fiona Harding, "and seeing the sun makes the time spent in the lab much more pleasant." For everyone else, the building features a "main street," where employees congregate to collaborate and interact throughout the day. CEO Jean-Jacques Bienaime believes that these employee-driven design features lead to a more stimulating workplace. "If you want employees to be productive, you have to create a nurturing environment and let them be creative," he says. Such a commitment to employee involvement in decision making is definitely paying off for the company. Its turnover rate was less than 4 percent (the national industry average is 18.5 percent), and its employees generate approximately $60,000 more revenue per employee than its largest competitor, Novozymes.[80]

Company vision is the business's purpose or reason for existing. In organizational cultures with a clear company vision, the organization's strategic purpose and direction are apparent to everyone in the company. When managers are uncertain about their business environments, the vision helps guide the discussions, decisions, and behavior of the people in the company. At F. H. Faulding & Company

company vision a company's purpose or reason for existing (a subsidiary of Mayne Group Limited), an Australia-based provider of health-care products and services doing business in 70 countries, the vision is "delivering innovative and valued solutions in health care."[81] This vision lets employees know why the company is in business (to deliver health-care solutions) and the values that really matter (innovative and valued solutions). To give its employees even more guidance, Faulding has clearly defined each of the key words in the vision statement. For example, "delivering" means targeting quality drugs, products, and services to the right place at the right time while concentrating on a global perspective. Likewise, "solutions" is defined as being focused, timely, and profitable by making quality products and services that satisfy customers' and partners' needs.

Specific vision statements strengthen organizational cultures by letting everyone know why the company is in business, what really matters (that is, the company's values), and how those values can be used to guide daily actions and behaviors.[82] Commenting on the value of Faulding's vision statement, Donna Martin, a former senior vice president of human resources, says, "A vision has to be more than a set of target revenue or profit numbers to meet. It has to be elevating, inspiring, with a strong emphasis on the future. A vision has to be a compelling and crystal-clear statement about where the organization is heading."[83] You will learn more about vision statements in Chapter 5 on planning and decision making.

Finally, in **consistent organizational cultures**, the company actively defines and teaches organizational values, beliefs, and attitudes. MCDONALD'S helps preserve its history and culture by having its executives work in its restaurants one day each year, on founder Ray Kroc's birthday. According to Kroc, this is to remind McDonald's executives that "if it's below [their] dignity to mop floors, clean toilets, and roll up [their] sleeves, then [they] are not going to succeed: [Their] attitude is wrong." McDonald's also has an exhibit called "Talk to Ray," in which, thanks to messages videotaped before his death, anyone can "ask" Ray questions about McDonald's values and history.[84]

Consistent organizational cultures are also called *strong cultures* because the core beliefs are widely shared and strongly held. Indeed, everyone who has ever worked at McDonald's has been taught its four core values: quality, service, cleanliness, and value.[85] Studies show that companies with consistent or strong corporate cultures will outperform those with inconsistent or weak cultures most of the time.[86] Why? The reason is that when core beliefs are widely shared and strongly held, it is easy for everyone to figure out what to do or not do to achieve organizational goals.

Having a consistent or strong organizational culture doesn't guarantee good company performance. When core beliefs are widely shared and strongly held, it is very difficult to bring about needed change. Consequently, companies with strong cultures tend to perform poorly when they need to adapt to dramatic changes in their external environments. Their consistency sometimes prevents them from adapting to those changes.[87] Indeed, McDonald's saw its sales and profits decline in the late 1990s as customer eating patterns began changing. To rescue falling performance, the company introduced its "Plan to Win," which focuses on the five elements that drive its business: people, products, place, price, and promotion. McDonald's developed hospitality and multilingual computer-training programs and expanded its menu

Source: D. R. Denison & A. K. Mishra, "Toward a Theory of Organizational Culture and Effectiveness," *Organization Science* 6 (1995): 204–223.

Exhibit 3.7
Successful Organizational Cultures

consistent organizational culture
a company culture in which the company actively defines and teaches organizational values, beliefs, and attitudes

to include more healthful and snack-oriented selections. Over 5,000 McDonald's restaurants were remodeled in a three-year period and now feature warmer lighting, upbeat music, flat-screen TVs, and Wi-Fi networks. And the company's promotional message "I'm lovin' it" went from being derided by advertising executives to one of the most recognizable jingles in any market. Only a few years into the plan, McDonald's achieved 32 consecutive months of positive sales (its longest streak in 25 years), reached record annual revenues of more than $20 billion, and tripled the cash dividend paid to stockholders.[88]

5.3 Changing Organizational Cultures

As shown in Exhibit 3.8, organizational cultures exist on three levels.[89] First, on the surface level, are the reflections of an organization's culture that can be seen and observed, such as symbolic artifacts (such as dress codes and office layouts), and workers' and managers' behaviors. Next, just below the surface, are the values and beliefs expressed by people in the company. You can't see these values and beliefs, but they become clear if you listen carefully to what people say and to how decisions are made or explained. Finally, unconsciously held assumptions and beliefs about the company are buried deep below the surface. These are the unwritten views and rules that are so strongly held and so widely shared that they are rarely discussed or even thought about unless someone attempts to change them or unknowingly violates them. Changing such assumptions and beliefs can be very difficult. Instead, managers should focus on the parts of the organizational culture they can control; these include observable surface-level items, such as workers' behaviors and symbolic artifacts, and expressed values and beliefs, which can be influenced through employee selection. Let's see how these can be used to change organizational cultures.

One way of changing a corporate culture is to use behavioral addition or behavioral substitution to establish new patterns of behavior among managers and employees. **Behavioral addition** is the process of having managers and employees perform a new behavior, while **behavioral substitution** is having managers and employees perform a new behavior in place of another behavior. The key in both instances is to choose behaviors that are central to and symbolic of the "old" culture you're changing and the "new" culture that you want to create. When Mike Ullman became *JCPenney*'s CEO, he thought the company's culture was stuck in the nineteenth century, when it was started: Employees called each other Mr. and Mrs., casual attire was unacceptable (even on Fridays), and any elaborate decoration of office cubicles was reported to a team of "office police" charged with enforcing corporate décor guidelines. Ullman quickly determined that the company's stringent code of conduct was, among other things, keeping it from recruiting the talent it needed. Mike Theilmann, the human resources officer, drafted a list of what he called "quick hits," small changes that would have a big impact on the culture. The first of

behavioral addition the process of having managers and employees perform new behaviors that are central to and symbolic of the new organizational culture that a company wants to create

behavioral substitution the process of having managers and employees perform new behaviors central to the "new" organizational culture in place of behaviors that were central to the "old" organizational culture

Exhibit 3.8

Three Levels of Organizational Culture

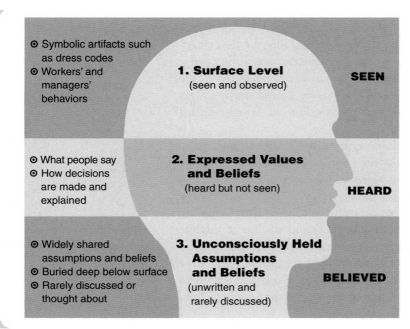

- ⊙ Symbolic artifacts such as dress codes
- ⊙ Workers' and managers' behaviors

1. Surface Level
(seen and observed)

SEEN

- ⊙ What people say
- ⊙ How decisions are made and explained

2. Expressed Values and Beliefs
(heard but not seen)

HEARD

- ⊙ Widely shared assumptions and beliefs
- ⊙ Buried deep below surface
- ⊙ Rarely discussed or thought about

3. Unconsciously Held Assumptions and Beliefs
(unwritten and rarely discussed)

BELIEVED

Theilmann's initiatives was a campaign titled "Just Call Me Mike," which he hoped would cure employees of the entrenched practice of calling executives and managers Mr. and Mrs. Three JCPenney officers are named Mike, along with nearly 400 other employees at headquarters. Theilmann created posters containing photos of the three executive Mikes along with a list of all the advantages of being on a first-name basis. Top of the list? "First names create a friendly place to shop and work."[90]

Another way in which managers can begin to change corporate culture is to change the **visible artifacts** of their old culture, such as the office design and layout, company dress code, and recipients (or nonrecipients) of company benefits and perks like stock options, personal parking spaces, or the private company dining room. To help anchor the internal culture change at JCPenney, Ullman issued all 150,000 JCPenney employees with new name badges. First names appear in large typeface; last names are printed much smaller. He also disbanded the office police, declared that suitable work attire was business casual, and sold or donated most of the 300 pieces in the company's art collection. (He replaced them with pictures of Penney's employees and other company-oriented art.) Most strikingly, Ullman updated founder James Cash Penney's code of conduct and replaced it with one that allows all employees—not just management—to receive the company's traditional Honor, Confidence, Service, Cooperation award for employee loyalty.[91]

Cultures can also be changed by hiring and selecting people with values and beliefs consistent with the company's desired culture. *Selection* is the process of gathering information about job applicants to decide who should be offered a job. As discussed in Chapter 11 on human resources, most selection instruments measure whether job applicants have the knowledge, skills, and abilities needed to succeed in their jobs. Today, however, companies are increasingly testing job applicants to determine how the fit with the company's desired culture (that is, values and beliefs). Management consultant Ram Charan says, "A poor job match is not only harmful to the individual but also to the company."[92] At BRISTOL-MYERS SQUIBB, people who didn't fit the culture tended to leave. According to Ben Dowell, who runs Bristol-Myers Squibb's Center for Leadership Development, "What came through was, those who left were uncomfortable in our culture or violated some core area of our value system."[93] The first step in hiring people who have values consistent with the desired culture is to define and describe that culture. Bristol-Myers Squibb hired an organizational psychologist who spent four months interviewing senior managers. He concluded that the company had a team-driven culture that focused on research and development, which meant that it valued self-motivated, intellectually curious people.

visible artifacts visible signs of an organization's culture, such as the office design and layout, company dress code, and company benefits and perks, like stock options, personal parking spaces, or the private company dining room

The second step is to ensure that applicants fit with the culture by using selection tests, instruments, and exercises to measure these values and beliefs in job applicants. (See Chapter 11 for a complete review of applicant and managerial selection.) At SOUTHWEST AIRLINES, humor and a good attitude are two of the most important requirements in its new hires. Chairman and former CEO Herb Kelleher says, "What's important is that a customer should get off the airplane feeling: 'I didn't just get from A to B. I had one of the most pleasant experiences I ever had and I'll be back for that reason.'"[94] For instance, on a flight from Houston to Dallas, a flight attendant addresses passengers over the speaker system, saying, "Could y'all lean in a little toward the center aisle, please?" Met with confused looks from passengers, he continues, "Just a bit, please. That's it. No, the other way, sir. Thanks. You see, the pilot has to pull out of this space here, and he needs to be able to check the rearview mirrors." On another Southwest plane, Yvonne Masters jokingly introduced her fellow flight attendants as her "former husband and his new girlfriend."[95] Southwest passenger Mark Rafferty said his favorite Southwest flight attendant joke was when "they told everyone on the plane's left side, toward the terminal, to put their faces in the window and smile so our competitors can see what a full flight looks like."[96] Corny, yes, but the humor is exactly what Southwest and its customers want, and the airline gets it by hiring people consistent with its hard-working, fun-loving culture. Says Kelleher, "We draft great attitudes. If you don't have a good attitude, we don't want you, no matter how skilled you are. We can change skill level through training. We can't change attitude."[97]

> "We draft great attitudes. If you don't have a good attitude, we don't want you, no matter how skilled you are. We can change skill level through training. We can't change attitude."
>
> HERB KELLEHER, CHAIRMAN AND FORMER CEO, SOUTHWEST AIRLINES

Corporate cultures are very difficult to change. Consequently, there is no guarantee that any one approach—changing visible cultural artifacts, using behavioral substitution, or hiring people with values consistent with a company's desired culture—will change a company's organizational culture. The best results are obtained by combining these methods. Together, these are some of the best tools managers have for changing culture because they send the clear message to managers and employees that "the accepted way of doing things" has changed.

Review 5: Organizational Cultures: Creation, Success, and Change

Organizational culture is the set of key values, beliefs, and attitudes shared by organizational members. Organizational cultures are often created by company founders and then sustained through the telling of organizational stories and the celebration of organizational heroes. Adaptable cultures that promote employee involvement, make clear the organization's strategic purpose and direction, and actively define and teach organizational values and beliefs can help companies achieve higher sales growth, return on assets, profits, quality, and employee satisfaction. Organizational cultures exist on three levels: the surface level, where cultural artifacts and behaviors can be observed; just below the surface, where values and beliefs are expressed; and deep below the surface, where unconsciously held assumptions and beliefs exist. Managers can begin to change company cultures by focusing on the top two levels and by using behavioral substitution and behavioral addition, changing visible artifacts, and selecting job applicants with values and beliefs consistent with the desired company culture.

Check Your Tolerance for Ambiguity

Think of the difference between playing chess (where you can see all the pieces and anticipate attacks and plan counterattacks) and playing poker (where no one knows anyone else's hand, and you have to make guesses based on your interpretation of opponents' betting patterns). In chess, there is little ambiguity, whereas in poker there is tremendous ambiguity. Although many people liken business to a game of chess, probably because of the strategic aspects of the game, business is actually more like poker. The business environment is complex and uncertain, and managers never *really* know all the cards the opposition is holding. Managers must learn to adapt to environmental shifts and new developments—sometimes on a daily basis. For some managers, however, this can be a challenging task because everyone has a different comfort level when it comes to ambiguity. For some, not knowing all the details can be a source of significant stress, whereas for others uncertainty can be energizing.

As a manager, you will need to develop an appropriate tolerance for ambiguity. For example, being stressed out every time interest rates change can be counterproductive, but completely ignoring the economic environment can be detrimental to your company's performance.

Complete the following questionnaire to get a sense of your tolerance for ambiguity.[98] Indicate the extent to which you agree with the statements using the following scale:

1 Strongly disagree
2 Moderately disagree
3 Slightly disagree
4 Neutral
5 Slightly agree
6 Moderately agree
7 Strongly agree

1. I don't tolerate ambiguous situations well.
   1   2   3   4   5   6   7

2. I find it difficult to respond when faced with an unexpected event.
   1   2   3   4   5   6   7

3. I don't think new situations are any more threatening than familiar situations.
   1   2   3   4   5   6   7

4. I am drawn to situations which can be interpreted in more than one way.
   1   2   3   4   5   6   7

5. I would rather avoid solving problems that must be viewed from several different perspectives.
   1   2   3   4   5   6   7

6. I try to avoid situations which are ambiguous.
   1   2   3   4   5   6   7

7. I am good at managing unpredictable situations.
   1   2   3   4   5   6   7

8. I prefer familiar situations to new ones.
   1   2   3   4   5   6   7

9. Problems which cannot be considered from just one point of view are a little threatening.
   1   2   3   4   5   6   7

10. I avoid situations which are too complicated for me to easily understand.
    1   2   3   4   5   6   7

11. I am tolerant of ambiguous situations.
    1   2   3   4   5   6   7

12. I enjoy tackling problems which are complex enough to be ambiguous.
    1   2   3   4   5   6   7

13. I try to avoid problems which don't seem to have only one "best" solution.
    1   2   3   4   5   6   7

14. I often find myself looking for something new, rather than trying to hold things constant in my life.
    1   2   3   4   5   6   7

15. I generally prefer novelty over familiarity.
    1   2   3   4   5   6   7

16. I dislike ambiguous situations.
    1   2   3   4   5   6   7

17. Some problems are so complex that just trying to understand them is fun.
    1   2   3   4   5   6   7

18. I have little trouble coping with unexpected events.
    1   2   3   4   5   6   7

19. I pursue problem situations which are so complex some people call them "mind-boggling."
    1   2   3   4   5   6   7

20. I find it hard to make a choice when the outcome is uncertain.
    1   2   3   4   5   6   7

21. I enjoy an occasional surprise.
    1   2   3   4   5   6   7

22. I prefer a situation in which there is some ambiguity.
    1   2   3   4   5   6   7

Scoring

Determine your score by entering your response to each survey item below, as follows. In blanks that say *regular score*, simply enter your response for that item. If your response was a 6, place a 6 in the *regular score* blank. In blanks that say *reverse score*, subtract your response from 8 and enter the result. So if your response was a 6, place a 2 (8 – 6 = 2) in the *reverse score* blank. Add up your total score.

1. regular score   ——
2. regular score   ——
3. reverse score   ——
4. reverse score   ——
5. regular score   ——
6. regular score   ——
7. reverse score   ——
8. regular score   ——
9. regular score   ——
10. regular score   ——
11. regular score   ——
12. reverse score   ——
13. regular score   ——
14. reverse score   ——
15. reverse score   ——
16. regular score   ——
17. reverse score   ——
18. reverse score   ——
19. reverse score   ——
20. regular score   ——
21. reverse score   ——
22. reverse score   ——
TOTAL =   ——

You can find the interpretation for your score on at: **academic.cengage.com/management/williams**

MANAGEMENT DECISION

Environmental Roller Coaster

It couldn't be a better day to be at Cedar Point amusement park. It's mid-September, sunny, and 75 degrees, and there's no one waiting in any of the lines. Passing by the Millennium Force roller coaster, you stop to get a slushee and then sit down at a nearby picnic table to start thinking about the annual environmental scan.

Since joining the management team of Cedar Point, a large regional amusement park located in Sandusky, Ohio, you've done this exercise 10 times. Each time, it is more difficult because the environment keeps changing, but doing the environmental assessment has kept Cedar

Point viable. You think to yourself "We've just finished a tight season, but we managed to come out ahead. We are facing some big shifts, though both in the general business environment and in the amusement industry, so we need to build a plan to meet those environmental challenges."

Pausing for a moment, you stare at the coaster's 80-degree drop. Your mind dives just as steeply into a flurry of issues: shifts toward year-round schooling; trends in the insurance industry; new forms of entertainment; new competition; the effect of changing demographics on your attendance and your work force; higher gasoline prices; and the impact of the economy in general. You've been able to increase the price of admission year after year, but how long can you continue to do that? Your straw makes a loud noise as you finish your slushee. "I guess that means it's time to head back to the office and figure out what trends are going to affect the park and how."

Questions

1. Consider the issues that you as the Cedar Point manager are examining as part of this exercise. What other issues should you examine?

2. Create a list of issues addressing each of the environmental factors discussed in the chapter (economy, technology, political/legal, sociocultural, customer, competitor, supplier, industry regulation). For each item on your list, explain how Cedar Point will face the challenges posed by that factor in its environment.

3. Based on the solutions you generated in question 2, how uncertain is the amusement park industry? Why do you think as you do? (Think about the environmental change, complexity, and resources of the amusement park industry. You may wish to use Exhibit 3.2 as a guide.)

MANAGEMENT TEAM DECISION

Dog Day Blues

One of the reasons you accepted a management position at MicroTek several years ago was the company's laid-back culture.[99] A loose organizational structure enables employees to move freely between projects, and the open office space encourages informal encounters and generates a feeling of teamwork. And among the very generous corporate perks is a policy allowing employees to bring their pets to work. It is not uncommon to see a small animal sitting in an employee's in-box drinking from a hamster lick. Several employees bring their dogs, large and small, to the office.

As the company has grown, thanks in part to its informal culture, more and more people are taking advantage of the pet policy, and problems are arising. Food is swiped from desks, animals are rooting through trash bins, and dogs are marking territory on the partitions that surround their owners' desks. Visiting customers often try to mask startled (at best) or disapproving (at worst) looks when they tour your facility for the first time—and even the second and third times. During a recent breakfast meeting, when a board member refused to share her bagel with the CFO's dog, the dog relieved itself on her briefcase. At least one employee has complained of allergic reactions due to the high levels of pet dander in the office air, but rather than change the policy, you installed a high-power air cleaner.

Despite the challenges, you have resisted changing the pet policy because it symbolizes both the company's relaxed culture and MicroTek's commitment to its employees' work-life balance. This afternoon, however, you were notified by the federal Occupational Safety and Health Administration (OSHA) that your office does not meet the required indoor air quality standards. Apparently, the cleaner you installed can't handle all the pet dander. To meet the standards, you'll need an even more powerful air cleaner that costs between $100,000 and $200,000. That would be a significant investment in the pet policy! And who knows if it would solve the allergy problem. Is the policy worth the cost?

In 2003, only 5,000 offices participated in "Bring Your Pet to Work Day," but the number doubled the very next year. Companies bigger than MicroTek have figured out how to make pet policies work: IAMS Pet Food; Replacements Ltd., the world's largest supplier of old and new china; and Netscape, to name a few. A quarter of Burton Snowboards' 230 employees bring their dogs to work every day! Anecdotal evidence from those companies indicates that pets can spur creativity and lower occupational stress. You ask yourself, "How committed am I to the pet policy?" Is the pet policy just trendy (or avant-garde), or does it say something deeper about your company?

For this Management Team Decision, assemble three or four students to act as the management team for MicroTek. Include both pet owners and people without pets to avoid any bias. Before you begin the exercise, have each team member privately write down answers to each of the following questions. By sharing your individual responses, you may be able to have a more varied and rounded discussion.

Questions

1. Do you buy the expensive air cleaner, or eliminate the pet policy? Why?

2. If you choose to stop allowing animals at the office, what effect, if any, do you think the change will have on the company's culture?

3. Can you think of a way to allow people to bring pets to work without upgrading the air cleaner or running afoul of OSHA?

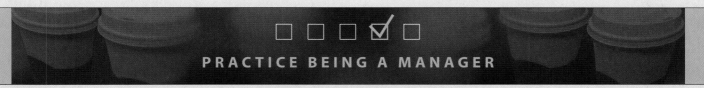

PRACTICE BEING A MANAGER

Navigating Different Organizational Cultures

Effective managers recognize that organizational culture is an important, often critical element of organizational health and performance. But recognizing and understanding culture, especially its less visible aspects, is often quite challenging. This exercise will give you some practice in recognizing cultural differences and the challenges and opportunities that managers face as they work with diverse cultures.

Suppose that major music recording company SonyBMG has announced plans to hire several college students to form a team that will invest in the "next big things in music." The selected students will be paid $50,000 per year for working part-time. SonyBMG will also allocate up to $10 million for hiring artists, producing records, and so on based on the team's recommendations.

The new team has been dubbed the Top Wave Team (TWT). If TWT's recommendations are fruitful, the company will sign each member of the team to $150,000 full-time contracts. The company also plans to keep the team together, and to give members bonuses and promotions based on their group performance.

Your class has been chosen as the representative college class. The music company is now asking you to form affinity groups by musical preferences in your class (for example, a Country Music group, an Urban/Hip-Hop group). Each group will nominate one of its members to receive the first $50,000 internship as a TWT team member at SonyBMG. The new TWT group will meet and discuss initial plans and investment recommendations, and then your class will discuss the process and outcomes.

Step 1: Choose your musical affinity. In the class session before this exercise, your professor will ask you to submit a survey form or sheet of paper with your name and your preferred musical genre/identity.

Identify yourself with one of the following musical genres based on (a) preference/affinity ("I prefer this music") and (b) knowledge/understanding ("Of all types of music, I know the most about _____ music/musicians"):

1. Rock
2. Country
3. Religious/Spiritual
4. Urban/Hip-Hop
5. Rap
6. Jazz/R&B
7. Pop/Mainstream
8. Classical
9. Folk/Bluegrass

Your professor will review your submitted preferences, and organize affinity groups for the next class session.

Step 2: Organize into groups. Your professor will organize you by musical affinity. If your class is heavily concentrated in one or a few of the musical genres, you may be asked to further divide into smaller groups by sub-categories (such as Rock—Heavy Metal and Rock—Popular/Hit).

Step 3: Prepare your recommendations. In groups, discuss what is important about your type of music, and what investments should be made by the TWT team. Keep in mind that the investments made by the TWT team could have a big impact on the future of your favorite music. Recommend a dollar amount or percentage of the $10 million that your representative ought to secure for investment in your genre.

Each group should then select one of its members to receive the internship from SonyBMG and represent the group on the TWT team.

Step 4: Discuss recommendations before the class. Nominees from the musical affinity groups should discuss their recommendations before the class. Those not on the TWT should observe the process and take notes on what happens in this meeting.

Step 5: Hold the team meeting. Your professor will allocate a short time for the initial meeting of the TWT. It may occur before or during the class meeting. After the TWT reaches agreement on how it might allocate its investments by genre (or by some alternative approach), reaches impasse, or reaches the time limit, your professor will call an end to the TWT meeting.

Step 6: Debrief and discuss. As a class, discuss the process and outcomes of this exercise. Consider the following questions and/or others posed by your professor.

- Did you sense some cultural affinity with others who shared your musical tastes? Why or why not?

- What expectations might be associated with choosing someone to "represent" a group on a team such as the TWT?

- What tensions and challenges might face each member of the TWT in a real-life setting of serving on a group that represents various cultures?

DEVELOP YOUR CAREER POTENTIAL

Dealing with the Press

In this age of 24-hour cable news channels, tabloid news shows, and aggressive local and national news reporters intent on exposing corporate wrongdoing, one of the most important skills for a manager to learn is how to deal effectively with the press.[100] Test your ability to deal effectively with the press by putting yourself in the following situations. To make the situation more realistic, read the scenario and then give yourself two minutes to write a response to each question.

Rats Take Over Manhattan Taco Bell

The release of Internet footage showed large rats running across the floors, over tables, and climbing onto countertops of a Manhattan Taco Bell. What is most surprising is that the day before the television crew filmed the rats through the restaurant window, New York City health inspectors had given the restaurant a passing grade! The broadcast prompted parent company Yum! Brands to temporarily close that and several other Taco Bell stores owned by franchisee ADF Companies. Based in New Jersey, ADF owns over 350 fast-food franchises in several states.

A TV reporter from Channel 5 has arrived with his camera crew at the Taco Bell you manage in Brooklyn. It's lunchtime, the restaurant is bustling, and the reporter walks right in with his crew and puts you on the spot, asking you if you would grant a short interview and let him ask questions of a few of your patrons. When you agree, he starts right in with these questions:

1. "Yesterday's filming of rats at an ADF-owned Taco Bell has caused consumers to question the cleanliness of the restaurants where they eat. This restaurant is also owned by ADF Companies. Do you also have problems with rodents?"

2. "Recent outbreaks of E. coli at other Taco Bells in the Northeast were finally attributed to contaminated lettuce, so Taco Bell changed suppliers." To the cameraman: "Get the camera in close here [camera zooms into the kitchen area, the slop sink, and the handwashing station] because I want our viewers to see the kitchen." Back to you: "How can consumers be sure that contamination occurred at the produce supplier and not inside filthy restaurants?"

3. "The health inspectors gave a passing grade to the rat-infested Taco Bell just a day before television crews filmed the rats running all over the restaurant. That doesn't instill our viewers with great confidence in the system. Would you be willing to let our camera crews accompany the health inspector during a full inspection of your restaurant so that viewers can see what an inspection entails?"

REEL TO REAL

BIZ FLIX
Brazil

Set somewhere in the twentieth century, the retro-futuristic world of *Brazil* is a gritty, urban cesspool patched over with cosmetic surgery and "designer ducts for your discriminating taste." Automation pervades every facet of life from toaster and coffee machine to doorways, but paperwork, inefficiency, and mechanical failures are the rule. *Brazil* stars Jonathan Pryce in the role of Sam, a low-level bureaucrat whose primary interests in life are his vivid dream fantasies to the tune of "Brazil," a 1940s big-band hit. In this scene, Sam is starting a new job and is being assigned an office and employee identification number.

What to Watch for and Ask Yourself

1. Describe the culture at Sam's new employer.
2. How easy would it be to change the culture at Sam's new company?
3. In which kind of business environment do you think the culture at Sam's employer is able to operate most successfully?

MANAGEMENT WORKPLACE
Lonely Planet's Travel Culture

When you think of corporate culture, the image of suits and ties, pantyhose and pumps often springs to mind. But at Lonely Planet, the values, beliefs, understandings, and norms of the firm are expressed by staff members and managers who wear T-shirts, khakis, soft skirts, and sandals or clogs to work. Lonely Planet is a publishing company based in Australia with offices in several other countries—including the United States—that produces travel books, guides, and language phrasebooks for people who want adventure.

Lonely Planet fosters an internal culture in which employees are free to be themselves—to exchange ideas and try new approaches to problems. Take a peek inside the management workplace of Lonely Planet.

What to Watch for and Ask Yourself

1. Create a list describing how each component of the general and specific external environment affects Lonely Planet. For example, under technology, you could write that the rise of the Internet has caused more people to research travel opportunities online rather than with guidebooks.
2. Which factors in the external environment could create uncertainty for Lonely Planet?
3. Give an example of Lonely Planet's corporate culture at each of the three levels identified in Exhibit 3.4.

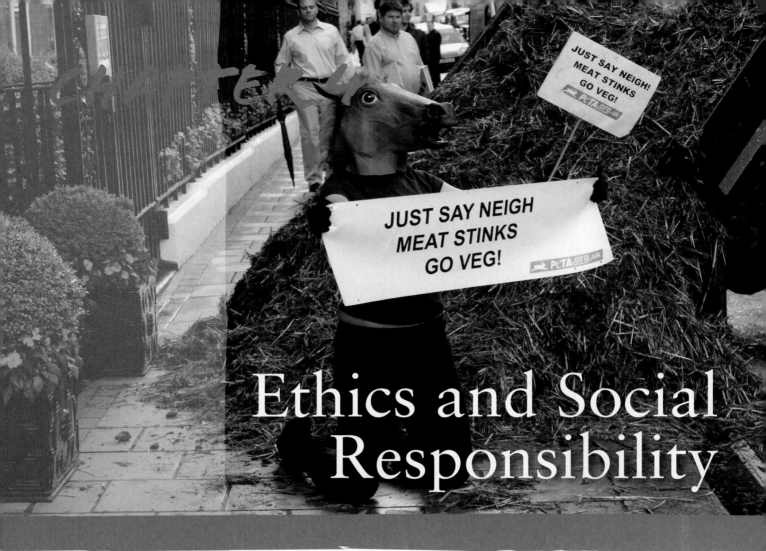

Ethics and Social Responsibility

WHAT WOULD YOU DO?

Procter & Gamble Headquarters, Cincinnati, Ohio.[1] "What's that?" you wonder as you look out your window. A small group of people are gathered on the sidewalk at the end of the wisteria gardens in front of the main headquarters of Procter & Gamble. If you squint, you can see they're holding signs, but the only text you can make out is the word "PETA" in big letters across the bottom. "Just great," you think to yourself.

People for the Ethical Treatment of Animals, the animal-rights group more commonly known as PETA, raises more than $25 million a year from its 1.6 million members and supporters. PETA not only campaigns for animal rights, but also funds lesser known animal-rights groups to engage in activism. PETA is extremely adept at organizing public campaigns and mobilizing the public to boycott companies. Its public-relations tactics include celebrity endorsements, traveling displays of animal abuse, and creative on-site demonstrations. Even large international companies like McDonald's, Burger King, and KFC have bowed to PETA's pressure, issuing strict guidelines for the humane treatment of animals, and then enforcing those standards with unannounced inspections of beef, pork, and chicken suppliers' production farms and processing plants.

PETA has been known to use aggressive tactics. In one instance, a viral ad featuring scantily clad women with cow udders instead of breasts was distributed in the UK as part of a campaign against milk drinking and production. PETA had hoped to air a television version of the ad on the ABC network in the United States during the Super Bowl, but was told that it "falls outside boundaries of good taste." Mimicking television shows like *Girls Gone Wild*, in which women are encouraged to disrobe for cameras, PETA's "Milk Gone Wild" ad shows models dancing in a bar, surrounded by men drinking glasses of milk. When the women tear off their tops, they expose cow udders. In another instance, PETA successfully launched a six-year campaign of intimidation against a farm that bred guinea pigs for scientific research. Their tactics, denounced as mob rule by some in the medical research community, included hate mail, malicious phone calls, death threats, fireworks, a pedophile smear campaign, car vandalism, arson attacks, and finally the theft of the remains of a relative of the farm owner from the churchyard cemetery.

Procter & Gamble (P&G) does not use animals to test the safety of its cosmetics, shampoos, detergents, cleansers, and paper goods; it does, however, use animals to test the safety of new drugs, health-care products, and products intended for use on babies and children. Nonetheless, P&G still draws protests from PETA in the form of PETA's "Died" advertising campaign, based on P&G's best-selling laundry detergent Tide. The "Died" ad shows a woman holding a box of "Died" detergent with the words "Thousands of Animals Died for Your Laundry" boldly written on the box. PETA is urging consumers to boycott all P&G products until the company ends all forms of animal testing.

From P&G's perspective, testing is critical to producing safe products for its customers. P&G has to know, for example, that a product will not cause injury if children accidentally swallow it or get it into their eyes. Furthermore, in the event that a product liability lawsuit is filed against the company, its best legal defense would be the scientific testing it performs on rats and rabbits.

As the CEO of P&G should you, as PETA demands, eliminate all animal testing? Or, by minimizing but not eliminating animal testing, has P&G achieved a reasonable balance that still allows it to make sure its products are safe? The last thing you need are product liability lawsuits accusing P&G of selling unsafe products. On the other hand, PETA's protests have pressured other companies to change, but how do you appease PETA while not compromising customer safety? There's also the risk that if PETA launches new campaigns and boycotts, it could turn some customers against the company, which in turn could hurt revenue, and declining revenues could affect stockholders, and might even lead to downsizing affecting employees. PETA's aggressive tactics and history of misrepresentation of facts are cause for concern. With so many tradeoffs to consider, what is the most socially responsible thing to do? **If you were the CEO of Procter & Gamble, what would you do?**

"WHAT'S NEW" COMPANIES

PROCTER & GAMBLE
PETA
CHICAGO SUN-TIMES
DAIMLERCHRYSLER
OMEGA ENGINEERING
GILLETTE
CAREMARK INTERNATIONAL
IBM
NORTEL
AND OTHERS . . .

Study Tip **Every chapter in this book contains diagrams and tables to illustrate the text material.** One good way to study is to try to recreate the exhibit from scratch on your own. Draw a blank diagram, fill it in, then check your work by comparing your worksheet with the original exhibit in the chapter.

The dilemma facing P&G's CEO is an example of the tough decisions involving ethics and social responsibility that managers face. Unfortunately, one of the "real-world" aspects of these decisions is that no matter what you decide, someone or some group will be unhappy with the outcome. Managers don't have the luxury of choosing theoretically optimal, win-win solutions that are obviously desirable to everyone involved. In practice, solutions to ethics and social responsibility problems aren't optimal. Often, managers must be satisfied with a solution that just "makes do" or "does the least harm." Crystal-clear rights and wrongs rarely reveal themselves to managers charged with "doing the right thing." The business world is much messier than that.

We begin this chapter by examining ethical behavior in the workplace and explaining how unethical behavior can expose a business to penalties under the U.S. Sentencing Commission Guidelines for Organizations. Second, we examine the influences on ethical decision making and review practical steps that managers can take to improve ethical decision making. We finish by considering to whom organizations are socially responsible, what organizations are socially responsible for, how they can respond to societal expectations for social responsibility, and whether social responsibility hurts or helps an organization's economic performance.

WHAT IS ETHICAL AND UNETHICAL WORKPLACE BEHAVIOR?

Ethics is the set of moral principles or values that defines right and wrong for a person or group. Unfortunately, numerous studies have consistently produced distressing results about the state of ethics in today's business world. According to an SHRM/CareerJournal.com survey, only 27 percent of employees felt that their organization's leadership was ethical.[2] In another study of 1,324 randomly selected workers, managers, and executives across multiple industries, 48 percent of the respondents admitted to actually committing an unethical or illegal act in the past year! These acts included cheating on an expense account, discriminating against coworkers, forging signatures, paying or accepting kickbacks, and "looking the other way" when environmental laws were broken.[3] Clearly, in an era with widely publicized corporate scandals at WorldCom, Tyco, and HealthSouth (where executives allegedly committed fraud by overstating company results by billions of dollars and used company funds for their personal gain), poor business ethics is a serious and widespread problem.[4]

The studies also contained good news, however. When people believe their work environment is ethical, they are six times more likely to stay with that company than if they believe they work in an unethical environment.[5] Furthermore, when 570 white-collar workers were asked which of 28 qualities were important in company leaders, honesty (24 percent) and integrity/morals/ethics (16 percent) ranked by far the highest (caring/compassion was third at 7 percent).[6] According to Dwight Reighard, the chief people officer at HomeBanc Mortgage Corp. in Atlanta, "people want to work for

ethics the set of moral principles or values that defines right and wrong for a person or group leaders they trust."[7] In short, much needs to be done to make workplaces more ethical, but—and this is very important—most managers and employees want this to happen.

Crystal-clear rights and wrongs rarely reveal themselves to managers charged with "doing the right thing."

After reading the next three sections, you should be able to

> 1 discuss how the nature of management jobs creates the possibility for ethical abuses.
>
> 2 identify common kinds of workplace deviance.
>
> 3 describe the U.S. Sentencing Commission Guidelines for Organizations and explain how they both encourage ethical behavior and punish unethical behavior by businesses.

1 Ethics and the Nature of Management Jobs

Ethical behavior follows accepted principles of right and wrong. By contrast, unethical management behavior, such as lying about company profits or knowingly producing an unsafe product, occurs when managers personally violate accepted principles of right and wrong or encourage others to do so. Because of the nature of their jobs, managers can be tempted to engage in unethical managerial behavior in four areas: authority and power, handling information, influencing the behavior of others, and setting goals.

The *authority and power* inherent in some management positions can tempt managers to engage in unethical practices. Because managers often control company resources, there is a risk that some managers will cross the line from legitimate use of company resources to personal use. For example, treating a client to dinner is a common and legitimate business practice in many companies. But what about treating a client to a ski trip? Taking the company jet to attend a business meeting in San Diego is legitimate. But how about using the jet to come home to Chicago by way of Honolulu? Human resources can be misused as well. For example, unless it's in an employee's job description, using an employee to do personal chores, like picking up the manager's dry cleaning, is unethical behavior. Even worse, though, is using one's managerial authority and power for direct personal gain, as some managers have done by using corporate funds to pay for extravagant personal parties, lavish home decorating, jewelry, or expensive works of art.

Handling information is another area in which managers must be careful to behave ethically. Information is a key part of management work. Managers collect it, analyze it, act on it, and disseminate it. In doing so, they are expected to be truthful and, when necessary, to keep confidential information confidential. Leaking company secrets to competitors, "doctoring" the numbers, wrongfully withholding information, and lying are some of the ways managers may misuse information entrusted to them. After thousands of customers canceled subscriptions because their papers weren't delivered on time (thanks to chronic problems at a new printing facility) and a "horrendous drop" in advertising dollars severely lowered revenues,

ethical behavior behavior that conforms to a society's accepted principles of right and wrong managers at the CHICAGO SUN-TIMES began inflating its daily sales numbers so that the newspaper could charge more for advertising and offset the declining revenues. By fraudulently padding the numbers by 50,000 papers per day, the *Sun-Times* tricked advertisers into paying much higher advertising rates. John Cruickshank, who became the paper's new publisher after the scandal was discovered, admitted, "Our appetite for fake numbers became greater and greater."[8]

Managers must also be careful to behave ethically in the way they *influence the behavior of others*, especially those they supervise. Managerial work gives managers significant power to influence others. If managers tell employees to perform unethical acts (or face punishment), such as "faking the numbers to get results," they are abusing their managerial power. This is sometimes called the "move it or lose it" syndrome. "Move it or lose it" managers tell employees, "Do it. You're paid to do it. If you can't do it, we'll find somebody who can."[9] A study of 400 managers found that the "move it or lose it" syndrome even affects top managers. Forty-seven percent of the corporate executives in this study said they would be willing to commit financial fraud by understating accounting write-offs that reduced company profits. Tulane University business professor Art Brief, who conducted the study, says, "People in subordinate roles will comply with their superiors even when that includes wrongdoing that goes against their individual moral code. I thought they would stick with their values, but most organizations are structured to produce obedience."[10]

When faced with plummeting subscription numbers, managers at the Chicago Sun-Times *opted to continue selling advertising based on old, higher subscription numbers.*

Setting goals is another way that managers influence the behavior of their employees. If managers set unrealistic goals, the pressure to perform and achieve those goals can influence employees to engage in unethical business behaviors, especially if they are just short of meeting their goals or a deadline.[11] DAIMLERCHRYSLER dismissed several employees after an internal bribery probe found that key officials made "improper payments" in Africa, Asia, and Eastern Europe to meet revenue targets. The U.S. Justice Department conducted a criminal investigation into the bribery allegations and whether senior executives were aware of the practice. In response, the company established a "corporate compliance department" to make sure that business practices are in compliance with anticorruption laws and the company's ethics standards. It has also set up a "sales-practices hotline" that employees can call to report "questionable activities."[12]

Review 1: **Ethics and the Nature of Management Jobs**

Ethics is the set of moral principles or values that define right and wrong. Ethical behavior occurs when managers follow those principles and values. Because they set the standard for others in the workplace, managers can model ethical behavior by using resources for company business and not personal gain. Furthermore, managers can encourage ethical behavior by handling information in a confidential and honest fashion, by not using their authority to influence others to engage in unethical behavior, by not creating policies that unintentionally reward employees for unethical behavior, and by setting reasonable rather than unreasonable goals.

2 Workplace Deviance

Depending on which study you look at, one-third to three-quarters of all employees admit that they have stolen from their employers, committed computer fraud, embezzled funds, vandalized company property, sabotaged company projects, faked injuries to receive workers' compensation benefits or insurance, or been "sick" from work when they weren't really sick. Experts estimate that unethical behaviors like these, which researchers call "workplace deviance" may cost companies as much as $660 billion a year, or roughly 6 percent of their revenues.[13]

More specifically, **workplace deviance** is unethical behavior that violates organizational norms about right and wrong. As Exhibit 4.1 shows, workplace deviance can be categorized by how deviant the behavior is, from minor to serious, and by the target of the deviant behavior, either the organization or particular people in the workplace.[14] One kind of workplace deviance, called **production deviance**, hurts the quality and quantity of work produced. Examples include leaving early, taking excessively long work breaks, intentionally working slower, or wasting resources.

Property deviance is unethical behavior aimed at company property or products. Examples include sabotaging, stealing, or damaging equipment or products, and overcharging for services and then pocketing the difference. For example, property deviance in the form of stealing was so bad at the telecommunications company where Bill Weiss worked that employees referred to the supply room as the "gift shop" where everything was available at "five-finger discount prices." Perforated boards, which were used to make prototypes for electronic devices, were taken by employees to finish the walls in their basements. Leather work gloves disappeared

workplace deviance unethical behavior that violates organizational norms about right and wrong

production deviance unethical behavior that hurts the quality and quantity of work produced

property deviance unethical behavior aimed at the organization's property or products

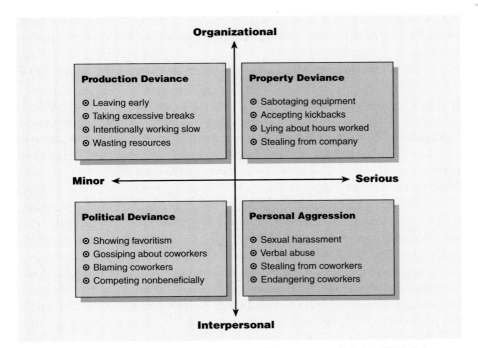

Exhibit 4.1

Types of Workplace Deviance

Source: Republished with permission of Academy of Management, P.O. Box 3020, Briar Cliff Manor, NY, 10510–8020. "A Typology of Deviant Workplace Behaviors," (Figure), S. L. Robinson & R. J. Bennett. *Academy of Management Journal*, 1995, Vol. 38. Reproduced by permission of the publisher via Copyright Clearance Center, Inc.

only to end up being used in employees' gardens. Says Weiss, "Every April, 4,000 pairs of these things used to disappear."[15] Fifty-eight percent of office workers acknowledge taking company property for personal use, according to a survey conducted for Lawyers.com.[16] Sometimes, property deviance involves the sabotage of company property. At OMEGA ENGINEERING, an employee planted a software bomb in the centralized file server containing the company's key programs and data. The code destroyed the programs and data that ran the machines in Omega's manufacturing plant. The company lost $10 million as a result, including $2 million in reprogramming costs. Eighty employees had to be laid off because of lost business resulting from the incident.[17]

The theft of company merchandise by employees, called **employee shrinkage**, is another common form of property deviance. Employee shrinkage, which costs U.S. retailers more than $15.8 billion a year and typically reduces store profits by 2 to 3 percent, takes many forms.[18] "Sweethearting" occurs when employees discount or don't ring up merchandise their family or friends bring to the cash register. In "dumpster diving," employees unload trucks, stash merchandise in a dumpster, and then retrieve it after work.[19] To help grocery stores reduce employee shrinkage, which costs the typical store approximately $350,000 per year, companies such as Procter & Gamble and GILLETTE, its subsidiary, are inserting radio frequency antitheft tags (see Chapter 17 for further information), some as small as the head of a pin, in low-cost household products like Bounty paper towels and Gillette blades and razors. The antitheft tags have built-in antennas that transmit unique identification numbers that enable a store to track a product and determine whether it "disappears" off the loading truck, falls off the shelf, is properly purchased, or is stolen by employees when they leave for the day.[20]

Workers compensation fraud is another example of property deviance aimed at defrauding and hurting the company. According to the National Insurance Crime Bureau (NICB), about 10 percent of insurance claims are fraudulent, resulting in $5 billion in sham workers' compensation claims annually. Abuses range from people who fake an injury while on the job in order to collect workers' compensation insurance to "organized criminal conspiracies of crooked physicians, attorneys, and patients who submit false and exaggerated medical claims to insurance companies."[21]

Whereas production and property deviance harm companies, political deviance and personal aggression are unethical behaviors that hurt particular people within companies. **Political deviance** is using one's influence to harm others in the company. Examples include making decisions based on favoritism rather than performance, spreading rumors about coworkers, or blaming others for mistakes they didn't make. **Personal aggression** is hostile or aggressive behavior toward others. Examples include sexual harassment, verbal abuse, stealing from coworkers, or personally threatening coworkers. One of the fastest-growing kinds of personal aggression is workplace violence. A former Navistar employee forced his way into a Chicago factory and fired 30 shots from an AK-47, killing four people. The day after Christmas, an employee of Edgewater Technology walked into the accounting department and shot seven people dead. In the worst mass murder in Hawaii's history, a frustrated copier repairman killed seven people outside a parts warehouse in Honolulu.[22] The violence isn't reserved for employees. A client entered a law firm on the 38th floor of a downtown Chicago office building and shot three people dead before he was killed by a SWAT officer.[23]

More than 2 million Americans are victims of some form of workplace violence each year. In a survey of 7.4 million U.S. companies, employing more than

employee shrinkage employee theft of company merchandise

political deviance using one's influence to harm others in the company

personal aggression hostile or aggressive behavior toward others

128 million workers, the U.S. Bureau of Labor Statistics (BLS) found that 5.4 percent of all employees suffered an incident of workplace violence each year.[24] Between 650 and 1,000 people are actually killed at work each year.[25] Though many victims, as might be expected, are police officers, security guards, or taxi drivers, store owners and company managers are killed most often.[26] For more information on workplace violence, see the BLS website, **http://www.bls.gov/iif/osh_wpvs.html**.

Review 2: **Workplace Deviance**

Workplace deviance is behavior that violates important organizational norms about right and wrong and harms the organization or its workers. Production deviance and property deviance harm the company, whereas political deviance and personal aggression harm individuals within the company.

3 U.S. Sentencing Commission Guidelines for Organizations

A male supervisor is sexually harassing female coworkers. A sales representative offers a $10,000 kickback to persuade an indecisive customer to do business with his company. A company president secretly meets with the CEO of her biggest competitor, and they agree not to compete in markets where the other has already established customers. Each of these behaviors is clearly unethical (and, in these cases, also illegal). Historically, if management was unaware of such activities, the company could not be held responsible for an employee's unethical acts. Since 1991, however, when the U.S. Sentencing Commission Guidelines for Organizations were established, companies can be prosecuted and *punished even if management didn't know about the unethical behavior*. Moreover, penalties can be substantial, with maximum fines approaching a whopping $300 million.[27] An amendment made in 2004 outlines much stricter ethics training requirements and emphasizes creating a legal and ethical company culture.[28]

> Let's examine **3.1 to whom the guidelines apply and what they cover** and **3.2 how, according to the guidelines, an organization can be punished for the unethical behavior of its managers and employees**.

3.1 Who, What, and Why?

Nearly all businesses, nonprofits, partnerships, labor unions, unincorporated organizations and associations, incorporated organizations and even pension funds, trusts, and joint stock companies are covered by the U.S. Sentencing Commission's guidelines. If your organization can be characterized as a business (remember, nonprofits count, too), then it is subject to the guidelines.[29]

The guidelines cover offenses defined by federal laws, such as invasion of privacy, price fixing, fraud, customs violations, antitrust violations, civil rights violations, theft, money laundering, conflicts of interest, embezzlement, dealing in stolen goods, copyright infringements, extortion, and more. It's not enough merely to stay "within the law," however. The purpose of the guidelines is not just to punish companies *after* they or their employees break the law, but rather to encourage companies to take proactive steps that will discourage or prevent white-collar crime *before* it happens. The guidelines also give companies an incentive to cooperate with and disclose illegal

© COMSTOCK/JUPITER IMAGES

activities to federal authorities.[30] Today, companies are revamping their ethics training programs to focus on encouraging a culture committed to ethics and compliance in which ethics is part of almost every business discussion, says Dov Seidman, chairman and CEO of LRN, a legal and educational consultancy in Los Angeles.[31]

3.2 Determining the Punishment

The guidelines impose smaller fines on companies that take proactive steps to encourage ethical behavior or voluntarily disclose illegal activities to federal authorities. Essentially, the law uses a carrot-and-stick approach. The stick is the threat of heavy fines that can total millions of dollars. The carrot is a greatly reduced fine, but only if the company has started an effective compliance program (discussed below) to encourage ethical behavior *before* the illegal activity occurs.[32] The method used to determine a company's punishment illustrates the importance of establishing a compliance program.

The first step is to compute the *base fine* by determining what *level of offense* has occurred. The level of the offense (that is, its seriousness) varies depending on the kind of crime, the loss incurred by the victims, and how much planning went into the crime. For example, simple fraud is a level 6 offense (there are 38 levels in all). But if the victims of that fraud lost more than $5 million, that level 6 offense becomes a level 22 offense. Moreover, anything beyond minimal planning to commit the fraud results in an increase of two levels to a level 24 offense. How much difference would this make to the company? As Exhibit 4.2 shows, crimes at or below level 6 incur a base fine of $5,000, whereas the base fine for level 24 is $2.1 million. So the difference is $2.095 million! The base fine for level 38, the top-level offense, is a hefty $72.5 million.

After assessing a *base fine*, the judge computes a culpability score, which is a way of assigning blame to the company. The culpability score can range from a minimum of 0.05 to a maximum of 4.0. The greater the corporate responsibility in conducting, encouraging, or sanctioning illegal or unethical activity, the higher the culpability score. A company that already has a compliance program and voluntarily reports the offense to authorities will incur a culpability score of 0.05. By contrast, a company whose management secretly plans, approves, and participates in illegal or unethical activity will receive the maximum score of 4.0.

The culpability score is critical because the total fine is computed by multiplying the base fine by the culpability score. Going back to our level 24 fraud offense, the left point of the upper arrow in Exhibit 4.2 shows that a company with a compliance program that turns itself in will be fined only $105,000 ($2,100,000 × 0.05). In contrast, a company that secretly planned, approved, and participated in illegal activity will be fined $8.4 million ($2,100,0003 × 4.0), as shown by the right point of the upper arrow. The difference is even greater for level 38 offenses. As shown by the left point of the bottom arrow, a company with a compliance program and a 0.05 culpability score is fined only $3.625 million, whereas a company with the maximum 4.0 culpability score is fined a whopping $290 million, as indicated by the right point of the bottom arrow. These differences clearly show the importance

> "The base fine for level 38, the top-level offense, is a hefty $72.5 million."

Offense Level	Base Fine	Culpability Score					
		0.05	0.5	1.0	2.0	3.0	4.0
6 or less	$ 5,000	$ 250	$ 2,500	$ 5,000	$ 10,000	$ 15,000	$ 20,000
7	7,500	375	3,750	7,500	15,000	22,500	30,000
8	10,000	500	5,000	10,000	20,000	30,000	40,000
9	15,000	750	7,500	15,000	30,000	45,000	60,000
10	20,000	1,000	10,000	20,000	40,000	60,000	80,000
11	30,000	1,500	15,000	30,000	60,000	90,000	120,000
12	40,000	2,000	20,000	40,000	80,000	120,000	160,000
13	60,000	3,000	30,000	60,000	120,000	180,000	240,000
14	85,000	4,250	42,500	85,000	170,000	255,000	340,000
15	125,000	6,250	62,500	125,000	250,000	375,000	500,000
16	175,000	8,750	87,500	175,000	350,000	525,000	700,000
17	250,000	12,500	125,000	250,000	500,000	750,000	1,000,000
18	350,000	17,500	175,000	350,000	700,000	1,050,000	1,400,000
19	500,000	25,000	250,000	500,000	1,000,000	1,500,000	2,000,000
20	650,000	32,500	325,000	650,000	1,300,000	1,950,000	2,600,000
21	910,000	45,500	455,000	910,000	1,820,000	2,730,000	3,640,000
22	1,200,000	60,000	600,000	1,200,000	2,400,000	3,600,000	4,800,000
23	1,600,000	80,000	800,000	1,600,000	3,200,000	4,800,000	6,400,000
24	2,100,000	105,000	1,050,000	2,100,000	4,200,000	6,300,000	8,400,000
25	2,800,000	140,000	1,400,000	2,800,000	5,600,000	8,400,000	11,200,000
26	3,700,000	185,000	1,850,000	3,700,000	7,400,000	11,100,000	14,800,000
27	4,800,000	240,000	2,400,000	4,800,000	9,600,000	14,400,000	19,200,000
28	6,300,000	315,000	3,150,000	6,300,000	12,600,000	18,900,000	25,200,000
29	8,100,000	405,000	4,050,000	8,100,000	16,200,000	24,300,000	32,400,000
30	10,500,000	525,000	5,250,000	10,500,000	21,000,000	31,500,000	42,000,000
31	13,500,000	675,000	6,750,000	13,500,000	27,000,000	40,500,000	54,000,000
32	17,500,000	875,000	8,750,000	17,500,000	35,000,000	52,500,000	70,000,000
34	28,500,000	1,425,000	14,250,000	28,500,000	57,000,000	85,500,000	114,000,000
35	36,000,000	1,800,000	18,000,000	36,000,000	72,000,000	108,000,000	144,000,000
36	45,500,000	2,275,000	22,750,000	45,500,000	91,000,000	136,500,000	182,000,000
37	57,500,000	2,875,000	28,750,000	57,500,000	115,000,000	172,500,000	230,000,000
38 or more	72,500,000	3,625,000	36,250,000	72,500,000	145,000,000	217,500,000	290,000,000

Source: "Chapter Eight—Part C—Fines," 2004 Federal Sentencing Guidelines, available at http://www.ussc.gov/2004guid/8c2_4.htm, 27 January 2005.

of having a compliance program in place. Over the last decade, 1,494 companies have been charged under the U.S. Sentencing Guidelines. Seventy-six percent of those charged were fined, with the average fine exceeding $2 million. Company fines are on average 20 times larger now than before the implementation of the guidelines in 1991.[33]

Fortunately, for companies that want to avoid paying these stiff fines, the U.S. Sentencing Guidelines clearly spell out the seven necessary components of an effective compliance program.[34] Exhibit 4.3 lists those components. CAREMARK INTERNATIONAL, a managed-care service provider in Delaware, pleaded guilty to criminal charges related to its physician contracts and improper patient referrals. When it was then sued by shareholders for negligence and poor management, the Delaware court dismissed the case, ruling that the company's ethics compliance program, built on the components described in Exhibit 4.3, was a "good-faith attempt" to monitor employees and that the company did not knowingly allow illegal and unethical behavior to occur. The court went on to rule that a compliance program

Exhibit 4.2

Offense Levels, Base Fines, Culpability Scores, and Possible Total Fines under the U.S. Sentencing Commission Guidelines for Organizations

"WHAT'S NEW" COMPANY

based on the U.S. Sentencing Guidelines was enough to shield the company from liability.[35]

For more information, see "An Overview of the Organizational Sentencing Guidelines" at **http://www.ussc.gov/training/corpover.PDF** and "Sentencing Guidelines Educational Materials" at **http://www.ussc.gov/training/educat.htm**.

Review 3: **U.S. Sentencing Commission Guidelines**

Under the U.S. Sentencing Commission Guidelines, companies can be prosecuted and fined up to $300 million for employees' illegal actions. Fines are computed by multiplying the base fine by a culpability score, which ranges from 0.05 to 4.0. Companies that establish compliance programs to encourage ethical behavior can reduce their culpability scores and their fines. Companies without compliance programs can face much heavier fines than companies with established programs. Compliance programs must establish standards and procedures, be run by top managers, encourage hiring and promotion of honest and ethical people, encourage employees to report violations, educate employees about compliance, punish violators, and find ways to improve the program after violations occur.

Exhibit 4.3

Compliance Program Steps for the U.S. Sentencing Guidelines for Organizations

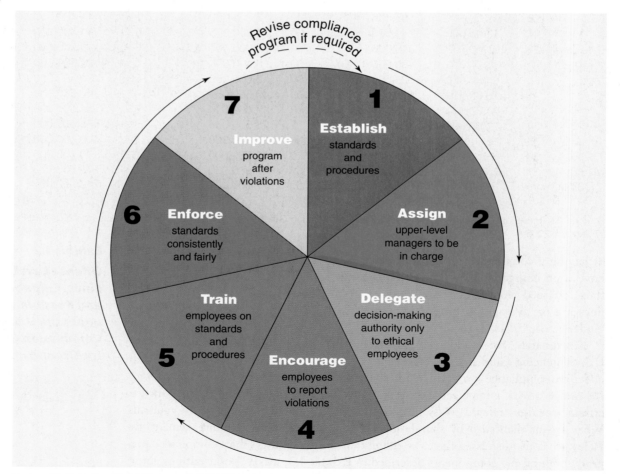

Source: D. R. Dalton, M. B. Metzger, & J. W. Hill, "The 'New' U.S. Sentencing Commission Guidelines: A Wake-up Call for Corporate America," *Academy of Management Executive* 8 (1994): 7–16.

HOW DO YOU MAKE ETHICAL DECISIONS?

On a cold morning in the midst of a winter storm, schools were closed and most people had decided to stay home from work. Nevertheless, Richard Addessi had already showered, shaved, and dressed for the office. He kissed his wife Joan goodbye, but before he could get to his car, he fell dead on the garage floor of a sudden heart attack. Addessi was four months short of his 30-year anniversary with the company. Having begun work at **IBM** at the age of 18, he was just 48 years old.[36]

You're the vice president in charge of benefits at IBM. Given that he was only four months short of full retirement, do you award full retirement benefits to Richard Addessi's wife and daughters? If the answer is yes, they will receive his full retirement benefits of $1,800 a month and free lifetime medical coverage. If you say no, his widow and two daughters will receive only $340 a month. They will also have to pay $473 a month just to continue their current medical coverage. As the VP in charge of benefits at IBM, what would be the ethical thing for you to do?

After reading the next two sections, you should be able to

> 4 describe what influences ethical decision making.
>
> 5 explain what practical steps managers can take to improve ethical decision making.

4 Influences on Ethical Decision Making

So, what did IBM decide to do? Since Richard Addessi had not completed 30 full years with the company, IBM officials felt they had no choice but to give Joan Addessi and her two daughters the smaller, partial retirement benefits. Do you think IBM's decision was ethical? Probably many of you don't. You wonder how the company could be so heartless as to deny Richard Addessi's family the full benefits to which you believe they were entitled. Yet others might argue that IBM did the ethical thing by strictly following the rules laid out in its pension benefit plan. After all, being fair means applying the rules to everyone. Although some ethical issues are easily solved, many do not have clearly right or wrong answers.

> *The ethical answers that managers choose depend on* **4.1 the ethical intensity of the decision,** *4.2 the moral development of the manager, and* **4.3 the ethical principles used to solve the problem.**

4.1 Ethical Intensity of the Decision

Managers don't treat all ethical decisions the same. The manager who has to decide whether to deny or extend full benefits to Joan Addessi and her family is going to treat that decision much more seriously than the decision of how to deal with an assistant who has been taking computer paper home for personal use. These decisions differ in their **ethical intensity**, or the degree of concern people have about an ethical issue. When addressing an issue of high ethical intensity, managers are more aware of the

ethical intensity the degree of concern people have about an ethical issue impact their decision will have on others. They are more likely to view the decision as an ethical or moral decision rather than as an economic decision. They are also more likely to worry about doing the "right thing."

Ethical intensity depends on six factors:[37]

- magnitude of consequences
- social consensus
- probability of effect
- temporal immediacy
- proximity of effect
- concentration of effect.

Magnitude of consequences is the total harm or benefit derived from an ethical decision. The more people who are harmed or the greater the harm to those people, the larger the consequences. **Social consensus** is agreement on whether behavior is bad or good. **Probability of effect** is the chance that something will happen and then result in harm to others. If we combine these factors, we can see the effect they can have on ethical intensity. For example, if there is *clear agreement* (social consensus) that a managerial decision or action is *certain* (probability of effect) to have *large negative consequences* (magnitude of effect) in some way, then people will be highly concerned about that managerial decision or action, and ethical intensity will be high.

Temporal immediacy is the time between an act and the consequences the act produces. Temporal immediacy is stronger if a manager has to lay off workers next week as opposed to three months from now. **Proximity of effect** is the social, psychological, cultural, or physical distance of a decision maker from those affected by his or her decisions. Thus, proximity of effect is greater when a manager lays off employees he knows than when he lays off employees that he doesn't know. Finally, whereas the magnitude of consequences is the total effect across all people, **concentration of effect** is how much an act affects the average person. Temporarily laying off 100 employees for 10 months without pay is a greater concentration of effect than temporarily laying off 1,000 employees for 1 month.

Which of these six factors has the most impact? Studies indicate that managers are much more likely to view decisions as ethical decisions when the magnitude of consequences (total harm) is high and there is a social consensus (agreement) that a behavior or action is bad.[38]

Many people will likely feel IBM was wrong to deny full benefits to Joan Addessi. Why? In this situation, IBM's decision met five of the six characteristics of ethical intensity. The difference in benefits, more than $23,000 per year, was likely to have serious consequences for the family. The decision was certain to affect them and would do so immediately. We can closely identify with Joan Addessi and her daughters as opposed to IBM's faceless, nameless corporate identity. And the decision would have a concentrated effect on the family in terms of their monthly benefits ($1,800 and free medical coverage if full benefits were awarded versus $340 a month and medical care that costs $473 per month if they weren't).

The exception, as we will discuss below, is social consensus. Not everyone will agree that IBM's decision was unethical. The judgment also depends on your level of moral development and which ethical principles you use to decide.

magnitude of consequences the total harm or benefit derived from an ethical decision

social consensus agreement on whether behavior is bad or good

probability of effect the chance that something will happen and then harm others

temporal immediacy the time between an act and the consequences the act produces

proximity of effect the social, psychological, cultural, or physical distance between a decision maker and those affected by his or her decisions

concentration of effect the total harm or benefit that an act produces on the average person

4.2 Moral Development

A friend of yours has given you the latest version of Microsoft Office. She stuffed the software disks in your backpack with a note saying that you should install it on your computer and get it back to her in a couple of days. You're tempted. You have papers to write, notes to take, and presentations to plan. Besides, all of your friends have the same version of Microsoft Office. They didn't pay for it either. Copying the software to your hard drive without buying your own copy clearly violates copyright laws. But no one would find out. Even if someone does, Microsoft probably isn't going to come after you. Microsoft goes after the big fish—companies that illegally copy and distribute software to their workers. Your computer has booted up, and you've got your mouse in one hand and the installation disk in the other. What are you going to do?[39]

In part, according to psychologist Lawrence Kohlberg, your decision will be based on your level of moral development. Kohlberg identified three phases of moral development, with two stages in each phase (see Exhibit 4.4).[40] At the **preconventional level of moral development**, people decide based on selfish reasons. For example, if you are in Stage 1, the punishment and obedience stage, your primary concern will be to avoid trouble for yourself. So, you won't copy the software because you are afraid of being caught and punished. Yet, in Stage 2, the instrumental exchange stage, you worry less about punishment and more about doing things that directly advance your wants and needs. So, you copy the software.

People at the **conventional level of moral development** make decisions that conform to societal expectations. In other words, they look outside themselves to others for guidance on ethical issues. In Stage 3, the good boy, nice girl stage, you normally do what the other "good boys" and "nice girls" are doing. If everyone else is illegally copying software, you will, too. But if they aren't, you won't either. In the law and order stage, Stage 4, you again look for external guidance and do whatever the law permits, so you won't copy the software.

People at the **postconventional level of moral development** always use internalized ethical principles to solve ethical dilemmas. In Stage 5, the social contract stage, you will refuse to copy the software because, as a whole, society is better off when the rights of others—in this case, the rights of software authors and manufacturers—are not violated. In Stage 6, the universal principle stage, you might or might not copy the software, depending on your principles of right and wrong. Moreover, you will stick to your principles even if your decision conflicts with the law (Stage 4) or what others believe is best for society (Stage 5). For example, those with socialist or communist beliefs would probably choose to copy the software because they believe goods and services should be owned by society rather than by individuals and corporations. (For information about the dos, don'ts, and legal issues concerning software piracy, see the Software & Information Industry Association's website at **http://www.siia.net/piracy/default.asp**.)

Kohlberg believed that as people became more educated and mature, they would progress sequentially from earlier stages to later stages. But only 20 percent of adults ever reach the postconventional stage of moral development where internal principles guide their decisions. By contrast, most adults are in the conventional stage of moral development in which they look outside themselves to others for

preconventional level of moral development the first level of moral development, in which people make decisions based on selfish reasons

conventional level of moral development the second level of moral development, in which people make decisions that conform to societal expectations

postconventional level of moral development the third level of moral development, in which people make decisions based on internalized principles

Exhibit 4.4

Kohlberg's Stages of Moral Development

Stage 1	Stage 2	Stage 3	Stage 4	Stage 5	Stage 6
Punishment and Obedience	Instrumental Exchange	Good Boy, Nice Girl	Law and Order	Social Contract	Universal Principle
Preconventional		Conventional		Postconventional	
Selfish		Societal Expectations		Internalized Principles	

Source: W. Davidson III & D. Worrell, "Influencing Managers to Change Unpopular Corporate Behavior through Boycotts and Divestitures," *Business & Society* 34 (1995): 171–196.

guidance on ethical issues. This means that most people in the workplace look to and need leadership when it comes ethical decision making.[41]

4.3 Principles of Ethical Decision Making

Besides an issue's ethical intensity and a manager's level of moral maturity, the particular ethical principles that managers use will also affect how they solve ethical dilemmas. Unfortunately, there is no one "ideal principle" to use in making ethical business decisions.

According to professor LaRue Hosmer, a number of different ethical principles can be used to make business decisions: long-term self-interest, personal virtue, religious injunctions, government requirements, utilitarian benefits, individual rights, and distributive justice.[42] All of these ethical principles encourage managers and employees to take others' interests into account when making ethical decisions. At the same time, however, these principles can lead to very different ethical actions, as we can see by using these principles to decide whether to award full benefits to Joan Addessi and her children.

According to the **principle of long-term self-interest**, you should never take any action that is not in your or your organization's long-term self-interest. Although this sounds as if the principle promotes selfishness, it doesn't. What we do to maximize our long-term interests (save more, spend less, exercise every day, watch what we eat) is often very different from what we do to maximize short-term interests (max out our credit cards, be couch potatoes, eat whatever we want). At any given time, IBM has nearly 1,000 employees who are just months away from retirement. Thus, because of the costs involved, it serves IBM's long-term interest to pay full benefits only after employees have put in their 30 years.

The **principle of personal virtue** holds that you should never do anything that is not honest, open, and truthful and that you would not be glad to see reported in the newspapers or on TV. Using the principle of personal virtue, IBM should have quietly awarded Joan Addessi her husband's full benefits. Had it done so, it could have avoided the publication of an embarrassing *Wall Street Journal* article on this topic.

The **principle of religious injunctions** holds that you should never take an action that is unkind or that harms a sense of community, such as the positive feelings that come from working together to accomplish a commonly accepted goal. Using this principle, IBM would have been concerned foremost with compassion and kindness. Thus, it would have awarded full benefits to Joan Addessi.

According to the **principle of government requirements**, the law represents the minimal moral standards of society, so you should never take any action that violates the law. Using this principle, IBM would deny full benefits to Joan Addessi because her husband did not work for the company for 30 years. Indeed, an IBM spokesperson stated that making exceptions would violate the federal Employee Retirement Income Security Act of 1974.

The **principle of utilitarian benefits** states that you should never take an action that does not result in greater good for society. In short, you should do whatever creates the greatest good for the greatest number. At first, this principle seems to suggest that IBM should award full benefits to Joan Addessi. If IBM did this with any regularity, however, the costs would be enormous, profits would shrink, and IBM would have to cut its stock dividend, harming countless shareholders,

principle of long-term self-interest an ethical principle that holds that you should never take any action that is not in your or your organization's long-term self-interest

principle of personal virtue an ethical principle that holds that you should never do anything that is not honest, open, and truthful and that you would not be glad to see reported in the newspapers or on TV

principle of religious injunctions an ethical principle that holds that you should never take any action that is not kind and that does not build a sense of community

principle of government requirements an ethical principle that holds that you should never take any action that violates the law, for the law represents the minimal moral standard

principle of utilitarian benefits an ethical principle that holds that you should never take any action that does not result in greater good for society

© REPORTAGE/GETTY IMAGES

many of whom rely on IBM dividends for retirement income. In this case, the principle does not lead to a clear choice.

The **principle of individual rights** holds that you should never take an action that infringes on others' agreed-upon rights. Using this principle, IBM would deny Joan Addessi full benefits. If it carefully followed the rules specified in its pension plan and granted Mrs. Addessi due process, meaning the right to appeal the decision, then IBM would not be violating her rights. In fact, it could be argued that providing full benefits to Mrs. Addessi would violate the rights of employees who had to wait 30 years to receive full benefits.

Finally, under the **principle of distributive justice**, you should never take any action that harms the least fortunate among us in some way. This principle is designed to protect the poor, the uneducated, and the unemployed. Although Joan Addessi could probably find a job, after 20 years as a stay-at-home mom it's unlikely that she could easily find one that would support her and her daughters in the manner to which they are accustomed. Using the principle of distributive justice, IBM would award her full benefits.

As mentioned at the beginning of this chapter, one of the "real-world" aspects of ethical decisions is that no matter *what* you decide, someone or some group will be unhappy. This corollary is also true: No matter *how* you decide, someone or some group will be unhappy. Consequently, although all of these ethical principles encourage managers to balance others' needs against their own, they can also lead to very different ethical actions. So even when managers strive to be ethical, there are often no clear answers when it comes to doing "the" right thing.

Review 4: *Influences on Ethical Decision Making*

Three factors influence ethical decisions: the ethical intensity of the decision, the moral development of the decision maker, and the ethical principles used to solve the problem. Ethical intensity is strong when decisions have large, certain, immediate consequences and when we are physically or psychologically close to those affected by the decision. There are three levels of moral maturity, each with two steps. At the preconventional level, decisions are made for selfish reasons. At the conventional level, decisions conform to societal expectations. At the postconventional level, internalized principles are used to make ethical decisions. Finally, managers can use a number of different principles when making ethical decisions: self-interest, personal virtue, religious injunctions, government requirements, utilitarian benefits, individual rights, and distributive justice.

5 Practical Steps to Ethical Decision Making

Managers can encourage more ethical decision making in their organizations by ***5.1 carefully selecting and hiring ethical employees***, ***5.2 establishing a specific code of ethics***, ***5.3 training employees to make ethical decisions***, *and* ***5.4 creating an ethical climate***.

5.1 Selecting and Hiring Ethical Employees

If you found a wallet containing $100, would you return it with the money? Informal studies typically show that 57 to 80 percent of people would, and that women and people in small towns are more likely to return the wallet with the money.[43]

principle of individual rights an ethical principle that holds that you should never take any action that infringes on others' agreed-upon rights

principle of distributive justice an ethical principle that holds that you should never take any action that harms the least fortunate among us: the poor, the uneducated, the unemployed

doing the right thing

If You Cheat in College, Will You Cheat in the Workplace?

Studies show that college students who cheat once are likely to cheat again. Students who cheat on exams are likely to cheat on assignments and projects. Furthermore, tolerance of cheating is widespread, as 70 percent of college students don't see cheating as a problem. Given these relaxed attitudes toward cheating, and with on-campus cheating at all-time highs, employers want to know whether someone who cheated in college will cheat in the workplace. Studies generally indicate that the answer is yes. The best predictor of cheating in medical school was cheating in high school or college. Likewise, students who cheated in school were much more likely to cheat on their taxes, in politics (by committing voter fraud or accepting illegal campaign contributions), in sports, and on the job. Why is this the case? Apparently, people who cheat and then cheat again come to see their behavior as normal and to rationalize it by telling themselves that cheating isn't wrong. In fact, 60 percent of the people who cheat their employers don't feel guilty about doing so. Cheating isn't situation-specific. Once you decide that cheating is acceptable, you're likely to cheat in most areas of your life.[48] Robert Hogan, a renowned personality psychologist, says there is an intrinsic link between cheating, embezzling, marital infidelity, public drunkenness, getting traffic tickets, fighting, vandalism, and so on. "All these things involve breaking the rules, and they're all motivated by hostility toward or disregard for authority."[49] If you want to do the right thing, don't cheat in college or tolerate cheating by others. Don't slide down the slippery slope of cheating.

As an employer, you can increase your chances of hiring the honest person who returns the wallet with the money if you give job applicants integrity tests. **Overt integrity tests** estimate job applicants' honesty by directly asking them what they think or feel about theft or about punishment of unethical behaviors.[44] For example, an employer might ask an applicant, "Would you ever consider buying something from somebody if you knew the person had stolen the item?" or "Don't most people steal from their companies?" Surprisingly, unethical people will usually answer "yes" to such questions, because they believe that the world is basically dishonest and that dishonest behavior is normal.[45]

Personality-based integrity tests indirectly estimate job applicants' honesty by measuring psychological traits such as dependability and conscientiousness. For example, prison inmates serving time for white-collar crimes (counterfeiting, embezzlement, and fraud) scored much lower than a comparison group of middle-level managers on scales measuring reliability, dependability, honesty, conscientiousness, and abiding by rules.[46] These results show that companies can selectively hire and promote people who will be more ethical.[47] For more on integrity testing, see the "What Really Works" feature in this chapter.

5.2 Codes of Ethics

Exhibit 4.5 displays the ethical code of conduct for Portland General Electric, a large electrical utility company in Oregon. The code urges employees to conduct themselves as "responsible and responsive corporate citizens," "respect the environment," "maintain high levels of legal and ethical conduct," and "deal honestly and fairly with customers."

Today, almost all large corporations have an ethics code in place. Still, two things must happen if those codes are to encourage ethical decision making and behavior.[50] First, a company must communicate its code to others both inside and outside the company. An excellent example of a well-communicated code of ethics can be found at Home Depot's website at **http://www.homedepot.com/governance/ethics**. With the click of a computer mouse, anyone inside or outside the company can obtain detailed information about the company's core values, specific ethical business practices, and much more. Second, executive sponsorship and involvement in ethics and compliance training is a must to create an ethical company culture.[51]

Second, in addition to having an ethics code with general guidelines like "do unto others as you would have others do unto you," management must also

One of the characteristics we value highly is the ability to make and keep commitments both to ourselves and to others. People who can make and keep commitments gain respect. They are known for their integrity, and it is the same with businesses.

Here is a list of commitments each of us needs to incorporate into our daily conduct of business:

- We will treat our fellow employees with honesty, respect, and dignity.

- We will strive to conduct our activities to protect the safety and health of our fellow employees.

- We will conduct ourselves as responsible and responsive corporate citizens in our communities.

- We will respect the environment and exercise good judgment concerning the impact of our activities on the environment.

- We will maintain high levels of legal and ethical conduct while pursuing our growth and earnings objectives.

- We will deal honestly and fairly with our customers and be responsive to their needs and requirements.

- We will strive to maintain the highest standards of excellence in the quality of the products and services we provide to our customers.

- We will strive to be the best customer we can be to our suppliers. We will emphasize fairness and integrity in all dealings with suppliers.

- We will respect and obey the law.

Source: "Law and Ethics: How We Do Business, A Compliance Guide for Portland General Electric Employees," Portland General Electric, available at http://www.portlandgeneral.com/about_pge/jobs/pdf/how_we_do_business.pdf, 20 March 2003.

Exhibit 4.5

Ethical Code of Conduct for Portland General Electric

develop practical ethical standards and procedures specific to the company's line of business. Visitors to NORTEL's website at **http://www.nortel.com/corporate/ community/ethics/guide.html** can instantly access references to very specific ethical standards on topics ranging from bribes and kickbacks to expense vouchers and illegal copying of software. For example, most businesspeople believe that it is wrong to take bribes or other gifts from a company that wants your business. Therefore, one of Nortel's ethical guidelines is "We do not accept or offer any form of bribe, kickback, improper or illegal inducement—even where the practice is widely considered a way of doing business."[52] And just to be sure there's no confusion over what constitutes, say, a gift, the guidelines are even more specific: "When we do give or receive gifts, they should be modest. T-shirts, mugs, and pens that carry the company logo are examples of gifts we would normally give or receive. If you give a gift, you must accurately account for it in your expense claim or department records."[53]

Specific codes of ethics such as this make it much easier for employees to decide what to do when they want to do the "right thing."

5.3 Ethics Training

The first objective of ethics training is to develop employees' awareness of ethics.[54] This means helping employees recognize which issues are ethical issues and then avoid rationalizing unethical behavior by thinking, "This isn't really illegal or immoral" or "No one will ever find out." Several companies have created board

overt integrity test a written test that estimates job applicants' honesty by directly asking them what they think or feel about theft or about punishment of unethical behaviors

personality-based integrity test a written test that indirectly estimates job applicants' honesty by measuring psychological traits, such as dependability and conscientiousness

INTEGRITY TESTS

U nder the 1991 and 2004 U.S. Sentencing Commission Guidelines, unethical employee behavior can lead to multimillion-dollar fines for corporations and fraudulent behavior of executives can lead to criminal prosecution. Moreover, workplace deviance like stealing, fraud, and vandalism costs companies an estimated $660 billion a year. One way to reduce workplace deviance and the chances of a large fine for unethical employee behavior is to use overt and personality-based integrity tests to screen job applicants.

One hundred eighty-one studies, with a combined total of 576,460 study participants, have examined how well integrity tests can predict job performance and various kinds of workplace deviance. These studies show that not only can integrity tests help companies reduce workplace deviance, but they provide the added bonus of helping companies hire workers who are better performers in their jobs.

WORKPLACE DEVIANCE (COUNTER-PRODUCTIVE BEHAVIORS)

Compared with job applicants who score poorly, there is an 82 percent chance that job applicants who score well on overt integrity tests will participate in less illegal activity, unethical behavior, drug abuse, or workplace violence.

Personality-based integrity tests also do a good job of predicting who will engage in workplace deviance. Compared with job applicants who score poorly, there is a 68 percent chance that job applicants who score well on personality-based integrity tests will participate in less illegal activity, unethical behavior, excessive absences, drug abuse, or workplace violence.

JOB PERFORMANCE

In addition to reducing unethical behavior and workplace deviance, integrity tests can help companies hire better performers. Compared with employees who score poorly, there is a 69 percent chance that employees who score well on overt integrity tests will be better performers.

The figures are nearly identical for personality-based integrity tests. Compared with those who score poorly, there is a 70 percent chance that employees who score well on personality-based integrity tests will be better at their jobs.

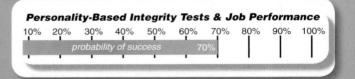

THEFT

Although integrity tests can help companies decrease most kinds of workplace deviance and increase employees' job performance, they have a smaller effect on a specific kind of workplace deviance: theft. Compared with employees who score poorly, there is a 57 percent chance that employees who score well on overt integrity tests will be less likely to steal. No theft data were available to assess personality-based integrity tests.

FAKING AND COACHING ON INTEGRITY TESTS

Although overt and personality-based integrity tests do a very good job of helping companies hire people of higher integrity, it is possible to improve scores on these tests through coaching and faking. In coaching, job applicants are taught the underlying rationale of an integrity test or given specific directions for improving their integrity scores. Faking occurs when applicants simply try to "beat the test" or try to fake a good impression. Unfortunately for the companies that use integrity tests, both strategies work. On average, coaching can improve scores on overt integrity tests by an astounding 1.5 standard deviations and on personality-based integrity tests by a meaningful .36 standard deviation. This would be the equivalent of increasing your total SAT score by 150 and 36 points, respectively (the SAT has a mean of 500 and a standard deviation of 100). Likewise, on average, faking can improve scores on overt integrity tests by an impressive 1.02 standard deviations and on personality-based integrity tests by a meaningful .59 standard deviation. Again, this would be the equivalent of increasing your SAT score by 102 and 59 points, respectively. Companies that want to avoid coaching and faking effects must maintain tight security over integrity tests so that applicants have little information regarding them, periodically check the validity of the tests to make sure they're accurately predicting workplace deviance and job performance, or periodically switch tests if they suspect that test security has been compromised.[55]

games to improve awareness of ethical issues.[56] Citigroup has a game called "The Work Ethic," in which players win or lose points depending on their answers to legal, regulatory, policy, and judgment questions. Defense contractor LOCKHEED MARTIN has created "The Ethics Challenge," which every employee, including the CEO, must play at least once a year. Lockheed workers sit around a table, roll dice, and then move their tokens ahead when they answer ethics questions correctly. Here's a sample question from the game:

A kickback may be in the form of:

A.   Cash
B.   Gift to a family member
C.   Donation to a charity at your request
D.   All of these (the correct answer)

The game has been very popular, except for one year when it was revised so that it did not indicate which answers were right. Brian Sears, an ethics officer for Lockheed's aeronautics division, comments that engineers, who are used to "correct answers," wanted more guidance. Says Sears, "They had a hard time with it," so the game was changed again to offer "preferred answers."[57]

The second objective for ethics training programs is to achieve credibility with employees. Not surprisingly, employees can be highly suspicious of management's reasons for offering ethics training. Some companies have hurt the credibility of their ethics programs by having outside instructors and consultants conduct the classes.[58] Employees often complain that outside instructors and consultants are teaching theory that has nothing to do with their jobs and the "real world." This is why Boeing has a vice president of ethics who employs 55 people to teach Boeing's 194,000 employees the difference between right and wrong in the aerospace industry.[59] And Boeing is not an exception. Almost every major corporation has a vice president of ethics and compliance. Ethics training becomes even more credible when top managers teach the initial ethics classes to their subordinates, who in turn teach their subordinates. In time, most managers will have both taken

In an effort to ensure that employees know how to act in an ethical manner, many companies have a code of ethics or ethical guidelines. Many companies use games to practice ethical decision making. There is even a game based on the popular cartoon character Dilbert.

Exhibit 4.6

A Basic Model of Ethical Decision Making

and taught the ethics classes, thereby pushing ethics training and principles throughout the entire company.[60] Unfortunately, though, 25 percent of large companies don't require top managers to attend, much less teach, ethics training.[61] The good news is that this scenario is changing, thanks to the 2004 amendment to the Sentencing Guidelines. Indeed, a recent survey shows that board involvement in ethics and compliance programs jumped from 21 percent in 1987 to 96 percent in 2005.[62]

The third objective of ethics training is to teach employees a practical model of ethical decision making. A basic model should help them think about the consequences their choices will have on others and consider how they will choose between different solutions. Exhibit 4.6 presents a basic model of ethical decision making.

5.4 Ethical Climate

In study after study, when researchers ask, "What is the most important influence on your ethical behavior at work?" the answer comes back, "My manager." The first step in establishing an ethical climate is for managers, especially top managers, to act ethically themselves. The National Business Ethics Survey found that unethical misconduct occurred in just 15 percent of the organizations where top managers talked about the importance of ethics, kept their promises to others, and modeled ethical behavior themselves. By contrast, unethical misconduct occurred in 56 percent of the organizations in which top management only talked about the importance of ethics, but did nothing else.[63]

1. **Identify the problem.** What makes it an ethical problem? Think in terms of rights, obligations, fairness, relationships, and integrity. How would you define the problem if you stood on the other side of the fence?

2. **Identify the constituents.** Who has been hurt? Who could be hurt? Who could be helped? Are they willing players, or are they victims? Can you negotiate with them?

3. **Diagnose the situation.** How did it happen in the first place? What could have prevented it? Is it going to get worse or better? Can the damage now be undone?

4. **Analyze your options.** Imagine the range of possibilities. Limit yourself to the two or three most manageable. What are the likely outcomes of each? What are the likely costs? Look to the company mission statement or code of ethics for guidance.

5. **Make your choice.** What is your intention in making this decision? How does it compare with the probable results? Can you discuss the problem with the affected parties before you act? Could you disclose without qualm your decision to your boss, the CEO, the board of directors, your family, or society as a whole?

6. **Act.** Do what you have to do. Don't be afraid to admit errors. Be as bold in confronting a problem as you were in causing it.

Source: L. A. Berger, "Train All Employees to Solve Ethical Dilemmas," *Best's Review—Life-Health Insurance Edition* 95 (1995): 70–80.

A second step in establishing an ethical climate is for top management to be active in and committed to the company ethics program.[64] Top managers who consistently talk about the importance of ethics and back up that talk by participating in their companies' ethics programs send the clear message that ethics matter. Business writer Dayton Fandray says, "You can have ethics offices and officers and training programs and reporting systems, but if the CEO doesn't seem to care, it's all just a sham. It's not surprising to find that the companies that really do care about ethics make a point of including senior management in all of their ethics and compliance programs."[65]

A third step is to put in place a reporting system that encourages managers and employees to report potential ethics violations. **Whistleblowing**, that is, reporting others' ethics violations, is a difficult step for most people to take.[66] Potential whistleblowers often fear that they, and not the ethics violators, will be punished.[67] Managers who have been interviewed about whistleblowing have said, "In every organization, someone's been screwed for standing up." "If anything, I figured that by taking a strong stand I might get myself in trouble. People might look at me as a goody two-shoes. Someone might try to force me out." This is exactly what happened to Sandy Baratta, who used to be a vice president at Oracle, which makes database software used by most large companies. Baratta was fired, she alleges, for complaining about Oracle's treatment of women and its unethical business practices. Under California's whistleblower protection laws, a jury awarded her $2.6 million in damages.[68]

Today, many federal and state laws protect the rights of whistleblowers (see **http://www.whistleblowers.org** for more information). In particular, the Sarbanes-Oxley Act of 2002 (see **http://www.aicpa.org/info/sarbanes_oxley_summary.htm**) made it a serious crime to retaliate in any way against corporate whistleblowers in publicly owned companies. Managers who punish whistleblowers can be imprisoned for up to 10 years.

Some companies, including defense contractor Northrop Grumman, have made it easier for whistleblowers to report possible violations by establishing anonymous, toll-free corporate ethics hot lines. Nortel, the telecommunications company, even publicizes which of its ethics hot lines don't have caller ID (so they can't identify the caller's phone number). The Sarbanes-Oxley Act also requires all publicly held companies to establish anonymous hot lines to encourage reporting of unethical and illegal behaviors, so it's not surprising that a recent survey found that 91 percent of companies have an anonymous reporting system whereby employees can report observed misconduct.[69] At HomeBanc, employees can call the "Associate Hotline" which goes directly to a voice mail in the CEO's office.

The factor that does the most to discourage whistleblowers from reporting problems, however, is lack of company action on their complaints.[70] Thus, the final step in developing an ethical climate is for management to fairly and consistently punish those who violate the company's code of ethics. For example, when an anonymous caller used hospital chain Columbia/HCA's toll-free ethics phone line to report that a supply clerk was stealing medical equipment and selling it online at eBay, the information was forwarded to company investigators who bid on and bought the equipment. Being a good eBay seller, the supply clerk quickly shipped the stolen goods directly from her home. When confronted with the stolen goods, she confessed and was immediately fired.[71] Amazingly, though, not all companies fire ethics violators. In fact, 8 percent of surveyed companies admit that they would promote top performers even if they violated ethical standards.[72]

whistleblowing reporting others' ethics violations to management or legal authorities

Employers can increase their chances of hiring ethical employees by administering overt integrity tests and personality-based integrity tests to all job applicants. Most large companies now have corporate codes of ethics. To affect ethical decision making, these codes must be known both inside and outside the organization. In addition to offering general rules, ethics codes must also provide specific, practical advice. Ethics training seeks to increase employees' awareness of ethical issues, make ethics a serious and credible factor in organizational decisions, and teach employees a practical model of ethical decision making. The most important factors in creating an ethical business climate are the personal examples set by company managers, involvement of management in the company ethics program, a reporting system that encourages whistleblowers to report potential ethics violations, and fair but consistent punishment of violators.

WHAT IS SOCIAL RESPONSIBILITY?

Social responsibility is a business's obligation to pursue policies, make decisions, and take actions that benefit society.[73] Unfortunately, because there are strong disagreements over to whom and for what in society organizations are responsible, it can be difficult for managers to know what is or will be perceived as socially responsible corporate behavior. In a recent McKinsey & Co. study of 1,144 top global executives, 79 percent predicted that at least some responsibility for dealing with future social and political issues would fall on corporations, but only 3 percent said they themselves do a good job of dealing with social pressures.[74] One thing is for sure: Corporate giving has increased 22 percent to $13.7 billion in cash and in-kind gifts. But checkbook philanthropy isn't enough, says Susan Puflea, senior vice president and director of GolinHarris Change.[75] Consider some examples. Former FORD MOTOR COMPANY CEO William C. Ford Jr. has championed green causes for years. He spent $2 billion overhauling Ford's sprawling River Rouge complex, installing a 10-acre grass roof to capture rainwater. The company also donated $25 million to Conservation International for an environmental center. But it kept churning out popular gas-guzzling SUVs and pickups desired by its customers. Wal-Mart Stores, long assailed for its labor and global-outsourcing practices, has made a series of high-profile investments to slash energy use overall, from its stores to its vast trucking fleets, and has promised to purchase more electricity derived from renewable sources.[76] These two examples illustrate the difficulties of acting in a socially responsible manner—balancing the needs of different groups in the face of limited resources and/or constraints.

> "WHAT'S NEW" COMPANY

The opening vignette also captured the dilemma of how to balance the needs of different groups. Is P&G obligated to eliminate all animal testing, as PETA believes? Or, by minimizing but not eliminating animal testing, has P&G achieved a reasonable balance that still allows it to make sure its products are safe? In the end, are P&G's actions regarding animal testing socially responsible or irresponsible?

social responsibility a business's obligation to pursue policies, make decisions, and take actions that benefit society

After reading the next four sections, you should be able to explain

> 6 to whom organizations are socially responsible.
>
> 7 for what organizations are socially responsible.
>
> 8 how organizations can choose to respond to societal demands for social responsibility.
>
> 9 whether social responsibility hurts or helps an organization's economic performance.

shareholder model a view of social responsibility that holds that an organization's overriding goal should be profit maximization for the benefit of shareholders

The U.S. Supreme Court ruled that the Boy Scouts of America do not have to accept homosexual troop leaders. As a result, corporate donations to the Boy Scouts dropped, while personal donations rose.

6 To Whom Are Organizations Socially Responsible?

There are two perspectives as to whom organizations are socially responsible: the shareholder model and the stakeholder model. According to the late Nobel Prize–winning economist Milton Friedman, the only social responsibility that organizations have is to satisfy their owners, that is, company shareholders. This view—called the **shareholder model**—holds that the only social responsibility that businesses have is to maximize profits. By maximizing profit, the firm maximizes shareholder wealth and satisfaction. More specifically, as profits rise, the company stock owned by shareholders generally increases in value.

Friedman argued that it is socially irresponsible for companies to divert time, money, and attention from maximizing profits to social causes and charitable organizations. The first problem, he believed, is that organizations cannot act effectively as moral agents for all company shareholders. Although shareholders are likely to agree on investment issues concerning a company, it's highly unlikely that they have common views on what social causes a company should or should not support. For example, corporate donations to the Boy Scouts dropped significantly after the U.S. Supreme Court ruled 5–4 that the Boy Scouts do not have to accept homosexual troop leaders. JPMorgan Chase, Levi-Strauss & Co., Textron, and Wells Fargo have all stopped donating to the Boy Scouts. Tom Unger of Wells Fargo explained, "The Boy Scouts are as American as apple pie, but this was an easy decision to make. We really have to, as a company, return to what our core vision and values are, and that's to not discriminate." Yet while corporate donations are down, overall donations to the Boy Scouts have risen.[77] Rather than act as moral agents, Friedman argued, companies should maximize profits for shareholders. Shareholders can then use their time and increased wealth to contribute to the social causes, charities, or institutions they want, rather than those that companies want.

The second major problem, Friedman said, is that the time, money, and attention diverted to social causes undermine market efficiency.[78] In competitive markets, companies compete for raw materials, talented workers, customers, and investment funds. A company that spends money on social causes will have less money to purchase quality materials or to hire talented workers who can produce a valuable product at a good price. If customers find the

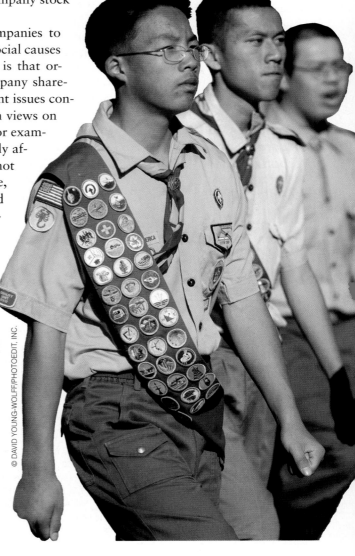

© DAVID YOUNG-WOLFF/PHOTOEDIT, INC.

company's product less desirable, its sales and profits will fall. If profits fall, the company's stock price will decline, and the company will have difficulty attracting investment funds that could be used to fund long-term growth. In the end, Friedman argues, diverting the firm's money, time, and resources to social causes hurts customers, suppliers, employees, and shareholders. Russell Roberts, an economist at George Mason University, agrees with this viewpoint. He says, "Doesn't it make more sense to have companies do what they do best, make good products at fair prices, and then let consumers use the savings for the charity of their choice?"[79]

By contrast, under the **stakeholder model**, management's most important responsibility is the firm's long-term survival (not just maximizing profits), which is achieved by satisfying the interests of multiple corporate stakeholders (not just shareholders).[80] **Stakeholders** are persons or groups with a legitimate interest in a company.[81] Since stakeholders are interested in and affected by the organization's actions, they have a "stake" in what those actions are. Consequently, stakeholder groups may try to influence the firm to act in their own interests. Exhibit 4.7 shows the various stakeholder groups that the organization must satisfy to assure its long-term survival.

Being responsible to multiple stakeholders raises two basic questions. First, how does a company identify organizational stakeholders? Second, how does a company balance the needs of different stakeholders? Distinguishing between primary and secondary stakeholders can help answer these questions.[82]

Some stakeholders are more important to the firm's survival than others. **Primary stakeholders** are groups on which the organization depends for its long-term sur-

stakeholder model a theory of corporate responsibility that holds that management's most important responsibility, long-term survival, is achieved by satisfying the interests of multiple corporate stakeholders

stakeholders persons or groups with a "stake" or legitimate interest in a company's actions

primary stakeholder any group on which an organization relies for its long-term survival

Exhibit 4.7

Stakeholder Model of Corporate Social Responsibility

Source: Republished with permission of Academy of Management, P.O. Box 3020, Briar Cliff Manor, NY, 10510–8020. "The Stakeholder Theory of the Corporation: Concepts, Evidence and Implications" (Figure), T. Donaldson & L. E. Preston, *Academy of Management Review*. 1995, Vol. 20. Reproduced by permission of the publisher via Copyright Clearance Center, Inc.

vival; they include shareholders, employees, customers, suppliers, governments, and local communities. When managers are struggling to balance the needs of different stakeholders, the stakeholder model suggests that the needs of primary stakeholders take precedence over the needs of secondary stakeholders. But among primary stakeholders, are some more important than others? According to the life-cycle theory of organizations, the answer is yes. Which groups are primary at any given time depends on which life-cycle stage an organization is in. Organizations' needs change as they go through the life-cycle stages of formation/start-up, growth, maturity, and decline or transition. At each stage, different primary stakeholders will be critical to organizational well-being, and their concerns and issues will take precedence over those of other primary stakeholders.[83] In practice, though, CEOs typically give somewhat higher priority to shareholders, employees, and customers than to suppliers, governments, and local communities, no matter the life-cycle stage.[84] Exhibit 4.8 lists issues that organizations will probably have to address to keep their primary stakeholders satisfied.

Addressing the concerns of primary stakeholders is important because if a stakeholder group becomes dissatisfied and terminates its relationship with the company, the company could be seriously harmed or go out of business. With 4,300 drugstores, WALGREENS was one of KODAK's key customers (and thus a stakeholder), selling two billion photo prints a year using Kodak paper and Kodak photo minilab machines. But with the growing popularity of digital photography, Kodak lost billions in sales because its film and film chemicals were no longer needed to make photos. Hoping to recapture lost sales, Kodak started Ofoto (http://www.ofoto.com), a website where customers can upload digital pictures to the Internet, view them, and then order prints directly from Kodak. Walgreens executives saw that Ofoto would cut them out of the print business. So even though it still had a $200 million agreement with Kodak, Walgreens installed 1,500 one-hour photo minilab machines (for traditional

Exhibit 4.8

Issues Important to Primary Stakeholders

Company	Company history, industry background, organization structure, economic performance, competitive environment, mission or purpose, corporate codes, and stakeholder and social issues management systems.
Employees	Benefits, compensation and rewards, training and development, career planning, employee assistance programs, health promotion, absenteeism and turnover, leaves of absence, relationships with unions, dismissal and appeal, termination, layoffs, retirement and termination counseling, employment equity and discrimination, women in management and on the board, day care and family accommodation, employee communication, occupational health and safety, and part-time, temporary, or contract employees.
Shareholders	Shareholder communications and complaints, shareholder advocacy, shareholder rights, and other shareholder issues.
Customers	Customer communications, product safety, customer complaints, special customer services, and other customer issues.
Suppliers	Relative power, general policy, and other supplier issues.
Public Stakeholders	Public health, safety, and protection, conservation of energy and materials, environmental assessment of capital projects, other environmental issues, public policy involvement, community relations, social investment and donations.

Source: M. B. E. Clarkson, "A Stakeholder Framework for Analyzing and Evaluating Corporate Social Performance," *Academy of Management Review* 20 (1995): 92–117.

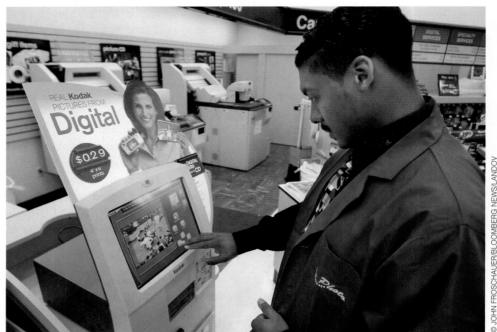

After Kodak launched its own Ofoto.com website to sell photos directly to customers, Walgreens canceled its contracts with Kodak and began installing film processing kiosks from Fuji. Walgreens returned to Kodak after several months, however, because of quality problems with Fuji.

© JOHN FROSCHAUER/BLOOMBERG NEWS/LANDOV

film prints) and digital photo kiosks (for digital film prints) from Fuji, Kodak's main competitor. As Walgreens' Gordon Addington observed at the time, "You have to earn your way in, but you also have to earn your way out . . . Kodak did its best to earn its way out."[85] Walgreens' switch to Fuji cost Kodak $500 million a year in sales.

Secondary stakeholders, such as the media and special interest groups, can influence or be influenced by the company. Unlike the primary stakeholders, however, they do not engage in regular transactions with the company and are not critical to its long-term survival. Consequently, meeting the needs of primary stakeholders is usually more important than meeting the needs of secondary stakeholders. Nevertheless, secondary stakeholders are still important because they can affect public perceptions and opinions about socially responsible behavior. For instance, after hundreds of protests by animal-rights activists, including groups such as the People for the Ethical Treatment of Animals (PETA), SMITHFIELD FOODS, the nation's largest pork producer, announced that it would phase out "gestation crates" at all of its company-owned sow farms over the next decade. Gestation crates, 2 feet wide by 7 feet long, are used to confine female pigs during their 16-week gestation period. In this case, a secondary stakeholder, animal-rights activists, was able to mobilize public opinion and convince Smithfield Foods' primary stakeholders and large customers, such as McDonald's and Wal-Mart, to exert pressure on Smithfield to discontinue the practice. Smithfield is the first major pork producer to move to ban the crates, and others are sure to follow.[86]

So, to whom are organizations socially responsible? Many commentators, especially economists and financial analysts, continue to argue that organizations are responsible only to shareholders. Increasingly, however, top managers have come to believe that they and their companies must be socially responsible to their stakeholders. This view has gained adherents since the Great Depression, when General Electric first identified shareholders, employees, customers, and the general public as its stakeholders. In 1947, Johnson & Johnson listed customers, employees, managers, and shareholders as its stakeholders; and in 1950, Sears Roebuck announced that its most important stakeholders were "customers, employees, community, and stockholders."[87]

"WHAT'S NEW" COMPANY

secondary stakeholder any group that can influence or be influenced by a company and can affect public perceptions about the company's socially responsible behavior

Today, surveys show that as many as 80 percent of top-level managers believe that it is unethical to focus just on shareholders. Twenty-nine states have changed their laws to allow company boards of directors to consider the needs of employees, creditors, suppliers, customers, and local communities, as well as those of shareholders.[88] So, although there is not complete agreement, a majority of opinion makers would argue that companies must be socially responsible to their stakeholders.

Review 6: **To Whom Are Organizations Socially Responsible?**

Social responsibility is a business's obligation to benefit society. To whom are organizations socially responsible? According to the shareholder model, the only social responsibility that organizations have is to maximize shareholder wealth by maximizing company profits. According to the stakeholder model, companies must satisfy the needs and interests of multiple corporate stakeholders, not just shareholders. However, the needs of primary stakeholders, on which the organization relies for its existence, take precedence over those of secondary stakeholders.

7 For What Are Organizations Socially Responsible?

If organizations are to be socially responsible to stakeholders, what are they to be socially responsible *for*? As Exhibit 4.9 illustrates, companies can best benefit their stakeholders by fulfilling their economic, legal, ethical, and discretionary responsibilities.[89] Exhibit 4.9 indicates that economic and legal responsibilities play a larger part in a company's social responsibility than do ethical and discretionary responsibilities. However, the relative importance of these various responsibilities depends on society's expectations of corporate social responsibility at a particular point in time.[90] A century ago, society expected businesses to meet their economic and legal responsibilities and little else. Today, when society judges whether businesses are socially responsible, ethical and discretionary responsibilities are considerably more important than they used to be.

Historically, **economic responsibility**, making a profit by producing a product or service valued by society, has been a business's most basic social responsibility. Organizations that don't meet their financial and economic expectations come under tremendous pressure. For example, company boards are very, very quick these days to fire CEOs. Typically, all it takes is two or three bad quarters in a row. Stagnant sales and declining profits led to Mary Forte's ouster as CEO of ZALES.[91] Kevin Rollins was relieved of his duties as CEO of Dell for a single bad quarter and for allowing arch-rival Hewlett-Packard to increase its lead over Dell.[92] Thomas Neff, who heads the executive recruiting firm Spencer Stuart, says, "It used to be a couple of years [and not two or three quarters]." William Rollnick, who became acting chairman of Mattel after the company fired its previous CEO, says, "There's zero forgiveness. You screw up and you're dead."[93] Indeed, in both Europe and the United States, nearly one-third of all CEOs are fired because of their inability to successfully change their companies.[94] In fact, CEOs are three times more likely to be fired today than two decades ago.

Legal responsibility is a company's social responsibility to obey society's laws and regulations as it tries to meet its economic responsibilities. For example, under

economic responsibility a company's social responsibility to make a profit by producing a valued product or service

legal responsibility a company's social responsibility to obey society's laws and regulations

Exhibit 4.9
Social Responsibilities

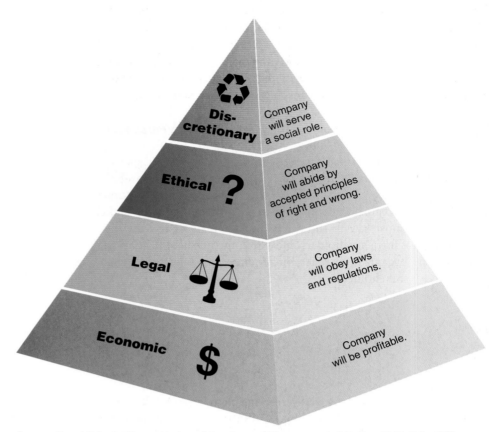

Source: Republished with permission of Academy of Management, P.O. Box 3020, Briar Cliff Manor, NY, 10510–8020. "A Three-Dimensional Conceptual Model of Corporate Performance." (Figure 3.3) A. B. Carroll, *Academy of Management Review*, 1979, Vol. 4. Reproduced by permission of the publisher via Copyright Clearance Center, Inc.

the 1990 Clean Air Act, the smell of fresh baked bread is now illegal. Actually, it's not the smell that is illegal, but the ethanol that is emitted when bread is baked.[95] Although ethanol itself is nontoxic, it contributes to pollution by promoting the formation of the harmful atmospheric compound ozone. Consequently, to meet the law, large bakery plants spent millions to purchase catalytic oxidizers that remove ethanol emissions.[96]

Ethical responsibility is a company's social responsibility not to violate accepted principles of right and wrong when conducting its business. For example, most people believe that **KFC** was wrong to run ads implying that its fried chicken was good for you and could help you lose weight. In one ad, one friend said to another, "Is that you? Man you look fantastic! What the heck you been doin'?" With his mouth full, the friend says, "Eatin' chicken." A voice-over then says, "So if you're watching carbs and going high protein, go KFC!" Pointing out that two fried chicken breasts contain 780 calories and 38 grams of fat, marketing consultant Marian Salzman says, "Marketers need to understand that you can't ask people to believe what isn't true."[97] Likewise, Michael Jacobsen, executive director of the Center for Science in the Public Interest, says, "These ads take the truth, dip it in batter and deep-fry it. Colonel Sanders himself would have a hard time swallowing this ad campaign."[98] After running the ads for a brief time, KFC quietly pulled them. Because different stakeholders may disagree about what is or is not ethical, meeting ethical responsibilities is more difficult than meeting economic or legal responsibilities.

ethical responsibility a company's social responsibility not to violate accepted principles of right and wrong when conducting its business

> Because different stakeholders may disagree about what is or is not ethical, meeting ethical responsibilities is more difficult than meeting economic or legal responsibilities.

Discretionary responsibilities pertain to the social roles that businesses play in society beyond their economic, legal, and ethical responsibilities. For example, dozens of companies support the fight against hunger at The Hunger Site, **http://www .thehungersite.com**. Each time someone clicks on the "donate free food" button (only one click per day per visitor), sponsors of The Hunger Site donate money to pay for food to be sent to Bosnia, Indonesia, Mozambique, or wherever people suffer from hunger. Thanks to the corporate sponsors and the clicks of 284 million visitors, nearly 49 million pounds of food have been distributed thus far.[99] Discretionary responsibilities such as these are voluntary. Companies are not considered unethical if they don't perform them. Today, however, corporate stakeholders expect companies to do much more than in the past to meet their discretionary responsibilities.

Review 7: **For What Are Organizations Socially Responsible?**

Companies can best benefit their stakeholders by fulfilling their economic, legal, ethical, and discretionary responsibilities. Being profitable, or meeting one's economic responsibility, is a business's most basic social responsibility. Legal responsibility consists of following a society's laws and regulations. Ethical responsibility means not violating accepted principles of right and wrong when doing business. Discretionary responsibilities are social responsibilities beyond basic economic, legal, and ethical responsibilities.

8 *Responses to Demands for Social Responsibility*

Social responsiveness refers to a company's strategy to respond to stakeholders' economic, legal, ethical, or discretionary expectations concerning social responsibility. A social responsibility problem exists whenever company actions do not meet stakeholder expectations. One model of social responsiveness, shown in Exhibit 4.10, identifies four strategies for responding to social responsibility problems: reactive, defensive, accommodative, and proactive. These strategies differ in the extent to which the company is willing to act to meet or exceed society's expectations.

A company using a **reactive strategy** will do less than society expects. It may deny responsibility for a problem or fight any suggestions that the company should solve a problem. For example, in an attempt to treat all charitable institutions the same way, *TARGET* created a social responsibility problem by banning Salvation Army bell ringers with their red kettles from soliciting donations in front

"WHAT'S NEW" COMPANY

discretionary responsibilities the social roles that a company fulfills beyond its economic, legal, and ethical responsibilities

social responsiveness refers to a company's strategy to respond to stakeholders' economic, legal, ethical, or discretionary expectations concerning social responsibility

reactive strategy a social responsiveness strategy in which a company does less than society expects

Exhibit 4.10

Social Responsiveness

Reactive	**Defensive**	**Accommodative**	**Proactive**
Fight all the way	Do only what is required	Be progressive	Lead the industry
Withdrawal	Public Relations Approach	Legal Approach	Bargaining	Problem Solving

DO NOTHING ⟷ DO MUCH

SOURCE: A.B. CARROLL, "A THREE-DIMENSIONAL CONCEPTUAL MODEL OF CORPORATE PERFORMANCE," *ACADEMY OF MANAGEMENT REVIEW*, 1979, VOL 4 497-505.

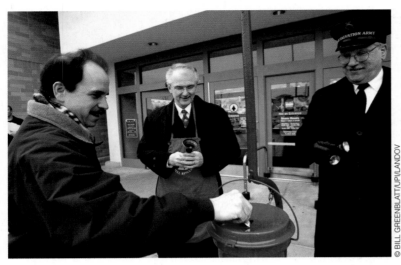

Even though Target maintains a policy against solicitation— even by the Salvation Army— Wal-Mart allows the holiday bell ringers to set up outside its stores and will match its customers' donations to the charity.

of its stores during the holiday season. A Target spokesperson says that because other nonprofit organizations made similar requests, "It's becoming increasingly difficult to have an exception to our policy, so we decided we would have no exceptions." Customer Phyllis McElaney spoke for many when she said this about Target's ban: "It's a disgrace. The bell ringers remind you of the meaning of Christmas, that it's about love, caring, and giving."[100] The ban also meant that the Salvation Army would have to find a way to replace the $9 million that Target customers typically donated each year. Wal-Mart, on the other hand, again welcomed the Salvation Army's bell ringers to its stores and pledged to match its customers' donations up to a total of $1 million.[101]

By contrast, a company using a **defensive strategy** would admit responsibility for a problem but would do the least required to meet societal expectations. *SECOND CHANCE BODY ARMOR* makes bulletproof vests for police officers. According to company founder Richard Davis, tests indicated that the protective material in its vests deteriorated quickly under high temperatures and humidity, conditions under which they're typically used. As a result, Davis concluded that even vests that were only two years old were potentially unsafe. Nevertheless, he couldn't convince the company's executive committee to recall the vests (an accommodative strategy). Davis says he told the committee that it had three choices: recall the vests and stop selling them, do nothing and wait "until a customer is injured or killed," or wait until the problem becomes public and "be forced to make excuses as to why we didn't recognize and correct the problem."[102] After two vests were pierced by bullets, killing one police officer and wounding another, Second Chance announced that it would fix or replace 130,000 potentially defective vests. Although the company finally admitted responsibility for the problem, management decided to do only the minimum of what society expects (fix a defective product). Second Chance, therefore, used a defensive strategy.

A company using an **accommodative strategy** will accept responsibility for a problem and take a progressive approach by doing all that could be expected to solve the problem. For example, when an F4 tornado with winds of over 200 mph struck *PARSONS MANUFACTURING* in Roanoke, Illinois, the metal-parts supplier's plant was completely destroyed. The owner, Bob Parsons, promised to rebuild. Workers continued to collect their paychecks as they helped with cleanup and reconstruction or with community service projects. A year later, the plant reopened and production was returned to 60 percent of its pre-tornado level. Dennis McCarthy, a director with the NOAA National Weather Service in Washington, D.C., presented Parsons with a Storm Ready Community Hero Award—only the second ever given. "It's important that we keep the Parsons story alive," McCarthy said. "I'm grateful. I'm humble," Bob Parsons said. "But I refuse to take all the credit for that. There were many other people involved." Parsons could have collected the insurance money and left, but he felt that workers were part of his extended family and the right thing to do was to rebuild.[103]

Finally, a company using a **proactive strategy** will anticipate responsibility for a problem before it occurs, do more than expected to address the problem, and lead the industry in its approach. Honda Motors announced that it will include side-curtain air

defensive strategy a social responsiveness strategy in which a company admits responsibility for a problem but does the least required to meet societal expectations

accommodative strategy a social responsiveness strategy in which a company accepts responsibility for a problem and does all that society expects to solve that problem

proactive strategy a social responsiveness strategy in which a company anticipates responsibility for a problem before it occurs and does more than society expects to address the problem bags (that drop from the roof and protect passengers' heads) and front-side air bags (that come out of the door to protect against side-impact collisions) as standard equipment on all of its cars. Although more expensive car brands, such as Lexus and Volvo, already included these safety features, Honda is the first to make them standard on all models. On most other cars, these features are optional, meaning that customers must pay extra for them. Brian O'Neill of the Insurance Institute for Highway Safety says, "This is a very positive development because we have been troubled by more and more manufacturers going the option route when it comes to safety equipment." Charlie Baker, Honda's vice president for U.S. research and development, says, "We are convinced this is the right direction and will save lives."[104]

Review 8: Responses to Demands for Social Responsibility

Social responsiveness is a company's response to stakeholders' demands for socially responsible behavior. There are four social responsiveness strategies. When a company uses a reactive strategy, it denies responsibility for a problem. When it uses a defensive strategy, it takes responsibility for a problem but does the minimum required to solve it. When a company uses an accommodative strategy, it accepts responsibility for problems and does all that society expects to solve them. Finally, when a company uses a proactive strategy, it does much more than expected to solve social responsibility problems.

9 Social Responsibility and Economic Performance

One question that managers often ask is, "Does it pay to be socially responsible?" Though understandable, asking whether social responsibility pays is a bit like asking if giving to your favorite charity will help you get a better-paying job. The obvious answer is no. There is not an inherent relationship between social responsibility and economic performance.[105] Nevertheless, this doesn't stop supporters of corporate social responsibility from claiming a positive relationship. For example, one study shows that the Domini 400 Social Index, which is a stock fund consisting of 400 socially responsible companies, has outperformed the Standard & Poor's 500 (an index of 500 stocks representative of the entire economy) by nearly 5 percent. At the same time, though, critics have plenty of facts to support their claim that social responsibility hurts economic performance. For example, another study of 42 socially responsible mutual funds found that they underperformed the Standard & Poor's 500 by 8 percent.[106]

When it comes to social responsibility and economic performance, the first reality is that being socially responsible can sometimes cost a company significantly. Boston-based *TIMBERLAND*, which makes an assortment of work and outdoor clothing and shoes, gives each of its employees a paid (yes, paid) week off each year to help local charities. For example, vice president Bonnie Monahan took four days off to organize a bike-a-thon that raised $50,000 to fight childhood cancer. Monahan, whose younger brother died from cancer, says, "Not too many companies will allow you to do this kind of stuff."[107] Each year, Timberland also gives four workers six months of paid leave so that they can work full-time for nonprofit organizations. Finally, Timberland closes the entire company for one day each year so that all of

"WHAT'S NEW" COMPANY

its 5,400 workers can spend the day working on charitable projects sponsored by the company. This commitment to giving back doesn't come cheap. Indeed, closing down for one day costs Timberland $2 million. Furthermore, assuming that the average employee makes $50,000 a year, the cost of giving each employee a paid week off to do charitable work is at least $5 million. That's $7 million a year that doesn't go to Timberland's bottom line.

The second reality of social responsibility and economic performance is that sometimes it does pay to be socially responsible. The mission of WORLDWISE, which sells environmentally friendly consumer products, is "to make environmentally responsible products that work as well or better, look as good or finer, and cost the same or less as the competition." For example, its water bowls for pets are made out of 125 recycled bottle caps. Likewise, its ecoplanter, which looks like a heavy terra-cotta planter, is light, cheap, and made from 100 percent recycled plastic. In short, Worldwise doesn't think you should have to pay more for environmentally friendly products. In fact, its products are priced competitively enough to be sold in Wal-Mart, Target, and Home Depot. CEO Aaron Lamstein says, "Part of our concept is that we must have an incredibly focused mission that includes equally environmental and social issues and economic issues—that is, making sure that we have a really solid, healthy, financially secure business. You can't put one in front of the other. You can't be successful if you can't do both." The company, which is only 13 years old, has been profitable each of the last eight years.[108]

The third reality of social responsibility and economic performance is that although socially responsible behavior may be "the right thing to do," it does not guarantee profitability. Socially responsible companies experience the same ups and downs in economic performance that traditional businesses do. A good example is BEN & JERRY'S, the ice cream people. Ben & Jerry's started in 1978 when founders Ben Cohen and Jerry Greenfield sent away for a $5 course on how to make ice cream. Ben & Jerry's is as famous for its commitment to social responsibility as for its super premium ice cream. The company donates 7.5 percent of its pretax profits to support AIDS patients, homeless people, and the environment.[109] Moreover, customers buy Ben & Jerry's ice cream because it tastes great *and* because they want to support a socially responsible company. As Ben Cohen says, "We see ourselves as somewhat of a social service agency and somewhat of an ice cream company."[110] But—and this is a big but—despite its outstanding reputation as a socially responsible company, Ben & Jerry's consistently had financial troubles after going public (selling shares of stock to the public) a decade ago. In fact, its financial problems became so severe that Ben and Jerry sold the company to British-based Unilever.[111] Being socially responsible may be the "right thing to do," but it doesn't guarantee business success.

While Ben & Jerry's struggled, Seattle-based STARBUCKS, which also markets itself as a socially responsible company, grew from 11 to more than 8,836 gourmet coffee shops just in the United States, not to mention its stores in some three dozen other countries. Starbucks pays its coffee shop workers much more than minimum wage, provides full health insurance coverage to anyone who works at least 20 hours a week, and gives employees with six or more months at the company the opportunity to participate in its stock options program. Besides taking good care of its employees, Starbucks also makes an annual six-figure charitable contribution to CARE, an international relief agency, for feeding, clothing, and educating poor people in the coffee-growing regions where it gets its coffee beans.[112] Workers from its thousands of stores worldwide are paid to volunteer in community service programs, such as Earth Day cleanups, regional AIDS walks, and local literacy organizations. For example, Starbucks workers in its 19 New Zealand stores donate about

Sometimes it does pay to be socially responsible.

100 hours of volunteer work each week. Aasha Murthy, Starbucks' general manager in New Zealand, says, "Any company can write out a check to a worthy cause, send it off, and think nothing more of it, but that isn't what Starbucks is about. We've got an enormous amount of talent, energy, and passion in our business and that comes from our staff. So we decided to donate their skills. We want Starbucks New Zealand to be a successful organization, not just a profitable one, and there's more than one dimension to success. We want to reach out to the community we're part of."[113]

In the end, if company management chooses a proactive or accommodative strategy toward social responsibility (rather than a defensive or reactive strategy), it should do so because it wants to benefit society and its corporate stakeholders, not because it expects a better financial return.

Review 9: Social Responsibility and Economic Performance

Does it pay to be socially responsible? Sometimes it pays, and sometimes it costs. Overall, there is no clear relationship between social responsibility and economic performance. Consequently, managers should not expect an economic return from socially responsible corporate activities. If your company chooses to practice a proactive or accommodative social responsibility strategy, it should do so to better society and not to improve its financial performance.

An Ethical Baseline

Most people think they are ethical, particularly when the right thing to do is seemingly obvious. But as you read in the chapter, 75 percent of the respondents in a nationwide survey indicated that they had witnessed unethical behavior at work. In another study across multiple industries, 48 percent of the respondents admitted to actually committing an unethical or illegal act in the past year! And recall that with so many ways to approach ethical decision making, ethical choices are not always cut and dried. To give you an idea of your ethical perspective, take this assessment.[114]

Answer each of the questions using the following scale:

1 Strongly agree
2 Agree
3 Not sure
4 Disagree
5 Strongly disagree

1. Did you ever think about taking money from where you worked, but didn't go through with it?
   1   2   3   4   5

2. Have you ever borrowed something from work without telling anyone?
   1   2   3   4   5

3. There are times I've been provoked into a fist fight.
   1   2   3   4   5

4. Is it okay to get around the law if you don't break it?
   1   2   3   4   5

5. I've had fellow employees show me how to take things from where I work.
   1   2   3   4   5

6. I will usually take someone up on a dare.
   1   2   3   4   5

7. I've always driven insured vehicles.
   1   2   3   4   5

8. If you were sent an extra item with an order, would you send it back?
   1   2   3   4   5

9. Would you say everyone is a little dishonest?
   1   2   3   4   5

10. Most supervisors treat their employees fairly.
   1   2   3   4   5

11. I worry about getting hurt at work.
   1   2   3   4   5

12. People say that I'm a workaholic.
   1   2   3   4   5

13. I like to plan things carefully ahead of time.
   1   2   3   4   5

14. Have you found a way a dishonest person in your job could take things from work?
   1   2   3   4   5

15. I often act quickly without stopping to think things through.
   1   2   3   4   5

16. It doesn't bother me what other people think.
   1   2   3   4   5

17. I have friends who are a little dishonest.
   1   2   3   4   5

18. I am not a thrill seeker.
   1   2   3   4   5

19. I have had my driver's license revoked.
   1   2   3   4   5

20. Are you too honest to steal?
   1   2   3   4   5

21. Do most employees take small items from work?
   1   2   3   4   5

22. Do most employees get along well with their supervisors?
   1   2   3   4   5

23. I'm lucky to avoid having accidents.
   1   2   3   4   5

24. I always finish what I start.
    1   2   3   4   5
25. I make sure everything is in its place before leaving home.
    1   2   3   4   5

Scoring

Determine your average score for each category by entering your response to each survey item below, as follows. In blanks that say *regular score*, simply enter your response for that item. If your response was a 4, place a 4 in the *regular score* blank. In blanks that say *reverse score*, subtract your response from 6 and enter the result. So if your response was a 4, place a 2 ($6 - 4 = 2$) in the *reverse score* blank. Total your scores then compute your average score for each section.

Antisocial Behavior

1. regular score   ——   14. regular score   ——
2. regular score   ——   15. regular score   ——
3. regular score   ——   16. regular score   ——
4. regular score   ——   17. regular score   ——
5. regular score   ——   18. reverse score   ——
6. regular score   ——   19. regular score   ——
7. reverse score   ——   20. reverse score   ——
8. reverse score   ——
TOTAL =   —— ÷ 15 = —— (your average for Antisocial Behavior)

Orderliness/Diligence

12. regular score   ——
13. regular score   ——
24. regular score   ——
25. regular score   ——
TOTAL =
—— ÷ 4 = ——
(your average for Orderliness/Diligence)

Positive Outlook

 9. reverse score   ——
10. regular score   ——
11. reverse score   ——
21. reverse score   ——
22. regular score   ——
23. regular score   ——
TOTAL =
—— ÷ 6 = ——
(your average for Positive Outlook)

You can find the interpretation for your scores at: **academic.cengage.com/management/williams**.

☐ ☑ ☐ ☐ ☐

MANAGEMENT DECISION

Implementing Sustainability

Your heart is racing as you stand in front of the gathering of customers.[115] Though not usually at a loss for words, you are having trouble answering their questions about the dangers of the materials and processes used by your company, Interface, Inc., a manufacturer of commercial-grade carpet and flooring. What's more, when you hesitate, they doggedly persist. And none of the questions are about things you know, like discounts, lower prices, or inventory!

After you conclude the meeting, you race back to the office and convene a task force to respond to your customers' questions. But as soon as you assign the team its task, its members turn around and ask you to explain the company's environmental vision. "What vision?" you think to yourself. Desperately looking for inspiration, you happen upon a book by Paul Hawken entitled *The Ecology of Commerce: A Declaration of Sustainability*. You open it, hoping to glean some good ideas that you can repackage for your task force (and your customers).

Interface generates billions of dollars in revenue each year, but in the process, it extracts over 1 billion pounds of raw materials from the earth. The company is also a profligate water user, requiring millions of gallons a year for its manufacturing process—not to mention the petroleum-based materials consumed and the greenhouse gases emitted during the process. Furthermore, your product, carpet, is not recyclable. When people install new carpet, the old carpet is dumped in a landfill.

But Interface is not alone. The entire carpet industry works to the same standards. Competitors like Shaw Walker, J & J Industries, and C&A Floorcoverings use the same amount of materials, have essentially the same manufacturing processes, and generate the same amount of waste, all for products that can't be (or aren't) recycled.

After reading Hawken's book, you realize that Interface will have to change. The question is, how much? How much can Interface change its processes to be environmentally friendly without compromising the company's growth? Sustainability requires that products either be able to easily reenter nature without depositing toxins or be recyclable into new materials. For a manufacturing process to be sustainable, its net effect on the environment must be zero. That might mean using renewable resources, redesigning the process to eliminate all waste streams, or even creating a product that can be infinitely recycled. That's a lot to ask. Can you sustain the company if you adopt environmental sustainability as a vision?

Questions

1. Which level of social responsibility best describes your company's current operations?

2. What environmental vision do you communicate to your task force? In other words, what social responsiveness strategy will you adopt at Interface?

3. Can sustainability be economically viable for Interface? Defend your answer.

MANAGEMENT TEAM DECISION

Sponsorship or Sellout

In the world of charitable organizations, the most grueling activity must certainly be fund-raising.[116] Although soliciting donations for popular causes can be easy, lesser-known nonprofits, which do very important work, may have difficulty consistently raising enough money to function. Sometimes, corporate sponsorship is necessary to obtain adequate funding. The obvious plus to corporate sponsorship is the cash, and perhaps greater visibility and legitimacy in the community (depending, of course, on the reputation of the sponsor). But corporate sponsorship can also have drawbacks. Potential donors may think that the charity no longer needs additional funding or withdraw support because they perceive that the charity has "sold out" to corporate financial inducements.

In considering a possible sponsorship, managers of charitable organizations can find themselves facing an ethical dilemma. Consider the following situation: A health-care foundation that is putting on a benefit concert to raise money to fund research on respiratory diseases signs up a popular regional band. Unable to cover the costs for the band, concert hall, decorations, and publicity, the foundation entertains an offer from operators of a new and controversial waste incineration plant, who are willing to put up $50,000 to become sponsors of the event.

Such situations are all too common in the world of nonprofit fund-raising, and getting these decisions right can often mean the difference between success and failure. To execute this management team decision, you will need to assemble a team of four to five students. Your management team will be working with the following scenario:

Women Against Violence (WAV) is a prominent local charity focused on providing victims of domestic violence with temporary housing, helping them cope with stress, and, in some cases, helping them begin a new life. During the 1990s, your management team was able to lift the fund-raising for WAV to all-time highs. Now, however, tight economic conditions have dried up donations. As WAV's management team is meeting to determine how and when to shut down operations, you receive a call from a local company, Famous Brewery and Bottling Company. Famous not only has its own brewery and specialty beers, but it also bottles and distributes beer for larger, nationally known beer brands. Famous is a progressive company with almost half its top management team comprised of women. But you also know that alcohol is involved in many domestic abuse situations.

You put the representative from Famous on speakerphone so the entire team can hear her. She proposes that Famous sponsor a spring festival to raise money for WAV. Famous will give WAV $40,000 to organize the festival (for advertising, tent and game rentals, concession stands, and so on), and WAV will receive all of the proceeds from the festival. In return, Famous wants to set up a booth at the festival and have its name and logo next to WAV's on any promotional materials, such as flyers, banners, and buttons. You thank the representative and turn off the phone. Turning to your team, you say, "So, do we take the money or not?"

You will be making a decision for or against corporate sponsorship for WAV by Famous Brewery and Bottling Company. Before beginning the exercise, review Exhibit 4.6.

Questions

1. Rank the ethical intensity of the decision. Consider assigning a numerical value to each of the six factors listed on page 124, on a scale of, say, 1 to 5. Add the six values together and assess the sum against a possible 30 points.

2. As a team, examine the situation through the lens of each of the principles of ethical decision making. What is your final decision?

3. What role did the ethical intensity of the decision play in your ultimate decision?

PRACTICE BEING A MANAGER

Discerning Unethical Behavior

Applying ethical judgment in an organizational setting can be challenging. This exercise offers you the opportunity to consider how you might approach such a situation as a manager in an investment firm.

Read the scenario and prepare your responses to the individual (homework) questions in advance of discussing this exercise in class.

Scenario

Imagine that you are a newly hired portfolio manager at Excalibur Funds. Although you're new to this job, you have eight years' experience in the mutual fund business. You left a larger and more established mutual fund company to join Excalibur because of its reputation as a bright, up-and-coming investment company, a place where someone like yourself could participate in building a new and dynamic investment company.

Your new fund, the Pioneer Fund, is a growth-oriented fund investing in small companies. Typically, the majority of the fund's stock investments is in high-technology companies. Pioneer is moving up fast in its peer group, and if the fund continues to perform well, you stand a good chance of being the manager recognized when it breaks into the top tier of performance.

One of the features that attracted you to this job is the opportunity to work with a seasoned group of traders, analysts, and staff professionals. The Pioneer Fund staff has averaged 10 percent turnover over the past five years, unusual in an industry where turnover commonly reaches 60 to 80 percent. After a month of working with your new team, however, you have noticed some troubling patterns. First, you felt that some of your staff were delaying or stonewalling you on several occasions when you requested more detailed information on particular trades. It took too long to get the information, and when you did receive it, the information looked a little *too* neat and well-organized. Second, the analysts have seemed guarded regarding their interaction with some of the technology companies in which the Pioneer Fund invests. On more than one occasion you've noticed analysts quickly ending phone calls when you entered the office, or minimizing computer screens when you walk by their desks. Finally, the group just seems a bit too *nice* when you are around. The investment business is often hectic and stressful. Shouting matches over investment decisions are not uncommon in this business, and grumbling is a second language. But all you get are smiles and charm.

So here you are at your desk on a Saturday evening, finishing off the last of a pot of coffee and planning for Monday morning. One thing is clear—you must begin to scratch below the surface of the Pioneer Fund team. Your gut tells you that something is wrong here, perhaps very wrong. For all you know you may be sitting on the next big investment scandal. Your head tells you that you have no hard evidence of unethical or illegal behavior, and that you'd better tread carefully. If your gut is wrong and you run around making hasty accusations you may lose what appears to be a very talented investment team.

What steps should you take starting Monday morning?

Preparing for Class Discussion

Complete the following steps individually in preparation for class discussion. Write your responses to the questions in each step.

Step 1: Understand the situation and key considerations. What considerations would be important to you in developing a plan of action in this situation? What resources might you draw upon to determine whether or not particular actions are unethical and/or illegal?

Step 2: Develop a plan of action. What steps would you follow in this scenario? What factors should you consider in planning your timing of these steps?

Step 3: Anticipate response(s). How might the Pioneer Fund employees respond to your plan of action? Develop a few scenarios.

Small Group and Class Discussion

Your professor will assign you to a small discussion group. Your group should discuss the following questions and be prepared to share your thoughts with the class:

1. What are the most difficult aspects of responding to a murky situation—those situations in which you sense the presence of unethical and/or illegal behavior, but you haven't seen unequivocal proof of wrongdoing?

2. What are the risks of waiting for unequivocal proof before beginning to take action? What are the risks of acting decisively based on your "gut" sense of a situation?

3. What is different about acting ethically/responsibly within an organizational environment/culture like that of the Pioneer Fund, versus acting ethically/responsibly as an individual? What are the particular challenges and dynamics associated with ethical and responsible behavior in an organization?

DEVELOP YOUR CAREER POTENTIAL

Examining Nonprofits

It is only the farmer who faithfully plants seeds in the Spring, who reaps a harvest in the Autumn.

—B. C. Forbes, founder of *Forbes* magazine

These assignments will help develop your present and future capabilities as a manager. Since stakeholders increasingly expect companies to do more to fulfill their discretionary responsibilities, chances are you and your company will be expected to support your community in some significant way. To begin learning about community needs and corporate social responsibility, visit a local charity or nonprofit organization of your choosing, perhaps a hospital, the Red Cross, Goodwill, Planned Parenthood, a soup kitchen, or a homeless shelter. Talk to the people who work or volunteer there. Gather the information you need to answer the following questions.

Questions

1. What is the organization's mission?

2. Who does the organization serve, and how does it serve them?

3. What percentage of the organization's donations is used for administrative purposes? What percentage is used to directly benefit those served by the organization? What is the ratio of volunteers to paid workers?

4. What job or task does a typical volunteer perform for the organization? How much time does a typical volunteer give to the organization each week? For what types of jobs does the organization need more volunteers?

5. How does the business community support the organization?

6. Why are you interested in the activities of this organization?

REEL TO REAL

Emperor's Club

William Hundert (Kevin Kline), a professor at Saint Benedict's preparatory school, believes in teaching his students about living a principled life as well as teaching them his beloved classical literature. Hundert's principled ways are challenged, however, by a new student, Sedgewick Bell (Emile Hirsch). Bell's behavior during the 73rd annual Julius Caesar competition causes Hundert to suspect that Bell leads a less than principled life.

Years later Hundert is the honored guest of his former student Sedgewick Bell (Joel Gretsch) at Bell's estate. Depaak Mehta (Rahul Khanna), Bell, and Louis Masoudi (Patrick Dempsey) compete in a reenactment of the Julius Caesar competition. Bell nearly wins the competition, but when Hundert notices that Bell is wearing an earpiece and is cheating with an assistant's help, he gives him a question he knows he cannot answer. Earlier in the film Hundert had suspected that the young Bell also cheated during the competition, but Headmaster Woodbridge (Edward Herrmann) had pressed him to ignore his suspicion.

This scene appears at the end of the film. It is an edited portion of the competition reenactment. Bell announced his candidacy for the U.S. Senate just before talking to Hundert in the bathroom. He carefully described his commitment to specific values that he would pursue if elected.

What to Watch for and Ask Yourself

1. Based on the clip, what ethical principles do you think most inform William Hundert's thinking?
2. Describe Sedgewick Bell's level of moral development.

Organic Valley—Socially Responsible Farming

Organic Valley Cooperative planted its seeds in the lands and barns of a half-dozen family farmers in Wisconsin nearly 20 years ago. And although U.S. family farms seem to be a dying breed—more than 6 million have failed during this time period—Organic Valley is growing. Driven by the belief that meat, produce, and dairy products should be free of pesticides, antibiotics, and synthetic hormones, the first group of Organic Valley farmers set up a cooperative with an office in tiny LaFarge, Wisconsin, whose population is still less than 800. More and more farmers are joining the cooperative—and as consumer demand for organic products is increasing, so are sales. As a result, Organic Valley is adding 30 to 50 organizational staff employees per year. Growth like that requires greater management, particularly in the highly risky business environment of agriculture.

What to Watch for and Ask Yourself

1. In addition to the farmers, who are Organic Valley's other stakeholders?
2. Does it pay for Organic Valley to be socially responsible?

two

PART 2
Planning

Chapter 5
Planning and Decision Making

This chapter examines the benefits and pitfalls of planning, making plans work, and the different plans used in organizations. You'll also learn the steps and limitations of rational decision making and review various group decision techniques.

Chapter 6
Organizational Strategy

This chapter examines how managers use strategies to obtain a sustainable competitive advantage. Then you learn the strategy-making process and how companies answer these questions: What business should we be in? How should we compete in this industry? How should we compete against a particular firm?

Chapter 7
Innovation and Change

This chapter reviews the issues associated with organizational innovation. The first part of this chapter shows you why innovation matters and how to manage innovation to create and sustain a competitive advantage. In the second part of the chapter, you will learn about organizational change and about the risk of not changing.

Chapter 8
Global Management

In this chapter, we examine the impact of global business on U.S. firms and review the basic rules and agreements that govern global trade. You'll learn how and when companies go global. And you'll read how companies decide where to expand globally and confront issues like business climates and cultural differences.

Planning and Decision Making

Learning Outcomes:

1 Discuss the benefits and pitfalls of planning.

2 Describe how to make a plan that works.

3 Discuss how companies can use plans at all management levels, from top to bottom.

4 Explain the steps and limits to rational decision making.

5 Explain how group decisions and group decision-making techniques can improve decision making.

In This Chapter:

WHAT WOULD YOU DO?

Ford Motor Company, Dearborn, Michigan.[1] Ford Motor Company has been one of the most prominent automobile producers in the world for almost 100 years. Founded by Henry Ford and eleven business associates in 1903, Ford Motor Company pioneered the moving assembly line, in which workers remained in place performing the same job on each automobile that came down the line. Henry Ford's vision was the production of cars that were affordable to the masses. Today, Ford's product lines include Ford, Lincoln, Mercury, Mazda, Aston Martin, Jaguar, Land Rover, and Volvo.

Despite the proliferation of nameplates, Ford Motor has been losing money for years, particularly in its North American operations. Ford produces more vehicles than it can sell and does so under very difficult personnel conditions that are part of the industry's history. Most of the company's production employees are represented by the United Auto Workers. Generous conditions for retirement, benefits, and job protection, which developed when the industry was doing well, now weigh down the company operations. Another issue that has you concerned is the Premium Automotive Group (PAG), which makes the company's Aston-Martin, Jaguar, Land Rover, and Volvo brands. Originally intended as the platform for the company to enter the luxury car market, this group loses billions year after year. Although the company has substantial cash reserves—over $20 billion—operating losses are steadily diminishing the company's financial safety net.

You've identified four options for the company. The first is to close down older plants in an effort to realign production and sales. You don't want to produce more cars than you sell; in fact, it might be good to produce a bit less than you could actually sell. There is an enormous cost to buying out the workers, shuttering the plants, and dealing with the political implications of a closure. A second option would be to produce only smaller cars, thus, eliminating or sharply reducing the SUV and truck lines. This has the advantage of getting back to Henry Ford's vision for the company as well as dealing quickly with products that are not selling because of high gas prices. Third, you could take the dramatic step of reducing your North American presence and focus your efforts on international markets where Ford has been very successful. Europe, South America, and China have been very receptive to Ford vehicles and the company is doing well in these markets. The fourth option is to sell the PAG group. What is the best way to evaluate these options? What criteria might you use to decide which of these four options is the best? No matter which option you choose, how might you build in some flexibility in case market conditions change? Once you do choose an option, what is the best way to put together an effective action plan and then track your progress? **If you were in charge at Ford Motor Company, what would you do?**

ACTIVITIES + VIDEOS

CengageNOW Audio study guide, electronic flashcards, author FAQ videos, On the Job and Biz Flix videos, concept tutorial, and concept exercise

Web (academic.cengage.com/management/williams) Quiz, PowerPoint slides, and glossary terms for this chapter

"WHAT'S NEW" COMPANIES

FORD MOTOR COMPANY

TOYOTA

McDONALD'S

SONY

OCEAN SPRAY

E.W. SCRIPPS

VIRGIN ATLANTIC AIRWAYS

AVON

NASA

PHILIP MORRIS

CHAPARRAL ENERGY

AIRBUS

U.S. CONGRESS

1-800-GOT-JUNK?

MERCK

ALTEON WEBSYSTEMS

BMW

AND OTHERS . . .

ven inexperienced managers know that planning and decision making are central parts of their jobs. Figure out what the problem is. Generate potential solutions or plans. Pick the best one. Make it work. Experienced managers, however, know how hard it really is to make good plans and decisions. One seasoned manager says: "I think the biggest surprises are the problems. Maybe I had never seen it before. Maybe I was protected by my management when I was in sales. Maybe I had delusions of grandeur, I don't know. I just know how disillusioning and frustrating it is to be hit with problems and conflicts all day and not be able to solve them very cleanly."[2]

This chapter begins by examining the benefits and pitfalls of planning. Next, you will learn how to make a plan that works. Then, you will look at the different kinds of plans that are used from the top to the bottom in most companies. In the second part of the chapter, we discuss the steps of rational decision making and also consider its limitations. We finish the chapter by discussing how managers can use groups and group decision techniques to improve decisions.

PLANNING

Planning is choosing a goal and developing a method or strategy to achieve that goal. Yuki Funo, who used to be in charge of TOYOTA's American sales division and is now CEO of Toyota Motor North America, says, "Once you grab a 10 percent share in most markets, consumers almost always put your product on their shopping list. My experience . . . tells me there's not a significant hurdle going from 10 percent to 20 percent."[3] Toyota established a goal to increase its U.S. market share to 15 percent by 2010. Achieving that goal would move Toyota, which at that time was the fourth largest car maker in the United States, ahead of DaimlerChrysler, which has a 14.1 percent market share. How did Toyota plan to meet its 15 percent market share goal? Two words: geography and trucks. In terms of geography, Toyota already had an 18 percent market share in California, but saw an opportunity in the Midwest where it had only 5 to 6 percent of the market. Funo believed that the only sure way for Toyota to get a 15 percent market share nationally was with pickup trucks. In 2006, Toyota rolled out its first full-size pickup truck, the Toyota Tundra, and saw its national market share jump to 13.3 percent, well on the way to the 15 percent goal. That same year, Toyota passed Ford Motor Company to become the number two automaker in the United States. Armed with more than $30 billion in cash, the company has built a new plant in Texas that when operating at full capacity will be able to produce 200,000 vehicles per year.[4]

planning choosing a goal and developing a strategy to achieve that goal

© GARY CAMERON/REUTERS/LANDOV

> **After reading the next three sections, you should be able to**
>
> 1 discuss the benefits and pitfalls of planning.
> 2 describe how to make a plan that works.
> 3 discuss how companies can use plans at all management levels, from top to bottom.

1 Benefits and Pitfalls of Planning

Are you one of those naturally organized people who always make a daily to-do list, write everything down so they won't forget, and never miss a deadline because they keep track of everything with their handy time management notebook or Palm PC? Or are you one of those flexible, creative, go-with-the-flow people who dislike planning and organizing because it restricts their freedom, energy, and performance? Some people are natural planners. They love it and can see only its benefits. Others dislike planning and can see only its disadvantages. It turns out that both views are have real value.

Planning has advantages and disadvantages. Let's learn about **1.1 the benefits** and **1.2 the pitfalls of planning**.

1.1 Benefits of Planning

Planning offers several important benefits: intensified effort, persistence, direction, and creation of task strategies.[5] First, as shown in Exhibit 5.1, managers and employees put forth greater effort when following a plan. Take two workers. Instruct one to "do your best" to increase production, and instruct the other to achieve a 2 percent increase in production each month. Research shows that the one with the specific plan will work harder.[6]

Second, planning leads to persistence, that is, working hard for long periods. In fact, planning encourages persistence even when there may be little chance of short-term success.[7] **McDonald's** founder Ray Kroc, a keen believer in the power of persistence, had this quotation from President Calvin Coolidge hung in all of his executives' offices: "Nothing in the world can take the place of persistence. Talent will not; nothing is more common than unsuccessful men with talent. Genius will not; unrewarded genius is almost a proverb. Education will not; the world is full of educated derelicts. Persistence and determination alone are omnipotent."[8]

The third benefit of planning is direction. Plans encourage managers and employees to direct their persistent efforts *toward* activities that help accomplish their goals and *away* from activities that don't.[9] For example, a large insurance company wanted to improve the performance evaluation feedback its managers gave employees. To help the managers improve, company trainers taught them 43 effective performance feedback behaviors, such as, "I will give my subordinate a clear understanding of the results I expect him or her to achieve" and "During the performance appraisal interview, I will be very supportive, stressing good points before discussing needed improvement." During the training, managers were instructed to choose just 12 behaviors (out of the 43) on which they wanted to make the most improvement. When subordinates rated their managers on the 43 behaviors, it became clear that no matter which 12 behaviors different managers chose to concentrate on, they improved only on those 12 behaviors. Thus, plans direct behavior toward activities that lead to goal accomplishment and away from those that don't.

The fourth benefit of planning is that it encourages the development of task strategies. In other words, planning not only encourages people to work hard for extended periods and to engage in behaviors directly related to goal accomplishment, it also encourages them to think of better ways to do their jobs.

Exhibit 5.1
Benefits of Planning

Finally, perhaps the most compelling benefit of planning is that it has been proved to work for both companies and individuals. On average, companies with plans have larger profits and grow much faster than companies that don't.[10] The same holds true for individual managers and employees: There is no better way to improve the performance of the people who work in a company than to have them set goals and develop strategies for achieving those goals.

1.2 Planning Pitfalls

Despite the significant benefits associated with planning, planning is not a cure-all. Plans won't fix all organizational problems. In fact, many management authors and consultants believe that planning can harm companies in several ways.[11]

As shown in Exhibit 5.2, the first pitfall of planning is that it can impede change and prevent or slow needed adaptation. Sometimes companies become so committed to achieving the goals set forth in their plans, or on following the strategies and tactics spelled out in them, that they fail to see that their plans aren't working or that their goals need to change. Ironically, SONY, one of the world's best known electronics innovators famous for its breakthrough Trinitron (picture tube) televisions, was one of the last major TV manufacturers to develop a line of flat-screen TVs. Sony's TV division was so committed to the old—and now outdated—Trinitron picture-tube technology that its engineers were reluctant to turn to Sony's audio, videogame, and computer monitor divisions for help and expertise in designing new flat-screen TVs. Makoto Kogure, who headed Sony's TV division, admits, "We did everything inside the TV group."[12]

The second pitfall is that planning can create a false sense of certainty. Planners sometimes feel that they know exactly what the future holds for their competitors, their suppliers, and their companies. However, all plans are based on assumptions. "The price of gasoline will increase by 4 percent per year." "Exports will continue to rise." For plans to work, the assumptions on which they are based must hold true. If the assumptions turn out to be false, then the plans based on them are likely to fail.

The third potential pitfall of planning is the detachment of planners. In theory, strategic planners and top-level managers are supposed to focus on the big picture and not concern themselves with the details of implementation, that is, carrying out the plan. According to management professor Henry Mintzberg, detachment leads planners to plan for things they don't understand.[13] Plans are meant to be guidelines for action, not abstract theories. Consequently, planners need to be familiar with the daily details of their businesses if they are to produce plans that can work.

If you doubt that the "details" are important to good execution of a plan, imagine that you're about to have coronary bypass surgery to replace four clogged arteries. You can have either an experienced surgeon or a first-year medical intern perform your surgery. The intern is a fully qualified M.D. who clearly understands the theory and the plan behind bypass surgery, but has never performed such an operation. As you lie on the operating table, who is the last person you'd like to see as the anesthesia kicks in, the first-year intern who knows the plan but has never done a bypass or the experienced surgeon who has followed the plan hundreds of times? Planning works better when the people developing the plan are not detached from the process of executing the plan.

Exhibit 5.2

Pitfalls of Planning

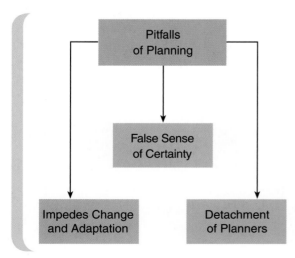

Review 1: **Benefits and Pitfalls of Planning**

Planning is choosing a goal and developing a method to achieve that goal. Planning is one of the best ways to improve organizational and individual performance. It encourages people to work harder (intensified effort), to work hard for extended periods (persistence), to engage in behaviors directly related to goal accomplishment (directed behavior), and to think of better ways to do their jobs (task strategies). Most importantly, companies that plan have larger profits and faster growth than companies that don't plan. However, planning also has three potential pitfalls. Companies that are overly committed to their plans may be slow to adapt to changes in their environment. Planning is based on assumptions about the future, and when those assumptions are wrong, the plans are likely to fail. Finally, planning can fail when planners are detached from the implementation of plans.

2 How to Make a Plan That Works

Planning is a double-edged sword. If done right, planning brings about tremendous increases in individual and organizational performance. If planning is done wrong, however, it can have just the opposite effect and harm individual and organizational performance.

*In this section, you will learn how to make a plan that works. As depicted in Exhibit 5.3, planning consists of **2.1 setting goals, 2.2 developing commitment to the goals, 2.3 developing effective action plans, 2.4 tracking progress toward goal achievement,** and **2.5 maintaining flexibility in planning.***

2.1 Setting Goals

Since planning involves choosing a goal and developing a method or strategy to achieve that goal, the first step in planning is to set goals. To direct behavior and increase effort, goals need to be specific and challenging.[14] For example, deciding to "increase sales this year" won't direct and energize workers as much as deciding to "increase North American sales by 4 percent in the next six months." Likewise, deciding to "drop a few pounds" won't motivate you as much as deciding to "lose 15 pounds." Specific, challenging goals provide a target for which to aim and a standard against which to measure success.

One way of writing effective goals for yourself, your job, or your company is to use the S.M.A.R.T. guidelines. **S.M.A.R.T. goals** are Specific, Measurable, Attainable, Realistic, and Timely.[15] Let's see how a heating, ventilation, and air-conditioning (HVAC) company might use S.M.A.R.T. goals in its business.

S.M.A.R.T. goals goals that are specific, measurable, attainable, realistic, and timely

Exhibit 5.3

How to Make a Plan That Works

| 1
Set goals | 2
Develop commitment | 3
Develop effective action plans
☑ Who ☑ What ☑ When ☑ How | 4
Track progress toward goal achievement | 5
Maintain flexibility |

Revise existing plan
or
Begin planning process anew

doing the right thing

Stretch Goals: Avoid the "15 Percent Delusion"

Stretch goals are extremely ambitious goals that you don't know how to reach. The purpose of stretch goals is to achieve extraordinary improvements in company performance. Stretch goals are so demanding that they force managers and workers to throw away old comfortable solutions and adopt radical, never-used solutions. Though stretch goals may encourage large improvements, they may also pressure people to do anything to meet "the numbers." The most common stretch goal CEOs set is "15 percent annual growth," the magical number that doubles corporate earnings every five years. But with earnings growth averaging just 8 percent over the last 40 years, the chances of achieving 15 percent growth every year are extremely low. So instead of promising generally unobtainable results, managers should set more realistic stretch goals. When Bob Eckert became CEO of Mattel, he dumped the company's stated goals of 15 percent annual earnings growth and 10 percent revenue growth. Says Eckert, "They were not realistic. We were not going to play that game anymore."[16]

The HVAC business is cyclical. It's extremely busy at the beginning of summer, when homeowners find that their air-conditioning isn't working, and at the beginning of winter, when furnaces and heat pumps need repair. During these times, most HVAC companies have more business than they can handle, while at other times of year their business can be very slow. So a *specific* goal would be to increase sales by 50 percent during the fall and spring, when business is slower. This goal could be *measured* by keeping track of the number of annual maintenance contracts sold to customers. This goal of increasing sales during the off-seasons is *attainable* because maintenance contracts typically include spring tune-ups (air-conditioning systems) and fall tune-ups (furnace or heating systems). Moreover, a 50 percent increase in sales during the slow seasons appears to be *realistic*. Because customers want their furnaces and air conditioners to work the first time it gets cold (or hot) each year, a well-designed pitch may make them very open to buying service contracts that ensure their equipment is in working order. Tune-up work can then be scheduled during the slow seasons, increasing sales at those times. Finally, this goal can be made *timely* by asking the staff to push sales of maintenance contracts before Labor Day, the traditional end of summer, when people start thinking about the cold days ahead, and in March, when winter-weary people start longing for hot days in air-conditioned comfort. The result should be more work during the slow fall and spring seasons.

2.2 Developing Commitment to Goals

Just because a company sets a goal doesn't mean that people will try to accomplish it. If workers don't care about a goal, that goal won't encourage them to work harder or smarter. Thus, the second step in planning is to develop commitment to goals.[17]

Goal commitment is the determination to achieve a goal. Commitment to achieve a goal is not automatic. Managers and workers must choose to commit themselves to a goal. Edwin Locke, professor emeritus of management at the University of Maryland and the foremost expert on how, why, and when goals work, tells a story about an overweight friend who finally lost 75 pounds. Locke says, "I asked him how he did it, knowing how hard it was for most people to lose so much weight." His friend responded, "Actually, it was quite simple. I simply decided that I *really wanted* to do it."[18] Put another way, goal commitment is really wanting to achieve a goal.

goal commitment the determination to achieve a goal

So how can managers bring about goal commitment? The most popular approach is to set goals participatively. Rather than assigning goals to workers ("Johnson, you've got till Tuesday of next week to redesign the flux capacitor so it gives us 10 percent more output"), managers and employees choose goals together. The goals are more likely to be realistic and attainable if employees participate in setting them.

Another technique for gaining commitment to a goal is to make the goal public. For example, college students who publicly communicated their semester grade goals ("This semester, I'm shooting for a 3.5") to significant others (usually a parent or sibling) were much more committed to achieving their grades. More important, those students earned grades that were nearly a half-grade higher than the grades of students who did not tell others about their grade goals. So, one way to increase commitment to goals is to "go public" by having individuals or work units tell others about their goals.

Another way to increase goal commitment is to obtain top management's support. Top management can show support for a plan or program by providing funds, speaking publicly about the plan, or participating in the plan itself.

2.3 Developing Effective Action Plans

The third step in planning is to develop effective action plans. An **action plan** lists the specific steps (how), people (who), resources (what), and time period (when) for accomplishing a goal. Unlike most CEOs, Randy Papadellis has a unique goal that requires an extraordinary action plan. As the CEO of OCEAN SPRAY, Papadellis has to buy all of the cranberries that his farmers produce (Ocean Spray is a farmer cooperative) and buy the crop at the highest possible price. Then, it's Papadellis's job to figure out how to sell the entire crop of high-cost berries. He says, "Imagine if Pepsi had to maximize the aluminum it used, and at the highest price it could afford!" Under Papadellis's direction, Ocean Spray began looking for alternative uses for cranberries beyond the traditional juice and canned products. The company invented dried-fruit Craisins by reinfusing juice into husks that used to be thrown away. Craisins have grown into a $100 million product line. Ocean Spray also developed a set of light drinks that had just 40 calories, mock berries that could be infused with other flavors (such as blueberry and strawberry) and used in muffins and cereals, and was the first company to introduce juice boxes. Because these plans have worked to perfection, Ocean Spray has been able to increase the price it pays its farmers over 100 percent in the past three years.[19]

2.4 Tracking Progress

The fourth step in planning is to track progress toward goal achievement. There are two accepted methods of tracking progress. The first is to set proximal goals and distal goals. **Proximal goals** are short-term goals or subgoals, whereas **distal goals** are long-term or primary goals.[20] The idea behind setting proximal goals is that achieving them may be more motivating and rewarding than waiting to reach far-off distal goals. In a

"WHAT'S NEW" COMPANY

action plan the specific steps, people, and resources needed to accomplish a goal

proximal goals short-term goals or subgoals

distal goals long-term or primary goals

Ocean Spray has been able to increase the price it pays its farmers over 100 percent in the past three years.

© MATTHIEU BELANGER/REUTERS/LANDOV

research study, Massachusetts Institute of Technology students were given a complex proofreading assignment; they were paid 10 cents for each error they found, but were penalized $1 a day for turning in their work late. One group of students was given a single deadline, that is, a distal goal, and told to turn in all of their work three weeks from the start of the study. A second group of students was given weekly deadlines, that is, proximal goals, and told to turn in one-third of their work each week. A third group of students was allowed to set their own deadlines; that is, they set their own proximal goals. The single-deadline students (those with no proximal goals, just a distal goal) were the worst performers: They turned in their work 12 days late and corrected only 70 errors. The students who were assigned weekly goals (proximal goals) were the best performers: They turned in their work only a half day late and corrected 136 errors. Next best were the students who set their own proximal goals: They turned in their work 6.5 days late and corrected 104 errors.[21] The lesson for managers is clear. If you want people to do a better job of tracking the quality and timeliness of their work, use proximal goals to set multiple deadlines.[22]

The second method of tracking progress is to gather and provide performance feedback. Regular, frequent performance feedback allows workers and managers to track their progress toward goal achievement and make adjustments in effort, direction, and strategies.[23] For example, Exhibit 5.4 shows the result of providing feedback on safety behavior to the makeup and wrapping workers in a large bakery company. The company had a worker safety record that was two-and-a-half

Exhibit 5.4

Effects of Goal Setting, Training, and Feedback on Safe Behavior in a Bread Factory

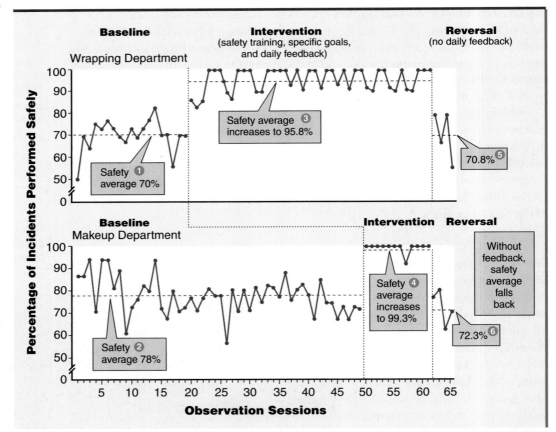

Source: © 1978 by the American Psychological Association. "A Behavioral Approach to Occupational Safety: Pinpointing and Reinforcing Safe Performance in a Food Manufacturing Plant." J. Komaki, K. D. Barwick, & L. R. Scott, *Journal of Applied Psychology*, 1978, V63. Reprinted with permission.

times worse than the industry average. During the baseline period, workers in the wrapping department, who measure and mix ingredients, roll the bread dough, and put it into baking pans, performed their jobs safely about 70 percent of the time (see ❶ in Exhibit 5.4). The baseline safety record for workers in the makeup department, who bag and seal baked bread and assemble, pack, and tape cardboard cartons for shipping, was somewhat better at 78 percent (see ❷). After the company gave workers 30 minutes of safety training, set a goal of 90 percent safe behavior, and then provided daily feedback (such as a chart similar to Exhibit 5.4), performance improved dramatically. During the intervention period, the percentage of safely performed behaviors rose to an average of 95.8 percent for wrapping workers (see ❸) and 99.3 percent for workers in the makeup department (see ❹), and never fell below 83 percent. Thus, the combination of training, a challenging goal, and feedback led to a dramatic increase in performance.

The importance of feedback alone can be seen in the reversal stage, when the company quit posting daily feedback on safe behavior. Without daily feedback, the percentage of safely performed behavior returned to baseline levels, 70.8 percent for the wrapping department (see ❺) and 72.3 percent for the makeup department (see ❻). For planning to be effective, workers need both a specific, challenging goal and regular feedback to track their progress. Indeed, additional research indicates that the effectiveness of goal setting can be doubled by the addition of feedback.[24]

2.5 Maintaining Flexibility

Because action plans are sometimes poorly conceived and goals sometimes turn out not to be achievable, the last step in developing an effective plan is to maintain flexibility. One method of maintaining flexibility while planning is to adopt an options-based approach.[25] The goal of **options-based planning** is to keep options open by making small, simultaneous investments in many options or plans. Then, when one or a few of these plans emerge as likely winners, you invest even more in these plans while discontinuing or reducing investment in the others. In part, options-based planning is the opposite of traditional planning. Whereas the purpose of an action plan is to commit people and resources to a particular course of action, the purpose of options-based planning is to leave those commitments open by maintaining **slack resources**, that is, a cushion of resources, such as extra time, people, money, or production capacity, that can be used to address and adapt to unanticipated changes, problems, or opportunities.[26] Holding options open gives you choices, and choices, combined with slack resources, gives you flexibility.

One example of options-based planning is *E.W. Scripps*'s *Naples Daily News*, which has aggressively tried to counter the national trend in the newspaper industry of decreasing sales as the audience turns to the Internet for its news. Nationally, sales of daily newspapers are falling at rate of almost 3 percent a year. To increase readership, the *Naples Daily News* offers content via TV, radio, magazines, cell phones, PlayStations, and iPods. The newspaper posts a 15-minute video newscast on its website each day and offers services like calling readers at the end of each quarter in a football game to update the score. Publisher John Fish says profits are "a good bit higher than our print margins. It's just going to grow in the future. And if we don't provide the services, someone else will come up under us."[27]

Another method of maintaining flexibility while planning is to take a learning-based approach. In contrast to traditional planning, which assumes that initial action plans are correct and will lead to success, **learning-based planning** assumes that action plans need to be continually tested, changed, and improved as com-

options-based planning maintaining planning flexibility by making small, simultaneous investments in many alternative plans

slack resources a cushion of extra resources that can be used with options-based planning to adapt to unanticipated change, problems, or opportunities

learning-based planning learning better ways of achieving goals by continually testing, changing, and improving plans and strategies

When a competitor came out with a better first-class seating option, Virgin Atlantic quickly changed its design plans and developed a first-class suite in advance of its original deadline.

"WHAT'S NEW" COMPANY

panies learn better ways of achieving goals.[28] For example, Joe Ferry's design team at VIRGIN ATLANTIC AIRWAYS was charged with coming up with a new reclining sleeper seat for use in both the first- and business-class sections. Even though sleeper seats were common in first class, no one was using them in business class. Virgin hoped its plan to move the plush seats into business class would give it an edge against the competition. But the year Virgin started design and development, chief competitor British Airways launched a truly flat bed (not just a reclining seat) in business class, making Virgin's plan all but useless. Compounding Virgin's woes were customers complaining about sliding and discomfort when using the seat in the reclining position. Ferry describes the situation like this: "We were an also-ran, which didn't really sit well with us." So Virgin changed the plan and decided to focus on overhauling its first class seating well before it needed to be. This time, the airline asked Ferry's team to change from designing a seat to designing a suite and allocated $127 million to the project. Different from the first attempt, the seats in Virgin's so-called upper-class suite have been a hit with customers. That's because the new suite seats use two types of foam—one for sitting, one for sleeping—so that passengers are comfortable in both positions (no more sliding). Virgin expected the change in plan to increase market share by 1 percent, but only two years after launch, the new seats have allowed the company to exceed that goal.[29]

Review 2: **How to Make a Plan That Works**

There are five steps to making a plan that works: (1) Set S.M.A.R.T. goals—goals that are **S**pecific, **M**easurable, **A**ttainable, **R**ealistic, and **T**imely. (2) Develop commitment to the goals from the people who contribute to goal achievement. Managers can increase workers' goal commitment by encouraging worker participation in goal setting, making goals public, and getting top management to show support for workers' goals. (3) Develop action plans for goal accomplishment. (4) Track progress toward goal achievement by setting both proximal and distal goals and by providing workers with regular performance feedback. (5) Maintain flexibility. Keeping options open through options-based planning and seeking continuous improvement through learning-based planning help organizations maintain flexibility as they plan.

3 Planning from Top to Bottom

Planning works best when the goals and action plans at the bottom and middle of the organization support the goals and action plans at the top of the organization. In other words, planning works best when everybody pulls in the same direction. Exhibit 5.5 illustrates this planning continuity, beginning at the top with a clear

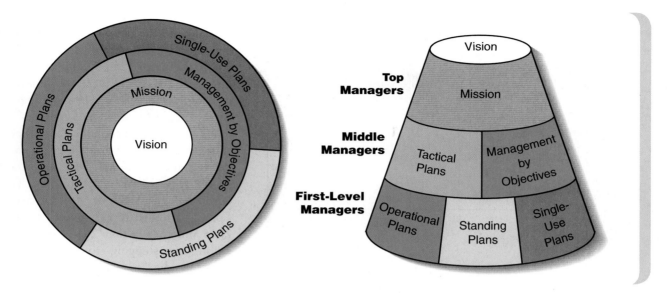

definition of the company vision and ending at the bottom with the execution of operational plans.

Let's see how **3.1 top managers create the organizational vision and mission, 3.2 middle managers develop tactical plans and use management by objectives to motivate employee efforts toward the overall vision and mission,** *and* **3.3 first-level managers use operational, single-use, and standing plans to implement the tactical plans.**

Exhibit 5.5

Planning from Top to Bottom

3.1 Starting at the Top

As shown in Exhibit 5.6, top management is responsible for developing long-term **strategic plans** that make clear how the company will serve customers and position itself against competitors in the next two to five years. (The strategic planning and management process is examined in its entirety in Chapter 6.) Strategic planning begins with the creation of an organizational vision and an organizational mission.

A **vision** is a statement of a company's purpose or reason for existing.[30] Vision statements should be brief—no more than two sentences. They should also be enduring, inspirational, clear, and consistent with widely shared company beliefs and values. An excellent example of a well-crafted vision statement is that of AVON, the cosmetics company, shown in Exhibit 5.7. It guides everyone in the organization and provides a focal point for the delivery of beauty products and services to the customer, women around the world. The vision is the same whether Avon is selling lipstick to women in India, shampoo packets to women in the Amazon, or jewelry to women in the United States. Understanding the needs of women—globally—does not change. Furthermore, Avon's vision is clear, inspirational, and consistent with Avon's company values and the principles that guide the company, also shown in Exhibit 5.7. Other examples of organizational visions that have been particularly effective include Walt Disney Company's "to make people happy" and Schlage Lock Company's "to make the world more secure."[31]

The **mission**, which flows from the vision, is a more specific goal that unifies company-wide efforts, stretches and challenges the organization, and possesses a finish line and a time frame. For example, in 1961, President John F. Kennedy

strategic plans overall company plans that clarify how the company will serve customers and position itself against competitors over the next two to five years

vision an inspirational statement of an organization's enduring purpose

mission a statement of a company's overall goal that unifies company-wide efforts toward its vision, stretches and challenges the organization, and possesses a finish line and a time frame

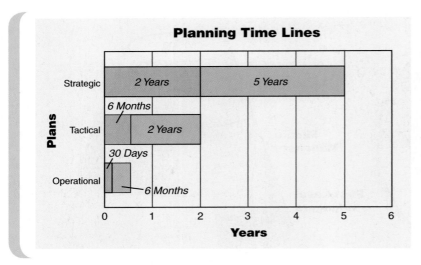

Planning Time Lines

Plans: Strategic, Tactical, Operational (vertical axis)

- Strategic: 2 Years, 5 Years
- 6 Months
- Tactical: 2 Years
- 30 Days
- Operational
- 6 Months

Years (horizontal axis): 0, 1, 2, 3, 4, 5, 6

Exhibit 5.6

Time Lines for Strategic, Tactical, and Operational Plans

"WHAT'S NEW" COMPANY

tactical plans plans created and implemented by middle managers that specify how the company will use resources, budgets, and people over the next six months to two years to accomplish specific goals within its mission

management by objectives (MBO) a four-step process in which managers and employees discuss and select goals, develop tactical plans, and meet regularly to review progress toward goal accomplishment

Exhibit 5.7

Avon's Vision and Values

established an organizational mission for **NASA** with this simple statement: "Achieving the goal, before this decade is out, of landing a man on the moon and returning him safely to earth."[32] NASA achieved this goal on July 20, 1969, when astronaut Neil Armstrong walked on the moon. Once a mission has been accomplished, a new one should be chosen. Again, however, the new mission must grow out of the organization's vision, which does not change significantly over time. For example, NASA's new mission is to return to the moon "as early as 2015 and no later than 2020" and to use the moon "as a stepping stone for more ambitious missions" to Mars and beyond."[33]

3.2 Bending in the Middle

Middle management is responsible for developing and carrying out tactical plans to accomplish the organization's mission. **Tactical plans** specify how a company will use resources, budgets, and people to accomplish specific goals within its mission. Whereas strategic plans and objectives are used to focus company efforts over the next two to five years, tactical plans and objectives are used to direct behavior, efforts, and attention over the next six months to two years. For example, Craig Knouf, CEO of Associated Business Systems, a 110-person business that sells office equipment in Portland, Oregon, reviews his company's 30-page business plan monthly, semiannually, and annually to compare the company's actual performance with the goals set forth in the plan. When Knouf noticed that over a six-month period the company had sold more high-volume scanners than before, he changed his business plan to put more emphasis on scanners and scanning software. As a result, sales of scanning products, which will double this year over last, now account for one-third of all sales. Working without his business plan, says Knouf, "would be like driving a car with no steering wheel."[34]

Management by objectives is a management technique often used to develop and carry out tactical plans. **Management by objectives**, or MBO, is a four-step process in which managers and their employees (1) discuss possible goals; (2) participatively select goals that are challenging, attainable, and consistent with the company's overall goals; (3) jointly develop tactical plans that lead to the accomplishment of tactical goals and objectives; and (4) meet regularly to review progress toward accomplishment of those goals. Lee Iacocca, the CEO who brought the former Chrysler Corporation back from the verge of bankruptcy, credits MBO (though he called it a "quarterly review system") for his 30 years of extraordinary success as a manager. Iacocca says, "Over the years, I've regularly asked my key people—and I've had

The Avon Vision	To be the company that best understands and satisfies the product, service and self-fulfillment needs of women—globally.
The Five Values of Avon	TRUST, RESPECT, BELIEF, HUMILITY, INTEGRITY.

Source: http://www.avoncompany.com/responsibility/values.html

MANAGEMENT BY OBJECTIVES

For years, both managers and management researchers have wondered how much effect planning has on organizational performance, or indeed if it has any effect at all. While proponents argued that planning encourages workers to work hard, persist in their efforts, engage in behaviors directly related to goal accomplishment, and develop better strategies for achieving goals, opponents argued that planning impedes organizational change and adaptation, creates the illusion of managerial control, and artificially separates thinkers and doers.

Now, however, the results from 70 different organizations strongly support the effectiveness of management by objectives (that is, short-term planning).

MANAGEMENT BY OBJECTIVES (MBO)

Management by objectives is a process in which managers and subordinates at all levels in a company sit down together to jointly set goals, share information and discuss strategies that could lead to goal achievement, and regularly meet to review progress toward accomplishing those goals. Thus, MBO is based on goals, participation, and feedback. On average, companies that effectively use MBO outproduce those that don't use MBO by an incredible 44.6 percent. And in companies where top management is committed to MBO, that is, where objective setting begins at the top, the average increase in performance is an even more astounding 56.5 percent. By contrast, when top management does not participate in or support MBO, the average increase in productivity is only 6.1 percent. In all, there is a 97 percent chance that companies that use MBO will outperform those that don't! Thus, MBO can make a very big difference to the companies that use it.[35]

When done right, MBO is an extremely effective method of tactical planning. Still, MBO is not without disadvantages.[36] Some MBO programs involve excessive paperwork, requiring managers to file annual statements of plans and objectives, plus quarterly or semiannual written reviews assessing goal progress. Today, however, electronic and web-based management systems and software make it easier for managers and employees to set goals, link them to the organization's strategic direction, and continuously track and evaluate their progress.[37] Another difficulty is that managers are frequently reluctant to give employees feedback about their performance. A third disadvantage is that managers and employees sometimes have difficulty agreeing on goals. And when employees are forced to accept goals that they don't want, goal commitment and employee effort suffer. Last, because MBO focuses on quantitative, easily measured goals, employees may neglect important but unmeasured parts of their jobs. In other words, if your job performance is judged only by whether you reduce costs by 3 percent or raise revenues by 5 percent, then you are unlikely to give high priority to the unmeasured but still important parts of your job, such as mentoring new employees or sharing knowledge and skills with coworkers.

them ask *their* key people, and so on down the line—a few basic questions: 'What are your objectives for the next ninety days? What are your plans, your priorities, your hopes? And how do you intend to go about achieving them?'"[38]

> **Working without his business plan, says Knouf, "would be like driving a car with no steering wheel."**

3.3 Finishing at the Bottom

Lower-level managers are responsible for developing and carrying out **operational plans**, which are the day-to-day plans for producing or delivering the organization's products and services. Operational plans direct the behavior, efforts, and priorities of operative employees for periods ranging from 30 days to six months. There are three kinds of operational plans: single-use plans, standing plans, and budgets.

Single-use plans deal with unique, one-time-only events. For example, PHILIP MORRIS is relocating its headquarters and 682 employees from Park Avenue in New York City to Henrico County, Virginia. Although the move will cost $120 million, the company will save $60 million a year in operating costs. While stressing that this was a "difficult decision to make because of our company's long corporate history in New York City and the impact it will have on our employees," Philip Morris's chairman and CEO says, "This move will help to streamline our business operations, increase efficiencies, and deliver significant cost savings over the long run."[39]

Unlike single-use plans that are created, carried out, and then never used again, **standing plans** save managers time because once the plans are created, they can be used repeatedly to handle frequently recurring events. If you encounter a problem that you've seen before, someone in your company has probably written a standing plan that explains how to address it. There are three kinds of standing plans: policies, procedures, and rules and regulations.

Policies indicate the general course of action that company managers should take in response to a particular event or situation. A well-written policy will also specify why the policy exists and what outcome the policy is intended to produce. Because the average employee surfs the Internet 11.1 hours per week, many companies have policies of either monitoring or blocking access to non-work-related websites. After its monitoring policy failed, CHAPARRAL ENERGY, an oil and gas company, switched to software that blocks access to religious, political, or sexually oriented websites. Systems engineer Richard Underwood explains, "Out in the field offices [where oil and gas exploration occurs], there was an established rule that they weren't going by the [monitoring] rule. We wanted to make sure policies were followed."[40] Employee web surfing has now dropped from an hour to less than 15 minutes a day.

Procedures are more specific than policies because they indicate the series of steps that should be taken in response to a particular event. A manufacturer's procedure for handling defective products might include the following steps. Step 1: Rejected material is locked in a secure area with "reject" documentation attached. Step 2: Material Review Board (MRB) identifies the defect and how far outside the standard the rejected products are. Step 3: MRB determines the disposition of the defective product as either scrap or as rework. Step 4: Scrap is either discarded or recycled, and rework is sent back through the production line to be fixed. Step 5: If delays in delivery will result, MRB member notifies customer.[41]

Rules and regulations are even more specific than procedures because they specify what must happen or not happen. They describe precisely how a particular action should be performed. For instance, many companies have rules and regulations forbidding managers from writing job reference letters for employees who have worked at their firms because a negative reference may prompt a former employee to sue for defamation of character.[42]

Budgets are the third kind of operational plan. **Budgeting** is quantitative planning because it forces managers to decide how to allocate available money to best accomplish company goals. According to Jan King, author of *Business Plans to Game*

operational plans day-to-day plans, developed and implemented by lower-level managers, for producing or delivering the organization's products and services over a 30-day to six-month period

single-use plans plans that cover unique, one-time-only events

standing plans plans used repeatedly to handle frequently recurring events

policy a standing plan that indicates the general course of action that should be taken in response to a particular event or situation

procedure a standing plan that indicates the specific steps that should be taken in response to a particular event

rules and regulations standing plans that describe how a particular action should be performed, or what must happen or not happen in response to a particular event

budgeting quantitative planning through which managers decide how to allocate available money to best accomplish company goals

Plans, "Money sends a clear message about your priorities. Budgets act as a language for communicating your goals to others." For example, Exhibit 5.8 shows the operating budget outlays for the U.S. federal government. Together, social programs (Social Security and income security, or welfare) and health-care programs (Medicare and health) account for nearly 60 percent of the federal budget. Budgeting is a critical management task—one that most managers could do better. For more detailed information about budgeting, see *Essential Managers: Managing Budgets* by Stephen Brookson or *Budgeting Basics & Beyond: A Complete Step-by-Step Guide for Nonfinancial Managers* by Jae K. Shim and Joel G. Siegel. Both books are written for budget beginners.

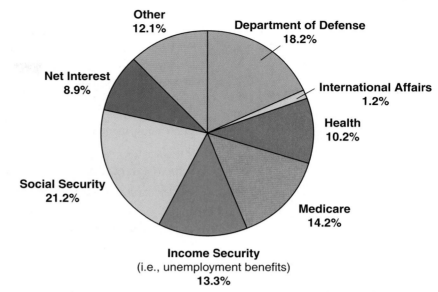

Source: "Table B-80. Federal Receipts and Outlays, by Major Category, and Surplus or Deficit, Fiscal Years 1940–2007," Economic Report of the President: 2006 Report Spreadsheet Tables, available at www.gpoaccess.gov/eop/2006/B80.xls.

Exhibit 5.8

2007 U.S. Federal Government Budget Outlays

Review 3: Planning from Top to Bottom

Proper planning requires that the goals at the bottom and middle of the organization support the objectives at the top of the organization. Top management develops strategic plans that indicate how a company will serve customers and position itself against competitors over a period of two to five years. Strategic planning starts with the creation of an organizational vision and mission. Middle managers use techniques like management by objectives to develop tactical plans that direct behavior, efforts, and priorities over the next six months to two years. Finally, lower-level managers develop operational plans that guide daily activities in producing or delivering an organization's products and services. Operational plans typically span periods ranging from 30 days to six months. There are three kinds of operational plans: single-use plans, standing plans (policies, procedures, and rules and regulations), and budgets.

WHAT IS RATIONAL DECISION MAKING?

Imagine that your boss asks you for a recommendation on outfitting the sales force, many of whom travel regularly, with new computers. She asks you to prepare a report that details the problems the sales team has been having with its computers and summarizes both current and future computer needs. You need to come up with at least five plans or options for getting computers to help members of the sales team do their job as efficiently as possible no matter where they are.

When your boss delegated this "computer problem," what she really wanted from you is a rational decision. **Decision making** is the process of choosing a solution from available alternatives.[43] **Rational decision making** is a systematic process in which managers define problems, evaluate alternatives, and choose optimal solutions that provide maximum benefits to their organizations. Thus, your boss expects you to define and analyze the computer problem and explore alternatives. Furthermore, your solution has to be "optimal," because the department is going to live with the computer equipment you recommend for the next three years.

After reading the next two sections, you should be able to

4 explain the steps and limits to rational decision making.

5 explain how group decisions and group decision-making techniques can improve decision making.

decision making the process of choosing a solution from available alternatives

rational decision making a systematic process of defining problems, evaluating alternatives, and choosing optimal solutions

problem a gap between a desired state and an existing state

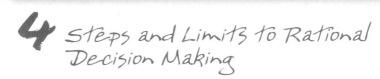

4 Steps and Limits to Rational Decision Making

Exhibit 5.9 shows the six steps of the rational decision-making process. Let's learn more about each of these steps: **4.1 define the problem, 4.2 identify decision criteria, 4.3 weight the criteria, 4.4 generate alternative courses of action, 4.5 evaluate each alternative,** *and* **4.6 compute the optimal decision.** *Then we'll consider* **4.7 limits to rational decision making.**

4.1 Define the Problem

The first step in decision making is identifying and defining the problem. A **problem** exists when there is a gap between a desired state (what is wanted) and an existing state (the situation you are actually facing). Because it can hold 550 to 850 passengers, AIRBUS's new A380 super-jumbo jetliner could generate tremendous revenues for airlines. But with wings larger than a small passenger jet and wheels so large that it takes a crane to move them, the A380 was several tons too heavy. Randy Baseler of Boeing, Airbus's competitor, says, "If the plane's heavier, it consumes more fuel. That drives up landing and navigation fees, and also maintenance costs, especially for wheels, tires and brakes."[44] Fearing exorbitant costs, the airlines told Airbus they wouldn't buy the A380 unless it was substantially lighter.[45]

The existence of a gap between an existing state and a desired state is no guarantee that managers will make decisions to solve problems. Three things must occur for this to happen.[46] First, managers have to be aware of the gap. They have to know there is a problem before they can begin solving it. For example, after noticing that people were spending more money on their pets, a new dog food company created an expensive, high-quality dog food. To emphasize its quality, the dog food was sold in cans and bags with gold labels, red letters, and detailed information about its benefits and nutrients. Yet the product did not sell very well, and the company went out of business in less than a year. Its founders didn't understand why. When they asked a manager at a competing dog food company what their biggest mistake had

Exhibit 5.9

Steps of the Rational Decision-Making Process

1 Define the Problem

2 Identify Decision Criteria

3 Weight the Criteria

4 Generate Alternative Courses of Action

5 Evaluate Each Alternative

6 Compute the Optimal Decision

been, the answer was, "Simple. You didn't have a picture of a dog on the package."[47] This problem would have been easy to solve, if management had only been aware of it.

Being aware of the gap between a desired state and an existing state isn't enough to begin the decision-making process. Managers also have to be motivated to reduce the gap. For example, businesspeople have complained for years about unreasonable workplace regulation. Nevertheless, the **U.S. CONGRESS** was not interested in solving this "problem" until the Congressional Accountability Act subjected Congress to the same laws as private businesses. Now, like any business, Congress must give overtime pay to anyone who works more than 40 hours a week. Legislative and office assistants, all of whom used to work 60 hours a week, are now limited by law to just 40. To limit hours and overtime pay, employees are not allowed to work during lunch (even if they want to). Computers are turned off. Phones go unanswered. Employees can't even watch C-Span while eating their sandwiches. At 6:00 PM, office managers walk through the offices, ringing loud bells and turning off lights to force employees who want to keep working to go home. Not surprisingly, these changes have motivated many in Congress to take a second look at the unintended effects that workplace laws and regulations have on businesses.[48]

REUTERS/LANDOV

The Airbus A380 is the largest passenger jet ever built. It's understandable that potential buyers of the two-story super-jumbo jet would be concerned about weight and fuel usage. Nose to tail, it's longer than this section of terminal where it's gated, and its 263-foot wingspan is nearly as long as a football field.

Finally, it's not enough to be aware of a problem and be motivated to solve it. Managers must also have the knowledge, skills, abilities, and resources to fix the problem. So, how did Airbus reduce the weight of its A380 super-jumbo jet? Engineers achieved the biggest weight savings by substituting a light carbon-fiber composite material for heavier aluminum in the rear fuselage and the large structural ribs in the wings. Altogether, these changes and others reduced the A380's weight by four tons.[49]

4.2 Identify Decision Criteria

Decision criteria are the standards used to guide judgments and decisions. Typically, the more criteria a potential solution meets, the better that solution will be.

Let's return to the employee who was given the responsibility for making a rational decision about the office computer setup. What general factors would be important when purchasing computers for the office? Reliability, price, warranty, on-site service, and compatibility with existing software, printers, and computers would all be important, but you must also consider the technical details. What specific factors would you want the office computers to have? Well, with technology changing so quickly, you'll probably want to buy computers with as much capability and flexibility as you can afford. Today, laptops account for over 25 percent of the market and their popularity is growing rapidly. They come in four distinct model types. There are budget models that are good for routine office work, but are usually saddled with a slower processor; workhorse models that are not lightweight, but have everything included; slim models for traveling but that usually require an external drive to read/write to a DVD/CD; and tablet models that include such items as handwriting-recognition software.[50] What will the users really need? Will they need to burn CDs and DVDs, or just read them? How much memory will the users need? How many files and programs will they need to store on their hard drive? What about Internet

"WHAT'S NEW" COMPANY

The existence of a gap between an existing state and a desired state is no guarantee that managers will make decisions to solve problems.

decision criteria the standards used to guide judgments and decisions connectivity? Answering questions like these will help you identify the criteria that will guide the purchase of the new equipment.

4.3 Weight the Criteria

After identifying decision criteria, the next step is deciding which criteria are more or less important. Although there are numerous mathematical models for weighting decision criteria, all require the decision maker to provide an initial ranking of the criteria. Some use **absolute comparisons**, in which each criterion is compared with a standard or ranked on its own merits. For example, *Consumer Reports* uses this checklist when it rates and recommends new cars: predicted reliability, previous owners' satisfaction, predicted depreciation (the price you could expect if you sold the car), ability to avoid an accident, fuel economy, crash protection, acceleration, ride, and front seat comfort.[51]

Exhibit 5.10 shows the absolute weights that someone buying a car might use. Because these weights are absolute, each criterion is judged on its own importance, using a five-point scale, with "5" representing "critically important" and "1" representing "completely unimportant." In this instance, predicted reliability, fuel economy, and front seat comfort were rated most important, and acceleration and predicted depreciation were rated least important.

Another method uses **relative comparisons**, in which each criterion is compared directly with every other criterion.[52] For example, Exhibit 5.11 shows six criteria that someone might use when buying a house. Moving down the first column of Exhibit 5.11, we see that the time of the daily commute has been rated less important (−1) than school system quality; more important (+1) than having an inground pool, sun room, or a quiet street, and just as important as the house being brand new (0). Total weights, which are obtained by summing the scores in each column, indicate that the daily commute and school system quality are the most important factors to this home buyer, while an inground pool, sun room, and a quiet street are the least important. So with relative comparison, criteria are directly compared with each other.

absolute comparisons a process in which each decision criterion is compared to a standard or ranked on its own merits

relative comparisons a process in which each decision criterion is compared directly with every other criterion

Exhibit 5.10

Absolute Weighting of Decision Criteria for a Car Purchase

Highlighted numbers indicate how important the particular criterion is to a hypothetical car buyer. Your rankings might be very different.					
5 critically important					
4 important					
3 somewhat important					
2 not very important					
1 completely unimportant					
1. Predicted reliability	1	2	3	4	**5**
2. Owner satisfaction	1	**2**	3	4	5
3. Predicted depreciation	**1**	2	3	4	5
4. Avoiding accidents	1	2	3	**4**	5
5. Fuel economy	1	2	3	4	**5**
6. Crash protection	1	2	3	**4**	5
7. Acceleration	**1**	2	3	4	5
8. Ride	1	2	**3**	4	5
9. Front seat comfort	1	2	3	4	**5**

4.4 Generate Alternative Courses of Action

After identifying and weighting the criteria that will guide the decision-making process, the next step is to identify possible courses of action that could solve the problem. In general, at this step, the idea is to generate as many alternatives as possible. For instance, let's assume that you're trying to select a city in Europe to be the location of a major office. After meeting with your staff, you generate a list of possible alternatives: Amsterdam, the Netherlands; Barcelona or Madrid, Spain; Berlin or Frankfurt, Germany; Brussels, Belgium; London, England; Milan, Italy; Paris, France; and Zurich, Switzerland.

4.5 Evaluate Each Alternative

The next step is to systematically evaluate each alternative against each criterion. Because of the amount of information that must be collected, this step can take much longer and be much more expensive than other steps in the decision-making process. For example, in selecting a European city for your office, you could contact economic development offices in each city, systematically interview businesspeople or executives who operate there, retrieve and use published government data on each location, or rely on published studies such as Cushman & Wakefield Healy & Baker's *European Cities Monitor*, which conducts an annual survey of more than 500 senior European executives who rate 30 European cities on 12 business-related criteria.[53]

No matter how you gather the information, once you have it, the key is to systematically use that information to evaluate each alternative against each criterion. For example, Exhibit 5.12 shows how each of the 10 cities on your staff's list fared on each of the 12 criteria (higher scores are better), from qualified staff to freedom from pollution. Although Paris has good access to markets and very good travel to and from the city, it has a poor business climate and relatively few different languages are spoken in its business community. On the other hand, Barcelona has the lowest costs for employing staff, but weak access to markets and poor ease of travel to and from the city.

HOME CHARACTERISTICS	DC	SSQ	IP	SR	QS	NBH
Daily commute (DC)		+1	−1	−1	−1	0
School system quality (SSQ)	−1		−1	−1	−1	−1
Inground pool (IP)	+1	+1		0	0	+1
Sun room (SR)	+1	+1	0		0	0
Quiet street (QS)	+1	+1	0	0		0
Newly built house (NBH)	0	+1	−1	0	0	
Total weight	+2	+5	−3	−2	−2	0

Exhibit 5.11

Relative Comparison of Home Characteristics

4.6 Compute the Optimal Decision

The final step in the decision-making process is to compute the optimal decision by determining each alternative's optimal value. This is done by multiplying the rating for each criterion (Step 5) by the weight for that criterion (Step 3), and then summing those scores for each alternative course of action that you generated (Step 4). For example, the 500 executives participating in Cushman & Wakefield Healy & Baker's survey of the best European cities for business rated the 12 decision criteria in terms of importance as follows: qualified staff (57 percent felt this was important), access to major markets (60 percent), travel to and from the city (52 percent), good telecommunications (50 percent), positive business climate (32 percent), cost of staff (35 percent), cost and value of office space (31 percent), availability of office space (30 percent), travel within the city (22 percent), languages spoken in the business community (24 percent), quality of life (16 percent), and freedom from pollution (13 percent). Those weights are then multiplied by the ratings in each category. For example, Amsterdam's optimal value of 1.68 (that is, its weighted average) is determined by the following calculation:

$$(0.57 \times 0.35) + (0.60 \times 0.39) + (0.52 \times 0.66) + (0.50 \times 0.32) +$$
$$(0.32 \times 0.34) + (0.35 \times 0.16) + (0.31 \times 0.28) + (0.30 \times 0.26) +$$
$$(0.22 \times 0.34) + (0.24 \times 1.00) + (0.16 \times 0.30) + (0.13 \times 0.41) = 1.68$$

The weighted average (or optimal) scores in the next to last row of Exhibit 5.12 show that London clearly ranks as the best location for your company's new European office

	WEIGHTS	Amsterdam	Barcelona	Berlin	Brussels	Frankfurt	London	Madrid	Milan	Paris	Zurich
QUALIFIED STAFF	57%	.35	.30	.40	.44	.58	1.32	.30	.33	.78	.41
ACCESS TO MARKETS	60%	.39	.30	.28	.54	.71	1.36	.41	.38	1.18	.24
TRAVEL TO/ FROM CITY	52%	.66	.26	.19	.55	1.19	1.74	.30	.23	1.42	.27
TELECOMMU- NICATIONS	50%	.32	.21	.33	.40	.58	1.22	.24	.20	.80	.34
BUSINESS CLIMATE	32%	.34	.40	.36	.35	.11	.51	.52	.11	.20	.51
COST OF STAFF	35%	.16	.73	.27	.19	.05	.15	.60	.21	.11	.07
COST & VALUE OF OFFICE SPACE	31%	.28	.57	.52	.44	.26	.18	.48	.17	.20	.18
AVAILABLE OFFICE SPACE	30%	.26	.46	.63	.42	.45	.55	.58	.21	.39	.25
TRAVEL WITHIN CITY	22%	.34	.45	.53	.34	.41	1.09	.38	.19	1.19	.38
LANGUAGES SPOKEN	24%	1.00	.22	.34	1.13	.53	1.41	.21	.17	.50	.66
QUALITY OF LIFE	16%	.30	1.21	.24	.38	.14	.39	.61	.26	.67	.55
FREEDOM FROM POLLUTION	13%	.41	.44	.17	.18	.12	.06	.16	.03	.10	.94
WEIGHTED AVERAGE SCORE		1.68	1.69	1.48	1.93	2.20	4.17	1.63	.99	3.07	1.36
RANKING		6	5	8	4	3	1	7	11	2	10

Source: "European Cities Monitor," Cushman & Wakefield Healy & Baker, available at http://www.cushmanwakefield.com/cwglobal/docviewer/European%20Cities%20Monitor.pdf?id=ca1500006&repositoryKey=CoreRepository&itemDesc=document.

Exhibit 5.12

Criteria Ratings Used to Determine the Best Locations in Europe for a New Office

because of its large number of qualified staff; easy access to markets; outstanding ease of travel to, from, and within the city; excellent telecommunications; and top-notch business climate.

4.7 Limits to Rational Decision Making

In general, managers who diligently complete all six steps of the rational decision-making model will make better decisions than those who don't. So, when they can, managers should try to follow the steps in the rational decision-making model, especially for big decisions with long-range consequences.

It's highly doubtful, however, that rational decision making can always help managers choose *optimal* solutions that provide *maximum* benefits to their organizations.

The terms *optimal* and *maximum* suggest that rational decision making leads to perfect or near-perfect decisions. Of course, for managers to make perfect decisions, they have to operate in perfect worlds with no real-world constraints. For example, in an optimal world, the manager who asked you to develop a computer strategy for the sales team would be able to clearly define which salespeople needed budget laptops, slim laptops, workhorse laptops, or tablet laptops and simply ensure that all team members received exactly what they needed to do their jobs effectively. In developing your solutions, you would not have been constrained by price or time. Furthermore, without any constraints, the manager could identify and weight an extensive list of decision criteria, generate a complete list of possible solutions, and then test and evaluate each computer against each decision criterion. Finally, the manager would have the necessary experience and knowledge with computers to easily make sense of all these sophisticated tests and information.

Of course, it never works like that in the real world. Managers face time and money constraints. They often don't have time to make extensive lists of decision criteria. And they often don't have the resources to test all possible solutions against all possible criteria.

The rational decision-making model describes the way decisions *should* be made. In other words, decision makers wanting to make optimal decisions *should not* have to face time and cost constraints. They *should* have unlimited resources and time to generate and test all alternative solutions against all decision criteria. And they *should* be willing to recommend any decision that produces optimal benefits for the company, even if that decision would harm their own jobs or departments. Of course, very few managers actually make rational decisions the way they *should*. The way in which managers actually make decisions is more accurately described as bounded (or limited) rationality. **Bounded rationality** means that managers try to take a rational approach to decision making, but are restricted by real-world constraints, incomplete and imperfect information, and their own limited decision-making capabilities.

In theory, fully rational decision makers **maximize** decisions by choosing the optimal solution. In practice, however, limited resources, along with attention, memory, and expertise problems, make it nearly impossible for managers to maximize decisions. Consequently, most managers don't maximize—they "satisfice." Whereas maximizing is choosing the best alternative, **satisficing** is choosing a "good enough" alternative. With 24 decision criteria, 50 alternative computers to choose from, two computer labs with hundreds of thousands of dollars of equipment, and unlimited time and money, the manager could test all alternatives against all decision criteria and choose the "perfect PC." In reality, however, the manager's limited time, money, and expertise mean that only a few alternatives will be assessed against a few decision criteria. In practice, the manager will visit two or three computer or electronic stores, read a couple of recent computer reviews, and get bids from a few local computer stores that sell complete computer systems at competitive prices, as well as from Dell, Lenovo, Gateway, and Hewlett-Packard. The decision will be complete when the manager finds a "good enough" laptop computer that meets a few decision criteria.

© EMPICS/LANDOV

bounded rationality a decision-making process restricted in the real world by limited resources, incomplete and imperfect information, and managers' limited decision-making capabilities

maximizing choosing the best alternative

satisficing choosing a "good enough" alternative

doing the right thing

PLUS—A Process for Ethical Decision Making

People are often unsure how to include ethics in their decision-making processes. To help them, the Ethics Resource Center recommends using the following PLUS guidelines throughout the various steps of the rational decision-making model:

- **P is for policies.** Is your decision consistent with your organization's policies, procedures, and guidelines?
- **L is for legal.** Is your decision acceptable under applicable laws and regulations?
- **U is for universal.** Is your decision consistent with your organization's values and principles?
- **S is for self.** Does your decision satisfy your personal sense of right, good, and fair?

The PLUS guidelines can't guarantee ethical decisions, but they can help employees be more attentive to ethical issues as they define problems, evaluate alternatives, and choose solutions.[54]

Review 4: Steps and Limits to Rational Decision Making

Rational decision making is a six-step process in which managers define problems, evaluate alternatives, and compute optimal solutions. The first step is identifying and defining the problem. Problems exist where there is a gap between desired and existing states. Managers won't begin the decision-making process unless they are aware of the gap, motivated to reduce it, and possess the necessary resources to fix it. The second step is defining the decision criteria that are used when judging alternatives. In Step 3, an absolute or relative comparison process is used to rate the importance of the decision criteria. Step 4 involves generating as many alternative courses of action (that is, solutions) as possible. Potential solutions are assessed in Step 5 by systematically gathering information and evaluating each alternative against each criterion. In Step 6, criterion ratings and weights are used to compute the optimal value for each alternative course of action. Rational managers then choose the alternative with the highest optimal value.

The rational decision-making model describes how decisions should be made in an ideal world without limits. However, bounded rationality recognizes that in the real world, managers' limited resources, incomplete and imperfect information, and limited decision-making capabilities restrict their decision-making processes. These limitations often prevent managers from being rational decision makers.

5 Using Groups to Improve Decision Making

According to a study reported in *Fortune* magazine, 91 percent of U.S. companies use teams and groups to solve specific problems (that is, make decisions).[55] Why so many? Because when done properly, group decision making can lead to much better decisions than decisions typically made by individuals. In fact, numerous studies show that groups consistently outperform individuals on complex tasks.

*Let's explore the **5.1 advantages and pitfalls of group decision making** and see how the following group decision-making methods—**5.2 structured conflict**, **5.3 the nominal group technique**, **5.4 the Delphi technique**, **5.5 the stepladder technique**, and **5.6 electronic brainstorming**—can be used to improve decision making.*

5.1 Advantages and Pitfalls of Group Decision Making

Groups can do a much better job than individuals in two important steps of the decision-making process: defining the problem and generating alternative solutions. Four reasons explain why.

First, because group members usually possess different knowledge, skills, abilities, and experiences, groups are able to view problems from multiple perspectives. Being able to view problems from different perspectives, in turn, can help groups perform better on complex tasks and make better decisions than individuals.[56]

Second, groups can find and access much more information than can individuals alone. At *1-800-Got-Junk?*, a national chain of over 200 locations that provides efficient, timely junk removal, applicants are not interviewed by one person at a time. Instead, each applicant is interviewed by a group of eight people with eight different areas of expertise, who, together, assess the candidate immediately following the interview. CEO Brian Scudamore believes there is wisdom in crowds, and relying on groups to conduct interviews has helped his company maintain a remarkably low employee turnover rate of only 1.4 percent.[57]

Third, the increased knowledge and information available to groups make it easier for them to generate more alternative solutions. Studies show that generating lots of alternative solutions is critical to improving the quality of decisions. Fourth, if groups are involved in the decision-making process, group members will be more committed to making chosen solutions work.

Although groups can do a better job of defining problems and generating alternative solutions, group decision making is subject to some pitfalls that can quickly erase these gains. One possible pitfall is groupthink. **Groupthink** occurs in highly cohesive groups when group members feel intense pressure to agree with each other so that the group can approve a proposed solution.[58] Because groupthink leads to consideration of a limited number of solutions and restricts discussion of any considered solutions, it usually results in poor decisions. Groupthink is most likely to occur under the following conditions:

- *The group is insulated from others with different perspectives.*
- *The group leader begins by expressing a strong preference for a particular decision.*
- *The group has no established procedure for systematically defining problems and exploring alternatives.*
- *Group members have similar backgrounds and experiences.*[59]

Groupthink may be one of the reasons that Merck's prescription drug Vioxx stayed on the market for over five years despite fatal side effects. Merck, one of the largest drug makers in the world, viewed Vioxx as a miracle pain reliever, and over 100 million prescriptions for the drug were written in the five years it was on the market. The *New England Journal of Medicine*, however, had reported that Vioxx users suffered from significant heart problems almost from the beginning, and the drug was eventually withdrawn from the market. Court documents revealed that Merck's internal studies showed an association between Vioxx usage and an elevated incidence of heart attacks. Litigants allege that because the drug generated a substantial profit, managers chose to listen to positive feedback about how well the drug worked as a painkiller rather than act on the information about the drug's risky side effects. Merck disputes this, but the company is involved in nearly 50,000 Vioxx lawsuits.[60]

A second potential problem with group decision making is that it takes considerable time. Reconciling schedules so that group members can meet takes time.

groupthink a barrier to good decision making caused by pressure within the group for members to agree with each other

Google's Marissa Mayer uses six guidelines to keep the 70 meetings she holds each week on track.

Furthermore, it's a rare group that consistently holds productive task-oriented meetings to effectively work through the decision process. Some of the most common complaints about meetings (and thus decision making) are that the meeting's purpose is unclear, participants are unprepared, critical people are absent or late, conversation doesn't stay focused on the problem, and no one follows up on the decisions that were made. As Google's vice president of search products and user experience, Marissa Mayer holds over 70 meetings a week and is the last executive to hear a pitch before it is made to the cofounders. To keep meetings on track, Mayer has set down six guidelines. Meetings must (1) have a firm agenda and (2) an assigned note-taker. Meetings must occur (3) during established office hours, and (4) preferably in short, 10-minute micromeetings. Those running the meeting should (5) discourage office politics and rely on data, and above all, they should (6) stick to the clock. Mayer's guidelines help meetings stay focused and productive.[61]

A third possible pitfall to group decision making is that sometimes one or two people, perhaps the boss or a strong-willed, vocal group member, dominate group discussion, restricting consideration of different problem definitions and alternative solutions. Another potential problem is that, unlike with their own decisions and actions, group members may not feel accountable for the decisions made and actions taken by the group.

Although these pitfalls can lead to poor decision making, this doesn't mean that managers should avoid using groups to make decisions. When done properly, group decision making can lead to much better decisions. The pitfalls of group decision making are not inevitable. Managers can overcome most of them by using the various techniques described next.

5.2 Structured Conflict

Most people view conflict negatively. Yet the right kind of conflict can lead to much better group decision making. **C-type conflict**, or "cognitive conflict," focuses on problem- and issue-related differences of opinion.[62] In c-type conflict, group members disagree because their different experiences and expertise lead them to view the problem and its potential solutions differently. C-type conflict is also characterized by a willingness to examine, compare, and reconcile those differences to produce the best possible solution. **Alteon WebSystems**, now a division of Nortel Networks, makes critical use of c-type conflict. Top manager Dominic Orr described Alteon's c-type conflict this way:

> *People arrive with a proposal or a solution—and with the facts to support it. After an idea is presented, we open the floor to objective, and often withering, critiques. And if the idea collapses under scrutiny, we move on to another: no hard feelings. We're judging the idea, not the person. At the same time, we don't really try to regulate emotions. Passionate conflict means that we're getting somewhere, not that the discussion is out of control. But one person does act as referee—by asking basic questions like "Is this good for the customer?" or "Does it keep our time-to-market advantage intact?" By focusing relentlessly on the facts, we're able to see the strengths and weaknesses of an idea clearly and quickly.*[63]

c-type conflict (cognitive conflict)
disagreement that focuses on problem- and issue-related differences of opinion

By contrast, **a-type conflict**, meaning "affective conflict," refers to the emotional reactions that can occur when disagreements become personal rather than professional. A-type conflict often results in hostility, anger, resentment, distrust, cynicism, and apathy. Unlike c-type conflict, a-type conflict undermines team effectiveness by preventing teams from engaging in the activities characteristic of c-type conflict that are critical to team effectiveness. Examples of a-type conflict statements are "your idea," "our idea," "my department," "you don't know what you are talking about," or "you don't understand our situation." Rather than focusing on issues and ideas, these statements focus on individuals.[64]

Two methods of introducing structured c-type conflict into the group decision-making process are devil's advocacy and dialectical inquiry. **Devil's advocacy** creates c-type conflict by assigning an individual or a subgroup the role of critic. The following five steps establish a devil's advocacy program:

1. *Generate a potential solution.*
2. *Assign a devil's advocate to criticize and question the solution.*
3. *Present the critique of the potential solution to key decision makers.*
4. *Gather additional relevant information.*
5. *Decide whether to use, change, or not use the originally proposed solution.*[65]

Dialectical inquiry creates c-type conflict by forcing decision makers to state the assumptions of a proposed solution (a thesis) and then generate a solution that is the opposite (antithesis) of the proposed solution. The following are the five steps of the dialectical inquiry process:

1. *Generate a potential solution.*
2. *Identify the assumptions underlying the potential solution.*
3. *Generate a conflicting counterproposal based on the opposite assumptions.*
4. *Have advocates of each position present their arguments and engage in a debate in front of key decision makers.*
5. *Decide whether to use, change, or not use the originally proposed solution.*[66]

BMW uses dialectical inquiry in its design process, typically creating six internal design teams to compete against each other to design a new car. After a front-runner or leading design emerges from one of the teams, another team is assigned to design a car that is "diametrically opposed" to the leading design (Step 3 of the dialectical inquiry method).[67]

When properly used, both the devil's advocacy and dialectical inquiry approaches introduce c-type conflict into the decision-making process. Further, contrary to the common belief that conflict is bad, studies show that these methods lead to less a-type conflict, improved decision quality, and greater acceptance of decisions once they have been made.[68] See the "What Really Works" feature for more information on both techniques.

5.3 Nominal Group Technique

"Nominal" means "in name only." Accordingly, the **nominal group technique** received its name because it begins with "quiet time," in which group members independently write down as many problem definitions and alternative solutions as possible. In other words, the nominal group technique begins by having group members

> *The right kind of conflict can lead to much better group decision making.*

a-type conflict (affective conflict) disagreement that focuses on individuals or personal issues

devil's advocacy a decision-making method in which an individual or a subgroup is assigned the role of a critic

dialectical inquiry a decision-making method in which decision makers state the assumptions of a proposed solution (a thesis) and generate a solution that is the opposite (antithesis) of that solution

nominal group technique a decision-making method that begins and ends by having group members quietly write down and evaluate ideas to be shared with the group act as individuals. After the "quiet time," the group leader asks each group member to share one idea at a time with the group. As they are read aloud, ideas are posted on flipcharts or wallboards for all to see. This step continues until all ideas have been shared. In the next step, the group discusses the advantages and disadvantages of the ideas. The nominal group technique closes with a second "quiet time," in which group members independently rank the ideas presented. Group members then read their rankings aloud, and the idea with the highest average rank is selected.[69]

The nominal group technique improves group decision making by decreasing a-type conflict. In doing so, however, it also restricts c-type conflict. Consequently, the nominal group technique typically produces poorer decisions than do the devil's advocacy and dialectical inquiry approaches. Nonetheless, more than 80 studies have found that nominal groups produce better ideas than those produced by traditional groups.[70]

5.4 Delphi Technique

In the **Delphi technique**, the members of a panel of experts respond to questions and to each other until reaching agreement on an issue. The first step is to assemble a panel of experts. Unlike other approaches to group decision making, however, it isn't necessary to bring the panel members together in one place. Because the Delphi technique does not require the experts to leave their offices or disrupt their schedules, they are more likely to participate. For example, a colleague and I were asked by a local government agency to use a Delphi-technique to assess the "10 most important steps for small businesses." The first step was to assemble a panel of local top-level managers and CEOs.

The second step is to create a questionnaire consisting of a series of open-ended questions for the experts. For example, we asked our panel to answer these questions: "What is the most common mistake made by small-business persons?" "Right now, what do you think is the biggest threat to the survival of most small businesses?" "If you had one piece of advice to give to the owner of a small business, what would it be?"

In Step 3, the panel members' written responses are analyzed, summarized, and fed back to the panel for reactions until the members reach agreement. In our Delphi study, it took about a month to get the panel members' written responses to the first three questions. Then we summarized their responses in a brief report (no more than two pages). We sent the summary to the panel members and asked them to explain why they agreed or disagreed with these conclusions from the first round of questions. Asking the members why they agree or disagree is important because it helps uncover their unstated assumptions and beliefs. Again, this process of summarizing panel feedback and obtaining reactions to that feedback continues until the panel members reach agreement. For our study, it took just one more round for the panel members' to reach a consensus. In all, it took approximately three and a half months to complete our Delphi study.

5.5 Stepladder Technique

The stepladder technique improves group decision making by ensuring that each member's contributions are independent, and are considered and discussed by the group. As shown in Exhibit 5.13, the **stepladder technique** begins with discussion between two group members who share their thoughts, ideas, and recommendations before jointly making a tentative decision. At each step, as other group members are added to the discussion one at a time, like a stepladder, the existing group members take the time to listen to each new member's thoughts, ideas, and

Delphi technique a decision-making method in which members of a panel of experts respond to questions and to each other until reaching agreement on an issue

stepladder technique a decision-making method in which group members are added to a group discussion one at a time (like a stepladder). The existing group members listen to each new member's thoughts, ideas, and recommendations; then the group shares the ideas and suggestions that it had already considered, discusses the new and old ideas, and makes a decision.

DEVIL'S ADVOCACY, DIALECTICAL INQUIRY, AND CONSIDERING NEGATIVE CONSEQUENCES

Ninety percent of the decisions managers face are well-structured problems that recur frequently under conditions of certainty. For example, for most retailers, a customer's request for a refund on a returned item without a receipt is a well-structured problem. It happens every day (recurs frequently), and it's easy to determine if a customer has a receipt (condition of certainty).

Well-structured problems are solved with programmed decisions, in which a policy, procedure, or rule clearly specifies how to solve the problem. Thus, there's no mystery about what to do when someone shows up without a receipt: allow the item to be exchanged for one of similar value, but don't give a refund.

In some sense, programmed decisions really aren't decisions because anyone with experience knows what to do. No thought is required. What keeps managers up at night is the other 10 percent of problems. Ill-structured problems that are novel (no one's seen them before) and exist under conditions of uncertainty are solved with nonprogrammed decisions. Nonprogrammed decisions do not involve standard methods of resolution. Every time managers make a nonprogrammed decision, they have to figure out a new way of handling a new problem. That's what makes the decisions so tough.

Both the devil's advocacy and dialectical inquiry approaches to decision making, along with a related approach, considering negative consequences, can be used to improve nonprogrammed decision making. All three work because they force decision makers to identify and criticize the assumptions underlying the nonprogrammed decisions that they hope will solve ill-structured problems.

DEVIL'S ADVOCACY

There is a 58 percent chance that decision makers who use the devil's advocacy approach to criticize and question their

solutions will produce decisions that are better than decisions based on the advice of experts.

DIALECTICAL INQUIRY

There is a 55 percent chance that decision makers who use the dialectical inquiry approach to criticize and question their solutions will produce decisions that are better than decisions based on the advice of experts.

Note that each technique has been compared with decisions obtained by following experts' advice. So, although these probabilities of success, 55 percent and 58 percent, seem small, they very likely understate the effects of both techniques. In other words, the probabilities of better decisions would have been much larger if both techniques had been compared with unstructured decision-making processes.

GROUP DECISION MAKING AND CONSIDERING NEGATIVE CONSEQUENCES

Considering negative consequences, such as with a devil's advocate or via critical inquiry, means pointing out the potential disadvantages of proposed solutions. There is an 86 percent chance that groups that consider negative consequences will produce better decisions than those that don't.[71]

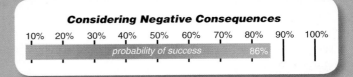

Managers should not use the Delphi technique for common decisions. Because it is a time-consuming, labor-intensive, and expensive process, the Delphi technique is best reserved for important long-term issues and problems. Nonetheless, the judgments and conclusions obtained from it are typically better than those you would get from one expert.

181

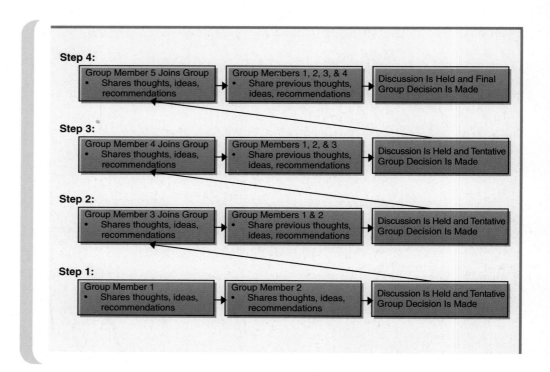

Exhibit 5.13

Stepladder Technique for Group Decision Making

recommendations. The existing members share the ideas and suggestions that they had already considered, and then the group discusses the new and old ideas and makes a tentative decision. This process (new member's ideas are heard, group shares previous ideas and suggestions, discussion is held, tentative group decision is made) continues until each group member's ideas have been discussed.

For the stepladder technique to work, group members must have enough time to consider the problem or decision on their own, to present their ideas to the group, and to thoroughly discuss all ideas and alternatives with the group at each step. Rushing through a step destroys the advantages of this technique. Also, groups must make sure that subsequent group members are completely unaware of previous discussions and suggestions. This will ensure that each member who joins the group brings truly independent thoughts and suggestions, thus greatly increasing the chances of making better decisions.

One study found that compared with traditional groups in which all group members are present for the entire discussion, groups using the stepladder technique produced significantly better decisions. Moreover, the stepladder groups performed better than the best individual member of their group 56 percent of the time, whereas traditional groups outperformed the best individual member of their group only 13 percent of the time.[72] Besides better performance, groups using the stepladder technique also generated more ideas and were more satisfied with the decision-making process. This technique also works particularly well with audio conferencing, in which geographically dispersed group members make decisions via a telephone conference call.[73]

5.6 Electronic Brainstorming

Brainstorming, in which group members build on others' ideas, is a technique for generating a large number of alternative solutions. Brainstorming has four rules:

1. The more ideas, the better.
2. All ideas are acceptable, no matter how wild or crazy they might seem.
3. Other group members' ideas should be used to come up with even more ideas.
4. Criticism or evaluation of ideas is not allowed.

Though brainstorming is great fun and can help managers generate a large number of alternative solutions, it does have a number of disadvantages. Fortunately, **electronic brainstorming**, in which group members use computers to communicate and generate alternative solutions, overcomes the disadvantages associated with face-to-face brainstorming.[74]

The first disadvantage that electronic brainstorming overcomes is **production blocking**, which occurs when you have an idea but have to wait to share it because someone else is already presenting an idea to the group. During this short delay, you may forget your idea or decide that it really wasn't worth sharing. With electronic brainstorming, production blocking doesn't happen. All group members are seated at computers, so everyone can type in ideas whenever they occur. There's no "waiting your turn" to be heard by the group.

The second disadvantage that electronic brainstorming overcomes is **evaluation apprehension**, that is, being afraid of what others will think of your ideas. With electronic brainstorming, all ideas are anonymous. When you type in an idea and hit the "Enter" key to share it with the group, group members see only the idea. Furthermore, many brainstorming software programs also protect anonymity by displaying ideas in random order. So if you laugh maniacally when you type "Cut top management's pay by 50 percent!" and then hit the "Enter" key, it won't show up immediately on everyone's screen. This makes it doubly difficult to determine who is responsible for which comments.

In the typical layout for electronic brainstorming, all participants sit in front of computers around a U-shaped table. This configuration allows them to see their computer screens, the other participants, a large main screen, and a meeting leader or facilitator. Exhibit 5.14 shows what the typical electronic brainstorming group member will see on his or her computer screen. The first step in electronic brainstorming is to anonymously generate as many ideas as possible. Groups commonly generate 100 ideas in a half-hour period. Step 2 is to edit the generated ideas, categorize them, and eliminate redundancies. Step 3 is to rank the categorized ideas in terms of quality. Step 4, the last step, has three parts: generate a series of action steps, decide the best order for accomplishing these steps, and identify who is responsible for each step. All four steps are accomplished with computers and electronic brainstorming software.[75]

Studies show that electronic brainstorming is much more productive than face-to-face brainstorming. Four-person electronic brainstorming groups produce 25 to 50 percent more ideas than four-person regular brainstorming groups, and 12-person electronic brainstorming groups produce 200 percent more ideas than regular groups of

brainstorming a decision-making method in which group members build on each others' ideas to generate as many alternative solutions as possible

electronic brainstorming a decision-making method in which group members use computers to build on each others' ideas and generate many alternative solutions

production blocking a disadvantage of face-to-face brainstorming in which a group member must wait to share an idea because another member is presenting an idea

evaluation apprehension fear of what others will think of your ideas

Source: Developing Consensus with Group Systems. © 2002 GroupSystems.com.

Exhibit 5.14

What You See on the Computer during Electronic Brainstorming

the same size! In fact, because production blocking (having to wait your turn) is not a problem for electronic brainstorming, the number and quality of ideas generally increase with group size.[76]

Even though it works much better than traditional brainstorming, electronic brainstorming has disadvantages, too. An obvious problem is the expense of computers, networks, software, and other equipment. As these costs continue to drop, however, electronic brainstorming will become cheaper.

Another problem is that the anonymity of ideas may bother people who are used to having their ideas accepted by virtue of their position (say, the boss). On the other hand, one CEO said, "Because the process is anonymous, the sky's the limit in terms of what you can say, and as a result it is more thought-provoking. As a CEO, you'll probably discover things you might not want to hear but need to be aware of."[77]

A third disadvantage is that outgoing individuals who are more comfortable expressing themselves verbally may find it difficult to express themselves in writing. Finally, the most obvious problem is that participants have to be able to type. Those who can't type, or who type slowly, may be easily frustrated and find themselves at a disadvantage to experienced typists. For example, one meeting facilitator was tipped off that an especially fast typist was pretending to be more than one person. Says the facilitator, "He'd type 'Oh, I agree' and then 'Ditto, ditto' or 'What a great idea,' all in quick succession, using different variations of uppercase and lowercase letters and punctuation. He tried to make it seem like a lot of people were concurring, but it was just him." Eventually, the person sitting next to him got suspicious and began watching his screen.[78]

Review 5: **Using Groups to Improve Decision Making**

When groups view problems from multiple perspectives, use more information, have a diversity of knowledge and experience, and become committed to solutions they help choose, they can produce better solutions than individual decision makers. However, group decisions can suffer from these disadvantages: groupthink, slowness, discussions dominated by just a few individuals, and unfelt responsibility for decisions. Group decisions work best when group members encourage c-type conflict. However, group decisions don't work as well when groups become mired in a-type conflict. The devil's advocacy and dialectical inquiry approaches improve group decisions because they bring structured c-type conflict into the decision-making process. By contrast, the nominal group technique and the Delphi technique both improve decision making by reducing a-type conflict through limited interactions between group members. The stepladder technique improves group decision making by adding each group member's independent contributions to the discussion one at a time. Finally, because it overcomes the problems of production blocking and evaluation apprehension, electronic brainstorming is a more effective method of generating alternatives than face-to-face brainstorming.

Self-Management

A key part of planning is setting goals and tracking progress toward their achievement. As a manager, you will be involved in some type of planning in an organization. But the planning process is also used in a personal context, where it is called self-management. Self-management involves setting goals for yourself, developing a method or strategy to achieve them, and then carrying it out. For some people, self-management comes naturally. Everyone seems to know someone who is highly organized, self-motivated, and disciplined. That someone may even be you. If that someone is not you, however, then you will need to develop your self-management skills as a means to becoming a better manager.

A part of planning, and therefore management, is setting goals and tracking progress toward goal achievement.[79] Answer each of the questions using the following scale:

1 Strongly disagree
2 Disagree
3 Not sure
4 Agree
5 Strongly Agree

1. I regularly set goals for myself.
   1   2   3   4   5

2. I keep track of how well I've been doing.
   1   2   3   4   5

3. I generally keep the resolutions that I make.
   1   2   3   4   5

4. I often seek feedback about my performance.
   1   2   3   4   5

5. I am able to focus on positive aspects of my work.
   1   2   3   4   5

6. I'll sometimes deny myself something until I've set my goals.
   1   2   3   4   5

7. I use a to-do list to plan my activities.
   1   2   3   4   5

8. I have trouble working without supervision.
   1   2   3   4   5

9. When I set my mind on some goal, I persevere until it's accomplished.
   1   2   3   4   5

10. I'm a self-starter.
    1   2   3   4   5

11. I make lists of things I need to do.
    1   2   3   4   5

12. I'm good at time management.
    1   2   3   4   5

13. I'm usually confident that I can reach my goals.
    1   2   3   4   5

14. I am careful about how I manage my time.
    1   2   3   4   5

15. I always plan my day.
    1   2   3   4   5

16. I often find I spend my time on trivial things and put off doing what's really important.
    1   2   3   4   5

17. Unless someone pushes me a bit, I have trouble getting motivated.
    1   2   3   4   5

18. I reward myself when I meet my goals.
    1   2   3   4   5

19. I tend to dwell on unpleasant aspects of the things I need to do.
    1   2   3   4   5

20. I tend to deal with life as it comes rather than to try to plan things.
    1   2   3   4   5

21. I generally try to find a place to work where I'll be free from interruptions.
    1   2   3   4   5

22. I'm pretty disorganized.
    1   2   3   4   5

KEY TERMS

absolute comparisons 172
action plan 161
a-type conflict (affective conflict) 179
bounded rationality 175
brainstorming 183
budgeting 168
c-type conflict (cognitive conflict) 178
decision criteria 171
decision making 170
Delphi technique 180
devil's advocacy 179
dialectical inquiry 179
distal goals 161
electronic brainstorming 183
evaluation apprehension 183
goal commitment 160
groupthink 177
learning-based planning 163
management by objectives (MBO) 166
maximizing 175
mission 165
nominal group technique 179
operational plans 168
options-based planning 163
planning 156
policy 168
problem 170
procedure 168
production blocking 183
proximal goals 161
rational decision making 170
relative comparisons 172
rules and regulations 168
satisficing 175
single-use plans 168
slack resources 163
S.M.A.R.T. goals 159
standing plans 168
stepladder technique 180
strategic plans 165
tactical plans 166
vision 165

23. The goals I set are quite specific.
1   2   3   4   5

24. Distractions often interfere with my performance.
1   2   3   4   5

25. I sometimes give myself a treat if I've done something well.
1   2   3   4   5

26. I am able to focus on positive aspects of my activities.
1   2   3   4   5

27. I use notes or other prompts to remind myself of schedules and deadlines.
1   2   3   4   5

28. I seem to waste a lot of time.
1   2   3   4   5

29. I use a day planner or other aids to keep track of schedules and deadlines.
1   2   3   4   5

30. I often think about how I can improve my performance.
1   2   3   4   5

31. I tend to lose track of the goals I've set for myself.
1   2   3   4   5

32. I tend to set difficult goals for myself.
1   2   3   4   5

33. I plan things for weeks in advance.
1   2   3   4   5

34. I try to make a visible commitment to my goals.
1   2   3   4   5

35. I set aside blocks of time for important activities.
1   2   3   4   5

Scoring

Determine your score by entering your response to each survey item below, as follows. In blanks that say *regular score*, simply enter your response for that item. If your response was a 4, place a 4 in the *regular score* blank. In blanks that say *reverse score*, subtract your response from 6 and enter the result. So if your response was a 4, place a 2 (6−4=2) in the *reverse score* blank. Add up your total score.

1. regular score _____
2. regular score _____
3. regular score _____
4. regular score _____
5. regular score _____
6. regular score _____
7. regular score _____
8. reverse score _____
9. regular score _____
10. regular score _____
11. regular score _____
12. regular score _____
13. regular score _____
14. regular score _____
15. regular score _____
16. reverse score _____
17. reverse score _____
18. regular score _____
19. reverse score _____
20. reverse score _____
21. regular score _____
22. reverse score _____
23. regular score _____
24. reverse score _____
25. regular score _____
26. regular score _____
27. regular score _____
28. reverse score _____
29. regular score _____
30. regular score _____
31. reverse score _____
32. regular score _____
33. regular score _____
34. regular score _____
35. regular score _____
TOTAL = _____

You can find the interpretation for your score at: **academic.cengage.com/management/williams**.

Drug Testing

The end of the week is always a relief, but this Friday, after everyone clocks out, you have a meeting with the company's frontline managers to discuss various problems that have been occurring in the warehouse. You've been bracing for the challenge since Monday.

Once all the managers are assembled, you begin to list the troubles that have been plaguing the warehouse. Petty theft and minor accidents have increased markedly in a relatively short period of time. Employees have run forklifts into walls and dropped pallets of boxes onto the floor as they were being moved. Items have disappeared from shipments being held by the company for its trucking customers. There have even been rumors that marijuana is being bought and sold on the premises. After you recite the laundry list of problems, you tell your managers that you don't think any single employee is the source of all these problems. Instead, you boldly state your suspicion: Drug use is probably the root of the problems in the warehouse.

A mumble circles the room, but no one wants to discuss the issue openly. Some managers look worried, others shocked, and the rest—you can't tell. So you begin slowly by saying, "I think we need to do drug testing. I'm sure we can't blame all our problems on drug use, but I'm convinced it's a contributing factor." You cite several successful companies that are committed to a drug-free workplace and some statistics on how much drug use costs U.S. businesses—$81 billion per year. Testing 100 employees over the course of a year will cost only about $5,000, but the average substance abuser costs his or her employer between $11,000 and $13,000 per year. Adding to the cost savings, the state gives a 5 percent rebate on workers' compensation insurance to certified drug-free workplaces. You conclude by saying, "I'll put together some materials for us to review next week."

Some of your managers nod perfunctorily, but others just raise an eyebrow. As they file out of the room in absolute silence, you murmur under your breath, "That went well," and let out a sigh. "I might as well get started now. Waiting is not going to make the task easier. But what do I really need to do? And how restrictive should I be?"[80]

Questions

1. What do you need to establish a drug-free workplace: a policy, a set of procedures, or rules and regulations—or maybe all three?

2. As the manager in question, draft the appropriate operational plan(s) for this situation. Think about issues like random versus regular testing, current employees versus future applicants only, all employees or only warehouse workers, the consequences of testing positive, and so forth.

3. Imagine that your drug-testing policy, whatever form it takes, has resulted in your company losing 40 percent of its work force. (That has actually happened to real companies.) What changes, if any, will you make as a result?

Selling to Wal-Mart

Because of your company's success, the end-of-the-year accounting review is usually an upbeat occasion, and this December is no different. Your company manufactures an innovative kickstand that reduces injuries by keeping a child's bike from falling all the way to the ground. After the device was written up in a parents' magazine recently, sales to specialty bike shops—your primary customers—have started to climb. Despite the increased demand, you can still make kickstands to order.

At a meeting with your management team, you remark that although sales are increasing at a slow but steady rate, the company still has a large amount of excess capacity. A colleague agrees and then enthusiastically announces, "I know how to take care of that. Let's sell to Wal-Mart!" A hush falls over the meeting. Becoming a Wal-Mart supplier would mean honing your current distribution process into a finely tuned, perfect delivery operation. The retailing behemoth gives suppliers a 30-second window to deliver their goods to Wal-Mart distribution centers;

you currently ship product via UPS ground. Wal-Mart requires severe price concessions from all its suppliers, a practice that has forced many American manufacturers to outsource production overseas in order to get their production costs low enough to meet Wal-Mart's pricing mandates. Master Lock, Carolina Mills, Levi's, and, a bit closer to home, Huffy Bicycle are a few examples. Your company uses local suppliers for metal, paint, plastics, and packaging, and it pays its 25 workers above-market wages. Thankfully, at the moment your company is the only manufacturer of the kickstand, so you have more freedom to set a competitive price on that item. If you begin selling through Wal-Mart, however, imitators will soon follow, and that would definitely affect your already modest margins. Not to mention that Wal-Mart uses historical price data about a company and its competitors to drive prices down across industries. Suppliers are rarely if ever granted a price increase; on the contrary, they are asked for regular price decreases!

In addition, if vendors want their products on Wal-Mart's shelves, they have to implement Wal-Mart's "customized business plans." Each year, the big retailer hands its suppliers detailed "strategic business planning packets." Wal-Mart grades its suppliers with weekly, quarterly, and annual report cards. And when it comes to discussion of price, there is no real negotiation even for household brands. Plus, Wal-Mart often requires its suppliers to underwrite the costs of the retailer's supply-chain productivity initiatives, like using radio-frequency identification (RFID) tags on their products for inventory tracking, a system that can cost between $13 million and $23 million to put in place. Trying to meet Wal-Mart's requirements has pushed many small- and medium-sized businesses into bankruptcy. Business that stay afloat have generally done so by outsourcing to China (in areas like shoes, housewares, and apparel, 80 to 90 percent of Wal-Mart's inventory comes from China).

But there are also benefits to selling to Wal-Mart. You have instant access to the world's largest global retailing network. Doing things the "Wal-Mart way" inevitably leads to more efficient operations. And the volume!

You could sell exponentially more kickstands through Wal-Mart than through the small specialty retailers to whom you currently sell. If doing business with Wal-Mart is so bad, why do Unilever, P&G, and Dial sell 6, 17, and 28 percent of their goods, respectively, to the giant retailer? A former president of Huffy Bicycle once said that Wal-Mart gives you "a chance to compete. If you can't compete, that's your problem." You agree, to a point. Before you can voice any of the pros and cons, another manager expertly sums up the dilemma by saying, "The only thing worse than selling to Wal-Mart is not selling to Wal-Mart."[81]

Before you begin this Management Team Decision, each team member will probably need to do some preliminary research on Wal-Mart's business practices; go to the campus library to find articles on topics like productivity, inventory management, and even Wal-Mart's business practices. A visit to the Wal-Mart stores website (**http://www.walmartstores.com**) can give you a wealth of information on how the company manages its suppliers. You may also wish to visit the PBS show *Frontline*'s web page "Is Wal-Mart Good for America?" (**http://www.pbs.org/wgbh/pages/frontline/shows/walmart/secrets**).

Questions

1. As a team, use this exercise to practice one of the group decision-making techniques discussed in the chapter. Work together to decide which technique to use.

2. Do you apply to become a Wal-Mart supplier, with all that entails? Why or why not?

3. If you become a Wal-Mart supplier, what key areas of your operations will need to change and how?

4. Think about how the decision-making technique you chose affected the outcome of your decision. Do you think your collective decision would have been different if you had used, say, dialectical inquiry instead of the stepladder technique?

Effective planning and decision making are crucial to the success of organizations. Your success as a manager will be determined in large part by your planning and decision-making capabilities. This exercise highlights some well-tested tools for strengthening your planning and decision-making skills.

Individual Preparation

Step 1: Identify your "best company." Suppose that you are going to develop a plan that will result in your being hired to work for the single BEST COMPANY possible. "Best company" has not been defined for you, so you must determine what this might mean. Identify your "best company," and make your plan. You need to consider such aspects as building the right academic and work profile, marketing yourself to the company, and effectively interviewing. Carefully record both your plan, and the steps that you took to develop it. In class you will be asked to share this information with a small discussion group.

Small Group Discussion

Step 2: Discuss your plan. Taking turns, individually share your plan with the members of your discussion group. Members should listen carefully, ask questions, and make notes regarding the similarities and differences of individual plans.

Step 3: Create a brochure. Now suppose that your group has been asked to develop a brochure for distribution in college career centers. The brochure will be titled "Getting a Job with Your Dream Company."

Using what you have learned from sharing your individual plans, work as a group to develop a sketch/outline of this brochure.

Class Discussion

Step 4: As a class discuss the following questions:

- Did you follow the rational decision-making process in identifying your *best company* and creating your plan for landing a job with this company? Why, or why not?

- What role might bounded rationality have played in your individual and/or team decision-making process?

- Does planning increase the likelihood of success in being hired by a great company? Why, or why not?

- If you were an editor assigned the project of developing the brochure "Getting a Job with Your Dream Company," would you be more likely to give the assignment to: 1) a qualified individual; or 2) a qualified group? Considering your recent experiences in this exercise, what are the tradeoffs of each approach (individual versus group decision making)?

□ □ □ □ ✓

DEVELOP YOUR CAREER POTENTIAL

What Do You Want To Be When You Grow Up?

What do you want to be when you grow up?[82] Still not sure? Ask around. You're not alone. Chances are, your friends and relatives aren't certain either. Sure, they may have jobs and careers, but you're likely to find that, professionally, many of them don't want to be where they are today. Sometimes people's interests change, or they may burn out. And some people are unhappy with their current job or career because they weren't in the right one to begin with.

Getting the job and career you want is not easy. It takes time, effort, and persistence. And even though you will probably follow multiple career paths in your life, your career-planning process will be easier (and more effective) if you take the time to develop a personal career plan.

Begin by answering the following questions. (*Hint*: Treat this seriously. If you do it effectively, this plan could guide your career decisions for the next five to seven years.)

1. Describe your strengths and weaknesses. Don't just rely on your opinions of your abilities. Ask your parents, relatives, friends, and employers what they think, too. Encourage them to be honest and then be prepared to hear some things that you may not

want to hear. Remember, though, this information can help you pick the right job or career.

2. Write an advertisement for the job you want to have five years from now. Be specific. Describe the company, title, responsibilities, required education, and experience, salary, and benefits. Use employment ads in the Sunday job listings as inspiration.

3. Create a detailed plan to obtain this job. In the short term, what classes do you need to take? Should you change your major? Do you need a business major or minor or maybe a minor in a foreign language? What kind of summer work experience will move you closer to getting the job you want five years from now? What job do you need to get right out of college to obtain the work experience you need? Create a specific plan for each of the five years in your career plan, keeping in mind that the plans for later years are likely to change. The value in planning is that it forces you to think about what you want and the steps you can take now to help achieve those goals.

4. Decide when you will monitor and evaluate the progress you're making with your plan. Career experts suggest that every six months is about right. Pick two dates and write them in your schedule. Furthermore, right now, before you forget, set five specific, challenging goals that you need to accomplish in the next six months in order to achieve your career plans.

REEL TO REAL

BIZ FLIX
The Bourne Identity

Jason Bourne (Matt Damon) cannot remember who he is, but others believe he is an international assassin. Bourne tries to learn his identity with the help of his new friend and lover Marie (Franka Potente). Meanwhile, while CIA agents pursue him across Europe trying to kill him, Bourne slowly discovers that he is an extremely well-trained and lethal agent. The story is loosely based on Robert Ludlum's 1981 novel.

This scene is an edited version of the "Bourne's Game" sequence near the end of the film. Jason Bourne kills the hired assassin who tried to kill him the day after Jason and Marie arrived at the home of Eamon (Tim Dutton). Eamon is Marie's friend but is a stranger to Jason. Jason uses the dead man's cell phone after returning to his apartment in Paris, France. He presses the redial button, which connects him to Conklin (Chris Cooper), the CIA manager who is looking for him. Listen carefully to Jason's conversation with Conklin.

What to Watch for and Ask Yourself

1. Does Bourne describe a plan to Conklin? If he does, what are the plan's elements? What is Bourne's goal?
2. Does Bourne assess the plan's execution to determine if it conforms to his goal? If so, what does he do?
3. Was Bourne's plan successfully carried out? Why or why not? How does this scene relate to organizational strategic planning?

MANAGEMENT WORKPLACE
Timbuk2—Undemocratic Group Decision Making

Making decisions is a big part of any manager's job. Making the decisions that determine the direction a company will take is the job of a CEO. Mark Dwight, CEO of Timbuk2, is comfortable with this role, even though it means sometimes making unpopular decisions—or even making mistakes. Timbuk2's 45 workers tend to be young, so Dwight sees himself as the senior manager in more ways than one. "I'm the experienced executive here, and it's my charter to manage the company," he explains. "It's not a democracy. I ask the people that I think have a good perspective on [an] issue, who are affected by the issue, we discuss it, and I make a command decision based on those inputs. Hopefully, people think I make educated, informed decisions. That's my job."

What to Watch for and Ask Yourself

1. What problems does Dwight identify at the opening of the Tag Junkie planning meeting?
2. How does the team incorporate flexibility into its product plan?
3. Does what you see in the video qualify as group decision making? Why or why not?

CHAPTER 6

Organizational Strategy

WHAT WOULD YOU DO?

StubHub, Inc., San Francisco, California.[1] Your management team at eBay just acquired rival upstart StubHub from its founders Jeff Fluhr and Eric Baker, who launched the company out of their Stanford dorm rooms. Fluhr and Baker wanted to use the Internet to replace scalping tickets at venue sites, so they developed a unique system comprised of ticket exchange, event information, and guaranteed delivery.

StubHub quickly signed contracts with Major League Baseball, the National Football League, National Hockey League, and National Basketball Association. Season-ticket holders used StubHub to safely sell their tickets for games they couldn't attend for whatever reason. To no one's surprise, StubHub acquired customers quickly and inexpensively, but once activity stabilized, the company became a slow-growth business—there are only so many season-ticket holders out there. That's when StubHub moved into direct consumer marketing.

StubHub started facilitating ticket sales between any two willing parties, a move that helped it become the second largest ticket resale auction site on the Internet. But as new companies entered (and filled) the market, companies like TicketsNow.com, RazorGator, eBay, and even Ticketmaster, StubHub watched its basic strategy and unique transaction capabilities begin to erode. And, industry powerhouse Ticketmaster launched a new lobbying effort to have states outlaw the reselling of tickets for more than their face value (the amount printed on the ticket).

Despite the competition, StubHub managed to attract 2.1 million unique visitors per month and generate over $100 million in annual revenue. Still, competition means lower prices means weakening revenues. You need a new strategy for growth and profit.

Could StubHub become an advertising medium for sporting and theatrical events? Huge revenues are possible, but advertisers are now regularly entering contracts with Google, YouTube, and Facebook. Should StubHub directly attack Ticketmaster's business of selling original tickets to concerts and sporting events? Finally, should you completely change the business model and actually buy tickets to resell on the open auction market? Buying the tickets would be costly and carry some risk, but if done well, you might end up with greater market power and the ability to maximize revenue. **If you had just bought StubHub and needed to spark additional growth, what would you do?**

ACTIVITIES + VIDEO

CengageNOW Audio study guide, electronic flashcards, author FAQ videos, On the Job and Biz Flix videos, concept tutorial, and concept exercise

Web (academic.cengage.com/management/williams) Quiz, PowerPoint slides, and glossary terms for this chapter

"WHAT'S NEW" COMPANIES

STUBHUB

APPLE COMPUTER

SONY

MICROSOFT

iTUNES

NAPSTER

YAHOO! MUSIC

KRAFT FOODS

WARNER MUSIC GROUP

MEMORIAL HOSPITAL

IKEA

HOME DEPOT

LOWE'S

ACE HARDWARE

84 LUMBER

CIBA-GEIGY

MENARDS

AND OTHERS . . .

In Chapter 5, you learned that *strategic plans* are overall company plans that clarify how a company intends to serve customers and position itself against competitors over the next two to five years. Although StubHub was the first online ticket reseller, it now faces challenges from numerous competitors and must develop a strategy to recapture its competitive advantage in this market. This chapter begins with an in-depth look at how managers create and use strategies to obtain a sustainable competitive advantage. Then you will learn the three steps of the strategy-making process. Next, you will learn about corporate-level strategies that help managers answer the question, What business or businesses should we be in? You will then examine the industry-level competitive strategies that help managers determine how to compete successfully within a particular line of business. The chapter finishes with a review of the firm-level strategies of direct competition and entrepreneurship.

BASICS OF ORGANIZATIONAL STRATEGY

"WHAT'S NEW" COMPANY

Before October 2001, **APPLE COMPUTER** was not in the portable digital music business, but that month, the company released its iPod, which quickly set the standard for all other digital music devices. Designed around a 1.8-inch-diameter hard drive, the iPod boasted low battery consumption and enough memory to hold literally thousands of songs, all packaged in a case smaller than a deck of cards and fashioned with style unparalleled in the technology market. Because Apple used existing and readily available technology, competitors were able to move quickly and aggressively to copy Apple's innovation. Powerhouses like Sony, Samsung, and even Dell Computer soon released their own iPod-like devices.

As the market has matured over the past several years, competitors have increasingly tried to steal—or at least minimize—Apple's competitive advantage by adding unique features to the standard set of features on an MP3 player. **SONY**'s new Walkman includes software that examines the user's taste in music and, at the push of a button labeled "Artist Link," the device will suggest new artists the user might like. SanDisk, best known as a maker of basic flash drive memory, has entered the MP3 market with its Sansa e280, which has twice the storage of an iPod Nano yet sells at roughly the same price. Another significant new entrant to the digital music space is **MICROSOFT**. Its Zune player can store

"WHAT'S NEW" COMPANY

the same number of songs as a video iPod, but Zune can also hold 100 hours of video (compared with the iPod's 40) and 25,000 pictures (same as an iPod). Plus the Zune allows users to wirelessly share music. Despite the creativity of the competition, however, Apple still holds a commanding 75 percent of the market for digital music players; SanDisk, its nearest competitor, has less than a 10 percent share.[2]

How can a company like Apple, which dominates a particular industry, maintain its competitive advantage as strong, well-financed competitors enter the market? What steps can Apple and other companies take to better manage their strategy-making process?

> **After reading the next two sections, you should be able to**
>
> 1 specify the components of sustainable competitive advantage and explain why it is important.
>
> 2 describe the steps involved in the strategy-making process.

1 Sustainable Competitive Advantage

Resources are the assets, capabilities, processes, employee time, information, and knowledge that an organization controls. Firms use their resources to improve organizational effectiveness and efficiency. Resources are critical to organizational strategy because they can help companies create and sustain an advantage over competitors.[3]

Organizations can achieve a **competitive advantage** by using their resources to provide greater value for customers than competitors can. For example, *iTunes* and iPod created competitive advantage for Apple and value for its customers by combining elements of design, price, and capability in a unique way. But the most important advantage was being the first company to make it easy to legally download music to digital devices. (Prior to the iTunes store, the only means of acquiring digital music was file swapping, which was illegal.) Apple negotiated agreements with virtually all of the major record labels to distribute their songs from a central online library, and iTunes quickly became the premier platform for music downloading. The easy-to-understand site came with free downloadable software customers could use to organize and manage their digital music library.[4]

The goal of most organizational strategies is to create and then sustain a competitive advantage. A competitive advantage becomes a **sustainable competitive advantage** when other companies cannot duplicate the value a firm is providing to customers. Sustainable competitive advantage is *not* the same as a long-lasting competitive advantage, though companies obviously want a competitive advantage to last a long time. Instead, a competitive advantage is *sustained* if competitors have tried unsuccessfully to duplicate the advantage and have, for the moment, stopped trying to duplicate it. It's the corporate equivalent of your competitors saying, "We give up. You win. We can't do what you do, and we're not even going to try to do it any more." As Exhibit 6.1 shows, four conditions must be met if a firm's resources are to be used to achieve a sustainable competitive advantage. The resources must be valuable, rare, imperfectly imitable, *and* nonsubstitutable.

"What's New" Company

resources the assets, capabilities, processes, employee time, information, and knowledge that an organization uses to improve its effectiveness and efficiency, create and sustain competitive advantage, and fulfill a need or solve a problem

competitive advantage providing greater value for customers than competitors can

sustainable competitive advantage a competitive advantage that other companies have tried unsuccessfully to duplicate and have, for the moment, stopped trying to duplicate

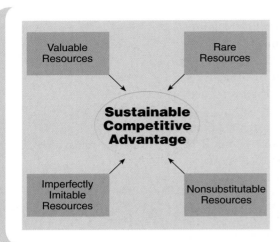

Exhibit 6.1

Four Requirements for Sustainable Competitive Advantage

Valuable resources allow companies to improve their efficiency and effectiveness. Unfortunately, changes in customer demand and preferences, competitors' actions, and technology can make once-valuable resources much less valuable. Throughout the 1980s, Sony controlled the portable music market with its ubiquitous Sony Walkman, which has sold over 230 million units worldwide since its introduction in 1979. For many years, Sony had the technology to produce a higher quality of music than any other portable format on the market. Sony leveraged the capabilities of its engineers and inventors (more resources) to make incremental changes to the Walkman that were unmatched by the competition—until the MP3 player came along. With the introduction of Apple's iPod to the market, Sony's previously valuable technology lost nearly all its value. Sony finally changed the Walkman to a portable digital device and created its own online music store (Connect), which does not match the iTunes store in either simplicity or availability of songs.[5]

For sustained competitive advantage, valuable resources must also be rare resources. Think about it: How can a company sustain a competitive advantage if all of its competitors have similar resources and capabilities? Consequently, **rare resources**, resources that are not controlled or possessed by many competing firms, are necessary to sustain a competitive advantage. When Apple introduced the iPod, no other portable music players on the market used existing hard-drive technology in their design. The iPod gained an immediate advantage over competitors because it was able to satisfy the desire of consumers to carry large numbers of songs in a portable device, something the newer MP3 systems and older individual CD players could not do. The technology that powered the iPod, however, was readily available, so competitors were able to quickly imitate iPod's basic storage capacity. As competitors began introducing their iPod look-alikes, Apple released a model with double the storage and replaced the original mechanical wheel with a solid-state touch wheel. Once again, Apple used its design talents (resources) to gain an advantage over the competition. One of Apple's truly rare resources is its ability to reconfigure existing technology into a package that is easy to use, elegantly designed, and therefore highly desired by customers.

As the example shows, valuable and rare resources can create temporary competitive advantage. For sustained competitive advantage, however, other firms must be unable to imitate or find substitutes for those valuable, rare resources. **Imperfectly imitable resources** are those resources that are impossible or extremely costly or difficult to duplicate. For example, despite numerous attempts by competitors to imitate it, iTunes has retained its competitive lock on the music download business. Capitalizing on Apple's reputation for developing customer-friendly software, and its library of music, movies, and podcasts, iTunes is still the market leader, although competition from Yahoo! Music and Zune is heating up. Because the company has developed a closed system for its iTunes and iPod, iPod owners cannot download music from sources other than Apple's iTunes store, but for many this is not a problem. Many devotees won't even consider another brand. Kelly Moore, a sales representative for a Texas software company, takes her pink iPod mini everywhere she goes and keeps it synchronized with her iBook laptop. She says, "Once I find something I like, I don't switch brands."[6] She's not alone: Since iTunes was launched, customers have downloaded over a billion songs. No other competitor comes close to those numbers.

valuable resource a resource that allows companies to improve efficiency and effectiveness

rare resource a resource that is not controlled or possessed by many competing firms

imperfectly imitable resource a resource that is impossible or extremely costly or difficult for other firms to duplicate

Valuable, rare, imperfectly imitable resources can produce sustainable competitive advantage only if they are also **nonsubstitutable resources**, meaning that no other resources can replace them and produce similar value or competitive advantage. To compete effectively against iTunes, competitors may need to change their business model. That is, competitors need to propose substitutes for iTunes that consumers will accept. For example, NAPSTER founders Shawn Fanning and Wayne Rosso have created a subscription-based service called Mashboxx that charges $15 a month for unlimited downloads. YAHOO! MUSIC uses a similar model but charges as little as $6 per month for complete access to its entire library of 2 million songs.[7] In addition to straight subscription models, some companies are experimenting with price. Where iTunes charges 99 cents per song, period, Amazon's online store will allow the record companies to charge different amounts for different songs based upon popularity. At Amie Street, a newly posted track can be downloaded for free, but as the number of downloads increases, so does the song's price, until it reaches the maximum of 98 cents.[8] In response to competitors' experimentation, Apple has stated that its one-flat-price model has been both effective and lucrative and has no plans to change. It will take years to find out whether these new means of purchase will constitute an effective substitute to iTunes.[9]

In summary, Apple has reaped the rewards of a first mover advantage from its interdependent iPod and iTunes. The company's history of developing customer-friendly software, the innovative capabilities of the iPod, the simple 99-cent-pay-as-you-go sales model of iTunes, and the unmatched list of music and movies available for download provide customers with a service that has been valuable, rare, relatively nonsubstitutable, and, in the past, imperfectly imitable. Past success is, however, no guarantee of future success: Apple needs to continually change and develop its offerings or risk being unseated by a more nimble competitor whose products are more relevant and have higher perceived value to the consumer.

Review 1: Sustainable Competitive Advantage

Firms can use their resources to create and sustain a competitive advantage, that is, to provide greater value for customers than competitors can. A competitive advantage becomes sustainable when other companies cannot duplicate the benefits it provides and have, for now, stopped trying. To provide a sustainable competitive advantage, the firm's resources must be valuable (capable of improving efficiency and effectiveness), rare (not possessed by many competing firms), imperfectly imitable (extremely costly or difficult to duplicate), and nonsubstitutable (competitors cannot substitute other resources to produce similar value).

There's a great deal of uncertainty in strategic business environments.

2 Strategy-Making Process

*Companies use a strategy-making process to create strategies that produce sustainable competitive advantage.[10] Exhibit 6.2 displays the three steps of the strategy-making process: **2.1 assess the need for strategic change**, **2.2 conduct a situational analysis**, and then **2.3 choose strategic alternatives**. Let's examine each of these steps in more detail.*

nonsubstitutable resource a resource that produces value or competitive advantage and has no equivalent substitutes or replacements

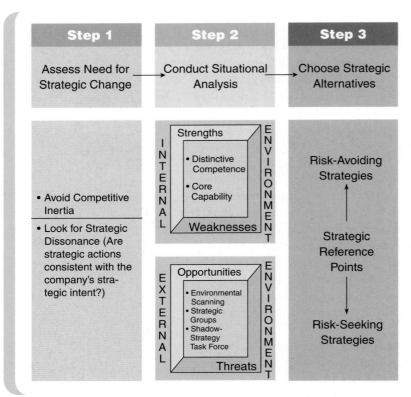

Step 1	Step 2	Step 3
Assess Need for Strategic Change	Conduct Situational Analysis	Choose Strategic Alternatives

Step 1
- Avoid Competitive Inertia
- Look for Strategic Dissonance (Are strategic actions consistent with the company's strategic intent?)

Step 2

INTERNAL ENVIRONMENT

Strengths
- Distinctive Competence
- Core Capability

Weaknesses

EXTERNAL ENVIRONMENT

Opportunities
- Environmental Scanning
- Strategic Groups
- Shadow-Strategy Task Force

Threats

Step 3

Risk-Avoiding Strategies

Strategic Reference Points

Risk-Seeking Strategies

Exhibit 6.2

Three Steps of the Strategy-Making Process

competitive inertia a reluctance to change strategies or competitive practices that have been successful in the past

strategic dissonance a discrepancy between a company's intended strategy and the strategic actions managers take when implementing that strategy

2.1 Assessing the Need for Strategic Change

The external business environment is much more turbulent than it used to be. With customers' needs constantly growing and changing, and with competitors working harder, faster, and smarter to meet those needs, the first step in strategy making is determining the need for strategic change. In other words, the company should determine whether it needs to change its strategy to sustain a competitive advantage.[11]

Determining the need for strategic change might seem easy to do, but in reality, it's not. There's a great deal of uncertainty in strategic business environments. Furthermore, top-level managers are often slow to recognize the need for strategic change, especially at successful companies that have created and sustained competitive advantages. Because they are acutely aware of the strategies that made their companies successful, they continue to rely on those strategies, even as the competition changes. In other words, success often leads to **competitive inertia**—a reluctance to change strategies or competitive practices that have been successful in the past.

For example, **KRAFT FOODS** makes some of the best-selling food brands around, such as Oreo cookies, Lunchables (prepackaged lunches for children), and Velveeta cheese. But Kraft hasn't introduced a successful new brand since it began selling DiGiorno frozen pizza in the mid-1990s. Instead, Kraft has focused on brand extensions, developing "new and improved" versions of its best-selling brands, such as mini Oreos, Chocolate Cream Oreos, Fudge Mint Oreos, Mint and Crème Oreos, and Uh-Oh Oreos.[12] Kraft now has 14 different varieties of the original Oreo cookie, the newest of which is the Thin Crisp, packaged in 100-calorie servings, and eight other Oreo-branded products such as ice-cream cones, Jello, and cereal.[13] And Kraft's competitive inertia—its reliance on extending already established brands and its reluctance to develop new ones—has hurt its performance. According to the *Wall Street Journal*, "years of failing to develop new categories and products has given Kraft a lineup that seems stuck in a time warp."[14] Indeed, former customer Jennifer Stoll, who used to buy Kraft's food brands, says, "My perception of Kraft is that they are the more expensive version of processed food 'junk.'"[15]

Besides being aware of the dangers of competitive inertia, what can managers do to improve the speed and accuracy with which they determine the need for strategic change? One method is to actively look for signs of strategic dissonance. **Strategic dissonance** is a discrepancy between a company's intended strategy and the strategic actions managers take when actually implementing that strategy.[16]

For example, when Edgar Bronfman, Jr., bought the struggling **WARNER MUSIC GROUP**, his strategy was to cut costs and change a company culture where excessive spending—not uncommon in the entertainment industry—was the norm. Accordingly, he hoped to send a strong message with his first move, laying off 1,200 employees to save $250 million. Then, to drive the point home, he cut remaining salaries by as much as 50 percent. Bronfman justified the cuts by saying that managers, lawyers, accountants, and salespeople shouldn't be earning double or triple their normal salaries just because they worked for a music company. A few weeks later, however, he contradicted his new cost-cutting strategy. First, he signed off on a $13,000 bill to charter a private jet to fly top company managers and the agents of the company's best-selling artists to the Grammy awards in Los Angeles. Then, despite his insistence that music industry professionals shouldn't be paid more than their counterparts in other industries, Bronfman quietly restored the salary cuts he had made after top executives complained.[17]

Finally, while strategic dissonance can indicate that managers are not doing what they should to carry out company strategy, it can also mean that the intended strategy is out of date and needs to be changed.

2.2 Situational Analysis

A situational analysis can also help managers determine the need for strategic change. A **situational analysis**, also called a **SWOT analysis** for *strengths*, *weaknesses*, *opportunities*, and *threats*, is an assessment of the strengths and weaknesses in an organization's internal environment and the opportunities and threats in its external environment.[18] Ideally, as shown in Step 2 of Exhibit 6.2, a SWOT analysis helps a company determine how to increase internal strengths and minimize internal weaknesses while maximizing external opportunities and minimizing external threats.

When MEMORIAL HOSPITAL of Fremont, Ohio, decided that the process it used to order all the necessary medical and administrative supplies was out of control, managers asked all the departments to work together to conduct a SWOT analysis. The process helped the hospital identify its strengths, such as the experience of the materials management group, and its weaknesses, which included allowing anyone in the organization to order anything he or she wanted from any vendor. The departments outlined opportunities to dramatically improve the quality and flow of supplies while controlling the related costs, and participants determined that one of the biggest threats was expired supplies. Using the SWOT analysis as a map, the hospital began requiring all vendors to register when they entered the building, wear a visitor's badge while on hospital premises, and process all orders through the central purchasing department. Soon, the hospital staff developed the right mix of products

doing the right thing

Is Ethics an Overlooked Source of Competitive Advantage?

Volvo's reputation for selling safe cars has been a source of competitive advantage for years. You didn't buy a boxy Volvo for its looks; you bought it because your family would be well protected in an accident. If safety can be a source of competitive advantage, could ethics be one, too? Though competitive advantage usually comes from physical capital (plant, equipment, finances), organizational capital (structure, planning, systems), and human capital (skills, judgment, adaptability of your work force), Johnson & Johnson is still widely admired, two decades afterward, for its response when several people died after someone put cyanide in Tylenol capsules. The company quickly pulled Tylenol from store shelves and introduced tamper-proof packaging. The move cost Johnson & Johnson half a billion dollars, but protected consumers from further harm. The company's market share was back to #1 within a year of the reintroduction. Should ethics be your first source of competitive advantage? Probably not. It makes more sense to start with low costs, good service, or unique product capabilities. But when you're looking for another way to create or sustain a competitive advantage, consider that a reputation as an ethical corporation may be an additional way to differentiate your company from the competition.[19]

situational (SWOT) analysis an assessment of the strengths and weaknesses in an organization's internal environment and the opportunities and threats in its external environment

STRATEGY MAKING FOR FIRMS, BIG AND SMALL

what *really* works.

Companies create strategies that produce sustainable competitive advantage by using the strategy-making process (assessing the need for strategic change, conducting a situational analysis, and choosing strategic alternatives). For years, it had been thought that strategy making was something that only large firms could do well. It was believed that small firms did not have the time, knowledge, or staff to do a good job of strategy making. However, two meta-analyses indicate that strategy making can improve the profits, sales growth, and return on investment of both big *and* small firms.

STRATEGY MAKING FOR BIG FIRMS

There is a 72 percent chance that big companies that engage in the strategy-making process will be more profitable than big companies that don't. Not only does strategy making improve profits, but it also helps companies grow. Specifically, there is a 75 percent chance that big companies that engage in the strategy-making process will have greater sales and earnings growth than big companies that don't. Thus, in practical terms, the strategy-making process can make a significant difference in a big company's profits and growth.

STRATEGY MAKING FOR SMALL FIRMS

Strategy making can also improve the performance of small firms. There is a 61 percent chance that small firms that engage

in the strategy-making process will have more sales growth than small firms that don't. Likewise, there is a 62 percent chance that small firms that engage in the strategy-making process will have a larger return on investment than small companies that don't. Thus, in practical terms, the strategy-making process can make a significant difference in a small company's profits and growth, too.

EXTERNAL GROWTH THROUGH ACQUISITIONS

One way to grow a company is through external growth, or buying other companies (see Section 3.1 on portfolio strategy). However, researchers have long debated whether buying other companies actually adds value to the acquiring company. A meta-analysis based on 103 studies and a sample of 25,205 companies indicates that, on average, acquiring other companies actually *hurts* the value of the acquiring firm. In other words, there is only a 45 percent chance that growing a company through external acquisitions will work![20]

and product inventories required for each area of the hospital and, at the same time, dramatically reduced the number of staff involved in purchasing and stocking supplies. Over the next two years the hospital saved more than $1 million, and administrators won praise from hospital departments for their ability to improve services.[21]

As this example illustrates, SWOT can be used to evaluate entire companies or individual operations within an organization. All companies will find that their competitive advantages can erode over time if internal strengths eventually become weaknesses. Consequently, an analysis of an organization's internal environment, that is, a company's strengths and weaknesses, often begins with an assessment of its distinctive competencies and core capabilities. A **distinctive competence** is something that a company can make, do, or perform better than its competitors. For example, *Consumer Reports* magazine consistently ranks Toyota cars number one in quality and reliability.[22] Similarly, for 13 of the last 15 years, *PC Magazine* readers have ranked Dell's desktop computers best in terms of service and reliability.[23]

Whereas distinctive competencies are tangible—for example, a product or service is faster, cheaper, or better—the core capabilities that produce distinctive competencies are not. **Core capabilities** are the less visible, internal decision-making routines, problem-solving processes, and organizational cultures that determine how efficiently inputs can be turned into outputs. Distinctive competencies cannot be sustained for long without superior core capabilities. *IKEA*'s core capability is the way it works with 1,800 suppliers in 55 countries that make products exclusively for IKEA. IKEA employees in 43 local trading offices work closely with these suppliers to improve quality, cut costs, and improve worker safety. When IKEA develops a new product, such as a $650 small kitchen, the trading offices, with the help of their suppliers, compete to earn the right to produce that product. IKEA uses the same approach for product design, encouraging its nine in-house designers and 80 freelance designers to compete to come up with the best design. This ability to work with so many suppliers and designers, to get them to compete to achieve the best design and the lowest-cost manufactured product, and to keep suppliers happy by guaranteeing them a high volume of work is the core capability that generates IKEA's distinctive competence, selling good-value, low-cost furniture, which it does better than anyone else in the world.[24]

After examining internal strengths and weaknesses, the second part of a situational analysis is to look outside the company and assess the opportunities and threats in the external environment. In Chapter 3, you learned that *environmental scanning* involves searching the environment for important events or issues that might affect the organization. Managers use environmental scanning to stay up-to-date on important factors in their environment, such as pricing trends and technology changes in the industry. In a situational analysis, however, managers use environmental scanning to identify specific opportunities and threats that can either improve or harm the company's ability to sustain its competitive advantage. Identification of strategic groups and formation of shadow-strategy task forces are two ways to do this.

Strategic groups are not actual groups; they are companies, usually competitors, that managers closely follow. More specifically, a **strategic group** is a group of other companies within an industry that top managers choose for comparing, evaluating, and benchmarking their company's strategic threats and opportunities.[25] (*Benchmarking* involves identifying outstanding practices, processes, and standards at other companies and adapting them to your own company.) Typically, managers include companies as part of their strategic group if they compete directly with those companies for customers or if those companies use strategies similar to theirs. The U.S. home improvement industry has annual sales in excess of

> *"* Distinctive competencies cannot be sustained for long without superior core capabilities. *"*

"WHAT'S NEW" COMPANY

distinctive competence what a company can make, do, or perform better than its competitors

core capabilities the internal decision-making routines, problem-solving processes, and organizational cultures that determine how efficiently inputs can be turned into outputs

strategic group a group of companies within an industry that top managers choose to compare, evaluate, and benchmark strategic threats and opportunities

IKEA's core capabilities help it keep its stores stocked with the merchandise customers want to buy.

	# of Stores	# of States	Countries	Size of Modern Store (Sq. Feet)
Home Depot	2,079	50	3	130,000
Lowe's	1,325	49	2	117,000
Ace Hardware	4,700	50	70	17,000
84 Lumber	500	40	1	33,000

Exhibit 6.3

Strategic Groups for Home Depot

core firms the central companies in a strategic group

secondary firms the firms in a strategic group that follow strategies related to but somewhat different from those of the core firms

transient firms the firms in a strategic group whose strategies are changing from one strategic position to another

$300 billion. It's likely that the managers at HOME DEPOT, the largest U.S. home improvement supply store operation with $12 billion in revenue, assess strategic threats and opportunities by comparing their company with a strategic group consisting of the other major home improvement supply companies. To assist in these comparisons, Exhibit 6.3 shows the number of stores, the size of the typical new store, and the overall geographic distribution (states, countries) of Home Depot stores compared with LOWE'S, 84 Lumber, and Ace Hardware.

In fact, when scanning the environment for strategic threats and opportunities, managers tend to categorize the different companies in their industries as core, secondary, and transient firms.[26] **Core firms** are the central companies in a strategic group. Home Depot operates 2,079 stores covering all 50 states, Puerto Rico, the U.S. Virgin Islands, Mexico, and all 10 provinces of Canada. The company has more than 350,000 employees and annual revenue of over $85 billion, Lowe's has more than 1,325 stores in 49 states, stocks more than 40,000 products in each store, and has annual revenues of more than $43 billion.[27] Clearly, Lowe's is the closest competitor to Home Depot and would probably be classified as the core firm in Home Depot's strategic group. And even though ACE HARDWARE has more stores than Home Depot and appears to be a bigger multinational player, Ace's franchise structure and small, individualized stores (each store is laid out differently and has a different mix of products) keeps it from being a core firm in Home Depot's strategic group.[28] Likewise, Home Depot's management probably doesn't concern itself much with Aubuchon Hardware. Aubuchon is a fine operation that has been family owned and operated for more than 100 years, but with only 140 stores in New England and upstate New York, Aubuchon would probably not be included in Home Depot's core strategic group.[29] When most managers scan their environments for strategic threats and opportunities, they concentrate on the strategic actions of core firms, not unrelated firms like Aubuchon.

Where does a firm like Ace Hardware fit in? The company has made significant efforts to position itself as a more helpful version of Home Depot. Ace's Vision 21 strategic plan aims to make franchisees the leaders in Ace's unique convenient-store approach to selling hardware. Ace operates stores in over 70 countries and has moved aggressively over the past decade to improve its supply chain operation.[30] Nonetheless, because of its small size—annual sales of less than $4 billion—Home Depot's managers might not classify it as a core firm.

Secondary firms are firms that use strategies related to but somewhat different from those of core firms. *84 LUMBER* has over 500 stores in 40 states, but the company focuses on supplying professional contractors. Stores are open to the public, but without the wide variety of products on the shelves or any assistance available to the average consumer, people without expertise in building or remodeling probably don't find 84 Lumber stores very navigable. In fact, the company sells more than 95 percent of its products to professional contractors. Home Depot would most likely classify 84 Lumber as a secondary firm in its strategic group analysis.[31] Managers are aware of the potential threats and opportunities posed by secondary firms, but they spend more time assessing the threats and opportunities associated with core firms.

Transient firms are companies whose strategies are changing from one strategic position to another. Ace Hardware is moving directly toward Home Depot's primary market. To compete more effectively with Home Depot and Lowe's, Ace recently increased the capacity of its warehouse operations, which now carries more than 65,000 products and makes them available to all Ace stores.[32] In other words, Ace Hardware is trying to become one of Home Depot's core competitors. Likewise, True Value Hardware has expanded to 6,200 stores in 54 countries. But rather than compete on the basis of assortment, True Value is attempting to compete with Home Depot and Lowe's on price and fast delivery.[33] Note, however, that because the strategies of transient firms are changing, managers may not know what to think about these firms. Consequently, managers may overlook or misjudge the potential threats and opportunities posed by transient firms.

Because top managers tend to limit their attention to the core firms in their strategic group, some companies have started using shadow-strategy task forces to more aggressively scan their environments for strategic threats and opportunities. A **shadow-strategy task force** actively seeks out its own company's weaknesses and then, thinking like a competitor, determines how other companies could exploit them for competitive advantage.[34] Furthermore, to make sure that the task force challenges conventional thinking, its members should be independent-minded, come from a variety of company functions and levels, and have the access and authority to question the company's current strategic actions and intent. For example, CIBA-GEIGY's Industrial Dye division makes color dyes used in carpet manufacturing. One of the difficulties in this business is ensuring color consistency, that is, making sure that the dark gray carpet manufactured next week will be the same dark gray color as the carpet manufactured today. Ciba-Geigy's shadow-strategy task force determined that if its competitors could find ways to consistently, precisely, and cheaply match color carpet dyes (so that carpet colors looked the same regardless of when and where they were manufactured), Ciba-Geigy would be at a considerable competitive disadvantage. After the shadow-strategy task force challenged top management with its conclusions, the company went about developing distinctive competencies in dye research and manufacturing, which allowed it to make dyes with scientific preciseness.[35]

In short, a situational analysis has two basic parts. The first is to examine internal strengths and weaknesses by focusing on distinctive competencies and core capabilities. The second is to examine external opportunities and threats by focusing on environmental scanning, strategic groups, and shadow-strategy task forces.

2.3 Choosing Strategic Alternatives

After determining the need for strategic change and conducting a situational analysis, the last step in the strategy-making process is to choose strategic alternatives that will help the company create or maintain a sustainable competitive advantage. According to strategic reference point theory, managers choose between two basic alternative strategies. They can choose a conservative, *risk-avoiding strategy* that aims to protect an existing competitive advantage. Or they can choose an aggressive, *risk-seeking strategy* that aims to extend or create a sustainable competitive advantage. For example, MENARDS is a hardware store chain with 170 locations throughout the Midwest.[36] When hardware giant Home Depot entered the Midwest, Menards faced a basic choice: Avoid risk by continuing with the strategy it had in place before Home Depot's arrival or seek risk by trying to further its competitive advantage against Home Depot, which is six times its size. Some of its competitors decided to fold. Kmart closed all of its Builders Square hardware stores when Home Depot came to Minneapolis. Handy Andy liquidated its 74 stores when Home Depot came to the Midwest. But Menards decided to fight, spending millions to open 35 new stores at the same time that Home Depot was opening 44 of its own.[37]

shadow-strategy task force a committee within a company that analyzes the company's own weaknesses to determine how competitors could exploit them for competitive advantage

When Home Depot came to Chicago, Menards implemented an aggressive strategy to expand its presence in the region. It opened more stores and stocked them with as much inventory as the national chain. Because Menards stores are built to resemble a grocery store more than a warehouse, however, the merchandise seems more accessible, and that has translated into greater sales per square foot than its rival.

"WHAT'S NEW" COMPANY

strategic reference points the strategic targets managers use to measure whether a firm has developed the core competencies it needs to achieve a sustainable competitive advantage

The choice to seek risk or avoid risk typically depends on whether top management views the company as falling above or below strategic reference points. **Strategic reference points** are the targets that managers use to measure whether their firm has developed the core competencies that it needs to achieve a sustainable competitive advantage. For example, if a hotel chain decides to compete by providing superior quality and service, then top management will track the success of this strategy through customer surveys or published hotel ratings, such as those provided by the prestigious *MOBIL TRAVEL GUIDE*. If a hotel chain decides to compete on price, it will regularly conduct market surveys to check the prices of other hotels. The competitors' prices are the hotel managers' strategic reference points against which to compare their own pricing strategy. If competitors can consistently underprice them, then the managers need to determine whether their staff and resources have the core competencies to compete on price.

As shown in Exhibit 6.4, when a company is performing above or better than its strategic reference points, top management will typically be satisfied with the company's strategy. Ironically, this satisfaction tends to make top management conservative and risk-averse. After all, since the company already has a sustainable competitive advantage, the worst thing that could happen would be to lose it. Consequently, new issues or changes in the company's external environments are viewed as threats. In contrast, when a company is performing below or worse than its strategic reference points, top management will typically be dissatisfied with the company's strategy. In this instance, managers are much more likely to choose a daring, risk-taking strategy. After all, if the current strategy is producing substandard results, the company has nothing to lose by switching to risky new strategies in the hopes that it can create a sustainable competitive advantage. Consequently, managers of companies in this situation view new issues or changes in external environments as opportunities for potential gain.

Strategic reference point theory is not deterministic, however. Managers are not predestined to choose risk-averse or risk-seeking strategies for their companies. Indeed, one of the most important elements of the theory is that managers *can* influence the strategies chosen by their company by *actively changing and adjusting* the strategic reference points they use to judge strategic performance. To illustrate, if a company has become complacent after consistently surpassing its strategic reference points, then top management can change from a risk-averse to a risk-taking orientation by raising the standards of performance (that is, the strategic reference points). Indeed, this is what happened at Menards.

Instead of being satisfied with just protecting its existing stores (a risk-averse strategy), founder John Menard changed the strategic reference points the company had been using to assess strategic performance. To encourage a daring, offensive-minded strategy that would allow the company to open nearly as many new stores as Home Depot, he determined that Menards would have to beat Home Depot on not one or two, but four strategic reference points: price, products, sales per square foot, and "friendly accessibility." The strategy appears to be succeeding. In terms of price, market research indicates that a 100-item shopping cart of goods is consistently cheaper at Menards.[38] In terms of products, Menards sells 50,000 products per store, the same as Home Depot. In terms of sales per square foot, Menards

Exhibit 6.4

Strategic Reference Points

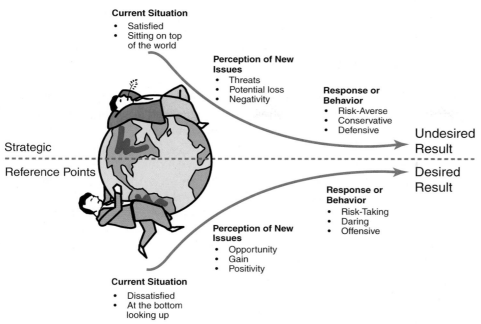

Current Situation
- Satisfied
- Sitting on top of the world

Perception of New Issues
- Threats
- Potential loss
- Negativity

Response or Behavior
- Risk-Averse
- Conservative
- Defensive

Undesired Result

Strategic

Reference Points

Desired Result

Response or Behavior
- Risk-Taking
- Daring
- Offensive

Perception of New Issues
- Opportunity
- Gain
- Positivity

Current Situation
- Dissatisfied
- At the bottom looking up

Source: A. Fiegenbaum, S. Hart, & D. Schendel, "Strategic Reference Point Theory," *Strategic Management Journal* 17 (1996): 219–235.

($407 per square foot) outsells Home Depot ($371 per square foot).[39] Finally, unlike Home Depot's warehouselike stores, Menards' stores are built to resemble grocery stores. Shiny tiled floors, wide aisles, and easy-to-reach products all make Menards a "friendlier" place for shoppers.[40] And now with Lowe's, the second-largest hardware store chain in the nation, also entering its markets, Menards has added a fifth strategic reference point, store size. At 225,000 square feet, most new Menards stores are more than double the size of Home Depot's stores and 75,000 square feet larger than Lowe's.[41] John Caulfield, who wrote a book about Home Depot and the hardware business, says, "Menards is clearly throwing the gauntlet down at Lowe's. They're saying, 'If you come into Chicago, here is what you're going to face.'"[42]

So even when (perhaps *especially* when) companies have achieved a sustainable competitive advantage, top managers must adjust or change strategic reference points to challenge themselves and their employees to develop new core competencies for the future. In the long run, effective organizations will frequently revise their strategic reference points to better focus managers' attention on the new challenges and opportunities that occur in their ever-changing business environments.

Review 2: *Strategy-Making Process*

The first step in strategy making is determining whether a strategy needs to be changed to sustain a competitive advantage. Because uncertainty and competitive inertia make this difficult to determine, managers can improve the speed and accuracy of this step by looking for differences between top management's intended strategy and the strategy actually implemented by lower-level managers (that is, looking for strategic dissonance). The second step is to conduct a situational analysis that examines internal strengths and weaknesses (distinctive competencies and core capabilities), as well as external threats and opportunities (environmental scanning, strategic groups, and shadow-strategy task forces). In the third step of strategy making, strategic reference point theory suggests that when companies are performing better than their strategic reference points, top management will typically choose a risk-averse strategy. When performance is below strategic reference points, risk-seeking strategies are more likely to be chosen. Importantly, however, managers can influence the choice of strategic alternatives by actively changing and adjusting the strategic reference points they use to judge strategic performance.

CORPORATE-, INDUSTRY-, AND FIRM-LEVEL STRATEGIES

To formulate effective strategies, companies must be able to answer these three basic questions:

- *What business are we in?*
- *How should we compete in this industry?*
- *Who are our competitors, and how should we respond to them?*

These simple but powerful questions are at the heart of corporate-, industry-, and firm-level strategies.

After reading the next three sections, you should be able to

3 explain the different kinds of corporate-level strategies.

4 describe the different kinds of industry-level strategies.

5 explain the components and kinds of firm-level strategies.

3 Corporate-Level Strategies

Corporate-level strategy is the overall organizational strategy that addresses the question "What business or businesses are we in or should we be in?" Garry Ridge, CEO of *WD-40* Corporation, explains how he changed its corporate-level strategy from a "Johnny one-note" business selling only WD-40 lubricant to an "innovation marketing and distribution company . . . [focused on] the squeak, smell, and dirt business."

"WHAT'S NEW" COMPANY

In the U.S., WD-40 had reached what I named "fortress status" as a brand. Back then, more people used WD-40 every day than used dental floss. We decided to turn up the volume on that opportunity to grow. And also, to position ourselves not just to be a marketing company (which we were back then) but what we are now, which is an innovation marketing and distribution company. We decided we were going to be in the squeak, smell, and dirt business. I listened to what Warren Buffet had said. He said you have to be in businesses that are going to be [around] in the future. I felt that

corporate-level strategy the overall organizational strategy that addresses the question "What business or businesses are we in or should we be in?"

there would always be squeaks. There will always be smells. And there would always be dirt. That was the strategy as we started looking for brands that we could acquire. We then formed a team called Team Tomorrow, which focused only on revenues of the future. Team Tomorrow has a goal of being able to generate $100 million worth of annual revenue from products developed and launched in the previous three-year period. We are doing $35 million now from zero dollars in 2002.[43]

Exhibit 6.5 shows the two major approaches to corporate-level strategy that companies use to decide which businesses they should be in: **3.1 portfolio strategy**[44] and **3.2 grand strategies**.

PORTFOLIO STRATEGY	GRAND STRATEGIES
• Acquisitions, unrelated diversification, related diversification, single businesses	• Growth
• Boston Consulting Group matrix	• Stability
• Stars	• Retrenchment/recovery
• Question marks	
• Cash cows	
• Dogs	

Exhibit 6.5
Corporate-Level Strategies

> Corporate-level strategy is the overall organizational strategy that addresses the question "What business or businesses are we in or should we be in?"

3.1 Portfolio Strategy

One of the standard strategies for stock market investors is **diversification**: owning stocks in a variety of companies in different industries. The purpose of this strategy is to reduce risk in the overall stock portfolio (the entire collection of stocks). The basic idea is simple: If you invest in 10 companies in 10 different industries, you won't lose your entire investment if one company performs poorly. Furthermore, because they're in different industries, one company's losses are likely to be offset by another company's gains. Portfolio strategy is based on these same ideas. We'll start by taking a look at the theory and ideas behind portfolio strategy and then proceed with a critical review that suggests that some of the key ideas behind portfolio strategy are *not* supported.

Portfolio strategy is a corporate-level strategy that minimizes risk by diversifying investment among various businesses or product lines. Just as a diversification strategy guides an investor who invests in a variety of stocks, portfolio strategy guides the strategic decisions of corporations that compete in a variety of businesses. For example, portfolio strategy could be used to guide the strategy of a company like *3M*, which makes 55,000 products for seven different business sectors: consumers and offices (Post-its, Scotch tape); display and graphics (for computers, cell phones, PDAs, TVs); electronics and communications (flexible circuits used in printers and electronic displays); health care (medical, surgical, dental, and personal care products); industrial (tapes, adhesives, supply chain software); safety, security, and protection services (glass safety, fire protection, respiratory products); and transportation (products and components for the manufacture, repair, and maintenance of autos, aircraft, boats, and other vehicles).[45] Similarly, portfolio strategy could be used by Johnson & Johnson, which has 200 divisions making health-care products for the pharmaceutical, diagnostic, consumer, and health-care-professionals markets.[46] Furthermore, just as investors consider the mix of stocks in their stock portfolio when deciding which stocks to buy or sell, managers following portfolio strategy try to acquire companies that fit well with the rest of their corporate portfolio and to sell

diversification a strategy for reducing risk by buying a variety of items (stocks or, in the case of a corporation, types of businesses) so that the failure of one stock or one business does not doom the entire portfolio

portfolio strategy a corporate-level strategy that minimizes risk by diversifying investment among various businesses or product lines those that don't. For example, when SARA LEE CORPORATION decided to revise its strategy to become a premier maker and distributor of food, beverage, household, and body care products, the company sold off multiple divisions that no longer fit with the new strategy, like Hanes, Champion, Playtex, Wonderbra, and other apparel companies.[47] Portfolio strategy provides the following guidelines to help companies make these difficult decisions.

First, according to portfolio strategy, the more businesses in which a corporation competes, the smaller its overall chances of failing. Think of a corporation as a stool and its businesses as the legs of the stool. The more legs or businesses added to the stool, the less likely it is to tip over. Using this analogy, portfolio strategy reduces 3M's risk of failing because the corporation's survival depends on essentially seven different business sectors. Because the emphasis is on adding "legs to the stool," managers who use portfolio strategy are often on the lookout for **acquisitions**, that is, other companies to buy.

Second, beyond adding new businesses to the corporate portfolio, portfolio strategy predicts that companies can reduce risk even more through **unrelated diversification**—creating or acquiring companies in completely unrelated businesses (more on the accuracy of this prediction later). According to portfolio strategy, when businesses are unrelated, losses in one business or industry should have minimal effect on the performance of other companies in the corporate portfolio. One of the best examples of unrelated diversification is SAMSUNG of Korea. Samsung has businesses in electronics (computer memory chips, computer and telecommunication equipment, color TV picture tubes, glass bulbs); machinery and heavy industries (shipbuilding, construction, airplane engine manufacturing, fiber optics, semiconductors); chemicals (engineering plastics, and specialty chemicals); financial services (life and accident insurance, credit cards, and financial securities and trusts); and other areas ranging from automobiles to hotels and entertainment.[48] Because most internally grown businesses tend to be related to existing products or services, portfolio strategy suggests that acquiring new businesses is the preferred method of unrelated diversification.

Third, investing the profits and cash flows from mature, slow-growth businesses into newer, faster-growing businesses can reduce long-term risk. The best-known portfolio strategy for guiding investment in a corporation's businesses is the BOSTON CONSULTING GROUP (BCG) matrix. The **BCG matrix** is a portfolio strategy that managers use to categorize their corporation's businesses by growth rate and relative market share, helping them decide how to invest corporate funds. The matrix, shown in Exhibit 6.6, separates businesses into four categories based on how fast the market is growing (high-growth or low-growth) and the size of the business's share of that market (small or large). **Stars** are companies that have a large share of a fast-growing market. To take advantage of a star's fast-growing market and its strength in that market (large share), the corporation must invest substantially in it. The investment is usually worthwhile, however, because many stars produce sizable future profits. **Question marks** are companies that have a small share of a fast-growing market. If the corporation invests in these companies, they may eventually become stars, but their relative weakness in the market (small share) makes investing in question marks more risky than investing in stars. **Cash cows** are companies that have a large share of a slow-growing market. Companies in this situation are often highly profitable, hence the name "cash cow." Finally, **dogs** are companies that have a small share of a slow-growing market. As the name "dogs" suggests, having a small share of a slow-growth market is often not profitable.

acquisition the purchase of a company by another company

unrelated diversification creating or acquiring companies in completely unrelated businesses

BCG matrix a portfolio strategy, developed by the Boston Consulting Group, that categorizes a corporation's businesses by growth rate and relative market share, and helps managers decide how to invest corporate funds

star a company with a large share of a fast-growing market

question mark a company with a small share of a fast-growing market

cash cow a company with a large share of a slow-growing market

dog a company with a small share of a slow-growing market

Since the idea is to redirect investment from slow-growing to fast-growing companies, the BCG matrix starts by recommending that while the substantial cash flows from cash cows last, they should be reinvested in stars (see ❶ in Exhibit 6.6) to help them grow even faster and obtain even more market share. Using this strategy, current profits help produce future profits. Over time, as their market growth slows, some stars may turn into cash cows (see ❷). Cash flows should also be directed to some question marks (see ❸). Though riskier than stars, question marks have great potential because of their fast-growing market. Managers must decide which question marks are most likely to turn into stars, and therefore warrant further investment, and which ones are too risky and should be sold. Over time, hopefully some question marks will become stars as their small markets become large ones (see ❹). Finally, because dogs lose money, the corporation should "find them new owners" or "take them to the pound." In other words, dogs should either be sold to other companies or be closed down and liquidated for their assets (see ❺).

Exhibit 6.6
Boston Consulting Group Matrix

Although the BCG matrix and other forms of portfolio strategy are relatively popular among managers, portfolio strategy has some drawbacks. The most significant is that contrary to the predictions of portfolio strategy, the evidence does *not* support the usefulness of acquiring unrelated businesses. As shown in Exhibit 6.7, there is a U-shaped relationship between diversification and risk. The left side of the curve shows that single businesses with no diversification are extremely risky (if the single business fails, the entire business fails). So, in part, the portfolio strategy of diversifying is correct—competing in a variety of different businesses can lower risk. However, portfolio strategy is partly wrong, too—the right side of the curve shows that conglomerates composed of completely unrelated businesses are even riskier than single, undiversified businesses.

A second set of problems with portfolio strategy has to do with the dysfunctional consequences that occur when companies are categorized as stars, cash cows, question marks, or dogs. Contrary to expectations, the BCG matrix often yields incorrect judgments about a company's potential. This is because it relies on past performance (previous market share and previous market growth), which is a notoriously poor predictor of

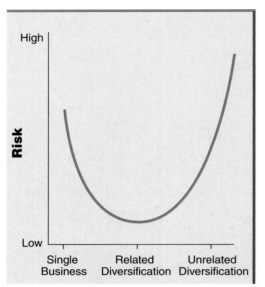

Source: Republished with permission of Academy of Management, P.O. Box 3020, Briar Cliff Manor, NY, 10510–8020. M. Lubatkin & P. J. Lane, "Psst … The Merger Mavens Still Have It Wrong!" *Academy of Management Executive* 10 (1996): 21–39. Reproduced with permission of the publisher via Copyright Clearance Center, Inc.

Exhibit 6.7

U-Shaped Relationship between Diversification and Risk

related diversification creating or acquiring companies that share similar products, manufacturing, marketing, technology, or cultures

future company performance. For example, from 1930 until about 10 years ago, Yellow Book, the yellow pages phone-directory publisher, was a tiny publisher of community phone directories in Long Island, New York. With phone companies such as Verizon and SBC accounting for 96 percent of the $14 billion yellow pages business, there was no reason, based on its undistinguished past, to expect Yellow Book to suddenly become successful. With only a sliver of a slow-growing market, Yellow Book was undoubtedly a "dog" according to the BCG matrix. In the last decade, however, Yellow Book has had remarkable growth. By aggressively cutting prices (in some markets, charging 40 percent to 50 percent less than Verizon's SuperPages), it increased its annual sales from $46 million to over $1 billion. Yellow Book now has a 10 percent share of the yellow pages directory market and sells 500+ yellow pages directories that are used by 72 million people in 42 states.[50]

Furthermore, using the BCG matrix can also weaken the strongest performer in the corporate portfolio, the cash cow. As funds are redirected from cash cows to stars, corporate managers essentially take away the resources needed to take advantage of the cash cow's new business opportunities. As a result, the cash cow becomes less aggressive in seeking new business or in defending its present business. For example, PROCTER & GAMBLE's Tide, the laundry detergent that P&G brought to market in 1946, is clearly a cash cow, accounting for billions in worldwide revenues. A few years ago, however, in a bid to bring new products to market—P&G hadn't introduced a top-selling new product since Pampers in 1961—the company was diverting up to half a billion dollars from cash cows like Tide to promote potential product blockbusters (that is, stars) such as Febreze, a spray that eliminates odors; Dryel, which dry-cleans clothes at home; Fit, a spray that kills bacteria on fruits and vegetables; and Impress, a high-tech plastic wrap.[51] Finally, labeling a top performer as a cash cow can harm employee morale. Cash-cow employees realize that they have inferior status and that instead of working for themselves, they are now working to fund the growth of stars and question marks. P&G ultimately reversed the diversion of funds as CEO A. G. Lafley refocused the company on its biggest brands (its cash cows).[52]

So, what kind of portfolio strategy does the best job of helping managers decide which companies to buy or sell? The U-shaped curve in Exhibit 6.7 indicates that, contrary to the predictions of portfolio strategy, the best approach is probably **related diversification**, in which the different business units share similar products, manufacturing, marketing, technology, or cultures. The key to related diversification is to acquire or create new companies with core capabilities that complement the core capabilities of businesses already in the corporate portfolio. We began this section with the example of 3M and its 55,000 products sold in over seven different business sectors. While seemingly different, most of 3M's product divisions are based in some fashion on its distinctive competencies in adhesives and tape (such as wet or dry sandpaper, Post-it notes, Scotchgard fabric protector, transdermal skin patches, and reflective material used in traffic signs). Furthermore, all of 3M's divisions share its strong corporate culture that promotes and encourages risk taking and innovation. In sum, in contrast to a single, undiversified business or unrelated diversification, related diversification reduces risk because the different businesses can work as a team, relying on each other for needed experience, expertise, and support.

Exhibit 6.8 details the problems associated with portfolio strategy and recommends ways that managers can increase their chances of success through related diversification.

3.2 Grand Strategies

A **grand strategy** is a broad strategic plan used to help an organization achieve its strategic goals.[53] Grand strategies guide the strategic alternatives that managers of individual businesses or subunits may use in deciding what businesses they should be in. There are three kinds of grand strategies: growth, stability, and retrenchment/recovery.

The purpose of a **growth strategy** is to increase profits, revenues, market share, or the number of places (stores, offices, locations) in which the company does business. Companies can grow in several ways. They can grow externally by merging with or acquiring other companies in the same or different businesses. Some of the largest mergers and acquisitions of recent years include Procter & Gamble acquiring Gillette (consumer products), Kmart acquiring Sears (retailing), Alcatel acquiring Lucent Technologies (telecommunications), Hewlett-Packard acquiring Compaq (computers), and McClatchy acquiring Tribune (publishing).[54]

Another way to grow is internally, directly expanding the company's existing business or creating and growing new businesses. For example, over the last decade, WALGREENS, one of the largest pharmacy chains in the United States, opened approximately 100 stores a year. With baby boomers aging and the

grand strategy a broad corporate-level strategic plan used to achieve strategic goals and guide the strategic alternatives that managers of individual businesses or subunits may use

growth strategy a strategy that focuses on increasing profits, revenues, market share, or the number of places in which the company does business

Exhibit 6.8
Portfolio Strategy: Problems and Recommendations

Problems with Portfolio Strategy	Recommendations for Making Portfolio Strategy Work
Unrelated diversification does not reduce risk.	Don't be so quick to sell dogs or question marks. Instead, management should commit to the markets in which it competes by strengthening core capabilities.
Present performance is used to predict future performance.	Put your "eggs in similar (not different) baskets" by acquiring companies in related businesses.
Assessments of a business's growth potential are often inaccurate	Acquire companies with complementary core capabilities.
Cash cows fail to aggressively pursue opportunities and defend themselves from threats.	Encourage collaboration and cooperation between related firms and businesses within the company.
Being labeled a "cash cow" can hurt employee morale.	"Date before you marry." Work with a business before deciding to acquire it.
Companies often overpay to acquire stars.	When in doubt, don't acquire new businesses. Mergers and acquisitions are inherently risky and difficult to make work. Only acquire firms that can help create or extend a sustainable competitive advantage.
Acquiring firms often treat acquired stars as "conquered foes." Key stars' managers, who once controlled their own destiny, often leave because they are now treated as relatively unimportant middle managers.	

Sources: M. Lubatkin, "Value-Creating Mergers: Fact or Folklore?" *Academy of Management Executive* 2 (1988): 295–302; M. Lubatkin & S. Chatterjee, "Extending Modern Portfolio Theory into the Domain of Corporate Diversification: Does It Apply?" *Academy of Management Journal* 37 (1994): 109–136. M. H. Lubatkin & P. J. Lane, "Psst . . . The Merger Mavens Still Have It Wrong!" *Academy of Management Executive* 10 (1996): 21–39.

need for more pharmacies to sell prescription drugs growing rapidly, Walgreens opened 425 new stores last year and will shoot for 500 this year. In fact, with 4,582 stores in 44 states, it hopes to have 7,000 stores by 2010.[55] Walgreens chairman David Bernauer says, "Growth is a huge challenge, but it's the right thing to do. And this is absolutely the right time in our history to do it." Because Walgreens stores tend to draw customers from only a one- to two-mile radius, each additional store should add significant revenues and profits without cannibalizing existing stores' sales.[56]

The purpose of a **stability strategy** is to continue doing what the company has been doing, but just do it better. Consequently, companies following a stability strategy try to improve the way in which they sell the same products or services to the same customers. For example, SUBARU has been making four-wheel-drive station wagons for 30 years. Over the last decade, it strengthened this focus by manufacturing only all-wheel-drive vehicles, like the Subaru Legacy and Outback (both come in four-door sedans or two-door coupes), which are popular in snowy and mountainous regions. Subaru's extremely loyal customers have rewarded the company with an average 7 percent annual increase in sales (extremely high for the auto industry) over the last 10 years.[57] Companies often choose a stability strategy when their external environment doesn't change much or after they have struggled with periods of explosive growth.

The purpose of a **retrenchment strategy** is to turn around very poor company performance by shrinking the size or scope of the business or, if a company is in multiple businesses, by closing or shutting down different lines of the business. The first step of a typical retrenchment strategy might include making significant cost reductions; laying off employees; closing poorly performing stores, offices, or manufacturing plants; or closing or selling entire lines of products or services.[58] For example, each time Home Depot, Menards, Lowe's, or Wal-Mart opened stores near Dave Umber's three Ace Hardware stores, the number of customers in his stores dropped by 10 percent. So, after losing $110,000 over two years, Umber began cutting. He says, "I had to walk up to people who've been employees of mine for years and say, 'I've got to let you go. You're a great person, but I can't afford to pay you anymore.' It was hard." He also reduced health benefits, eliminated bonuses, chopped his advertising budget by $20,000, saved $500 a month by using efficient fluorescent light bulbs, and made sure prices were within 10 percent of his competitors. Says Umber, "If it's the difference between $1.09 and $1.29, customers don't care, particularly if it saves them from having to run across town to Home Depot. But if something is $10 more, they will."[59]

After cutting costs and reducing a business's size or scope, the second step in a retrenchment strategy is recovery. **Recovery** consists of the strategic actions that a company takes to return to a growth strategy. This two-step process of cutting and recovery is analogous to pruning roses. Prior to each growing season, roses should be cut back to two-thirds their normal size. Pruning doesn't damage the roses; it makes them stronger and more likely to produce beautiful, fragrant flowers. The retrenchment-and-recovery process is similar. Cost reductions, layoffs, and plant closings are sometimes necessary to restore companies to "good health." But like pruning, those cuts are intended to allow companies to eventually return to growth strategies (that is, recovery). So, when company performance drops significantly, a strategy of retrenchment and recovery may help the company return to a successful growth strategy.

stability strategy a strategy that focuses on improving the way in which the company sells the same products or services to the same customers

retrenchment strategy a strategy that focuses on turning around very poor company performance by shrinking the size or scope of the business

recovery the strategic actions taken after retrenchment to return to a growth strategy

Review 3: Corporate-Level Strategies

Corporate-level strategies, such as portfolio strategy and grand strategies, help managers determine what businesses they should be in. Portfolio strategy focuses on lowering business risk by being in multiple, unrelated businesses and by investing the cash flows from slow-growth businesses into faster-growing businesses. One portfolio strategy, the BCG matrix, suggests that cash flows from cash cows should be reinvested in stars and in carefully chosen question marks. Dogs should be sold or liquidated. Portfolio strategy has several problems, however. Acquiring unrelated businesses actually increases risk rather than lowering it. The BCG matrix is often wrong when predicting companies' futures (as dogs or cash cows, for example). And redirecting cash flows can seriously weaken cash cows. The most successful way to use the portfolio approach to corporate strategy is to reduce risk through related diversification.

The three kinds of grand strategies are growth, stability, and retrenchment/recovery. Companies can grow externally by merging with or acquiring other companies, or they can grow internally through direct expansion or creating new businesses. Companies choose a stability strategy—selling the same products or services to the same customers—when their external environment changes very little or after they have dealt with periods of explosive growth. Retrenchment strategy, shrinking the size or scope of a business, is used to turn around poor performance. If retrenchment works, it is often followed by a recovery strategy that focuses on growing the business again.

4 Industry-Level Strategies

Industry-level strategy addresses the question "How should we compete in this industry?"

Let's find out more about industry-level strategies, shown in Exhibit 6.9, by discussing **4.1 the five industry forces that determine overall levels of competition in an industry** *and* **4.2 the positioning strategies** *and* **4.3 adaptive strategies that companies can use to achieve sustained competitive advantage and above-average profits**.

4.1 Five Industry Forces

According to Harvard professor Michael Porter, five industry forces—character of the rivalry, threat of new entrants, threat of substitute products or services, bargaining power of suppliers, and bargaining power of buyers—determine an industry's

Five Industry Forces	Positioning Strategies	Adaptive Strategies
Character of the rivalry	Cost leadership	Defenders
Threat of new entrants	Differentiation	Prospectors
Threat of substitute products or services	Focus	Analyzers
Bargaining power of suppliers		Reactors
Bargaining power of buyers		

Industry-level strategy addresses the question "How should we compete in this industry?"

industry-level strategy a corporate strategy that addresses the question "How should we compete in this industry?"

Exhibit 6.9
Industry-Level Strategies

overall attractiveness and potential for long-term profitability. The stronger these forces, the less attractive the industry becomes to corporate investors because it is more difficult for companies to be profitable. Porter's industry forces are illustrated in Exhibit 6.10. Let's examine how these industry forces are bringing changes to several kinds of industries.

Character of the rivalry is a measure of the intensity of competitive behavior between companies in an industry. Is the competition among firms aggressive and cutthroat, or do competitors focus more on serving customers than on attacking each other? Both industry attractiveness and profitability decrease when rivalry is cutthroat. For example, selling cars is a highly competitive business. Pick up a local newspaper on Friday, Saturday, or Sunday morning, and you'll find dozens of pages of car advertising ("Anniversary Sale-A-Bration," "Ford March Savings!" and "$99 Down, You Choose!"). In fact, competition in new car sales is so intense that if it weren't for used-car sales, repair work, and replacement parts, many auto dealers would actually lose money.

The **threat of new entrants** is a measure of the degree to which barriers to entry make it easy or difficult for new companies to get started in an industry. If new companies can easily enter the industry, then competition will increase, and prices and profits will fall. However, if there are sufficient barriers to entry, such as large capital requirements to buy expensive equipment or plant facilities or the need for specialized knowledge, then competition will be weaker, and prices and profits will generally be higher. For instance, high costs and intense competition make it very difficult to enter the video-game business. With today's average video game taking 12 to 36 months to create, $5 million to $10 million to develop, and teams of high-paid creative workers that have the skills to develop realistic graphics, captivating story lines, and innovative game capabilities while also being disciplined enough to meet budgets and very strict deadlines and still produce efficient, reliable, bug-free code, the barriers to entry for this business are obviously extremely high. And with already dominant firms like *EA SPORTS* chalking up $3 billion in sales, 60 percent profit margins, 254 percent annual growth over the last three years, $2.4 billion in cash, and no debt, it will be extremely difficult to enter the video-game industry and be successful.[60]

The **threat of substitute products or services** is a measure of the ease with which customers can find substitutes for an industry's products or services. If customers can easily find substitute products or services, the competition will be greater, and profits will be lower. If there are few or no substitutes, competition will be weaker, and profits will be higher. Generic medicines are some of the best-known examples of substitute products. Under U.S. patent law, a company that develops a drug has exclusive rights to produce and market that drug for 20 years. During this time, if the drug sells well, prices and profits are generally high. After 20 years, however, the patent will expire, and any pharmaceutical company can manufacture and sell the same drug. When this happens, drug prices

character of the rivalry a measure of the intensity of competitive behavior between companies in an industry

threat of new entrants a measure of the degree to which barriers to entry make it easy or difficult for new companies to get started in an industry

threat of substitute products or services a measure of the ease with which customers can find substitutes for an industry's products or services

Exhibit 6.10

Porter's Five Industry Forces

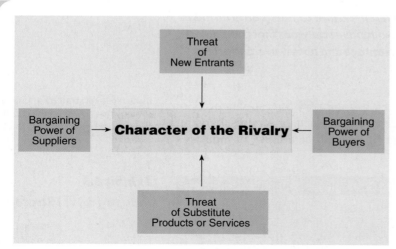

Source: Adapted with permission of The Free Press, a Division of Simon & Schuster, Inc. M. E. Porter, *Competitive Strategy: Techniques for Analyzing Industries and Competitors* (New York: Free Press, 1980). © 1980 by the Free Press.

drop substantially, and the company that developed the drug typically sees its revenues drop sharply. For example, Prozac, a medication that fights depression, cost $30 a pill and returned $2.7 billion in sales revenues to **ELI LILLY & CO.** the last year it was under patent. In contrast, fluoxetine, a generic version of Prozac made by Merck-Medco that became available the day the patent for Prozac expired, costs only $5 per pill. As a result, Eli Lilly lost 90% of its Prozac business within one year. It faced a similar loss of revenue when patent protection ended for Zyprexa, its even more successful schizophrenia drug.[61]

© SUSAN VAN ETTEN

Bargaining power of suppliers is a measure of the influence that suppliers of parts, materials, and services to firms in an industry have on the prices of these inputs. When companies can buy parts, materials, and services from numerous suppliers, the companies will be able to bargain with the suppliers to keep prices low. On the other hand, if there are few suppliers, or if a company is dependent on a supplier with specialized skills and knowledge, then the suppliers will have the bargaining power to dictate price levels. Today, there are so many suppliers of inexpensive, standardized parts, computer chips, and video screens that dozens of new companies are beginning to manufacture flat-screen TVs. One of those companies is **XOCECO** (ZO-say-co), a Chinese company that has made inexpensive, low-quality TVs for two decades. But with dozens of companies able to supply the high-tech parts it needs, Xoceco was able to enter the flat-screen TV market without having to spend millions of dollars on research and development. Instead, it is simply buying the parts and software it needs directly from suppliers, assembling the TVs in its Chinese factories, and then undercutting the prices of now-struggling market leaders like Sony.[62]

Bargaining power of buyers is a measure of the influence that customers have on the firm's prices. If a company sells a popular product or service to multiple buyers, then the company has more power to set prices. By contrast, if a company is dependent on just a few high-volume buyers, those buyers will typically have enough bargaining power to dictate prices. For example, with more than 6,200 stores and 176 million weekly shoppers, **WAL-MART** is the largest single buyer in the history of retailing.[63] Wal-Mart buys 30 percent of all toothpaste, shampoo, and paper towels made by retail suppliers; 15 to 20 percent of all CDs, videos, and DVDs; 15 percent of all magazines; 14 percent of all groceries; and 20 percent of all toys. And, of course, Wal-Mart uses its purchasing power as a buyer to push down prices. Wal-Mart's Gary Meyers, a vice president of global procurement, admits that "as things get more competitive [in the retail industry], the pressure that comes along with that, yeah, we try to take advantage of it."[64]

4.2 Positioning Strategies

After analyzing industry forces, the next step in industry-level strategy is to protect your company from the negative effects of industry-wide competition and to create a sustainable competitive advantage. According to Michael Porter, there are three positioning strategies: cost leadership, differentiation, and focus.

Cost leadership means producing a product or service of acceptable quality at consistently lower production costs than competitors so that the firm can offer the

bargaining power of suppliers a measure of the influence that suppliers of parts, materials, and services to firms in an industry have on the prices of these inputs

bargaining power of buyers a measure of the influence that customers have on a firm's prices

cost leadership the positioning strategy of producing a product or service of acceptable quality at consistently lower production costs than competitors can, so that the firm can offer the product or service at the lowest price in the industry product or service at the lowest price in the industry. Cost leadership protects companies from industry forces by deterring new entrants, who will have to match low costs and prices. Cost leadership also forces down the prices of substitute products and services, attracts bargain-seeking buyers, and increases bargaining power with suppliers, who have to keep their prices low if they want to do business with the cost leader. For example, although it sells the occasional $106,000 diamond ring or $11,000 Lalique crystal vase, thousands of $1,500 42-inch plasma televisions, and too many cases of $90 Dom Perignon champagne to count, COSTCO, the second-largest warehouse chain (behind Sam's), has a simple strategy—ultra-low costs. At Costco, nothing, not even the $106,000 diamond ring, is marked up more than 14 percent over the wholesale price. By contrast, low-priced Wal-Mart uses an average 33 percent markup. "This is not a tricky business. We just try to sell high-quality merchandise at a cost lower than everybody else," says Costco CEO Jim Sinegal, who, to keep overhead costs low, still answers his own phone and eats lunch at the same desk he had when he started the company two decades ago.[65]

Differentiation means making your product or service sufficiently different from competitors' offerings so that customers are willing to pay a premium price for the extra value or performance that it provides. Differentiation protects companies from industry forces by reducing the threat of substitute products. It also protects companies by making it easier to retain customers and more difficult for new entrants trying to attract new customers. For example, why would anyone pay $2,300 for WHIRLPOOL's Duet, a deluxe washer-dryer combination, when they could purchase a regular washer-dryer combination for $700 or less? The answer is that the Duet washer does huge loads, almost twice what normal washers hold, with just 16 gallons of water, compared with 40 gallons for conventional washers. So it's incredibly efficient in terms of water and energy. But most importantly, the Duet saves time. Whirlpool brand manager Ali Evans says, "By doing larger loads, women can do fewer loads, and the chore of doing laundry is minimized tremendously. It's giving them back some freedom and time."[66] And, according to Evans, customers love the Duet. She says, "We've been surprised by the passion women have when they talk about it. They call it their 'buddy' or their 'baby.' They invite people over to see it and use it. People say it's changing their lives."[67]

With a **focus strategy**, a company uses either cost leadership or differentiation to produce a specialized product or service for a limited, specially targeted group of customers in a particular geographic region or market segment. Focus strategies typically work in market niches that competitors have overlooked or have difficulty serving. With 38 stores nationwide, the CONTAINER STORE sells products to reorganize and rebuild your closets, sort out your kitchen drawers and cabinets, or add shelves, hooks, and storage anywhere in your home, office, or dorm room.[68] But, unlike Wal-Mart or Target, that's all it does. President Kip Tindell says, "The fact is, we don't sell Bounty paper towels or Coca-Cola Classic. We sell complicated stuff like those Elfa storage systems [for closets or garages]. . . . But selling stuff that's hard to sell is a key business strategy for us. It ends up giving us incredible differentiation from other retailers, because they just can't seem to sell the hard stuff. That's why we give our first-year employees 235 hours of training, as opposed to the industry average of 7 hours."[69]

4.3 Adaptive Strategies

Adaptive strategies are another set of industry-level strategies. Whereas the aim of positioning strategies is to minimize the effects of industry competition and build a sustainable competitive advantage, the purpose of adaptive strategies is to choose

differentiation the positioning strategy of providing a product or service that is sufficiently different from competitors' offerings that customers are willing to pay a premium price for it

focus strategy the positioning strategy of using cost leadership or differentiation to produce a specialized product or service for a limited, specially targeted group of customers in a particular geographic region or market segment an industry-level strategy that is best suited to changes in the organization's external environment. There are four kinds of adaptive strategies: defenders, prospectors, analyzers, and reactors.[70]

Defenders seek moderate, steady growth by offering a limited range of products and services to a well-defined set of customers. In other words, defenders aggressively "defend" their current strategic position by doing the best job they can to hold on to customers in a particular market segment. At Manoj Patel's small grocery in India, laundry detergent sales soared when Procter & Gamble drastically cut prices. Patel says, "It's so inexpensive now, my customers are buying more." Market leader Hindustan Lever responded by matching P&G's detergent price cuts and by cutting its shampoo prices, too. It also introduced a detergent that needs only half as much water to clean clothes, a considerable advantage since most Indians don't have running water. M.S. Banga, the company's chairman, says, "We have a very strong position that was built up over years. We are determined not just to defend it, but to strengthen our market share."[71] Despite P&G's price cuts, the strategy is working: Hindustan Lever's market share has increased from 27.8 to 29.5 percent in laundry detergent, and from 48.9 to 52.5 percent in shampoo.[72]

Prospectors seek fast growth by searching for new market opportunities, encouraging risk taking, and being the first to bring innovative new products to market. Prospectors are analogous to gold miners who "prospect" for gold nuggets (new products) in hopes that the nuggets will lead them to a rich deposit of gold (fast growth). 3M has long been known for its innovative products, particularly in the areas of adhesives. Since 1904, it has invented sandpaper; masking, cellophane, electrical, and scotch tapes; the first commercially available audio and video tapes; and its most famous invention, Post-It notes. Lately, 3M has invented a film that increases the brightness of LCD displays on laptop computers, developed a digital system for construction companies to detect underground telecommunication, gas, water, sewer, or electrical lines without digging, and created a pheromone spray that, by preventing harmful insects from mating, will protect apple, walnut, tomato, cranberry, and grape crops. For more on 3M's innovative products, see the 3M innovation archive (**http://solutions.3m.com/wps/portal/_l/en_US/_s.155/123515**).[73]

Analyzers are a blend of the defender and prospector strategies. Analyzers seek moderate, steady growth *and* limited opportunities for fast growth. Analyzers are rarely first to market with new products or services. Instead, they try to simultaneously minimize risk and maximize profits by following or imitating the proven successes of prospectors. India-based RANBAXY PHARMACEUTICALS follows an analyzer strategy by making low-priced generic copies of already popular patented drugs, such as GlaxoSmithKline's antibiotic Ceftin and Eli Lilly and Company's Ceclor. With $80 billion of patented drugs losing their patent protection in the next four years, Ranbaxy plans to file applications with the U.S. Food and Drug Administration to make 20 more generic drugs.[74] Says Brian Tempest, president of Ranbaxy's pharmaceuticals division, "Our [drug] pipeline is getting stronger."[75] Since Ranbaxy spends very little on research and marketing, and its costs in India are one-fifth those of U.S. pharmaceutical firms, its profit margins are 16 percent, very close to the 20 percent margins of companies like Eli Lilly that have the high risk approach of researching and developing new drugs. Finally, unlike defenders, prospectors, or analyzers, **reactors** do not follow a consistent strategy. Rather than anticipating and preparing for external opportunities and threats, reactors tend to "react" to changes in their external environment after they occur. Not

"WHAT'S NEW" COMPANY

defenders companies using an adaptive strategy aimed at defending strategic positions by seeking moderate, steady growth and by offering a limited range of high-quality products and services to a well-defined set of customers

prospectors companies using an adaptive strategy that seeks fast growth by searching for new market opportunities, encouraging risk taking, and being the first to bring innovative new products to market

analyzers companies using an adaptive strategy that seeks to minimize risk and maximize profits by following or imitating the proven successes of prospectors

reactors companies using an adaptive strategy of not following a consistent strategy, but instead reacting to changes in the external environment after they occur surprisingly, reactors tend to be poorer performers than defenders, prospectors, or analyzers. A reactor approach is inherently unstable, and firms that fall into this mode of operation must change their approach or face almost certain failure. *FIAT*, the Italian automaker, the largest automaker in Europe just 15 years ago, fell into a reactor strategy with predictably bad results.[76] Protected from competition by quotas that kept high-quality foreign cars out of Italy until 10 years ago, and repeatedly bailed out of financial crises by Italian banks and the Italian government, Fiat underinvested in research and design and didn't begin serious efforts to improve quality or bring out new models until quotas had expired and Japanese and German companies had exported dozens of stylish, higher-quality cars to Italy. As a result of this reactive strategy, Fiat's share of the Italian market alone dropped from 44 percent to 32 percent. Recently Fiat has attempted to become more competitive and adopt a different posture with some limited success. Despite its efforts, Fiat remains not only the weakest competitor in the industry, but also the one with the lowest profit margins.[77]

Review 4: **Industry-Level Strategies**

Industry-level strategies focus on how companies choose to compete in their industry. Five industry forces determine an industry's overall attractiveness to corporate investors and its potential for long-term profitability. Together, a high level of new entrants, substitute products or services, bargaining power of suppliers, bargaining power of buyers, and rivalry between competitors combine to increase competition and decrease profits. Three positioning strategies can help companies protect themselves from the negative effects of industry-wide competition. Under a cost leadership strategy, firms try to keep production costs low so that they can sell products at prices lower than competitors'. Differentiation is a strategy aimed at making a product or service sufficiently different from competitors' that it can command a premium price. Using a focus strategy, firms seek to produce a specialized product or service for a limited, specially targeted group of customers. The four adaptive strategies help companies adapt to changes in the external environment. Defenders want to "defend" their current strategic positions. Prospectors look for new market opportunities by bringing innovative new products to market. Analyzers minimize risk by following the proven successes of prospectors. Reactors do not follow a consistent strategy, but instead react to changes in their external environment after they occur.

Firm-level strategy addresses the question "How should we compete against a particular firm?"

5 Firm-Level Strategies

Microsoft brings out its Xbox 360 video-game console; Sony counters with its PlayStation 3. Sprint Nextel drops prices and increases monthly cell phone minutes; Verizon strikes back with better reception and even lower prices and more minutes. FedEx, the overnight delivery company, buys Kinko's copying and printing stores and turns them into FedEx Kinko's Office and Print Centers to provide a convenient place for businesspeople to drop off and pick up packages; UPS buys Mail Boxes, Etc. and turns its outlets into UPS Stores for exactly the same purpose. Starbucks Coffee opens a store, and nearby locally run coffeehouses respond by improving service, increasing portions, and holding the line on prices. Attack and respond, respond and attack. **Firm-level strategy** addresses the question "How should we compete against a particular firm?"

*Let's find out more about the firm-level strategies (direct competition between companies) shown in Exhibit 6.11 by reading about **5.1 the basics of direct competition**, **5.2 the strategic moves involved in direct competition between companies**, and **5.3 entrepreneurship and intrapreneurship**.*

5.1 Direct Competition

Although Porter's five industry forces indicate the overall level of competition in an industry, most companies do not compete directly with all the firms in their industry. For example, MᴄDᴏɴᴀʟᴅ's and Red Lobster are both in the restaurant business, but no one would characterize them as competitors. McDonald's offers low-cost, convenient fast food in a "seat yourself" restaurant, while Red Lobster offers mid-priced, sit-down seafood dinners complete with servers and a bar.

Instead of "competing" with the industry, most firms compete directly with just a few companies. **Direct competition** is the rivalry between two companies offering similar products and services that acknowledge each other as rivals and take offensive and defensive positions as they act and react to each other's strategic actions.[78] Two factors determine the extent to which firms will be in direct competition with each other: market commonality and resource similarity. **Market commonality** is the degree to which two companies have overlapping products, services, or customers in multiple markets. The more markets in which there is product, service, or customer overlap, the more intense the direct competition between the two companies. **Resource similarity** is the extent to which a competitor has similar amounts and kinds of resources, that is, similar assets, capabilities, processes, information, and knowledge used to create and sustain an advantage over competitors. From a competitive standpoint, resource similarity means that your direct competitors can probably match the strategic actions that your company takes.

Exhibit 6.12 shows how market commonality and resource similarity interact to determine when and where companies are in direct competition.[79] The overlapping area in each quadrant (between the triangle and the rectangle, or between the differently colored rectangles) depicts market commonality. The larger the overlap, the greater the market commonality. Shapes depict resource similarity, with rectangles representing one set of competitive resources and triangles representing another. Quadrant I shows two companies in direct competition because they have similar resources at their disposal and a high degree of market commonality. These companies try to sell similar products and services to similar customers. McDonald's and Bᴜʀɢᴇʀ Kɪɴɢ would clearly fit here as direct competitors.

In Quadrant II, the overlapping parts of the triangle and rectangle show two companies going after similar customers with some similar products or services,

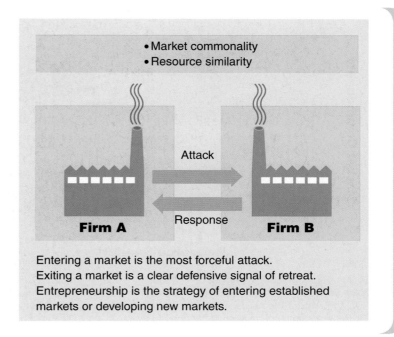

- Market commonality
- Resource similarity

Firm A — Attack → Response → **Firm B**

Entering a market is the most forceful attack. Exiting a market is a clear defensive signal of retreat. Entrepreneurship is the strategy of entering established markets or developing new markets.

Exhibit 6.11

Firm-Level Strategies (Direct Competition)

firm-level strategy a corporate strategy that addresses the question "How should we compete against a particular firm?"

direct competition the rivalry between two companies that offer similar products and services, acknowledge each other as rivals, and act and react to each other's strategic actions

market commonality the degree to which two companies have overlapping products, services, or customers in multiple markets

resource similarity the extent to which a competitor has similar amounts and kinds of resources

Source: Republished with permission of Academy of Management, P.O. Box 3020, Briar Cliff, NY, 10510–8020. M. Chen, "Competitor Analysis and Interfirm Rivalry: Toward a Theoretical Integration," *Academy of Management Review* 21. Reproduced by permission of the publisher via Copyright Clearance Center, Inc.

Exhibit 6.12

A Framework of Direct Competition

but doing so with different competitive resources. McDonald's and Wendy's restaurants would fit here. Wendy's is after the same lunchtime and dinner crowds that McDonald's is. Nevertheless, with its more expensive hamburgers, fries, shakes, and salads, Wendy's is less of a direct competitor to McDonald's than Burger King is. For example, Wendy's Garden Sensation salads (using fancy lettuce varieties, grape tomatoes, and mandarin oranges) bring in customers who would have eaten at more expensive casual dining restaurants like Applebee's.[80] A representative from Wendy's says, "We believe you win customers by consistently offering a better product at a strong, everyday value."[81]

In Quadrant III, the very small overlap shows two companies with different competitive resources and little market commonality. McDonald's and Luby's cafeterias fit here. Although both are in the fast-food business, there's almost no overlap in terms of products and customers. For example, Luby's sells baked chicken, turkey, roasts, meat loaf, and vegetables, none of which are available at McDonald's. Furthermore, Luby's customers aren't likely to eat at McDonald's. In fact, Luby's is not really competing with other fast-food restaurants, but with eating at home. Company surveys show that close to half of its customers would have eaten at home, not at another restaurant, if they hadn't come to Luby's.[82]

Finally, in Quadrant IV, the small overlap between the two rectangles shows that McDonald's and Subway compete with similar resources but with little market commonality. In terms of resources, McDonald's sales are much larger, but Subway, with its 27,270 stores worldwide, much faster growth, and plans to have 30,000 stores worldwide by 2010, will soon approach McDonald's 31,129 stores worldwide (just 13,000 in the United States).[83] Though Subway and McDonald's compete, they aren't direct competitors in terms of market commonality in the way that McDonald's and Burger King are, because Subway, unlike McDonald's, sells itself as a provider of healthy fast food. Thus, the overlap is much smaller in Quadrant IV than in Quadrant I. With its advertising featuring "Jared," who lost 245 pounds eating at Subway, the detailed nutritional information available in its stores, and its close relationship with the American Heart Association, Subway's goal "is to emphasize that the Subway brand represents all that is good about health and well-being."[84] And while fast-food customers tend to eat at both restaurants, Subway's customers are twice as loyal as McDonald's customers, most likely because of Subway's healthier food.[85]

5.2 Strategic Moves of Direct Competition

While corporate-level strategies help managers decide what business to be in and industry-level strategies help them determine how to compete within an industry, firm-level strategies help managers determine when, where, and what strategic actions should be taken against a direct competitor. Firms in direct competition can make two basic strategic moves: attacks and responses. These moves occur all the time in virtually every industry, but they are most noticeable in industries where multiple large competitors are pursuing customers in the same market space.

An **attack** is a competitive move designed to reduce a rival's market share or profits. For example, hoping to increase its market share at Burger King's expense, McDonald's began a brutal price war by putting eight items on a new $1 value menu, including two sandwiches, the Big N' Tasty quarter-pounder and the McChicken sandwich, that usually sold for $1.99.[86] Sales of those sandwiches doubled within weeks. The attack worked very well at first, as Robert Doughty, a Burger King spokesperson, complained: "They've created a senseless price war. That has put a lot of competitive pressure on us and others, too."[87] By contrast, a **response** is a countermove, prompted by a rival's attack, that is designed to defend or improve a company's market share or profit. There are two kinds of responses.[88] The first is to match or mirror your competitor's move. This is what Burger King did to McDonald's by selling 11 menu items at 99 cents each, including its popular double cheeseburgers. The second kind of response, however, is to respond along a different dimension from your competitor's move or attack. For example, instead of cutting prices, Burger King could have introduced a new menu item to attract customers away from McDonald's.

Market commonality and resource similarity determine the likelihood of an attack or response, that is, whether a company is likely to attack a direct competitor or to strike back with a strong response when attacked. When market commonality is strong and companies have overlapping products, services, or customers in multiple markets, there is less motivation to attack and more motivation to respond to an attack. The reason for this is straightforward: When firms are direct competitors in a large number of markets, they have a great deal at stake. So when McDonald's launched an aggressive price war with its value menu, Burger King had no choice but to respond by cutting its own prices.

Whereas market commonality affects the likelihood of an attack or a response to an attack, resource similarity largely affects response capability, that is, how quickly and forcefully a company can respond to an attack. When resource similarity is strong, the responding firm will generally be able to match the strategic moves of the attacking firm. Consequently, a firm is less likely to attack firms with similar levels of resources because it is unlikely to gain any sustained advantage when the responding firms strike back. On the other hand, if one firm is substantially stronger than another (that is, there is low resource similarity), then a competitive attack is more likely to produce sustained competitive advantage. With over 30,000 stores to Burger King's 11,000 stores and much greater financial resources, McDonald's hoped its price war would inflict serious financial damage on Burger King while suffering minimal financial damage itself. This strategy worked to some extent. Although Burger King already sold 11 menu items for 99 cents, it wasn't willing or able to cut the price of its best-selling Whopper sandwiches to 99 cents (from $1.99). Basically admitting that it couldn't afford to match McDonald's price cuts on more expensive sandwiches, a Burger King spokesperson insisted, "McDonald's can't sell those sandwiches at $1 without losing money. It isn't sustainable." Thanks to its much larger financial resources, McDonald's had the funds to outlast Burger King in the price war. As often happens, though, the price war ended up hurting both companies' profits.[89]

attack a competitive move designed to reduce a rival's market share or profits

response a competitive countermove, prompted by a rival's attack, to defend or improve a company's market share or profit

McDonald's ended the price war when it became clear that lower prices didn't draw more customers to its restaurants.

In general, the more moves (attacks) a company initiates against direct competitors, and the greater a company's tendency to respond when attacked, the better its performance. More specifically, attackers and early responders (companies that are quick to launch a retaliatory attack) tend to gain market share and profits at the expense of late responders. This is not to suggest that a "full attack" strategy always works best. In fact, attacks can provoke harsh retaliatory responses. When **KIMBERLY-CLARK** cut the price of Huggies diapers below $10 a box (by reducing the number of diapers), Procter & Gamble, maker of Pampers diapers, retaliated by cutting prices 15 percent and printing "Compare" on Pampers boxes to point out that it had *not* reduced the number of diapers, only the price. In the end, Kimberly-Clark had to undo its price cut and increase the number of diapers per box. The price war was so damaging that profits declined, leading to a 12 percent drop in Kimberly-Clark's stock price.[90] Consequently, when deciding when, where, and what strategic actions to take against a direct competitor, managers should always consider the possibility of retaliation.

5.3 Entrepreneurship and Intrapreneurship: Entering New Markets

As the McDonald's–Burger King and Huggies-Pampers examples illustrate, attacks and responses can include smaller, more tactical moves, like price cuts, specially advertised sales or promotions, or improvements in service. On a larger scale, they can also involve resource-intensive strategic moves, such as expanding service and production facilities, introducing new products or services within the firm's existing business, or entering a completely new line of business for the first time.

Of these, *market entries* and *market exits* are probably the most important kinds of attacks and responses. Entering a market is perhaps the most forceful attack or response because it sends the clear signal that the company is committed to gaining or defending market share and profits at a direct competitor's expense. By contrast, exiting a market is an equally clear defensive signal that your company is retreating.[91]

Since **entrepreneurship** is the process of entering new or established markets with new goods or services, entrepreneurship is also a firm-level strategy. In fact, the basic strategic act of entrepreneurship is new entry—creating a new business from a brand-new startup firm. For example, Scott Griffith created a new rental car company called **ZIPCAR** to compete with such established companies as Enterprise, Hertz, and Avis. Zipcar is able to do this by offering more and doing it cheaply. After reserving a Zipcar (for an hour, day, or longer) online or via a toll-free phone number, Zipcar members simply go to a Zipcar location and use their access card to unlock their reserved car—but the wireless access system allows entry only during the time period that the car is reserved. That way, no one else can use the car during that time. When finished, the renter simply returns the car to its original location. Gas and insurance are included in the price (about $60 a day, or $8.50 to $12 an hour), so the car doesn't have to be filled up before it is returned. And all of this is done without filling out forms, dealing with people at a rental counter, and

"Entering a market is perhaps the most forceful attack or response."

entrepreneurship the process of entering new or established markets with new goods or services

Using entrepreneurial strategies, Zipcar entered an established market with a competitive product. Shown here is a member holding her membership card, which acts as an electronic car key.

GETTY IMAGES

having the paperwork and car inspected by security personnel before leaving the rental car lot.[92]

Established firms can be entrepreneurial, too, by entering new or established markets with new goods or services. When existing companies are entrepreneurial, it's called **intrapreneurship**.[93] Think "coffee," and chances are you'll end up at a *DUNKIN' DONUTS*, which sells more regular coffee than anybody else. Think "latte," and you'll end up at Starbucks Coffee instead. Dunkin' Donuts, however, is branching out from its regular coffee and donuts and entering a new market. It wants to sell you a tall, medium, or large latte for 25 percent less than Starbucks. Rather than hire and train new staff to be coffee baristas, Dunkin' Donuts had a Swiss company produce an $8,000 automated, "idiot-proof" machine that consistently makes a good cappuccino or latte in less than 60 seconds. Boston lawyer Kathleen Brown, who has switched from Starbucks to Dunkin' Donuts, says, "I can order a plain medium caramel latte and not deal with all that fancy stuff."[94] Customer Leslie Bello agrees: "Both are good, but Starbucks takes too long."[95] With sales surging, Dunkin' Donuts plans to triple its stores to 15,000 over the next decade. As an executive at Dunkin' Donuts points out, "Espresso has become mainstream in America. And who does mainstream better than Dunkin' Donuts?" Accordingly, Dunkin' Donuts advertising proclaims, "Latte for Every Tom, Dick, and Lucciano."[96]

Whereas the goal of an intrapreneurial strategy is new entry, the process of carrying out an intrapreneurial strategy depends on the ability of the company's founders or existing managers to foster an entrepreneurial orientation (remember, intrapreneurship is entrepreneurship in an existing organization). An **entrepreneurial orientation** is the set of processes, practices, and decision-making activities that lead to new entry. Five key dimensions characterize an entrepreneurial orientation:[97]

- *Risk taking*. Entrepreneurial firms are willing to take some risks by making large resource commitments that may result in costly failure. Another way to conceptualize risk taking is to think of it as a managerial preference for bold rather than cautious acts.

- *Autonomy*. If a firm wants to successfully develop new products or services to enter new markets, it must foster creativity among employees. To be creative, employees need the freedom and control to develop a new idea into a new product or service opportunity without interference from others. In other words, they need autonomy.

- *Innovativeness*. Entrepreneurial firms also foster innovativeness by supporting new ideas, experimentation, and creative processes that might produce new products, services, or technological processes.

- *Proactiveness*. Entrepreneurial firms have the ability to anticipate future problems, needs, or changes by developing new products or services that may not be related to their current business, by introducing new products or services before the competition does, and by dropping products or services that are declining (and likely to be replaced by new products or services).[98]

- *Competitive aggressiveness*. Because new entrants are more likely to fail than existing firms are, they must be aggressive if they want to succeed. A new firm often must be willing to use unconventional methods to directly challenge competitors for their customers and market share.

Without these five key characteristics, an entrepreneurial orientation is unlikely to be created, and an intrapreneurial strategy is unlikely to succeed.

intrapreneurship entrepreneurship within an existing organization

entrepreneurial orientation the set of processes, practices, and decision-making activities that lead to new entry, characterized by five dimensions: risk taking, autonomy, innovativeness, proactiveness, and competitive aggressiveness

Review 5: *Firm-Level Strategies*

Firm-level strategies are concerned with direct competition between firms. Market commonality and resource similarity determine whether firms are in direct competition and thus likely to attack each other or respond to each other's attacks. In general, the more markets in which there is product, service, or customer overlap, and the greater the resource similarity between two firms, the more intense the direct competition between them. When firms are direct competitors in a large number of markets, attacks are less likely because responding firms are highly motivated to quickly and forcefully defend their profits and market share. By contrast, resource similarity affects response capability, meaning how quickly and forcefully a company responds to an attack. When resource similarity is strong, attacks are much less likely to produce a sustained advantage because the responding firm is capable of striking back with equal force.

Market entries and exits are the most important kinds of attacks and responses. Entering a new market is a clear offensive signal, while exiting a market is a clear signal that a company is retreating. Market entry is perhaps the most forceful attack or response because it sends the clear signal that the company is committed to gaining or defending market share and profits at a direct competitor's expense. In general, attackers and early responders gain market share and profits at the expense of late responders. Attacks must be carefully planned and carried out, however, because they can provoke harsh retaliatory responses.

Finally, the basic strategic act of entrepreneurship is new entry. To carry out an entrepreneurial strategy, a company must create an entrepreneurial orientation by encouraging risk taking, autonomy, innovativeness, proactiveness, and competitive aggressiveness.

Strategy Questionnaire

Generally speaking, a strategy is a plan of action that is designed to help you achieve a goal. Strategies are not limited to grand plans that help you accomplish grand goals. You probably use strategies every day in simple ways. For example, think of a route you regularly drive. Do you know how fast (or slow) you need to go to catch all the lights on green? Or where to swerve to avoid a pothole? Or even when to take a side street to shave a few minutes off your commute? Speeding up for one block in order to catch the green lights at the next five intersections is a strategy. Strategy, then, involves thinking about how you are going to accomplish what you set out (that is, have planned) to do.

This assessment will provide some baseline information on attitudes you might have that will relate to your management skills.[99] Answer each of the questions either true or false. Try not to spend too much time on any one item, and be sure to answer all the questions.

1. I get satisfaction from competing with others.
2. It's usually not important to me to be the best.
3. Competition destroys friendships.
4. Games with no clear-cut winners are boring.
5. I am a competitive individual.
6. I will do almost anything to avoid an argument.
7. I try to avoid competing with others.
8. I would like to be on a debating team.
9. I often remain quiet rather than risk hurting another person.
10. I find competitive situations unpleasant.
11. I try to avoid arguments.
12. In general, I will go along with the group rather than create conflict.
13. I don't like competing against other people.
14. I don't like games that are winner-take-all.
15. I dread competing against other people.
16. I enjoy competing against an opponent.
17. When I play a game, I like to keep score.
18. I often try to outperform others.
19. I like competition.
20. I don't enjoy challenging others even when I think they are wrong.

To determine your score, count the number of responses marked "True" and enter it here _____. You can find the interpretation for your score at: academic.cengage.com/management/williams.

KEY TERMS

acquisition 208
analyzers 217
attack 221
bargaining power of buyers 215
bargaining power of suppliers 215
BCG matrix 208
cash cow 208
character of the rivalry 214
competitive advantage 195
competitive inertia 198
core capabilities 201
core firms 202
corporate-level strategy 206
cost leadership 215
defenders 217
differentiation 216
direct competition 219
distinctive competence 201
diversification 207
dog 208
entrepreneurial orientation 223
entrepreneurship 222
firm-level strategy 218
focus strategy 216
grand strategy 211
growth strategy 211
imperfectly imitable resource 196
industry-level strategy 213
intrapreneurship 223
market commonality 219
nonsubstitutable resources 198
portfolio strategy 207
prospectors 217
question mark 208
rare resources 196
reactors 217
recovery 212
related diversification 210
resource similarity 219
resources 195

How Does Your Garden (Company) Grow?

The Scotts Company is older than dirt. Well, almost. O.M. Scott founded the company in 1868 as a premium seed company for U.S. farmers, who, to his mind, needed and should have clean, weed-free fields.[100] The company began selling grass seed in 1907 and launched a dedicated research division in 1947. Throughout the 20th century and still today, Scotts has been associated with the Turf Builder line of consumer grass seed, professional turf seed (think golf courses and football fields), and numerous fertilizer products.

In 1995, the $100 million plant-food company Miracle-Gro, started by your grandfather, merged with Scotts to form Scotts Miracle-Gro. Since the merger was finalized, you've seen Scotts Miracle-Gro buy companies that make everything from fertilizer to insecticides. When conglomerate ITT, which primarily makes electronics and fluid controls and equipment, bought Burpee, the seed company, ITT asked Scotts to manage it. In addition, Scotts introduced a line of fertilizer spreaders under its own name, solidified relationships with big-box retail stores like Lowe's and Home Depot, and began selling products in the United Kingdom countries, known for their love of and knack for gardening.

Over the years Scotts Miracle-Gro has bought dozens of companies, and as a result, Scotts Miracle-Gro is huge. Now with $2.5 billion in annual sales, Scotts dominates lawn care like Budweiser dominates beer. (Your grandfather would never have imagined this.) So now that you're on top, how do you keep growing? Or *should* you keep growing? The lawn and garden market is a $35 billion annual market, so there could be plenty of upside, but drawing from your weed-killing technology, you know it's possible to grow a plant to death.

Questions

1. What strategic alternative—risk seeking or risk avoiding—do you think Scotts Miracle-Gro should pursue? Answer in terms of strategic reference point theory.

2. Using portfolio theory, map out a diversification plan that would help Scotts grow without straying too far from its distinctive competencies in turf, seed, and fertilizer.

3. Do you continue following a growth strategy, or do you shift to a stability strategy? Explain.

Playing the Game

When you first started in the business of inventing video-game systems, it was fresh and exhilarating.[101] Nintendo had revolutionized the home video-game industry by making arcade-quality graphics available on home game consoles. By the mid 1990s, the company's Super Nintendo Entertainment System was a market leader, selling 49 million units, and your Sega Genesis system was no slacker, selling 30 million units globally. Today, however, video games and consoles have little in common with Nintendo's groundbreaking Mario Brothers and Donkey Kong games, let alone Atari's Pong.

The video-game industry is a $17 billion industry and consoles sell hundreds of millions of units. Sony's first PlayStation sold 102.5 million units worldwide, and its PlayStation 2, which was so powerful the Japanese government feared it could be used to make advanced weaponry, has sold 111.3 million units since its launch. Microsoft's first-generation Xbox sold roughly 25 million units and used chip technology that made it more powerful than Sony's market leader. Then Microsoft upped the ante with the Xbox 360, whose new-generation microchip transmits data 3.5 times faster than the original Xbox. Then Sony trumped Microsoft by making its PlayStation 3 even more powerful; it contains a chip able to perform 218 billion calculations per second—speed on par with a supercomputer!

All this one-upmanship comes at a heavy price that pushes smaller players out of the market. For example, Sony spent $1.8 billion just to develop the microchip that powers its PlayStation 3 console, which retails for approximately $500. Even at that price, though, Sony is selling the PlayStation hardware at a loss and counting on making up the money on the sale of related video games, which it expects will take three years! The same is true of Microsoft, whose Xbox console retails for nearly $300 but hadn't earned Microsoft a single penny after six years on the market.

You wonder if all these big investments make sense. After all, despite the general increase in the number of consoles sold, the same folks tend to buy the consoles year after year. Game playing in Japan is declining about 10 percent a year, and in the United States game consoles have been in the same percentage of households (36 percent, to be exact) for years. That means competitors are all vying for the same customers, those 18-to-34-year-old men who get a rush from the screamingly fast action of complex games.

That is, until Nintendo came out with Wii, a simple console designed to play simple games and priced at a relatively reasonable $250. Wii was designed to attract new customers to video-gaming, like women and older consumers. As for handheld video games, Nintendo's DS is simpler than the Sony equivalent PSP3 and has sold more units. The cost to develop a game for DS is one tenth the cost to develop games for other platforms, which means Nintendo recoups its investments more quickly.

In the end, the industry is still exhilarating—not so much from the excitement of creating something new, but in a swimming-with-sharks kind of way. Sega hasn't been a serious force in the industry for over 20 years. If you're going to get back into the game, so to speak, how should you do it?

Assemble a team of four to five students to play the management team at Sega trying to reestablish itself in the gamer market.

Questions

1. Using Porter's Five Industry Forces, map the video-game industry.

2. What are the risks and opportunities of the strategies followed by Sony and Xbox? Of Nintendo?

3. Do you try to reestablish Sega by participating in the attack-and-respond dynamic of escalating technology, or do you try to follow Nintendo's go-simple path out of the video arms race? Explain.

PRACTICE BEING A MANAGER

Organizational strategy is aimed at achieving sustainable competitive advantage over rivals in a particular market. This exercise will offer you the opportunity to consider how companies in the restaurant industry might develop a strategy and attempt to gain sustainable competitive advantage.

For purposes of this exercise, your professor will organize your class into small teams. Each team will be competing for the title of "Most Likely to Succeed." One team will be designated as judges for this competition.

Step 1 (15 minutes): Develop a concept for a new restaurant business. You may choose to develop your concept as a local, regional, or national company—but in all cases, you must plan to open a restaurant in your local area. Your concept should include the following: (a) name of your restaurant/chain; (b) description of your menu, layout, and any other distinguishing features; and (c) likely direct competitors of your new concept. Prepare an informal presentation of not more than two minutes.

Step 2 (20 minutes): Present the concepts. Each team will make an informal two-minute presentation of the restaurant concepts.

Step 3 (5 minutes): Judge the presentations. Judges will confer and reach a decision regarding the top concepts on the basis of "Most Likely to Succeed." Judges should apply the Sustainable Competitive Advantage concept/factors in making their selections. While the judges are conferring, each team should discuss and evaluate the concepts presented by the competing teams. Teams should apply the tools and concepts in this chapter in evaluating these concepts.

Step 4: Discuss as a class.

- What are the challenges of achieving sustainable competitive advantage in the restaurant business? Consider cases of failure and success in your local market—what factors seemed to play a role in determining success or failure?

- What *strategic groups*, or clusters of direct competitors (for example, fast-food burger), were identified in the team presentations? Which strategic groups might be tougher to enter in your local area? Which might be easier to enter?
- Do major restaurant chains have a built-in sustainable competitive advantage over local

competition in your area? If you think so, what is the source of this advantage, and is it more pronounced in some strategic groups than in others (for example, greater in tacos than in fine dining)? If not, what strategies have the "locals" used to successfully compete with larger restaurant chains?

DEVELOP YOUR CAREER POTENTIAL

An Individual SWOT Analysis

In order to maintain and sustain a competitive advantage, companies continue to analyze their overall strategy in light of their current situation.[102] In doing so, they often use a SWOT analysis, which focuses on the strengths and weaknesses in the firm's internal environment and the opportunities and threats present in the firm's external environment. One way to gain experience in conducting a SWOT analysis is to perform one on yourself—in other words, conduct a personal SWOT analysis.

Assume you have just completed your college education and are ready to apply for a job as a manager of a small- to medium-sized facility. Perform a personal SWOT analysis to determine if your current situation matches your overall strategy. Identifying your strengths will probably be the easiest step in the analysis. They will most likely be the skills, abilities, experience, and knowledge that help differentiate you from your competitors. Take care to be realistic and honest in analyzing your strengths and weaknesses.

One way to identify both strengths and weaknesses is to look at previous job evaluation comments and talk to former and present employers and coworkers. Their comments will typically focus on objective strengths and weaknesses that you have exhibited on the job. You may also gather information about your strengths and weaknesses by analyzing your personal interests and learning more about your personality type. Most college placement offices have software to help students identify their interests and personality types and then match that information to certain career paths. This type of assessment can help ensure that you do not choose a career path that is incongruent with your personality and interests.

Probably the hardest portion of the personal SWOT analysis will be the identification of your weaknesses. As humans, we are often reluctant to focus on our deficiencies; nonetheless, being aware of potential weaknesses can help

us reduce them or improve upon them. Since you are preparing for a career in management, you should research what skills, abilities, knowledge, and experience are needed to be a successful manager. Comparing your personal strengths against those needed as a manager can help you identify potential weaknesses. Once you identify weaknesses, develop a plan to overcome them. Remember that most annual evaluations will include both strengths and weaknesses, so don't forget to include them in your analysis.

You can identify opportunities now by looking at employment possibilities for entry-level managers. In this part of the analysis, it helps to match your personal strengths with opportunities. For example, if you have experience in manufacturing, you may initially choose to apply only to manufacturing-type businesses.

The last step of the analysis involves identifying potential threats. Threats are barriers that can prevent you from obtaining your goals. Threats may include events such as an economic recession that reduces the number of job openings for entry-level managers. By knowing what the barriers are and by assembling proactive plans to help deal with them, you can reduce the possibility of your strategy becoming ineffective.

Focusing on a personal SWOT analysis can be a practical way to prepare for an actual company analysis, and it also allows you to learn more about yourself and your long-term plans.

Questions

1. In light of the SWOT analysis, what plans might you propose for yourself that will help you maximize your strengths, exploit your opportunities, and minimize your weaknesses and threats? Write three S.M.A.R.T. goals (remember Chapter 5) that will help you implement your plans.

2. How might this assignment prepare you for both your academic and your professional career?

BIZ FLIX
Seabiscuit

Seabiscuit is a 2003 American drama film based on the best-selling book *Seabiscuit: An American Legend*, by Laura Hillenbrand. The film stars Tobey Maguire as Red Pollard, the jockey for Seabiscuit, an undersized and overlooked Thoroughbred race horse whose unexpected successes made him a popular sensation in the United States near the end of the Great Depression. In this scene, a hospitalized Pollard is unable to ride during the final leg of the Triple Crown, so he tries to communicate to his friend and replacement jockey Charley Kurtsinger (played by Chris McCarron) what he needs to do to win the race.

What to Watch for and Ask Yourself

1. What aspects of strategic planning can you identify in the clip?
2. Which strategic alternative (risk seeking or risk avoiding) does Red Pollard advocate that his friend use during the race? Explain.

MANAGEMENT WORKPLACE
Timbuk2—Setting a New Course

"We want to make the *Swirl* as famous as the *Swoosh*," says Timbuk2's CEO Mark Dwight with a chuckle. While he may be joking by comparing his firm's logo to the Nike *Swoosh*, Dwight isn't kidding. When Dwight took over as head of Timbuk2 a few years ago, the company was on a downward slide, losing money because it had only one product to offer to a narrow market—a bag for bicycle messengers. Granted, the bag came in several sizes and colors, but Dwight realized that Timbuk2 couldn't survive, let alone grow, on the strength of one messenger bag. So Dwight and his managers developed corporate- and firm-level strategies to achieve the goal of turning the company around and then achieving growth: increasing and broadening the product line to reach into new markets, developing the brand while remaining true to the company's heritage, finding new distribution channels, creating alliances with other firms, and outsourcing some production to maintain quality but reduce costs.

Watch how Dwight transformed Timbuk2's management workplace with a strong strategy.

What to Watch for and Ask Yourself

1. In which category would you place Timbuk2's grand strategy? Why?
2. How would you define Timbuk2's core competency?
3. Identify one strength, weakness, opportunity, and threat for Timbuk2.

CHAPTER 7

Innovation and Change

Learning Outcomes:

1 Explain why innovation matters to companies.

2 Discuss the different methods that managers can use to effectively manage innovation in their organizations.

3 Discuss why *not* changing can lead to organizational decline.

4 Discuss the different methods that managers can use to better manage change as it occurs.

In This Chapter:

Organizational Innovation

WHAT WOULD YOU DO?

Whirlpool Headquarters, Benton Harbor, Michigan.
Standing in the showroom of a local appliance store, you realize the problem almost immediately. Virtually all of the washers, dryers, refrigerators, freezers, and dishwashers are white. It is tough to tell one company's product from another, and the biggest signs in the place announce the low prices on this versus that model. This is why Whirlpool's senior management team developed the "Brand-Focused Value Creation" strategy: to create innovative, branded solutions that consumers will find appealing, that will generate brand loyalty, and, most important, that will command a premium price. During its 95-year history, Whirlpool has become an expert in manufacturing excellence. Its machines are among the most reliable in the industry, and its products have been in almost every household in the United States at one time or another. Periodically its products have gotten a facelift or a small improvement in performance or function, but no more than that.

How can you make a company like Whirlpool innovative? How can you teach your people to be creative and innovative, especially when your core capability is manufacturing reliable products? Corporate director Nancy Snyder said, "Over the years people have used many nice adjectives to describe Whirlpool. But 'innovative' has rarely been among them." Worse yet, J.C. Anderson, your VP of group manufacturing, proclaimed, "It's cost reduction that has made Whirlpool great."

Nonetheless, you can see that without significant innovation, Whirlpool will be mired in a never-ending price-cutting battle. Generic-looking products are compared on price, and your cost-cutting measures will only take the company so far. The first effort at innovation within the company produced some new product lines, but expenses far exceeded the positive results of those innovations. During that effort, the former CEO pushed all 61,000 employees to unleash their creativity for the future of the company. Most employees saw the effort as a waste of time and employee morale dipped severely, making the next effort all the more difficult for you.

There is no real financial crisis at Whirlpool. The company is performing well for now, but future success will be limited if it can't differentiate its products from the pack. How can you develop a culture of innovation at Whirlpool? If the company produces a commodity item such as a standard, white clothes washer, how can that be changed so that it produces a premium-priced product? With manufacturing as Whirlpool's core strength, how will you develop a customer focus?

As you stand in the appliance store, you realize that these questions need to be addressed and need to be addressed quickly. You can't afford to have another failure in this effort at the company. Beyond managing for innovation, how might you implant innovation as a standard of your business? What role should the company's leaders play in this effort? **If you were in charge at Whirlpool, what would you do?**

ACTIVITIES + VIDEOS

CengageNOW Audio study guide, electronic flashcards, author FAQ videos, On the Job and Biz Flix videos, concept tutorial, and concept exercise

Web (academic.cengage.com/management/williams) Quiz, PowerPoint slides, and glossary terms for this chapter

Study Tip

On a separate sheet, write the titles of the exhibits in this chapter. Then, with your book closed, try to reproduce the diagrams exactly as they are in the text. Write a short description of what each diagram depicts; then open your book to check your work.

"WHAT'S NEW" COMPANIES

WHIRLPOOL

INTEL

EASTMAN KODAK

MICROSOFT

TRACTOR SUPPLY COMPANY

ROYAL PHILIPS ELECTRONICS

BEST BUY

AVERY DENNISON

INNOCENTIVE

FORD MOTOR COMPANY

NINTENDO

SONY

BOMBARDIER AEROSPACE

FASTCAR

INCREDIBLE UNIVERSE

GENERAL MOTORS

BARNEYS NEW YORK

AND OTHERS . . .

We begin this chapter by reviewing the issues associated with organizational innovation, the problem facing Whirlpool. **Organizational innovation** is the successful implementation of creative ideas in an organization.[2] **Creativity**, which is a form of organizational innovation, is the production of novel and useful ideas.[3] In the first part of this chapter, you will learn why innovation matters and how to manage innovation to create and sustain a competitive advantage.

In the second half of this chapter, you will learn about organizational change. **Organizational change** is a difference in the form, quality, or condition of an organization over time.[4] You will also learn about the risk of not changing and the ways in which companies can manage change.

ORGANIZATIONAL INNOVATION

"When you're done, be sure to turn off the lights and lock the doors. We don't want anyone breaking into the tent." The tent? Because of their low cost and interesting architectural features, organizations are increasingly using tents as buildings. A church in Colorado Springs spent $1.6 million to erect a 20,000-square-foot tent with tiled bathrooms, a second-floor mezzanine, and 32 aluminum arches for its chapel and youth facility. The facility has heavy vinyl walls and ceilings instead of canvas, huge metal frames instead of tent poles, windows and doors that lock instead of zippered openings, central heating and air-conditioning instead of campfires, and wood floors and carpeting instead of hard, uneven ground, leading architect Todd Dalland, who has designed tents for 30 years, to ask, "At what point is it a tent? At what point is it a building?"[5] Nine years ago, Trump Hotel & Casino Resorts put up a two-story, 80,000-square-foot "hospitality and entertainment center" at its Buffington Harbor riverboat casino in Gary, Indiana. From the inside, viewing its crystal chandeliers, marble walls and floors, elevator, numerous restaurants, and high-tech water display, you wouldn't know you were in a tent.

Organizational innovation is the successful implementation of creative ideas, like using tents for buildings, in an organization.[6]

After reading the next two sections on organizational innovation, you should be able to

1 *explain why innovation matters to companies.*

2 *discuss the different methods that managers can use to effectively manage innovation in their organizations.*

organizational innovation the successful implementation of creative ideas in organizations

creativity the production of novel and useful ideas

organizational change a difference in the form, quality, or condition of an organization over time

1 Why Innovation Matters

When was the last time you used a record player to listen to music, tuned up your car, baked cookies from scratch, or manually changed the channel on your TV? Because of product innovations and advances in technology, it's hard to remember, isn't it? In fact, since compact discs began replacing vinyl record albums more than a decade ago, many of you may *never* have played a record album. Lots of people used to tune up their own cars because doing a tune-up was easy, quick, and cheap. Change the points, spark plugs, and distributor cap, and your car was good for another six months or 12,000 miles. Today, with advanced technology and computerized components, tuning up a car is far too complex for most people. Hardly anybody makes cookies from scratch anymore, either. Millions of kids think that baking cookies means adding water to a powdered mix or getting premade cookie dough out of the refrigerator. As for manually changing the channels on your TV, you may have done that recently, but only because you couldn't find the remote.

We can only guess what changes technological innovations will bring in the next 20 years. Maybe we'll be listening to compact chips instead of compact discs. (Come to think of it, with iPods, we already do.) Maybe cars won't need tune-ups. Maybe we'll use the Internet to have cookies delivered hot to our homes like pizza. And maybe TVs will be voice activated, so it won't matter if you lose the remote (just don't lose your voice). Who knows? The only thing we do know about the next 20 years is that innovation will continue to change our lives. For a fuller appreciation of how technological innovation has changed our lives, see Exhibit 7.1.

*Let's begin our discussion of innovation by learning about **1.1 technology cycles** and **1.2 innovation streams**.*

1.1 Technology Cycles

In Chapter 3, you learned that technology is the knowledge, tools, and techniques used to transform inputs (such as raw materials and information) into outputs (products and services). A **technology cycle** begins with the "birth" of a new technology and ends when that technology reaches its limits and "dies" as it is replaced by a newer, substantially better technology.[7] For example, technology cycles occurred when air-conditioning supplanted fans, when Henry Ford's Model T replaced horse-drawn carriages, when planes replaced trains as a means of cross-country travel, when vaccines that prevented diseases replaced medicines designed to treat them, and when battery-powered wristwatches replaced mechanically powered, stem-wound wristwatches.

From Gutenberg's invention of the printing press in the 1400s to the rapid advance of the Internet, studies of hundreds of technological innovations have shown that nearly all technology cycles follow the typical **S-curve pattern of innovation** shown in Exhibit 7.2.[8] Early in a technology cycle, there is still much to learn, so progress is slow, as depicted by point A on the S-curve. The flat slope indicates that increased effort (in terms of money or research and development) brings only small improvements in technological performance. *INTEL*'s technology cycles have followed this pattern. Intel spends billions to develop new computer chips and to build new production facilities to produce them. Intel has found that the technology cycle for its integrated circuits is about three years. In each three-year cycle, Intel introduces a new chip, improves the chip by making it a little bit faster each year, and then replaces that chip at the end of the cycle with a brand new, different chip that is substantially faster than the old chip. At first, though, the billions Intel spends typically produce only small improvements in performance. For instance, as shown in Exhibit 7.3, Intel's first 60 megahertz (MHz) Pentium processors ran at a speed of 51 based on the iComp Index.[9] (The iComp Index is a benchmark test for measuring relative computer speed. For example, a computer with an iComp score of 200 is twice as fast as a computer with an iComp score of 100.) Yet, six months later, Intel's new 75 MHz Pentium was only slightly faster, with an iComp speed of 67.

"WHAT'S NEW" COMPANY

technology cycle a cycle that begins with the "birth" of a new technology and ends when that technology reaches its limits and is replaced by a newer, substantially better technology

S-curve pattern of innovation a pattern of technological innovation characterized by slow initial progress, then rapid progress, and then slow progress again as a technology matures and reaches its limits

Exhibit 7.1

Technological Innovation since 1900

There's no better way to understand how technology has repeatedly and deeply changed modern life than to read a decade-by-decade list of innovations since 1900. The first time through the list, simply appreciate the amount of change that has occurred. The second time through, look at each invention and ask yourself two questions: What brand new business or industry was created by this innovation? And what old business or industry was made obsolete by this innovation?

1900–1910
- electric typewriter
- air conditioner
- airplane
- reinforced concrete skyscraper
- vacuum tube
- plastic
- chemotherapy
- electric washing machine

1911–1920
- artificial kidney
- mammography
- 35mm camera
- zipper
- sonar
- tank
- Band-Aid
- submachine gun

1921–1930
- self-winding watch
- TB vaccine
- frozen food
- commercial fax service
- talking movies
- black and white television
- penicillin
- jet engine
- supermarket

1931–1940
- defibrillator
- radar
- Kodachrome film
- helicopter
- nylon
- ballpoint pen
- first working computer
- fluorescent lighting
- color television

1941–1950
- aerosol can
- nuclear reactor
- atomic bomb
- first modern herbicide
- microwave oven
- bikini
- disposable diaper
- ENIAC computer
- mobile phone
- transistor
- credit card

1951–1960
- Salk's polio vaccine
- DNA's structure deciphered
- oral contraceptive
- solar power
- Tylenol
- Sputnik
- integrated circuit
- breast implants

1961–1970
- measles vaccine
- navigation satellite
- miniskirt
- video recorder
- soft contact lenses
- coronary bypass
- handheld calculator
- computer mouse
- Arpanet (prototype Internet)
- bar-code scanner
- lunar landing

1971–1980
- compact disc
- Pong (first computer game)
- word processor
- gene splicing
- Post-it note
- Ethernet (computer network)
- laser printer
- personal computer
- VHS video recording
- fiber optics
- linked ATMs
- magnetic resonance imaging

1981–1990
- MS-DOS
- space shuttle
- clone of IBM personal computer
- cell phone network
- computer virus
- camcorder
- human embryo transfer
- CD-ROM
- Windows software
- 3-D video game
- disposable contact lenses
- Doppler radar
- RU-486 (abortion pill)
- global positioning system (GPS) by satellite
- stealth bomber
- World Wide Web

1991–2000
- baboon-human liver transplant
- Taxol (cancer drug)
- mapping of the male chromosome
- Pentium processor
- Channel tunnel opens
- HIV protease inhibitor
- gene for obesity discovered
- Java (computer language)
- MP3s
- cloning of an adult mammal

2001–Today
- mapping of human genome
- first cloning of human embryo
- inexpensive global positioning tracking/ mapping/guidance systems
- Abiocor artificial heart

Source: T. Gideonse, "Decade by Decade: A Rich Century of Better Mousetraps," *Newsweek Special Issue: The Power of Invention*, Winter 1997–1998, 12–15.

Fortunately, as the new technology matures, researchers figure out how to get better performance from it. This is represented by point B of the S-curve in Exhibit 7.2. The steeper slope indicates that small amounts of effort will result in significant increases in performance. Again, Intel's technology cycles have followed this pattern. In fact, after six months to a year with a new chip design, Intel's engineering and production people typically figure out how to make the new chips much faster than they were initially. For example, as shown in Exhibit 7.3, Intel soon rolled out 100 MHz, 120 MHz, 133 MHz, 150 MHz, and 166 MHz Pentium chips that, based on their iComp scores, were 76 percent, 96 percent, 117 percent, 124 percent, and 149 percent faster than the original 60 MHz speed.

At point C in Exhibit 7.2, the flat slope again indicates that further efforts to develop this particular technology will result in only small increases in performance. More importantly, however, point C indicates that the performance limits of that particular technology are being reached. In other words, additional significant improvements in performance are highly unlikely. For example, Exhibit 7.3 shows that with iComp speeds of 127 and 142, Intel's 166 MHz and 200 MHz Pentiums were 2.49 and 2.78 times as fast as its original 60 MHz Pentiums. Yet, despite these impressive gains in performance, Intel was unable to make its Pentium chips run any faster because the basic Pentium design had reached its limits.

After a technology has reached its limits at the top of the S-curve, significant improvements in performance usually come from radical new designs or new performance-enhancing materials. In Exhibit 7.2, that new technology is represented by the second S-curve. The changeover or discontinuity between the old and new technologies is represented by the dotted line. At first, the old and new technologies will likely coexist. Eventually, however, the new technology will replace the old technology. When that happens, the old technology cycle will be complete, and a new one will have started. The changeover between Intel's Pentium processors, the old technology, and its Pentium II processors, the new technology (despite their similar names, these chips used significantly different technologies), took approximately one year. Exhibit 7.3 shows this changeover or discontinuity between the two technologies. With an iComp speed of 267, the first Pentium II (233 MHz) was 88 percent faster than the last and fastest 200 MHz Pentium processor. And because their design and performance were significantly different from (and faster than) Pentium II chips, Intel's Pentium III chips represented the beginning

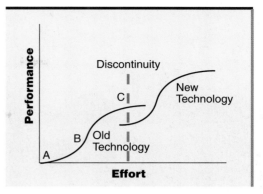

Source: R. N. Foster, *Innovation: The Attacker's Advantage* (New York: Summit, 1986).

Exhibit 7.2

S-Curves and Technological Innovation

Exhibit 7.3

iComp Index 2.0 Comparing the Relative Performance of Different Intel Microprocessors

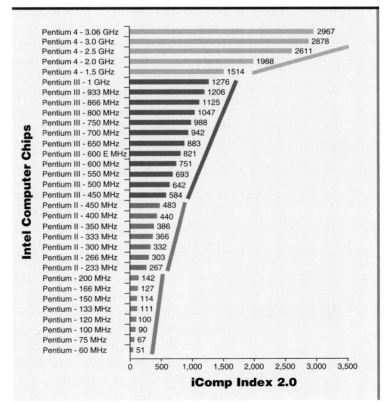

Intel Computer Chips	iComp Index 2.0
Pentium 4 - 3.06 GHz	2967
Pentium 4 - 3.0 GHz	2878
Pentium 4 - 2.5 GHz	2611
Pentium 4 - 2.0 GHz	1988
Pentium 4 - 1.5 GHz	1514
Pentium III - 1 GHz	1276
Pentium III - 933 MHz	1206
Pentium III - 866 MHz	1125
Pentium III - 800 MHz	1047
Pentium III - 750 MHz	988
Pentium III - 700 MHz	942
Pentium III - 650 MHz	883
Pentium III - 600 E MHz	821
Pentium III - 600 MHz	751
Pentium III - 550 MHz	693
Pentium III - 500 MHz	642
Pentium III - 450 MHz	584
Pentium II - 450 MHz	483
Pentium II - 400 MHz	440
Pentium II - 350 MHz	386
Pentium II - 333 MHz	366
Pentium II - 300 MHz	332
Pentium II - 266 MHz	303
Pentium II - 233 MHz	267
Pentium - 200 MHz	142
Pentium - 166 MHz	127
Pentium - 150 MHz	114
Pentium - 133 MHz	111
Pentium - 120 MHz	100
Pentium - 100 MHz	90
Pentium - 75 MHz	67
Pentium - 60 MHz	51

Sources: "Intel iComp (Full List)," Ideas International, available at http://www.ideasinternational.com, 16 May 2002; "Benchmark Resources: iComp Index3.0," Intel, available at http://developer.intel.com, 13 October 2001, "PC CPU Benchmarks, News, Prices and Reviews," *CPU Scorecard*, available at http://www.cpuscorecard.com, 17 March 2003.

© GETTY IMAGES EDITORIAL

Technological change doesn't just mean computers. Building sewer lines to carry waste away from London represented a tremendous technological breakthrough. Pictured here is Joseph Bazalgette, father of the London sewer system, surveying work on the project.

of yet another S-curve technology cycle in integrated circuits. A 450 MHz Pentium III chip was 21 percent faster than a 450 MHz Pentium II chip. Over time, improving existing technology (tweaking the performance of the current technology cycle), combined with replacing old technology with new technology cycles (the Pentium 4 replacing the Pentium III replacing the Pentium II replacing the Pentium), has increased the speed of Pentium computer processors by a factor of 58 in just 17 years and all computer processors by a factor of 300!

Though the evolution of Intel's Pentium chips has been used to illustrate S-curves and technology cycles, it's important to note that technology cycles and technological innovation don't necessarily mean "high technology." Remember, *technology* is simply the knowledge, tools, and techniques used to transform inputs into outputs. So a technology cycle occurs whenever there are major advances or changes in the *knowledge*, *tools*, and *techniques* of a field or discipline. For example, one of the most important technology cycles in the history of civilization occurred in 1859, when 1,300 miles of central sewer line were constructed throughout London to carry human waste to the sea more than 11 miles away. This extensive sewer system replaced the widespread practice of dumping raw sewage directly into streets, where people walked through it and where it drained into public wells that supplied drinking water. Though the relationship wasn't known at the time, preventing waste runoff from contaminating water supplies stopped the spread of cholera that had killed millions of people for centuries in cities throughout the world.[10] Safe water supplies immediately translated into better health and longer life expectancies. Indeed, the water you drink today is safe thanks to this "technology" breakthrough. So, when you think about technology cycles, don't automatically think "high technology." Instead, broaden your perspective by considering advances or changes in knowledge, tools, and techniques.

1.2 Innovation Streams

In Chapter 6, you learned that organizations can create *competitive advantage* for themselves if they have a *distinctive competence* that allows them to make, do, or perform something better than their competitors. Furthermore, a competitive advantage becomes sustainable if other companies cannot duplicate the benefits obtained from that distinctive competence. Technological innovation, however, not only can enable competitors to duplicate the benefits obtained from a company's distinctive advantage but also can quickly turn a company's competitive advantage into a competitive disadvantage. For more than 110 years, *EASTMAN KODAK* was the dominant producer of photographic film worldwide. Retailers often dedicated an entire aisle for the yellow and red boxes containing Kodak film in a variety of speeds and exposures for all types of cameras. The Kodak brand was associated with quality, availability, and value, and consumers purchased rolls of film by the billions. That is, until Kodak invented the digital camera (patent number 4,131,919). But Kodak itself was unprepared for the rapid acceptance of its new technology by the market, and managers watched film quickly become obsolete for the majority of camera users. Technological innovation turned Kodak's competitive advantage into a competitive disadvantage. This technology shift has had a significant impact on Kodak, which

"WHAT'S NEW" COMPANY

is in the process of reducing its film operation to a quarter of its former size by laying off over 27,000 employees. To adjust to the new marketplace, Kodak has been bolstering investments in its digital camera division and in the chemicals, paper, and kiosks used for picture printing.[11]

As the Kodak example shows, companies that want to sustain a competitive advantage must understand and protect themselves from the strategic threats of innovation. Over the long run, the best way for a company to do that is to create a stream of its own innovative ideas and products year after year. Consequently, we define **innovation streams** as patterns of innovation over time that can create sustainable competitive advantage.[12] Exhibit 7.4 shows a typical innovation consisting of a series of technology cycles. Recall that a technology cycle begins with a new technology and ends when that technology is replaced by a newer, substantially better technology. The innovation stream in Exhibit 7.4 shows three such technology cycles.

An innovation stream begins with a **technological discontinuity**, in which a scientific advance or a unique combination of existing technologies creates a significant breakthrough in performance or function. For example, minimally invasive techniques are revolutionizing brain surgery. When Douglas Baptist had a golf ball–sized tumor, his surgeon cut a tiny opening through his eyebrow, removed the tumor, and sewed up the opening, leaving practically no trace of the operation. Previously, his skull would have been sawed open. Dr. John Mangiardi, who did the procedure, says, "We used to have to shave off half the head. We don't do that anymore."[13] Today, surgeons use endoscopes (tiny cameras with lights attached to minisurgical tools) and MRI and CT scans (which create 3-D maps of the brain) to remove brain tumors with precision and little physical trauma. As a result, the cost and length of hospital stays associated with these surgeries have been cut in half.

Technological discontinuities are followed by a **discontinuous change**, which is characterized by technological substitution and design competition. **Technological substitution** occurs when customers purchase new technologies to replace older technologies. For example, in the first half of the 1800s, letters, messages, and news traveled by boat, train, or horseback, such as the famous Pony Express, which, using a large number of fresh riders and fresh horses, could deliver mail from St. Joseph, Missouri, to Sacramento, California, in 10 days.[14] Between 1840 and 1860, however, many businesses began using the telegraph, which could transmit messages and news cross-country (or even around the world) in minutes rather than days, weeks, or months.[15] Indeed, telegraph companies were so successful that the Pony Express went out of business almost immediately

innovation streams patterns of innovation over time that can create sustainable competitive advantage

technological discontinuity the phase of an innovation stream in which a scientific advance or unique combination of existing technologies creates a significant breakthrough in performance or function

discontinuous change the phase of a technology cycle characterized by technological substitution and design competition

technological substitution the purchase of new technologies to replace older ones

Exhibit 7.4
Innovation Streams: Technology Cycles over Time

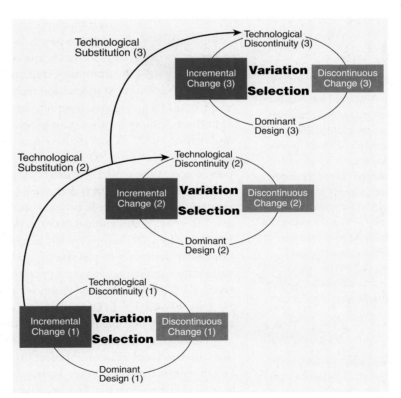

Source: Adapted from M. L. Tushman, P. C. Anderson, & C. O'Reilly, "Technology Cycles, Innovation Streams, and Ambidextrous Organizations," in *Managing Strategic Innovation and Change*, ed. M. L. Tushman & P. Anderson (1997), 3–23. © 1997 by Oxford University Press, Inc. Used by permission of Oxford University Press, Inc.

Whereas Whirlpool has begun a process of innovation focusing on design, competitor Bosch—whose products already had an aesthetically appealing look—has innovated on energy usage. Appliances requiring significantly less energy to function, like those invented by Bosch, are becoming increasingly popular and may ultimately displace current dominant designs for appliances that consume significantly more energy resources.

"WHAT'S NEW"
COMPANY

design competition competition between old and new technologies to establish a new technological standard or dominant design

dominant design a new technological design or process that becomes the accepted market standard

after the completion of the transcontinental telegraph, which linked telegraph systems from coast to coast.

Discontinuous change is also characterized by **design competition**, in which the old technology and several different new technologies compete to establish a new technological standard or dominant design. Because of large investments in old technology, and because the new and old technologies are often incompatible with each other, companies and consumers are reluctant to switch to a different technology during a design competition. Indeed, the telegraph was so widely used as a means of communication in the late 1800s that at first almost no one understood why telephones would be a better way to communicate. As Edwin Schlossberg explains in his book *Interactive Excellence*: "People could not imagine why they would want or need to talk immediately to someone who was across town or, even more absurdly, in another town. Although people could write letters to one another, and some could send telegraph messages, the idea of sending one's voice to another place and then instantly hearing another voice in return was simply not a model that existed in people's experience. They also did not think it was worth the money to accelerate sending or hearing a message."[16] In addition, during design competition, the older technology usually improves significantly in response to the competitive threat from the new technologies; this response also slows the changeover from older to newer technologies.

Discontinuous change is followed by the emergence of a **dominant design**, which becomes the new accepted market standard for technology.[17] Dominant designs emerge in several ways. One is critical mass, meaning that a particular technology can become the dominant design simply because most people use it. For example, even though Apple's AAC and MICROSOFT's WMA digital music file formats are arguably better (better sound, smaller file sizes), the MP3 digital file format became dominant because millions of people across the world first used Napster to exchange MP3 digital music files.[18] As a result, today, nearly all new digital file formats are compatible with the MP3 format. If they weren't, digital music lovers wouldn't use them.

Likewise, a design can become dominant if it solves a practical problem. For example, the QWERTY keyboard (named for the top left line of letters) became the dominant design for typewriters because it slowed typists who, by typing too fast, caused mechanical typewriter keys to jam. Though computers can easily be switched to the DVORAK keyboard layout, which doubles typing speed and cuts typing errors by half, QWERTY lives on as the standard keyboard. Thus, the best technology doesn't always become the dominant design.

Dominant designs can also emerge through independent standards bodies. The International Telecommunication Union (**http://www.itu.ch**) is an independent organization that establishes standards for the communications industry. The ITU was founded in Paris in 1865 because European countries all had different telegraph systems that could not communicate with each other. Messages crossing borders had to be transcribed from one country's system before they could be coded and delivered on another. After three months of negotiations, 20 countries signed the International Telegraph Convention, which standardized equipment and instructions, enabling telegraph messages to flow seamlessly from country to country. Today, as in 1865, various standards are proposed, discussed, negotiated, and changed until agreement is reached on a final set of standards that communication industries (Internet, telephony, satellites, radio) will follow worldwide. For example, within a few years, multibeam, or spot-beam, technology should double or triple the speed and capacity with which satellites deliver data streams to users on Earth.[19] Likewise, China has developed a new standard for third-generation (3G) mobile phone networks that is fast enough for graphics, video, and other high-speed Internet functions.[20] Eventually, the ITU will choose an official standard from several competing standards for both of those technologies.[21]

No matter how it happens, the emergence of a dominant design is a key event in an innovation stream. First, the emergence of a dominant design indicates that there are winners and losers. Technological innovation is both competence enhancing and competence destroying. Companies that bet on the now-dominant design usually prosper. In contrast, when companies bet on the wrong design or the old technology, they may experience **technological lockout**, which occurs when a new dominant design (that is, a significantly better technology) prevents a company from competitively selling its products or makes it difficult to do so.[22] In fact, more companies are likely to go out of business in a time of discontinuous change and changing standards than in an economic recession or slowdown. Second, the emergence of a dominant design signals a shift from design experimentation and competition to **incremental change**, a phase in which companies innovate by lowering the cost and improving the functioning and performance of the dominant design. For example, during a technology cycle, manufacturing efficiencies enable Intel to cut the cost of its chips by one-half to two-thirds, while doubling or tripling their speed. This focus on improving the dominant design continues until the next technological discontinuity occurs.

Review 1: *Why Innovation Matters*

Technology cycles typically follow an S-curve pattern of innovation. Early in the cycle, technological progress is slow, and improvements in technological performance are small. As a technology matures, however, performance improves quickly. Finally, as the limits of a technology are reached, only small improvements occur. At this point, significant improvements in performance must come from new technologies. The best way to protect a competitive advantage is to create a stream of innovative ideas and products. Innovation streams begin with technological discontinuities that create significant breakthroughs in performance or function. Technological discontinuities are followed by discontinuous change, in which customers purchase new technologies (technological substitution) and companies compete to establish the new dominant design (design competition). Dominant designs emerge because of critical mass, because they solve a practical problem, or because of the negotiations of independent standards bodies. Because technological innovation is both competence enhancing and competence destroying, companies that bet on the wrong design often struggle (technological lockout), while companies that bet on the eventual dominant design usually prosper. Emergence of a dominant design leads to a focus on incremental change, lowering costs and making small, but steady improvements in the dominant design. This focus continues until the next technological discontinuity occurs.

> A design can become dominant if it solves a practical problem.

technological lockout the inability of a company to competitively sell its products because it relied on old technology or a nondominant design

incremental change the phase of a technology cycle in which companies innovate by lowering costs and improving the functioning and performance of the dominant technological design

2 Managing Innovation

As the discussion of technology cycles and innovation streams showed, managers must be equally good at managing innovation in two very different circumstances. First, during discontinuous change, companies must find a way to anticipate and survive the technological changes that can suddenly transform industry leaders into losers and industry unknowns into powerhouses. Companies that can't manage innovation following technological discontinuities risk quick organizational decline and dissolution. Second, after a new dominant design emerges following discontinuous change, companies must manage the very different process of incremental improvement and innovation. Companies that can't manage incremental innovation slowly deteriorate as they fall farther behind industry leaders.

Unfortunately, what works well when managing innovation during discontinuous change doesn't work well when managing innovation during periods of incremental change (and vice versa).

*Consequently, to successfully manage innovation streams, companies need to be good at three things: **2.1 managing sources of innovation**, **2.2 managing innovation during discontinuous change**, and **2.3 managing innovation during incremental change**.*

2.1 Managing Sources of Innovation

Innovation comes from great ideas. So a starting point for managing innovation is to manage the sources of innovation, that is, where new ideas come from. One place that new ideas originate is with brilliant inventors. For example, do you know who invented the telephone, the light bulb, a way to collect and store electricity, air-conditioning, radio, television, automobiles, the jet engine, computers, and the Internet? Respectively, these innovations were created by Alexander Graham Bell, Thomas Edison, Pieter van Musschenbroek, Willis Carrier, Guglielmo Marconi, John Baird and Philo T. Farnsworth, Gottlieb Daimler and Wilhelm Maybach, Sir Frank Whittle, Charles Babbage, and Vint Cerf and Robert Kahn. These innovators and their innovations forever changed the course of modern life. Only a few companies, however, have the likes of an Edison, Marconi, or Graham Bell working for them. Given that great thinkers and inventors are in short supply, what might companies do to ensure a steady flow of good ideas?

Well, when we say that innovation begins with great ideas, we're really saying that innovation begins with creativity. Creativity is the production of novel and useful ideas.[23] Although companies can't command employees to be creative ("You will be more creative!"), they can jump-start innovation by building **creative work environments**, in which workers perceive that creative thoughts and ideas are welcomed and valued. As Exhibit 7.5 shows, creative work environments have six components that encourage creativity: challenging work, organizational encouragement, supervisory encouragement, work group encouragement, freedom, and a lack of organizational impediments.[24]

Work is *challenging* when it requires effort, demands attention and focus, and is perceived as important to others in the organization. According to researcher Mihaly Csikszentmihalyi (pronounced ME-high-ee CHICK-sent-me-high-ee), challenging work promotes creativity because it creates a rewarding psychological experience known as "flow." **Flow** is a psychological state of effortlessness, in which you

creative work environments workplace cultures in which workers perceive that new ideas are welcomed, valued, and encouraged

flow a psychological state of effortlessness, in which you become completely absorbed in what you're doing and time seems to pass quickly become completely absorbed in what you're doing and time seems to fly. When flow occurs, who you are and what you're doing become one. Csikszentmihalyi first encountered flow when studying artists: "What struck me by looking at artists at work was their tremendous focus on the work, this enormous involvement, this forgetting of time and body. It wasn't justified by expectation of rewards, like, 'Aha, I'm going to sell this painting.'"[25] Csikszentmihalyi has found that chess players, rock climbers, dancers, surgeons, and athletes regularly experience flow, too. A key part of creating flow experiences, and thus creative work environments, is to achieve a balance between skills and task challenge. When workers can do more than is required of them, they become bored, and when their skills aren't sufficient to accomplish a task, they become anxious. When skills and task challenge are balanced, however, flow and creativity can occur.

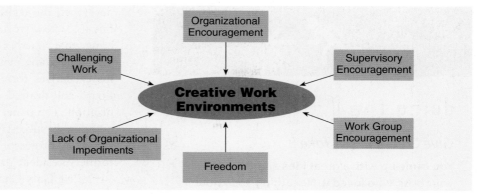

Sources: T. M. Amabile, R. Conti, H. Coon, J. Lazenby, & M. Herron, "Assessing the Work Environment for Creativity," *Academy of Management Journal* 39 (1996): 1154–1184.

Exhibit 7.5
Components of Creative Work Environments

A creative work environment requires three kinds of encouragement: organizational, supervisory, and work group encouragement. *Organizational encouragement* of creativity occurs when management encourages risk taking and new ideas, supports and fairly evaluates new ideas, rewards and recognizes creativity, and encourages the sharing of new ideas throughout different parts of the company. *Supervisory encouragement* of creativity occurs when supervisors provide clear goals, encourage open interaction with subordinates, and actively support development teams' work and ideas. *Work group encouragement* occurs when group members have diverse experience, education, and backgrounds and the group fosters mutual openness to ideas, positive, constructive challenge to ideas, and shared commitment to ideas. For further discussion of these ideas, see Chapter 10 on managing teams,.

An example of organizational and supervisory encouragement can be found at TRACTOR SUPPLY COMPANY, which sells farm supplies, equipment, and tools. Tractor Supply encourages employees to take calculated risks, and it doesn't punish them if those risks don't work out. Chairman Joe Scarlett explains what happened after a company buyer took a gamble on a new line of "Iron Smith" power tools for its stores: "It was well put together as a program. But we imported the product and it was junk. We could have fired the buyer. But he did a wonderful job conceptually. We took our punch in the mouth and our financial losses. Today, that buyer is our VP of marketing. The only reason the line didn't work was because the outside people we relied on for a piece of the execution didn't work out. Most people who take risks are not doing crazy things. We just tell them to fix the problem. Nobody gets chewed out."[26]

Freedom means having autonomy over one's day-to-day work and a sense of ownership and control over one's ideas. Numerous studies have indicated that creative ideas thrive under conditions of freedom. ROYAL PHILIPS ELECTRONICS (Philips) embraced this freedom in its drive to both simplify its products and make everything sensible. All groups within the company have been given complete freedom to rethink every product with the goal of making it simpler for the end user to install and use. Says Andrea Ragnetti, chief marketing officer for Philips, "In the past, companies just

> When skills and task challenge are balanced, however, flow and creativity can occur.

developed the technology and hoped someone would buy it . . . now we are starting from the point of discovering what exactly consumers want a product to do." To ensure that any new ideas are on the right track, Philips executives formed the Philips Simplicity Advisory Board and drafted only people from outside the organization. The panel includes Sara Berman, head of her own highly successful clothing label; Peggy Fritzsche, a radiology professor at Loma Linda University and the former president of the Radiological Society of North Armerica; Gary Chang, an architect in China; and John Maeda, a professor of design at MIT. The eclectic panel works with any of Philips's work groups to help them think through the practicality of every product.[28]

To foster creativity, companies may also have to *remove impediments* to creativity from their work environments. Internal conflict and power struggles, rigid management structures, and a conservative bias toward the status quo can all discourage creativity. They create the perception that others in the organization will decide which ideas are acceptable and deserve support. BEST BUY developed a unique, somewhat risky program called ROWE (results-only work environment). All of the 4,000 employees at the company's headquarters in Minneapolis work on their own schedule. There are no office hours, no set meetings, and no need to come into the office at all—provided you get your work done. Employees are strictly evaluated on output measures that are determined by the management of the company. Since its inception, productivity has risen 35 percent, turnover has dropped dramatically, and employee satisfaction has skyrocketed. As pointed out by *BusinessWeek*, "the most innovative new product may be the structure of the workplace itself."[29]

2.2 Experiential Approach: Managing Innovation during Discontinuous Change

A study of 72 product-development projects (that is, innovation) in 36 computer companies across the United States, Europe, and Asia found that companies that succeeded in periods of discontinuous change (characterized by technological substitution and design competition, as described earlier) typically followed an experiential approach to innovation.[30] The **experiential approach to innovation** assumes that innovation is occurring within a highly uncertain environment and that the key to fast product innovation is to use intuition, flexible options, and hands-on experience to reduce uncertainty and accelerate learning and understanding. As Exhibit 7.6 shows, the experiential approach to innovation has five aspects: design iterations, testing, milestones, multifunctional teams, and powerful leaders.[31]

An "iteration" is a repetition. So a **design iteration** is a cycle of repetition in which a company tests a prototype of a new product or service, improves on the design, and then builds and tests the improved product or service prototype. A **product prototype** is a full-scale working model that is being tested for design, function, and reliability. **Testing** is a systematic comparison of different product

experiential approach to innovation an approach to innovation that assumes a highly uncertain environment and uses intuition, flexible options, and hands-on experience to reduce uncertainty and accelerate learning and understanding

design iteration a cycle of repetition in which a company tests a prototype of a new product or service, improves on that design, and then builds and tests the improved prototype

product prototype a full-scale working model that is being tested for design, function, and reliability

testing the systematic comparison of different product designs or design iterations

	Experiential Approach to Innovation: Managing Innovation During Discontinuous Change	Compression Approach to Innovation: Managing Innovation during Incremental Change

Environment	Highly uncertain
	    discontinuous change—technological substitution and design competition
		Certain
		    incremental change—established technology (i.e., dominant design)

Goals	Speed Significant improvements in performance Establishment of new dominant design	Speed Lower costs Incremental improvements in performance of dominant design
Approach	Build something new, different, and substantially better	Compress time and steps needed to bring about small improvements
Steps	Design iterations Testing Milestones Multifunctional teams Powerful leaders	Planning Supplier involvement Shortening the time of individual steps Overlapping steps Multifunctional teams

Exhibit 7.6

Comparing the Experiential and Compression Approaches to Managing Innovation

designs or design iterations. Companies that want to create a new dominant design following a technological discontinuity quickly build, test, improve, and retest a series of different product prototypes. When *AVERY DENNISON* decided to build a new label printer for offices, focus groups complained about paper cuts, the difficulty of peeling labels, the ends of labels sticking together, and labels that got dirty or wrinkled with handling. Office worker Heather Wilson said, "If all you had to do is just grab a label off and stick it on, it would save a lot of time."[32] Accordingly, Avery designed a prototype printer that prints and then partially peels each label. When Avery tested the prototype in offices, workers said that it was too heavy to move, its large electrical plug wouldn't fit a standard surge protector strip, and it was too loud. After numerous design iterations, Avery's Quick Peel Automatic Label Peeler is quiet, weighs just seven pounds, and can print 500 labels in just 30 minutes, as opposed to 54 minutes for earlier printers.

By trying a number of very different designs, or by making successive improvements and changes in the same design, frequent design iterations reduce uncertainty and improve understanding. Simply put, the more prototypes you build, the more likely you are to learn what works and what doesn't. Also, when designers and engineers build a number of prototypes, they are less likely to "fall in love" with a particular prototype. Instead, they'll be more concerned with improving the product or technology as much as they can. Testing speeds up and improves the innovation process, too. When two very different design prototypes are tested against each other, or the new design iteration is tested against the previous iteration, product design strengths and weaknesses quickly become apparent. Likewise, testing uncovers errors early in the design process when they are easiest to correct. Finally, testing accelerates learning and understanding by forcing engineers and product designers to examine hard data about product performance. When there's hard evidence that prototypes are testing well, the confidence of the design team grows. Also, personal conflict between design team members is less likely when testing focuses on hard measurements and facts rather than personal hunches and preferences.

"WHAT'S NEW"
COMPANY

"WHAT'S NEW"
COMPANY

milestones formal project review points used to assess progress and performance

multifunctional teams work teams composed of people from different departments

Milestones are formal project review points used to assess progress and performance. For example, a company that has put itself on a 12-month schedule to complete a project might schedule milestones at the 3-month, 6-month, and 9-month points on the schedule. By making people regularly assess what they're doing, how well they're performing, and whether they need to take corrective action, milestones provide structure to the general chaos that follows technological discontinuities. Milestones also shorten the innovation process by creating a sense of urgency that keeps everyone on task. For example, when Florida Power & Light was building its first nuclear power facility, the company's construction manager passed out 2,000 desk calendars to company employees, construction contractors, vendors, and suppliers to ensure that everyone involved in the project was aware of the construction timeline. Contractors that regularly missed deadlines were replaced.[33] Finally, milestones are beneficial for innovation because meeting regular milestones builds momentum by giving people a sense of accomplishment.

Multifunctional teams are work teams composed of people from different departments. Multifunctional teams accelerate learning and understanding by mixing and integrating technical, marketing, and manufacturing activities. By involving all key departments in development from the start, multifunctional teams speed innovation through early identification of new ideas or problems that would typically not have been generated or addressed until much later. FORD MOTOR COMPANY relied on multifunctional teams to design its hybrid sport utility vehicle (SUV) that runs on gas and battery power. The hybrid version of the Ford Escape is powerful enough to tow a boat, but still gets 36 miles per gallon. At Ford, researchers, who dream up and test ideas, and product engineers, who find ways to get them to work, usually work in separate buildings. But to design the hybrid Escape, they worked side by side in cubicles for over three years. Team member Tom Gee says, "Before, it might have been a half mile apart, but even one building away is a barrier compared with what we have now. It makes a huge difference."[35] Working side by side was critical to figuring out how to prevent the battery from being damaged by overcharging in cold weather. Ford's researchers and engineers solved the problem by designing sensors and software that monitor the energy sent to the battery (when the gas engine is being used) 50,000 times per second, making sure that the energy is sufficient to recharge the battery but not enough to damage it.

Powerful leaders provide the vision, discipline, and motivation to keep the innovation process focused, on time, and on target. Powerful leaders are able to get resources when they are needed, are typically more experienced, have high status in the company, and are held directly responsible for the products' success or failure. On average, powerful leaders can get innovation-related projects done nine months faster than leaders with little power or influence. One such powerful leader was Phil Martens, the former head of Ford's product development. With a year to go before introduction and Ford's hybrid Escape months behind schedule, he told the team, "We are going to deliver on time. . . . Anything you need you'll get."[36] Martens said, "You could have heard a pin drop." But he followed this declaration by strongly supporting the team. Despite daily inquiries "from above," he promised no interruptions or interference from anyone—even top management. When the team members needed something, they got it without waiting. When language differences created problems with the Japanese company that made the hybrid's batteries, "a Ford battery expert fluent in Japanese was dispatched to Japan within 24 hours."[37] Martens said, "I allowed them to be entrepreneurial, and they doubled their productivity." Mary Ann Wright, the launch manager charged with making sure the project stayed on schedule, said, "The same people who had been coming into my office saying, 'I don't know how we're going to get there,' were saying within weeks and months, 'My God, we can get there.'"[38]

2.3 Compression Approach: Managing Innovation during Incremental Change

As Exhibit 7.6 shows, whereas the experiential approach is used to manage innovation in highly uncertain environments during periods of discontinuous change, the compression approach is used to manage innovation in more certain environments during periods of incremental change. Whereas the goals of the experiential approach are significant improvements in performance and the establishment of a *new* dominant design, the goals of the compression approach are lower costs and incremental improvements in the performance and function of the *existing* dominant design.

The general strategies in each approach are different, too. With the experiential approach, the general strategy is to build something new, different, and substantially better. Because there's so much uncertainty—no one knows which technology will become the market leader—companies adopt a winner-take-all approach by trying to create the market-leading, dominant design. With the compression approach, the general strategy is to compress the time and steps needed to bring about small, consistent improvements in performance and functionality. Because a dominant technology design already exists, the general strategy is to continue improving the existing technology as rapidly as possible.

In short, a **compression approach to innovation** assumes that innovation is a predictable process, that incremental innovation can be planned using a series of steps, and that compressing the time it takes to complete those steps can speed up innovation. As Exhibit 7.6 shows, the compression approach to innovation has five aspects: planning, supplier involvement, shortening the time of individual steps, overlapping steps, and multifunctional teams.[39]

In Chapter 5, *planning* was defined as choosing a goal and a method or strategy to achieve that goal. When *planning for incremental innovation*, the goal is to squeeze or compress development time as much as possible, and the general strategy is to create a series of planned steps to accomplish that goal. Planning for incremental innovation helps avoid unnecessary steps and enables developers to sequence steps in the right order to avoid wasted time and delays between steps. Planning also reduces misunderstandings and improves coordination.

Most planning for incremental innovation is based on the idea of generational change. **Generational change** occurs when incremental improvements are made to a dominant technological design such that the improved version of the technology is fully backward compatible with the older version.[40] Software is backward compatible if a new version of the software will work with files created by older versions. One of the expected and important features of gaming machines, like PlayStation 3, Xbox 360 and the NINTENDO Wii, is their ability to play games purchased for

"WHAT'S NEW" COMPANY

compression approach to innovation an approach to innovation that assumes that incremental innovation can be planned using a series of steps and that compressing those steps can speed innovation

generational change change based on incremental improvements to a dominant technological design such that the improved technology is fully backward compatible with the older technology earlier machines. In fact, the latest Game Boy can play games released more than 20 years ago.[41] Backward compatibility is an important component to ensuring the success of new technology. When developing its PlayStation 3 (PS3), SONY decided to reduce the game machine's backward compatibility with its predecessor, the Play-Station 2 (PS2) because of production costs. Making the PS3 units fully compatible would have required including a high-end technology chip for PS2 games and one for PS3 games, which would have significantly added to the costs of the new unit. Designers opted instead to load software into the PS3 chip that would allow the new system to play older games. But not all PS2 games worked with the software, and often when PS2 games were played on the PS3 machines, the screens would freeze or the system would lock up. Adding to that frustration, dedicated PS3 games were not rolled out as quickly as expected. As you can imagine, Sony paid the price in reduced sales and angry consumers.[42]

Because the compression approach assumes that innovation can follow a series of preplanned steps, one of the ways to shorten development time is *supplier involvement*. Delegating some of the preplanned steps in the innovation process to outside suppliers reduces the amount of work that internal development teams must do. Plus, suppliers provide an alternative source of ideas and expertise that can lead to better designs. When BOMBARDIER AEROSPACE designed its new Continental business jet, it relied heavily on 30 suppliers to design and test new parts and share in the $500 million development cost. In today's jets, it is essential that the various electronic components, most of which are computer controlled, do not interfere with each other (this is why you're asked to turn off all electrical devices before takeoff and touchdown). Instead of handling this itself, Bombardier relied on supplier Rockwell Collins, which built an electronics integration testing unit to ensure that the electronic controls for the throttles, wings and rudders, radar, and other components were compatible.[43] In general, the earlier suppliers are involved, the quicker they catch and prevent future problems, such as unrealistic designs or mismatched product specifications.

Another way to shorten development time is simply to *shorten the time of individual steps* in the innovation process. A common way to do that is through computer-aided design (CAD). CAD speeds up the design process by allowing designers and engineers to make and test design changes using computer models rather than physically testing expensive prototypes. CAD also speeds innovation by making it easy to see how design changes affect engineering, purchasing, and production. Karenann Terrell, director of e-business strategy at DaimlerChrysler, explains how the company's CAD system, FASTCAR, works:

> *FastCar takes a virtual CAD/CAM design and teams it with all the other information that we already have on hand about the part or vehicle. So, no longer do we change a part and then ask: "How much do those new components cost? What are the quality implications?" As we make changes, all that information is integrated into the new designs. Think of the side of a sedan where the hood and fender come together . . . when we brought them together in a digital mock-up, there was a bigger gap than we wanted. Using FastCar technology, we were able to work out the effects of a proposed design change before it was made. In this case, we notified the engineers of the fender and hood, as well as the supplier of a plastic attachment in the wheel well. That vendor said: "If you make that change, I need to cut a new tool, which will cost you lots of money. Why don't I just move my fastening point? Then you don't have a gap." So we didn't have to make a design change. In the old world, it would have been four or five weeks before we knew about the supplier's tool change.*[44]

In a sequential design process, each step must be completed before the next step begins. But sometimes multiple development steps can be performed at the same time. *Overlapping steps* shorten the development process by reducing delays or waiting time between steps. For example, Warner Bros. is using overlapping steps to reduce the time it will take to make the entire series of seven Harry Potter films—one for each of the seven books in J.K. Rowling's series chronicling the seven years the title character is at Hogwarts School of Witchcraft and Wizardry. Unfortunately, it was taking Warner Bros. more than two years to write, shoot, and produce each movie. All the actors were aging, and the core cast of young actors would soon resemble adults more than high school students. So Warner Bros. decided to use new directors and new production teams for each of the movies in the *Harry Potter* series. That way, the company could begin shooting the next film while the previous one was in postproduction and the one prior to that was in the theaters. Without this effort, young Harry Potter might be in his early 30s by the time of the seventh and final movie.[45]

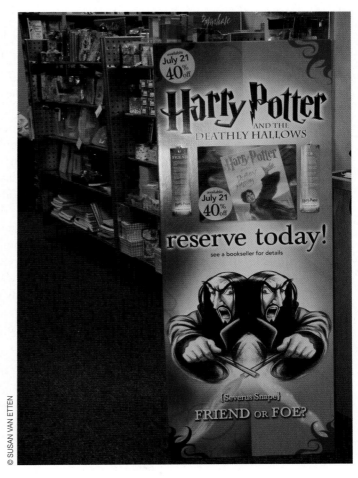

© SUSAN VAN ETTEN

Review 2: **Managing Innovation**

To successfully manage innovation streams, companies must manage the sources of innovation and learn to manage innovation during both discontinuous and incremental change. Since innovation begins with creativity, companies can manage the sources of innovation by supporting a creative work environment in which creative thoughts and ideas are welcomed, valued, and encouraged. Creative work environments provide challenging work; offer organizational, supervisory, and work group encouragement; allow significant freedom; and remove organizational impediments to creativity.

Companies that succeed in periods of discontinuous change typically follow an experiential approach to innovation. The experiential approach assumes that intuition, flexible options, and hands-on experience can reduce uncertainty and accelerate learning and understanding. This approach involves frequent design iterations, frequent testing, regular milestones, creation of multifunctional teams, and use of powerful leaders to guide the innovation process.

A compression approach to innovation works best during periods of incremental change. This approach assumes that innovation can be planned using a series of steps and that compressing the time it takes to complete those steps can speed up innovation. The five aspects of the compression approach are planning (generational change), supplier involvement, shortening the time of individual steps (computer-aided design), overlapping steps, and multifunctional teams.

ORGANIZATIONAL CHANGE

The idea was simple. Build a series of electronics superstores and watch the customers and profits pour in. For a while, it seemed to work. Sales at **INCREDIBLE UNIVERSE** grew to $725 million in less than four years as the company grew to 17 stores, each of which stocked an average of 85,000 products in a 185,000-square-foot building. That's more than four times the size of rival Circuit City stores. Incredible Universe stores had a carnival atmosphere that featured laser shows, karaoke contests, and door prizes. Because of the size, inventory, and extras, the breakeven point for each store was $70 million in sales per year, so despite rapid growth, the company was losing money at record rates. Managers were unable to change the store concept quickly enough to reverse the situation, so the parent company, Tandy Corporation, closed Incredible Universe just four years after its founding. All told, the stores lost over $230 million and completely wiped out Tandy's profits for the year.

The company's collapse wasn't a surprise. Incredible Universe and everyone else in the industry knew it was hemorrhaging cash. Yet the company was unable to change its business quickly enough to stop the bleeding. That inability to change, to figure out ways to bring in more customers for higher end appliances and electronics, eventually led to its demise.[46]

After reading the next two sections on organizational change, you should be able to

    3 *discuss why not changing can lead to organizational decline.*

    4 *discuss the different methods that managers can use to better manage change as it occurs.*

3 Organizational Decline: The Risk of Not Changing

Businesses operate in a constantly changing environment. Recognizing and adapting to internal and external changes can mean the difference between continued success and going out of business. Companies that fail to change run the risk of organizational decline.[47]

Organizational decline occurs when companies don't anticipate, recognize, neutralize, or adapt to the internal or external pressures that threaten their survival.[48] In other words, decline occurs when organizations don't recognize the need for change. **GENERAL MOTORS'** loss of market share in the automobile industry (from 50 percent to 25 percent) is an example of organizational decline. There are five stages of organizational decline: blinded, inaction, faulty action, crisis, and dissolution.[49]

In the *blinded stage*, decline begins because key managers fail to recognize the internal or external changes that will harm their organizations. This "blindness" may be due to a simple lack of awareness about changes or an inability to understand their significance. It may also come from the overconfidence that can develop when a company has been successful. For example, **BARNEYS NEW YORK** started as a tiny men's discount clothing store in New York City and grew into an international phenomenon with stores in Beverly Hills, Chicago, London, Tokyo, and a dozen other cities. Barneys sold some of the most expensive and fashionable designer clothes in the world until the overconfidence of the founder's grandsons, Gene and Bob Pressman, eventually led to the company's demise.[50] In his book *The Rise and Fall of the House of Barneys: A Family Tale of Chutzpah, Glory, and Greed*, Joshua Levine of

organizational decline a large decrease in organizational performance that occurs when companies don't anticipate, recognize, neutralize, or adapt to the internal or external pressures that threaten their survival

Forbes magazine described how overconfidence led the Pressmans to spend more time working out at the gym than running the company.[51] Sure of their success, the Pressmans blindly overspent and overbuilt the company. Indeed, just three years after opening a luxurious $270 million store on Madison Avenue in New York City, complete with marble floors, silver-plated windows, and an extravagantly priced restaurant, espresso bar, beauty salon, and health club, Barneys filed for bankruptcy.

In the *inaction stage*, as organizational performance problems become more visible, management may recognize the need to change but still take no action. The managers may be waiting to see if the problems will correct themselves. Or, they may find it difficult to change the practices and policies that previously led to success. Possibly, too, they wrongly assume that they can easily correct the problems, so they don't feel the situation is urgent. For example, when Barneys expanded from men's into women's clothing, management budgeted $12 million to buy and convert a building into a 70,000-square-foot women's clothing store. When the store ended up costing $25 million, more than double the estimate—a prospect that would have worried most managers—one of Barneys' top managers exclaimed, "What's money?"[52]

In the *faulty action stage*, faced with rising costs and decreasing profits and market share, management will announce "belt-tightening" plans designed to cut costs, increase efficiency, and restore profits. In other words, rather than recognizing the need for fundamental changes, managers assume that if they just run a "tighter ship," company performance will return to previous levels. Barneys fit this pattern, too. Rather than reexamine the basic need for change, Barneys' management focused on cost cutting. Company managers and staff were no longer allowed to spend hundreds of thousands of dollars a year on perks such as cell phones, cars, clothing allowances, and entertainment.[53] Unfortunately for Barneys, this belt-tightening move was too little too late.

In the *crisis stage*, bankruptcy or dissolution (breaking up the company and selling its parts) is likely to occur unless the company completely reorganizes the way it does business. At this point, however, companies typically lack the resources to fully change how they run their businesses. Cutbacks and layoffs will have reduced the level of talent among employees. Furthermore, talented managers who were savvy enough to see the crisis coming will have found jobs with other companies (often with competitors). Because of rising costs and lower sales, cash is tight. And lenders and suppliers are unlikely to extend further loans or credit to ease the cash crunch. For example, after lending Barneys more than $180 million, its bankers refused to extend the company any more credit.

In the *dissolution stage*, after failing to make the changes needed to sustain the organization, the company is dissolved through bankruptcy proceedings or by selling assets in order to pay suppliers, banks, and creditors. At this point, a new CEO may be brought in to oversee the closing of stores, offices, and manufacturing facilities, the final layoff of managers and employees, and the sale of assets. After filing for bankruptcy, Barneys closed four stores, including the original location.[54] Three years later, Barneys was sold to two investment companies that brought in new management to rebuild the company.[55]

Finally, note that because decline is reversible at each of the first four stages, not all companies in decline reach final dissolution as Barneys did. For example, GM is trying to aggressively cut costs, stabilize its shrinking market share, and use innovative

When key managers fail to recognize the internal or external changes that will harm their organizations, decline is sure to follow. Sure of their success, the Pressmans blindly overspent and overbuilt Barneys, only to have to file for bankruptcy three years into their extravagant corporate spending spree.

© LYNN GOLDSMITH/CORBIS

production techniques in an effort to reverse a decline that has lasted nearly a decade and resulted in all-time-low stock prices.

Review 3: **Organizational Decline: The Risk of Not Changing**

The five-stage process of organizational decline begins when organizations don't recognize the need for change. In the blinded stage, managers fail to recognize the changes that threaten their organization's survival. In the inaction stage, management recognizes the need to change, but doesn't act, hoping that the problems will correct themselves. In the faulty action stage, management focuses on cost cutting and efficiency rather than facing up to the fundamental changes needed to ensure survival. In the crisis stage, failure is likely unless fundamental reorganization occurs. Finally, in the dissolution stage, the company is dissolved through bankruptcy proceedings, by selling assets to pay creditors, or through the closing of stores, offices, and facilities. If companies recognize the need to change early enough, however, dissolution may be avoided.

4 Managing Change

According to social psychologist Kurt Lewin, change is a function of the forces that promote change and the opposing forces that slow or resist change.[56] **Change forces** lead to differences in the form, quality, or condition of an organization over time.

By contrast, **resistance forces** support the status quo, that is, the existing conditions in organizations. Change is difficult under any circumstances. Indeed, in a study of heart bypass patients, doctors told participants straightforwardly to change their eating and health habits or they would die. Unbelievably, a full 90 percent of participants did *not* change their habits at all![57] This fierce resistance to change also applies to organizations. A few years ago, XEROX was facing certain bankruptcy if it didn't change the method it used to sell its products and services. So, the senior management changed Xerox's sales system from a transaction-based model, which focused on the quantity of sales made, to a relationship-based model, which focused on partnering with clients to determine how Xerox could help them be more efficient and successful. James Firestone, president of Xerox North America, says succinctly, "Their whole careers, salespeople had done one thing. They would knock on doors, look at copiers, see how old they were, and sell a refresh." But under the new system, salespeople were expected to build relationships with clients and spend considerable time understanding their business. That meant it would take longer to get a sale. The salespeople resisted the changes, complaining that it took months to schedule training in the new approach. They also complained that the compensation system still rewarded salespeople for the number and value of sales made (transactions); they would be making less money because they were going to be spending more time making each sale (building relationships). It took the company more than two years to realign the incentive pay system to match the new relationship-based sales approach, and once the entire transformation was complete—four years later—Xerox returned to profitability. To prevent any tendency toward stagnation, Xerox now runs regular "alignment workshops" to outline ways its existing systems might inhibit change in the future.[58]

Resistance to change, like that shown by the Xerox employees, is caused by self-interest, misunderstanding and distrust, and a general intolerance for change.[59] People resist change out of *self-interest* because they fear that change will cost or

"WHAT'S NEW" COMPANY

change forces forces that produce differences in the form, quality, or condition of an organization over time

resistance forces forces that support the existing state of conditions in organizations

resistance to change opposition to change resulting from self-interest, misunderstanding and distrust, or a general intolerance for change deprive them of something they value. For example, resistance might stem from a fear that the changes will result in a loss of pay, power, responsibility, or even perhaps one's job. People also resist change because of *misunderstanding and distrust*; they don't understand the change or the reasons for it, or they distrust the people, typically management, behind the change. Resistance isn't always visible at first, however. In fact, some of the strongest resisters may initially support the changes in public, nodding and smiling their agreement, but then ignore the changes in private and do their jobs as they always have. Management consultant Michael Hammer calls this deadly form of resistance the "Kiss of Yes."[60]

Resistance may also come from a generally low tolerance for change. Some people are simply less capable of handling change than others. People with a *low tolerance for change* feel threatened by the uncertainty associated with change and worry that they won't be able to learn the new skills and behaviors needed to successfully negotiate change in their companies.

*Because resistance to change is inevitable, successful change efforts require careful management. In this section you will learn about: **4.1 managing resistance to change**, **4.2 what not to do when leading organizational change**, and **4.3 different change tools and techniques**.*

4.1 Managing Resistance to Change

According to Kurt Lewin, managing organizational change is a basic process of unfreezing, change intervention, and refreezing. **Unfreezing** is getting the people affected by change to believe that change is needed. During the **change intervention** itself, workers and managers change their behavior and work practices. **Refreezing** is supporting and reinforcing the new changes so that they "stick."

Resistance to change, as shown by Xerox's salespeople, is an example of frozen behavior. Given the choice between changing and not changing, most people would rather not change. Because resistance to change is natural and inevitable, managers need to unfreeze resistance to change to create successful change programs. The following methods can be used to manage resistance to change: education and communication, participation, negotiation, top management support, and coercion.[61]

When resistance to change is based on insufficient, incorrect, or misleading information, managers should *educate* employees about the need for change and *communicate* change-related information to them. Managers must also supply the information and funding or other support employees need to make changes. For example, resistance to change can be particularly strong when one company buys another company. Jeff Boyd, who worked for a large Canadian company that was acquired, describes the first meeting between his department and the same department from the acquiring company: "It wasn't a friendly meeting. It wasn't hostile or anything like that, but everybody was on their guard a little bit. Right now, everybody's wondering if they'll be able to get along with the other employees, because there's a big difference in both companies' cultures and in the way both companies operate." Boyd concludes, "There's a lot of tension down at the employee level. We're still being kept in the dark about certain things. Everything seems to be up in the air right now."[62] By contrast, NEW YORK–PRESBYTERIAN HEALTHCARE SYSTEM reduced resistance to change by designating mentors to coach individuals, groups, and departments in newly acquired companies about its procedures and practices. New York–Presbyterian's Diane Iorfida said at the time, "Keeping employees informed every step of the way is so important. It's also important to tell the truth, whatever you do. If you don't know, say you don't know."[63]

unfreezing getting the people affected by change to believe that change is needed

change intervention the process used to get workers and managers to change their behavior and work practices

refreezing supporting and reinforcing new changes so that they "stick"

Another way to reduce resistance to change is to have those affected by the change *participate in planning and implementing the change process*. Employees who participate have a better understanding of the change and the need for it. Furthermore, employee concerns about change can be addressed as they occur if employees participate in the planning and implementation process. As you learned in Chapter 6, CEO A. G. Lafley turned around *PROCTER & GAMBLE* by refocusing the company on its billion-dollar brands (Tide and Pantene, among others). Martin Nuechtern, then chief of global hair care, said, "A. G. made things very clear: Make sure you focus on Pantene."[64] While Lafley clearly shifted the focus to P&G's best brands, the strategies to reenergize those brands were generated through employee participation. At an informal luncheon with midlevel managers, Lafley said, "I don't have a speech planned. I thought we could talk. I'm searching for meaty issues. Give me some meaty issues."[65] Then, he listened to their ideas. Vice president Chris Start said, "You can tell him bad news or things you'd be afraid to tell other bosses."[66] As a result, there was little resistance to Lafley's sweeping changes at P&G.

Employees are also less likely to resist change if they are allowed *to discuss and agree on who will do what* after change occurs. The *CHUGACH SCHOOL DISTRICT* in Anchorage, Alaska, had some of the lowest test scores in the state. For superintendent Richard DeLorenzo, that was a clear sign that change was needed. After designing a system that would allow each student to advance at his or her own learning pace, DeLorenzo turned to teacher compensation. But rather than make wholesale changes himself, he went to the teacher's union for input. Together, DeLorenzo and the union developed a program that based teachers' pay on the average improvement of the entire district's students, rather than seniority. Four years later, after enthusiastic support from teachers and students, the district's standardized test scores improved from the 28th to the 71st percentile in the state.[67]

Resistance to change also decreases when change efforts receive *significant managerial support*. Managers must do more than talk about the importance of change, though. They must provide the training, resources, and autonomy needed to make change happen. For example, with a distinguished 70-year history of hand-drawing Hollywood's most successful animated films (*Snow White, Bambi, The Little Mermaid, Beauty and the Beast*), animators at *WALT DISNEY COMPANY* naturally resisted the move to computer-generated (CG) animation. David Stainton, chief of animation, says his animators "fundamentally worry that, 20 years from now, nobody will know how to draw. They're afraid they won't be able to express their skill to the same level."[68] Animator Glen Keane worried that "I would have to go backwards from what I do by hand."[69] So Stainton told his animators, "Your talent really lies in . . . your ability to bring characters to life," and that can be done through drawing or computers.[70] Disney supported the difficult change by putting all of its animators through a six-month "CG Boot Camp," where they learned how to "draw" animated characters with computers.

Finally, resistance to change can be managed through **coercion**, or the use of formal power and authority to force others to change. Because of the intense negative reactions it can create (for example, fear, stress, resentment, sabotage of company products), coercion should be used only when a crisis exists or when all other attempts to reduce resistance to change have failed. Exhibit 7.7 summarizes some additional suggestions for what managers can do when employees resist change.

4.2 What Not to Do When Leading Change

So far, you've learned about the basic change process (unfreezing, change, refreezing) and managing resistance to change. However, Harvard Business School

coercion the use of formal power and authority to force others to change

UNFREEZING	
• Share reasons	Share the reasons for change with employees.
• Empathize	Be empathetic to the difficulties that change will create for managers and employees.
• Communicate	Communicate the details simply, clearly, extensively, verbally, and in writing.
CHANGE	
• Explain benefits	Explain the benefits, "what's in it for them."
• Champion	Identify a highly respected manager to manage the change effort.
• Seek input	Allow the people who will be affected by change to express their needs and offer their input.
• Choose timing	Don't begin change at a bad time, for example, during the busiest part of the year or month.
• Maintain security	If possible, maintain employees' job security to minimize fear of change.
• Offer training	Offer training to ensure that employees are both confident and competent to handle new requirements.
• Pace yourself	Change at a manageable pace. Don't rush.

Source: G. J. Iskat & J. Liebowitz, "What to Do When Employees Resist Change," *Supervision*, 1 August 1996.

Exhibit 7.7

What to Do When Employees Resist Change

professor John Kotter argues that knowing what *not* to do is just as important as knowing what to do when it comes to achieving successful organizational change.[71]

Exhibit 7.8 shows the most common errors that managers make when they lead change. The first two errors occur during the unfreezing phase, when managers try to get the people affected by change to believe that change is really needed. The first and potentially most serious error is *not establishing a great enough sense of urgency*. Indeed, Kotter estimates that more than half of all change efforts fail because the people affected are not convinced that change is necessary. People will feel a greater sense of urgency if a leader in the company makes a public, candid assessment of the company's problems and weaknesses. For example, KMART stores had (and maybe still have) a reputation for being dingy. After the company merged with Sears, *Chain Store Age* conducted an online survey to find out what its readership of retail professionals thought about the prospects of the combined company. Many thought that postmerger, Sears stores would become as dumpy as Kmarts. The company acknowledged its bad image when Sears's new CEO, Aylwin Lewis, told the managers of the recently acquired Kmart chain, "Our worst stores are dungeons! Well, who wants to work in a dungeon? Who wants to shop in a dungeon? Who wants to walk into an environment that is so dull and lifeless that it is sucking the air out of your body?" At the end of his speech there was a spontaneous standing ovation. They got it.[72]

Exhibit 7.8

Errors Managers Make When Leading Change

UNFREEZING
1. Not establishing a great enough sense of urgency.
2. Not creating a powerful enough guiding coalition.
CHANGE
3. Lacking a vision.
4. Undercommunicating the vision by a factor of 10.
5. Not removing obstacles to the new vision.
6. Not systematically planning for and creating short-term wins.
REFREEZING
7. Declaring victory too soon.
8. Not anchoring changes in the corporation's culture.

Source: J. P. Kotter, "Leading Change: Why Transformation Efforts Fail," *Harvard Business Review* 73, no. 2 (March–April 1995): 59.

The second mistake that occurs in the unfreezing process is *not creating a powerful enough coalition*. Change often starts with one or two people, but to build enough momentum to change an entire department, division, or company, change has to be supported by a critical and growing group of people. Besides top management, Kotter recommends that key employees, managers, board members, customers, and even union leaders be members of a *core change coalition*, which guides and supports organizational change. Procter & Gamble's CEO A. G. Lafley says, "I put together the guiding coalition—the leaders who would go with me. If you are going to make a significant change, you have to declare where are we going and why are we going there. Then you have to put together this guiding coalition. You have to put the true disciples together—the prophets who believe in it as passionately as you do. And they help you to carry the organization, because you can't carry a 100,000-person organization spread across 80 to 100 countries by yourself."[73] Furthermore, it's important to strengthen this group's resolve by periodically bringing its members together for off-site retreats.

The next four errors that managers make occur during the change phase, when a change intervention is used to try to get workers and managers to change their behavior and work practices. *Lacking a vision* for change is a significant error at this point. As you learned in Chapter 5, a *vision* is a statement of a company's purpose or reason for existing. A vision for change makes clear where a company or department is headed and why the change is occurring. Change efforts that lack vision tend to be confused, chaotic, and contradictory. By contrast, change efforts guided by visions are clear and easy to understand and can be effectively explained in five minutes or less. At Sears, rather than use the industry standards of market share and sales volume, CEO Aylwin Lewis focuses on profitability and giving "our customers reasons to shop our stores more frequently."[74] In the first year after the merger, Sears Holdings' profit rose over 230 percent.[75]

During his weekly store visits, Sears CEO Aylwin Lewis questions managers about their knowledge of the profit margins for various products. He asks them how they would run their stores better and pushes them to be financially literate. This is one way he's anchoring the changes he's making.

© ASSOCIATED PRESS

Undercommunicating the vision by a factor of 10 is another mistake in the change phase. According to Kotter, companies mistakenly hold just one meeting to announce the vision. Or, if the new vision receives heavy emphasis in executive speeches or company newsletters, senior management then undercuts the vision by behaving in ways contrary to it. Successful communication of the vision requires that top managers link everything the company does to the new vision and that they "walk the talk" by behaving in ways consistent with the vision.

Furthermore, even companies that begin change with a clear vision sometimes make the mistake of *not removing obstacles to the new vision*. They leave formidable barriers to change in place by failing to redesign jobs, pay plans, and technology to support the new way of doing things. One way CEO Lewis removed obstacles to Sears's new vision was by reorganizing how the work of store employees gets done so that they could spend less time with inventory in the back of the store and more time with customers in the front. Many employees at headquarters had never worked at a Sears store, so Lewis began requiring all 3,800 staff members at company headquarters to spend a day each year working in a store. Lewis himself spends every Thursday through Saturday visiting company stores. Without these store visits, management would be isolated from customers and less able to understand how customers perceive and use the store. Store visits help connect the staff at headquarters to the store employees and reinforce the sense that they are all working toward the same strategic goals.[76]

Another error in the change phase is *not systematically planning for and creating short-term wins*. Most people don't have the discipline and patience to wait two years to see if the new change effort works. Change is threatening and uncomfortable, so people need to see an immediate payoff if they are to continue to support it. Kotter recommends that managers create short-term wins by actively picking people and projects that are likely to work extremely well early in the change process. Even though Ford Motor Company posted a $12.7 billion loss in 2006, CEO Alan Mulally announced that he would award blue-collar employees year-end bonuses ranging from $300 to $800. Admitting that the company did not meet profit or market share goals for the year, Mulally acknowledged that workers did improve quality levels and reduce costs, and that those improvements are an important part of turning things around at what used to be America's second largest automaker (it has been surpassed by Toyota). "These awards underscore the importance of working together as a unified team," Mulally said in an e-mail. "That's the only way we'll make more progress down the road."[77]

The last two errors that managers make occur during the refreezing phase, when attempts are made to support and reinforce changes so that they "stick." *Declaring victory too soon* is a tempting mistake in the refreezing phase. Managers typically declare victory right after the first large-scale success in the change process. For instance, it would have been easy for Sears to declare victory the first time that it posted an increase in profits. Declaring success too early has the same effect as draining the gasoline out of a car: It stops change efforts dead in their tracks. With success declared, supporters of the change process stop pushing to make change happen. After all, why push when success has been achieved? Rather than declaring victory, managers should use the momentum from short-term wins to push for even bigger or faster changes. This maintains urgency and prevents change supporters from slacking off before the changes are frozen into the company's culture. During his weekly store visits, Sears CEO Lewis questions managers about their knowledge of the profit margins for various products. He asks them how they would run their stores better and pushes them to be financially literate. At today's Sears, one of the highest complements is to be called "commercial," meaning that the employee understands how to make money.[78]

The last mistake that managers make is *not anchoring changes in the corporation's culture*. An o*rganization's culture* is the set of key values, beliefs, and attitudes shared by organizational members that determines the "accepted way of doing things" in a company. As you learned in Chapter 3, changing cultures is extremely difficult and slow. According to Kotter, two things help anchor changes in a corporation's culture. The first is directly showing people that the changes have actually improved performance. At Sears, this was easily demonstrated by the company's ability to drastically increase profits despite declining sales. The year after Lewis became CEO and Sears began seriously focusing on cost-cutting and profitability, the company tripled its annual profits. The second is to make sure that the people who get promoted fit the new culture. If they don't, it's a clear sign that the changes were only temporary. To anchor its budding customer focus, Sears created a new executive position, chief customer officer, and hired the former head of Best Buy's online division, John Walden, to fill the position. He is in charge of customer strategies and new business development.[79] Lewis is also anchoring cultural change by identifying 500 future leaders at Sears who will attend his day-long course called "Sowing the Seeds of Our Culture." When they come for the class, Lewis tells them, "Make no mistake, we have to change" and either they can "drink the Kool-Aid" or leave.[80]

4.3 Change Tools and Techniques

Imagine that your boss came to you and said, "All right, genius, you wanted it. You're in charge of turning around the division." How would you start? Where would you begin? How would you encourage change-resistant managers to change? What would you do to include others in the change process? How would you get the change process off to a quick start? Finally, what long-term approach would you use to promote long-term effectiveness and performance? Results-driven change, the GENERAL ELECTRIC workout, transition management teams, and organizational development are different change tools and techniques that can be used to address these issues.

One of the reasons that organizational change efforts fail is that they are activity oriented rather than results oriented, meaning that they focus primarily on changing company procedures, management philosophy, or employee behavior. Typically, there is much buildup and preparation as consultants are brought in, presentations are made, books are read, and employees and managers are trained. There's a tremendous emphasis on "doing things the new way." But, with all the focus on activities, on "doing," almost no attention is paid to results, to seeing if all this activity has actually made a difference.

By contrast, **results-driven change** supplants the emphasis on activity with a laserlike focus on quickly measuring and improving results.[81] For example, top managers at HYUNDAI knew that if they were to compete successfully against the likes of Honda and Toyota, they would have to substantially improve the quality of their cars. So top managers guided the company's results-driven change process by first increasing the number of quality teams from 100 to 865. Then, all employees were required to attend seminars on quality improvement and use the results of industry quality studies, like those published annually by J. D. POWER AND ASSOCIATES, as their benchmark. Hyundai then measured the effects of the focus on quality. Before the change, a new Hyundai averaged 23.4 initial quality problems; after the results-driven change efforts, that number dropped to 9.6.[82]

Another advantage of results-driven change is that managers introduce changes in procedures, philosophy, or behavior only if they are likely to improve measured performance. In other words, managers and workers actually test to see if changes make a difference. Consistent with this approach, Chairman Chung invested $30 million in a test center where cars could be subjected to a sequence of extremely harsh conditions for as long as they could withstand, allowing engineers to pinpoint defects and fix the problems.[83] A third advantage of results-driven change is that quick, visible improvements motivate employees to continue to make additional changes to improve measured performance. A few years into Hyundai's change process, DaimlerChrysler and Mitsubishi

results-driven change change created quickly by focusing on the measurement and improvement of results

Motors announced that they would use Hyundai-designed four-cylinder engines in their small and midsized cars, reinforcing that all the changes Hyundai had made to the way it measured and improved car quality had been worth the effort.[84] As at Hyundai, the quick successes associated with results-driven change can be particularly effective at reducing resistance to change. Exhibit 7.9 describes the basic steps of results-driven change.

The **General Electric workout** is a special kind of results-driven change. It is a three-day meeting that brings together managers and employees from different levels and parts of an organization to quickly generate and act on solutions to specific business problems.[85] On the first morning of a workout, the boss discusses the agenda and targets specific business problems that the group is to try to solve. Then, the boss leaves, and an outside facilitator breaks the group, typically 30 to 40 people, into five or six teams and helps them spend the next day and a half discussing and debating solutions. On day three, in what GE calls a "town meeting," the teams present specific solutions to their boss, who has been gone since day one. As each team's spokesperson makes specific suggestions, the boss has only three options: agree on the spot, say no, or ask for more information so that a decision can be made by a specific, agreed-on date. GE boss Armand Lauzon sweated his way through a town meeting. To encourage him to say yes, his workers set up the meeting room so that Lauzon couldn't make eye contact with his boss. He says, "I was wringing wet within half an hour. They had 108 proposals, I had about a minute to say yes or no to each one, and I couldn't make eye contact with my boss without turning around, which would show everyone in the room that I was chicken."[86] In the end, Lauzon agreed to all but eight suggestions. Furthermore, once those decisions were made, no one at GE was allowed to overrule them.

While the GE workout clearly speeds up change, it may also fragment change, if different managers approve conflicting suggestions in separate town meetings across a company. By contrast, a transition management team provides a way to coordinate change throughout an organization. A **transition management team (TMT)** is a team of 8 to 12 people whose full-time job is to manage and coordinate a company's change process.[87] One member of the TMT is assigned to anticipate and manage the emotions and behaviors related to resistance to change. Despite their importance, many companies overlook the impact that negative emotions and resistant behaviors can have on the change process. TMT members report to the CEO every day, decide which change projects are approved and funded, select and evaluate the people in charge of different change projects, and make sure that different change projects complement one another.

For example, when FleetBoston Financial merged with *BANK OF AMERICA* (BoA), a TMT was used to quickly implement Six Sigma quality programs (see Chapter 18 for an explanation) throughout the entire merged organization. Six Sigma programs, which eliminate mistakes and improve quality, had already saved BoA $2 billion by cutting the time required to open a new branch from 500 to 350 days, reducing the number of ATM and deposit errors by 88 percent, and cutting the response time on individual retirement accounts from three days to 10 minutes. Since BoA had been

- Management should create measurable, short-term goals to improve performance.
- Management should use action steps only if they are likely to improve measured performance.
- Management should stress the importance of immediate improvements.
- Consultants and staffers should help managers and employees achieve quick improvements in performance.
- Managers and employees should test action steps to see if they actually yield improvements. Action steps that don't should be discarded.
- It takes few resources to get results-driven change started.

Source: R. H. Schaffer & H. A. Thomson, J.D, "Successful Change Programs Begin with Results," *Harvard Business Review on Change* (Boston: Harvard Business School Press, 1998), 189–213.

Exhibit 7.9
Results-Driven Change Programs

General Electric workout a three-day meeting in which managers and employees from different levels and parts of an organization quickly generate and act on solutions to specific business problems

transition management team (TMT) a team of 8 to 12 people whose full-time job is to manage and coordinate a company's change process

Transition management teams helped Bank of America better integrate Six Sigma practices at its acquisition of Fleet Boston. TMTs helped the company save money by cutting the number of days it takes to open a new branch from 500 to 350 days.

using Six Sigma for four years and FleetBoston for just two, the goal of the TMT was to ensure that the Six Sigma programs for FleetBoston's half of the merged company would catch up as quickly as possible. The team accomplished this by assigning a Six Sigma expert from BoA to each of FleetBoston's key lines of business. Jim Buchanan, who is in charge of the team, says, "We expect that within two years Fleet will be caught up."[88]

It is also important to say what a TMT is not. A TMT is not an extra layer of management further separating upper management from lower managers and employees. A TMT is not a steering committee that creates plans for others to carry out. Instead, the members of the TMT are fully involved with making change happen on a daily basis. Furthermore, it's not the TMT's job to determine how and why the company will change. That responsibility belongs to the CEO and upper management. Finally, a TMT is not permanent. Once the company has successfully changed, the TMT is disbanded. Indeed, Bank of America won't need a TMT anymore once everyone in the merged companies has been trained in Six Sigma practices. Exhibit 7.10 lists the primary responsibilities of TMTs.

Organizational development is a philosophy and collection of planned change interventions designed to improve an organization's long-term health and performance. Organizational development takes a long-range approach to change; assumes that top management support is necessary for change to succeed; creates change by educating workers and managers to change ideas, beliefs, and behaviors so that problems can be solved in new ways; and emphasizes employee participation in diagnosing, solving, and evaluating problems.[89] As shown in Exhibit 7.11, organizational development interventions begin with the recognition of a problem. Then, the company designates a **change agent** to be formally in charge of guiding the change effort. This person can be someone from the company or a professional consultant. The change agent clarifies the problem, gathers information, works with decision makers to create and implement an action plan, helps to evaluate the plan's effectiveness, implements the plan throughout the company, and then leaves (if from outside the company) after making sure the change intervention will continue to work.

For example, change agent Hajime Oba is one of the key reasons that Toyota cars are tops in quality and reliability. Oba's job is to work closely with Toyota suppliers, showing them how to increase quality and decrease costs. For example, Michigan Summit Polymers installed a $280,000 paint system with robots and a paint oven to bake paint onto the dashboard vents that went into Toyota cars, but Oba showed that a $12 hair dryer did the job better and faster (3 minutes versus 90 minutes for the robots and paint oven). Because of Oba's demonstration, Summit replaced the robots with simple but effective $150 spray guns and the paint oven with intense light bulbs. Overall, Oba has helped Summit cut its defects from 3,000 parts

organizational development a philosophy and collection of planned change interventions designed to improve an organization's long-term health and performance

change agent the person formally in charge of guiding a change effort

Exhibit 7.10
Primary Responsibilities of Transition Management Teams

1. Establish a context for change and provide guidance.
2. Stimulate conversation.
3. Provide appropriate resources.
4. Coordinate and align projects.
5. Ensure congruence of messages, activities, policies, and behaviors.
6. Provide opportunities for joint creation.
7. Anticipate, identify, and address people problems.
8. Prepare the critical mass.

Source: J. D. Duck, "Managing Change: The Art of Balancing," *Harvard Business Review on Change* (Boston: Harvard Business School Press, 1998), 55–81.

1.	**Entry**	A problem is discovered and the need for change becomes apparent. A search begins for someone to deal with the problem and facilitate change.
2.	**Startup**	A change agent enters the picture and works to clarify the problem and gain commitment to a change effort.
3.	**Assessment & feedback**	The change agent gathers information about the problem and provides feedback about it to decision makers and those affected by it.
4.	**Action planning**	The change agent works with decision makers to develop an action plan.
5.	**Intervention**	The action plan, or organizational development intervention, is carried out.
6.	**Evaluation**	The change agent helps decision makers assess the effectiveness of the intervention.
7.	**Adoption**	Organizational members accept ownership and responsibility for the change, which is then carried out through the entire organization.
8.	**Separation**	The change agent leaves the organization after first ensuring that the change intervention will continue to work.

Source: W. J. Rothwell, R. Sullivan, & G. M. McLean, *Practicing Organizational Development: A Guide for Consultants* (San Diego: Pfeiffer & Co., 1995).

Exhibit 7.11

General Steps for Organizational Development Interventions

per million to less than 60 parts per million.[90] Oba's efforts as a change agent have significantly improved the quality of parts at Toyota's other suppliers as well. That, in turn, has helped Toyota reach the top of the quality rankings issued by J. D. Power and Associates and *Consumer Reports* magazine.[91]

Organizational development interventions are aimed at changing large systems, small groups, or people.[92] More specifically, the purpose of *large system interventions* is to change the character and performance of an organization, business unit, or department. *Small group intervention* focuses on assessing how a group functions and helping it work more effectively to accomplish its goals. *Person-focused intervention* is intended to increase interpersonal effectiveness by helping people become aware of their attitudes and behaviors and acquire new skills and knowledge. Exhibit 7.12 describes the most frequently used organizational development interventions for large systems, small groups, and people. For additional information about changing systems, groups, and people, see the "What Really Works" feature.

Exhibit 7.12

Different Kinds of Organizational Development Interventions

LARGE SYSTEM INTERVENTIONS	
Sociotechnical systems	An intervention designed to improve how well employees use and adjust to the work technology used in an organization.
Survey feedback	An intervention that uses surveys to collect information from the members, reports the results of that survey to the members, and then uses those results to develop action plans for improvement.
SMALL GROUP INTERVENTIONS	
Team building	An intervention designed to increase the cohesion and cooperation of work group members.
Unit goal setting	An intervention designed to help a work group establish short- and long-term goals.
PERSON-FOCUSED INTERVENTIONS	
Counseling/coaching	An intervention designed so that a formal helper or coach listens to managers or employees and advises them on how to deal with work or interpersonal problems.
Training	An intervention designed to provide individuals with the knowledge, skills, or attitudes they need to become more effective at their jobs.

Source: W. J. Rothwell, R. Sullivan, & G. M. McLean, *Practicing Organizational Development: A Guide for Consultants* (San Diego: Pfeiffer & Co., 1995).

CHANGE THE WORK SETTING OR CHANGE THE PEOPLE? DO BOTH!

what *really* *works.*

Let's assume that you believe that your company needs to change. Congratulations! Just recognizing the need for change puts you ahead of 80 percent of the companies in your industry. But now that you've recognized the need for change, how do you make change happen? Should you focus on changing the work setting or the behavior of the people who work in that setting? It's a classic chicken-or-egg type of question. Which would you do?

A recent meta-analysis based on 52 studies and a combined total of 29,611 study participants indicated that it's probably best to do both!

CHANGING THE WORK SETTING

An organizational work setting has four parts: organizing arrangements (control and reward systems, organizational structure), social factors (people, culture, patterns of interaction), technology (how inputs are transformed into outputs), and the physical setting (the actual physical space in which people work). Overall, there is a 55 percent chance that organizational change efforts will successfully bring changes to a company's work setting. Although the odds are 55–45 in your favor, this is a much lower probability of success than you've seen with the management techniques discussed in other chapters. This simply reflects how strong resistance to change is in most companies.

CHANGING THE PEOPLE

Changing people means changing individual work behavior. The idea is powerful. Change the decisions people

make. Change the activities they perform. Change the information they share with others. And change the initiatives they take on their own. Change these individual behaviors and collectively you change the entire company. Overall, there is a 57 percent chance that organizational change efforts will successfully change people's individual work behavior. If you're wondering why the odds aren't higher, consider how difficult it is to change personal behavior. It's incredibly difficult to quit smoking, change your diet, or maintain a daily exercise program. Not surprisingly, changing personal behavior at work is also difficult. Viewed in this context, a 57 percent chance of success is a notable achievement.

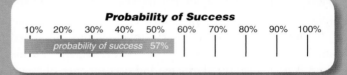

CHANGING INDIVIDUAL BEHAVIOR AND ORGANIZATIONAL PERFORMANCE

The point of changing individual behavior is to improve organizational performance (increase profits, market share, and productivity, and lower costs). Overall, there is a 76 percent chance that changes in individual behavior will produce changes in organizational outcomes. So, if you want to improve your company's profits, market share, or productivity, focus on changing the way that your people behave at work.[93]

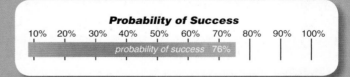

Review 4: **Managing Change**

The basic change process is unfreezing, change, and refreezing. Resistance to change, which stems from self-interest, misunderstanding and distrust, and a general intolerance for change, can be managed through education and communication, participation, negotiation, top management support, and coercion. Knowing what not to do is as important as knowing what to do to achieve successful change. Managers should avoid these errors when leading change: not establishing urgency, not creating a guiding coalition, lacking a vision, undercommunicating the vision, not removing obstacles to the vision, not creating short-term wins, declaring victory too soon, and not anchoring changes in the corporation's culture.

Finally, managers can use a number of change techniques. Results-driven change and the GE workout reduce resistance to change by getting change efforts off to a fast start. Transition management teams, which manage a company's change process, coordinate change efforts throughout an organization. Organizational development is a collection of planned change interventions (large system, small group, person-focused), guided by a change agent, that are designed to improve an organization's long-term health and performance.

Mind-Benders

Innovation is a key to corporate success. Companies that innovate and embrace the changes in their business environment tend to outperform those that stand still. Even so, innovative companies don't simply rely on the creativity of their own workforce. They often contract with outside providers to generate new ideas for everything from operations to new products. In other words, innovative companies fill gaps in their own creativity by looking outside the organization.

As a manager, you will benefit from understanding how you are creative (not *if* you are creative). And just as important as your own creativity is your attitude toward creative endeavors.

This assessment will provide some baseline information you can use as you develop your managerial skills.[94] Indicate the extent to which each of the following statements is true of either your actual behavior or your intentions at work. That is, describe the way you are or the way you intend to be on the job. Use this scale for your responses:

1 Almost never true
2 Seldom true
3 Not applicable
4 Often true
5 Almost always true

1. I openly discuss with my supervisor how to get ahead.
   1   2   3   4   5

2. I try new ideas and approaches to problems.
   1   2   3   4   5

3. I take things or situations apart to find out how they work.
   1   2   3   4   5

4. I welcome uncertainty and unusual circumstances related to my tasks.
   1   2   3   4   5

5. I negotiate my salary openly with my supervisor.
   1   2   3   4   5

6. I can be counted on to find a new use for existing methods or equipment.
   1   2   3   4   5

7. Among my colleagues and coworkers, I will be the first or nearly the first to try out a new idea or method.
   1   2   3   4   5

8. I take the opportunity to translate communications from other departments for my work group.
   1   2   3   4   5

9. I demonstrate originality.
   1   2   3   4   5

10. I will work on a problem that has caused others great difficulty.
    1   2   3   4   5

11. I provide critical input toward a new solution.
    1   2   3   4   5

12. I provide written evaluations of proposed ideas.
    1   2   3   4   5

13. I develop contacts with experts outside my firm.
    1   2   3   4   5

14. I use personal contacts to maneuver into choice work assignments.
    1   2   3   4   5

15. I make time to pursue my own pet ideas or projects.
    1   2   3   4   5

16. I set aside resources for the pursuit of a risky project.
    1   2   3   4   5

17. I tolerate people who depart from organizational routine.
    1   2   3   4   5

18. I speak out in staff meetings.

    1   2   3   4   5

19. I work in teams to try to solve complex problems.

    1   2   3   4   5

20. If my coworkers are asked, they will say I am a wit.

    1   2   3   4   5

=TOTAL

You can find an interpretation of your score at: **academic .cengage.com/management/williams**.

MANAGEMENT DECISION

Change Costs More than Pennies

As you wipe your feet, you can't help but notice how messy the carpet is. "Well, that's what it's for," you think. "This is a factory, not a bookstore." But seeing all those metal chips in the rug makes you think about the plant floor. You turn back around and survey the shop. Everywhere you look, parts are stacked in metal bins on wooden palettes, next to the palettes, on tables by machines, encroaching into the aisles—which are marked off with vibrant yellow striping to remind workers to keep them clear. It looks like there is much more work than the roughly $500,000 worth of parts that are actually in process.

Slowly, you begin to wend your way through the machines. Your plant uses five basic types of machines to make hundreds of thousands of different parts for everything from motorcycles to hospital beds to nail guns to industrial water purifiers. You make the mechanism that fills Downy bottles at Procter & Gamble and the tumblers that spit the movie tickets out from under the counter at theaters across the country. Machines are organized by type, so as a job moves through the plant, it will hit any number of machines in a particular order. A job with multiple operations might get moved around the plant from area to area up to seven times. Even though things are always moving, many areas of the plant seem crowded, as jobs line up waiting for their turn on the next machine. Red tickets in pans scattered around the shop and in a designated area are a reminder that there's still quite a bit of scrap (or bad) work being run. Twenty-five percent of jobs going through the shop have to be fixed or rerun because the parts are the wrong size, if only by 0.001 inch. When you make it to the scheduling area, colored Post-it notes show how many jobs are rush, how many are late, and how many haven't even been started. The on-time delivery rate is only 70 percent. For a precision machine shop that can cut metal to measurements in the ten-thousandths of an inch, the overall operations aren't so precise.

Everywhere you look, you see disorder. Maybe those consultants were right: To be competitive, really to survive, you need to approach your operations in a more systematic fashion. A large percentage of companies with your capabilities have gone out of business, but even though there is less competition, there are fewer customers. The types of parts you manufacture are either being designed out of products or are being outsourced to China and Mexico. Without significant change, you're not going to be able to survive the decade, let alone double your size in two years (which is your secret stretch goal).

Last week, a local manufacturing consultancy sent a few members to your shop to present a preliminary proposal on how they could help you run a more efficient operation. The company would assign a team to help your workers learn new, leaner processes of doing work; promises of increased productivity, profitability, and morale were made, with references galore. The consultants even invited you and your management team to take a plant tour of one (or more) of their most recent clients. Ultimately, the consultants would provide materials, workshops, and follow-up support to your shop employees every day all day for several days over a period of six months—for approximately $200,000. Right out of the gate, they would send two consultants to your shop for five consecutive weeks. But at $250 per hour per consultant, that's a quick $100,000 to spend on teaching communication skills and showing workers how to identify waste issues that prevent them from doing their jobs effectively and efficiently.

With only $8 million in revenue in a business where labor and the costs of goods sold are high, your profits are slim. Spending money on the outsiders could very well mean finishing the year in the red instead of the black. Maybe you could hire someone to do the job full-time for half that amount. For $100,000, you could hire someone to do the same job full-time for a year. That might be better than having some consultants come, give their workshops, and leave the rest up to you after they head home. And will telling your employees that "things are going to change around here" be the best way to get things in order? Maybe it would be better if change initiatives started from the bottom. The majority of your 65 workers have been with you for over 20 years (turnover is not one of your problems), but with tenure comes intractability. In general, your employees are set in their ways. Still, they want the company to succeed, so maybe that concern will be a strong enough motivator.

Questions

1. Consider the above situation. What are the benefits to hiring outsiders to manage your change efforts?

2. Do you pay the $200,000 for the consultancy, do you hire a dedicated change agent, or do you try to marshal internal teams to spearhead a change effort?

MANAGEMENT TEAM DECISION

Brushing Up at Colgate

Ever since Procter & Gamble merged with Gillette, your phone has been ringing off the hook from investment bankers wanting your company, Colgate, to make a deal with Alberto-Culver, S.C. Johnson, Reckitt Benckiser, or Clorox, and today is no exception.[95] Your management team has assembled to listen to yet another set of bankers outline some grandiose proposal. You've got another plan for Colgate, however, and it doesn't involve a big acquisition. Quite the opposite, in fact. For the first time in nearly a decade, Colgate's earnings shrank last quarter (by 10 percent), and you are planning to cut 4,400 jobs, restructure the company, and save $300 million in the process.

Colgate's problems are no secret. In a decades-long tug-of-war, P&G has regained the edge thanks to its innovation machine. In the last five years, P&G has aggressively expanded in the oral care markets where it competes most heavily with Colgate. New flavors of Crest whitening toothpastes, Crest Whitestrips, SpinBrush, and a licensing arrangement with W.L. Gore for Glide floss have all helped Crest reemerge as the leader in the markets it serves. Colgate's most recent innovations—Colgate Total, Motion and Actibrush electric toothbrushes, and Simply White tooth whitener—are now either fading memories or also-rans. And even though Colgate has a strong reputation as a reliable brand, it has been slow to develop new products for developing and existing markets. Perhaps it's just gun-shy. The company's most aggressive innovation was the tooth-whitening system Simply White. Regardless of the product's quality, the bottle and applicator looked like Liquid Paper and proved no match for P&G's Crest Whitestrips. After that near debacle, Colgate managers apparently decided that going for big hits wasn't a workable strategy. The company now seems to be playing catch-up to P&G and GlaxoSmithKline, a new competitor in the oral care market. In fact, in a recent year, P&G spent $229 million on its toothpaste and tooth-whitening products; Colgate spent only $80 million.

Innovation isn't the only area where Colgate has failed to invest. The company's annual ad budget of $1 billion pales in comparison with the $5 billion P&G spends each year to promote its consumer products. Heavy spending has helped P&G capture 51 percent of unit sales and 70 percent of dollar sales in the tooth-whitening segment. Colgate weighs in with 21 percent and 10 percent, respectively. P&G's innovative approach to advertising has helped catapult its products to the forefront of consumers' minds. For example, advertising and sales for Whitestrips began on the web, where the demand was overwhelming. Once the product was rolled out on the market, the day after Colgate's Simply White, P&G had a blockbuster. Simply White hit the shelves and stayed there.

After hanging up from yet another conference call with investment bankers urging your management team to consider a merger, you lean back in your chair and look around the table. "I think we all know what we're *not* going to do," you begin cautiously. "The real question is what we *are* going to do. Now that we have announced measures to conserve resources, we need to decide how to invest what we save."

For this exercise, assemble a team of four to five students to play the role of the management team at Colgate.

Questions

1. Is innovation really necessary at Colgate? In other words, in a market saturated with innovation, is there something to be said for the "keep it simple" approach? Explain.

2. Do you use the $300 million saved from operational cuts to fund innovation, or do you use the money to better market current products?

3. Where do you suggest Colgate look for sources of innovation?

4. As Colgate begins implementing a new innovation strategy, do you recommend that the company follow a compression approach to innovation or an experiential approach? Why?

PRACTICE BEING A MANAGER

Successfully managing innovation is challenging. Companies must find ways to support creativity and invention, while at the same time screening their investments in support of innovation. This exercise will give you an opportunity to experience a bit of the organizational dynamic regarding innovation and investment.

Step 1: Assign roles. Your professor will assign you to a pair or small group, and give your team a role as either "Inventors" or "Investors."

Regardless of role, assume that you work for a large clothing and accessories company that targets college students. Your company makes some traditional clothing and gear (such as backpacks and folios), but also prides itself on developing new and innovative products. And recently there has been some interest in considering new services that the company might offer to the college market, things like event or trip planning.

Step 2: Work with your partner(s) on the following tasks depending upon your assigned role.

Inventors: Brainstorm and work to develop a new product or service concept. Be prepared to explain your concept to those inside the company who screen ideas and recommend investments.

Investors: Discuss and agree upon some criteria that your company should use to screen new product and service concepts and to identify which ones to recommend to senior management. Be prepared to listen to one or more concept presentations, ask questions, and then to use your criteria to evaluate the concept(s).

Step 3: Pair up. As instructed by your professor, Inventor and Investor groups should pair up. Inventors will now present their new concept, and investors will ask questions and then use their criteria to rate the concept.

Step 4: Change roles. As time allows, your professor will rotate Inventor and Investor pairings through a few rounds of concept presentation and investor evaluation.

Step 5: Debrief. Return to your original Inventor or Investor pair/group, and discuss your experiences in this role play. What are some of the challenges of playing this role? What was it like to interact with the "other side" of the presentation/evaluation process?

Step 6: Discuss challenges. As a class, discuss the challenges likely faced by companies as they try to successfully manage innovation. Some items for discussion might include:

1. What is the impact of an "evaluation/rating" on the creative process?

2. Do you think that "inventor units" (such as product development and R&D) and "investor units" (finance) often clash over new-product investment decisions? Why or why not?

3. What role might organizational culture (and subculture) play in the innovation and investment processes?

4. How might managers support healthy innovation and wise investment?

DEVELOP YOUR CAREER POTENTIAL

Spark Your Own Creativity

Creativity is a vital part of every organization—and not just the whiz-bang, multimillion-dollar type of creativity.[96] Even banal tasks can benefit from a new approach: an office assistant may think creatively about how to manage the company's filing system or figure out a simple way to keep track of who is in and out of the office. A Chicago company called Inventables has developed innovation kits—boxes containing disparate items to spark creativity—which it sells to clients like Procter & Gamble and Motorola four times a year. The idea is that designers and engineers will be inspired by tinkering with the contents of the kits.

You don't need Inventables to become inspired, however. Nor do you have to wait for your company to develop a creative work environment before you can become creative. You can spark your own creativity and think "outside the box" on your own. Eureka! Ranch, a Cincinnati-based innovation consultancy company, uses toys to help adults remember how to be imaginative, and its long client list of *Fortune* 500 companies is a testament to founder Doug Hall's methods. Another company, Mindware, specializes in educational activities and toys that can help adults regain access to their imaginations. Just looking through its catalog of erector sets, science sets, puzzle books, strategy games, and tangrams may be enough to get your juices flowing.

Activities

1. Visit **http://www.eurekaranch.com** and search for the audio clip of what the company does and how it does it. Listen to the clip. What do you think of the three dimensions of creativity?

2. At the Eureka Ranch website, find the page on Brain Brew. What is Brain Brew Radio? Is it available in your area? If it is, consider listening to it once a month to hear the creative ideas that people across the country are working on.

3. Visit **http://www.mindwareonline.com** and peruse some of the products the company sells. Which products do you find most appealing? If it's in your budget, order one of the items as a tool to help you develop and refine your creative side.

REEL TO REAL

BIZ FLIX
October Sky

The movie *October Sky* is based on the autobiographical book *Rocket Boys* by Homer Hickam. The talented cast is led by Jake Gyllenhaal, who plays Homer Hickam. As a teenager, Homer is facing a dreary future as a coal miner until he sees the Soviet satellite *Sputnik* pass over his small mining town of Coalwood, West Virginia. A new interest in rockets infects Homer, who begins to experiment with model rockets in the summer of 1957. Soon, Homer has convinced several of his friends to join him in designing a rocket to enter in the National Science Fair, where they hope to win college scholarships as a result.

What to Watch for and Ask Yourself

1. Are Homer and his friends working toward discontinuous change or incremental change? Explain.
2. Which approach to innovation best describes what the "Rocket Boys" are doing? Identify the elements of the approach you choose that are evident in the clip.

MANAGEMENT WORKPLACE
Original Penguin—Innovating a 50-Year-Old Brand

Original Penguin was a 1950s icon—the penguin logo appeared on Munsingwear Penguin knit sport shirts for men, mostly golfers. Eventually, its popularity faded, and Perry Ellis International later acquired the brand. Chris Kolbe was working in merchandising at retailer Urban Outfitters when he conceived the idea of rejuvenating the penguin—but with a new twist and for a new market. Starting with a few new shirts, which sold out almost immediately, the "new" Original Penguin began to grow. Watch the video to see how Kolbe has created a completely new management workplace for a 50-year-old brand.

What to Watch for and Ask Yourself

1. How can you apply the concept of innovation streams to the fashion industry?
2. Based on the tour of the store, what kind of work environment would you expect to find at Original Penguin?
3. What role does Kolbe play in the Perry Ellis organization?

CHAPTER 8

Global Management

Learning Outcomes:

1 Discuss the impact of global business and the trade rules and agreements that govern it.

2 Explain why companies choose to standardize or adapt their business procedures.

3 Explain the different ways that companies can organize to do business globally.

4 Explain how to find a favorable business climate.

5 Discuss the importance of identifying and adapting to cultural differences.

6 Explain how to successfully prepare workers for international assignments.

In This Chapter:

WHAT WOULD YOU DO?

Tommy Hilfiger Headquarters, New York, New York.[1] Over the last five years, Tommy Hilfiger's fashion, cosmetics, and accessories business has struggled. U.S. revenues, which peaked at $1.9 billion in 2000, fell to $1.1 billion in 2003, and now stand at a comparatively paltry $260 million. Thirty Tommy Hilfiger stores had to be closed in the United States. The company's children's wear and Tommy Jeans divisions, both based in the United States were shut down. At corporate headquarters, 230 people were let go. Business reporters began referring to the company as a "fading and mature brand."

There are a number of reasons that things changed so quickly. To start, U.S. clothing sales, which accounted for most of the company's sales, have grown less than 5 percent per year. But that's not enough to explain Tommy Hilfiger

Inc.'s astounding 86 percent drop in U.S. revenues. A more damaging factor has been consolidation in U.S. retail stores. A decade ago, Tommy Hilfiger products were sold in hundreds of different department stores and discount stores in the United States. Today, many of those stores have either closed or been purchased by large department store chains. Macy's and Kohl's, which account for more than a third of U.S. clothing sales, sell their own private-label brands to increase profits, thus squeezing out opportunities for companies like Tommy Hilfiger."

The result, as one of your top managers says, is, "You become vulnerable if you are going to operate just in the U.S. marketplace." So growth in Europe and Asia is critical for future success, but the company has a poor track record over seas. At the height of its U.S. popularity, Hilfiger opened a large store on Bond Street in London, filling it with too much merchandise originally destined for U.S. stores. The Bond Street store closed a year later because Europeans have different fashion tastes from Americans.

If Tommy Hilfiger is to reduce its dependence on the U.S. market, it must grow in Europe and Asia. But how? How much should Tommy Hilfiger, which was unable to push its U.S. products overseas, adapt its products to different cultures in Europe and Asia? Can it have a standard set of products or should they be different in each market and culture? Similarly, who should make key decisions for the company? Should managers at headquarters make these decisions, or should managers in different countries make them? Should Tommy Hilfiger run its business around the world the same way it runs its business in the United States? Finally, *how* should Hilfiger expand internationally? Should it license its brands to local businesses, form strategic alliances with key foreign business partners, or bear the risk itself and wholly own and control each Tommy Hilfiger operation throughout the world? **If you were in charge at Tommy Hilfiger, what would you do?**

ACTIVITIES + VIDEO

CengageNOW Audio study guide, electronic flashcards, author FAQ videos, On the Job and Biz Flix videos, concept tutorial, and concept exercise

Web (academic.cengage.com/management/williams) Quiz, PowerPoint slides, and glossary terms for this chapter

Study Tip

Review your class notes. Do they give you enough information? Do they give you the right information? If not, visit your campus study center to learn how to take good notes.

"WHAT'S NEW" COMPANIES

TOMMY HILFIGER

WAL-MART

INFOSYS

MTV

FREMANTLEMEDIA (AMERICAN IDOL)

CADBURY SCHWEPPES

MCDONALD'S

YUM! BRANDS

FUJI XEROX

POWEREX

VENYON

SHANGHAI AUTOMOTIVE

HONDA MOTORS OF AMERICA

FORD MOTOR COMPANY

VODAFONE

VISTA PRINT

COCA-COLA

AND OTHERS . . .

Tommy Hilfiger's struggle with international expansion is an example of the key issue in global business: How can you be sure that the way you run your business in one country is the right way to run that business in another? This chapter discusses how organizations make those decisions. We start by examining global business in two ways: first by exploring its impact on U.S. businesses, and then by reviewing the basic rules and agreements that govern global trade. Next, we examine how and when companies go global by examining the tradeoff between consistency and adaptation and by discussing how to organize a global company. Finally, we look at how companies decide where to expand globally. Here, we examine how to find the best business climate, how to adapt to cultural differences, and how to better prepare employees for international assignments.

WHAT IS GLOBAL BUSINESS?

"WHAT'S NEW" COMPANY

Business is the buying and selling of goods or services. Buying this textbook was a business transaction. So was selling your first car. So was getting paid for babysitting or for mowing lawns. **Global business** is the buying and selling of goods and services by people from different countries. The Timex watch on my wrist as I write this chapter was purchased at a *WAL-MART* in Texas. But since it was made in the Philippines, I participated in global business when I wrote Wal-Mart a check. Wal-Mart, for its part, had already paid Timex, which had paid the company that employs the Filipino managers and workers who made my watch.

Of course, there is more to global business than buying imported products at Wal-Mart. After reading the next section, you should be able to

1 *discuss the impact of global business and the trade rules and agreements that govern it.*

1 Global Business, Trade Rules, and Trade Agreements

If you want a simple demonstration of the impact of global business, look at the tag on your shirt, the inside of your shoes, and the inside of your cell phone (take your battery out). Chances are, all of these items were made in different places around the world. As I write this, my shirt, shoes, and cell phone were made in Thailand, China, and Korea. Where were yours made?

*Let's learn more about **1.1 the impact of global business**, **1.2 how tariff and non-tariff trade barriers have historically restricted global business**, **1.3 how today global and regional trade agreements are reducing those trade barriers worldwide**, and **1.4 how consumers are responding to those changes in trade rules and agreements**.*

global business the buying and selling of goods and services by people from different countries

1.1 The Impact of Global Business

Thomas Friedman, author and *New York Times* columnist, observed global business in action when he visited Infosys, a consulting and information technology company, in India:

> *I guess the eureka moment came on a visit to the campus of Infosys Technologies, one of the crown jewels of the Indian outsourcing and software industry. Nandan Nilekani, the Infosys CEO, was showing me his global video-conference room, pointing with pride to a wall-size flat-screen TV, which he said was the biggest in Asia. Infosys, he explained, could hold a virtual meeting of the key players from its entire global supply chain for any project at any time on that supersize screen. So its American designers could be on the screen speaking with their Indian software writers and their Asian manufacturers all at once. That's what globalization is all about today, Nilekani said. Above the screen there were eight clocks that pretty well summed up the Infosys workday: 24/7/365. The clocks were labeled United States West, United States East, G.M.T., India, Singapore, Hong Kong, Japan, Australia.*[2]

"WHAT'S NEW" COMPANY

Today, there are 77,175 multinational corporations, nearly 11.25 times as many as in 1970.

multinational corporation a corporation that owns businesses in two or more countries

direct foreign investment a method of investment in which a company builds a new business or buys an existing business in a foreign country

Infosys does global business by selling products and services worldwide with managers and employees from different continents working together as seamlessly as if they were next door to each other. But Infosys isn't unique. There are thousands of other multinational companies just like it.

Multinational corporations are corporations that own businesses in two or more countries. In 1970, more than half of the world's 7,000 multinational corporations were headquartered in just two countries: the United States and the United Kingdom. Today, there are 77,175 multinational corporations, nearly 11.25 times as many as in 1970, and only 2,418, or 2.8 percent, are based in the United States.[3] Today, 53,072 multinationals, or 68.8 percent, are based in other developed countries (such as Germany, Italy, Canada, and Japan), while 20,238, or 26.2 percent, are based in developing countries (such as Colombia, South Africa, and Tunisia). So, today, multinational companies can be found by the thousands all over the world!

Another way to appreciate the impact of global business is by considering direct foreign investment. **Direct foreign investment** occurs when a company builds a new business or buys an existing business in a foreign country. Brazilian steelmaker Gerdau S.A. made a direct foreign investment when it began purchasing U.S. steel companies such as International Steel Group. Over the last five years, these U.S. acquisitions have made Gerdau SA the fourth-largest steelmaker in the United States and the 16th-largest in the world.[4] Of course, companies from many other countries also own businesses in the United States. As Exhibit 8.1 shows, companies from the United Kingdom, Japan, Germany, the Netherlands, Canada, France, Switzerland, and Luxembourg have the largest direct foreign investment in the United States. Overall, foreign companies invest more than $1.6 trillion a year to do business in the United States.

Exhibit 8.1

Direct Foreign Investment in the United States

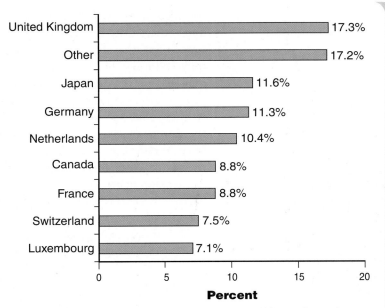

Country	Percent
United Kingdom	17.3%
Other	17.2%
Japan	11.6%
Germany	11.3%
Netherlands	10.4%
Canada	8.8%
France	8.8%
Switzerland	7.5%
Luxembourg	7.1%

Percent

Source: J. Koncz & D. Yorgason, "Direct Investment Positions for 2005: Country and Industry Detail," available at http://www.bea.gov/bea/ARTICLES/2006/07July/0706_DIP_WEB.pdf, 7 February 2007.

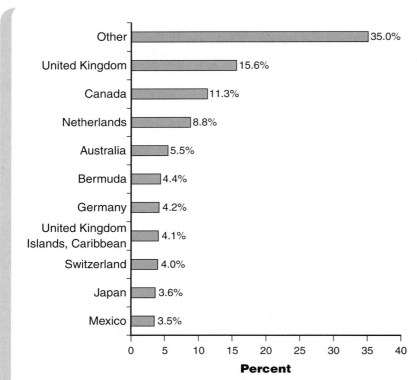

Source: J. Koncz & D. Yorgason, "Direct Investment Positions for 2005: Country and Industry Detail," available at http://www.bea.gov/bea/ARTICLES/2006/07July/0706_DIP_WEB.pdf, 7 February 2007.

Exhibit 8.2

U.S. Direct Foreign Investment Abroad

At the same time, direct foreign investment in the United States is just half the picture. U.S. companies also have made large direct foreign investments in countries throughout the world. For example, Anheuser-Busch, the brewer of Budweiser beer, paid $700 million to acquire Harbin Brewery Group, the fourth-largest beer company in China.[5] As Exhibit 8.2 shows, U.S. companies have made their largest direct foreign investments in the United Kingdom, Canada, the Netherlands, and Australia. Overall, U.S. companies invest more than $2 trillion a year to do business in other countries.

So, whether foreign companies invest in the United States or U.S. companies invest abroad, direct foreign investment is an increasingly important and common method of conducting global business.

1.2 Trade Barriers

Although today's consumers usually don't care where the products they buy come from (more on this in Section 1.4), national governments have traditionally preferred that consumers buy domestically made products in hopes that such purchases would increase the number of domestic businesses and workers. Indeed, governments have done much more than hope that you will buy from domestic companies. Historically, governments have actively used **trade barriers** to make it much more expensive or difficult (or sometimes impossible) for consumers to buy or consume imported goods. For example, countries throughout the world restrict the number and kind of imported television shows and movies. The French government requires that 40 percent of all TV shows be French and that at least 60 percent be European; the Chinese government permits only 20 foreign films to be imported each year.[6] Likewise, the European Union places a 34 percent tax on frozen strawberries imported from China.[7] And the U.S. government imposes a tariff of 54 cents a gallon on imported ethanol, which is blended with gasoline for use in automobiles.[8] By establishing these restrictions and taxes, the European Union and the French, Chinese, and U.S. governments are engaging in **protectionism**, which is the use of trade barriers to protect local companies and their workers from foreign competition.

Governments have used two general kinds of trade barriers: tariff and nontariff barriers. A **tariff** is a direct tax on imported goods. Like the U.S. government's 54-cent-per-gallon tax on imported ethanol, tariffs increase the cost of imported goods relative to that of domestic goods. For example, the U.S. import tax on trucks is 25 percent. This means that U.S. buyers must pay $25,000 for a $20,000 imported truck, with the $5,000 tariff going to the U.S. government. As a result, less than 10,000 pickup trucks are imported by the United States each year.[9] **Nontariff barriers** are nontax methods of increasing the cost or reducing the volume of imported goods. There are five types of nontariff barriers: quotas, voluntary export restraints, government import standards, government subsidies, and customs valuation/classification. Because there are so many

trade barriers government-imposed regulations that increase the cost and restrict the number of imported goods

protectionism a government's use of trade barriers to shield domestic companies and their workers from foreign competition

tariff a direct tax on imported goods

nontariff barriers nontax methods of increasing the cost or reducing the volume of imported goods different kinds of nontariff barriers, they can be an even more potent method of shielding domestic industries from foreign competition.

Quotas are specific limits on the number or volume of imported products. For example, because of strict import quotas, raw sugarcane imports into the United States are limited to approximately 1.2 million metric tons per year.[10] Since this is well below the demand for sugar in the United States, domestic U.S. sugar prices are twice as high as sugar prices in the rest of the world.[11] Like quotas, **voluntary export restraints** limit the amount of a product that can be imported annually. The difference is that the exporting country, rather than the importing country, imposes restraints. Usually, however, the "voluntary" offer to limit exports occurs because the importing country has implicitly threatened to impose quotas. For example, to protect South African textile manufacturers from cheap and plentiful Chinese textile products, the South African government convinced China to "voluntarily" restrict the textiles it exports to South Africa each year.[12] According to the World Trade Organization (see the discussion in Section 1.3), however, voluntary export restraints are illegal and should not be used to restrict imports.[13]

In theory, **government import standards** are established to protect the health and safety of citizens. In reality, such standards are often used to restrict or ban imported goods. For example, Japan banned the importation of nearly all U.S. apples, which are one-third the cost of Japanese apples. Ostensibly, the ban was to prevent transmission of fire blight bacteria to Japanese apple orchards, but research conducted *jointly* by U.S. and Japanese scientists "does not support Japan's assertion that mature, symptomless apples can transmit" the fire blight bacteria.[14] The Japanese government was actually using this government import standard to protect the economic health of its apple farmers, rather than the biological health of its apple orchards. Only after the World Trade Organization ruled that there was no scientific basis for the ban did Japan allow U.S. apples to be imported without restrictions.[15]

Many nations also use **subsidies**, such as long-term, low-interest loans, cash grants, and tax deferments, to develop and protect companies in special industries. Not surprisingly, businesses complain about unfair trade practices when foreign companies receive government subsidies. Boeing, the U.S. jet manufacturer, protested when Airbus received $4.5 billion in "launch aid" from nine European countries to build its new A380 superjumbo jet. In a formal complaint to the World Trade Organization, the U.S. Trade Representative argued that "Airbus governments thus enable Airbus to launch aircraft at an otherwise unsustainable scale and pace, if it could have launched them at all. Thus they expand the range of the Airbus product family against which U.S. producers must compete, and lower the price at which Airbus is able to offer those products. . . . The subsidization of Airbus jeopardizes the durability of any recent improvement in Boeing's competitive situation."[16]

© SUSAN VAN ETTEN

France is only one of many countries that restrict the number of imported television shows and movies as a means of protecting its domestic entertainment industry.

© INSIDE OUT/JUPITER IMAGES

quota a limit on the number or volume of imported products

voluntary export restraints voluntarily imposed limits on the number or volume of products exported to a particular country

government import standard a standard ostensibly established to protect the health and safety of citizens but, in reality, often used to restrict imports

subsidies government loans, grants, and tax deferments given to domestic companies to protect them from foreign competition

The last type of nontariff barrier is **customs classification**. As products are imported into a country, they are examined by customs agents, who must decide into which of nearly 9,000 categories they should classify a product (see the Official Harmonized Tariff Schedule of the United States at **http://www.usitc.gov/tata/hts/index.htm** for more information). Classification is important because the category assigned by customs agents can greatly affect the size of the tariff and whether the item is subject to import quotas. For example, the U.S. Customs Service has several customs classifications for imported shoes. Tariffs on imported leather or "nonrubber" shoes are about 8.5 percent, whereas tariffs on imported rubber shoes, such as athletic footwear or waterproof shoes, range from 20 to 67 percent.[17] The difference is large enough that some importers try to make their rubber shoes look like leather in hopes of receiving the nonrubber customs classification and lower tariff.

1.3 Trade Agreements

Thanks to the trade barriers described above, buying imported goods has often been much more expensive and difficult than buying domestic goods. During the 1990s, however, the regulations governing global trade were transformed. The most significant change was that 124 countries agreed to adopt the **General Agreement on Tariffs and Trade (GATT)**. Although GATT itself was replaced by the **World Trade Organization (WTO)** in 1995, the changes that it made continue to encourage international trade.

Through tremendous decreases in tariff and nontariff barriers, GATT made it much easier and cheaper for consumers in all countries to buy foreign products. First, tariffs were cut 40 percent on average worldwide by 2005. Second, tariffs were eliminated in 10 specific industries: beer, alcohol, construction equipment, farm machinery, furniture, medical equipment, paper, pharmaceuticals, steel, and toys. Third, stricter limits were put on government subsidies. For example, GATT put limits on how much national governments can subsidize company research in electronic and high-technology industries (see the discussion of subsidies in Section 1.2). Fourth, GATT established protections for intellectual property, such as trademarks, patents, and copyrights. Protection of intellectual property has become an increasingly important issue in global trade because of widespread product piracy. For example, 90 percent of the computer software and 95 percent of the video games in China are illegal pirated copies.[18] Likewise, Chinese bootleggers regularly sell illegal DVD copies of movies, such as *Borat* or *The Da Vinci Code*, months before the movie studios release official copies to stores in the United States.[19] Product piracy like this costs movie companies $6 billion in lost revenue each year.[20] Finally, trade disputes between countries now are fully settled by arbitration panels from the WTO. In the past, countries could use their veto power to cancel a panel's decision.

---

customs classification a classification assigned to imported products by government officials that affects the size of the tariff and imposition of import quotas

General Agreement on Tariffs and Trade (GATT) a worldwide trade agreement that reduced and eliminated tariffs, limited government subsidies, and established protections for intellectual property

World Trade Organization (WTO) the successor to GATT; the only international organization dealing with the global rules of trade between nations. Its main function is to ensure that trade flows as smoothly, predictably, and freely as possible.

Exhibit 8.3

World Trade Organization

☑ **FACT FILE**   WORLD TRADE ORGANIZATION

Location: Geneva, Switzerland
Established: 1 January 1995
Created by: Uruguay Round negotiations (1986–1994)
Membership: 150 countries (as of 11 October 2007)
Budget: 175 million Swiss francs for 2006
Secretariat staff: 635
Head: Pascal Lamy (director-general)

Functions:
- Administering WTO trade agreements
- Forum for trade negotiations
- Handling trade disputes
- Monitoring national trade policies
- Technical assistance and training for developing countries
- Cooperation with other international organizations

Source: "WTO: About the Organization," World Trade Organization, available at http://www.wto.org/english/thewto_e/whatis_e/whatis_e.htm, 7 February 2007.

For instance, the French government routinely vetoed rulings that its large cash grants to French farmers constituted unfair subsidies. Now, however, countries that are members of the WTO (every country that agreed to GATT is a member) no longer have veto power. Thus, WTO rulings are complete and final. For more information about GATT and the WTO, go to the WTO's Web site at **http://www.wto.org.** Exhibit 8.3 provides a brief overview of the WTO and its functions.

The second major development that has reduced trade barriers has been the creation of **regional trading zones**, in which tariff and nontariff barriers are reduced or eliminated for countries within the trading zone. The largest and most important trading zones are in Europe (the Maastricht Treaty), North America (the North American Free Trade Agreement, or NAFTA), Central America (Central America Free Trade Agreement, or CAFTA-DR), South America (Mercosur, and the proposed South American Community of Nations, or SACN), and Asia (the Association of Southeast Asian Nations, or ASEAN, and Asia-Pacific Economic Cooperation, or APEC). The map in Exhibit 8.4 shows the extent to which free trade agreements govern global trade.

regional trading zones areas in which tariff and nontariff barriers on trade between countries are reduced or eliminated

Exhibit 8.4
Global Map of Regional Trade Agreements

Maastricht Treaty of Europe Austria, Belgium, Cyprus, the Czech Republic, Denmark, Estonia, Finland, France, Germany, Greece, Hungary, Ireland, Italy, Latvia, Lithuania, Luxembourg, Malta, the Netherlands, Poland, Portugal, Slovakia, Slovenia, Spain, Sweden, and the United Kingdom.

ASEAN Brunei Darussalam, Cambodia, Indonesia, Laos, Malaysia, Myanmar, the Philippines, Singapore, Thailand, and Vietnam.

APEC Australia, Canada, Chile, the People's Republic of China, Hong Kong (China), Japan, Mexico, New Zealand, Papua New Guinea, Peru, Russia, South Korea, Taiwan, the United States, and all members of ASEAN except Cambodia, Laos, and Myanmar.

NAFTA (North American Free Trade Agreement)
United States, Canada, and Mexico.

CAFTA-DR (Central America-Dominican Republic Free Trade Agreement)
Costa Rica, the Dominican Republic, El Salvador, Guatemala, Honduras, Nicaragua, and the United States.

SACN (South American Community of Nations)
Argentina, Bolivia, Brazil, Chile, Colombia, Ecuador, Guyana, Paraguay, Peru, Suriname, Uruguay, and Venezuela

Mercosur
Argentina, Brazil, Paraguay, and Uruguay

In 1992, Belgium, Denmark, France, Germany, Greece, Ireland, Italy, Luxembourg, the Netherlands, Portugal, Spain, and the United Kingdom implemented the **Maastricht Treaty of Europe**. The purpose of this treaty was to transform their 12 different economies and 12 currencies into one common economic market, called the European Union (EU), with one common currency. Austria, Finland, and Sweden joined the EU in 1995, followed by Cyprus, the Czech Republic, Estonia, Hungary, Latvia, Lithuania, Malta, Poland, Slovakia, and Slovenia in 2004, bringing the total membership to 25 countries.[21] Bulgaria and Romania joined in 2007; Croatia, Macedonia, and Turkey are now being considered for membership.[22] On 1 January 2002, a single common currency, the euro, went into circulation in 12 of the EU's members (Austria, Belgium, Finland, France, Germany, Greece, Ireland, Italy, Luxembourg, the Netherlands, Portugal, and Spain).

Prior to the treaty, trucks carrying products were stopped and inspected by customs agents at each border. Furthermore, since the required paperwork, tariffs, and government product specifications could be radically different in each country, companies often had to file 12 different sets of paperwork, pay 12 different tariffs, produce 12 different versions of their basic product to meet various government specifications, and exchange money in 12 different currencies. Likewise, open business travel from state to state, which we take for granted in the United States, was complicated by inspections at each border crossing. If you lived in Germany but worked in Luxembourg, your car was stopped and your passport was inspected twice every day, as you traveled to and from work. Also, every business transaction required a currency exchange, for example, from German deutsche marks to Italian lira, or from French francs to Dutch guilders. Imagine all of this happening to millions of trucks, cars, and businesspeople, and you can begin to appreciate the difficulty and cost of conducting business across Europe before the Maastricht Treaty. For more information about the Maastricht Treaty and the EU, go to **http://europa .eu.int/index-en.htm**. For more about Europe's new common currency, the euro, see **http://www.ecb.int/ecb/educational/html/index.en.html**.

NAFTA, the **North American Free Trade Agreement** between the United States, Canada, and Mexico, went into effect on 1 January 1994. More than any other regional trade agreement, NAFTA has liberalized trade between countries so that businesses can plan for one market, North America, rather than for three separate markets, the United States, Canada, and Mexico. One of NAFTA's most important achievements was to eliminate most product tariffs *and* prevent the three countries from increasing existing tariffs or introducing new ones. Before NAFTA, Wal-Mart used expensive intermediaries to distribute goods to its stores, and Mexican officials often pressured managers for bribes. Because of burdensome paperwork, deliveries sometimes took months to clear customs. This all changed with NAFTA. Before NAFTA, Wal-Mart sold a Sony flat-screen TV imported from Japan with a 23 percent tariff for $1,600 in Mexico. After NAFTA, Sony built a new factory in Mexico, enabling it to ship the TVs duty-free anywhere in the United States, Canada, or Mexico. With shipping costs now next to nothing and the 23 percent tariff eliminated, Wal-Mart sells the flat-screen TVs for $600 in Mexico, or about what they sell for in the United States.[23]

Overall, both Mexican and Canadian exports to the United States have doubled since NAFTA went into effect. U.S. exports to Mexico and Canada have doubled, too, growing twice as fast as U.S. exports to any other part of the world.[24] In fact, Mexico and Canada now account for 36 percent of all U.S. exports.[25] For more information about NAFTA, see the Office of NAFTA & Inter-American Affairs at **http://www.ustr.gov/Trade_Agreements/Regional/NAFTA/Section_Index.html**.

Maastricht Treaty of Europe a regional trade agreement between most European countries

North American Free Trade Agreement (NAFTA) a regional trade agreement between the United States, Canada, and Mexico

CAFTA-DR, the new **Central America Free Trade Agreement** between the United States, the Dominican Republic, and the Central American countries of Costa Rica, El Salvador, Guatemala, Honduras, and Nicaragua went into effect in August 2005. With a combined population of 347.6 million (302.3 million in the United States), the CAFTA-DR countries together are the 10th-largest U.S. export market in the world, and the second-largest U.S. export market in Latin America, after Mexico. U.S. companies export more than $16 billion in goods each year to the CAFTA-DR countries. Furthermore, U.S. exports to CAFTA-DR countries, which are increasing at 16 percent per year, are by far the fastest growing export market for U.S. companies.[26] For more information about CAFTA-DR, see **http://www.fas.usda.gov/itp/ CAFTA/cafta.asp**.

One of the goals of the proposed SACN, the South American Community of Nations, is to establish a free trade zone throughout South America for the countries of Argentina, Bolivia, Brazil, Chile, Colombia, Ecuador, Guyana, Paraguay, Peru, Suriname, Uruguay, and Venezuela. If created, the SACA would likely supplant Mercosur, a free trade agreement between Brazil, Argentina, Uruguay, and Paraguay, which have been granted associate membership in SACN. For more information about Mercosur, see **http://www.sice.oas.org/agreemts/ Mercin_e.asp#MERCOSUR**. If approved, SACN would become one of the largest trading zones in the world, encompassing 361 million people in 12 countries in South America with a combined gross domestic product of $1 trillion.[27] For more information about SACN, see **http://www.comunidadandina.org/ingles/ sudamerican.htm**.

ASEAN, the **Association of Southeast Asian Nations**, and **APEC**, the **Asia-Pacific Economic Cooperation**, are the two largest and most important regional trading groups in Asia. ASEAN is a trade agreement between Brunei Darussalam, Cambodia, Indonesia, Lao PDR, Malaysia, Myanmar, the Philippines, Singapore, Thailand, and Vietnam, which form a market of more than 558 million people. U.S. trade with ASEAN countries exceeds $153 billion a year.[28] In fact, the United States is ASEAN's largest trading partner, and ASEAN'S member nations constitute the fifth-largest trading partner of the United States. ASEAN's members have agreed to create an ASEAN free trade area beginning in 2015 for the six original countries (Brunei Darussalam, Indonesia, Malaysia, the Philippines, Singapore, and Thailand) and in 2018 for the newer member countries (Cambodia, Lao PDR, Myanmar, and Vietnam).[29] For more information about ASEAN, see **http://www.aseansec.org**.

APEC is a broader agreement that includes Australia, Canada, Chile, the People's Republic of China, Hong Kong (China), Japan, Mexico, New Zealand, Papua New Guinea, Peru, Russia, South Korea, Taiwan, the United States, and all the members of ASEAN except Cambodia, Lao PDR, and Myanmar.[30] APEC's 21 member countries contain 2.6 billion people, account for 47 percent of all global trade, and have a combined gross domestic product of over $19 trillion.[31] APEC countries began reducing trade barriers in 2000, though all the reductions will not be completely phased in until 2020. For more information about APEC, see **http://www.apecsec.org.sg**.

1.4 Consumers, Trade Barriers, and Trade Agreements

In Tokyo, a Coke costs $1.33.[32] In Geneva, Switzerland, a small cup of regular coffee costs $1.70. In the United States, each of these items costs about a dollar. A McDonald's Big Mac sandwich costs an average of $3.22 in the United States, $3.90 in the United Kingdom, and $5.05 in Switzerland.[33] Although not all products are more expensive in other countries (in some, they are cheaper; for example, a Big Mac costs $1.41 in China and $2.66 in Mexico), international studies find

Central America Free Trade Agreement (CAFTA-DR) a regional trade agreement between Costa Rica, the Dominican Republic, El Salvador, Guatemala, Honduras, Nicaragua, and the United States

Association of Southeast Asian Nations (ASEAN) a regional trade agreement between Brunei Darussalam, Cambodia, Indonesia, Laos, Malaysia, Myanmar, the Philippines, Singapore, Thailand, and Vietnam

Asia-Pacific Economic Cooperation (APEC) a regional trade agreement between Australia, Canada, Chile, the People's Republic of China, Hong Kong, Japan, Mexico, New Zealand, Papua New Guinea, Peru, Russia, South Korea, Taiwan, the United States, and all the members of ASEAN, except Cambodia, Laos, and Myanmar

One of the most widely known methods of comparing the purchasing power of nations is the Big Mac Index assembled yearly by **The Economist.** **In China, a Big Mac costs the equivalent of a mere $1.41.**

that American consumers get much more for their money than most other consumers in the world. For example, the average worker earns nearly $54,930 a year in Switzerland, $59,590 in Norway, $38,980 in Japan, and $43,749 in America.[34] Yet, after adjusting these incomes for how much they can buy, the Swiss income is equivalent to just $37,080, the Norwegian income to $40,420, and the Japanese income to $31,410![35] This is the same as saying that $1 of income can buy you only 68 cents worth of goods in Switzerland and Norway, and 81 cents worth in Japan. In other words, Americans can buy much more with their incomes than those in other countries can.

One reason that Americans get more for their money is that the U.S. marketplace has been one of the easiest for foreign companies to enter. Although some U.S. industries, such as textiles, have been heavily protected from foreign competition by trade barriers, for the most part, American consumers (and businesses) have had plentiful choices among American-made and foreign-made products. More important, the high level of competition between foreign and domestic companies that creates these choices helps to keep prices low in the United States. Furthermore, it is precisely the lack of choice and the low level of competition that keep prices higher in countries that have not been as open to foreign companies and products. For example, Japanese trade barriers are estimated to cost Japanese consumers more than $100 billion a year. In fact, Japanese trade barriers amount to a 51 percent tax on food for the average Japanese family.[36]

So why do trade barriers and free trade agreements matter to consumers? They're important because free trade agreements increase choices, competition, and purchasing power and thus decrease what people pay for food, clothing, necessities, and luxuries. Accordingly, today's consumers rarely care where their products and services come from. For example, Mark Sneed, president of Phillips Foods, which imports blue crab from its Asian processing factories at one-third the cost of crab caught and processed in the United States, says, "I've never once had a customer ask me if we served domestic or imported crabs, just like they never ask if we have foreign shrimp."[37] Peter Germano, a New York jeweler who sells diamonds, says people don't care where the diamonds are from; they "just want to know which is cheaper."[38] Finally, Luis de Anda, who visits one of Wal-Mart's Sam's Wholesale Clubs in Mexico once a month to purchase diapers and toilet paper in bulk for his family and friends, says, "Why should I care where they're from? With the money I save, I take my family to the movies."[39]

> Free trade agreements increase choices, competition, and purchasing power and thus decrease what people pay for food, clothing, necessities, and luxuries.

And why do trade barriers and free trade agreements matter to managers? The reason, as you're about to read, is that while free trade agreements create new business opportunities, they also intensify competition, and addressing that competition is a manager's job.

Review 1: *Global Business, Trade Rules, and Trade Agreements*

Today, there are more than 77,175 multinational corporations worldwide; just 3.1 percent are based in the United States. Global business affects the United States in two ways: through direct foreign investment in the United States by foreign companies, and through U.S. companies' investment in business in other countries. U.S. direct foreign investment throughout the world typically amounts to about $2 trillion per year, whereas direct foreign investment by foreign companies in the United States amounts to $1.6 trillion per year. Historically, tariffs and nontariff trade barriers, such as quotas, voluntary export restraints, government import standards, government subsidies, and customs classifications, have made buying foreign goods much harder or more expensive than buying domestically produced products. In recent years, however, worldwide trade agreements, such as GATT, along with regional trading agreements, like the Maastricht Treaty of Europe, NAFTA, CAFTA-DR, Mercosur, SACN, ASEAN, and APEC, have substantially reduced tariff and nontariff barriers to international trade. Companies have responded by investing in growing markets in Asia, eastern Europe, and Latin America. Consumers have responded by purchasing products based on value, rather than geography.

HOW TO GO GLOBAL?

Once a company has decided that it *will* go global, it must decide *how* to go global. For example, if you decide to sell in Singapore, should you try to find a local business partner who speaks the language, knows the laws, and understands the customs and norms of Singapore's culture, or should you simply export your products from your home country? What do you do if you are also entering eastern Europe, perhaps starting in Hungary? Should you use the same approach in Hungary that you used in Singapore?

> **Although there is no magical formula for answering these questions, after reading the next two sections, you should be able to**
>
> 2 explain why companies choose to standardize or adapt their business procedures.
>
> 3 explain the different ways that companies can organize to do business globally.

2 Consistency or Adaptation?

In this section, we return to a key issue: How can you be sure that the way you run your business in one country is the right way to run that business in another? In other words, how can you strike the right balance between global consistency and local adaptation? **Global consistency** means that when a multinational company has offices, manufacturing plants, and distribution facilities in different countries, it will use the same rules, guidelines, policies, and procedures to run those offices, plants, and facilities. Managers at company headquarters value global consistency because it simplifies decisions. In contrast, a company with a **local adaptation** policy modifies its standard operating procedures to adapt to differences in foreign customers, governments, and

global consistency when a multinational company has offices, manufacturing plants, and distribution facilities in different countries and runs them all using the same rules, guidelines, policies, and procedures

local adaptation modifying rules, guidelines, policies, and procedures to adapt to differences in foreign customers, governments, and regulatory agencies regulatory agencies. Local adaptation is typically more important to local managers who are charged with making the international business successful in their countries.

If companies lean too much toward global consistency, they run the risk of using management procedures poorly suited to particular countries' markets, cultures, and employees (that is, not enough local adaptation). *MTV* made this mistake when going global. According to Divya Gupta, president of Media Edge, which helps companies buy advertising in India, "MTV, when it first entered the country, made the mistake of coming in as MTV. No changes." So MTV quickly learned from this mistake and stopped showing Western videos in international locations and started featuring local music and shows. In Brazil, it developed *Mochilão*, a travel show hosted by a popular model who backpacks to famous sites.[40] In China, it developed *Mei Mei Sees MTV*, in which an animated, "virtual" video disc jockey introduces music videos.[41] And in India it developed *Silly Point*, a humor show that takes a lighthearted view of India's most popular sport, cricket.[42]

"WHAT'S NEW" COMPANY

If companies focus too much on local adaptation, however, they run the risk of losing the cost efficiencies and productivity that result from using standardized rules and procedures throughout the world. A decade into its development, MTV International was profitable, but not by much. While it had access to huge markets—in fact, 80 percent of MTV viewers were outside the United States—access to those markets was slow to translate into large profits. Why? Because of the enormous cost of building new studios, acquiring new talent, and developing local content for so many different international markets.

Review 2: Consistency or Adaptation?

Global business requires a balance between global consistency and local adaptation. Global consistency means using the same rules, guidelines, policies, and procedures in each location. Managers at company headquarters like global consistency because it simplifies decisions. Local adaptation means adapting standard procedures to individual markets. Local managers prefer a policy of local adaptation because it gives them more control. Not all businesses need the same combinations of global consistency and local adaptation. Some thrive by emphasizing global consistency and ignoring local adaptation. Others succeed by ignoring global consistency and emphasizing local adaptation.

3 Forms for Global Business

Besides determining whether to adapt organizational policies and procedures, a company must also determine how to organize itself for successful entry into foreign markets.

*Historically, companies have generally followed the phase model of globalization, in which a company makes the transition from a domestic company to a global company in the following sequential phases: **3.1 exporting**, **3.2 cooperative contracts**, **3.3 strategic alliances**, and **3.4 wholly owned affiliates**. At each step, the company grows much larger, uses those resources to enter more global markets, is less dependent on home country sales, and is more committed in its orientation to global business. Some companies, however, do not follow the phase model of globalization.[43] Some skip phases on their way to becoming more global and less domestic. Others don't follow the phase model at all. These are known as **3.5 global new ventures**. This section reviews these forms of global business.[44]*

3.1 Exporting

When companies produce products in their home countries and sell those products to customers in foreign countries, they are **exporting**. For example, FREMANTLEMEDIA, the London-based company that originally developed the *Pop Idol* TV show in Britain and then exported a nearly identical version to the United States as *American Idol*, now has exported similar versions of the show to 35 different countries.[45]

Exporting as a form of global business offers many advantages. It makes the company less dependent on sales in its home market and provides a greater degree of control over research, design, and production decisions. Sheldon Bailey is a "flying producer" who helps FremantleMedia set up *Idol* in different countries and cultures. Bailey allows for some adaptation to local cultures. In Germany, for example, the word *Idol* is associated with Hitler, so the show is called *Germany Seeks the Superstar*; likewise, since popular Arabic songs last eight or nine minutes, three times as long as in the rest of the world, contestants get three minutes to sing, compared with 90 seconds in other versions of *Idol*. For the most part, however, the show is basically the same worldwide—find undiscovered talents and turn them into major recording artists—and it's Bailey's job to ensure that consistency. When local Russian producers claimed that Russians want to see celebrities and pushed to have them on the show, Bailey refused: "We told them this is not about celebrities, it's about kids. They're your stars."

Though advantageous in a number of ways, exporting also has its disadvantages. The primary disadvantage is that many exported goods are subject to tariff and nontariff barriers that can substantially increase their final cost to consumers. A second disadvantage is that transportation costs can significantly increase the price of an exported product. For example, because of special safety requirements such as maintaining particular temperatures and pressures, the ships that transport liquefied natural gas can cost up to $350 million to build. Consequently, shipping costs account for as much as 20 to 30 percent of the total cost of liquefied natural gas.[46] Another disadvantage is that companies that export depend on foreign importers for product distribution. This means that if, for example, the foreign importer makes a

doing the right thing

Fair and Safe Working Conditions in Foreign Factories

Requiring workers to work 15-hour days or to work seven days a week with no overtime pay, beating them for arriving late, requiring them to apply toxic materials with their bare hands, charging them excessive fees for food and lodging—these are just a few of the workplace violations found in the overseas factories that make shoes, clothes, bicycles, and other goods for large U.S. and multinational companies. The Fair Labor Association, which inspects overseas factories for Adidas-Salomon, Levi Strauss, Liz Claiborne, Nike, Reebok, Polo Ralph Lauren, and others, recommends the following workplace standards for foreign factories.

- Make sure there is no forced labor or child labor; no physical, sexual, psychological, or verbal abuse or harassment; and no discrimination.

- Provide a safe and healthy working environment to prevent accidents.

- Respect the right of employees to freedom of association and collective bargaining. Compensate employees fairly by paying the legally required minimum wage or the prevailing industry wage, whichever is higher.

- Provide legally required benefits. Employees should not be required to work more than 48 hours per week and 12 hours of overtime (for which they should receive additional pay), and they should have at least one day off per week.

Do the right thing. Investigate and monitor the working conditions of overseas factories where the goods sold by your company are made. Insist that improvements be made. Find another supplier if they aren't.[47]

exporting selling domestically produced products to customers in foreign countries

Local adaptation is a necessary consideration of global business. For example, since Germans associate the word 'idol' with Hitler, producers exporting the popular American Idol television show opted to change the name to Deutschland sucht den SuperStar ("Germany Seeks the Superstar").

cooperative contract an agreement in which a foreign business owner pays a company a fee for the right to conduct that business in his or her country

licensing an agreement in which a domestic company, the licensor, receives royalty payments for allowing another company, the licensee, to produce the licensor's product, sell its service, or use its brand name in a specified foreign market

franchise a collection of networked firms in which the manufacturer or marketer of a product or service, the franchisor, licenses the entire business to another person or organization, the franchisee

mistake on the paperwork that accompanies a shipment of imported goods, those goods can be returned to the foreign manufacturer at the manufacturer's expense.

3.2 Cooperative Contracts

When an organization wants to expand its business globally without making a large financial commitment to do so, it may sign a **cooperative contract** with a foreign business owner, who pays the company a fee for the right to conduct that business in his or her country. There are two kinds of cooperative contracts: licensing and franchising.

Under a **licensing** agreement, a domestic company, the *licensor*, receives royalty payments for allowing another company, the *licensee*, to produce its product, sell its service, or use its brand name in a particular foreign market. For example, brands such as Peter Paul Mounds and Almond Joy, which consumers associate with American companies, are not really American products. A British company, CADBURY SCHWEPPES, licenses those candy bars to Hershey for U.S. production.

One of the most important advantages of licensing is that it allows companies to earn additional profits without investing more money. As foreign sales increase, the royalties paid to the licensor by the foreign licensee increase. Moreover, the licensee, not the licensor, invests in production equipment and facilities to produce the licensed product. Licensing also helps companies avoid tariff and nontariff barriers. Since the licensee manufactures the product within the foreign country, tariff and nontariff barriers don't apply. For example, Britvic Corona is licensed to bottle and distribute Pepsi-Cola within the United Kingdom. Because it bottles the soft drink in Britain, tariff and nontariff barriers do not apply.

The biggest disadvantage associated with licensing is that the licensor gives up control over the quality of the product or service sold by the foreign licensee. Unless the licensing agreement contains specific restrictions, the licensee controls the entire business, from production to marketing to final sales. Many licensors include inspection clauses in their license contracts, but closely monitoring product or service quality from thousands of miles away can be difficult. An additional disadvantage is that licensees can eventually become competitors, especially when a licensing agreement includes access to important technology or proprietary business knowledge.

A **franchise** is a collection of networked firms in which the manufacturer or marketer of a product or service, the *franchisor*, licenses the entire business to another person or organization, the *franchisee*. For the price of an initial franchise fee plus royalties, franchisors provide franchisees with training, assistance with marketing and advertising, and an exclusive right to conduct business in a particular location. Most franchise fees run between $5,000 and $35,000. Franchisees pay McDONALD'S, one of the largest franchisors in the world, an initial franchise fee of $45,000. Another $610,750 to $1,210,000 is needed beyond that to pay for food inventory, kitchen equipment, construction, landscaping, and other expenses (the cost varies per country). While franchisees typically borrow part of this cost from a bank, McDonald's requires that they invest $200,000 of their own money into a new McDonald's restaurant.[48] Since typical royalties range from 2.0 to 12.5 percent of gross sales, franchisors are well rewarded for the help they provide to franchisees. More than 400 U.S. companies franchise their businesses to foreign franchise partners.

Overall, franchising is a fast way to enter foreign markets. Over the last 20 years, U.S. franchisors have more than doubled their global franchises for a total of more than 100,000 global franchise units. Because it gives the franchisor additional cash flows from franchisee fees and royalties, franchising can be a good strategy when a company's domestic sales have slowed. For example, YUM! BRANDS, which owns and runs Pizza Hut, Taco Bell, KFC (formerly Kentucky Fried Chicken), A&W Restaurants, and Long John Silver's, is accepting very few new franchises in the United States because the U.S. market is saturated with fast-food outlets. McDonald's opens only 50 to 100 new restaurants a year in the United States.[49] Outside the United States, however, these restaurants are experiencing much stronger growth. In the last decade, McDonald's nearly doubled the number of its overseas restaurants and continues to add approximately 700 to 800 new international restaurants per year.[50] Between Pizza Hut, Taco Bell, KFC, A&W Restaurants, and Long John Silvers, Yum! Brands opens nearly 700 new international franchise restaurants a year.[51]

"WHAT'S NEW" COMPANY

Despite franchising's many advantages, franchisors face a loss of control when they sell businesses to franchisees who are thousands of miles away. Franchising specialist Cheryl Scott says, "One franchisor I know was wondering why the royalties coming from India were so small when he knew the shop was always packed. It was because the franchisee wasn't putting all of the sales through the cash register."[52]

Although there are exceptions, franchising success may be somewhat culture-bound. Because most global franchisors begin by franchising their businesses in similar countries or regions (Canada is by far the first choice for American companies taking their first step into global franchising), and because 65 percent of franchisors make absolutely no change in their business for overseas franchisees, that success may not generalize to cultures with different lifestyles, values, preferences, and technological infrastructures. When Jim Bryant began opening Subway sandwich shops in China 10 years ago, Americans living there were elated (one kissed the floor), but Chinese customers didn't know how to order (he had to make signs explaining how) or how to eat a sandwich (they peeled it like a banana because they didn't want to physically touch their food). Likewise, because the tuna in the tuna salad didn't have a visible head or a tail, they didn't believe it was actually fish.[53] Management consultant Dennis Custage says, "The number one mistake companies make is trying to run everything the way it was in their home country, with a bunch of expatriates."[54] Furthermore, unlike McDonald's, which added a new spicy chicken burger, and KFC, which replaced coleslaw with shredded carrots, fungus, or bamboo shoots, Subway didn't change its menu for Chinese tastes. Luo Bing Ling, who runs a Subway store in Beijing, says, "Subway should have at least one item tailored to Chinese tastes to show they are respecting the local culture."[55]

3.3 Strategic Alliances

Companies forming **strategic alliances** combine key resources, costs, risks, technology, and people. The most common strategic alliance is a **joint venture**, which occurs when two existing companies collaborate to form a third company. The two founding companies remain intact and unchanged, except that together they now own the newly created joint venture.

One of the oldest and most successful global joint ventures is FUJI XEROX, which is a joint venture between Fuji Film of Japan and U.S.-based Xerox Corporation, which makes copiers and automated office systems. More than 45 years after its creation, Fuji Xerox employs nearly 37,000 employees and has close to $9.1 billion in revenues. Fuji Xerox is largely responsible for copier sales in Asia, whereas Xerox is responsible for North American sales. Rank Xerox, a Xerox subsidiary, is responsible for sales in Europe.[56]

"WHAT'S NEW" COMPANY

strategic alliance an agreement in which companies combine key resources, costs, risk, technology, and people

joint venture a strategic alliance in which two existing companies collaborate to form a third, independent company

One of the advantages of global joint ventures is that, like licensing and franchising, they help companies avoid tariff and nontariff barriers to entry. Another advantage is that companies participating in a joint venture bear only part of the costs and the risks of that business. Many companies find this attractive because of the expense of entering foreign markets or developing new products. For example, General Electric and Mitsubishi Electric have formed POWEREX, an international joint venture to share the high development costs of designing and making parts for hybrid cars that run on both gasoline and electric power. Powerex makes electronic parts that help convert brake heat into power that is stored in batteries; the batteries run the electric motor when the car starts and during acceleration. Once the car attains a stable speed, the gasoline engine takes over and recharges the batteries. Hybrid cars are capable of getting 70 percent more miles per gallon than standard cars in city driving.[57]

Global joint ventures can be especially advantageous to smaller local partners that link up with larger, more experienced foreign firms that can bring advanced management, resources, and business skills to the joint venture. For instance, VENYON is a global joint venture between Finland-based cell phone giant Nokia and Germany-based Giesecke & Devrient (G&D), which specializes in secure smart cards, telecommunications, electronic payments and identification, and IT security. Through their combined efforts in Venyon, Nokia and G&D will enable consumers to securely use their cell phones, Blackberrys, or personal digital assistants to buy airline, rail, or taxi service, or to make credit card purchases from retailers, banks, and providers of digital services and media.[58] In short, if you can purchase something via the Internet, you should, thanks to Venyon, be able to purchase it securely via your cell phone.

Global joint ventures are not without problems, though. Because companies share costs and risks with their joint venture partners, they must also share profits. At one time, sharing of profits created some tension at Fuji Film, Xerox, and their joint venture, Fuji Xerox. In fact, until Xerox's recent turnaround, the company struggled for so long that business experts joked that Fuji Xerox, which has been highly profitable, should purchase Xerox.

Managing global joint ventures can also be difficult because they represent a merging of four cultures: the country and the organizational cultures of the first partner, and the country and the organizational cultures of the second partner. Oftentimes, to be "fair" to all involved, each partner in the global joint venture will have equal ownership and power. But this can result in power struggles and a lack of leadership. Because of these problems, companies forming global joint ventures should carefully develop detailed contracts that specify the obligations of each party. Toshiba, which participated in its first global joint ventures in the early 1900s by making light bulb filaments with General Electric, treats joint ventures like a marriage of the two companies and views the contract as a prenuptial agreement. The joint venture contract specifies how much each company will invest, what its rights and responsibilities are, and what it is entitled to if the joint venture does not work out. These steps are important, because the rate of failure for global joint ventures is estimated to be as high as 50 percent.[59]

When companies involved in global joint ventures don't carefully specify the obligations of each party, difficulties can occur. SHANGHAI AUTOMOTIVE, an auto manufacturer owned by the Chinese government that has global joint ventures with General Motors and Volkswagen, builds hundreds of thousands of Buicks, Chevys, Santanas, and Passats each year for Chinese consumers. Now, however, Shanghai Automotive has announced that it will build its own cars to the Chinese market to compete directly with its partners. Michael Dunne, president of Automotive

Resources Asia, says, "The Chinese formed joint ventures for one purpose: to learn how to do it themselves one day. That day is here."[60]

3.4 Wholly Owned Affiliates (Build or Buy)

Approximately one-third of multinational companies enter foreign markets through wholly owned affiliates. Unlike licensing arrangements, franchises, or joint ventures, **wholly owned affiliates** are 100 percent owned by the parent company. For example, HONDA MOTORS OF AMERICA in Marysville, Ohio, is 100 percent owned by Honda Motors of Japan. Ford Motor of Germany in Cologne is 100 percent owned by the FORD MOTOR COMPANY in Detroit, Michigan.

The primary advantage of wholly owned businesses is that the parent company receives all of the profits and has complete control over the foreign facilities. The biggest disadvantage is the expense of building new operations or buying existing businesses. While the payoff can be enormous if wholly owned affiliates succeed, the losses can be immense if they fail because the parent company assumes all of the risk. Two years after VODAFONE, the world's largest cell phone company, paid $2.2 billion to acquire J-Phone, the third-largest Japanese cell phone company, annual revenues continue to fall, and the number of new subscribers has dropped by 87 percent—a bad sign for future sales. The problem is that Vodafone focuses on selling small, reliable phones that work anywhere in the world, but most Japanese customers don't care whether their phones work outside the country. They want stylish, flashy, high-tech G3 cell phones that can download music, games, videos, and e-mail. And because Vodafone wholly owns J-Phone, it is bearing all the risk. Darryl Green, president of Vodafone in Japan, says, "We're losing our share of heavy users," the most profitable customers in the cell phone business.[61]

3.5 Global New Ventures

Companies used to evolve slowly from small operations selling in their home markets to large businesses selling to foreign markets. Furthermore, as companies went global, they usually followed the phase model of globalization. Recently, however, three trends have combined to allow companies to skip the phase model when going global. First, quick, reliable air travel can transport people to nearly any point in the world within one day. Second, low-cost communication technologies, such as international e-mail, teleconferencing, phone conferencing, and the Internet, make it easier to communicate with global customers, suppliers, managers, and employees. Third, there is now a critical mass of businesspeople with extensive personal experience in all aspects of global business.[62] This combination of developments has made it possible to start companies that are global from inception. With sales, employees, and financing in different countries, **global new ventures** are companies that are founded with an active global strategy.[63]

Although there are several different kinds of global new ventures, all share two common factors. First, the company founders successfully develop and communicate the company's global vision from inception. Winphoria Networks, which specializes in wireless networks, was global the day it started. Company investor Promod Haque explains: "Sales and marketing and the CEO were in Boston," but "the center of gravity was outside the United States. By having our employees based in Madrid and Bangalore, we were bidding contracts in Europe and Asia" during a time when sales were slow in the United States.[64] Winphoria's global launch was so successful that Motorola bought it only a few years after the start-up.

wholly owned affiliates foreign offices, facilities, and manufacturing plants that are 100 percent owned by the parent company

global new ventures new companies that are founded with an active global strategy and have sales, employees, and financing in different countries

Second, rather than going global one country at a time, new global ventures bring a product or service to market in several foreign markets at the same time. While headquartered in Lexington, Massachusetts, VISTAPRINT receives 15,000 orders a day from customers in 120 different countries who design their business cards, brochures, and invitations online using 17 different VistaPrint websites, each representing a different language or location. Printing happens at two automated production facilities, one in the Netherlands and the other in Canada. Once printed, the products are cut and sized by robots, and then packaged and delivered just three days after ordering. Regarding VistaPrint's commitment to worldwide customers, founder Robert Keane says, "The United States is blessed and cursed with a huge domestic market. It's often hard for startups to find their way out of their home nation. But you have to—it's not that type of world anymore."[65]

Review 3: Forms for Global Business

The phase model of globalization says that as companies move from a domestic to a global orientation, they use these organizational forms in sequence: exporting, cooperative contracts (licensing and franchising), strategic alliances, and wholly owned affiliates. Yet not all companies follow the phase model. For example, global new ventures are global from their inception.

WHERE TO GO GLOBAL?

Deciding where to go global is just as important as deciding how your company will go global. After reading the next three sections, you should be able to

4 explain how to find a favorable business climate.

5 discuss the importance of identifying and adapting to cultural differences.

6 explain how to successfully prepare workers for international assignments.

4 Finding the Best Business Climate

When deciding where to go global, companies try to find countries or regions with promising business climates.

> An attractive global business climate **4.1 positions the company for easy access to growing markets, 4.2 is an effective but cost-efficient place to build an office or manufacturing facility, and 4.3 minimizes the political risk to the company.**

4.1 Growing Markets

The most important factor in an attractive business climate is access to a growing market. For example, no product is known and purchased by as many people throughout the world as COCA-COLA. Yet, even Coke, which is available in over 200 countries, still has tremendous potential for further global growth. Currently, the Coca-Cola Company gets about 80 percent of its sales from its 16 largest markets.[66] The remaining 20 percent is spread across the other 200 countries in which Coke does business.

Two factors help companies determine the growth potential of foreign markets: purchasing power and foreign competitors. **Purchasing power** is measured by comparing the relative cost of a standard set of goods and services in different countries. Earlier in the chapter we noted that a Coke costs $1.33 in Tokyo. Because a Coke costs only about $1.00 in the United States, the average American would have more purchasing power than the average Japanese. Purchasing power is strong in countries like Mexico, India, and China, which have low average levels of income. This is because basic living expenses, such as food, shelter, and transportation, are very inexpensive in those countries, so consumers still have money to spend after paying for necessities. For example, Mexican newlyweds Lucia Jiminez, a clothing store clerk, and Benjamin Macias, an office worker for an eyeglass store, earn just $650 a month. But that modest income easily qualifies them for a 30-year mortgage because the cost of their brand-new two-bedroom house 30 minutes outside Mexico City is just $25,200.[67] Because basic living expenses are so low in China, Mexico, and India and incomes are rising, purchasing power is strong, and millions of Chinese, Mexican, and Indian consumers increasingly have extra money to spend on what they want, in addition to what they need.[68]

Consequently, countries with high and growing levels of purchasing power are good choices for companies looking for attractive global markets. As Exhibit 8.5 shows, Coke has found that the per capita consumption of Coca-Cola, or the number of Cokes a person drinks per year, rises directly with purchasing power. For example, in China, Colombia, and Argentina, where the average person earns $7,600, $9,100, and $15,000 annually, the respective number of Coca-Cola soft drinks increases from 18 to 80 to 253. The more purchasing power people have, the more likely they are to purchase soft drinks.[69]

The second part of assessing the growth potential of global markets involves analyzing the degree of global competition, which is determined by the number

> The number of Cokes a person drinks per year rises directly with purchasing power.

purchasing power the relative cost of a standard set of goods and services in different countries

Exhibit 8.5

How Consumption of Coca-Cola Varies with Purchasing Power around the World

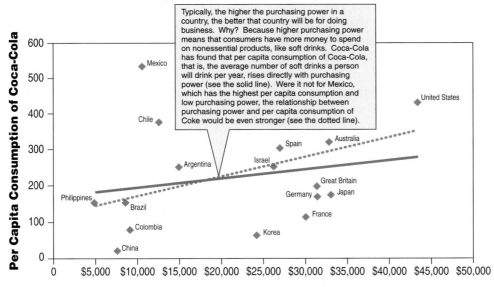

Sources: "Rank Order—GDP—Per Capita," *The World Factbook*, available at https://www.cia.gov/library/publications/the-world-factbook/rankorder/2004rank.html, 12 February 2007; "2005 Annual Per Capita Consumption of All Company Beverage Products," *The Coca-Cola Company 2005 Annual Review*, available at http://www.thecocacolacompany.com/investors/annualandotherreports/2005/companyToday_chart.html, 12 February 2007.

Sources: "Customer Care in the Netherlands," The Netherlands Foreign Investment Agency, available at http://www.nfia.com/solutions.php?pageid=11, 13 February 2007; "Customer Care Centers," *Netherlands Foreign Investment Agency Information Manual*, 13 February 2007, available at http://www.nfia.com/downloads/customercare.htm.

Exhibit 8.6

Quality of the Netherlands Work Force for Call Center Jobs

In today's environment, companies are not the only entities looking into global business. With the world's busiest airport and nonstop flights to 40 international destinations, the state of Georgia is positioning itself as an attractive gateway to doing "business with the world."

Go global.

GEORGIA DEPARTMENT OF ECONOMIC DEVELOPMENT

and quality of companies that already compete in a foreign market. Intel has been in China for 20 years not only because of the size of the potential market—China has 1.3 billion people and 95 percent of Chinese homes still don't have a computer—but also because there was almost no competition. But now that China is the third-largest computer chip market in the world, Intel faces competition from AMD, Intel's primary U.S. competitor, which entered China four years ago, and Shanghai Semiconductor Manufacturing International, a five-year-old Chinese company that manufactures low-end chips. Intel's 20-year head start, however, has given it a dominating 84 percent share of the Chinese market.[70]

4.2 Choosing an Office/Manufacturing Location

Companies do not have to establish an office or manufacturing location in each country they enter. They can license, franchise, or export to foreign markets, or they can serve a larger region from one country. Thus, the criteria for choosing an office/manufacturing location are different from the criteria for entering a foreign market.

Rather than focusing on costs alone, companies should consider both qualitative and quantitative factors. Two key qualitative factors are work force quality and company strategy. Work force quality is important because it is often difficult to find workers with the specific skills, abilities, and experience that a company needs to run its business. Work force quality is one reason that many companies doing business in Europe locate their customer call centers in the Netherlands. As shown in Exhibit 8.6, workers in the Netherlands are the most linguistically gifted in Europe, with 73 percent speaking two languages, 44 percent speaking three languages, and 12 percent speaking more than three. Of course, with employees who speak several languages, call centers located in the Netherlands can handle calls from more countries and generally employ 30 to 50 percent fewer employees than those located in other parts of Europe. Another advantage of locating a call center in the Netherlands is that 60 percent of call center workers have university or advanced degrees in technology or management.[71]

A company's strategy is also important when choosing a location. For example, a company pursuing a low-cost strategy may need plentiful raw materials, low-cost transportation, and low-cost labor. A company pursuing a differentiation strategy (typically a higher-priced, better product or service) may need access to high-quality materials and a highly skilled and educated work force.

Quantitative factors, such as the kind of facility being built, tariff and nontariff barriers, exchange rates, and transportation and labor costs, should also be considered when choosing an office/manufacturing location. Regarding the kind of facility being built, a real estate specialist in company location decisions explains: "If it's an assembly plant, a company might be inclined to look for incentives that would subsidize its hiring. With a distribution facility, an adequate transportation network will likely be critical. A corporate headquarters will need a good communications network, a multilingual labor force, and easy access by air. On the other hand, a research and development operation will require proximity to a high-tech infrastructure and access to good universities."[72]

Exhibit 8.7 shows the world's top cities for global business. This information is a good starting point if your company is trying to decide where to put an international office or manufacturing plant.

4.3 Minimizing Political Risk

When managers think about political risk in global business, they envision burning factories and riots in the streets. Although political events such as these receive dramatic and extended coverage from the media, the political risks that most companies face usually are not covered as breaking stories on Fox News and CNN. Nonetheless, the negative consequences of ordinary political risk can be just as devastating to companies that fail to identify and minimize that risk.[73]

When conducting global business, companies should attempt to identify two types of political risk: political uncertainty and policy uncertainty.[74] **Political uncertainty** is associated with the risk of major changes in political regimes that can result from

political uncertainty the risk of major changes in political regimes that can result from war, revolution, death of political leaders, social unrest, or other influential events

Exhibit 8.7

World's Best Cities for Business

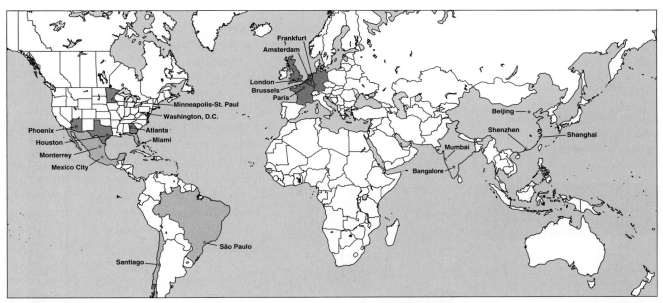

North America	Latin America	Europe	Asia Pacific
1. Washington, D.C.	1. Santiago	1. London	1. Shanghai
2. Atlanta	2. Miami	2. Paris	2. Beijing
3. Phoenix	3. São Paulo	3. Frankfurt	3. Shenzhen
4. Houston	4. Monterrey	4. Amsterdam	4. Bangalore
5. Minneapolis-St. Paul	5. Mexico City	5. Brussels	5. Mumbai

Sources: "European Cities Monitor 2006," *Cushman & Wakefield*, http://www.cushmanwakefield.com/cwglobal/jsp/publication. jsp?Country=EMEA&Language=EN, 13 February 2007. K. Badenhausen, "Best Places for Business and Careers," http://www.forbes. com/lists/2005/05/05/05bestplaces.html, 17 February 2007. "Shanghai, Beijing, Shenzhen Top 3 in Best City Survey," *Fortune China*, http://www.fortunechina.com/pdf/Best%20Cities%20Press%20Release%20(English)%202004.12.01.pdf, 13 February 2007. R. Sridharan, "Best Cities, Really?" *Business Today*, 13 August 2006, 62. "Miami Is the Best City for Doing Business in Latin America, According to AmericaEconomia Magazine," *PR Newswire*, 24 April 2003;

war, revolution, death of political leaders, social unrest, or other influential events. **Policy uncertainty** refers to the risk associated with changes in laws and government policies that directly affect the way foreign companies conduct business.

Policy uncertainty is the most common form of political risk in global business and perhaps the most frustrating, especially when changes in laws and government policies directly undercut sizable investments made by foreign companies. ROYAL DUTCH SHELL joined with Russia-based Gazprom, a state-owned company controlled by the Kremlin, to develop Sakhalin-2, one of the world's largest liquefied natural gas fields. Shell and its partners took the lead role with 55 percent ownership, and fronted a correspondingly larger amount of the estimated $20 billion in development costs. However, after years of development and billions in investment, the Russian government banned foreign companies from owning more than 49 percent of any energy development project. In the end, to avoid losing its investment, Royal Dutch Shell relinquished majority ownership to Gazprom in return for a $7.45 billion payment, well short of the $12 billion Shell had already invested. Furthermore, the deal significantly reduced Shell's access to develop and sell gas reserves in the Sakhalin-2 gas field and in the Zapolyarnoye gas field, which Shell had contracted to develop a year before.[75]

Several strategies can be used to minimize or adapt to the political risk inherent in global business. An *avoidance strategy* is used when the political risks associated with a foreign country or region are viewed as too great. If firms are already invested in high-risk areas, they may divest or sell their businesses. If they have not yet invested, they will likely postpone their investment until the risk shrinks. Exhibit 8.8 shows the long-term political stability for various countries in the Middle East (higher scores indicate less political risk). The following factors, which were used to compile these ratings, indicate greater political risk: government instability, poor socioeconomic conditions, internal or external conflict, military involvement in politics, religious and ethnic tensions, high foreign debt as a percentage of gross domestic product, exchange rate instability, and high inflation.[76] An avoidance strategy would likely be used for the riskiest countries shown in Exhibit 8.8, such as Iran and Lebanon, but would probably not be needed for the least risky countries, such as Israel, Jordan, or Oman. Risk conditions and factors change, so be sure to make risk decisions with the latest available information from resources such as the PRS Group, **http://www.prsgroup.com**, which supplies information about political risk to 80 percent of the *Fortune* 500 companies.

Control is an active strategy to prevent or reduce political risks. Firms using a control strategy lobby foreign governments or international trade agencies to change laws, regulations, or trade barriers that hurt their business in that country.

Another method for dealing with political risk is *cooperation*, which involves using joint ventures and collaborative contracts, such as franchising and licensing. Although cooperation does not eliminate the political risk of doing business in a country, it can limit the risk associated with foreign ownership of

policy uncertainty the risk associated with changes in laws and government policies that directly affect the way foreign companies conduct business

Ceding to political pressure, Royal Dutch Shell relinquished its majority ownership in Russia's Gazprom. Oil companies are facing similar problems in Venezuela.

Новая глава в истории проекта «Сах
New Chapter in the Sakhalin II Project

Mitsubishi Co

MIT & CO.,

© DENIS SINAKOV/REUTERS/LANDOV

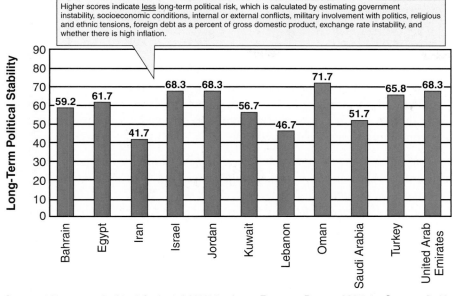

Higher scores indicate less long-term political risk, which is calculated by estimating government instability, socioeconomic conditions, internal or external conflicts, military involvement with politics, religious and ethnic tensions, foreign debt as a percent of gross domestic product, exchange rate instability, and whether there is high inflation.

Exhibit 8.8

Long-Term Political Stability in the Middle East

Source: "Chapter 1: Political Outlook," *UAE Business Forecast Report*, 2007 1st Quarter, 5–10.

a business. For example, a German company forming a joint venture with a Chinese company to do business in China may structure the joint venture contract so that the Chinese company owns 51 percent or more of the joint venture. Doing so qualifies the joint venture as a Chinese company and exempts it from Chinese laws that apply to foreign-owned businesses. However, as we saw with Shell and Gazprom, the state-controlled Russian oil company, cooperation cannot always protect against *policy risk* if a foreign government changes its laws and policies to directly affect the way foreign companies conduct business.

Review 4: Finding the Best Business Climate

The first step in deciding where to take your company global is finding an attractive business climate. Look for a growing market where consumers have strong purchasing power and foreign competitors are weak. When locating an office or manufacturing facility, consider both qualitative and quantitative factors. In assessing political risk, be sure to examine political uncertainty and policy uncertainty. If the location you choose has considerable political risk, you can avoid it, try to control the risk, or use a cooperation strategy.

doing the right thing

Foreign Corrupt Business Practices Act

The Foreign Corrupt Business Practices Act (FCPA) prohibits company managers, employees, or agents from offering money or anything else of value to bribe officials of foreign governments or political parties to use their influence to help that firm acquire new business or keep existing business in that country. Individuals violating the FCPA can be fined up to $100,000 and imprisoned for up to 10 years. Companies that violate the FCPA can be fined up to $2 million, suspended from government contracts, denied export licensing privileges, and investigated by the Securities and Exchange Commission. U.S. businesspeople often worry that the FCPA puts them at a disadvantage because other countries have permitted bribes to be deducted as business expenses. Recently, however, 33 major trading partners of the United States agreed to enact laws similar to the FCPA.[77]

5 Becoming Aware of Cultural Differences

Some of the more interesting and amusing aspects of global business are the unexpected confrontations that people have with cultural differences, "the way they do things over there." *Wall Street Journal* columnist Geoffrey Fowler relates the following story from Hong Kong, where he works:

> I was riding the elevator a few weeks ago with a Chinese colleague here in the Journal's Asian headquarters. I smiled and said, "Hi." She responded, "You've gained weight."
>
> I might have been appalled, but at least three other Chinese coworkers also have told me I'm fat. I probably should cut back on the pork dumplings.[78]

Uttered in the United States, such comments would be considered rude. Fowler indicates that in China, where people openly talk about people's weight, body shapes, and salaries, such comments are probably just friendliness. Likewise, the Chinese colleagues of American Jennifer Gallo, who works in Beijing, have commented on her clothing ("very nice, could be European"), her muscle tone ("flabby"), and her likeliness to bear children ("certain to have many boys").[79] So what does Fowler say when his friendly Chinese colleagues tell him he's fat? "There's so much good food here."

National culture is the set of shared values and beliefs that affects the perceptions, decisions, and behavior of the people from a particular country. The first step in dealing with culture is to recognize that there are meaningful differences in national cultures. Professor Geert Hofstede spent 20 years studying cultural differences in 53 different countries. His research shows that there are five consistent cultural dimensions across countries: power distance, individualism, masculinity, uncertainty avoidance, and short-term versus long-term orientation.[80]

Power distance is the extent to which people in a country accept that power is distributed unequally in society and organizations. In countries where power distance is weak, such as Denmark and Sweden, employees don't like their organization or their boss to have power over them or tell them what to do. They want to have a say in decisions that affect them. As Exhibit 8.9 shows, Russia and China, with scores of 95 and 80 respectively, are much stronger in power distance than Germany (35), the Netherlands (38), and the United States (40).

Individualism is the degree to which societies believe that individuals should be self-sufficient. In individualistic societies, employees put loyalty to themselves first and loyalty to their company and work group second. In Exhibit 8.9, the United States (91), the Netherlands (80), France (71), and Germany (67) are the strongest in individualism, while Indonesia (14), West Africa (20), and China (20) are the weakest.

Masculinity and *femininity* capture the difference between highly assertive and highly nurturing cultures. Masculine cultures emphasize assertiveness, competition, material success, and achievement, whereas feminine cultures emphasize the importance of relationships, modesty, caring for the weak, and quality of life. In Exhibit 8.9, Japan (95), Germany (66), and the United States (62) have the most masculine orientations, while the Netherlands (14) has the most feminine orientation.

The cultural difference of *uncertainty avoidance* is the degree to which people in a country are uncomfortable with unstructured, ambiguous, unpredictable situations. In countries with strong uncertainty avoidance, like Greece and Portugal, people tend to be aggressive and emotional and seek security (rather than uncertainty). In Exhibit 8.9,

> The first step in dealing with culture is to recognize that there are meaningful differences in national cultures.

national culture the set of shared values and beliefs that affects the perceptions, decisions, and behavior of the people from a particular country

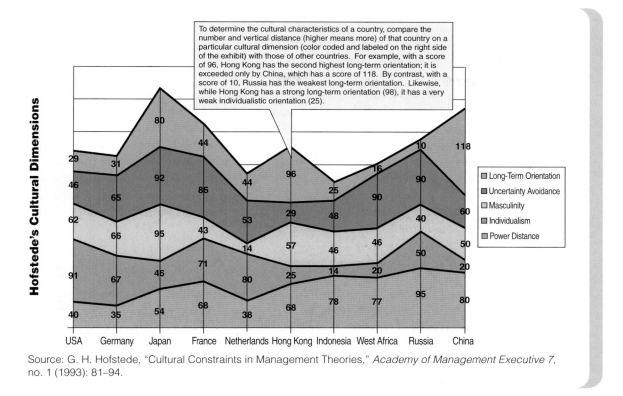

To determine the cultural characteristics of a country, compare the number and vertical distance (higher means more) of that country on a particular cultural dimension (color coded and labeled on the right side of the exhibit) with those of other countries. For example, with a score of 96, Hong Kong has the second highest long-term orientation; it is exceeded only by China, which has a score of 118. By contrast, with a score of 10, Russia has the weakest long-term orientation. Likewise, while Hong Kong has a strong long-term orientation (98), it has a very weak individualistic orientation (25).

Hofstede's Cultural Dimensions

- Long-Term Orientation
- Uncertainty Avoidance
- Masculinity
- Individualism
- Power Distance

USA Germany Japan France Netherlands Hong Kong Indonesia West Africa Russia China

Source: G. H. Hofstede, "Cultural Constraints in Management Theories," *Academy of Management Executive 7,* no. 1 (1993): 81–94.

Exhibit 8.9

Hofstede's Five Cultural Dimensions

Japan (92), France (86), West Africa (90), and Russia (90) are strongest in uncertainty avoidance, while Hong Kong (29) is the weakest.

Short-term/long-term orientation addresses whether cultures are oriented to the present and seek immediate gratification, or to the future and defer gratification. Not surprisingly, countries with short-term orientations are consumer driven, whereas countries with long-term orientations are savings driven. In Exhibit 8.9, China (118) and Hong Kong (96) have very strong long-term orientations, while Russia (10), West Africa (16), Indonesia (25), the United States (29), and Germany (31) have very strong short-term orientations. To generate a graphical comparison of two different country's cultures, go to **http://www.geert-hofstede.com/hofstede_dimensions.php.** Select a "home culture." Then select a "host culture." A graph comparing the countries on each of Hofstede's five cultural differences will automatically be generated.

Cultural differences affect perceptions, understanding, and behavior. Recognizing cultural differences is critical to succeeding in global business. Nevertheless, as Hofstede pointed out, descriptions of cultural differences are based on averages—the average level of uncertainty avoidance in Portugal, the average level of power distance in Argentina, and so forth. Accordingly, says Hofstede, "If you are going to spend time with a Japanese colleague, you shouldn't assume that overall cultural statements about Japanese society automatically apply to this person."[81] Similarly, cultural beliefs may differ significantly from one part of a country to another.[82]

After becoming aware of cultural differences, the second step is deciding how to adapt your company to those differences. Unfortunately, studies investigating the effects of cultural differences on management practice point more to difficulties than to easy solutions. One problem is that different cultures will probably perceive management policies and practices differently. For example, blue-collar workers in France and Argentina, all of whom performed the same factory jobs for the same multinational company, perceived its company-wide safety policy differently.[83]

French workers perceived that safety wasn't very important to the company, but Argentine workers thought that it was. The fact that something as simple as a safety policy can be perceived differently across cultures shows just how difficult it can be to standardize management practices across different countries and cultures.

Another difficulty is that cultural values are changing, albeit slowly, in many parts of the world. The fall of communism in eastern Europe and the former Soviet Union and the broad economic reforms in China have produced sweeping changes on two continents in the last decade. Thanks to increased global trade resulting from GATT and other regional free trade agreements, major economic transformations are also under way in India, Mexico, Central America, and South America. Consequently, when trying to adapt management practices to cultural differences, companies must ensure that they are not basing their adaptations on outdated and incorrect assumptions about a country's culture.

Review 5: **Becoming Aware of Cultural Differences**

National culture is the set of shared values and beliefs that affects the perceptions, decisions, and behavior of the people from a particular country. The first step in dealing with culture is to recognize meaningful differences, such as power distance, individualism, masculinity, uncertainty avoidance, and short-term/long-term orientation. Cultural differences should be carefully interpreted because they are based on averages, not individuals. Adapting managerial practices to cultural differences is difficult because policies and practices can be perceived differently in different cultures. Another difficulty is that cultural values may be changing in many parts of the world. Consequently, when companies try to adapt management practices to cultural differences, they need to be sure that they are not using outdated assumptions about a country's culture.

mgmt: fact

Bilingualism—A Growing Trend

Over 50 million people in the United States speak more than one language. This number is double what it was just 20 years ago, and it continues to grow. In Europe even more value is placed on the ability to speak multiple languages; more Europeans are multilingual, speaking three or more languages, than are just bilingual. Being able to communicate in multiple languages is an important asset in any business and can help give a company the edge it needs to succeed in a competitive market.

Source: "Two Languages Spoken Here," Talaris Research Institute, April 2006, http://www.talaris.org/spotlight_bilingual.htm.

6 Preparing for an International Assignment

Around a conference table in a large U.S. office tower, three American executives sat with their new boss, Akiro Kusumoto, the newly appointed head of a Japanese firm's American subsidiary, and two of his Japanese lieutenants. The meeting was called to discuss ideas for reducing operating costs. Kusumoto began by outlining his company's aspirations for its long-term U.S. presence. He then turned to the budgetary matter. One Japanese manager politely offered one suggestion, and an American then proposed another. After gingerly discussing the alternatives for quite some time, the exasperated American blurted out: "Look, that idea is just not going to have much impact. Look at the numbers!" In the face of such bluntness, uncommon and unacceptable in Japan, Kusumoto fell silent. He leaned back, drew air between his teeth, and felt a deep longing to return home.

He realized his life in this country would be filled with many such jarring encounters and lamented his posting to a land of such rudeness.[84]

Akiro Kusumoto is a Japanese **expatriate**, someone who lives and works outside his or her native country. The cultural shock that he was experiencing is common. The difficulty of adjusting to language, cultural, and social differences is the primary reason for expatriate failure in overseas assignments. For example, although there have recently been disagreements among researchers about these numbers, it is probably safe to say that 5 to 20 percent of American expatriates sent abroad by their companies will return to the United States before they have successfully completed their assignments.[85] Of those who do complete their international assignments, about one-third are judged by their companies to be no better than marginally effective.[86]

Since the average cost of sending an employee on a three-year international assignment is $1 million, failure in those assignments can be extraordinarily expensive.[87]

The chances for a successful international assignment can be increased through **6.1 language and cross-cultural training** *and* **6.2 consideration of spouse, family, and dual-career issues**.

6.1 Language and Cross-Cultural Training

Predeparture language and cross-cultural training can reduce the uncertainty that expatriates feel, the misunderstandings that take place between expatriates and natives, and the inappropriate behaviors that expatriates unknowingly commit when they travel to a foreign country. Indeed, simple things like using a phone, locating a public toilet, asking for directions, finding out how much things cost, exchanging greetings, or understanding what people want can become tremendously complex when expatriates don't know a foreign language or a country's customs and cultures. In his book *Blunders in International Business*, David Ricks tells the story of an American manager working in the South Pacific who, by hiring too many local workers from one native group, unknowingly upset the balance of power in the island's traditional status system. The islanders met on their own and quickly worked out a solution to the problem. After concluding their meeting at 3 AM, they calmly went to the manager's home to discuss their solution with him (time was not important in their culture). But since the American didn't speak their language and didn't understand why they had shown up en masse outside his home at 3 AM, he called in the Marines, who were stationed nearby, to disperse what he thought was a riot.

Expatriates who receive predeparture language and cross-cultural training make faster adjustments to foreign cultures and perform better on their international assignments.[88] Unfortunately, only a third of the managers who go on international assignments are offered any kind of predeparture training, and only half of those actually participate in the training![89] Suzanne Bernard, director of international mobility at **BOMBARDIER AEROSPACE** in Canada, says, "We always offer cross-cultural training, but it's very seldom used by executives leaving in a rush at the last minute."[90] This is somewhat surprising given the failure rates for expatriates and the high cost of those failures. Furthermore, with the exception of some language courses, predeparture training is not particularly expensive or difficult to provide. Three methods can be used to prepare workers for international assignments: documentary training, cultural simulations, and field experiences.

Documentary training focuses on identifying specific critical differences between cultures. For example, when 60 workers at **AXCELIS TECHNOLOGIES** in Beverly, Massachusetts, were preparing to do business in India, they learned that while

expatriate someone who lives and works outside his or her native country

Americans make eye contact and shake hands firmly when greeting others, Indians, as a sign of respect, do just the opposite, avoiding eye contact and shaking hands limply.[91]

After learning specific critical differences through documentary training, trainees can then participate in *cultural simulations*, in which they practice adapting to cultural differences. After the workers at Axcelis Technologies learned about key differences between their culture and India's, they practiced adapting to those differences by role playing: Some Axcelis workers would take the roles of Indian workers, while other Axcelis workers would play themselves and try to behave in a way consistent with Indian culture. As they role-played, Indian music played loudly in the background, and they were coached on what to do or not do by Bidhan Chandra, an international consultant. Chandra says, "When people understand these differences, they're less likely to make mistakes with each other." Axcelis human resources director Randy Longo says, "At first, I was skeptical and wondered what I'd get out of the class. But it was enlightening for me. Not everyone operates like we do in America."

Finally, *field simulation* training, a technique made popular by the **U.S. PEACE CORPS**, places trainees in an ethnic neighborhood for three to four hours to talk to residents about cultural differences. For example, a U.S. electronics manufacturer prepared workers for assignments in South Korea by having trainees explore a nearby South Korean neighborhood and talk to shopkeepers and people on the street about South Korean politics, family orientation, and day-to-day living practices.

6.2 Spouse, Family, and Dual-Career Issues

When Ford Motor Company manager John Larsen moved his wife, Laurel, and their children, ages 2, 4, and 6, to Chongqing, China, his children became a "crowd-stopping spectacle" as local people, who had never seen Westerners, much less their children, stopped to gawk. Laurel Larsen says, "It's not very fun and my kids hate it. . . . When we go home [to the 19th-floor Hilton hotel suite in which they live] and close the door, we feel like we are back in America."[92]

Not all international assignments are as difficult for expatriates and their families, but the evidence clearly shows that how well an expatriate's spouse and family adjust to the foreign culture is the most important factor in determining the success or failure of an international assignment.[93] Barry Kozloff of Selection Research International says, "The cost of sending a family on a foreign assignment is around $1 million and their failure to adjust is an enormous loss."[94] Unfortunately, despite its importance, there has been little systematic research on what does and does not help expatriates' families successfully adapt. A number of companies, however, have found that adaptability screening and intercultural training for families can lead to more successful overseas adjustment.

Adaptability screening is used to assess how well managers and their families are likely to adjust to foreign cultures. For example, **PRUDENTIAL RELOCATION MANAGEMENT**'s international division has developed an "Overseas Assignment Inventory" to assess a spouse and family's open-mindedness, respect for others' beliefs, sense of humor, and marital communication. Likewise, Pennsylvania-based AMP, a worldwide producer of electrical connectors, conducts extensive psychological screening on expatriates and their spouses when making international assignments. But adaptability screening does not just involve a company assessing an employee; it can also involve an employee screening international assignments for desirability. Since more employees are becoming aware of the costs of international assignments (spouses having to give up or change jobs, children having to change schools, everyone having to learn a new language), some companies are willing to pay for a preassignment trip so the employee and his or her spouse can investigate the country *before* accepting the international assignment.[95]

CROSS-CULTURAL TRAINING

Most expatriates will tell you that cross-cultural training helped them adjust to foreign cultures. Such anecdotal data, however, are not as convincing as systematic studies. Twenty-one studies, with a combined total of 1,611 participants, have examined whether cross-cultural training affects the self-development, relationships, perceptions, adjustment, and job performance of expatriates. Overall, they show that cross-cultural training works extremely well in most instances.

SELF-DEVELOPMENT

When you first arrive in another country, you must learn how to make decisions that you took for granted in your home country: how to get to work, how to get to the grocery, how to pay your bills, and so on. If you've generally been confident about yourself and your abilities, an overseas assignment can challenge that sense of self. Cross-cultural training helps expatriates deal with these and other challenges. Expatriates who receive cross-cultural training are 79 percent more likely to report healthy psychological well-being and self-development than those who don't receive training.

FOSTERING RELATIONSHIPS

One of the most important aspects of an overseas assignment is establishing and maintaining relationships with host nationals. If you're in Brazil, you need to make friends with Brazilians. Many expatriates, however, make the mistake of making friends only with other expatriates from their home country. In effect, they become social isolates in a foreign country. They work and live there, but as much as they can, they speak their native language, eat their native foods, and socialize with other expatriates from their home country. Cross-cultural training makes a big difference in whether expatriates establish relationships with host nationals. Expatriates who receive

cross-cultural training are 74 percent more likely to establish such relationships.

ACCURATE PERCEPTIONS OF CULTURE

Another characteristic of successful expatriates is that they understand the cultural norms and practices of the host country. For example, many Americans do not understand the famous pictures of Japanese troops turning their backs to American military commanders on V-J Day, when Japan surrendered to the United States at the end of World War II. Americans viewed this as a lack of respect, when, in fact, in Japan turning one's back in this way is a sign of respect. Cross-cultural training makes a big difference in the accuracy of perceptions concerning host country norms and practices. Expatriates who receive cross-cultural training are 74 percent more likely to have accurate perceptions.

RAPID ADJUSTMENT

New employees are most likely to quit in the first six months because this initial period requires the most adjustment: learning new names, new faces, new procedures, and new information. It's tough. Of course, expatriates have a much harder time adjusting to their new jobs because they are also learning new languages, new foods, new customs, and often new lifestyles. Expatriates who receive cross-cultural training are 74 percent more likely to make a rapid adjustment to a foreign country.

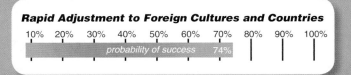

JOB PERFORMANCE

It's good that cross-cultural training improves self-development, fosters relationships, improves the accuracy of perceptions, and helps expatriates make rapid adjustments to foreign cultures. From an organizational standpoint, however, the ultimate test of cross-cultural training is whether it improves expatriates' job performance. The evidence shows that cross-cultural training makes a significant difference in expatriates' job performance, although the difference is not quite as large as for the other factors. Nonetheless, it is estimated that cross-cultural training for 100 managers could bring about $390,000 worth of benefits to a company, or nearly $4,000 per manager. This is an outstanding return on investment, especially when you consider the high rate of failure for expatriates. Expatriates who have received cross-cultural training are 71 percent more likely to have better on-the-job performance than those who did not receive cross-cultural training.[96]

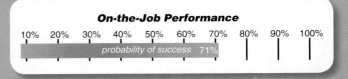

Only 40 percent of expatriates' families receive language and cross-cultural training, yet such training is just as important for the families of expatriates as for the expatriates themselves. In fact, it may be more important because, unlike expatriates, whose professional jobs often shield them from the full force of a country's culture, spouses and children are fully immersed in foreign neighborhoods and schools. Households must be run, shopping must be done, and bills must be paid. Unfortunately, expatriate spouse Laurel Larsen, despite two hours of Chinese lessons a week, hasn't learned enough of the language to communicate with the family's babysitter. She has to phone her husband, who became fluent in Chinese in his teens, to translate. Expatriates' children must deal with different cultural beliefs and practices, too. While the Larsens' three daughters love the private, international school that they attend, they still have had difficulty adapting to, from their perspective, the incredible differences in inner China. Six-year-old Emma taped this poem to her parents nightstand: "Amarica is my place! I love Amarica. It was fun. It was so fun. I miss it."[97] In addition to helping families prepare for the cultural differences they will encounter, language and cross-cultural training can help reduce uncertainty about how to act and decrease misunderstandings between expatriates and their families and locals.

> "Training is just as important for the families of expatriates as for the expatriates themselves."

Review 6: Preparing for an International Assignment

Many expatriates return prematurely from international assignments because of poor performance. However, premature return is much less likely to happen if employees receive language and cross-cultural training, such as documentary training, cultural simulations, or field experiences, before going on assignment. Adjustment of expatriates' spouses and families, which is the most important determinant of success in international assignments, can be improved through adaptability screening and intercultural training.

Are You Nation-Minded or World-Minded?

Attitudes about global business are as varied as managers are numerous. It seems that the business press can always find someone who is for globalization and someone who is against it. But regardless of your opinion on the subject, managers will increasingly confront issues related to the globalization of the business environment. It is probable that, as a manager, you will need to develop global sensibilities (if you don't already have them). Understanding your own cultural perspective is the first step in doing so.

This assessment has three parts: Step 1, Complete the questionnaire shown below; Step 2, Determine your score; Step 3, Develop a plan to increase your global managerial potential.[98]

Step 1: Use the six-point rating scale to complete the 32-question inventory shown below.

Rating Scale

1	Strongly Disagree
2	Disagree
3	Mildly Disagree
4	Mildly Agree
5	Agree
6	Strongly Agree

1. Our country should have the right to prohibit certain racial and religious groups from entering it to live.
   1   2   3   4   5   6

2. Immigrants should not be permitted to come into our country if they compete with our own workers.
   1   2   3   4   5   6

3. It would set a dangerous precedent if every person in the world had equal rights that were guaranteed by an international charter.
   1   2   3   4   5   6

4. All prices for exported food and manufactured goods should be set by an international trade committee.
   1   2   3   4   5   6

5. Our country is probably no better than many others.
   1   2   3   4   5   6

6. Race prejudice may be a good thing for us because it keeps many undesirable foreigners from coming into this country.
   1   2   3   4   5   6

7. It would be a mistake for us to encourage certain racial groups to become well educated because they might use their knowledge against us.
   1   2   3   4
   5   6

8. We should be willing to fight for our country without questioning whether it is right or wrong.
   1   2   3   4
   5   6

9. Foreigners are particularly obnoxious because of their religious beliefs.
   1   2   3   4
   5   6

10. Immigration should be controlled by a global organization rather than by each country on its own.
    1   2   3   4
    5   6

11. We ought to have a world government to guarantee the welfare of all nations irrespective of the rights of any one.
    1   2   3   4
    5   6

12. Our country should not cooperate in any global trade agreements that attempt to better world economic conditions at our expense.
    1   2   3   4
    5   6

13. It would be better to be a citizen of the world than of any particular country.
    1   2   3   4
    5   6

KEY TERMS

APEC (Asia-Pacific Economic Cooperation) 277
ASEAN (Association of Southeast Asian Nations) 277
CAFTA-DR (Central America Free Trade Agreement) 277
cooperative contract 282
customs classification 274
direct foreign investment 271
expatriate 295
exporting 281
franchise 282
General Agreement on Tariffs and Trade (GATT) 274
global business 270
global consistency 279
global new ventures 285
government import standards 273
joint venture 283
licensing 282
local adaptation 279
Maastricht Treaty of Europe 276
multinational corporation 271
NAFTA (North American Free Trade Agreement) 276
national culture 292
nontariff barriers 272
policy uncertainty 290
political uncertainty 289
protectionism 272
purchasing power 287
quota 273
regional trading zones 275
strategic alliance 283
subsidies 273
tariff 272
trade barriers 272
voluntary export restraints 273
wholly owned affiliates 285
World Trade Organization (WTO) 274

14. Our responsibility to people of other races ought to be as great as our responsibility to people of our own race.

   1   2   3   4   5   6

15. A global committee on education should have full control over what is taught in all countries about history and politics.

   1   2   3   4   5   6

16. Our country should refuse to cooperate in a total disarmament program even if some other nations agree to it.

   1   2   3   4   5   6

17. It would be dangerous for our country to make international agreements with nations whose religious beliefs are antagonistic to ours.

   1   2   3   4   5   6

18. Any healthy individual, regardless of race or religion, should be allowed to live wherever he or she wants to in the world.

   1   2   3   4   5   6

19. Our country should not participate in any global organization that requires that we give up any of our national rights or freedom of action.

   1   2   3   4   5   6

20. If necessary, we ought to be willing to lower our standard of living to cooperate with other countries in getting an equal standard for every person in the world.

   1   2   3   4   5   6

21. We should strive for loyalty to our country before we can afford to consider world brotherhood.

   1   2   3   4   5   6

22. Some races ought to be considered naturally less intelligent than ours.

   1   2   3   4   5   6

23. Our schools should teach the history of the whole world rather than of our own country.

   1   2   3   4   5   6

24. A global police force ought to be the only group in the world allowed to have armaments.

   1   2   3   4   5   6

25. It would be dangerous for us to guarantee by international agreement that every person in the world should have complete religious freedom.

   1   2   3   4   5   6

26. Our country should permit the immigration of foreign peoples, even if it lowers our standard of living.

   1   2   3   4   5   6

27. All national governments ought to be abolished and replaced by one central world government.

   1   2   3   4   5   6

28. It would not be wise for us to agree that working conditions in all countries should be subject to international control.

   1   2   3   4   5   6

29. Patriotism should be a primary aim of education so that our children will believe our country is the best in the world.

   1   2   3   4   5   6

30. It would be a good idea if all the races were to intermarry until there was only one race in the world.

   1   2   3   4   5   6

31. We should teach our children to uphold the welfare of all people everywhere, even though it may be against the best interests of our own country.

   1   2   3   4   5   6

32. War should never be justifiable, even if it is the only way to protect our national rights and honor.

   1   2   3   4   5   6

Step 2: Determine your score by entering your response to each survey item below, as follows. In blanks that say *regular score*, simply enter your response for that item. If your response was a 4, place a 4 in the *regular score* blank. In blanks that say *reverse score*, subtract your response from 7 and enter the result. So if your response was a 4, place a 3 (7 − 4 = 3) in the *reverse score* blank.

1. reverse score   _____
2. reverse score   _____
3. reverse score   _____
4. regular score   _____
5. regular score   _____
6. reverse score   _____
7. reverse score   _____
8. reverse score   _____
9. reverse score   _____
10. regular score   _____
11. regular score   _____
12. reverse score   _____
13. regular score   _____
14. regular score   _____
15. regular score   _____
16. reverse score   _____
17. reverse score   _____
18. regular score   _____
19. reverse score   _____
20. regular score   _____
21. reverse score   _____
22. reverse score   _____

23. regular score	_____
24. regular score	_____
25. reverse score	_____
26. regular score	_____
27. regular score	_____
28. reverse score	_____
29. reverse score	_____
30. regular score	_____

31. regular score _____
32. regular score _____
Total your scores from items 1–16 _____
Total your scores from items 17–32 _____
Add together to compute TOTAL = _____
You can find an interpretation of your score at: **academic.cengage.com/management/williams**.

MANAGEMENT DECISION

Forbidden Lattes?

There's no denying Starbucks is an international force.[99] The company had over 13,000 stores at the beginning of 2007, over 3,400 of them outside the United States, and is shooting for a long-term goal of 30,000 stores (international and domestic).

Starbucks opened its first overseas store in Tokyo in 1996. Asia was chosen as the point of entry because the company decided that the European coffee market was extremely mature and wasn't going to change much over the years. In contrast, the Asian market was still developing. Starbucks had the opportunity to position itself as the leader of a new industry. The table shows the operating regions for Starbucks retail stores and licenses as of October 2006.

Starbucks quickly jumped from Japan into other Asian countries, most notably China, where its presence has been nearly doubling on a yearly basis. But some troubles remain. In 2000, Starbucks opened a kiosk in Beijing's Forbidden City. Once home only to the emperor, his family, and his concubines, the Forbidden City is now a key tourist attraction in China's capital and still a symbol of Chinese heritage and culture. A Chinese newspaper criticized Starbucks for operating a kiosk there, so shortly after opening, Starbucks removed its hallmark signage from the outside of the building. A sign simply points to a "Coffee Bar."

Business as usual continued until 2007, when comments from a Chinese blogger reignited

ASIA-PACIFIC		EUROPE/MIDDLE EAST/AFRICA		AMERICAS	
Japan	650	United Kingdom	520	Canada	686
China	261	Germany	68	Mexico	101
Taiwan	175	Spain	55	Puerto Rico	17
South Korea	174	Turkey	51	Chile	16
Philippines	98	Greece	50	Peru	9
Thailand	85	Saudi Arabia	46	The Bahamas	5
Australia	83	United Arab Emirates	44		
Malaysia	71	Kuwait	36		
New Zealand	45	Switzerland	27		
Indonesia	45	France	26		
Singapore	37	Austria	11		
		Lebanon	11		
		Bahrain	8		
		Qatar	8		
		Cyprus	7		
		Jordan	5		
		Oman	4		
		Ireland	9		
TOTAL	**1,714**		**986**		**834**

Source: Starbucks Annual Report, 2006, 4–6.

the debate about whether Starbucks should be allowed to continue operating inside the Forbidden City. About one third of the retailers that formerly operated inside the Forbidden City have closed as the museum plans a renovation, and Starbucks is only one of several retailers still open inside the museum site; the other retailers, however, are Chinese.

Popular opinion is divided. Some Chinese see the presence of Starbucks as against the spirit of the Forbidden City as emblematic of Chinese heritage. Others think having a Starbucks at the museum is a nice feature for tourists and support Starbucks' presence there as just another retailer. Still others consider the world to be global in nature and take a "Mi Starbucks, su Starbucks" attitude.

In South Korea, Starbucks opened up shop in the Insadong area of Seoul, famous for traditional Korean antiques and crafts. Even though the company sign is in Korean—not the standard board in English posted elsewhere around the world—owners of other shops in the district were upset. They posted signs of their own reading "Starbucks' invasion of Korea's pride, Insadong." Nonetheless, Starbucks doubled the number of stores in Korea and in China over a two-year period, and demand continues to rise.

Questions

1. Should Starbucks pursue areas near national historic sites and tourist attractions of foreign countries for placement of new international locations?

2. Using Hofstede's Cultural Dimensions and the information in Exhibit 8.9, outline an explanation for Starbucks's Forbidden City problems based on cultural differences between the United States and China.

3. If you were in charge, would you keep the Starbucks in Beijing's Forbidden City (and the Insadong district of Seoul, for that matter), or would you close those outlets and pursue growth elsewhere?

MANAGEMENT TEAM DECISION

Men or Women, Who Goes Abroad?

As a member of the regional sales management team for a multinational corporation with offices located on almost every continent, you've made some tough decisions throughout your career.[100] Unfortunately, you feel that today's decision might possibly be the team's hardest yet. Sales in Asia have been dropping lately, and the team has been charged with choosing one of its salespersons to take over as the new regional manager for that area.

Two salespeople immediately come to mind. Laura, one of the potential candidates, has been a sales representative for the North American region for seven years. She has a master's degree in business administration and was a foreign exchange student in Hong Kong for two years during college. She is extremely competent, knowledgeable, and confident and has consistently been a top performer at the company since she was hired. Adam, the other possible candidate, has been with the North American region for only four years, but before that he served three and a half years as a sales representative for the European region of a well-known competitor. He too is qualified, with a master's degree in business and considerable experience in international assignments, but his performance has not been quite as stellar as Laura's. Neither candidate speaks any Asian languages.

Lingering in the back of your mind is a conversation you had with a colleague a few days ago. You and John, a fellow team member, were discussing international assignments, and the subject of sending women abroad came up. John said that in his experience, women do not make good expatriate candidates for several reasons. First, they are not as willing as men to take assignments in foreign countries due to family obligations and other personal reasons. Second, women are typically not as successful as men in foreign assignments because certain cultures tend to view women as inferior to men. (Including some Asian cultures, you think to yourself.) Last, John said that women are more likely to be subjected to discrimination or sexual harassment than men are. Although you initially agreed with John's perception, you later conclude that times have changed: after all, the world is much smaller and more culturally diverse today than it was when you went on your first international assignment.

You can't stop thinking about John's comments, though. You enter the meeting room weighing the pros and cons of each candidate and wondering if Laura would be accepted by her Asian counterparts.

To work this Management Team Decision, you will need to assemble a team of four to six students to represent the sales management team in the scenario.

Questions

1. Use either the stepladder technique or the nominal group technique (see Chapter 5) to decide which candidate the company should send abroad. Defend your decision.

2. Did the decision-making process change your mind? How so?

3. Determine what, if anything, the company should do to prepare the chosen candidate for the Asian assignment.

PRACTICE BEING A MANAGER

One of the major dilemmas in global management concerns the degree to which a multinational firm should adapt its business practices to particular locations and cultures versus the degree to which it should maintain consistency across all its operations. In general, firms prefer consistency because it streamlines operations and may result in global economies of scale. At the same time, multinational firms cannot gloss over differences without running the risk of losing a particular market to more responsive (local) competition. In this exercise, you will interpret your "hometown" culture for a large multinational company.

Suppose that a large multinational equipment company (based outside your country of origin) is planning to open a major production facility and retail dealership in your hometown. This company has hired you as a consultant to help them successfully establish operations in your hometown.

Step 1: Describe your hometown. Write a brief sketch (1–2 pages, using bullet points will suffice) in which you describe the important cultural features of your hometown, including such aspects as language, dress, courtesy/customs, and attitudes toward "foreignness" and newcomers. Try as much as possible to capture aspects of the location and culture of your hometown

that would be important for newcomers to recognize and respect.

Step 2: Form a team. Your professor will assign you to small discussion groups of three to five students.

Step 3: Share your description. Take turns in your discussion groups introducing yourselves, identifying your hometown, and sharing the highlights of your brief sketch of your hometown. Listen for similarities and differences across your hometowns.

Step 4: Make recommendations. As a group, agree on some recommendations to the multinational company. Assume that the company is planning to enter all of your hometowns simultaneously. To what degree might the company use a consistent (same) approach in entering your hometowns? Is one or more of your hometowns likely to require a foreign multinational to make more particular adaptations?

Step 5: Share findings with class. Each group should share its list of hometowns and its recommendations with the class.

Step 6: Consider challenges. As a class discuss the challenges of entering global markets, particularly in regards to achieving the appropriate mix of consistency and adaptation.

DEVELOP YOUR CAREER POTENTIAL

Building Cultural Bridges inside American Business

All savvy managers seem to be familiar with the Japanese custom of exchanging business cards, the French custom of the two-hour lunch, and the South American custom of getting to know potential business partners on a personal level before discussing business.[101] But how many managers

are aware of the cultural differences that exist within the United States? For example, how many Manhattanites know that in some parts of the country, businesses close down on the first day of hunting season?

Political rhetoric often refers to "two Americas" and the differences between the heartland and the coasts, but many other oppositional geographic pairings also represent different sets of cultural norms. Some other obvious examples are North–South, East–West, and the more general urban–rural. How many businesspeople know how to be effective in all these American cultures? Much has been made of the political and cultural implications of these divides, but not enough attention has been paid to what it means for business.

Cultural differences were addressed in Chapter 3 (Organizational Environments and Cultures) and will be again in Chapter 15 (Managing Communication). In the context of this chapter, however, it is important to note that many of the issues related to global management are applicable in any geographic context. Deciding whether to locate a firm in Alabama versus Oregon requires the same due diligence as deciding between Madrid and Madagascar. Managers need to assess the best business climate, identify and adapt to cultural differences, and prepare workers who will be transferred to the new location.

Activities

1. Think of yourself as a member of a particular geographical cultural group. (In the United States, we are conditioned to think of cultural groups based on ethnicity and race, but for this exercise, think in terms of location.) What are the characteristics of this group?

2. Once you have an outline of your geographic culture, try to identify the group most opposite to your own. For example, if you consider yourself a New Yorker, you may think of a Mississippian or a Californian.

3. Research regional and local periodicals to learn about the norms in the other culture. You might also talk with a friend who attends college in a different region or state to get a more personal understanding of norms in other parts of the country. List of some of the norms in the other location, and compare them with the norms in your area of the country.

REEL TO REAL

BIZ FLIX
Mr. Baseball

The New York Yankees trade aging baseball player Jack Elliot (Tom Selleck) to the Chunichi Dragons, a Japanese team. This lighthearted comedy traces Elliot's bungling entry into Japanese culture where he almost loses everything, including Hiroko Uchiyama (Aya Takanashi). As Elliot slowly begins to understand Japanese culture and Japanese baseball, he finally is accepted by his teammates. This film shows many examples of Japanese culture, especially the Japanese love for baseball.

Unknown to Hiroko's father, she and Jack develop an intimate relationship. Meanwhile, Jack does not know that Hiroko's father is "The Chief" (Ken Takakura), the manager of the Chunichi Dragons. This scene takes place after "The Chief" has removed Jack from a baseball game. The scene shows Jack dining with Hiroko and her grandmother (Mineko Yorozuyo), grandfather (Jun Hamamura), and father.

What to Watch for and Ask Yourself

1. Does Jack Elliot behave as if he had had cross-cultural training before arriving in Japan?
2. Is he culturally sensitive or insensitive?
3. What do you propose that Elliot do for the rest of his time in Japan?

MANAGEMENT WORKPLACE
Lonely Planet—Global from the Start

For a company such as Lonely Planet, the idea of a borderless world is nothing new. Founded in Australia by Tony and Maureen Wheeler so that they could fund their own travel dreams, the travel publisher now has offices in Australia, the United States, the United Kingdom, and France, with a total of about 450 employees. Its writers, photographers, and marketers span the globe on a regular basis in search of the best destinations for their customers to explore. However, despite the fact that the idea of globalization is built into the firm's culture, its managers still face international challenges every day. Watch the video to see how Lonely Planet grapples with global issues in its management workplace.

What to Watch for and Ask Yourself

1. To what extent does Lonely Planet practice global consistency versus adaptation?
2. How does the image being proposed for the global campaign illustrate the need to be aware of cultural differences?
3. Which of the forms for global business do you think Lonely Planet is using? Explain.

three

PART 3
Organizing

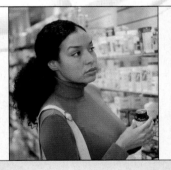

Chapter 9
Designing Adaptive Organizations

This chapter shows you the traditional organizational structure approach to organizational design (the vertical and horizontal configuration of departments, authority, and jobs within a company), as well as how contemporary organizations are redesigning their processes to better transform inputs into outputs.

Chapter 10
Managing Teams

Chapter 10 reviews the advantages and disadvantages of teams and explores when companies should use them. You'll also read about the different types of work teams and the characteristics common to all teams and learn practical steps to managing teams—team goals and priorities, and organizing, training, and compensating teams.

Chapter 11
Managing Human Resource Systems

This chapter covers the key aspects of human resource systems: determining your human resource needs; finding qualified employees; developing the knowledge, skills, and abilities of the work force; implementing effective compensation practices; and effectively managing separation.

Chapter 12
Managing Individuals and a Diverse Work Force

In this chapter, you'll learn what diversity is and why it matters. We'll go over surface-level diversity (how age, gender, race/ethnicity, and disabilities affect people at work) and deep-level diversity (how core personality differences influence behavior and attitudes). And you will learn how diversity can be managed.

CHAPTER 9

Designing Adaptive Organizations

WHAT WOULD YOU DO?

Alcan Headquarters, Montreal, Canada.[1] On a beautiful spring morning that is unusually warm for this time of year, you find yourself once again contemplating whether your company is organized in the best manner possible. With almost 70,000 employees in 55 countries, Alcan has been one of the best performers in a slow-growth industry, aluminum. That said, aligning the organization for the best performance possible is an ongoing process, and having so many separate companies in so many different areas is a constant challenge.

The company was founded in 1902 as a producer of aluminum. Today, in addition to supplying basic metals, Alcan produces food and beauty product packaging and engineered products for the automobile and aerospace industries. The size and complexity of the organization has grown as the company has developed. Alcan currently has five corporate-wide staff operations (corporate development, external affairs, finance, human resources, and corporate headquarters), which work with all areas of the organization. The company also has four operating divisions: Bauxite and Alumina, Primary Metal, Engineered Products, and Packaging. Each of these divisions has its own staff operations, including such functions as finance, human resources, procurement, and information technology. And each division is also organized into sales groups; the Packaging division, for example, is grouped into Food Packaging—Europe, Food Packaging—Americas, Food Packaging—Asia, Global Pharmaceutical Packaging, Global Beauty Packaging, and Global Tobacco Packaging.

The company has made great strides to control its costs, divesting areas that it could not run profitably and moving into areas where it felt they had a competitive advantage. But beyond cost cutting, Alcan has found it difficult to raise net income as a percentage of sales. You realize that organizing the company to take advantage of growth opportunities and move it away from being a basic metals supplier is the key to the company's future. Would it make sense to organize the entire company geographically to focus on the needs of local markets? Or would an organizational structure geared toward new product development and marketing be more appropriate? The company could also organize exclusively around its customers and become experts in customer solutions. Other structuring options include a functional structure such that all of manufacturing is under one arm and all sales another; or a matrix structure that has employees reporting both functionally and geographically.

Another significant concern in an organization like Alcan that is seeking new areas of growth is how to manage creativity and communication within a company spread over 55 countries. What should you do about the informal organizational culture, part of which is critical to innovation and attracting and retaining topflight employees? **If you were in charge at Alcan, what would you do?**

ACTIVITIES + VIDEO

CengageNOW Audio study guide, electronic flashcards, author FAQ videos, On the Job and Biz Flix videos, concept tutorial, and concept exercise

Web (academic.cengage.com/management/williams) Quiz, PowerPoint slides, and glossary terms for this chapter

Study Tip

Think about your favorite company and imagine how you think it could be organized. Draw an organizational structure that you think makes sense for the business and the industry it's in. Try the exercise with a variety of company types and then see if the companies you used have organizational information on their websites. Practicing building organizational structures will help you better understand the different elements covered in the chapter.

"WHAT'S NEW" COMPANIES

ALCAN
MICROSOFT
SARA LEE CORPORATION
UNITED TECHNOLOGIES
SPRINT NEXTEL
COCA-COLA ENTERPRISES
PROCTER & GAMBLE
UNILEVER
NIKE
GLAXOSMITHKLINE
GENERAL MOTORS
MCDONALD'S
AES
IBM CREDIT
LEVI STRAUSS
WEGMANS
CHIPOTLE MEXICAN GRILL
AND OTHERS . . .

N̶o one builds a house without first looking at the design. Put a window there. Take out a wall here. Soon you've got the design you want. Only then do you start building. These days, the design of a company is just as important as the design of a house. As Alcan's case shows, even successful companies must constantly examine their organizational design.

organizational structure the vertical and horizontal configuration of departments, authority, and jobs within a company

Exhibit 9.1

Microsoft Corporation's Organizational Chart

This chapter begins by reviewing the traditional organizational structure approach to organizational design. **Organizational structure** is the vertical and horizontal configuration of departments, authority, and jobs within a company. As an example, Exhibit 9.1 shows **MICROSOFT**'s organizational chart. From this chart, you can see the vertical dimensions of the company—who reports to whom, the number of management levels, who has authority over what, and so forth. Founder Bill Gates is the chairman and chief software architect. In this role, Gates focuses on Microsoft's product and technology strategies. CEO Steve Ballmer reports directly to him.[2] Three division presidents, each responsible for one of Microsoft's core businesses, report directly to Ballmer. In turn, each division has several group vice presidents who oversee a number of operations.[3] For instance, the group vice president for Information Worker works with managers and employees to develop and improve Microsoft's Office Suite (Word, Excel, PowerPoint, Outlook, and Access), Microsoft Publisher (for business publishing and marketing materials), Microsoft Visio (for drawing and diagramming business and technical concepts), Microsoft Project (project management software), and stand-alone desktop products.

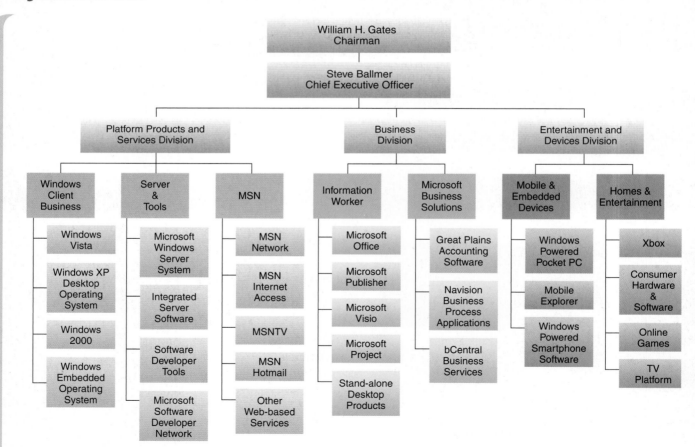

Source: "Our Commitment to Our Customers: The Business of Microsoft," Microsoft, available at http://www.microsoft.com/about/companyinformation/ourbusinesses/business.mspx.

The organizational chart also displays Microsoft's horizontal dimensions—who does what jobs, the number of different departments, and so forth. For instance, in addition to Information Worker, Microsoft's groups include Windows Client Business (where software such as Windows XP is written); Server and Tools (server software and development tools); MSN (the MSN online network, Internet access, TV, Hotmail e-mail services, and other web-based services); Microsoft Business Solutions (accounting and portals); Mobile and Embedded Devices (software for handheld computers and mobile phones); and Homes and Entertainment (Xbox game machine, consumer products, online games, and software for TVs). In the first half of the chapter, you will learn about the traditional vertical and horizontal approaches to organizational structure, including departmentalization, organizational authority, and job design.

In the second half of the chapter, you will learn how contemporary organizations are becoming more adaptive by redesigning their internal and external processes. An **organizational process** is the collection of activities that transform inputs into outputs that customers value.[4] For example, Microsoft uses basic internal and external processes to write computer software, shown in Exhibit 9.2. The process starts when Microsoft gets feedback from customers through Internet newsgroups, e-mail, phone calls, or letters. This information helps Microsoft understand customers' needs and problems and identify important software issues and needed changes and functions. Microsoft then rewrites the software, testing it internally at the company and then externally through its beta-testing process.

In beta testing, early versions of software are distributed to beta testers (customers who volunteer or are selected by Microsoft), who give the company extensive feedback, which is then used to make improvements. The beta-testing process may take as long as a year and involve thousands of knowledgeable people. After "final" corrections are made to the software, the company distributes and sells it to customers, who start the process again by giving Microsoft more feedback.

This process view of Microsoft, which focuses on how things get done, is very different from the hierarchical view of Microsoft (go back to Microsoft's organizational chart in Exhibit 9.1), which focuses on accountability, responsibility, and positions within the chain of command. In the second half of the chapter, you will learn how companies are using reengineering, empowerment, and behavioral informality to redesign their internal organizational processes. The chapter ends with a discussion about the ways in which companies are redesigning their external processes, that is, how they are changing to improve their interactions with those outside the company. In that discussion, you will explore the basics of modular and virtual organizations.

organizational process the collection of activities that transform inputs into outputs that customers value

Exhibit 9.2

Process View of Microsoft's Organization

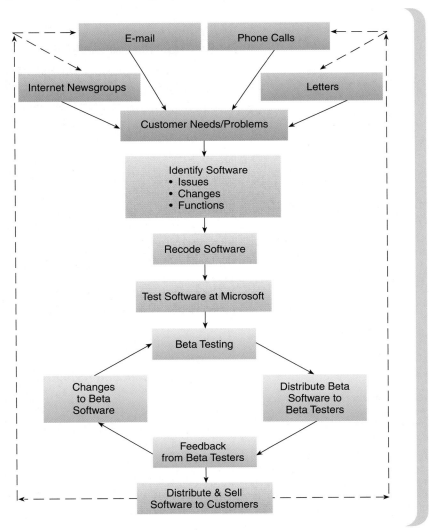

DESIGNING ORGANIZATIONAL STRUCTURES

With offices and operations in 58 countries, products in over 200, and more than 150,000 employees worldwide, SARA LEE CORPORATION owns some of the best-known brands (Sara Lee, Hillshire Farm, Ball Park, and Jimmy Dean) in the world. Nevertheless, in hopes of improving company performance, Sara Lee changed its organizational structure to focus on three key customer/geographic markets: North American retail (bakery, packaged meats, and Senseo coffee), North American food service (bakery goods, coffee, and meats sold to restaurants), and Sara Lee International (bakery and beverage businesses outside North America and global household products). Companies or divisions that didn't fit with the new structure, like the European meats division and the branded apparel businesses (including Hanes, Champion, and Playtex) were sold. As a result of the transformation plan, Sara Lee is now focused on its core businesses—food, beverage, and household and body care.[5]

Why would a large company like Sara Lee with 150,000 employees and $20 billion in annual revenues completely restructure its organizational design? What does it expect to gain from this change?

> **After reading the next three sections, you should be able to**
>
> 1 describe the departmentalization approach to organizational structure.
> 2 explain organizational authority.
> 3 discuss the different methods for job design.

1 Departmentalization

Traditionally, organizational structures have been based on some form of departmentalization. **Departmentalization** is a method of subdividing work and workers into separate organizational units that take responsibility for completing particular tasks.[6] Sony, for example, has separate departments or divisions for electronics, music, movies, computer games and game consoles, and theaters.[7] Likewise, Bayer, a Germany-based company, has separate departments or divisions for health care, crop science, material science, and services.[8]

*Traditionally, organizational structures have been created by departmentalizing work according to five methods: **1.1 functional**, **1.2 product**, **1.3 customer**, **1.4 geographic**, and **1.5 matrix**.*

1.1 Functional Departmentalization

departmentalization subdividing work and workers into separate organizational units responsible for completing particular tasks

functional departmentalization organizing work and workers into separate units responsible for particular business functions or areas of expertise

The most common organizational structure is functional departmentalization. Companies tend to use this structure when they are small or just starting out. **Functional departmentalization** organizes work and workers into separate units responsible for particular business functions or areas of expertise. A common functional structure might have individuals organized into accounting, sales, marketing, production, and human resources departments.

Not all functionally departmentalized companies have the same functions, however. The insurance company and the advertising agency shown in Exhibit 9.3 both have sales, accounting, human resources, and information systems departments, as indicated by the orange boxes. The purple and red boxes indicate the functions that are different. As would be expected, the insurance company has separate departments for life, auto, home, and health insurance. The advertising agency has departments for artwork, creative work, print advertising, and Internet advertising. So the kind of functional departments in a functional structure depends, in part, on the business or industry a company is in.

Functional departmentalization has some advantages. First, it allows work to be done by highly qualified specialists. While the accountants in the accounting department take responsibility for producing accurate revenue and expense figures, the engineers in research and development can focus their efforts on designing a product that is reliable and simple to manufacture. Second, it lowers costs by reducing duplication. When the engineers in research and development come up with that fantastic new product, they don't have to worry about creating an aggressive advertising campaign to sell it. That task belongs to the advertising experts and sales representatives in marketing. Third, with everyone in the same department having similar work experience or training, communication and coordination are less problematic for departmental managers.

At the same time, functional departmentalization has a number of disadvantages. To start, cross-department coordination can be difficult. Managers and employees are often more interested in doing what's right for their function than in doing what's right for the entire organization. A good example is the traditional conflict between marketing and manufacturing. Marketing typically pushes for spending more money to make more products with more accessories and capabilities to meet customer needs. By contrast, manufacturing pushes for fewer products with simpler designs so that manufacturing facilities can ship finished products on time and keep costs within expense budgets. As companies grow, functional departmentalization may also lead to slower decision making and produce managers and workers with narrow experience and expertise.

1.2 Product Departmentalization

Product departmentalization organizes work and workers into separate units responsible for producing particular products or services. Exhibit 9.4 shows the product departmentalization structure used by UNITED TECHNOLOGIES. United Technologies is organized along seven different product lines: Carrier (heating, ventilating, and air-conditioning); Chubb (security, monitoring, and fire protection systems); Hamilton Sundstrand (aircraft electrical power generation and distribution systems); Otis (design, manufacture, installation, maintenance, and servicing of elevators and escalators); Pratt & Whitney (commercial and military jet aircraft engines); Sikorsky (military and commercial helicopters); and UTC Power (heating, cooling, and power systems for commercial and industrial applications and fuel cell systems).[9]

One of the advantages of product departmentalization is that, like functional departmentalization, it allows managers and workers to specialize in one area of expertise. Unlike the narrow expertise and experiences in functional departmentalization,

Exhibit 9.3
Functional Departmentalization

product departmentalization
organizing work and workers into separate units responsible for producing particular products or services

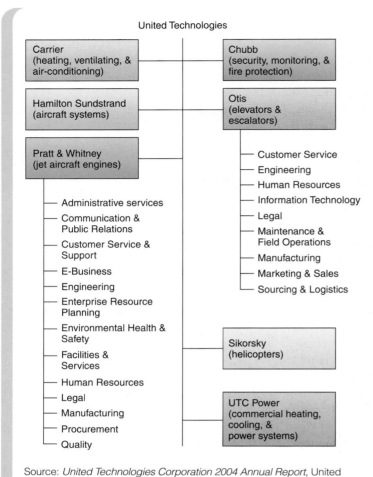

United Technologies

| Carrier (heating, ventilating, & air-conditioning) | Chubb (security, monitoring, & fire protection) |

Hamilton Sundstrand (aircraft systems)

Otis (elevators & escalators)
— Customer Service
— Engineering
— Human Resources
— Information Technology
— Legal
— Maintenance & Field Operations
— Manufacturing
— Marketing & Sales
— Sourcing & Logistics

Pratt & Whitney (jet aircraft engines)
— Administrative services
— Communication & Public Relations
— Customer Service & Support
— E-Business
— Engineering
— Enterprise Resource Planning
— Environmental Health & Safety
— Facilities & Services
— Human Resources
— Legal
— Manufacturing
— Procurement
— Quality

Sikorsky (helicopters)

UTC Power (commercial heating, cooling, & power systems)

Source: *United Technologies Corporation 2004 Annual Report,* United Technologies, available at http://www.utc.com/annual_reports/2004/2004_ar.pdf, 1 May 2005.

Exhibit 9.4

Product Departmentalization: United Technologies

customer departmentalization
organizing work and workers into separate units responsible for particular kinds of customers

however, managers and workers develop a broader set of experiences and expertise related to an entire product line. Likewise, product departmentalization makes it easier for top managers to assess work-unit performance. Because of the clear separation of their seven different product divisions, United Technologies' top managers can easily compare the performance of, for example, its Otis elevators product division and its Pratt & Whitney aircraft engines division. The divisions had similar revenues— almost $8.99 billion for Otis and $8.3 billion for Pratt & Whitney—but Otis had a profit of $1.54 billion (a 17 percent profit margin) compared with just $1.1 billion (a 13 percent profit margin) for Pratt & Whitney. Finally, decision making should be faster because managers and workers are responsible for the entire product line rather than for separate functional departments, and thus there are fewer conflicts (compared to functional departmentalization).

The primary disadvantage of product departmentalization is duplication. You can see in Exhibit 9.4 that the Otis elevators and Pratt & Whitney divisions both have customer service, engineering, human resources, legal, manufacturing, and procurement (similar to sourcing and logistics) departments. Duplication like this often results in higher costs.

A second disadvantage is the challenge of coordinating across the different product departments. United Technologies would probably have difficulty standardizing its policies and procedures in product departments as different as the Carrier (heating, ventilating, and air-conditioning) and Sikorsky (military and commercial helicopters) divisions.

1.3 Customer Departmentalization

Customer departmentalization organizes work and workers into separate units responsible for particular kinds of customers. For example, as Exhibit 9.5 shows, the telecommunications company *SPRINT NEXTEL*, is organized into departments that cater to businesses (local, long-distance, and data and wireless services for U.S. and international businesses); consumers (local, long-distance, and wireless services for individuals, sold separately or bundled together); Mobile Broadband Operations (Network Design, Operations and Servicing); and product development.[11]

The primary advantage of customer departmentalization is that it focuses the organization on customer needs rather than on products or business functions. Furthermore, creating separate departments to serve specific kinds of customers allows companies to specialize and adapt their products and services to customer needs and problems.

The primary disadvantage of customer departmentalization is that, like product departmentalization, it leads to duplication of resources. Furthermore, as with product departmentalization, it can be difficult to achieve coordination across different customer departments. Finally, the emphasis on meeting customers' needs may lead workers to make decisions that please customers but hurt the business.

1.4 Geographic Departmentalization

Geographic departmentalization organizes work and workers into separate units responsible for doing business in particular geographic areas. Exhibit 9.6 shows the geographic departmentalization used by COCA-COLA ENTERPRISES (CCE), the largest bottler and distributor of Coca-Cola products in the world. (The Coca-Cola Company develops and advertises soft drinks. CCE, which is a separate company with its own stock, buys the soft drink concentrate from the Coca-Cola Company, combines it with other ingredients, and then distributes the final product in cans, bottles, or fountain containers.) As shown in Exhibit 9.6, CCE has two regional groups: North America and Europe. As the table in the exhibit shows, each of these regions would be a sizable company by itself. The European Group alone serves a population of 146 million people in Belgium, Great Britain, France, Luxembourg, Monaco, and the Netherlands; sells one billion cases of soft drinks a year; employs 11,000 people; runs 32 bottling facilities; and has a customer base that drinks an average of 174 soft drinks per year per person.

The primary advantage of geographic departmentalization is that it helps companies respond to the demands of different markets. This can be especially important when the company sells in different countries. For example, CCE's geographic divisions sell products suited to taste preferences in different countries. CCE bottles and distributes the following products in Europe but not in the United States: Aquarius, Bonaqua, and Burn, Coca-Cola Light (which is somewhat different from Diet Coke), Cresta flavors, Five Alive, Kia-Ora, Kinley, Lilt, Malvern, and Oasis.[12] Another advantage is that geographic departmentalization can reduce costs by locating unique organizational resources closer to customers. For instance, it is cheaper in the long run for CCE to build bottling plants in Belgium than to bottle Coke in England and then transport it across the English Channel to Belgium.

The primary disadvantage of geographic departmentalization is that it can lead to duplication of resources. For example, while it may be necessary to adapt products and marketing to different geographic locations, it's doubtful that CCE needs significantly different inventory tracking systems from location to location. Also, even more than with the other forms of departmentalization, it can be difficult to coordinate departments that are literally thousands of miles from each other and whose managers have very limited contact with each other.

1.5 Matrix Departmentalization

Matrix departmentalization is a hybrid structure in which two or more forms of departmentalization are used together. The most common matrix combines the product and functional forms of departmentalization, but other forms may also be

Sprint Nextel Corporation

Source: "Overview," Sprint, available at http://www.sprint.com/sprint/fastfacts/overview/index.html, 1 May 2005.

Exhibit 9.5

Customer Departmentalization: Sprint Corporation

geographic departmentalization organizing work and workers into separate units responsible for doing business in particular geographic areas

matrix departmentalization a hybrid organizational structure in which two or more forms of departmentalization, most often product and functional, are used together

Territories of Operation

	POPULATION	PER CAPITA CONSUMPTION[1]	EMPLOYEES	FACILITIES[2]
North American Group	263 M	300	63,000	399
European Group	146 M	174	11,000	32
Total Company	409 M	255	74,000	431

(1) Number of 8-ounce servings consumed per person per year.
(2) Facilities include 18 production, 335 sales/distribution, and 46 combination sales and production plants in North America, and 3 production, 17 sales/distribution, and 12 combination plants in Europe.

Source: "Territories of Operation, 2004 Annual Report," Coca-Cola Enterprises, available at http://ir.cokecce.com/annuals.cfm, 1 May 2005.

Exhibit 9.6

Geographic Departmentalization: Coca-Cola Enterprises

used. Exhibit 9.7 shows the matrix structure used by **PROCTER & GAMBLE**, which has 98,000 employees working in 80 different countries. Across the top of Exhibit 9.7, you can see that the company uses a product unit structure with managers responsible for the global efforts of their branded products. The left side of the figure, however, shows that the company is also using a geographic structure. Geographic managers are responsible for taking P&G's globally positioned products and adapting them to fit the cultures of the countries where they are sold—more than 140 countries in all. P&G's roster of brands includes Pampers (diapers), Tide (laundry detergent), Always (feminine protection), Pantene (shampoo), Bounce (dryer sheets), Folgers (coffee), Pringles (snack food), Charmin (toilet paper), Downy (fabric softener), Iams (dog and cat food), Crest (toothpaste), Actonel (prescription drug) and Olay (body care).[13] The company also has two groups that cut across the entire matrix taking care of customer service and administration.

The boxes in the figure represent the matrix structure, created by the combination of the geographic and product structures. For example, in the health-care business in Central-Eastern Europe, Middle East, and Africa, country managers in Hungary, United Arab Emirates, and Kenya are responsible for developing P&G's business in products such as Metamucil, Pepto-Bismol, Prilosec OTC, and Vicks. Likewise, in the snack and beverage business in Asia/India/Australia, country managers in China, Australia, and South Korea are responsible for developing P&G's business in products such as Folgers coffee, Millstone coffee, and Pringles potato chips in those countries.

Several things distinguish matrix departmentalization from the other traditional forms of departmentalization.[14] First, most employees report to two bosses, one from each core part of the matrix. For example, in Exhibit 9.7, the manager responsible for Charmin in France would report both to the president for Global Baby Care/Family Care and to the president for Western Europe. Second, by virtue of their hybrid design, matrix structures lead to much more cross-functional interaction than other forms of departmentalization. In fact, while matrix workers are typically members of only one functional department (based on their work experience and expertise), they are also commonly members of several ongoing project, product, or customer groups. Third, because of the high level of cross-functional interaction, matrix departmentalization requires significant coordination between managers in the different parts of the matrix. In particular, managers have the complex job of tracking and managing the multiple demands (project, product, customer, or functional) on employees' time.

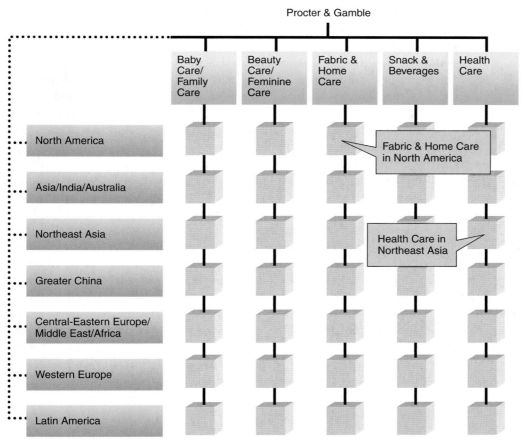

Procter & Gamble

Baby Care/ Family Care

Beauty Care/ Feminine Care

Fabric & Home Care

Snack & Beverages

Health Care

North America

Asia/India/Australia

Northeast Asia

Greater China

Central-Eastern Europe/ Middle East/Africa

Western Europe

Latin America

Fabric & Home Care in North America

Health Care in Northeast Asia

Source: "Corporate Info: Corporate Structure—Four Pillars," Procter & Gamble, http://www.pg.com/jobs/corporate_structure/four_pillars.jhtml; "P&G Management," Procter & Gamble, http://www.pg.com/news/management/bios_photos.jhtml.

Exhibit 9.7

Matrix Departmentalization: Procter & Gamble

The primary advantage of matrix departmentalization is that it allows companies to efficiently manage large, complex tasks like researching, developing, and marketing pharmaceuticals or carrying out complex global businesses. Efficiency comes from avoiding duplication. For example, rather than having an entire marketing function for each project, the company simply assigns and reassigns workers from the marketing department as they are needed at various stages of product completion. More specifically, an employee from a department may simultaneously be part of five different ongoing projects, but may be actively completing work on only a few projects at a time.

Another advantage is the pool of resources available to carry out large, complex tasks. Because of the ability to quickly pull in expert help from all the functional areas of the company, matrix project managers have a much more diverse set of expertise and experience at their disposal than do managers in the other forms of departmentalization.

The primary disadvantage of matrix departmentalization is the high level of coordination required to manage the complexity involved with running large, ongoing projects at various levels of completion. Matrix structures are notorious for confusion and conflict between project bosses in different parts of the matrix. At P&G, such confusion or conflict might occur between managers in the Global Fabric and Home Care division and the president of operations in Greater China. Disagreements or misunderstandings about schedules, budgets, available resources, and the availability of employees with particular functional expertise are common. Another disadvantage is that matrix structures require much more management skill than the other forms of departmentalization.

Because of these problems, many matrix structures evolve from a **simple matrix**, in which managers in different parts of the matrix negotiate conflicts and resources directly, to a **complex matrix**, in which specialized matrix managers and departments are added to the organizational structure. In a complex matrix, managers from different parts of the matrix might report to the same matrix manager, who helps them sort out conflicts and problems.

Sometimes, however, even these steps aren't enough to alleviate the problems that can occur in matrix structures. For example, Europe-based *UNILEVER*, maker and marketer of such well-known products as Dove soap, Vaseline Intensive Care lotions, Hellman's mayonnaise, I Can't Believe It's Not Butter, Lipton teas, Wishbone salad dressings, Skippy peanut butter, and Lawry's seasonings, was run using a complex matrix structure. The company even had dual headquarters in Rotterdam, the Netherlands, and London, England. The confusion and conflict associated with having two sets of management located in two headquarters were so great, however, that Unilever has now switched to just one CEO and one headquarters. In addition, the company has moved to a simpler organizational structure based on geography, with three regional chiefs (in Europe, the Americas, and Asia/Africa), plus two global divisions: foods and soaps.[15] Patrick Cescau, the new CEO, says, "We have recognized the need for greater clarity of leadership and we are moving to a simpler leadership structure that will provide a sharper operational focus."[16] In short, because everyone now reports to just one boss, "we have clarified who calls the shots," says Cescau.

Review 1: **Departmentalization**

The five traditional departmental structures are functional, product, customer, geographic, and matrix. Functional departmentalization is based on the different business functions or expertise used to run a business. Product departmentalization is organized according to the different products or services a company sells. Customer departmentalization focuses its divisions on the different kinds of customers a company has. Geographic departmentalization is based on the different geographic areas or markets in which the company does business. Matrix departmentalization is a hybrid form that combines two or more forms of departmentalization, the most common being the product and functional forms. There is no "best" departmental structure. Each structure has advantages and disadvantages.

simple matrix a form of matrix departmentalization in which managers in different parts of the matrix negotiate conflicts and resources

complex matrix a form of matrix departmentalization in which managers in different parts of the matrix report to matrix managers, who help them sort out conflicts and problems

authority the right to give commands, take action, and make decisions to achieve organizational objectives

2 Organizational Authority

The second part of traditional organizational structures is authority. **Authority** is the right to give commands, take action, and make decisions to achieve organizational objectives.[17]

*Traditionally, organizational authority has been characterized by the following dimensions: **2.1 chain of command**, **2.2 line versus staff authority**, **2.3 delegation of authority**, and **2.4 degree of centralization**.*

2.1 Chain of Command

Turn back a few pages to Microsoft's organizational chart in Exhibit 9.1. If you place your finger on any position in the chart, say, Central Business Services (under Business Division), you can trace a line upward to the company's CEO, Steve Ballmer. This line, which vertically connects every job in the company to higher levels of management, represents the chain of command. The **chain of command** is the vertical line of authority that clarifies who reports to whom throughout the organization. People higher in the chain of command have the right, *if they so choose*, to give commands, take action, and make decisions concerning activities occurring anywhere below them in the chain. In the following discussion about delegation and decentralization, you will learn that managers don't always choose to exercise their authority directly.[18]

One of the key assumptions underlying the chain of command is **unity of command**, which means that workers should report to just one boss.[19] In practical terms, this means that only one person can be in charge at a time. Matrix organizations, in which employees have two bosses, or—as in the Unilever example you just read about—two headquarters, automatically violate this principle. This is one of the primary reasons that matrix organizations are difficult to manage. The purpose of unity of command is to prevent the confusion that might arise when an employee receives conflicting commands from two different bosses. For example, when Bill Gates became chairman of Microsoft (after being CEO) and Steve Ballmer became CEO, there was confusion about the chain of command at Microsoft. In one meeting, Gates approved a budget increase for a project. Ballmer then denied the increase, shouting at Gates, "You put me in charge of the company. Let me run it."[20] With their different styles and approaches, with Gates not planning to leave active management until July 2008, and with managers and employees used to deferring to Gates over the 20 years that he was CEO, it's not surprising that the chain of command was unclear and that Gates and Ballmer had trouble adjusting to their new roles.

2.2 Line versus Staff Authority

A second dimension of authority is the distinction between line and staff authority. **Line authority** is the right to command immediate subordinates in the chain of command. For example, in the Microsoft organizational chart in Exhibit 9.1, CEO Steve Ballmer has line authority over the manager of the Business Division. Ballmer can issue orders to that division president and expect them to be carried out. In turn, the Business Division president can issue orders to the manager of the Information Worker group and expect them to be carried out.

Staff authority is the right to advise, but not command, others who are not subordinates in the chain of command. For example, at Microsoft, a manager in human resources might advise the vice president of MSN on a hiring decision but cannot order him or her to hire a certain applicant.

The terms *line* and *staff* are also used to describe different functions within the organization. A **line function** is an activity that contributes directly to creating or selling the company's products. So activities that take place within the manufacturing and marketing departments would be considered line functions. A **staff function**, such as accounting, human resources, or legal services, does not contribute directly to creating or selling the company's products, but instead supports line activities. For example, marketing managers might consult with the legal staff to make sure the wording of a particular advertisement is legal.

chain of command the vertical line of authority that clarifies who reports to whom throughout the organization

unity of command a management principle that workers should report to just one boss

line authority the right to command immediate subordinates in the chain of command

staff authority the right to advise, but not command, others who are not subordinates in the chain of command

line function an activity that contributes directly to creating or selling the company's products

staff function an activity that does not contribute directly to creating or selling the company's products, but instead supports line activities

2.3 Delegation of Authority

Managers can exercise their authority directly by completing the tasks themselves, or they can choose to pass on some of their authority to subordinates. **Delegation of authority** is the assignment of direct authority and responsibility to a subordinate to complete tasks for which the manager is normally responsible.

When a manager delegates work, three transfers occur, as illustrated in Exhibit 9.8. First, the manager transfers full responsibility for the assignment to the subordinate. Many managers find giving up full responsibility somewhat difficult. For example, Phil Knight, the charismatic founder of NIKE, has made three unsuccessful attempts at turning over the reigns of his multibillion-dollar corporation. According to former CEO William Perez, Knight's name belongs near the top of the list of CEO's who can't delegate. Perez says, "From virtually the day I arrived, Phil was as engaged in the company as he ever was. He was talking to my direct reports. It was confusing for the people and frustrating for me."[21]

Another problem is that managers often fear that the task won't be done as well as if they did it themselves. However, one CEO says, "If you can delegate a task to somebody who can do it 75 percent to 80 percent as well as you can today, you delegate it immediately." Why? The reason is that many tasks don't need to be done perfectly; they just need to be done. And delegating tasks that someone else can do frees managers to assume other important responsibilities.

Sometimes managers delegate only to later interfere with how the employee is performing the task. "Why are you doing it that way? That's not the way I do it." In contrast, delegating full responsibility means that the employee—not the manager—is now completely responsible for task completion.

The second transfer that occurs with delegation is that the manager gives the subordinate full authority over the budget, resources, and personnel needed to do the job. To do the job effectively, subordinates must have the same tools and information at their disposal that managers had when they were responsible for the same task. In other words, for delegation to work, delegated authority must be commensurate with delegated responsibility. Historically, pharmaceutical research at GLAXOSMITHKLINE followed a process common to nearly all drug companies: A panel of research and development chiefs far removed from the laboratory determined which drugs to develop and then decided how much money to invest in each. Research scientists in the labs had limited or no say in the drugs selected for research, and each scientist worked on only a single aspect of a drug, passing the resultant compounds onto the next researcher in line, who would do the next step. This assembly-line process led to fewer drugs in the pipeline and scientists who weren't particularly enthusiastic about their work. In order to improve the flow of new drugs as well as to retain the best talent, Glaxo began to delegate to its frontline researchers the ability to set research priorities and allocate the resources required to see a drug through development. Glaxo scientists are now organized into "pods" that focus on specific disease categories. Employees control their own budgets, decide which projects to pursue, and receive funding based on the number of useful compounds their labs have created. Delegating at Glaxo has worked. Not only has the number of drugs entering human trials tripled since the company began using "pods," Glaxo is now expanding into treatment areas where it previously had no presence.[22]

The third transfer that occurs with delegation is the transfer of accountability. The subordinate now has the authority and responsibility to do the job and in return is accountable for getting the job done. In other words, managers delegate their managerial authority

delegation of authority the assignment of direct authority and responsibility to a subordinate to complete tasks for which the manager is normally responsible

Exhibit 9.8
Delegation: Responsibility, Authority, and Accountability

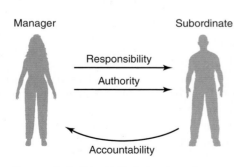

Manager   Subordinate

Responsibility →
Authority →
← Accountability

Source: C. D. Pringle, D. F. Jennings, & J. G. Longenecker, *Managing Organizations: Functions and Behaviors* © 1990. Adapted by permission of Pearson Education, Inc., Upper Saddle River, NJ.

and responsibility to subordinates in exchange for results. *Forbes* magazine columnist John Rutledge calls delegation "MBB," Managing by Belly Button. He says, "The belly button is the person whose belly you point your finger at when you want to know how the work is proceeding, i.e., the person who will actually be accountable for each step. . . . The belly button is not a scapegoat—a person to blame later when things go wrong. He or she is the person who makes sure that things go right."[23] Exhibit 9.9 gives some tips on how to be an effective delegator.

> *The belly button is not a scapegoat—a person to blame later when things go wrong. He or she is the person who makes sure that things go right.*
>
> **JOHN RUTLEDGE,** COLUMNIST, *FORBES* MAGAZINE

2.4 Degree of Centralization

If you've ever called a company's toll-free number with a complaint or a special request and been told by the customer service representative, "I'll have to ask my manager," or "I'm not authorized to do that," you know that centralization of authority exists in that company. **Centralization of authority** is the location of most authority at the upper levels of the organization. In a centralized organization, managers make most decisions, even the relatively small ones. That's why the customer service representative you called couldn't make a decision without first asking the manager.

If you are lucky, however, you may have talked to a customer service representative at another company who said, "I can take care of that for you right now." In other words, the person was able to handle your problem without any input from or consultation with company management. **Decentralization** is the location of a significant amount of authority in the lower levels of the organization. An organization is decentralized if it has a high degree of delegation at all levels. In a decentralized organization, workers closest to problems are authorized to make the decisions necessary to solve the problems on their own.

Decentralization has a number of advantages. It develops employee capabilities throughout the company and leads to faster decision making and more satisfied customers and employees. Furthermore, a study of 1,000 large companies found that companies with a high degree of decentralization outperformed those with a low degree of decentralization in terms of return on assets (6.9 percent versus 4.7 percent), return on investment (14.6 percent

centralization of authority the location of most authority at the upper levels of the organization

decentralization the location of a significant amount of authority in the lower levels of the organization

Exhibit 9.9

How to Be a More Effective Delegator

1. Trust your staff to do a good job. Recognize that others have the talent and ability to complete projects.

2. Avoid seeking perfection. Establish a standard of quality and provide a time frame for reaching it.

3. Give effective job instructions. Make sure employees have enough information to complete the job successfully.

4. Know your true interests. Delegation is difficult for some people who actually prefer doing the work themselves rather than managing it.

5. Follow up on progress. Build in checkpoints to help identify potential problems.

6. Praise the efforts of your staff.

7. Don't wait to the last minute to delegate. Avoid crisis management by routinely delegating work.

8. Ask questions, expect answers, and assist employees to help them complete the work assignments as expected.

9. Provide the resources you would expect if you were doing an assignment yourself.

10. Delegate to the lowest possible level to make the best possible use of organizational resources, energy, and knowledge.

Source: S. B. Wilson, "Are You an Effective Delegator?" *Female Executive*, 1 November 1994, 19.

versus 9.0 percent), return on equity (22.8 percent versus 16.6 percent), and return on sales (10.3 percent versus 6.3 percent). Surprisingly, the same study found that few large companies actually are decentralized. Specifically, only 31 percent of employees in these 1,000 companies were responsible for recommending improvements to management. Overall, just 10 percent of employees received the training and information needed to support a truly decentralized approach to management.[24]

With results like these, the key question is no longer whether companies should decentralize, but where they should decentralize. One rule of thumb is to stay centralized where standardization is important and to decentralize where standardization is unimportant. **Standardization** is solving problems by consistently applying the same rules, procedures, and processes. Each year, GENERAL MOTORS purchases roughly $85 billion worth of wheels, seats, bolts, and other automotive parts, many of which are only slight variations of the same thing. For instance, GM makes 26 different types of seat frames (the steel latticework that provides support for seat cushions), 20 different fuel pumps, and a dozen V6 engines. In contrast, highly profitable Toyota uses just two types of seat frames and a few models of V6 engines. One reason for GM's part redundancies is that the company used to have completely separate engineering groups for each of its cars and trucks. To become more competitive, however, GM has started standardizing the parts it uses across its product lines and wants to share as much technology and engineering across the company as possible. Today, GM uses only six types of fuel pump, and management wants to cut that number to five.[25]

Review 2: *Organizational Authority*

Organizational authority is determined by the chain of command, line versus staff authority, delegation, and the degree of centralization in a company. The chain of command vertically connects every job in the company to higher levels of management and makes clear who reports to whom. Managers have line authority to command employees below them in the chain of command, but have only staff, or advisory, authority over employees not below them in the chain of command. Managers delegate authority by transferring to subordinates the authority and responsibility needed to do a task; in exchange, subordinates become accountable for task completion. In centralized companies, most authority to make decisions lies with managers in the upper levels of the company. In decentralized companies, much of the authority is delegated to the workers closest to problems, who can then make the decisions necessary for solving the problems themselves. Centralization works best for tasks that require standardized decision making. When standardization isn't important, decentralization can lead to faster decisions, greater employee and customer satisfaction, and significantly better financial performance.

3 Job Design

Imagine that MCDONALD'S decided to pay $50,000 a year to its drive-through window cashiers. That's $50,000 for saying, "Welcome to McDonald's. May I have your order please?" Would you take the job? Sure you would. Work a couple of years. Make a hundred grand. Why not? Let's assume, however, that to get this outrageous salary, you have to be a full-time McDonald's drive-through window cashier for the next 10 years. Would you still

standardization solving problems by consistently applying the same rules, procedures, and processes take the job? Just imagine, 40 to 60 times an hour, you repeat the same basic process:

1. *"Welcome to McDonald's. May I have your order please?"*
2. *Listen to the order. Repeat it for accuracy. State the total cost. "Please drive to the second window."*
3. *Take the money. Make change.*
4. *Give customers drinks, straws, and napkins.*
5. *Give customers food.*
6. *"Thank you for coming to McDonald's."*

This two-window drive-thru in Monroe, Washington, is typical of McDonald's (and other fast-food restaurants) around the country. But even though this way of organizing the work is extremely efficient, it can be less than stimulating for employees.

Could you stand to do the same simple tasks an average of 50 times per hour, 400 times per day, 2,000 times per week, 8,000 times per month? Few can. Fast-food workers rarely stay on the job more than six months. Indeed, McDonald's and other fast-food restaurants have well over 100 percent employee turnover each year.[26]

*In this next section, you will learn about **job design**—the number, kind, and variety of tasks that individual workers perform in doing their jobs. You will learn **3.1 why companies continue to use specialized jobs like the McDonald's drive-through job** and **3.2 how job rotation, job enlargement, job enrichment**, and **3.3 the job characteristics model** are being used to overcome the problems associated with job specialization.*

3.1 Job Specialization

Job specialization occurs when a job is composed of a small part of a larger task or process. Specialized jobs are characterized by simple, easy-to-learn steps, low variety, and high repetition, like the McDonald's drive-through window job just described. One of the clear disadvantages of specialized jobs is that, being so easy to learn, they quickly become boring. This, in turn, can lead to low job satisfaction and high absenteeism and employee turnover, all of which are very costly to organizations.

Why, then, do companies continue to create and use specialized jobs? The primary reason is that specialized jobs are very economical. Once a job has been specialized, it takes little time to learn and master. Consequently, when experienced workers quit or are absent, the company can replace them with new employees and lose little productivity. For example, next time you're at McDonald's, notice the pictures of the food on the cash registers. These pictures make it easy for McDonald's trainees to quickly learn to take orders. Likewise, to simplify and speed operations, the drink dispensers behind the counter are set to automatically fill drink cups. Put a medium cup below the dispenser. Punch the medium drink button. The soft drink machine then fills the cup to within a half-inch of the top, while that same worker goes to get your fries. At McDonald's, every task has been simplified in this way. Because the work is designed to be simple, wages can remain low since it isn't necessary to pay high salaries to attract highly experienced, educated, or trained workers.

3.2 Job Rotation, Enlargement, and Enrichment

Because of the efficiency of specialized jobs, companies are often reluctant to eliminate them. Consequently, job redesign efforts have focused on modifying jobs to keep the benefits of specialized jobs, while reducing their obvious costs and disadvantages.

job design the number, kind, and variety of tasks that individual workers perform in doing their jobs

job specialization a job composed of a small part of a larger task or process

> *The more you increase individual responsibility, the better the chances for incremental improvements in operations.*
>
> **DENNIS BAKKE,**
> CEO, AES

job rotation periodically moving workers from one specialized job to another to give them more variety and the opportunity to use different skills

job enlargement increasing the number of different tasks that a worker performs within one particular job

job enrichment increasing the number of tasks in a particular job and giving workers the authority and control to make meaningful decisions about their work

job characteristics model (JCM) an approach to job redesign that seeks to formulate jobs in ways that motivate workers and lead to positive work outcomes

Three methods—job rotation, job enlargement, and job enrichment—have been used to try to improve specialized jobs.[27]

In factory work or even some office jobs, many workers perform the same task all day long. For example, if you attach side mirrors in an auto factory, you probably complete this task 45 to 60 times an hour. If you work as the cashier at a grocery store, you check out a different customer every two to three minutes. And if you work as an office receptionist, you may answer and direct phone calls up to 200 times an hour.

Job rotation attempts to overcome the disadvantages of job specialization by periodically moving workers from one specialized job to another to give them more variety and the opportunity to use different skills. For example, the office receptionist who does nothing but answer phones could be systematically rotated to a different job, such as typing, filing, or data entry, every day or two. Likewise, the "mirror attacher" in the automobile plant might attach mirrors in the first half of the day's work shift and then install bumpers during the second half. Because employees simply switch from one specialized job to another, job rotation allows companies to retain the economic benefits of specialized work. At the same time, the greater variety of tasks makes the work less boring and more satisfying for workers.

Another way to counter the disadvantages of specialization is to enlarge the job. **Job enlargement** increases the number of different tasks that a worker performs within one particular job. Instead of being assigned just one task, workers with enlarged jobs are given several tasks to perform. For example, an enlarged "mirror attacher" job might include attaching the mirror, checking to see that the mirror's power adjustment controls work, and then cleaning the mirror's surface. Though job enlargement increases variety, many workers report feeling more stress when their jobs are enlarged. Consequently, many workers view enlarged jobs as simply "more work," especially if they are not given additional time to complete the additional tasks.

Job enrichment attempts to overcome the deficiencies in specialized work by increasing the number of tasks *and* by giving workers the authority and control to make meaningful decisions about their work.[28]

At **AES**, an independent power company that sells electricity to public utilities and steam (for power) to industrial organizations, workers have been given an extraordinary level of authority and control. For example, with his hands still blackened after unloading coal from a barge, employee Jeff Hatch calls a broker to determine which Treasury bills the company should buy to maximize the short-term return on its available cash. Hatch asks his broker, "What kind of rate can you give me for $10 million at 30 days?" When the broker tells him, "6.09 percent," he responds, "But I just got a 6.13 percent quote from Chase."[29] Indeed, at AES, ordinary plant technicians are given budgets worth several million dollars and are trusted to purchase everything from mops to gas turbines. In most companies, such tasks would be entrusted only to managers, but CEO Dennis Bakke says, "The more you increase individual responsibility, the better the chances for incremental improvements in operations." Paul Burdick, an engineer entrusted with the ability to purchase billions of dollars of coal, agrees, adding, "You're given a lot of leeway and a lot of rope. You can use it to climb or you can hang yourself."[30]

3.3 Job Characteristics Model

In contrast to job rotation, job enlargement, and job enrichment, which focus on providing variety in job tasks, the **job characteristics model (JCM)** is an approach to job redesign that seeks to formulate jobs in ways that motivate workers and lead to positive work outcomes.[31] As shown in Exhibit 9.10, the primary goal of the model is to create jobs that result in positive personal and work outcomes such as internal work motivation, satisfaction with one's job, and work effectiveness. Of these, the central concern of the JCM is internal motivation. **Internal motivation** is motivation that comes from the job itself rather than from outside rewards, such as a raise or praise from the boss. If workers feel that performing the job well is itself rewarding, then the job has internal motivation. Statements such as "I get a nice sense of accomplishment" or "I feel good about myself and what I'm producing" are examples of internal motivation.

Moving to the left in Exhibit 9.10, you can see that the JCM specifies three critical psychological states that must occur for work to be internally motivating. First, workers must *experience the work as meaningful*; that is, they must view their job as being important. Second, they must *experience responsibility for work outcomes*—they must feel personally responsible for the work being done well. Third, workers must have *knowledge of results*; that is, they must know how well they are performing their jobs. All three critical psychological states must occur for work to be internally motivating.

For example, let's return to our grocery store cashier. Cashiers usually have knowledge of results. When you're slow, your checkout line grows long. If you make a mistake, customers point it out: "No, I think that's on sale for $2.99, not $3.99." Likewise, cashiers experience responsibility for work outcomes. At the end of the day, the register is totaled and the money is counted. Ideally, the money matches the total sales in the register. If the money in the till is less than what's recorded in the register, most stores make the cashier pay the difference. Consequently, most cashiers are very careful to avoid being caught short at the end of the day. Nonetheless, despite knowing the results and experiencing responsibility for work outcomes, most grocery store cashiers (at least where I shop) aren't internally motivated because they don't experience the work as meaningful. With scanners, it takes little skill to learn or do the job. Anyone can do it. In addition, cashiers have few decisions to make, and the job is highly repetitive.

internal motivation motivation that comes from the job itself rather than from outside rewards

Exhibit 9.10
Job Characteristics Model

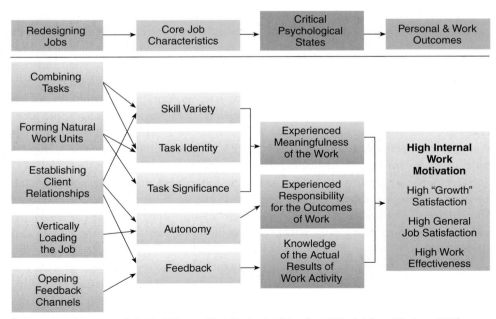

Source: J. R. Hackman & G. R. Oldham, *Work Redesign* (Reading, MA: Addison-Wesley, 1980). Reprinted by permission of Addison-Wesley Longman.

Of course, this raises the question: What kinds of jobs produce the three critical psychological states? Moving another step to the left in Exhibit 9.10, you can see that these psychological states arise from jobs that are strong on five core job characteristics: skill variety, task identity, task significance, autonomy, and feedback. **Skill variety** is the number of different activities performed in a job. **Task identity** is the degree to which a job, from beginning to end, requires completion of a whole and identifiable piece of work. **Task significance** is the degree to which a job is perceived to have a substantial impact on others inside or outside the organization. **Autonomy** is the degree to which a job gives workers the discretion, freedom, and independence to decide how and when to accomplish the work. Finally, **feedback** is the amount of information the job provides to workers about their work performance.

To illustrate how the core job characteristics work together, let's use them to more thoroughly assess why the McDonald's drive-through window job is not particularly satisfying or motivating. To start, skill variety is low. Except for the size of an order or special requests ("no onions"), the process is the same for each customer. At best, task identity is moderate. Although you take the order, handle the money, and deliver the food, others are responsible for a larger part of the process—preparing the food. Task identity will be even lower if the McDonald's has two drive-through windows because each drive-through window worker will have an even more specialized task. The first is limited to taking the order and making change, while the second just delivers the food. Task significance, the impact you have on others, is probably low. Autonomy is also very low: McDonald's has strict rules about dress, cleanliness, and procedures. But the job does provide immediate feedback, such as positive and negative customer comments, car horns honking, the amount of time it takes to process orders, and the number of cars in the drive-through. With the exception of feedback, the low levels of the core job characteristics show why the drive-through window job is not internally motivating for many workers.

What can managers do when jobs aren't internally motivating? The far left column of Exhibit 9.10 lists five job redesign techniques that managers can use to strengthen a job's core characteristics. *Combining tasks* increases skill variety and task identity by joining separate, specialized tasks into larger work modules. For example, some trucking firms are now requiring truck drivers to load their rigs as well as drive them. The hope is that involving drivers in loading will ensure that trucks are properly loaded, thus reducing damage claims.

Work can be formed into *natural work units* by arranging tasks according to logical or meaningful groups. Although many trucking companies randomly assign drivers to trucks, some have begun assigning drivers to particular geographic locations (for example, the Northeast or Southwest) or to truckloads that require special driving skill (such as oversized loads or hazardous chemicals). Forming natural work units increases task identity and task significance.

Establishing client relationships increases skill variety, autonomy, and feedback by giving employees direct contact with clients and customers. In some companies, truck drivers are expected to establish business relationships with their regular customers. When something goes wrong with a shipment, customers are told to call drivers directly.

Vertical loading means pushing some managerial authority down to workers. For truck drivers, this means that they have the same authority as managers to resolve customer problems. In some companies, if a late shipment causes problems for a customer, the driver has the authority to fully refund the cost of that shipment (without first obtaining management's approval).

skill variety the number of different activities performed in a job

task identity the degree to which a job, from beginning to end, requires the completion of a whole and identifiable piece of work

task significance the degree to which a job is perceived to have a substantial impact on others inside or outside the organization

autonomy the degree to which a job gives workers the discretion, freedom, and independence to decide how and when to accomplish the job

feedback the amount of information the job provides to workers about their work performance

The last job redesign technique offered by the model, *opening feedback channels*, means finding additional ways to give employees direct, frequent feedback about their job performance. For example, with advances in electronics, many truck drivers get instantaneous data as to whether they're on schedule and driving their rigs in a fuel-efficient manner. Likewise, the increased contact with customers also means that many drivers now receive monthly data on customer satisfaction. For additional information on the JCM, see this chapter's "What Really Works" feature.

© DIGITAL VISION/GETTY IMAGES

By allowing truck drivers to interact with customers and resolve customers' complaints, driving a truck can become more internally motivating.

Review 3: **Job Design**

Companies use specialized jobs because they are economical and easy to learn and don't require highly paid workers. However, specialized jobs aren't motivating or particularly satisfying for employees. Companies have used job rotation, job enlargement, job enrichment, and the job characteristics model to make specialized jobs more interesting and motivating. With job rotation, workers move from one specialized job to another. Job enlargement simply increases the number of different tasks within a particular job. Job enrichment increases the number of tasks in a job and gives workers authority and control over their work. The goal of the job characteristics model is to make jobs intrinsically motivating. For this to happen, jobs must be strong on five core job characteristics (skill variety, task identity, task significance, autonomy, and feedback), and workers must experience three critical psychological states (knowledge of results, responsibility for work outcomes, and meaningful work). If jobs aren't internally motivating, they can be redesigned by combining tasks, forming natural work units, establishing client relationships, vertical loading, and opening feedback channels.

DESIGNING ORGANIZATIONAL PROCESSES

More than 40 years ago, Tom Burns and G. M. Stalker described how two kinds of organizational designs, mechanistic and organic, are appropriate for different kinds of organizational environments.[32] **Mechanistic organizations** are characterized by specialized jobs and responsibilities; precisely defined, unchanging roles; and a rigid chain of command based on centralized authority and vertical communication. This type of organization works best in stable, unchanging business environments. By contrast, **organic organizations** are characterized by broadly defined jobs and responsibility; loosely defined, frequently changing roles; and decentralized authority and horizontal communication based on task knowledge. This type of organization works best in dynamic, changing business environments.

mechanistic organization an organization characterized by specialized jobs and responsibilities; precisely defined, unchanging roles; and a rigid chain of command based on centralized authority and vertical communication

organic organization an organization characterized by broadly defined jobs and responsibility; loosely defined, frequently changing roles; and decentralized authority and horizontal communication based on task knowledge

THE JOB CHARACTERISTICS MODEL: MAKING JOBS MORE INTERESTING AND MOTIVATING

Think of the worst job you ever had. Was it factory work where you repeated the same task every few minutes? Was it an office job requiring a lot of meaningless paperwork? Or was it a job so specialized that it took no effort or thinking whatsoever to do?

The job characteristics model reviewed in this chapter suggests that workers will be more motivated or satisfied with their work if their jobs have greater task identity, task significance, skill variety, autonomy, and feedback. Eighty-four studies, with a combined total of 22,472 participants, found that, on average, these core job characteristics make jobs more satisfying for most workers. In addition, jobs rich with the five core job characteristics are especially satisfying for workers who possess an individual characteristic called *growth need strength*. Read on to see how well the JCM really increases job satisfaction and reduces workplace absenteeism.

JOB SATISFACTION

There is a 66 percent chance that workers will be more satisfied with their work when their jobs have task identity, the chance to complete an entire job from beginning to end, than when they don't.

On average, there is a 69 percent chance that workers will be more satisfied with their work when their jobs have task significance—a substantial impact on others—than when they don't.

On average, there is a 70 percent chance that workers will be more satisfied with their work when their jobs have skill variety—a variety of activities, skills, and talents—than when they don't.

On average, there is a 73 percent chance that workers will be more satisfied with their work when their jobs have autonomy—the discretion to decide how and when to accomplish the work—than when they don't.

On average, there is a 70 percent chance that workers will be more satisfied with their work when their jobs provide feedback—information about their work performance—than when they don't.

These statistics indicate that, on average, the JCM has at worst a 66 percent chance of improving workers' job satisfaction. In all, this is impressive evidence that the model works. In general, you can expect these results when redesigning jobs based on the model.

We can be more accurate about the effects of the JCM, however, if we split workers into two groups: those with high growth need strength and those with low growth need strength. *Growth need strength* is the need or desire to achieve personal growth and development through one's job. Workers high in growth need strength respond well to jobs designed according to the JCM because they enjoy work that challenges them and allows them to learn new skills and knowledge. In fact, there is an 84 percent chance that workers with high growth need strength will be more satisfied with their work when their jobs are redesigned according to the JCM.

By comparison, because they aren't as interested in being challenged or learning new things at work, there is only a 69 percent chance that workers low in growth need strength will be satisfied with jobs that have been redesigned according to the principles of the JCM. This is still a favorable percentage, but it is weaker than the 84 percent chance of job satisfaction that occurs for workers high in growth need strength.

WORKPLACE ABSENTEEISM

Although not shown in the job characteristics model displayed in Exhibit 9.10, workplace absenteeism is an important personal or work outcome affected by a job's core job characteristics. In general, the "richer" your job is with task identity, task significance, skill variety, autonomy, and feedback, the more likely you are to show up for work every day.

Workers are 63 percent more likely to attend work when their jobs have task identity than when they don't.

Workers are 68 percent more likely to attend work when their jobs have task significance than when they don't.

Workers are 72 percent more likely to attend work when their jobs have skill variety than when they don't.

Workers are 74 percent more likely to attend work when their jobs have autonomy than when they don't.

Workers are 72 percent more likely to attend work when their jobs provide feedback than when they don't.[33]

The organizational design techniques described in the first half of this chapter—departmentalization, authority, and job design—are better suited for mechanistic organizations and the stable business environments that were more prevalent before 1980. In contrast, the organizational design techniques discussed next, in the second part of the chapter, are more appropriate for organic organizations and the increasingly dynamic environments in which today's businesses compete.

The key difference between these approaches is that whereas mechanistic organizational designs focus on organizational structure, organic organizational designs are concerned with organizational process, the collection of activities that transform inputs into outputs valued by customers. After reading the next two sections, you should be able to

4 *explain the methods that companies are using to redesign internal organizational processes (that is, intraorganizational processes).*

5 *describe the methods that companies are using to redesign external organizational processes (that is, interorganizational processes).*

4 Intraorganizational Processes

An **intraorganizational process** is the collection of activities that take place within an organization to transform inputs into outputs that customers value. The steps involved in an automobile insurance claim are a good example of an intraorganizational process:

1. *Document the loss (the accident).*
2. *Assign an appraiser to determine the dollar amount of damage.*
3. *Make an appointment to inspect the vehicle.*
4. *Inspect the vehicle.*
5. *Write an appraisal and get the repair shop to agree to the damage estimate.*
6. *Pay for the repair work.*
7. *Return the repaired car to the customer.*

*Let's take a look at how companies are using **4.1 reengineering**, **4.2 empowerment**, and **4.3 behavioral informality** to redesign intraorganizational processes like these.*

4.1 Reengineering

In their best-selling book *Reengineering the Corporation*, Michael Hammer and James Champy define **reengineering** as "the *fundamental* rethinking and *radical* redesign of business *processes* to achieve *dramatic* improvements in critical, contemporary measures of performance, such as cost, quality, service and speed."[34] Hammer and Champy further explained the four key words shown in italics in this definition. The first key word is *fundamental*. When reengineering organizational designs, managers must ask themselves, "Why do we do what we do?" and "Why do we do it the way we do?" The usual answer is, "Because that's the way we've always done it." The second key word is *radical*. Reengineering is about significant change, about starting over by throwing out the old ways of getting work done. The third key word is *processes*. Hammer and Champy noted that "most business people are not process oriented; they are focused on tasks, on jobs, on people, on structures, but not on processes." The fourth key word is *dramatic*. Reengineering is about achieving "quantum" improvements in company performance.

"WHAT'S NEW" COMPANY

I wasn't smart enough about that [the people issues].
I was reflecting my engineering background and was
insufficiently appreciative of the human dimension. I've
[now] learned that's critical.

MICHAEL HAMMER, CO-AUTHOR, *REENGINEERING THE CORPORATION*

An example from **IBM CREDIT**'s operation illustrates how work can be reengineered.[35] IBM Credit lends businesses money to buy IBM computers. Previously, the loan process began when an IBM salesperson called the home office to obtain credit approval for a customer's purchase. The first department involved in the process took the credit information over the phone from the salesperson and recorded it on the credit form. The credit form was sent to the credit checking department, then to

intraorganizational process the collection of activities that take place within an organization to transform inputs into outputs that customers value

reengineering fundamental rethinking and radical redesign of business processes to achieve dramatic improvements in critical measures of performance, such as cost, quality, service, and speed the pricing department (where the interest rate was determined), and on through a total of five departments. In all, it took the five departments six days to approve or deny the customer's loan. Of course, this delay cost IBM business. Some customers got their loans elsewhere. Others, frustrated by the wait, simply canceled their orders.

Finally, two IBM managers decided to walk a loan straight through each of the departments involved in the process. At each step, they asked the workers to stop what they were doing and immediately process their loan application. They were shocked by what they found. From start to finish, the entire process took just 90 minutes! The six-day turnaround time was almost entirely due to delays in handing off the work from one department to another. The solution: IBM redesigned the process so that one person, not five people in five separate departments, now handles the entire loan approval process without any handoffs. The results were indeed "dramatic." Reengineering the credit process reduced approval time from six days to four hours and allowed IBM Credit to increase the number of loans it handled by a factor of 100!

Reengineering changes an organization's orientation from vertical to horizontal. Instead of "taking orders" from upper management, lower- and middle-level managers and workers "take orders" from a customer who is at the beginning and end of each process. Instead of running independent functional departments, managers and workers in different departments take ownership of cross-functional processes. Instead of simplifying work so that it becomes increasingly specialized, reengineering complicates work by giving workers increased autonomy and responsibility for complete processes.

In essence, reengineering changes work by changing **task interdependence**, the extent to which collective action is required to complete an entire piece of work. As shown in Exhibit 9.11, there are three kinds of task interdependence.[36] In **pooled interdependence**, each job or department independently contributes to the whole. In **sequential interdependence**, work must be performed in succession, as one group's or job's outputs become the inputs for the next group or job. Finally, in **reciprocal interdependence**, different jobs or groups work together in a back-and-forth manner to complete the process. By reducing the handoffs between different jobs or groups, reengineering decreases sequential interdependence. Likewise, reengineering decreases pooled interdependence by redesigning work so that formerly independent jobs or departments now work together to complete processes. Finally, reengineering increases reciprocal interdependence by making groups or individuals responsible for larger, more complete processes in which several steps may be accomplished at the same time.

As an organizational design tool, reengineering promises big rewards, but it has also come under severe criticism. The most serious complaint is that because it allows a few workers to do the work formerly done by many, reengineering is simply a corporate code word for cost cutting and worker layoffs.[37] Likewise, for that reason, detractors claim that reengineering hurts morale and performance. For example, even though ordering times were reduced from three weeks to three days, *LEVI STRAUSS* ended an $850 million reengineering project because of the fear and turmoil it created in the company's work force. One low point occurred when Levi management, encouraged by its reengineering consultants, told 4,000 workers that they would have to "reapply for their jobs" as the company shifted from its traditional vertical structure to a process-based form of

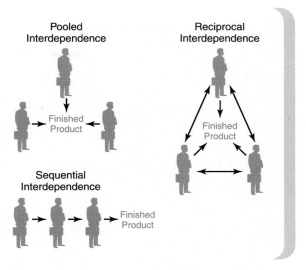

Exhibit 9.11

Reengineering and Task Interdependence

task interdependence the extent to which collective action is required to complete an entire piece of work

pooled interdependence work completed by having each job or department independently contribute to the whole

sequential interdependence work completed in succession, with one group's or job's outputs becoming the inputs for the next group or job

reciprocal interdependence work completed by different jobs or groups working together in a back-and-forth manner

As managers at Levi Strauss discovered, reengineering must make sense for the kind of work being done.

organizing. Thomas Kasten, Levi Strauss's vice president for reengineering and customer service, says, "We felt the pressure building up [over reengineering efforts], and we were worried about the business."[38] Today, even reengineering gurus Hammer and Champy admit that roughly 70 percent of all reengineering projects fail because of the effects on people in the workplace. Says Hammer, "I wasn't smart enough about that [the people issues]. I was reflecting my engineering background and was insufficiently appreciative of the human dimension. I've [now] learned that's critical."[39]

4.2 Empowerment

Another way of redesigning interorganizational processes is through empowerment. **Empowering workers** means permanently passing decision-making authority and responsibility from managers to workers. For workers to be fully empowered, companies must give them the information and resources they need to make and carry out good decisions, and then reward them for taking individual initiative.[40] Unfortunately, this doesn't happen often enough. As Michael Schrage, author and MIT researcher, wrote:

A warehouse employee can see on the intranet that a shipment is late but has no authority to accelerate its delivery. A project manager knows—and can mathematically demonstrate—that a seemingly minor spec change will bust both her budget and her schedule. The spec must be changed anyway. An airline reservations agent tells the Executive Platinum Premier frequent flier that first class appears wide open for an upgrade. However, the airline's yield management software won't permit any upgrades until just four hours before the flight, frequent fliers (and reservations) be damned. In all these cases, the employee has access to valuable information. Each one possesses the "knowledge" to do the job better. But the knowledge and information are irrelevant and useless. Knowledge isn't power; the ability to act on knowledge is power.[41]

When workers are given the proper information and resources and are allowed to make good decisions, they experience strong feelings of empowerment. **Empowerment** is a feeling of intrinsic motivation, in which workers perceive their work to have meaning and perceive themselves to be competent, having an impact, and capable of self-determination.[42] Work has meaning when it is consistent with personal standards and beliefs. Workers feel competent when they believe they can perform an activity with skill. The belief that they are having an impact comes from a feeling that they can affect work outcomes. A feeling of self-determination arises from workers' belief that they have the autonomy to choose how best to do their work.

Empowerment can lead to changes in organizational processes because meaning, competence, impact, and self-determination produce empowered employees who take active, rather than passive, roles in their work. WEGMANS Food Market Inc., a perennial top company on the *Fortune* ranking of the best businesses to work for is a classic example of employee empowerment. Wegmans has 69 stores in New York, Pennsylvania, New Jersey and Virginia. Employees are encouraged to do just about anything to keep customers loyal to the organization and to do so on the spot, without consulting a higher-up. One day it could mean sending a chef to a customer's home to clear up a botched food order or it could mean cooking a family's Thanksgiving turkey in the store because the one bought was too big for the customer's oven. This approach leads to what operations chief Jack DePeters jokingly says is a "$3 billion company run by 16-year-old cashiers."[43]

empowering workers permanently passing decision-making authority and responsibility from managers to workers by giving them the information and resources they need to make and carry out good decisions

empowerment feelings of intrinsic motivation, in which workers perceive their work to have impact and meaning and perceive themselves to be competent and capable of self-determination

	FORMAL	INFORMAL
LANGUAGE USAGE	Fully articulated speech ("What are you doing?") Grammatically complete phrasing ("Would you like some coffee?") Use of formal word choices ("Would you care to dine?") Use of honorifics ("Ms.," "Sir," "Dr.") Elimination of "I" and "you" ("It is requested that…")	Phonological slurring ("Whatcha doin'?") Use of elliptical expressions ("Coffee?") Use of colloquial and slang expressions ("Wanna grab a bite to eat?") Use of the vivid present ("So I come down the stairs, and she says…") First name, in-group names ("Mac," "Bud")
CONVERSATIONAL TURN TAKING AND TOPIC SELECTION	Turn taking well regulated Few interruptions or overlaps Few changes of topic Generally serious topics	Turn taking relatively unregulated Many interruptions or overlaps Many shifts of topic possible Joking or conversational levity possible
EMOTIONAL AND PROXEMIC GESTURES	Sober facial demeanor Much interpersonal distance No touching; postural attention	Greater latitude of emotional expression Small interpersonal distance Touching, postural relaxation allowed
PHYSICAL AND CONTEXTUAL CUES	Formal clothing, shoes, etc. Central focus of attention Symmetric arrangement of chairs/furniture Artifacts related to official status Hushed atmosphere, little background noise	Informal clothing, shoes, etc. Decentralized, multiple centers of attention possible Asymmetric arrangement of chairs/furniture Informal trappings: flowers, art, food, soft furniture Background noise acceptable

Source: Republished with permission of Academy of Management, P.O. Box 3020, Briar Cliff Manor, NY, 10510–8020. D. A. Morland, "The Role of Behavioral Formality and Informality in the Enactment of Bureaucratic versus Organic Organizations," *Academy of Management Review* 20 (1995): 831–872. Reproduced by permission of the publisher via Copyright Clearance Center, Inc.

4.3 Behavioral Informality

How would you describe the atmosphere in the office where you last worked? Was it a formal, by-the-book, follow-the-rules, address-each-other-by-last-names atmosphere? Or was it more informal, with an emphasis on results rather than rules, casual business dress rather than suits, and first names rather than last names and titles? Or was it somewhere in between?

Behavioral informality (or formality) is a third influence on intraorganizational processes. **Behavioral informality** refers to workplace atmospheres characterized by spontaneity, casualness, and interpersonal familiarity. By contrast, **behavioral formality** refers to workplace atmospheres characterized by routine and regimen, specific rules about how to behave, and impersonal detachment. As Exhibit 9.12 shows, behavioral formality and informality are characterized by four factors: language usage, conversational turn taking and topic selection, emotional and proxemic gestures, and physical and contextual cues. Let's examine each in more detail.[44]

Compared with formal work atmospheres, the language in informal workplaces is often slurred ("Whatcha doin'?"), elliptical ("Coffee?" versus "Would you like some coffee?"), and filled with slang terms and vivid descriptions. People use first names and perhaps nicknames to address each other, rather than Mr., Ms., Dr., or formal titles. When it comes to conversations in informal workplaces, people jump right in when they have something to say (known as unregulated turn taking); conversations shift

Exhibit 9.12

Differences between Formal and Informal Workplaces

behavioral informality a workplace atmosphere characterized by spontaneity, casualness, and interpersonal familiarity

behavioral formality a workplace atmosphere characterized by routine and regimen, specific rules about how to behave, and impersonal detachment

Chipotle's unusual employee titles may be an extreme, but behavioral informality can help nearly any company unleash worker creativity.

from topic to topic, many of which are unrelated to business; and joking and laughter are common. From joy to disappointment, people show much more emotion in informal workplaces. Relaxed behavior, such as putting your feet on your desk or congregating in hallways for impromptu discussions, is more common, too. In terms of physical and contextual cues, informal workplaces de-emphasize differences in hierarchical status or rank to encourage more frequent interaction between organizational members. Consequently, to make their organizations feel less formal, many companies have eliminated such management perks as executive dining rooms, reserved parking spaces, and large corner offices separated from most workers by virtue of their location on a higher floor of the company building (the higher the floor, the greater one's status). *CHIPOTLE MEXICAN GRILL* de-emphasizes differences in hierarchical rank through an innovative employee title system that speaks volumes about the company's informal culture. The "Manager of Duct Tape and Plungers" is in charge of customer service. The "Director of Hoopla, Hype, and Ballyhoo" is the company's spokesman, and the leader of the creative services department is the "Head of Special Weapons and Tactics." Even though the title system has never received an official corporate blessing, the offbeat titles are still sanctioned: They are used on business cards and in formal business correspondence, reinforcing how seriously Chipotle takes behavioral informality.[45]

Casual dress policies and open office systems are two of the most popular methods for increasing behavioral informality. In fact, a survey conducted by the Society for Human Resource Management indicates that casual dress policies (no suits, ties, jackets, dresses, or formal clothing required) are extremely popular.[46] Today, 86 percent of companies have some form of casual dress code, up from 63 percent seven years ago and 24 percent 12 years ago.[47] Similarly, 42 percent of all companies permit casual dress at least one day a week, compared with 17 percent five years ago. Moreover, 33 percent of companies permit casual dress every day of the week, up from 20 percent seven years ago.

Although sales of formal business wear, such as men's suits, increased last year for the first time in eight years and some companies, such as retailer Target Corporation, have instituted formal dress codes that ban "business casual," "no study shows that productivity goes up with better dress," says John Challenger, chief executive of Challenger, Gray & Christmas, a Chicago-based outplacement company.[48] Indeed, casual dress appears to improve employee attitudes. For example, Colin Stanbridge, the chief executive of London's Chamber of Commerce, says, "People tend to work at their best when they feel most comfortable. And today I think the vast majority of people feel at their most comfortable when wearing casual dress."[49] In fact, 85 percent of human resources directors believe that casual dress can improve office morale, and 79 percent say that employees are very satisfied with casual dress codes.[50] Moreover, nearly two-thirds of the human resources directors believe that casual dress policies are an important tool for attracting qualified employees in tight labor markets. Michael Losey, president of the Society for Human Resource Management, concludes that "for the majority of corporations and industries, allowing casual dress can have clear advantages at virtually no cost."[51]

While casual dress increases behavioral informality by having managers and workers at all levels dress in a more relaxed manner, open office systems increase behavioral informality by significantly increasing the level of communication and interaction among employees. By definition, **open office systems** try to increase interaction by removing physical barriers

open office systems offices in which the physical barriers that separate workers have been removed in order to increase communication and interaction that separate workers. One characteristic of open office systems is that they have much more shared space than private space. **Shared spaces** are areas used by and open to all employees. Cubicles with low-to-the-ground partitions (used by 75 percent of office workers), offices with no doors or with glass walls, collections of comfortable furniture that encourage people to congregate, and common areas with tables and chairs that encourage people to meet, work, or eat together are examples of shared space.[52] In contrast, **private spaces**, such as private offices with doors, are used by and open to just one employee.

DIGITAL VISION

The advantage of an open office with extensive shared space is that it dramatically increases the amount of unplanned, spontaneous, and chance communication between employees.[53] People are much more likely to plan meetings and work together when numerous "collaboration spaces" with conference tables, white boards, and computers are readily available. With no office walls, inviting common areas, and different departments mixed together in large open spaces, spontaneous communication occurs more often. After RADIO SHACK moved from two traditional, 19-story office towers into a new headquarters with open offices, cubicles, and immense amounts of shared space, the volume of corporate e-mail dropped by 37 percent because people were much more likely to run into and actually talk to each other. Senior vice president Laura Moore says, "For somebody to stick his or her head over your workplace [cubicle] is accepted protocol. That has made executives much more approachable."[54] Also, open office systems increase chance encounters by making it much more likely that people from different departments or areas will run into each other. When SIGMA-ALDRICH, a biotechnology firm, built a new office with a three-story, open staircase at the center of the building, the main goal, according to Keld Sorensen, director of research and development, was increasing "interaction."[55] In fact, the open staircase, which is complemented by benches and expansive landings on each story (so people would sit and talk) has led to 156 percent more chance encounters than at the old building, which had elevators and an enclosed stairwell. Indeed, soon after the move to the new office, two scientists from opposite sides of the building ran into each other on the stairs, stopped to talk, and ended up generating a significant new reagent for scientific testing.

Not everyone is enthusiastic about open offices, however. For example, Ingrid Tischer, who sits in a cubicle next to the kitchen in her office, says she can't help being distracted by others' conversations and frequently joins in. Because of the location of her cubicle, "I know things about my colleagues' lives, and they know things about mine."[56] In fact, cubicle dwellers are interrupted by "noise, visual distractions, and chatty visitors" up to 21 times a day. And, since it takes about three minutes each time to refocus on what they were doing, cubicle workers can lose an hour a day to these interruptions.[57] Attorney Phillip Fisher says, "I honestly don't know how people can concentrate in a cubicle."[58] For this reason, SUN MICROSYSTEMS and Microsoft give their employees private offices. William Agnello, Sun's vice president of real estate and the workplace, says, "We have researched the heck out of this. Our studies show that, for our engineers, there are just too many distractions and interruptions."[59] Microsoft's John Pinette agrees: "Private offices allow our employees to concentrate on their work and to avoid unnecessary distractions—[which is] obviously critical when you're doing something that requires as much focus as developing software does."[60]

Indeed, because there is so much shared space and so little private space, companies with open systems have to take steps to give employees privacy when they need to concentrate on individual work. One step is simply to use taller cubicles. Indeed, Herman

Open-offices encourage communication and interaction throughout an organization, but they have their drawbacks as well. In fact, sales of taller cube walls, like those shown here, are increasing, while sales of traditional four-foot walls are decreasing.

shared spaces spaces used by and open to all employees

private spaces spaces used by and open to just one employee

Miller, a manufacturer of office furniture and systems, has seen sales of its 62-inch-high cubicle panels increase by 18 percent while sales of its 46-inch-high panels have dropped by 19 percent. Another approach is to install white-noise machines to prevent voices and other noises from disrupting others.[62] At Procter & Gamble's headquarters in Cincinnati, white noise from two interior waterfalls provides a constant background sound that mutes other noises. Yet another approach is to make conference rooms available. In contrast to traditional offices, where such rooms are used for meetings, many employees in open systems reserve conference rooms when they need private time to work. Another possibility is to turn a cubicle into a more private space. When Mark Saunders, of GlaxoSmithKline Consumer Healthcare, moved from a private office to a cubicle at the end of a busy hallway, he "felt sensory overload." To make it easier for him to concentrate, the company's office design team created a nylon screen that can be placed around his cubicle to block out visual distractions.[63] If your office doesn't provide such screens, you can always fork out $39.95 for the Cube-a-Door, a free-standing cardboard partition stamped with the words "Work in Progress. Do Not Disturb," that will serve as a "door" to your cubicle when you need to screen out interruptions.

doing the right thing

Don't Scavenge That Office if Somebody Is Still in It

It's like roadkill in the animal kingdom. As soon as the word gets out that someone is leaving the company, coworkers start scheming to scavenge the office leftovers—chairs, computer monitors, filing cabinets, even staplers. "This issue is practically everywhere," says Mary Wong, president of a human resources consulting company. "Professionals—anyone you and I would normally consider to be very adult—turn into children" over the prospect of picking an empty office clean of its "goodies." Sometimes—and this is where it gets disrespectful—office scavengers move in even before the employee, who's often been laid off, has left. Ethics consultant Steve Lawler tells the story of a laid-off manager who, just hours after hearing the bad news, was already getting requests for the expensive Herman Miller Aeron chair in which he was still sitting. Office scavenging is a strange and predictable aspect of office life. It happens everywhere. But if you're going to scavenge, and you probably will, do the right thing by maintaining the dignity of departing coworkers: Wait until the office is empty before you strike.[61]

Review 4: Intraorganizational Processes

Today, companies are using reengineering, empowerment, and behavioral informality to change their intraorganizational processes. Through fundamental rethinking and radical redesign of business processes, reengineering changes an organization's orientation from vertical to horizontal. Reengineering changes work processes by decreasing sequential and pooled interdependence and by increasing reciprocal interdependence. Reengineering promises dramatic increases in productivity and customer satisfaction, but it has been criticized as simply an excuse to cut costs and lay off workers. Empowering workers means taking decision-making authority and responsibility from managers and giving it to workers. Empowered workers develop feelings of competence and self-determination and believe that their work has meaning and impact. Workplaces characterized by behavioral informality are spontaneous and casual. The formality or informality of a workplace depends on four factors: language usage, conversational turn taking and topic selection, emotional and proxemic gestures, and physical and contextual cues. Casual dress policies and open office systems are two of the most popular methods for increasing behavioral informality.

5   Interorganizational Processes

An **interorganizational process** is a collection of activities that occur *among companies* to transform inputs into outputs that customers value. In other words, many companies work together to create a product or service that keeps customers happy. For example, when you purchase a Liz Claiborne outfit, you're not just buying from LIZ CLAIBORNE; you're also buying from a network of 250 suppliers in 35 countries from Saipan, to Mexico, to Cambodia, to China that make those clothes for Liz Claiborne. After Liz Claiborne's New York–based designers come up with a concept, it is shipped to a "sourcing" team in Hong Kong, which changes the design as needed to keep costs low and then finds companies that can produce the right fabrics and the entire line of clothing. Those companies then manufacture the first product prototypes and send them back to the New York designers for final inspection and possibly last-minute changes.[64]

> In this section, you'll explore interorganizational processes by learning about **5.1 modular organizations** and **5.2 virtual organizations.**[65]

5.1 Modular Organizations

Stephen Roach, chief economist for investment bank Morgan Stanley, says that companies increasingly want to take "functions that aren't central to their core competency," and outsource them.[66] Except for the core business activities that they can perform better, faster, and cheaper than others, **modular organizations** outsource all remaining business activities to outside companies, suppliers, specialists, or consultants. The term *modular* is used because the business activities purchased from outside companies can be added and dropped as needed, much like adding pieces to a three-dimensional puzzle. Exhibit 9.13 depicts a modular organization in which the company has chosen to keep training, human resources, sales, product design, manufacturing, customer service, research and development, and information technology as core business activities, but it has outsourced the noncore activities of product distribution, web page design, advertising, payroll, accounting, and packaging.

Modular organizations have several advantages. First, because modular organizations pay for outsourced labor, expertise, or manufacturing capabilities only when needed, they can cost significantly less to run than traditional organizations. For example, when APPLE came up with its iPod digital music player, it outsourced the audio chip design and manufacture to SigmaTel in Austin, Texas, and final assembly to Asutek Computers in Taiwan. Doing so not only reduced costs and sped up production (beating Sony's Network Walkman to market), but also allowed Apple to do what it does best—design innovative products with easy-to-use software.[67] Furthermore, after other companies imitated Apple by producing their own digital music

interorganizational process a collection of activities that take place among companies to transform inputs into outputs that customers value

modular organization an organization that outsources noncore business activities to outside companies, suppliers, specialists, or consultants

Exhibit 9.13
Modular Organization

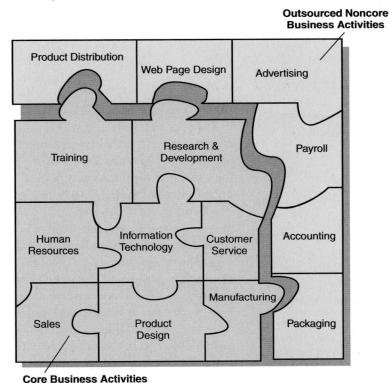

Outsourced Noncore Business Activities

Core Business Activities

PUBLIC DOMAIN

Trivia: What was the original Mechanical Turk? See page 344 for the answer.

mgmt:trend

Crowdsourcing

Companies are tapping into an army of people willing to work for literally pennies. At AMAZON's Mechanical Turk, companies or individuals (called "requesters") post repetitive tasks that can be completed only by human intelligence, such as identifying the best of a set of photos, writing product descriptions, and color-coding clothing sold by online retailers. Most of these jobs take only a few minutes and pay just a few cents. But requesters can also post tasks that are more involved. One manager originally paid a consultant $2,000 for a flow chart of his company's repair process. When the company needed additional work, however, it enlisted a "Turker." The second flow chart cost $5. Keep your eye on the trend of crowdsourcing.

Sources: Jeff Howe, "The Rise of Crowdsourcing," *Wired*, June 2006, 176; Katherine Mieszkowski, "I Make $1.45 a Week, and I Love It!," http://www.salon.com, August 2006; http://www.wikipedia.org, August 2006.

players, Apple was able to take advantage of its lower costs by aggressively cutting prices.[68] To obtain these advantages, however, modular organizations need reliable partners—vendors and suppliers that they can work closely with and can trust.

Modular organizations have disadvantages, too. The primary disadvantage is the loss of control that occurs when key business activities are outsourced to other companies. Also, companies may reduce their competitive advantage in two ways if they mistakenly outsource a core business activity. First, as a result of competitive and technological change, the noncore business activities a company has outsourced may suddenly become the basis for competitive advantage. Second, related to that point, suppliers to whom work is outsourced can sometimes become competitors.

5.2 Virtual Organizations

In contrast to modular organizations in which the interorganizational process revolves around a central company, a **virtual organization** is part of a network in which many companies share skills, costs, capabilities, markets, and customers with each other. Exhibit 9.14 shows a virtual organization in which, for "today," the parts of a virtual company consist of product design, purchasing, manufacturing, advertising, and information technology. Unlike modular organizations, in which the outside organizations are tightly linked to one central company, virtual organizations work with some companies in the network alliance, but not with all. So, whereas a puzzle with various pieces is a fitting metaphor for a modular organization, a potluck dinner is an appropriate metaphor for a virtual organization. All participants bring their finest food dish, but eat only what they want.

Another difference is that the working relationships between modular organizations and outside companies tend to be more stable and longer lasting than the shorter, often temporary relationships found among the virtual companies in a network alliance. The composition of a virtual organization is always changing. The combination of network partners that a virtual corporation has at any one time depends on the expertise needed to solve a particular problem or provide a specific product or service. This is why the businessperson in the network organization shown in Exhibit 9.14 is saying, "Today, I'll have. . . ." Tomorrow, the business could want something completely different. In this sense, the term *virtual organization* means the organization that exists "at the moment." For example, 19 small companies in Pennsylvania have formed a network of virtual organizations that they call the AGILE WEB.[69] Together,

"WHAT'S NEW" COMPANY

virtual organization an organization that is part of a network in which many companies share skills, costs, capabilities, markets, and customers to collectively solve customer problems or provide specific products or services

"WHAT'S NEW" COMPANY

the companies have expertise in product development and design, machining, metal fabrication, die casting, plastic-injection molding, finishing and coating, and the design and manufacture of electronic components. Tony Nickel, who coordinates business opportunities for the 19 Agile Web members, says, "We do have multiple machine shops and multiple sheet-metal shops. If only one is needed, I make the decision based on the nature of the [customer's] request and the areas of specialization of the member firms." He adds, "We've already had one occasion where, while negotiating with a customer, we discovered that we really didn't have the right Web member for a particular part—so we changed members."[70]

Exhibit 9.14
Virtual Organization

Virtual organizations have a number of advantages. They let companies share costs. And, because members can quickly combine their efforts to meet customers' needs, they are fast and flexible. For example, Tony Nickel of the Agile Web says, "Where we think we really can have rapid response is when a customer wants help in the design and building of an assembly or system. Then I can bring members of the Web to the table—or to the customer's facility—right away; the next day, if required. We are able to assemble a team from the Web within 24 hours if that is what the customer wants."[71] Finally, because each member of the network alliance is the "best" at what it does, virtual organizations should in theory provide better products and services in all respects.

As with modular organizations, a disadvantage of virtual organizations is that once work has been outsourced, it can be difficult to control the quality of work done by network partners. The greatest disadvantage, however, is that tremendous managerial skills are required to make a network of independent organizations work well together, especially since their relationships tend to be short and based on a single task or project. Virtual organizations are using two methods to solve this problem. The first is to use a *broker*, like Tony Nickel. In traditional, hierarchical organizations, managers plan, organize, and control. But with the horizontal, interorganizational processes that characterize virtual organizations, the job of a broker is to create and assemble the knowledge, skills, and resources from different companies for outside parties, such as customers.[72] The second way to make networks of virtual organizations more manageable is to use a *virtual organization agreement* that, somewhat like a contract, specifies the schedules, responsibilities, costs, payouts, and liabilities for participating organizations.[73] The AgileWeb has operationalized its virtual organization agreement on a day-to-day basis through web-based software that is used by all 19 companies to schedule work, share design specifications, and provide anything else they need to complete their work for particular customers.[74] For more information on how a virtual organization works, see **http://www.g5technologies.com/agileweb/overview/index.html**.

Review 5: *Interorganizational Processes*

Organizations are using modular and virtual organizations to change interorganizational processes. Because modular organizations outsource all noncore activities to other businesses, they are less expensive to run than traditional companies. However, modular organizations require extremely close relationships with suppliers, may result in a loss of control, and could create new competitors if the wrong business activities are outsourced. Virtual organizations participate in a network in which they share skills, costs, capabilities, markets, and customers. As customer problems, products, or services change, the combination of virtual organizations that work together changes. Virtual organizations can reduce costs, respond quickly, and, if they can successfully coordinate their efforts, produce outstanding products and service.

KEY TERMS

Flexibility and Structure

Every organization needs some degree of flexibility and standardization. In other words, companies need to have enough flexibility in their organizations to respond to changes in their business environment, but firms also must have certain structures in place to ensure smooth operations. For example, if someone gets hurt on company property, clear procedures about what to do in the case of an accident help managers respond quickly and confidently. But being overly committed to following rules can hamstring an organization and keep it from growing. As a manager, you will probably encounter both types of situations, and to respond appropriately you will need to have an idea of how comfortable you are in a formal environment versus a more loosely structured workplace. Every organization needs some degree of flexibility to adapt to new situations, and some degree of standardization to make routine tasks and decisions as efficient and effective as possible.[75] In this assessment, indicate the extent to which you agree or disagree with the following statements. Use this scale for your responses:

1	Strongly disagree
2	Disagree
3	Slightly disagree
4	Neutral
5	Slightly agree
6	Agree
7	Strongly agree

1. If a written rule does not cover some situation, we make up informal rules for doing things as we go along.

   1   2   3   4   5   6   7

2. I feel that I am my own boss in most matters.

   1   2   3   4   5   6   7

3. There are many things in my business that are not covered by some formal procedure.

   1   2   3   4   5   6   7

4. A person can make his or her own decisions without checking with somebody else.

   1   2   3   4   5   6   7

5. Usually, my contact with my company and its representatives involves doing things "by the rule book."

   1   2   3   4   5   6   7

6. How things are done here is left up to the person doing the work.

   1   2   3   4   5   6   7

7. Contacts with my company and its representatives are on a formal, pre-planned basis.

   1   2   3   4   5   6   7

8. People here are allowed to do almost anything as they please.

   1   2   3   4   5   6   7

9. I ignore the rules and reach informal agreements to handle some situations.

1   2   3   4   5   6   7

10. Most people here make their own rules on the job.

1   2   3   4   5   6   7

11. When rules and procedures exist in my company, they are usually written agreements.

1   2   3   4   5   6   7

12. The employees are constantly being checked on for rule violations.

1   2   3   4   5   6   7

13. People here feel as though they are constantly being watched, to see that they obey all the rules

1   2   3   4   5   6   7

Scoring

Determine your score by entering your response to each survey item below, as follows. In blanks that say *regular score*, simply enter your response for that item. If your response was a 6, place a 6 in the *regular* score blank. In blanks that say *reverse score*, subtract your response from 8 and enter the result. So if your response was a 6, place a 2 (8 − 6 = 2) in the *reverse score* blank.

1. reverse score   _____
2. reverse score   _____
3. reverse score   _____
4. reverse score   _____
5. regular score   _____
6. reverse score   _____
7. regular score   _____
8. reverse score   _____
9. reverse score   _____
10. reverse score   _____
11. regular score   _____
12. regular score   _____
13. regular score   _____

TOTAL = _____

You can see where you fall on the formality continuum and find the interpretation of your score at: **academic .cengage.com/ management/williams.**

□ ☑ □ □ □

MANAGEMENT DECISION

Garbage Jobs

Glancing at the newspaper machine in the lobby, you are happy to see the headline proclaiming the end of the garbage collectors' strike in a nearby city.[76] That kind of strike tends to have a ripple effect on neighboring areas, and as the manager of a private waste collection company in the region, you breathe a sigh of relief.

Nonetheless, as you walk to your office, you can't help thinking about the job of your garbage collectors. It's repetitive, hot (or cold, depending on the season), anonymous, and relatively thankless. Your employees work in pairs, so each truck has one driver and one "thrower"—not much variety for either worker. There's not much on-the-job interaction either, as the driver is in the cab and the thrower rides on the back of the truck. And with the company looking into purchasing newer trucks that automatically lift and dump the garbage cans, you may even go to one person per truck.

In addition, to minimize the time it takes to collect the trash, you assign each team to the same neighborhood week after week. That ensures maximum efficiency: drivers subconsciously time traffic lights, pace themselves for starts and stops, and know the route without needing to consult a map. Even when collectors know the route, the work can be grueling. Each route has to be finished each day; no one will tolerate garbage left on the curb after the assigned pickup day. So even if a traffic accident or construction brings traffic to a standstill, the garbage has to be collected each day according to schedule.

The more you think about it, the more the job sounds dull—and somewhat stressful. As you fire up your computer and begin to look at your favorite industry blog, you wonder if you can make the job more interesting for your employees. Scanning the screen, you link to an article about a region in Britain that is putting defibrillators in garbage trucks to complement the ambulance service in rural areas. Well, that's not quite what you had in mind for making garbage collecting interesting for your employees, but still, it's something.

Questions

1. Can you use the job characteristics model (JCM) to redesign the job of the trash collector to be internally motivating? How?

2. Assume that the trash collection job is not internally motivating. Identify areas where you can strengthen the job's core characteristics and give specific examples.

3. Is it possible to redesign the very specialized job of a garbage collector to make it more satisfying? Is a redesign feasible? In other words, do you redesign the job or keep it as is? Explain your reasoning.

MANAGEMENT TEAM DECISION

Letting Go at Lego

By definition, toys should be fun. Unfortunately for you, competing in today's toy industry is anything but.[77] Cutthroat competition and children's changing interests have pushed toymakers to consolidate, cut costs, and grow through licensing agreements with media giants like Disney and Nickelodeon, something many toymakers consider to be selling out.

No one needs to explain the crushing pressure to you—you're the new CEO of Lego, the first outsider in the company's history to run the family-owned business—because you were hired to save the company from sure decline. Last year, Lego had over $1 billion in sales. Its proprietary manufacturing operation pumps out 15 billion components a year—that's 1.7 million bricks, Lego people, and other elements per hour. By the numbers, Lego is the world's leading tire maker, producing 306 million tiny rubber tires a year for its sets. Lego's iconic bricks are so versatile that with a pack of only six bricks, a child can create 915,103,765 unique configurations. It's no wonder that Lego beat out Barbie and the teddy bear to be named Toy of the Century by *Fortune* magazine and by the British Toy Retailers Association.

Despite the volume of product being produced, the perennial accolades, and a reputation for nurturing creativity in children, Lego is losing money at an alarming rate. On last year's $1 billion in sales, the company lost a whopping $240 million. It also carries about $750 million in debt. That means you begin your stint as CEO squarely behind the eight ball. First on your list of things to do: change the company mission from "nurturing the child" to "I'm here to make money for the company."

Part of what's weighing Lego down is the fact that the company does it all. Lego uses its own designers to develop new products; other companies use a combination of in-house talent and innovation labs to come up with new product ideas. Lego manufactures its bricks (and other products) on extruding machines it developed itself at company-owned factories in Denmark and Switzerland, where labor costs are stratospheric; 70 percent of the world's toys are manufactured in China by contract manufacturers hired just to produce the toys and with labor that costs pennies on the kroner. Lego distributes all of its own products; other companies use third-party logistics companies like DHL and UPS to manage distribution. Lego even books $5.2 million in travel a year through an in-house travel agency that uses proprietary software; most companies use dedicated travel services, like American Express Travel.

To bring Lego back into the black, you've got to cut costs, and the fastest way to cut costs is outsourcing. The biggest savings would come from outsourcing your production, but that also carries the biggest risks. Controlling your manufacturing would be difficult. You'd have to share your machinery technology—what if a contractor started using your technology and specifications to make black-market Legos, something not at all inconceivable if you outsourced to China? And there's the fact that Legos are part of the fabric of Billund, the Danish town of 6,500 where the bricks were invented and where Lego's headquarters employs most of the company's 8,000 workers. Most of the people in Billund work for Lego. Still, savings from outsourcing manufacturing alone would bring the company to nearly break-even levels.

Controlling distribution helps you manage inventories and track sales trends, but should Lego really operate its own distribution network? So many companies specialize in this area that it's hard to equal their capabilities. Even something that is as seemingly easy to outsource as travel is not so easy. In-house travel agents know the ins and outs of Lego's travel policy; an outside provider is not always able to recognize a breach in the policy. Lego managers book 10,000 air tickets a year, and the head of the travel department says her team saves the company $325,000 in administrative costs alone over working with an outside company.

One thing is certain: You're not going to be able to make a decision on what to outsource (if anything) without consulting your management team. Form a team of four or five students to act as the management team for Lego. You may want to refer to Exhibit 9.13 as you work through the following questions.

Questions

1. What risks, if any, does outsourcing pose to Lego's corporate identity?

2. What do you think Lego's core and noncore business activities should be?

3. Do you outsource production, which will by itself achieve your cost-cutting goal, or do you outsource a smattering of other functions and keep Lego a "toymaker" rather than a "toy marketer"?

PRACTICE BEING A MANAGER

Effective organization is vital to the accomplishment of company objectives. Two critical aspects of effective organization are departmentalization and the design of jobs. In this role play exercise you will have the opportunity to experience some of the work dynamics surrounding the grouping of workers and the design of jobs.

Step 1: Form work groups. Your professor will form groups, and give you a role assignment.

Step 2: Review your role. Read your role assignment carefully and prepare to begin working per your role assignment.

Step 3 (10–20 minutes): Begin acting. When your professor directs you to begin you should start working as assigned by your role.

Step 4: Compile your results. Total your results by work group, and compare across the teams.

Step 5: Debrief as a class. Discuss the results as a class. What factors seemed to play a role in the efficiency and effectiveness of the work groups? What role did organization and job design play? If this were an actual organizational work group, what might you do to improve performance and worker satisfaction?

DEVELOP YOUR CAREER POTENTIAL

"Work" in Someone Else's Shoes

Why is learning to see things from someone else's perspective one of the most difficult things to do in today's workplace? Sometimes, the inability to see things as others see them has to do with the people involved. Inexperience, ignorance, and selfishness can all play a role. In most organizations, however, the inability to see things from someone else's perspective results from the jobs themselves, not the people who do them. Because jobs limit who we talk to, what we talk about, what we think about, and what we care about at work, it should not be a surprise that people who perform different jobs have very different views about each other and the workplace.

For example, at Southwest Airlines the pilots who fly the planes and the ground crews who unload, load,

and refuel them had little appreciation for each other. The ground crews felt that the pilots treated them like second-class citizens. The pilots couldn't understand why the ground crews weren't doing more to get their planes out of the gates and in the air as fast as possible. To improve understanding and help them see things from each other's perspective, Southwest created a program called Cutting Edge, in which the captains and ground crews learned a lot about each other's jobs. For example, the pilots brought the ground crews into their cockpits and showed them the detailed processes they were required to follow to get planes ready for departure. The pilots, on the other hand, gained appreciation and understanding by actually working as members of Southwest's ground crews. After several days of demanding ground crew work, Southwest pilot Captain Mark Boyter said:

> I remember one time when I was working the ramp [as a member of a ground crew] in Los Angeles. I was dead tired. I had flown that morning and had a couple of legs in, so I got out of my uniform and jumped into my ramp clothes. That afternoon was very hot. It was in the 80s—I can't imagine how they do it on a 120-degree day in Phoenix. I was tired and hungry and hadn't had a break. Then I saw this pilot sitting up there in the cockpit eating his frozen yogurt. I said to myself, "Man, I'd like to be up there now." Then I caught myself. I'm up there every day. Now, I know that pilot has been up since 3:00 in the morning. I know that he's been flying an airplane since 6:00 AM. I know it's 3:00 in the afternoon and he hasn't had a chance to get off and have a meal yet today. I know all that, and yet, the yogurt still looks really good to me. Then I thought, "How can a ramp agent [on the ground crew] in Los Angeles who works his butt off for two or three years, working double shifts two or three times a week, understand this? It hit me that there's a big gap in understanding here."[78]

The misunderstandings between Southwest's pilots and ground crews are not unique. All organizations experience them. Nurses and doctors, teachers and students, and managers and employees all have difficulty seeing things from each other's perspective. As Southwest's Cutting Edge program shows, however, you can minimize differences and build understanding by "working" in someone else's shoes.

Questions

1. Describe the job-related differences or tensions where you work. Who is involved? What jobs do they do? Explain why the job-related differences or tensions exist.

2. Since the best way to see things from someone else's perspective is to "work" in his or her shoes, see if you can spend a day, a morning, or even two hours performing one of these jobs. If that's not possible, spend some time carefully observing the jobs and then interview several people who perform them. Describe your boss's reaction to this request. Was he or she supportive? Why or why not?

3. Answer the following questions after you have worked the job or conducted your interviews. What most surprised you about this job? What was easiest? What was hardest? Explain. Now that you've had the chance to see things as others see them, what do you think would happen, good or bad, from letting other people in your organization work in someone else's shoes? Explain.

Trivia answer: The original Mechanical Turk was an 18th-century chess playing automaton that purportedly could beat anyone at chess. The Turk was a mannequin, but the machine concealed a human chess master who would actuate the Turk with mechanical controls. The Turk beat many statesmen and luminaries, including Napoleon Bonaparte and Benjamin Franklin. Read more in Tom Standage's book The Mechanical Turk.

REEL TO REAL

Reality Bites

Reality Bites is an American film starring Winona Ryder, Ethan Hawke, Ben Stiller, Steve Zahn, Janeane Garofalo, and David Spade. The plot follows the life of recent college graduate Lelaine Pierce (Ryder), who wants to make a documentary about her friends as a way to capture the strife and problems confronting her generation. In this scene, she is applying for a job at Wienerschnitzel, a fast-food restaurant managed by David Spade.

What to Watch for and Ask Yourself

1. Using the terms from the chapter, outline the job of cashier as Spade is describing it in the clip.
2. Is the cashier position a line or staff function?
3. Describe the atmosphere at the restaurant.

MANAGEMENT WORKPLACE
Lonely Planet's World Is Flat

When travelers Tony and Maureen Wheeler founded Lonely Planet in the early 1970s, they didn't intend to create a globe-spanning company. They didn't necessarily plan to start a publishing company. As newlyweds, they had just completed an overland trip from London through Asia, winding up in Australia. All they really wanted to do was finance their next trip—it never occurred to them to stop traveling around the world. So they wrote and published the first Lonely Planet guidebook, *Across Asia on the Cheap*; it was an instant bestseller among world wanderers.

With just two people, the Wheelers naturally didn't think about organization. They traveled, wrote, and published whatever they wanted. By the mid-1970s, they had completed *Nepal and Trekking in the Himalayas* and were working on a group of guides covering Australia, Europe, Africa, and New Zealand. In 1981, *Lonely Planet India* was published and became a travel best-seller. By then, Lonely Planet had a staff of 10. Watch the video to see how the Wheelers organized Lonely Planet's management workplace.

What to Watch for and Ask Yourself

1. In what ways is Lonely Planet decentralized? In what ways is it centralized?
2. What type of departmentalization does Lonely Planet use? Do you think another type of departmentalization would be as or more successful? Which one? Why?
3. How does Lonely Planet benefit from its flat organizational structure (limited hierarchy)? What does a flat structure indicate about the organization?

CHAPTER 10

Managing Teams

Learning Outcomes:

1 Explain the good and bad of using teams.

2 Recognize and understand the different kinds of teams.

3 Understand the general characteristics of work teams.

4 Explain how to enhance work team effectiveness.

In This Chapter:

WHAT WOULD YOU DO?

Kaiser Permanente, Oakland, California.[1] With 8.5 million health plan members in nine states and Washington, D.C., 148,884 employees, 12,879 physicians, 37 medical centers, 400 medical offices, and $31.1 billion in operating revenues, Kaiser Permanente is the largest not-for-profit managed care organization in the U.S. Overall, Kaiser has a solid reputation. Consumer Reports ranks Kaiser Permanente as an average or better hospital system. U.S. News and World Report ranks Kaiser Permanente Northern California 58th out of 257 health plans and Kaiser Permanente Southern California as 88th.

But lately Kaiser has come under intensive scrutiny for a series of management and patient care issues. For example, after Northern California Kaiser Permanente began an in-house program that required kidney transplant candidates to obtain medical treatment through their local Kaiser medical center, 56 people received kidney transplants, but twice that many died waiting for a kidney. In contrast, at other California transplant centers, more than twice as many people received kidneys than died during the same period. Another serious problem came to light when the California Office of Statewide Health Planning and Development determined that Kaiser had 5 of the 28 hospitals with the highest pneumonia death rates in the state. This was particularly troubling because pneumonia, the sixth-leading cause of death in the U.S., can be prevented with good care. "Timely diagnosis and treatment can greatly improve a patient's chances of surviving," said Mary Tran, a patient data analysis manager who helped with the study for the state agency. In other words, frequent pneumonia in your hospitals means that your medical control processes are breaking down. A well-run hospital system like Kaiser should not have problems treating pneumonia. Something is going wrong. But what?

You immediately pull your top managers together to analyze the problem and come up with potential solutions. One of your vice presidents mentioned that she had read that a number of hospitals use teams to improve patient care and service, maintain a clean and sanitary environment, manage costs, reduce patient mortality rate, and reduce medical errors. For instance, Baptist Memphis Hospital in Memphis, Tennessee, empowered Rapid Response Teams to call in the hospital's Medical Emergency Team to care for seriously ill patients whose condition was worsening. After doing so, the number of cardiac arrests dropped by 26 percent, and survival rates nearly doubled from 13 percent to 24 percent. Likewise, Stanford University Hospital uses Patient-Centered Care Teams, who are responsible for everything from admission to discharge, and Process-Centered Care Teams, who are charged with identifying hospital processes and making them effective and efficient.

Successful teams might help Kaiser reduce medical errors, increase quality of patient care, increase customer satisfaction, and could help reduce costs. And, you have to try new approaches, because not taking any action is no longer an option. You realize if you are going to use teams that you'll have to do your homework by answering these questions. First, does it make sense for Kaiser to use teams, and, if so, what kind of teams should it use and where? Second, how should people who work on teams be trained and paid? You have to find a way to encourage individual initiative, while at the same time encouraging people to work together on teams. Also, it's incredibly difficult to attract and retain nurses and highly trained medical personnel, so don't overlook that as you consider what to do. Third, who leads the teams, physicians, managers, or employees? And what roles should those leaders play? Finally, how large or small should the teams be and how do you build cohesion and make sure the team norms are functional and productive. **If you were in charge at Kaiser, what would you do?**

"WHAT'S NEW" COMPANIES

THREE COUNTIES

LONGABERGER COMPANY

WHOLE FOODS

INDUSTRIAL LIGHT & MAGIC

FORD MOTOR COMPANY

ORPHEUS CHAMBER ORCHESTRA

GENERAL ELECTRIC

EATON CORPORATION

AND OTHERS . . .

A growing number of organizations are significantly improving their effectiveness by establishing work teams. In fact, 91 percent of U.S. companies use teams and groups of one kind or another to solve specific problems.[2] Nonetheless, with the exception of early adopters such as Procter & Gamble and Cummins Engine, which began using teams in 1962 and 1973, respectively, many companies did not establish work teams until the mid to late 1980s. Boeing, Caterpillar, Champion International, Ford Motor Company, and General Electric, for example, set up their first teams in the 1980s.[3] So, most companies have been using teams for only 20 to 25 years, if that long. In other words, teams are a relatively new phenomenon in companies, and there's still much for organizations to learn about managing them.

We begin this chapter by reviewing the advantages and disadvantages of teams and exploring when companies should use them instead of more traditional approaches. Next, we discuss the different types of work teams and the characteristics common to all teams. The chapter ends by focusing on the practical steps to managing teams—team goals and priorities, and organizing, training, and compensating teams.

WHY WORK TEAMS?

Work teams consist of a small number of people with complementary skills who hold themselves mutually accountable for pursuing a common purpose, achieving performance goals, and improving interdependent work processes.[4] By this definition, computer programmers working on separate projects in the same department of a company would not be considered a team. To be a team, the programmers would have to be interdependent and share responsibility and accountability for the quality and amount of computer code they produced.[5] In many industries, teams are growing in importance because they help organizations respond to specific problems and challenges. Though work teams are not the answer for every situation or organization, if the right teams are used properly and in the right settings, teams can dramatically improve company performance over more traditional management approaches and instill a sense of vitality in the workplace that is otherwise difficult to achieve.

> **After reading the next two sections, you should be able to**
>
> 1 explain the good and bad of using teams.
>
> 2 recognize and understand the different kinds of teams.

1 The Good and Bad of Using Teams

Let's begin our discussion of teams by learning about **1.1 the advantages of teams**, **1.2 the disadvantages of teams**, and **1.3 when to use and not use teams**.

1.1 The Advantages of Teams

Companies are making greater use of teams because teams have been shown to improve customer satisfaction, product and service quality, speed and efficiency in

work team a small number of people with complementary skills who hold themselves mutually accountable for pursuing a common purpose, achieving performance goals, and improving interdependent work processes product development, employee job satisfaction, and decision making.[6] For example, one survey indicated that 80 percent of companies with more than 100 employees use teams, and 90 percent of all U.S. employees work part of their day in a team.[7]

Teams help businesses increase *customer satisfaction* in several ways. One way is to create work teams that are trained to meet the needs of specific customers. Hewitt Associates, a consulting firm, manages benefits administration for hundreds of multinational client firms. To ensure customer satisfaction, Hewitt reengineered its customer service center and created specific teams to handle benefits-related questions posed by employees of specific client organizations.[8] Similarly, THREE COUNTIES, a fund and portfolio management company, uses a team structure in which specific teams are responsible for specific groups of customers, thereby ensuring high quality service necessary for customer satisfaction.[9]

Businesses also create problem-solving teams and employee involvement teams to study ways to improve overall customer satisfaction and make recommendations for improvements. Teams like these typically meet on a weekly or monthly basis. Every day at the LONGABERGER COMPANY, 2,500 skilled weavers make over 40,000 high-quality baskets (which sell for $30 to $260). When productivity began to drop, management turned to an employee involvement group to solve the problem. After studying 40 basket makers for three weeks, the team found that the weavers often had the wrong materials. The team came up with a solution that makes sure each weaver has the proper kinds of wood veneers used to make the different baskets. Before the new system, workers ran out of the proper materials 53 times per day. Now, that happens only 9 times per day. And because the new system has also cut scrap (leftover, unusable materials) by 75 percent, the company is saving $3 million per year.[10]

Teams also help firms improve *product and service quality* in several ways.[11] In contrast to traditional organizational structures where management is responsible for organizational outcomes and performance, teams take direct responsibility for the quality of the products and service they produce. At WHOLE FOODS, a supermarket chain that sells groceries and health foods, the 10 teams that manage each store are responsible for store quality and performance; they are also directly accountable because the size of their team bonus depends on the store's performance. Productive teams get an extra $1.50 to $2.00 per hour in every other paycheck. As a result, Whole Food teams don't want friends on their teams—they want talented, productive workers.[12] And making teams directly responsible for service and product quality pays off. At Whole Foods, comparable store sales, meaning a particular store's sales this year compared with its sales last year, are increasing between 7.7 and 10 percent per year on average! Likewise, a survey by *Industry Week* found that 42 percent of the companies that use teams report revenues of more than $250,000 per employee, compared with only 25 percent of the companies that don't use teams.[13]

A team-based structure is part of the reason for the resounding success of Whole Foods Market. Employee teams are responsible for all aspects of the store's operations. This Whole Foods team is in charge of preparing the seafood section for the opening of the New York City store.

As you learned in Chapter 7, companies that are slow to innovate or integrate new features and technologies into their products are at a competitive disadvantage. Therefore, a third reason that teams are increasingly popular is that they can increase *speed and efficiency when designing and manufacturing products.*[14] Traditional product design proceeds sequentially, meaning that one department, such as engineering or manufacturing, has to finish its work on the design before the next department, such as

GETTY IMAGES

marketing, can start. Unfortunately, not only is sequential development slow, but it also encourages departments to work in isolation from one another.[15] A faster and better way to design products is to use *overlapping development phases*, which often requires the use of teams. With overlapping development phases, teams of employees, consisting of members from the different functional areas in a firm (such as engineering, manufacturing, and marketing), work on the product design at the same time. Because all of the different functional areas are involved in the design process from the start, the company can avoid most of the delays and frustration associated with sequential development. INDUSTRIAL LIGHT & MAGIC (ILM), founded by George Lucas, the originator and producer of *Star Wars*, has won 19 Academy Awards for visual effects and technical achievement. ILM uses overlapping development phases to quickly produce specialized computer effects for movies. Teams of artists and animators work simultaneously on different scenes, such as the opening and closing of a movie, to speed up production. Visual-effects producer Jacqui Lopez says, "When we get down to the wire, our artists need every second they can get in front of their computers."[16] Oftentimes, she says, "Being late is not an option. The publicity is already locked in, and the studios have schedules to keep. We can't be late."[17] And ILM has *never* been late. Indeed, whether the movie is *Harry Potter* or *Pirates of the Caribbean*, when film studios and directors fall behind, they regularly come to ILM to avoid missing deadlines.

"*Being late is not an option. The publicity is already locked in, and the studios have schedules to keep. We can't be late.*"

JACQUI LOPEZ, VISUAL-EFFECTS PRODUCER, INDUSTRIAL LIGHT & MAGIC

Another reason for using teams is that teamwork often leads to increased *job satisfaction*.[18] One reason that teamwork can be more satisfying than traditional work is that it gives workers a chance to improve their skills. This is often accomplished through **cross-training**, in which team members are taught how to do all or most of the jobs performed by the other team members. Mary Keene used to stand in one spot for eight hours a day using a power chisel to chip cast iron from Ford automobile engines. She says, "You thought your arms would fall off. It was the worst job I had there." Today, thanks to cross-training, Mary and her Plant 2 coworkers at FORD MOTOR COMPANY's Brook Park, Ohio, manufacturing facility perform seven different jobs each shift, such as installing ignition coils, taking apart engines, restarting machinery after it breaks down, and contacting suppliers if engine parts are of subpar quality.[19] The advantage for the organization is that cross-training allows a team to function normally when one member is absent, quits, or is transferred. The advantage for workers is that cross-training broadens their skills and increases their capabilities while also making their work more varied and interesting. Indeed, Ford's Mary Keene says, "Plant 2 is the best we've ever had it." Huck Granakis, the United Auto Workers' building chairman and a member of Plant 2's operating committee, says, "They love it. I know of no one who has quit to go to another job."[20]

A second reason that teamwork is satisfying is that work teams often receive proprietary business information that is available only to managers at most companies. For example, at Whole Foods, the supermarket chain that sells groceries and health foods, team members are given full access to their store's financial information and everyone's salaries, including those of the store manager and the

"WHAT'S NEW" COMPANY

"WHAT'S NEW" COMPANY

cross-training training team members to do all or most of the jobs performed by the other team members

CEO.[21] Each day, next to the time clock, Whole Foods employees can see the previous day's sales for each team, as well as the sales on the same day from the previous year. Each week, team members can examine the same information, broken down by team, for all of the Whole Foods stores in their region. And each month, store managers review information on profitability, including sales, product costs, wages, and operating profits, with each team in the store. Since team members decide how much to spend, what to order, what things should cost, and how many team members should work each day, this information is critical to making teams work at Whole Foods.[22] Whole Foods creates an empowering work environment to honor one of its core values: "supporting team member excellence and happiness."[23]

Team members also gain job satisfaction from unique leadership responsibilities that typically are not available in traditional organizations. For example, in contrast to most orchestras, which are led by one conductor who is clearly in charge, at the award-winning, New York City–based ORPHEUS CHAMBER ORCHESTRA, the concertmaster's role, as they call it, is rotated among different members of the orchestra. Flutist Susan Palma-Nidel says that assuming the concertmaster's role "has allowed me to discover strengths that I didn't know I had. Not only have I helped lead the group, but I've also been interviewed by the media—something I never thought I'd do. If I hadn't been forced to do those things, I'm not sure that I ever would have."[24] Furthermore, rotating leadership among team members can lead to more participation and cooperation in team decision making and improved team performance.[25]

Finally, teams share many of the advantages of group decision making discussed in Chapter 5. For instance, because team members possess different knowledge, skills, abilities, and experiences, a team is able to view problems from multiple perspectives. This diversity of viewpoints increases the odds that team decisions will solve the underlying causes of problems and not just address the symptoms. The increased knowledge and information available to teams also make it easier for them to generate more alternative solutions, which is a critical part of improving the quality of decisions. Because team members are involved in decision-making processes, they are also likely to be more committed to making those decisions work. In short, teams can do a much better job than individuals in two important steps of the decision-making process: defining the problem and generating alternative solutions. Exhibit 10.1 summarizes the advantages and disadvantages of teams (disadvantages are discussed in the next section).

Exhibit 10.1

Advantages and Disadvantages of Teams

ADVANTAGES 👍	DISADVANTAGES 👎
☺ Customer satisfaction	☹ Initially high employee turnover
☺ Product and service quality	☹ Social loafing
☺ Speed and efficiency in product development	☹ Disadvantages of group decision making (groupthink, inefficient meetings, domination by a minority, lack of accountability)
☺ Employee job satisfaction	
☺ Better decision making and problem solving (multiple perspectives, more alternative solutions, increased commitment to decisions)	

doing the right thing

Don't Be a Team Slacker—Do Your Share

Given the amount of teamwork required in business classes, most of you have encountered slackers in student groups. Perhaps you've even "slacked" yourself from time to time. From an ethical perspective, though, slacking is clearly wrong. In reality, it's no different from cheating on an exam. When you slack, you're relying on others to do your work. You benefit without putting forth effort. And "your" team's project, paper, or presentation hasn't benefited from your contributions. In fact, it's very likely that your slacking may have significantly hurt "your" team's performance. Furthermore, in the real world, the consequences of team slacking, such as lost sales, poorer decisions, lower-quality service or products, or lower productivity, are much larger. So, do the right thing. Whether it's in class or in business, don't be a slacker. Don't cheat your teammates. Pull your share of the "rope."

social loafing behavior in which team members withhold their efforts and fail to perform their share of the work

1.2 The Disadvantages of Teams

Although teams can significantly improve customer satisfaction, product and service quality, speed and efficiency in product development, employee job satisfaction, and decision making, using teams does not guarantee these positive outcomes. In fact, if you've ever participated in team projects in your classes, you're probably already aware of some of the problems inherent in work teams. Despite all of their promise, teams and teamwork are also prone to these significant disadvantages: initially high turnover, social loafing, and the problems associated with group decision making.

The first disadvantage of work teams is *initially high turnover*. Teams aren't for everyone, and some workers balk at the responsibility, effort, and learning required in team settings. When **GENERAL ELECTRIC**'s Salisbury plant switched to teams, the turnover rate jumped from near zero to 14 percent. Plant manager Roger Gasaway says of teams and teamwork, "It's not all wonderful stuff."[26] Other people may quit because they object to the way team members closely scrutinize each other's job performance, particularly when teams are small. Randy Savage, who works for **EATON CORPORATION**, a manufacturer of car and truck parts, said, "They say there are no bosses here, but if you screw up, you find one pretty fast." Beverly Reynolds, who quit Eaton's team-based system after nine months, says her coworkers "weren't standing watching me, but from afar, they were watching me." And even though her teammates were willing to help her improve her job performance, she concludes, "As it turns out, it just wasn't for me at all."[27]

Social loafing is another disadvantage of work teams. **Social loafing** occurs when workers withhold their efforts and fail to perform their share of the work.[28] A 19th-century French engineer named Maximilian Ringlemann first documented social loafing when he found that one person pulling on a rope alone exerted an average of 63 kilograms of force on the rope. In groups of three, the average force dropped to 53 kilograms per person. In groups of eight, the average dropped to just 31 kilograms per person. Ringlemann concluded that the larger the team, the smaller the individual effort. In fact, social loafing is more likely to occur in larger groups where identifying and monitoring the efforts of individual team members can be difficult.[29] In other words, social loafers count on being able to blend into the background, where their lack of effort isn't easily spotted. From team-based class projects, most students already know about social loafers or "slackers," who contribute poor, little, or no work whatsoever. Not surprisingly, a study of 250 student teams found that the most talented students are typically the least satisfied with teamwork because of having to carry "slackers" and do a disproportionate share of their team's work.[30] Perceptions of fairness are negatively related to the extent of social loafing within teams.[31]

How prevalent is social loafing on teams? One study found that when team activities were not mandatory, only 25 percent of manufacturing workers volunteered to join problem-solving teams, 70 percent were quiet, passive supporters (that is, they didn't put forth effort), and 5 percent were actively opposed to these activities.[32] Another study found that on management teams, 56 percent of the managers, or more than half, withheld their effort in one way or another. Exhibit 10.2 lists the factors that encourage people to withhold effort in teams.

Finally, teams share many of the *disadvantages of group decision making* discussed in Chapter 5, such as groupthink. In *groupthink*, members of highly cohesive groups feel intense pressure not to disagree with each other so that the group can approve a proposed solution. Because groupthink restricts discussion and leads to consideration of a limited number of alternative solutions, it usually results in poor decisions. Also, team decision making takes considerable time, and team meetings can often be unproductive and inefficient. Another possible pitfall is *minority domination*, where just one or two people dominate team discussions, thus restricting consideration of different problem definitions and alternative solutions. Finally, team members may not feel accountable for the decisions and actions taken by the "team."

1.3 When to Use Teams

As the two previous subsections made clear, teams have significant advantages *and* disadvantages. Therefore, the question is not whether to use teams, but when and where to use teams for maximum benefit and minimum cost. As Doug Johnson, associate director at the Center for Collaborative Organizations at the University of North Texas, puts it, "Teams are a means to an end, not an end in themselves. You have to ask yourself questions first. Does the work require interdependence? Will the team philosophy fit company strategy? Will management make a long-term commitment to this process?"[33] Exhibit 10.3 provides some additional guidelines on when to use or not use teams.[34]

Exhibit 10.2

Factors That Encourage People to Withhold Effort in Teams

1.	**The presence of someone with expertise**. Team members will withhold effort when another team member is highly qualified to make a decision or comment on an issue.
2.	**The presentation of a compelling argument**. Team members will withhold effort if the arguments for a course of action are very persuasive or similar to their own thinking.
3.	**Lacking confidence in one's ability to contribute**. Team members will withhold effort if they are unsure about their ability to contribute to discussions, activities, or decisions. This is especially so for high-profile decisions.
4.	**An unimportant or meaningless decision**. Team members will withhold effort by mentally withdrawing or adopting a "who cares" attitude if decisions don't affect them or their units, or if they don't see a connection between their efforts and their team's successes or failures.
5.	**A dysfunctional decision-making climate**. Team members will withhold effort if other team members are frustrated or indifferent or if a team is floundering or disorganized.

Source: P. W. Mulvey, J. F. Veiga, & P. M. Elsass, "When Teammates Raise a White Flag," *Academy of Management Executive* 10, no. 1 (1996): 40–49.

USE TEAMS WHEN . . .	**STOP** DON'T USE TEAMS WHEN . . .
✓ there is a clear, engaging reason or purpose.	✗ there isn't a clear, engaging reason or purpose.
✓ the job can't be done unless people work together.	✗ the job can be done by people working independently.
✓ rewards can be provided for teamwork and team performance.	✗ rewards are provided for individual effort and performance.
✓ ample resources are available.	✗ the necessary resources are not available.
✓ teams will have clear authority to manage and change how work gets done.	✗ management will continue to monitor and influence how work gets done.

Source: R. Wageman, "Critical Success Factors for Creating Superb Self-Managing Teams," *Organizational Dynamics* 26, no. 1 (1997): 49–61.

Exhibit 10.3

When to Use or Not Use Teams

First, teams should be used when there is a clear, engaging reason or purpose for using them. Too many companies use teams because they're popular or because the companies assume that teams can fix all problems. Teams are much more likely to succeed if they know why they exist and what they are supposed to accomplish, and more likely to fail if they don't. For example, at **CBS**, chief information officer Amy Berkowitz has split a sizable information technology staff into four different groups that support four kinds of company software—finance and administration, sales and traffic, programming and production, and interactive systems. Project managers oversee three to five dedicated work teams in each area. Berkowitz says, "The key is to make sure [the work teams] have a very focused purpose. And that they're very outcome-based."[35] Consequently, each support team is now measured on adaptability, speed, and innovation. Jon Katzenbach, coauthor of *The Wisdom of Teams*, supports Berkowitz's approach, saying, "If groups want to achieve team performance, the most important factor is not the leader of the team; it is the clarity around the performance purpose for that group. The more clear and compelling that is, the more naturally those people will function as a team."[36]

> If groups want to achieve team performance, the most important factor is not the leader of the team; it is the clarity around the performance purpose for that group. The more clear and compelling that is, the more naturally those people will function as a team.

JON KATZENBACH, COAUTHOR, *THE WISDOM OF TEAMS*

Second, teams should be used when the job can't be done unless people work together. This typically means that teams are needed when tasks are complex, require multiple perspectives, or require repeated interaction with others to complete. For example, contrary to stories of legendary programmers who write software programs by themselves, **MICROSOFT** uses teams to write computer code because of the enormous complexity of today's software. Most software simply has too many options and features for one person (or even one team) to complete it all. Likewise, Microsoft uses teams because writing good software requires repeated interaction with others. Microsoft ensures this interaction by having its teams "check in" their computer code every few days. The different pieces of code written by the different teams are then compiled to create an updated working build or prototype of the software. The next day, all the teams and team members begin testing and debugging the new build. Over and over again, the computer code is compiled, sent back to the teams to be tested and improved, and then compiled and tested again.[37]

If tasks are simple and don't require multiple perspectives or repeated interaction with others, however, teams should not be used.[38] For instance, production levels dropped by 23 percent when LEVI STRAUSS introduced teams in its factories. Levi Strauss's mistake was assuming that teams were appropriate for garment work, where workers perform single, specialized tasks, like sewing zippers or belt loops. Because this kind of work does not require interaction with others, Levi Strauss unwittingly pitted the faster workers against the slower workers on each team. Arguments, infighting, insults, and threats were common between faster workers and the slower workers who held back team performance. One seamstress even had to physically restrain an angry coworker who was about to throw a chair at a faster worker who constantly nagged her about her slow pace.[39]

Third, teams should be used when rewards can be provided for teamwork and team performance. Team rewards that depend on team performance, rather than individual performance, are the key to rewarding team behaviors and efforts. You'll read more about team rewards later in the chapter, but for now it's enough to know that if the level of rewards (individual versus team) is not matched to the level of performance (individual versus team), groups won't work. This was the case with Levi Strauss, where a team structure was superimposed on individual jobs that didn't require interaction between workers. After the switch to teams, faster workers placed tremendous pressure on slower workers to increase their production speed. And since pay was determined by team performance, top individual performers saw their pay drop by several dollars an hour, while slower workers saw their pay increase by several dollars an hour—all while overall productivity dropped in the plant.[40] Systems that reward individual performance but hope for high team-level performance are sure to fail.[41]

Review 1: *The Good and Bad of Using Teams*

In many industries, teams are growing in importance because they help organizations respond to specific problems and challenges. Teams have been shown to increase customer satisfaction (specific customer teams), product and service quality (direct responsibility), speed and efficiency in product development (overlapping development phases), and employee job satisfaction (cross-training, unique opportunities, and leadership responsibilities). Although teams can produce significant improvements in these areas, using teams does not guarantee these positive outcomes. Teams and teamwork have the disadvantages of initially high turnover and social loafing (especially in large groups). Teams also share many of the advantages (multiple perspectives, generation of more alternatives, and more commitment) and disadvantages (groupthink, time-consuming, poorly run meetings, domination by a few team members, and weak accountability) of group decision making. Finally, teams should be used for a clear purpose, when the work requires that people work together, when rewards can be provided for both teamwork and team performance, when ample resources can be provided, and when teams can be given clear authority over their work.

2 Kinds of Teams

Companies use different kinds of teams for different purposes. Google uses teams to innovate and develop new products and to tweak and improve its search algorithms and functions.[42] At Children's Hospital Boston, the use of teams and team-based rewards helped shorten the billing cycle by reducing the average number of days a bill spent in the accounts receivable department from 100 to just 65 days.[43]

*Let's continue our discussion of teams by learning about the different kinds of teams that companies like Google and Maytag use to make themselves more competitive. We look first at **2.1 how teams differ in terms of autonomy, which is the key dimension that makes one team different from another**, and then at **2.2 some special kinds of teams**.*

2.1 Autonomy, the Key Dimension

Teams can be classified in a number of ways, such as permanent or temporary, or functional or cross-functional. However, studies indicate that the key dimension that makes teams different from each another is the amount of autonomy possessed by a team.[44] *Autonomy* is the degree to which workers have the discretion, freedom, and independence to decide how and when to accomplish their jobs.

Exhibit 10.4 shows how five kinds of teams differ in terms of autonomy. Moving left to right across the autonomy continuum at the top of the exhibit, traditional work groups and employee involvement groups have the least autonomy, semi-autonomous work groups have more autonomy, and, finally, self-managing teams and self-designing teams have the most autonomy. Moving from bottom to top along the left side of the exhibit, note that the number of responsibilities given to each kind of team increases directly with its autonomy. Let's review each of these kinds of teams and their autonomy and responsibilities in more detail.

The smallest amount of autonomy is found in **traditional work groups**, where two or more people work together to achieve a shared goal. In these groups, workers are responsible for doing the work or "executing the task," but they do not have direct responsibility or control over their work. Workers report to managers, who are responsible for their performance and have the authority to hire and fire them, make job assignments, and control resources. For instance, suppose that an experienced worker blatantly refuses to do his share of the work, saying, "I've done my time. Let the younger employees do the work." In a team with high autonomy, the responsibility of getting this employee to put forth his fair share of effort would belong to his teammates. But in a traditional work group, that responsibility belongs to the boss or supervisor. The supervisor in this situation calmly confronted the employee and told him, "We need your talent, [and] your knowledge of these machines. But if you won't work, you'll have to go elsewhere." Within days, the employee's behavior improved.[45]

Employee involvement teams, which have somewhat more autonomy, meet on company time on a weekly or monthly basis to provide advice or make suggestions to management concerning specific issues, such as plant safety, customer relations, or product quality.[46] Though they offer advice and suggestions, they do not have the authority to make decisions. Membership on these teams is often voluntary, but members may be selected because of their expertise. The idea behind employee involvement teams is that the people closest to the problem or situation are best able to recommend solutions. When a large hospital found that it could

traditional work group a group composed of two or more people who work together to achieve a shared goal

employee involvement team team that provides advice or makes suggestions to management concerning specific issues

RESPONSIBILITIES	TRADITIONAL WORK GROUPS	EMPLOYEE INVOLVEMENT GROUPS	SEMI-AUTONOMOUS WORK GROUPS	SELF-MANAGING TEAMS	SELF-DESIGNING TEAMS
Control Design of					
Team					✓
Tasks					✓
Membership					✓
All Production/Service Tasks					
Make Decisions				✓	✓
Solve Problems				✓	✓
Major Production/Service Tasks					
Make Decisions			✓	✓	✓
Solve Problems			✓	✓	✓
Receive Information			✓	✓	✓
Give Advice/Make Suggestions		✓	✓	✓	✓
Execute Task	✓	✓	✓	✓	✓

Sources: R. D. Banker, J. M. Field, R. G. Schroeder, & K. K. Sinha, "Impact of Work Teams on Manufacturing Performance: A Longitudinal Field Study," *Academy of Management Journal* 39 (1996): 867–890; J. R. Hackman, "The Psychology of Self-Management in Organizations," in *Psychology and Work: Productivity, Change, and Employment*, ed. M. S. Pallak & R. Perlof (Washington, DC: American Psychological Association), 85–136.

Exhibit 10.4

Team Autonomy Continuum

no longer afford its expensive employee retirement plan, it turned to six employee involvement groups representing 3,000 workers for a solution. The groups analyzed the problem and then worked with retirement consultants (chosen by the groups) to generate new retirement options that were affordable, protected the retirement benefits that employees had already earned, and, in the end, were even better for employees.[47]

Semi-autonomous work groups not only provide advice and suggestions to management, but also have the authority to make decisions and solve problems related to the major tasks required to produce a product or service. Semi-autonomous groups regularly receive information about budgets, work quality and performance, and competitors' products. Furthermore, members of semi-autonomous work groups are typically cross-trained in a number of different skills and tasks. In short, semi-autonomous work groups give employees the authority to make decisions that are typically made by supervisors and managers.

That authority is not complete, however. Managers still play a role, though much reduced compared with traditional work groups, in supporting the work of semi-autonomous work groups. The role a manager plays on a team usually evolves over time.

semi-autonomous work group a group that has the authority to make decisions and solve problems related to the major tasks of producing a product or service

"It may start with helping to transition problem-solving responsibilities to the team, filling miscellaneous requests for the team, and doing ad hoc tasks," says Steven Hitchcock, president of Axis Performance Advisors in Portland, Oregon. Later, the team may develop into a "mini-enterprise" and the former manager becomes externally focused—sort of an account manager for the customer. Managers have to adjust what they do based on the sophistication of the team, she explains.[48] A lot of what managers of semi-autonomous work groups do is ask good questions, provide resources, and facilitate performance of group goals.

Self-managing teams differ from semi-autonomous work groups in that team members manage and control *all* of the major tasks *directly related* to production of a product or service without first getting approval from management. This includes managing and controlling the acquisition of materials, making a product or providing a service, and ensuring timely delivery. At a CROWN CORK aluminum can factory in Texas, "The teams make and implement decisions regarding production, product quality, training, attendance, safety, maintenance, and certain types of discipline. The teams can stop production lines without management approval, stop delivery of cans that do not meet quality standards, decide which workers should receive training, decide whether to grant leave requests, and investigate and correct safety problems."[49] Seventy-two percent of *Fortune* 1,000 companies have at least one self-managing team, up from 28 percent in 1987.[50]

Self-designing teams have all the characteristics of self-managing teams, but they can also control and change the design of the teams themselves, the tasks they do and how and when they do them, and the membership of the teams. Two engineers, Roger Jellicoe and Gary Weiss, assembled a team of 20 for the "thin calm" project at MOTOROLA. Money and resources were no object, but secrecy and speed were. The team had complete control over all aspects of the project, and it delivered the Motorola RAZR V3. Since RAZR's launch in late 2004, it has sold almost as many units as Apple's iPod.[51]

2.2 Special Kinds of Teams

Companies are also increasingly using several other kinds of teams that can't easily be categorized in terms of autonomy: cross-functional teams, virtual teams, and project teams. Depending on how these teams are designed, they can be either low- or high-autonomy teams.

Cross-functional teams are intentionally composed of employees from different functional areas of the organization.[52] Because their members have different functional backgrounds, education, and experience, cross-functional teams usually attack problems from multiple perspectives and generate more ideas and alternative solutions, all of which are especially important when trying to innovate or do creative problem solving.[53] Cross-functional teams can be used almost anywhere in an organization and are often used in conjunction with matrix and product organizational structures (see Chapter 9). They can also be used either with part-time or temporary team assignments or with full-time, long-term teams.

CESSNA, which manufactures airplanes, created cross-functional teams for purchasing parts. With workers from purchasing, manufacturing engineering,

self-managing team a team that manages and controls all of the major tasks of producing a product or service

self-designing team a team that has the characteristics of self-managing teams but also controls team design, work tasks, and team membership

cross-functional team a team composed of employees from different functional areas of the organization quality engineering, product design engineering, reliability engineering, product support, and finance, each team addressed make-versus-buy decisions (make it themselves or buy from others), sourcing (who to buy from), internal plant and quality improvements, and the external training of suppliers to reduce costs and increase quality. The teams looked at every major parts category, from engines to wings to electronics. In the end, they came up with parts groups, such as sheet and plate aluminum, that could be completely outsourced to suppliers at lower cost and higher quality.[54]

Virtual teams are groups of geographically and/or organizationally dispersed coworkers who use a combination of telecommunications and information technologies to accomplish an organizational task.[55] Members of virtual teams rarely meet face-to-face; instead, they use e-mail, videoconferencing, and group communication software. For example, PLOTDEVMULTIMEDIA DEVELOPERS is a website-development company of 12 people that does work for Sean Jean, P. Diddy's clothing label, among others. Yet the people in the company have never met. As Max Oshman, who started the company, describes it, "Some of them live in the U.K., two in Croatia, two in Sweden, and the rest are scattered around in southern California, New York, Texas, and Amsterdam." How do they communicate? Oshman says, "Mostly by e-mail. When we have a big project, we communicate via phone. We also have group talks using MSN Messenger."[56] Virtual teams can be employee involvement teams, self-managing teams, or nearly any kind of team discussed in this chapter. Virtual teams are often (but not necessarily) temporary teams that are set up to accomplish a specific task.[57]

The principal advantage of virtual teams is their flexibility. Employees can work with each other, regardless of physical location, time zone, or organizational affiliation.[58] Because the team members don't meet in a physical location, virtual teams also find it much easier to include other key stakeholders, such as suppliers and customers. Plus, virtual teams have certain efficiency advantages over traditional team structures. Because the teammates do not meet face-to-face, a virtual team typically requires a smaller time commitment than a traditional team does. Moreover, employees can fulfill the responsibilities of their virtual team membership from the comfort of their own offices, without the travel time or downtime typically required for face-to-face meetings.[59]

A drawback of virtual teams is that the team members must learn to express themselves in new contexts.[60] The give-and-take that naturally occurs in face-to-face meetings is more difficult to achieve through video conferencing or other methods of virtual teaming. For example, when an English-speaking member of a virtual, multinational website-development team e-mailed a Russian-speaking member that the website design she had developed was "awesome," the Russian-speaking member took offense and flamed an emotional e-mail back. At that point, other members of the team, all in different locations, started sending their own nasty e-mails. What caused the problem? The English-to-Russian website on which they relied incorrectly translated "awesome" as "awful." Chances are, this problem would not have occurred if the team members were working face-to-face.[61] Consistent with this example, several studies have shown that physical proximity enhances information processing.[62] Therefore, some companies bring virtual team members together on a regular basis to try to minimize these problems. Pat O'Day, who manages a five-person virtual team at accounting firm KPMG with members living in the states of Washington, Maryland, and Texas, says, "We communicate through e-mail and conference calls and meet in person four times a year."[63] Exhibit 10.5 provides a number of tips for successfully managing virtual teams.

virtual team a team composed of geographically and/or organizationally dispersed coworkers who use telecommunication and information technologies to accomplish an organizational task

- Select people who are self-starters and strong communicators.

- Keep the team focused by establishing clear, specific goals and by explaining the consequences and importance of meeting these goals.

- Provide frequent feedback so that team members can measure their progress.

- Keep team interactions upbeat and action-oriented by expressing appreciation for good work and completed tasks.

- "Personalize" the virtual team by periodically bringing team members together and by encouraging team members to share information with each other about their personal lives. This is especially important when the virtual team first forms.

- Improve communication through increased telephone calls, e-mails, and Internet messaging and video conference sessions.

- Periodically ask team members how well the team is working and what can be done to improve performance.

- Empower virtual teams so they have the discretion, freedom, and independence to decide how and when to accomplish their jobs.

Sources: W. F. Cascio, "Managing a Virtual Workplace," *Academy of Management Executive* 14 (2000): 81–90; B. Kirkman, B. Rosen, P. Tesluk, & C. Gibson, "The Impact of Team Empowerment on Virtual Team Performance: The Moderating Role of Face-to-Face Interaction," *Academy of Management Journal* 47 (2004): 175–192; S. Furst, M. Reeves, B. Rosen, & R. Blackburn, "Managing the Life Cycle of Virtual Teams," *Academy of Management Executive* (May 2004): 6–20; C. Solomon, "Managing Virtual Teams," *Workforce* 80 (June 2001), 60.

Exhibit 10.5

Tips for Managing Successful Virtual Teams

Project teams are created to complete specific, one-time projects or tasks within a limited time.[64] Project teams are often used to develop new products, significantly improve existing products, roll out new information systems, or build new factories or offices. The project team is typically led by a project manager, who has the overall responsibility for planning, staffing, and managing the team, which usually includes employees from different functional areas. Effective project teams demand both individual and collective responsibility.[65] One advantage of project teams is that drawing employees from different functional areas can reduce or eliminate communication barriers. In turn, as long as team members feel free to express their ideas, thoughts, and concerns, free-flowing communication encourages cooperation among separate departments and typically speeds up the design process.[66] For example, GXS, a supply chain management provider, used a cross-functional team to design its website so that it would have the same simple, intuitive feel in English, French, Spanish, German, and Italian. This website is equally effective across all of these languages and cultures because, according to GE employee Doug Irwin, the company used a "cross-functional, cross-geography tiger team" during development. Says Irwin, "Every Wednesday morning for an hour, we'd meet on a global conference call. There were 5 to 15 of us, from all areas of the business and from all across the globe."[67] Today, GXS uses its website (**http://www.gxs.com**) in 58 countries to operate one of the world's largest business-to-business e-commerce networks, with more than 100,000 trading partners.

Another advantage of project teams is their flexibility. When projects are finished, project team members either move on to the next project or return to their functional units. For example, publication of this book required designers, editors, page compositors, and web designers, among others. When the task was finished, these people applied their skills to other textbook projects. Because of this flexibility, project teams are often used with the matrix organizational designs discussed in Chapter 9.

project team a team created to complete specific, one-time projects or tasks within a limited time

Review 2: *Kinds of Teams*

Companies use different kinds of teams to make themselves more competitive. Autonomy is the key dimension that makes teams different. Traditional work groups (which execute tasks) and employee involvement groups (which make suggestions) have the lowest levels of autonomy. Semi-autonomous work groups (which control major direct tasks) have more autonomy, while self-managing teams (which control all direct tasks) and self-designing teams (which control membership and how tasks are done) have the highest levels of autonomy. Cross-functional, virtual, and project teams are common, but are not easily categorized in terms of autonomy. Cross-functional teams combine employees from different functional areas to help teams attack problems from multiple perspectives and generate more ideas and solutions. Virtual teams use telecommunications and information technologies to bring coworkers "together," regardless of physical location or time zone. Virtual teams reduce travel and work time, but communication may suffer since team members don't work face-to-face. Finally, project teams are used for specific, one-time projects or tasks that must be completed within a limited time. Project teams reduce communication barriers and promote flexibility; teams and team members are reassigned to their department or new projects as old projects are completed.

MANAGING WORK TEAMS

"Why did I ever let you talk me into teams? They're nothing but trouble."[68] Lots of managers have this reaction after making the move to teams. Many don't realize that this reaction is normal, both for them and for workers. In fact, such a reaction is characteristic of the *storming* stage of team development (discussed in Section 3.5). Managers who are familiar with these stages and with the other important characteristics of teams will be better prepared to manage the predictable changes that occur when companies make the switch to team-based structures.

After reading the next two sections, you should be able to

> 3 understand the general characteristics of work teams.
>
> 4 explain how to enhance work team effectiveness.

3 Work Team Characteristics

*Understanding the characteristics of work teams is essential for making teams an effective part of an organization. Therefore, in this section you'll learn about **3.1 team norms**, **3.2 team cohesiveness**, **3.3 team size**, **3.4 team conflict**, and **3.5 the stages of team development**.*

3.1 Team Norms

Over time, teams develop **norms**, informally agreed-on standards that regulate team behavior.[69] Norms are valuable because they let team members know what is expected of them. At Nucor Steel, work groups expect their members to get to work on time. To reinforce this norm, anyone who is late to work will not receive the team bonus

norms informally agreed-on standards that regulate team behavior for that day (assuming the team is productive). A worker who is more than 30 minutes late will not receive the team bonus for the entire week. At Nucor losing a bonus matters because work group bonuses can easily double the size of a worker's take-home pay.[70]

Studies indicate that norms are one of the most powerful influences on work behavior. Team norms are often associated with positive outcomes, such as stronger organizational commitment, more trust in management, and stronger job and organizational satisfaction.[71] In general, effective work teams develop norms about the quality and timeliness of job performance, absenteeism, safety, and honest expression of ideas and opinions. The power of norms also comes from the fact that they regulate the everyday behaviors that allow teams to function effectively. To encourage the development of team norms, trainer Tom Ruddy created a deck of 35 playing cards describing problems that *XEROX*'s customer service teams usually encounter. Ruddy has teams discuss each card/problem. When they agree what to do, they write their solution on the card along with the word *norm*. Everyone then gets a copy of the deck with the team's norms on them. When a team norm is broken, such as one teammate cutting off another's point, the card with the violated norm is played, in this case "everyone's opinion will be heard." It's a little corny at first, but, says Ruddy, "After a while, team members internalize the proper behavior. That's when the team really starts to click."[72]

Norms can also influence team behavior in negative ways. For example, most people would agree that damaging organizational property; saying or doing something to hurt someone at work; intentionally doing one's work badly, incorrectly, or slowly; griping about coworkers; deliberately bending or breaking rules; or doing something to harm the company or boss are negative behaviors. Nonetheless, a study of workers from 34 teams in 20 different organizations found that teams with negative norms strongly influenced their team members to engage in these negative behaviors. In fact, the longer individuals were members of a team with negative norms and the more frequently they interacted with their teammates, the more likely they were to perform negative behaviors. Since team norms typically develop early in the life of a team, these results indicate how important it is for teams to establish positive norms from the outset.[73]

3.2 Team Cohesiveness

Cohesiveness is another important characteristic of work teams. **Cohesiveness** is the extent to which team members are attracted to a team and motivated to remain in it.[74] Burlington Northern Santa Fe Railway's intermodal team, which was charged with finding efficient ways to combine transportation through trucks and trains, was a particularly cohesive team. Dave Burns, a member of that team, says, "In my mind, the key word to this team was 'shared.' We shared everything. There was a complete openness among us. And the biggest thing that we shared was an objective and a strategy that we had put together jointly. That was our benchmark every day. Were we doing things in support of *our* plan?"[75] The same was true of the team that came up with *MASTERCARD*'s endearing "Priceless" ad campaigns. Each ad in the series features a list of ordinary transactions and the dollar amounts associated with those purchases. The final item in the series, however, is always pitched as "priceless." Joyce Thomas, one of the three-member team that conceived of and created those ads, says, "We were very comfortable working together, so we debated everything freely."[76]

"WHAT'S NEW" COMPANY

"WHAT'S NEW" COMPANY

We were very comfortable working together, so we debated everything freely.

JOYCE THOMAS,
TEAM MEMBER,
"PRICELESS" AD CAMPAIGNS, MASTERCARD

cohesiveness the extent to which team members are attracted to a team and motivated to remain in it

COHESION AND TEAM PERFORMANCE

Have you ever worked in a really cohesive group where everyone liked and enjoyed each other and was glad to be part of the group? It's great. By contrast, have you ever worked in a group where everyone really disliked each other and was unhappy to be part of the group? It's terrible. Anyone who has had either of these experiences can appreciate how important group cohesion is and the effect it can have on team performance. Indeed, 46 studies based on 1,279 groups confirm that cohesion does matter.

TEAM PERFORMANCE

On average, there is a 66 percent chance that cohesive teams will outperform less cohesive teams.

TEAM PERFORMANCE WITH INTERDEPENDENT TASKS

Teams work best for interdependent tasks that require people to work together to get the job done. When teams perform

interdependent tasks, there is a 73 percent chance that cohesive teams will outperform less cohesive teams.

TEAM PERFORMANCE WITH INDEPENDENT TASKS

Teams generally are not suited for independent tasks that people can accomplish by themselves. When teams perform independent tasks, there is a only a 60 percent chance that cohesive teams will outperform less cohesive teams.

Some caution is warranted in interpreting these results. For example, there is always the possibility that a team could become so cohesive that its team goals become more important than organizational goals. Also, teams sometimes unite around negative goals and norms that are harmful rather than helpful to organizations. Nonetheless, there is also room for even more optimism about cohesive teams. Teams that are cohesive *and* committed to the goals they are asked to achieve should have an even higher probability of success than the numbers shown here.[77]

The level of cohesiveness in a group is important for several reasons. To start, cohesive groups have a better chance of retaining their members. As a result, cohesive groups typically experience lower turnover.[78] In addition, team cohesiveness promotes cooperative behavior, generosity, and a willingness on the part of team members to assist each other.[79] When team cohesiveness is high, team members are more motivated to contribute to the team because they want to gain the approval of other team members. For these reasons and others, studies have clearly established that cohesive teams consistently perform better.[80] Furthermore, cohesive teams quickly achieve high levels of performance. By contrast, teams low in cohesion take much longer to reach the same levels of performance.[81]

What can be done to promote team cohesiveness? First, make sure that all team members are present at team meetings and activities. Team cohesiveness suffers when members are allowed to withdraw from the team and miss team meetings and events.[82] Second, create additional opportunities for teammates to work together by rearranging work schedules and creating common workspaces. When task interdependence is high and team members have lots of chances to work together, team cohesiveness tends to increase.[83] Third, engaging in nonwork activities as a team can help build cohesion. At a company where teams put in extraordinarily long hours coding computer software, the software teams maintained cohesion by doing "fun stuff" together. Team leader Tammy Urban says, "We went on team outings at least once a week. We'd play darts, shoot pool. Teams work best when you get to know each other outside of work—what people's interests are, who they are. Personal connections go a long way when you're developing complex applications in our kind of time frames."[84] Finally, companies build team cohesiveness by making employees feel that they are part of a "special" organization. For example, all the new hires at Disney World in Orlando are required to take a course entitled "Traditions One," where they learn the traditions and history of the WALT DISNEY COMPANY (including the names of the seven dwarfs!). The purpose of Traditions One is to instill a sense of team pride in working for Disney.

3.3 Team Size

There appears to be a curvilinear relationship between team size and performance. Very small or very large teams may not perform as well as moderately sized teams. For most teams, the right size is somewhere between six and nine members.[85] This size is conducive to high team cohesion, which has a positive effect on team performance, as discussed above. A team of this size is small enough for the team members to get to know each other and for each member to have an opportunity to contribute in a meaningful way to the success of the team. At the same time, the team is also large enough to take advantage of team members' diverse skills, knowledge, and perspectives. It is also easier to instill a sense of responsibility and mutual accountability in teams of this size.[86]

By contrast, when teams get too large, team members find it difficult to get to know one another, and the team may splinter into smaller subgroups. When this occurs, subgroups sometimes argue and disagree, weakening overall team cohesion. As teams grow, there is also a greater chance of *minority domination*, where just a few team members dominate team discussions. Even if minority domination doesn't occur, larger groups may not have time for all team members to share their input. And when team members feel that their contributions are unimportant or not needed, the result is less involvement, effort, and accountability to the team.[87] Large teams also face logistical problems, such as finding an appropriate time or place to meet. Finally, the incidence of social loafing, discussed earlier in the chapter, is much higher in large teams.

Just as team performance can suffer when a team is too large, it can also be negatively affected when a team is too small. Teams with just a few people may lack the diversity of skills and knowledge found in larger teams. Also, teams that are too small are unlikely to gain the advantages of team decision making (multiple perspectives, generating more ideas and alternative solutions, and stronger commitment) found in larger teams.

What signs indicate that a team's size needs to be changed? If decisions are taking too long, if the team has difficulty making decisions or taking action, if a few members dominate the team, or if the commitment or efforts of team members are weak, chances are the team is too big. In contrast, if a team is having difficulty coming up with ideas or generating solutions, or if the team does not have the expertise to address a specific problem, chances are the team is too small.

3.4 Team Conflict

Conflict and disagreement are inevitable in most teams. But this shouldn't surprise anyone. From time to time, people who work together are going to disagree about what and how things get done. What causes conflict in teams? Although almost anything can lead to conflict—casual remarks that unintentionally offend a team member or fighting over scarce resources—the primary cause of team conflict is disagreement over team goals and priorities.[88] Other common causes of team conflict include disagreements over task-related issues, interpersonal incompatibilities, and simple fatigue.

Though most people view conflict negatively, the key to dealing with team conflict is not avoiding it, but rather making sure that the team experiences the right kind of conflict. In Chapter 5, you learned about *c-type conflict*, or *cognitive conflict*, which focuses on problem-related differences of opinion, and *a-type conflict*, or *affective conflict*, which refers to the emotional reactions that can occur when disagreements become personal rather than professional.[89] Cognitive conflict is strongly associated with improvements in team performance, whereas affective conflict is strongly associated with decreases in team performance.[90] Why does this happen? With cognitive conflict, team members disagree because their different experiences and expertise lead them to different views of the problem and solutions. Indeed, managers who participated on teams that emphasized cognitive conflict described their teammates as "smart," "team players," and "best in the business." They described their teams as "open," "fun," and "productive." One manager summed up the positive attitude that team members had about cognitive conflict by saying, "We scream a lot, then laugh, and then resolve the issue."[91] Thus, cognitive conflict is also characterized by a willingness to examine, compare, and reconcile differences to produce the best possible solution.

By contrast, affective conflict often results in hostility, anger, resentment, distrust, cynicism, and apathy. Managers who participated on teams that emphasized affective conflict described their teammates as "manipulative," "secretive," "burned out," and "political."[92] Not surprisingly, affective conflict can make people uncomfortable and cause them to withdraw and decrease their commitment to a team.[93] Affective conflict also lowers the satisfaction of team members, may lead to personal hostility between coworkers, and can decrease team cohesiveness.[94] So, unlike cognitive conflict, affective conflict undermines team performance by preventing teams from engaging in the kinds of activities that are critical to team effectiveness.

So, what can managers do to manage team conflict? First, managers need to realize that emphasizing cognitive conflict alone won't be enough. Studies show that cognitive and affective conflicts often occur together in the same teams! Therefore, sincere attempts to reach agreement on a difficult issue can quickly deteriorate from cognitive to affective conflict if the discussion turns personal and tempers and emotions flare. So, while cognitive conflict is clearly the better approach to take, efforts to engage in cognitive conflict should be approached with caution.

Can teams disagree and still get along? Fortunately, they can. In an attempt to study this issue, researchers examined team conflict in 12 high-tech companies. In four of the companies, work teams used cognitive conflict to address work problems but did so in a way that minimized the occurrence of affective conflict. Exhibit 10.6 shows the steps these teams took to be able to have a "good fight."[95]

First, work with more, rather than less, information. If data are plentiful, objective, and up-to-date, teams will focus on issues, not personalities. Second, develop multiple alternatives to enrich debate. Focusing on multiple solutions diffuses conflict by getting the team to keep searching for a better solution. Positions and opinions are naturally more flexible with five alternatives than with just two. Third, establish common goals. Remember, most team conflict arises from disagreements over team

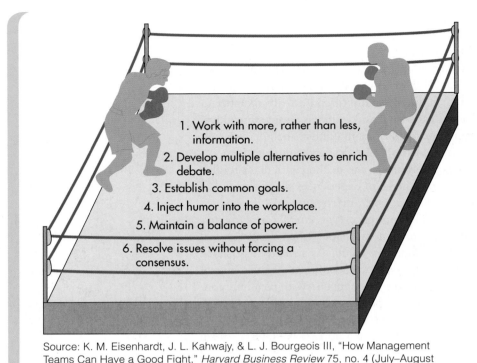

1. Work with more, rather than less, information.
2. Develop multiple alternatives to enrich debate.
3. Establish common goals.
4. Inject humor into the workplace.
5. Maintain a balance of power.
6. Resolve issues without forcing a consensus.

Source: K. M. Eisenhardt, J. L. Kahwajy, & L. J. Bourgeois III, "How Management Teams Can Have a Good Fight," *Harvard Business Review* 75, no. 4 (July–August 1997): 77–85.

Exhibit 10.6

How Teams Can Have a Good Fight

goals and priorities. Therefore, common goals encourage collaboration and minimize conflict over a team's purpose. Steve Jobs, CEO of **APPLE**, explains it this way: "It's okay to spend a lot of time arguing about which route to take to San Francisco when everyone wants to end up there, but a lot of time gets wasted in such arguments if one person wants to go to San Francisco and another secretly wants to go to San Diego."[96] Fourth, inject humor into the workplace. Humor relieves tension, builds cohesion, and just makes being in teams fun. Fifth, maintain a balance of power by involving as many people as possible in the decision process. And sixth, resolve issues without forcing a consensus. Consensus means that everyone must agree before decisions are finalized. Effectively, requiring consensus gives everyone on the team veto power. Nothing gets done until everyone agrees, which, of course, is nearly impossible. As a result, insisting on consensus usually promotes affective rather than cognitive conflict. If team members can't agree after constructively discussing their options, it's better to have the team leader make the final choice. Most team members can accept the team leader's choice if they've been thoroughly involved in the decision process.

3.5 Stages of Team Development

As teams develop and grow, they pass through four stages of development. As shown in Exhibit 10.7, those stages are forming, storming, norming, and performing.[97] Although not every team passes through each of these stages, teams that do tend to be better performers.[98] This holds true even for teams composed of seasoned executives. After a period of time, however, if a team is not managed well, its performance may start to deteriorate as the team begins a process of decline and progresses through the stages of de-norming, de-storming, and de-forming.[99]

Forming is the initial stage of team development. This is the getting-acquainted stage, when team members first meet each other, form initial impressions, and try to get a sense of what it will be like to be part of the team. Some of the first team norms will be established during this stage, as team members begin to find out what behaviors will and won't be accepted by the team. During this stage, team leaders should allow time for team members to get to know each other, set early ground rules, and begin to set up a preliminary team structure.

Conflicts and disagreements often characterize the second stage of team development, **storming**. As team members begin working together, different personalities and work styles may clash. Team members become more assertive at this stage and more willing to state opinions. This is also the stage when team members jockey for position and try to establish a favorable role for themselves on the team. In addition, team members are likely to disagree about what the group should do and how it

forming the first stage of team development, in which team members meet each other, form initial impressions, and begin to establish team norms

storming the second stage of development, characterized by conflict and disagreement, in which team members disagree over what the team should do and how it should do it should do it. Team performance is still relatively low, given that team cohesion is weak and team members are still reluctant to support each other. Since teams that get stuck in the storming stage are almost always ineffective, it is important for team leaders to focus the team on team goals and on improving team performance. Team members need to be particularly patient and tolerant with each other in this stage.

During **norming**, the third stage of team development, team members begin to settle into their roles as team members. Positive team norms will have developed by this stage, and teammates should know what to expect from each other. Petty differences should have been resolved, friendships will have developed, and group cohesion will be relatively strong. At this point, team members will have accepted team goals, be operating as a unit, and, as indicated by the increase in performance,

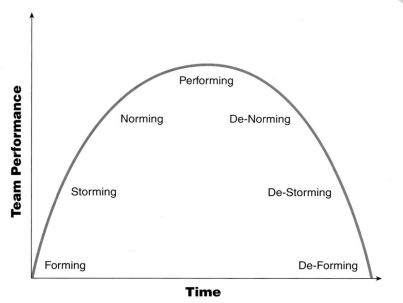

Sources: J. F. McGrew, J. G. Bilotta, & J. M. Deeney, "Software Team Formation and Decay: Extending the Standard Model for Small Groups," *Small Group Research* 30, no. 2 (1999): 209–234; B. W. Tuckman, "Development Sequence in Small Groups," *Psychological Bulletin* 63, no. 6 (1965): 384–399.

Exhibit 10.7
Stages of Team Development

be working together effectively. This stage can be very short and is often characterized by someone on the team saying, "I think things are finally coming together." Note, however, that teams may also cycle back and forth between storming and norming several times before finally settling into norming.

In the last stage of team development, **performing**, performance improves because the team has finally matured into an effective, fully functioning team. At this point, members should be fully committed to the team and think of themselves as "members of a team" and not just "employees." Team members often become intensely loyal to one another at this stage and feel mutual accountability for team successes and failures. Trivial disagreements, which can take time and energy away from the work of the team, should be rare. At this stage, teams get a lot of work done, and it is fun to be a team member.

The team should not become complacent, however, because without effective management, its performance may begin to decline as the team passes through the stages of de-norming, de-storming, and de-forming.[100] Indeed, John Puckett, manufacturing vice president for circuit-board manufacturer **XEL COMMUNICATIONS**, says, "The books all say you start in this state of chaos and march through these various stages, and you end up in this state of ultimate self-direction, where everything is going just great. They never tell you it can go back in the other direction, sometimes just as quickly."[101]

In **de-norming**, which is a reversal of the norming stage, team performance begins to decline as the size, scope, goal, or members of the team change. With new members joining the group, older members may become defensive as established ways of doing things are questioned and challenged. Expression of ideas and opinions becomes less open. New members change team norms by actively rejecting or passively neglecting previously established team roles and behaviors.

In **de-storming**, which is a reversal of the storming phase, the team's comfort level decreases. Team cohesion weakens as more group members resist conforming to team norms and quit participating in team activities. Angry emotions flare as the group explodes in conflict and moves into the final stage of de-forming.

norming the third stage of team development, in which team members begin to settle into their roles, group cohesion grows, and positive team norms develop

performing the fourth and final stage of team development, in which performance improves because the team has matured into an effective, fully functioning team

de-norming a reversal of the norming stage, in which team performance begins to decline as the size, scope, goal, or members of the team change

de-storming a reversal of the storming phase, in which the team's comfort level decreases, team cohesion weakens, and angry emotions and conflict may flare

In **de-forming**, which is a reversal of the forming stage, team members position themselves to gain control of pieces of the team. Team members begin to avoid each other and isolate themselves from team leaders. Team performance rapidly declines as the members quit caring about even minimal requirements of team performance.

If teams are actively managed, decline is not inevitable. However, managers need to recognize that the forces at work in the de-norming, de-storming, and de-forming stages represent a powerful, disruptive, and real threat to teams that have finally made it to the performing stage. Getting to the performing stage is half the battle. Staying there is the second half.

Review 3: **Work Team Characteristics**

The most important characteristics of work teams are team norms, cohesiveness, size, conflict, and development. Norms let team members know what is expected of them and can influence team behavior in positive and negative ways. Positive team norms are associated with organizational commitment, trust, and job satisfaction. Team cohesiveness helps teams retain members, promotes cooperative behavior, increases motivation, and facilitates team performance. Attending team meetings and activities, creating opportunities to work together, and engaging in nonwork activities can increase cohesiveness. Team size has a curvilinear relationship with team performance: Teams that are very small or very large do not perform as well as moderate-sized teams of six to nine members. Teams of this size are cohesive and small enough for team members to get to know each other and contribute in a meaningful way, but are large enough to take advantage of team members' diverse skills, knowledge, and perspectives. Conflict and disagreement are inevitable in most teams. The key to dealing with team conflict is to maximize cognitive conflict, which focuses on issue-related differences, and minimize affective conflict, the emotional reactions that occur when disagreements become personal rather than professional. As teams develop and grow, they pass through four stages of development: forming, storming, norming, and performing. After a period of time, however, if a team is not managed well, its performance may decline as the team regresses through the stages of de-norming, de-storming, and de-forming.

 Enhancing Work Team Effectiveness

*Making teams work is a challenging and difficult process. Nonetheless, companies can increase the likelihood that teams will succeed by carefully managing **4.1 the setting of team goals and priorities** and **4.2 how work team members are selected**, **4.3 trained**, and **4.4 compensated**.*[102]

4.1 Setting Team Goals and Priorities

In Chapter 5, you learned that having specific, measurable, attainable, realistic, and timely (S.M.A.R.T.) goals is one of the most effective means for improving individual job performance. Fortunately, team goals also improve team performance. In fact, team goals lead to much higher team performance 93 percent of the time.[103] For example, Nucor Steel sets specific, challenging *hourly* goals for each of its production teams, which consist of first-line supervisors and production and maintenance workers. The average in the steel industry is 10 tons of steel per hour. Nucor production teams have an hourly goal of 8 tons per hour, but get a 5 percent

de-forming a reversal of the forming stage, in which team members position themselves to control pieces of the team, avoid each other, and isolate themselves from team leaders bonus for every ton over 8 tons that they produce. With no limit on the bonuses they can receive, Nucor's production teams produce an average of 35 to 40 tons of steel per hour![104]

Why is setting specific, challenging team goals so critical to team success? One reason is that increasing a team's performance is inherently more complex than just increasing one individual's job performance. For instance, consider that any team is likely to involve at least four different kinds of goals: each member's goal for the team, each member's goal for himself or herself on the team, the team's goal for each member, and the team's goal for itself.[105] In other words, without a specific, challenging goal for the team itself (the last of the four goals listed), team members may head off in all directions at once pursuing these other goals. Consequently, setting a specific, challenging goal *for the team* clarifies team priorities by providing a clear focus and purpose.

Specific, challenging team goals also affect how hard team members work. In particular, challenging team goals greatly reduce the incidence of social loafing. When faced with difficult goals, team members necessarily expect everyone to contribute. Consequently, they are much more likely to notice and complain if a teammate isn't doing his or her share. In fact, when teammates know each other well, when team goals are specific, when team communication is good, and when teams are rewarded for team performance (discussed below), there is only a 1 in 16 chance that teammates will be social loafers.[106]

What can companies and teams do to ensure that team goals lead to superior team performance? One increasingly popular approach is to give teams stretch goals. *Stretch goals* are extremely ambitious goals that workers don't know how to reach.[107] SONY's hardware is unrivaled, as are its movies and music. The bridge between content and hardware is software, an area in which Sony is far behind its rivals. Consequently, Sir Howard Stringer, CEO of Sony, says the company's most important priority, or stretch goal, is the "conquest of software." But Sony is so far behind that Stringer anticipates it will take years to make Sony a world-class software company. "We will succeed," he concludes, "because we must."[108] The purpose of stretch goals is to achieve extraordinary improvements in performance by forcing managers and workers to throw away old, comfortable solutions and adopt radical, never-used-before solutions.[109]

Four things must occur for stretch goals to effectively motivate teams.[110] First, teams must have a high degree of autonomy or control over how they achieve their goals. At CSX's railroad division, top management challenged the new management team at its Cumberland, Maryland, office to increase productivity by 16 percent. The goal was specific and challenging: Ship the same amount of coal each month, but do it with 4,200 railcars instead of 5,000 railcars. The local team, consisting of five new managers, quickly figured out that the trains were spending too much time sitting idly in the rail yards. Finance director Peter Mills says, "We'd look out our office windows at the tracks and wonder, 'Why aren't the cars moving?'" The problem? Headquarters wouldn't let the trains run until they had 160 full railcars to pull, but amassing that many cars could take nearly a week. Since the local management team had the autonomy to pay for the extra crews to run the trains more

"We'd look out our office windows at the tracks and wonder, "Why aren't the cars moving?"

PETER MILLS,
FINANCE DIRECTOR, CSX

*"WHAT'S NEW" ×2
COMPANY*

By setting specific and challenging goals, CSX was able to ship the same amount of coal with 16 percent fewer rail cars.

© GRAPHISTOCK IMAGE/JUPITER IMAGES

structural accommodation the ability to change organizational structures, policies, and practices in order to meet stretch goals

bureaucratic immunity the ability to make changes without first getting approval from managers or other parts of an organization

frequently, it started running trains with as few as 78 cars. Now, coal cars never wait more than a day to be transported to customers, and rail productivity has skyrocketed.[111]

Second, teams must be empowered with control resources, such as budgets, workspaces, computers, or whatever else they need to do their jobs. Steve Kerr, Goldman Sachs' chief learning officer, says, "We have a moral obligation to try to give people the tools to meet tough goals. I think it's totally wrong if you don't give employees the tools to succeed, then punish them when they fail."[112]

Third, teams need structural accommodation. **Structural accommodation** means giving teams the ability to change organizational structures, policies, and practices if doing so helps them meet their stretch goals. *Pfizer* CEO Jeffrey Kindler has established five stretch goals for his top management team, one of which is to reduce costs by $2 billion by the end of 2008, while—and here's where the goal really stretches—maintaining rich funding for research and development, business development, and cultivating emerging markets. Structural accommodation is one of the key mechanisms the team will use to facilitate the accomplishment of these stretch goals. The team intends to cut down on bureaucracy and reduce management layers, and eliminate unnecessary committees, policies, and procedures. Kindler acknowledges that this change won't happen overnight and notes that it will take time, discipline, and persistence.[113]

Finally, teams need bureaucratic immunity. **Bureaucratic immunity** means that teams no longer have to go through the frustratingly slow process of multilevel reviews and sign-offs to get management approval before making changes. Once granted bureaucratic immunity, teams are immune from the influence of various organizational groups and are accountable only to top management. Therefore, teams can act quickly and even experiment with little fear of failure. Motorola gave the "thin calm" project team that invented the sleek RAZR V3 bureaucratic immunity. The team violated most existing bureaucratic checks and balances within Motorola, and reported directly to top management. The team leaders were given complete control over recruiting new team members and structuring and running the team.[114]

4.2 Selecting People for Teamwork

University of Southern California management professor Edward Lawler says, "People are very naive about how easy it is to create a team. Teams are the Ferrari of work design. They're high performance but high maintenance and expensive."[115] It's almost impossible to have an effective work team without carefully selecting people who are suited for teamwork or for working on a particular team. A focus on teamwork (individualism-collectivism), team level, and team diversity can help companies choose the right team members.[116]

Are you more comfortable working alone or with others? If you strongly prefer to work alone, you may not be well suited for teamwork. Indeed, studies show that job satisfaction is higher in teams when team members prefer working with others.[117] An indirect way to measure someone's *preference for teamwork* is to assess the person's degree of individualism or collectivism. **Individualism-collectivism** is the degree to which a person believes that people should be self-sufficient and that loyalty to one's self is more important than loyalty to one's team or company.[118] *Individualists*, who put their own welfare and interests first, generally prefer independent tasks in which they work alone. In contrast, *collectivists*, who put group or team interests ahead of self-interests, generally prefer interdependent tasks in which they work with others. Collectivists would also rather cooperate than compete and are fearful of disappointing team members or of being ostracized from teams. Given these differences, it makes sense to select team members who are collectivists rather than individualists. Indeed, many companies use individualism-collectivism as an initial screening device for team members. For example, when selecting workers for its team-based approach to manufacturing single-engine planes, Cessna focuses exclusively on team skills. If tests indicate that you aren't a "team player" with an aptitude and willingness to take on responsibility and work with others, Cessna doesn't hire you.[119] If team diversity is desired, however, individualists may also be appropriate, as discussed below. To determine your preference for teamwork, take the Team Player Inventory shown in Exhibit 10.8.

Team level is the average level of ability, experience, personality, or any other factor on a team. For example, a high level of team experience means that a team has particularly experienced team members. This does not mean that every member of the team has considerable experience, but that enough team members do to significantly raise the average level of experience on the team. Team level is used to guide selection of teammates when teams need a particular set of skills or capabilities to do their jobs well. For example, at GE's Aerospace Engines manufacturing plant in Durham, North Carolina, only applicants who have an FAA-certified mechanic's

© STEPHANIE SINCLAIR/CORBIS

For the U.S. Marine Corps, effective team work on the battlefield begins with effective team work in the barracks.

individualism-collectivism the degree to which a person believes that people should be self-sufficient and that loyalty to one's self is more important than loyalty to team or company

team level the average level of ability, experience, personality, or any other factor on a team

Exhibit 10.8
The Team Player Inventory

	STRONGLY DISAGREE				STRONGLY AGREE
1. I enjoy working on team/group projects.	1	2	3	4	5
2. Team/group project work easily allows others to not pull their weight.	1	2	3	4	5
3. Work that is done as a team/group is better than the work done individually.	1	2	3	4	5
4. I do my best work alone rather than in a team/group.	1	2	3	4	5
5. Team/group work is overrated in terms of the actual results produced.	1	2	3	4	5
6. Working in a team/group gets me to think more creatively.	1	2	3	4	5
7. Teams/groups are used too often, when individual work would be more effective.	1	2	3	4	5
8. My own work is enhanced when I am in a team/group situation.	1	2	3	4	5
9. My experiences working in team/group situations have been primarily negative.	1	2	3	4	5
10. More soultions/ideas are generated when working in a team/group situation than when working alone.	1	2	3	4	5

Reverse-score items 2, 4, 5, 7, and 9. Then add the scores for items 1 to 10. Higher scores indicate a preference for teamwork, whereas lower total scores indicate a preference for individual work.

Source: T. J. B. Kline, "The Team Player Inventory: Reliability and Validity of a Measure of Predisposition Toward Organizational Team-Working Environments," *Journal for Specialists in Group Work* 24, no. 1 (1999): 102–112.

license are considered for hire. Following that, all applicants are tested in 11 different areas, only one of which involved those technical skills. Keith McKee, who works at the plant, says, "You have to be above the bar in all 11 of the areas: helping skills, team skills, communication skills, diversity, flexibility, coaching ability, work ethic, and so forth. Even if just one thing out of the 11 knocks you down, you don't come to work here."[120]

Whereas team level represents the average level or capability on a team, **team diversity** represents the variances or differences in ability, experience, personality, or any other factor on a team.[121] From a practical perspective, why is team diversity important? Professor John Hollenbeck explains, "Imagine if you put all the extroverts together. Everyone is talking, but nobody is listening. [By contrast,] with a team of [nothing but] introverts, you can hear the clock ticking on the wall."[122] Strong teams not only have talented members (that is, a high team level), but those talented members are also different in terms of ability, experience, or personality. For example, teams with strong team diversity on job experience have a mix of team members, ranging from seasoned veterans to people with three or four years of experience to rookies with little or no experience. When Cessna built a brand new manufacturing plant for its single-engine Skyhawk planes in a new location, none of the new workers it hired for its teams had any manufacturing experience whatsoever. Having passed Cessna's team skills tests, they were all great team players, but none had ever worked in a factory. Consequently, Cessna diversified the teams by bringing in 60 retirees who had built Skyhawks before. The mentors worked with the teams, teaching them basic manufacturing skills and instilling confidence.[123] As in this example, team diversity is used to guide the selection of team members when teams must complete a wide range of different tasks or when tasks are particularly complex.

Once the right team has been put together in terms of individualism-collectivism, team level, and team diversity, it's important to keep the team together as long as practically possible. Interesting research by the National Transportation Safety Board shows that 73 percent of the serious mistakes made by jet cockpit crews are made the very first day that a crew flies together as a team and that 44 percent of serious mistakes occur on their very first flight together (pilot teams fly two to three flights per day). Moreover, research has shown that fatigued pilot crews who have worked together before make significantly fewer errors than rested crews who have never worked together.[124] Their experience working together helps them overcome their fatigue and outperform new teams that have not worked together before. So, once you've created effective teams, keep them together as long as possible.

4.3 Team Training

After selecting the right people for teamwork, you need to train them. And, to be successful, teams need significant training, particularly in interpersonal skills, decision making and problem solving, conflict resolution, and technical training. Team leaders need training, too.

Organizations that create work teams *often underestimate the amount of training* required to make teams effective. This mistake occurs frequently in successful organizations, where managers assume that if employees can work effectively on their own, they can work effectively in teams. In reality, companies that successfully use teams provide thousands of hours of training to make sure that teams work. Stacy Myers, a consultant who helps companies implement teams, says, "When we help companies move to teams, we also require that employees take basic quality and business knowledge classes as well. Teams must know how their work affects the company, and how their success will be measured."[125]

team diversity the variances or differences in ability, experience, personality, or any other factor on a team

Most commonly, members of work teams receive training in interpersonal skills. **Interpersonal skills**, such as listening, communicating, questioning, and providing feedback, enable people to have effective working relationships with others.

Because of teams' autonomy and responsibility, many companies also give team members training in *decision-making and problem-solving skills* to help them do a better job of cutting costs and improving quality and customer service. At GENERAL MOTORS' automobile assembly plant in Lansing, Michigan, each employee working on the assembly line receives 250 classroom hours of training, most of it in problem solving. According to Tim Lee, the group director of manufacturing for GM's North American car group, "Problem solving is not an easy task. Typically, in a plant we treat the symptoms, not the problem."[126] Many organizations also teach teams *conflict resolution skills*. "Teams at Delta Faucet have specific protocols for addressing conflict. For example, if an employee's behavior is creating a problem within a team, the team is expected to work it out without involving the team leader. Two team members will meet with the 'problem' team member and work toward a resolution. If this is unsuccessful, the whole team meets and confronts the issue. If necessary, the team leader can be brought in to make a decision, but . . . it is a rare occurrence for a team to reach that stage."[127]

Firms must also provide team members with the *technical training* they need to do their jobs, particularly if they are being cross-trained to perform all of the different jobs on the team. Before teams were created at Milwaukee Mutual Insurance, separate employees performed the tasks of rating, underwriting, and processing insurance policies. After extensive cross-training, however, each team member can now do all three jobs.[128] Cross-training is less appropriate for teams of highly skilled workers. For instance, it is unlikely that a group of engineers, computer programmers, and systems analysts would be cross-trained for each other's jobs.

Finally, companies need to provide *training for team leaders*, who often feel unprepared for their new duties. Exhibit 10.9 shows the top 10 problems reported by new team leaders. These range from confusion about their new roles as team leaders (compared with their old jobs as managers or employees) to not knowing where to go for help when their teams have problems. The solution is extensive training for team leaders.

4.4 Team Compensation and Recognition

Compensating teams correctly is very difficult. For instance, one survey found that only 37 percent of companies were satisfied with their team compensation plans and even fewer, just 10 percent, reported being "very positive."[129] One of the problems,

"WHAT'S NEW" COMPANY

interpersonal skills skills, such as listening, communicating, questioning, and providing feedback, that enable people to have effective working relationships with others

Exhibit 10.9
Top 10 Problems Reported by Team Leaders

1.	Confusion about their new roles and about what they should be doing differently.
2.	Feeling they've lost control.
3.	Not knowing what it means to coach or empower.
4.	Having personal doubts about whether the team concept will really work.
5.	Uncertainty about how to deal with employees' doubts about the team concept.
6.	Confusion about when a team is ready for more responsibility.
7.	Confusion about how to share responsibility and accountability with the team.
8.	Concern about promotional opportunities, especially about whether the "team leader" title carries any prestige.
9.	Uncertainty about the strategic aspects of the leader's role as the team matures.
10.	Not knowing where to turn for help with team problems, as few, if any, of their organization's leaders have led teams.

Source: B. Filipczak, M. Hequet, C. Lee, M. Picard, & D. Stamps, "More Trouble with Teams," *Training*, October 1996, 21.

according to Susan Mohrman of the Center for Effective Organizations at the University of Southern California, is that "there is a very strong set of beliefs in most organizations that people should be paid for how well they do. So when people first get put into team-based organizations, they really balk at being paid for how well the team does. It sounds illogical to them. It sounds like their individuality and their sense of self-worth are being threatened."[130] Consequently, companies need to carefully choose a team compensation plan and then fully explain how teams will be rewarded. One basic requirement for team compensation to work is that the level of rewards (individual versus team) must match the level of performance (individual versus team).

Employees can be compensated for team participation and accomplishments in three ways: skill-based pay, gainsharing, and nonfinancial rewards. **Skill-based pay** programs pay employees for learning additional skills or knowledge.[131] These programs encourage employees to acquire the additional skills they will need to perform multiple jobs within a team and to share knowledge with others within their work groups.[132] For example, at XEL Communications, the circuit-board manufacturer, the number of skills each employee has mastered determines his or her individual pay. An employee who takes a class and on-the-job training in advanced soldering will earn 30 cents more per hour. Passing a written test or satisfactorily performing a skill or job for a supervisor or trainer certifies mastery of new skills and results in increased pay. Eastman Chemical uses a similar approach with its teams, but team members also have to demonstrate that they use their new skills at least 10 percent of the time. Otherwise, they lose their pay increase.[133]

In **gainsharing** programs, companies share the financial value of performance gains, such as productivity increases, cost savings, or quality improvements, with their workers.[134] Over the last 25 years, the **U.S. POSTAL SERVICE** (USPS) has lost $9 billion. Recently, however, a gainsharing program for its 84,000 supervisors produced annual savings of $497 million for the USPS and average annual gainsharing payments of $3,100 for each supervisor. Thanks to cost-saving suggestions, improved productivity, and better management, on-time delivery of first class mail increased by 10 percent, the number of workdays lost to injury dropped significantly, and, most impressively of all, the USPS had five straight years of positive net income. Nonetheless, Congress killed the USPS gainsharing program by passing a law prohibiting payment of gainsharing savings to employees for any year that the USPS lost money (which it has done the last few years).[135]

Nonfinancial rewards are another way to reward teams for their performance. These rewards, which can range from vacation trips to T-shirts, plaques, and coffee mugs, are especially effective when coupled with management recognition, such as awards, certificates, and praise.[136] Nonfinancial awards tend to be most effective when teams or team-based interventions, such as total quality management (see Chapter 18), are first introduced.[137]

Which team compensation plan should your company use? In general, skill-based pay is most effective for self-managing and self-directing teams performing complex tasks. In these situations, the more each team member knows and can do, the better the whole team performs. By contrast, gainsharing works best in relatively stable environments where employees can focus on improving the productivity, cost savings, or quality of their current work system.

Finally, given the level of dissatisfaction with most team compensation systems, what compensation plans would today's managers like to use with the teams in their companies? As shown in Exhibit 10.10,

Plantwide Profit Sharing (based on overall company or division performance, but with *equal* payouts to all teams and team members)

Gainsharing (*different* payouts to teams depending on how much each saved the company, but with *equal* payouts within teams)

Merit-Based Team Pay (*adjust within teams* for differences in individual performance)

Gainsharing (*equal* payouts to all teams and team members)

Merit-Based Team Pay (*equal* shares within teams)

12.2%

14.5%

40.5%

19.1%

13.7%

Source: J. H. Sheridan, "'YES' to Team Incentives," *Industry Week*, 4 March 1996, 63.

Exhibit 10.10
Managers' Preferences for Team-Based Pay

40.5 percent of managers would directly link merit-pay increases to team performance, but allow adjustments within teams for differences in individual performance. By contrast, 13.7 percent would also link merit-based increases directly to team performance but give each team member an equal share of the team's merit-based reward. Also, 19.1 percent would use gainsharing plans based on quality, delivery, productivity, or cost reduction and then provide equal payouts to all teams and team members. Another 14.5 percent would also use gainsharing, but they would vary the team gainsharing award, depending on how much money the team saved the company. Payouts would still be equally distributed within teams. Finally, 12.2 percent of managers would opt for plantwide profit-sharing plans tied to overall company or division performance.[138] In this case, there would be no payout distinctions between or within teams.

Review 4: *Enhancing Work Team Effectiveness*

Companies can make teams more effective by setting team goals and managing how team members are selected, trained, and compensated. Team goals provide a clear focus and purpose, reduce the incidence of social loafing, and lead to higher team performance 93 percent of the time. Extremely difficult stretch goals can be used to motivate teams as long as teams have autonomy, control over resources, structural accommodation, and bureaucratic immunity. Not everyone is suited for teamwork. When selecting team members, companies should select people who have a preference for teamwork (individualism-collectivism) and should consider team level (average ability on a team) and team diversity (different abilities on a team). Organizations that successfully use teams provide thousands of hours of training to make sure that teams work. The most common types of team training are for interpersonal skills, decision-making and problem-solving skills, conflict resolution, technical training to help team members learn multiple jobs (that is, cross-training), and training for team leaders. Employees can be compensated for team participation and accomplishments in three ways: skill-based pay, gainsharing, and nonfinancial rewards.

Working in Groups

From sports to school to work to civic involvement, working in teams is increasingly part of our experience. Even though teams are increasingly used to get work done, people still have widely varying opinions of their value. Think of your own situation. When a professor divides the class into groups to complete a project, do you respond with an inward smile or a heavy sigh? Do you enjoy team projects, or would you rather just do your own work? The following 20-question survey assesses your thoughts about working in teams.[139] Indicate the extent to which you agree with each of the following statements. Try not to spend too much time on any one item, and be sure to answer all the questions. Use this scale for your responses:

1   Strongly disagree
2   Disagree
3   Slightly disagree
4   Neutral
5   Slightly agree
6   Agree
7   Strongly agree

1. Only those who depend on themselves get ahead in life.
    1   2   3   4   5   6   7

2. To be superior, a person must stand alone.
    1   2   3   4   5   6   7

3. If you want something done right, you've got to do it yourself.
    1   2   3   4   5   6   7

4. What happens to me is my own doing.
    1   2   3   4   5   6   7

5. In the long run, the only person you can count on is yourself.
    1   2   3   4   5   6   7

6. Winning is everything.
    1   2   3   4   5   6   7

7. I feel that winning is important in both work and games.
    1   2   3   4   5   6   7

8. Success is the most important thing in life.
    1   2   3   4   5   6   7

9. It annoys me when other people perform better than I do.
    1   2   3   4   5   6   7

10. Doing your best isn't enough; it is important to win.
    1   2   3   4   5   6   7

11. I prefer to work with others in a group rather than working alone.
    1   2   3   4   5   6   7

12. Given the choice, I would rather do a job where I can work alone rather than doing a job where I have to work with others in a group.
    1   2   3   4
    5   6   7

13. Working with a group is better than working alone.
    1   2   3   4
    5   6   7

14. People should be made aware that if they are going to be part of a group, then they are sometimes going to have to do things they don't want to do.
    1   2   3   4
    5   6   7

15. People who belong to a group should realize that they're not always going to get what they personally want.
    1   2   3   4
    5   6   7

16. People in a group should realize that they sometimes are going to have to make sacrifices for the sake of the group as a whole.
    1   2   3   4
    5   6   7

17. People in a group should be willing to make sacrifices for the sake of the group's well-being.
    1   2   3   4
    5   6   7

KEY TERMS

18. A group is more productive when its members do what they want to do rather than what the group wants them to do.

    1   2   3   4   5   6   7

19. A group is most efficient when its members do what they think is best rather than doing what the group wants them to do.

    1   2   3   4   5   6   7

20. A group is more productive when its members follow their own interests and desires.

    1   2   3   4   5   6   7

Scoring

Determine your score by entering your response to each survey item below, as follows. In blanks that say *regular score*, simply enter your response for that item. If your response was a 3, place a 3 in the *regular score* blank. In blanks that say *reverse score*, subtract your response from 8 and enter the result. So if your response was a 3, place a 5 (8 − 3 = 5) in the *reverse score* blank.

1. reverse score _____
2. reverse score _____
3. reverse score _____
4. reverse score _____
5. reverse score _____
6. reverse score _____
7. reverse score _____
8. reverse score _____
9. reverse score _____
10. reverse score _____
11. regular score _____
12. reverse score _____
13. regular score _____
14. regular score _____
15. regular score _____
16. regular score _____
17. regular score _____
18. reverse score _____
19. reverse score _____
20. reverse score _____

TOTAL = _____

You can find the interpretation of your score at: **academic.cengage.com/management/williams.**

□ ☑ □ □ □

MANAGEMENT DECISION

Do You Assemble a Team of Stars or Ordinary Players?

What criteria will you use to assemble a work team?[140] Is a team composed of all-stars better than one composed of ordinary players? Recall that the United States baseball team that included Roger Clemens, Derek Jeter, Alex Rodriguez and Johnny Damon lost to Mexico, South Korea, and Canada and failed to reach the semifinals of the World Baseball Classic. The 2004 U.S. Olympic basketball team consisting of NBA star players finished third and lost to Lithuania. How could a *Fortune* 500 company that was run by a brilliant former McKinsey consultant and that only hired graduates of America's elite business schools dissolve into fraud and bankruptcy? It happened at Enron. "Some of the worst teams I've ever seen have been those where everybody was a potential CEO," says David Nadler, chief of the Mercer Delta consulting firm, who has worked with executive teams for more than 30 years.

The most important lesson about team performance is that the basic theory of the dream team is wrong, says Geoffrey Colvin, senior editor at *Fortune*. Consider the 1980 U.S. hockey team that beat the Soviets at the Lake Placid Olympics; it was built entirely on anti-dream-team principles. Coach Herb Brooks based his picks on personal chemistry: "I'm not looking for the best players, I'm looking for the right players," he said at the time. CEO John McConnell of Worthington Industries, the Ohio-based steel processor, says, "Give us people who are dedicated to making the team work, as opposed to a bunch of talented people with big egos, and we'll win every time." That's the philosophy that powers teams such as the New England Patriots, which is only the second team in NFL history to win three Super Bowls in four years.

Questions

1. Briefly discuss the advantages and disadvantages of assembling a team composed of (a) star players, and (b) ordinary players.

2. If you were to include star players on your team, what should you do to make sure the team is not dysfunctional and is able to perform as well as expected? Explain.

Taking a Chance on Teams at IBM

Evenings at home are the only time you can look over your management team's monthly reports without interruptions.[141] Tonight, you're quietly sipping coffee (decaf, naturally) as you review the reports in the comfort of your favorite chair. You are suddenly jarred, however, by a single line deep in one report, which might have gone unnoticed if you hadn't carved out this time away from the office. In discussing the prospects for a new opportunity, one of your managers wrote, "Pressures in the current quarter have forced us to cut costs by discontinuing efforts in this promising new area." Unbelievable! As you continue reading, you can't get this line out of your head. Why is the company abandoning "promising" avenues of growth and revenue because of external pressures? You finish reading the reports and resolve to discuss the issue with all of your managers—not just the one who wrote the report.

The next morning, you ask your senior vice president to investigate, and in short order, he discovers a pattern of nonconversion. In other words, even though your company, *IBM*, obtains thousands of patents each year, management seems to have tremendous difficulties turning its basic research into functioning businesses. The reason apparently stems from the company's focus on existing markets and short-term results. Rather than focusing on turning new ideas into new products and services, IBM's most talented and experienced executives are being rewarded based on how much revenue their divisions generate and the number of employees reporting to them. Not surprisingly, they're more concerned with growing existing products and services than they are with developing new products and services for the future. As a result, IBM has left many innovations on the table for

outsiders to scoop up. For example, IBM invented the relational database and the router, but it was Oracle and Cisco that built huge companies around them.

You call your management team together and pose this problem: "How are we going to transform the work of our research scientists into new businesses? We need to figure out how to recognize and nurture these emerging business opportunities. IBM has hundreds of thousands of employees and billions of dollars in revenue. Surely, we have enough resources to commercialize our great ideas!"

In response, your VP for strategy says, "I wonder if we could do it with teams."

For this Management Team Decision, assemble five to six students to act as the management team at IBM.

Questions

1. Are teams a good idea for IBM's emerging business opportunities (EBOs) given the company's culture and well-defined organization? Why or why not?

2. If you do use teams, what kind of team would be best in the situation described? In other words, how much autonomy should teams working on EBOs have?

3. Who would you choose to lead the EBO teams—experienced executives who are successfully managing established divisions or less experienced managers who want to prove themselves? Explain your rationale. (You may want to review Chapter 1, Section 3, "Kinds of Managers.")

4. What will your management team need to do to help EBO teams be successful? Remember, the whole point of looking into EBOs is to increase IBM's revenue and reach.

Teamwork is vital to the success of organizations. And this makes creating high-performance teams an important management challenge. In this exercise, you will work with fellow students to brainstorm the creation of a high-performing team. Pay particular attention to the assumptions that you and your

peers bring to this process regarding what works, and what doesn't work, in relation to creating a high-performance team. At the conclusion of the exercise, you will have an opportunity to discuss the theory and common assumptions regarding effective team building.

Step 1: Get into groups. Your professor will organize small groups.

Step 2: Review the situation. Assume that your group has been hand-picked by the president of your college or university to work for one semester as a "campus improvement" team. At the end of the year you will submit your recommendations to the president and the board of your institution. These leaders have assured you that they will make every effort to implement your recommendations.

Step 3: Develop a plan. Brainstorm and develop a plan for working as a team to achieve the objective of delivering a set of quality recommendations to the president and the board. You should consider the following in developing your plan:

- Working well together as a team
- Establishing criteria for "quality recommendations" (such as representing the various important constituencies and interests on campus)
- Outlining steps, areas and types of work, and assignments for each member that are most likely to take full advantage of the capabilities and resources in your team

Step 4: Discuss your plans as a class. Is this the sort of project that is well-suited to using a work team? Why, or why not? How might work team characteristics such as norms, cohesiveness, and team size play a role in this team effort? What conflicts might be likely down the road, and at what stage of the process are these conflicts most likely to occur?

☐ ☐ ☐ ☐ ☑

DEVELOP YOUR CAREER POTENTIAL

Evaluate Your Team Skills

Step 1: Answer the following questions the way that you think *other members of your team* would if they were describing your actions.[142] Use this scale for your responses:

1 Almost never
2 Seldom
3 Sometimes
4 Usually
5 Almost always

I. Honor Team Values and Agreements

As a team member, (your name):

_____ a. shows appreciation for other team members' ideas.

_____ b. helps other team members cope with change.

_____ c. encourages others to use their strengths.

_____ d. helps the team develop a productive relationship with other teams.

_____ e. willingly assumes a leadership role when needed.

Total for Section I: _____

II. Promote Team Development

As a team member, (your name):

_____ a. volunteers for all types of tasks, including the hard ones.

_____ b. helps orient and train new team members.

_____ c. helps organize and run effective meetings.

_____ d. helps examine how we are doing as a team and makes any necessary changes in the way we work together.

_____ e. helps identify milestones and mini-successes to celebrate.

Total for Section II: _____

III. Help Make Team Decisions

As a team member, (your name):

_____ a. analyzes what a decision entails.

_____ b. ensures that the team selects and includes the appropriate people in the decision process.

_____ c. clearly states his or her concerns.

_____ d. searches for common ground when team members have different views.

_____ e. actively supports the team's decisions.

Total for Section III: _____

IV. Coordinate and Carry Out Team Tasks

As a team member, (your name):

_____ a. helps identify the information, skills, and resources necessary to accomplish team tasks.

_____ b. helps formulate and agree on a plan to meet performance goals.

_____ c. stays abreast of what is happening in other parts of the organization and brings that information to the team.

_____ d. finds innovative ways to meet the needs of the team and of others in the organization.

_____ e. maintains a win-win outlook in all dealings with other teams.

Total for Section IV: _____

V. Handle Difficult Issues with the Team

As a team member, (your name):

_____ a. brings team issues and problems to the team's attention.

_____ b. encourages others on the team to state their views.

_____ c. helps build trust among team members by speaking openly about the team's problems.

_____ d. gives specific, constructive, and timely feedback to others.

_____ e. admits when he or she has made a mistake.

Total for Section V: _____

Step 2: Transfer the section totals to this table:

Category	Total Score
Honor team values and agreements.	———
Promote team development.	———
Help make team decisions.	———
Coordinate and carry out team tasks.	———
Handle difficult issues with the team.	———

Interpreting Scores

- A score of 20 or above in any activity indicates an area of strength.
- A score of below 20 in any activity indicates an area that needs more attention.

Questions to Ask Yourself

Looking at your scores, what areas are strengths? How can you maintain these strengths? What areas are weaknesses? What steps can you take to turn these areas into strengths?

REEL TO REAL

BIZ FLIX
Apollo 13

This film re-creates the heroic efforts of astronaut Jim Lovell (Tom Hanks), his crew, NASA, and Mission Control to return the damaged Apollo spacecraft to earth. Examples of both problem solving and decision making occur in almost every scene.

This scene takes place during day 5 of the mission, about two-thirds of the way through the film. Early in Apollo 13's mission Jack Swigert (Kevin Bacon) stirred the oxygen tanks at the request of Mission Control. After this procedure, an explosion occurred, causing unknown damage to the command module. Before the scene takes place, the damage has forced the crew to move into the LEM (Lunar Exploration Module), which becomes their lifeboat for return to earth.

What to Watch for and Ask Yourself

1. What triggers the conflict in this scene?
2. Is this intergroup conflict or intragroup conflict? What effects can such conflict have on the group dynamics on board Apollo 13?
3. Does mission commander Jim Lovell successfully manage the group dynamics to return the group to a normal state?

MANAGEMENT WORKPLACE
NEADS—Unconventional Teams

All the teams you have encountered in this chapter have been teams of people. NEADS, the National Education for Assistance Dog Services, functions with teams of people as well. But another type of teamwork is central to the mission of NEADS: the team of human and dog. NEADS acquires, raises, trains, and matches service dogs to meet the needs of people with limited physical mobility or who are deaf. A typical service dog may be trained to respond to a blaring smoke alarm or ringing telephone, nudge a light switch on or off with its nose, or retrieve items for an owner. Since this partnership is intended to last a lifetime, it is important for the match to be perfect. Step into the management workplace of NEADS to find out how this unique organization implements teams—both human and canine.

What to Watch for and Ask Yourself

1. Describe the characteristics of a typical NEADS team, using the criteria discussed in the chapter.
2. What factors determine the cohesiveness of NEADS teams?
3. Describe a situation in which conflict might arise in a NEADS team.

Managing Human Resource Systems

Learning Outcomes:

1 Describe the basic steps involved in human resource planning.

2 Explain how different employment laws affect human resource practice.

3 Explain how companies use recruiting to find qualified job applicants.

4 Describe the selection techniques and procedures that companies use when deciding which applicants should receive job offers.

5 Describe how to determine training needs and select the appropriate training methods.

6 Discuss how to use performance appraisal to give meaningful performance feedback.

7 Describe basic compensation strategies and explain how they affect human resource practice.

8 Discuss the four kinds of employee separations: termination, downsizing, retirements, and turnover.

In This Chapter:

WHAT WOULD YOU DO?

RadioShack, Fort Worth, Texas.[1] "Radio Sacked," read the headline in the *Vancouver Sun*. "Read this E-Mail—Then Scram," wrote the *Los Angeles Times*. In an article published in the *Washington Post*, psychologist Ken Siegel said "To almost everyone who observes or reads about this, it represents a stupefying new low in the annals of management practice." These and other such headlines are referring to the manner in which layoffs were communicated to affected employees at RadioShack.

RadioShack needed to lay off over 400 employees, mostly at its corporate headquarters. It delivered the following e-mail to those selected for termination: *The work force reduction notification is currently in progress. Unfortunately your position is one that been eliminated.*

Workers who received the notification had 30 minutes to collect their thoughts and say their goodbyes before they went to meet with senior leaders. Workers who survived the layoff were shocked and demoralized.

This is not the first time RadioShack's reputation has taken a beating. Just a few months prior to this e-mail, CEO David J. Edmondson was fired after a newspaper

investigation revealed that he had not, as he had claimed, earned degrees in theology and psychology from the Heartland Baptist Bible College; in fact, according to the school's records, he had completed only two semesters and had never even taken a single psychology class. What kind of message does that send to employees about the ethics of RadioShack's top executives?

But RadioShack's human resource troubles don't stop there. The company also made the news for race discrimination in hiring practices and for its controversial "Fix 1500 Initiative." In that program, store managers were subjectively assessed relative to other store managers, and the bottom 1,500 were given 90 days to improve. As a result, in one six-month period, a total of 1,734 store managers were demoted to sales associates or fired. Executives also eliminated the stock purchase plan for employees but retained it for management, which did little to improve the company's image, especially among employees.

All the while, the company is struggling to compete with big-box retailers like Best Buy, Circuit City, Costco, and Wal-Mart. Total sales have fallen by 12 percent, 530 stores have been closed, and same-store sales fell 6.8 percent in one year. Credit Suisse analyst Gary Balter wrote in a report

that the results, which were "weaker than the weak results we had expected, raise a number of questions, none of which we expect to get answers to from this company."

You knew this would be a tough job. But as the new Vice President of Human Resources you are committed to making things better at RadioShack; a lot of things. Should you focus on building trust and enhancing employee morale? What about recruiting and hiring processes? You wonder if RadioShack is hiring the right people. Background checks would be a good start, you think. But even if you hire good people, how are you going to tell if they're doing a good job? The performance-appraisal system of relative grading has got to go, but what should replace it? And there's surely going to be more restructuring, so you'll need to establish procedures to communicate layoffs, and guidelines for dealing with laid-off employees and survivors. Finally, what can you do about RadioShack's poor reputation? You know it will affect your ability to recruit high-quality applicants for management jobs. Human Resources can make a positive impact on Radio Shack's future and bottom line, but where do you start? **As the new VP of HR, what would you do?**

ACTIVITIES + VIDEO

CengageNOW Audio study guide, electronic flashcards, author FAQ videos, On the Job and Biz Flix videos, concept tutorial, and concept exercise

Web (academic.cengage.com/management/williams) Quiz, PowerPoint slides, and glossary terms for this chapter

Study Tip

Use the chapter outline on the preceding page as a study tool. After reading the whole chapter, return to the list and write a summary of each item. Check your work by reading the actual review paragraphs on pages 388, 393, 398, 408, 413, 417, 421, and 425.

"WHAT'S NEW" COMPANIES

RADIOSHACK

BEHLEN MANUFACTURING

CORNING GLASS

HOOTERS

MORGAN STANLEY

BRITISH PETROLEUM

COCA-COLA

BAKER & MCKENZIE

QUICK CHEK FOOD STORES

FUJISAWA PHARMACEUTICALS

AND OTHERS . . .

As the problems facing RadioShack show, **human resource management (HRM)**, or the process of finding, developing, and keeping the right people to form a qualified work force, is one of the most difficult and important of all management tasks. This chapter is organized around the four parts of the human resource management process shown in Exhibit 11.1: determining human resource needs and attracting, developing, and keeping a qualified work force.

Accordingly, the chapter begins by reviewing how human resource planning determines human resource needs, such as the kind and number of employees a company requires to meet its strategic plans and objectives. Next, we explore how companies use recruiting and selection techniques to attract and hire qualified employees to fulfill those needs. The third part of the chapter discusses how training and performance appraisal can develop the knowledge, skills, and abilities of the work force. The chapter concludes with a review of compensation and employee separation, that is, how companies can keep their best workers through effective compensation practices and how they can manage the separation process when employees leave the organization.

DETERMINING HUMAN RESOURCE NEEDS

Should we hire more workers? What should we pay our current employees to slow employee turnover? What kinds of training do our new employees need to be prepared to do a good job, and what's the best way to deliver that training? In other words, what are our human resource needs, and what's the best way to address them? The human resource management process, shown in Exhibit 11.1, can provide answers to these questions.

We can see how the HRM process works by examining what hospitals are doing to address the shortage of qualified nurses around the world. How acute is this shortage? Hospitals in London, England, find it so difficult to attract British nurses that they have sent managers all the way to Jamaica to recruit English-speaking nurses. But Jamaica has lost so many nurses to English hospitals that it now prevents the British government (which runs the health system in Britain) from hiring its nurses. And why do British hospitals have such a hard time finding nurses? Because Canadian nurses take higher-paying jobs in the United States, which forces Canadian hospitals to hire British nurses and British hospitals to hire nurses from Ghana (since they can no longer hire Jamaican nurses). The nursing shortage is so severe worldwide that even U.S. hospitals now recruit directly in many countries. In South Africa and the Philippines, nurses are encouraged to come to the United States by ads that say, "Nurses! Think of it as your seat in America. Gain invaluable experience, learn the latest medical techniques, and live a fuller life in a relaxed environment."[2] And, like all workers, nurses who work in poor conditions for poor pay are willing to move to other countries for better-paying jobs in good companies. So, for the hospitals around the world that struggle to hire nurses, the

human resource management (HRM) the process of finding, developing, and keeping the right people to form a qualified work force

© CORBISRF/JUPITER IMAGES

HRM process, as shown in Exhibit 11.1, comes full circle as attracting, developing, and then keeping qualified nurses affect their human resource needs.

> **After reading the next two sections, you should be able to**
> 1 describe the basic steps involved in human resource planning.
> 2 explain how different employment laws affect human resource practice.

1 Human Resource Planning

Human resource planning (HRP) is the process of using an organization's goals and strategy to forecast the organization's human resource needs in terms of attracting, developing, and keeping a qualified work force.[3] Importantly, companies that don't use HRP or that do it poorly may end up with either a surplus of employees that has to be corrected with layoffs or a shortage of employees that leads to increased overtime costs and an inability to meet demand for the company's product or service.

> Let's explore human resource planning by examining how to
> **1.1 forecast the demand and supply of human resources** and
> **1.2 use human resource information systems to improve those forecasts**.

1.1 Forecasting Demand and Supply

Work force forecasting is the process of predicting the number and kind of workers with specific skills and abilities that an organization will need in the future.[4] There are two kinds of work force forecasts, internal and external forecasts, and three kinds of forecasting methods—direct managerial input, best guess, and statistical/historical ratios.

Internal forecasts are projections about factors within the organization that affect the supply and demand for human resources. These factors include the financial performance of the organization, its productivity, its mission, changes in technology or the way the work is performed, and terminations, promotions, transfers, retirements, resignations, and deaths of current employees. For example, according to Mark Young, senior research associate for the Conference Board, Corning Glass focuses on trends over a period of three to four years, rather than a precise headcount and short-term plans. It then segments jobs based on how critical the jobs are to accomplishing its mission, and makes different levels of workforce investment in each segment.[5] Exhibit 11.2 provides a more complete list of factors that influence internal forecasts.

External forecasts are projections about factors outside the organization that affect the supply and demand for human resources. These factors include the labor supply for specific types of workers, the economy (unemployment rate), labor unions, demographics of the labor force (proportion of labor force in, for example, various age groups), geographic movement of the labor force, strength of competitors, and growth in particular businesses and markets.

Exhibit 11.1

The Human Resource Management Process

Determining Human Resource Needs — Human Resource Planning

Attracting Qualified Employees — Recruiting → Selection

Developing Qualified Employees — Training → Performance Appraisal

Keeping Qualified Employees — Compensation → Employee Separation

human resource planning (HRP) using an organization's goals and strategy to forecast the organization's human resource needs in terms of attracting, developing, and keeping a qualified work force

work force forecasting the process of predicting the number and kind of workers with specific skills and abilities that an organization will need in the future

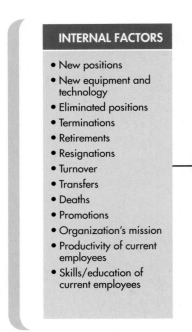

INTERNAL FACTORS	EXTERNAL FACTORS

INTERNAL FACTORS
- New positions
- New equipment and technology
- Eliminated positions
- Terminations
- Retirements
- Resignations
- Turnover
- Transfers
- Deaths
- Promotions
- Organization's mission
- Productivity of current employees
- Skills/education of current employees

Work Force Forecast

EXTERNAL FACTORS
- Demographics of labor supply
- Geographic population shifts
- Shift from manufacturing- to service- to information-based economy
- General economic conditions
- Unemployment rate
- Labor unions
- Availability of applicants with specific skills and education
- Technological advances
- Strength and number of competitors
- Growth in particular businesses and markets

Exhibit 11.2

Internal and External Factors That Influence Work Force Forecasting

For example, when the economy slowed, BEHLEN MANUFACTURING switched its 400 factory workers from full-time to part-time work and cut the pay of its salaried workers by 10 percent. CEO Tony Raimondo said during the change, "This year, we've been reducing hours and telling people we believed it was short-term. We think we saved a lot of jobs by doing that."[6] When the economy strengthened and sales began increasing again, he quickly switched his factory workers back to full-time hours and removed the 10 percent pay cut. Exhibit 11.2 provides a more complete list of factors that influence external forecasts.

Three kinds of forecasting methods—direct managerial input, best guess, and statistical/historical ratios—are often used to predict the number and kind of workers with specific skills and abilities that an organization will need in the future.[7] The most common forecasting method, *direct managerial input*, is based on straightforward projections of cash flows, expenses, or financial measures, such as return on capital. Though financial indicators are relatively quick to calculate and can help managers determine how many workers might be needed, they don't help managers decide which critical skills new employees should possess.

The *best guess* forecasting method is based on managers' assessment of current head count, plus a best guess of how internal factors and external factors will affect that head count. A recent survey reported that managers typically overestimate future staffing levels needed to achieve business goals. The survey also found that organizations are more accurate when it comes to forecasting employment increases than when forecasting employment decreases.[8]

Finally, the *statistical/historical ratios* forecasting method uses statistical methods, such as multiple regression, in combination with historical data to predict the number and kind of workers a company should hire. For example, a manager might run a regression analysis using data from the last two years. In this analysis, the number of employees that need to be hired is the dependent (predicted) variable, and the number of items manufactured, number of clients, average increase in sales, and similar factors are the independent (predictor) variables. The regression analysis produces a simple equation that indicates how many more employees should be added for each increase in the independent variables, such as items manufactured or increased sales. This approach takes advantage of existing data and can be much more accurate than best guess predictions, but only if a company's internal and external environments have not changed significantly.

CORNING GLASS uses a variety of statistical tools to help predict its work force needs, a process it calls human capital planning. Corning uses human capital planning to improve its ability to identify human resource requirements of corporate strategy and reshape HR services to better support the business. "We've already realized considerable value from the human capital planning process," says Kurt Fischer, vice president of human resources at Corning.[9]

1.2 Human Resource Information Systems

Human resource information systems (HRISs) are computerized systems for gathering, analyzing, storing, and disseminating information related to attracting, developing, and keeping a qualified work force.[10] Exhibit 11.3 shows some of the data that are commonly used in HRISs, such as personal and educational data, company employment history, performance appraisal information, work history, and promotions.

Human resource information systems can be used for transaction processing, employee self-service, and decision support. For HRISs, *transaction processing* usually involves employee payroll checks, taxes, and benefit deductions. For example, when ER One, a Michigan-based company that provides physicians and other clinicians for hospital emergency rooms, was small, it used paper files and different computer spreadsheets and databases to keep track of compensation and benefits for its employees. But now that the company has 180 employees in seven different locations, it uses an HRIS to keep track of its employees. This system quickly provides accurate, up-to-date information about employee compensation and benefits and can be easily accessed from any of the seven locations, says Pat Brainard, the company's director of human resources.[11] HRISs can also reduce administrative costs by preparing certain routine reports, such as the EEOC (Equal Employment Opportunity Commission) or OSHA (Occupational Safety and Health Administration) reports that are required of many companies.

Though typically used to give managers and HR staffers access to human resource data, today's secure web-based HRISs also give employees immediate, 24-hour *self-service* access to personal data, such as benefits and retirement packages. By entering a user name and a password, employees can access and change their medical insurance plan, adjust the mix of investments in their 401(k) retirement plan, or check on the status of medical or child-care reimbursements. Hewitt Associates is a global HR consulting and benefits outsourcing firm that provides its customers with secure access to HR data and applications using web-services technology, 24/7. Customers, meaning, employees of client organizations, can access and change their current health care enrollment, check on their retirement benefits, and reallocate their 401(k) investments.[12]

In addition to gathering and storing information, HRISs also help managers by serving as decision support systems for critical HR decisions.[13] In Chapter 17, you will learn that *decision support systems (DSSs)* help managers understand problems and potential solutions by acquiring and analyzing information with sophisticated models and tools. For instance, an HRIS can help managers make HR decisions from the moment job applicants submit résumés to the company. Those résumés are scanned into the HRIS, where they are analyzed for the quality of the writing and for

> "This year, we've been reducing hours and telling people we believed it was short-term. We think we saved a lot of jobs by doing that."
>
> — TONY RAIMONDO,
> CEO, BEHLEN MANUFACTURING

human resource information system (HRIS) a computerized system for gathering, analyzing, storing, and disseminating information related to the HRM process

Exhibit 11.3

Common Data Categories in Human Resource Information Systems

Personal Data
- Name
- Address/telephone number
- Employee identification number
- Social Security number
- Medical plan/coverage
- Retirement/investment plan

Promotion Data
- Geographic preferences
- Personal interests
- Awards
- Job preferences
- Special skills/knowledge
- Foreign language(s)

Work History
- Previous employers
- Previous positions
- Duties in previous positions
- Supervisory experience

HRIS

Educational Data
- High school diploma
- College degrees
- Special courses training

Performance Appraisal
- Date of last performance appraisal
- Productivity measures
- Disciplinary action
- Tardiness
- Absenteeism
- Last performance rating
- Quality measures

Company Employment History
- Previous job assignments
- Current position
- Date of initial employment
- Seniority date
- Salary/pay history
- Current salary/pay
- Fringe benefit package
- Last pay raise

key words that match the organization's job database. For instance, to identify experienced tax preparers, tax preparation company H&R Block looks for key phrases like "certified financial planner" and "insurance license."[14]

An HRIS can even be used to do preemployment testing or background screening. At Sprint Nextel, when job applicants apply at **http://www.sprint.com/careers/index.html**, they are asked to answer screening questions, such as "Do you know C++ programming?" or "Have you sold to *Fortune* 500 companies?"[15] Sprint's HRIS then automatically ranks the applicants based on their responses. Recruiters then review the top 25 percent of applicants for job openings.

An HRIS can also be used effectively to screen *internal applicants* on particular qualifications, to match the qualifications of external applicants against those of internal applicants, to compare salaries within and between departments, and to review and change employees' salaries instantaneously without lengthy paperwork. In short, today's HRISs can help managers make any number of critical human resource decisions.

Review 1: **Human Resource Planning**

Human resource planning (HRP) uses organizational goals and strategies to determine what needs to be done to attract, develop, and keep a qualified work force. Work force forecasts are used to predict the number and kind of workers with specific skills and abilities that an organization needs. Work force forecasts consider both internal and external factors that affect the supply and demand for workers and can be formulated using three kinds of forecasting methods: direct managerial input, best guess, and statistical/historical ratios. Computerized human resource information systems improve HRP by gathering, analyzing, storing, and disseminating information (personal, educational, work history, performance, and promotions) related to human resource management activities. Human resource information systems can be used for transaction processing (payroll checks and routine reports), employee self-service (24-hour web access allowing instant changes to benefit and retirement packages), and decision support for human resource decisions (analyzing résumés, background screening, and preemployment testing).

2 Employment Legislation

Since their inception, **HOOTERS** restaurants have hired only female servers. Moreover, consistent with the company's marketing theme, the servers wear short nylon shorts and cutoff T-shirts that show their midriffs. The Equal Employment Opportunity Commission (EEOC) began an investigation of Hooters when a Chicago man filed a sex-based discrimination charge. The man alleged that he had applied for a server's job at a Hooters restaurant and was rejected because of his sex. The dispute between Hooters and the EEOC quickly gained national attention. One sarcastic letter to the EEOC printed in *Fortune* magazine read as follows:

Dear EEOC:

Hi! I just wanted to thank you for investigating those Hooters restaurants, where the waitresses wear those shorty shorts and midriffy T-shirts. I think it's a great idea that you have decided to make Hooters hire men as—how do you say it?—waitpersons. Gee, I never knew so many men wanted to be waitpersons at Hooters. No reason to let them sue on their own either. You're right, the government needs to take the lead on this one.[16]

This letter characterized public sentiment at the time. Given its backlog of 100,000 job discrimination cases, many wondered if the EEOC didn't have better things to do with its scarce resources.

Three years after the initial complaint, the EEOC ruled that Hooters had violated antidiscrimination laws and offered to settle the case if the company would agree to pay $22 million to the EEOC for distribution to male victims of the "Hooters Girl" hiring policy, establish a scholarship fund to enhance opportunities or education for men, and provide sensitivity training to teach Hooters' employees how to be more sensitive to men's needs. Hooters responded with a $1 million publicity campaign criticizing the EEOC's investigation. Billboards featuring "Vince," a man dressed in a Hooters Girl uniform and blond wig, sprang up all over the country. Hooters customers were given postcards to send complaints to the EEOC. Of course, Hooters paid the postage. As a result of the publicity campaign, restaurant sales increased by 10 percent. Soon thereafter, the EEOC announced that it would not pursue discriminatory hiring charges against Hooters.[17] Nonetheless, the company ended up paying $3.75 million to settle a class-action suit brought by seven men who claimed that their inability to get a job at Hooters violated federal law.[18] Under the settlement, Hooters maintained its women-only policy for server jobs, but had to create additional support jobs, such as hosts and bartenders, that would also be open to men.

As the Hooters example illustrates, the human resource planning process occurs in a very complicated legal environment. Let's explore employment legislation by reviewing **2.1 the major federal employment laws that affect human resource practice**, **2.2 how the concept of adverse impact is related to employment discrimination**, *and* **2.3 the laws regarding sexual harassment in the workplace**.

2.1 Federal Employment Laws

Exhibit 11.4 lists the major federal employment laws and their websites, where you can find more detailed information. Except for the Family and Medical Leave Act and the Uniformed Services Employment and Reemployment Rights Act, which are administered by the Department of Labor (**http://www.dol.gov**), all of these laws are administered by the EEOC (**http://www.eeoc.gov**). The general effect of this body of law, which is still evolving through court decisions, is that employers may not discriminate in employment decisions on the basis of sex, age, religion, color, national origin, race, or disability. The intent is to make these factors irrelevant in employment decisions. Stated another way, employment decisions should be based on factors that are "job related," "reasonably necessary," or a "business necessity" for successful job performance. The only time that sex, age, religion, and the like can be used to make employment decisions is when they are considered a bona fide occupational qualification.[19] Title VII of the 1964 Civil Rights Act says that it is not unlawful to hire and

Despite a favorable ruling, Hooters was still required to create more support jobs that would be open to men—even on its failed airline.

© TAMMY CHAPPELL/REUTERS/LANDOV

Equal Pay Act of 1963	http://www.eeoc.gov/policy/epa.html	Prohibits unequal pay for males and females doing substantially similar work.
Civil Rights Act of 1964	http://www.eeoc.gov/policy/vii.html	Prohibits discrimination on the basis of race, color, religion, sex, or national origin.
Age Discrimination in Employment Act of 1967	http://www.eeoc.gov/policy/adea.html	Prohibits discrimination in employment decisions against persons age 40 and over.
Pregnancy Discrimination Act of 1978	http://www.eeoc.gov/facts/fs-preg.html	Prohibits discrimination in employment against pregnant women.
Americans with Disabilities Act of 1990	http://www.eeoc.gov/policy/ada.html	Prohibits discrimination on the basis of physical or mental disabilities.
Civil Rights Act of 1991	http://www.eeoc.gov/policy/cra91.html	Strengthened the provisions of the Civil Rights Act of 1964 by providing for jury trials and punitive damages.
Family and Medical Leave Act of 1993	http://www.dol.gov/esa/whd/fmla//index.html	Permits workers to take up to 12 weeks of unpaid leave for pregnancy and/or birth of a new child, adoption or foster care of a new child, illness of an immediate family member, or personal medical leave.
Uniformed Services Employment and Reemployment Rights Act of 1994	http://www.osc.gov/userra.htm	Prohibits discrimination against those serving in the Armed Forces Reserve, the National Guard, or other uniformed services; guarantees that civilian employers will hold and then restore civilian jobs and benefits for those who have completed uniformed service.

Exhibit 11.4

Summary of Major Federal Employment Laws

bona fide occupational qualification (BFOQ) an exception in employment law that permits sex, age, religion, and the like to be used when making employment decisions, but only if they are "reasonably necessary to the normal operation of that particular business." BFOQs are strictly monitored by the Equal Employment Opportunity Commission.

employ someone on the basis of sex, religion, or national origin when there is a **bona fide occupational qualification (BFOQ)** that is "reasonably necessary to the normal operation of that particular business." For example, a Baptist church hiring a new minister can reasonably specify that being a Baptist rather than a Catholic or Presbyterian is a BFOQ for the position. However, it's unlikely that the church could specify race or national origin as a BFOQ. In general, the courts and the EEOC take a hard look when a business claims that sex, age, religion, color, national origin, race, or disability is a BFOQ. For instance, the EEOC disagreed with Hooters' claim that it was "in the business of providing vicarious sexual recreation" and that "female sexuality is a bona fide occupational qualification."[20]

It is important to understand, however, that these laws apply to the entire HRM process and not just to selection decisions (hiring or promotion). These laws also cover all training and development activities, performance appraisals, terminations, and compensation decisions. Employers who use sex, age, race, or religion to make employment-related decisions when those factors are unrelated to an applicant's or employee's ability to perform a job may face charges of discrimination from employee lawsuits or the EEOC. For example, MORGAN STANLEY, an investment bank, agreed to pay $54 million in damages after the EEOC filed a sex discrimination suit on behalf of 300 of the firm's female employees. The women were paid less and promoted less often than comparable male employees with whom they worked.[21] Boeing, the jet plane manufacturer, paid $72.5 million to settle a similar lawsuit brought by a group of its female employees.[22]

In addition to the laws presented in Exhibit 11.4, there are two other important sets of federal laws: labor laws and laws and regulations governing safety standards. Labor laws regulate the interaction between management and labor unions that represent groups of employees. These laws guarantee employees the right to form and join unions of their own choosing. For more information about labor laws, see the National Labor Relations Board at **http://www.nlrb.gov**. The Occupational Safety and Health Act (OSHA) requires that employers provide employees with a workplace that is "free from recognized hazards that are causing or are likely to cause death or serious physical harm." This law is administered by the Occupational Safety and Health Administration (which, like the act, is referred to as OSHA). OSHA sets safety and health standards for employers and conducts inspections to determine whether those standards are being met. Employers who do not meet OSHA standards may be fined.[23] For example, OSHA fined BRITISH PETROLEUM $23.8 million after a refinery explosion in Texas City, Texas, killed 15 workers and injured 180 employees.[24] OSHA announced the fine for "egregious, willful violations" of safety standards that led to the fatal explosion.[25] The U.S. Chemical Safety and Hazard Investigation Board, a government agency that investigates major workplace accidents, accused BP of knowing about "widespread safety problems" prior to the accident, which it said was the result of "drastic cost-cutting at the Texas refinery, where maintenance and infrastructure deteriorated over time, setting the stage for the disaster."[26] For more information about OSHA, see **http://www.osha.gov**.

2.2 Adverse Impact and Employment Discrimination

The EEOC has investigatory, enforcement, and informational responsibilities. Therefore, it investigates charges of discrimination, enforces the employment discrimination laws in federal court, and publishes guidelines that organizations can use to ensure they are in compliance with the law. One of the most important guidelines jointly issued by the EEOC, the Department of Labor, the U.S. Justice Department, and the federal Office of Personnel Management is the *Uniform Guidelines on Employee Selection Procedures*, which can be read in their entirety at **http://www.dol.gov/esa/regs/cfr/41cfr/toc_Chapt60/60_3_toc.htm**. These guidelines define two important criteria, disparate treatment and adverse impact, that are used in determining whether companies have engaged in discriminatory hiring and promotion practices.

Disparate treatment, which is *intentional* discrimination, occurs when people, despite being qualified, are *intentionally* not given the same hiring, promotion, or membership opportunities as other employees, because of their race, color, age, sex, ethnic group, national origin, or religious beliefs.[27] For example, COCA-COLA paid $192.5 million to settle a class-action disparate treatment lawsuit in which it was accused of purposely not giving African American employees equal opportunities in pay, promotions, and performance reviews.[28] Likewise, Rent-A-Center paid $12.3 million to settle a class-action disparate treatment lawsuit in which it was accused of not providing fair hiring and promotion opportunities to 4,600 female employees and job applicants.[29]

Legally, a key element of discrimination lawsuits is establishing motive, meaning that the employer intended to discriminate. If no motive can be established, then a claim of disparate treatment may actually be a case of adverse impact. **Adverse impact**, which is *unintentional* discrimination, occurs when members of a particular race, sex, or ethnic group are *unintentionally* harmed or disadvantaged because they are hired, promoted, or trained (or any other employment decision) at substantially lower rates than others. The courts and federal agencies use the **four-fifths (or 80 percent) rule** to determine if adverse impact has occurred. Adverse

disparate treatment intentional discrimination that occurs when people are purposely not given the same hiring, promotion, or membership opportunities because of their race, color, sex, age, ethnic group, national origin, or religious beliefs

adverse impact unintentional discrimination that occurs when members of a particular race, sex, or ethnic group are unintentionally harmed or disadvantaged because they are hired, promoted, or trained (or any other employment decision) at substantially lower rates than others

four-fifths (or 80 percent) rule a rule of thumb used by the courts and the EEOC to determine whether there is evidence of adverse impact. A violation of this rule occurs when the selection rate for a protected group is less than 80 percent or four-fifths of the selection rate for a nonprotected group.

impact occurs if the decision rate for a protected group of people is less than four-fifths (or 80 percent) of the decision rate for a nonprotected group (usually white males). So, if 100 white applicants and 100 black applicants apply for entry-level jobs, and 60 white applicants are hired (60/100 = 60%), but only 20 black applicants are hired (20/100 = 20%), adverse impact has occurred (0.20/0.60 = 0.33). The criterion for the four-fifths rule in this situation is 0.48 (0.60 × 0.80 = 0.48). Since 0.33 is less than 0.48, the four-fifths rule has been violated.

Violation of the four-fifths rule is not an automatic indication of discrimination, however. If an employer can demonstrate that a selection procedure or test is valid, meaning that the test accurately predicts job performance or that the test is job related because it assesses applicants on specific tasks actually used in the job, then the organization may continue to use the test. If validity cannot be established, however, then a violation of the four-fifths rule may likely result in a lawsuit brought by employees, job applicants, or the EEOC itself.

2.3 Sexual Harassment

According to the EEOC, **sexual harassment** is a form of discrimination in which unwelcome sexual advances, requests for sexual favors, or other verbal or physical conduct of a sexual nature occurs. From a legal perspective, there are two kinds of sexual harassment, quid pro quo and hostile work environment.[30]

Quid pro quo sexual harassment occurs when employment outcomes, such as hiring, promotion, or simply keeping one's job, depend on whether an individual submits to being sexually harassed. For example, in a quid pro quo sexual harassment lawsuit against Costco, a female employee alleged that her boss groped her and bumped into her from behind to simulate sex. "He would tell her: 'You work with me and I'll work with you,' motioning to his private area."[31] The supervisor also allegedly told her that he would fire her if she reported his activities to upper management. In quid pro quo cases requests for sexual acts are linked to economic outcomes (such as keeping a job). A **hostile work environment** occurs when unwelcome and demeaning sexually related behavior creates an intimidating, hostile, and offensive work environment. In contrast to quid pro quo cases, a hostile work environment may not result in economic injury; however, it can lead to psychological injury. The world's largest law firm, *BAKER & McKENZIE*, was fined $3.5 million for creating a sexually hostile work environment. Former secretary Rena Weeks accused partner Martin Greenstein of dropping candies in the pocket of her blouse, groping her breasts, pressing against her from behind, and pulling her arms back to "see which one is bigger." A number of women had already complained to supervisors that Greenstein harassed them, but the firm took no action against Greenstein in those cases. This fact, together with Greenstein's conduct toward Weeks, led the court to penalize the law firm.[32]

What common mistakes do managers make when it comes to sexual harassment laws?[33] First, many assume that the victim and harasser must be of opposite sexes. According to the courts, they do not. Sexual harassment can also occur between people of the same sex. Second, managers often assume that sexual harassment can occur only between coworkers or between supervisors and subordinates. Not so. Agents of employers, such as consultants, and even nonemployees can be sexual harassers. The key is not employee status but whether the harassment takes place while company business is being conducted. Third, it is often assumed that only people who have themselves been harassed can file complaints or lawsuits. In fact, especially in hostile work environments, anyone affected by offensive conduct can file a complaint or lawsuit.

sexual harassment a form of discrimination in which unwelcome sexual advances, requests for sexual favors, or other verbal or physical conduct of a sexual nature occurs while performing one's job

quid pro quo sexual harassment a form of sexual harassment in which employment outcomes, such as hiring, promotion, or simply keeping one's job, depend on whether an individual submits to sexual harassment

hostile work environment a form of sexual harassment in which unwelcome and demeaning sexually related behavior creates an intimidating and offensive work environment

Finally, what should companies do to make sure that sexual harassment laws are followed and not violated?[34] First, respond immediately when sexual harassment is reported. A quick response encourages victims of sexual harassment to report problems to management rather than to lawyers or the EEOC. Furthermore, a quick and fair investigation may serve as a deterrent to future harassment. A lawyer for the EEOC says, "Worse than having no sexual harassment policy is a policy that is not followed. It's merely window dressing. You wind up with destroyed morale when people who come forward are ignored, ridiculed, retaliated against, or nothing happens to the harasser."[35] Next, take the time to write a clear, understandable sexual harassment policy that is strongly worded, gives specific examples of what constitutes sexual harassment, spells outs sanctions and punishments, and is widely publicized within the company. This lets potential harassers and victims know what will not be tolerated and how the firm will deal with harassment should it occur.

Next, establish clear reporting procedures that indicate how, where, and to whom incidents of sexual harassment can be reported. The best procedures ensure that a complaint will receive a quick response, that impartial parties will handle the complaint, and that the privacy of the accused and accuser will be protected. At DuPont, Avon, and Texas Industries, employees can call a confidential hotline 24 hours a day, 365 days a year.[36]

Finally, managers should also be aware that most states and many cities or local governments have their own employment-related laws and enforcement agencies. So compliance with federal law is often not enough. In fact, organizations can be in full compliance with federal law and at the same time be in violation of state or local sexual harassment laws.

Review 2: Employment Legislation

Human resource management is subject to the following major federal employment laws: Equal Pay Act, Civil Rights Acts of 1964 and 1991, Age Discrimination in Employment Act, Pregnancy Discrimination Act, Americans with Disabilities Act, Family and Medical Leave Act, and Uniformed Services Employment and Reemployment Rights Act. Human resource management is also subject to review by these federal agencies: Equal Employment Opportunity Commission, Department of Labor, Occupational Safety and Health Administration, and National Labor Relations Board. In general, these laws state that sex, age, religion, color, national origin, race, disability, and pregnancy may not be considered in employment decisions unless these factors reasonably qualify as BFOQs. Two important criteria, disparate treatment (intentional discrimination) and adverse impact (unintentional discrimination), are used to decide whether companies have wrongly discriminated against someone. While motive is a key part of determining disparate treatment, the courts and federal enforcement agencies use the four-fifths rule to determine if adverse impact has occurred. The two kinds of sexual harassment are quid pro quo and hostile work environment. Managers often wrongly assume that the victim and harasser must be of the opposite sex, that sexual harassment can only occur between coworkers or between supervisors and their employees, and that only people who have themselves been harassed can file complaints or lawsuits. To ensure compliance with sexual harassment laws, companies should respond immediately when harassment is reported; write a clear, understandable sexual harassment policy; establish clear reporting procedures; and be aware of and follow city and state laws concerning sexual harassment.

"Worse than having no sexual harassment policy is a policy that is not followed.
— EEOC LAWYER

FINDING QUALIFIED WORKERS

Technical Materials, which sells electroplating and metal-bonding processes to car manufacturers and high-tech industries, was enjoying record sales but could not find enough qualified employees to work in its factories. Its pool of prospective employees was so weak that one in six applicants failed its drug test; the usual failure rate was one in 25. Company president Al Lubrano made numerous strong job offers, added more pay and benefits to those offers when applicants asked for more, and still couldn't hire anybody. Finally, Lubrano says, "When it got ridiculous, we walked away."[37] Likewise, the nursing shortage mentioned at the beginning of the chapter is why Mary Viney, director of patient care services at Seton Northwest Hospital in Austin, Texas, found herself in Manila, trying to encourage Filipino nurses to work for her hospital in Austin, Texas. In Texas, says Viney, "it's a day-to-day, shift-to-shift challenge to get enough nurses."[38]

As these examples illustrate, finding qualified workers can be an increasingly difficult task. Finding qualified applicants is just the first step, however. Deciding which applicants to hire is the second. Gail Hyland-Savage, CEO of real estate and marketing firm Michaelson, Connor & Boul, says, "Staffing is absolutely critical to the success of every company. To be competitive in today's economy, companies need the best people to create ideas and execute them for the organization. Without a competent and talented workforce, organizations will stagnate and eventually perish. The right employees are the most important resources of companies today."[39]

> **After reading the next two sections, you should be able to**
>
> 3 explain how companies use recruiting to find qualified job applicants.
>
> 4 describe the selection techniques and procedures that companies use when deciding which applicants should receive job offers.

3 Recruiting

Recruiting *is the process of developing a pool of qualified job applicants. Let's examine* **3.1 what job analysis is and how it is used in recruiting** *and* **3.2 how companies use internal recruiting** *and* **3.3 external recruiting to find qualified job applicants**.

3.1 Job Analysis and Recruiting

Job analysis is a purposeful, systematic process for collecting information on the important work-related aspects of a job.[40] Typically, a job analysis collects four kinds of information:

- *Work activities, such as what workers do and how, when, and why they do it*
- *The tools and equipment used to do the job*
- *The context in which the job is performed, such as the actual working conditions or schedule*
- *The personnel requirements for performing the job, meaning the knowledge, skills, and abilities needed to do a job well*[41]

recruiting the process of developing a pool of qualified job applicants

job analysis a purposeful, systematic process for collecting information on the important work-related aspects of a job

Job analysis information can be collected by having job incumbents and/or supervisors complete questionnaires about their jobs, by direct observation, by interviews, or by filming employees as they perform their jobs.

Job descriptions and job specifications are two of the most important results of a job analysis. A **job description** is a written description of the basic tasks, duties, and responsibilities required of an employee holding a particular job. **Job specifications**, which are often included as a separate section of a job description, are a summary of the qualifications needed to successfully perform the job. Exhibit 11.5 shows a job description and the job specifications for a helicopter pilot for the city of Little Rock, Arkansas.

Because a job analysis specifies what a job entails, as well as the knowledge, skills, and abilities that are needed to do the job well, companies must complete a job analysis *before* beginning to recruit job applicants. Exhibit 11.6 shows that job analysis, job descriptions, and job specifications are the foundation on which all critical human resource activities are built. They are used during recruiting and selection to match applicant qualifications with the requirements of the job. They are used throughout the staffing process to ensure that selection devices and the decisions based on these devices are job related. For example, the questions asked in an interview should be based on the most important work activities identified by a job analysis. Likewise, during performance appraisals, employees should be evaluated in areas that a job analysis has identified as the most important in a job.

Job analyses, job descriptions, and job specifications also help companies meet the legal requirement that their human resource decisions be job related. To be judged *job related*, recruitment, selection, training, performance appraisals, and employee separations must be valid and be directly related to the important aspects of the job, as identified by a careful job analysis. In fact, in *Griggs v. Duke Power Co.* and *Albemarle Paper Co. v. Moody*, the U.S. Supreme Court stated that companies should use job analyses to help establish the job relatedness of their human resource

job description a written description of the basic tasks, duties, and responsibilities required of an employee holding a particular job

job specifications a written summary of the qualifications needed to successfully perform a particular job

Exhibit 11.5

Job Description and Job Specifications for a Helicopter Pilot for the City of Little Rock, Arkansas

DESCRIPTION FOR HELICOPTER PILOT

To provide assistance for air searches, river rescues, high-rise building rescues, and other assignments, by providing air survey and aviation response. Pilots a rotary-wing aircraft, serving as pilot or copilot, to assist in air searches, river rescues, high-rise building rescues, and other assignments. Ensures that aircraft is properly outfitted for each assignment (equipment, rigging tools, supplies, etc.). Performs preflight inspection of aircraft; checks rotors, fuel, lubricants, controls, etc. Prepares written reports on assignments; maintains flight logs. Obtains weather reports; determines to proceed with assignments given forecasted weather conditions. Operates a radio to maintain contact with and to report information to airport personnel and police department personnel.

JOB SPECIFICATIONS FOR HELICOPTER PILOT

Must possess a valid Commercial Pilot's License for rotary-wing aircraft before employment and maintain licensure for the duration of employment in this position. Must have considerable knowledge of Federal Aviation Administration (FAA) laws and regulations, rotary-wing aircraft operating procedures, air traffic safety, flying procedures and navigational techniques, and FAA and police radio operation and procedures. Must have some knowledge of preventive maintenance methods, repair practices, safety requirements, and inspection procedures. Must have skill in the operation of a rotary-wing aircraft and radio equipment and the ability to conduct safety inspections of aircraft, to maintain aircraft maintenance logs and prepare reports, to detect and identify aircraft malfunction symptoms, to detect and recognize ground conditions and characteristics (utility line breaks, river currents, etc.), to read maps and air navigation charts, and to communicate effectively, both orally and in writing. Must have completed high school; at least one thousand hours of flight time experience in piloting rotary-wing aircraft; OR any equivalent combination of experience and training that provides the required knowledge, skills, and abilities.

Source: "Job Description: Helicopter Pilot," City of Little Rock, Arkansas, http://www.littlerock.org, 31 May 2003.

HR Decisions

Recruiting
Selection
Training
Performance
Appraisal
Separation

HR Subsystems

• Job Description
• Job Specification

← Job Analysis →

Exhibit 11.6

Importance of Job Analysis to Human Resource Management

internal recruiting the process of developing a pool of qualified job applicants from people who already work in the company

external recruiting the process of developing a pool of qualified job applicants from outside the company

procedures.[42] The EEOC's *Uniform Guidelines on Employee Selection Procedures* also recommend that companies base their human resource procedures on job analysis.

3.2 Internal Recruiting

Internal recruiting is the process of developing a pool of qualified job applicants from people who already work in the company. Internal recruiting, sometimes called "promotion from within," improves employee commitment, morale, and motivation. Recruiting current employees also reduces recruitment startup time and costs, and because employees are already familiar with the company's culture and procedures, they are more likely to succeed in new jobs. This is why, according to Bob Graczyk, director of human resources, that **QUICK CHEK FOOD STORES**' goal is to hire "100 percent" of its new store managers through internal recruiting. Graczyk says, "We try to find people whose personal values align with the company values."[43] And, of course, it's easier to do that when the applicants already work for the company. Job posting and career paths are two methods of internal recruiting.

Job posting is a procedure for advertising job openings within the company to existing employees. A job description and requirements are typically posted on a bulletin board, in a company newsletter, or in an internal computerized job bank that is accessible only to employees. For example, under Japan-based **FUJISAWA PHARMACEUTICALS**' "Job Challenge" policy, all Fujisawa departments and divisions recruit internally by posting job openings to the company's intranet for all employees to see.[44] Job posting helps organizations discover hidden talent, allows employees to take responsibility for career planning, and makes it easier for companies to retain talented workers who are dissatisfied in their current jobs and would otherwise leave the company.[45] Fujisawa Pharmaceuticals also has a "Free Agent" policy, which encourages employees who want to change jobs to post their résumés to the same intranet. When Fujisawa's departments and divisions have openings, the first place they look to fill the positions is the company intranet.[46]

A *career path* is a planned sequence of jobs through which employees may advance within an organization. For example, a person who starts as a sales representative may move up to sales manager and then to district or regional sales manager. Career paths help employees focus on long-term goals and development while also helping companies increase employee retention. **ECHOSTAR COMMUNICATIONS** developed a "career path" program designed to persuade call-center workers to stick around longer and cut the costs of hiring and training new workers. Employees who participate in training and meet required skill levels are eligible for rapid promotions and pay increases. EchoStar executives say the program is working—the average call-center agent now stays for 19 months, up from 9 months two years ago. Jessica Nicolo, an early participant in EchoStar's program, was promoted four times in two years and her pay is now 27 percent higher than when she started. Nicolo, a mother of two, says she doesn't expect to leave EchoStar for a long time because now she doesn't feel trapped in another dead-end job.[47]

3.3 External Recruiting

External recruiting is the process of developing a pool of qualified job applicants from outside the company. For example, as part of its strategic plan for long-term success, **ELECTRONIC ARTS**, the maker of top-selling video games such as *Madden NFL*, has put together a "top 40" list of the most talented managers in the industry (including senior executives, game directors and producers) that it hopes to eventually recruit to the company.[48] José Martin, head of human resources for EA's 13 game-production studios, says, "The challenge for companies now is not identifying talented people but persuading those people to join your company."[49]

© RISER/GETTY IMAGES

External recruitment methods include advertising (newspapers, magazines, direct mail, radio, or television), employee referrals (asking current employees to recommend possible job applicants), walk-ins (people who apply on their own), outside organizations (universities, technical/trade schools, professional societies), employment services (state or private employment agencies, temporary help agencies, and professional search firms), special events (career conferences or job fairs), and Internet job sites. Which external recruiting method should you use? Studies show that employee referrals, walk-ins, newspaper advertisements, and state employment agencies tend to be used most frequently for office/clerical and production/service employees. By contrast, newspaper advertisements and college/university recruiting are used most frequently for professional/technical employees. When recruiting managers, organizations tend to rely most heavily on newspaper advertisements, employee referrals, and search firms.[50]

In the last few years, the biggest changes in external recruiting has been the increased use of the Internet. Some companies now recruit applicants through Internet job sites such as **MONSTER.COM**, **HOTJOBS.COM**, Hire.com, and **CAREERBUILDER .COM**. Companies can post job openings for 30 days on one of these sites for about half of the cost of running an advertisement just once in a Sunday newspaper. Plus, Internet job listings generate nine times as many résumés as one ad in the Sunday newspaper.[51] And because these sites attract so many applicants and offer so many services, companies save by finding qualified applicants without having to use more expensive recruitment and search firms, which typically charge one-third of a new hire's salary.[52] Monica Albano, executive vice president of human resources for the Americas at Reuters, the news and information company, says, "Utilizing Hire.com, we're able to attract the best available talent, be specific about the data we retain on people, and utilize that data as openings become available. Overall, we saved in excess of $1.5 million worldwide."[53]

Despite their many benefits, job websites have a significant drawback: Companies may receive hundreds, if not thousands, of applications from *unqualified* applicants. The sheer volume increases the importance of proper screening and selection. For example, when IMLogic, which makes instant messaging software, advertised job openings on Monster.com and CareerBuilder.com, the company was flooded with 200 résumés the first hour the jobs were posted and nearly 750 résumés within two days. CEO Francis deSouza says, "We weren't ready for that."[54]

Call centers are known to have high turnover rates. To reduce that churn, EchoStar developed career paths to help employees see how they could move up the corporate ladder. The result is that the average tenure of a call-center agent has more than doubled.

"WHAT'S NEW" COMPANY

"WHAT'S NEW" COMPANY

"WHAT'S NEW" COMPANY

"WHAT'S NEW" COMPANY

Therefore, assuming that the most qualified applicants will learn something about the company before applying, many organizations now advertise job openings directly on their websites. For example, Subway accepts applications for part-time work at its 27,868 restaurants in 86 countries at its website (**http://www.subway .com/applications/InStoreJobs/index.aspx**).[55] In fact, 60 percent of the people hired via the Internet have applied at a company website.

Today, between 82 percent and 92 percent of companies use the Internet to fill job openings. In fact, Internet recruiting is now second to newspaper advertising in terms of the number of applicants it generates.[56] And with the addition of the ".jobs" Internet top-level domain (for example, **http://www.dell.jobs** for jobs at Dell, Inc.), more and more companies will use their websites to attract, recruit, and screen job applicants.[57] That's because job seekers tend to first visit company websites before looking for a job through more general sites. In fact, 95 percent of *Fortune* 500 companies have career portals on their corporate websites.[58]

Review 3: **Recruiting**

Recruiting is the process of finding qualified job applicants. The first step in recruiting is to conduct a job analysis to collect information about the important work-related aspects of the job. The job analysis is then used to write a job description of basic tasks, duties, and responsibilities and to write job specifications indicating the knowledge, skills, and abilities needed to perform the job. Job analyses, descriptions, and specifications help companies meet the legal requirement that their human resource decisions be job related. Internal recruiting, or finding qualified job applicants from inside the company, can be done through job posting and career paths. External recruiting, or finding qualified job applicants from outside the company, is done through advertising, employee referrals, walk-ins, outside organizations, employment services, special events, and Internet job sites. The Internet is a particularly promising method of external recruiting because of its low cost, wide reach, and ability to communicate and receive unlimited information.

"WHAT'S NEW" COMPANY

Selecting qualified applicants is especially critical for police departments. That's why in East Providence, Rhode Island, the police department uses the "rule of three."

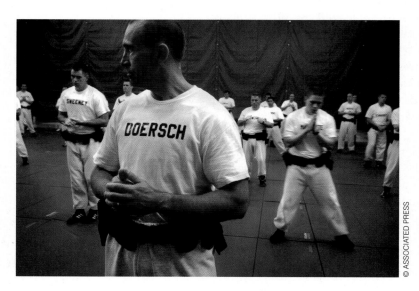

© ASSOCIATED PRESS

4 Selection

Once the recruitment process has produced a pool of qualified applicants, the selection process is used to determine which applicants have the best chance of performing well on the job. When the ***EAST PROVIDENCE, RHODE ISLAND POLICE DEPARTMENT*** has job openings, it follows a "rule of three," meaning that no matter how many candidates it has for an opening, it looks at only the top three applicants, as determined by a standardized written test. Those top three applicants for every position must then pass a physical fitness test and a background check. Every applicant who makes it that far is then put on a list of official candidates for police jobs for two years. Only the best candidates on that list participate in group interviews with the city manager, police chief, deputy chief, a police captain, and the department's personnel director and affirmative action officer, each of whom privately ranks the candidates after each interview. Applicants with the highest rankings from the group interviews are offered positions in the Police Academy. The remaining applicants from the group interviews may be considered two more times before being rejected.[59]

As this example illustrates, **selection** is the process of gathering information about job applicants to decide who should be offered a job. To make sure that selection decisions are accurate and legally defensible, the EEOC's *Uniform Guidelines on Employee Selection Procedures* recommend that all selection procedures be validated. **Validation** is the process of determining how well a selection test or procedure predicts future job performance. The better or more accurate the prediction of future job performance, the more valid a test is said to be. See the "What Really Works" feature later in this chapter for more on the validity of common selection tests and procedures.

*Let's examine common selection procedures, such as **4.1 application forms and résumés**, **4.2 references and background checks**, **4.3 selection tests**, and **4.4 interviews**.*

4.1 Application Forms and Résumés

The first selection devices that most job applicants encounter when they seek a job are application forms and résumés. Both contain similar information about an applicant, such as name, address, job and educational history, and so forth. Though an organization's application form often asks for information already provided by the applicant's résumé, most organizations prefer to collect this information in their own format for entry into a human resource information system.

Employment laws apply to application forms, just as they do to all selection devices. Application forms may ask applicants for only valid, job-related information. Nonetheless, application forms commonly ask applicants for non-job-related information, such as marital status, maiden name, age, or date of high school graduation. Indeed, one study found that 73 percent of organizations had application forms that violated at least one federal or state law.[60] Exhibit 11.7 lists the kinds of information that companies may not request in application forms, during job interviews, or in any other part of the selection process. Courts will assume that

selection the process of gathering information about job applicants to decide who should be offered a job

validation the process of determining how well a selection test or procedure predicts future job performance. The better or more accurate the prediction of future job performance, the more valid a test is said to be.

doing the right thing

Don't Embellish Your Résumé

Your résumé is supposed to help you get the interview that can get you a job. So where do you draw the line between making yourself look attractive to a potential employer and lying? Despite the strong temptation to improve your odds of getting a job, embellishing your résumé is wrong. Moreover, the information on your résumé is legally binding. If you misrepresent information or lie on your résumé—and many people do—you're breaking the law and can be fired. But where should you draw the line? In general, if what you put on your résumé feels wrong, don't do it. More specifically, don't embellish job titles, responsibilities, employment dates, college degrees, certifications, general qualifications, or previous experience in any way. Do the right thing: Tell the truth on your résumé.[61]

1. *Children.* Don't ask applicants if they have children, plan to have them, or have or need child care. Questions about children can unintentionally single out women.

2. *Age.* Because of the Age Discrimination in Employment Act, employers cannot ask job applicants their age during the hiring process. Since most people graduate high school at the age of 18, even asking for high school graduation dates could violate the law.

3. *Disabilities.* Don't ask if applicants have physical or mental disabilities. According to the Americans with Disabilities Act, disabilities (and reasonable accommodations for them) cannot be discussed until a job offer has been made.

4. *Physical characteristics.* Don't ask for information about height, weight, or other physical characteristics. Questions about weight could be construed as leading to discrimination toward overweight people, who studies show are less likely to be hired in general.

5. *Name.* Yes, you can ask an applicant's name, but you cannot ask a female applicant for her maiden name because it indicates marital status. Asking for a maiden name could also lead to charges that the organization was trying to establish a candidate's ethnic background.

6. *Citizenship.* Asking applicants about citizenship could lead to claims of discrimination on the basis of national origin. However, according to the Immigration Reform and Control Act, companies may ask applicants if they have a legal right to work in the United States.

7. *Lawsuits.* Applicants may not be asked if they have ever filed a lawsuit against an employer. Federal and state laws prevent this to protect whistleblowers from retaliation by future employers.

8. *Arrest records.* Applicants cannot be asked about their arrest records. Arrests don't have legal standing. However, applicants can be asked whether they have been convicted of a crime.

9. *Smoking.* Applicants cannot be asked if they smoke. Smokers might be able to claim that they weren't hired because of fears of higher absenteeism and medical costs. However, they can be asked if they are aware of company policies that restrict smoking at work.

10. *AIDS/HIV.* Applicants can't be asked about AIDS, HIV, or any other medical condition. Questions of this nature would violate the Americans with Disabilities Act, as well as federal and state civil rights laws.

Source: J. S. Pouliot, "Topics to Avoid with Applicants," *Nation's Business* 80, no. 7 (1992): 57.

Exhibit 11.7

Topics That Employers Should Avoid in Application Forms, Interviews, or Other Parts of the Selection Process

you consider all of the information you request of applicants, even if you don't. Be sure to ask only those questions that directly relate to the candidate's ability and motivation to perform the job.

Companies should also be aware that employment laws in other countries may differ from U.S. laws. For instance, in France, employers may ask applicants for non-job-related personal information such as their age or the number of children. And most French employers expect applicants to include a picture with their curriculum vitae (another term for résumé).[62] Consequently, companies should closely examine their application forms, interview questions, and other selection procedures for compliance with the law wherever they do business.

Résumés also pose problems for companies, but in a different way. Studies show that as many as one-third of job applicants intentionally falsify some information on their résumés and that 80 percent of the information on résumés may be misleading. A study of 200,000 job applicants found that 20 percent listed college degrees they hadn't earned, 30 percent changed the dates of their employment, 40 percent reported much higher salaries, 30 percent incorrectly described their previous jobs, 27 percent falsified their references, and 25 percent reported working at nonexistent or no longer existing companies, so the fact that they never worked there couldn't be discovered.[63]

Therefore, managers should verify the information collected via résumés and application forms by comparing it with additional information collected during interviews and other stages of the selection process, such as references and background checks, which are discussed next.

4.2 References and Background Checks

Nearly all companies ask an applicant to provide **employment references**, such as previous employers or coworkers, that they can contact to learn more about the candidate. **Background checks** are used to verify the truthfulness and accuracy of information that applicants provide about themselves and to uncover negative, job-related background information not provided by applicants. Background checks are conducted by contacting "educational institutions, prior employers, court records, police and governmental agencies, and other informational sources, either by telephone, mail, remote computer access, or through in-person investigations."[64]

Unfortunately, previous employers are increasingly reluctant to provide references or background check information for fear of being sued by previous employees for defamation. If former employers provide potential employers with unsubstantiated information that damages applicants' chances of being hired, applicants can (and do) sue for defamation. As a result, 54 percent of employers will not provide information about previous employees.[65] Many provide only dates of employment, positions held, and date of separation.

When previous employers decline to provide meaningful references or background information, they put other employers at risk of *negligent hiring* lawsuits, in which an employer is held liable for the actions of an employee who would not have been hired if the employer had conducted a thorough reference search and background check.[66] In Florida, the TALLAHASSEE FURNITURE COMPANY hired a worker to make home furniture deliveries but did not conduct a background check or even ask him to complete an application form. After being hired, he attacked a woman in her home with a knife. When she sued the company, it discovered that he had a history of drug use, violent assault, and mental illness. The courts awarded the woman $2.5 million in damages.[67]

With previous employers generally unwilling to give full, candid references and with negligent hiring lawsuits awaiting companies that don't get such references and background information, what can companies do? Conduct criminal record checks, especially if the job for which the person is applying involves money, drugs, control over valuable goods, or access to the elderly, people with disabilities, or people's homes.[68] According to the Society for Human Resource Management, 96 percent of companies conduct background checks and 80 percent of companies go further and conduct criminal record checks.[69]

Next, dig deeper for more information. Ask references to provide references. VOCA CORPORATION, based in Columbus, Ohio, has 2,500 employees in six states who care for people with mental retardation and developmental disabilities. Hilary Franklin, director of human resources, says she not only checks references, but also asks the references to provide references and then asks those references for still others. She says, "As you get two or three times removed, you get more detailed, honest information."[70]

employment references sources such as previous employers or coworkers who can provide job-related information about job candidates

background checks procedures used to verify the truthfulness and accuracy of information that applicants provide about themselves and to uncover negative, job-related background information not provided by applicants

Next, ask applicants to sign a waiver that permits you to check references, run a background check, or contact anyone else with knowledge of their work performance or history. Likewise, ask applicants if there is anything they would like the company to know or if they expect you to hear anything "unusual" when contacting references.[71] This in itself is often enough to get applicants to share information that they typically withhold. When you've finished checking, keep the findings confidential to minimize the chances of a defamation charge.

© IMAGE SOURCE PINK/JUPITER IMAGES

Before hiring, make sure to conduct thorough background checks.

Always document all reference and background checks, noting who was called and what information was obtained. And to reduce the likelihood that negligent hiring lawsuits will succeed, it's particularly important to document which companies and people refused to share reference check and background information.

Finally, consider hiring private investigators to conduct background checks. They can often uncover surprising information not revealed by traditional background checks. When an American investment company was looking for a Japanese manager to run its Tokyo office, it quickly found a strong applicant who claimed to have experience with dozens of initial public offerings, or IPOs (the process of bringing privately held companies public so that shares of company stock can be sold in financial markets). In multiple interviews, this applicant clearly had detailed information about each IPO deal. However, a background check soon revealed that he was the Japanese translator and not the financier behind each deal.[72]

4.3 Selection Tests

We're all aware that some people do well in jobs while other people do poorly, but how do you determine into which category an applicant falls? Selection tests give organizational decision makers a chance to know who will likely do well in a job and who won't. The basic idea behind selection testing is to have applicants take a test that measures something directly or indirectly related to doing well on the job. The selection tests discussed here are specific ability tests, cognitive ability tests, biographical data, personality tests, work sample tests, and assessment centers.

Specific ability tests measure the extent to which an applicant possesses the particular kind of ability needed to do a job well. Specific ability tests are also called **aptitude tests** because they measure aptitude for doing a particular task well. For example, if you took the SAT to get into college, then you've taken the aptly named Scholastic Aptitude Test, which is one of the best predictors of how well students will do in college (that is, their scholastic performance). Specific ability tests also exist for mechanical, clerical, sales, and physical work. For example, clerical workers have to be good at accurately reading and scanning numbers as they type or enter data. Exhibit 11.8 shows items similar to the Minnesota Clerical Test; applicants have only a short time to determine if the two columns of numbers and letters are identical. Applicants who are good at this are likely to do well as clerical or data-entry workers.

Cognitive ability tests measure the extent to which applicants have abilities in perceptual speed, verbal comprehension, numerical aptitude, general reasoning, and spatial aptitude. In other words, these tests indicate how quickly and how well people understand words, numbers, logic, and spatial dimensions. Whereas specific ability tests predict job performance in only particular types of jobs, cognitive ability tests accurately predict job performance in almost all kinds of jobs.[73] Why is this so? The reason is that people with strong cognitive or mental abilities are usually good at learning new things, processing complex information, solving problems, and making decisions, and these abilities are important in almost all jobs.[74] In fact, cognitive ability tests are almost always the best predictors of job performance. Consequently, if you were allowed to

specific ability tests (aptitude tests) tests that measure the extent to which an applicant possesses the particular kind of ability needed to do a job well

cognitive ability tests tests that measure the extent to which applicants have abilities in perceptual speed, verbal comprehension, numerical aptitude, general reasoning, and spatial aptitude

Exhibit 11.8

Clerical Test Items Similar to Those Found on the Minnesota Clerical Test

	NUMBERS/LETTERS		SAME	
1.	3468251	3467251	Yes	No
2.	4681371	4681371	Yes	No
3.	7218510	7218520	Yes	No
4.	ZXYAZAB	ZXYAZAB	Yes	No
5.	ALZYXMN	ALZYXNM	Yes	No
6.	PRQZYMN	PRQZYMN	Yes	No

Source: N. W. Schmitt & R. J. Klimoski, *Research Methods in Human Resource Management* (Mason, OH: South-Western, 1991). Used with permission.

use just one selection test, cognitive ability tests would be the one to use.[75] (In practice, though, companies use a battery of different tests because doing so leads to much more accurate selection decisions.)

Biographical data, or **biodata**, are extensive surveys that ask applicants questions about their personal backgrounds and life experiences. The basic idea behind biodata is that past behavior (personal background and life experience) is the best predictor of future behavior. For example, during World War II, the **U.S. Air Force** had to quickly test tens of thousands of men without flying experience to determine who was likely to be a good pilot. Since flight training took several months and was very expensive, selecting the right people for training was important. After examining extensive biodata, it found that one of the best predictors of success in flight school was whether students had ever built model airplanes that actually flew. This one biodata item was almost as good a predictor as the entire set of selection tests that the Air Force was using at the time.[76]

Most biodata questionnaires have over 100 items that gather information about habits and attitudes, health, interpersonal relations, money, what it was like growing up in your family (parents, siblings, childhood years, teen years), personal habits, current home (spouse, children), hobbies, education and training, values, preferences, and work.[78] In general, biodata are very good predictors of future job performance, especially in entry-level jobs.

You may have noticed that some of the information requested in biodata surveys also appears in Exhibit 11.7 as topics employers should avoid in applications, interviews, or other parts of the selection process. This information can be requested in biodata questionnaires provided that the company can demonstrate that the information is job related (that is, valid) and does not result in adverse impact against protected groups of job applicants. Biodata surveys should be validated and tested for adverse impact before they are used to make selection decisions.[79]

Personality is the relatively stable set of behaviors, attitudes, and emotions displayed over time that makes people different from each other. **Personality tests** measure the extent to which applicants possess different kinds of job-related personality dimensions. In Chapter 12, you will learn that there are five major

doing the right thing

Don't Use Psychics, Lie Detectors, or Handwriting Analysis to Make HR Decisions

The Coronado Bay Resort in San Diego hired a psychic to work with its 18-member management team as a way of "moving the managers to the next step." Seventy-five percent of the organizations in France and Switzerland use handwriting analysis for hiring and promotion decisions. In the past, employers in the United States regularly used polygraphs (lie detectors) for preemployment screening. What do these methods have in common? Companies use them, but they don't work. For example, there is no scientific evidence that handwriting analysis works, yet managers continue to use it. Lie detectors are no more accurate than a coin flip in screening out unethical employees. Fortunately, the Employee Polygraph Protection Act now prevents organizations from using polygraphs for hiring and promotion decisions. As for psychics at work, well, enough said. So, when you're hiring and promoting people, do the right thing. Stay away from fads. Use the reliable, valid, scientifically proven selection and assessment procedures discussed here to hire the right workers and promote the right people into management.[77]

biographical data (biodata) extensive surveys that ask applicants questions about their personal backgrounds and life experiences

personality tests tests that measure the extent to which applicants possess different kinds of job-related personality dimensions personality dimensions (the Big Five)—extraversion, emotional stability, agreeableness, conscientiousness, and openness to experience—related to work behavior.[80] Of these, only conscientiousness, the degree to which someone is organized, hardworking, responsible, persevering, thorough, and achievement oriented, predicts job performance across a wide variety of jobs.[81] Conscientiousness works especially well in combination with cognitive ability tests, allowing companies to select applicants who are organized, hardworking, responsible, and smart!

Work sample tests, also called *performance tests*, require applicants to perform tasks that are actually done on the job. So, unlike specific ability, cognitive ability, biographical data, and personality tests, which are indirect predictors of job performance, work sample tests directly measure job applicants' capability to do the job. For example, a computer-based work sample test has applicants assume the role of a real estate agent who must decide how to interact with "virtual clients" in a gamelike scenario. And, as in real life, the clients can be frustrating, confusing, demanding, or indecisive. In one situation, the wife loves the "house" but the husband hates it. The applicants, just like actual real estate agents, must demonstrate what they would do in these realistic situations.[82] This work sample simulation gives real estate companies direct evidence of whether applicants can do the job if they are hired. Work sample tests are generally very good at predicting future job performance; however, they can be expensive to administer and can be used for only one kind of job. For example, an auto dealership could not use a work sample test for mechanics as a selection test for sales representatives.

Assessment centers use a series of job-specific simulations that are graded by multiple trained observers to determine applicants' ability to perform managerial work. Unlike the previously described selection tests that are commonly used for specific jobs or entry-level jobs, assessment centers are most often used to select applicants who have high potential to be good managers. Assessment centers often last two to five days and require participants to complete a number of tests and exercises that simulate managerial work.

Some of the more common assessment center exercises are in-basket exercises, role-plays, small-group presentations, and leaderless group discussions. An *in-basket exercise* is a paper-and-pencil test in which an applicant is given a manager's "in-basket" containing memos, phone messages, organizational policies, and other communications normally received by and available to managers. Applicants have a limited time to read through the in-basket, prioritize the items, and decide how to deal with each item. Experienced managers then score the applicants' decisions and recommendations. Exhibit 11.9 shows an item that could be used in an assessment center for evaluating applicants for a job as a store manager.

In a *leaderless group discussion*, another common assessment center exercise, a group of six applicants is given approximately two hours to solve a problem, but no one is put in charge (hence the name "leaderless" group discussion). Trained observers watch and score each participant on the extent to which he or she facilitates discussion, listens, leads, persuades, and works well with others.

---

work sample tests tests that require applicants to perform tasks that are actually done on the job

assessment centers a series of managerial simulations, graded by trained observers, that are used to determine applicants' capability for managerial work

Exhibit 11.9

In-Basket Item for an Assessment Center for Store Managers

```
February 28
Sam & Dave's Discount Warehouse
Orange, California


Dear Store Manager,

Last week, my children and I were shopping in your store.
After doing our grocery shopping, we stopped in the
electronics department and asked the clerk, whose name
is Donald Block, to help us find a copy of the latest
version of the Madden NFL video game. Mr. Block was rude,
unhelpful, and told us to find it for ourselves as he
was busy.


I've been a loyal customer for over six years and expect
you to immediately do something about Mr. Block's
behavior. If you don't, I'll start doing my shopping
somewhere else.


Sincerely,
Margaret Quinlan
```

Source: Adapted from N. W. Schmitt & R. J. Klimoski, *Research Methods in Human Resource Management* (Mason, OH: South-Western 1991).

Are tests perfect predictors of job performance? No, they aren't. Some people who do well on selection tests will do poorly in their jobs. Likewise, some people who do poorly on selection tests (and therefore weren't hired) would have been very good performers. Nonetheless, valid tests will minimize these selection errors (hiring people who should not have been hired, and not hiring people who should have been hired) while maximizing correct selection decisions (hiring people who should have been hired, and not hiring people who should not have been hired). In short, tests increase the chances that you'll hire the right person for the job, that is, someone who turns out to be a good performer. So, although tests aren't perfect, almost nothing predicts future job performance as well as the selection tests discussed here. For more on how well selection tests increase the odds of hiring the right person for the job, see the "What Really Works" feature.

4.4 Interviews

Sharon Ball, director of recruiting and administration for Epitec Group, has interviewed all kinds of mistake-prone job candidates: one with food on his sweater, another with breath that "smelled like bile," one who reeked of marijuana, and one who stopped the interview to talk on his cell phone for five minutes. Only the applicant with bad breath was hired. She says, "Nice guy. We had to pump him full of Tic Tacs."[83] In **interviews**, company representatives ask job applicants job-related questions to determine whether they are qualified for the job. Interviews are probably the most frequently used and relied on selection device. There are several basic kinds of interviews: unstructured, structured, and semistructured.

In **unstructured interviews**, interviewers are free to ask applicants anything they want, and studies show that they do. Because interviewers often disagree about which questions should be asked during interviews, different interviewers tend to ask applicants very different questions.[84] Furthermore, individual interviewers even seem to have a tough time asking the same questions from one interview to the next. This high level of inconsistency lowers the validity of unstructured interviews as a selection device because comparing applicant responses can be difficult. As a result, unstructured interviews are about half as accurate as structured interviews at predicting which job applicants should be hired.

By contrast, with **structured interviews**, standardized interview questions are prepared ahead of time so that all applicants are asked the same job-related questions.[85] Four kinds of questions are typically asked in structured interviews:

- Situational questions, *which ask applicants how they would respond in a hypothetical situation ("What would you do if …?"). These questions are more appropriate for hiring new graduates, who are unlikely to have encountered real-work situations because of their limited work experience.*

- Behavioral questions, *which ask applicants what they did in previous jobs that were similar to the job for which they are applying ("In your previous jobs, tell me about …"). These questions are more appropriate for hiring experienced individuals.*

- Background questions, *which ask applicants about their work experience, education, and other qualifications ("Tell me about the training you received at …").*

- Job-knowledge questions, *which ask applicants to demonstrate their job knowledge (for example, nurses might be asked, "Give me an example of a time when one of your patients had a severe reaction to a medication. How did you handle it?")*[86]

The primary advantage of structured interviews is that comparing applicants is much easier because they are all asked the same questions. Structuring interviews also

interviews a selection tool in which company representatives ask job applicants job-related questions to determine whether they are qualified for the job

unstructured interviews interviews in which interviewers are free to ask the applicants anything they want

structured interviews interviews in which all applicants are asked the same set of standardized questions, usually including situational, behavioral, background, and job-knowledge questions

USING SELECTION TESTS TO HIRE GOOD WORKERS

iring new employees is always something of a gamble. When you say, "We'd like to offer you the job," you never know how it's going to turn out. Nonetheless, the selection tests discussed in this chapter can go a long way toward taking the gambling aspect out of the hiring process. Indeed, more than 1,000 studies based on over 100,000 study participants strongly indicate that selection tests can give employers a much better than average (50–50) chance of hiring the right workers. If you had odds like these working for you in Las Vegas, you'd make so much money the casinos wouldn't let you in the door.

COGNITIVE ABILITY TESTS

There is a 76 percent chance that applicants who do well on cognitive ability tests will be much better performers in their jobs than applicants who do not do well on such tests.

WORK SAMPLE TESTS

There is a 77 percent chance that applicants who do well on work sample tests will be much better performers in their jobs than applicants who do not do well on such tests.

ASSESSMENT CENTERS

There is a 69 percent chance that applicants who do well on assessment center exercises will be much better managers than applicants who do not do well on such exercises.

STRUCTURED INTERVIEWS

There is a 76 percent chance that applicants who do well in structured interviews will be much better performers in their jobs than applicants who do not do well in such interviews.

COGNITIVE ABILITY + WORK SAMPLE TESTS

When deciding whom to hire, most companies use a number of tests to make even more accurate selection decisions. There is an 82 percent chance that applicants who do well on a combination of cognitive ability tests and work sample tests will be much better performers in their jobs than applicants who do not do well on both tests.

COGNITIVE ABILITY + INTEGRITY TESTS

There is an 83 percent chance that applicants who do well on a combination of cognitive ability tests and integrity tests (see Chapter 4 for a discussion of integrity tests) will be much better performers in their jobs than applicants who do not do well on both tests.

COGNITIVE ABILITY + STRUCTURED INTERVIEWS

There is an 82 percent chance that applicants who do well on a combination of cognitive ability tests and structured interviews will be much better performers in their jobs than applicants who do not do well on both tests.[87]

ensures that interviewers ask only for important, job-related information. Not only are the accuracy, usefulness, and validity of the interview improved, but the chances that interviewers will ask questions about topics that violate employment laws (go back to Exhibit 11.7 for a list of these topics) are reduced.

Semistructured interviews are in between structured and unstructured interviews. A major part of the semistructured interview (perhaps as much as 80 percent) is based on structured questions, but some time is set aside for unstructured interviewing to allow the interviewer to probe into ambiguous or missing information uncovered during the structured portion of the interview.

How well do interviews predict future job performance? Contrary to what you've probably heard, recent evidence indicates that even unstructured interviews do a fairly good job.[88] When conducted properly, however, structured interviews can lead to much more accurate hiring decisions than unstructured interviews. In some cases, the validity of structured interviews can rival that of cognitive ability tests. But even more important, because interviews are especially good at assessing applicants' interpersonal skills, they work particularly well with cognitive ability tests. Therefore, using structured interviews together with cognitive ability tests (that is, smart people who work well in conjunction with others) leads to even better selection decisions than using either alone.[89] Exhibit 11.10 provides a set of guidelines for conducting effective structured employment interviews.

Exhibit 11.10

Guidelines for Conducting Effective Structured Interviews

Interview Stage	What to Do

Planning the Interview

- Identify and define the knowledge, skills, abilities, and other (KSAO) characteristics needed for successful job performance.
- For each essential KSAO, develop key behavioral questions that will elicit examples of past accomplishments, activities, and performance.
- For each KSAO, develop a list of things to look for in the applicant's responses to key questions.

Conducting the Interview

- Create a relaxed, nonstressful interview atmosphere.
- Review the applicant's application form, résumé, and other information.
- Allocate enough time to complete the interview without interruption.
- Put the applicant at ease; don't jump right into heavy questioning.
- Tell the applicant what to expect. Explain the interview process.
- Obtain job-related information from the applicant by asking those questions prepared for each KSAO.
- Describe the job and the organization to the applicant. Applicants need adequate information to make a selection decision about the organization.

After the Interview

- Immediately after the interview, review your notes and make sure they are complete.
- Evaluate the applicant on each essential KSAO.
- Determine each applicant's probability of success and make a hiring decision.

Source: B. M. Farrell, "The Art and Science of Employment Interviews," *Personnel Journal* 65 (1986): 91–94.

Review 4: *Selection*

Selection is the process of gathering information about job applicants to decide who should be offered a job. Accurate selection procedures are valid, are legally defendable, and improve organizational performance. Application forms and résumés are the most common selection devices. Because many application forms request illegal, non-job-related information, and as many as one-third of job applicants falsify information on résumés, these procedures are often of little value in making hiring decisions. References and background checks can also be problematic, given that previous employers are reluctant to provide such information for fear of being sued for defamation. Unfortunately, without this information, other employers are at risk of negligent hiring lawsuits. Selection tests generally do the best job of predicting applicants' future job performance. In general, cognitive ability tests, work sample tests, biographical data, and assessment centers are the most valid tests, followed by personality tests and specific ability tests, which are still good predictors. Selection tests aren't perfect predictors of job performance, but almost nothing predicts future job performance as well as selection tests. The three kinds of job interviews are unstructured, structured, and semistructured interviews. Of these, structured interviews work best because they ensure that all applicants are consistently asked the same situational, behavioral, background, or job-knowledge questions, in the same order.

DEVELOPING QUALIFIED WORKERS

According to a recent survey by Mercer Human Resource Consulting, 49 percent of companies are increasing their training budgets. For instance, Hewlett-Packard recently increased its training budget to a whopping $300 million.[90] What is driving the infusion of dollars into training and development budgets of companies? Companies like HP recognize that it is more cost-efficient and competitive to develop talent from within rather than compete for talent on the open market.[91] In addition, according to the American Society for Training and Development, a typical investment in training increases productivity by an average of 17 percent, reduces employee turnover, and makes companies more profitable.[92]

Giving employees the knowledge and skills they need to improve their performance is just the first step in developing employees, however. The second step, and not enough companies do this, is giving employees formal feedback about their actual job performance. A CEO of a large telecommunications company hired an outside consultant to assess and coach (provide feedback to) the company's top 50 managers. To the CEO's surprise, 75 percent of those managers indicated that the feedback they received from the consultant regarding their strengths and weaknesses was the only substantial feedback they had received about their performance in the last five years. On a more positive note, as a result of that feedback, two-thirds of the managers then took positive steps to improve their skills, knowledge, and job performance and expressed a clear desire for more feedback, especially from their boss, the CEO.[93] So, in today's competitive business environment, even top managers understand the importance of formal performance feedback to their growth and development.

After reading the next two sections, you should be able to

> 5 describe how to determine training needs and select the appropriate training methods.
>
> 6 discuss how to use performance appraisal to give meaningful performance feedback.

5 Training

Training means providing opportunities for employees to develop the job-specific skills, experience, and knowledge they need to do their jobs or improve their performance. American companies spend more than $60 billion a year on training. To make sure those training dollars are well spent, companies need to **5.1 determine specific training needs**, **5.2 select appropriate training methods**, and **5.3 evaluate training**.

5.1 Determining Training Needs

Needs assessment is the process of identifying and prioritizing the learning needs of employees. Needs assessments can be conducted by identifying performance deficiencies, listening to customer complaints, surveying employees and managers, or formally testing employees' skills and knowledge.

The Work Keys method created by American College Testing (maker of the ACT test used for college admissions) in Iowa City, Iowa, is a needs assessment tool used for 7,000 different jobs by more than 1,400 companies nationwide.[94] Work Keys is a series of tests that can be used to determine employees' knowledge and skill levels in communication (listening, reading for information, and writing), problem solving (applied mathematics, applied technology, locating information, and observation), and interpersonal skills (teamwork). As shown in Step 1 of Exhibit 11.11, a needs assessment using Work Keys begins with a job analysis (what ACT calls "job profiling") to determine the knowledge and skill levels required to perform a job successfully. Step 1 shows that a worker needs a skill level of 4 in reading for information, a 5 in applied mathematics, a 3 in applied technology, and a 4 in teamwork (skill levels range from 1 to 6) to do well in a manufacturing job. Following the job analysis, employees are tested to see how well their skills match those required for the job, as shown in Step 2 of Exhibit 11.11. Then, as shown in Step 3 of the exhibit, employees' skill levels are compared with the requirements for the job. The greater the difference between an employee's skill levels and those required, the greater the need for training. Based on the Work Keys needs assessment, this employee needs some training in reading for information, applied mathematics, and teamwork.

Note that training should never be conducted without first performing a needs assessment. Sometimes, training isn't needed at all or isn't needed for all employees. Since the needs assessment shown in Exhibit 11.11 indicates that the employee's applied technology skills match those required for the job, it would be a waste of time and money to send this employee for training in that area.

training developing the skills, experience, and knowledge employees need to perform their jobs or improve their performance

needs assessment the process of identifying and prioritizing the learning needs of employees

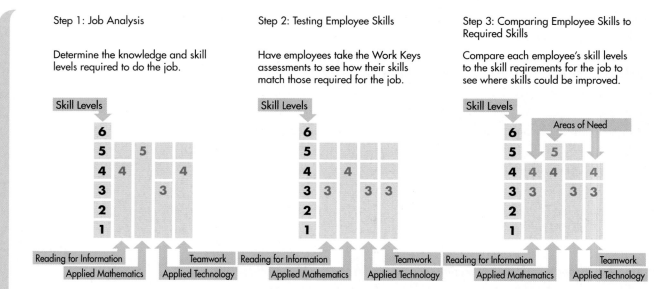

Step 1: Job Analysis

Determine the knowledge and skill levels required to do the job.

Step 2: Testing Employee Skills

Have employees take the Work Keys assessments to see how their skills match those required for the job.

Step 3: Comparing Employee Skills to Required Skills

Compare each employee's skill levels to the skill reqirements for the job to see where skills could be improved.

Exhibit 11.11

Work Keys Needs Assessment for a Manufacturing Job

Unfortunately, however, many organizations simply require all employees to attend training, whether they need to or not. As a result, employees who are not interested or don't need the training may react negatively during or after training. Likewise, employees who should be sent for training but aren't may also react negatively. Consequently, a needs assessment is an important tool for deciding who should or should not attend training. In fact, employment law restricts employers from discriminating on the basis of age, sex, race, color, religion, national origin, or disability when selecting training participants. Just like hiring decisions, the selection of training participants should be based on job-related information.

5.2 Training Methods

Assume that you're a training director for a bank and that you're in charge of making sure that all bank employees know what to do in case of a robbery. Exhibit 11.12 lists a number of training methods you could use: films and videos, lectures, planned readings, case studies, coaching and mentoring, group discussions, on-the-job training, role-playing, simulations and games, vestibule training, and computer-based learning. Which method would be best?

To choose the best method, you should consider a number of factors, such as the number of people to be trained, the cost of training, and the objectives of the training. For instance, if the training objective is to impart information or knowledge to trainees, then you should use films and videos, lectures, and planned readings. In our robbery training example, trainees would hear, see, or read about what to do in case of a robbery.

If developing analytical and problem-solving skills is the objective, then use case studies, coaching and mentoring, and group discussions. In our example, trainees would read about a real robbery, talk to people who had been through robberies, and discuss what to do.

If practicing, learning, or changing job behaviors is the objective, then use on-the-job training, role-playing, simulations and games, and vestibule training. In our example, trainees would learn about robbery situations on the job, pretend that they were in a robbery situation, or participate in a highly realistic mock robbery.

TRAINING OBJECTIVE	TRAINING METHOD
Impart Information and Knowledge	• **Films and videos.** Films and videos share information, illustrate problems and solutions, and effectively hold trainees' attention.
	• **Lectures.** Trainees listen to instructors' oral presentations.
	• **Planned readings.** Trainees read about concepts or ideas before attending training.
Develop Analytical and Problem-Solving Skills	• **Case studies.** Cases are analyzed and discussed in small groups. The cases present a specific problem or decision, and trainees develop methods for solving the problem or making the decision.
	• **Coaching and mentoring.** Coaching and mentoring of trainees by managers involves informal advice, suggestions, and guidance. This method is helpful for reinforcing other kinds of training and for trainees who benefit from support and personal encouragement.
	• **Group discussions.** Small groups of trainees actively discuss specific topics. The instructor may perform the role of discussion leader.
Practice, Learn, or Change Job Behaviors	• **On-the-job training (OJT).** New employees are assigned to experienced employees. The trainee learns by watching the experienced employee perform the job and eventually by working alongside the experienced employee. Gradually, the trainee is left on his or her own to perform the job.
	• **Role-playing.** Trainees assume job-related roles and practice new behaviors by acting out what they would do in job-related situations.
	• **Simulations and games.** Experiential exercises place trainees in realistic job-related situations and give them the opportunity to experience a job-related condition in a relatively low-cost setting. The trainee benefits from "hands-on experience" before actually performing the job where mistakes may be more costly.
	• **Vestibule training.** Procedures and equipment similar to those used in the actual job are set up in a special area called a vestibule. The trainee is then taught how to perform the job at his or her own pace without disrupting the actual flow of work, making costly mistakes, or exposing the trainee and others to dangerous conditions.
Impart Information and Knowledge; Develop Analytical and Problem-Solving Skills; and Practice, Learn, or Change Job Behaviors	• **Computer-based learning.** Interactive videos, software, CD-ROMs, personal computers, teleconferencing, and the Internet may be combined to present multimedia-based training.

Source: A. Fowler, "How to Decide on Training Methods," *People Management* 25, no. 1 (1995): 36.

Exhibit 11.12

Training Objectives and Methods

If training is supposed to meet more than one of these objectives, then your best choice may be to combine one of the previous methods with computer-based training. *CDW* (Computer Discount Warehouse) now uses avatar-based training. An avatar is a computerized depiction of a person. If you've ever played a video game, you've encountered an avatar. When CDW account manager Danielle Paden took a sales course, the avatar first described a situation: an unhappy customer whose computer won't connect to her high-speed Internet hookup. Then, a picture of the customer appeared on the screen, accompanied by audio of the customer speaking. Finally, with help from the avatar when she needed it (just click on the avatar), Paden decided what to do and then received feedback from the avatar and another response from the customer. Paden describes the training as "the closest thing you can get to [actual] client interactions," because "the avatar went through almost every situation you will run across."[95]

"[Avatar training is] the closest thing you can get to [actual] client interactions [because] the avatar went through almost every situation you will run across.

DANIELLE PADEN, ACCOUNT MANAGER, CDW

These days, many companies are adopting Internet training, or "e-learning." For instance, **DOW CHEMICAL** now has the ability to provide electronic learning or training to all 40,000 employees in 70 countries using its **Learn@dow.now** web-based training system.[96] Likewise, Cisco Systems offers 4,500 e-learning courses to its managers and employees.[97] E-learning can offer several advantages. Because employees don't need to leave their jobs, travel costs are greatly reduced. Also, because employees can take training modules when it is convenient (in other words, they don't have to fall behind at their jobs to attend week-long training courses), workplace productivity should increase and employee stress should decrease. Finally, if the company's technology infrastructure can support it, e-learning can be much faster than traditional training methods. For example, British Telecom used an avatar-based course to train 4,500 salespeople in just over a month. Traditional classroom training would have cost twice as much and taken twice as long to deliver.[98]

There are, however, several disadvantages to e-learning. First, despite its increasing popularity, it's not always the appropriate training method. E-learning can be a good way to impart information, but it isn't always as effective for changing job behaviors or developing problem-solving and analytical skills. Second, e-learning requires a significant investment in computers and high-speed Internet and network connections for all employees. Finally, though e-learning can be faster, many employees find it so boring and unengaging that they may choose to do their jobs rather than complete e-learning courses when sitting alone at their desks. E-learning may become more interesting, however, as more companies incorporate gamelike features in training, such as avatars and competition, into their e-learning courses.

5.3 Evaluating Training

After selecting a training method and conducting the training, the last step is to evaluate the training. Training can be evaluated in four ways: on *reactions*, how satisfied trainees were with the program; on *learning*, how much employees improved their knowledge or skills; on *behavior*, how much employees actually changed their on-the-job behavior because of training; or on *results*, how much training improved job performance, such as increased sales or quality, or decreased costs.[99] In general, if done well, training provides meaningful benefits for most companies. For example, a study by the American Society for Training and Development shows that a training budget as small as $680 per employee can increase a company's total return on investment by 6 percent.[100]

Review 5: Training

Training is used to give employees the job-specific skills, experience, and knowledge they need to do their jobs or improve their job performance. To make sure training dollars are well spent, companies need to determine specific training needs, select appropriate training methods, and then evaluate the training. Needs assessments can be conducted by identifying performance deficiencies, listening to customer complaints, surveying employees and managers, or formally testing employees' skills and knowledge. Selection of an appropriate training method depends on a number of factors, such as the number of people to be trained, the cost of training, and the objectives of the training. If the objective is to impart information or knowledge, then films and videos, lectures, and planned readings should be used. If developing analytical and problem-solving skills is the objective, then case studies, coaching and mentoring, and group discussions should be used. If practicing, learning, or changing job behaviors is the objective, then on-the-job training, role-playing, simulations and games, and vestibule training should be used. If training is supposed to meet more than one of these objectives, then it may be best to combine one of the previous methods with computer-based training. Training can be evaluated on reactions, learning, behavior, or results.

6 Performance Appraisal

Performance appraisal is the process of assessing how well employees are doing their jobs. Most employees and managers intensely dislike the performance appraisal process. One manager says, "I hate annual performance reviews. I hated them when I used to get them, and I hate them now that I give them. If I had to choose between performance reviews and paper cuts, I'd take paper cuts every time. I'd even take razor burns and the sound of fingernails on a blackboard."[101] Unfortunately, attitudes like this are all too common. In fact, 70 percent of employees are dissatisfied with the performance appraisal process in their companies. Likewise, according to the Society for Human Resource Management, 90 percent of human resource managers are dissatisfied with the performance appraisal systems used by their companies.[102]

Performance appraisals are used for four broad purposes: making administrative decisions (such as pay increase, promotion, retention); providing feedback for employee development (such as performance feedback, developing career plans); evaluating Human Resource programs (such as validating selection systems); and for documentation purposes (such as documenting performance ratings and decisions based on those ratings).[103]

*Let's explore how companies can avoid some of these problems with performance appraisals by **6.1 accurately measuring job performance** and **6.2 effectively sharing performance feedback with employees**.*

6.1 Accurately Measuring Job Performance

Workers often have strong doubts about the accuracy of their performance appraisals—and they may be right. For example, it's widely known that assessors are prone to errors when rating worker performance. Three of the most common rating errors are central tendency, halo, and leniency. *Central tendency error* occurs when assessors rate all workers as average or in the middle of the scale. *Halo error* occurs when assessors rate all workers as performing at the same level (good, bad, or average) in all parts of their jobs. *Leniency error* occurs when assessors rate all workers as performing particularly well. One of the reasons that managers make these errors is that they often don't spend enough time gathering or reviewing performance data.

performance appraisal the process of assessing how well employees are doing their jobs

Winston Connor, the former vice president of human resources at Huntsman Chemical, says, "Most of the time, it's just a ritual that managers go through. They pull out last year's review, update it and do it quickly."[104]

What can be done to minimize rating errors and improve the accuracy with which job performance is measured? In general, two approaches have been used: improving performance appraisal measures themselves and training performance raters to be more accurate.

One of the ways companies try to improve performance appraisal measures is to use as many objective performance measures as possible. **Objective performance measures** are measures of performance that are easily and directly counted or quantified. Common objective performance measures include output, scrap, waste, sales, customer complaints, and rejection rates.

But when objective performance measures aren't available, and frequently they aren't, subjective performance measures have to be used instead. **Subjective performance measures** require that someone judge or assess a worker's performance. The most common kind of subjective performance measure is the Graphic Rating Scale (GRS) shown in Exhibit 11.13. Graphic rating scales are most widely used because they are easy to construct, but they are very susceptible to rating errors.

A popular alternative to graphic rating scales is the **Behavior Observation Scale (BOS)**. BOS requires raters to rate the frequency with which workers perform specific behaviors representative of the job dimensions that are critical to successful job performance. Exhibit 11.13 shows a BOS for two important job dimensions for a retail salesperson: customer service and money handling. Notice that each dimension lists several specific behaviors characteristic of a worker who excels in that dimension of job performance. (Normally, the scale would list 7 to 12 items per dimension, not 3, as in the exhibit.). Notice also, that the behaviors are good behaviors, meaning they indicate good performance, and the rater is asked to judge how frequently an employee engaged in those good behaviors. The logic behind the BOS is that better performers engage in good behaviors more often.

Not only do BOSs work well for rating critical dimensions of performance, but studies also show that managers strongly prefer BOSs for giving performance feedback; accurately differentiating between poor, average, and good workers; identifying training needs; and accurately measuring performance. And in response to the statement, "If I were defending a company, this rating format would be an asset to my case," attorneys strongly preferred BOSs over other kinds of subjective performance appraisal scales.[105]

The second approach to improving the measurement of workers' job performance is **rater training**. The most effective is frame-of-reference training, in which a group of trainees learn how to do performance appraisals by watching a videotape of an employee at work. Next, they evaluate the performance of the person in the videotape. A trainer (an expert in the subject matter) then shares his or her evaluations, and trainees' evaluations are compared with the expert's. The expert then explains the rationales behind his or her evaluations. This process is repeated until the difference in evaluations given by trainees and evaluations by the expert are minimized. The underlying logic behind the frame-of-reference training is that by adopting the frame of reference

objective performance measures measures of job performance that are easily and directly counted or quantified

subjective performance measures measures of job performance that require someone to judge or assess a worker's performance

behavior observation scales (BOSs) rating scales that indicate the frequency with which workers perform specific behaviors that are representative of the job dimensions critical to successful job performance

rater training training performance appraisal raters in how to avoid rating errors and increase rating accuracy used by an expert, trainees will be able to accurately observe, judge and use the scale to evaluate performance of others.[106]

6.2 Sharing Performance Feedback

After gathering accurate performance data, the next step is to share performance feedback with employees. Unfortunately, even when performance appraisal ratings are accurate, the appraisal process often breaks down at the feedback stage. Employees become defensive and dislike hearing any negative assessments of their work, no matter how small. Managers become defensive, too, and dislike giving appraisal feedback as much as employees dislike receiving it. One manager says, "I myself don't go as far as those who say performance reviews are inherently destructive and ought to be abolished, but I agree that the typical annual-review process does nothing but harm. It creates divisions. It undermines morale. It makes people angry, jealous, and cynical. It unleashes a whole lot of negative energy, and the organization gets nothing in return."[107]

What can be done to overcome the inherent difficulties in performance appraisal feedback sessions? Since performance appraisal ratings have traditionally been the judgments of just one person, the boss, one possibility is to use **360-degree feedback**. In this approach, feedback comes from four sources: the boss, subordinates, peers and coworkers, and the employees themselves. The data, which are obtained anonymously (except for the boss's), are compiled into a feedback report comparing the employee's self-ratings with those of the boss, subordinates, and peers and coworkers. Usually, a consultant or human resource specialist discusses the results with the employee. The advantage of 360-degree programs is that negative feedback ("You don't listen") is often more credible when it comes from several people. For example, one boss who received 360-degree feedback thought he was a great writer, so he regularly criticized and corrected his subordinates' reports. Though the subordinates had never discussed this among themselves, they all complained about it in the 360-degree feedback and asked that he stop rewriting their reports. After receiving the feedback, he apologized and stopped.[108]

Graphic Rating Scale

	Very Poor	Poor	Average	Good	Very Good
Example 1:					
1. Quality of work performed is........	1	2	3	4	5

	Very Poor (20% errors)	Poor (15% errors)	Average (10% errors)	Good (5% errors)	Very Good (less than 5% errors)
Example 2:					
2. Quality of work performed is........	1	2	3	4	5

Behavioral Observation Scale

Dimension: Customer Service

	Almost Never				Almost Always
1. Greets customers with a smile and a "hello."	1	2	3	4	5
2. Calls other stores to help customers find merchandise that is not in stock.	1	2	3	4	5
3. Promptly handles customer concerns and complaints.	1	2	3	4	5

Dimension: Money Handling

	Almost Never				Almost Always
1. Accurately makes change from customer transactions.	1	2	3	4	5
2. Accounts balance at the end of the day, no shortages or surpluses.	1	2	3	4	5
3. Accurately records transactions in computer system.	1	2	3	4	5

Exhibit 11.13

Subjective Performance Appraisal Scales

360-degree feedback a performance appraisal process in which feedback is obtained from the boss, subordinates, peers and coworkers, and the employees themselves

A word of caution, though: About half of the companies using 360-degree feedback for performance appraisal now use the feedback only for developmental purposes. They found that sometimes when raises and promotions were on the line, peers and subordinates would give high ratings in order to get high ratings from others, and that they would also distort ratings to harm competitors or help people they liked. A senior manager at a New York City marketing company agrees, saying that 360-degree feedback "also allows people to vent their frustrations and anger on bosses and colleagues in an insensitive way."[109] On the other hand, studies clearly show that ratees prefer to receive feedback from multiple raters, so 360-degree feedback is likely to continue to grow in popularity.[110]

Herbert Meyer, who has been studying performance appraisal feedback for more than 30 years, recommends a list of topics for discussion in performance appraisal feedback sessions (see Exhibit 11.14)[111] First, managers should separate developmental feedback, which is designed to improve future performance, from administrative feedback, which is used as a reward for past performance, such as for raises. When managers give developmental feedback, they're acting as coaches, but when they give administrative feedback, they're acting as judges. These roles, coaches and judges, are clearly incompatible. As coaches, managers are encouraging, pointing out opportunities for growth and improvement, and employees are typically open and receptive to feedback. But as judges, managers are evaluative, and employees are typically defensive and closed to feedback.

Second, Meyer suggests that performance appraisal feedback sessions be based on self-appraisals, in which employees carefully assess their own strengths, weaknesses, successes, and failures in writing. Because employees play an active role in the review of their performance, managers can be coaches rather than judges. Also, because the focus is on future goals and development, both employees and managers are likely to be more satisfied with the process and more committed to future plans and changes. And, because the focus is on development and not administrative assessment, studies show that self-appraisals lead to more candid self-assessments than traditional supervisory reviews.[112] See Exhibit 11.14 for a list of topics that Meyer recommends for discussion in performance appraisal feedback sessions.

Finally, what people do with the performance feedback they receive matters. A study of 1,361 senior managers found that managers who reviewed their 360-degree feedback with an executive coach (hired by the company) were more likely to set specific goals for improvement, ask their bosses for ways to improve, and subsequently improve their performance.[113] Also, a five-year study of 252 managers found that their performance improved dramatically if they met with their subordinates to discuss their 360-degree feedback ("You don't listen") and how they were going to address it ("I'll

Exhibit 11.14

What to Discuss in a Performance Appraisal Feedback Session

- ✔ Overall progress—an analysis of accomplishments and shortcomings.
- ✔ Problems encountered in meeting job requirements.
- ✔ Opportunities to improve performance.
- ✔ Long-range plans and opportunities—for the job and for the individual's career.
- ✔ General discussion of possible plans and goals for the coming year.

Source: H. H. Meyer, "A Solution to the Performance Appraisal Feedback Enigma," *Academy of Management Executive* 5, no. 1 (1991): 68–76.

restate what others have said before stating my opinion"). Performance was dramatically lower for managers who never discussed their 360-degree feedback with subordinates and for managers who did not routinely do so (some managers did not review their 360-degree feedback with subordinates each year of the study). Why is discussing 360-degree feedback with subordinates so effective? These discussions help managers better understand their weaknesses, force them to develop a plan to improve, and demonstrate to the subordinates the managers' public commitment to improving.[114] In short, it helps to have people discuss their performance feedback with others, but it particularly helps to have them discuss their feedback with the people who provided it.

It is clear that organizations, and specifically managers, must take the task of providing feedback seriously. Recent studies have reported that employees' satisfaction with feedback they receive influences not only their job satisfaction but also their future performance.[115] An employee's satisfaction with feedback is influenced by his or her perceptions of how well the manager knows the employee's job, the extent to which evaluations were based on job-related factors, whether the feedback process included goal setting, and whether the manager provided insights on how to improve future performance.[116]

Review 6: Performance Appraisal

Most employees and managers intensely dislike the performance appraisal process. Some of the problems associated with appraisals can be avoided, however, by accurately measuring job performance and effectively sharing performance feedback with employees. Organizations should develop good performance appraisal scales, preferably use behavior observation scales. They should train raters to accurately evaluate performance, perhaps by providing frame-of-reference training. They should impress upon managers the value of providing feedback in a clear, consistent, and fair manner, and of setting goals and monitoring progress toward those goals.

One way to overcome the inherent difficulties in performance appraisal feedback is to provide 360-degree feedback, in which feedback is obtained from four sources: the boss, subordinates, peers and coworkers, and the employees themselves. Feedback tends to be more credible if it is heard from several sources. Finally, especially for managers, it's helpful to have people discuss the feedback they received with executive coaches or the people who provided it.

KEEPING QUALIFIED WORKERS

China has a population of 1.3 billion people, but in the Pearl River delta there aren't enough workers to meet the skyrocketing demand for manufacturing workers. Consequently, companies such as *CHIGO AIR-CONDITIONING* are having to work hard to keep their employees. In the last five years, Chigo has raised salaries, started giving bonuses to workers who stay longer than three years, and built brand new housing with TV sets and swimming pools to entice workers to stay.[117] All this may not be enough, however, as Chinese economists estimate that companies will have to

> The typical annual-review process does nothing but harm. It creates divisions. It undermines morale. It makes people angry, jealous, and cynical. It unleashes a whole lot of negative energy, and the organization gets nothing in return.
>
> **A MANAGER**

"WHAT'S NEW" COMPANY

pay wages 40 to 50 percent higher to keep the workers they have and to fill the two million job openings in this part of China.

MASSEY ENERGY, in Richmond, Virginia, faces similar problems keeping workers. With coal prices increasing 60 percent over the last two years, coal producers like Massey are running full out to meet demand. The rise in coal prices has been accompanied by a rise in demand for miners. Turnover is high as employees jump ship to work for Massey's competitors at better pay and benefits. As a result, Massey has given all of its production workers raises ranging from 3 to 15 percent over the last year. Furthermore, it offered a $3 an hour raise to electricians who already make $27 an hour and can earn $90,000 a year with overtime pay. And, like Chigo Air-Conditioning, Massey offers bonuses to workers who stay longer. Finally, Massey also gives its supervisors stock options to encourage them to stay.[118]

> **After reading the next two sections, you should be able to**
>
> 7 describe basic compensation strategies and explain how they affect human resource practice.
>
> 8 discuss the four kinds of employee separations: termination, downsizing, retirements, and turnover.

 7 Compensation

*Compensation includes both the financial and the nonfinancial rewards that organizations give employees in exchange for their work. Let's learn more about compensation by examining the **7.1 compensation decisions that managers must make** and **7.2 the role that employment benefits play in compensating today's employees**.*

7.1 Compensation Decisions

As Exhibit 11.15 shows, there are four basic kinds of compensation decisions: pay level, pay variability, pay structure, and employment benefits. We'll discuss employment benefits in the next subsection.[119]

Pay-level decisions are decisions about whether to pay workers at a level that is below, above, or at current market wages. Companies use job evaluation to set their pay structures. **Job evaluation** determines the worth of each job by determining the market value of the knowledge, skills, and requirements needed to perform it. After conducting a job evaluation, most companies try to pay the "going rate," meaning the current market wage. There are always companies, however, whose financial situation causes them to pay considerably less than current market wages. The child-care industry, for example, has chronic difficulties filling jobs because it pays well below market wages. Also, because

compensation the financial and nonfinancial rewards that organizations give employees in exchange for their work

job evaluation a process that determines the worth of each job in a company by evaluating the market value of the knowledge, skills, and requirements needed to perform it

Exhibit 11.15

Kinds of Compensation Decisions

Pay Level	Pay Variability	Pay Structure	Employment Benefits
	• Piecework • Commission • Profit Sharing • Employee Stock Ownership Plans		
• Job Evaluation	• Stock Options	• Hierarchical • Compressed	• Cafeteria Plans • Flexible Plans • Payroll Deductions

wages are so low (an average of $7.86 an hour, or $16,350 a year), the applicants it attracts are increasingly less qualified.[120] Donna Krause, who runs Creative Learning and Child Care in Dundalk, Maryland, lost five child-care teachers one August when all were hired away by higher-paying public school systems. All of the teachers who left had college degrees, but none of their replacements did.[121]

Some companies choose to pay above-average wages to attract and keep employees. *Above-market wages* can attract a larger, more qualified pool of job applicants, increase the rate of job acceptance, decrease the time it takes to fill positions, and increase the time that employees stay.[122] For example, the severe nursing shortage discussed at the beginning of the chapter has begun to ease because, as Vanderbilt University nursing professor Peter Buerhaus explains, "Hospitals recognized that all their previous attempts weren't working so they had to raise wages."[123] Three years ago, 13 percent of the nursing positions at the Ochsner Clinic in New Orleans were open. After raising salaries substantially and giving nurses more flexible schedules (for example, $50,000+per year to work three 12-hour days per week), only 2.4 percent of its nursing positions were open, compared with a national average of 8.4 percent.

Pay-variability decisions concern the extent to which employees' pay varies with individual and organizational performance. Linking pay to performance is intended to increase employee motivation, effort, and job performance. Piecework, sales commissions, profit sharing, employee stock ownership plans, and stock options are common pay-variability options. For instance, under **piecework** pay plans, employees are paid a set rate for each item produced up to some standard (for example, 35 cents per item produced for output up to 100 units per day). Once productivity exceeds the standard, employees are paid a set amount for each unit of output over the standard (for example, 45 cents for each unit above 100 units). Under a sales **commission** plan, salespeople are paid a percentage of the purchase price of items they sell. The more they sell, the more they earn.

Because pay plans such as piecework and commissions are based on individual performance, they can reduce the incentive that people have to work together. Therefore, companies also use group incentives (discussed in Chapter 10) and organizational incentives, such as profit sharing, employee stock ownership plans, and stock options, to encourage teamwork and cooperation.

With **profit sharing**, employees receive a portion of the organization's profits over and above their regular compensation. The more profitable the company, the more profit is shared. Renault SAS, the French automaker, has a profit sharing agreement that distributes 6 percent of its net income to employees, with a minimum payout of 2,134 euros per employee.[124] **Employee stock ownership plans (ESOPs)** compensate employees by awarding them shares of the company stock in addition to their regular compensation. At MCKAY NURSERY in Waterloo, Wisconsin, Joe Hernandez, a 41-year-old migrant worker, makes $20,000 a year working from April to November. But Joe also gets an additional 20 to 25 percent in company stock. So far, he's accumulated more than $80,000 through the company ESOP.[125]

Stock options give employees the right to purchase shares of stock at a set price. Options work like this. Let's say that you are awarded the right (or option) to buy 100 shares of stock from the company for $5 a share. If the company's stock price rises to

piecework a compensation system in which employees are paid a set rate for each item they produce

commission a compensation system in which employees earn a percentage of each sale they make

profit sharing a compensation system in which a company pays a percentage of its profits to employees in addition to their regular compensation

employee stock ownership plan (ESOP) a compensation system that awards employees shares of company stock in addition to their regular compensation

stock options a compensation system that gives employees the right to purchase shares of stock at a set price, even if the value of the stock increases above that price

McKay Nursery includes company stock in its compensation program. The result is that employee ownership and commitment to the company grows.

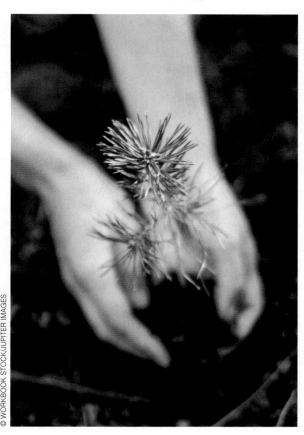

© WORKBOOK STOCK/JUPITER IMAGES

$15 a share, you can exercise your options and make $1,000. When you exercise your options, you pay the company $500 (100 shares at $5 a share), but because the stock is selling for $15 in the stock market, you can sell your 100 shares for $1,500 and make $1,000. Of course, as the company's profits and share values increase, stock options become even more valuable to employees. Stock options have no value, however, if the company's stock falls below the option "grant price," the price at which the options have been issued to you. For instance, the options you have on 100 shares of stock with a grant price of $5 aren't going to do you a lot of good if the company's stock is worth $2.50. Why exercise your stock options and pay $5 a share for stock that sells for $2.50 a share in the stock market? (Stock options are said to be "underwater" when the grant price is lower than the market price.) Proponents of stock options argue that this gives employees and managers a strong incentive to work hard to make the company successful. If they do, the company's profits and stock price increase, and their stock options increase in value. If they don't, profits stagnate or turn into losses, and their stock options decrease in value or become worthless. To learn more about ESOPs and stock options, see the National Center for Employee Ownership (**http://www.nceo.org**).

Pay-structure decisions are concerned with internal pay distributions, meaning the extent to which people in the company receive very different levels of pay.[126] With *hierarchical pay structures*, there are big differences from one pay level to another. The highest pay levels are for people near the top of the pay distribution. The basic idea behind hierarchical pay structures is that large differences in pay between jobs or organizational levels should motivate people to work harder to obtain those higher-paying jobs. Many publicly owned companies have hierarchical pay structures by virtue of the huge amounts they pay their top managers and CEOs. For example, the average CEO now makes 289 times as much as the average worker, down from 475 times the pay of average workers just five years ago. But with CEO pay packages averaging $9.6 million per year and average workers earning just $33,176, the difference is still incredible.[127]

By contrast, *compressed pay structures* typically have fewer pay levels and smaller differences in pay between levels. Pay is less dispersed and more similar across jobs in the company. The basic idea behind compressed pay structures is that similar pay levels should lead to higher levels of cooperation, feelings of fairness and a common purpose, and better group and team performance.

So should companies choose hierarchical or compressed pay structures? The evidence isn't straightforward, but studies seem to indicate that there are significant problems with the hierarchical approach. The most damaging finding is that there appears to be little link between organizational performance and the pay of top managers.[128] Furthermore, studies of professional athletes indicate that hierarchical pay structures (for example, paying superstars 40 to 50 times as much as the lowest-paid athlete on the team) hurt the performance of teams and individual players.[129] Likewise, managers are twice as likely to quit their jobs when their companies have very strong hierarchical pay structures (that is, when they're paid dramatically less than the people above them).[130] For now, it seems that hierarchical pay structures work best for independent work, where it's easy to determine the contributions of individual performers and little coordination with others is needed to get the job done. In other words, hierarchical pay structures work best when clear links can be drawn between individual performance and individual rewards. By contrast, compressed pay structures, in which everyone receives similar pay, seem to work best for interdependent work, which requires employees to work together. Some companies are pursuing a middle ground: combining hierarchical and compressed pay structures by giving ordinary workers the chance to earn more through ESOPs, stock options, and profit sharing.

7.2 Employment Benefits

Employment benefits include virtually any kind of compensation other than direct wages paid to employees.[131] Three employee benefits are mandated by law: Social Security, workers' compensation insurance, and unemployment insurance. To attract and retain a good work force, however, most organizations offer a wide variety of benefits, including retirement plans and pensions, paid holidays, paid vacations, sick leave, health insurance, life insurance, dental care, eye care, day-care facilities, paid personal days, legal assistance, physical fitness facilities, educational assistance, and discounts on company products and services. Currently, benefits cost organizations about 29.3 percent of their payroll, with an average cost of $15,000 per employee for a basic benefit plan.[132]

Managers should understand that although benefits are unlikely to improve employee motivation and performance, they do affect job satisfaction, employee decisions about staying or leaving the company, and the company's attractiveness to job applicants.[133] One way that organizations make their benefit plans more attractive is by offering **cafeteria benefit plans** or **flexible benefit plans**, which allow employees to choose which benefits they receive, up to a certain dollar value.[134] Many cafeteria or flexible benefit plans start with a core of benefits, such as health insurance and life insurance, that are available to all employees. Then employees are allowed to select the other benefits that best fit their needs, up to a predetermined dollar amount. Some organizations allow employees to choose from several packages of benefits. The packages are of equivalent value, but offer a different mix of benefits. For example, older employees may prefer more benefit dollars spent on retirement plans, while younger employees may prefer additional vacation days.

Pretax payroll deductions, which enable employees to pay for expenses such as medical care, day care, and commuting out of pretax dollars, are one of the more popular benefits options because they provide significant tax savings for employees and organizations. Nevertheless, only 18 percent of eligible employees participate in their company's pretax payroll deduction plan. The problem, as employee Kate Morrison explained, has been that "by the time you filled out the paperwork and mailed it off and they processed it, it could take up to 45 days to get your money back [from your pretax account]."[135] Some companies have solved these problems by giving employees a debit card attached to their pretax spending accounts that they can use to pay expenses directly, thereby avoiding the paperwork and the wait for reimbursement.

The drawback to flexible benefit plans has been the high cost of administering them. With advances in information processing technology and HRISs, however, the cost has begun to drop in recent years.

Review 7: Compensation

Compensation includes both the financial and the nonfinancial rewards that organizations give employees in exchange for their work. There are four basic kinds of compensation decisions: pay level, pay variability, pay structure, and employment benefits. Pay-level decisions determine whether workers will receive wages below, above, or at current market levels. Pay-variability decisions concern the extent to which pay varies with individual and organizational performance. Piecework, sales commissions, profit sharing, employee stock ownership plans, and stock options are common pay-variability options. Pay-structure decisions concern the extent to which people in the company receive very different levels of pay. Hierarchical pay structures work best for independent work, while compressed pay structures work best for interdependent work.

employment benefits a method of rewarding employees that includes virtually any kind of compensation other than wages or salaries

cafeteria benefit plans (flexible benefit plans) plans that allow employees to choose which benefits they receive, up to a certain dollar value

Employee benefits include virtually any kind of compensation other than direct wages paid to employees. Flexible or cafeteria benefit plans offer employees a wide variety of benefits, improve job satisfaction, increase the chances that employees will stay with companies, and make organizations more attractive to job applicants. The cost of administering flexible benefit plans has begun to drop in recent years.

8 Employee Separations

Employee separation is a broad term covering the loss of an employee for any reason. *Involuntary separation* occurs when employers terminate or lay off employees. *Voluntary separation* occurs when employees quit or retire. Because employee separations affect recruiting, selection, training, and compensation, organizations should forecast the number of employees they expect to lose through terminations, layoffs, turnover, or retirements when doing human resource planning.

*Let's explore employee separation by examining **8.1 terminations**, **8.2 downsizing**, **8.3 retirements**, and **8.4 turnover**.*

8.1 Terminating Employees

Hopefully, the words "You're fired!" have never been directed at you. Lots of people hear them, however, as more than 400,000 people a year get fired from their jobs. Getting fired is a terrible thing, but many managers make it even worse by bungling the firing process, needlessly provoking the person who was fired and unintentionally inviting lawsuits. For example, one worker learned he had been fired only after a restaurant told him that his company credit card was no longer active. The top office manager for a professional sports team returned to the office to find his parking space taken by someone interviewing for his job. The CEO of a clothing store company gave all of his top managers a fruit basket one holiday season, except his top finance manager, who was soon fired.[136] A computer systems engineer was fired on "Take Your Daughter to Work Day," with his eight-year-old daughter sitting next to him in the human resource manager's office. He and his daughter were both escorted from the building.[137] Recall from the beginning of the chapter how 400 employees at the Fort Worth headquarters of RadioShack got the following e-mail message: "The work force reduction notification is currently in progress. Unfortunately your position is one that has been eliminated."[138] How would you feel if you had been fired in one of these ways? Though firing is never pleasant (and managers hate firings nearly as much as employees do), managers can do several things to minimize the problems inherent in firing employees.

First, in most situations, firing should not be the first option. Instead, employees should be given a chance to change their behavior. When problems arise, employees should have ample warning and must be specifically informed as to the nature and seriousness of the trouble they're in. After being notified, they should be given sufficient time to change. If the problems continue, the employees should again be counseled about their job performance, what could be done to improve it, and the possible consequences if things don't change (such as a written reprimand, suspension without pay, or firing). Sometimes this is enough to solve the problem. If the problem isn't corrected after several rounds of warnings and discussions, however, the employee may be terminated.[139]

Second, employees should be fired only for a good reason. Employers used to hire and fire employees under the legal principle of "employment at will," which allowed them to fire employees for a good reason, a bad reason, or no reason at all. (Employees could also quit for a good reason, a bad reason, or no reason whenever they desired.)

employee separation the voluntary or involuntary loss of an employee

As employees began contesting their firings in court, however, the principle of wrongful discharge emerged. **Wrongful discharge** is a legal doctrine that requires employers to have a job-related reason to terminate employees. In other words, like other major human resource decisions, termination decisions should be made on the basis of job-related factors, such as violating company rules or consistently poor performance. And with former employees winning 68 percent of wrongful discharge cases and the average wrongful termination award at $532,000 and climbing, managers should record the job-related reasons for the termination, document specific instances of rule violations or continued poor performance, and keep notes and documents from the counseling sessions held with employees.[140]

Finally, to reduce the chances of a wrongful discharge suit, employees should always be fired in private. State the reason for discharge, but don't go into detail or engage in a lengthy discussion with the employee. Make every attempt to be as kind and respectful as possible when informing someone that he or she is being fired. It is permissible, and sometimes a good idea, to have a witness present. This person should be from human resources or part of the employee's chain of command, such as the supervisor's boss. Company security may be nearby, but should not be in the room unless the employee has made direct threats toward others. Finally, managers should be careful not to publicly criticize the employee who has just been fired, as this can also lead to a wrongful discharge lawsuit. In general, unless someone has a "business reason to know" why an employee was fired, the reasons and details related to the firing should remain confidential.[141]

8.2 Downsizing

Downsizing is the planned elimination of jobs in a company. Whether it's because of cost cutting, declining market share, previous overaggressive hiring and growth, or outsourcing, companies typically eliminate 1 million to 1.9 million jobs a year.[142] Two-thirds of companies that downsize will downsize a second time within a year. For example, Eastman Kodak recently announced that it would be eliminating 21 percent of its work force—12,000 to 15,000 jobs—over the next two years. Previously, because of the long-term decline in its core photography business, Kodak had laid off 50,000 workers in an effort to cut costs.[143] FORD MOTOR COMPANY's "Way Forward" plan calls for shedding 25,000 to 30,000 jobs and closing 14 plants by 2012 to help return its North American automotive operations to profitability.[144] Does downsizing work? In theory, downsizing is supposed to lead to higher productivity and profits, better stock performance, and increased organizational flexibility. However, numerous studies demonstrate that it doesn't. For instance, a 15-year study of downsizing found that downsizing 10 percent of a company's work force produced only a 1.5 percent decrease in costs; that firms that downsized increased their stock price by only 4.7 percent over three years, compared with 34.3 percent for firms that didn't; and that profitability and productivity were generally not improved by downsizing.[145] These results make it clear that the best strategy is to conduct effective human resource planning and avoid downsizing altogether. Indeed, downsizing should always be a last resort.

If companies do find themselves in financial or strategic situations where downsizing is required for survival, however, they should train managers in how to break the news to downsized employees, have senior managers explain in detail why downsizing is necessary, and time the announcement so that employees hear it from the company and not from other sources, such as TV or newspaper reports.[146] Finally, companies should do everything they can to help downsized employees find other jobs. One of the best ways to do this is to use **outplacement services** that provide employment-counseling services for employees faced with downsizing. Outplacement services often include advice and training in preparing résumés, getting ready for job interviews, and even

wrongful discharge a legal doctrine that requires employers to have a job-related reason to terminate employees

downsizing the planned elimination of jobs in a company

outplacement services employment-counseling services offered to employees who are losing their jobs because of downsizing identifying job opportunities in other companies. Fifty-five percent of companies provide outplacement services for laid-off employees, 76 percent provide extended health coverage, and 45 percent offer extended access to employee assistance programs.[147] Exhibit 11.16 provides additional guidelines for conducting layoffs.

Companies also need to pay attention to the "survivors," the employees remaining after layoffs have occurred. University of Pennsylvania management professor Peter Cappelli says that survivors "may feel like they could just as easily be the next person laid off."[148] Management consultant Diane Durken agrees: "The people who are left behind start looking behind their backs and saying, 'Am I next?' They need to be rejuvenated, so they can refocus on the future. Honesty and integrity are the core of this."[149] The key to working with layoff survivors, according to Barry Nickerson, president of Dallas-based Marlow Industries, which downsized from 800 to 200 employees, is "Communicate. Communicate. Communicate." Nickerson says, "Every time we had a change we had a meeting to explain exactly what we were doing. We were very open with our employees about where we were financially. We would explain exactly the current status and where we were."[150]

8.3 Retirement

Early retirement incentive programs (ERIPs) offer financial benefits to employees to encourage them to retire early. Companies use ERIPs to reduce the number of employees in the organization, to lower costs by eliminating positions after employees retire, to lower costs by replacing high-paid retirees with lower-paid, less-experienced employees, or to create openings and job opportunities for people inside the company. For example, the state of Wyoming offered its employees a lump-sum bonus, additional insurance benefits, and increased monthly retirement payments to encourage early retirement. Its ERIP must have been fairly attractive, because 56 percent of the state employees eligible for early retirement accepted. Thirty percent of the 437 positions vacated by the early retirees remained empty, saving the state $23.2 million over the first 46 months of the program and a projected $65 million over eight years. After accounting for the costs of the increased early retirement benefits, the predicted savings came to more than $148,000 per retiree.[151]

Although ERIPs can save companies money, they can pose a big problem for managers if they fail to accurately predict which employees—the good performers or the poor performers—and how many will retire early. Consultant Ron Nicol says, "The thing that doesn't work is just asking for volunteers. You get the wrong volunteers. Some of your best people will feel they can get a job anywhere. Or you have people who are close to retirement and are a real asset to the company."[152] When Ameritech Corporation (now part of AT&T) offered an ERIP, it carefully identified the number of employees near retirement age and estimated that 5,000 to 6,000 of its 48,000 employees would take advantage of the program. Instead, nearly 22,000 employees accepted the ERIP offer and applied for early retirement![153]

early retirement incentive programs (ERIPs) programs that offer financial benefits to employees to encourage them to retire early

Exhibit 11.16

Guidelines for Conducting Layoffs

1. Provide clear reasons and explanations for the layoffs.
2. To avoid laying off employees with critical or irreplaceable skills, knowledge, and expertise, get input from human resources, the legal department, and several levels of management.
3. Train managers in how to tell employees that they are being laid off (stay calm; make the meeting short; explain why, but don't be personal; and provide information about immediate concerns, such as benefits, job search, and collecting personal goods).
4. Give employees the bad news early in the day, and try to avoid laying off employees just before holidays.
5. Provide outplacement services and counseling to help laid-off employees find new jobs.
6. Communicate with survivors to explain how the company and their jobs will change.

Source: M. Boyle, "The Not-So-Fine Art of the Layoff," *Fortune*, 19 March 2001, 209.

Because of the problems associated with ERIPs, many companies are now offering **phased retirement**, in which employees transition to retirement by working reduced hours over a period of time before completely retiring. The advantage for employees is that they have more free time, but continue to earn salaries and benefits without changing companies or careers. The advantage for companies is that it allows them to reduce salaries and hiring and training costs and retain experienced, valuable workers.[154]

8.4 Employee Turnover

Employee turnover is the loss of employees who voluntarily choose to leave the company. In general, most companies try to keep the rate of employee turnover low to reduce recruiting, hiring, training, and replacement costs. Not all kinds of employee turnover are bad for organizations, however. In fact, some turnover can actually be good. For instance, **functional turnover** is the loss of poor-performing employees who choose to leave the organization.[155] Functional turnover gives the organization a chance to replace poor performers with better workers. In fact, one study found that simply replacing poor-performing leavers with average workers would increase the revenues produced by retail salespeople in an upscale department store by $112,000 per person per year.[156] By contrast, **dysfunctional turnover**, the loss of high performers who choose to leave, is a costly loss to the organization.

Employee turnover should be carefully analyzed to determine whether good or poor performers are choosing to leave the organization. If the company is losing too many high performers, managers should determine the reasons and find ways to reduce the loss of valuable employees. The company may have to raise salary levels, offer enhanced benefits, or improve working conditions to retain skilled workers. One of the best ways to influence functional and dysfunctional turnover is to link pay directly to performance. A study of four sales forces found that when pay was strongly linked to performance via sales commissions and bonuses, poor performers were much more likely to leave (that is, functional turnover). By contrast, poor performers were much more likely to stay when paid large, guaranteed monthly salaries and small sales commissions and bonuses.[157]

Review 8: *Employee Separations*

Employee separation is the loss of an employee, which can occur voluntarily or involuntarily. Before firing or terminating employees, managers should give employees a chance to improve. If firing becomes necessary, it should be done because of job-related factors, such as violating company rules or consistently performing poorly. Downsizing is supposed to lead to higher productivity and profits, better stock performance, and increased organizational flexibility, but studies show that it doesn't. The best strategy is to downsize only as a last resort. Companies that do downsize should offer outplacement services to help employees find other jobs. Companies use early retirement incentive programs to reduce the number of employees in the organization, lower costs, and create openings and job opportunities for people inside the company. The biggest problem with ERIPs is accurately predicting who and how many will accept early retirement. Companies generally try to keep the rate of employee turnover low to reduce costs. Functional turnover can be good for organizations, however, because it offers the chance to replace poor performers with better workers. Managers should analyze employee turnover to determine who is resigning and take steps to reduce the loss of good performers.

phased retirement employees transition to retirement by working reduced hours over a period of time before completing retiring

employee turnover loss of employees who voluntarily choose to leave the company

functional turnover loss of poor-performing employees who voluntarily choose to leave a company

dysfunctional turnover loss of high-performing employees who voluntarily choose to leave a company

Interview Anxiety

How would you feel if you got a call to interview for your dream job? Excited? Nervous? Or downright panicked? It's not uncommon to get butterflies in your stomach at the prospect of a job interview, but some candidates have more than weak knees and sweaty palms. Complete the assessment below by indicating the extent to which you agree with each of the following statements.[158] Your score will be a baseline as you begin working on the skills you'll need during your job hunt. Try not to spend too much time on any one item, and be sure to answer all the questions. Use this scale for your responses:

1 Strongly disagree
2 Disagree
3 Neutral
4 Agree
5 Strongly agree

1. I become so apprehensive in job interviews that I am unable to express my thoughts clearly.
   1   2   3   4   5
2. I often feel uneasy about my appearance when I am being interviewed for a job.
   1   2   3   4   5
3. While taking a job interview, I become concerned that the interviewer will perceive me as socially awkward.
   1   2   3   4   5
4. In job interviews, I get very nervous about whether my performance is good enough.
   1   2   3   4   5
5. During job interviews, my hands shake.
   1   2   3   4   5
6. I get so anxious while taking job interviews that I have trouble answering questions that I know.
   1   2   3   4   5
7. Before a job interview I am so nervous that I spend an excessive amount of time on my appearance.
   1   2   3   4   5
8. I become very uptight about having to socially interact with a job interviewer.
   1   2   3   4   5
9. I am overwhelmed by thoughts of doing poorly when I am in job interview situations.
   1   2   3   4   5
10. My heartbeat is faster than usual during job interviews.
    1   2   3   4   5
11. During job interviews, I often can't think of a thing to say.
    1   2   3   4   5
12. In job interviews, I worry that the interviewer will focus on what I consider to be my least attractive physical features.
    1   2   3   4   5
13. I get afraid about what kind of personal impression I am making on job interviews.
    1   2   3   4   5
14. I worry that my job interview performance will be lower than that of other applicants.
    1   2   3   4   5
15. It is hard for me to avoid fidgeting during a job interview.
    1   2   3   4   5
16. I feel that my verbal communication skills are strong.
    1   2   3   4   5
17. If I do not look my absolute best in a job interview, I find it very hard to be relaxed.
    1   2   3   4   5
18. During a job interview, I worry that my actions will not be considered socially appropriate.
    1   2   3   4   5

19. During a job interview, I am so troubled by thoughts of failing that my performance is reduced.
1   2   3   4   5

20. Job interviews often make me perspire (e.g., sweaty palms and underarms).
1   2   3   4   5

21. During job interviews, I find it hard to understand what the interviewer is asking me.
1   2   3   4   5

22. I feel uneasy if my hair is not perfect when I walk into a job interview.
1   2   3   4   5

23. I worry about whether job interviewers will like me as a person.
1   2   3   4   5

24. During a job interview, I worry about what will happen if I don't get the job.
1   2   3   4   5

25. My mouth gets very dry during job interviews.
1   2   3   4   5

26. I find it easy to communicate my personal accomplishments during a job interview.
1   2   3   4   5

27. During a job interview, I worry about whether I have dressed appropriately.
1   2   3   4   5

28. When meeting a job interviewer, I worry that my handshake will not be correct.
1   2   3   4   5

29. While taking a job interview, I worry about whether I am a good candidate for the job.
1   2   3   4   5

30. I often feel sick to my stomach when I am interviewed for a job.
1   2   3   4   5

Scoring

Reverse your score on items 16 and 26. That is, if you wrote in a "5," change it to a "1" and vice versa; if you wrote in a "4," change it to a "2" and vice versa.
TOTAL = _____
You can find the interpretation of your score at: **academic.cengage.com/ management/williams**.

MANAGEMENT DECISION

Open for Abuse

This isn't the first time you've had an employee who wanted to take leave under the Family and Medical Leave Act (FMLA). The act has been in place for over a decade, and you've had employees take leave for childbirth, for elder care, and to recover from surgery or injuries. In general, most people have used the FMLA as it was intended and have been relieved that they didn't have to choose between their job and caring for a family member. As with most things, however, there are always abuses, and you have occasionally had to grapple with a request for time off that you considered questionable. Today, you've received one of those requests.

You operate two upscale restaurants, one in the financial district and one in the entertainment district. Last week, you had to tell Cal, one of your experienced bartenders in the financial district location, that he would be moving from the happy hour to the lunch hour because you needed his experience there. Although Cal would now be the team leader on the day shift, he was angry about the change, insisting that it amounted to a pay reduction because no one has three-martini lunches anymore. He said he'd only be serving soda and coffee, and tips on those drinks weren't going to pay his rent. Even without drinks, lunchtime checks generally average $75 per table, so you assure Cal that once the five waitresses tip out (give a portion of their tips to the bartenders and table clearers), his pay should be the same. You reiterate that you really need him on days because the new crew is having trouble keeping up, even though they are just serving soda and coffee. But Cal announced his resignation. Before leaving at the end of his shift, however, he told you he had changed his mind. Today he came in late, with a doctor's note saying he required a 12-week leave for stress!

Under the FMLA, stress is considered a serious health condition, so you have to grant Cal's request and continue his health coverage. Legally, you can ask that he get a second opinion, but you can't question a doctor's recommendation for time off. Cal has requested the maximum time allowed—12 weeks of unpaid leave per year—and if he decides to come back after that, you have to keep his job for him. You are convinced, however, that he intends to quit when the 12 weeks are up.

What are you going to do? Asking other employees to pick up the slack will create morale problems for both the day and evening shifts (they get testy enough when someone is on leave for a legitimate situation), but hiring a temporary replacement may not solve your problem. If you do hire a temp, you might find a great new employee whom you'd have to let go in 12 weeks if Cal does come back. Maybe you should just be thankful that Cal requested the leave in one block, instead of taking it in daily or hourly increments, which, according to the law, he could have done.

Questions

1. How do you handle Cal's three-month absence with the least disruption?

2. Do you have a frank discussion with Cal and ask him if he plans to return after his leave, or do you just plan around him?

3. How can businesses mitigate the unintended impact of the FMLA?

MANAGEMENT TEAM DECISION

Hire or Holdout?

When your systems engineer left to have a baby, you had no idea how hard it would be to replace her.[159] You'd heard the labor market for engineers was tight, but you thought it wouldn't be too tough to find a new hire for a company as well known as Raytheon. That was six months ago.

Today, your team is sitting down again with another crop of 200 résumés to compare against the job specifications: Ph.D in science or computer engineering; experience in manufacturing; knowledge of the manufacturing software you use and with Pro/Engineer Wildfire, a computer-aided design (CAD) software package; able to get top-secret government security clearance; willingness to relocate to Waltham, Massachusetts, where Raytheon is headquartered; and more technical competency requirements. Really, when you look over the list, you don't think the requirements are that stringent, particularly when you consider that Raytheon designs and manufactures aircraft, missile systems, and intelligence and information systems for the U.S. Department of Defense.

And your pool of applicants is nowhere near that of some other companies. Microsoft receives 60,000 résumés a month, but it has only 2,000 openings for software-development jobs. Of the 100,000 résumés it received from graduating students last year, it screened only 15,000, interviewed 3,500, and hired 1,000. Come to think of it, though, your chances of getting hired at Microsoft are better than your chances of filling your systems engineer opening.

As you sit down with your team and begin to sift through the 200 résumés, you see right away that 100 don't have a Ph.D. Of the remaining 100 candidates, 40 wouldn't be able to get security clearance, 23 are overqualified, and 18 don't have manufacturing experience, and 10 only have experience on 2001i, an earlier version CAD software. So out of your 200 applicants, only 9 are left, and you haven't even broached the question about relocating.

You've gone through seven similar piles of résumés in the past six months. The whole point of specifying the exact qualifications you want in an applicant was to save time getting the person up and running at the company. Maybe you'd have been better off loosening up the requirements and developing appropriate training programs. What if none of the applicants left standing after this round wants to relocate? Then you'll be starting with another pile next month—or sooner.

Form a team of four to five students to play the role of the hiring team at Raytheon and work through the following questions to come to a decision.

Questions

1. What are the risks to keeping the job requirements tightly structured?

2. What are the risks to loosening up the job specifications?

3. How would loosening up the job specifications affect your training needs?

4. Do you hire an applicant who meets a good number of the job requirements and is generally compatible with the corporate culture; or do you wait for the perfect candidate, even if that means another six months of interviewing?

PRACTICE BEING A MANAGER

Managing human resources in today's complex business and legal environment is not easy. Not only must companies hire the creative and hard-working employees that will fuel growth and competitive advantage, but they must be careful to do so legally and ethically. Unfair discrimination in any HR process will result in poor placement, turnover, and legal woes. This exercise will give you some practice in navigating the challenges of legal and effective recruitment and selection of employees.

Step 1: Get into groups. Your professor will assign you to groups of four or five students. One student will be given the role of HR attorney for the applicants, two students the role of nursing shift (day/night) managers at Montclair Hospital, and the remaining student(s) will be assigned the role of senior hospital administrator at Montclair Hospital.

Scenario: Montclair Hospital needs to hire new nurses. In fact, the hospital is in a bit of a crisis. Three nurses were recently fired for using drugs while on duty. In the ensuing publicity, a journalist uncovered that two of these nurses were convicted felons. As if these problems were not enough, nurse turnover is up 20 percent this year over last, and productivity of the remaining staff is substandard. Absences are also up lately, particularly those related to child-care or elder-care issues.

Both the day and the night nursing shift managers need to hire some quality nurses—and fast. Hospital administrators have made it abundantly clear that they do not want a repeat of the headline "Felons and Drug Users among Montclair Nursing Staff." Your compensation and benefits are competitive, and, with the exception of the recent news coverage, your hospital enjoys a strong reputation. The nursing labor market is tight (there are fewer nurses than openings), and most new hires are recent nursing school graduates.

Nursing shift managers need to work together to develop a plan to achieve the following:

1. Hire top-flight nurses to fill vacancies left by recent firings and resignations.
2. Stem the turnover of quality nurses already employed by Montclair.

3. Reduce absenteeism, especially unplanned "emergency" absences that wreak havoc with planning the work of an upcoming shift.

Step 2a: Outline a plan. The day and the night nursing shift managers should work together to sketch out a plan for making progress on the three concerns of Montclair Hospital administration (hiring, turnover, absenteeism). Some elements of this plan might include

- Where and how to recruit top nursing candidates
- Screening applicants to reduce risks of turnover, criminal/behavioral problems, and disruptive absenteeism
- Dealing with the turnover, absenteeism, and productivity problems of existing nursing staff

Step 2b: Review the plan. Students in the roles of hospital administrator and HR attorney should listen to the nursing managers as they sketch out their plans. Do not offer comments unless one of the managers asks you for your input. Take careful notes regarding what you hear, with particular attention to concerns and questions. Those in the HR attorney role should consider what you hear from the perspective of both potential applicants (and litigants) and Montclair Hospital (defense of HR practices).

Are the nursing managers developing a plan likely to successfully address the three concerns related to hiring, turnover, and absenteeism? Why, or why not? Do you hear anything that might raise a legal concern (such as inappropriate interview question, possible discrimination)?

Step 3: Debrief as a class. Students should open with comments from each perspective: (1) HR attorneys, (2) hospital administrators, and (3) nursing shift managers. What are some of the particular concerns or questions that arose in your mind as you played your particular role? What are some of the tensions that face the managers and administrators in this situation? How might the HR system of a hospital be improved? Why might nurses represent a particularly challenging set of HR concerns?

360-Degree Feedback

Whereas most performance appraisal ratings have traditionally come from just one person, the boss, 360-degree feedback is obtained from four sources: the boss, subordinates, peers and coworkers, and the employees themselves. In this assignment, you will be gathering 360-degree feedback from people that you work with or from a team or group that you're a member of for a class.

Here are some guidelines for obtaining your 360-degree feedback:

- *Carefully select respondents.* One of the keys to good 360-degree feedback is getting feedback from the right people. In general, the people you ask for feedback should interact with you on a regular basis and should have the chance to regularly observe your behavior. Also, be sure to get a representative sample of opinions from a similar number of coworkers and subordinates (assuming you have some).

- *Get a large enough number of responses.* In addition to your boss, you should have a minimum of three peers and three subordinates giving you feedback. Five or six respondents in each of those categories is even better.

- *Ensure confidentiality.* Respondents are much more likely to be honest if they know that their comments are confidential and anonymous. So, when you ask respondents for feedback, have them return their comments to someone other than yourself. This person, your "feedback facilitator," will remove the names and any other information that would identify who made particular comments.

- *Explain how the 360-degree feedback will be used.* In this case, explain that the feedback is for a class assignment, that the results will be used for your own personal growth and development, and that the feedback they give you will not affect your grade or formal assessment at work.

- *Ask respondents to make their feedback as specific as possible.* For instance, "bad attitude" isn't very good feedback. "Won't listen to others' suggestions" is much better because it would let you know how to improve your behavior. Have your respondents use the feedback form below to provide your feedback.

Here's what you need to turn in for this assignment:

1. The names and relationships (boss, peers, subordinates, classmates, teammates) of those whom you've asked for feedback.

2. The name of the person you've asked to be your feedback facilitator.

3. Copies of all written feedback that was returned to you.

4. A one-page summary of the written feedback.

5. A one-page description of your specific goals and action plans for responding to the feedback you received.

360-Degree Feedback Form

As part of a class assignment, I, _____, am collecting feedback from you about my performance. What you say or write will not affect my grade. The purpose of this assignment is for me to receive honest feedback from the people I work with in order to identify the things I'm doing well and the things that I need to improve. So please be honest and direct in your evaluation.

When you have completed this feedback form, please return it to _____. He or she has been selected as my feedback facilitator and is responsible for ensuring that your confidentiality and anonymity are maintained. After all feedback forms have been returned to _____, he or she will make sure that your particular responses cannot be identified. Only then will the feedback be shared with me.

Please provide the following feedback.

Continue doing . . .

Describe three things that _____ is doing that are a positive part of his or her performance and that you want him or her to continue doing.

1.

2.

3.

Start doing . . .

Describe three things that _____ needs to start doing that would significantly improve his or her performance.

1.

2.

3.

Please make your feedback as specific and behavioral as possible. For instance, "needs to adjust attitude" isn't very good feedback. "Needs to begin listening to others' suggestions" is much better because the person now knows exactly how to change his or her behavior. So please be specific. Also, please write more than one sentence per comment. This will help the feedback recipient better understand your comments.

REEL TO REAL

BIZ FLIX
Bowfinger

This film, which brought Steve Martin and Eddie Murphy together for the first time, offers a funny look at Hollywood filmmaking. Bobby Bowfinger (Martin), perhaps the least successful director in films, wants to produce a low-budget film with top star Kit Ramsey (Murphy). Bowfinger's problem: recruit a crew and cast with almost no budget and trick Kit into appearing in his film. So he decides to hire a lookalike.

Bowfinger interviews several candidates for the Kit Ramsey lookalike role. He rejects everyone until Jif-ferson (Jiff) Ramsey (also played by Murphy) auditions. This scene is an edited version of the "The Lookalike" sequence early in the film. It includes Jiff's audition and interview, and a brief look at his first day at work.

What to Watch for and Ask Yourself

1. Does Bobbie Bowfinger have a set of valid selection criteria for filling the role of a Kit Ramsey lookalike? Does Bowfinger apply the criteria uniformly to each applicant?
2. Is there a good person-job fit of Jiff Ramsey in the screen role of Kit Ramsey?
3. Do you predict that Jiff Ramsey will be successful as a Kit Ramsey substitute?

MANAGEMENT WORKPLACE
PepsiCo—Employee Champions

Whether a company employs five or five thousand people, its greatest resource is those workers. Many of today's companies view their workforces as part of their overall competitive strategy—the best people producing the best products. Human resource managers at large firms such as PepsiCo may be viewed as strategic business partners. No longer do they simply sign paychecks, approve vacations, and process health benefit claims. At PepsiCo, HR managers play an integral role in the day-to-day success of the business.

Headquartered in Purchase, New York, PepsiCo is a global organization, with more than 143,000 employees worldwide. The company produces and markets such brands as PepsiCo beverages, Frito-Lay snacks, Gatorade and Tropicana drinks, and Quaker Foods. PepsiCo brand products are available in nearly 200 countries and territories. But recruiting, selecting, training, and managing more than 100,000 workers requires planning to meet the career needs of so many people. Let's look inside the management work-place at PepsiCo to see how the company does it.

Questions

1. What do you think the role of the employee champion is in terms of the human resource (HR) function discussed in the chapter?
2. Which areas of human resources are handled by PepsiCo's administrative experts?
3. What do you think is the advantage of dividing HR functions into four distinct quadrants?

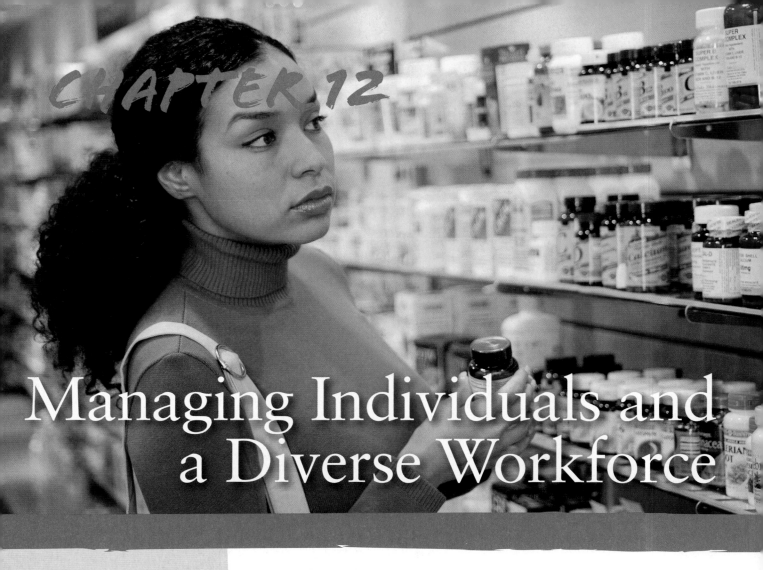

CHAPTER 12

Managing Individuals and a Diverse Workforce

Learning Outcomes:

1 Describe diversity and explain why it matters.

2 Understand the special challenges that the dimensions of surface-level diversity pose for managers.

3 Explain how the dimensions of deep-level diversity affect individual behavior and interactions in the workplace.

4 Explain the basic principles and practices that can be used to manage diversity.

In This Chapter:

WHAT WOULD YOU DO?

Walgreens, Deerfield, Illinois. Walgreens is the nation's largest drugstore chain, with annual sales of $47.4 billion. It operates 5,584 stores in 47 states and Puerto Rico and plans to have 7,000 stores by 2010.[1]

The Equal Employment Opportunity Commission (EEOC) has filed an employment discrimination class-action lawsuit against Walgreens, alleging widespread racial bias against thousands of African American workers. The EEOC charges that company management assigns African American managers, management trainees, and pharmacists to low-performing stores in African American communities because of their race. Additionally, the EEOC asserts that Walgreens denies these managers and professionals promotional opportunities based on race—all in violation of federal law. The EEOC case started when a group of current and former African American managers filed a private lawsuit making similar allegations. Since then, more than 20 current and former employees have complained to the EEOC, alleging racial discrimination by Walgreens in employment decisions. An EEOC investigation offered enough evidence to file a class-action suit in federal court. With your guidance, the company issued a statement saying, "As a company with a history of commitment to fairness, diversity, and opportunity, we are saddened and disappointed by the EEOC's decision. Our commitment is to providing opportunity to all employees—not only because it is the right thing to do but because our business was built on this principle." The statement continued, "Fairness and equality always have been the cornerstone of our business. We're the nation's best represented retailer in urban areas, and managers of all backgrounds are promoted to senior levels from those locations." Obviously, data must suggest otherwise to file a class-action suit. "Black managers are assigned to stores in black neighborhoods more often than one would expect, and black employees are not being promoted to management and within management as often as similar white employees," said EEOC attorney Robert Johnson. Attorneys who filed the private lawsuit said that the employees not only "faced discrimination, but faced segregation. The segregation is a throwback that most of us thought was gone from American life."

The trial, the appeals that are sure to follow, and any final settlement may take years to resolve. The question now is, what do you do in the interim? Certainly, pressure is building to address these issues. Even stockholders are not happy, especially since the stock price dropped following the EEOC announcement.

So, what should you do to address these issues as you wait for the case to wind its way through the court system? First, what should you do when it comes to placements, that is, assigning managers and pharmacists to stores? Should store location not be considered when making placement decisions? Should management make a conscious attempt to completely disregard race and other demographics when assigning people to stores? Second, what about promotion decisions? Should you reserve a percentage of promotions for minorities or base promotions strictly on performance with no regard to race? Some in the company argue that making changes now is tantamount to an admission of guilt and would weaken your court case. Others argue that both Walgreens' minority employees and the public perceive the promotion differences as real and problematic, and that something needs to be done regardless of the class-action suit. So, what, if anything, should you do? Finally, what changes does Walgreens need to make in its organizational structure and company leadership so that these issues aren't problems in the future? When all this started, Walgreens didn't have a senior vice president of diversity, a leadership position that many companies of Walgreens' size and revenue have. **If you were in charge of diversity at Walgreens, what would you do?**

Study Tip

In the margin next to each paragraph or section in the chapter, write the question that the section answers. For example, "What is the difference between surface- and deep-level diversity?" could go on page 440. Once you have questions throughout the chapter, you can quiz yourself by using a blank piece of paper to cover the content. To check yourself, reveal each paragraph after you have answered the corresponding question.

Workplace diversity as we know it today is changing. Exhibit 12.1 shows predictions from the U.S. Bureau of the Census of how the U.S. population will change over the next 65 years. The percentage of white, non-Hispanic Americans in the general population is expected to decline from 69.3 percent in 2005 to 46.8 percent by the year 2070. By contrast, the percentage of African Americans will increase (from 12.3 percent to 13.2 percent), as will the percentage of Asian Americans (from 4.3 percent to 10.6 percent). Meanwhile the proportion of Native Americans will hold steady (at 0.8 percent). The fastest-growing group by far, though, is Hispanics, who are expected to increase from 13.3 percent of the total population in 2005 to 28.6 percent by 2070.

Other significant changes have already occurred, as Walgreens' situation in the opening case illustrates. For example, today women hold half the jobs in the United States, up from 38.2 percent in 1970.[2] Furthermore, white males, who composed 63.9 percent of the work force in 1950, hold just 38.2 percent of today's jobs.[3]

These rather dramatic changes have taken place in a relatively short time. And, as these trends clearly show, the workforce of the near future will be increasingly Hispanic, Asian American, African American, and female. According to Hewitt Associates, by 2008, women and minorities will represent 70 percent of the new labor force entrants, and by 2010, 34 percent of the U.S. workforce will be non-Caucasian.[4] It will also be older, as the average baby boomer approaches the age of 60 around 2010. Since many boomers are likely to postpone retirement and work well into their 70s to offset predicted reductions in Social Security and Medicare benefits, the workforce may become even older than expected.[5] For instance, Hewitt Associates estimates that by 2010 the U.S. workforce will have a 29 percent increase in the 45–64 age group and a 14 percent increase in the 65+ age group, but a 1 percent decline in the 18–44 age group.[6] This chapter begins with a review of workforce diversity—what it is and why it matters. Next, you will learn about two basic dimensions of diversity: surface-level diversity, or how age, sex, race/ethnicity, and mental and physical disabilities affect people at

Exhibit 12.1

Predicted U.S. Population, Distributed by Race, 2005–2070

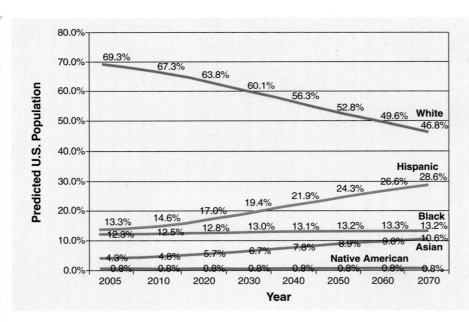

Sources: "Projections of the Resident Population by Race, Hispanic Origin, and Nativity: Middle Series, 2001–2005, 2006–2010, 2011–2015, 2016–2020, 2025–2045, 2050–2070," U.S. Census Bureau, available at http://www.census.gov/population/projections/nation/summary/np-t5-b.txt, http://www.census.gov/population/projections/nation/summary/np-t5-c.txt, http://www.census.gov/population/projections/nation/summary/np-t5-e.txt, http://www.census.gov/population/projections/nation/summary/np-t5-f.txt, http://www.census.gov/population/projections/nation/summary/np-t5-g.txt.

work; and deep-level diversity, or how core personality differences influence behavior and attitudes. In the last section, you will learn how diversity can be managed. Here, you'll read about diversity paradigms, principles, and practices that help managers strengthen the diversity *and* the competitiveness of their organizations.

DIVERSITY AND WHY IT MATTERS

Diversity means variety. Therefore, **diversity** exists in organizations when there is a variety of demographic, cultural, and personal differences among the people who work there and the customers who do business there. For example, step into *LONGO TOYOTA* in El Monte, California, one of Toyota's top-selling dealerships, and you'll find diversity in the form of salespeople who speak Spanish, Korean, Arabic, Vietnamese, Hebrew, and Mandarin Chinese. In fact, the 60 salespeople at Longo Toyota speak 30 different languages. Surprisingly, this level of diversity was achieved without a formal diversity plan in place.[7]

By contrast, some companies lack diversity, in their work force, their customers, or both. For example, *DENNY'S* restaurants paid $54.4 million to settle a class-action lawsuit alleging discriminatory treatment of black customers at its restaurants. Edison International, a California-based utility company, paid more than $11 million for wrongly rejecting job applicants on the basis of race. And phone company Bell Atlantic paid a whopping $500 million to African American employees who were unfairly passed over for promotions.[8] (Bell Atlantic and GTE have now merged and become *VERIZON* Communications.) In recent years, Tyson Foods, Coca-Cola, Los Alamos National Laboratory, and many other companies have settled class-action discrimination lawsuits.[9]

Today, however, Denny's, Edison International, Verizon, and Coca-Cola have made great improvements in their level of diversity. At Denny's, all of the company's charitable contributions now go to organizations that benefit minorities. Furthermore, minorities now constitute 29.1 percent, 28.6 percent, and 24.6 percent of managers at Denny's, Edison International, and Verizon, respectively, and 47.4 percent, 44.9 percent, and 32 percent, respectively, of their workers.[10] And Coca-Cola received a glowing report for its efforts to improve diversity.[11] In fact, these four companies have increased their diversity so much that they consistently make *Fortune* magazine's list of the 50 best companies for minorities.[12]

After reading the next section, you should be able to

> 1 describe diversity and explain why it matters.

1 Diversity: Differences That Matter

*You'll begin your exploration of diversity by learning **1.1 that diversity is not affirmative action** and **1.2 how to build a business case for diversity**.*

diversity a variety of demographic, cultural, and personal differences among an organization's employees and customers

1.1 Diversity Is Not Affirmative Action

A common misconception is that workplace diversity and affirmative action are the same, yet these concepts differ in several critical ways. To start, **affirmative action** refers to purposeful steps taken by an organization to create employment opportunities for minorities and women.[13] By contrast, diversity exists in organizations when there is a variety of demographic, cultural, and personal differences among the people who work there and the customers who do business there. So one key difference is that affirmative action is more narrowly focused on demographics such as sex and race, while diversity has a broader focus that includes demographic, cultural, and personal differences. Furthermore, diversity can exist even if organizations don't take purposeful steps to create it. For example, as mentioned earlier, Longo Toyota achieved a high level of diversity without having a formal affirmative action program. Likewise, a local restaurant located near a university in a major city is likely to have a more diverse group of employees than one located in a small town. So, organizations can achieve diversity without affirmative action. Likewise, organizations that take affirmative action to create employment opportunities for women and minorities may not yet have diverse workforces.

Another important difference is that affirmative action is required by law for private employers with 15 or more employees, while diversity is not. Affirmative action originated with the 1964 Civil Rights Act, which bans discrimination in voting, public places, federal government programs, federally supported public education, and employment. Title VII of the Civil Rights Act (**http://www.eeoc.gov/policy/vii.html**) requires that workers have equal employment opportunities when being hired or promoted. More specifically, Title VII prohibits companies from discriminating on the basis of race, color, religion, sex, or national origin. Furthermore, Title VII created the Equal Employment Opportunity Commission, or EEOC (**http://www.eeoc.gov**), to administer these laws. By contrast, there is no federal law or agency to oversee diversity. Organizations that pursue diversity goals and programs do so voluntarily. "Until recently, the commitment many companies had to diversity was fundamentally based on moral, ethical and compliance reasons," says Rudy Mendez, vice president for diversity and inclusion at MCDONALD'S. "But now that we can add business impact, diversity executives are being given a much bigger role."[14]

"WHAT'S NEW"
COMPANY

> ❝ Until recently, the commitment many companies had to diversity was fundamentally based on moral, ethical and compliance reasons. But now that we can add business impact, diversity executives are being given a much bigger role. ❞

RUDY MENDEZ, VICE PRESIDENT FOR DIVERSITY AND INCLUSION, MCDONALD'S

Affirmative action programs and diversity programs also have different purposes. The purpose of affirmative action programs is to compensate for past discrimination, which was widespread when legislation was introduced in the 1960s; to prevent ongoing discrimination; and to provide equal opportunities to all, regardless of race, color, religion, sex, or national origin. Organizations that fail to uphold these laws may be required to

affirmative action purposeful steps taken by an organization to create employment opportunities for minorities and women

Consequently, affirmative action is basically a punitive approach.[16] By contrast, as shown in Exhibit 12.2, the general purpose of diversity programs is to create a positive work environment where no one is advantaged or disadvantaged, where "we" is everyone, where everyone can do his or her best work, where differences are respected and not ignored, and where everyone feels comfortable.[17] So, unlike affirmative action, which punishes companies for not achieving specific sex and race ratios in their work forces, diversity programs seek to benefit both organizations and their employees by encouraging organizations to value all kinds of differences.

Despite affirmative action's overall success in making workplaces much fairer than they used to be,[18] many people argue that some affirmative action programs unconstitutionally offer preferential treatment to females and minorities at the expense of other employees—a view accepted by some courts.[19] In California, voters approved Proposition 209, which bans race- and sex-based affirmative action in college admissions, government hiring, and government contracting programs. Jake Weiss, a white worker in Jericho, New York, expressed a typical complaint when he said, "It used to be if you were white, you got everything in America and that wasn't right. But now [with affirmative action], all that's left for people like me are the crumbs."[20] And Christopher Katzenbach, an attorney in a San Francisco law firm, said, "I think people want to be evaluated on their merits, not their race or gender, and that is the driving force behind a lot of this [reverse discrimination] litigation."[21] Furthermore, research shows that people who have gotten a job or promotion as a result of affirmative action are frequently viewed as unqualified, even when clear evidence of their qualifications exists.[22] For example, one woman said, "I won a major prize [in my field], and some of the guys in my lab said it was because I was a woman. I'm certain they didn't choose me because I was a woman. But it gave some disgruntled guys who didn't get the prize a convenient excuse."[23] So, while affirmative action programs have created opportunities for minorities and women, those same minorities and women are frequently presumed to be unqualified when others believe they obtained their jobs as a result of affirmative action.

In summary, affirmative action and diversity are not the same thing. Not only are they fundamentally different, but they also differ in purpose, practice, and the reactions they produce.

1.2 Diversity Makes Good Business Sense

Those who support the idea of diversity in organizations often ignore its business aspects altogether, claiming instead that diversity is simply the "right thing to do." Yet diversity actually makes good business sense in several ways: cost savings, attracting and retaining talent, and driving business growth.[24]

Diversity helps companies with *cost savings* by reducing turnover, decreasing absenteeism, and avoiding expensive

Exhibit 12.2

General Purpose of Diversity Programs

To create a positive work environment where
• No one is advantaged or disadvantaged.
• "We" is everyone.
• Everyone can do his or her best work.
• Differences are respected and not ignored.
• Everyone feels comfortable.

Source: T. Roosevelt, "From Affirmative Action to Affirming Diversity," *Harvard Business Review* 68, no. 2 (1990): 107–117.

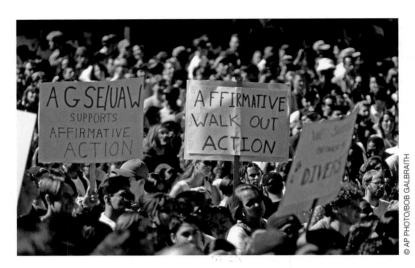

Affirmative action programs are substantially more controversial than diversity programs, but the former are finding some surprising proponents.

lawsuits.[25] Because of lost productivity and the cost of recruiting and selecting new workers, companies lose substantial amounts of money when employees quit their jobs. In fact, turnover costs typically amount to more than 90 percent of employees' salaries. By this estimate, if an executive who makes $200,000 leaves, the organization will have to spend approximately $180,000 to find a replacement, and even the lowest-paid hourly workers can cost the company as much as $10,000 when they quit. Since turnover rates for African Americans average 40 percent higher than for whites, and since women quit their jobs at twice the rate men do, companies that manage diverse workforces well can cut costs by reducing the turnover rates of these employees.[26] And, with women absent from work 60 percent more often than men, primarily because of family responsibilities, diversity programs that address the needs of female workers can also reduce the substantial costs of absenteeism.

Diversity programs also save companies money by helping them avoid discrimination lawsuits, which have increased by a factor of 20 since 1970 and quadrupled just since 1995. In one survey conducted by the Society of Human Resource Management, 78 percent of respondents reported that diversity efforts helped them avoid lawsuits and litigation costs.[27] Indeed, because companies lose two-thirds of all discrimination cases that go to trial, the best strategy from a business perspective is not to be sued for discrimination at all. When companies lose, the average individual settlement amounts to more than $600,000.[28] And settlement costs can be substantially higher in class-action lawsuits, in which individuals join together to sue a company as a group. For example, COCA-COLA paid $192.5 million to settle a class-action suit brought by 2,200 African American workers who were discriminated against in pay, promotions, and performance reviews; a similar lawsuit brought by 1,300 African American workers cost Texaco $176 million.[29] Boeing paid $72.5 million to settle a sex discrimination lawsuit with female employees who were paid less and not promoted because they were women.[30] And Dial Corporation, the soap manufacturer, paid $10 million to settle a sex discrimination lawsuit filed by 90 female employees at its manufacturing plants.[31] In fact, the average class-action lawsuit costs companies $58.9 million for racial discrimination and $24.9 million for sex discrimination.[32] According to the EEOC, companies paid $420 million in damages in 2004 for discrimination lawsuits.[33]

Diversity also makes business sense by helping companies *attract and retain talented workers*.[34] Indeed, diversity-friendly companies tend to attract better *and* more diverse job applicants. Very simply, diversity begets more diversity. Companies that make *Fortune* magazine's list of the 50 best companies for minorities already attract a diverse and talented pool of job applicants. But, after being recognized by *Fortune* for their efforts, they experience even bigger increases in both the quality and the diversity of people who apply for jobs. Indeed, research shows that companies with acclaimed diversity programs not only attract more talented workers, but also have higher stock market performance.[35]

Just as important, however, is that these companies also create opportunities that encourage workers to stay. For example, Anne Shen Smith, vice president of support services for PACIFIC ENTERPRISES, a California-based utility holding company, said that the company created opportunities by replacing the "old-boy network," in which only bosses could nominate employees for promotions, with a program called "Readiness for Management," in which employees nominate themselves. Workers begin the process by taking a number of self-assessment tests to determine their strengths and weaknesses. Then they take training courses to improve their skills and knowledge. The Readiness for Management program works because it gives people who were previously overlooked a chance to move up and makes employees responsible for improving their skills and knowledge.[36] Employees who don't take that responsibility don't get promoted.

The third way that diversity makes business sense is by *driving business growth*. Diversity helps companies grow by improving their understanding of the marketplace. When companies have diverse workforces, they are better able to understand the needs of their increasingly diverse customer bases. For example, at FRITO LAY, the Latino Employee Network proved invaluable during the development of Doritos' guacamole-flavored tortilla chips. Members of the network, called Adelante, provided feedback on the taste and packaging to help ensure that the product would be regarded as authentic in the Latino community. The Adelante members' insights helped make the guacamole-flavored Doritos one of the most successful new-product launches in the company's history, generating more than $100 million in sales in its first year alone.[37]

In the United States today there are 36 million African Americans, 41 million Hispanic Americans, and 12 million Asian Americans, who, together, represent 30 percent of U.S. consumers. Indeed, according to the U.S. Bureau of Labor Statistics, "America's population will increase 50 percent over the next 50 years, with almost 90 percent of that increase in the minority community."[38] By 2050, Hispanics will make up one-quarter of the population and will nearly triple in number to 97 million. Accordingly, the U.S. Department of Commerce expects minority purchasing power to grow fivefold to $6,080 billion.[39] In fact, a recent survey conducted by the Society for Human Resource Management found that tapping into "diverse customers and markets" was the number one reason managers gave for implementing diversity programs.[40] Diversity also helps companies grow through higher-quality problem solving. Though diverse groups initially have more difficulty working together than homogeneous groups, after several months diverse groups do a better job of identifying problems and generating alternative solutions, the two most important steps in problem solving.[41] Ernest Drew, former CEO of HOECHST CELANESE, a chemical company, recalls a company conference in which the company's top 125 managers, mostly white males, were joined by 50 lower-level employees, mostly minorities and women. Problem-solving teams were formed to discuss how the company's corporate culture affected business and how it could be changed. Half the teams were composed of white males, while the other half were of mixed sex and race. Drew says, "It was so obvious that the diverse teams had the broader solutions. They had ideas I hadn't even thought of. For the first time, we realized that diversity is a strength as it relates to problem solving. Before, we just thought of diversity as the total number of minorities and women in the company, like affirmative action. Now we knew we needed diversity at every level of the company where decisions are made."[42]

"It was so obvious that the diverse teams had the broader solutions. They had ideas I hadn't even thought of.

ERNEST DREW, FORMER CEO, HOECHST CELANESE

In short, "diversity is no longer about counting heads; it's about making heads counts," says Amy George, vice president of diversity and inclusion at Pepsico.[43]

Review 1: **Diversity: Differences That Matter**

Diversity exists in organizations when there is a variety of demographic, cultural, and personal differences among the people who work there and the customers who do business there. A common misconception is that workplace diversity and affirmative action are the same. However, affirmative action is more narrowly focused on demographics, is required by law, and is used to punish companies that discriminate on the basis of race, color, religion, sex, or national origin. By contrast, diversity is broader in focus (going beyond demographics), voluntary, more positive in that it encourages companies to value all kinds of differences, and, at the same time, substantially less controversial than affirmative action. Thus, affirmative action and diversity differ in purpose, practice, and the reactions they produce. Diversity also makes good business sense in terms of cost savings (reducing turnover, decreasing absenteeism, and avoiding lawsuits), attracting and retaining talent, and driving business growth (improving marketplace understanding and promoting higher-quality problem solving).

DIVERSITY AND INDIVIDUAL DIFFERENCES

A survey that asked managers, "What is meant by diversity to decision-makers in your organization?" found that they most frequently mentioned race, culture, sex, national origin, age, religion, and regional origin.[44] When managers describe workers this way, they are focusing on surface-level diversity. **Surface-level diversity**, as illustrated in Exhibit 12.3, consists of differences that are immediately observable, typically unchangeable, and easy to measure.[45] In other words, independent observers can usually agree on dimensions of surface-level diversity, such as another person's age, sex, race/ethnicity, or physical capabilities.

And while most people start by using easily observable characteristics, such as surface-level diversity, to categorize or stereotype other people, those initial, surface-level categorizations typically give way to deeper impressions formed from knowledge of others' behavior and psychological characteristics, such as personality and attitudes.[46] When you think of others this way, you are focusing on deep-level diversity. **Deep-level diversity** consists of differences that are communicated through verbal and nonverbal behaviors and are learned only through extended interaction with others.[47] Examples of deep-level diversity include personality differences, attitudes, beliefs, and values. In other words, as people in diverse

surface-level diversity differences such as age, sex, race/ethnicity, and physical disabilities that are observable, typically unchangeable, and easy to measure

deep-level diversity differences such as personality and attitudes that are communicated through verbal and nonverbal behaviors and are learned only through extended interaction with others workplaces get to know each other, the initial focus on surface-level differences such as age, race/ethnicity, sex, and physical capabilities is replaced by deeper, more accurate knowledge of coworkers.

If managed properly, the shift from surface- to deep-level diversity can accomplish two things.[48] First, coming to know and understand each other better can result in reduced prejudice and conflict. Second, it can lead to stronger social integration. **Social integration** is the degree to which group members are psychologically attracted to working with each other to accomplish a common objective, or, as one manager put it, "working together to get the job done."

Exhibit 12.3
Surface- and Deep-Level Diversity

After reading the next two sections, you should be able to

2 understand the special challenges that the dimensions of surface-level diversity pose for managers.

3 explain how the dimensions of deep-level diversity affect individual behavior and interactions in the workplace.

2 Surface-Level Diversity

Because age, sex, race/ethnicity, and disabilities are usually immediately observable, many managers and workers use these dimensions of surface-level diversity to form initial impressions and categorizations of coworkers, bosses, customers, or job applicants. Whether intentionally or not, sometimes those initial categorizations and impressions lead to decisions or behaviors that discriminate. Consequently, these dimensions of surface-level diversity pose special challenges for managers who are trying to create positive work environments where everyone feels comfortable and no one is advantaged or disadvantaged.

Let's learn more about those challenges and the ways that **2.1 age, 2.2 sex, 2.3 race/ethnicity**, and **2.4 mental or physical disabilities can affect decisions and behaviors in organizations**.

2.1 Age

Age discrimination is treating people differently (e.g., in hiring and firing, promotion, and compensation decisions) because of their age. The victims of age discrimination are almost always "older" workers, based on the idea that "You can't teach an old dog new tricks." It's commonly believed that older workers can't learn how to use computers and technology, won't adapt to change, are sick more often, and, in general, are much more expensive to employ than younger workers. One manager explains his preference for younger workers over older workers this way: "The way I look at it, for $40,000 or $50,000, I can get a smart, raw kid right out of undergrad who's going to work seven days a week for me for the next two years. I'll train him the way I want him, he'll grow with me, and I'll pay him long-term options so I own him, for lack of a better word. He'll do exactly what I want—and if he doesn't, I'll fire him. . . . The alternative is to pay twice as much for some 40-year-old who does half the amount of work, has been trained improperly, and doesn't listen to what I say."[49]

social integration the degree to which group members are psychologically attracted to working with each other to accomplish a common objective

age discrimination treating people differently (e.g., in hiring and firing, promotion, and compensation decisions) because of their age

Unfortunately, attitudes like this are all too common.[50] According to the Society for Human Resource Management, 53 percent of 428 surveyed managers believed that older workers "didn't keep up with technology," and 28 percent said that older workers were "less flexible."[51] For example, when 57-year old Sam Horgan, a former chief financial officer, was interviewing for a job, he was asked by a 30-something job interviewer, "Would you have trouble working with young bright people?"[52] Not surprisingly, 80 percent of human resource managers surveyed by *Personnel Management* magazine said that age discrimination was a major problem in their organizations and that older employees were not receiving the same training and promotional opportunities as younger workers.[53] Likewise, two-thirds of 10,000 people surveyed by AARP (American Association of Retired Persons) felt that they had been wrongly discharged from a job because of their age. In fact, a study by the Society for Human Resource Management found that 20 percent of all companies had been sued for age discrimination in the preceding five years.[54] Normally, somewhere between 17,000 and 20,000 age discrimination cases are filed with the EEOC each year (**http://www.eeoc.gov/stats/ adea.html**). And these numbers may increase, given a U.S. Supreme Court ruling that employees may sue for age discrimination even if the discrimination was not intentional (see Chapter 11's discussion of disparate treatment and adverse impact).[55] What's really sad is that it takes older workers not months, but years to find a suitable job.[56] Thankfully, in recent years, a number of companies have started specializing in recruiting and placing applicants who are 50 years and older.[57]

So, what's reality and what's myth? Do older employees actually cost more? In some ways, they do. The older people are and the longer they stay with a company, the more the company pays for salaries, pension plans, and vacation time. But older workers cost companies less, too, because they show better judgment, care more about the quality of their work, and are less likely to quit, show up late, or be absent, the cost of which can be substantial.[58] A survey by Chicago outplacement firm Challenger, Gray & Christmas found that only 3 percent of employees age 50 and over changed jobs in any given year, compared with 10 percent of the entire work force and 12 percent of workers ages 25 to 34. The study also found that while older workers make up about 14 percent of the work force, they suffer only 10 percent of all workplace injuries and use fewer healthcare benefits than younger workers with school-age children.[59] As for the widespread belief that job performance declines with age, the scientific evidence clearly refutes this stereotype. Performance does not decline with age, regardless of the type of job.[60]

What can companies do to reduce age discrimination?[61] To start, managers need to recognize that age discrimination is much more pervasive than they probably think. Whereas "old" used to mean mid-50s, in today's workplace, "old" is closer to 40. When 773 CEOs were asked, "At what age does a worker's productivity peak?" the average age they gave was 43. Thus, age discrimination may be affecting more workers because perceptions about age have changed. In addition, with the aging of the baby boomers, age discrimination is more likely to occur simply because there are millions more older workers than there used to be. And, because studies show that interviewers rate younger job candidates as more qualified (even when they aren't), companies need to train managers and recruiters to make hiring and promotion decisions on the basis of qualifications, not age. Companies also need to monitor the extent to which

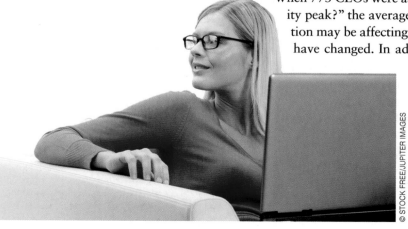

© STOCK FREE/JUPITER IMAGES

older workers receive training. The Bureau of Labor Statistics found that the number of training courses and number of hours spent in training drops dramatically after employees reach the age of 44.[62] Finally, companies need to ensure that younger and older workers interact with each other. One study found that younger workers generally hold positive views of older workers and that the more time they spent working with older coworkers, the more positive their attitudes became.[63]

2.2 Sex

Sex discrimination occurs when people are treated differently because of their sex. Sex discrimination and racial/ethnic discrimination (discussed in the next section) are often associated with the so-called **glass ceiling**, the invisible barrier that prevents women and minorities from advancing to the top jobs in organizations.

To what extent do women face sex discrimination in the workplace? Almost every year, the EEOC receives between 21,000 and 26,000 charges of sex-based discrimination (**http://www.eeoc.gov/stats/sex.html**). In some ways, there is much less sex discrimination than there used to be. For example, whereas women held only 17 percent of managerial jobs in 1972, today they now outnumber men with 50.6 percent of managerial jobs, a percentage that is nearly equal to their representation in the workforce.[64] Likewise, women own 47 percent of all U.S. businesses.[65] Whereas women owned 700,000 businesses in 1977 and 4.1 million businesses in 1987, today they own 9 million![66] Finally, though women still earn less than men on average, the differential is narrowing. As Exhibit 12.4 shows, women earned 79.5 percent of what men did in 2003, up from 63 percent in 1979.

Although progress is being made, sex discrimination continues to operate via the glass ceiling at higher levels in organizations. For instance, as shown in Exhibit 12.5, in 2002/2003 a woman had the highest salary (that is, was the top earner) in only 5.2 percent of *Fortune* 500 companies, and only 15.7 percent of corporate officers (top management) were women. Indeed, only 9 of the 500 largest companies in the United States have women CEOs.[67] Similarly, just 13.6 percent of the members of corporate boards of directors are women.[68]

Is sex discrimination the sole reason for the slow rate at which women have been promoted to middle and upper levels of management and corporate boards? Some studies indicate that it's not.[69] In some instances, the slow progress appears to be due to career and job choices. Whereas men's career and job choices are often driven by the search for higher pay and advancement, women are more likely to choose jobs or careers that also give them a greater sense of accomplishment, more control over their work schedules, and easier movement in and out of the workplace.[70] Furthermore, women are historically much more likely than men to prioritize family over work at some time in their careers. For example, 96 percent of 600 female Harvard MBAs held jobs while they were in their 20s. That dropped to 71 percent in their late 30s when they had children, but then increased to 82.5 percent in their late 40s as their children became older.[71]

sex discrimination treating people differently because of their sex

glass ceiling the invisible barrier that prevents women and minorities from advancing to the top jobs in organizations

Exhibit 12.4

Women's Earnings as a Percentage of Men's

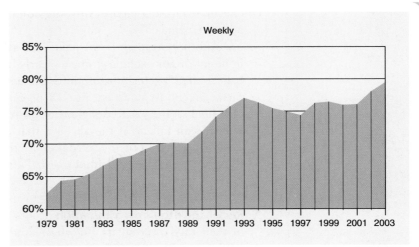

Sources: "Highlights of Women's Earnings in 2001, 2002, 2003," U.S. Department of Labor, Bureau of Labor Statistics, available at http://www.bls.gov/cps/cpswom2001 .pdf and http://www.bls.gov/opub/ted/2004/oct/wk4/art01.htm, 25 May 2005.

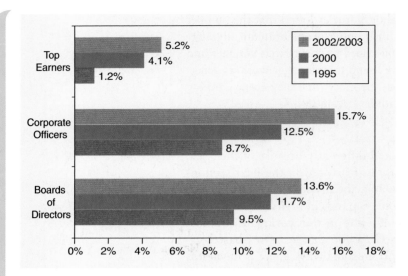

Sources: "Census of Women Corporate Officers and Top Earners"
Catalyst, available at http://www.catalystwomen.org/knowledge/titles/title
.php?page=cen_WOTE02, 26 May 2005; "2003 Catalyst Census of Women
Board Directors of the *Fortune* 1000," Catalyst, available at http://www
.catalystwomen.org/knowledge/titles/title.php?page=cen_WBD03, 26 May
2005.

Exhibit 12.5

*Women at Fortune 500
and 1000 Companies*

Beyond these reasons, however, it's likely that sex discrimination does play a role in women's slow progress into the higher levels of management. And even if you don't think so, many of the women you work with probably do. Indeed, one study found that more than 90 percent of executive women believed that the glass ceiling had hurt their careers.[72] In another study, 80 percent of women said they left their last organization because the glass ceiling had limited their chances for advancement.[73] A third study indicated that the glass ceiling is prompting more and more women to leave companies to start their own businesses.[74] Anita Borg, a senior researcher at a *Fortune* 500 company, sums up the frustrations of many professional women when she says, "You run into subtle sexism every day. It's like water torture. It wears you down."[75] Very few professional women achieve the same status as their male counterparts even in advanced economies, such as the United States, Canada, the United Kingdom, and Japan.[76]

In a Catalyst study of *Fortune* 1000 organizations, about two-thirds of the executives and half of the CEOs surveyed noted the failure of senior leadership to assume accountability for women's advancement to be the key barrier preventing professional women from progressing to senior executive positions.[77] So, what can companies do to make sure that women have the same opportunities for development and advancement as men? One strategy is mentoring, or pairing promising female executives with senior executives from whom they can seek advice and support. A vice president at a utility company says, "I think it's the single most critical piece to women advancing career-wise. In my experience you need somebody to help guide you and . . . go to bat for you."[78] In fact, 91 percent of female executives have a mentor at some point and feel their mentor was critical to their advancement.

Another strategy is to make sure that male-dominated social activities don't unintentionally exclude women. Nearly half (47 percent) of women in the workforce believe that "exclusion from informal networks" makes it more difficult to advance their careers. By contrast, just 18 percent of CEOs thought this was a problem.[79] One final strategy is to designate a "go-to person," other than their supervisors, that women can talk to if they believe that they are being held back or discriminated against because of their sex. Make sure this person has the knowledge and authority to conduct a fair, confidential internal investigation.[80]

2.3 Race/Ethnicity

Racial and ethnic discrimination occurs when people are treated differently because of their race or ethnicity. To what extent is racial and ethnic discrimination a factor in the workplace? Every year, the EEOC receives between 26,000 and 30,000 charges of race discrimination, which is more than any other type of charge of discrimination (**http://www.eeoc.gov/stats/race.html**). However, it is true that since

racial and ethnic discrimination
treating people differently because of
their race or ethnicity

the passage of the 1964 Civil Rights Act and Title VII, there is much less racial and ethnic discrimination than there used to be. For example, 18 *Fortune* 500 firms had an African American or Hispanic CEO in 2005, whereas none did in 1988.[81] Nonetheless, strong racial and ethnic disparities still exist. For instance, whereas about 12 percent of Americans are black, only 5.9 percent of managers and 3.2 percent of top managers are black. Similarly, about 13 percent of Americans are Hispanic, but only 6.3 percent are managers and 3.7 percent are CEOs. By contrast, Asians, who constitute about 4 percent of the population, are better represented holding 4 percent of management jobs and 3.4 percent of CEO jobs.[82]

What accounts for the disparities between the percentages of minority groups in the general population and their smaller representation in management positions? Some studies have found that the disparities are due to preexisting differences in training, education, and skills; when African Americans, Hispanics, Asian Americans, and whites have similar skills, training, and education, they are much more likely to have similar jobs and salaries.[83]

Other studies, however, provide increasingly strong direct evidence of racial or ethnic discrimination in the workplace. For example, one study directly tested hiring discrimination by sending pairs of black and white males and pairs of Hispanic and non-Hispanic males to apply for the same jobs. Each pair had résumés with identical qualifications, and all were trained to present themselves in similar ways to minimize differences during interviews. The researchers found that the white males got three times as many job offers as the black males, and that the non-Hispanic males got three times as many offers as the Hispanic males.[84]

Another study, which used similar methods to test hiring procedures at 149 different companies, found that whites received 10 percent more interviews than blacks. Half of the whites interviewed received job offers, but only 11 percent of the blacks. And when job offers were made, blacks were much more likely to be offered lower-level positions, while whites were more likely to be offered jobs at higher levels than the jobs they had applied for.[85]

Critics of these studies point out that it's nearly impossible to train different applicants to give identical responses in job interviews and that differences in interviewing skills may have somehow accounted for the results. However, British researchers found similar kinds of discrimination just by sending letters of inquiry to prospective employers. As in the other studies, the letters were identical except for the applicant's race. Employers frequently responded to letters from Afro-Caribbean, Indian, or Pakistani "applicants" by

Pepsi's Diversity Culture

It's not surprising that when it came time for PepsiCo to choose a new CEO, the board picked the Indian-born female executive, Indra Nooyi. PepsiCo has a long history of diversity, stretching back to the end of World War II, when president Walter Mack hired Edward Boyd away from the National Urban League to head a team charged with launching a marketing program for African American consumers. In every area of the country where Boyd's team ran a marketing blitz, Pepsi sales increased, and soon Pepsi-Cola was able to overtake market leader Coca-Cola in cities like Cleveland and Chicago. One of the most successful campaigns was a series of print advertisements titled "Leaders in Their Fields," which profiled the accomplishments of professional and successful African Americans. Pepsi's print campaign was the first to shun the stereotypical images of African Americans used in advertising.

Source: S. Capparell, "How Pepsi Opened Door to Diversity," *Wall Street Journal*, 9 January 2007, B1.

© SUSAN VAN ETTEN

indicating that the positions had been filled. By contrast, they often responded to white, Anglo-Saxon "applicants" by inviting them to face-to-face interviews. Similar results were found with Vietnamese and Greek "applicants" in Australia.[86] In short, the evidence strongly indicates that there is strong and persistent racial and ethnic discrimination in the hiring processes of many organizations.

What can companies do to make sure that people of all racial and ethnic backgrounds have the same opportunities?[87] Start by looking at the numbers. Compare the hiring rates of whites with the hiring rates for racial and ethnic applicants. Do the same thing for promotions within the company. (Had Walgreens done this, it could have avoided the class-action suit filed by the EEOC.) See if nonwhite workers quit the company at higher rates than white workers. Also, survey employees to compare white and nonwhite employees' satisfaction with jobs, bosses, and the company, as well as their perceptions concerning equal treatment. Next, if the numbers indicate racial or ethnic disparities, consider employing a private firm to test your hiring system by having applicants of different races with identical qualifications apply for jobs in your company.[88] Although disparities aren't proof of discrimination, it's much better to investigate hiring and promotion disparities yourself than to have the EEOC or a plaintiff's lawyer do it for you.

Another step companies can take is to eliminate unclear selection and promotion criteria. Vague criteria allow decision makers to focus on non-job-related characteristics that may unintentionally lead to employment discrimination. Instead, selection and promotion criteria should spell out the specific knowledge, skills, abilities, education, and experience needed to perform a job well.

Finally, train managers and others who make hiring and promotion decisions. At Tower Records, the human resources staff assembles on a giant game board that covers a conference room floor. Tower store managers then answer questions about hiring situations. If they answer a question correctly, they move forward on the board. If they answer it incorrectly, they stay in place, and the group discusses what should have been done instead. The number of grievances about hiring procedures has dropped significantly since the training began.[89]

2.4 Mental or Physical Disabilities

HABITAT INTERNATIONAL, a leading supplier of artificial-grass and indoor-outdoor carpet products for Home Depot, Lowe's, and other retailers, is also socially responsible business: It employs hard-to-place workers. In fact, 75 percent of Habitat's workers have a physical or mental disability, or both. Over the years the company has also employed recovering alcoholics, homeless people, non-English-speaking refugees, and others who, when given a chance, work hard to overcome the stereotypes about them. Launched by David Morris and his father Saul in 1981, the Chattanooga, Tennessee, company has become a role model for other businesses, disability advocates, and the general public. At Habitat, people matter most and its philosophy of love, kindness, and compassion honor the special diversity of the people who work at Habitat International (**http://www .habitatinc.com**).[90] According to the Americans with Disabilities Act (**http://www.ada .gov**), a **disability** is a mental or physical impairment that substantially limits one or more major life activities.[91] One in every five Americans, or more than 54 million people, has a disability.[92] **Disability discrimination** occurs when people are treated differently because of their disabilities.

To what extent is disability discrimination a factor in the workplace? According to the U.S. Census Bureau, 80 percent of able men have jobs, compared with only 60 percent of those with disabilities. For women, the statistic shows a similar pattern, with 67 percent of able women being employed versus only 51 percent of

disability a mental or physical impairment that substantially limits one or more major life activities

disability discrimination treating people differently because of their disabilities disabled women. More specifically, only 47 percent of those who have a sensory disability, 32 percent of those who have a physical disability, and 28 percent of those who have a mental disability have jobs.[93] Furthermore, people with disabilities are disproportionately employed in low-status or part-time jobs, have little chance for advancement, and, on average, are twice as likely to live in poverty as able people.[94] Numerous studies also indicate that managers and the general public believe that discrimination against people with disabilities is common and widespread.[95]

What accounts for the disparities between the employment and income levels of able people and people with disabilities? Contrary to popular opinion, it has nothing to do with the ability of people with disabilities to do their jobs well. Studies show that as long as companies make reasonable accommodations for disabilities (such as changing procedures or equipment), people with disabilities perform their jobs just as well as able people. Furthermore, they have better safety records and are not any more likely to be absent or quit their jobs.[96]

What can companies do to make sure that people with disabilities have the same opportunities as everyone else? Beyond educational efforts to address incorrect stereotypes and expectations, a good place to start is to commit to reasonable workplace accommodations such as changing work schedules, reassigning jobs, acquiring or modifying equipment, or providing assistance when needed. Accommodations for disabilities needn't be expensive. According to the Job Accommodation Network, 71 percent of accommodations cost employers $500 or less, and 20 percent of accommodations don't cost anything at all.[97] For example, rather than rebuild its offices, the U.S. Postal Service used inexpensive ramps to raise wheelchair-bound clerks to counter level so they could wait on customers. Other examples of low-cost accommodations include a telephone sound amplifier ($48) for a hearing-impaired factory worker; a card system with streets filed alphabetically with ZIP codes ($150) for a learning-impaired mail room worker who couldn't remember which streets had which ZIP codes; lateral filing cabinets ($450 each) for a clerk who couldn't reach the vertical filing cabinets from her wheelchair; and a personal paging device ($350) that vibrated to let a grocery store worker with Down syndrome who couldn't hear the public address system know when he was to go to the store office.[98] For further information about reasonable accommodations, visit the Job Accommodation Network (**http://janweb .icdi.wvu.edu**), which provides free help and has a database of 26,000 successful accommodations.[99] Exhibit 12.6 provides a list of common, inexpensive accommodations that companies can make for disabled workers.

Some of the accommodations just described involve *assistive technology* that gives workers with disabilities the tools they need to overcome their disabilities. Providing workers with assistive technology is also an effective strategy to

Exhibit 12.6

Reasonable Accommodations for Disabled Workers

- Physical changes, such as installing a ramp or modifying a workspace or restroom.
- A quieter workspace or other changes that reduce noisy distractions for someone with a mental disability.
- Training and other written materials in an accessible format, such as in Braille, on audio tape, or on computer disk.
- TTYs for use with telephones by people who are deaf, and hardware and software that make computers accessible to people who have vision impairments or who have difficulty using their hands.
- Time off for someone who needs treatment for a disability.

Source: "Americans with Disabilities Act: A Guide for People with Disabilities Seeking Employment," U.S. Department of Justice, available at http://www.usdoj.gov/crt/ada/workta.htm, 2 October 2003.

recruit, retain, and enhance productivity of people with disabilities. According to the National Council on Disability, 92 percent of workers with disabilities who use assistive technology report that it helps them work faster and better, 81 percent indicate that it helps them work longer hours, and 67 percent say that it is critical to getting a job.[100] To learn about assistive technologies that can help workers with disabilities, see Abledata (**http://www.abledata.com**), which lists 25,000 products from 3,000 organizations, or the National Rehabilitation Information Center (**http://www.naric.com**), which provides information for specific disabilities.

Finally, companies should actively recruit qualified workers with disabilities. Numerous organizations, such as Mainstream, Kidder Resources, the American Council of the Blind (**http://www.acb.org**), the National Federation of the Blind (**http://www.nfb.org**), the National Association of the Deaf (**http://www.nad.org**), the Epilepsy Foundation (**http://www.epilepsyfoundation.org**), and the National Amputation Foundation (**http://www.nationalamputation.org**), actively work with employers to find jobs for qualified people with disabilities. Companies can also place advertisements in publications, such as *Careers and the Disabled*, that specifically target workers with disabilities.[101]

Review 2: **Surface-Level Diversity**

Age, sex, race/ethnicity, and physical and mental disabilities are dimensions of surface-level diversity. Because those dimensions are (usually) easily observed, managers and workers tend to rely on them to form initial impressions and stereotypes. Sometimes this can lead to age, sex, racial/ethnic, or disability discrimination (that is, treating people differently) in the workplace. In general, older workers, women, people of color or different national origins, and people with disabilities are much less likely to be hired or promoted than white males. This disparity is often due to incorrect beliefs or stereotypes, such as "job performance declines with age," or "women aren't willing to travel on business," or "workers with disabilities aren't as competent as able workers." To reduce discrimination, companies can determine the hiring and promotion rates for different groups, train managers to make hiring and promotion decisions on the basis of specific criteria, and make sure that everyone has equal access to training, mentors, reasonable work accommodations, and assistive technology. Finally, companies need to designate a "go-to person" that employees can talk to if they believe they have suffered discrimination.

3 Deep-Level Diversity

Have you ever taken an instant dislike to someone—perhaps because of the way the person talked, acted, or treated you—only to decide, after spending some time working or interacting with this person, that your initial impressions were wrong and that he or she wasn't so bad after all?

If you've had this experience, then you understand the difference between surface- and deep-level diversity. As you just learned, people often use the dimensions of surface-level diversity to form initial impressions about others. Over time, however, as people have a chance to get to know each other, initial impressions based on age, sex, race/ethnicity, and mental or physical disabilities give way to deeper impressions based on behavior and psychological characteristics. When we think of others this way, we are focusing on deep-level diversity. *Deep-level diversity* represents differences that can be learned only through extended interaction with others. Examples of deep-level diversity include differences in personality, attitudes, beliefs, and values. In short, recognizing deep-level diversity requires getting to know and understand one another better. And that matters, because it can result in less prejudice, discrimination, and conflict in the workplace. These changes can then lead to better *social integration*, the degree to which organizational or group members are psychologically attracted to working with each other to accomplish a common objective.

Let's examine deep-level diversity by exploring **3.1 the "Big Five" dimensions of personality** and **3.2 other significant work-related aspects of personality**.

3.1 Big Five Dimensions of Personality

Stop for a second and think about your boss (or the boss you had in your last job). What words would you use to describe him or her? Is your boss introverted or extraverted? Emotionally stable or unstable? Agreeable or disagreeable? Organized or disorganized? Open or closed to new experiences? When you describe your boss or others in this way, what you're really doing is describing dispositions and personality.

A **disposition** is the tendency to respond to situations and events in a predetermined manner. **Personality** is the relatively stable set of behaviors, attitudes, and emotions displayed over time that makes people different from each other.[102] For example, which of your aunts or uncles is a little offbeat, a little out of the ordinary? What was that aunt or uncle like when you were small? What is she or he like now? Chances are she or he is pretty much the same wacky person. In other words, the person's core personality hasn't changed. For years, personality researchers studied hundreds of different ways to describe people's personalities. In the last decade, however, personality research conducted in different cultures, different settings, and different languages has shown that five basic dimensions of personality account for most of the differences in peoples' behaviors, attitudes, and emotions (or for why your boss is the way he or she is!). The *Big Five Personality Dimensions* are extraversion, emotional stability, agreeableness, conscientiousness, and openness to experience.[103]

Extraversion is the degree to which someone is active, assertive, gregarious, sociable, talkative, and energized by others. In contrast to extraverts, introverts are less active, prefer to be alone, and are shy, quiet, and reserved. For the best results in the workplace, introverts and extraverts should be correctly matched to their jobs. Tim Burke, CEO of QUEST, a technology consulting and management company based in Sacramento, California, has had trouble finding the right people for jobs. He says the biggest challenge is "when we've hired a person who has all the necessary skills but still is not right for the job." Now Quest uses personality assessment to match people to jobs, matching for instance, extraverts to outside sales jobs and introverts to technical jobs.[104]

Emotional stability is the degree to which someone is not angry, depressed, anxious, emotional, insecure, or excitable. People who are emotionally stable respond well to stress. In other words, they can maintain a calm, problem-solving attitude in even the toughest situations (such as conflict, hostility, dangerous conditions, or extreme time pressures). By contrast, under only moderately stressful situations, emotionally unstable people find it difficult to handle the most basic demands of their jobs and become distraught, tearful, self-doubting, and anxious. Emotional stability is particularly important for high-stress jobs, such as police work, fire fighting,

"WHAT'S NEW" COMPANY

disposition the tendency to respond to situations and events in a predetermined manner

personality the relatively stable set of behaviors, attitudes, and emotions displayed over time that makes people different from each other

extraversion the degree to which someone is active, assertive, gregarious, sociable, talkative, and energized by others

emotional stability the degree to which someone is not angry, depressed, anxious, emotional, insecure, and excitable emergency medical treatment, piloting planes, or commanding rockets. The firing of astronaut Lisa Nowak by NASA illustrates the importance of emotional stability and the failure of employers to adequately screen potential employees for important characteristics. Nowak was charged with trying to kidnap a woman she regarded as her romantic rival for the affection of a space shuttle pilot. She allegedly pepper-sprayed the woman, and police found a BB gun, a steel mallet, a knife, and rubber tubing in her possession. The inability to handle stressful situations is a clear sign of emotional instability.[105] As you learned in Chapter 1, emotional stability is also important for managers. Indeed, the number one mistake managers make is intimidating, bullying, and being abrasive to the people who work for them.

Agreeableness is the degree to which someone is cooperative, polite, flexible, forgiving, good-natured, tolerant, and trusting. Basically, agreeable people are easy to work with and be around, whereas disagreeable people are distrusting and difficult to work with and be around. A number of companies have made general attitude or agreeableness the most important factor in their hiring decisions. Small-business owner Roger Cook says, "Hire nice people. I'm looking for personal—not professional—traits. I want a good or nice person. I can teach the skills. I call their references and ask, 'Is he or she a nice person?' I take a close look at how applicants answer questions and carry themselves. Why nice people? Because they're trustworthy; they get along with other crew members: they are good with customers and they are usually hard workers."[106]

Conscientiousness is the degree to which someone is organized, hardworking, responsible, persevering, thorough, and achievement oriented. One management consultant wrote about his experiences with a conscientious employee: "He arrived at our first meeting with a typed copy of his daily schedule, a sheet bearing his home and office phone numbers, addresses, and his e-mail address. At his request, we established a timetable for meetings for the next four months. He showed up on time every time, day planner in hand, and carefully listed tasks and due dates. He questioned me exhaustively if he didn't understand an assignment and returned on schedule with the completed work or with a clear explanation as to why it wasn't done."[107]

Openness to experience is the degree to which someone is curious, broad-minded, and open to new ideas, things, and experiences; is spontaneous; and has a high tolerance for ambiguity. Most companies need people who are strong in terms of openness to experience to fill certain positions, but for other positions, this dimension is less important. People in marketing, advertising, research, or other creative jobs need to be curious, open to new ideas, and spontaneous. By contrast, openness to experience is not particularly important to accountants, who need to consistently apply stringent rules and formulas to make sense out of complex financial information.

Which of the Big Five Personality Dimensions has the largest impact on behavior in organizations? The cumulative results indicate that conscientiousness is related to job performance across five different occupational groups (professionals, police, managers, sales, and skilled or semiskilled jobs).[108] In short, people who are dependable, persistent, goal directed, and organized tend to be higher performers on virtually any job; viewed negatively, those who are careless, irresponsible, low-achievement striving, and impulsive tend to

agreeableness the degree to which someone is cooperative, polite, flexible, forgiving, good-natured, tolerant, and trusting

conscientiousness the degree to which someone is organized, hardworking, responsible, persevering, thorough, and achievement oriented

openness to experience the degree to which someone is curious, broad-minded, and open to new ideas, things, and experiences; is spontaneous; and has a high tolerance for ambiguity

People who are hardworking, responsible, persevering, and thorough are conscientious; this personality trait alone is a strong indicator of motivation and high performance.

© AMY ETRA/PHOTOEDIT, INC.

CONSCIENTIOUSNESS: THE ORGANIZED, HARDWORKING, RESPONSIBLE PERSONALITY

Conscientious people are organized, hardworking, responsible, persevering, thorough, and achievement oriented. Who wouldn't want to hire people with these personality traits? Indeed, 92 studies across five occupational groups (professionals, police, managers, sales, and skilled/semiskilled jobs) with a combined total of 12,893 study participants indicated that, on average, conscientious people are inherently more motivated and are better at their jobs.

MOTIVATIONAL EFFORT

There is a 71 percent chance that conscientious workers will be more motivated and will work harder than less conscientious workers.

Probability of Success

| 10% | 20% | 30% | 40% | 50% | 60% | 70% | 80% | 90% | 100% |

probability of success   71%

JOB PERFORMANCE

There is a 66 percent chance that conscientious workers will be better at their jobs than less conscientious workers.[109]

Probability of Success

| 10% | 20% | 30% | 40% | 50% | 60% | 70% | 80% | 90% | 100% |

probability of success   66%

---

be lower performers on virtually any job.[110] See the "What Really Works" feature in this chapter for further explanation. The results also indicate that extraversion is related to performance in jobs that involve significant interaction with others, such as sales and management. In people-intensive jobs like these, it helps to be sociable, assertive, and talkative and to have energy and be able to energize others. Finally, people who are extraverted and open to experience seem to do much better in training. Being curious and open to new experiences, as well as sociable, assertive, talkative, and full of energy, helps people perform better in learning situations.[111]

3.2 Work-Related Personality Dimensions

Does the way you keep your desk reveal something about your personality? Lots of people think so. For example, people with ultra-neat desks tend to believe that a desk buried under mounds of paper, food wrappers, and old magazines is a sign that its owner is lazy, disorganized, undependable, and a dreamer. On the other hand, people with messy desks believe that a spotless desk with everything in its place is a sign that its owner is impatient, critical, controlling, analytical, and a perfectionist. Who knows, maybe if your desk is somewhere between operating-room clean and the aftermath of a tornado, it is a sign that you have a good-natured, flexible, and fun-loving personality.[112]

Although studies indicate that extraversion, emotional stability, agreeableness, conscientiousness, and openness to experience are the five basic dimensions of personality in any culture, setting, or language, research has also identified additional personality dimensions that directly affect workplace attitudes and behaviors. These additional personality dimensions are authoritarianism, Machiavellian tendencies, Type A/B personality, locus of control, and positive/negative affectivity.

Authoritarianism is the extent to which an individual believes there should be power and status differences within the organization.[113] Authoritarian employees are likely to prefer a direct leadership style, in which the boss tells them exactly what to do. While this sounds desirable, one disadvantage is that even when they know a better solution or are aware of problems, authoritarian employees may simply carry out their boss's orders without question. Also, authoritarian employees may not perform well on ambiguous tasks or for managers who encourage employees to use their own initiative and judgment.

Authoritarian leaders are highly demanding and expect employees to unquestioningly obey their orders. One such boss, a body builder who liked to show off his strength to managers by doing 25 pushups at the start of meetings, used to call the vice president of marketing at all hours to scream about things that had gone wrong. A second bully boss, the CEO of a semiconductor-network start-up, ridiculed employees publicly. "He'd pick up something I'd written and say, 'Who wrote this? A second grader? It's the stupidest thing I've ever read,'" says the firm's marketing vice president. Business executives who are too demanding or who ridicule and scream at employees undermine productivity, discourage innovation and may cause a talent drain at their companies, says James Clifton, CEO of the *GALLUP ORGANIZATION*.[114]

People with **Machiavellian** personalities believe that virtually any type of behavior is acceptable if it helps satisfy needs or accomplish goals.[115] In other words, people with Machiavellian personalities believe that the ends justify the means. For example, "high Machs" are generally more willing to use lies and deceit to get their way than are "low Machs," even in situations where the chances of being caught in a lie are high.[116] High Machs believe that most people are gullible and can be manipulated. High Machs are also more effective at persuading others than low Machs are and tend to be resistant to others' efforts to persuade them.[117] One reason high Machs are more effective at persuading others is that low Machs (meaning most people) may be distracted by emotions or issues unrelated to winning. By contrast, high Machs are difficult to persuade because they ignore emotions and secondary issues and focus only on the things that move them closer to their goals. Also, because they are out for themselves and no one else, high Machs don't do well in work teams. High Machs often cause conflicts within teams and sometimes cause teams to break up. The *Wall Street Journal* offers this vivid description of High Machs: "They tend to be narcissistic, arrogant, manipulative, and goal-oriented. They trust no one and refuse to collaborate. They lack a capacity for empathy but are skilled at politics. Though they purposely disregard how they're coming off to colleagues or subordinates, they're often very good at sweet-talking bosses, who remain oblivious to their dastardly ways."[118] One study found that employees stuck with such manipulative bosses experienced more exhaustion, job tension, nervousness, depressed mood, and mistrust.[119]

The **Type A/B personality dimension** is the extent to which people tend toward impatience, hurriedness, competitiveness, and hostility.[120] **Type A personalities** try to complete as many tasks as possible in the shortest possible time and are hard driving, competitive, impatient, perfectionistic, angry, and unable to relax.[121] Type As have a high need for achievement and are also likely to be aggressive, self-confident, dominant, and extraverted. In contrast, **Type B personalities** are easygoing, patient, and able to relax and engage in leisure activities. Unlike Type A personalities, they are neither highly competitive nor excessively driven to accomplishment.

authoritarianism the extent to which an individual believes there should be power and status differences within organizations

Machiavellian the extent to which individuals believe that virtually any type of behavior is acceptable in trying to satisfy their needs or meet their goals

Type A/B personality dimension the extent to which people tend toward impatience, hurriedness, competitiveness, and hostility

Type A personality a person who tries to complete as many tasks as possible in the shortest possible time and is hard driving, competitive, impatient, perfectionistic, angry, and unable to relax

Type B personality a person who is relaxed, easygoing, and able to engage in leisure activities without worrying about work

What do we know about the Type A/B personality dimension and the workplace? Contrary to what you'd expect, Type As don't always outperform Type Bs on the job. Type As tend to perform better on tasks that demand quick decisions made at a rapid work pace under time pressure, whereas Type Bs tend to perform better at tasks requiring well-thought-out decisions when there is little time pressure. And despite the characteristic Type A ambition to succeed, top managers are much more likely to have Type B personalities.[122] Ironically, the task complexity and psychological challenge inherent in management jobs actually work against many Type A managers by dramatically increasing their stress levels.[123] Type Bs, on the other hand, do a much better job of handling and responding to the stress of managerial jobs.

A recent study involving 6,148 people aged 14 to 102 conducted by a group of researchers and the U.S. National Institute of Aging found absolutely no connection between a hard-driving personality and heart disease, contrary to previous studies and conventional wisdom. This study clearly establishes that Type A personality in itself is not related to heart disease.[124] However, individuals who are Type A and also "hostile and angry," may be at risk of heart attack. For example, businessperson Matt Sicinski gets extremely hostile and angry when his coworkers miss deadlines or don't follow directions. Says Sicinski, "My feet get cold, and I get a throbbing in my head. I can feel every muscle in my body tense up." If he gets angry with someone on the phone, sometimes he presses the mute button so he can't be heard and begins "cursing somebody up one side and down the other."[125] How dangerous is angry, hostile behavior to your health? A long-term study at Duke University followed a group of lawyers for 25 years and found that those with higher hostility scores were 4.2 times as likely to have died over that period as those with low scores.[126] This does not bode well for Sicinski, who at age 30 already has dangerously high blood pressure, which he admits is not responding well to his blood pressure medications.

You do poorly on an exam. Quick: Who do you blame, yourself or the professor? The answer to that question may, to some extent, indicate whether you have an internal or external locus of control. **Locus of control** is the degree to which people believe that their actions influence what happens to them. **Internal locus of control** is the belief that what happens to you is largely under your control. Therefore, students with an internal locus of control are more likely to hold themselves accountable for their exam performance ("I studied the wrong material" or "I didn't study enough."). Besides believing that what happens to them is largely under their control, internals are also easier to motivate (especially when rewards are linked to performance), more difficult to lead, more independent, and better able to handle complex information and solve complex problems.[127] In contrast, an **external locus of control** is the belief that what happens to you is primarily due to factors beyond your control, such as luck, chance, or powerful people.[128] Therefore, students with an external locus of control are more likely to attribute their poor exam performance to luck ("If only it had been an essay exam instead of multiple choice"), chance ("I didn't get enough sleep"), or the professor (a powerful person). In general, externals are more compliant and conforming and therefore are easier to lead than internals. For example, internals may question directives from their managers, while externals are likely to quietly accept them. Finally, internals are likely to perform better on complex tasks that require initiative and independent decision making, whereas externals tend to perform better on simple, repetitive tasks that are well structured.

Affectivity is the stable tendency to experience positive or negative moods and to react to things in a generally positive or negative way.[129] People with **positive affectivity** consistently notice and focus on the positive aspects of themselves and

locus of control the degree to which individuals believe that their actions can influence what happens to them

internal locus of control the belief that what happens to you is largely the result of your own actions

external locus of control the belief that what happens to you is largely the result of factors beyond your control

affectivity the stable tendency to experience positive or negative moods and to react to things in a generally positive or negative way

positive affectivity a personality trait in which individuals tend to notice and focus on the positive aspects of themselves and their environments their environments. In other words, they seem to be in a good mood most of the time and are predisposed to being optimistic, cheerful, and cordial. By contrast, people with **negative affectivity** consistently notice and focus on the negative in themselves and their environments. They are frequently in bad moods, consistently expect the worst to happen, and are often irritated or pessimistic.

How stable are the positive or negative moods associated with positive/negative affectivity? A 10-year study by the National Institute of Aging found that even when people changed jobs or companies, the people who were the happiest at the beginning of the study were still the happiest at the end of the study 10 years later.[130] Likewise, a much longer study found that high school counselors' ratings of student cheerfulness predicted how satisfied these people were with their jobs 30 years later.[131] Since dispositions toward positive or negative affectivity are long lasting and very stable, some companies have begun measuring affectivity during the hiring process. Providing superior customer service is crucial to achieving a firm's goals, says Walter Timoshenko, chief marketing officer at the accounting firm Weiser LLP, adding that "people make the difference."[132] Indeed, a recent survey of 1,000 customers conducted by Accenture indicates that poor customer service drives nearly half of consumers to take their business elsewhere. Many experts agree that hiring people who are enthusiastic and have a positive outlook is important for providing world-class customer service.[133] Studies also show that employees with positive affectivity are absent less often, report feeling less stress, are less likely to be injured in workplace accidents, and are less likely to retaliate against management and the company when they believe that they have been treated unfairly.[134] Affectivity is also important because of **mood linkage**, a phenomenon in which one worker's negative affectivity and bad moods can spread to others. Studies of nurses and accountants show a strong relationship between individual workers' moods and the moods of their coworkers.[135] Finally, people with positive affectivity are better decision makers, are rated as having much higher managerial potential, and are more successful in sales jobs.[136] Indeed, numerous studies show that happy individuals are successful across multiple domains, including marriage, friendship, income, work performance and health.[137]

Review 3: **Deep-Level Diversity**

Deep-level diversity matters because it can reduce prejudice, discrimination, and conflict while increasing social integration. It consists of dispositional and personality differences that can be learned only through extended interaction with others. Research conducted in different cultures, settings, and languages indicates that there are five basic dimensions of personality: extraversion, emotional stability, agreeableness, conscientiousness, and openness to experience. Of these, conscientiousness is perhaps the most important to companies because conscientious workers tend to be better performers on virtually any job. Extraversion is also related to performance in jobs that require significant interaction with others. Studies also show that the personality dimensions of authoritarianism, Machiavellian tendencies, Type A/B personality, locus of control, and positive/negative affectivity are important in the workplace. These personality dimensions are related to honesty, trust, teamwork, persuasive abilities, job performance, decision making, stress, heart disease, adaptability, promotions, interpersonal skills, motivation, initiative, job satisfaction, absenteeism, accidents, retaliatory behavior, mood linkage, and management potential.

negative affectivity a personality trait in which individuals tend to notice and focus on the negative aspects of themselves and their environments

mood linkage a phenomenon in which one worker's negative affectivity and bad moods can spread to others

HOW CAN DIVERSITY BE MANAGED?

How much should companies change their standard business practices to accommodate the diversity of their workers? For example, at WHIRLPOOL's Lavergne, Tennessee, appliance factory, 10 percent of the work force is Muslim. Many Muslim men have long beards and wear skullcaps, while Muslim women traditionally wear flowing headscarves and modest, loose-fitting, form-hiding clothes. For safety reasons, long hair, hats of any kind, and loose clothing are prohibited on the factory floor. (Imagine any of these getting caught in moving machinery.) How should Whirlpool's managers deal with the obvious conflict between Muslim religious practices and the company's safety procedures that are designed to prevent injury? Furthermore, at noon on Fridays, observant Muslims attend 45- to 90-minute religious services at their mosques. With a typical Monday to Friday workweek and lunch breaks of just 30 minutes, how can Whirlpool's managers accommodate this Friday service without hurting the production schedule and without giving the Muslims special treatment (that may be resented by the 90 percent of workers who aren't Muslim)?[138]

Likewise, what do you do when a talented top executive has a drinking problem that only seems to affect his behavior at company business parties (for entertaining clients), where he has made inappropriate advances toward female employees? What do you do when, despite aggressive company policies against racial discrimination, employees continue to tell racial jokes and publicly post cartoons displaying racial humor? And, since many people confuse diversity with affirmative action, what do you do to make sure that your company's diversity practices and policies are viewed as benefiting all workers and not just some workers?

No doubt about it, questions like these make managing diversity one of the toughest challenges that managers face.[139] Nonetheless, there are steps companies can take to begin to address these issues.

After reading the next section, you should be able to

4 explain the basic principles and practices that can be used to manage diversity.

*As discussed earlier, diversity programs try to create a positive work environment where no one is advantaged or disadvantaged, where "we" is everyone, where everyone can do his or her best work, where differences are respected and not ignored, and where everyone feels comfortable. Let's begin to address those goals by learning about **4.1 different diversity paradigms, 4.2 diversity principles,** and **4.3 diversity training and practices**.*

4.1 Diversity Paradigms

As shown in Exhibit 12.7, there are several different methods or paradigms for managing diversity: the discrimination and fairness paradigm, the access and legitimacy paradigm, and the learning and effectiveness paradigm.[140] The *discrimination and fairness paradigm*, which is the most common method of approaching

"" If you don't measure something, it doesn't count You measure your market share. You measure your profitability. The same should be true for diversity. ""

A MANAGER

diversity, focuses on equal opportunity, fair treatment, recruitment of minorities, and strict compliance with the equal employment opportunity laws. Under this approach, success is usually measured by how well companies achieve recruitment, promotion, and retention goals for women, people of different racial/ethnic backgrounds, or other underrepresented groups. According to a recent workplace diversity practices survey conducted by the Society of Human Resource Management, 66 percent to 91 percent of companies use specialized strategies to recruit, retain and promote talented women and minorities. The percentages increase with company size, with companies of more than 500 employees the most likely to use these strategies. And 77 percent of companies with more than 500 employees systematically collect measurements on diversity-related practices.[141] One manager says, "If you don't measure something, it doesn't count. You measure your market share. You measure your profitability. The same should be true for diversity. There has to be some way of measuring whether you did, in fact, cast your net widely, and whether the company is better off today in terms of the experience of people of color than it was a few years ago. I measure my market share and my profitability. Why not this?"[142] The primary benefit of the discrimination and fairness paradigm is that it generally brings about fairer treatment of employees and increases demographic diversity. The primary limitation is that the focus of diversity remains on the surface-level diversity dimensions of sex, race, and ethnicity.

Exhibit 12.7

Paradigms for Managing Diversity

DIVERSITY PARADIGM	FOCUS	SUCCESS MEASURED BY	BENEFITS	LIMITATIONS
Discrimination & Fairness	Equal opportunity Fair treatment Recruitment of minorities Strict compliance with laws	Recruitment, promotion, and retention goals for underrepresented groups	Fairer treatment Increased demographic diversity	Focus on surface-level diversity
Access & Legitimacy	Acceptance and celebration of differences	Diversity in company matches diversity of primary stakeholders	Establishes a clear business reason for diversity	Focus on surface-level diversity
Learning & Effectiveness	Integrating deep-level differences into organization	Valuing people on the basis of individual knowledge, skills, and abilities	Values common ground Distinction between individual and group differences Less conflict, backlash, and divisiveness Bringing different talents and perspectives together	Focus on deep-level diversity is more difficult to measure and quantify

The *access and legitimacy paradigm* focuses on the acceptance and celebration of differences to ensure that the diversity within the company matches the diversity found among primary stakeholders, such as customers, suppliers, and local communities. This is similar to the *business growth* advantage of diversity discussed earlier in the chapter. The basic idea behind this approach is to create a demographically diverse work force and gain access to different ethnic customer groups.[143] Consistent with this goal, Ed Adams,

vice president of human resources for Enterprise Rent-a-Car, says, "We want people who speak the same language, literally and figuratively, as our customers. We don't set quotas. We say [to our managers], 'Reflect your local market.'"[144] The primary benefit of this approach is that it establishes a clear business reason for diversity. Like the discrimination and fairness paradigm, however, it focuses only on the surface-level diversity dimensions of sex, race, and ethnicity. Furthermore, employees who are assigned responsibility for customers and stakeholders on the basis of their sex, race, or ethnicity may eventually feel frustrated and exploited.

The most common method of managing diversity is the discrimination and fairness paradigm, which increases demographic diversity in even large companies.

While the discrimination and fairness paradigm focuses on assimilation (having a demographically representative workforce), and the access and legitimacy paradigm focuses on differentiation (having demographic differences inside the company match those of key customers and stakeholders), the *learning and effectiveness paradigm* focuses on integrating deep-level diversity differences, such as personality, attitudes, beliefs, and values, into the actual work of the organization. AETNA's 28,000 employees are diverse not only in terms of sex, ethnicity and race, but also by age group, sexual orientation, work styles and levels, perspective, education, skills and other characteristics. Raymond Arroyo, head of diversity at Aetna, says, "Diversity at Aetna means treating individuals individually, leveraging everyone's best, and maximizing the powerful potential of our workforce." He adds, "Part of a top diversity executive's role in any organization is to integrate diversity into every aspect of a business, including the workforce, customers, suppliers, products, services and even into the community a business serves."[145] Exhibit 12.8 shows the necessary preconditions for creating a learning and effectiveness diversity paradigm within an organization.

The learning and effectiveness paradigm is consistent with achieving organizational plurality. **Organizational plurality** is a work environment where (1) all members are empowered to contribute in a way that maximizes the benefits to the organization, customers, and themselves, and (2) the individuality of each member is respected by not segmenting or polarizing people on the basis of their membership in a particular group.[146]

The learning and effectiveness diversity paradigm offers four benefits.[147] First, it values common ground. Dave Thomas of the Harvard Business School explains: "Like the fairness paradigm, it promotes equal opportunity for all individuals. And like the access paradigm, it acknowledges cultural differences among people and recognizes the value in those differences. Yet this new model for managing diversity lets the organization internalize differences among employees so that it learns

organizational plurality a work environment where (1) all members are empowered to contribute in a way that maximizes the benefits to the organization, customers, and themselves, and (2) the individuality of each member is respected by not segmenting or polarizing people on the basis of their membership in a particular group

1.	The leadership must understand that a diverse workforce will embody different perspectives and approaches to work, and must truly value variety of opinion and insight.
2.	The leadership must recognize both the learning opportunities and the challenges that the expression of different perspectives presents for an organization.
3.	The organizational culture must create an expectation of high standards of performance for everyone.
4.	The organizational culture must stimulate personal development.
5.	The organizational culture must encourage openness and a high tolerance for debate and support constructive conflict on work-related matters.
6.	The culture must make workers feel valued.
7.	The organization must have a well-articulated and widely understood mission. This keeps discussions about work differences from degenerating into debates about the validity of people's perspectives.
8.	The organization must have a relatively egalitarian, nonbureaucratic structure.

Source: D. A. Thomas & R. J. Ely, "Making Differences Matter: A New Paradigm for Managing Diversity," *Harvard Business Review* 74 (September–October 1996): 79–90.

Exhibit 12.8

Creating a Learning and Effectiveness Diversity Paradigm in an Organization

and grows because of them. Indeed, with the model fully in place, members of the organization can say, 'We are all on the same team, with our differences—not despite them.'"[148]

Second, this paradigm makes a distinction between individual and group differences. When diversity focuses only on differences between groups, such as females versus males, large differences within groups are ignored.[149] For example, think of the women you know at work. Now, think for a second about what they have in common. After that, think about how they're different. If your situation is typical, the list of differences should be just as long as the list of commonalties, if not longer. In short, managers can achieve a greater understanding of diversity and their employees by treating them as individuals and by realizing that not all African Americans, Hispanics, women, or white males want the same things at work.[150]

Third, because the focus is on individual differences, the learning and effectiveness paradigm is less likely to encounter the conflict, backlash, and divisiveness sometimes associated with diversity programs that focus only on group differences. Taylor Cox, one of the leading management writers on diversity, says, "We are concerned here with these more destructive forms of conflict which may be present with diverse work forces due to language barriers, cultural clash, or resentment by majority-group members of what they may perceive as preferential and unwarranted treatment of minority-group members."[151] And Ray Haines, a consultant who has helped companies deal with the aftermath of diversity programs that became divisive, says, "There's a large amount of backlash related to diversity training. It stirs up a lot of hostility, anguish, and resentment but doesn't give people tools to deal with [the backlash]. You have people come in and talk about their specific ax to grind."[152] Certainly, not all diversity programs are divisive or lead to conflict. But, by focusing on individual rather than group differences, the learning and effectiveness paradigm helps to minimize these potential problems.

Finally, unlike the other diversity paradigms that simply focus on surface-level diversity, the learning and effectiveness paradigm focuses on bringing different talents and perspectives *together* (that is, deep-level diversity) to make the best organizational decisions and to produce innovative, competitive products and services.

4.2 Diversity Principles

While diversity paradigms represent general approaches or strategies for managing diversity, the diversity principles shown in Exhibit 12.9 will help managers do a better job of *managing company diversity programs*, no matter which diversity paradigm they choose.[153]

Begin by *carefully and faithfully following and enforcing federal and state laws regarding equal opportunity employment*. Diversity programs can't and won't succeed if the company is being sued for discriminatory actions and behavior. Faithfully following the law will also reduce the time and expense associated with EEOC investigations or lawsuits. Start by learning more at the EEOC website (**http://www.eeoc.gov**). Following the law also means strictly and fairly enforcing company policies.

Treat group differences as important, but not special. Surface-level diversity dimensions such as age, sex, and race/ethnicity should be respected, but should not be treated as more important than other kinds of differences (that is, deep-level diversity). Remember, the shift from surface- to deep-level diversity helps people know and understand each other better, reduces prejudice and conflict, and leads to stronger social integration with people wanting to work together and get the job done. Also, *find the common ground*. While respecting differences is important, it's just as important, especially with diverse workforces, to actively find ways for employees to see and share commonalties.

Tailor opportunities to individuals, not groups. Special programs for training, development, mentoring, or promotions should be based on individual strengths and weaknesses, not on group status. Instead of making mentoring available for just one group of workers, create mentoring opportunities for everyone who wants to be mentored. For example, at Pacific Enterprises, all programs, including Career Conversations forums, in which upper-level managers are publicly interviewed about themselves and how they got their jobs, are open to all employees.[154]

Reexamine, but maintain, high standards. Companies have a legal and moral obligation to make sure that their hiring and promotion procedures and standards are fair to all. At the same time, in today's competitive markets, companies should not lower standards to promote diversity. This not only hurts the organizations, but also feeds the stereotype that applicants who are hired or promoted in the name of affirmative action or diversity are less qualified. Monica Emerson, executive director

1.	Carefully and faithfully follow and enforce federal and state laws regarding equal employment opportunity.
2.	Treat group differences as important, but not special.
3.	Find the common ground.
4.	Tailor opportunities to individuals, not groups.
5.	Reexamine, but maintain, high standards.
6.	Solicit negative as well as positive feedback.
7.	Set high but realistic goals.

Source: L. S. Gottfredson, "Dilemmas in Developing Diversity Programs," in *Diversity in the Workplace*, ed. S. E. Jackson & Associates (New York: Guildford Press, 1992).

Exhibit 12.9
Diversity Principles

doing the right thing

Don't Break the Law in the Name of Diversity

As you learned in Chapter 11 on human resource management, the general effect of employment law, which is still evolving through court decisions, is that employers may not discriminate in employment decisions on the basis of sex, age, religion, color, national origin, race, or disability. Employment decisions should be based on factors that are "job related," "reasonably necessary," or a "business necessity" for successful job performance. With one exception (see Chapter 11 for further explanation), employers who use sex, age, race, or religion to make employment-related decisions when those factors are unrelated to an applicant's or employee's ability to perform a job may face charges of discrimination from employee lawsuits or the Equal Employment Opportunity Commission. So, do the right thing. Stay within the law as you build a diverse work force.

"WHAT'S NEW"
COMPANY

of diversity at **DAIMLERCHRYSLER**, says, "As a diversity executive, I not only have to have solid business capabilities, I need to be very knowledgeable of the different businesses in my organization to align diversity initiatives to support the needs of the businesses. Maintaining high standards when making employment decisions and involving the top-management and the board in diversity-initiatives is critical to the success of workplace diversity parctices."[155]

"WHAT'S NEW"
COMPANY

Solicit negative as well as positive feedback. Diversity is one of the most difficult management issues. No company or manager gets it right from the start. Consequently, companies should aggressively seek positive and negative feedback about their diversity programs. One way to do that is to use a series of measurements to see if progress is being made. *L'ORÉAL*, the cosmetics firm, has goals and measurements to track its progress in diversity with respect to recruitment, retention, and advancement, as well as the extent to which the company buys goods and services from minority- and women-owned suppliers.[156]

Set high but realistic goals. Just because diversity is difficult doesn't mean that organizations shouldn't try to accomplish as much as possible. The general purpose of diversity programs is to try to create a positive work environment where no one is advantaged or disadvantaged, where "we" is everyone, where everyone can do his or her best work, where differences are respected and not ignored, and where everyone feels comfortable. Even if progress is slow, companies should not shrink from these goals.

4.3 Diversity Training and Practices

Organizations use diversity training and several common diversity practices to manage diversity. There are two basic types of diversity training programs. **Awareness training** is designed to raise employees' awareness of diversity issues, such as the dimensions discussed in this chapter, and to get employees to challenge underlying assumptions or stereotypes they may have about others. As a starting point in awareness training, some companies have begun using the Implicit Association Test (IAT), which measures the extent to which people associate positive or negative thoughts (that is, underlying assumptions or stereotypes) with blacks or whites, men or women, homosexuals or heterosexuals, young or old, or other groups. For example, test takers are shown black or white faces that they must instantly pair with various words. Response times (shorter responses generally indicate stronger associations) and the pattern of associations indicates the extent to which people are biased. Most people are, and strongly so. For example, 88 percent of whites have a more positive mental association toward whites than toward blacks, but, surprisingly, so do blacks, 48 percent of whom show the same bias. Taking the IAT is a good way to increase awareness of diversity issues. To take the IAT and to learn more about the decade of research behind it, go to **https://implicit.harvard.edu**.[157] By contrast, **skills-based diversity training** teaches employees the practical skills they need for managing a diverse work force, such as flexibility and adaptability, negotiation, problem solving, and conflict resolution.[158]

Companies also use diversity audits, diversity pairing, and minority experiences for top executives to better manage diversity. **Diversity audits** are formal assessments that measure employee and management attitudes, investigate the extent to which people are advantaged or disadvantaged with respect to hiring and promotions, and review companies' diversity-related policies and procedures. For example, the results of a formal diversity audit prompted BRW,

awareness training training that is designed to raise employees' awareness of diversity issues and to challenge the underlying assumptions or stereotypes they may have about others

skills-based diversity training training that teaches employees the practical skills they need for managing a diverse work force, such as flexibility and adaptability, negotiation, problem solving, and conflict resolution

diversity audits formal assessments that measure employee and management attitudes, investigate the extent to which people are advantaged or disadvantaged with respect to hiring and promotions, and review companies' diversity-related policies and procedures an architecture and engineering firm, to increase job advertising in minority publications, set up a diversity committee to make recommendations to upper management, provide diversity training for all employees, and rewrite the company handbook to make a stronger statement about the company's commitment to a diverse work force.[159]

Earlier in the chapter you learned that *mentoring*, pairing a junior employee with a senior employee, is a common strategy for creating learning and promotional opportunities for women. Diversity pairing is a special kind of mentoring. In **diversity pairing**, people of different cultural backgrounds, sexes, or races/ethnicities are paired for mentoring. The hope is that stereotypical beliefs and attitudes will change as people get to know each other as individuals.[160] Consultant Tom McGee, who has set up mentoring programs for numerous companies, supports diversity pairing, saying "the assumption that people participating in diversity mentoring programs are looking for someone of the same race or gender has been proved wrong in many cases."[161] Pat Carmichael, an African American female vice president at *JPMORGAN CHASE*, who was mentored early in her career by a white male, mentors men and women of all backgrounds. Regarding a current mentee, John Imperiale, a white assistant branch manager, she says, "My hope is that the exposure John has to me will give him insights when he's managing a diverse group of employees."[162]

Finally, because top managers are still overwhelmingly white and male, a number of companies believe that it is worthwhile to *have top executives experience what it is like to be in the minority*. This can be done by having top managers go to places or events where nearly everyone else is of a different sex or racial/ethnic background. At Hoechst Celanese (which has now split into two companies), top managers would join two organizations in which they were a minority. For instance, the CEO, a white male, joined the board of Hampton University, a historically African American college, and Jobs for Progress, a Hispanic organization that helps people prepare for jobs. Commenting on his experiences, he said, "The only way to break out of comfort zones is to be exposed to other people. When we are, it becomes clear that all people are similar." A Hoechst vice president who joined three organizations in which he was in the minority said, "Joining these organizations has been more helpful to me than two weeks of diversity training."[163]

diversity pairing a mentoring program in which people of different cultural backgrounds, sexes, or races/ethnicities are paired together to get to know each other and change stereotypical beliefs and attitudes

More and more companies are embracing diversity because it makes good business sense. As this ad for Cargill puts it, "no one has a monopoly on good ideas."

REPRINTED WITH PERMISSION FROM CARGILL. © 2007, CARGILL INCORPORATED

Good business is built on diversity.

Each day Cargill does business around the world in food, nutrition, agriculture, and supply chain management. Our work in diverse communities has made us very aware of the importance of diversity in our supply chain. We've learned that no one has a monopoly on good ideas and that they can come from anyone, anywhere. We're committed to supplier diversity because we know it's good business. It adds value to what we do for our customers, as well as promoting prosperity in communities where we live and work. For more information, visit www.cargill.com/about

©2005 Cargill, Incorporated

Cargill
Nourishing Ideas. Nourishing People.

Review 4: *Managing Diversity*

The three paradigms for managing diversity are the discrimination and fairness paradigm (equal opportunity, fair treatment, strict compliance with the law), the access and legitimacy paradigm (matching internal diversity to external diversity), and the learning and effectiveness paradigm (achieving organizational plurality by integrating deep-level diversity into the work of the organization). Unlike the other paradigms, which focus on surface-level differences, the learning and effectiveness program values common ground, distinguishes between individual and group differences, minimizes conflict and divisiveness, and focuses on bringing different talents and perspectives together. What principles can companies use when managing diversity? Follow and enforce federal and state laws regarding equal employment opportunity. Treat group differences as important, but not special. Find the common ground. Tailor opportunities to individuals, not groups. Reexamine, but maintain, high standards. Solicit negative as well as positive feedback. Set high but realistic goals. The two types of diversity training are awareness training and skills-based diversity training. Companies also manage diversity through diversity audits and diversity pairing and by having top executives experience what it is like to be in the minority.

Do You Know Your Mind?

Do you always speak your mind? Chances are that you probably don't—at least not always. In some cases, you may not even know your mind. Our conscious mind is not always aligned with our subconscious, and we may be motivated by deeply held beliefs that diverge from our image of who we are or want to be. Researchers at Harvard have developed a series of assessments to help you identify your implicit associations about a variety of topics, many related to the diversity issues you learned about in this chapter. Unlike the other assessments in this book, this one requires you to go online. Each Project Implicit test, which is also called an Implicit Association Test (IAT), takes about 10 minutes to complete. However, you'll find it worthwhile to complete all of the different IATs. The researchers ask that you complete the initial surveys so that they can further enrich their data, but you needn't worry about privacy issues. They are only interested in the raw data and not in who actually contributed it.

1. To begin, go to **https://implicit.harvard.edu** and click on **"Demonstration."**

2. You will then be given a brief description of the project and prompted to **"Go to the demonstration tests."** Click on that hot link.

3. The front page of the demonstration tests is a more detailed synopsis of the project and a disclaimer. Read the information and then click on **"I wish to proceed."**

4. You will then reach the list of all the tests: age, gender-science, race, presidents, sexuality, gender-career, Arab-Muslim, weight, religion, disability, Native, Asian, weapons, and skin-tone. The tests most closely related to Chapter 12's content on diversity are age, race, sexuality, gender-career, weight, disability, Native, Asian, and skin-tone. Each time you complete an IAT, return to the list to select the next relevant test for this course. We'll use the age IAT as the basis for these instructions. Once you get the hang of it, you will be able to move through the preliminaries on any of IATs. To begin, click on **"Age IAT."**

5. You will be directed to a page of technical information related to your computer settings. If you can see the green check mark, then click to begin. At the next page, click on **"Continue."**

6. A survey of general information will pop up. The survey for each IAT is slightly different, except for the main demographic information at the bottom (age, race, etc.). Once you complete the survey, click on **"Proceed."**

7. Read the instructions carefully. In essence, each time a certain word or image appears, you will need to either respond by typing an "e" or an "i." The words used are purposely set to be obviously good or bad. For example, few people would dispute that *evil* goes in the category labeled "bad," and *love* goes in the category labeled "good." Don't get caught up in semantics; just classify the terms as they are understood in the common language.

8. The test will ask you to classify the words and images several times, switching the words and images from the left hand to the right hand. That way, your right hand isn't always typing an "i" for good and your left an "e" for bad. Pay attention to the changes.

9. Once you have finished the IAT on a particular topic, you will receive a results page. Check with your professor if he or she wants you to print it out or keep track of results in any way. Your instructor may want to average class results.

After completing the IATs, think about your results. Do any surprise you, or were you aware that you were making the unconscious associations the software identified?

KEY TERMS

affectivity 455
affirmative action 438
age discrimination 443
agreeableness 452
authoritarianism 454
awareness training 462
conscientiousness 452
deep-level diversity 442
disability 448
disability discrimination 448
disposition 451
diversity 437
diversity audits 462
diversity pairing 463
emotional stability 451
external locus of control 455
extraversion 451
glass ceiling 445
internal locus of control 455
locus of control 455
Machiavellian 454
mood linkage 456
negative affectivity 456
openness to experience 452
organizational plurality 459
personality 451
positive affectivity 455
racial and ethnic
    discrimination 446
sex discrimination 445
skills-based diversity
    training 462
social integration 443
surface-level diversity 442
Type A personality 454
Type A/B personality
    dimension 454
Type B personality 454

Company of INTJs Seeks ESFP Employee

Every business magazine you've picked up recently has had some kind of article on personality testing in the workplace.[164] You've read about the Caliper, used by FedEx, the Chicago Cubs, and the WNBA's Phoenix Mercury. Anne Mariucci, part-owner of the Mercury, uses the test to evaluate potential draft picks and make coaching assignments. With the help of a consultant, venerable retailer Neiman Marcus designed a test to identify the characteristics needed to be a successful sales associate; as a result, it has increased sales per associate by 42 percent and reduced staff turnover by 18 percent. Today, you're reading about a personality test originally designed for Olympic teams and military units (small groups in high-pressure situations with a single, focused goal).

As you close your magazine, you can't help thinking about diversity. As the manager in a medium-sized candy company, you have always made sure that your work force was diverse with respect to minorities and women, but until now you've never considered managing based on personalities. Even though personality tests sound like a good idea (lots of reputable companies are using them), you wonder about the drawbacks. There must be some, in addition to the several hundred dollars it would cost to test each of your 75 employees, or you would have started testing a long time ago.

The stack of articles you've read, however, is prompting you to think that personality testing might be a good idea. It looks like the only way to ensure deep-level diversity. New wave of tests, like the NEO Personality Inventory (Neuroticism, Extroversion, and Openness) and the Occupational Personality Questionnaire, make less sweeping generalizations than their predecessors. By using narrower indicators, the NEO and OPQ can identify how people will behave in certain situations and, ultimately, how well an employee's personality is suited to the tasks his or her job requires.

Testing is already a $400 million industry in the United States, and it's growing at 8 percent a year. The amount spent on personality testing alone has increased 10 to 15 percent each of the last three years. Most *Fortune* 500 companies use the venerable Myers-Briggs test. A recent study found that poorly performing employees cost U.S. employers $100 billion a year, so perhaps it's time to jump on the bandwagon.

Questions

1. If you knew the personality profiles of your workers, how would you actually use the information to benefit the company? Can personality testing help you achieve the company's goal of becoming one of the largest candy makers in North America?

2. Does personality testing help cultivate deep-level diversity, or does it do the opposite, ensuring a company staffed with people who are the same? Is there another way to cultivate deep-level diversity besides personality testing?

3. Do you see any drawbacks to personality testing? In addition to a diverse work force, what benefits could a manager derive from personality testing?

4. Do you begin personality testing? Explain your answer.

Is Older Necessarily Wiser?

Two weeks ago, you were pleased to receive a fat envelope from the U.S. government awarding your aeronautics company several hefty contracts with the Department of Defense.[165] As a result of the contracts, you'll have to increase production, so you immediately placed ads in the local paper for four skilled mechanics.

Résumés have been flooding in, and to your surprise, the prospective applicants fall into one of two groups. In addition to the usual crop of inexperienced youngsters eager to start their careers, you have an equally large pool of retired mechanics, many of them older than 65. They've spent their entire lives building planes and now want to work only 15 to 20 hours a week.

Flipping through the second pile, you realize that you face a difficult decision. Younger hires would require more training and supervision, but they could eventually become productive full-timers with the potential to stay at the company for most (if not all) of their careers. On the other hand, older veterans would be able to jump in feet first, but they would work fewer hours and probably have much shorter careers with the company. Whereas the veterans will expect pay commensurate with their experience, the newbies will accept much lower starting salaries

Between 2000 and 2010, the number of Americans between the ages of 55 and 64 will jump 47 percent, compared with a scant 2.8 percent increase in the number of those aged 25 to 34. The group that makes up the bulk of most companies' management talent, those aged 35 to 45, will actually shrink by 13.7 percent! With the graying of the workforce, this may be the first time you have to decide whether to hire older or younger workers, but it certainly won't be the last.

For this exercise, assemble a team of three to four students to represent the senior management team at the aeronautics firm in the scenario. Try using the dialectical inquiry technique discussed in Chapter 5 (Planning and Decision Making) on page 179.

Questions

1. Do you hire older workers or younger workers? Explain your choice.

2. What challenges can you foresee in managing a multigenerational work force?

PRACTICE BEING A MANAGER

Diversity may contribute a richness of perspective and understanding to a work group or organization. But to unlock these riches, it is essential that we develop tools of understanding individuals and cultures different from our own. Not all college students have experienced crossing a cultural boundary to live in another country. But most have encountered subcultures in the context of their middle or high school years. Teen subcultures are often quite pronounced and diverse. This exercise will offer practice in recognizing and understanding diversity.

Step 1: Get into groups. Your professor will organize you in small groups of three or four students.

Step 2: Identify teen subcultures. Think back to your middle school or high school experiences and identify some of the major subcultures you observed (Athletes, Toughs, and so on). Share descriptions of these subcultures with the members of your group.

Step 3: Conduct diversity training. Take turns training each other on what it would be like to be a member of one of the subcultures which you knew well. It is not necessary that you belonged to this subculture, but only that you can recall it vividly. Teach your fellow group members what a young person would need to

know to fit in with this subculture, including such dimensions as

- Clothing
- Manner of speech, common slang, or "code language"
- Music
- Value of the subculture to members; what it means to be "in" this group

Step 4: Discuss how teen subcultures are diverse. Discuss as a group the impact of teen subcultures on valuing diversity. In what ways do teen subcultures bond diverse people (athletes of different races, for example) together, and help them to understand one another better? In what ways do teen subcultures separate people into "cliques" or foster stereotyping ("us" vs. "them")?

Step 5: Debrief as a class. Based on your group discussions, what are the challenges for organizations who are seriously attempting to value diversity? What are the benefits to these organizations? How do organizations train people about cultural (and subcultural) differences without falling into stereotyping?

From Majority to Minority and Back Again

Do you know what it feels like to walk into a room where, because of your sex, race/ethnicity, religion, language, or some other dimension, you are intensely aware of being different from everyone else?[166] Some of you do. Most of you probably don't. And, since most managers are white and male, it's a good bet that they don't know either. The experience can be unsettling, especially the first time it happens.

Some companies have begun broadening perspectives and understanding by having their managers join groups or attend events where they are different from everyone else. As you read in Section 4.3, at Hoechst Celanese, the CEO, a white male, joined the board of Hampton University, a historically African American college, and Jobs for Progress, a Hispanic organization that helps people prepare for jobs.

For more than 30 years, UPS has required its top managers to participate in community service programs in inner cities or poor rural areas. James Casey, UPS's founder, started the program in 1968 to expose his white male managers to diverse experiences, people, and communities. Casey also hoped that the experience would increase empathy, break down stereotypes, and encourage volunteer and community service. Today, managers with 10 to 30 years of experience are assigned to community service tasks in inner cities or rural areas. Don Wofford, who directs the program, says, "We choose managers on the fast track, people who'll be positioned to influence their work force and the community for years to come." The managers spend two weeks doing community service, followed by a weekend at home and then two more weeks of community service. Wofford says, "This format gives them a chance to digest the experience—they tend to come back renewed after the break, with a new focus, sometimes even more bewildered, but still ready to go for it."

Your assignment is to attend an event, meeting, or activity where you are different from almost everyone else in terms of your sex, race/ethnicity, religion, language, or some other dimension. You can choose a church service, local community group, volunteer organization, or student group on campus. Ask your professor for ideas. You should probably contact the group beforehand to arrange your visit. Answer the following questions after your visit.

Questions

1. Describe the event, meeting, activity, or organization you visited.

2. How were you different from others in attendance? Describe what it was like to be different from everyone else.

3. In what ways was this experience actually similar to previous experiences that you've had? In other words, while question 2 focuses on differences, this question focuses on similarities and commonalties.

4. What did you learn from this experience?

REEL TO REAL

In Good Company

In Good Company, a 2004 film, stars Dennis Quaid as Dan Foreman, a seasoned advertising sales executive at the magazine *Sports America*. A corporate takeover results in Dan having a new supervisor named Carter Duryea. On his first day on the job, Carter confesses to a young woman he meets on the elevator that he doesn't know what he's doing. In this scene, Dan and Carter meet for the first time.

What to Watch for and Ask Yourself

1. How does this scene relate to diversity?
2. Review the Chapter 2 clip from the same movie. How diverse is the advertising department at *Sports America*? Explain.
3. Consider the two clips together and think about deep-level diversity. Why do you think *Sports America* hired Carter Duryea?

PepsiCo

Imagine trying to manage and accommodate the needs of more than 140,000 people at once. Imagine a variety of voices, languages, cultures, ethnic backgrounds, families, lifestyles, ages, and geographies all vying for attention, all bearing the name PepsiCo. That's the challenge of managers throughout PepsiCo. From the top down, PepsiCo embraces diversity and inclusion in its worldwide workforce. Top executives, including former CEO Steve Reinemund, believe that nurturing diversity in the organization is not only a matter of responsible ethics but also good business. Because PepsiCo offers products to such a diverse array of customers, it makes sense for the PepsiCo workforce to mirror the market. In addition, a facility's workforce will likely reflect the local population. However, embracing a philosophy of diversity is entirely different from implementing it. Watch the video to see how PepsiCo takes on this global task.

What to Watch for and Ask Yourself

1. Why is it important for upper-level managers at PepsiCo to receive diversity and inclusion training?
2. Do you think that PepsiCo's encouragement of employee networks actually works against diversity and formation of multicultural teams? Why or why not?

467

four

PART 4
Leading

Chapter 13
Motivation

This chapter covers the basics of motivation—effort, needs, and intrinsic and extrinsic rewards. As we progress through the chapter, we build on that basic model of motivation by adding concepts of equity, expectancy, reinforcement, and goal-setting theories. There's also a summary of practical, theory-based actions that managers can take to motivate their workers.

Chapter 14
Leadership

This chapter discusses what leadership is, what characteristics are common of leaders, and what leaders do that makes them different from people who aren't leaders. We examine major contingency theories of leadership and review strategic leadership issues, such as charismatic and transformational leadership.

Chapter 15
Managing Communication

This chapter examines perception in communication, the communication process, and the kinds of organizational communication. You'll also learn about effective one-on-one communication as well as techniques for organization-wide communication.

CHAPTER 13

Motivation

Learning Outcomes:

1 Explain the basics of motivation.
2 Use equity theory to explain how employees' perceptions of fairness affect motivation.
3 Use expectancy theory to describe how workers' expectations about rewards, effort, and the link between rewards and performance influence motivation.
4 Explain how reinforcement theory works and how it can be used to motivate.
5 Describe the components of goal-setting theory and how managers can use them to motivate workers.
6 Discuss how the entire motivation model can be used to motivate workers.

In This Chapter:

WHAT WOULD YOU DO?

Nucor Corporation, Charlotte, North Carolina.[1] You love working for Nucor Corporation, whose mission is to "Take Care of Our Customers" by being the safest, highest-quality, lowest-cost, most productive, and most profitable steel and steel products company in the world. Nucor operates with one of the leanest corporate staffs in the nation. A typical *Fortune* 500 company has a triple-digit corporate staff. By contrast, Nucor's staff is just 65 corporate employees, which means that the staff serves the operating managers and employees, and not the other way around. Likewise, Nucor's streamlined chain of command, with just five levels of management (president and CEO, executive vice president, general manager, department manager, and supervisory/professional), allows general managers like you to operate your steel plant like an independent business. Since the day-to-day decisions are made at the steel plants, and not headquarters, you can quickly respond to suppliers, customers, and employees without waiting for a decision from the corporate office.

Operating employees also love working at Nucor because the company makes few distinctions between management and hourly employees. Another reason that hourly employees love Nucor is that the company is committed to not laying off employees. Indeed, since its entry into the steelmaking business, Nucor has not laid off a single worker. The result is a committed team of Nucor employees.

One of the things that has made it easier for you to be a general manager at Nucor is its aggressive use of bonuses to motivate employees. Employees involved directly in manufacturing are paid weekly bonuses based on the production of their work groups. Bonuses typically average 80–170 percent of the base wage, but can go higher as there is no limit. If productivity and production increase, bonuses will continue to rise. Department managers earn annual incentive bonuses based primarily on the return on investment of their facility. These bonuses can be as much as 100 percent of base salary. Professional and staff employees, such as accountants, engineers, clerks, and receptionists, can earn bonuses up to 28 percent of salary. As for manufacturing employees, their base pay is actually well below industry average, but their productivity bonuses make them among the highest-paid steel workers in the world. And Nucor's employees have responded positively to Nucor's production incentives, and produce high-quality products at the lowest possible cost. In short, Nucor has established itself as one of the best-run steel companies in the United States.

Part of that success, however, is due to the unprecedented domestic and international demand for steel, particularly in China. Now, though, China has become self-sufficient and not only produces enough steel to meet local demand but also is emerging as a major exporter of steel. As this chapter is being written, Chinese steelmakers are negotiating with Indian steel companies to start joint ventures to produce high-quality steel. Worldwide supply of steel is catching with demand, and current inventories are higher than industry analysts consider appropriate.

With increased competition, Nucor's sales could slow, which would mean that bonuses would decrease and total compensation (base pay plus bonus) could fall below the industry average. If sales and bonuses drop, how will you motivate your workforce? Are there any non-monetary steps you could take? What if the demand for steel decreases so much that Nucor is forced to revoke its "no layoff" policy? If you had to conduct layoffs for the first time in company history, what steps would you take to treat employees fairly and with dignity? Finally, what might you do to avoid layoffs or to postpone them as long as possible? You've got to come up with a plan. **If you were a general manager at Nucor, what would you do?**

What makes people happiest and most productive at work? Is it money, benefits, opportunities for growth, interesting work, or something else altogether? And if people desire different things, how can a company keep everyone motivated? It takes insight and hard work to motivate workers to join the company, perform well, and then stay with the company. Indeed, when asked to name their biggest management challenge, nearly one-third of executives polled by Creative Group, a specialized staffing service in Menlo Park, California, cited "motivating employees."[2]

This chapter begins by reviewing the basics of motivation—effort, needs, and intrinsic and extrinsic rewards. We will start with a basic model of motivation and add to it as we progress through each section in the chapter. Next, we will explore how employees' equity perceptions and reward expectations affect their motivation. If you're familiar with the phrase "perception is reality," you're off to a good start in understanding the importance of perceptions and expectations in motivation. The third part of the chapter reviews the role that rewards and goals play in motivating employees. You'll see that finding the right combination of goals and rewards is much harder in practice than it looks. The chapter finishes with a summary of practical, theory-based actions that managers can take to motivate their workers.

WHAT IS MOTIVATION?

Motivation is the set of forces that initiates, directs, and makes people persist in their efforts to accomplish a goal.[3] In terms of this definition, *initiation of effort* is concerned with the choices that people make about how much effort to put forth in their jobs. ("Do I really knock myself out for these performance appraisals or just do a decent job?") *Direction of effort* is concerned with the choices that people make in deciding where to put forth effort in their jobs. ("I should be spending time with my high-dollar accounts instead of learning this new computer system!") *Persistence of effort* is concerned with the choices that people make about how long they will put forth effort in their jobs before reducing or eliminating those efforts. ("I'm only halfway through the project, and I'm exhausted. Do I plow through to the end, or just call it quits?") As Exhibit 13.1 shows, initiation, direction, and persistence are at the heart of motivation.

motivation the set of forces that initiates, directs, and makes people persist in their efforts to accomplish a goal

Exhibit 13.1

The Components of Motivation

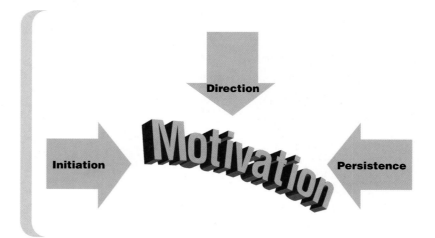

1 Basics of Motivation

Take your right hand and point the palm toward your face. Keep your thumb and pinky finger straight and bend the three middle fingers so the tips are touching your palm. Now rotate your wrist back and forth. If you were in the *REGENT SQUARE TAVERN* in Pittsburgh, Pennsylvania, that hand signal would tell waitress Marjorie Landale that you wanted a Yuengling beer. Marjorie, who isn't deaf, would not have understood that sign a few years ago. But with a state school for the deaf nearby, the tavern always has its share of deaf customers, so she decided on her own to take classes to learn how to sign. At first, deaf customers would signal for a pen and paper to write out their orders. But after Marjorie signaled that she was learning to sign, "their eyes [would] light up, and they [would] finger-spell their order." Word quickly spread as the students started bringing in their friends, classmates, teachers, and hearing friends as well. Says Marjorie, "The deaf customers are patient with my amateur signing. They appreciate the effort."[4]

What would motivate an employee like Marjorie to voluntarily learn a new language like American Sign Language? (Sign language is every bit as much a language as French or Spanish.) She wasn't paid to take classes in her free time. She chose to do it on her own. And while she undoubtedly makes more tip money with a full bar than with an empty one, it's highly unlikely that she began her classes with the objective of making more money. Just what is it that motivates employees like Marjorie Landale?

Let's learn more about motivation by building a basic model of motivation out of **1.1 effort and performance**, **1.2 need satisfaction**, *and* **1.3 extrinsic and intrinsic rewards** *and then discussing* **1.4 how to motivate people with this basic model of motivation**.

1.1 Effort and Performance

When most people think of work motivation, they think that working hard (effort) should lead to a good job (performance). Exhibit 13.2 shows a basic model of work motivation and performance, displaying this process.

The first thing to notice about Exhibit 13.2 is that this is a basic model of work motivation *and* performance. In practice, it's almost impossible to talk about one without mentioning the other. Not surprisingly, managers often assume motivation to be the only determinant of performance, saying things such as "Your performance was really terrible last quarter. What's the matter? Aren't you as motivated as you used to be?" In fact, motivation is just one of three primary determinants of job performance. In industrial psychology, job performance is frequently represented by this equation:

Job Performance = Motivation × Ability × Situational Constraints

In this formula, *job performance* is how well someone performs the requirements of the job. *Motivation*, as defined above, is effort, the degree to which someone works hard to do the job well. *Ability* is the degree to which workers possess the knowledge, skills, and talent needed to do a job well. And *situational constraints* are factors beyond the control of

© MICHAEL NEWMAN/PHOTOEDIT, INC.

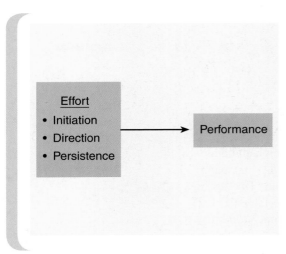

Exhibit 13.2

A Basic Model of Work Motivation and Performance

individual employees, such as tools, policies, and resources that have an effect on job performance.

Since job performance is a multiplicative function of motivation times ability times situational constraints, job performance will suffer if any one of these components is weak. For example, in 1988, the East German bobsled team was fully funded by the East German government and had state-of-the-art coaching and equipment (no situational constraints). The team members were recruited and selected from a large pool of talented athletes (ability) who had trained year-round for most of their lives (motivation) for a chance to make the highly prestigious team. By contrast, consider the *JAMAICAN BOBSLED TEAM* that Disney made famous in the movie *Cool Runnings*. In 1988 at its first Winter Olympics, the team had limited funding, a coach with bobsledding experience (a five-time U.S. champion) but no coaching experience, and an old bobsled that couldn't compete with the world-class equipment used by the best teams (high situational constraints). Furthermore, its members had been raised in tropical Jamaica and had almost no bobsledding or winter sports experience (very little ability). Nonetheless, they dreamed of competing in the Olympics and did what they could to train for several months, considering their limited circumstances (strong motivation).

It's not hard to guess which team did better, is it? With ample motivation, ability, and almost no situational constraints, you'd expect the East Germans to be competitive, and they were—finishing second and third in the two-man competition and second in the four-man competition.[5] By contrast, with strong motivation, little ability, and extremely high situational constraints, the Jamaican two-man team finished in 35th place, while the four-man team crashed spectacularly and had to push the bobsled across the line to complete the final run on the course.

Does this mean that motivation doesn't matter? No, not at all. It just means that all the motivation in the world won't translate into high performance when you have little ability and high situational constraints. In fact, prior to the 1996 Winter Olympics, the Jamaican team spent six weeks working with Sam Bock, who also worked with the elite Canadian team. Bock put the Jamaicans through their paces at a special bobsled training center in Oberhof, Germany. After training for four to eight hours a day in world-class conditions under world-class tutelage, the Jamaican four-man team finished in 14th place, ahead of the Americans, French, Russians, and one of the two Swiss and Italian teams. The two-man team did even better, finishing 10th.[6]

1.2 Need Satisfaction

In Exhibit 13.2, we started with a very basic model of motivation in which effort leads to job performance. However, managers want to know, "What leads to effort?" And they will try almost anything they can to find the answer. For example, *CHECKERS DRIVE-IN RESTAURANTS* pays highly competitive salaries and has a great benefits package, but it also offers out-of-this world rewards for outstanding performance, including cars, cruises, and consumer electronics. One year, Checkers took the top general managers, area managers, top-performing corporate employees, *and* their spouses on a week-long cruise.[7] At Seattle-based *ZILLOW*, the online real-estate valuation service, teams have had to work overtime to add new features to the company's website. So, the company added foosball, ping pong, and air-hockey tables and free all-you-can-drink soft drinks, juice, and milk to its downtown offices.[8] Envision Technology, a Seattle software company, offers a variety of health-oriented perks, including on-site massages and "Business Boxes" of fresh fruit and healthy snacks.[9] At Parker LePla, a Seattle marketing and branding company, the employees regularly spend an afternoon playing WhirlyBall, lawn bowling, or kayaking on Lake Union.[10] As you can see, employers will do almost anything to motivate employees to put forth extra effort into their jobs.

Needs are the physical or psychological requirements that must be met to ensure survival and well-being.[11] As shown on the left side of Exhibit 13.3, a person's unmet need creates an uncomfortable, internal state of tension that must be resolved. For example, if you normally skip breakfast, but then have to work through lunch, chances are you'll be so hungry by late afternoon that the only thing you'll be motivated to do is find something to eat. So, according to needs theories, people are motivated by unmet needs. But once a need is met, it no longer motivates. When this occurs, people become satisfied, as shown on the right side of Exhibit 13.3.

Note: Throughout the chapter, as we build on this basic model, the parts of the model that we've already discussed will appear shaded in color. For example, since we've already discussed the effort → performance part of the model, those components are shown with a colored background. When we add new parts to the model, they will have a white background. For instance, since we're adding need satisfaction to the model at this step, the need-satisfaction components of unsatisfied need, tension, energized to take action, and satisfaction are shown with a white background. This shading convention should make it easier to understand the work motivation model as we add to it in each section of the chapter.

Since people are motivated by unmet needs, managers must learn what those unmet needs are and address them. This is not always a straightforward task, however, because different needs theories suggest different needs categories. Exhibit 13.4 shows needs from three well-known needs theories. Maslow's Hierarchy of Needs suggests that people are motivated by *physiological* (food and water), *safety* (physical and economic), *belongingness* (friendship, love, social interaction), *esteem* (achievement and recognition), and *self-actualization* (realizing your full potential) needs.[12] Alderfer's ERG Theory collapses Maslow's five needs into three: *existence* (safety and physiological needs), *relatedness* (belongingness), and *growth* (esteem and self-actualization).[13] McClelland's Learned Needs Theory suggests that people are motivated by the need for *affiliation* (to be liked and accepted), the need for *achievement* (to accomplish challenging goals), or the need for *power* (to influence others).[14]

doing the right thing

Faking It, Not Making It

With technological assistance, you may be tempted to engage in "impression management" to try to convince your boss and coworkers that you're working hard when you're really not. For instance, a tech support worker who enjoyed three-hour lunches used a program on his Palm personal computer to remotely control his office computer. He would open, close, and move files so it would look as if he had just stepped away from his desk. Other employees write e-mails before they go home and then "send" them after midnight (we won't tell you how this is done) to make it look as though they are still at work. Some people leave early and, on their way home, send e-mails via their Blackberry device so it will appear they are still at the office. You may be thinking that these ruses are harmless, but 59 percent of human resource managers and 53 percent of supervisors have caught employees lying about the hours they work. Furthermore, if you're using technology to fake it, you're usually leaving high-tech tracks and footprints along the way. That tech worker who controlled his office computer with his Palm PC at lunch was fired for habitual lateness. Motivation is all about effort. So, do the right thing. Work hard for your company, your customers, and yourself.[15]

needs the physical or psychological requirements that must be met to ensure survival and well-being

As shown on the left side of this exhibit, a person's unsatisfied need creates an uncomfortable, internal state of tension that must be resolved. So, according to needs theories, people are motivated by unmet needs. But once a need is met, it no longer motivates. When this occurs, people become satisfied, as shown on the right side of the exhibit.

Exhibit 13.3

Adding Need Satisfaction to the Model

Things become even more complicated when we consider the different predictions made by these theories. According to Maslow, needs are arranged in a hierarchy from low (physiological) to high (self-actualization). Within this hierarchy, people are motivated by their lowest unsatisfied need. As each need is met, they work their way up the hierarchy from physiological to self-actualization needs. By contrast, Alderfer says that people can be motivated by more than one need at a time. Furthermore, he suggests that people are just as likely to move down the needs hierarchy as up, particularly when they are unable to achieve satisfaction at the next higher need level. McClelland argues that the degree to which particular needs motivate varies tremendously from person to person, with some people being motivated primarily by achievement and others by power or affiliation. Moreover, McClelland says that needs are learned, not innate. For instance, studies show that children whose parents own a small business or hold a managerial position are much more likely to have a high need for achievement.[16]

So, with three different sets of needs and three very different ideas about how needs motivate, how do we provide a practical answer to managers who just want to know "What leads to effort?" Fortunately, the research evidence simplifies things a bit. To start, studies indicate that there are two basic kinds of needs categories.[17] As shown in Exhibit 13.4, *lower-order needs* are concerned with safety and with physiological and existence requirements, whereas *higher-order needs* are concerned with relationships (belongingness, relatedness, and affiliation); challenges and accomplishments (esteem, self-actualization, growth, and achievement); and influence (power). Studies generally show that higher-order needs will not motivate people as long as lower-order needs remain unsatisfied.[18]

For example, imagine that you graduated from college six months ago and are still looking for your first job. With money running short (you're probably living on your credit cards) and the possibility of having to move back in with your parents looming (if this doesn't motivate you, what will?), your basic needs for food, shelter, and security drive your thoughts, behavior, and choices at this point.

Exhibit 13.4

Needs Classification of Different Theories

But once you land that job, find a great place (of your own!) to live, and put some money in the bank, these basic needs should decrease in importance as you begin to think about making new friends and taking on challenging work assignments. In fact, once lower-order needs are satisfied, it's difficult for

	MASLOW'S HIERARCHY	ALDERFER'S ERG	McCLELLAND'S LEARNED NEEDS
Higher-Order Needs	Self-Actualization Esteem Belongingness	Growth Relatedness	Power Achievement Affiliation
Lower-Order Needs	Safety Physiological	Existence	

managers to predict which higher-order needs will motivate behavior.[19] Some people will be motivated by affiliation, while others will be motivated by growth or esteem. Also, the relative importance of the various needs may change over time, but not necessarily in any predictable pattern. So, what leads to effort? In part, needs do. After we discuss rewards in Subsection 1.3, in Subsection 1.4 we discuss how managers can use what we know from need-satisfaction theories to motivate workers.

1.3 Extrinsic and Intrinsic Rewards

No discussion of motivation would be complete without considering rewards. Let's add two kinds of rewards, extrinsic and intrinsic, to the model, as shown in Exhibit 13.5.[20]

Extrinsic rewards are tangible and visible to others and are given to employees contingent on the performance of specific tasks or behaviors.[21] External agents (managers, for example) determine and control the distribution, frequency, and amount of extrinsic rewards, such as pay, company stock, benefits, and promotions. For example, 80 percent of 1,000 large and medium-sized U.S. companies surveyed by Hewitt Associates, a consulting company based in Lincolnshire, Illinois, offer incentives or bonuses to reward employees.[22] The payout from *Boeing*'s employee incentive plan is determined by how well Boeing meets financial targets. One year, the incentive plan paid $439 million to about 109,000 workers companywide.[23] Likewise, *Wal-Mart* paid $529.8 million in bonuses to 813,759 hourly U.S. employees at Wal-Mart and Sam's Club stores. Lois Honeycutt, a 46-year old customer service manager at Wal-Mart in Altamonte Springs, Florida, says the bonus program will help increase employee performance and boost employee spirits and morale.[24] As described in the chapter-opening "What Would You Do?," manufacturing employees at Nucor Corporation can earn bonuses of up to 170 percent of base pay.[25]

Why do companies need extrinsic rewards? To get people to do things they wouldn't otherwise do. Companies use extrinsic rewards to motivate people to perform four basic behaviors: join the organization, regularly attend their jobs, perform their jobs well, and stay with the organization.[26] Think about it. Would you show up to work every day to do the best possible job that you could just out of the goodness of your heart? Very few people would. This is why *CDW* (Computer Discount Warehouse) rewards its employees for staying with the company. CDW found that new employees are only one-third as productive as employees who have at least three years of experience with the company. Accordingly, CDW has an "old-timers" program that rewards employees who have been with the company at least three years with a four-day trip for themselves and their families anywhere in the continental United States. There is one catch: The company has to meet its sales goals. But if it does, the company pays for the airline tickets and hotel costs associated with those trips. And CDW pays for such trips every year that employees stay with the company beyond three years.[27] At CDW's expense, account manager Brigid Brindley has taken her family to California and Washington, D.C., and is planning a trip to Seattle. Brindley says this about CDW: "They recognize that there are other things in life that you do besides just work." CDW's approach makes sense in light of a Maritz Incentives poll of 1,002 full-time employees, which concluded that employees who feel their value is recognized are seven times more likely to stay with their present company than employees who don't feel valued.[28]

extrinsic reward a reward that is tangible, visible to others, and given to employees contingent on the performance of specific tasks or behaviors

Join Cognex—and Stay—and Travel the World

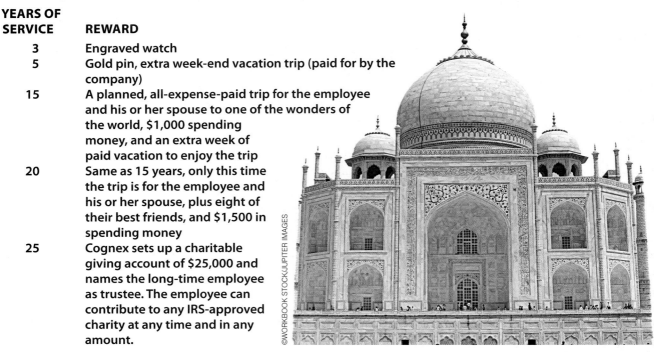

YEARS OF SERVICE	REWARD
3	Engraved watch
5	Gold pin, extra week-end vacation trip (paid for by the company)
15	A planned, all-expense-paid trip for the employee and his or her spouse to one of the wonders of the world, $1,000 spending money, and an extra week of paid vacation to enjoy the trip
20	Same as 15 years, only this time the trip is for the employee and his or her spouse, plus eight of their best friends, and $1,500 in spending money
25	Cognex sets up a charitable giving account of $25,000 and names the long-time employee as trustee. The employee can contribute to any IRS-approved charity at any time and in any amount.

©WORKBOOK STOCK/JUPITER IMAGES

SOURCE: J. S. LUBLIN, "CREATIVE COMPENSATION: A CEO TALKS ABOUT HIS COMPANY'S INNOVATIVE PAY IDEAS. FREE ICE CREAM, ANYONE?" *WALL STREET JOURNAL*, 10 APRIL 2006, R6.

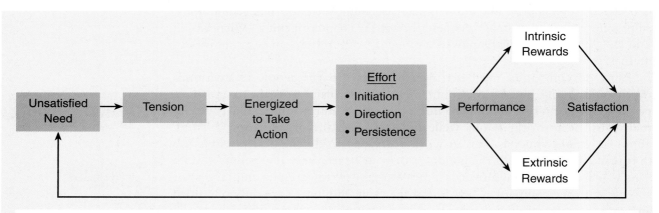

Performing a job well can be rewarding intrinsically (the job itself is fun, challenging, or interesting) or extrinsically (as you receive better pay or promotions, etc.). Intrinsic and extrinsic rewards lead to satisfaction of various needs.

Exhibit 13.5

Adding Rewards to the Model

intrinsic reward a natural reward associated with performing a task or activity for its own sake

By contrast, **intrinsic rewards** are the natural rewards associated with performing a task or activity for its own sake. For example, aside from the external rewards management offers for doing something well, employees often find the activities or tasks they perform interesting and enjoyable. Examples of intrinsic rewards include a sense of accomplishment or achievement, a feeling of responsibility, the chance to learn something new or interact with others, or simply the fun that comes from performing an interesting, challenging, and engaging task. For instance, researcher Mark Rise works for Medtronic, a leading medical technology company. Rise, one of Medtronic's most creative inventors, could have a more prestigious job at a university or make more money starting his own company, but he doesn't want to test theory or develop marketing plans or raise venture capital. What matters most to him is developing products that make a difference in people's lives. Says Rise, "That's what keeps me tied to what I'm doing now." Indeed, Rise thrives on the intrinsic aspects of his work such as being able to work with physicians, medical researchers, software developers, and engineers to identify new treatments and design and manufacture new products.[29]

Which types of rewards are most important to workers in general? A number of surveys suggest that both extrinsic and intrinsic rewards are important. One survey found that the most important rewards were good benefits and health insurance, job security, a week or more of vacation (all extrinsic rewards), interesting work, the opportunity to learn new skills, and independent work situations (all intrinsic rewards). And employee preferences for intrinsic and extrinsic rewards appear to be relatively stable. Studies conducted over the last three decades have consistently found that employees are twice as likely to indicate that "important and meaningful work" matters more to them than what they are paid.[30]

1.4 Motivating with the Basics

So, given the basic model of work motivation in Exhibit 13.5, what practical steps can managers take to motivate employees to increase their effort?

As shown in Exhibit 13.6, *start by asking people what their needs are*. If managers don't know what workers' needs are, they won't be able to provide them the opportunities and rewards that can satisfy those needs. Linda Connor, vice president of corporate culture at TECHNOLOGY PROFESSIONALS CORP. (TPC) in Grand Rapids, Michigan, keeps careful notes about TPC employees' needs. She says, "I sit down at employees' 30-day reviews and ask specific questions about hobbies and interests for each member of their families."[31] For instance, her notes about top performer Phil Mayrose indicated that he loves college football, oldies music, and, more than anything else, golf. Armed with this information, Connor and TPC rewarded Mayrose with a weekend vacation at a dude ranch with a great golf course. Connor's notes also include ideas for helping employees deal with stress.[32] So, if you want to meet employees' needs, do what Linda Connor does and just ask.

Next, *satisfy lower-order needs first*. Since higher-order needs will not motivate people as long as lower-order needs remain unsatisfied, companies should satisfy lower-order needs first. In practice, this means providing the equipment, training, and knowledge to create a safe workplace free of physical risks, paying employees well enough to provide financial security, and offering a benefits package that will protect employees and their families through good medical coverage and health and disability insurance. Indeed, a survey based on a representative sample of Americans found that when people choose jobs or organizations, three of the four most important factors—starting pay/salary (62 percent), employee benefits (57 percent), and job security (47 percent)—are lower-order needs.[33]

Third, managers should *expect people's needs to change*. As some needs are satisfied or situations change, what motivated people before may not motivate them now. Likewise, what motivates people to accept a job may not necessarily motivate them once they have the job. For instance, David Stum, president of the Loyalty Institute, says, "The [attractive] power of pay and benefits is only [strong] during the recruitment stage. After employees take the job, pay and benefits become entitlements to them. They think: 'Now that I work here, you owe me that.'"[34] Managers should also expect needs to change as people mature.[35]

Exhibit 13.6

Motivating to Increase Effort

- Start by asking people what their needs are.
- Satisfy lower-order needs first.
- Expect people's needs to change.
- As needs change and lower-order needs are satisfied, create opportunities for employees to satisfy higher-order needs.

For older employees benefits are as important as pay, which is always ranked as more important by younger employees. Also, older employees rank job security as more important than personal and family time, which is more important to younger employees.[36]

Finally, *as needs change and lower-order needs are satisfied, create opportunities for employees to satisfy higher-order needs.* Recall that intrinsic rewards, such as accomplishment, achievement, learning something new, and interacting with others, are the natural rewards associated with performing a task or activity for its own sake. And, with the exception of influence (power), intrinsic rewards correspond very closely to higher-order needs that are concerned with relationships (belongingness, relatedness, and affiliation) and challenges and accomplishments (esteem, self-actualization, growth, and achievement). Therefore, one way for managers to meet employees' higher-order needs is to create opportunities for employees to experience intrinsic rewards by providing challenging work, encouraging employees to take greater responsibility for their work, and giving employees the freedom to pursue tasks and projects they find naturally interesting. For example, we began this section by asking what would motivate an employee like Marjorie Landale to voluntarily learn American Sign Language. Marjorie wasn't paid to do this. In fact, she even spent her own money and free time to learn how to sign. The reason that Marjorie learned to sign is that doing so met her higher-order needs. It gave her a sense of accomplishment, and it allowed her to interact with deaf customers with whom she had previously been unable to interact. And Marjorie's boss was smart enough to encourage her to pursue a project that she found naturally interesting.

mgmt: trend

Motivating the Multigenerational Work Force

Now that Generation Y (also known as millennials) is entering the work force, managers must juggle four generations of workers with distinctly different work styles, ambitions, and values. Gen Y-ers have grown up immersed in technology and have largely been insulated from negative feedback by overinvolved boomer parents. These workers tend to be fearless and blunt, believe that old-school ways don't necessarily generate the best results, and are more committed to work-life balance than previous generations. Today's managers need to adapt if they want to attract, retain, and motivate Gen Y-ers, who will conceivably dominate the work force for the next 70 years. What motivated older generations is probably not going to work as well with Gen Y.

Sources: Danielle Sacks, "Scenes from the Culture Clash: Companies Are Now Waking Up to the Havoc That the Newest Generation of Workers Is Causing in Their Offices," *Fast Company*, January–February 2006, 73–77; Claire Raines, "Managing Millennials," *Connecting Generations: The Sourcebook for the Workplace* (Menlo Park, CA: Crisp Publications, 2003).

Review 1: Basics of Motivation

Motivation is the set of forces that initiates, directs, and makes people persist in their efforts over time to accomplish a goal. Managers often assume motivation to be the only determinant of performance, but job performance is a multiplicative function of motivation times ability times situational constraints. If any one of these components is weak, job performance will suffer. Needs are the physical or psychological requirements that must be met to ensure survival and well-being. When needs are not met, people experience an internal state of tension. But once a particular need is met, it no longer motivates. When this occurs, people become satisfied and are then motivated by other unmet needs. Different motivational theories, such as Maslow's Hierarchy of Needs (physiological, safety, belongingness, esteem, and self-actualization), Alderfer's ERG Theory (existence, relatedness, and growth), and McClelland's Learned Needs Theory (affiliation, achievement, and power), specify a number of different needs. However, studies show that there are only two general kinds of needs, lower-order needs and higher-order needs, and that higher-order needs will not motivate people as long as lower-order needs remain unsatisfied. Both extrinsic and intrinsic rewards motivate people. Extrinsic rewards, which include pay, company stock, benefits, and promotions, are used to motivate people to join organizations and attend and perform their jobs. The basic model of motivation suggests that managers can motivate employees by asking them what their needs are, satisfying lower-order needs first, expecting people's needs to change, and satisfying higher-order needs through intrinsic rewards.

© BANANA STOCK/JUPITER IMAGES

Managing the multiple styles of multigenerational workforces is proving to be a delicate balancing act for managers.

> The [attractive] power of pay and benefits is only [strong] during the recruitment stage. After employees take the job, pay and benefits become entitlements to them. They think: "Now that I work here, you owe me that."

DAVID STUM, PRESIDENT, LOYALTY INSTITUTE

HOW PERCEPTIONS AND EXPECTATIONS AFFECT MOTIVATION

When employees perceive that they will be unable to perform at a level necessary to obtain rewards, whether extrinsic or intrinsic, they are likely to be *de-motivated*. Reward systems at many organizations are geared toward top performers and ignore the mid-level performers. Most banks, for instance, reward the top 10 percent of the sales force; other sales representatives, who don't believe they can generate enough sales to end up in the top category, simply give up. Stephen O'Malley, an independent consultant, says that one way to avoid this scenario is to create an open-ended incentive program that keeps the top-performer programs intact while offering awards for mid-level performers who surpass their annual sales goals by 10 percent. This system implemented at a large U.S.-based financial services institution was successful in influencing perceptions and expectations of mid-level performers and resulted in better performance from all employees and increased revenue for the company. Specifically, two-thirds of the company's mid-level performers qualified for rewards by collectively contributing almost 80 percent of the total sales growth and creating $14 million in incremental profit. The contributions of these mid-level performers as a group outpaced the growth of top performers by 16 percent. By influencing perceptions and expectations of the entire sales force, the company was able to achieve a 47 percent overall increase in sales growth, three times the industry average.[37]

> **After reading the next two sections, you should be able to**
>
> 2 use equity theory to explain how employees' perceptions of fairness affect motivation.
>
> 3 use expectancy theory to describe how workers' expectations about rewards, effort, and the link between rewards and performance influence motivation.

2 Equity Theory

Finnish businessman Jaako Rytsola was out driving in his car one evening. "The road was wide and I was feeling good. It was nice to be driving when there was no one in sight." Unfortunately for Rytsola, he wasn't really alone. A police officer pulled him over and issued him a speeding ticket for driving 43 miles per hour in a 25 mph zone. The cost of the ticket: $71,400! Janne Rajala, a college student, was also pulled over for driving 18 mph over the speed limit. However, Rajala's ticket cost him only $106. The $71,294 difference occurred because Finland bases traffic fines on the severity of the offense, which was identical in this case, *and* the income of the driver, which clearly wasn't.

Is Finland's method of determining speeding fines fair or unfair? Most Americans would argue that Finland's approach is unfair, that fairness requires that fines be proportional to the offense and that everyone who breaks the law to the same degree should pay the same fine. By contrast, most Finns believe that fines proportional to income are fair. Erkki Wuouma of Finland's Ministry of the Interior says, "This is a Nordic tradition. We have progressive taxation and progressive punishments. So the more you earn, the more you pay." Rytsola pays more because he is a high-earning Internet entrepreneur. Rajala pays less because he's a low-earning college student.[38]

Fairness, or what people perceive to be fair, is also a critical issue in organizations. **Equity theory** says that people will be motivated at work when they *perceive* that they are being treated fairly. In particular, equity theory stresses the importance of perceptions. So, regardless of the actual level of rewards people receive, they must also perceive that, relative to others, they are being treated fairly. For example, you learned in Chapter 11 that the average CEO now makes 289 times more than the average worker.[39] On average, CEOs of the 500 largest U.S. companies make $10.9 million,[40] CEOs of the Standard & Poor's 500 make $13.51 million.[41] And many CEOs make in the $200 million range. For instance, Terry Semel, former CEO of Yahoo made $230.6 million

equity theory a theory that states that people will be motivated when they perceive that they are being treated fairly

Equity theory is not an absolute. It is dependent on many factors, including culture. Jaako Rytsola, pictured here with his Lamborghini, was fined $71,400 for speeding because in Finland traffic fines are based on a person's income. People of other cultures may not have the same view of equity as the Finns!

© AP PHOTO/SARI GUSTAFSSON/LEHTIKUVA

one year.[42] Many people believe that CEO pay is obscenely high and unfair. Others believe that CEO pay is fair because the supply and demand for executive talent largely determine what CEOs are paid. They argue that if it were easier to find good CEOs, then CEOs would be paid much less.

As explained below, equity theory doesn't focus on objective equity (that is, that CEOs make 289 times more than blue-collar workers). Instead, equity theory says that equity, like beauty, is in the eye of the beholder.

*Let's learn more about equity theory by examining **2.1 the components of equity theory**, **2.2 how people react to perceived inequities**, and **2.3 how to motivate people using equity theory**.*

2.1 Components of Equity Theory

The basic components of equity theory are inputs, outcomes, and referents. **Inputs** are the contributions employees make to the organization. Inputs include education and training, intelligence, experience, effort, number of hours worked, and ability. **Outcomes** are what employees receive in exchange for their contributions to the organization. Outcomes include pay, fringe benefits, status symbols, and job titles and assignments. And, since perceptions of equity depend on comparisons, **referents** are others with whom people compare themselves to determine if they have been treated fairly. The referent can be a single person (comparing yourself with a coworker), or a generalized other (comparing yourself with "students in general," for example), or could be yourself over time ("I was better off last year than I am this year"). Usually, people choose to compare themselves with referents who hold the same or similar jobs or who are otherwise similar in gender, race, age, tenure, or other characteristics.[43] For instance, by any objective measure, it's hard to argue that the best professional athletes, who make as much as $30 million a year (and no doubt more by the time you read this), are treated unfairly, given that the typical American earns $43,318 a year.[44] Nonetheless, most top athletes' contracts include escalator clauses specifying that if another top player at the same position (that is, their referent) receives a larger contract, then their contract will automatically be increased to that amount.

According to the equity theory process shown in Exhibit 13.7, employees compare their outcomes, the rewards they receive from the organization, with their inputs, their contributions to the organization. This comparison of outcomes with inputs is called the **outcome/input (O/I) ratio**. After an internal comparison in which they compare their outcomes with their inputs, employees then make an external comparison in which they compare their O/I ratio with the O/I ratio of a referent.[45] When people perceive that their O/I ratio is equal to the referent's O/I ratio, they conclude that they are being treated fairly. But when people perceive that their O/I ratio is different from their referent's O/I ratio, they conclude that they have been treated inequitably or unfairly.

Inequity can take two forms, underreward and overreward. **Underreward** occurs when a referent's O/I ratio is better than your O/I ratio. In other words, you are getting fewer outcomes relative to your inputs than the referent you compare yourself with is getting. When people perceive that they have been underrewarded, they tend to experience anger or frustration. For example, when a manufacturing company received notice that some important contracts had been canceled, management cut employees' pay by 15 percent in one plant but not in another. Just as equity theory predicts, theft doubled in the plant that received the pay cut. Likewise, employee turnover increased from 5 percent to 23 percent.[46]

inputs in equity theory, the contributions employees make to the organization

outcomes in equity theory, the rewards employees receive for their contributions to the organization

referents in equity theory, others with whom people compare themselves to determine if they have been treated fairly

outcome/input (O/I) ratio in equity theory, an employee's perception of how the rewards received from an organization compare with the employee's contributions to that organization

underreward a form of inequity in which you are getting fewer outcomes relative to inputs than your referent is getting

Exhibit 13.7
Outcome/Input Ratios

$$\frac{\text{OUTCOMES}_{\text{SELF}}}{\text{INPUTS}_{\text{SELF}}} = \frac{\text{OUTCOMES}_{\text{REFERENT}}}{\text{INPUTS}_{\text{REFERENT}}}$$

By contrast, **overreward** occurs when a referent's O/I ratio is worse than your O/I ratio. In this case, you are getting more outcomes relative to your inputs than your referent is. In theory, when people perceive that they have been overrewarded, they experience guilt. But, not surprisingly, people have a very high tolerance for overreward. It takes a tremendous amount of overpayment before people decide that their pay or benefits are more than they deserve.

2.2 How People React to Perceived Inequity

As a child do you ever remember calling for a do-over? Even as children, we have a strong desire for fairness, for being treated equitably. When this need isn't met, we are strongly motivated to find a way to restore equity and be fair, hence the "do-over." Not surprisingly, equity is just as important at the office as it is on the playground.

So what happens when people perceive that they have been treated inequitably at work? Exhibit 13.8 shows that perceived inequity affects satisfaction. In the case of underreward, this usually translates into frustration or anger; with overreward, the reaction is guilt. These reactions lead to tension and a strong need to take action to restore equity in some way. At first, a slight inequity may not be strong enough to motivate an employee to take immediate action. If the inequity continues or there are multiple inequities, however, tension may build over time until a point of intolerance is reached, and the person is energized to take action.[47] For example, when *THE ACCIDENT GROUP*, an insurance company, laid off 2,500 employees in Manchester, Birmingham, and Liverpool, England,

overreward a form of inequity in which you are getting more outcomes relative to inputs than your referent

Exhibit 13.8

Adding Equity Theory to the Model

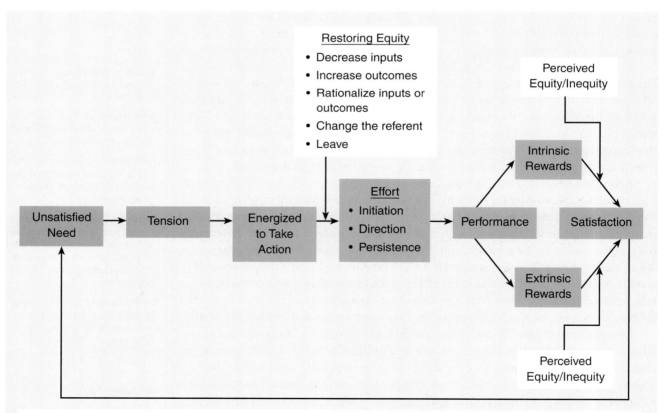

When people perceive that they have been treated inequitably at work because of the intrinsic or extrinsic rewards they receive relative to their efforts, they are dissatisfied (or frustrated or angry), because their needs aren't met. Those reactions lead to tension and a strong need to take action to restore equity in some way (as explained in the "Restoring Equity" box).

it made the announcement in an impersonal, insensitive way. Employees received text messages on their cell phones telling them to not go into work, that their final paychecks could not be issued, and that a more thorough explanation would be provided by e-mail. In addition, this message was left on everyone's office voice mail: "All staff who are being retained will be contacted today. If you have not been spoken to, you are therefore being made redundant [laid off] with immediate effect." Angry employees *and* managers ransacked offices, taking computers, phones, and anything else they could carry off. Claims assessor Andy Potton says, "I could hardly believe what I saw. There were people walking out of the office with computers. One chap quite high up in the company had loaded up his car with laptops and driven off."[48]

When people perceive that they have been treated unfairly, they may try to restore equity by reducing inputs, increasing outcomes, rationalizing inputs or outcomes, changing the referent, or simply leaving. We will discuss these possible responses in terms of the inequity associated with underreward, which is much more common than the inequity associated with overreward.

People who perceive that they have been underrewarded may try to restore equity by *decreasing or withholding their inputs (that is, effort)*. For example, when IBERIA, the Spanish airline, was near bankruptcy, it pressured its pilots to take substantial pay cuts. When Iberia's finances improved, the pilots requested that the pay cuts, which had cost them $140 million, be reversed. They also asked for annual pay increases substantially higher than the rate of inflation. When Iberia management refused, the pilots staged a work slowdown at the peak of the busy summer tourism season. Over the course of 10 separate days throughout the summer, 30 to 40 percent of Iberia's pilots called in sick, disrupting the airline's flight schedule, customers, and profits.[49]

Increasing outcomes is another way people try to restore equity. This might include asking for a raise or pointing out the inequity to the boss and hoping that he or she takes care of it. Sometimes, however, employees may go to external organizations, such as labor unions, federal agencies, or the courts for help in increasing outcomes to restore equity. For instance, the U.S. Department of Labor estimates that 10 percent of workers are not getting the extra overtime pay they deserve when they work more than 40 hours a week.[50] In fact, more than 30,000 such cases are brought each year, and employees win two-thirds of them.[51] For example, the managers of Waffle House restaurants sued the company because they were working an average of 89 hours a week without any overtime pay (managers at Radio Shack and Wal-Mart have sued their companies for similar reasons).[52] The company contended that as managers they were exempt from the Fair Labor Standards Act (FLSA), which mandates that workers be paid time and a half for any work beyond 40 hours a week. But because Waffle House managers were required to perform and be proficient in the duties of hourly workers in addition to their managerial responsibilities, the courts ruled that Waffle House managers were really employees who deserved overtime pay. As a result, they were awarded $2,868,841.50 in back overtime pay.[53]

Another method of restoring equity is to *rationalize or distort inputs or outcomes*. Instead of decreasing inputs or increasing outcomes, employees restore equity by making mental or emotional "adjustments" in their O/I ratios or the O/I ratios of their referents. For example, suppose that a company downsizes 10 percent of its work force. It's likely that the survivors, the people who still have jobs, will be angry or frustrated with company management because of the layoffs. If alternative jobs are difficult to find, however, these survivors may rationalize or distort their O/I ratios and conclude, "Well, things could be worse. At least I still have my job." Rationalizing or distorting outcomes may be used when other ways to restore equity aren't available.

Changing the referent is another way of restoring equity. In this case, people compare themselves with someone other than the referent they had been using for previous O/I ratio comparisons. Since people usually choose to compare themselves with others who hold the same or similar jobs or who are otherwise similar (such as friends, family members, neighbors who work at other companies), they may change referents to restore equity when their personal situations change, such as a decrease in job status or pay.[54]

Finally, when none of these methods—reducing inputs, increasing outcomes, rationalizing inputs or outcomes, or changing referents—are possible or restore equity, *employees may leave* by quitting their jobs, transferring, or increasing absenteeism.[55] For example, attorneys and accountants at the Securities and Exchange Commission (SEC) quit their jobs at twice the rate of employees in other federal agencies. Why? One reason is that the SEC's attorneys and accountants are paid 40 percent less than their counterparts at other government agencies. Furthermore, they can get jobs in the private sector that pay $180,000 to $250,000 per year.[56]

2.3 Motivating with Equity Theory

What practical steps can managers take to use equity theory to motivate employees? As Exhibit 13.9 shows, they can *start by looking for and correcting major inequities*. Among other things, equity theory makes us aware that an employee's sense of fairness is based on subjective perceptions. What one employee considers grossly unfair may not affect another employee's perceptions of equity at all. Although these different perceptions make it difficult for managers to create conditions that satisfy all employees, it's critical that they do their best to take care of major inequities that can energize employees to take disruptive, costly, or harmful actions, such as decreasing inputs or leaving. So, whenever possible, managers should look for and correct major inequities. Junior accountant Monica DiCenso supervised three auditors and regularly put in 80-hour weeks certifying the financial statements of PRICEWATERHOUSECOOPERS' corporate clients. After receiving a $2,000 annual bonus (effectively paying her $2.86 an hour for overtime work), DiCenso quit, as did 20 of the 35 accountants who started when she did. DiCenso says, "I could have made more working at a fast-food restaurant."[57] With turnover up significantly, the Big Four accounting firms have begun addressing those inequities by paying bigger bonuses and giving junior accountants more vacation time. To help with the long hours, the firms are offering concierge services, which pick up and drop off dry cleaning and take care of other daytime tasks that workers don't have time to do. Frequent "town hall" meetings also give junior accountants a chance to gripe to senior partners about the difficulties in their jobs.

Second, managers can *reduce employees' inputs*. Increasing outcomes is often the first and only strategy that companies use to restore equity, yet reducing employee inputs is just as viable a strategy. In fact, with dual-career couples working 50-hour weeks, more and more employees are looking for ways to reduce stress and restore a balance between work and family. Consequently, it may make sense to ask employees to do less, not more; to have them identify and eliminate the 20 percent of their jobs that doesn't increase productivity or add value for customers; and to eliminate company-imposed requirements that really aren't critical to the performance of managers, employees, or the company (for example, unnecessary meetings and reports). In addition to higher pay, more vacation time, concierge services, and town hall sessions, the Big Four accounting firms are trying to make the jobs of junior accountants more equitable by reducing the hours (that is, inputs) they must work. To shrink the workload, the firms are hiring more accountants, adding staff from other departments to help, and even actually turning away business that they lack the staff to handle. Bob Moritz, a senior partner at PriceWaterhouseCoopers, says,

Exhibit 13.9

Motivating with Equity Theory

- Look for and correct major inequities.
- Reduce employees' inputs.
- Make sure decision-making processes are fair.

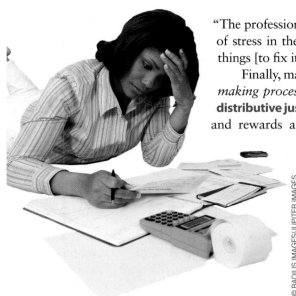
© RADIUS IMAGES/JUPITER IMAGES

"The profession has recognized that we have a lot of stress in the system, and we're doing a lot of things [to fix it]."[58]

Finally, managers should *make sure decision-making processes are fair*. Equity theory focuses **distributive justice**, the degree to which outcomes and rewards are fairly distributed or allocated. However, **procedural justice**, the fairness of the procedures used to make reward allocation decisions, is just as important.[59] Procedural justice matters because even when employees are unhappy with their outcomes (that is, low pay), they're much less likely to be unhappy with company management if they believe that the procedures used to allocate outcomes were fair. For example, employees who are laid off tend to be hostile toward their employer when they perceive that the procedures leading to the layoffs were unfair. By contrast, employees who perceive layoff procedures to be fair tend to continue to support and trust their employers.[60] Also, if employees perceive that their outcomes are unfair (that is, distributive injustice), but that the decisions and procedures leading to those outcomes were fair (that is, procedural justice), they are much more likely to seek constructive ways of restoring equity, such as discussing these matters with their manager. In contrast, if employees perceive both distributive and procedural injustice, they may resort to more destructive tactics, such as withholding effort, absenteeism, tardiness, or even sabotage and theft.[61] *Interactional justice* refers to the fairness of interpersonal treatment that individuals receive during the enactment of organizational procedures. Two elements central to perceptions of interactional justice are (1) whether the reasons underlying the resource allocation decisions are clearly, truthfully, and adequately explained to affected parties, and (2) whether those responsible for implementing the decision treat the affected individuals with dignity and respect.[62] Recent studies indicate that interactional justice perceptions are at least as important as perceptions of procedural justice and distributive justice.[63] In addition, most managers are likely to have more control over interactional justice perceptions than, for example, fairness of organizational procedures or reward allocations in organizations.

Review 2: **Equity Theory**

The basic components of equity theory are inputs, outcomes, and referents. After an internal comparison in which employees compare their outcomes with their inputs, they then make an external comparison in which they compare their O/I ratio with the O/I ratio of a referent, a person who works in a similar job or is otherwise similar. When their O/I ratio is equal to the referent's O/I ratio, employees perceive that they are being treated fairly. But when their O/I ratio is different from their referent's O/I ratio, they perceive that they have been treated inequitably or unfairly. There are two kinds of inequity, underreward and overreward. Underreward, which occurs when a referent's O/I ratio is better than the employee's O/I ratio, leads to anger or frustration. Overreward, which occurs when a referent's O/I ratio is worse than the employee's O/I ratio, can lead to guilt, but only when the level of overreward is extreme. When employees perceive that they

distributive justice the perceived degree to which outcomes and rewards are fairly distributed or allocated

procedural justice the perceived fairness of the process used to make reward allocation decisions have been treated inequitably (underrewarded), they may try to restore equity by reducing inputs, increasing outcomes, rationalizing inputs or outcomes, changing the referent, or simply leaving. Managers can use equity theory to motivate workers by looking for and correcting major inequities, reducing employees' inputs, and emphasizing procedural as well as distributive justice. Most importantly, they should treat workers in an interpersonally sensitive manner and work to make sure that organizational procedures are fair and are applied in a consistent manner.

3 Expectancy Theory

How attractive do you find each of the following rewards? A company concierge service that will pick up your car from the mechanic and send someone to be at your house when the cable guy or repair person shows up. A "7 to 7" travel policy stipulating that no one has to leave home for business travel before 7 AM on Mondays and that everyone should be home from business travel by 7 PM on Fridays. The opportunity to telecommute so that you can feed your kids breakfast, pick them up after school, and tuck them into bed at night.[64]

If you have kids, you might love the chance to telecommute; but if you don't, you may not be interested. If you don't travel much on business, you won't be interested in the "7 to 7" travel policy; but if you do, you'll probably love it. One of the hardest things about motivating people is that rewards that are attractive to some employees are unattractive to others. **Expectancy theory** says that people will be motivated to the extent to which they believe that their efforts will lead to good performance, that good performance will be rewarded, and that they will be offered attractive rewards.[65]

*Let's learn more about expectancy theory by examining **3.1 the components of expectancy theory** and **3.2 how to use expectancy theory as a motivational tool**.*

3.1 Components of Expectancy Theory

Expectancy theory holds that people make conscious choices about their motivation. The three factors that affect those choices are valence, expectancy, and instrumentality.

Valence is simply the attractiveness or desirability of various rewards or outcomes. Expectancy theory recognizes that the same reward or outcome, say, a promotion, will be highly attractive to some people, will be highly disliked by others, and will not make much difference one way or the other to still others. Accordingly, when people are deciding how much effort to put forth, expectancy theory says that they will consider the valence of all possible rewards and outcomes that they can receive from their jobs. The greater the sum of those valences, each of which can be positive, negative, or neutral, the more effort people will choose to put forth on the job.

Expectancy is the perceived relationship between effort and performance. When expectancies are strong, employees believe that their hard work and efforts will result in good performance, so they work harder. By contrast, when expectancies are weak, employees figure that no matter what they do or how hard they work, they won't be able to perform their jobs successfully, so they don't work as hard.

Instrumentality is the perceived relationship between performance and rewards. When instrumentality is strong, employees believe that improved performance will lead to better and more rewards, so they choose to work harder. When instrumentality is weak, employees don't believe that better performance will result in more or better rewards, so they choose not to work as hard.

expectancy theory the theory that people will be motivated to the extent to which they believe that their efforts will lead to good performance, that good performance will be rewarded, and that they will be offered attractive rewards

valence the attractiveness or desirability of a reward or outcome

expectancy the perceived relationship between effort and performance

instrumentality the perceived relationship between performance and rewards

Expectancy theory holds that for people to be highly motivated, all three variables—valence, expectancy, and instrumentality—must be high. Thus, expectancy theory can be represented by the following simple equation:

$$\text{Motivation} = \text{Valence} \times \text{Expectancy} \times \text{Instrumentality}$$

If any one of these variables (valence, expectancy, or instrumentality) declines, overall motivation will decline, too.

Exhibit 13.10 incorporates the expectancy theory variables into our motivation model. Valence and instrumentality combine to affect employees' willingness to put forth effort (that is, the degree to which they are energized to take action), while expectancy transforms intended effort ("I'm really going to work hard in this job") into actual effort. If you're offered rewards that you desire and you believe that you will in fact receive these rewards for good performance, you're highly likely to be energized to take action. However, you're not likely to actually exert effort unless you also believe that you can do the job (that is, that your efforts will lead to successful performance).

KIMBERLY-CLARK, known for its brand name products such as Kleenex, Scott, Huggies, and Cottonelle, revamped its performance management system to integrate valence, expectancy, and instrumentality into its employee motivation program. First, Kimberly-Clark offers a wide variety of rewards, including international assignments, employee recognition programs, incentives, bonuses, and stock options, so that all of its employees can receive highly valent rewards that they desire. The company manages expectancies through rigorous selection, orientation, and placement

Exhibit 13.10

Adding Expectancy Theory to the Model

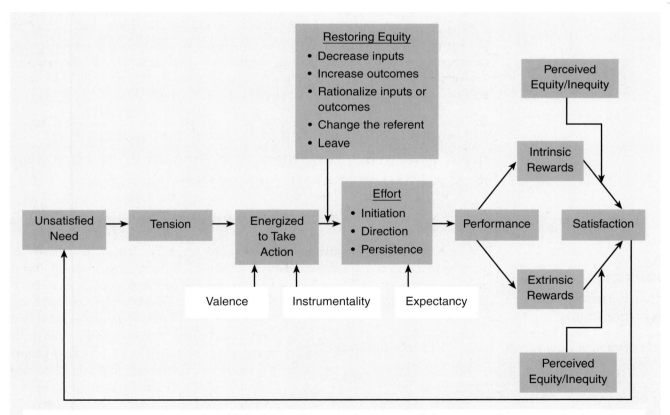

If rewards are attractive (valence) and linked to performance (instrumentality), then people are energized to take action. In other words, good performance gets them rewards that they want. Intended effort (i.e., energized to take action) turns into actual effort when people believe that their hard work and efforts will result in good performance. After all, why work hard if that hard work is wasted?

for new employees and through training and development opportunities for continuing employees. Finally, Kimberly-Clark manages instrumentality by linking rewards to the specific results, behaviors, and values it wants to reward. One of the primary goals of the new system was to treat the determination of compensation as "fully integrated business process, as opposed to an HR process," notes Liz Gottung, Kimberly-Clark's chief human resources officer. Employees know that base pay as well as consideration for stock options and variable pay are tied to performance, which is tied to the objectives, which are tied to the business plan.[66]

3.2 Motivating with Expectancy Theory

What practical steps can managers take to use expectancy theory to motivate employees? First, as Exhibit 13.11 shows, they can *systematically gather information to find out what employees want from their jobs*. In addition to individual managers directly asking employees what they want from their jobs (see Subsection 1.4 "Motivating with the Basics"), companies need to survey their employees regularly to determine their wants, needs, and dissatisfactions. Since people consider the valence of all the possible rewards and outcomes that they can receive from their jobs, regular identification of wants, needs, and dissatisfactions gives companies the chance to turn negatively valent rewards and outcomes into positively valent rewards and outcomes, thus raising overall motivation and effort. Mark Peterman, vice president of client solutions at *MARITZ INCENTIVES*, says that individual employees are motivated in vastly different ways; for example, he says, "For some, being honored in front of one's peers is a great award, but for others, the thought of being put on display in front of peers embarrasses them." And companies have a long way to go to ensure their employees feel valued, Peterman says. A Maritz survey found that only 27 percent of employees who want to be recognized by nonmonetary incentives are recognized that way.[67] Such findings suggest that employers should routinely survey employees to identify not only the range of rewards that are valued by most employees but also understand preferences of specific employees.

"WHAT'S NEW" COMPANY

> For some, being honored in front of one's peers is a great award, but for others, the thought of being put on display in front of peers embarrasses them.

MARK PETERMAN, VICE PRESIDENT OF CLIENT SOLUTIONS, MARITZ INCENTIVES

Second, managers can *take specific steps to link rewards to individual performance in a way that is clear and understandable to employees*. Unfortunately, most employees are extremely dissatisfied with the link between pay and performance in their organizations. In one study, based on a representative sample, 80 percent of the employees surveyed wanted to be paid according to a different kind of pay system! Moreover, only 32 percent of employees were satisfied with how their annual pay raises were determined, and only 22 percent were happy with the way the starting salaries for their jobs were determined.[68] One way to make sure that employees see the connection between pay and performance (see Chapter 11 for a discussion of compensation strategies) is for managers to publicize the way in which pay decisions

Exhibit 13.11

Motivating with Expectancy Theory

- Systematically gather information to find out what employees want from their jobs.
- Take specific steps to link rewards to individual performance in a way that is clear and understandable to employees.
- Empower employees to make decisions if management really wants them to believe that their hard work and effort will lead to good performance.

are made. This is especially important given that only 41 percent of employees know how their pay increases are determined.[69] Kerry Solomon, an HR executive, faced this challenge when she joined SecureWorks, an Atlanta-based Internet security services provider. She gathered accurate, comparable salary information and launched an aggressive educational enlightenment program to show employees how pay rates and increases are determined and how their pay compares with pay at other comparable firms. She believes that such information sharing is important because it allows employees to gain an accurate sense of where they stand—and to appreciate their employer's generosity.[70] Employees at Nucor Corporation know exactly how bonuses are computed and are able to calculate their bonus accurately, to the nearest dollar.

Finally, managers should *empower employees to make decisions if management really wants them to believe that their hard work and effort will lead to good performance*. If valent rewards are linked to good performance, people should be energized to take action. However, this works only if they also believe that their efforts will lead to good performance. One of the ways that managers destroy the expectancy that hard work and effort will lead to good performance is by restricting what employees can do or by ignoring employees' ideas. In Chapter 9, you learned that *empowerment* is a feeling of intrinsic motivation, in which workers perceive their work to have meaning and perceive themselves to be competent, to have an impact, and to be capable of self-determination.[71] So, if managers want workers to have strong expectancies, they should empower them to make decisions. Doing so will motivate employees to take active rather than passive roles in their work.

Review 3: Expectancy Theory

Expectancy theory holds that three factors affect the conscious choices people make about their motivation: valence, expectancy, and instrumentality. Valence is simply the attractiveness or desirability of various rewards or outcomes. Expectancy is the perceived relationship between effort and performance. Instrumentality is the perceived relationship between performance and rewards. Expectancy theory holds that for people to be highly motivated, all three factors must be high. If any one of these factors declines, overall motivation will decline, too. Managers can use expectancy theory to motivate workers by systematically gathering information to find out what employees want from their jobs, by linking rewards to individual performance in a way that is clear and understandable to employees, and by empowering employees to make decisions, which will increase their expectancies that hard work and effort will lead to good performance.

HOW REWARDS AND GOALS AFFECT MOTIVATION

When used properly, rewards motivate and energize employees. But when used incorrectly, they can demotivate, baffle, and even anger them. For example, consider the dot-com company that gave *every* employee a plaque for "outstanding performance." Then it compounded that mistake (how can every employee be "outstanding?") by firing one of those "outstanding" employees, James Finkel, two weeks after awarding him his plaque. Says Finkel, "My reward for outstanding performance was getting canned. I left the plaque sitting on my desk."[72]

© IMAGE SOURCE PINK/JUPITER IMAGES

Goals are also supposed to motivate employees. But leaders who focus blindly on meeting goals at all costs often find that they destroy motivation. For instance, a president of a technology company calls his vice president of sales *daily* and asks, "Did you make your numbers *today*?" Consultant Richard Hapburg, who works with the vice president who receives these daily calls, says that the VP should be focusing on long-term solutions that increase sales, but "he's under enormous pressure to meet certain sales and profit targets on a *daily basis* now." The clear danger to using goals in this way, says Hapburg, is "that it's hard to capture employees' hearts, and best efforts, with numbers alone."[73]

Sometimes rewards aren't as motivating as managers hope, and in fact, can work opposite to what managers intend.

After reading the next three sections, you should be able to

> 4 *explain how reinforcement theory works and how it can be used to motivate.*
>
> 5 *describe the components of goal-setting theory and how managers can use them to motivate workers.*
>
> 6 *discuss how the entire motivation model can be used to motivate workers.*

4 Reinforcement Theory

Reinforcement theory says that behavior is a function of its consequences, that behaviors followed by positive consequences (that is, reinforced) will occur more frequently, and that behaviors followed by negative consequences, or not followed by positive consequences, will occur less frequently.[74] Therefore, to improve its safety record, Monsanto decided to reinforce safe behaviors. Chuck Davis, a safety consultant, says, "It's better to recognize a guy for success than beat him up for failure. It's amazing how little reward a guy needs so he doesn't stick his arm in a machine."[75] More specifically, **reinforcement** is the process of changing behavior by changing the consequences that follow behavior.[76]

Reinforcement has two parts: reinforcement contingencies and schedules of reinforcement. **Reinforcement contingencies** are the cause-and-effect relationships between the performance of specific behaviors and specific consequences. For example, if you get docked an hour's pay for being late to work, then a reinforcement contingency exists between a behavior, being late to work, and a consequence, losing an hour's pay. A **schedule of reinforcement** is the set of rules regarding reinforcement contingencies, such as which behaviors will be reinforced, which consequences will follow those behaviors, and the schedule by which those consequences will be delivered.[77]

Exhibit 13.12 incorporates reinforcement contingencies and reinforcement schedules into our motivation model. First, notice that extrinsic rewards and the schedules of reinforcement used to deliver them are the primary method for creating reinforcement contingencies in organizations. In turn, those reinforcement contingencies directly affect valences (the attractiveness of rewards), instrumentality (the perceived link between rewards and performance), and effort (how hard employees will work).

reinforcement theory the theory that behavior is a function of its consequences, that behaviors followed by positive consequences will occur more frequently, and that behaviors followed by negative consequences, or not followed by positive consequences, will occur less frequently

reinforcement the process of changing behavior by changing the consequences that follow behavior

reinforcement contingencies cause-and-effect relationships between the performance of specific behaviors and specific consequences

schedule of reinforcement rules that specify which behaviors will be reinforced, which consequences will follow those behaviors, and the schedule by which those consequences will be delivered

Let's learn more about reinforcement theory by examining **4.1 the components of reinforcement theory, 4.2 the different schedules for delivering reinforcement, and 4.3 how to motivate with reinforcement theory**.

4.1 Components of Reinforcement Theory

As just described, *reinforcement contingencies* are the cause-and-effect relationships between the performance of specific behaviors and specific consequences. There are four kinds of reinforcement contingencies: positive reinforcement, negative reinforcement, punishment, and extinction.

Positive reinforcement strengthens behavior (that is, increases its frequency) by following behaviors with desirable consequences. Harry Kraemer, the CEO of

positive reinforcement reinforcement that strengthens behavior by following behaviors with desirable consequences

Exhibit 13.12

Adding Reinforcement Theory to the Model

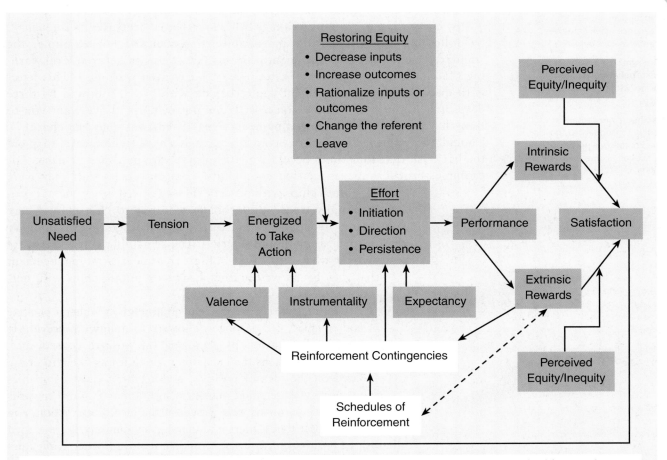

Extrinsic rewards and the schedules of reinforcement used to deliver them are the primary method for creating reinforcement contingencies in organizations. In turn, those reinforcement contingencies directly affect valences (the attractiveness of rewards), instrumentality (the perceived link between rewards and performance), and effort (how hard employees will work).

"What's New" Company

BAXTER INTERNATIONAL, a pharmaceutical firm, included this story about his four-year-old son in Baxter's company newsletter to illustrate the power of incentives and positive reinforcement:

> He had got a hold of his sister's bead set and he somehow got one of them stuck up his nose. He tried to get it out, and the thing kept getting higher up his nose. I got him in the car to take him to the emergency room, and right as I was getting ready to park I said to him, "Andrew, Daddy loves you a lot. We've got to get this thing out. If we go to the emergency room, this is going to cost Dad about $150. But here's the deal: If you can figure out a way to blow that out of your nose [the goal], first, we'll go to Blockbuster and you can buy any tape you want. And second, we'll go to Bakers Square, and you and I will split a French silk pie [the positive rewards]." Well, he blew the thing out, and it almost cracked my windshield.[78]

negative reinforcement reinforcement that strengthens behavior by withholding an unpleasant consequence when employees perform a specific behavior

punishment reinforcement that weakens behavior by following behaviors with undesirable consequences

extinction reinforcement in which a positive consequence is no longer allowed to follow a previously reinforced behavior, thus weakening the behavior

Negative reinforcement strengthens behavior by withholding an unpleasant consequence when employees perform a specific behavior. Negative reinforcement is also called *avoidance learning* because workers perform a behavior to *avoid* a negative consequence. For example, at the Florist Network, a small business in Buffalo, New York, company management instituted a policy of requiring good attendance for employees to receive their annual bonuses. Employee attendance has improved significantly now that excessive absenteeism can result in the loss of $1,500 or more.[79]

By contrast, **punishment** weakens behavior (that is, decreases its frequency) by following behaviors with undesirable consequences. For example, the standard disciplinary or punishment process in most companies is an oral warning ("Don't ever do that again"), followed by a written warning ("This letter is to discuss the serious problem you're having with . . ."), followed by three days off without pay ("While you're at home not being paid, we want you to think hard about . . ."), followed by being fired ("That was your last chance"). Though punishment can weaken behavior, managers have to be careful to avoid the backlash that sometimes occurs when employees are punished at work. For example, Frito-Lay began getting complaints from customers that they were finding potato chips with obscene messages written on them. Frito-Lay eventually traced the problem to a potato chip plant where supervisors had fired 58 out of the 210 workers for disciplinary reasons over a nine-month period. The remaining employees were so angry over what they saw as unfair treatment from management that they began writing the phrases on potato chips with felt-tipped pens.[80]

Extinction is a reinforcement strategy in which a positive consequence is no longer allowed to follow a previously reinforced behavior. By removing the positive consequence, extinction weakens the behavior, making it less likely to occur. Based on the idea of positive reinforcement, most companies give company leaders and managers substantial financial rewards when the company performs well. Based on the idea of extinction, you would then expect that leaders and managers would not be rewarded (that is, the positive consequence would be removed) when companies perform poorly. If companies really want pay to reinforce the right kinds of behaviors, then rewards have to be removed when company management doesn't produce successful performance. For example, with a $1 billion loss, sales down 28 percent, and the stock price down

© FOOD PIX/JUPITER IMAGES

35 percent, AGILENT's board of directors cut CEO Ned Barnholt's base pay by 10 percent and didn't award him a cash or stock bonus. Says Barnholt, "I don't expect anything different. If the company doesn't perform, I shouldn't be getting any rewards."[81] By contrast, even though the WALT DISNEY COMPANY's income dropped from $1.9 billion to $1.4 billion in four years, Disney rewarded then-CEO Michael Eisner with a large increase in salary, options for 2 million shares of stock worth $37.7 million, a $5 million restricted stock bonus, and an $11.5 million cash bonus.[82]

4.2 Schedules for Delivering Reinforcement

As mentioned earlier, a *schedule of reinforcement* is the set of rules regarding reinforcement contingencies, such as which behaviors will be reinforced, which consequences will follow those behaviors, and the schedule by which those consequences will be delivered. There are two categories of reinforcement schedules: continuous and intermittent.

With **continuous reinforcement schedules**, a consequence follows every instance of a behavior. For example, employees working on a piece-rate pay system earn money (consequence) for every part they manufacture (behavior). The more they produce, the more they earn. By contrast, with **intermittent reinforcement schedules**, consequences are delivered after a specified or average time has elapsed or after a specified or average number of behaviors has occurred. As Exhibit 13.13 shows, there are four types of intermittent reinforcement schedules. Two of these are based on time and are called *interval reinforcement schedules*, while the other two, known as *ratio schedules*, are based on behaviors.

With **fixed interval reinforcement schedules**, consequences follow a behavior only after a fixed time has elapsed. For example, most people receive their paychecks on a fixed interval schedule (for example, once or twice per month). As long as they work (behavior) during a specified pay period (interval), they get a paycheck (consequence). With **variable interval reinforcement schedules**, consequences follow a behavior after different times, some shorter and some longer, that vary around a specified average time. On a 90-day variable interval reinforcement schedule, you might receive a bonus after 80 days or perhaps after 100 days, but the average interval between performing your job well (behavior) and receiving your bonus (consequence) would be 90 days.

With **fixed ratio reinforcement schedules**, consequences are delivered following a specific number of behaviors. For example, a car salesperson might receive a $1,000 bonus after every 10 sales. Therefore, a salesperson with only 9 sales would not receive the bonus until he or she finally sold a 10th car.

With **variable ratio reinforcement schedules**, consequences are delivered following a different number of behaviors, sometimes more and sometimes less, that vary around a specified average number of behaviors. With a 10-car variable ratio

continuous reinforcement schedule a schedule that requires a consequence to be administered following every instance of a behavior

intermittent reinforcement schedule a schedule in which consequences are delivered after a specified or average time has elapsed or after a specified or average number of behaviors has occurred

fixed interval reinforcement schedule an intermittent schedule in which consequences follow a behavior only after a fixed time has elapsed

variable interval reinforcement schedule an intermittent schedule in which the time between a behavior and the following consequences varies around a specified average

fixed ratio reinforcement schedule an intermittent schedule in which consequences are delivered following a specific number of behaviors

variable ratio reinforcement schedule an intermittent schedule in which consequences are delivered following a different number of behaviors, sometimes more and sometimes less, that vary around a specified average number of behaviors

Exhibit 13.13

Intermittent Reinforcement Schedules

INTERMITTENT REINFORCEMENT SCHEDULES		
	FIXED	**VARIABLE**
INTERVAL (TIME)	Consequences follow behavior after a fixed time has elapsed.	Consequences follow behavior after different times, some shorter and some longer, that vary around a specific average time.
RATIO (BEHAVIOR)	Consequences follow a specific number of behaviors.	Consequences follow a different number of behaviors, sometimes more and sometimes less, that vary around a specified average number of behaviors.

reinforcement schedule, a salesperson might receive the bonus after 7 car sales, or after 12, 11, or 9 sales, but the average number of cars sold before receiving the bonus would be 10 cars.

Students often have trouble envisioning how these schedules can actually be used in work settings, so a couple of examples will help. In a study designed to increase employee attendance, employees who came to work participated in an innovative variable ratio schedule in which they drew a card from a deck of playing cards every day they came to work. At the end of each week, the employee with the best poker hand from those cards received a $20 bonus.[83] In another variable reinforcement system, ELECTRIC BOAT, which builds nuclear submarines, uses a lottery that gives workers with good attendance a chance to win sizable rewards. Eligibility for the various rewards depends on the level of attendance. For example, 933 workers with two years of perfect attendance were placed in a lottery in which 20 of them would win $2,500. Likewise, 1,400 workers with a year of perfect attendance were placed in a lottery where 75 would win $1,000, 50 would win $500, 25 would win prime parking spaces, and all would win a $25 gift certificate for the company store. Greg Angelini, who won a $1,000 prize, says, "I'm not a gambler, but it sure was nice to get that check right before Christmas. And it was just as nice that the powers that be noticed that I've had perfect attendance."[84] Electric Boat's lottery system is so rewarding that on average an amazing 41 percent of its workers have perfect attendance.

Which reinforcement schedules work best? In the past, the standard advice was to use continuous reinforcement when employees were learning new behaviors because reinforcement after each success leads to faster learning. Likewise, the standard advice was to use intermittent reinforcement schedules to maintain behavior after it is learned because intermittent rewards are supposed to make behavior much less subject to extinction.[85] Research shows, however, that except for interval-based systems, which usually produce weak results, the effectiveness of continuous reinforcement, fixed ratio, and variable ratio schedules differs very little.[86] In organizational settings, all three produce consistently large increases over noncontingent reward schedules. So managers should choose whichever of these three is easiest to use in their companies.

4.3 Motivating with Reinforcement Theory

What practical steps can managers take to use reinforcement theory to motivate employees? University of Nebraska business professor Fred Luthans, who has been studying the effects of reinforcement theory in organizations for more than a quarter of a century, says that there are five steps to motivating workers with reinforcement theory: *identify*, *measure*, *analyze*, *intervene*, and *evaluate* critical performance-related behaviors.[87]

Identify means identifying critical, observable, performance-related behaviors. These are the behaviors that are most important to successful job performance. In addition, they must also be easily observed so that they can be accurately measured. *Measure* means measuring the baseline frequencies of these behaviors. In other words, find out how often workers perform them. *Analyze* means analyzing the causes and consequences of these behaviors. Analyzing the causes helps managers create the conditions that produce these critical behaviors, and analyzing the consequences helps them determine if these behaviors produce the results that they want. *Intervene* means changing the organization by using positive and negative reinforcement to increase the frequency of these critical behaviors. *Evaluate* means evaluating the extent to which the intervention actually changed workers' behavior. This is done by comparing behavior after the intervention to the original baseline of behavior before the intervention. For more on the effectiveness of reinforcement theory, see the "What Really Works?" feature in this chapter.

In addition to these five steps, Exhibit 13.14 lists three other things that managers should remember when motivating with reinforcement theory. *Don't reinforce the wrong behaviors*. Although reinforcement theory sounds simple, it's actually very difficult to put into practice. One of the most common mistakes is accidentally reinforcing the wrong behaviors. In fact, sometimes managers reinforce behaviors that they don't want! If you want to become a merit-based company, stop rewarding behavior that is not exceptional, says Dave Anderson, a management consultant. According to him, "the average car salesperson in the United States sells 10 cars per month, but many pay plans begin to pay bonuses at 7, 8, 9, or 10 cars. Under a typical plan, an employee who sells 8 cars gets a $200 bonus, another $250 for selling 2 additional cars, and $300 for selling 2 more cars. The total bonus for selling 12 cars in a month is $750." Anderson notes, "Based on national averages, such a pay plan financially rewards average and below-average results." Many of his clients have revised their system and only pay an $800 bonus to an employee *after* he or she has sold 12 cars, thus ending bonus payments for employees who sell fewer than the target amount of cars.[88] In this system, you pay more for better performance but don't fall into the trap of rewarding and endorsing the wrong things, rewarding below average performance.

Managers should also *correctly administer punishment at the appropriate time*. Many managers believe that punishment can change workers' behavior and help them improve their job performance. Furthermore, managers believe that fairly punishing workers also lets other workers know what is or isn't acceptable.[89] A danger of using punishment is that it can produce a backlash against managers and companies, but if administered properly, punishment can weaken the frequency of undesirable behaviors without creating a backlash.[90] To be effective, the punishment must be strong enough to stop the undesired behavior and must be administered objectively (same rules applied to everyone), impersonally (without emotion or anger), consistently and contingently (each time improper behavior occurs), and quickly (as soon as possible following the undesirable behavior). In addition, managers should clearly explain what the appropriate behavior is and why the employee is being punished. Employees typically respond well when punishment is administered this way.[91]

Finally, managers should *choose the simplest and most effective schedule of reinforcement*. When choosing a schedule of reinforcement, managers need to balance effectiveness against simplicity. In fact, the more complex the schedule of reinforcement, the more likely it is to be misunderstood and resisted by managers and employees. For example, a forestry and logging company experimented with a unique variable ratio schedule. When tree-planters finished planting a bag of seedlings (about 1,000 seedlings per bag), they got to flip a coin. If they called the coin flip correctly (heads or tails), they were paid $4, double the regular rate of $2 per bag. If they called the coin flip incorrectly, they got nothing. The company began having problems when several workers and a manager, who was a part-time minister, claimed that the coin flip was a form of gambling. Then, another worker found that the company was taking out too much money for taxes from workers' paychecks. Since the workers didn't really understand

Exhibit 13.14

Motivating with Reinforcement Theory

- Identify, measure, analyze, intervene, and evaluate critical performance-related behaviors.
- Don't reinforce the wrong behaviors.
- Correctly administer punishment at the appropriate time.
- Choose the simplest and most effective schedule of reinforcement.

FINANCIAL, NONFINANCIAL, AND SOCIAL REWARDS

what *really* works.

Throughout this chapter, we have been making the point that there is more to motivating people than money. But we haven't yet examined how well financial (money or prizes), nonfinancial (performance feedback), and social (recognition and attention) rewards motivate workers by themselves or in combination. However, the results of two meta-analyses, one with 19 studies based on more than 2,800 people (study 1) and another based on 72 studies and 13,301 people (study 2), clearly indicate that rewarding and reinforcing employees greatly improve motivation and performance, especially when combined.

FINANCIAL REWARDS

On average, there is a 68 percent chance that employees whose behavior is reinforced with financial rewards will outperform employees whose behavior is not reinforced. This increases to 84 percent in manufacturing organizations but drops to 61 percent in service organizations.

NONFINANCIAL REWARDS

On average, there is a 58 percent chance that employees whose behavior is reinforced with nonfinancial rewards will outperform employees whose behavior is not reinforced. This increases to 87 percent in manufacturing organizations but drops to 54 percent in service organizations.

SOCIAL REWARDS

On average, there is a 63 percent chance that employees whose behavior is reinforced with social rewards will outperform employees whose behavior is not reinforced.

FINANCIAL AND NONFINANCIAL REWARDS

On average, there is a 62 percent chance that employees whose behavior is reinforced with a combination of financial and nonfinancial rewards will outperform employees whose behavior is not reinforced.

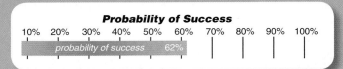

FINANCIAL AND SOCIAL REWARDS

On average, there is only a 52 percent chance that employees whose behavior is reinforced with a combination of financial and social rewards will outperform employees whose behavior is not reinforced.

NONFINANCIAL AND SOCIAL REWARDS

On average, there is a 61 percent chance that employees whose behavior is reinforced with a combination of nonfinancial and social rewards will outperform employees whose behavior is not reinforced.

FINANCIAL, NONFINANCIAL, AND SOCIAL REWARDS

On average, there is a 90 percent chance that employees whose behavior is reinforced with a combination of financial, nonfinancial, and social rewards will outperform employees whose behavior is not reinforced.[92]

the reinforcement schedule, they blamed the payment plan associated with it and accused the company of trying to cheat them out of their money. After all of these problems, the researchers who implemented the variable ratio schedule concluded that "the results of this study may not be so much an indication of the relative effectiveness of different schedules of reinforcement as they are an indication of the types of problems that one encounters when applying these concepts in an industrial setting."[93] In short, choose the simplest, most effective schedule of reinforcement. Since continuous reinforcement, fixed ratio, and variable ratio schedules are about equally effective, continuous reinforcement schedules may be the best choice in many instances by virtue of their simplicity.

Review 4: *Reinforcement Theory*

Reinforcement theory says that behavior is a function of its consequences. Reinforcement has two parts: reinforcement contingencies and schedules of reinforcement. The four kinds of reinforcement contingencies are positive reinforcement and negative reinforcement, which strengthen behavior, and punishment and extinction, which weaken behavior. There are two kinds of reinforcement schedules, continuous and intermittent; intermittent schedules, in turn, can be divided into fixed and variable interval schedules and fixed and variable ratio schedules. Managers can use reinforcement theory to motivate workers by following five steps (identify, measure, analyze, intervene, and evaluate critical performance-related behaviors); not reinforcing the wrong behaviors; correctly administering punishment at the appropriate time; and choosing a reinforcement schedule, such as continuous reinforcement, that balances simplicity and effectiveness.

5 Goal-Setting Theory

The basic model of motivation with which we began this chapter showed that individuals feel tension after becoming aware of an unfulfilled need. Once they experience tension, they search for and select courses of action that they believe will eliminate this tension. In other words, they direct their behavior toward something. This something is a goal. A **goal** is a target, objective, or result that someone tries to accomplish. For example, one of the goals of discount airline *JetBlue* is that all the baggage on a plane be delivered to the baggage pickup area no later than 20 minutes after the plane reaches the gate. Why? Because, as JetBlue CEO Dave Barger explains, "The 45 minutes you wait for your bags is your last impression," and a strongly negative one at that.[94] JetBlue also has specific goals for completion rate (the percentage of flights that aren't canceled) and on-time arrivals. Last year, JetBlue was first in the industry in completion rate and second in on-time arrivals.

"What's New" Company

Goal-setting theory *says that people will be motivated to the extent to which they accept specific, challenging goals and receive feedback that indicates their progress toward goal achievement. Let's learn more about goal setting by examining **5.1 the components of goal-setting theory** and **5.2 how to motivate with goal-setting theory**.*

goal a target, objective, or result that someone tries to accomplish

goal-setting theory the theory that people will be motivated to the extent to which they accept specific, challenging goals and receive feedback that indicates their progress toward goal achievement

5.1 Components of Goal-Setting Theory

The basic components of goal-setting theory are goal specificity, goal difficulty, goal acceptance, and performance feedback.[95] **Goal specificity** is the extent to which goals are detailed, exact, and unambiguous. Specific goals, such as "I'm going to have a 3.0 average this semester," are more motivating than general goals, such as "I'm going to get better grades this semester."

Goal difficulty is the extent to which a goal is hard or challenging to accomplish. Difficult goals, such as "I'm going to have a 3.5 average and make the Dean's List this semester," are more motivating than easy goals, such as "I'm going to have a 2.0 average this semester."

Goal acceptance, which is similar to the idea of goal commitment discussed in Chapter 5, is the extent to which people consciously understand and agree to goals. Accepted goals, such as "I really want to get a 3.5 average this semester to show my parents how much I've improved," are more motivating than unaccepted goals, such as "My parents really want me to get a 3.5 average this semester, but there's so much more I'd rather do on campus than study!"

Performance feedback is information about the quality or quantity of past performance and indicates whether progress is being made toward the accomplishment of a goal. Performance feedback, such as "My prof said I need a 92 on the final to get an 'A' in that class," is more motivating than no feedback, "I have no idea what my grade is in that class." In short, goal-setting theory says that people will be motivated to the extent to which they accept specific, challenging goals and receive feedback that indicates their progress toward goal achievement.

How does goal setting work? To start, challenging goals focus employees' attention (that is, direction of effort) on the critical aspects of their jobs and away from unimportant areas. Goals also energize behavior. When faced with unaccomplished goals, employees typically develop plans and strategies to reach those goals. Goals also create tension between the goal, which is the desired future state of affairs, and where the employee or company is now, meaning the current state of affairs. This tension can be satisfied only by achieving or abandoning the goal. Finally, goals influence persistence. Since goals only "go away" when they are accomplished, employees are more likely to persist in their efforts in the presence of goals. Exhibit 13.15 incorporates goals into the motivation model by showing how goals directly affect tension, effort, and the extent to which employees are energized to take action.

5.2 Motivating with Goal-Setting Theory

What practical steps can managers take to use goal-setting theory to motivate employees? Exhibit 13.16 lists three suggestions beginning with *assign specific, challenging goals*. One of the simplest, most effective ways to motivate workers is to give them specific, challenging goals.

For example, although CDW (Computer Discount Warehouse) offers fantastic benefits and rewards, senior publicist Gary Ross says, "It's not a cushy place to work." According to vice president Art Friedson, CDW sets company-wide "Big Hairy Aggressive Goals," such as "A Million for a Billion," in which everyone in the company would split $1 million in bonuses (about $500 per employee at the time) when CDW booked $1 billion in annual sales.[96] With that accomplished, the next BHAG was $3 billion in annual sales with a payout of $5 million in bonuses (about $2,500 per employee at the time). And with that accomplished, the BHAG is now $10 billion in annual sales (sales were $6.8 billion last year). For more information on assigning specific, challenging goals, see the discussion in Chapter 5 on S.M.A.R.T. goals.

goal specificity the extent to which goals are detailed, exact, and unambiguous

goal difficulty the extent to which a goal is hard or challenging to accomplish

goal acceptance the extent to which people consciously understand and agree to goals

performance feedback information about the quality or quantity of past performance that indicates whether progress is being made toward the accomplishment of a goal

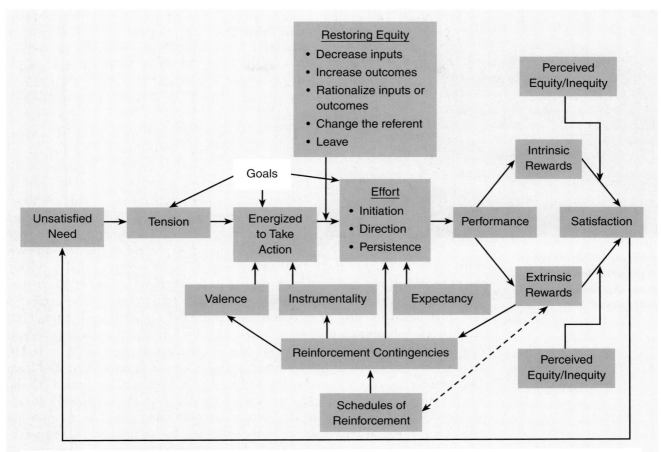

Goals create tension between the goal, which is the desired future state of affairs, and where the employee or company is now, meaning the current state of affairs. This tension can be satisfied only by achieving or abandoning the goal. Goals also energize behavior. When faced with unaccomplished goals, employees typically develop plans and strategies to reach those goals. Finally, goals influence persistence.

Second, managers should *make sure workers truly accept organizational goals*. Specific, challenging goals won't motivate workers unless they really accept, understand, and agree to the organization's goals. For this to occur, people must see the goals as fair and reasonable. Plus, they must trust management and believe that managers are using goals to clarify what is expected from them rather than to exploit or threaten them ("If you don't achieve these goals . . . "). Participative goal setting, in which managers and employees generate goals together, can help increase trust and understanding and thus acceptance of goals. Furthermore, providing workers with training can help increase goal acceptance, particularly when workers don't believe they are capable of reaching the organization's goals.[97]

Finally, managers should *provide frequent, specific, performance-related feedback*. Once employees have accepted specific, challenging goals, they should receive frequent performance-related feedback so that they can track their progress toward goal completion. Feedback leads to stronger motivation and effort in three ways.[98] Receiving specific feedback that indicates how well they're performing can encourage employees who don't have specific,

Exhibit 13.15
Adding Goal-Setting Theory to the Model

Exhibit 13.16
Motivating with Goal-Setting Theory

- Assign specific, challenging goals.
- Make sure workers truly accept organizational goals.
- Provide frequent, specific, performance-related feedback.

What increased the safe behavior on the oil rig was setting goals and tracking progress toward reaching them.

© STOCK CONNECTION/JUPITER IMAGES

challenging goals to set goals to improve their performance. Once people meet goals, performance feedback often encourages them to set higher, more difficult goals. And feedback lets people know whether they need to increase their efforts or change strategies in order to accomplish their goals.

For example, in an effort to improve worker safety on offshore oil-drilling platforms, an oil company generated a list of dangerous work behaviors by analyzing previous accident reports, reviewing industry safety manuals, and interviewing and observing workers. Following detailed safety training, each work crew set goals to engage in safe behaviors 100 percent of the time on each shift. To help workers track their improvement, management posted a weekly safety record in the galley of each rig, where workers would see it when they gathered for meals and coffee breaks. Previously, employees were engaging in safe work behaviors just 76 percent of the time. After a year of goal setting (100 percent safe behavior on each shift) and weekly performance feedback at two oil rigs, however, workers behaved safely over 90 percent of the time. As a result, accident rates dropped from 21.1 percent to 6.1 percent at the first rig and from 14.2 percent to 12.1 percent at the second rig. By contrast, at a third oil rig, where training, goal setting, and feedback were not used, the total accident rate *increased* from 11.6 percent to 20.3 percent over the same time.[99] So, to motivate employees with goal-setting theory, make sure they receive frequent performance-related feedback so that they can track their progress toward goal completion.

Review 5: Goal-Setting Theory

A goal is a target, objective, or result that someone tries to accomplish. Goal-setting theory says that people will be motivated to the extent to which they accept specific, challenging goals and receive feedback that indicates their progress toward goal achievement. The basic components of goal-setting theory are goal specificity, goal difficulty, goal acceptance, and performance feedback. Goal specificity is the extent to which goals are detailed, exact, and unambiguous. Goal difficulty is the extent to which a goal is hard or challenging to accomplish. Goal acceptance is the extent to which people consciously understand and agree to goals. Performance feedback is information about the quality or quantity of past performance and indicates whether progress is being made toward the accomplishment of a goal. Managers can use goal-setting theory to motivate workers by assigning specific, challenging goals, making sure workers truly accept organizational goals, and providing frequent, specific, performance-related feedback.

6 Motivating with the Integrated Model

We began this chapter by defining motivation as the set of forces that initiates, directs, and makes people persist in their efforts to accomplish a goal. We also asked the basic question that managers ask when they try to figure out how to

MOTIVATING WITH	MANAGERS SHOULD...
THE BASICS	• Ask people what their needs are. • Satisfy lower-order needs first. • Expect people's needs to change. • As needs change and lower-order needs are satisfied, create opportunities for employees to satisfy higher-order needs.
EQUITY THEORY	• Look for and correct major inequities. • Reduce employees' inputs. • Make sure decision-making processes are fair.
EXPECTANCY THEORY	• Systematically gather information to find out what employees want from their jobs. • Take specific steps to link rewards to individual performance in a way that is clear and understandable to employees. • Empower employees to make decisions if management really wants them to believe that their hard work and efforts will lead to good performance.
REINFORCEMENT THEORY	• Identify, measure, analyze, intervene, and evaluate critical performance-related behaviors. • Don't reinforce the wrong behaviors. • Correctly administer punishment at the appropriate time. • Choose the simplest and most effective schedule of reinforcement.
GOAL-SETTING THEORY	• Assign specific, challenging goals. • Make sure workers truly accept organizational goals. • Provide frequent, specific, performance-related feedback.

Exhibit 13.17
Motivating with the Integrated Model

motivate their workers: "What leads to effort?" Though the answer to that question is likely to be somewhat different for each employee, Exhibit 13.17 helps you begin to answer it by consolidating the practical advice from the theories reviewed in this chapter in one convenient location. So, if you're having difficulty figuring out why people aren't motivated where you work, Exhibit 13.17 provides a useful, theory-based starting point.

What Do You Need?

What people want out of their jobs is as varied as the jobs themselves.[100] And as you would expect, need theories show why not everyone wants to be CEO. Take the example of the woman who is extremely organized and efficient in her job as an assistant. She is so effective that she is offered a promotion to management, but she turns it down flatly, saying that she has no interest in moving up the ladder, that she is happy doing what she does. What she needs from work clearly differs from the needs of the person who jumps at every opportunity to move up the corporate hierarchy. Not everyone needs or wants the same things from their jobs.[101] Indicate the extent to which you agree with each of the following statements. Try not to spend too much time on any one item, and be sure to answer all the questions. Use this scale for your responses:

1 Strongly disagree

2 Disagree

3 Slightly disagree

4 Neutral

5 Slightly agree

6 Agree

7 Strongly agree

1. I get enough money from my job to live comfortably.

    1   2   3   4

    5   6   7

2. Our benefits cover many of the areas they should.

    1   2   3   4

    5   6   7

3. My boss encourages people to make suggestions.

1   2   3   4   5   6   7

4. I can count on my coworkers to give me a hand when I need it.

1   2   3   4   5   6   7

5. I always get the feeling of learning new things from my work.

1   2   3   4   5   6   7

6. I often think about how to improve my job performance.

1   2   3   4   5   6   7

7. My pay is adequate to provide for the basic things in life.

1   2   3   4   5   6   7

8. The benefit program here gives nearly all the security I want.

1   2   3   4   5   6   7

9. My boss takes account of my wishes and desires.

1   2   3   4   5   6   7

10. My coworkers will speak out in my favor if justified.

1   2   3   4   5   6   7

11. My job requires that a person use a wide range of abilities.

1   2   3   4   5   6   7

12. I will actively try to improve my job performance in the future.

1   2   3   4   5   6   7

13. Considering the work required, the pay is what it should be.

1   2   3   4   5   6   7

14. Compared to other places, our benefits are excellent.

1   2   3   4   5   6   7

15. My boss keeps me informed about what is happening in the company.

1   2   3   4   5   6   7

16. I can tell my coworkers how I honestly feel.

1   2   3   4   5   6   7

17. My job requires making one (or more) important decision(s) every day.

1   2   3   4   5   6   7

18. I intend to do a lot more at work in the future.

1   2   3   4   5   6   7

19. Compared to the rates for similar work, here, my pay is good.

   1   2   3   4   5   6   7

20. The benefit program here is adequate.

   1   2   3   4   5   6   7

21. My boss lets me know when I could improve my performance.

   1   2   3   4   5   6   7

22. My coworkers welcome opinions different from their own.

   1   2   3   4   5   6   7

23. I have the opportunity to do challenging things at work.

   1   2   3   4   5   6   7

24. I will probably do my best to perform well on the job in the future.

   1   2   3   4   5   6   7

Scoring

(A) Add together your scores for items 1, 2, 7, 8, 13, 14, 19, and 20: _____

(B) Add together your scores for items 3, 4, 9, 10, 15, 16, 21, and 22: _____

(C) Add together your scores for items 5, 6, 11, 12, 17, 18, 23, and 24: _____

You can find the interpretation for your score at: **academic.cengage.com/management/williams.**

MANAGEMENT DECISION

Motivating an "A" Who's Getting "Fs"

You have definitely reached a low point. Frustrated by an employee who is uncooperative, unmotivated, and sloppy about his work, you have resorted to writing a "Dear Abby" style letter to a columnist in a popular business magazine. Letting out a heavy sigh, you scroll back to the top of your screen to review your work:

Dear Business Guru,

A few months ago, I was promoted into my first management job at the greeting card company where I work. I inherited a whiz-bang team, full of talent and energy, with the exception of one person—Let's call him David. Unlike the others on our team, he is uncooperative and unmotivated, and his work is sloppy, even though I know he can do better! Several veteran employees have told me David used to be the crown jewel in the team, working hard, collaborating, and generating great ideas. But now he's altogether different. I'm reluctant to fire him for two reasons: from a technical standpoint, he would be difficult to replace; and our division is under an indefinite hiring freeze. But his attitude and performance are having a negative impact on the rest of the team. What can I do to pull this guy out of a slump? Evidently, he was quite the employee—and I need him to be that star employee again.

Pausing for a moment before hitting "send," your eyes fall on an old management book in your overhead. Grabbing it, you say to yourself, "There's got to be something in there to help me." But as you flip through the pages, you can't help thinking of all the time you've already spent on this guy. Maybe you should just fire him and be done.

Questions

1. Which motivational theory discussed in the chapter do you think would be most successful in helping David rekindle his spark? Why?

2. Which motivational theory will be most helpful in refocusing the efforts of your entire team? Explain.

3. Do you fire David or keep him on your team?

Mining Human Capital

Labor is probably the single largest expense of any business.[102] According to some estimates, labor costs average about 60 percent of sales. In addition to salaries, labor costs include health insurance, paid time off, child-care benefits, tuition reimbursements, and any number of other programs designed to extrinsically motivate the work force. Many companies offer the same types of benefits across their organizations without knowing whether the benefits really motivate employees at all. In other words, companies often don't know what return they are getting on their labor investment. The same is true where you work.

As you head back to your desk from a meeting on cafeteria-style benefit plans, your boss intercepts you and says she wants to talk with you about cutting labor costs. As she plops into your side chair, she is already describing a new type of software that applies data-mining technology to employee information to determine what is the best motivator. "We can get rid of one-size-fits-all benefit programs and tailor the benefits to each employee. This software lets you slice and dice employee data, like age, seniority, education, commute time, residential ZIP code, even the age and condition of the person's office," she says. "We could find out if we could pay someone, say, 20 percent less if we gave a three-month sabbatical every couple of years. Or we could predict the reaction of certain employees if we cut our 401(k) match. Maybe that's not as important to everyone as we think. We could find out who would quit if we did that and who couldn't care less. Basically, we could find out what incentives would spike productivity the most with each employee, and that way we could cut costs without sabotaging morale. It would reduce the guesswork of rewarding our employees. Here is some literature on the various programs. I'd like your team to draft a recommendation to top management by next Monday. I'm really excited about this." She leaves a small stack of brochures on your desk corner and leaves your office.

All you can do is wonder, "What will the employees think of this idea?"

Assemble a team of three to four students to review the issue of mining human resource data for information to help you customize incentives.

Questions

1. Which motivational theory provides the biggest justification for employee data mining? Explain.

2. Does employee data mining violate any of the motivational theories? If so, which ones and how?

3. Will your team recommend mining employee data or, despite your boss's enthusiasm, will you present reasons not to begin mining employee data? Explain your choice, using the motivational theories in the chapter as support for your recommendation.

Motivation is an invisible and powerful force. Strong motivation can drive individuals and organizations to remarkable heights of achievement. A loss of motivation can leave us dispirited and ineffective. One of the fundamental responsibilities of managers is to support healthy worker motivation. This exercise will allow you to practice designing support for worker motivation.

Step 1: Divide intro groups. Your professor will organize you in pairs or groups of three.

Step 2: Prepare interviews. Between this class session and the target date set by your professor, you and your partner(s) will each interview two individuals about motivation at work. You should brainstorm about possible types of work, interesting individuals, and so on, and then agree on each partner's list of interviewees/job-holders.

Some considerations for brainstorming include jobs or types of work that you consider particularly interesting, appealing, or mysterious; jobs or types of work that you consider particularly uninteresting, dull, or monotonous (how does a person do that work day after day?); and self-employed or creative work (how do such workers manage their own motivation without a boss or supervisor?)

Step 3: Conduct interviews. Outside of class each student should complete their assigned interviews. Inform the potential interviewee that you are interested in talking about workplace motivation. Set a time that is convenient and ensure that you arrive on time and prepared. Make the interview brief, with 15–20 minutes a good target. Go beyond 20 minutes only if the interviewee gives permission and the discussion is lively. Be sure to thank the interviewee for taking the time to visit with you.

Your instructor may give additional instructions for these interviews, and you should carefully follow these guidelines in conducting the interview.

Interview questions might include the following:

1. How would you describe your work? What are some of the things that you particularly like about your work?

2. We are currently studying the topic of motivation in one of my classes. What boosts your motivation at work? If you have ever experienced a period of low motivation, can you identify things that might have contributed to your losing steam in your work?

3. What kinds of rewards or incentives work best to motivate individuals and/or teams who do your type of work? What kinds of rewards or incentives don't work so well?

Step 4: Summarize your findings. Write a one-page paper summarizing your interview findings. Be prepared to compare notes with your partners, and to contribute to class discussion.

Step 5: Debrief as a class. Pairs/small groups report their findings and discuss as a class. What did you learn from your interviews? Did you notice common themes or issues across the interviews you conducted? Did you notice any striking differences across individuals or types of work? What are some possible implications of these interview findings for managers who are responsible for cultivating healthy motivation in a particular work setting?

DEVELOP YOUR CAREER POTENTIAL

Cut Your Costs, Not Your Morale

Management textbooks abound with discussions of the importance of honest and open communication when disseminating negative information to employees.[103] One study suggests that the best way to ruin morale and motivation is to spring bad news on employees without explaining the reasoning or rationale. Yet, despite the need to maintain a high level of motivation and morale during a receding economy, many companies cut perks without communicating the need to their employees. During the high-tech boom at the end of the 20th century, many companies implemented programs to increase productivity, motivation, and job satisfaction. Some of the perks provided were minor, such as free soft drinks, catered lunches, snacks, and tickets to events such as a baseball game or the opera. Other free perks were more extravagant, such as concierge services to run errands for employees, service their vehicles, and pick up their laundry. Some firms even provided their employees with in-house massages and annual Caribbean cruises. Obviously, cutting these non-value-added expenses can save tremendous money for a struggling firm. In fact, many firms cut out both the extravagant perks and the basics as a way to conserve much-needed cash. Cutting perks, however, doesn't have to be forever. Perks can be powerful motivational tools that companies can reintegrate into their performance reward systems.

For this assignment, consider your own budget and expenses in terms of revenue and perks. Imagine that like so many companies, you experience a cash crunch. Your revenue (income) shrinks 25 percent, so you must trim some fat from your budget.

Exercises

1. First, you will need to review your expenditures. What "perks" have you built into your budget as a student? (Think pizza and beer.) Make a list of all your non-value-added expenses. This includes anything not directly related to your studies (like books, tuition, enrollment fees, pens, paper) or your fixed expenses (like rent, car payments, insurance).

2. If you experienced a 25 percent reduction in your income—as numerous firms did after the tech bubble burst—which perks would you eliminate? In addition, are there items that you previously considered necessities that you could cut out? An example would be selling your car (thereby

eliminating car payments and related insurance) and taking public transportation or catching a ride with a friend. What about getting a roommate, moving into the dorms, or living with your parents?

3. Often employees develop a sense of entitlement about perks, and when the perks are trimmed, great dissatisfaction can result. Companies even lose employees when perks are cut. In this exercise, let's consider that cutting out your non-value-added (that is, fun) expenditures may put a crimp in your social life. In fact, you may have trouble staying in the loop. What can you do to "retain" your social friends as you cut down on your personal perks? Do you think that "retention" will even be an issue for you? Why or why not?

4. Once you have taken the ax to your perks, how can you reincorporate them into your budget, this time as motivational tools? Which perks would motivate you to have perfect attendance in class? To make an A? Straight As? Be creative. The purpose is to see if you can modify your own behavior by using your perks.

REEL TO REAL

For Love of the Game

Billy Chapel (Kevin Costner), a 20-year veteran pitcher with the Detroit Tigers, learns just before the season's last game that the team's new owners want to trade him. He also learns that his partner, Jane Aubrey (Kelly Preston), intends to leave him. Faced with these daunting blows, Chapel, who decides to retire, wants to pitch a perfect final game. Director Sam Raimi's love of baseball shines through in some striking visual effects.

This scene is a slightly edited version of the "Just Throw" sequence, which begins the film's exciting closing scenes in which Chapel pitches his last game. In this scene, the Tigers' catcher Gus Sinski (John C. Reilly) comes out to the pitching mound to talk to Billy.

What to Watch for and Ask Yourself

1. How would you describe Billy Chapel's esteem needs at this point in the game?
2. Do you expect Gus Sinski's talk to have any effect on Chapel? If it will, what will be the effect? Why?
3. What rewards potentially exist for Billy Chapel? Remember, this is the last baseball game of his career.

P. F. Chang's—Motivating Workers Who Already Like Their Jobs

What motivates you—money, prestige, fear, vacation, recognition, or something else altogether different? Not everyone is motivated by the same things. The same is true for workers everywhere, including P. F. Chang's bistros. It's easy to see what motivates managers and executives at P. F. Chang's: They want customers to love the food and atmosphere, they want their business to succeed and grow, and they want to earn a good living in return for their investment and hard work. "We are truly glad you are here," says P. F. Chang's motto, "and we will do everything possible to make you want to come back again." This is the biggest motivation of all—to have customers come back. But what motivates the employees at P. F. Chang's—the wait staff, bartenders, hosts, chefs and kitchen crew, bussers, and dishwashers?

Questions

1. P. F. Chang's offers a menu of extrinsic rewards to its workers. What are some of the intrinsic rewards?
2. In what ways might managers at P. F. Chang's use positive reinforcement for their kitchen crew or wait staff?
3. Do you think managers at P. F. Chang's would be successful using expectancy theory? Explain.

CHAPTER 14

HP Digital Publishing Solutions
Demand more. Get more.

Leadership

Learning Outcomes:

1 Explain what leadership is.
2 Describe who leaders are and what effective leaders do.
3 Explain Fiedler's contingency theory.
4 Describe how path-goal theory works.
5 Discuss Hersey and Blanchard's Situational Leadership theory.
6 Explain the normative decision theory.
7 Explain how visionary leadership (that is, charismatic and transformational leadership) helps leaders achieve strategic leadership.

In This Chapter:

WHAT WOULD YOU DO?

Hewlett-Packard Headquarters, Palo Alto, California.[1] As CEO at your previous company, you had to make plenty of tough decisions to turn things around. And not everyone was happy when you did. A laid-off employee tracked you down after hours on a basketball court, pushed you around, and later made repeated death threats against you and your family. Then, after another round of cost-cutting decisions, your and your top management team's car tires were slashed in the parking lot. But compared to the mess that you're in now as CEO of Hewlett-Packard, those were the good old days.

Since your predecessor, Carly Fiorina, was fired by the board, you expected to find a number of significant problems, the first of which was HP's strategic vision, which Fiorina had repeatedly described as "digital, virtual, mobile, personal." While this sounded good, no one was quite sure what it meant. But was it a bad strategy, or was HP just doing a poor job of executing it? This would take some time to figure out. Another problem was the confusing matrix structure, which blurred lines of accountability and slowed decision making. For example, HP's sales force was separate from the printing, computing, and corporate products divisions that were at the heart of the company. This meant that HP's salespeople sold everything from high-end corporate servers to low-end personal computers for consumers. Effectively, it also meant that instead of reporting to just one division, HP salespeople reported to people in four or more divisions, such as sales, printing, computing, and corporate. Carol Potts, one of your sales vice presidents in Chicago, complained, "We were very matrixed." A third problem was the reward system, which was so complex in its calculation that no one understood how their performance affected their bonuses. A fourth well-known problem was that HP was struggling financially. Under Fiorina's guidance, HP had paid $19 billion to acquire Compaq Computers, but then incurred, according to some estimates, more than $10 billion in expenses to integrate Compaq into HP. In short, expenses had risen too much, revenues and market share had risen too little, and HP was earning profits far below its competition.

But what worried you most of all was the deep sense of distrust that pervaded HP. The first sentence in the "HP Way," a set of corporate objectives written by founders Bill Hewlett and Dave Packard in 1957, says, "We have trust and respect for individuals." At HP, people were supposed to be as important as profits, but that was no longer the case. Some employees toasted Fiorina's departure with champagne, but the HP Way had been deteriorating long before she became CEO. Plus, top executives were leaving left and right and HP was unable to attract talented replacements. Finally, the board of directors was a dysfunctional soap opera. Patricia Dunn, the board chair, authorized an investigation to spy on board members' phone records to determine who was leaking confidential information to the press. When the leaker was confronted, another board member angrily resigned and contacted the press to air the story.

So, where do you start? Given HP's current problems, should you focus on what the company is doing or not doing, meaning its current strategy, or should you simply focus on doing what HP is doing, but doing it better Or should you follow your predecessor's strategy of HP being "digital, virtual, mobile, and personal"? Or do you reexamine the company's strategy and start anew? Finally, there are two key problems at HP: distrust, which is accompanied by poor morale; and poor company performance in terms of product innovation, market share, and profits. Which is more important and which should you fix first? **If you were in charge at HP, what would you do?**

"WHAT'S NEW" COMPANIES

HEWLETT-PACKARD
SOUTHWEST AIRLINES
McDONALD'S
CITIGROUP
HOME DEPOT
HYPERSPACE COMMUNICATIONS
PEPSICO
XEROX
JPMORGAN CHASE
AND OTHERS . . .

Do I have what it takes to lead? What are the most important things leaders do? How can I transform a poorly performing department, division, or company? Do I need to adjust my leadership depending on the situation and the employee? Why doesn't my leadership inspire people? If you've ever been "in charge," or even just thought about it, chances are you've considered similar questions. Well, you're not alone—millions of leaders in organizations across the world struggle with these fundamental leadership issues on a daily basis.

We begin this chapter by discussing what leadership is, who leaders are (meaning their traits and characteristics), and what leaders do that makes them different from people who aren't leaders. Next we examine four major contingency theories of leadership that specify which leaders are best suited for which situations or how leaders should change their behavior to lead different people in different circumstances. The chapter ends with a review of strategic leadership issues, such as charismatic and transformational leadership, which are concerned with working with others to meet long-term goals and with creating a viable future for an organization.

WHAT IS LEADERSHIP?

SOUTHWEST AIRLINES flies two to three times as many passengers per employee as other airlines at a cost 25 to 40 percent below its competitors.[2] One of the keys to Southwest's performance is that it empties its planes; refills them with passengers, crews, fuel, and food (peanuts and soft drinks); and has them back on the runway in 20 minutes, one-third the time of most airlines. This allows Southwest to keep each of its planes filled with paying passengers about three more hours a day. Why is Southwest able to achieve such incredible results? It takes care of its employees. For instance, with most ticket sales moving to its website, Southwest closed reservation centers in Dallas, Little Rock, and Salt Lake City. But instead of laying off employees, it paid for them to commute or relocate to places it had jobs. Regarding layoffs, Colleen Barrett, Southwest's president, says, "We don't do those kind of things. That's what our competitors do. At Southwest, our employees come first."[3] The result, says Southwest spokesperson Paula Berg, is, "We work hard. I'll stay here until 10 PM, if necessary. . . . But we do it because the company takes care of us, so we want to take care of the company."[4] As Colleen Barrett and the rest of the managers at Southwest Airlines have discovered, **leadership** is the process of influencing others to achieve group or organizational goals.

> *After reading the next two sections, you should be able to*
>
> 1 *explain what leadership is.*
> 2 *describe who leaders are and what effective leaders do.*

1 Leadership

leadership the process of influencing others to achieve group or organizational goals

In Chapter 1, we defined *management* as getting work done through others. In other words, managers don't do the work themselves. Managers help others do their jobs better. By contrast, *leadership* is the process of influencing others to achieve group or organizational goals. What then are the key differences between leaders and managers? Another question that goes to the nature of leadership is whether it's required in every situation. Does leadership always matter? Or are there situations when leadership isn't needed or may even make things worse?

*Let's learn more about leadership by exploring **1.1 the differences between leaders and managers** and **1.2 substitutes for leadership**.*

1.1 Leaders versus Managers

According to University of Southern California business professor Warren Bennis, the primary difference between leaders and managers, as shown in Exhibit 14.1, is that leaders are concerned with doing the right thing, while managers are concerned with doing things right.[5] In other words, leaders begin with the question, "What should we be doing?" while managers start with "How can we do what we're already doing better?" Leaders focus on vision, mission, goals, and objectives, while managers focus on productivity and efficiency. Managers see themselves as preservers of the status quo, while leaders see themselves as promoters of change and challengers of the status quo in that they encourage creativity and risk taking. Four years ago, MCDONALD'S was losing money and closing down stores. Today, with faster, friendlier service, healthier, better-tasting food, and a focus on quality rather than growth, McDonald's stock is up 45 percent. Furthermore, 50 million customers walk into its restaurants each day, 3.5 million more per day than four years ago. Despite these successes, CEO Jim Skinner is not happy with the status quo. Says Skinner, "I worry about complacency. We're not satisfied. We have a lot [more] work to do."[6]

Another difference is that managers have a relatively short-term perspective, while leaders take a long-term view. After financial improprieties in investment banking, bond trading, consumer lending, and corporate financing led to investigations and penalties in Europe, Japan, and the United States, new CITIGROUP CEO Charles Prince replaced the company's focus on short-term goals, such as fast growth, acquisitions, and quarterly earnings gains, with longer-term goals to improve ethics and financial controls and to grow its international business and replace aging technology systems.[7] Says Prince, "You can never sacrifice your long-term growth, your long-term reputation, to the short term."[8] Managers are also more concerned with *means*, how to get things done, while leaders are more concerned with *ends*, what gets done. Managers are concerned with control and limiting the choices of others, while leaders are more concerned with expanding people's choices and options.[9] Finally, managers solve problems so that others can do their work, while leaders inspire and motivate others to find their own solutions.

Exhibit 14.1

Managers versus Leaders

Though leaders are different from managers, organizations need them both. Managers are critical to getting out the day-to-day work, and leaders are critical to inspiring employees and setting the organization's long-term direction. The key issue for any organization is the extent to which it is properly led and properly managed. As Warren Bennis said in summing up the difference between leaders and managers, "American organizations

Managers

- Do things right
- Status quo
- Short term
- Means
- Builders
- Problem solving

Leaders

- Do the right things
- Change
- Long term
- Ends
- Architects
- Inspiring & motivating

doing the right thing

The Three M's: Mission, Mentor, and Mirror

Doctors take the Hippocratic oath. Lawyers swear to protect and enforce the law. Leaders . . . well, there's no equivalent for business leaders. That's why Harvard professor Howard Gardner says that business leaders can develop personal ethics by focusing on their mission, a mentor, and the mirror.

First, leaders need to develop a personal mission statement by asking themselves these questions: *Why am I doing what I'm doing? What do I want from work? What are my personal goals?* Let your personal mission statement, and not the company's, guide your ethical behavior.

Second, take care in choosing a mentor. An interesting study compared 20 business leaders selected at random with 20 "good" business leaders nominated by businesspeople, business school professors, and deans. The randomly selected business leaders focused on short-term goals exclusively, worrying only about next quarter's results. By contrast, 18 of the 20 "good" executives focused on the long term, on doing what was right for the company in the long run. So, if you want to be a good leader, choose a "good" mentor.

Third, periodically stand in front of the mirror to assess your ethical performance as a business leader. Are you proud or ashamed of what you accomplished and how you accomplished it? Are you proud or ashamed of your company? What needs to change to make you proud?

So, do the right thing. Develop a personal mission statement. Choose the right mentor. And look hard at yourself in the mirror.[11]

(and probably those in much of the rest of the industrialized world) are under led and over managed. They do not pay enough attention to doing the right thing, while they pay too much attention to doing things right."[10]

1.2 Substitutes for Leadership: Do Leaders Always Matter?

One of the basic assumptions about leadership is that leaders always matter. According to this thinking, without sound leadership, organizations are sure to fail. In fact, when companies struggle, their leaders are almost always blamed for their poor performance. When **HOME DEPOT** fired CEO Robert Nardelli, *BusinessWeek* wrote:

Nardelli's "numbers were quite good," says Matthew J. Fassler, an analyst at Goldman Sachs Group Inc. But "the fact is that this retail organization never really embraced his leadership style." The CEO's reputation also suffered because of Wall Street's affection for Home Depot's smaller archrival, Lowe's Companies, whose stock price has soared more than 200 percent since 2000, while Home Depot's shares declined 6 percent. . . . "He's not a very humble guy. He seems to have enormous energy but needs to be front and center, and that can wear on the board and the employees after a while," says Edward E. Lawler, director of the Center for Effective Organizations at the University of Southern California's Marshall School of Business. . . .

. . . [T]he Nardelli departure was already brightening the mood at some company stores. "It's amazing the reaction of people on my floor. People are openly ecstatic. High-fiving," said an Atlanta store operations manager only hours after the Jan. 3 announcement.[12]

In some situations and circumstances, however, leadership isn't necessary, is unlikely to make much of a difference, or isn't to blame for poor performance. These are known as leadership substitutes and leadership neutralizers.[13] Exhibit 14.2 lists a number of subordinate, task, or organizational characteristics that can act as leadership substitutes or neutralizers (some can act as both) for either people-related or task-related leader behaviors. Leaders' people-related behaviors, such as being approachable, supportive, or showing concern for employees, affect how satisfied people are with their jobs. Leaders' task-related behaviors, such as setting goals, giving directions, and providing resources, affect the extent to which people are able to perform their jobs well.

> American organizations (and probably those in much of the rest of the industrialized world) are under led and over managed.

WARREN BENNIS, BUSINESS PROFESSOR, UNIVERSITY OF SOUTHERN CALIFORNIA

Leadership substitutes are subordinate, task, or organizational characteristics that make leaders redundant or unnecessary. For instance, when subordinates have ability, experience, training, and knowledge about their jobs (see subordinate characteristics in Exhibit 14.2), task-related leader behavior that specifies goals, task assignments, and how to do the job is unlikely to improve a subordinate's work performance. Think about it. Workers already have the capability to do their jobs. And the job itself provides enough information to let them know how well they're doing or what they might do to correct performance problems. In situations like this, where leadership substitutes are strong, leaders don't need to tell workers what to do or how to do their jobs.

Leadership neutralizers are subordinate, task, or organizational characteristics that can interfere with a leader's actions or make it impossible for a leader

leadership substitutes subordinate, task, or organizational characteristics that make leaders redundant or unnecessary

leadership neutralizers subordinate, task, or organizational characteristics that can interfere with a leader's actions or make it impossible for a leader to influence followers' performance

Exhibit 14.2

Leadership Substitutes and Neutralizers

Characteristics	People-Related Leadership Behaviors	Task-Related Leadership Behaviors
SUBORDINATE		
• Ability, experience, training, knowledge	Neutralize	Substitute, Neutralize
• Need for independence	Neutralize	Neutralize
• Professional orientation	Substitute, Neutralize	Substitute, Neutralize
• Indifference toward organizational rewards	Neutralize	Neutralize
TASK		
• Unambiguous and routine tasks	No effect	Substitute, Neutralize
• Performance feedback provided by the work itself	No effect	Substitute, Neutralize
• Intrinsically satisfying work	Substitute, Neutralize	Neutralize
ORGANIZATIONAL		
• Formalization, meaning specific plans, goals, and areas of responsibility	No effect	Neutralize
• Inflexibility, meaning rigid, unbending rules and procedures	No effect	Neutralize
• Highly specified staff functions	No effect	Neutralize
• Cohesive work groups	Substitute, Neutralize	Substitute, Neutralize
• Organizational rewards beyond a leader's	Neutralize	Neutralize control
• Spatial distance between supervisors and subordinates	Neutralize	Neutralize

Source: S. Kerr & J. M. Jermier, "Substitutes for Leadership: Their Meaning and Measurement," *Organizational Behavior and Human Performance* 22 (1978): 375–403.

to influence followers' performance. Unlike substitutes, which simply take the place of leaders, leadership neutralizers create an "influence vacuum." In other words, leadership neutralizers actually create a need for leadership by preventing leadership from working. For example, when subordinates are indifferent toward organizational rewards (see subordinate characteristics in Exhibit 14.2), there may be nothing that a leader can do to reward them for good performance. Likewise, inflexible rules and procedures (see organizational characteristics in Exhibit 14.2), such as union contracts that specify that all employees be paid the same, organizational policies that reward employees by seniority, and salary and raise processes that don't give leaders enough money to substantially reward good performers, effectively neutralize the ability of leaders to reward workers.

Spatial distance (see organizational characteristics in Exhibit 14.2) can also neutralize leadership. Spatial distance arises when supervisors and subordinates don't work in the same place, as occurs with telecommuters or people working thousands of miles away in overseas offices. Spatial distance typically results in infrequent feedback, little or no face-to-face contact, and being "out of sight and out of mind," all of which make it very difficult for leaders to lead. Because of those problems, John Yeros, founder and CEO of software company HYPERSPACE COMMUNICATIONS, lets only one of his employees, a programmer, work from home. Yeros says that when everyone is at the office, it's easier to "keep on the same page." Plus, it's easier for him as a leader. "I like to see them, feel them, touch them, and have them around," he says.[14] In fact, some companies find telecommuting to be so disruptive to leadership processes that they require their telecommuters to come into the office at least once or twice a week.

So do leaders *always* matter? Leadership substitutes and neutralizers indicate that sometimes they don't. This doesn't mean that leaders never matter, though. Quite the opposite. Leaders do matter, but they're not superhuman. They can't do it all by themselves. And they can't fix every situation. In short, leadership is very important. But poor leadership isn't the cause of every organizational crisis, and changing leaders isn't the solution to every company problem.

Review 1: *Leadership*

Leadership is the process of influencing others to achieve group or organizational goals. Leaders are different from managers. The primary difference is that leaders are concerned with doing the right thing, while managers are concerned with doing things right. Furthermore, managers have a short-term focus and are concerned with the status quo, with means rather than ends, and with solving others' problems. By contrast, leaders have a long-term focus and are concerned with change, with ends rather than means, and with inspiring and motivating others to solve their own problems. Organizations need both managers and leaders. But in general, companies are overmanaged and underled. While leadership is important, leadership substitutes and neutralizers create situations in which leadership isn't necessary or is unlikely to make much of a difference. Leadership substitutes are subordinate, task, or organizational characteristics that make leaders redundant or unnecessary. By contrast, leadership neutralizers are subordinate, task, or organizational characteristics that interfere with a leader's actions or make it impossible for a leader to influence followers' performance.

2 Who Leaders Are and What Leaders Do

Indra Nooyi, **PepsiCo**'s new CEO, talks straight, has a sharp sense of humor, and sings in the hallways wherever she is. She's commonly described as a "force." By contrast, J.C. Penney's CEO, Mike Ullman, is soft-spoken and easy to approach.[15] Nooyi is an extrovert. Ullman is an introvert. Which one is likely to be successful as a CEO? According to a survey of 1,542 senior managers, it's the extrovert. Forty-seven percent of those 1,542 senior managers felt that extroverts make better CEOs, while 65 percent said that being an introvert hurts a CEO's chances of success.[16] So clearly senior managers believe that extroverted CEOs are better leaders. But are they? Not necessarily. In fact, a relatively high percentage of CEOs, 40 percent, are introverts. Sara Lee CEO Brenda Barnes says, "I've always been shy. . . . People wouldn't call me that [an introvert], but I am."[17] Indeed, Barnes turns down all speaking requests and rarely gives interviews.

So, what makes a good leader? Does leadership success depend on who leaders are, such as introverts or extroverts, or on what leaders do and how they behave? Let's learn more about who leaders are by investigating 2.1 leadership traits and 2.2 leadership behaviors.

2.1 Leadership Traits

Trait theory is one way to describe who leaders are. **Trait theory** says that effective leaders possess a similar set of traits or characteristics. **Traits** are relatively stable characteristics, such as abilities, psychological motives, or consistent patterns of behavior. For example, according to trait theory, leaders are taller and more confident and have greater physical stamina (that is, higher energy levels) than nonleaders. Indeed, while just 14.5 percent of men are six feet tall, 58 percent of Fortune 500 CEOs are six foot or taller.[18] Author Malcolm Gladwell says, "We have this sense of what a leader is supposed to look like. And that stereotype is so powerful that when someone fits it, we simply become blind to other considerations."[19] Trait theory is also known as the "great person" theory because early versions of the theory stated that leaders are born, not made. In other words, you either have the "right stuff" to be a leader, or you don't. And if you don't, there is no way to get "it."

For some time, it was thought that trait theory was wrong and that there are no consistent trait differences between leaders and nonleaders, or between effective and ineffective leaders. However, more recent evidence shows that "successful leaders are not like other people," that successful leaders are indeed different from the rest of us.[20] More specifically, as shown in Exhibit 14.3, leaders are different from nonleaders in the following traits: drive, the desire to lead, honesty/integrity, self-confidence, emotional stability, cognitive ability, and knowledge of the business.[21]

Drive refers to high levels of effort and is characterized by achievement, motivation, initiative, energy, and tenacity. In terms of achievement and ambition, leaders always try

trait theory a leadership theory that holds that effective leaders possess a similar set of traits or characteristics

traits relatively stable characteristics, such as abilities, psychological motives, or consistent patterns of behavior

Because we think we know what a leader should look like, we become blind to other considerations.

© DIGITAL VISION/GETTY

Exhibit 14.3

Leadership Traits

to make improvements or achieve success in what they're doing. Because of their initiative, they have strong desires to promote change or solve problems. Leaders typically have more energy, and they have to, given the long hours they put in and followers' expectations that they be positive and "up." Thus, leaders must have physical, mental, and emotional vitality. Leaders are also more tenacious than nonleaders and are better at overcoming obstacles and problems that would deter most of us.

Successful leaders also have a stronger *desire to lead*. They want to be in charge and think about ways to influence or convince others about what should or shouldn't be done. *Honesty/integrity* is also important to leaders. *Honesty*, being truthful with others, is a cornerstone of leadership. Without honesty, leaders won't be trusted. When leaders have it, subordinates are willing to overlook other flaws. For example, one follower said this about the leadership qualities of his manager: "I don't like a lot of the things he does, but he's basically honest. He's a genuine article, and you'll forgive a lot of things because of that. That goes a long way in how much I trust him."[22] *Integrity* is the extent to which leaders do what they said they would do. Leaders may be honest and have good intentions, but if they don't consistently deliver on what they promise, they won't be trusted.

Self-confidence, believing in one's abilities, also distinguishes leaders from nonleaders. Self-confident leaders are more decisive and assertive and are more likely to gain others' confidence. Moreover, self-confident leaders will admit mistakes because they view them as learning opportunities rather than a refutation of their leadership capabilities. This also means that leaders have *emotional stability*. Even when things go wrong, they remain even-tempered and consistent in their outlook and in the way they treat others. Leaders who can't control their emotions, who anger quickly or attack and blame others for mistakes, are unlikely to be trusted.

Leaders are also smart. Leaders typically have strong *cognitive abilities*. This doesn't mean that leaders are geniuses, far from it. But it does mean that leaders have the capacity to analyze large amounts of seemingly unrelated, complex information and see patterns, opportunities, or threats where others might not see them. Finally, leaders also "know their stuff," which means they have superior technical knowledge about the businesses they run. Leaders who have a good *knowledge of the business* understand the key technological decisions and concerns facing their companies. More often than not, studies indicate that effective leaders have long, extensive experience in their industries.

How does Anne Mulcahy, the CEO who turned around **XEROX**, measure up on these traits? In general, quite well. *Fortune* magazine said this about her: "She is straightforward, hard-working, disciplined. She is fiercely loyal to Xerox—the company, the brand, the people. She has the integrity of the Catholic schoolgirl she was for 16 years. Her coworkers describe her as both compassionate and tough. She is not afraid of bad news. . . . Her willingness to work shoulder to shoulder with subordinates gives her unusual credibility and the ability to galvanize her team."[23]

Initially, however, Mulcahy had a clear weakness: Because her experience was limited to sales, she lacked knowledge of the entire business. And since Xerox was $14.1 billion in debt and had only $154 million in cash on hand, she had to learn fast. So she asked Joe Mancini, Jr., the director of corporate financial analysis, to give her a course in "Balance Sheet 101." Mulcahy says, "It was an unusual situation for me—tutoring the CEO. But there wasn't a lot of time for false pride."[24] Every night she took home binders full of information to study, and eventually she transformed her knowledge of the financial side of the business from a weakness into a strength.

what really works.

For decades, researchers assumed that leadership traits, such as drive, emotional stability, cognitive ability, and charisma were *not* related to effective leadership. More recent evidence, however, shows that there are reliable trait differences between leaders and nonleaders. In fact, 54 studies based on more than 6,000 people clearly indicate that in terms of leadership traits, "successful leaders are not like other people."

TRAITS AND PERCEPTIONS OF LEADERSHIP EFFECTIVENESS

Several leadership models argue that in order to be successful, leaders must be viewed as good leaders by their followers. (This is completely different from determining whether leaders actually improve organizational performance.) Consequently, one test of trait theory is whether leaders with particular traits are viewed as more or less effective leaders by their followers.

Intelligence. On average, there is a 75 percent chance that intelligent leaders will be seen as better leaders than less intelligent leaders.

Dominance. On average, there is only a 57 percent chance that leaders with highly dominant personalities will be seen as better leaders than those with less dominant personalities.

Extroversion. On average, there is a 63 percent chance that extroverts will be seen as better leaders than introverts.

CHARISMA AND LEADERSHIP EFFECTIVENESS

As discussed at the end of the chapter, *charismatic leadership* is the set of behavioral tendencies and personal characteristics of leaders that creates an exceptionally strong relationship between leaders and their followers. More specifically, charismatic leaders articulate a clear vision for the future that is based on strongly held values or morals; model those values by acting in a way consistent with the company's vision; communicate high performance expectations to followers; and display confidence in followers' abilities to achieve the vision.

Charisma and Performance. On average, there is a 72 percent chance that charismatic leaders will have better-performing followers and organizations than less charismatic leaders.

Charisma and Perceived Leader Effectiveness. On average, there is an 89 percent chance that charismatic leaders will be perceived as more effective leaders than less charismatic leaders.

Charisma and Leader Satisfaction. On average, there is a 90 percent chance that the followers of charismatic leaders will be more satisfied with their leaders than the followers of less charismatic leaders.[25]

2.2 Leadership Behaviors

Thus far, you've read about who leaders *are*. Traits alone are not enough to make a successful leader, however, though they are a precondition for success. After all, it's hard to imagine a truly successful leader who lacks all of these qualities. Leaders who have these traits (or many of them) must then take actions that encourage people to achieve group or organizational goals.[26] Accordingly, we now examine what leaders *do*, meaning the behaviors they perform or the actions they take to influence others to achieve group or organizational goals.

Researchers at the University of Michigan, Ohio State University, and the University of Texas examined the specific behaviors that leaders use to improve subordinate satisfaction and performance. Hundreds of studies were conducted and hundreds of leader behaviors were examined. At all three universities, two basic leader behaviors emerged as central to successful leadership: initiating structure (called *job-centered leadership* at the University of Michigan and *concern for production* at the University of Texas) and considerate leader behavior (called *employee-centered leadership* at the University of Michigan and *concern for people* at the University of Texas).[27] These two leader behaviors form the basis for many of the leadership theories discussed in this chapter.

Initiating structure is the degree to which a leader structures the roles of followers by setting goals, giving directions, setting deadlines, and assigning tasks. A leader's ability to initiate structure primarily affects subordinates' job performance. When Jamie Dimon became CEO of *JPMORGAN CHASE*, the financial services company had four different computer systems from previously acquired companies. Branch bankers couldn't access checking histories, or determine whether customers qualified for credit cards or mortgages. Dimon initiated structure by telling his executives to put one system in place, and, "If you don't do it in six weeks, I'll make all the choices myself."[28] The deadline was met. Now, with just one software system, the annual cost of processing credit card statements has dropped from $80 to $52 a customer. Furthermore, with a new system that calculates which credit card deals are best for particular customers, Morgan has increased its open credit card accounts by 55 percent.

Consideration is the extent to which a leader is friendly, approachable, and supportive and shows concern for employees. Consideration primarily affects subordinates' job satisfaction. Specific leader consideration behaviors include listening to employees' problems and concerns, consulting with employees before making decisions, and treating employees as equals. Twenty-five years ago *WAL-MART*'s CEO, Lee Scott, received a lesson in the importance of consideration from founder Sam Walton. Scott, who was then in charge of a transportation unit, was known for his tough management style and for sending "blistering memos." When "Mr. Sam" called him into his office, Scott found nine of his truck drivers there waiting for him. The drivers, who were taking advantage of Wal-Mart's open-door policy, had complained to Walton about the way Scott treated them and asked that he be fired. According to Scott, "They just wanted to do their work and be appreciated for it. So Mr. Walton asked me, with them there, if I could do it differently."[29] After agreeing that he could, Scott said that Walton "had me stand at the door as they were leaving and thank each one for having the courage to use the open door, which is one of the very basic principles of Wal-Mart."[30] That office is now Scott's, and Wal-Mart has the same open door through which any Wal-Mart employee can walk to talk with the CEO.

Although researchers at all three universities generally agreed that initiating structure and consideration were basic leader behaviors, they differed on the interaction and effectiveness of these behaviors. The University of Michigan studies

"WHAT'S NEW" COMPANY

"WHAT'S NEW" COMPANY

initiating structure the degree to which a leader structures the roles of followers by setting goals, giving directions, setting deadlines, and assigning tasks

consideration the extent to which a leader is friendly, approachable, and supportive and shows concern for employees indicated that initiating structure and consideration were mutually exclusive behaviors on opposite ends of the same continuum. In other words, leaders who wanted to be more considerate would have to do less initiating of structure (and vice versa). The University of Michigan studies also indicated that only considerate leader behaviors (that is, employee-centered behaviors) were associated with successful leadership. By contrast, researchers at Ohio State University and the University of Texas found that initiating structure and consideration were independent behaviors, meaning that leaders can be considerate and initiate structure at the same time. Additional evidence confirms this finding.[31] The same researchers also concluded that the most effective leaders were strong on both initiating structure and considerate leader behaviors.

This "high-high" approach can be seen in the upper right corner of the Blake/ Mouton leadership grid, shown in Exhibit 14.4. Blake and Mouton used two leadership behaviors, concern for people (that is, consideration) and concern for production (that is, initiating structure), to categorize five different leadership styles. Both behaviors are rated on a 9-point scale with 1 representing "low" and 9 representing "high." Blake and Mouton suggest that a "high-high" or 9,9 leadership style is the best. They call this style *team management* because leaders who use it display a high concern for people (9) and a high concern for production (9).

By contrast, leaders use a 9,1 *authority-compliance* leadership style when they have a high concern for production and a low concern for people. A 1,9 *country*

Exhibit 14.4

Blake/Mouton Leadership Grid

Source: R. R. Blake & A. A. McCanse, "The Leadership Grid®," *Leadership Dilemmas—Grid Solutions* (Houston: Gulf Publishing Company), 21. Copyright © 1991, by Scientific Methods, Inc. Reproduced by permission of the owners.

A fun work environment where little attention is paid to production or performance is a country club style.

club style occurs when leaders care about having a friendly enjoyable work environment but don't really pay much attention to production or performance. The worst leadership style, according to the grid, is the 1,1 *impoverished* leader, who shows little concern for people or production and does the bare minimum needed to keep his or her job. Finally, the 5,5 *middle-of-the-road* style occurs when leaders show a moderate amount of concern for both people and production.

Is the team management style, with a high concern for production and a high concern for people, the "best" leadership style? Logically, it would seem so. Why wouldn't you want to show high concern for both people and production? Nonetheless, nearly 50 years of research indicates that there isn't one "best" leadership style. The "best" leadership style depends on the situation. In other words, no one leadership behavior by itself and no one combination of leadership behaviors works well across all situations and employees.

Review 2: **Who Leaders Are and What Leaders Do**

Trait theory says that effective leaders possess traits or characteristics that differentiate them from nonleaders. Those traits are drive, the desire to lead, honesty/integrity, self-confidence, emotional stability, cognitive ability, and knowledge of the business. Traits alone aren't enough for successful leadership, however; leaders who have these traits (or many of them) must also behave in ways that encourage people to achieve group or organizational goals. Two key leader behaviors are initiating structure, which improves subordinate performance, and consideration, which improves subordinate satisfaction. There is no "best" combination of these behaviors. The "best" leadership style depends on the situation.

SITUATIONAL APPROACHES TO LEADERSHIP

After leader traits and behaviors, the situational approach to leadership is the third major method used in the study of leadership. There are four major situational approaches to leadership—Fiedler's contingency theory, path-goal theory, Hersey and Blanchard's Situational Leadership theory, and Vroom and Yetton's normative decision model. All assume that the effectiveness of any **leadership style**, the way a leader generally behaves toward followers, depends on the situation.[32] Stanford Business School professor Jeffrey Pfeffer agrees: "Situations differ, often wildly, in the extent to which one individual can make a difference and in the set of attributes required to be successful. . . . But utopia is impossible, which is why management consultants and authors should stop talking so much about how to find an ideal leader and instead focus on placing people into jobs that play to their strengths—and where their flaws won't be fatal."[33]

leadership style the way a leader generally behaves toward followers

> Management consultants and authors should stop talking so much about how to find an ideal leader and instead focus on placing people into jobs that play to their strengths.

JEFFREY PFEFFER, PROFESSOR, STANFORD BUSINESS SCHOOL

According to situational leadership theories, there is no one "best" leadership style. But, one of these situational theories differs from the other three in one significant way. Fiedler's contingency theory assumes that leadership styles are consistent and difficult to change. Therefore, leaders must be placed in or "matched" to a situation that fits their leadership style. In contrast, the other three situational theories all assume that leaders are capable of adapting and adjusting their leadership styles to fit the demands of different situations.

After reading the next four sections, you should be able to

3 explain Fiedler's contingency theory.

4 describe how path-goal theory works.

5 discuss Hersey and Blanchard's Situational Leadership theory.

6 explain the normative decision theory.

3 Putting Leaders in the Right Situation: Fiedler's Contingency Theory

Fiedler's **contingency theory** states that in order to maximize work group performance, leaders must be matched to the right leadership situation.[34] More specifically, as shown in Exhibit 14.5, the first basic assumption of Fiedler's theory is that leaders are effective when the work groups they lead perform well. So, instead of judging leaders' effectiveness by what the leaders do (initiating structure and consideration) or who they are (trait theory), Fiedler assesses leaders by the conduct and performance of the people they supervise. Second, Fiedler assumes that leaders are generally unable to change their leadership styles and that they will be more effective when their styles are matched to the proper situation. Third, Fiedler assumes that the favorableness of a situation for a leader depends on the degree to which the situation permits the leader to influence the behavior of group members. Thus, Fiedler's third assumption is consistent with our definition of leadership, which is the process of influencing others to achieve group or organizational goals.

*Let's learn more about Fiedler's contingency theory by examining **3.1 the least preferred coworker and leadership styles**, **3.2 situational favorableness**, and **3.3 how to match leadership styles to situations**.*

3.1 Leadership Style: Least Preferred Coworker

When Fiedler refers to *leadership style*, he means the way that leaders generally behave toward their followers. Do the

contingency theory a leadership theory that states that in order to maximize work group performance, leaders must be matched to the situation that best fits their leadership style

Exhibit 14.5
Fiedler's Contingency Theory

Good fit makes for higher performance levels.

leaders yell and scream and blame others when things go wrong? Or do they correct mistakes by listening and then quietly but directly make their point? Do they take credit for others' work when things go right? Or do they make sure that those who did the work receive the credit they rightfully deserve? Do they let others make their own decisions and hold them accountable for the results? Or do they micromanage, insisting that all decisions be approved first by them? Fiedler also assumes that leadership styles are tied to leaders' underlying needs and personalities. And since personality and needs are relatively stable, he assumes that leaders are generally incapable of changing their leadership styles. In other words, the way that leaders treat people now is probably the way they've always treated others. So, according to Fiedler, if your boss's first instinct is to yell and scream and blame others, chances are he or she has always done that.

Fiedler uses a questionnaire called the Least Preferred Coworker (LPC) scale to measure leadership style (sample shown in Exhibit 14.6). When completing the LPC scale, people are instructed to consider all of the people with whom they have ever worked and then to choose the one person with whom they have worked *least* well. Fiedler explains, "This does not have to be the person you liked least well, but should be the one person with whom you have the most trouble getting the job done."[35]

Would you describe your LPC as pleasant, friendly, supportive, interesting, cheerful, and sincere? Or would you describe the person as unpleasant, unfriendly, hostile, boring, gloomy, and insincere? (The Self-Assessment at the end of this chapter contains the full LPC scale.) People who describe their LPC in a positive way (scoring 64 and above) have *relationship-oriented* leadership styles. After all, if they can still be positive about their least preferred coworker, they must be people oriented. By contrast, people who describe their LPC in a negative way (scoring 57 or below) have *task-oriented* leadership styles. Given a choice, they'll focus first on getting the job done and second on making sure everyone gets along. Finally, those with moderate scores (from 58 to 63) have a more flexible leadership style and can be somewhat relationship oriented or somewhat task oriented.

3.2 Situational Favorableness

Fiedler assumes that leaders will be more effective when their leadership styles are matched to the proper situation. Specifically, Fiedler defines **situational favorableness**

situational favorableness the degree to which a particular situation either permits or denies a leader the chance to influence the behavior of group members

Exhibit 14.6

Sample from Fiedler's Least Preferred Coworker Scale

Pleasant									Unpleasant
	8	7	6	5	4	3	2	1	
Friendly									Unfriendly
	8	7	6	5	4	3	2	1	
Supportive									Hostile
	8	7	6	5	4	3	2	1	
Boring									Interesting
	1	2	3	4	5	6	7	8	
Gloomy									Cheerful
	1	2	3	4	5	6	7	8	
Insincere									Sincere
	1	2	3	4	5	6	7	8	

Source: F. E. Fiedler & M. M. Chemers, *Improving Leadership Effectiveness: The Leader Match Concept,* 2nd ed. (New York: Wiley, 1984). Available at http://depts.washington.edu/psych/faculty/*cv/fiedler_cv.pdf, 23 March 2002. Reprinted by permission of the authors.

as the degree to which a particular situation either permits or denies a leader the chance to influence the behavior of group members.[36] In highly favorable situations, leaders find that their actions influence followers, but in highly unfavorable situations, leaders have little or no success influencing the people they are trying to lead.

Three situational factors determine the favorability of a situation: leader-member relations, task structure, and position power. The most important situational factor is **leader-member relations**, which refers to how well followers respect, trust, and like their leaders. When leader-member relations are good, followers trust the leader and there is a friendly work atmosphere. Such was the case under Gordon Bethune, CEO of Continental Airlines for 10 years. Joe Caudle, a Continental employee, says, "I've worked under a lot of presidents and CEOs. When the others came around, the employees would be ducking out. But with him, it's 'Hey, Bethune's upstairs!' They start smiling and want to shake his hand."[37] **Task structure** is the degree to which the requirements of a subordinate's tasks are clearly specified. With highly structured tasks, employees have clear job responsibilities, goals, and procedures. **Position power** is the degree to which leaders are able to hire, fire, reward, and punish workers. The more influence leaders have over hiring, firing, rewards, and punishments, the greater their power.

Exhibit 14.7 shows how leader-member relations, task structure, and position power can be combined into eight situations that differ in their favorability to leaders. In general, Situation I, on the left side of Exhibit 14.7, is the most favorable leader situation. Followers like and trust their leaders and know what to do because their tasks are highly structured. Also, the leaders have the formal power to influence workers through hiring, firing, rewarding, and punishing them. Therefore, in Situation I, it's relatively easy for a leader to influence followers. By contrast, Situation VIII, on the right side of Exhibit 14.7, is the least favorable situation for leaders. Followers don't like or trust their leaders. Plus, followers are not sure what they're supposed to be doing, given that their tasks or jobs are highly unstructured. Finally, leaders find it difficult to influence followers because they don't have the ability to hire, fire, reward, or punish the people who work for them. In short, it's very difficult to influence followers given the conditions found in Situation VIII.

3.3 Matching Leadership Styles to Situations

After studying thousands of leaders and followers in hundreds of different situations, Fiedler found that the performance of relationship- and task-oriented leaders followed the pattern displayed in Exhibit 14.8.

Relationship-oriented leaders with high LPC scores were better leaders (that is, their groups performed more effectively) under moderately favorable situations. In moderately favorable situations, the leader may be liked somewhat, tasks may be somewhat structured, and the leader may have some position power. In this situation, a relationship-oriented leader improves leader-member relations, which is the most

leader-member relations the degree to which followers respect, trust, and like their leaders

task structure the degree to which the requirements of a subordinate's tasks are clearly specified

position power the degree to which leaders are able to hire, fire, reward, and punish workers

Exhibit 14.7

Situational Favorableness

Leader-Member Relations	Good	Good	Good	Good	Poor	Poor	Poor	Poor
Task Structure	High	High	Low	Low	High	High	Low	Low
Position Power	Strong	Weak	Strong	Weak	Strong	Weak	Strong	Weak
Situation	I	II	III	IV	V	VI	VII	VIII
	Favorable			**Moderately Favorable**			**Unfavorable**	

Leader-Member Relations	Good	Good	Good	Good	Poor	Poor	Poor	Poor
Task Structure	High	High	Low	Low	High	High	Low	Low
Position Power	Strong	Weak	Strong	Weak	Strong	Weak	Strong	Weak
Situation	I	II	III	IV	V	VI	VII	VIII

Favorable **Moderately Favorable** **Unfavorable**

Exhibit 14.8

Matching Leadership Styles to Situations

important of the three situational factors. In turn, morale and performance improve. How did Gordon Bethune turn around Continental Airlines and its previously poisonous labor-management relations? Bethune explains it this way: "When I was a mechanic, I knew how much faster I could fix an airplane when I wanted to fix it than when I didn't. I've tried to make it so our guys want to do it."[38] By contrast, as Exhibit 14.8 shows, task-oriented leaders with low LPC scores are better leaders in highly favorable and unfavorable situations. Task-oriented leaders do well in favorable situations where leaders are liked, tasks are structured, and the leader has the power to hire, fire, reward, and punish. In these favorable situations, task-oriented leaders effectively step on the gas of a well-tuned car that's in perfect running condition. Their focus on performance sets the goal for the group, which then charges forward to meet it. But task-oriented leaders also do well in unfavorable situations where leaders are disliked, tasks are unstructured, and the leader doesn't have the power to hire, fire, reward, and punish. In these unfavorable situations, the task-oriented leader sets goals, which focus attention on performance, and clarifies what needs to be done, thus overcoming low task structure. This is enough to jump-start performance, even if workers don't like or trust the leader. Finally, though not shown in Exhibit 14.8, people with moderate LPC scores, who can be somewhat relationship oriented or somewhat task oriented, tend to do fairly well in all situations because they can adapt their behavior. Typically, though, they don't perform quite as well as relationship-oriented or task-oriented leaders whose leadership styles are well matched to the situation.

Recall, however, that Fiedler assumes that leaders are incapable of changing their leadership styles. Accordingly, the key to applying Fiedler's contingency theory in the workplace is to accurately measure and match leaders to situations or to teach leaders how to change situational favorableness by changing leader-member relations, task structure, or position power. Though matching or placing leaders in appropriate situations works particularly well, practicing managers have had little luck with "reengineering situations" to fit their leadership styles. The primary problem, as you've no doubt realized, is the complexity of the theory. In a study designed to teach leaders how to reengineer their situations to fit their leadership styles, Fiedler found that most of the leaders simply did not understand what they were supposed to do to change their leadership situations. Furthermore, if they didn't like their LPC profile (perhaps they felt they were more relationship oriented than their scores indicated), they arbitrarily changed it to better suit their view of themselves. Of course, the theory won't work as well if leaders are attempting to change situational factors to fit their perceived leadership style and not their real leadership style.[39]

Fiedler's theory assumes that leaders are effective when their work groups perform well, that leaders are unable to change their leadership styles, that leadership styles must be matched to the proper situation, and that favorable situations permit leaders to influence group members. According to the Least Preferred Coworker (LPC) scale, there are two basic leadership styles. People who describe their LPC in a positive way have relationship-oriented leadership styles. By contrast, people who describe their LPC in a negative way have task-oriented leadership styles. Situational favorableness, which occurs when leaders can influence followers is determined by leader-member relations, task structure, and position power. In general, relationship-oriented leaders with high LPC scores are better leaders under moderately favorable situations, while task-oriented leaders with low LPC scores are better leaders in highly favorable and unfavorable situations. Since Fiedler assumes that leaders are incapable of changing their leadership styles, the key is to accurately measure and match leaders to situations or to teach leaders how to change situational factors. Though matching or placing leaders in appropriate situations works well, "reengineering situations" to fit leadership styles doesn't because of the complexity of the model, which makes it difficult for people to understand.

4 Adapting Leader Behavior: Path-Goal Theory

"WHAT'S NEW" COMPANY

Just as its name suggests, **path-goal theory** states that leaders can increase subordinate satisfaction and performance by clarifying and clearing the paths to goals and by increasing the number and kinds of rewards available for goal attainment. Said another way, leaders need to clarify how followers can achieve organizational goals, take care of problems that prevent followers from achieving goals, and then find more and varied rewards to motivate followers to achieve those goals.[40]

For path clarification, path clearing, and rewards to increase followers' motivation and effort, however, leaders must meet two conditions. First, leader behavior must be a source of immediate or future satisfaction for followers. Therefore, the things you do as a leader must please your followers today or lead to activities or rewards that will satisfy them in the future. For example, Carla Jones, who works in marketing for EDWARD JONES, the St. Louis–based investment company that has been near the top of *Fortune*'s list of the top 100 companies to work for, hasn't looked outside the company for career opportunities since she joined the company 14 years ago. Indeed, Edward Jones' management does such a good job of satisfying its workers that a phenomenal 83 percent of its associates plan to work there until they retire.[41]

Second, while providing the coaching, guidance, support, and rewards necessary for effective work performance, leader behaviors must

path-goal theory a leadership theory that states that leaders can increase subordinate satisfaction and performance by clarifying and clearing the paths to goals and by increasing the number and kinds of rewards available for goal attainment

Exhibit 14.9
Basic Assumptions of Path-Goal Theory

- Clarify paths to goals.
- Clear paths to goals by solving problems and removing roadblocks.
- Increase the number and kinds of rewards available for goal attainment.
- Do things that satisfy followers today or will lead to future rewards or satisfaction.
- Offer followers something unique and valuable beyond what they're experiencing or can already do for themselves.

Source: R. J. House & T. R. Mitchell, "Path-Goal Theory of Leadership," *Journal of Contemporary Business* 3 (1974): 81–97.

complement and not duplicate the characteristics of followers' work environments. Thus, leader behaviors must offer something unique and valuable to followers beyond what they're already experiencing as they do their jobs or what they can already do for themselves. Exhibit 14.9 summarizes these basic assumptions of path-goal theory.

In contrast to Fiedler's contingency theory, path-goal theory assumes that leaders can change and adapt their leadership styles. Exhibit 14.10 illustrates this process, showing that leaders change and adapt their leadership styles contingent on their subordinates or the environment in which those subordinates work.

*Let's learn more about path-goal theory by examining **4.1 the four kinds of leadership styles that leaders use, 4.2 the subordinate and environmental contingency factors that determine when different leader styles are effective,** and **4.3 the outcomes of path-goal theory in improving employee satisfaction and performance**.*

4.1 Leadership Styles

As illustrated in Exhibit 14.10, the four leadership styles in path-goal theory are directive, supportive, participative, and achievement oriented.[42] **Directive leadership** involves letting employees know precisely what is expected of them, giving them specific guidelines for performing tasks, scheduling work, setting standards of performance, and making sure that people follow standard rules and regulations. For example, "each month, *Audi*'s compulsive chief executive, Martin Winterkorn, rolls up his sleeves and leads a trouble-shooting session with managers and engineers at the company's electronics center, zeroing in on faulty systems and problem parts. Winterkorn's rules: no shifting the blame to anyone else, such as suppliers. No phone calls to subordinates—the brains to remedy the defects better be in the room. And no one leaves until a fix is found."[43] Why is Winterkorn so demanding (that is, directive)? As he explains, "We want [Audi] to be the No. 1 premium [car] brand," and you don't achieve that goal easily when you're competing with Lexus, Mercedes, BMW, and Acura.

Supportive leadership involves being friendly to and approachable by employees, showing concern for them and their welfare, treating them as equals, and creating a friendly climate. Supportive leadership is very similar to considerate leader behavior. Supportive leadership often results in employee satisfaction with the job and with leaders. This leadership style may also result in improved performance when it increases employee confidence, lowers employee job stress, or improves relations and trust between employees and leaders.[44] For example, husband and wife Shane and Allison Alexander both work for Wal-Mart in Madisonville, Kentucky. Over the years, the Wal-Mart managers in their store have shown concern for them in a number of important ways. For example, since the Alexanders had only one car, Wal-Mart managers scheduled them for alternating shifts, which also allowed them to care for their baby without outside help, and made sure the couple had some Saturdays off to spend time as a family.[45]

directive leadership a leadership style in which the leader lets employees know precisely what is expected of them, gives them specific guidelines for performing tasks, schedules work, sets standards of performance, and makes sure that people follow standard rules and regulations

supportive leadership a leadership style in which the leader is friendly to and approachable, shows concern for employees and their welfare, treats them as equals, and creates a friendly climate

Exhibit 14.10

Path-Goal Theory

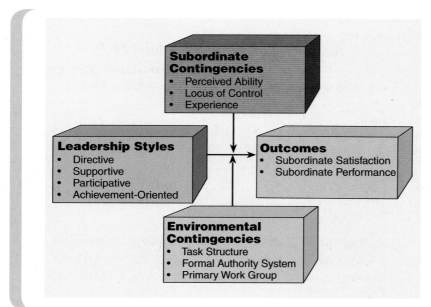

Participative leadership involves consulting employees for their suggestions and input before making decisions. Participation in decision making should help followers understand which goals are most important and clarify the paths to accomplishing them. Furthermore, when people participate in decisions, they become more committed to making them work. At the customer call center at United Kingdom–based Kwik-Fit Financial Services, managers were overly aggressive, employees were not consulted about anything, and annual employee turnover was 52 percent. When Kwik-Fit changed to a highly participative approach, managers met with all 650 employees in small groups and asked them what it would take to make the call center a good place to work. After those initial discussions, seven project groups, which included people from across the company, began addressing problems in facilities, incentives, pay, management style, management processes, and customer service. Today, because of those project groups, Kwik-Fit has an improved flexible benefits plan; flextime work scheduling; a "chillout" room with a TV, video game machine, pool table, and air hockey table; a concierge to take care of employees' nonwork tasks (dry cleaning, running to the bank); and new phone/customer software for doing their jobs. As a result of these employee-suggested changes, employee turnover has fallen to 35 percent, 66 percent of employees (up from 40 percent) recommend Kwik-Fit as a place to work, customer complaints are down 50 percent, customer satisfaction has risen from 90 to 94 percent, and profits are up by 50 percent.[46]

Achievement-oriented leadership means setting challenging goals, having high expectations of employees, and displaying confidence that employees will assume responsibility and put forth extraordinary effort. Simon Cooper, president and COO of the *RITZ-CARLTON* luxury hotel chain, uses the phrase "He who says it, does" to describe achievement-oriented leadership, Cooper explains, "I use this phrase whenever someone convinces me that they can achieve something I consider to be unachievable. In the past I've been known to add focus to a goal by making a bet to see if they can make it—sometimes with amusing consequences. I remember being at a mountain resort in Canada and proposing an incredible goal for the season. The team convinced me that they could achieve it, and I offered to jump into the lake if they did. It's a long story, but they made it. There's a great scene of a hole being cut in the ice and an ambulance on standby while I gave a whole new meaning to the term 'dunking.' The cognac [afterwards] was very welcome."[47]

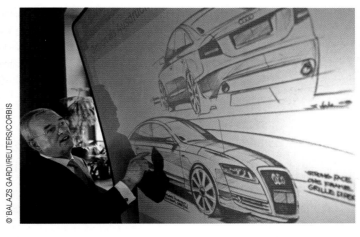

In addition to being a directive leader, Audi president Martin Winterkorn has deep technical knowledge in his field, which gives him credibility when he assigns work and sets goals and procedures. Winterkorn is shown here giving a lecture on car design concepts at the Budapest Technical University.

4.2 Subordinate and Environmental Contingencies

As shown in Exhibit 14.10, path-goal theory specifies that leader behaviors should be fitted to subordinate characteristics. The theory identifies three kinds of subordinate contingencies: perceived ability, experience, and locus of control. *Perceived ability* is simply how much ability subordinates believe they have for doing their jobs well. Subordinates who perceive that they have a great deal of ability will be dissatisfied with directive leader behaviors. Experienced employees are likely to react in a similar way. Since they already know how to do their jobs (or perceive that they do), they don't need or want close supervision. By contrast, subordinates with little experience or little perceived ability will welcome directive leadership.

Locus of control is a personality measure that indicates the extent to which people believe that they have control over what happens to them in life. *Internals* believe

participative leadership a leadership style in which the leader consults employees for their suggestions and input before making decisions

achievement-oriented leadership a leadership style in which the leader sets challenging goals, has high expectations of employees, and displays confidence that employees will assume responsibility and put forth extraordinary effort that what happens to them, good or bad, is largely a result of their choices and actions. *Externals*, on the other hand, believe that what happens to them is caused by external forces beyond their control. Accordingly, externals are much more comfortable with a directive leadership style, while internals greatly prefer a participative leadership style because they like to have a say in what goes on at work.

> In the past I've been known to add focus to a goal by making a bet to see if they can make it—sometimes with amusing consequences.

SIMON COOPER, PRESIDENT AND COO, RITZ-CARLTON

Path-goal theory specifies that leader behaviors should complement rather than duplicate the characteristics of followers' work environments. There are three kinds of environmental contingencies: task structure, the formal authority system, and the primary work group. As in Fiedler's contingency theory, *task structure* is the degree to which the requirements of a subordinate's tasks are clearly specified. When task structure is low and tasks are unclear, directive leadership should be used because it complements the work environment. When task structure is high and tasks are clear, however, directive leadership is not needed because it duplicates what task structure provides. Alternatively, when tasks are stressful, frustrating, or dissatisfying, leaders should respond with supportive leadership.

The *formal authority system* is an organization's set of procedures, rules, and policies. When the formal authority system is unclear, directive leadership complements the situation by reducing uncertainty and increasing clarity. But when the formal authority system is clear, directive leadership is redundant and should not be used.

Primary work group refers to the amount of work-oriented participation or emotional support that is provided by an employee's immediate work group. Participative leadership should be used when tasks are complex and there is little existing work-oriented participation in the primary work group. When tasks are stressful, frustrating, or repetitive, supportive leadership is called for.

Finally, since keeping track of all of these subordinate and environmental contingencies can get a bit confusing, Exhibit 14.11 provides a summary of when directive, supportive, participative, and achievement-oriented leadership styles should be used.

Exhibit 14.11

Path-Goal Theory: When to Use Directive, Supportive, Participative, or Achievement-Oriented Leadership

DIRECTIVE LEADERSHIP	SUPPORTIVE LEADERSHIP	PARTICIPATIVE LEADERSHIP	ACHIEVEMENT-ORIENTED LEADERSHIP
Unstructured tasks	Structured, simple, repetitive tasks	Experienced workers	Unchallenging tasks
Inexperienced workers	Stressful, frustrating tasks	Workers with high perceived ability	
Workers with low perceived ability	When workers lack confidence	Workers with internal locus of control	
Workers with external locus of control	Clear formal authority system	Workers not satisfied with rewards	
Unclear formal authority system		Complex tasks	

4.3 Outcomes

Does following path-goal theory improve subordinate satisfaction and performance? Preliminary evidence suggests that it does.[48] In particular, people who work for supportive leaders are much more satisfied with their jobs and their bosses. Likewise, people who work for directive leaders are more satisfied with their jobs and bosses (but not quite as much as when their bosses are supportive) and perform their jobs better, too. Does adapting one's leadership style to subordinate and environmental characteristics improve subordinate satisfaction and performance? At this point, because of the difficulty of completely testing this complex theory, it's too early to tell.[49] However, since the data clearly show that it makes sense for leaders to be both supportive *and* directive, it also makes sense that leaders could improve subordinate satisfaction and performance by adding participative and achievement-oriented leadership styles to their capabilities as leaders.

mgmt: fact

Executive Turnover

In 2005, 1,322 CEOs changed at U.S. companies, for an average of five exits per business day. The first half of 2006 proved just as robust, with 728 CEOs leaving (or losing) their positions—an average of six per day. The health-care industry alone accounted for 124 of those exits.

Source: Telis Demos, "Leading Indicators," *Fortune*, August 7, 2006, 15.

Review 4: *Adapting Leader Behavior: Path-Goal Theory*

Path-goal theory states that leaders can increase subordinate satisfaction and performance by clarifying and clearing the paths to goals and by increasing the number and kinds of rewards available for goal attainment. For this to work, however, leader behavior must be a source of immediate or future satisfaction for followers and must complement and not duplicate the characteristics of followers' work environments. In contrast to Fiedler's contingency theory, path-goal theory assumes that leaders can and do change and adapt their leadership styles (directive, supportive, participative, and achievement oriented), depending on their subordinates (experience, perceived ability, internal or external) or the environment in which those subordinates work (task structure, formal authority system, or primary work group).

5 Adapting Leader Behavior: Hersey and Blanchard's Situational Leadership® Theory*

Have you ever had a new job that you didn't know how to do and your boss was not around to help you learn it? Conversely, have you ever known exactly how to do your job but your boss kept treating you as though you didn't? Hersey and Blanchard's Situational Leadership theory is based on the idea of follower readiness. Hersey and Blanchard argue that employees have different levels of readiness for handling different jobs, responsibilities, and work assignments. Accordingly, Hersey

---

* Situational Leadership® is a registered trademark of the Center for Leadership Studies.

and Blanchard's **situational theory** states that leaders need to adjust their leadership styles to match followers' readiness.[50]

Let's learn more about Hersey and Blanchard's situational theory by examining **5.1 worker readiness** *and* **5.2 different leadership styles**.

5.1 Worker Readiness

Worker readiness is the ability and willingness to take responsibility for directing one's behavior at work. Readiness is composed of two components. *Job readiness* consists of the amount of knowledge, skill, ability, and experience people have to perform their jobs. As you would expect, people with greater skill, ability, and experience do a better job of supervising their own work. *Psychological readiness*, on the other hand, is a feeling of self-confidence or self-respect. Likewise, confident people are better at guiding their own work than insecure people are. Job readiness and psychological readiness are combined to produce four different levels of readiness in Hersey and Blanchard's Situational Leadership theory. The lowest level, R1, represents insecure people who are neither willing nor able to take responsibility for guiding their own work. R2 represents people who are confident and willing but not able to take responsibility for guiding their own work. R3 represents people who are insecure and able but not willing to take responsibility for guiding their own work. And R4 represents people who are confident and willing and able to take responsibility for guiding their own work. It's important to note that a follower's readiness is usually task specific. For example, you may be highly confident and capable when it comes to personal computers, but know nothing about setting up budgets for planning purposes. Thus, you would possess readiness (R4) with respect to computers but not with respect to budgets.

5.2 Leadership Styles

Similar to Blake and Mouton's managerial grid, situational theory defines leadership styles in terms of task behavior (that is, concern for production) and relationship behavior (that is, concern for people). These two behaviors can be combined to form four different leadership styles: telling, selling, participating, and delegating. Leaders choose one of these styles depending on the readiness a follower has for a specific task.

A *telling* leadership style (high task behavior and low relationship behavior) is based on one-way communication, in which followers are told what, how, when, and where to do particular tasks. Telling is used when people are at the R1 stage. For instance, someone using a telling leadership style would identify all the steps in a project and give explicit instructions on exactly how to execute each one.

A *selling* leadership style (high task behavior and high relationship behavior) involves two-way communication and psychological support to encourage followers to "own" or "buy into" particular ways of doing things. Selling is used most appropriately at the R2 stage. For instance, someone using a selling leadership style might say, "We're going to start a company newsletter. I really think that's a great idea, don't you? We're going to need some cost estimates from printers and some comments from each manager. But that's pretty straightforward. Oh, don't forget that we need the CEO's comments, too. She's expecting you to call. I know that you'll do a great job on this. We'll meet next Tuesday to see if you have any questions once you've dug into this. By the way, we need to have this done by next Friday."

A *participating* style (low task behavior and high relationship behavior) is based on two-way communication and shared decision making. Participating is used with

situational theory a leadership theory that states that leaders need to adjust their leadership styles to match their followers' readiness

worker readiness the ability and willingness to take responsibility for directing one's behavior at work employees at R3. Since the problem is with motivation and not ability, someone using a participating leadership style might solicit ideas from a subordinate about a project, let the subordinate get started, but ask to review progress along the way.

A *delegating* style (low task behavior and low relationship behavior) is used when leaders basically let workers "run their own show" and make their own decisions. Delegating is used for people at R4. For instance, someone using a delegating leadership style might say, "We're going to start a company newsletter. You've got 10 days to do it. Run with it. Let me know when you've got it done. I'll e-mail you a couple of ideas, but other than that, do what you think is best. Thanks."

In general, as people become more "ready," and thus more willing and able to guide their own behavior, leaders should become less task oriented and more relationship oriented. Then, as people become even more "ready," leaders should become both less task oriented and less relationship oriented until people eventually manage their own work with little input from their leaders.

How well does Hersey and Blanchard's situational theory work? Despite its intuitive appeal (managers and consultants tend to prefer it over Fiedler's contingency theory because of its underlying logic and simplicity), most studies don't support situational theory.[51] While managers generally do a good job of judging followers' readiness levels, the theory doesn't seem to work well, except at lower levels, where a telling style is recommended for people who are insecure and neither willing nor able to take responsibility for guiding their own work.[52]

Review 5: Adapting Leader Behavior: Hersey and Blanchard's Situational Leadership Theory

According to situational theory, leaders need to adjust their leadership styles to match their followers' readiness, which is the ability (job readiness) and willingness (psychological readiness) to take responsibility for directing one's work. Job readiness and psychological readiness combine to produce four different levels of readiness (R1–R4), which vary based on people's confidence, ability, and willingness to guide their own work. Situational theory combines task and relationship behavior to create four leadership styles—telling (R1), selling (R2), participating (R3), and delegating (R4)—that are used with employees at different readiness levels.

6 Adapting Leader Behavior: Normative Decision Theory

For years, your company has insisted on formal business attire for men and women. Now, however, you want to make a change to casual wear. Do you make the decision yourself and announce it, or do you consult your employees before making the decision?

To keep up with the exponential growth in one of your sales regions, you're going to cut the region in half, add staff, and effectively reduce the earnings of its sales representatives and managers. Do you make the decision yourself, announce it, and then live with the backlash? Do you consult all of your regional managers before making this decision? Or do you go straight to the salespeople in the region to let them know about your concerns?

Many people believe that making tough decisions is at the heart of leadership. Yet experienced leaders will tell you that deciding how to make decisions is just as important. The **normative decision theory** (also known as the *Vroom-Yetton-Jago model*) helps leaders decide how much employee participation (from none to letting employees make the entire decision) should be used when making decisions.[53]

*Let's learn more about normative decision theory by investigating **6.1 decision styles** and **6.2 decision quality and acceptance**.*

6.1 Decision Styles

Unlike nearly all of the other leadership theories discussed in this chapter, which have specified leadership styles, that is, the way a leader generally behaves toward followers, the normative decision theory specifies five different decision styles, or ways of making decisions. (See Chapter 5 for a more complete review of decision making in organizations.) As shown in Exhibit 14.12, those styles vary from *autocratic decisions* (AI or AII) on the left, in which leaders make the decisions by themselves, to *consultative decisions* (CI or CII), in which leaders share problems with subordinates but still make the decisions themselves, to *group decisions* (GII) on the right, in which leaders share the problems with subordinates and then have the group make the decisions. **GE AIRCRAFT ENGINES** in Durham, North Carolina, uses a similar approach when making decisions. According to *Fast Company* magazine, "At GE/Durham, every decision is either an 'A' decision, a 'B' decision, or a 'C' decision. An 'A' decision is one that the plant manager makes herself, without consulting anyone."[54] Plant manager Paula Sims says, "I don't make very many of those, and when I do make one, everyone at the plant knows it. I make maybe 10 or 12 a year."[55] "B" decisions are also made by the plant manager, but with input from the people affected. "C" decisions, the most common type, are made by consensus, by the people directly involved, with plenty of discussion. With "C" decisions, the view of the plant manager doesn't necessarily carry more weight than the views of those affected."[56]

"WHAT'S NEW" COMPANY

normative decision theory a theory that suggests how leaders can determine an appropriate amount of employee participation when making decisions

Exhibit 14.12

Decision Styles and Levels of Employee Participation

Leader solves the problem or makes the decision				**Leader is willing to accept any decision supported by the entire group**
AI	**AII**	**CI**	**CII**	**GII**
Using information available at the time, the leader solves the problem or makes the decision.	The leader obtains necessary information from employees, and then selects a solution to the problem. When asked to share information, employees may or may not be told what the problem is.	The leader shares the problem and gets ideas and suggestions from relevant employees on an individual basis. Individuals are not brought together as a group. Then the leader makes the decision, which may or may not reflect their input.	The leader shares the problem with employees as a group, obtains their ideas and suggestions, and then makes the decision, which may or may not reflect their input.	The leader shares the problem with employees as a group. Together, the leader and employees generate and evaluate alternatives and try to reach an agreement on a solution. The leader acts as a facilitator and does not try to influence the group. The leader is willing to accept and implement any solution that has the support of the entire group.

Source: Adapted from V. H. Vroom & P. W. Yetton, *Leadership and Decision Making* (Pittsburgh: University of Pittsburgh Press, 1973),

6.2 Decision Quality and Acceptance

According to the normative decision theory, using the right degree of employee participation improves the quality of decisions and the extent to which employees accept and are committed to decisions. Exhibit 14.13 lists the decision rules that normative decision theory uses to increase decision quality and employee acceptance and commitment. The quality, leader information, subordinate information, goal congruence, and problem structure rules are used to increase decision quality. For example, the leader information rule states that if a leader doesn't have enough information to make a decision on his or her own, then the leader should not use an autocratic decision style.

The commitment probability, subordinate conflict, and commitment requirement rules shown in Exhibit 14.13 are used to increase employee acceptance and commitment to decisions. For example, the commitment requirement rule says that if decision acceptance and commitment are important, and the subordinates share the organization's goals, then you shouldn't use an autocratic or consultative style. In other words, if followers want to do what's best for the company and you need their acceptance and commitment to make a decision work, then use a group decision style and let them make the decision.

As you can see, these decision rules help leaders improve decision quality and follower acceptance and commitment by eliminating decision styles that don't fit the decision or situation they're facing. Normative decision theory then operationalizes these decision rules in the form of yes/no questions, which are shown in the decision tree displayed in Exhibit 14.14. You start at the left side of the model and answer the first question, "How important is the technical quality of this decision?" by choosing "high" or "low." Then you continue by answering each question as you proceed along the decision tree until you get to a recommended decision style.

Exhibit 14.13

Normative Theory Decision Rules

DECISION RULES TO INCREASE DECISION QUALITY

Quality Rule. If the quality of the decision is important, then don't use an autocratic decision style.

Leader Information Rule. If the quality of the decision is important, and if the leader doesn't have enough information to make the decision on his or her own, then don't use an autocratic decision style.

Subordinate Information Rule. If the quality of the decision is important, and if the subordinates don't have enough information to make the decision themselves, then don't use a group decision style.

Goal Congruence Rule. If the quality of the decision is important, and subordinates' goals are different from the organization's goals, then don't use a group decision style.

Problem Structure Rule. If the quality of the decision is important, the leader doesn't have enough information to make the decision on his or her own, and the problem is unstructured, then don't use an autocratic decision style.

DECISION RULES TO INCREASE DECISION ACCEPTANCE

Commitment Probability Rule. If having subordinates accept and commit to the decision is important, then don't use an autocratic decision style.

Subordinate Conflict Rule. If having subordinates accept the decision is important and critical to successful implementation and subordinates are likely to disagree or end up in conflict over the decision, then don't use an autocratic or consultative decision style.

Commitment Requirement Rule. If having subordinates accept the decision is absolutely required for successful implementation and subordinates share the organization's goals, then don't use an autocratic or consultative style.

Sources: Adapted from V. H. Vroom, "Leadership," in *Handbook of Industrial and Organizational Psychology*, ed. M. D. Dunnette (Chicago: Rand McNally, 1976); V. H. Vroom & A. G. Jago, *The New Leadership: Managing Participation in Organizations* (Englewood Cliffs, NJ: Prentice Hall, 1988).

Exhibit 14.14

Normative Decision Theory Tree for Determining the Level of Participation in Decision Making

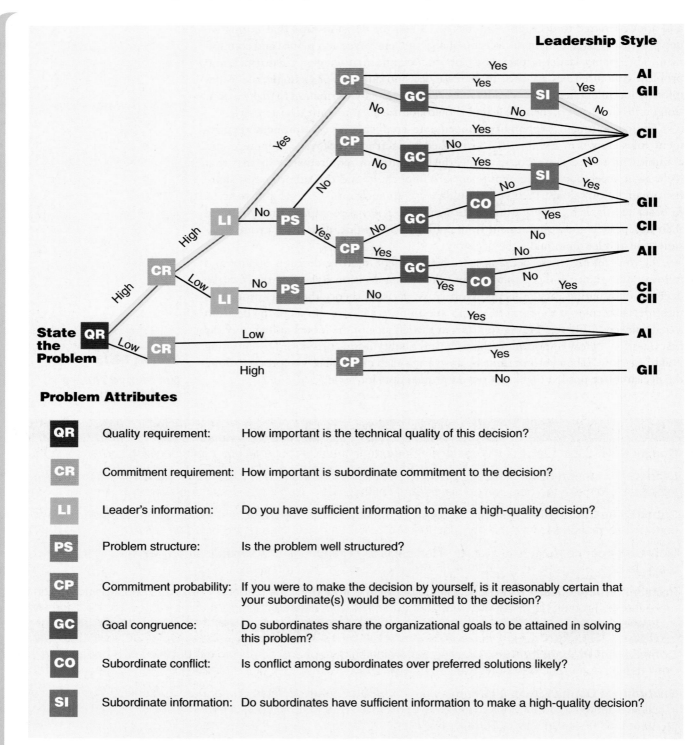

Leadership Style

Problem Attributes

QR	Quality requirement:	How important is the technical quality of this decision?	
CR	Commitment requirement:	How important is subordinate commitment to the decision?	
LI	Leader's information:	Do you have sufficient information to make a high-quality decision?	
PS	Problem structure:	Is the problem well structured?	
CP	Commitment probability:	If you were to make the decision by yourself, is it reasonably certain that your subordinate(s) would be committed to the decision?	
GC	Goal congruence:	Do subordinates share the organizational goals to be attained in solving this problem?	
CO	Subordinate conflict:	Is conflict among subordinates over preferred solutions likely?	
SI	Subordinate information:	Do subordinates have sufficient information to make a high-quality decision?	

Source: V. H. Vroom & P. W. Yetton, *Leadership and Decision Making* (Pittsburgh: University of Pittsburgh Press, 1973). Adapted and reprinted by permission of University of Pittsburgh Press.

Let's use the model to make the decision of whether to change from a formal business attire policy to a casual wear policy. The problem sounds simple, but it is actually more complex than you might think. Follow the yellow line in Exhibit 14.14 as we work through the decision in the discussion below.

Problem: Change to Casual Wear?

1. *Quality requirement: How important is the technical quality of this decision?* High. This question has to do with whether there are quality differences in the alternatives and whether those quality differences matter. Although most people would assume that quality isn't an issue here, it really is, given the overall positive changes that generally accompany changes to casual wear.

2. *Commitment requirement: How important is subordinate commitment to the decision?* High. Changes in culture, like dress codes, require subordinate commitment or they fail.

3. *Leader's information: Do you have sufficient information to make a high-quality decision?* Yes. Let's assume that you've done your homework. Much has been written about casual wear, from how to make the change to the effects it has in companies (almost all positive).

4. *Commitment probability: If you were to make the decision by yourself, is it reasonably certain that your subordinate(s) would be committed to the decision?* No. Studies of casual wear find that employees' reactions are almost uniformly positive. Nonetheless, employees are likely to be angry if you change something as personal as clothing policies without consulting them.

How much involvement should employees have in creating the company dress code? Use Exhibit 14.14 as you think through the issue.

5. *Goal congruence: Do subordinates share the organizational goals to be attained in solving this problem?* Yes. The goals that usually accompany a change to casual dress policies are a more informal culture, better communication, and less money spent on business attire.

6. *Subordinate information: Do subordinates have sufficient information to make a high-quality decision?* No. Most employees know little about casual wear policies or even what constitutes casual wear in most companies. Consequently, most companies have to educate employees about casual wear practices and policies before making a decision.

7. *CII is the answer:* With a CII, or consultative decision process, the leader shares the problem with employees as a group, obtains their ideas and suggestions, and then makes the decision, which may or may not reflect their input. So, given the answers to these questions (remember, different managers won't necessarily answer these questions the same way), the normative decision theory recommends that leaders consult with their subordinates before deciding whether to change to a casual wear policy.

How well does the normative decision theory work? A prominent leadership scholar has described it as the best supported of all leadership theories.[57] In general, the more managers violate the decision rules in Exhibit 14.13, the less effective their decisions are, especially with respect to subordinate acceptance and commitment.[58]

Review 6: Adapting Leader Behavior: Normative Decision Theory

The normative decision theory helps leaders decide how much employee participation should be used when making decisions. Using the right degree of employee participation improves the quality of decisions and the extent to which employees accept and are committed to decisions. The theory specifies five different decision styles or ways of making decisions: autocratic decisions (AI or AII), consultative decisions (CI or CII), and group decisions (GII). The theory improves decision quality via the quality, leader information, subordinate information, goal congruence, and unstructured problem decision rules. The theory improves employee commitment and acceptance via the commitment probability, subordinate conflict, and commitment requirement decision rules. These decision rules help leaders improve decision quality and follower acceptance and commitment by eliminating decision styles that don't fit the decision or situation they're facing. Normative decision theory then operationalizes these decision rules in the form of yes/no questions, as shown in the decision tree displayed in Exhibit 14.14.

STRATEGIC LEADERSHIP

Thus far, you have read about three major leadership ideas: traits, behaviors, and situational theories. Leader *traits* are relatively stable characteristics, such as abilities or psychological motives. Traits capture who effective leaders are. Leader *behaviors* are the actions leaders take to influence others to achieve group or organizational goals. Behaviors capture what effective leaders do (that is, initiate structure and consideration). And *situational theories* indicate that the effectiveness of a leadership style, the way a leader generally behaves toward followers, depends on the situation. Situational theories capture what leaders need to do or not do in particular situations or circumstances. This final part of the chapter introduces a fourth major leadership idea—strategic leadership—and its components: visionary, charismatic, and transformational leadership.

Strategic leadership is the ability to anticipate, envision, maintain flexibility, think strategically, and work with others to initiate changes that will create a positive future for an organization.[59] GENERAL ELECTRIC is one of the best run and most profitable companies in the world. Yet since taking charge seven years ago, CEO Jeffrey Immelt has led GE through a series of strategic changes that have made the company more global, more customer-oriented, and more focused on developing new technology for new markets.[60] Immelt explains his strategic leadership this way, "In my case, I was taking over a well-known company that had been led by a famous and excellent CEO [Jack Welch]. But I never wanted to run *that* company, and I never wanted to be *that* CEO. [But] I knew the company had to change. I would say most of us were trained to have a pretty healthy disrespect for history. We respect performance, respect integrity, but everybody was trained to have a look-forward attitude instead of look-backward. I inherited a company that had great strengths for a long time—good risk management, good cost control, good productivity—and I viewed the mission for my generation as not to lose those things but to build capability around growth, which we didn't have."[61] Thus, strategic leadership captures how leaders inspire their companies to change and their followers to give extraordinary effort to accomplish organizational goals.

strategic leadership the ability to anticipate, envision, maintain flexibility, think strategically, and work with others to initiate changes that will create a positive future for an organization

After reading the next section, you should be able to

7 *explain how visionary leadership (that is, charismatic and transformational leadership) helps leaders achieve strategic leadership.*

7 Visionary Leadership

In Chapter 5, we defined *vision* as a statement of a company's purpose or reason for existing. Similarly, **visionary leadership** creates a positive image of the future that motivates organizational members and provides direction for future planning and goal setting.[62]

*Two kinds of visionary leadership are **7.1 charismatic leadership** and **7.2 transformational leadership**.*

7.1 Charismatic Leadership

Charisma is a Greek word meaning "divine gift." The ancient Greeks saw people with charisma as inspired by the gods and capable of incredible accomplishments. German sociologist Max Weber viewed charisma as a special bond between leaders and followers.[63] Weber wrote that the special qualities of charismatic leaders enable them to strongly influence followers. For example, Richard Scrushy, a founder and the former CEO of HealthSouth, a worldwide provider of health care (outpatient surgery, diagnostic imaging, and rehabilitation), was undoubtedly a charismatic leader. Scrushy, who had a magnetic personality, personally recruited many of HealthSouth's employees and top managers. Says one employee, "When he was talking, you could be hypnotized by him."[64] Dean Thomas Ratcliffe of Troy State University's business school says, "Heck, I [got] goosebumps listening to him."[65] Weber also noted that charismatic leaders tend to emerge in times of crisis and that the radical solutions they propose enhance the admiration that followers feel for them. Indeed, charismatic leaders tend to have incredible influence over their followers, who may be inspired by their leaders and become fanatically devoted to them. From this perspective, charismatic leaders are often seen as larger-than-life or uniquely special.

Charismatic leaders have strong, confident, dynamic personalities that attract followers and enable the leaders to create strong bonds with their followers. Followers trust charismatic leaders, are loyal to them, and are inspired to work toward the accomplishment of the leader's vision. Followers who become devoted to charismatic leaders may go to extraordinary lengths to please them. Therefore, we can define **charismatic leadership** as the behavioral tendencies and personal characteristics of leaders that create an exceptionally strong relationship between them and their followers. Charismatic leaders also

- *Articulate a clear vision for the future that is based on strongly held values or morals*
- *Model those values by acting in a way consistent with the vision*
- *Communicate high performance expectations to followers*
- *Display confidence in followers' abilities to achieve the vision[66]*

Does charismatic leadership work? Studies indicate that it often does. In general, the followers of charismatic leaders are more committed and satisfied, are better performers, are more likely to trust their leaders, and simply work harder.[67] Nonetheless, charismatic leadership also has risks that are at least as large as its benefits. The problems are likely to occur with ego-driven charismatic leaders who take advantage of fanatical followers.

In general, there are two kinds of charismatic leaders, ethical charismatics and unethical charismatics.[68] **Ethical charismatics** provide developmental opportunities for followers, are open to positive and negative feedback, recognize others' contributions, share information, and have moral standards that emphasize the larger interests of the group, organization, or society. Jim McNerney, *BOEING*'s CEO, believes that providing development opportunities for followers should be a leader's highest priority. Says

visionary leadership leadership that creates a positive image of the future that motivates organizational members and provides direction for future planning and goal setting

charismatic leadership the behavioral tendencies and personal characteristics of leaders that create an exceptionally strong relationship between them and their followers

ethical charismatics charismatic leaders who provide developmental opportunities for followers, are open to positive and negative feedback, recognize others' contributions, share information, and have moral standards that emphasize the larger interests of the group, organization, or society

unethical charismatics
charismatic leaders who control and manipulate followers, do what is best for themselves instead of their organizations, want to hear only positive feedback, share only information that is beneficial to themselves, and have moral standards that put their interests before everyone else's

Six CEOs a day leave their position.

McNerney, "I don't start with the company's strategy or products. I start with people's growth because I believe that if the people who are running and participating in a company grow, then the company's growth will in many respects take care of itself. I have this idea in my mind—all of us get 15 percent better every year. . . . Usually that means your ability to lead, and that's all about your ability to chart the course for [your employees], to inspire them to reach for performance—the values you bring to the job, with a focus on the courage to do the right thing. I tend to think about this in terms of helping others get better."[69] As you would expect, ethical charismatics produce stronger commitment, higher satisfaction, more effort, better performance, and greater trust.

By contrast, **unethical charismatics** control and manipulate followers, do what is best for themselves instead of their organizations, want to hear only positive feedback, share only information that is beneficial to themselves, and have moral standards that put their interests before everyone else's. Because followers can become just as committed to unethical charismatics as to ethical characteristics, unethical characteristics pose a tremendous risk for companies. Why? According to *Fast Company*, "We're worshipful of top executives who seem charismatic, visionary, and tough. So long as they're lifting profits and stock prices, we're willing to overlook that they can also be callous, cunning, manipulative, deceitful, verbally and psychologically abusive, remorseless, exploitative, self-delusional, irresponsible, and megalomaniacal."[70]

John Thompson, a management consultant, warns, "Often what begins as a mission becomes an obsession. Leaders can cut corners on values and become driven by self-interest. Then they may abuse anyone who makes a mistake."[71] In terms of cutting corners and self-interest, it's hard to top the unethical charismatic behavior of former ENRON chief financial officer Andrew Fastow, whom *Fast Company* described as follows: "He pressured his bosses for a promotion to CFO even though he had a shaky grasp of the position's basic responsibilities, such as accounting and treasury operations. Suffering delusions of grandeur after just a little time on the job, Fastow ordered Enron's PR people to lobby *CFO* magazine to make him its CFO of the Year. But Fastow's master manipulation was a scheme to loot Enron. He set up separate partnerships, secretly run by himself, to engage in deals with Enron. The deals quickly made tens of millions of dollars for Fastow—and prettified Enron's financials in the short run by taking unwanted assets off its books. But they left Enron with time bombs that would ultimately cause the company's total implosion—and lose shareholders billions. When Enron's scandals were exposed, Fastow pleaded guilty to securities fraud and agreed to pay back nearly $24 million and serve 10 years in prison."[72]

Exhibit 14.15 shows the stark differences between ethical and unethical charismatics on several leader behaviors: exercising power, creating the vision, communicating with followers, accepting feedback, stimulating followers intellectually, developing followers, and living by moral standards. For example, in terms of creating a vision, ethical charismatics include followers' concerns and wishes by having them participate in the development of the company vision. By contrast, unethical charismatics develop a vision by themselves solely to meet their personal agendas. One unethical charismatic said, "The key thing is that it is my idea; and I am going to win with it at all costs."[73]

So, what can companies do to reduce the risks associated with unethical charismatics?[74] To start, they need a clearly written code of conduct that is fairly and consistently enforced for all managers. Next, companies should recruit, select, and promote managers with high ethical standards. Also, companies need to train leaders to value, seek, and use diverse points of view. Leaders and subordinates also need training regarding

© POLKA DOT IMAGES/JUPITER IMAGES

CHARISMATIC LEADER BEHAVIORS	ETHICAL CHARISMATICS	UNETHICAL CHARISMATICS
Exercising power	Power is used to serve others.	Power is used to dominate or manipulate others for personal gain.
Creating the vision	Followers help develop the vision.	Vision comes solely from leader and serves his or her personal agenda.
Communicating with followers	Two-way communication: Seek out viewpoints on critical issues.	One-way communication: Not open to input and suggestions from others.
Accepting feedback	Open to feedback. Willing to learn from criticism.	Inflated ego thrives on attention and admiration of sycophants. Avoid or punish candid feedback.
Stimulating followers	Want followers to think and question status quo as well as leader's views.	Don't want followers to think. Want uncritical, intellectually unquestioning acceptance of leader's ideas.
Developing followers	Focus on developing people with whom they interact. Express confidence in them and share recognition with others.	Insensitive and unresponsive to followers' needs and aspirations.
Living by moral standards	Follow self-guided principles that may go against popular opinion. Have three virtues: courage, a sense of fairness or justice, and integrity.	Follow standards only if they satisfy immediate self-interests. Manipulate impressions so that others think they are "doing the right thing." Use communication skills to manipulate others to support their personal agenda.

Source: J. M. Howell & B. J. Avolio, "The Ethics of Charismatic Leadership: Submission or Liberation?" *Academy of Management Executive* 6, no. 2 (1992): 43–54.

Exhibit 14.15

Ethical and Unethical Charismatics

ethical leader behaviors so that abuses can be recognized and corrected. Finally, companies should celebrate and reward people who exhibit ethical behaviors, especially ethical leader behaviors.[75]

7.2 Transformational Leadership

While charismatic leaders are able to articulate a clear vision, model values consistent with that vision, communicate high performance expectations, and establish very strong relationships with their followers, **transformational leadership** goes further by generating awareness and acceptance of a group's purpose and mission and by getting employees to see beyond their own needs and self-interest for the good of the group.[76] Like charismatic leaders, transformational leaders are visionary, but they transform their organizations by getting their followers to accomplish more than they intended and even more than they thought possible.

Transformational leaders are able to make their followers feel that they are a vital part of the organization and help them see how their jobs fit with the organization's vision. By linking individual and organizational interests, transformational leaders encourage followers to make sacrifices for the organization because they know that they will prosper when the organization prospers. As Exhibit 14.16 shows, transformational leadership has four components: charismatic leadership or idealized influence, inspirational motivation, intellectual stimulation, and individualized consideration.[77]

Charismatic leadership or idealized influence means that transformational leaders act as role models for their followers. Because transformational leaders put others' needs

transformational leadership
leadership that generates awareness and acceptance of a group's purpose and mission and gets employees to see beyond their own needs and self-interests for the good of the group

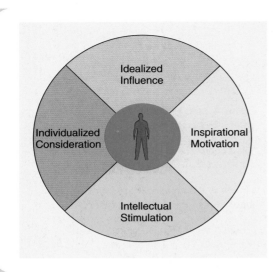

Exhibit 14.16

Components of Transformational Leadership

© BLOOMBERG NEWS/LANDOV

ahead of their own and share risks with their followers, they are admired, respected, and trusted, and followers want to emulate them. Thus, in contrast to purely charismatic leaders (especially unethical charismatics), transformational leaders can be counted on to do the right thing and maintain high standards for ethical and personal conduct. After Jim McNerney became Boeing's third CEO in three years, he pushed company lawyers to settle ethics violations that occurred under his predecessors. Under the settlement with the U.S. Justice Department, Boeing agreed to pay a $615 million penalty. But for McNerney, that wasn't enough. He apologized before a Senate committee and refused to take a $200 million tax deduction to which Boeing was entitled for its costs in obtaining the settlement. Critics charge that McNerney's decision to not take the tax deduction wrongly cost Boeing shareholders $200 million. McNerney, who was responsible for restoring the company's commitment to ethical behavior, said, "I thought it was the right thing to do."[78] McNerney also instituted a new organization-wide ethics program and has linked bonuses and promotion to ethical behavior.

Inspirational motivation means that transformational leaders motivate and inspire followers by providing meaning and challenge to their work. By clearly communicating expectations and demonstrating commitment to goals, transformational leaders help followers envision future states, such as the organizational vision or mission. In turn, this leads to greater enthusiasm and optimism about the future. MEDTRONIC's mission is "To contribute to human welfare by application of biomedical engineering in the research, design, manufacture, and sale of instruments or appliances that *alleviate pain, restore health, and extend life*."[79] Because Medtronic designs and makes life-altering products, it has an opportunity to inspire the managers and workers who work there. Every December for the holiday party, Medtronic flies in six patients to demonstrate that the company is accomplishing its mission to "alleviate pain, restore health, and extend life." The patients give testimonials describing the difference that Medtronic's products have made to them and their loved ones. Production supervisor Karen McFadzen says, "We have patients who come in who would be dead if it wasn't for us. I mean, they sit right up there and they tell us what their lives are like. You don't walk away from them not feeling anything." *Fortune* magazine described the annual event this way: "It's a teary, communal reminder that what goes on here day after day is not the same as making VCRs."[80]

Intellectual stimulation means that transformational leaders encourage followers to be creative and innovative, to question assumptions, and to look at problems and situations in new ways, even if their ideas are different from the leader's. CEO Anne Mulcahy encourages a questioning approach by regularly meeting with Xerox's 500 top managers in groups of 80 managers at a time. Mulcahy says that the meetings, which last for several days, are "designed to be critical," to encourage honest, unfiltered discussions, and to realistically face up to problems that need solving. She asks the managers to tell her what Xerox's weaknesses are and what their major concerns are. In general, says Mulcahy, "They worry about growth, and whether our strategy is sufficient to deliver growth, especially with the economy we're in."[81] In return, Mulcahy uses these meetings to be brutally candid with her managers regarding their performance and where Xerox stands. Says one manager, "Part of her DNA is to tell you the good, the bad, and the ugly."[82]

Individualized consideration means that transformational leaders pay special attention to followers' individual needs by creating learning opportunities, accepting and tolerating individual differences, encouraging two-way communication, and being good listeners. Roy Pelaez, who supervises 426 ARAMARK employees who clean airplanes, believes in attending to employees' needs. He says, "Managers are not supposed to get involved with the personal problems of their employees, but I take the opposite view."[83] With morale low and turnover high, he hired a tutor to improve his employees' English skills. To keep absences low, he found government programs that provided certified babysitters for his low-paid employees. And he set up three computers so that employees could teach each other to use word processors and spreadsheets. Says Pelaez, "All of these things are important, because we want employees who really feel connected to the company." Clearly, they do. Turnover, once almost 100 percent per year, dropped to 12 percent after Pelaez began paying attention to his employees' needs.

Finally, a distinction needs to be drawn between transformational leadership and transactional leadership. While transformational leaders use visionary and inspirational appeals to influence followers, **transactional leadership** is based on an exchange process, in which followers are rewarded for good performance and punished for poor performance. When leaders administer rewards fairly and offer followers the rewards that they want, followers will often reciprocate with effort. A problem, however, is that transactional leaders often rely too heavily on discipline or threats to bring performance up to standards. Though this may work in the short run, it's much less effective in the long run. Also, as discussed in Chapters 11 and 13, many leaders and organizations have difficulty successfully linking pay practices to individual performance. As a result, studies consistently show that transformational leadership is much more effective on average than transactional leadership. In the United States, Canada, Japan, and India, and at all organizational levels, from first-level supervisors to upper-level executives, followers view transformational leaders as much better leaders and are much more satisfied when working for them. Furthermore, companies with transformational leaders have significantly better financial performance.[84]

Review 7: **Visionary Leadership**

Strategic leadership requires visionary, charismatic, and transformational leadership. Visionary leadership creates a positive image of the future that motivates organizational members and provides direction for future planning and goal setting. Charismatic leaders have strong, confident, dynamic personalities that attract followers, enable the leader to create strong bonds, and inspire followers to accomplish the leader's vision. Followers of ethical charismatic leaders work harder, are more committed and satisfied, are better performers, and are more likely to trust their leaders. Followers can be just as supportive and committed to unethical charismatics, but these leaders can pose a tremendous risk for companies. Unethical charismatics control and manipulate followers and do what is best for themselves instead of their organizations. To reduce the risks associated with unethical charismatics, companies need to enforce a clearly written code of conduct; recruit, select, and promote managers with high ethical standards; train leaders to value, seek, and use diverse points of view; teach everyone in the company to recognize unethical leader behaviors; and celebrate and reward people who exhibit ethical behaviors. Transformational leadership goes beyond charismatic leadership by generating awareness and acceptance of a group's purpose and mission and by getting employees to see beyond their own needs and self-interest for the good of the group. The four components of transformational leadership are charisma or idealized influence, inspirational motivation, intellectual stimulation, and individualized consideration.

transactional leadership leadership based on an exchange process, in which followers are rewarded for good performance and punished for poor performance

Leadership Orientation

Think of everyone you have ever worked with in jobs, clubs, volunteer positions, student projects—everything. Now that you have all those situations in mind, try to identify the one person with whom you least liked to work. Who was the most difficult person to work with to get a job done? For whatever reason, you had trouble working with this person. The person can be a peer, boss, or subordinate. Once you have that person in mind, think of how you would describe him or her to another person. The Least Preferred Coworker scale uses 18 oppositional adjective pairs to help you build your description.[85] For each pair, choose the number closest to the word that best describes your LPC.

Pleasant	8	7	6	5	4	3	2	1	Unpleasant
Friendly	8	7	6	5	4	3	2	1	Unfriendly
Rejecting	1	2	3	4	5	6	7	8	Accepting
Tense	1	2	3	4	5	6	7	8	Relaxed
Distant	1	2	3	4	5	6	7	8	Close
Cold	1	2	3	4	5	6	7	8	Warm
Supportive	8	7	6	5	4	3	2	1	Hostile
Boring	1	2	3	4	5	6	7	8	Interesting
Quarrelsome	1	2	3	4	5	6	7	8	Harmonious
Gloomy	1	2	3	4	5	6	7	8	Cheerful
Open	8	7	6	5	4	3	2	1	Guarded
Backbiting	1	2	3	4	5	6	7	8	Loyal
Untrustworthy	1	2	3	4	5	6	7	8	Trustworthy
Considerate	8	7	6	5	4	3	2	1	Inconsiderate
Nasty	1	2	3	4	5	6	7	8	Nice
Agreeable	8	7	6	5	4	3	2	1	Disagreeable
Insincere	1	2	3	4	5	6	7	8	Sincere
Kind	8	7	6	5	4	3	2	1	Unkind
TOTAL = _____									

Scoring

Determine your leadership style by totaling all the numbers you selected into a single sum. Your score will fall between 18 and 96.

You can find the interpretation for your score at: **academic.cengage.com/management/williams.**

Are New Offices Necessary?

Everyone says that when business is good, you're supposed to be able to relax a little. Whoever said that never set foot in the office of your magazine.[86]

When you launched the magazine, the staff consisted of you (editor and publisher), an advertising salesperson (who also handled distribution), an art director, a page designer, and a production director. All writing was by freelancers. As circulation has grown, so has the number of pages in the magazine and the frequency with which you publish issues. That core of six people has quadrupled, causing the space all of you occupy to become cramped. At 6,000 square feet, the office is comfortably full with 25 people. Your problem is that you have more work than your 25 employees can comfortably handle, and you need to hire about five more people. Where will you put them?

The way you see it, you have a couple of options. First, you could move. Pack everyone's desk up, all the equipment, and find a space that will accommodate a larger and growing workforce. Moving, though, would be costly. Companies typically charge upwards of $50 per hour per mover, plus you'd have to get insurance to cover the move. The Better Business Bureau received complaints about companies in over 1,000 industries; the moving industry received over 5,000 complaints, putting them 11th on that list. Finding a reputable, high-quality moving company could take time away from magazine work. And managing the logistics could be a nightmare. You can't just shut down, turn off the phones, and move in peace. You'd still have to conduct business, sell ads, edit copy, handle subscriptions, lay out pages, shoot photos, and do dozens of other day-to-day activities. Plus, the sheer volume of paper archives related to five years of magazine publishing, not to mention all the technology hardware, would make packing and unpacking a big endeavor for each of your workers.

The second option: Stay put and let workers telecommute. Although you'd avoid the headache of a move, you'd trade the management of a one-time event (moving offices) for regular management of everyone's on-site and off-site schedules. Telecommuting is on the verge of being a widely accepted form of scheduling despite the very real danger of work and home life blending into one big pot of time. Already 40 percent of Americans work evenings, weekends, or on rotating shifts, and the numbers of full-time workers who work from home at least one day a month rose 30 percent in a single year, proving the trend is toward working from home. People tend to romanticize working from home, however, and forget that there are real challenges (like not having access to convenient photocopying or shipping, lack of quiet space, not enough space, and, yes, no social interaction).

You're primarily concerned about a drop in creativity as fewer people are on site to collaborate and give feedback on article ideas, layouts, and other decisions that come up nearly every hour. Statistically, 14 percent of U.S. workers who could telecommute if they wanted still prefer to work in an office. That means you could be left with only four people in the office! But offering telecommuting would let you tap into a larger talent pool and help you retain workers who are looking for flexibility with their schedules and work locations. If your employees could work from home, you wouldn't lose as much time during inclement weather either—no more snow days.

Even though your choice is between two options—move or offer telecommuting—you also need to consider how involved your employees should be in the decision. Telecommuting affects their work and home lives, but the expense and the responsibility for managing the project will be yours.

Questions

1. How involved should your employees be in making the decision? (Hint: Consider using the decision tree in Exhibit 14.14 to determine the appropriate level of employee participation in this decision.)

2. Because everyone has worked closely in the same open office, you've been able to use an achievement-oriented leadership style. Would a shift to telecommuting require a change in style? Explain.

3. How do you manage space issues as your business grows?

Transition at Habitat for Humanity

With 500 full-time employees, roughly 500,000 unpaid volunteers, 2,303 affiliates worldwide, and upwards of $160 million in annual donations, Habitat for Humanity International (HFHI) is the 19th largest nonprofit organization in the United States.[87] Since it was founded in 1976 by Millard and Linda Fuller, HFHI has built some 175,000 houses around the world, more than 20,000 of them in a single year. Clearly, what started as a straightforward, ecumenical Christian ministry has grown into a global force for housing the poor and one of the world's most renowned nonprofit organizations. And that success is due in large part to the efforts of Millard Fuller, an avid fund-raiser, prolific author (he has written nine books), sought-after public speaker, and an all-around passionate spokesperson for the cause.

When Fuller's tenure as president was set to end after 28 years at the helm of HFHI, he and the board of directors had serious disagreements about the transition of leadership. Fuller feared that the board was moving toward a culture of "bean-counting" and away from a strong Christian commitment. He charged that many board members were not spiritually grounded. The board defended its Christian focus, but recognized that the organization's mission had become much larger than the influence of a single individual.

After 11 months of wrangling, Fuller, who was approaching 70 years of age, agreed to step down as CEO and hire an interim CEO. Fuller took a new position with the title Founder/President and became the chief spokesperson for Habitat. Taking the CEO position was Paul Leonard, who couldn't have been more different from his predecessor. Leonard, a retired real estate and construction industry executive, had expertise in organizational development and a deep knowledge of the construction industry. He accepted the position and with it responsibility for the overall management of HFHI for a period of two years.

Only three months after naming Leonard as CEO, however, the HFHI board of directors fired Fuller altogether for a pattern of "divisive and disruptive" public comments and went so far as to lock him out of the HFHI building. In the face of soaring land costs and growing housing regulations, Leonard will have to contend with a changing external environment that requires more careful planning. At the same time, HFHI's five-year plan calls for the organization to seek exponential annual growth, rather than the 5 to 10 percent annual growth it has been experiencing in recent years.

As a member of the board, you face significant challenges as well. Even though Leonard was a solid choice for interim CEO, the board is conducting an executive search to fill the permanent position. Should the permanent CEO be more like Fuller, a passionate and charismatic evangelist not afraid of setting tremendous stretch goals (like eradicating substandard housing in 20 years), or like Leonard, a methodical executive who can manage and grow Habitat's sprawling, decentralized organization? Or should the permanent CEO fit an altogether different profile?

Assemble a team of four to five students to act as the board of directors of Habitat for Humanity International. As a group, discuss each of the following questions to identify the chief characteristics the new CEO of HFHI will need to possess.

Questions

1. Does Habitat for Humanity need a leader or a seasoned manager? In other words, do you look to fill the CEO position with a visionary leader (like Fuller) or a seasoned manager (like Leonard) whose strengths lie more in organizational development than charismatic passion?

2. The new CEO will need to work with both the employees of HFHI and its hundreds of thousands of volunteers and donors. What leadership style will you look for in prospective candidates to meet the needs of those two constituencies?

Leadership is a highly prized process and capability. Organizations invest billions of dollars each year in recruiting and developing leadership talent. As more companies compete primarily on the basis of how well they employ their human capabilities, the importance of leadership continues to grow. This exercise will provide you with an opportunity to play coach to a leader entering a challenging situation.

Step 1: Get into groups. Your professor will assign you to pairs or small groups.

Scenario: The opening "What would you do?" segment in this chapter focused on the challenges facing the new CEO of Hewlett-Packard (HP). HP is a company with a remarkable tradition of product and management innovations, including a much-admired business philosophy known as the "HP Way." But as the opening segment makes clear, over the past several years HP seems to have lost its way. As the new CEO scans the situation, it is difficult to know how to prioritize. Where to begin?

Assume that the members of your small team are a group of consultants working with HP's new CEO. Your job is behind the scenes—you are simply helping the CEO to brainstorm and think carefully about how to lead this company, improve performance, and restore the once-vibrant HP culture.

Step 2: Outline leadership criteria. Work as a team to develop a set of leadership recommendations that are well-matched to the HP situation. What do you think employees need most from their new leader? Should the CEO help employees to look back and learn from the company's past, or should the CEO encourage employees to move on and focus on the future? What are the tradeoffs of each approach? The opening segment highlights some key areas of concern: (a) structural issues (for example, problems with the matrix structure); (b) unclear vision; (c) declining financial and marketing performance; (d) distrust and low morale. So how would you recommend that the CEO prioritize these issues? Are there creative possibilities for tackling some of these concerns simultaneously?

Step 3: Determine a coaching plan. Prepare to coach the CEO during the process of transforming HP. How might path-goal thinking help the CEO guide HP employees through the transition? What should the CEO keep in mind regarding such situational factors as worker readiness, situation favorableness, and environmental contingencies? Assuming the CEO possesses charismatic capabilities, would you recommend relying upon a charismatic leadership style in this situation? Why, or why not?

Step 4: Debrief as a class. Share some of the highlights of your recommendations, and discuss what leadership consultants/coaches need to know to effectively advise their clients.

The Role of Humility in Leadership

Everybody makes mistakes; today's media-saturated culture makes everyone's mistakes everyone else's news.[88] This is particularly true of leaders, who are less able (perhaps simply unable) to hide from the media microscope than in times past. We want our leaders to have an unshakable integrity, so when their mistakes turn into front-page news, it provides a unique look at the mettle of those who lead our governments, institutions, and businesses. One of the functions of leadership is to assume responsibility for company actions, even when those actions are dubious at best or downright shameful at worst. But how can leaders—who are supposed to always take the high road—work through mistakes that they or their organizations have made?

The answer is simple: a sincere apology. Okay, so the answer is not so simple. Everyone knows that apologizing is not so easy, as proved by the associated lump-in-the-throat and the awful feeling that comes from knowing that something you did caused someone else pain, embarrassment, loss, or hardship. But as you read in the chapter, a critical element of what leaders do and how leaders succeed is consideration, which is akin to empathy, the engine of a sincere apology.

How do *you* apologize for mistakes? Do you use the word "sorry" so often that it is devoid of meaning? Or do you apologize profusely, which comes to the same effect? Do you wait until you have time to think things over, or do you apologize immediately if briefly? The biggest mistake that leaders make when apologizing is passing the buck and using the word "regret" instead of "apologize." Leaders take responsibility for actions and should assume blame even if it is not their own. Making an unqualified assumption of responsibility helps demonstrate that your apology is sincere, as does going beyond a basic "I'm sorry." According to Karen Friedman, a communication coach, " 'I'm sorry' doesn't cut it.... It's empty, hollow, and quite frankly, pathetic: 'I'm sorry I cooked the books.' 'I'm sorry I beat my wife. I won't do it again.' You have to say, 'I made a terrible mistake. I offended people. I lied. I was stupid.'"[89] So, one of the marks of a true leader is not hubris, but humility. In other words, the best way to *appear* sincere is to *be* sincere.

Questions

1. Describe a time when something you did or said had a profound negative impact on a person, group, or situation.

2. Did you take responsibility for your actions, or did you try to blame circumstances or other people?

3. Did you apologize? How do you think the person who was receiving the apology took it?

4. What was the most difficult thing about apologizing?

5. Think about some high-profile blunders in recent news, whether in the world of sports, business, or entertainment. How do you think the company or individual involved did at delivering a public apology? Explain why you thought it was—or was not—sincere.

BIZ FLIX
U-571

This action-packed thriller deals with a U.S. submarine crew's efforts to retrieve an Enigma encryption device from a disabled German submarine during World War II. After the crew gets the device, the U.S. submarine sinks, and they must use the German submarine to escape from enemy destroyers. The film's nonstop action and extraordinary special effects powerfully illustrate the challenges facing the leadership on board the submarine.

This scene is an edited composite of scenes that appear early in the film. The S33, an older U.S. submarine, is embarking on a secret mission. Before departure, the S33's officers receive a briefing on their mission from Office of Naval Intelligence representatives on board. Executive officer Lt. Andrew Tyler (Matthew McConaughey) reports on the submarine's status to Lt. Commander Mike Dahlgren (Bill Paxton). The film continues with the S33 finding the disabled German submarine.

What to Watch for and Ask Yourself

1. What aspects of leadership does Dahlgren say are important for a submarine commander?
2. Which leadership behaviors or traits does he emphasize?
3. Are these traits or behaviors right for this situation? Why or why not?

MANAGEMENT WORKPLACE
P. F. Chang's—Leading by Involvement

How do you manage 97 bistros and 33 diners at once? This isn't a riddle. It is actually the daily challenge of Rick Federico, CEO of P. F. Chang's, which owns and operates a chain of Asian-style restaurants across the country. During the time he has been head of the company, Federico has taken on the huge tasks of taking the company public and launching Pei Wei, the firm's chain of diners. In addition, he has developed management teams and laid out clear expectations for his employees. He has earned the respect of his managers, his workers, his customers, and even his competitors. He has won accolades and leadership awards. "Rick has done a great job of building a strong team culture and has built an organization that is based upon quality of execution," notes one colleague. Watch the video to see Federico's leadership style in action at P. F. Chang's.

What to Watch for and Ask Yourself

1. Describe some of Rick Federico's personal leadership traits.
2. What leadership style does he use with his chefs? Why do you think so?
3. Would you characterize Rick Federico as a charismatic or a transformational leader? Why?

CHAPTER 15

Managing Communication

WHAT WOULD YOU DO?

Sony Headquarters, Tokyo, Japan.[1] Since becoming Sony's CEO, you've spent 10 days a month in Tokyo, 10 days a month at Sony's New York City office, and 10 days a month at home in London. So after yet another long international flight, you return exhausted to your Tokyo hotel room. When the travel wears you down, you sometimes question why you took this job. You didn't actively campaign for the position. However, the board and the previous CEO picked you because they felt an "outsider" was needed to shake Sony out of it funk. As head of Sony's U.S. operations, you restored profitability by cutting $700 million in costs and laying off one-third of the employees. More importantly, though, you were able to get Sony's entertainment, electronics, and games units to work together. So why are you an outsider if you turned around a Sony Division? Well, it's simple. Unlike Sony's previous CEOs, you're not Japanese and you're not an engineer.

Sony was in terrible shape when you took over, posting its first loss in more than a decade after a series of embarrassing business mistakes, including

Sony BMG's music copy protection software (which installed itself on computers when music was played and unintentionally made computers vulnerable to hackers), and flawed laptop batteries (which overheated and occasionally caught fire). The most visible and expensive mistake, though, was the long delay in introducing Sony's new PlayStation 3 videogame console. By the time the PlayStation 3 came out, Microsoft had already sold 10 million of its competing Xbox 360 game stations, cutting significantly into Sony's market share. And, with the Xbox 360 priced at a relatively cheap $400, Sony's $700 price for the PlayStation 3 will barely cover costs. So, not only was the PS3 late, it won't be adding the $2 billion in annual profits to the bottom line that it was supposed to.

Some of Sony's problems lie in its competitive corporate culture, which celebrates the success of maverick innovators who did what was needed, including going around their bosses, to bring new, innovative products to market. Consequently, working independently, not communicating, and not collaborating became the norm. That worked when Sony was a smaller and primarily Japanese company, but it no longer works given Sony's size and global scale (just 25 percent of Sony's revenues come from Japan). With over 1,000 products, one

manager put it best when he said, "Sony's gotten so big that things don't connect any more." One of your top executives explained the problem this way: "I have 35 Sony devices at home. I have 35 battery chargers. That's all you need to know." Other signs of the poor communication and collaboration included actively discouraging designers and engineers from listening to customers; the Walkman and PC groups—without consultation—simultaneously bringing new MP3 players to market; and the head of Sony's videogames division going over his budget by hundreds of millions of dollars without telling the then CEO.

None of those problems are going to get solved unless you can convince your Japanese managers and employees, who criticize you for spending too little time in Tokyo, to follow your lead. Despite your success at Sony's U.S. division, you're seen as an outsider because you don't speak Japanese. So what can you do to improve cross-cultural communication? Beyond that, how do you get Sony's different divisions to talk to each other and work together? Sony will fail if these groups ignore each other. Finally, how do you change the culture of organizational silence that encourages Sony's independent managers and employees to not keep their bosses informed about problems? Problems are opportunities, but only if you know about them. **If you were in charge at Sony, what would you do?**

It's estimated that managers spend over 80 percent of their day communicating with others.[2] Indeed, much of the basic management process—planning, organizing, leading, and controlling—cannot be performed without effective communication. If this weren't reason enough to study communication, consider that effective oral communication, such as listening, following instructions, conversing, and giving feedback, is the most important skill for college graduates who are entering the work force.[3] Furthermore, across all industries, poor communication skills rank as the single most important reason that people do not advance in their careers.[4] Finally, communication is especially important for top managers like Sony's CEO. As Mark DeMichele, former CEO of Arizona Public Service Company, puts it, "Communication is the key to success. CEOs can have good ideas, a vision, and a plan. But they also have to be able to communicate those plans to people who work for them."[5]

This chapter begins by examining the role of perception in communication and how perception can make it difficult for managers to achieve effective communication. Next, you'll read about the communication process and the various kinds of communication found in most organizations. In the last half of the chapter, the focus is on improving communication in organizations. You'll learn about one-on-one communication and then about how to communicate and listen to others effectively organization-wide.

WHAT IS COMMUNICATION?

Whenever Kristy Keith's boss said, "Today is a good day for change," she knew that bad news, such as layoffs or a lost client, was sure to follow. Keith says, "It was comforting to some people who didn't know better," but the experienced employees went "back to their offices and huddled" to discuss what her boss's announcement really meant (and it usually wasn't good).[6] Many bosses try to make bad news sound good with phrases like "rightsizing" for layoffs, "merger of equals" for another company has acquired ours, "pursuing other interests" for employees who were fired, and "cost efficiencies" for your job is being outsourced to India. Why do managers sugarcoat bad news when communicating? Because, says Dartmouth management professor Paul Argenti, they think "they'll get less flak."

Communication is the process of transmitting information from one person or place to another. While some bosses sugarcoat bad news, smart managers understand that in the end effective, straightforward communication between managers and employees is essential for success.

> *After reading the next two sections, you should be able to*
>
> 1 *explain the role that perception plays in communication and communication problems.*
>
> 2 *describe the communication process and the various kinds of communication in organizations.*

communication the process of transmitting information from one person or place to another

1 Perception and Communication Problems

One study found that when *employees* were asked whether their supervisor gave recognition for good work, only 13 percent said their supervisor gave a pat on the back, and a mere 14 percent said their supervisor gave sincere and thorough praise. But when the *supervisors* of these employees were asked if they gave recognition for good work, 82 percent said they gave pats on the back, while 80 percent said that they gave sincere and thorough praise.[7] Given that these managers and employees worked closely together, how could they have had such different perceptions of something as simple as praise?

Let's learn more about perception and communication problems by examining **1.1 the basic perception process**, **1.2 perception problems**, **1.3 how we perceive others**, *and* **1.4 how we perceive ourselves**. *We'll also consider how all of these factors make it difficult for managers to achieve effective communication.*

1.1 Basic Perception Process

As shown in Exhibit 15.1, **perception** is the process by which individuals attend to, organize, interpret, and retain information from their environments. And since communication is the process of transmitting information from one person or place to another, perception is obviously a key part of communication. Yet, perception can also be a key obstacle to communication.

As people perform their jobs, they are exposed to a wide variety of informational stimuli, such as e-mails, direct conversations with the boss or coworkers, rumors heard over lunch, stories about the company in the press, or a video broadcast of a speech from the CEO to all employees. Just being exposed to an informational stimulus, however, is no guarantee that an individual will pay attention or attend to that stimulus. People experience stimuli through their own **perceptual filters**—the personality-, psychology-, or experience-based differences that influence them to ignore or pay attention to particular stimuli. Because of filtering, people exposed to the same information will often disagree about what they saw or heard. For example, every major stadium in the *NATIONAL FOOTBALL LEAGUE* has a huge TV monitor on which fans can watch replays. As the slow motion video is replayed on the monitor, you can often hear cheers *and* boos, as fans of both teams perceive the same replay in completely different ways. This happens because the fans' perceptual filters predispose them to attend to stimuli that support their team and not their opponents.

And the same perceptual filters that affect whether we believe our favorite team was "robbed" by the referees also affect communication, that is, the transmitting of information from one person or place to another. As shown in Exhibit 15.1, perceptual filters affect each part of the *perception process*: attention, organization, interpretation, and retention.

Attention is the process of noticing or becoming aware of particular stimuli. Because of perceptual filters, we attend to some stimuli and not others. *Organization* is the process of incorporating new information (from the stimuli that you notice) into your existing knowledge. Because of perceptual filters, we are more likely

perception the process by which individuals attend to, organize, interpret, and retain information from their environments

perceptual filters the personality-, psychology-, or experience-based differences that influence people to ignore or pay attention to particular stimuli

Exhibit 15.1
Basic Perception Process

This play probably elicited both cheers and boos. The same perceptual filters that affect whether we think our team was "robbed" also affect management communication.

to incorporate new knowledge that is consistent with what we already know or believe. *Interpretation* is the process of attaching meaning to new knowledge. Because of perceptual filters, our preferences and beliefs strongly influence the meaning we attach to new information ("This must mean that top management supports our project."). Finally, *retention* is the process of remembering interpreted information. In other words, retention is what we recall and commit to memory after we have perceived something. Of course, perceptual filters also affect retention, that is, what we're likely to remember in the end.

For instance, imagine that you miss the first 10 minutes of a TV show and turn on your TV to see two people talking to each other in a living room. As they talk, they walk around the room, picking up and putting down various items; some items, such as a ring, watch, and credit card, appear to be valuable, and others appear to be drug related, such as a water pipe for smoking marijuana. In fact, this situation was depicted on videotape in a well-known study that manipulated people's perceptual filters.[8] Before watching the video, one-third of the study participants were told that the people were there to rob the apartment. Another third of the participants were told that police were on their way to conduct a drug raid and that the people in the apartment were getting rid of incriminating evidence. The remaining third of the participants were told that the people were simply waiting for a friend.

After watching the video, participants were asked to list all of the objects from the video that they could remember. Not surprisingly, the different perceptual filters (theft, drug raid, and waiting for a friend) affected what the participants attended to, how they organized the information, how they interpreted it, and ultimately which objects they remembered. Participants who thought a theft was in progress were more likely to remember the valuable objects in the video. Those who thought a drug raid was imminent were more likely to remember the drug-related objects. There was no discernible pattern to the items remembered by those who thought that the people in the video were simply waiting for a friend.

In short, because of perception and perceptual filters, people are likely to pay attention to different things, organize and interpret what they pay attention to differently, and, finally, remember things differently. Consequently, even when people are exposed to the same communications (for example, organizational memos, discussions with managers or customers), they can end up with very different perceptions and understandings. This is why communication can be so difficult and frustrating for managers. Let's review some of the communication problems created by perception and perceptual filters.

1.2 Perception Problems

Perception creates communication problems for organizations because people exposed to the same communication and information can end up with completely different ideas and understandings. Two of the most common perception problems in organizations are selective perception and closure.

At work, we are constantly bombarded with sensory stimuli—phones ringing, people talking in the background, computers dinging as new e-mail arrives, people calling our names, and so forth. As limited processors of information, we cannot possibly notice, receive, and interpret all of this information. As a result, we attend to and accept some stimuli but screen out and reject others. This isn't a random process, however. **Selective perception** is the tendency to notice and accept objects and information consistent with our values, beliefs, and expectations, while ignoring or screening out inconsistent information. For example, when Jack Smith, the former CEO of GENERAL MOTORS, was a junior-level executive, he traveled to Japan to learn why Toyota's cars were so reliable and why Toyota was so productive. When he learned that Toyota could build a car with half as many people as GM, he wrote a report and shared his findings with GM's all-powerful executive committee. But no one on the committee believed what he told them. The executives just couldn't accept that a Japanese company was so much more effective than GM. Says Smith, "Never in my life have I been so quickly and unceremoniously blown out of the water."[9]

Once we have initial information about a person, event, or process, **closure** is the tendency to fill in the gaps where information is missing, that is, to assume that what we don't know is consistent with what we already know. If employees are told that budgets must be cut by 10 percent, they may automatically assume that 10 percent of employees will lose their jobs, too, even if that isn't the case. Not surprisingly, when closure occurs, people sometimes "fill in the gaps" with inaccurate information, and this can create problems for organizations.

For example, one of the first decisions faced by a new CEO was whether to approve a marketing campaign to launch a new product. Promotional materials, advertising, and a sales and distribution plan had all been completed. The only thing missing was the CEO's approval. Though he liked the campaign, he wanted to send a strong message that the company needed to change. So he killed the campaign, which demoralized the marketing manager and team that had spent a year developing it. Because they didn't know why the CEO canceled the marketing campaign, his top managers assumed (that is, closure) that the CEO didn't have confidence in any of them either. Fearing that their decisions would be overturned, too, they began seeking the CEO's approval on everything from capital expenditures to personnel decisions to lower-level issues such as where, when, and whether to hold a conference for customers. After the marketing manager quit to take a job at another company, the CEO called his top managers together, assured them they had his confidence, told them he probably should have approved the marketing campaign, and said that he wouldn't repeat his mistake by doing anything to undermine their confidence or their authority.[10]

1.3 Perceptions of Others

Attribution theory says that we all have a basic need to understand and explain the causes of other people's behavior.[11] In other words, we need to know why people do what they do. According to attribution theory, we use two general reasons or attributions to explain people's behavior: an *internal attribution*, in which behavior is thought to be voluntary or under the control of the individual, and an *external attribution*, in which behavior is thought to be involuntary and outside of the control of the individual.

For example, have you ever seen someone changing a flat tire on the side of the road and thought to yourself, "What rotten luck—somebody's having a bad day"? If you did, you perceived the person through an external attribution known as the defensive bias. The **defensive bias** is the tendency for people to perceive themselves as personally and situationally similar to someone who is having difficulty or trouble.[12] And, when we identify with the person in a situation, we tend to use external attributions (the situation) to explain the person's behavior. For instance,

selective perception the tendency to notice and accept objects and information consistent with our values, beliefs, and expectations, while ignoring or screening out or not accepting inconsistent information

closure the tendency to fill in gaps of missing information by assuming that what we don't know is consistent with what we already know

attribution theory the theory that we all have a basic need to understand and explain the causes of other people's behavior

defensive bias the tendency for people to perceive themselves as personally and situationally similar to someone who is having difficulty or trouble since flat tires are common, it's easy to perceive ourselves in that same situation and put the blame on external causes, such as running over a nail.

Now, let's assume a different situation, this time in the workplace:

A utility company worker puts a ladder on a utility pole and then climbs up to do his work. As he's doing his work, he falls from the ladder and seriously injures himself.[13]

Answer this question: Who or what caused the accident? If you thought, "It's not the worker's fault. Anybody could fall from a tall ladder," then you're still operating from a defensive bias in which you see yourself as personally and situationally similar to someone who is having difficulty or trouble. In other words, you made an external attribution by attributing the accident to an external cause, meaning the situation.

In reality, however, most accident investigations initially blame the worker (an internal attribution) and not the situation (an external attribution). Typically, 60 to 80 percent of workplace accidents each year are blamed on "operator error," that is, the employees themselves. More complete investigations, however, usually show that workers are responsible for only 30 to 40 percent of all workplace accidents.[14] Why are accident investigators so quick to blame workers? The reason is that they are committing the **fundamental attribution error**, which is the tendency to ignore external causes of behavior and to attribute other people's actions to internal causes.[15] In other words, when investigators examine the possible causes of an accident, they're much more likely to assume that the accident is a function of the person and not the situation.

Which attribution, the defensive bias or the fundamental attribution error, are workers likely to make when something goes wrong? In general, as shown in Exhibit 15.2, employees and coworkers are more likely to perceive events and explain behavior from a defensive bias. Because they do the work themselves and see themselves as similar to others who make mistakes, have accidents, or are otherwise held responsible for things that go wrong at work, employees and coworkers are likely

fundamental attribution error the tendency to ignore external causes of behavior and to attribute other people's actions to internal causes

Exhibit 15.2

Defensive Bias and Fundamental Attribution Error

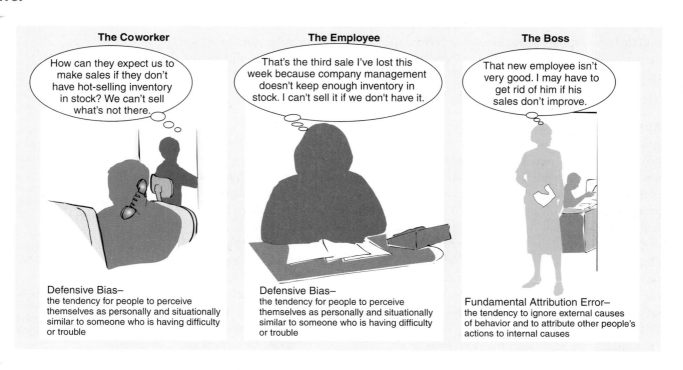

to attribute problems to external causes, such as failed machinery, poor support, or inadequate training. By contrast, because they are typically observers (who don't do the work themselves) and see themselves as situationally and personally different from workers, managers (that is, the boss) tend to commit the fundamental attribution error and blame mistakes, accidents, and other things that go wrong on workers (an internal attribution).

Consequently, in most workplaces, when things go wrong, workers and managers can be expected to take opposite views. Therefore, together, the defensive bias, which is typically used by workers, and the fundamental attribution error, which is typically made by managers, present a significant challenge to effective communication and understanding in organizations.

1.4 Self-Perception

Cindy Pruit is a professional development and recruiting manager at the law firm of Womble Carlyle Sandridge & Rice. Pruitt works frequently with the firm's summer associates, law school students who are interning with the company during summer break. Pruitt was surprised when one of the summer associates broke down in tears after being told that the writing structure on a memo he had written was "a little too loose." Says Pruitt, "They're simply stunned when they get any kind of negative feedback. I practically had to walk him off the ledge."[16]

The **self-serving bias** is the tendency to overestimate our value by attributing successes to ourselves (internal causes) and attributing failures to others or the environment (external causes).[17] As the example with the upset summer law associate illustrates, the self-serving bias can make it especially difficult for managers to talk to employees about performance problems. In general, people have a need to maintain a positive self-image. This need is so strong that when people seek feedback at work, they typically want verification of their worth (rather than information about performance deficiencies) or assurance that mistakes or problems weren't their fault.[18] And, when managerial communication threatens people's positive self-image, they can become defensive and emotional. They quit listening, and communication becomes ineffective. In the second half of the chapter, which focuses on improving communication, we'll explain ways in which managers can minimize this self-serving bias and improve effective one-on-one communication with employees.

Review 1: Perception and Communication Problems

Perception is the process by which people attend to, organize, interpret, and retain information from their environments. Perception is not a straightforward process, however. Because of perceptual filters, such as selective perception and closure, people exposed to the same information stimuli often end up with very different perceptions and understandings. Perception-based differences can also lead to differences in the attributions (internal or external) that managers and workers make when explaining workplace behavior. In general, workers are more likely to explain behavior from a defensive bias, in which they attribute problems to external causes (the situation). Managers, on the other hand, tend to commit the fundamental attribution error, attributing problems to internal causes (the worker associated with a mistake or error). Consequently, when things go wrong, it's common for managers to blame workers and for workers to blame the situation or context in which they do their jobs. Finally, this problem is compounded by a self-serving bias that leads people to attribute successes to internal causes and failures to external causes. So, when workers receive

> *They're simply stunned when they get any kind of negative feedback. I practically had to walk him off the ledge.*
>
> **CINDY PRUIT,**
> PROFESSIONAL DEVELOPMENT AND
> RECRUITING MANAGER, WOMBLE CARLYLE
> SANDRIDGE & RICE

self-serving bias the tendency to overestimate our value by attributing successes to ourselves (internal causes) and attributing failures to others or the environment (external causes) negative feedback from managers, they may become defensive and emotional and not hear what their managers have to say. In short, perceptions and attributions represent a significant challenge to effective communication and understanding in organizations.

2 Kinds of Communication

Each year, on the anniversary of your hiring date, you receive a written assessment of your performance from your boss. This year, after receiving your performance appraisal, you gripe about it to your best friend, a coworker in a cubicle down the hall. Despite your griping, however, you appreciate that your boss cut you some slack, allowing you extra days off when you went through a divorce earlier this year. How did your boss know you were having personal problems? He knew something was wrong from your nonverbal communication—your rounded shoulders, the bags under your eyes, and your overall lack of energy. There are many kinds of communication—formal, informal, coaching/counseling, and nonverbal—but they all follow the same fundamental process.

Let's learn more about the different kinds of communication by examining **2.1 the communication process**, **2.2 formal communication channels**, **2.3 informal communication channels**, **2.4 coaching and counseling, or one-on-one communication**, *and* **2.5 nonverbal communication**.

2.1 The Communication Process

Earlier in the chapter, we defined *communication* as the process of transmitting information from one person or place to another. Exhibit 15.3 displays a model of the communication process and its major components: the sender (message to be conveyed, encoding the message, transmitting the message); the receiver (receiving message, decoding message, and the message that was understood); and noise, which interferes with the communication process.

The communication process begins when a *sender* thinks of a message he or she wants to convey to another person. For example, a few years ago, the CEO of a phone company turned a corner near his house, saw a pay phone booth sitting there, and thought, "That's an odd location for a phone booth. I wonder how much money it earns us."[19] The next step is to encode the message. **Encoding** means putting a message into a written, verbal, or symbolic form that can be recognized and understood by the receiver. The sender then *transmits the message* via *communication channels*. In the case of the CEO and the phone booth, the CEO ran into a midlevel employee the next day and said, "I'm curious. How much do we make on that phone booth near my house? It's not a big deal. Don't spend a lot of time on it. Just send me a note."[20] With some communication channels such as the telephone and face-to-face communication, the sender

encoding putting a message into a written, verbal, or symbolic form that can be recognized and understood by the receiver

Exhibit 15.3

The Interpersonal Communication Process

Sender | Feedback to Sender | Receiver

Message to be conveyed → Message that was understood

Encode message | Decode message

NOISE | NOISE | NOISE

Transmit message | Communication channel | Receive message

receives immediate feedback, whereas with others such as e-mail (text messages and file attachments), fax, beepers, voice mail, memos, and letters, the sender must wait for the receiver to respond.

Unfortunately, because of technical difficulties (for example, fax down, dead battery on the mobile phone, inability to read e-mail attachments) or people-based transmission problems (for example, forgetting to pass on the message), messages aren't always transmitted. If the message is transmitted and received, however, the next step is for the receiver to decode it. **Decoding** is the process by which the receiver translates the written, verbal, or symbolic form of the message into an understood message. However, the message, as understood by the receiver, isn't always the same message that was intended by the sender. Because of different experiences or perceptual filters, receivers may attach a completely different meaning to a message than was intended. With respect to the phone booth, the midlevel employee was writing that quick note that the CEO wanted when his manager walked up and asked, "What are you doing?" The employee explained, "Oh, this is for the CEO. He stopped by and wanted to know how much we make on that phone booth near his house." At this point the manager said—and this is where the message is improperly decoded—"You can't send him a little note. There's no comparison between that phone booth and other booths in the area."

The last step of the communication process occurs when the receiver gives the sender feedback. **Feedback to sender** is a return message to the sender that indicates the receiver's understanding of the message (of what the receiver was supposed to know, to do, or to not do). Feedback makes senders aware of possible miscommunications and enables them to continue communicating until the receiver understands the intended message. Unfortunately, feedback doesn't always occur in the communication process. In the case of the CEO and the phone booth, two months after his inquiry about the phone booth near his house, the midlevel employee to whom he posed the question and that employee's executive vice president walked into his office. When they presented the CEO with a three-ring binder containing a report and detailed analysis and charts regarding the phone booth near his house, he looked at them and said, "I have no idea what you're talking about."[21]

Complacency and overconfidence about the ease and simplicity of communication can lead senders and receivers to simply assume that they share a common understanding of the message and to not use feedback to improve the effectiveness of their communication. This is a serious mistake, especially since messages and feedback are always transmitted with and against a background of noise. **Noise** is anything that interferes with the transmission of the intended message. Noise can occur in any of the following situations:

1. *The sender isn't sure what message to communicate.*
2. *The message is not clearly encoded.*
3. *The wrong communication channel is chosen.*
4. *The message is not received or decoded properly.*
5. *The receiver doesn't have the experience or time to understand the message.*

Any idea what "rightsizing," "delayering," "unsiloing," and "knowledge acquisition" mean? Rightsizing means laying off workers. Delayering means firing managers, or getting rid of layers of management. Unsiloing means getting workers in different parts of the company (that is, different vertical silos) to work with others outside their own areas. Knowledge acquisition means teaching workers new knowledge or

decoding the process by which the receiver translates the written, verbal, or symbolic form of a message into an understood message

feedback to sender in the communication process, a return message to the sender that indicates the receiver's understanding of the message

noise anything that interferes with the transmission of the intended message skills. **Jargon**, which is vocabulary particular to a profession or group, is another form of noise that interferes with communication in the workplace. Unfortunately, the business world is rife with jargon. Carol Hymowitz of the *Wall Street Journal* points out, "A new crop of buzzwords usually sprouts every three to five years, or about the same length of time many top executives have to prove themselves. Some can be useful in swiftly communicating, and spreading, new business concepts. Others are less useful, even devious."[22]

 A new crop of buzzwords usually sprouts every three to five years, or about the same length of time many top executives have to prove themselves. "

CAROL HYMOWITZ, *WALL STREET JOURNAL*

When managers wrongly assume that communication is easy, they reduce communication to something called the "conduit metaphor."[23] Strictly speaking, a conduit is a pipe or tube that protects electrical wire. The **conduit metaphor** refers to the mistaken assumption that senders can pipe their intended messages directly into the heads of receivers with perfect clarity and without noise or perceptual filters interfering with the receivers' understanding of the message. However, this just isn't possible. Even if managers could telepathically direct their thoughts straight into receivers' heads, misunderstandings and communication problems would still occur because words and symbols typically have multiple meanings, depending on how they're used. For example, Exhibit 15.4 shows several meanings of an extremely common word, *fine*. Depending on how you use it, *fine* can mean a penalty; a good job; that something is delicate, small, pure, or flimsy; or that something is okay.

In summary, the conduit metaphor causes problems in communication by making managers too complacent and confident in their ability to easily and accurately transfer messages to receivers. Managers who want to be effective communicators need to carefully choose words and symbols that will help receivers derive the intended meaning of a message. Furthermore, they need to be aware of all steps of the communication process, beginning with the sender (message to be conveyed, encoding the message, transmitting the message) and ending with the receiver (receiving message, decoding message, understanding the message, and using feedback to communicate what was understood).

jargon vocabulary particular to a profession or group that interferes with communication in the workplace

conduit metaphor the mistaken assumption that senders can pipe their intended messages directly into the heads of receivers with perfect clarity and without noise or perceptual filters interfering with the receivers' understanding of the message

formal communication channel the system of official channels that carry organizationally approved messages and information

Exhibit 15.4

Meanings of the Word Fine

1. If you exceed the 55 mph speed limit, you may have to pay a *fine* (penalty).
2. During the playoffs, Shaquille O'Neal turned in a *fine* performance (excellent).
3. The machine has to run at a slow speed because the tolerance is extremely *fine* (tight).
4. Putting this puzzle together is difficult because many of the pieces are so *fine* (small).
5. Recently, experiments have been conducted on manufacturing certain drugs in space. It is hoped that these drugs, as compared with those manufactured on Earth, will be extremely *fine* (pure).
6. Be careful when you handle that antique book. Its pages are extremely *fine* (flimsy).
7. That's *fine* with me (okay).

2.2 Formal Communication Channels

An organization's **formal communication channel** is the system of official channels that carry organizationally approved messages and information. Organizational objectives, rules, policies, procedures, instructions, commands, and requests for information are all transmitted via the formal communication system or "channel." There are three formal communication channels: downward communication, upward communication, and horizontal communication.[24]

Downward communication flows from higher to lower levels in an organization. Downward communication is used to issue orders down the organizational hierarchy, to give organizational members job-related information, to give managers and workers performance reviews from upper managers, and to clarify organizational objectives and goals.[25] When an economic downturn quickly caused a significant drop in sales at AGILENT, a technology company, then-CEO Ned Barnholt summoned his top managers. Together, they decided that their first strategy would be to freeze hiring, cut expenses, and cut temporary workers. Then, through e-mails, the twice-weekly company newsletter, and a speech played over the public-address system at all Agilent facilities, Barnholt explained why the cuts were necessary and how they would help the company; then he encouraged the troops to cut costs any way they could. Agilent managers reinforced the message at "coffee talks," the regular brainstorming meetings that they hold with their employees. Employees responded by using websites to house data electronically (to avoid printing costs), staying with friends and family when on company travel (to avoid hotel charges), and bringing bags of potato chips to company recruiting events (to avoid costly catering charges). Within months, thanks to effective downward communicating, Agilent's travel expenses had dropped by 50 percent, and the company's purchases of personal computers had dropped by 70 percent.[26]

Upward communication flows from lower levels to higher levels in an organization. Upward communication is used to give higher-level managers feedback about operations, issues, and problems; to help higher-level managers assess organizational performance and effectiveness; to encourage lower-level managers and employees to participate in organizational decision making; and to give those at lower levels the chance to share their concerns with higher-level authorities. At CISCO SYSTEMS, the manufacturer of the switches, routers, and computer equipment that form the backbone of the Internet and company computer networks, CEO John Chambers uses monthly birthday breakfasts to create upward communication. Says Chambers, "As for how I hear from employees, I host a monthly birthday breakfast. Anybody who has a birthday in that month gets to come and quiz me for an hour and 15 minutes. No directors or VPs in the room. It's how I keep my finger on the pulse of what's working and what's not. It's brutal, but it's my most enjoyable session."[27]

Horizontal communication flows among managers and workers who are at the same organizational level, such as when a day shift nurse comes in at 7:30 AM for a half-hour discussion with the midnight nurse supervisor who leaves at 8:00 AM. Horizontal communication helps facilitate coordination and cooperation between different parts of a company and allows coworkers to share relevant information. It also helps people at the same level resolve conflicts and solve problems without involving high levels of management. Studies show that communication breakdowns, which occur most often during horizontal communication, such as when patients are handed over from one nurse or doctor to another, are the largest source of medical errors in hospitals. Different communication styles, time pressures, and a general lack of standardized procedures for sharing information during patient handoffs are the likely causes. Medical organizations like KAISER PERMANENTE, which has 30 patient care facilities, are changing that by requiring all of its doctors and nurses to communicate SBAR information (situation, background, assessment, and recommendation) about each patient in 60 seconds. Since its adoption at Kaiser's St. Joseph Medical Center in Bloomington, Illinois, the number of unexpected medical problems fell

downward communication
communication that flows from higher to lower levels in an organization

upward communication
communication that flows from lower to higher levels in an organization

horizontal communication
communication that flows among managers and workers who are at the same organizational level

from 89.9 per 1,000 patient days to 39.6 per 1,000 patient days. Using the SBAR protocol significantly reduces the horizontal communication problems associated with patient handoffs.[28]

In general, what can managers do to improve formal communication? First, decrease reliance on downward communication. Second, increase chances for upward communication by increasing personal contact with lower-level managers and workers. Third, as at Kaiser Permanente, encourage much better use of horizontal communication. Finally, be aware of the problems associated with downward, upward, and horizontal communication, some of which are listed in Exhibit 15.5.

2.3 Informal Communication Channels

An organization's **informal communication channel**, sometimes called the **grapevine**, is the transmission of messages from employee to employee outside of formal communication channels. The grapevine arises out of curiosity, that is, the need to know what is going on in an organization and how it might affect you or others. To satisfy this curiosity, employees need a consistent supply of relevant, accurate, in-depth information about "who is doing what and what changes are occurring within the organization."[29] Employee Paul Haze agrees, saying, "If employees don't have a definite explanation from management, they tend to interpret for themselves."[30]

For example, at the **UNIVERSITY OF TEXAS MEDICAL BRANCH** (part of the UT system), any of the 13,000 employees wanting to know the truth about rumors working their way through the campus grapevine can log on to the school's website and click on "Rumors or Trumors." Campus administrators comment on each posted rumor and rate it using the "kernel of truth" system. As shown in Exhibit 15.6, one kernel of corn indicates a little bit of truth. Two kernels indicate that more of the rumor is accurate, but it's still not entirely true. Three kernels indicate that the rumor is accurate. Wildly inaccurate rumors, such as the one in Exhibit 15.6 about new ID tags being able to track employees' location, are rated with a spaceship, indicating that they're too far out to be believed. Reaction thus far has been positive. Lecturer

informal communication channel ("grapevine") the transmission of messages from employee to employee outside of formal communication channels

Exhibit 15.5

Common Problems with Downward, Upward, and Horizontal Communication

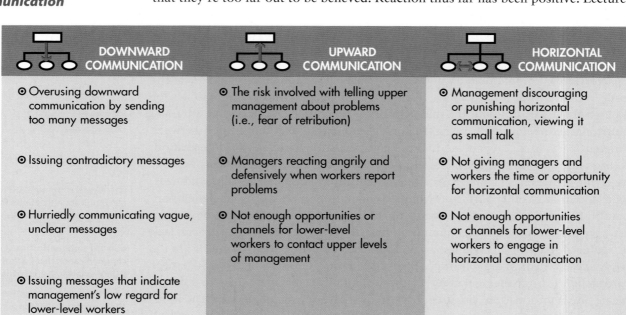

DOWNWARD COMMUNICATION	UPWARD COMMUNICATION	HORIZONTAL COMMUNICATION
⊙ Overusing downward communication by sending too many messages	⊙ The risk involved with telling upper management about problems (i.e., fear of retribution)	⊙ Management discouraging or punishing horizontal communication, viewing it as small talk
⊙ Issuing contradictory messages	⊙ Managers reacting angrily and defensively when workers report problems	⊙ Not giving managers and workers the time or opportunity for horizontal communication
⊙ Hurriedly communicating vague, unclear messages	⊙ Not enough opportunities or channels for lower-level workers to contact upper levels of management	⊙ Not enough opportunities or channels for lower-level workers to engage in horizontal communication
⊙ Issuing messages that indicate management's low regard for lower-level workers		

Source: G. L. Kreps, *Organizational Communication: Theory and Practice* (New York: Longman, 1990).

Sheryl Prather says, "It looks sincere. I've found that everything thus far has been pretty factual. It at least shows that somebody's listening to some of the talk that goes on around here and [is] putting it down on the computer where we can all see it."[31]

Grapevines arise out of informal communication networks, such as the gossip or cluster chains shown in Exhibit 15.7. In a *gossip chain*, one "highly connected" individual shares information with many other managers and workers. By contrast, in a *cluster chain*, numerous people simply tell a few of their friends. The result in both cases is that information flows freely and quickly through the organization. Some believe that grapevines are a waste of employees' time, that they promote gossip and rumors that fuel political speculation, and that they are sources of highly unreliable, inaccurate information. Yet studies clearly show that grapevines are highly accurate sources of information for a number of reasons.[32] First, because grapevines typically carry "juicy" information that is interesting and timely, information spreads rapidly. At Meghan De Goyler Hauser's former company, the word on the grapevine was that her boss drank on the job, the company accountant was stealing the company blind, and that one of her coworkers was a nude model. She says, "The rumors all turned out to be true."[33] Second, since information is typically spread by face-to-face conversation, receivers can send feedback to make sure they understand the message that is being communicated. This reduces misunderstandings and increases accuracy. Third, since most of the information in a company moves along the grapevine, as opposed to formal communication channels, people can usually verify the accuracy of information by "checking it out" with others.

What can managers do to "manage" organizational grapevines? The very worst thing managers can do is withhold information or try to punish those who share information with others. The grapevine abhors a vacuum, and in the absence of information from company management, rumors and anxiety will flourish. Why does this occur? According to workplace psychologist Nicholas DiFonzo, "The main focus of rumor is to figure out the truth. It's the group trying to make sense of something that's important to them."[34] A better strategy is to embrace the grapevine and keep employees informed about possible changes and strategies. Failure to do so will just make things work.

Rumor: I heard that the new "smart" ID badges will store all kinds of my private information, and worse, they can be used to track where I am at UTMB. True?

Rating:

TRUTH-O-METER

= Want to buy some swampland?

= A "kernel" of truth

= Maybe, but...

= The whole truth

Response: No, the cards will not contain anything but the most basic information, much as ID cards do today. No personal data, no employment history, no critical financial info or medical records. The cards will primarily verify identity (your photo and name help do that) and access, the same way magnetic strips and keys do now. In the future, they will also enable a user, at his/her discretion, to use them as a debit card for campus purchases, like a pre-paid phone card, and will help manage access to computer resources.

The cards can't track your location. The proximity readers are designed with a narrow sensitivity field (you wouldn't want doors unexpectedly unlocking because someone with access is walking in a nearby hallway). However, the system does register when you are in or out of a restricted area. This is no different than is currently the case with the magnetic key cards, and is an important aspect of maintaining security in sensitive research, clinical, and business areas.

Source: "Rumors or Trumors," *The University of Texas Medical Branch*, available at http://www.utmb.edu/impact/rumors/default.htm, 1 March 2007.

Exhibit 15.6

"Rumors or Trumors" at the University of Texas Medical Branch

Exhibit 15.7

Grapevine Communication Networks

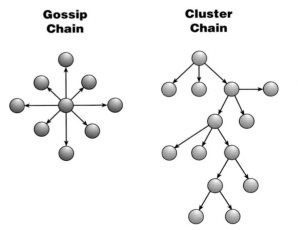

Source: K. Davis & J. W. Newstrom, *Human Behavior at Work: Organizational Behavior*, 8th ed. (New York: McGraw-Hill, 1989).

An employee who works in a company where management maintains a "culture of silence" says, "They [management] think that not communicating the tough stuff will keep employees unaware of it. Of course, it doesn't work. It just fuels the grapevine. . . ."[35]

Finally, in addition to using the grapevine to communicate with others, managers should not overlook the grapevine as a tremendous source of valuable information and feedback. In fact, information flowing through organizational grapevines is estimated to be 75 to 95 percent accurate.[36] For this reason, managers should gather their courage and be willing to read the anonymous comments that angry, frustrated employees post on Internet "gripe sites" like untied.com (about United Airlines) or stainedapron.com (for griping restaurant workers), where employees post gripes about hundreds of different companies. Bob Rosner, who runs a gripe site called workingwounded.com, suggests managers look for themes rather than responding to any particular message. And Jeff Jarvis, author of *The Blog BuzzMachine*, says, "There should be someone at every company whose job is to put into Google and blog search engines the name of the company or the brand, followed by the word 'sucks,' just to see what customers [and employees] are saying."[37]

Exhibit 15.8 lists other strategies that today's managers can use in dealing with gripe sites and blogs, the newest forms of the traditional organizational grapevine. See Section 4.2 for more on how managers can use blogs to do a better job of hearing what employees and customers feel and think about their companies.

2.4 Coaching and Counseling: One-on-One Communication

When the Wyatt Company surveyed 531 U.S. companies undergoing major changes and restructuring, it asked their CEOs, "If you could go back and change one thing, what would it be?" The answer? "The way we communicated with our employees." The CEOs said that instead of flashy videos, printed materials, or formal meetings, they would make greater use of one-on-one communication, especially with employees' immediate supervisors instead of with higher-level executives that employees didn't know.[38]

Coaching and counseling are two kinds of one-on-one communication. **Coaching** is communicating with someone for the direct purpose of improving the person's on-the-job performance or behavior.[39] Managers tend to make several mistakes when coaching employees, however. First, they wait for a problem before coaching. Jim Concelman, who is manager for leadership development at Development Dimensions International, says, "Of course, a boss has to coach an employee if a mistake has been made, but they shouldn't be waiting for the error. While it is a lot easier to see a mistake and correct it, people learn more through success than through failure, so bosses should ensure that employees are experiencing as many successes as possible. Successful employees lead to a more successful organization."[40] Second, when mistakes *are* made, managers wait much too long before talking to the

coaching communicating with someone for the direct purpose of improving the person's on-the-job performance or behavior

Exhibit 15.8

Organizational Grapevines: Dealing with Internet Gripe Sites

1.	Correct misinformation. Put an end to false rumors and set the record straight. Don't be defensive.
2.	Don't take angry comments personally.
3.	Give your name and contact number to show employees that you're concerned and that they can contact you directly.
4.	Hold a town meeting to discuss the issues raised on the gripe site.
5.	Set up anonymous internal discussion forums on the company server. Then encourage employees to gripe anonymously on the company intranet, rather than on the Web.

Source: J. Simons, "Stop Moaning about Gripe Sites and Log On," *Fortune*, 2 April 2001, 181.

employee about the problem. Management professor Ray Hilgert says, "A manager must respond as soon as possible after an incident of poor performance. Don't bury your head. . . . When employees are told nothing, they assume everything is okay."[41] When Jay Whitehead, now president of Outsourcing Today, was a manager at a previous company, one of his employees accidentally copied an e-mail to a customer that insulted the customer. Whitehead immediately talked to the employee, who offered to quit. Whitehead told him, "No, instead you're going to do something much harder. You're going to apologize." He did, and, according to White, "all was forgiven."[42] The key to this successful result was that Whitehead acted immediately to coach the employee on his mistake. In Section 3, you'll learn a number of specific steps for effective one-on-one communication and coaching.

By contrast, **counseling** is communicating with someone about non-job-related issues that may be affecting or interfering with the person's performance. However, counseling does not mean that managers should try to be clinicians, even though an estimated 20 percent of employees are dealing with personal problems at any one time. Dana Kiel, who works for *CIGNA BEHAVIORAL HEALTH*, says, "We call it the quicksand. If you're a good supervisor, you do care about your employees, but it's not your job to be a therapist."[43] Instead, managers should discuss specific performance problems, listen if the employee chooses to share personal issues, and then recommend that the employee call the company's *Employee Assistance Program (EAP)*. EAPs are typically free when provided as part of a company's benefit package. In emergencies or times of crisis, EAPs can offer immediate counseling and support; they can also provide referrals to organizations and professionals that can help employees and their family members address personal issues. Exhibit 15.9 lists the standard services provided by EAPs.

2.5 Nonverbal Communication

When people talk, they send both verbal and nonverbal messages. Verbal messages are sent and received through the words we speak. "That was a great presentation." By contrast, nonverbal messages are sent through body language, facial expressions, or tone of voice. For instance, hearing "*That* was a *great* presentation!" is very different from hearing "ahem [clearing throat], that was, ahem, ahem, a great presentation."

More specifically, **nonverbal communication** is any communication that doesn't involve words. Nonverbal communication and messages almost always accompany verbal communication and may support and reinforce the verbal message or contradict it. The importance of nonverbal communication is well established. Researchers have estimated that as much as 93 percent of any message is transmitted nonverbally, with 55 percent coming from body language and facial expressions and 38 percent coming from the tone and pitch of the voice.[44] Since many nonverbal cues are unintentional, receivers often consider nonverbal communication to be a more accurate representation of what senders are

counseling communicating with someone about non-job-related issues that may be affecting or interfering with the person's performance

nonverbal communication any communication that doesn't involve words

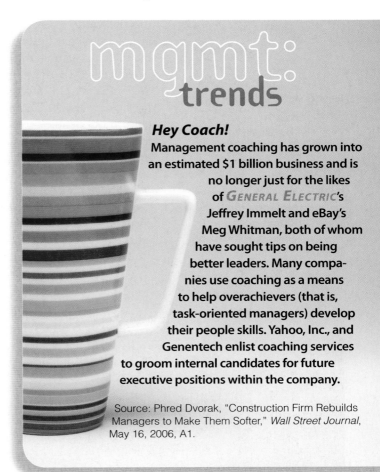

mgmt: trends

Hey Coach!
Management coaching has grown into an estimated $1 billion business and is no longer just for the likes of *GENERAL ELECTRIC*'s Jeffrey Immelt and eBay's Meg Whitman, both of whom have sought tips on being better leaders. Many companies use coaching as a means to help overachievers (that is, task-oriented managers) develop their people skills. Yahoo, Inc., and Genentech enlist coaching services to groom internal candidates for future executive positions within the company.

Source: Phred Dvorak, "Construction Firm Rebuilds Managers to Make Them Softer," *Wall Street Journal*, May 16, 2006, A1.

PROBLEM OR NEED	SERVICE PROVIDED
Stress, depression, relationships, substance abuse	Counseling
Pregnancy, adoption, day care, nutrition, fertility	Child care
Health and nutrition, care options, Alzheimer's disease	Senior care
Wills, leases, estate plans, adoptions	Legal services
Referrals and discounts on chiropractic care, acupuncture, massage therapy, vitamins	Health/lifestyle assistance
Pet-sitting resources, obedience training, veterinarians	Pet care
Retirement planning, debt consolidation, budgeting	Financial services

Source: "You Can Do It. We Can Help," CIGNA Behavioral Health, available at http://www.hr.tcu.edu/eappages/core/html/default.html, 30 March 2002.

Exhibit 15.9

Services Provided by Employee Assistance Programs (EAPs)

"WHAT'S NEW" COMPANY

kinesics movements of the body and face

paralanguage the pitch, rate, tone, volume, and speaking pattern (i.e., use of silences, pauses, or hesitations) of one's voice

Body language can be one of the most telling methods of communicating, particularly when the message is "I'm not listening."

thinking and feeling than the words they use. If you have ever asked someone out on a date and been told "yes," but realized that the real answer was "no," then you understand the importance of paying attention to nonverbal communication.

Kinesics and paralanguage are two kinds of nonverbal communication.[45] **Kinesics** (from the Greek word *kinesis*, meaning "movement") are movements of the body and face.[46] These movements include arm and hand gestures, facial expressions, eye contact, folding arms, crossing legs, and leaning toward or away from another person. For example, people tend to avoid eye contact when they are embarrassed or unsure of the message they are sending. Crossed arms or legs usually indicate defensiveness or that the person is not receptive to the message or the sender. Also, people tend to smile frequently when they are seeking someone's approval.

It turns out that kinesics play an incredibly important role in communication. Studies of married couples' kinesic interactions can predict whether they will stay married with 93 percent accuracy.[47] The key is the ratio of positive to negative kinesic interactions that husbands and wives make as they communicate. Negative kinesic expressions such as eye rolling suggest contempt, whereas positive kinetic expressions such as maintaining eye contact and nodding suggest listening and caring. When the ratio of positive to negative interactions drops below 5 to 1, the chances for divorce quickly increase. Kinesics operate similarly in the workplace, providing clues about people's true feelings, over and beyond what they say (or don't say). For instance, Louis Giuliano, former CEO of *ITT*, which makes heavy use of teams, says, "When you get a team together and say to them we're going to change a process, you always have people who say, 'No, we're not.'" They usually don't say it out loud, but "the body language is there," making it clear that their real answer is "no."[48]

Paralanguage includes the pitch, rate, tone, volume, and speaking pattern (use of silences, pauses, or hesitations) of one's voice. For example, when people are unsure what to say, they tend to decrease their communication effectiveness by speaking softly. When people are nervous, they tend to talk faster and louder. These characteristics have a tremendous influence on whether listeners are receptive to what speakers are saying. For example, Vinya Lynch believes that her "timid and sing-songy" voice is why others don't take her seriously and cut her off when she makes presentations. Lynch says, "When I listen to myself, it doesn't sound intelligent." She began working with a speech coach ($2,250 for 10 sessions) because, as she says, "I want my voice to be charismatic and confident all at the same time."[49]

In short, because nonverbal communication is so informative, especially when it contradicts verbal communication, managers need to learn how to monitor and control their nonverbal behavior.

© IMAGE SOURCE BLACK/JUPITER IMAGES

Review 2: *Kinds of Communication*

Organizational communication depends on the communication process, formal and informal communication channels, one-on-one communication, and nonverbal communication. The major components of the communication process are the sender, the receiver, noise, and feedback. The conduit metaphor refers to the mistaken assumption that senders can pipe their intended messages directly into receivers' heads with perfect clarity. With noise, perceptual filters, and little feedback, however, this just isn't possible. Formal communication channels, such as downward, upward, and horizontal communication, carry organizationally approved messages and information. By contrast, the informal communication channel, called the grapevine, arises out of curiosity and is carried out through gossip or cluster chains. Managers should use the grapevine to keep employees informed and to obtain better, clearer information for themselves. There are two kinds of one-on-one communication. Coaching is used to improve on-the-job performance while counseling is used to communicate about non-job-related issues affecting job performance. Nonverbal communication, such as kinesics and paralanguage, accounts for as much as 93 percent of a message's content and understanding. Since nonverbal communication is so informative, managers need to learn how to monitor and control their nonverbal behavior.

HOW TO IMPROVE COMMUNICATION

An employee comes in late every day, takes long lunches, and leaves early. His coworkers resent his tardiness and having to do his share of the work. Another employee makes as many as 10 personal phone calls a day on company time. Still another employee's job performance has dropped significantly in the last three months. How do you communicate with these employees to begin solving these problems? Or suppose that you supervise a division of 50, 100, or even 1,000 people. How can you communicate effectively with everyone in that division? Moreover, how can top managers communicate effectively with everyone in the company when employees work in different offices, states, countries, and time zones? Turning that around, how can managers make themselves

doing the right thing

Protect Personal, Confidential Information

By virtue of their jobs, managers are privy to information that others aren't. Although much of that information will be about the company, some of it will be personal and confidential information about employees. As a manager, you have a moral and legal obligation to protect employees' privacy. Moreover, sharing others' personal, confidential information may dissuade employees from confiding in managers or seeking help from a company's employee assistance program. Does this mean that if employees confide in you that you can't tell anyone else? No, if you're a manager, sometimes you may have to inform your boss or human resources about a situation. But inform only those who have a need to know and who are also obligated to protect employee privacy. Furthermore, not all information that employees disclose to you should be protected. Information about discrimination, sexual harassment, potential workplace violence, or conflicts of interest between employees and the company may need to be shared with upper management to protect the rights and well-being of others. So, when employees disclose personal, confidential information, do the right thing. Don't discuss it with others unless it falls into one of the exceptions discussed here.[50]

accessible so that they can hear what employees feel and think throughout the organization?

When it comes to improving communication, managers face two primary tasks, managing one-on-one communication and managing organization-wide communication.

After reading the next two sections, you should be able to

> 3 explain how managers can manage effective one-on-one communication.
>
> 4 describe how managers can manage effective organization-wide communication.

3 Managing One-on-One Communication

In Chapter 1, you learned that, on average, first-line managers spend 57 percent of their time with people, middle managers spend 63 percent of their time directly with people, and top managers spend as much as 78 percent of their time dealing with people.[51] These numbers make it clear that managers spend a great deal of time in one-on-one communication with others.

> Learn more about managing one-on-one communication by reading how to **3.1 choose the right communication medium**, **3.2 be a good listener**, **3.3 give effective feedback**, and **3.4 improve cross-cultural communication**.

3.1 Choosing the Right Communication Medium

Sometimes messages are poorly communicated simply because they are delivered using the wrong **communication medium**, which is the method used to deliver a message. For example, the wrong communication medium is being used when an employee returns from lunch, picks up the note left on her office chair, and learns she has been fired. The wrong communication medium is also being used when an employee pops into your office every 10 minutes with a simple request. (An e-mail would be better.)

There are two general kinds of communication media: oral and written communication. *Oral communication* includes face-to-face and group meetings through telephone calls, videoconferencing, or any other means of sending and receiving spoken messages. Studies show that managers generally prefer oral communication over written because it provides the opportunity to ask questions about parts of the message that they don't understand. Oral communication is also a rich communication medium because it allows managers to receive and assess the nonverbal communication that accompanies spoken messages (body language, facial expressions, and the voice characteristics associated with paralanguage).

Furthermore, you don't need a personal computer and an Internet connection to conduct oral communication. Simply schedule an appointment, track someone down in the hall, or catch someone on the phone. In fact, *WALL STREET JOURNAL* columnist Jason Fry worries that with voice mail and e-mail, managers are not as willing to engage in meaningful, face-to-face oral communication as they once were. In fact, 67 percent of managers admit to using e-mail as a substitute for face-to-face conversations.[52] While there are advantages to e-mail—it creates a record of what's been said—it's often better to talk to people instead of just e-mailing them. Jason Fry writes, "If you're close enough that the person you're e-mailing uses the plonk of your return key as a cue to look for the little Outlook envelope, [it's] best [to]

communication medium the method used to deliver an oral or written message think carefully about whether you should be typing instead of talking."[53] Oral communication should not be used for all communication, however. In general, when the message is simple, such as a quick request or a presentation of straightforward information, a memo or e-mail is often the better communication medium.

Written communication includes letters, e-mail, and memos. Although most managers still like and use oral communication, e-mail in particular is changing how they communicate with workers, customers, and each other. E-mail is the fastest-growing form of communication in organizations primarily because of its convenience and speed. For instance, because people read six times faster than they can listen, they usually can read 30 e-mail messages in 10 to 15 minutes.[54] By contrast, dealing with voice messages can take a considerable amount of time. Fred DeLuca, founder of the **SUBWAY** sandwich shop franchise, says, "I get about 60 messages a day from employees and franchisees, and I listen to all of them. For my sanity, I set a time limit of 75 seconds, because people can be long-winded when they're excited. When I hear, 'You have 30 messages,' I know right away that I'll spend 60 minutes on voice mail. I take two minutes per message, listening and returning or forwarding."[55]

Written communication, such as e-mail, is well suited for delivering straightforward messages and information. Furthermore, with e-mail accessible at the office, at home, and on the road (by laptop computer, cell phone, or web-based e-mail), managers can use e-mail to stay in touch from anywhere at almost any time. And since e-mail and other written communications don't have to be sent and received simultaneously, messages can be sent and stored for reading at any time. Consequently, managers can send and receive many more messages using e-mail than using oral communication, which requires people to get together in person or by phone or video conference.

Although written communication is well suited for delivering straightforward messages and information, it is not well suited to complex, ambiguous, or emotionally laden messages, which are better delivered through oral communication. Neal Patterson, CEO of **CERNER CORPORATION**, which develops health-care software, learned this lesson when he sent the following e-mail to 400 company managers:

> *We are getting less than 40 hours of work from a large number of our KC-based EMPLOYEES.... The parking lot is sparsely used at 8 AM, likewise at 5 PM. As managers—you either do not know what your EMPLOYEES are doing or YOU do not CARE. You have created expectations on the work effort which allowed this to happen inside Cerner, creating a very unhealthy environment. In either case, you have a problem and you will fix it or I will replace you.*
>
> *NEVER in my career have I allowed a team which worked for me to think they had a 40-hour job. I have allowed YOU to create a culture which is permitting this. NO LONGER.*[56]

Patterson continued: "We passed a Stock Purchase Program, allowing for the EMPLOYEE to purchase Cerner stock at a 15 percent discount, at Friday's BOD [board of directors] meeting. Hell will freeze over before this CEO implements ANOTHER EMPLOYEE benefit in this Culture."[57] He concluded by saying, "I will hold you accountable. You have allowed this to get to this state. You have two weeks. Tick, tock."[58]

Reaction to the message was so strong that, in just over a week, the e-mail had been leaked to the entire company. And then someone, nobody knows who, posted the e-mail on a Yahoo.com discussion board about Cerner. As word spread about the negative e-mail, Cerner's stock price dropped from $44 to $31 per share in just three days. By the end of the week, Patterson issued another e-mail, offering an apology.

Not surprisingly, that e-mail began, "Please treat this memo with the utmost confidentiality. It is for internal dissemination only. Do not copy or e-mail to anyone else."[59]

3.2 Listening

Are you a good listener? You probably think so. But in fact most people, including managers, are terrible listeners, retaining only about 25 percent of what they hear.[60] You qualify as a poor listener if you frequently interrupt others, jump to conclusions about what people will say before they've said it, hurry the speaker to finish his or her point, are a passive listener (not actively working at your listening), or simply don't pay attention to what people are saying.[61] On this last point, attentiveness, college students were periodically asked to record their thoughts during a psychology course. On average, 20 percent of the students were paying attention (only 12 percent were actively working at being good listeners), 20 percent were thinking about sex, 20 percent were thinking about things they had done before, and the remaining 40 percent were thinking about other things unrelated to the class (for example, worries, religion, lunch, daydreaming).[62]

How important is it to be a good listener? In general, about 45 percent of the total time you spend communicating with others is spent listening. Furthermore, listening is important for managerial and business success, even for those at the top of an organization. According to *Fortune* magazine, listening is one of the reasons that CEO A. G. Lafley has been able to turn around Procter & Gamble so quickly: "He's a listener, not a storyteller. He's likable but not awe inspiring. He's the type of guy who gets excited in the mop aisle of a grocery store. His plan to fix P&G isn't anything groundbreaking, but rather a straightforward, back-to-basics tack. And so far it's worked. He has rallied his troops not with big speeches and dazzling promises, but by *hearing them out* (practically) one at a time."[63]

As Feargal Quinn, CEO of Irish grocery chain SUPERQUINN'S, points out, "Listening is not an activity you can delegate—no matter who you are."[64] In fact, managers with better listening skills are rated as better managers by their employees and are much more likely to be promoted.[65]

So, what can you do to improve your listening ability? First, understand the difference between hearing and listening. According to *Webster's New World Dictionary*, **hearing** is the "act or process of perceiving sounds," whereas **listening** is "making a conscious effort to hear." In other words, we react to sounds, such as bottles breaking or music being played too loud, because hearing is an involuntary physiological process. By contrast, listening is a voluntary behavior. So, if you want to be a good listener, you have to choose to be a good listener. Typically, that means choosing to be an active, empathetic listener.[66]

Active listening means assuming half the responsibility for successful communication by actively giving the speaker nonjudgmental feedback that shows you've accurately heard what he or she said. Active listeners make it clear from their behavior that they are listening carefully to what the speaker has to say. Active listeners put the speaker at ease, maintain eye contact, and show the speaker that they are attentively listening by nodding and making short statements.

Several specific strategies can help you be a better active listener. First, *clarify responses* by asking the speaker to explain confusing or ambiguous statements.

hearing the act or process of perceiving sounds

listening making a conscious effort to hear

active listening assuming half the responsibility for successful communication by actively giving the speaker nonjudgmental feedback that shows you've accurately heard what he or she said

Part of what makes A.G. Lafley so successful as Procter & Gamble's CEO is his ability to listen intently.

© RICHARD DREW/ASSOCIATED PRESS

Second, when there are natural breaks in the speaker's delivery, use this time to paraphrase or summarize what has been said. *Paraphrasing* is restating what has been said in your own words. *Summarizing* is reviewing the speaker's main points or emotions. Paraphrasing and summarizing give the speaker the chance to correct the message if the active listener has attached the wrong meaning to it. Paraphrasing and summarizing also show the speaker that the active listener is interested in the speaker's message. Exhibit 15.10 lists specific statements that listeners can use to clarify responses, paraphrase, or summarize what has been said.

> **[CEO A. G. Lafley's]** plan to fix P&G isn't anything groundbreaking, but rather a straightforward, back-to-basics tack. And so far it's worked. He has rallied his troops not with big speeches and dazzling promises, but by *hearing them out* (practically) one at a time.

FORTUNE MAGAZINE

Active listeners also avoid evaluating the message or being critical until the message is complete. They recognize that their only responsibility during the transmission of a message is to receive it accurately and derive the intended meaning from it. Evaluation and criticism can take place after the message is accurately received. Finally, active listeners also recognize that a large portion of any message is transmitted nonverbally and thus pay very careful attention to the nonverbal cues transmitted by the speaker.

Empathetic listening means understanding the speaker's perspective and personal frame of reference and giving feedback that conveys that understanding to the speaker. Empathetic listening goes beyond active listening because it depends on our ability to set aside our own attitudes or relationships to be able to see and understand things through someone else's eyes. Empathetic listening is just as important as active listening, especially for managers, because it helps build rapport and trust with others.

The key to being a more empathetic listener is to show your desire to understand and to reflect people's feelings. You can *show your desire to understand* by listening, that is, asking people to talk about what's most important to them and then by giving them sufficient time to talk before responding or interrupting. Altera Corp., which makes computer chips, uses empathetic listening as the key sales tool for its salesforce. When salesperson Mike Dionne first met with an information technology manager from a medical company, he told him he was there to find out how Altera could expand its business in the medical field. During the 90-minute meeting, Dionne

empathetic listening understanding the speaker's perspective and personal frame of reference and giving feedback that conveys that understanding to the speaker

Exhibit 15.10

Clarifying, Paraphrasing, and Summarizing Responses for Active Listeners

CLARIFYING RESPONSES	PARAPHRASING RESPONSES	SUMMARIZING RESPONSES
Could you explain that again?	What you're really saying is . . .	Let me summarize . . .
I don't understand what you mean.	If I understand you correctly . . .	Okay, your main concerns are . . .
I'm not sure how . . .	In other words . . .	To recap what you've said . . .
I'm confused. Would you run through that again?	So your perspective is that . . .	Thus far, you've discussed . . .
	Tell me if I'm wrong, but what you're saying is . . .	

Source: E. Atwater, *I Hear You*, revised ed. (New York: Walker, 1992).

rarely spoke and never said that Altera wanted to sell him computer chips. Instead, Dionne listened quietly and didn't interrupt as the manager described the kinds of technology (using computer chips) that his company wanted to buy. Dionne says, "You could tell [he] was jazzed. He was comfortable, leaning back in his chair and talking freely."[67]

Reflecting feelings is also an important part of empathetic listening because it demonstrates that you understand the speaker's emotions. Unlike active listening, in which you restate or summarize the informational content of what has been said, the focus is on the affective part of the message. As an empathetic listener, you can use the following statements to reflect the speaker's emotions:

- *So, right now it sounds like you're feeling....*
- *You seem as if you're....*
- *Do you feel a bit...?*
- *I could be wrong, but I'm sensing that you're feeling....*

In the end, says management consultant Terry Pearce, empathetic listening can be boiled down to these three steps. First, wait 10 seconds before you answer or respond. It will seem an eternity, but waiting prevents you from interrupting others and rushing your response. Second, to be sure you understand what the speaker wants, ask questions to clarify the speaker's intent. Third, only then should you respond first with feelings and then facts (notice that facts *follow* feelings).[68]

3.3 Giving Feedback

In Chapter 11, you learned that performance appraisal feedback (that is, judging) should be separated from developmental feedback (that is, coaching).[69] At this point, we now focus on the steps needed to communicate feedback one-on-one to employees.

To start, managers need to recognize that feedback can be constructive or destructive. **Destructive feedback** is disapproving without any intention of being helpful and almost always causes a negative or defensive reaction in the recipient. When business reporter Margaret Heffernan worked in television, her boss Tim frequently gave destructive feedback. Says Heffernan, "Standard procedure required that all films be seen in an early rough cut by the program editor. These viewings filled me with dread. Not only was I revealing my carefully nurtured work to the outside world for the first time; I also happened to work for a screamer. Tim almost never liked the first cut of anything, and his displeasure took the form of tantrums: yelling, screaming, throwing phones against the wall, occasionally dragging in other producers to see what a miserable piece of dumb garbage I'd wasted his budget on. The only (very slight) compensation was knowing that he treated everyone this way."[70] Heffernan eventually quit her job because of her boss's behavior. Some employees, however, will push back when their bosses behave this way. In fact, one study found that 98 percent of employees responded to destructive feedback from their bosses with either verbal aggression (two-thirds) or physical aggression (one-third).[71]

By contrast, **constructive feedback** is intended to be helpful, corrective, and/or encouraging. It is aimed at correcting performance deficiencies and motivating employees. When providing constructive feedback, Jenet Noriega Schwind, vice president and chief people officer of Zantaz, an e-business archiving company, tells employees, "What I'm going to tell you may be upsetting to you—but it's important to your success." She says, "When you are telling people things they don't necessarily want to hear, you have to deliver your message in a way that gets their attention and acceptance."[72]

destructive feedback feedback that disapproves without any intention of being helpful and almost always causes a negative or defensive reaction in the recipient

constructive feedback feedback intended to be helpful, corrective, and/or encouraging

For feedback to be constructive rather than destructive, it must be immediate, focused on specific behaviors, and problem oriented. *Immediate feedback* is much more effective than delayed feedback because manager and worker can recall the mistake or incident more accurately and discuss it in detail. For example, if a worker is rude to a customer and the customer immediately reports the incident to management, and the manager, in turn, immediately discusses the incident with the employee, there should be little disagreement over what was said or done. By contrast, if the manager waits several weeks to discuss the incident, it's unlikely that either the manager or the worker will be able to accurately remember the specifics of what occurred. When that happens, it's usually too late to have a meaningful conversation.

Specific feedback focuses on particular acts or incidents that are clearly under the control of the employee. For instance, instead of telling an employee that he or she is "always late for work," it's much more constructive to say, "In the last three weeks, you have been 30 minutes late on four occasions and more than an hour late on two others." Furthermore, specific feedback isn't very helpful unless employees have control over the problems that the feedback addresses. Indeed, giving negative feedback about behaviors beyond someone's control is likely to be seen as unfair. Similarly, giving positive feedback about behaviors beyond someone's control may be viewed as insincere.

Last, *problem-oriented feedback* focuses on the problems or incidents associated with the poor performance rather than on the worker or the worker's personality. Giving feedback does not give managers the right to personally attack workers. Though managers may be frustrated by a worker's poor performance, the point of problem-oriented feedback is to draw attention to the problem in a nonjudgmental way so that the employee has enough information to correct it. For example, if an employee has body odor, a surprisingly common workplace problem, don't leave deodorant, soap, or shampoo on the person's desk (for all to see) or say, "You stink." *HR Magazine* advises handling the problem this way: "Because this is a sensitive issue and the employee will likely be uncomfortable and embarrassed in discussing it, keep the meeting private and confidential. Be compassionate but direct. Treat it as you would handle any other job-related performance issue. Explain the problem and the need to correct it. Be specific about expectations....If the employer has a dress and grooming policy, refer to the policy and provide the employee with a copy."[73]

3.4 Improving Cross-Cultural Communication

As you know by now, effective communication is very difficult to accomplish. **Cross-cultural communication**, which involves transmitting information from a person in one country or culture to a person from another country or culture, is even more difficult. For example, when a French company bought a U.S. company, it found that the American managers would not implement the new strategy that it recommended. As tensions grew worse, the American managers challenged their new French boss's strategy and explained why they hadn't followed it. Meanwhile, the French, who now owned the company, couldn't understand why the American managers, who, after all, worked for them, didn't just do as they were told.[74] Exhibit 15.11, which shows the rather different views that French and American workers have about work, gives us some insight into the difficulty of cross-cultural communication in this situation. Overall, the French are much more likely to believe that managers need to have precise answers to subordinates' questions (53 percent versus 18 percent), that organizations would be better off without conflict (24 percent versus 5 percent), and that managers are more motivated by power than by achieving objectives (56 percent

cross-cultural communication
transmitting information from a person in one country or culture to a person from another country or culture

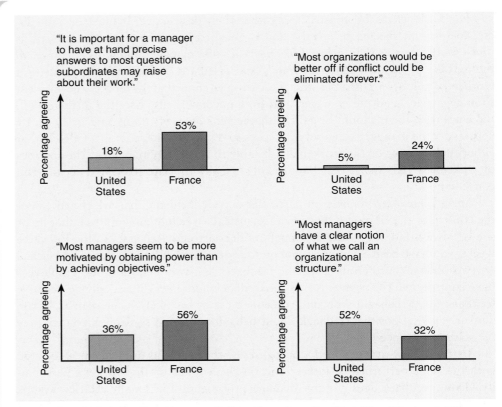

Exhibit 15.11

A Comparison of French and American Views of Work

Source: From N. J. Adler, *From Boston to Beijing: Managing with a World View* (Cincinnati, OH: South-Western, 2002), based on A. Laurent, "The Cultural Diversity of Western Conceptions of Management," in *International Studies of Management and Organization*, vol. 13, no. 1–2 (Spring–Summer 1983): 75–96.

versus 36 percent).[75] With such different views on these basic topics, no wonder there were communication difficulties.

You can do a number of things to increase your chances for successful cross-cultural communication: familiarize yourself with a culture's general work norms; determine whether a culture is emotionally affective or neutral; develop respect for other cultures; and understand how address terms and attitudes toward time (polychronic versus monochronic time, and appointment, schedule, discussion, and acquaintance time) differ from culture to culture.

In Chapter 8, you learned that expatriates who receive predeparture language and cross-cultural training make faster adjustments to foreign cultures and perform better on their international assignments.[76] Therefore, the first step for successful cross-cultural communication is *familiarizing yourself with a culture's general work norms*, that is, the shared values, beliefs, and perceptions toward work and how it should be done. (See Chapter 8 for a more complete discussion of international cultures.) And don't assume that it will be easy. British engineer Mike Cantelo says, "In Europe, people are neighbors and they kind of look the same and it's not far to travel and 'I have been there on vacation and so it's no big deal.' But working in a culture is a hugely different thing."[77] Yet, no matter how difficult, you should work hard to learn different cultures and languages. When New Yorker Donald Dowling was working in his law firm's Paris office, his boss came up to him at a Christmas party hugged him, and declared, "I love this guy because he speaks French." Dowling says, "It took me a minute to figure out he wasn't making fun of me. I think he just appreciated that I tried, unlike one American stationed in that office for two years who managed to pick up a total of three words."[78]

> It took me a minute to figure out he wasn't making fun of me. I think he just appreciated that I tried, unlike one American stationed in that office for two years who managed to pick up a total of three words.

DONALD DOWLING, NEW YORKER WORKING IN PARIS

Fortunately, books such as *Kiss, Bow, or Shake Hands: How to Do Business in 60 Countries* (by Terri Morrison, Wayne Conaway, George Borden, and Hans Koehler), *Do's and Taboos Around the World* (by Roger E. Axtell), and *Dun & Bradstreet's Guide to Doing Business Around the World* (by Terri Morrison, Wayne Conaway, and Joseph Douress) and websites such as BusinessCulture.com and ExecutivePlanet.com provide a wealth of information about countries, their cultures, and their work and communication norms.

Determining whether a culture is emotionally affective or neutral is also important to cross-cultural communication. People in **affective cultures** tend to display their emotions and feelings openly when communicating, whereas people in **neutral cultures** do not.[79] For example, while Italians are prone to strong bursts of emotion (positive and negative), Chinese don't show strong emotions because doing so is thought to disrupt harmony and lead to conflict. Likewise, a smiling American is displaying happiness, but a smiling Japanese may be trying to hide another emotion or avoid answering a question.[80] The mistake most managers make is misunderstanding the differences between affective and neutral cultures. People from neutral cultures aren't by definition cold and unfeeling. They just don't show their emotions in the same way or with the same intensity as people from affective cultures. The key is to recognize the differences and then make sure your judgments are not based on the lack or presence of emotional reactions. Exhibit 15.12 provides a more detailed explanation of the differences between affective and neutral cultures.

Respecting other cultures is also an important part of improving cross-cultural communication. Because we use our own culture as the standard of comparison,

affective cultures cultures in which people display emotions and feelings when communicating

neutral cultures cultures in which people do not display emotions and feelings when communicating

Exhibit 15.12

Affective and Neutral Cultures

IN AFFECTIVE CULTURES, PEOPLE	IN NEUTRAL CULTURES, PEOPLE
1. Reveal thoughts and feelings through verbal and nonverbal communication	1. Don't reveal what they are thinking or feeling
2. Express and show feelings of tension	2. Hide tension and only show it accidentally in face or posture
3. Let their emotions flow easily, intensely, and without inhibition	3. Suppress emotions, leading to occasional "explosions"
4. Admire heated, animated, and intense expression of emotion	4. Admire remaining cool, calm, and relaxed
5. Are used to touching, gesturing, and showing strong emotions through facial expressions (all are common)	5. Resist touching, gesturing, and showing strong emotions through facial expressions
6. Make statements with emotion	6. Often make statements in an unexpressive manner

Source: F. Trompenaars, *Riding the Waves of Culture: Understanding Diversity in Global Business* (London: Economist Books, 1994).

it's very easy to make the common mistake of assuming that "different" means "inferior."[81] Take this example:

> *A Swiss executive waits more than an hour past the appointed time for his Spanish colleague to arrive and to sign a major supply contract. In his impatience he concludes that the Spaniard must be lazy and totally unconcerned about business.*[82]

According to Professor Nancy J. Adler,

> *The Swiss executive has misevaluated his colleague by negatively comparing the colleague's behavior to his own culture's standard for business punctuality. Implicitly, he has labeled his own culture's behavior as good ("The Swiss arrive on time, especially for important meetings, and that is good.") and the other culture's behavior as bad ("The Spanish do not arrive on time and that is bad.").*[83]

According to Adler, "Evaluating others' behavior rarely helps in trying to understand, communicate with, or conduct business with people from another culture."[84] The key, she says, is taking a step back and realizing that you don't know or understand everything that is going on and that your assumptions and interpretations of others' behavior and motives may be wrong. So, instead of judging or evaluating your international business colleagues, observe what they do. Also, delay your judgments until you have more experience with your colleagues and their culture. Lastly, treat any judgments or conclusions you do make as guesses, and then double-check those judgments or conclusions with others.[85] The more patient you are in forming opinions and drawing conclusions, the better you'll be at cross-cultural communication.

Next, you can improve cross-cultural communication by *knowing the address terms* that different cultures use to address each other in the workplace.[86] **Address terms** are the cultural norms that establish whether you address businesspeople by their first names, family names, or titles. When meeting for the first time, Americans and Australians tend to be informal and address each other by first names, even nicknames. Such immediate informality is not accepted in many cultures, however.

For instance, an American manager working in one of his company's British subsidiaries introduced himself as "Chuck" to his British employees and coworkers. Nonetheless, even after six months on the job, his British counterparts still referred to him as "Charles." And the more he insisted they call him "Chuck," the more they seemed to dig in their heels and call him "Charles."[87] So, to decrease defensiveness, know your address terms before addressing your international business counterparts.

Understanding different cultural attitudes toward time is another major consideration for effective cross-cultural communication. Cultures tend to be either monochronic or polychronic in their orientation toward time.[88] In **monochronic cultures**, people tend to do one thing at a time and view time as linear, meaning that time is the passage of sequential events. You may have heard the saying, "There are three stages in people's lives: when they believe in Santa Claus, when they don't believe in Santa Claus, and when they are Santa Claus." The progression from childhood, to young adulthood, to parenthood (when they are Santa Claus) reflects a linear view of time. Schedules are important in monochronic cultures because you schedule time to get a particular thing done. Professor Frons Trompenaars, a noted researcher on international cultures and business, gives these examples of monochronic cultures:

> *In London I once saw a long queue of people waiting for a bus when it started pouring rain. They all stood stolidly, getting soaked even though cover was*

address terms cultural norms that establish whether you should address business-people by their first names, family names, or titles

monochronic cultures cultures in which people tend to do one thing at a time and view time as linear *close by, lest they lose their sequential order. They preferred to do things right rather than do the right thing. In the Netherlands, you could be the queen, but if you are in a butcher's shop with number 46 and you step up for service when number 12 is called, you are still in deep trouble. Nor does it matter if you have an emergency; order is order.*[89]

By contrast, in **polychronic cultures**, people tend to do more than one thing at a time and view time as circular, meaning that time is a combination of the past, present, and future. Consider the following example from a polychronic culture:

In the Bahamas, bus service is managed similarly to many taxi systems. Drivers own their own buses and collect passenger fares for their income. There is no set schedule nor set time when buses will run or arrive at a particular location. Everything depends on the driver.

Bus drivers in the Bahamas are present-oriented; what they feel like doing on a particular day at a particular hour dictates what they will actually do. If the bus driver feels hungry, for example, the driver will go home to eat lunch without waiting for a preset lunch hour. Drivers see no need to repeat yesterday's actions today, nor to set tomorrow's schedule according to the needs and patterns of yesterday.[90]

As you can easily imagine, businesspeople from monochronic cultures are driven to distraction by what they perceive as the laxness of polychronic cultures, while people from polychronic cultures chafe under what they perceive as the strict regimentation of monochronic cultures. Conflicts between these two views of time occur rather easily. Let's go back to Trompenaars's butcher shop for an example:

At my local butcher shop in Amsterdam, the butcher calls a number, unwraps, cuts, rewraps each item the customer wants, and then calls the next number. Once I ventured a suggestion, "While you have the salami out, cut a pound for me, too." Customers and staff went into shock. The system may be inefficient, but they were not about to let some wise guy change it.

Researchers Edward and Mildred Hall summed up the conflicts between these different views of time by saying, "It is impossible to know how many millions of dollars have been lost in international business because monochronic and polychronic people do not understand each other or even realize that two such different time systems exist."[91] Exhibit 15.13 provides a more detailed explanation of the differences between monochronic and polychronic cultures.

Differences in monochronic and polychronic time show up in four important temporal concepts that affect cross-cultural communication: appointment time, schedule time, discussion time, and acquaintance time.[92] **Appointment time** refers to how punctual you must be when showing up for scheduled appointments or meetings. In the United States, you are considered "late" if you arrive more than five minutes after the appointed time. Swedes don't even allow five minutes, expecting others to arrive "on the dot." By contrast, in Latin countries people can arrive 20 to 30 minutes after a scheduled appointment and still not be considered late.

Schedule time is the time by which scheduled projects or jobs should actually be completed. In the United States and other Anglo cultures, a premium is placed on completing things on time. By contrast, more relaxed attitudes toward schedule time can be found throughout Asia and Latin America.

Discussion time concerns how much time should be spent in discussion with others. In the United States, we carefully manage discussion time to avoid "wasting"

polychronic cultures cultures in which people tend to do more than one thing at a time and view times as circular

appointment time a cultural norm for how punctual you must be when showing up for scheduled appointments or meetings

schedule time a cultural norm for the time by which scheduled projects or jobs should actually be completed

discussion time a cultural norm for how much time should be spent in discussion with others

PEOPLE IN MONOCHRONIC CULTURES	PEOPLE IN POLYCHRONIC CULTURES
• Do one thing at a time	• Do many things at once
• Concentrate on the job	• Are highly distractible and subject to interruptions
• Take time commitments (deadlines, schedules) seriously	• Meet time commitments only if possible without extreme measures
• Are committed to the job	• Are committed to people
• Adhere scrupulously to plans	• Change plans easily and often
• Are concerned about not disturbing others (privacy is to be respected)	• Are more concerned with relationships (family, friends, business associates) than with privacy
• Show respect for private property (rarely lend or borrow things)	• Frequently borrow and lend things
• Emphasize promptness	• Vary their promptness by the relationship
• Are accustomed to short-term relationships	• Tend to build lifetime relationships

Source: E. T. Hall & M. R. Hall, *Understanding Cultural Differences* (Yarmouth, ME: Intercultural Press, 1990).

Exhibit 15.13

Monochronic versus Polychronic Cultures

time on nonbusiness topics. In Brazil, though, because of the emphasis on building relationships, as much as two hours of general discussion on nonbusiness topics can take place before moving on to business issues.

Finally, **acquaintance time** is how much time you must spend getting to know someone before the person is prepared to do business with you. Again, in the United States, people quickly get down to business and are willing to strike a deal on the same day if the terms are good and initial impressions are positive. In the Middle East, however, it may take two or three weeks of meetings before reaching this comfort level. The French also have a different attitude toward acquaintance time. Polly Platt, author of *French or Foe*, a book that explains French culture and people for travelers and businesspeople, says, "Know that things are going to take longer and don't resent it. Realize that the time system is different. Time is not a quantity for them. We save time, we spend time, we waste time; all this comes from money. The French don't. They pass time. It's a totally different concept."[93]

*Review 3: **Managing One-on-One Communication***

One-on-one communication can be managed by choosing the right communication medium, being a good listener, giving effective feedback, and understanding cross-cultural communication. Managers generally prefer oral communication because it provides the opportunity to ask questions and assess nonverbal communication. Oral communication is best suited to complex, ambiguous, or emotionally laden topics. Written communication is best suited for delivering straightforward messages and information. Listening is important for managerial success, but most people are terrible listeners. To improve your listening skills, choose to be an active listener (clarify responses, paraphrase, and summarize) and an empathetic listener (show your desire to understand, reflect feelings). Feedback can be constructive or destructive. To be constructive, feedback must be immediate, focused on specific behaviors, and problem oriented. Finally, to increase the chances for successful cross-cultural communication, familiarize yourself with a culture's general work norms, determine whether a culture is emotionally affective or neutral, develop respect for other cultures, and understand how address terms and attitudes toward time (polychronic versus monochronic time, and appointment, schedule, discussion, and acquaintance time) differ from culture to culture.

acquaintance time a cultural norm for how much time you must spend getting to know someone before the person is prepared to do business with you

4 Managing Organization-Wide Communication

Although managing one-on-one communication is important, managers must also know how to communicate effectively with a larger number of people throughout an organization. When Bill Zollars became CEO of **YELLOW CORPORATION**, a trucking company, he decided that he needed to communicate directly with all 25,000 of the company's employees, most of whom did not work at company headquarters in Overland Park, Kansas. For a year and a half, he traveled across the country conducting small, "town hall" meetings. Zollars says, "When I first got to Yellow, we were in a bad state. So I spent 85 percent of my time on the road talking to people one-on-one or in small groups. I would start off in the morning with the sales force, then talk to drivers, and then the people on the docks. At the end of the day I would have a customer dinner. I would say the same thing to every group and repeat it ad nauseam. The people traveling with me were ready to shoot me. But you have to be relentless in terms of your message."[94] Effective leaders, however, don't just communicate to others; they also make themselves accessible so that they can hear what employees throughout their organizations are feeling and thinking.

*Learn more about organization-wide communication by reading the following sections about **4.1 improving transmission by getting the message out** and **4.2 improving reception by finding ways to hear what others feel and think**.*

4.1 Improving Transmission: Getting the Message Out

Several methods of electronic communication—e-mail, online discussion forums, televised/videotaped speeches and conferences, corporate talk shows, and broadcast voice mail—now make it easier for managers to communicate with people throughout the organization and "get the message out."

Although we normally think of *e-mail*, the transmission of messages via computers, as a means of one-on-one communication, it also plays an important role in organization-wide communication. With the click of a button, managers can send e-mail to everyone in the company via e-mail distribution lists. Many CEOs now use this capability regularly to keep employees up-to-date on changes and developments. On his first day as CEO of **DIEBOLD**, which makes ATM machines, Thomas Swidarski e-mailed Diebold's 14,500 employees a message about improving customer loyalty, increasing the speed with which products were manufactured and delivered, and "providing quality products and outstanding service." Swidarski concluded his e-mail by writing that leading Diebold, "does not rest with one person—it rests with each and every one of us."[95]

Many CEOs and top executives make their e-mail addresses public and encourage employees to contact them directly. On his first day as the new CEO of Quest Communications, Richard Notebaert sent this simple e-mail to his 50,000 employees, "I'm here. Talk to me." Since then he has received 200,000 e-mails, most of which he has "reacted to" by taking some action.[96]

Discussion forums are another means of electronically promoting organization-wide communication. **Online discussion forums** are the in-house equivalent of Internet newsgroups; by using web- or software-based discussion tools that are available across the company, employees can easily ask questions and share knowledge with each other. The point is to share expertise and not duplicate solutions

online discussion forums the in-house equivalent of Internet newsgroups. By using Web- or software-based discussion tools that are available across the company, employees can easily ask questions and share knowledge with each other.

already "discovered" by others in the company. Furthermore, because online discussion forums remain online, they provide a historical database for people who are dealing with particular problems for the first time.

Online discussion forums are typically organized by topic. For example, at ERNST & YOUNG, a major accounting firm, accountants who have questions about multinational tax analysis can simply log on to the E&Y tax forum (one of dozens of forums). They can either post new questions and wait for others to respond with answers or read previously posted questions and answers to see if the information they need has already been discussed. If both of these options fail, they will at least learn the names of people in the organization that they can contact for help.[97]

Exhibit 15.14 lists the steps companies need to take to establish successful online discussion forums. First, pinpoint your company's top intellectual assets through a knowledge audit; then spread that knowledge throughout the organization. Second, create an online directory detailing the expertise of individual workers and make it available to all employees. Third, set up discussion groups on the intranet so that managers and workers can collaborate on problem solving. Finally, reward information sharing by making the online sharing of knowledge a key part of performance ratings.

Televised/videotaped speeches and meetings are a third electronic method of organization-wide communication. **Televised/videotaped speeches and meetings** are simply speeches and meetings originally made to a smaller audience that are either simultaneously broadcast to other locations in the company or videotaped for subsequent distribution and viewing. Cisco's John Chambers describes how, over his 15 years as CEO, he's added televised messages to his communication strategies:

> I started off with classic communication methods when I got here 15 years ago. I'd walk around and talk to small groups and larger groups. I'd see who was here in the evening. To this day I can tell you whose car is out in the parking lot. Then e-mail became very effective, because it gave me the ability to send a message to the whole group. But I'm a voice person. I communicate with emotion that way. I like to listen to emotion too. It's a lot easier to listen to a key customer if I hear how they're describing a problem to me. I'll leave 40 or 50 voice mails a day. I do them on the way to work and coming back from work. The newest thing for me is video on demand, which is my primary communication vehicle today. We have a small studio downstairs. We probably tape 10 to 15 videos a quarter. That way employees, and customers, can watch them when they want.[98]

televised/videotaped speeches and meetings speeches and meetings originally made to a smaller audience that are either simultaneously broadcast to other locations in the company or videotaped for subsequent distribution and viewing

corporate talk shows televised company meetings that allow remote audiences (employees) to pose questions to the show's host and guests

Corporate talk shows are a variant on televised/videotaped speeches and meetings. But instead of simply being watched, **corporate talk shows** allow remote audience members, all of whom are typically workers or managers, to pose questions to the show's host and guests. For example, once a month, Emma Carrasco, vice president of marketing and communication, and Dan Hunt, president of Caribbean and Latin American operations, host the Virtual Leadership Academy, which is a corporate talk show for NORTEL NETWORKS. Typically, 2,000 employees in 46 countries watch the live broadcast and can call in with questions about Nortel and its competitors. Why a corporate talk show? Carrasco says, "We're always looking for ways to break down barriers in the company, and people are comfortable with the talk-show format. People watch talk shows in every country in the region, and they've learned that it's okay to say what's on their mind. In fact, it's expected."[99]

Voice messaging, or voice mail, is a telephone answering system that records audio messages. In one survey, 89 percent of respondents said that voice messaging is critical to business communication,

Exhibit 15.14

Establishing Online Discussion Forums

Source: Based on G. McWilliams & M. Stepanek, "Knowledge Management: Taming the Info Monster," *BusinessWeek*, 22 June 1998, 170.

78 percent said that it improves productivity, and 58 percent said they would rather leave a message on a voice messaging system than with a receptionist.[100] Nonetheless, most people are unfamiliar with the ability to *broadcast voice mail* by sending a recorded message to everyone in the company. Broadcast voice mail gives top managers a quick, convenient way to address their work forces via oral communication. Harry Kraemer, CEO of pharmaceutical giant BAXTER INTERNATIONAL, describes Baxter's broadcast voice mail system: "We have more than 30,000 Baxter team members hooked onto the same voice-mail system. That includes everybody but the folks on the factory line. This is hooked up in over 50 countries."[101] At Ernst & Young, the company-wide broadcast voice mails of chairman Phil Laskawy were so well known and well liked that E & Y employees called them "Travels with Phil." No matter where he was traveling on business for the company—and he traveled all over the world—Phil would begin his voice mails, most of which lasted 5 to 10 minutes, with a weather report, a couple of bad jokes, and an update on his beloved New York Yankees baseball team; then came the core part of his message.[102]

© ASSOCIATED PRESS

Corporate talk shows are an increasingly popular — and effective — way to get the word out about and to hear what people throughout the company are thinking.

4.2 Improving Reception: Hearing What Others Feel and Think

When people think of "organization-wide" communication, they think of the CEO and top managers getting their message out to people in the company. But organization-wide communication also means finding ways to hear what people throughout the organization are feeling and thinking. This is important because most employees and managers are reluctant to share their thoughts and feelings with top managers. Surveys indicate that only 29 percent of first-level managers feel that their companies encourage employees to express their opinions openly. Another study of 22 companies found that 70 percent of the people surveyed were afraid to speak up about problems they knew existed at work.

Withholding information about organizational problems or issues is called **organizational silence**. Organizational silence occurs when employees believe that telling management about problems won't make a difference or that they'll be punished or hurt in some way for sharing such information.[103] For example, the norm in most operating rooms is that the surgeon is clearly in charge. At first look, there doesn't seem to be anything wrong with that. After all, if the surgeon wasn't in charge, who would be? However, at 20 hospitals, 60 percent of the operating room staffers—nurses, technicians, and other doctors—agreed with this statement, "In the ORs here, it is difficult to speak up if I perceive a problem with patient care."[104] And when nurses and other operating room staffers don't speak up (organizational silence), serious mistakes can occur. *VHA* Inc., which helps 2,400 hospitals coordinate best practices, has a new program called "Transformation of the Operating Room," in which operating teams use "safety pauses" and "time-outs." The surgical team pauses for a moment, is asked if anyone has concerns or comments, and then addresses them if need be. Studies show that programs such as this are not only changing the norms in operating rooms but also reducing mistakes, such as operating on the wrong leg or noticing that key surgical instruments are missing prior to beginning surgery.

Company hotlines, survey feedback, frequent informal meetings, surprise visits, and blogs are additional ways of overcoming organizational silence. **Company hotlines** are phone numbers that anyone in the company can call anonymously to leave information for upper management. For example, DELOITTE TOUCHE TOHMATSU has a toll-free

organizational silence when employees withhold information about organizational problems or issues

company hotlines phone numbers that anyone in the company can call anonymously to leave information for upper management hotline for employees to call to report any kind of problem or issue within the company. Hotlines are particularly important because 44 percent of employees will not report misconduct. Why not? The reason is twofold: They don't believe anything will be done, *and* they "fear that the report will not be kept confidential."[105] David Childers, CEO of ETHICSPOINT, which runs hotlines for corporations, says that companies can expect 1 to 1.5 percent of their employees to call their hotlines and that 10 to 15 percent of the calls will involve serious problems that require immediate company action.[106]

Survey feedback is information that is collected by survey from organization members and then compiled, disseminated, and used to develop action plans for improvement. Many organizations make use of survey feedback by surveying their managers and employees several times a year. FEDEX, for example, runs its own Survey Feedback Action program. The survey, which is administered online and is completely anonymous, includes sections for employees to evaluate their managers and the overall environment at FedEx, including benefits, incentives, and working conditions. After the surveys are completed, the results are compiled and then fed back to each FedEx work group. Each group then uses the results to decide where changes and improvements need to be made and to develop specific action plans to address those problems. The final step is to look for improvements in subsequent employee surveys to see if those plans worked. John Allison, vice president of HR for FedEx Asia Pacific, says, "It's a means of engaging all of our employees so that they can participate in expressing concerns about issues and at the same time participate in solving any problems that might arise."[107]

Frequent, *informal meetings* between top managers and lower-level employees are one of the best ways for top managers to hear what others feel and think. Many people assume that top managers are at the center of everything that goes on in organizations, but top managers commonly feel isolated from most of their lower-level managers and employees. Consequently, more and more top managers are scheduling frequent, informal meetings with people throughout their companies. At JETBLUE, founder and chairman David Neeleman uses informal meetings to listen to customers and employees. On an almost daily basis, Neeleman can be found on a JetBlue flight talking to customers. Neeleman listens, writing thoughts and customer comments on airplane napkins that he stuffs in his pockets to be turned into organizational to-do's once the flight is over. However, Neeleman also flies to work with and listen to his company's flight crews. Says Neeleman, "I want them to know that I value what they do. I value it so much that I'm not too good to do it. I fly with 8 to 12 crew-members a week, but the other 1,200 flight attendants know about it."[108] Al Spain, senior vice president of operations, emphasizes how important these visits are, saying, "There is no 'they' here. It's 'we' and 'us.' We succeed together or we fail together."[109]

Have you ever been around when a supervisor learns that upper management is going to be paying a visit? First, there's shock. Next, there's anxiety. And then there's panic, as everyone is told to drop what he or she is doing to polish, shine, and spruce up the workplace so that it looks perfect for the visit. Of course, when visits are conducted under these conditions, top managers don't get a realistic look at what's going on in the company. Consequently, one of the ways to get an accurate picture is to pay *surprise visits* to various parts of the organization. These visits should not just be surprise inspections, but should also be used as an opportunity to encourage meaningful upward communication from those who normally don't get a chance to communicate with upper management. Such surprise visits are now part of the culture at the ROYAL MAIL, the United Kingdom's postal service. Chairman Allan Leighton frequently shows up announced at Royal Mail delivery offices. Leighton says the initial reaction is always the same, "Oh s***, it's the chairman." However, Leighton isn't there to catch his employees doing something wrong. He's there to find out, right or wrong, what's really going on. Says Leighton, "Those

---

"WHAT'S NEW" COMPANY

"WHAT'S NEW" COMPANY

"There is no "they" here. It's "we" and "us." We succeed together or we fail together."

AL SPAIN,
SENIOR VICE PRESIDENT OF OPERATIONS,
JETBLUE

"WHAT'S NEW" COMPANY

"WHAT'S NEW" COMPANY

survey feedback information that is collected by surveys from organizational members and then compiled, disseminated, and used to develop action plans for improvement visits at half past five in the morning [with employees] are the most important part" of turning around the Royal Mail, which was once losing 1.5 million pounds a day.[110] Today, thanks in part to his communication with employees, the Royal Mail delivers 95 percent of first-class mail in one day, better than any other postal service in the world, and now earns a profit of 1.5 million pounds per day.

Blogs are another way to hear what people are thinking and saying, both inside and outside the organization. A **blog** is a personal website that provides personal opinions or recommendations, news summaries, and reader comments. At Google, which owns the blog-hosting service Blogger, hundreds of employees are writing *internal blogs*. One employee even wrote a blog for posting all the notes from the brainstorming sessions used to redesign the search page used by millions each day. Staffer Marissa Mayer says, "Our legal department loves the blogs, because it basically is a written-down, backed-up, permanent time-stamped version of the scientist's notebook. When you want to file a patent, you can now show in blogs where this idea happened."[111]

External blogs, written by people outside the company, can be a good way to find out what others are saying or thinking about your organization or its products or actions. Tim Holmes, Ford's executive director of public affairs, believes that companies have to pay attention to what is being said about them online. Says Holmes, "Like most big companies, we monitor the press, but the problem with that is it's always retrospective, everything's a few weeks old. The real value of searching the net, including blogs, is that you get a live picture of what people are thinking about certain issues. It means that you can predict if there is going to be an issue that's going to grow and become something you need to respond to before it gets to the mainstream press."[112] Some companies have created the new position of chief blogging officer to manage internal company blogs and to monitor what it said about the company and its products on external blogs.[113]

PROCTER & GAMBLE is also turning to the Internet to do a better job of hearing what people outside the company are feeling and thinking. P&G is working with PlanetFeedback to find out what consumers are saying about P&G's two biggest brands, Tide detergent and Pampers diapers. PlanetFeedback collects consumer comments on its website about various companies and their products. It will also search online message boards, discussion websites, Usenet user groups, and blogs to find out what people are saying about P&G's brands.[114]

"WHAT'S NEW" COMPANY

Review 4: **Managing Organization-Wide Communication**

Managers need methods for managing organization-wide communication and for making themselves accessible so that they can hear what employees throughout their organizations are feeling and thinking. E-mail, online discussion forums, televised/videotaped speeches and conferences, corporate talk shows, and broadcast voice mail make it much easier for managers to improve message transmission and "get the message out." By contrast, anonymous company hotlines, survey feedback, frequent informal meetings, and surprise visits help managers avoid organizational silence and improve reception by hearing what others in the organization feel and think. Monitoring internal and external blogs is another way to find out what people are saying and thinking about your organization.

blog a personal Web site that provides personal opinions or recommendations, news summaries, and reader comments

How Do You Listen?

Have you ever been eager to tell someone a funny story, only to have that person interrupt you repeatedly to ask for details or clarification? And have you ever said in exasperation, "Will you just listen?" Some people prefer an inquisitive listening style, whereas others prefer a contemplative listening style. What listening style best describes you? This listening styles inventory will help you establish a baseline to use as a foundation for developing your listening skills.

The following items relate to listening style.[115] Circle the appropriate responses. Please be candid.

	Almost always	Often	Sometimes	Seldom	Almost never
1. I want to listen to what others have to say when they are talking.	5	4	3	2	1
2. I do not listen at my capacity when others are talking.	1	2	3	4	5
3. By listening, I can guess a speaker's intent or purpose without being told.	5	4	3	2	1
4. I have a purpose for listening when others are talking.	5	4	3	2	1
5. I keep control of my biases and attitudes when listening to others speak so that these factors won't affect my interpretation of the message.	5	4	3	2	1
6. I analyze my listening errors so as not to make them again.	5	4	3	2	1
7. I listen to the complete message before making judgments about what the speaker has said.	5	4	3	2	1
8. I cannot tell when a speaker's biases or attitudes are affecting his or her message.	1	2	3	4	5
9. I ask questions when I don't fully understand a speaker's message.	5	4	3	2	1
10. I am aware of whether or not a speaker's meaning of words and concepts is the same as mine.	5	4	3	2	1

SUBTOTAL = _____ + _____ + _____ + _____ + _____ =

GRAND TOTAL = _____

You can find the interpretation of your score at:
academic.cengage.com/management/williams.

To Blog or Not to Blog

Just this month, your company, AeroPrecision, a manufacturer of aircraft engine components, completed the upgrade of its computer system—the first upgrade in nearly 15 years.[116] Everyone cheered when the DOS-based operating software was replaced with the newest Windows-based version. Now, for the first time data are being electronically collected directly from the factory floor, and the engineering, tooling, and maintenance departments are connected. You and the other top managers expect to reap terrific gains in productivity—and profitability—as a result of the upgrade. As the operations manager, you were ultimately responsible for revamping the entire system, and the process has left you motivated to adopt even more technological advances.

Over the course of the upgrade, you came across several short articles and references to *blogs*, which you learned was short for "Web logs." Not too savvy about these things at the time, you turned to asked your IT consultant, and she told you that blogs are web pages that serve as publicly accessible journals. That didn't help you much, so she directed you to a variety of blogs to find out what they were all about. After only a few visits you started thinking about creating a blog for AeroPrecision.

Some managers use blogs to communicate with employees, and others use them as marketing tools to "get the message out" about their companies. The question for you is how AeroPrecision would use blogs. Only 30 of AeroPrecision's 100 employees have computers at their desks (only 30 have desks). The rest of the employees are shop-floor workers who use the 20 terminals located on stands throughout the factory to record their personal production information. Shop-floor terminals don't have Internet access. Could you justify connecting the 20 factory terminals to the Internet? And do you really want employees standing around the shop-floor terminals reading a company blog? But then you wonder, "Would that be any different from them hovering around the bulletin board by the time clock reading the company's biweekly newsletter? And with a blog, the information would be more timely."

Or would it? You pause to think about the time required to maintain a blog. And what would you link out to? A public blog would need to be an authoritative voice on, well, what? You could hook up to links about aerodynamics, metal prices, and travel statistics. If you could leverage AeroPrecision's technical expertise, you would be able to position the company as a premier provider of component parts for aircraft engines. You may even be able to convert the research you do for the blog into new customers or products for new industries. If you put your mind to it, you are confident that you can brainstorm enough valuable resources for a blog, but you come back to the issue of time. Would the time spent be worth it?

(continued)

online discussion
    forums 579
organizational silence 581
paralanguage 566
perception 553
perceptual filters 553
polychronic cultures 577
schedule time 577
selective perception 555
self-serving bias 557
survey feedback 582
televised/videotaped
    speeches and
    meetings 580
upward communication 562

Questions

1. Does it make sense for AeroPrecision to create a company blog for employees only? In other words, is a blog the best medium to get the company's message out to employees and to hear what they feel and think? Explain.

2. Brainstorm possible items for inclusion on an AeroPrecision blog destined for public viewing. Can you think of any topics that you would want to avoid linking to?

3. How could a blog play a role in designing a company's strategy? (Recall the issues discussed in Chapter 6, Organizational Strategy.)

4. Do you create a public blog for AeroPrecision? Why or why not?

Communication Dilemmas and Decisions

As you watch the falling snow, you can't help thinking about the way the fax machine coughs out legal missives into a collection bin. You are a partner at Shaw Walker Theobald, a law firm with offices across the United States, and your office sits right next to the constantly humming fax machine. You're at your wit's end from the incessant buzzing. Documents of all lengths and levels of importance come through the fax; sometimes, a lawyer on one floor will write a question on a cover letter, send it by fax to a lawyer on another floor at your firm, and then request the answer by fax! While you pack your briefcase before heading home, you think, "What a drain on productivity! And the client ends up footing the bill. There has to be a more efficient way to communicate."

After you finish dinner, you open your work, and are again distracted—not by a fax, but by the pinging of your teenager's instant messaging on the computer in the den. Immediately, you think you've hit on a solution for the office. If the firm used instant messaging, you could save the energy used by the fax, eliminate all the paper, and have answers in an instant. Communication would reach terminal speed! Unfortunately, you can't just implement your idea when you walk in tomorrow morning. You're only one of many partners, and they all have to approve anything that affects the management of the firm. How are you going to persuade a team of people trained to object? Instead of pulling a brief out of your bag, you flip to a clean sheet on your legal pad and begin drafting a convincing memo.

Getting Started

This exercise will give you practice in writing memos and giving verbal feedback. You will begin by writing a memo on your own based on the scenario you just read. Then assemble a team of five to six students. Make enough copies of your memo so that each team member can have one. The job of the team is to review and critique all the memos. You will want to review Section 3.3 on giving feedback before convening the team to evaluate the memos. Choose one team member to be the moderator. The moderator will be in charge of keeping the discussion on track and ensuring that it doesn't disintegrate into subjective attacks.

Activities

1. Write a memo to your colleagues proposing the use of instant messaging to speed communication.

2. Convene the team and critique the members' memos. Try to use descriptive terms to give feedback about the memos. Avoid words like "good" and "bad"—they don't give the writer any real information about the effectiveness of the memo. Here are some adjectives that you might find useful as a starting point:
    - Convincing
    - Persuasive
    - Condescending
    - Concise
    - Wordy
    - Informative
    - Detailed
    - Sparse
    - Neat
    - Hard to follow
    - Clear
    - Sloppy
    - Off-putting
    - Effective
    - Inappropriate
    - Unprofessional

    Don't limit your comment to a negative adjective, either. If you say a memo is hard to follow, explain *why*. What makes it hard to follow? If you say a memo is wordy, explain how it is wordy. And be specific: point out which phrases are redundant, unnecessary, or repetitive.

3. Assume that your individual proposal was accepted, and the partners (your team) have asked you to announce the new capabilities and outline the rules for their use. Determine the best way to communicate the instant messaging plan to the junior partners, associates, paralegals, and office staff. Using whatever medium you think is best, write out your communication. For example, if you think e-mail is best, draft a relevant e-mail. If you think a memo would be appropriate, then draft one. If you think oral communication would be a better choice, draft the speech you will give. Regardless of your medium, you will need to remember your audience.

4. If you have time, repeat the group critique session with the second communication. You may also wish to discuss as a team which medium would be the best for telling everyone at the firm about the new instant messaging initiative.

When problems occur in organizations, they are frequently attributed to a breakdown in communication. The communication process may get more than its share of the blame for some breakdowns that result from organizational or leadership problems. But there is some truth to the common perception that communication is problematic. In this exercise you will have the opportunity to consider how you might improve your own communication from two sides of the table—coaching/disciplining an employee; and receiving coaching/disciplining from a manager.

Step 1: Get into groups and read the scenario. Your professor will organize you in small groups of three or four students.

Scenario: Chalet is a fine dining restaurant in a ski resort setting. The restaurant is well known for its gourmet cuisine, fine wine selection, and outstanding service. Dinner for two at Chalet would typically cost $100 or more. A key management responsibility at Chalet is the training and development of wait staff. Service quality is carefully monitored and standards rigorously maintained. In exchange for meeting these demanding standards, Chalet wait staff are well-compensated and enjoy good benefits. As time permits, you should complete conversations in which you play each of the following roles: Dennis/Denise (new wait staff member with three months of experience at Chalet); Christy/Chris (service manager); and D.J./R.J. (communication consultant to Chalet).

Here are some basic facts of the situation:

- The service manager has not directly observed any problems with Dennis/Denise interacting with customers of the restaurant.

- Over this past busy weekend three tables of customers reported problems with the service they received from Dennis/Denise. Only one other table received any negative feedback at all during the weekend, and that concerned the quality of a particular dessert item.

- The reports about Dennis/Denise were rather vague—"server seemed distant, unresponsive" and "acted aloof, like we were a bother."

- Christy/Chris, the service manager, did catch the tail end of what seemed like an argument between Dennis/Denise and one of the cooks on Friday night. When the cook was asked about the incident, she said, "It was nothing…usual cook versus server stuff."

- Dennis/Denise needs this job to pay for college, and is taking a full load of classes.

The role play should involve a brief conversation (five to seven minutes) initiated by Christy/Chris on Monday afternoon prior to opening. The focus of this conversation should be to coach and/or discipline regarding the concerns of the previous weekend. Those playing the role of communication consultant should take notes and provide feedback on the communication in this conversation (strengths and areas for improvement). As time allows, rotate roles after completing a conversation and hearing consultant feedback.

Step 2: Do the role play. Complete a role play conversation with one person playing the role of the service manager (Christy/Chris) and another person playing the role of the wait staffer (Dennis/Denise). Communication consultant(s) should listen and take notes in order to provide feedback to the two individuals who are role-playing the coaching/discipline conversation.

Step 3: Give feedback. Communication consultant(s) should give feedback to the role players at the conclusion of the conversation, considering key aspects of communication discussed in this chapter.

Step 4: Switch roles. Switch roles and repeat the role-play conversation and post-conversation feedback as time allows.

Step 5: Debrief as a class. What challenges face the communicators in this scenario? Which role was most difficult for you, and why? Why is it important for managers to do coach and discipline effectively? Why might managers avoid (or underutilize) this form of communication?

I Don't Agree, but I'm Listening

Being a good listener is a critical part of effective communication. Without it, you're unlikely to be a good manager. Therefore, the purpose of this assignment is to help you develop your listening skills. And there's no better way to do that than to talk to someone whose views are quite different from yours. In the best of situations, being a good listener is difficult. Because of perceptual filters, distractions, or daydreams, we retain only about 25 percent of what we hear. When we're talking with people who have very different views and opinions, it can be almost impossible to be good listeners. We tend to interrupt, jump to conclusions about what they'll say, and hurry them to finish their points (which we don't want to listen to anyway) so that we can "correct" their thinking with our own opinions.

To complete this assignment, you'll have to find someone who has different views or opinions on some topic (handgun control, abortion, capital punishment, and euthanasia are just some of the topics on which you can always find someone with a different viewpoint). Once you've found someone, conduct a 10-minute listening session, following this simple rule: Before stating your opinion, you must first accurately reflect or paraphrase the statement that your listening partner just made (be sure to reread Subsection 3.2 on listening).

For example, suppose that your listening partner says, "Women shouldn't have to ask anyone for permission for what they do to their bodies. If they decide they want an abortion, they should go ahead and have it." Before making your point or disagreeing with your partner's, you will have to accurately paraphrase that statement in your own words. If you don't paraphrase it correctly, your listening partner will tell you. If you or your partner has difficulty accurately paraphrasing a statement, ask the other person to repeat the statement, and try again. Also, don't parrot the statement by repeating it word for word. Good listening isn't mimicry. It's capturing the essence of what others have said in your own words. And before your listening partner responds, he or she, too, has to accurately paraphrase what you say. Continue this listening-based discussion for 10 minutes.

Questions

1. Was this discussion different from the way you normally discuss contentious topics with other people? Why or why not?

2. Was it difficult to reflect or paraphrase your listening partner's perspectives? Explain and give an example.

3. Did active listening techniques or empathetic listening techniques lead to more effective listening for you? Explain.

REEL TO REAL

The Paper

This engaging film shows the ethical dilemmas and stress of producing the *New York Sun,* a daily metropolitan newspaper. Metro editor Henry Hackett (Michael Keaton) races against the clock to publish a story about a major police scandal that could send two young African American men to jail. He is in constant conflict with managing editor Alicia Clark (Glenn Close), who is more concerned about controlling the budget than about running accurate stories. Hackett is also under constant pressure from his wife Marty (Marisa Tomei), who is pregnant with their first child. While Hackett tries to get his story, Marty urges him to take a less demanding job at the *Sentinel*.

This scene occurs early in *The Paper*. It shows a staff meeting that takes place the day after the *Sun* missed a story about a murder and other shootings with racial overtones. Instead, the *Sun* ran a front-page story about parking problems. At the meeting, senior editor Bernie White (Robert Duvall) discusses his preferences in front-page stories.

What to Watch for and Ask Yourself

1. Use the model of the communication process to diagram what is occurring in the clip.
2. What types of communication do you see in the video?
3. Discuss the paralanguage used in the clip. What mood or attitude does it convey?

NEADS—Communicating with and without Voice

Suppose you woke up one day and couldn't see. Or perhaps you couldn't hear, couldn't speak, or couldn't walk. How would you communicate and interact with the world around you? Today's technology provides solutions to some of these challenges, but there is a live solution as well: assistance dogs. National Education for Assistance Dog Services (NEADS) acquires, trains, and matches dogs with people who need assistance. Founded in 1976 as a nonprofit organization, NEADS is based in the rural community of Princeton, Massachusetts, where it adopts and trains dogs to serve their new owners. Watch the video to see why communication is a central part of success at this unique management workplace.

What to Watch for and Ask Yourself

1. How does perception affect the communication process at NEADS?
2. What role does nonverbal communication play at NEADS?
3. Why are listening skills so important at NEADS?

five

PART 5
Controlling

Chapter 16
Control

This chapter examines the basic and in-depth methods that companies use to achieve control, as well as those things that companies choose to control (finances, customer retention, and product quality, among others).

Chapter 17
Managing Information

This chapter explains why information matters, the value of strategic information to companies, and the cost and characteristics of good information. We investigate how companies capture, process, and protect information, and how information, knowledge, and expertise are shared.

Chapter 18
Managing Service and Manufacturing Operations

This chapter discusses the daily production of goods and services, starting with the basics of productivity and quality. Next, you will read about managing service and manufacturing operations, and the measures, costs, and methods for managing inventory.

CHAPTER 16

Control

Learning Outcomes:

1 Describe the basic control process.

2 Discuss the various methods that managers can use to maintain control.

3 Describe the behaviors, processes, and outcomes that today's managers are choosing to control in their organizations.

In This Chapter:

WHAT WOULD YOU DO?

Gap Headquarters, San Francisco, CA[1]—Standing outside one of Gap's mall stores, you realize how difficult it will be to turn around this venerable chain. The company consists of more than 3,200 locations worldwide, and same-store sales have been flat or declining in 29 of the past 31 months. Furthermore, same-store sales have dropped 9 percent each of the last two years. You have been hired to change the pattern and bring glory back to the operation.

Donald and Doris Fisher opened the first Gap store in 1969 in San Francisco. Over the next few decades they grew the business into America's largest fashion retailer. In 1983 they took over Banana Republic and in 1994 they launched Old Navy. Old Navy became the first fashion retailer to reach $1 billion in annual sales in less than four years from their founding. Mickey Drexler, the brilliant CEO who grew

the business for two decades, was known as a fashion icon who let the financial part of the business slip as he focused on the fashion side. All of this was fine while the business grew at astronomical rates. However, the wheels came off the machine when sales slumped across the board as the company's efforts to attract teenagers alienated their main group of customers (people in their 20s and 30s). Frustrated with out-of-control costs and a burgeoning inventory, the Fishers fired Drexler and brought in Paul Pressler, who had a long history of strict organizational control at Disney. Pressler rapidly closed underperforming stores, reduced inventory, and cleaned up the finances of the organization. Unfortunately, the fashion side of the business had no real direction and although the organization was carefully managing its finances, foot traffic fell in its stores. (Pressler was ultimately replaced.)

You knew when you took over that fashion is a difficult business. Consistently attracting profitable customers is your goal, but how can the Gap do that? Financial

controls and efficient operations are crucial, but so is presenting desirable fashions, because numerous competitors do the same thing extraordinarily well. Abercrombie & Fitch, which made a significant turnaround after being spun off from Limited Brands, is now one of the hottest stores in the teen market. Even old-line retailer JCPenney turned its clothing line into a strength again behind the fashion expertise of merchandiser Vanessa Castagna.

The top companies in any industry benchmark the best practices of their competitors, effectively understand and manage their financial and human resources, and consistently deliver innovative products that attract customers. So what companies should Gap benchmark in order to turn around its operations and increase customer traffic? With these things in mind, should Gap hire a fashion head to focus on the products in its stores, or should it hire someone who will focus on controlling the organization's costs, schedules, and operations? How much control and what types of controls should be in place? How do you achieve a balance between control and creativity? What techniques might help you achieve this balance? **If you were in charge at Gap, what would you do?**

"WHAT'S NEW" COMPANIES

- GAP
- COVENTRY MALL
- IROBOT
- CADILLAC
- GOOGLE
- MICROSOFT
- KMART
- WAL-MART
- NIKE
- APPLE
- PHONES4U
- STATE OF CALIFORNIA
- MOTOROLA
- SMITHFIELD FOODS
- NORDSTROM
- NUCOR
- DUKE CHILDREN'S HOSPITAL
- AND OTHERS . . .

Study Tip — **The list of key terms on page 621 can be a valuable study aid.** Write down the definition of each term on a separate piece of paper without consulting the margin terms in the chapter. Cement your understanding by also writing an example if possible.

As Gap's situation shows, past success is no guarantee of future success. Even successful companies fall short, face challenges, and have to make changes. **Control** is a regulatory process of establishing standards to achieve organizational goals, comparing actual performance against the standards, and taking corrective action when necessary, as at Gap, to restore performance to those standards. Control is achieved when behavior and work procedures conform to standards and company goals are accomplished.[2] Control is not just an after-the-fact process, however. Preventive measures are also a form of control.

We begin this chapter by examining the basic control process used in organizations. In the second part of the chapter, we go beyond the basics to an in-depth examination of the different methods that companies use to achieve control. We conclude the chapter by looking at the things that companies choose to control (finances, customer retention, and product quality, among others).

BASICS OF CONTROL

"WHAT'S NEW" COMPANY

With many empty stores and a dated look, COVENTRY MALL in Pottstown, Pennsylvania, just 22 miles from the gigantic King of Prussia Mall, *was* dying, but mall manager Rene Daniel has it on the mend. The first step was fixing the food. With the mall down to just six food vendors (for example, Hot Dogs & More and Egg Roll Hut), he convinced McDonald's, Subway, and Saladworks to open restaurants. When the lease expired on the "Everything 99 Cent" store, he convinced Gap to lease the adjacent space, knock out the wall, and replace the aging blue Formica with blond wood and modern glass. Changes like this have increased mall sales by a third, and they are now above the national average. Nevertheless, despite the changes, Vickey Sihler, who started shopping at the Coventry Mall again because of Gap and the new Children's Place store, still sees room for improvement. "This place really needs to be fixed up," she says.[3] So, by working the control process (standards, comparison to standards, and corrective action), Rene Daniel is slowly but surely fixing Coventry Mall.

> **After reading the next section, you should be able to**
>
> 1 describe the basic control process.

1 The Control Process

control a regulatory process of establishing standards to achieve organizational goals, comparing actual performance against the standards, and taking corrective action, when necessary

The basic control process **1.1 begins with the establishment of clear standards of performance, 1.2 involves a comparison of performance to those standards, 1.3 takes corrective action, if needed, to repair performance deficiencies, 1.4 is a dynamic, cybernetic process,** and **1.5 consists of three basic methods: feedback control, concurrent control, and feedforward control.** However, as much as managers would like, **1.6 control isn't always worthwhile or possible.**

1.1 Standards

The control process begins when managers set goals, such as satisfying 90 percent of customers or increasing sales by 5 percent. Companies then specify the performance standards that must be met to accomplish those goals. **Standards** are a basis of comparison for measuring the extent to which organizational performance is satisfactory or unsatisfactory. For example, many pizzerias use 30–40 minutes as the standard for delivery times. Since anything longer is viewed as unsatisfactory, they'll typically reduce the price if they can't deliver a hot pizza to you within that time period.

So how do managers set standards? How do they decide which levels of performance are satisfactory and which are unsatisfactory? The first criterion for a good standard is that it must enable goal achievement. If you're meeting the standard, but still not achieving company goals, then the standard may have to be changed. For example, hospital patients are typically billed a month or two after treatment. But with the amount of unreimbursed care totaling $22.3 billion nationwide, many hospitals are changing payment standards by asking that insurance copayments be paid before the patient leaves the hospital. Anyone who can't afford the entire copayment at once is asked to at least make a down payment (those who do are much more likely to pay their entire bill). Karen Dostart, at Marshall Medical Center in Placerville, California, says, "My goal is to reduce elective services that go to bad debt by 50 percent within a year."[4]

Companies also determine standards by listening to customers or observing competitors. After hearing from consumers that they were interested in machines that would automate routine household tasks, *iRobot*, a manufacturer of industrial and government (military) robots, created the Scooba, a robot that washes floors. Founder Colin Angle says, "People just hated to mop, so we saw a real opportunity."[5] The Scooba vacuums up dirt and debris, sprays a bleach cleaning solution, and then squeegees and sucks up the dirty water from the floor. At about $250, the Scooba can mop a typical kitchen in 45 minutes.

Standards can also be determined by benchmarking other companies. **Benchmarking** is the process of determining how well other companies (though not just competitors) perform business functions or tasks. In other words, benchmarking is the process of determining other companies' standards.

When setting standards by benchmarking, the first step is to determine what to benchmark. Companies can benchmark anything, from cycle time (how fast) to quality (how well) to price (how much). The next step is to identify the companies against which to benchmark your standards. The last step is to collect data to determine other companies' performance standards. *Cadillac* sales dropped for three straight decades because car buyers saw Cadillacs as big, bloated, poor-quality, luxury cars. Then, several years ago, after losing most of its luxury car market share, Cadillac began systematically benchmarking its quality and driving performance against Mercedes, BMW, Audi, and Lexus cars. Because of the changes made as a result of that benchmarking, Cadillac's STS sedan is now giving those luxury automakers' cars a run for their money. The *Wall Street Journal* concluded, "We'd have been impressed if the STS had matched these European cars' performance, but what surprised us was that in some ways it was better. The STS felt more nimble and fun to drive than heavier-feeling models including the Mercedes E-Class or Audi A6. It kept us feeling connected to the road, while a Lexus LS430 left us feeling isolated. And up against BMW's 5 Series,

> ❝My goal is to reduce elective services that go to bad debt by 50 percent within a year.❞
>
> **KAREN DOSTART,**
> MARSHALL MEDICAL CENTER,
> PLACERVILLE, CALIFORNIA

"WHAT'S NEW" COMPANY

"WHAT'S NEW" COMPANY

standards a basis of comparison for measuring the extent to which various kinds of organizational performance are satisfactory or unsatisfactory

benchmarking the process of identifying outstanding practices, processes, and standards in other companies and adapting them to your company considered the benchmark in the class? We'd call it a draw."[6] Cadillac now consistently sells more cars than Mercedes in the all-important luxury car market.[7]

1.2 Comparison to Standards

The next step in the control process is to compare actual performance against performance standards. Although this sounds straightforward, the quality of the comparison largely depends on the measurement and information systems a company uses to keep track of performance. The better the system, the easier it is for companies to track their progress and identify problems that need to be fixed. One way for retailers to verify that performance standards are being met is to use "secret shoppers." Retail stores spend $600 million a year to hire these consultants, who visit the stores pretending to be customers, to determine whether employees provide helpful customer service. The "secret shoppers" make detailed observations of the service provided (or not). Secret shopper Cliff Fill recalls the fast-food restaurant where the workers discussed their dating plans as he stood in front of them ready to order. After ignoring him for 90 seconds (secret shoppers often carry timers with them), they turned to him and said, "We'll be done with our conversation in a minute and be with you."[8] Mystery shoppers also note great service. Mike Bare, cofounder of the Mystery Shopping Providers Association, says, "It used to be about catching people doing something wrong. But, more and more, it's validating people who do things right."[9] Indeed, Intrawest, a ski resort, gives $100 bills to employees praised in its secret shopper reports.

1.3 Corrective Action

The next step in the control process is to identify performance deviations, analyze those deviations, and then develop and implement programs to correct them. This is similar to the planning process discussed in Chapter 5: regular, frequent performance feedback allows workers and managers to track their performance and make adjustments in effort, direction, and strategies.

"WHAT'S NEW" COMPANY

"WHAT'S NEW" COMPANY

Beta versions of software programs are a classic tool that developers use to monitor deviations from the standard and take corrective action—before the product is released on the market. GOOGLE used a beta version of its Google Groups software for close to a decade as managers mined users' comments to improve the product.[10] Likewise, MICROSOFT has an internal program called Software Quality Metrics (SQM) that company software developers use when creating new software releases. SQM helps the developers determine how each change in the software code will affect the functionality of the program and uses a system of comparison charts to show how the changes will affect users of new software.[11]

1.4 Dynamic, Cybernetic Process

As shown in Exhibit 16.1, control is a continuous, dynamic, cybernetic process. Control begins by setting standards, measuring performance, and then comparing performance to the standards. If the performance deviates from the standards, then managers and employees analyze the deviations and develop and implement corrective programs that (hopefully) achieve the desired performance by meeting the standards. Managers must repeat the entire process again and again in an endless feedback loop (a continuous process). Thus, control is not a onetime achievement or result. It continues over time (that is, it is dynamic) and requires daily, weekly, and monthly attention from managers to maintain performance levels at the standard (that is, it is cybernetic). **Cybernetic** derives from the Greek word *kubernetes*, meaning "steersman," that is, one who steers or keeps on course.[12] Therefore, the

cybernetic the process of steering or keeping on course

control process shown in Exhibit 16.1 is cybernetic because of the feedback loop in which actual performance is compared against standards so that deviations from those standards can be minimized or corrected.

Keeping control of business expenses is an example of a continuous, dynamic, cybernetic process. A company that doesn't closely monitor expenses usually finds that they quickly get out of control, even for the smallest things. For example, when Eddie Lampert became chairman of *KMART*, everywhere he looked, he saw expenses that could be cut. He demanded that everyone stop looking at sales and instead focus on profitability. He told all of his store managers that he was willing to spend money, but only when they could assure the company of a big return. He didn't allow a proposal to improve lighting in stores that would have cost more than $2 million; declaring, "It doesn't matter what Target and Wal-Mart do," he wanted to know the positive value of every investment. He quickly eliminated what he referred to as "crazy promotions" that were designed to clear out inventory. Kmart stopped pricing DVDs at *WAL-MART* levels (that is, heavily discounted) and began selling DVDs only at full price. Lampert knew the stores would sell less in terms of volume but make more profit on each sale. Lampert says, "For the first year or so, we had declining same-store sales, but more stores made a profit. To some people, it looked like a plane that was going from 40,000 feet to 20,000 feet, and in five minutes from now, it's going to hit the ground. We said, 'We're going to land this plane' and we did."[13]

Sure, it's a cliché, but it's just as true in business as in sports: If you take your eye off the ball, you're going to strike out. Control is an ongoing, dynamic, cybernetic process.

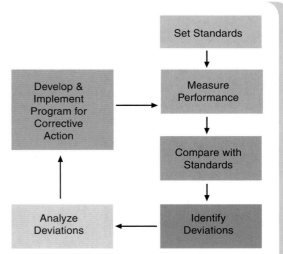

| Set Standards |
| Measure Performance |
| Compare with Standards |
| Identify Deviations |
| Analyze Deviations |
| Develop & Implement Program for Corrective Action |

Source: H. Koontz & R. W. Bradspies, "Managing through Feedforward Control: A Future-Directed View," *Business Horizons*, June 1972, 25–36. Reprinted with permission from *Business Horizons*, © 1972 by the Trustees at Indiana University, Kelley School of Business.

Exhibit 16.1
Cybernetic Control Process

1.5 Feedback, Concurrent, and Feedforward Control

The three basic control methods are feedback control, concurrent control, and feedforward control.[12] **Feedback control** is a mechanism for gathering information about performance deficiencies *after* they occur. This information is then used to correct or prevent performance deficiencies. Study after study has clearly shown that feedback improves both individual and organizational performance. In most instances, any feedback is better than no feedback.

If there is a downside to feedback, however, it is that it is always after the fact. Wal-Mart instituted a new feedback system when it began building more stores closer to urban areas. The company engaged the services of business analysts whose job it is to roam Wal-Mart stores and competitors' stores looking for opportunities to increase sales. This new feedback system is designed to help Wal-Mart managers and merchandisers tailor store floor plans to produce maximum sales per square foot, a standard metric in retailing. One business analyst noticed that a Wal-Mart in a mostly Hispanic neighborhood was out of women's shoes in size 5½ and concluded that the buyers at headquarters were not "aware of the store's large base of Hispanic women, who tend to have small feet—an insight that could aid buying decisions." Wal-Mart's feedback system helps it identify problems on the floor with merchandise locations and displays, as well as opportunities to sell products the analysts discover in other stores. Still, the feedback is always lagging the actual opportunity.[14]

Concurrent control is a mechanism for gathering information about performance deficiencies *as* they occur. Thus, it is an improvement over feedback because

feedback control a mechanism for gathering information about performance deficiencies after they occur

concurrent control a mechanism for gathering information about performance deficiencies as they occur, thereby eliminating or shortening the delay between performance and feedback

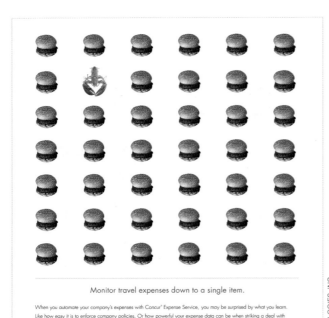

Monitor travel expenses down to a single item.

When you automate your company's expenses with Concur® Expense Service, you may be surprised by what you learn. Like how easy it is to enforce company policies. Or how powerful your expense data can be when striking a deal with commonly used travel service providers. Instead of guessing on the details, a few clicks can reveal spending patterns all the way down to a specific employee. Which streamlines the process, eliminates paperwork, and most important, saves you a whole lot of money. Call 888.800.4883 or visit www.ExpenseTour.com to take a free Concur Expense Service tour.

Concur Technologies has developed software to help companies automate their expenses and keep track of expenditures and all the spending patterns way down to a specific employee. Without controls for business expenses (like travel), companies would soon be unwittingly paying for luxuries (like lobster) rather than basic business necessities (like meals). Imagine the costs associated with 41 lobsters and 1 hamburger!

"What's New" × 3
Company

feedforward control a mechanism for monitoring performance inputs rather than outputs to prevent or minimize performance deficiencies before they occur

control loss the situation in which behavior and work procedures do not conform to standards

it attempts to eliminate or shorten the delay between performance and feedback about the performance. Apple and **NIKE** teamed up to create a real-time exercise feedback system called Nike + iPod. After a runner installs the system in her shoes, it transmits concurrent information to her iPod. The system measures time, distance, calories burned, and pace. Runners can actually track their efforts every moment of their run and make changes on the fly. Greg Joswiak, **APPLE**'s vice president of worldwide iPod marketing, says, "We've enabled people to have a much better running experience than ever before."[15]

Feedforward control is a mechanism for gathering information about performance deficiencies *before* they occur. In contrast to feedback and concurrent control, which provide feedback on the basis of outcomes and results, feedforward control provides information about performance deficiencies by monitoring inputs, not outputs. Thus, feedforward control seeks to prevent or minimize performance deficiencies *before* they happen. Microsoft uses feedforward controls to try to prevent software problems before they occur. For example, when developing the latest version of its Windows Server software (for network and Internet computer servers), Microsoft taught 8,500 experienced programmers new methods for writing more reliable software code *before* asking them to develop new features for Windows Server software. Microsoft has also developed new software testing tools that let the programmers thoroughly test the code they've written (that is, input) before passing the code on to others to be used in beta testing and then in final products.[16] Exhibit 16.2 lists guidelines that companies can follow to get the most out of feedforward control.

1.6 Control Isn't Always Worthwhile or Possible

Control is achieved when behavior and work procedures conform to standards and goals are accomplished. By contrast, **control loss** occurs when behavior and work procedures do not conform to standards.[17] John Caudwell, owner of **PHONES4U**, one of the United Kingdom's largest mobile phone chains, felt that his company had control loss with respect to e-mail. Managers and employees were averaging three hours per day on e-mail and, according to Caudwell, not spending enough time with customers. So he completely banned e-mail. "The policy came from me. The staff was initially slightly shocked that I should make such a revolutionary move," said Caudwell. "We have email paralysis. If you have a cancer, you have to cut it out. That's what I've done."[18]

Maintaining control is important because control loss prevents goal achievement (in the Phones4U example, not spending enough time with customers). When control loss occurs managers need to find out what, if anything, they could have done to prevent it. Usually, as discussed above, that means identifying deviations from standard performance, analyzing the causes of those deviations, and taking corrective action. Implementing controls, however, isn't always worthwhile or possible. For example, it's debatable whether, in the long run, Phones4U's e-mail ban is a net plus for the company. Indeed, Tanno Massar, director of media relations at TPG, a logistics company, said "It would be a serious setback for the company if we could no longer use e-mail, and we are not considering it."[19] Let's look at regulation costs and cybernetic feasibility to see why implementing controls isn't always worthwhile or possible.

To determine whether control is worthwhile, managers need to carefully assess **regulation costs**, that is, whether the costs and both the intended and unintended consequences of control exceed its benefits. Initially enacted with the very best of intentions, the corporate average fuel economy (CAFE) standards have not been increased since 1985. The standards require that the entire fleet of a particular automaker achieve an average miles per gallon standard. That standard has been 27.5 mpg highway with a reduced requirement of 22.2 mpg for light trucks. With the dramatic increases in gasoline over the past few years there has been added pressure to increase the CAFE standards. In his 2007 State of the Union address, President George Bush proposed an increase of 4 percent per year through 2017 as a means of increasing U.S. independence and providing a boost to the ecology of the country. Later that year the Senate passed a new fleetwide standard of 35 mpg. The impact on the automakers is extreme. A recent estimate is that the new standards will cost the automakers more than $114 billion over the next ten years. The automakers feel that the market is not demanding sufficient numbers of high-mileage cars and the CAFE standards are a distortion and detriment to their business model. Ford Motor Chief Executive Alan Mulally called CAFE the most "market-distorting" policy he had ever come across. This all comes at a time when the big Detroit-based automakers are suffering through enormous financial losses and are in the process of radically working their business models to remain competitive.[20]

| 1. Thorough planning and analysis are required. |
| 2. Careful discrimination must be applied in selecting input variables. |
| 3. The feedforward system must be kept dynamic. |
| 4. A model of the control system should be developed. |
| 5. Data on input variables must be regularly collected. |
| 6. Data on input variables must be regularly assessed. |
| 7. Feedforward control requires action. |

Source: H. Koontz & R. W. Bradspies, "Managing through Feedforward Control: A Future Directed View," *Business Horizons*, June 1972, 25–36. Reprinted with permission from *Business Horizons*, © 1972 by the Trustees at Indiana University, Kelley School of Business.

Exhibit 16.2
Guidelines for Using Feedforward Control

> *We have email paralysis. If you have a cancer, you have to cut it out. That's what I've done.*

JOHN CAUDWELL, OWNER, PHONES4U

An often-overlooked factor in determining the cost of control is that *unintended consequences* sometimes accompany increased control. Control systems help companies, managers, and workers accomplish their goals, but at the same time that control systems help solve some problems, they can create others. For example, Six Sigma is a quality control system originally developed by MOTOROLA, that manufacturers use to achieve the goal of producing only 3.4 defective or nonstandard parts per million parts made. Clearly, manufacturers who reach Six Sigma consistently produce extremely high-quality products. But aligning the very constrictive process needed to attain Six Sigma with the need for out-of-the box thinking and innovation can be a feat. For example, Motorola's focus on achieving near-perfect production (99.9997 percent error-free) was stifling the company's creativity and innovation, both of which are critical for organizations to grow. In the late 1990s, Motorola lost its lead in mobile phones to Nokia, in part because tight manufacturing control systems were crushing efforts to develop new products. To mitigate the unintended consequences of Six Sigma, Motorola designers are now given a free hand to design, but the process engineers are always on hand to help ensure that even the coolest

regulation costs the costs associated with implementing or maintaining control innovation—like the RAZR—can actually be manufactured to perfection. In fact, the RAZR helped Motorola climb from a 15.4 percent market share to 22.4 percent in a two-year period.[21]

Another factor to consider is **cybernetic feasibility**, the extent to which it is possible to implement each step in the control process: clear standards of performance, comparison of performance against standards, and corrective action. If one or more steps cannot be implemented, then maintaining effective control may be difficult or impossible. For example, many retail companies provide significant employee discounts, which can be used by entering special codes at the company's online store. However, those codes, meant for employee use, have leaked out via e-mail to nonemployees and are also published at websites such as **http://www .quicktoclick.com**. Amy Krasuna doesn't work for Old Navy or Banana Republic, but she has the employee codes for each company. Says Krasuna, "I'm being bombarded with them."[22]

Is it possible to control these discounts so that only employees can use them? Yes, with sufficient money, technical expertise, and the proper software tools (the costs of control), online retailers can create unique online discount codes that work only once and e-mail them to employees. A spokesperson for Gap, which uses such codes, says, "We want to make sure we're protecting the integrity of the [sales] event. We really consider it a benefit to our employees." However, at Banana Republic, which is owned by Gap, a spokesperson said that "technological challenges" prevented the company from using unique onetime codes. As a result, Banana Republic's 25 percent employee discount was being widely used by people who aren't employees, like Amy Krasuna.

Review 1: **The Control Process**

The control process begins by setting standards, measuring performance, and then comparing performance against the standards. The better a company's information and measurement systems, the easier it is to make these comparisons. The control process continues by identifying and analyzing performance deviations, and then developing and implementing programs for corrective action. However, control is a continuous, dynamic, cybernetic process, not a onetime achievement or result. Control requires frequent managerial attention. The three basic control methods are feedback control (after-the-fact performance information), concurrent control (simultaneous performance information), and feedforward control (preventive performance information). Control, however, has regulation costs and unanticipated consequences and therefore isn't always worthwhile or possible.

HOW AND WHAT TO CONTROL

At about 10 percent of Sam's Club and Wal-Mart stores, the doors are locked on midnight-shift employees to keep out robbers and, some say, also to prevent employee theft. According to Mona Williams, Wal-Mart's vice president for communications, "Wal-Mart secures these stores just as any other business does that has employees working overnight. Doors are locked to protect associates and the store from intruders."[23] But many employees dislike the policy. When Michael Rodriguez

cybernetic feasibility the extent to which it is possible to implement each step in the control process injured his ankle at 3 AM, he had to wait an hour for a store manager to show up to unlock the doors. Says Rodriguez, "Being locked in in an emergency like that, that's not right."[24] Wal-Mart's Mona Williams responds, "Fire doors are always accessible [and unlocked from the inside] for safety, and there will always be at least one manager in the store with a set of keys to unlock the doors."[25]

If you managed a Wal-Mart store, would you lock in your midnight employees? Would doing so jeopardize or improve their safety? Kmart, Sears, Home Depot, and Costco don't lock in their employees, so is Wal-Mart being overly restrictive? Or is this policy a reasonable response to employee theft, which can often exceed a store's profits? Former Sam's Club manager Tom Lewis says of the lock-in practice, "They're concerned about the bottom line, and the bottom line is affected by shrinkage in the store."[26] If you were a Wal-Mart or Sam's Club store manager, what would you do?

After reading the next two sections, you should be able to

> 2 discuss the various methods that managers can use to maintain control.
> 3 describe the behaviors, processes, and outcomes that today's managers are choosing to control in their organizations.

2 Control Methods

Managers can use five different methods to achieve control in their organizations: **2.1 bureaucratic**, **2.2 objective**, **2.3 normative**, **2.4 concertive**, and **2.5 self-control**.

2.1 Bureaucratic Control

When most people think of managerial control, what they have in mind is bureaucratic control. **Bureaucratic control** is top-down control, in which managers try to influence employee behavior by rewarding or punishing employees for compliance or noncompliance with organizational policies, rules, and procedures. Most employees, however, would argue that bureaucratic managers emphasize punishment for noncompliance much more than rewards for compliance. For instance, when visiting the company's regional offices and managers, the president of a training company, who was known for his temper and for micromanaging others, would get some toilet paper from the restrooms and aggressively ask, "What's this?" When the managers answered, "Toilet paper," the president would scream that it was two-ply toilet paper that the company couldn't afford. When told of a cracked toilet seat in one of the women's restrooms, he said, "If you don't like sitting on that seat, you can stand up like I do!"[27]

Ironically, bureaucratic management and control were created to prevent just this type of managerial behavior. By encouraging managers to apply well-thought-out rules, policies, and procedures in an impartial, consistent manner to everyone in the organization, bureaucratic control is supposed to make companies more efficient, effective, and fair. Perversely, it frequently has just the opposite effect. Managers who use bureaucratic control often emphasize following the rules above all else. When an employee collapsed from chest pains, her boss, fearing a heart attack, helped carry her to an ambulance. Yet when the employee was diagnosed with indigestion and not a heart attack and returned to work several hours later, her boss filed a disciplinary action accusing her of an unexcused absence. Employees complained to the company

bureaucratic control the use of hierarchical authority to influence employee behavior by rewarding or punishing employees for compliance or noncompliance with organizational policies, rules, and procedures

CEO, who then took steps to correct the situation. The boss subsequently apologized to the employee and to his entire 25-person staff, explaining that he was wrong for taking the company's absence policy "too literally."[28]

Another characteristic of bureaucratically controlled companies is that due to their rule- and policy-driven decision making, they are highly resistant to change and slow to respond to customers and competitors. Recall from Chapter 2 that even Max Weber, the German philosopher who is largely credited with popularizing bureaucratic ideals in the late 19th century, referred to bureaucracy as the "iron cage." He said, "Once fully established, bureaucracy is among those social structures which are the hardest to destroy."[29] Of course, the national government, with hundreds of bureaus, agencies, and departments, is typically the largest bureaucracy in most countries. In the United States, because of the thousands of career bureaucrats who staff the offices of the federal government, even presidents and Congress have difficulty making changes. When General Dwight Eisenhower became president, his predecessor, Harry Truman, quipped, "Poor Ike. It won't be a bit like the army. He'll sit here and he'll say, 'Do this, do that,' and nothing will happen."[30]

2.2 Objective Control

In many companies, bureaucratic control has evolved into **objective control**, which is the use of observable measures of employee behavior or output to assess performance and influence behavior. Whereas bureaucratic control focuses on whether policies and rules are followed, objective control focuses on the observation or measurement of worker behavior or output. Three employees at Kwik Trip Convenience stores were fired for postings they made about the company on the social networking website Facebook. Because the employees' postings were complaints about rude customers and their jobs in general, the company determined that their behavior was not appropriate, especially given that an employee can be let go for treating customers badly in the store.[31] There are two kinds of objective control: behavior control and output control.

Behavior control is regulating behaviors and actions that workers perform on the job. The basic assumption of behavior control is that if you do the right things (that is, the right behaviors) every day, then those things should lead to goal achievement. Behavior control is still management-based, however, which means that managers are responsible for monitoring and rewarding or punishing workers for exhibiting desired or undesired behaviors. Companies that use global positioning satellite (GPS) technology to track where workers are and what they're doing are using behavior control. For example, after getting complaints that his Clinton Township, New Jersey, police officers weren't always on the job, Sergeant John Kuczynski quietly put GPS tracking devices in his officers' cars. Contrary to the officers' reports indicating that they were patrolling streets or using radar to catch speeding drivers, the GPS tracking software soon showed that five officers were sitting for long periods in parking lots or taking long breaks for meals. All five are now barred from law enforcement jobs.[32] Likewise, some organizations, worried that employees are wasting time on nonproductive behaviors, are removing Solitaire and Mine Sweeper games from employees' computers. The reason? Researchers at the Internal Revenue Service have found that half the time IRS employees are using computers they're playing games, gambling, or shopping on the Internet.[33]

Instead of measuring what managers and workers do, **output control** measures the results of their efforts. Whereas behavior control regulates, guides, and measures how workers behave on the job, output control gives managers and workers the freedom to behave as they see fit as long as they accomplish prespecified, measurable

"Poor Ike. It won't be a bit like the army. He'll sit here and he'll say, "Do this, do that," and nothing will happen.

HARRY TRUMAN

objective control the use of observable measures of worker behavior or outputs to assess performance and influence behavior

behavior control the regulation of the behaviors and actions that workers perform on the job

output control the regulation of workers' results or outputs through rewards and incentives results. Output control is often coupled with rewards and incentives.

Three things must occur for output control and rewards to lead to improved business results. First, output control measures must be reliable, fair, and accurate. Second, employees and managers must believe that they can produce the desired results. If they don't, then the output controls won't affect their behavior. Third, the rewards or incentives tied to outcome control measures must truly be dependent on achieving established standards of performance. For example, SMITHFIELD FOODS CEO Joseph Luter doesn't earn a bonus unless pretax profits exceed $100 million. Ray Goldberg, chairman of the company's compensation committee, says that the performance requirements shouldn't "be so low that you get a bonus no matter what you do."[35] Goldberg explains, "We were trying to make sure [Luter's] rewards are based on the ups and downs of the company."[36] So, with pretax profits of $227.1 million, Luter's bonus, based on 2 percent of earnings between $100 million and $300 million, and 3 percent of profits over $300 million, would total just over $2.5 million. For output control to work with rewards, the rewards must truly be at risk if performance doesn't measure up.

2.3 Normative Control

Rather than monitoring rules, behavior, or output, another way to control what goes on in organizations is to use normative control to shape the beliefs and values of the people who work there. With **normative controls**, a company's widely shared values and beliefs guide workers' behavior and decisions. For example, at NORDSTROM, a Seattle-based department store chain, one value permeates the entire work force from top to bottom: extraordinary customer service. On the first day of work at Nordstrom, trainees begin their transformation to the "Nordstrom way" by reading the employee handbook. Sounds boring, doesn't it? But Nordstrom's handbook is printed on one side of a 3-by-5-inch note card. In its entirety, it reads:

> *Welcome to Nordstrom's. We're glad to have you with our company. Our Number One goal is to provide outstanding customer service. Set both your personal and professional goals high. We have great confidence in your ability to achieve them. Nordstrom Rules: Rule #1: Use your good judgment in all situations. There will be no additional rules. Please feel free to ask your department manager, store manager, or division general manager any question at any time.*[37]

That's it. No lengthy rules. No specifics about what behavior is or is not appropriate. Use your judgment.[38]

Normative controls are created in two ways. First, companies that use normative controls are very careful about whom they hire. While many companies screen potential applicants on the basis of their abilities, normatively controlled companies

doing the right thing

Don't Cheat on Travel Expense Reports

Workers are often tempted to pad their travel expense reports. As one puts it, "After a while you feel that they owe it to ya, so the hell with 'em. I'm going to expense it." Frank Navran of the Ethics Resource Center says that people justify this by telling themselves, "I'm not really stealing from the company—I'm just getting back what I feel I'm entitled to." However, Joel Richards, executive vice president and chief administrative officer of El Paso Corporation, says, "You learn a lot about people from their expense reports. If you can't trust an employee to be truthful on an expense report, if you can't trust them with small dollars, how can you trust them with making decisions involving millions of dollars?" So, do the right thing: Don't cheat on your travel expense reports.[34]

normative control the regulation of workers' behavior and decisions through widely shared organizational values and beliefs

Nordstrom sets the retailing industry's benchmark for customer service by using normative control. Here an employee is helping customers in Nordstrom's Costa Mesa, California, store.

are just as likely to screen potential applicants based on their attitudes and values. For example, before building stores in a new city, Nordstrom sends its human resource team into town to interview prospective applicants. In a few cities, the company canceled its expansion plans when it could not find enough qualified applicants who embodied the service attitudes and values for which Nordstrom is known. Nordstrom would rather give up potential sales in lucrative markets than do business using people who cannot provide Nordstrom's level of service.[39]

Second, with normative controls, managers and employees learn what they should and should not do by observing experienced employees and by listening to the stories they tell about the company. At Nordstrom, many of these stories, which employees call "heroics," have been inspired by the company motto, "Respond to Unreasonable Customer Requests!"[40] "Nordies," as Nordstrom employees call themselves, like to tell the story about a customer who just had to have a pair of burgundy Donna Karan slacks that had gone on sale, but she could not find her size. The sales associate who was helping her contacted five nearby Nordstrom stores, but none had the customer's size. So rather than leave the customer dissatisfied with her shopping experience, the sales associate went to her manager for petty cash and then went across the street and paid full price for the slacks at a competitor's store. She then resold them to the customer at Nordstrom's lower sale price.[41] Obviously, Nordstrom would quickly go out of business if this were the norm. Nevertheless, this story makes clear the attitude that drives employee performance at Nordstrom in ways that rules, behavioral guidelines, or output controls could not.

2.4 Concertive Control

Whereas normative controls are based on beliefs that are strongly held and widely shared throughout a company, **concertive controls** are based on beliefs that are shaped and negotiated by work groups.[42] Whereas normative controls are driven by strong organizational cultures, concertive controls usually arise when companies give autonomous work groups complete autonomy and responsibility for task completion (see Chapter 10, Managing Teams, for a complete discussion of the role of autonomy in teams and groups). The most autonomous groups operate without managers and are completely responsible for controlling work group processes, outputs, and behavior. Such groups do their own hiring, firing, worker discipline, work schedules, materials ordering, budget making and meeting, and decision making.

Concertive control is not established overnight. Highly autonomous work groups evolve through two phases as they develop concertive control. In phase one, group members learn to work with each other, supervise each other's work, and develop the values and beliefs that will guide and control their behavior. And because they develop these values and beliefs themselves, work group members feel strongly about following them.

In the steel industry, NUCOR was long considered an upstart compared with the "biggies" U.S. Steel and Bethlehem Steel. Today, however, not only has Nucor managed to outlast many other mills, the company has bought out 13 other mills in the past five years. But Nucor has a unique culture that gives real power to employees on the line and fosters teamwork throughout the organization. This type of teamwork can be a difficult thing for a newly acquired group of employees to get used to. For

concertive control the regulation of workers' behavior and decisions through work group values and beliefs example, at Nucor's first big acquisition in Auburn, New York, David Hutchins is a frontline supervisor or "lead man" in the rolling mill, where steel from the furnace is spread thin enough to be cut into sheets. When the plant was under the previous ownership, if the guys doing the cutting got backed up, the guys doing the rolling—including Hutchins—would just take a break. He says, "We'd sit back, have a cup of coffee, and complain: 'Those guys stink.'" It took six months to convince the employees at the Auburn plant that the Nucor teamwork way was better than the old way. Now, Hutchins says, "At Nucor, we're not 'you guys' and 'us guys.' It's all of us guys. Wherever the bottleneck is, we go there, and everyone works on it."[43]

> " At Nucor, we're not "you guys" and "us guys." It's all of us guys. Wherever the bottleneck is, we go there, and everyone works on it. "
>
> **DAVID HUTCHINS**, FRONTLINE SUPERVISOR, NUCOR

The second phase in the development of concertive control is the emergence and formalization of objective rules to guide and control behavior. The beliefs and values developed in phase one usually develop into more objective rules as new members join teams. The clearer those rules, the easier it becomes for new members to figure out how and how not to behave.

Before Nucor finalizes an acquisition, it sends a team of long-time employees to the new plant. People at all levels, from managers to steelworkers, visit with their counterparts at the mill being acquired and tell them about the "Nucor way." Getting new employees on board quickly helps preserve everyone's bonus and performance-based pay. By following the "program" of working together and increasing output, Dave Hutchins saw his annual pay of $53,000 rise to $67,000 the year after Nucor acquired his plant, then to $92,000 only four years after that.[44] Again, the key difference in concertive control is that the teams—and not management—enforce these rules, but a system based upon team equality permeates the best companies.

Ironically, concertive control may lead to even more stress for workers to conform to expectations than bureaucratic control. Under bureaucratic control, most workers only have to worry about pleasing the boss. But with concertive control, their behavior has to satisfy the rest of their team members. For example, one team member says, "I don't have to sit there and look for the boss to be around; and if the boss is not around, I can sit there and talk to my neighbor or do what I want. Now the whole team is around me and the whole team is observing what I'm doing."[45] Plus, with concertive control, team members have a second, much more stressful role to perform—that of making sure that their team members adhere to team values and rules.

2.5 Self-Control

Self-control, also known as **self-management**, is a control system in which managers and workers control their own behavior.[46] Self-control does not result in anarchy in which everyone gets to do whatever he or she wants. In self-control or self-management, leaders and managers provide workers with clear boundaries within which they may guide and control their own goals and behaviors.[47] Leaders and managers also contribute to self-control by teaching others the skills they need to maximize and monitor their own work effectiveness. In turn, individuals who manage and lead themselves establish self-control by setting their own goals, monitoring their own progress, rewarding or punishing themselves for achieving or for not achieving

self-control (self-management) a control system in which managers and workers control their own behavior by setting their own goals, monitoring their own progress, and rewarding themselves for goal achievement their self-set goals, and constructing positive thought patterns that remind them of the importance of their goals and their ability to accomplish them.[48]

For example, let's assume you need to do a better job of praising and recognizing the good work that your staff does for you. You can use goal setting, self-observation, and self-reward to self-manage this behavior. For self-observation, write "praise/ recognition" on a 3-by-5-inch card. Put the card in your pocket. Put a check on the card each time you praise or recognize someone (wait until the person has left before you do this). Keep track for a week. This serves as your baseline or starting point. Simply keeping track will probably increase how often you do this. After a week, assess your baseline or starting point, and then set a specific goal. For instance, if your baseline was twice a day, you might set a specific goal to praise or recognize others' work five times a day. Continue monitoring your performance with your cards. Once you've achieved your goal every day for a week, give yourself a reward (perhaps a CD, a movie, lunch with a friend at a new restaurant) for achieving your goal.[49]

As you can see, the components of self-management, self-set goals, self-observation, and self-reward have their roots in the motivation theories you read about in Chapter 13. The key difference, though, is that the goals, feedback, and rewards originate from employees themselves and not from their managers or organizations.

Review 2: *Control Methods*

The five methods of control are bureaucratic, objective, normative, concertive, and self-control (self-management). Bureaucratic and objective controls are top-down, management-based, and measurement-based. Normative and concertive controls represent shared forms of control because they evolve from company-wide or team-based beliefs and values. Self-control, or self-management, is a control system in which managers turn much, but not all, control over to the individuals themselves.

Bureaucratic control is based on organizational policies, rules, and procedures. Objective controls are based on reliable measures of behavior or outputs. Normative control is based on strong corporate beliefs and careful hiring practices. Concertive control is based on the development of values, beliefs, and rules in autonomous work groups. Self-control is based on individuals' setting their own goals, monitoring themselves, and rewarding or punishing themselves with respect to goal achievement.

We end this section by noting that each of these control methods may be more or less appropriate depending on the circumstances. Examine Exhibit 16.3 to find out when each of these five control methods should be used.

3 What to Control?

In the first section of this chapter, we discussed the basics of the control process and that control isn't always worthwhile or possible. In the second section, we looked at the various ways in which control can be obtained. In this third and final section, we address an equally important issue, "What should managers control?" The way managers answer this question has critical implications for most businesses. In the midst of an economic slowdown, a medium-sized financial company created a huge upheaval when it tried to cut costs by eliminating company-paid-for cell phones. Salespeople were furious, claiming, "No other group in the company had their cell phone use restricted." Lynda Ford, a consultant who was working with the

BUREAUCRATIC CONTROL	• When it is necessary to standardize operating procedures
	• When it is necessary to establish limits
BEHAVIOR CONTROL	• When it is easier to measure what workers do on the job than what they accomplish on the job
	• When "cause-effect" relationships are clear, that is, when companies know which behaviors will lead to success and which won't
	• When good measures of worker behavior can be created
OUTPUT CONTROL	• When it is easier to measure what workers accomplish on the job than what they do on the job
	• When good measures of worker output can be created
	• When it is possible to set clear goals and standards for worker output
	• When "cause-effect" relationships are unclear
NORMATIVE CONTROL	• When organizational culture, values, and beliefs are strong
	• When it is difficult to create good measures of worker behavior
	• When it is difficult to create good measures of worker output
CONCERTIVE CONTROL	• When responsibility for task accomplishment is given to autonomous work groups
	• When management wants workers to take "ownership" of their behavior and outputs
	• When management desires a strong form of worker-based control
SELF-CONTROL	• When workers are intrinsically motivated to do their jobs well
	• When it is difficult to create good measures of worker behavior
	• When it is difficult to create good measures of worker output
	• When workers have or are taught self-control and self-leadership skills

Sources: L. J. Kirsch, "The Management of Complex Tasks in Organizations: Controlling the Systems Development Process," *Organization Science* 7 (1996): 1–21; S. A. Snell, "Control Theory in Strategic Human Resource Management: The Mediating Effect of Administrative Information," *Academy of Management Journal* 35 (1992): 292–327.

Exhibit 16.3

When to Use Different Methods of Control

company at the time, says that canceling cell phones "became the straw that broke the camel's back." As a result, salespeople started quitting and productivity dropped significantly. Several months later, realizing the policy was wrong, the company reinstated company cell phones.[50]

This financial company lost salespeople and productivity because it worried about (that is, controlled) only one thing—reducing costs. Companies need to have a clear vision. They can't be everything to everybody. Most companies successfully carry out their visions and missions by finding a balance that comes from doing a multitude of small things right, like managing costs, providing value, and keeping customers and employees satisfied.

*After reading this section, you should be able to explain **3.1 the balanced scorecard approach to control** and how companies can achieve balanced control of company performance by choosing to control **3.2 budgets, cash flows, and economic value added, 3.3 customer defections, 3.4 quality**, and **3.5 waste and pollution**.*

3.1 The Balanced Scorecard

Most companies measure performance using standard financial and accounting measures such as return on capital, return on assets, return on investments, cash flow, net income, and net margins. The **balanced scorecard** encourages managers to look beyond traditional financial measures to four different perspectives on company performance. How do customers see us (the customer perspective)? At what must we excel (the internal perspective)? Can we continue to improve and create value (the innovation and learning perspective)? How do we look to shareholders (the financial perspective)?[51]

The balanced scorecard has several advantages over traditional control processes that rely solely on financial measures. First, it forces managers at each level of the company to set specific goals and measure performance in each of the four areas. For example, Exhibit 16.4 shows that Southwest Airlines uses nine different measures in its balanced scorecard. Of those, only three, market value, seat revenue, and plane lease costs (at various compounded annual growth rates, or CAGR), are standard financial measures of performance. In addition, Southwest measures its Federal Aviation Administration (FAA) on-time arrival rating and the cost of its airfares compared with competitors (customer perspective); how much time each plane spends on the ground after landing and the percentage of planes that depart on time (internal business perspective); and the percentage of its ground crew workers, such as mechanics and luggage handlers, who own company stock and have received job training (learning perspective).

The second major advantage of the balanced scorecard approach to control is that it minimizes the chances of **suboptimization**, which occurs when performance improves in one area, but at the expense of decreased performance in others. Jon Meliones, chief medical director at *DUKE CHILDREN'S HOSPITAL*, says, "We explained the [balanced scorecard] theory to clinicians and administrators like this.... if you sacrifice too much in one quadrant to satisfy another, your organization as a whole is thrown out of balance. We could, for example, cut costs to improve the financial quadrant by firing half the staff, but that would hurt quality of service, and the customer quadrant would fall out of balance. Or we could increase productivity in the internal business quadrant by assigning more patients to a nurse, but doing so would raise the likelihood of errors—an unacceptable trade-off."[52]

balanced scorecard measurement of organizational performance in four equally important areas: finances, customers, internal operations, and innovation and learning

suboptimization performance improvement in one part of an organization but only at the expense of decreased performance in another part

Exhibit 16.4
Southwest Airlines' Balanced Scorecard

	OBJECTIVES	MEASURES	TARGETS	INITIATIVES
FINANCIAL	Profitability	Market Value	30% CAGR	
	Increased Revenue	Seat Revenue	20% CAGR	
	Lower Costs	Plane Lease Cost	5% CAGR	
CUSTOMER	On-Time Flights	FAA On-Time Arrival Rating	#1	Quality Management, Customer Loyalty Program
	Lowest Prices	Customer Ranking (Market Survey)	#1	
INTERNAL	Fast Ground Turnaround	Time on Ground	30 Minutes	Cycle Time Optimization Program
		On-Time Departure	90%	
LEARNING	Ground Crew Alignment with Company Goals	% Ground Crew Shareholders	Year 1: 70% Year 3: 90% Year 5: 100%	Employee Stock Option Plan Ground Crew Training
		% Ground Crew Trained		

Sources: G. Anthes, "ROI Guide: Balanced Scorecard," *Computer World* available at http://www.computerworld.com/managementtopics/roi/story/0,10801,78512,00.html, 5 May 2003.

Let's examine some of the ways in which companies are controlling the four basic parts of the balanced scorecard: the financial perspective (budgets, cash flows, and economic value added), the customer perspective (customer defections), the internal perspective (total quality management), and the innovation and learning perspective (waste and pollution).

3.2 The Financial Perspective: Controlling Budgets, Cash Flows, and Economic Value Added

The traditional approach to controlling financial performance focuses on accounting tools, such as cash flow analysis, balance sheets, income statements, financial ratios, and budgets. **Cash flow analysis** predicts how changes in a business will affect its ability to take in more cash than it pays out. **Balance sheets** provide a snapshot of a company's financial position at a particular time (but not the future). **Income statements**, also called profit and loss statements, show what has happened to an organization's income, expenses, and net profit (income less expenses) over a period of time. Exhibit 16.5 shows the basic steps or parts for cash flow analyses, balance sheets, and income statements. **Financial ratios** are typically used to track a business's liquidity (cash), efficiency, and profitability over time compared with other businesses in its industry. Exhibit 16.6 lists a few of the most common financial ratios and explains how they are calculated, what they mean, and when to use them. Finally, **budgets** are used to project costs and revenues, prioritize and control spending, and ensure that expenses don't exceed available funds and revenues. Exhibit 16.7 reviews the different kinds of budgets managers can use to track and control company finances.

By themselves, none of these tools—cash flow analyses, balance sheets, income statements, financial ratios, or budgets—tell the whole financial story of a business. They must be used together when assessing a company's financial performance. Since these tools are reviewed in detail in your accounting and finance classes, only a brief overview is provided here. Still, these are necessary tools for controlling organizational finances and expenses, and they should be part of your business toolbox. Unfortunately, most managers don't (but should) have a good understanding of these accounting tools.[53] When *Boeing*'s new chief financial officer attended her first company retreat with other Boeing executives, she assumed that her discussion of financial ratios, like those shown in Exhibit 16.6, would be a boring review for everyone present. Afterwards, she was shocked when dozens of the 280 executives attending the retreat told her that for the very first time they finally understood what the formulas meant.[54]

So if, like those experienced executives, you struggle to understand how financial ratios can be used where you work, you might find help in the following books: *Accounting the Easy Way*, by Peter J. Eisen; *Accounting for Dummies* and *How to Read a Financial Report: Wringing Vital Signs Out of the Numbers*, both by John A. Tracy; *Schaum's Quick Guide to Business Formulas: 201 Decision-Making Tools for Business, Finance, and Accounting Students*, by Joel G. Siegel, Jae K. Shim, and Stephen W. Hartman; *The Vest-Pocket Guide to Business Ratios*, by Michael R. Tyran; *Essential Managers: Managing Budgets*, by Stephen Brookson; or *Forecasting Budgets: 25 Keys to Successful Planning (The New York Times Pocket MBA Series)*, by Norman Moore and Grover Gardner.

Though no one would dispute the importance of cash flow analyses, balance sheets, income statements, financial ratios, or budgets for

"WHAT'S NEW" COMPANY

© IMAGE SOURCE/JUPITER IMAGES

STEPS FOR A BASIC CASH FLOW ANALYSIS

1. Forecast sales (steady, up, or down).
2. Project changes in anticipated cash inflows (as a result of changes).
3. Project anticipated cash outflows (as a result of changes).
4. Project net cash flows by combining anticipated cash inflows and outflows.

PARTS OF A BASIC BALANCE SHEET (ASSETS = LIABILITIES + OWNER'S EQUITY)

1. Assets
   a. Current Assets (cash, short-term investment, marketable securities, accounts receivable, etc.)
   b. Fixed Assets (land, buildings, machinery, equipment, etc.)
2. Liabilities
   a. Current Liabilities (accounts payable, notes payable, taxes payable, etc.)
   b. Long-Term Liabilities (long-term debt, deferred income taxes, etc.)
3. Owner's Equity
   a. Preferred stock and common stock
   b. Additional paid-in capital
   c. Retained earnings

BASIC INCOME STATEMENT

SALES REVENUE

– sales returns and allowances

+ other income

= NET REVENUE

– cost of goods sold (beginning inventory, costs of goods purchased, ending inventory)

= GROSS PROFIT

– total operating expenses (selling, general, and administrative expenses)

= INCOME FROM OPERATIONS

– interest expense

= PRETAX INCOME

– income taxes

= NET INCOME

Exhibit 16.5

Basic Accounting Tools for Controlling Financial Performance

economic value added (EVA) the amount by which company profits (revenues, minus expenses, minus taxes) exceed the cost of capital in a given year

determining the financial health of a business, accounting research also indicates that the complexity and sheer amount of information contained in these accounting tools can shut down the brain and glaze over the eyes of even the most experienced manager.[55] Sometimes, there's simply too much information to make sense of. The balanced scorecard simplifies things by focusing on one simple question when it comes to finances: How do we look to shareholders? One way to answer that question is through something called economic value added.

Conceptually, **economic value added (EVA)** is not the same thing as profits. It is the amount by which profits exceed the cost of capital in a given year. It is based on the simple idea that capital is necessary to run a business and that capital comes at a cost. Although most people think of capital as cash, capital, once invested (that is, spent), is more likely to be found in a business in the form of computers, manufacturing plants, employees, raw materials, and so forth. And just like the interest that a homeowner pays on a mortgage or that a college student pays on a student loan, there is a cost to that capital.

The most common costs of capital are the interest paid on long-term bank loans used to buy all those resources, the interest paid to bondholders (who lend organizations their money), and the dividends (cash payments) and growth in stock value that accrue to shareholders. EVA is positive when company profits (revenues minus expenses minus taxes) exceed the cost of capital in a given year. In other words, if a business is to truly grow, its revenues must be large enough to cover both short-term costs (annual expenses and taxes) and long-term costs (the cost of borrowing capital from bondholders and shareholders). If you're a bit confused, the late Roberto Goizueta, the former CEO of Coca-Cola, explained it this way: "You borrow money at a certain rate and invest it at a higher rate and pocket the difference. It is simple. It is the essence of banking."[56]

RATIOS	FORMULA	WHAT IT MEANS	WHEN TO USE
LIQUIDITY RATIOS			
Current Ratio	$\dfrac{\text{Current Assets}}{\text{Current Liabilities}}$	• Whether you have enough assets on hand to pay for short-term bills and obligations. • Higher is better. • Recommended level is two times as many current assets as current liabilities.	• Track monthly and quarterly. • Basic measure of your company's health.
Quick (Acid Test) Ratio	$\dfrac{\text{(Current Assets–Inventories)}}{\text{Current Liabilities}}$	• Stricter than current ratio • Whether you have enough (i.e., cash) to pay short-term bills and obligations. • Higher is better. • Recommended level is one or higher.	• Track monthly. • Also calculate quick ratio with potential customers to evaluate whether they're likely to pay you in a timely manner.
LEVERAGE RATIOS			
Debt to Equity	$\dfrac{\text{Total Liabilities}}{\text{Total Equity}}$	• Indicates how much the company is leveraged (in debt) by comparing what is owed (liabilities) with what is owned (equity). • Lower is better. A high debt-to-equity ratio could indicate that the company has too much debt. • Recommended level depends on industry.	• Track monthly. • Lenders often use this to determine the creditworthiness of a business (i.e., whether to approve additional loans).
Debt Coverage	$\dfrac{\text{(Net Profit + Noncash Expense)}}{\text{Debt}}$	• Indicates how well cash flow covers debt payments. • Higher is better.	• Track monthly. • Lenders look at this ratio to determine if there is adequate cash to make loan payments.
EFFICIENCY RATIOS			
Inventory Turnover	$\dfrac{\text{Cost of Goods Sold}}{\text{Average Value of Inventory}}$	• Whether you're making efficient use of inventory. • Higher is better, indicating that inventory (dollars) isn't purchased (spent) until needed. • Recommended level depends on industry.	• Track monthly by using a 12-month rolling average.
Average Collections Period	$\dfrac{\text{Accounts Receivable}}{\text{(Annual Net Credit Sales Divided by 365)}}$	• Shows on average how quickly your customers are paying their bills. • Lower is better. • Recommended level is no more than 15 days longer than credit terms. If credit is net 30 days, then average should not be longer than 45 days.	• Track monthly. • Use to determine how long company's money is being tied up in customer credit.
PROFITABILITY RATIOS			
Gross Profit Margin	$\dfrac{\text{Gross Profit}}{\text{Total Sales}}$	• Shows how efficiently a business is using its materials and labor in the production process. • Higher is better, indicating that a profit can be made if fixed costs are controlled.	• Track monthly. • Analyze when unsure about product or service pricing. • Low margin compared with competitors means you're underpricing.
Return on Equity	$\dfrac{\text{Net Income}}{\text{Owner's Equity}}$	• Shows what was earned on your investment in the business during a particular period. Often called "return on investment." • Higher is better.	• Track quarterly and annually. • Use to compare what you might have earned on the stock market, bonds, or government Treasury bills during the same period.

Exhibit 16.6

Common Financial Ratios

Revenue Budgets—used to project or forecast future sales.	• Accuracy of projection depends on economy, competitors, sales force estimates, etc. • Determined by estimating future sales volume and sales prices for all products and services
Expense Budgets—used within departments and divisions to determine how much will be spent on various supplies, projects, or activities.	• One of the first places that companies look for cuts when trying to lower expenses
Profit Budgets—used by profit centers, which have "profit and loss" responsibility.	• Profit budgets combine revenue and expense budgets into one budget • Typically used in large businesses with multiple plants and divisions
Cash Budgets—used to forecast how much cash a company will have on hand to meet expenses.	• Similar to cash flow analyses • Used to identify cash shortfalls, which must be covered to pay bills, or cash excesses, which should be invested for a higher return
Capital Expenditure Budgets—used to forecast large, long-lasting investments in equipment, buildings, and property.	• Help managers identify funding that will be needed to pay for future expansion or strategic moves designed to increase competitive advantage
Variable Budgets—used to project costs across varying levels of sales and revenues.	• Important because it is difficult to accurately predict sales revenue and volume • Lead to more accurate budgeting with respect to labor, materials, and administrative expenses, which vary with sales volume and revenues • Build flexibility into the budgeting process

Exhibit 16.7

Common Kinds of Budgets

Exhibit 16.8 shows how to calculate EVA. First, starting with a company's income statement, you calculate the net operating profit after taxes (NOPAT) by subtracting taxes owed from income from operations (see Exhibit 16.5 for a review of an income statement). The NOPAT shown in Exhibit 16.8 is $3,500,000. Second, identify how much capital the company has invested (that is, spent). Total liabilities (what the company owes) less accounts payable and less accrued expenses, neither of which you pay interest on, provides a rough approximation of this amount. In Exhibit 16.8, total capital invested is $16,800,000. Third, calculate the cost (that is, rate) paid for capital by determining the interest paid to bondholders (who lend organizations their money), which is usually somewhere between 5 and 8 percent, and the return that stockholders want in terms of dividends and stock price appreciation, which is historically about 13 percent. Take a weighted average of the two to determine the overall cost of capital. In Exhibit 16.8, the cost of capital is 10 percent. Fourth, multiply the total capital ($16,800,000) from Step 2 by the cost of capital (10 percent) from Step 3. In Exhibit 16.8, this amount is $1,680,000. Fifth, subtract the total dollar cost of capital in Step 4 from the NOPAT in Step 1. In Exhibit 16.8, this value is $1,820,000, which means that our example company has created economic value or wealth this year. If our EVA number had been negative, meaning that the company didn't make enough profit to cover the cost of capital from bondholders and shareholders, then the company would have destroyed economic value or wealth by taking in more money than it returned.[57]

But why is EVA so important? First and most importantly, because it includes the cost of capital, it shows whether a business, division, department, profit center, or product is really paying for itself. The key is to make sure that managers and employees can see how their choices and behavior affect the company's EVA.

1. Calculate net operating profit after tax (NOPAT).	$3,500,000
2. Identify how much capital the company has invested (i.e., spent).	$16,800,000
3. Determine the cost (i.e., rate) paid for capital (usually between 5 percent and 13 percent).	10 percent
4. Multiply capital used (Step 2) times cost of capital (Step 3).	(10% × $16,800,000) = $1,680,000
5. Subtract the total dollar cost of capital from net profit after taxes.	$3,500,000 NOPAT −$1,680,000 Total cost of capital $1,820,000 Economic value added

Exhibit 16.8

Calculating Economic Value Added (EVA)

For example, because of EVA training and information systems, factory workers at Herman Miller, a leading office furniture manufacturer, understand that using more efficient materials, such as less expensive wood-dust board instead of real wood sheeting, contributes an extra dollar of EVA from each desk the company makes.[58]

Second, because EVA can easily be determined for subsets of a company, such as divisions, regional offices, manufacturing plants, and sometimes even departments, it makes managers and workers at all levels pay much closer attention to their segment of the business. When company offices were being refurbished at Genesco, a shoe company, a worker who had EVA training handed CEO Ben Harris $4,000 in cash. The worker explained that he now understood the effect his job had on the company's ability to survive and prosper. And since the company was struggling, he had sold the old doors that had been removed during remodeling so that the company could have the cash.[59] In other words, EVA motivates managers and workers to think like small-business owners who must scramble to contain costs and generate enough business to meet their bills each month. And, unlike many kinds of financial controls, EVA doesn't specify what should or should not be done to improve performance. Thus, it encourages managers and workers to be creative in looking for ways to improve EVA performance.

Exhibit 16.9 shows the top 10 U.S. companies in terms of EVA and market value added (MVA), as measured by the Stern Stewart Performance 1000 index. Remember that EVA is the amount by which profits exceed the cost of capital in a given year. So the more that EVA exceeds the total dollar cost of capital, the better a company has used investors' money that year. MVA is simply the cumulative EVA created by a company over time. Thus, MVA indicates how much value or wealth a company has

Exhibit 16.9

Leading Companies by Market Value Added and Economic Value Added

MVA RANKING IN 2004	MVA RANKING IN 2003	COMPANY	MARKET VALUE ADDED ($ MILLIONS)	ECONOMIC VALUE ADDED/(LOST) ($ MILLIONS)
1	1	General Electric	$299,810	$5,288
2	9	ExxonMobil	197,782	14,456
3	3	Microsoft	178,032	6,426
4	2	Wal-Mart	161,693	4,972
5	10	Johnson & Johnson	138,199	5,655
6	15	United Health Group	112,755	1,897
7	7	Procter & Gamble	105,858	3,951
8	4	CitiGroup	99,485	4,536
9	5	Intel	97,468	1,720
10	13	Dell	88,086	1,891

Source: R. Grizzetti, "U.S. Performance 1000," Stern Stewart & Co, available by request, http://www.sternstewart.com, 20 June 2005.

created or destroyed in total during its existence. As indicated by the MVA figures in Exhibit 16.9, over time the top 10 companies have created considerable wealth, ranging from almost $88 billion at Dell to $300 billion at General Electric; thus, they have returned substantially more than they took in. All of the top 10 in MVA had positive EVAs in the most recent year. However, this doesn't always happen. Good businesses sometimes have years with negative EVAs.

3.3 The Customer Perspective: Controlling Customer Defections

The second aspect of organizational performance that the balanced scorecard helps managers monitor is customers. It does so by forcing managers to address the question, "How do customers see us?" Unfortunately, most companies try to answer this question through customer satisfaction surveys, but these are often misleadingly positive. Most customers are reluctant to talk about their problems because they don't know who to complain to or think that complaining will not do any good. Indeed, a study by the federal Office of Consumer Affairs found that 96 percent of unhappy customers never complain to anyone in the company.[60]

One reason that customer satisfaction surveys can be misleading is that sometimes even very satisfied customers will leave to do business with competitors. Another challenge is getting effective feedback when there is a problem. Jon Piot, co-founder of **IMPACT INNOVATIONS GROUP**, an IT solutions provider, sent a team of 20 employees to work with a client at the client's facility. He thought everything was going well: All of the feedback from the client's CIO (chief information officer) was positive. So Piot was shocked when the client did not renew Impact's contract. As it turned out, the rest of the client's organization was very dissatisfied with the performance of Impact's employees. Piot says, "This was pretty painful for us; we had a pretty big team there, and it was a prestigious client."[61]

Rather than pouring over customer satisfaction surveys from current customers, studies indicate that companies may do a better job of answering the question "How do customers see us?" by closely monitoring **customer defections**, that is, by identifying which customers are leaving the company and measuring the rate at which they are leaving. Unlike the results of customer satisfaction surveys, customer defections and retention do have a great effect on profits.

For example, very few managers realize that obtaining a new customer costs five times as much as keeping a current one. In fact, the cost of replacing old customers with new ones is so great that most companies could double their profits by increasing the rate of customer retention by just 5 to 10 percent per year.[62] And if a company can keep a customer for life, the benefits are even larger. According to Stew Leonard, owner of the Connecticut-based **STEW LEONARD'S** grocery store chain, "The lifetime value of a customer in a supermarket is about $246,000. Every time a customer comes through our front door I see, stamped on their forehead in big red numbers, '$246,000.' I'm never going to make that person unhappy with me. Or lose her to the competition."[63]

Beyond the clear benefits to the bottom line, the second reason to study customer defections is that customers who have left are much more likely than current customers to tell you what you are doing wrong. Perhaps the best way to tap into this source of good feedback is to have top-level managers from various departments talk directly to customers who have left. It's also worthwhile to have top managers talk to dissatisfied customers who are still with the company. Every day, John Chambers, CEO of **CISCO SYSTEMS**, has 15 to 20 voice mails from dissatisfied Cisco customers forwarded to his phone. Chambers says, "E-mail would be more efficient, but I want to hear

customer defections a performance assessment in which companies identify which customers are leaving and measure the rate at which they are leaving

Customer retention is critical for the grocery industry. Margins are razor thin and incapable of underwriting the expense involved with finding new customers, which can be tremendous.

© GOODSHOOT/JUPITER IMAGES

the emotion, I want to hear the frustration, I want to hear the caller's level of comfort with the strategy we're employing. I can't get that through e-mail." Likewise, at Vanguard, a leading investment fund company, CEO Jack Brennan visits the customer call center and, working alongside call representatives, answers customer questions and addresses customer complaints.[64] Some might argue that it's a waste of valuable executive time to have upper-level managers make or listen to these calls, but there's no faster way for the people in charge to learn what needs to be done than to hear it directly from customers who are unhappy with the company's performance.

> "Every time a customer comes through our front door I see, stamped on their forehead in big red numbers, "$246,000."

STEW LEONARD, OWNER, STEW LEONARD'S GROCERY STORE CHAIN

Finally, companies that understand why customers leave can not only take steps to fix ongoing problems, but can also identify which customers are likely to leave and make changes to prevent them from leaving.

3.4 The Internal Perspective: Controlling Quality

The third part of the balanced scorecard, the internal perspective, consists of the processes, decisions, and actions that managers and workers make within the organization. In contrast to the financial perspective of EVA and the outward-looking customer perspective, the internal perspective asks the question "At what must we excel?" For McDonald's, the answer would be consistent, quick, low-cost food. For Toyota, the answer would be reliability—when you turn on your car it starts, no matter whether the car has 20,000 or 200,000 miles on it. Yet no matter what area a company chooses, the key is to excel in that area. Consequently, the internal perspective of the balanced scorecard usually leads managers to a focus on quality.

Quality is typically defined and measured in three ways: excellence, value, and conformance to expectations.[65] When the company defines its quality goal as *excellence*, then managers must try to produce a product or service of unsurpassed performance and features. For example, by almost any standard, *SINGAPORE AIRLINES* is the best airline in the world. It has been named "best" 18 years in a row by readers of *Conde Nast Traveler* magazine.[66] It has also received various "best airline" awards from the *Asian Wall Street Journal, Business Traveler International, Germany Business Traveler, Travel and Leisure*, and *Fortune*.[67] Whereas many airlines try to cram passengers into every available inch on a plane, Singapore Airlines delivers creature comforts to encourage repeat business and customers willing to pay premium prices. On its newer planes, the first-class cabin is divided into

mgmt: trends

An Old Standby Is a Hot Trend
Vertical integration is making a comeback. In an effort to better control resources—namely, raw materials—some companies are buying suppliers who furnish critical components for important product lines. In 2006, Armor Holdings bought the North Carolina textile manufacturer that supplied the super-strong fibers used in its armored cars. Toyota took control of a key battery supplier for hybrid gasoline-electric engines, and Bridgestone Tire bought a rubber plantation in Indonesia. Watch the business press for articles on companies expanding vertically rather than horizontally.

Source: Timothy Aeppel, "A Hot Commodities Market Spurs Buying Spree by Manufacturers," *Wall Street Journal*, August 14, 2006, A1, A7.

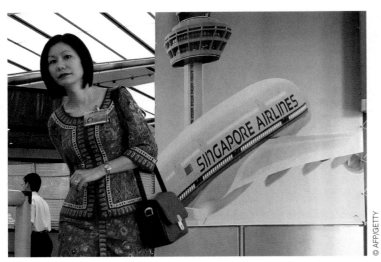

eight private mini-rooms, each with an unusually wide leather seat that folds down flat for sleeping, a 23-inch LCD TV that doubles as a computer monitor, and an adjustable table. These amenities and services are common for private jets but truly unique in the commercial airline industry.[68] Singapore Airlines was the first airline, in the 1970s, to introduce a choice of meals, complimentary drinks, and earphones in coach class. It was the first to introduce worldwide video, news, telephone, and fax services, and the first to feature personal video monitors for movies, news, documentaries, and games. Singapore Airlines has had AC power for laptop computers for some time, and recently it became the first airline to introduce on-board, high-speed Internet access.[69]

Singapore Airlines excels at providing high-quality amenities for its customers. By incorporating many elements of private air travel into a regular plane ride, the airline offers its passengers a luxurious travel experience.

"WHAT'S NEW" COMPANY

value customer perception that the product quality is excellent for the price offered

Value is the customer perception that the product quality is excellent for the price offered. At a higher price, for example, customers may perceive the product to be less of a value. When a company emphasizes value as its quality goal, managers must simultaneously control excellence, price, durability, or other features of a product or service that customers strongly associate with value. ALDI, a grocery store company with 7,500 stores worldwide, operates on the single principle of bringing maximum value to customers. Aldi stocks only 3 percent of the products that a typical grocery store carries, and most of its products are store brands. Customers bring their own bags and pick products off pallets rather than store shelves. Yet Aldi's store brands have consistently beaten the name-brand rivals in taste and quality, and in Germany, Aldi was voted the most trusted name in the grocery business.[70]

When a company defines its quality goal as conformance to specifications, employees must base decisions and actions on whether services and products measure up to standard specifications. In contrast to excellence and value-based definitions of quality that can be somewhat ambiguous, measuring whether products and services are "in spec" is relatively easy. Furthermore, while conformance to specifications (that is, precise tolerances for a part's weight or thickness) is usually associated with manufacturing, it can be used equally well to control quality in nonmanufacturing jobs. Exhibit 16.10 shows a checklist that a cook or restaurant owner would use to ensure quality when buying fresh fish.

Exhibit 16.10

Conformance to Specifications Checklist for Buying Fresh Fish

QUALITY CHECKLIST FOR BUYING FRESH FISH		
FRESH WHOLE FISH	**ACCEPTABLE**	**NOT ACCEPTABLE**
Gills	✓ bright red; free of slime; clear mucus	✗ brown to grayish; thick, yellow mucus
Eyes	✓ clear, bright, bulging, black pupils	✗ dull, sunken, cloudy, gray pupils
Smell	✓ inoffensive, slight ocean smell	✗ ammonia or putrid smell
Skin	✓ opalescent sheen; scales adhere tightly to skin	✗ dull or faded color; scales missing or easily removed
Flesh	✓ firm and elastic to touch, tight to the bone	✗ soft and flabby, separating from the bone
Belly cavity	✓ no viscera or blood visible; lining intact; no bone protruding	✗ incomplete evisceration; cuts or protruding bones; off-odor

Sources: "A Closer Look: Buy It Fresh, Keep It Fresh," *Consumer Reports Online*, available at http://www.seagrant.sunysb.edu/SeafoodTechnology/SeafoodMedia/CR02–2001/CR-SeafoodII020101.htm, 20 June 2005; National Fisheries Institute, "How to Purchase: Buying Fish," http://www.aboutseafood.com, 20 June 2005.

QUALITY MEASURE	ADVANTAGES	DISADVANTAGES
Excellence	Promotes clear organizational vision.	Provides little practical guidance for managers.
	Being/providing the "best" motivates and inspires managers and employees.	Excellence is ambiguous. What is it? Who defines it?
	Appeals to customers, who "know excellence when they see it."	Difficult to measure and control.
Value	Customers recognize differences in value.	Can be difficult to determine what factors influence whether a product/service is seen as having value.
	Easier to measure and compare whether products/services differ in value.	Controlling the balance between excellence and cost (i.e., affordable excellence) can be difficult.
Conformance to Specifications	If specifications can be written, conformance to specifications is usually measurable.	Many products/services cannot be easily evaluated in terms of conformance to specifications.
	Should lead to increased efficiency.	Promotes standardization, so may hurt performance when adapting to changes is more important.
	Promotes consistency in quality.	May be less appropriate for services, which are dependent on a high degree of human contact.

Source: Republished with permission of Academy of Management, PO Box 3020, Briar Cliff Manor, NY, 10510–8020. C. A. Reeves & D. A. Bednar, "Defining Quality: Alternatives and Implications," *Academy of Management Review* 19 (1994): 419–445. Reproduced by permission of the publisher via Copyright Clearance Center, Inc.

Exhibit 16.11

Advantages and Disadvantages of Different Measures of Quality

The way in which a company defines quality affects the methods and measures that workers use to control quality. Accordingly, Exhibit 16.11 shows the advantages and disadvantages associated with the excellence, value, and conformance to specification definitions of quality.

3.5 The Innovation and Learning Perspective: Controlling Waste and Pollution

The last part of the balance scorecard, the innovation and learning perspective, addresses the question "Can we continue to improve and create value?" Thus, the innovation and learning perspective involves continuous improvement in ongoing products and services (discussed in Chapter 18), as well as relearning and redesigning the processes by which products and services are created (discussed in Chapter 7). Since these are discussed in more detail elsewhere in the text, this section reviews an increasingly important topic, waste and pollution minimization. Exhibit 16.12 shows the four levels of waste minimization, from waste disposal, which produces the smallest minimization of waste, to waste prevention and reduction, which produces the greatest minimization.[71] The goals of the top level, *waste prevention and reduction*, are to prevent waste and pollution before they occur, or to reduce them when they do occur. There are three strategies for waste prevention and reduction.

1. *Good housekeeping*—performing regularly scheduled preventive maintenance for offices, plants, and equipment. Quickly fixing leaky valves and making sure machines are running properly so that they don't use more fuel than necessary are examples of good housekeeping. For example, Doug Goulding, a maintenance

"WHAT'S NEW" COMPANY

"WHAT'S NEW" COMPANY

"WHAT'S NEW" COMPANY

"WHAT'S NEW" COMPANY

supervisor at CANADA CORDAGE, a producer of synthetic and natural fiber ropes, reduced the water bills at the company's factory in Kitchener, Canada, from $1,200 to $200 per month by systematically plugging leaks in machines and pipes and installing water-saving devices.[72]

2. *Material/product substitution*—replacing toxic or hazardous materials with less harmful materials. As part of its Pollution Prevention Pays program over the last 30 years, *3M* eliminated 2.2 billion pounds of pollutants and saved $1 billion by using benign substitutes for toxic solvents in its manufacturing processes.[73]

3. *Process modification*—changing steps or procedures to eliminate or reduce waste. *TERRACYCLE* is a manufacturer of plant food made from the castings (that is, the droppings) of red worms that have feasted on various types of organic waste. But rather than package the plant food in new bottles, Terracycle packages its product in used beverage containers and ships the bottles in recycled boxes to the retailers. The company's entire process operation is 100 percent geared toward reducing or eliminating waste.[74]

At the second level of waste minimization, *recycle and reuse*, wastes are reduced by reusing materials as long as possible or by collecting materials for on- or off-site recycling. *RECYCLINE* recycles more than 50,000 pounds of plastic each year and provides recycled material to business customers and recyclable products to consumers. The company recycles all manner of plastic waste, including its own products, into new toothbrushes, plastic dinnerware, razors, and toothpicks. In addition to the waste plastic the company receives from other manufacturers and garbage collectors, Recycline receives about 15 percent of its own products back each year for recycling, which it heats to over 400 degrees to thoroughly sterilize. Partners like Stonyfield Farm, a maker of yogurt, donate their plastic cups to Recycline and give Recycline advertising space on their lids.[75]

A growing trend in recycling is *design for disassembly*, where products are designed from the start for easy disassembly, recycling, and reuse once they are no longer usable. For example, the European Union (EU) is moving toward prohibiting companies from selling products unless most of the product and its packaging can be recycled.[76] Since companies, not consumers, will be held responsible for recycling the products they manufacture, they must design their products from the start with recycling in mind.[77] At reclamation centers throughout Europe, companies will have to be able to recover and recycle 80 percent of the parts that go into their original products.[78] Already, under the EU's end-of-life vehicle program, all cars built in Europe since June 2002 are subject to the 80 percent requirement, which rose to 85 percent in 2006 and will be 95 percent by 2015 for autos. Moreover, effective in 2007, the EU requires auto manufacturers to pay to recycle all the cars they made

Exhibit 16.12
Four Levels of Waste Minimization

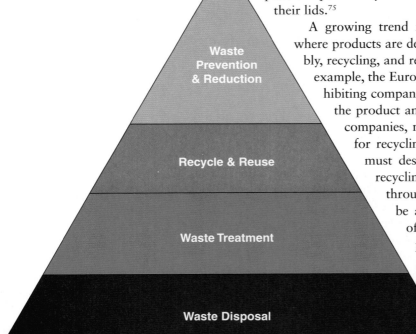

Source: D. R. May & B. L. Flannery, "Cutting Waste with Employee Involvement Teams," *Business Horizons*, September–October 1995, 28–38. Reprinted with permission from *Business Horizons*, © 1995 by the Trustees at Indiana University, Kelley School of Business.

between 1989 and 2002.[79] Roughly 160 million cars in Europe are covered by these strict end-of-life regulations, and although rising prices for recycled steel have made the regulations less burdensome than they might have been otherwise, the high level of composite plastics that make up today's lighter, more environmentally friendly cars are more difficult to recycle. One critic calls the 95 percent threshold "utopian," but others are more optimistic. DaimlerChrysler, for example, has begun to replace fiberglass in some of its car exterior panels with a type of banana-plant fiber.[80]

At the third level of waste minimization, *waste treatment*, companies use biological, chemical, or other processes to turn potentially harmful waste into harmless compounds or useful by-products. For example, during "pickling," a process in the manufacture of steel sheets, the steel is bathed in an acid solution to clean impurities and oxides (which would rust) from its surface. Getting rid of the "pickle juice" has always been a problem. Not only is the juice an acid, but it also contains ferric chloride and other metals, so steelmakers can't dump it into local water supplies. Fortunately, MAGNETICS INTERNATIONAL has found a safe, profitable way to treat the pickle juice. It sprays the juice into a 100-foot-high chamber at 1,200 degrees Fahrenheit. The iron chloride in the juice reacts with oxygen at that temperature to form pure iron oxide, which can be transformed into a useful magnetic powder. Inland Steel is now using this process to transform pickle juice into 25,000 tons of magnetic powder that can be reused in electric motors, stereo speakers, and refrigerator gaskets.[81]

The fourth and lowest level of waste minimization is *waste disposal*. Wastes that cannot be prevented, reduced, recycled, reused, or treated should be safely disposed of in processing plants or in environmentally secure landfills that prevent leakage and contamination of soil and underground water supplies. Contrary to common belief, all businesses, not just manufacturing firms, have waste disposal problems. For example, with the average computer lasting just three years, approximately 60 million computers come out of service each year, creating disposal problems for offices all over the world.[82] But with lead-containing cathode ray tubes in the monitors, toxic metals in the circuit boards, paint-coated plastic, and metal coatings that can contaminate ground water, organizations can't just throw old computers away.[83] Many companies give old computers and computer equipment to local computer recycling centers that distribute usable computers to nonprofit organizations or safely dispose of lead and other toxic materials. HEWLETT-PACKARD has started a unique computer disposal program that allows individual computer users to recycle PCs and electronic equipment.. The service is available at **http://www .hp.com/hpinfo/globalcitizenship/environment/recycle/index.html**. With three clicks and a credit card number (prices range from $13 to $34 per item), the old PC equipment will be picked up and properly disposed of.[84] HP makes no profit from this service.

Review 3: What to Control?

Deciding what to control is just as important as deciding whether to control or how to control. In most companies, performance is measured using financial measures alone. However, the balanced scorecard encourages managers to measure and control company performance from four perspectives: financial, customers, internal operations, and innovation and learning. Traditionally, financial control has been achieved through cash flow analysis, balance sheets, income statements, financial ratios, and budgets. Another way to measure and control financial performance is through economic value added (EVA). Unlike traditional financial measures, EVA helps managers assess whether they are performing well enough to pay the cost of the capital needed to run the business. Instead of using customer satisfaction surveys to measure performance, companies should pay attention to customer defectors, who are more likely to speak up about what the company is doing wrong. Performance of internal operations is often measured in terms of quality, which is defined in three ways: excellence, value, and conformance to expectations.[85] Minimization of waste has become an important part of innovation and learning in companies. The four levels of waste minimization are waste prevention and reduction, recycling and reuse, waste treatment, and waste disposal.

Too Much Information?

Imagine that your professor handed back term papers, and the only mark on yours was the grade. Would you be content, or would you feel gypped? People have different comfort about receiving feedback: Some thrive on it; others are ambivalent. What about you? Would you rather see comments in the margins of your term paper or not? This Self Assessment will give you insights into your perceptions of feedback. Understanding your preferences in this area will help you develop the skills you'll need as a manager.[86]

As you complete this feedback inventory, be candid as you circle the appropriate responses.

		Extremely Untrue				Extremely True	
1.	It is important for me to obtain useful information about my performance.	1	2	3	4	5	6
2.	If I receive negative feedback, I would have a negative attitude towards myself, so I try to avoid criticism.	1	2	3	4	5	6
3.	I am not really worried about what people will think of me if I ask for feedback about my performance.	1	2	3	4	5	6
4.	I like people to hear about my good performance at work (or at college).	1	2	3	4	5	6
5.	Receiving feedback about my performance helps me to improve my skills.	1	2	3	4	5	6
6.	Negative feedback doesn't really lower my self worth, so I don't go out of my way to avoid it.	1	2	3	4	5	6
7.	I'm concerned about what people would think of me if I were to ask for feedback.	1	2	3	4	5	6
8.	Seeking feedback from my supervisor (instructor) is one way to show that I want to improve my performance.	1	2	3	4	5	6
9.	I would like to obtain more information to let me know how I am performing.	1	2	3	4	5	6
10.	Receiving negative feedback wouldn't really change the way I feel about myself.	1	2	3	4	5	6
11.	I am worried about the impression I would make if I were to ask for feedback.	1	2	3	4	5	6
12.	I want people to know when I ask for feedback so I can show my responsible nature.	1	2	3	4	5	6
13.	I would like to receive more useful information about my performance.	1	2	3	4	5	6
14.	It's hard to feel good about myself when I receive negative feedback.	1	2	3	4	5	6
15	I don't really worry about what others would think of me if I asked for feedback.	1	2	3	4	5	6

KEY TERMS

balance sheets 609
balanced scorecard 608
behavior control 602
benchmarking 595
budgets 609
bureaucratic control 601
cash flow analysis 609
concertive control 604
concurrent control 597
control 594
control loss 598
customer defections 614
cybernetic 596
cybernetic feasibility 600
economic value added (EVA) 610
feedback control 597
feedforward control 598
financial ratios 509
income statements 509
normative control 603
objective control 602
output control 602
regulation costs 599
self-control (self-management) 605
standards 595
suboptimization 608
value 616

		Extremely Untrue					Extremely True
16.	I don't really care if people hear the good feedback that is given to me.	1	2	3	4	5	6
17.	I'm not really concerned about whether I receive useful information about my performance.	1	2	3	4	5	6
18.	I don't really worry about getting negative feedback because I still feel I am a person of worth.	1	2	3	4	5	6
19.	I don't really care if people know the type of feedback I get.	1	2	3	4	5	6
20.	When I receive praise, I don't really want others to hear it.	1	2	3	4	5	6
21.	Feedback is not really useful to help me improve my performance.	1	2	3	4	5	6
22.	I try to avoid negative feedback because it makes me feel bad about myself.	1	2	3	4	5	6
23.	If I sought feedback about my performance, I wouldn't want other people to know what type of feedback I received.	1	2	3	4	5	6
24.	I don't care either way if people see me asking my supervisor (instructor) for feedback.	1	2	3	4	5	6
25.	Obtaining useful feedback information is not very important to me.	1	2	3	4	5	6
26.	I worry about receiving feedback that is likely to be negative because it hurts to be criticized.	1	2	3	4	5	6
27.	I am usually concerned about other people hearing the content of the individual feedback I receive.	1	2	3	4	5	6
28.	I hope positive feedback about my performance will make a good impression on others.	1	2	3	4	5	6
29.	I don't really require more feedback to let me know how I am performing.	1	2	3	4	5	6
30.	Negative feedback doesn't really worry me because I still have a positive attitude towards myself.	1	2	3	4	5	6
31.	It doesn't worry me if people know how I've performed at something.	1	2	3	4	5	6
32.	I don't really need to impress others by letting them know about the positive feedback I receive regarding my performance.	1	2	3	4	5	6

Scoring

Determine your average score for each category by entering your response to each survey item below, as follows. In blanks that say *regular score*, simply enter your response for that item. If your response was a 4, place a 4 in the *regular score* blank. In blanks that say *reverse score*, subtract your response from 7 and enter the result. So if your response was a 4, place a 3 (7 − 4 = 3) in the *reverse score* blank. Total your scores, then compute each average score.

Desire for Useful Information
1. regular score _____
5. regular score _____
9. regular score _____
13. reverse score _____
17. reverse score _____
21. reverse score _____
25. reverse score _____
29. reverse score _____
TOTAL = _____

Ego Defense
2. regular score _____
6. reverse score _____
10. regular score _____
14. regular score _____
18. reverse score _____
22. reverse score _____
26. regular score _____
30. regular score _____
TOTAL = _____

Defensive Impression Management
3. reverse score _____
7. reverse score _____
11. reverse score _____
15. reverse score _____
19. reverse score _____
23. reverse score _____
27. reverse score _____
31. reverse score _____
TOTAL = _____

Assertive Impression Management
4. reverse score _____
8. reverse score _____
12. reverse score _____
16. reverse score _____
20. reverse score _____
24. reverse score _____
28. reverse score _____
32. reverse score _____
TOTAL = _____

You can find the interpretation for your score at: **academic.cengage.com/management/williams**.

Too Many Machines

You've just looked at your company's total spending and it's way too high, particularly in the areas of energy and supplies.[87] Top managers have ordered you to cut costs, so you sit down to assess the situation. The main culprits are the nearly 3,000 printers, copiers, scanners, and fax machines crowding your 200 office sites. A recent inventory shows that you have one machine for every four employees.

Running so many machines racks up huge operating costs for your company (buying supplies like ink and paper, electricity, and renting enough office space to contain them). Machine breakdowns, a frequent occurrence because of the sheer number of machines, eat up even more time and money with maintenance and repairs. Mechanical breakdowns are also mucking up your organization's chain-of-command, since no one knows who is responsible for which machines.

Even when the machines themselves are running efficiently, they generate confusion. Employees are printing too many documents and making too many copies—so many, in fact, that people are loosing track of them. Every office you visit is filled with humming machines and flurries of paper. This makes it hard to find paper files when they are needed. Even worse, you're in danger of accidentally leaking confidential information. Still, having such a high machine-employee ratio means that employees don't spend a lot of time collecting copies (and collecting coffee and conversation on the way).

Clearly, your company's printing is out of control. But how to get it back into control? You can reduce the number of machines and save on costs, or you can implement more controls on employees in the way of policies and procedures.

Questions

1. Can you control employees' printing and copying habits?

2. What control measures can you implement that relate only to controlling the machines?

3. What control measures can you implement that relate only to controlling employee behavior?

4. How do you get your printing problem under control: controlling machines, controlling employees, or both?

Is H & R Block Taxed to Its Limits?

When you first came to H & R Block four years ago, you had a vision: increase the scope of the company and transform it from a simple tax preparation service to a full-service financial services provider.[88] And why not? Block has roughly 17 million customers, and converting only a fraction of them to financial services clients would mean substantial growth for the 60-year-old company. Couple that with the company's recent expansion into mortgage financing, and Block could become a financial services powerhouse.

Eagerly you set about mapping the company's growth. You bought Olde Financial, a discount-brokerage business, and quickly found yourself with around $50 billion in assets under management. You hired financial advisers, and then to get them more clients, you instructed tax preparers to refer new financial prospects to them.

Another way you planned to fuel growth was by aggressively opening new tax preparation outlets. Today, Block has more U.S. storefronts (over 11,000) than Barnes & Noble (2,356), Gap (3,051), and even growth-happy Starbucks (6,409)! Over 1,000 outlets were added just this year to expand coverage during tax-filing season.

Despite all the good ideas, H & R Block is not producing the results you expected. In fact, it is struggling. Assets under management in the financial services division have declined by more than 30 percent since the division was acquired, and its advisers are leaving faster than they can be replaced. Outwardly, you say that the economic upswing is creating more demand for junior advisers, the largest percentage of your financial managers, but you also know that even new advisers are going to follow the money. And the money seems to be flowing out of Block.

Mortgage refinancing, which at its peak contributed an incredible 70 percent of pretax income, now contributes only 28 percent per year, or $112 million. Mortgage activity has dropped since the Federal Reserve began increasing interest rates, and competitive pricing among lenders has not subsided as you expected it would.

On the tax front, the company faces serious competition from smaller upstarts like Jackson Hewitt and Liberty Tax Service, which are both experiencing increases in the number of returns prepared at Block's expense. This tax season Jackson Hewitt handled nearly 6 percent more returns than last year. Compare that with Block, which has lost over one million customers in the past three years. Aggressive cost cutting is minimizing damage to the bottom line, but it is also having some adverse effects, including waits as long as two to three hours for some customers. Digitally, Block is being surpassed by Intuit's TurboTax software. Even though Intuit's TurboTax costs 50 percent more than Block's competing TaxCut software, Intuit has three times the market share of TaxCut, and is growing by double digits each tax season. All this trouble has caused Block's revenues to slide over 5 percent from last year.

As you hang up the phone from yet another apologetic conference call with Wall Street analysts, during which you revised your expectations for earnings per share sharply downward, you sigh and sink back into your chair. You are getting tired of announcing quarterly losses. Plans should be flexible enough to change if expected results don't materialize, but you really believe in the growth strategy. One analyst even said, "It seems like a smart strategy, and they seem to have the right infrastructure, but for some reason it's just not happening." You think to yourself, "There's got to be a way to get things back on track!"

Form a team of four students to answer the following questions.

Questions

1. As a team, identify where more control is needed at H & R Block. Is control in these areas possible? Explain.
2. Build a balanced scorecard for H & R Block that proposes objectives and measures for each the four quadrants of the card (financial, customer, internal, and learning).

PRACTICE BEING A MANAGER

Control is one of the most controversial aspects of management. Exercising too much control can foster employee resentment and bureaucratic delays. Exercising too little control can raise employee stress and breed organizational chaos. And not only must managers work to achieve a healthy *level* of control, but they must also strive to set controls around the *right targets*. The control process is about more than charts and feedback loops—it is about focusing personal and organizational efforts toward desired outcomes. This exercise will allow you an opportunity to try your hand at developing a control system that is tailored to a particular company and type of work.

Step 1: Get into groups. Your professor will organize your class into teams of three or four students per team. One team will be designated as Company Leadership.

Scenario: Razor's Edge (RE) is a young and growing company that serves the needs of those who engage in extreme sports, adventure/exploration, and guiding services. Some examples of RE's core market include

expert/professional mountain climbers, white-water rafting guides, and polar explorers. The founders of RE are the husband and wife team of Dan and Alice Connors, world-famous mountain climbers and explorers. Dan and Alice have both reached the summit of Mount Everest and each is well-respected in the rather small and close-knit community of adventurers and explorers. RE is an eclectic company of employees who, like Dan and Alice, share a passion for adventure and extreme sports. The company not only designs and sells its own lines of specialized products such as mountain-climbing shoes and ropes, but also develops software designed to support expedition planning, communication and navigation, and simulation and scenario response (that is, training tools for guides and newer expedition members). For the first five years of its development, RE did not worry too much about organizational policies or controls. Employees were encouraged to climb, trek, and guide, and attendance issues were addressed on a case-by-case basis. Although officially all employees were given two weeks of paid vacation, many employees were allowed to take up to two months off at half-pay so that they could complete an expedition. Sick days were jokingly referred to as "mountain flu" days, and it was not unusual for the small company to be thinly staffed on Mondays and Fridays.

But in the past three years RE has grown from 25 employees to 85. The company is too big, and the jobs too diverse, for Dan and Alice to deal with each employee request for "expedition time" away from work. And the "mountain flu" has occasionally weakened the company's response to customers. Dan and Alice have also become victims of their own success as they attracted other climbers to join their company—most climbers want time off in the peak climbing seasons. But this also happens to be a peak time for RE orders and service requests.

The company has organized all employees into teams and announced a contest. Each team should come up with an approach for controlling staffing levels to meet or exceed customer expectations for responsiveness, while at the same time preserving RE's tradition as a company of active adventurers and explorers. The company has announced that each member of the employee team that develops the winning solution will receive $2,500 worth of RE gear of their choice.

Step 2: Determine staffing levels. You are a team of workers at RE. Design an approach to controlling daily staffing levels so that RE is able to meet customer or exceed customer expectations for responsiveness without sacrificing its own identity as a company of adventurers and explorers. Keep in mind that RE is somewhat unusual in that even its accounting staff members (five full-time employees) are experienced adventurers and explorers,

and are expected to answer customer questions and handle their service needs. You should consider the following elements:

- Paid vacation
- Expedition time
- Sick days and "mountain flu" (Monday/Friday absences)
- Dealing with peak times, and/or most desirable times for vacation or expedition
- Knowing whether customers are pleased with RE's responsiveness to their needs

Step 3: Outline a proposal. Submit a one-page handwritten outline of your proposal to the Company Leadership team.

Step 4: Present the proposal. Each team will briefly present their proposal to the Company Leadership team, and members of the Company Leadership team may ask questions.

Step 5: Vote. The Company Leadership will confer, vote, and announce the winning proposal.

Step 6: Debrief as a class. What tensions confronted you as you worked to design an approach to staffing control for Razor's Edge? What tradeoffs and challenges might you anticipate for the company when it implements the winning proposal? In what ways is control related to employee motivation? In what ways is control related to organizational culture? Do you think that the winning RE proposal would be well-suited for use by a major outdoor and casual clothing company such as Lands' End? Why, or why not?

DEVELOP YOUR CAREER POTENTIAL

Learning from Failure

There is the greatest practical benefit of making a few failures early in life.

—T. H. Huxley

No one wants to fail.[89] Everyone wants to succeed. Nevertheless, some businesspeople believe that failure can have enormous value. At Microsoft, founder and chairman Bill Gates encourages his managers to hire people who have made mistakes in their jobs or careers. A Microsoft vice president says, "We look for somebody who learns, adapts, and is active in the process of learning from mistakes. We always ask, what was a

major failure you had? What did you learn from it?" Another reason that failure is viewed positively is that it is often a sign of risk taking and experimentation, both of which are in short supply in many companies. Harvard Business School professor John Kotter says, "I can imagine a group of executives 20 years ago discussing a candidate for a top job and saying, 'This guy had a big failure when he was 32.' Everyone else would say, 'Yep, yep, that's a bad sign.' I can imagine that same group considering a candidate today and saying, 'What worries me about this guy is that he's never failed.' " Jack Matson, who teaches a class at the University of Michigan called Failure 101, says, "If you are doing something innovative, you are going to trip and fumble. So the more failing you do faster, the quicker you can get to success."

One of the most common mistakes that occurs after failure is the *attribution error*. To *attribute* is to assign blame or credit. When we succeed, we take credit for the success by claiming it was due to our strategies, how we behaved, and how hard we worked. When we fail, however, we ignore our strategies, how we behaved, and how hard we worked (or didn't). Instead, when we fail, we assign the blame to other people, or to the circumstances, or to bad luck. In other words, the basic attribution error is that success is our fault but failure isn't. The disappointment we feel when we fail often prevents us from learning from our failures.

This means that attribution errors disrupt the control process. The three basic steps of control are to set goals and performance standards, to compare actual performance against the performance standards, and to identify and correct performance deviations. When we put all of the blame on external forces rather than our own actions, we stop ourselves from identifying and correcting performance deviations.

Furthermore, by not learning from our mistakes, we make it even more likely that we will fail again. Your task in this exercise is to begin the process of learning from failure. This is not an easy thing to do. When *Fortune* magazine writer Patricia Sellers wrote an article called "So You Fail," she found that most of the people she contacted were reluctant to talk about their failures. She wrote:

Compiling this story required months of pleading and letter writing to dozens of people who failed and came back. "If it weren't for the 'F' word, I'd talk," lamented one senior executive who got fired twice, reformed his know-it-all management style, and considered bragging about his current hot streak. Others cringed at hearing the word "failure" in the same breath as "your career."

Questions

1. Identify and describe a point in your life when you failed. Don't write about simple or silly mistakes. The difference between a failure and a mistake is how bad you felt afterwards. A real failure still makes you cringe when you think about it years later. What was the situation? What were your goals? And how did it turn out?

2. Describe your initial reaction to the failure. Were you shocked, surprised, angry, or depressed? Initially, who or what did you blame for the failure? Explain.

3. One purpose of control is to identify and correct performance deviations. With that in mind, describe three mistakes that you made that contributed to your failure. Now that you've had time to think about it, what could you have done differently to prevent these mistakes? Finally, summarize what you learned from your mistakes that will increase your chances of success the next time around.

REEL TO REAL

Brazil

*B*razil takes place in a retro-futuristic world in which automation pervades every facet of life, but paperwork, inefficiency, and mechanical failures are the rule. *Brazil* stars Jonathan Pryce in the role of Sam, a low-level bureaucrat. In this scene, Sam inadvertently gets wrapped up in an intrigue surrounding the so-called terrorist Harry Tuttle (played by Robert DeNiro), who is actually a renegade heating technician for whom the Ministry of Central Services has issued an arrest order. The clip moves quickly, so you may need to review it several times to grasp all the nuances in the conversation.

What to Watch for and Ask Yourself

1. What kind of control is being used by Central Services?
2. Tuttle describes a paradox of control. What is it?
3. What kind of control does Tuttle seem to prefer? Explain.

MANAGEMENT WORKPLACE

Peapod—Controlling the Process to Ensure the Outcome

*T*he grocery industry is a like a food fight without the mess. It is so competitive that only the strongest survive. Now imagine trying to survive in the online grocery industry, where customers can't see, smell, or touch the goods, and they expect their orders to be accurate and arrive on time. Finally, picture being one of the few companies to ride out the original dot-com storm. Those are daunting challenges for any firm. But Peapod, the online grocery service founded in 1989 by brothers Andrew and Thomas Parkinson, is succeeding on all three fronts.

Peapod introduced a new concept 15 years ago: the convenience of shopping for groceries online. Plenty of skeptics said the idea wouldn't fly, but some consumers and businesses were intrigued and began to order their groceries online. When many dot-coms of the era began to fail, Peapod hung on. Step into the management workplace at Peapod to see how the company maintained control during such challenging and turbulent times.

What to Watch for and Ask Yourself

1. What types of feedforward controls might Peapod use in the next few years?
2. Using the feedback control model, identify at least two standards that Peapod might establish.
3. What elements would you expect to be in each quadrant of Peapod's balanced scorecard?

627

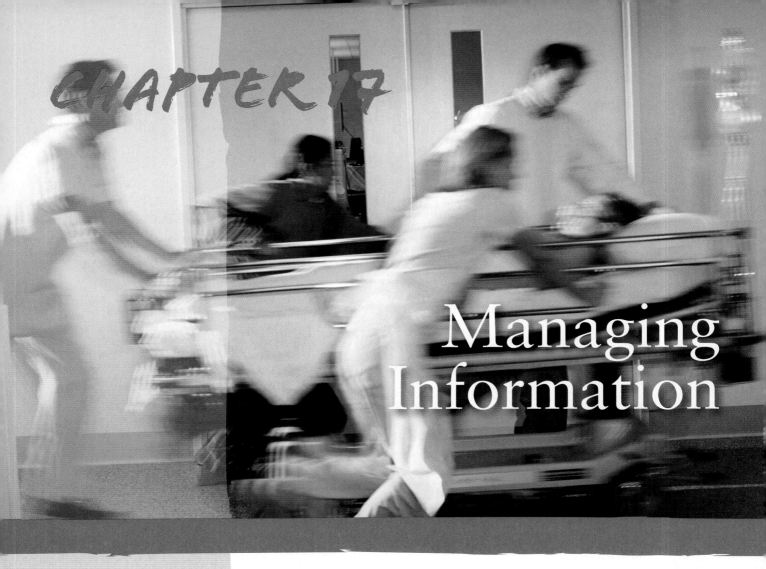

CHAPTER 17

Managing Information

Learning Outcomes:

1 Explain the strategic importance of information.

2 Describe the characteristics of useful information (that is, its value and costs).

3 Explain the basics of capturing, processing, and protecting information.

4 Describe how companies can access and share information and knowledge.

In This Chapter:

WHAT WOULD YOU DO?

University of Pittsburgh **Medical Center, Pittsburgh, Pennsylvania.**[1] The University of Pittsburgh Medical Center, which has a $5 billion annual budget, includes 19 hospitals with 3,340 beds, 4,500 physicians spread across 400 offices, 50 outpatient facilities, and 43,000 employees. Each year, it handles 167,000 inpatient admissions, three million outpatient visits, 400,000 emergency visits, 130,000 surgeries, and one million home care visits.

You've been chief information officer (CIO) for 18 months now, but with so many problems it seems like 18 years. To start, the hospital's databases contain information on over four million patients whose data are spread across 162 Unix servers, 624 Windows/Intel servers, and 40 storage systems, which are often incapable of sharing data or "talking to each other." That means that doctors, nurses, therapists, and patients frequently don't have the right information when they need it. For example, a doctor in one of the suburban offices who sends a patient to the downtown UPMC hospital for an MRI scan will be frustrated when the results are not received in time for the patient's next appointment. This is unfortunately the norm and not the exception.

Another problem, this one assigned to you by the CEO, is that departments regularly overspend their budgets. Normally, this would be the chief financial officer's problem, but at UPMC, purchasing procedures, which rely on carbon copy forms straight out of the 1960s, make it difficult to get up-to-date budget information. Since no one is sure what's been ordered or whether they're over or under their budgets, it's your problem. Furthermore, UPMC's employees use the carbon copy forms to make "rogue" purchases, bypassing UPMC's 70-member purchasing staff, which is supposed to approve or deny all purchase requests. Says one manager, "Unfortunately, anybody can file a form, call a supplier, and get whatever they want delivered."

Another significant issue is medication errors, many of which are created by illegible prescription orders. In hospitals, the average patient is exposed to a medication error every day, though most mistakes are caught by staff, the patient, or a family member before any harm is done. Nationwide each year, however, medication errors harm 1.5 million patients and cause 9,000 deaths. Fixing medication errors with additional medical treatments, and settling related legal settlements, costs hospitals an estimated $2 billion to $3.5 billion per year. Illegible hand-written prescriptions and medical orders are a significant problem at UPMC, too. There's no doubt in your mind that electronic medical records and a computer physician order entry (CPOE) system, in which doctors

electronically record their orders, treatment, and prescriptions, will solve these problems. Doctors and nurses would be able to quickly access patients' medical records any time from any location. And doctors' orders would be typed and thus legible.

Creating electronic patient records and a CPOE from scratch won't be easy. Doctors are incredibly resistant to change, especially if they don't see how it benefits them. So, the most important question you face is how to create an electronic system that doctors will use. You could have the most advanced computerized system in the world, but if the doctors don't buy in, it won't work. Next, what steps do you need to take to consolidate those 162 Unix servers, 624 Windows/Intel servers, and 40 storage systems? While it's tempting to centralize everything into one large system managed by your IT staff, doctors, nurses, and other caregivers want to easily process, store, retrieve, and communicate their patients' medical information. How can you do that while shrinking the number of servers and storage systems? Finally, how will you fix the budgeting problems and get rid of those 1960s carbon copy order forms? With the cost of medical services increasing 8 to 10 percent per year, and the employers and HMOs who pay those bills pressuring you to keep costs down, what's the best way to fix this? **If you were the Chief Information Officer of the University of Pittsburgh Medical Center, what would you do?**

ACTIVITIES + VIDEO

CengageNOW Audio study guide, electronic flashcards, author FAQ videos, On the Job and Biz Flix videos, concept tutorial, and concept exercise

Web (academic.cengage.com/management/williams) Quiz, PowerPoint slides, and glossary terms for this chapter

"WHAT'S NEW" COMPANIES

UNIVERSITY OF PITTSBURGH MEDICAL CENTER

CRATE AND BARREL

PIER 1

WAL-MART

PORTSMOUTH TRAFFIC SYSTEMS GROUP

AVERO

CON-WAY

HEALTH DECISIONS

AND OTHERS . . .

A generation ago, computer hardware and software had little to do with managing business information. Rather than storing information on hard drives, managers stored it in filing cabinets. Instead of uploading daily sales and inventory levels by satellite to corporate headquarters, they mailed hard-copy summaries to headquarters at the end of each month. Instead of word processing, reports were typed on an electric typewriter. Instead of spreadsheets, calculations were made on adding machines. Managers communicated by sticky notes, not e-mail. Phone messages were written down by assistants and coworkers, not left on voice mail. Workers did not use desktop or laptop computers as a daily tool to get work done; they scheduled limited access time to run batch jobs on the mainframe computer (and prayed that the batch job computer code they wrote would work).

Today, a generation later, computer hardware and software are an integral part of managing business information. In large part, this is due to something called **Moore's law**. Gordon Moore is one of the founders of Intel Corporation, which makes 75 percent of the integrated processors used in personal computers. In 1965, Moore predicted that about every two years, computer-processing power would double and its cost would drop by 50 percent.[2] As Exhibit 17.1 shows, Moore was right. Every few years, computer power, as measured by the number of transistors per computer chip, *has* more than doubled. Consequently, the computer sitting in your lap or your desk is not only smaller, but also much cheaper and more powerful than the large mainframe computers used by *Fortune* 500 companies 15 years ago. In fact, if car manufacturers had achieved the same power increases and cost decreases attained by computer manufacturers, a fully outfitted Lexus or Mercedes sedan would cost less than $1,000!

We begin this chapter by explaining why information matters. In particular, you will learn the value of strategic information to companies, as well as the cost and characteristics of good information. Next, you will investigate how companies capture, process, and protect information. Finally, you'll learn how information is accessed and shared with those within and outside the company, and how knowledge and expertise (not just information or data) are shared, too.

WHY INFORMATION MATTERS

Moore's law the prediction that about every two years, computer-processing power would double and its cost would drop by 50 percent

raw data facts and figures

information useful data that can influence people's choices and behavior

Raw data are facts and figures. For example, 11, $452, 4, and 26,100 are some data that I used the day I wrote this section of the chapter. However, facts and figures aren't particularly useful unless they have meaning. For example, you probably can't guess what these four pieces of raw data represent, can you? And if you can't, these data are useless. That's why researchers make the distinction between raw data and information. Whereas raw data consist of facts and figures, **information** is useful data

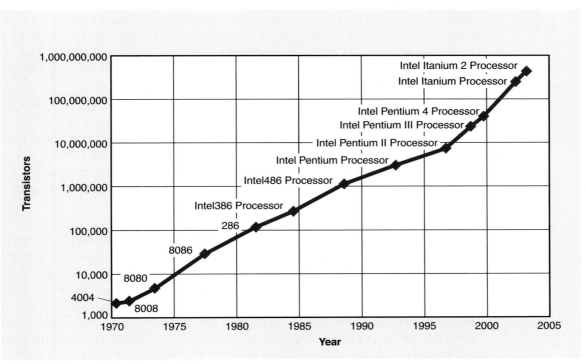

Source: "Moore's Law: Overviews," © Intel Corporation, available at http://www.intel.com/technology/mooreslaw, 27 June 2005.

Exhibit 17.1

Moore's Law

that can influence someone's choices and behavior. So what did those four pieces of data mean to me? Well, 11 stands for Channel 11, the local CBS affiliate on which I watched part of the men's PGA golf tournament; $452 is how much it would cost me to rent a minivan for a week if I go skiing over spring break; 4 is for the 4-gigabyte storage card that I want to add to my digital camera (prices are low, so I'll probably buy it); and 26,100 means that it's time to get the oil changed in my car.

After reading the next two sections, you should be able to

> 1 explain the strategic importance of information.
> 2 describe the characteristics of useful information (that is, its value and costs).

1 Strategic Importance of Information

Each year 15,000 customers file formal complaints over late, bungled deliveries of their furniture. If it was promised to be delivered in a month, it actually shows up in eight weeks, but with only three of the four pieces you ordered. Then, on the day the furniture is finally scheduled for delivery, the furniture truck shows up late or doesn't show at all, leaving furious customers who were required to be home from 9 AM to 5 PM to receive delivery. The strategic use of technology, however, is beginning to address these problems. *CRATE AND BARREL* and *PIER 1* now use their websites to give customers instant access to estimated completion dates using inventory tracking programs that follow the construction of furniture through the factory. This way customers don't have to guess when their furniture will be ready. Sophisticated route-tracking software, which determines the fastest and most efficient combination of directions and deliveries for each furniture truck, joined with global positioning systems that track each truck's progress and location is reducing costs and scheduled delivery windows. As a result, Crate and Barrel charges only $69 for delivery within 50 miles, no matter how much furniture you order. Likewise, Pottery Barn requires furniture customers to be home for just a two-hour delivery window instead of all day.[3]

*In today's hypercompetitive business environments, information, whether it's about furniture delivery, product inventory, pricing, or costs, is as important as capital (that is, money) for business success. It takes money to get businesses started, but businesses can't survive and grow without the right information. Information has strategic importance for organizations because it can be used to **1.1 obtain first-mover advantage** and **1.2 sustain a competitive advantage once it has been created**.*

1.1 First-Mover Advantage

First-mover advantage is the strategic advantage that companies earn by being the first in an industry to use new information technology to substantially lower costs or to differentiate a product or service from that of competitors. By investing $90 billion over the last decade to replace copper coaxial lines with digital lines that fed high-speed cable modems and digital TV cable channels, cable companies convinced two out of every three high-speed Internet subscribers to choose "cable" over DSL service provided by phone companies.[4] While the phone companies are beginning to catch up—they now sign up more new high-speed Internet subscribers than cable providers—does that mean that cable companies' first-mover advantage is slipping away? Well, not yet, as 57 percent of high-speed Internet subscribers still choose cable.[5] And with a growing subscriber base for residential phone service, the cable companies are now going after the phone companies' business customers, offering them high-speed Internet and business phone service.[7]

In all, first-mover advantages, like those established by high-speed Internet cable companies, can be sizable. On average, first movers earn a 30 percent market share, compared with 19 percent for the companies that follow.[8] Likewise, over 70 percent of market leaders started as first movers.[9]

1.2 Sustaining a Competitive Advantage

As described above, companies that use information technology to establish first-mover advantage usually have higher market shares and profits. According to the resource-based view of information technology shown in Exhibit 17.2, companies need to address three critical issues in order to sustain a competitive advantage through information technology. First, does the information technology create value for the firm by lowering costs or providing a better product or service? If an information technology doesn't add value, then investing in it would put the firm at a competitive disadvantage to companies that choose information technologies that do add value.

Second, is the information technology the same or different across competing firms? If all the firms have access to the same information technology and use it in the same way, then no firm has an advantage over another (there is competitive parity).

Third, is it difficult for another company to create or buy the information technology used by the firm? If so, then the firm has established a sustainable competitive advantage over competitors through information technology. If not, then the competitive advantage is just temporary, and competitors should eventually be able to duplicate the advantages the leading firm has gained from information technology. For more about sustainable competitive advantage and its sources, see Chapter 6 on organizational strategy.

first-mover advantage the strategic advantage that companies earn by being the first to use new information technology to substantially lower costs or to make a product or service different from that of competitors

In short, the key to sustaining a competitive advantage is not faster computers, more memory, and larger hard drives. The key is using information technology to continuously improve and support the core functions of a business. Ron Ireland, a former *WAL-MART* manager, says, "Wal-Mart has always considered information technology as a competitive advantage, never as a business expense."[10] Thanks to innovative use of information technology and the largest private satellite network and database system in the world, Wal-Mart's costs are 10 percent lower than its competitors'.[11] Wal-Mart was one of the first retailers to use computers and bar codes to track sales and inventory data and then share those data with suppliers. Today, Wal-Mart's $4 billion supplier network, Retail Link, allows vendors like Ted Haedicke of Coca-Cola to "look at how much [and what kind of] Coke [has] sold ... and at what prices at any store in the Wal-Mart system." He went on to say, "You can't do that with any other retailer today."[12]

Companies like Wal-Mart that achieve first-mover advantage with information technology and then sustain it with continued investment create a moving target that competitors have difficulty hitting.

Review 1: **Strategic Importance of Information**

The first company to use new information technology to substantially lower costs or differentiate products or services often gains first-mover advantage, which can lead to higher profits and larger market share. Creating a first-mover advantage can be difficult, expensive, and risky, however. According to the resource-based view of information technology, sustainable competitive advantage occurs when information technology adds value, is different across firms, and is difficult to create or acquire.

Does the information technology create value?

No → Competitive Disadvantage

Yes → **Is the information technology different across competing firms?**

No → Competitive Parity

Yes → **Is it difficult for another firm to create or buy the information technology?**

No → Temporary Competitive Advantage

Yes → Sustained Competitive Advantage

Source: Adapted from F. J. Mata, W. L. Fuerst, & J. B. Barney, "Information Technology and Sustained Competitive Advantage: A Resource-Based Analysis," *MIS Quarterly* 19, no. 4, December 1995, 487–505. Reprinted by special permission by the Society for Information Management and the Management Information Systems Research Center at the University of Minnesota.

Exhibit 17.2

Using Information Technology to Sustain a Competitive Advantage

2 Characteristics and Costs of Useful Information

Portsmouth, a scenic city of 190,000 on the southern coast of England, attracts 6.5 million visitors a year, primarily because of its historic role as the home of the British Royal Navy. To handle the crush of visitors, Portsmouth relies on 320 buses, all equipped with computers and QDMA (quad-division multiple access)

radio communication, which works reliably at speeds up to 250 miles per hour. Because the buses are networked, passengers waiting at bus stops can access a weatherproof computer terminal to find out when the next bus will arrive and what route that bus is taking. They can also check their e-mail, use trip planning software to determine which bus routes to take, or swipe a credit card to purchase tickets. John Domblides, who works for Portmouth's TRAFFIC SYSTEMS GROUP, says, "The response from the public using the new facilities has been very positive, largely due to the quality of both the information displayed and the infrastructure used—stainless-steel and glass bus shelters with bright displays."[13] The initial cost was £3.2 million (about $6.4 million), and the annual cost is £200,000 ($400,000).

*As Portsmouth's bus system demonstrates, information is useful when it is **2.1 accurate**, **2.2 complete**, **2.3 relevant**, and **2.4 timely**. However, there can be significant **2.5 acquisition**, **2.6 processing**, **2.7 storage**, **2.8 retrieval**, and **2.9 communication** costs associated with useful information.*

2.1 Accurate Information

Information is useful when it is accurate. Before relying on information to make decisions, you must know that the information is correct. But what if it isn't? For example, the restaurant business is notoriously difficult for two reasons. First, it's extremely competitive. Customers in any location typically have hundreds of restaurants from which to choose when dining out. Second, 60 percent of restaurants go out of business within three years. Why? Restaurant owners and managers typically have little accurate information about their businesses. Sure, they know whether they're losing money or not, but they don't know why. Most restaurants don't have accurate information regarding how much alcohol they sell, for example, wine versus beer versus hard liquor, nor do they have information regarding which food dishes, lobster versus swordfish, sell more or are more expensive to prepare. With AVERO's Slingshot software, however, restaurants can track this information and more. John Stinson, the head chef at Antonio's in Las Vegas, says, "My bosses keep asking, 'How many did you sell? How many did you sell?' I constantly need to provide the numbers." So Stinson uses Slingshot to examine the data and plan his menus accordingly. For instance, he found out that sea bass sold 196 times in one month, whereas ahi tuna sold 89 times. Since they both cost the same and sell for $29, Stinson reduced costs and eliminated unsold food by cutting his ahi tuna orders from suppliers in half.[14]

> My bosses keep asking, "How many did you sell? How many did you sell?" I constantly need to provide the numbers.

JOHN STINSON, HEAD CHEF, ANTONIO'S, LAS VEGAS

2.2 Complete Information

Information is useful when it is complete. Incomplete or missing information makes it difficult to recognize problems and identify potential solutions. For example, dispatchers at CON-WAY, a freight transportation company, are responsible for choosing truck routes that maximize trailer loads, minimize expenses (time, miles, and fuel), and get drivers home as soon as possible. On a typical day, Con-way's dispatchers must consider the number of trucks (2,100) and available drivers (varies), locations (200 across 25 states), shipments (typically 50,000), and the tonnage and trailer capacity for that day. Though Con-way's dispatchers do extremely well, they typically have only 85 percent of the information they need. Because they lack information about last-minute changes in orders, weather, accidents, driver no-shows, and breakdowns, they end up assigning longer, less efficient truck routes with less than full trucks that ultimately increase costs by $5 million per year.[15]

2.3 Relevant Information

You can have accurate, complete information, but if it doesn't pertain to the problems you're facing, then it's irrelevant and not very useful. Con-way dispatchers not only lacked complete information, they also lacked relevant information about their problems. To address these issues, the company spent $3 million over five years to build a computerized truck route optimization system. This system tracks all customer shipment requests (which can be made as late as 5:15 PM each day for the next day's delivery) and communicates by satellite with each truck to monitor truck availability, loads, miles, fuel, weather, and accidents. Then, armed with all of this relevant information, it cranks out optimal truck routes in just seven minutes. On an average day, this system allows Con-way to use 111 fewer trucks and 68 fewer drivers, drive 26,000 fewer miles, and increase the load in each truck by 370 revenue-generating pounds. Route optimization analyst Marty Robinson says, "It saves us a lot of time each night, which we use to make sure we've got accurate order information, look into problems and handle changes."[16]

2.4 Timely Information

Finally, information is useful when it is timely. To be timely, the information must be available when needed to define a problem or to begin to identify possible solutions. If you've ever thought, "I wish I had known that earlier," then you understand the importance of timely information and the opportunity cost of not having it. For instance, *HEALTH DECISIONS* is a company that designs and runs clinical drug-testing trials for pharmaceutical companies. To provide timely access to study results, it records data using specially designed bubble forms (like multiple-choice test Scantrons). By scanning a form every second, the company can read up to 8,000 per day— entering the same amount of data by hand would take months. This allows medical clinics and labs to verify and correct their data just four days after sending the data to Health Decisions. By contrast, the industry average is 122 days. How much does this matter? A Health Decisions study of a potential Alzheimer's drug based on 450,000 pages of data was completed in three and a half years rather than seven. Although the Food and Drug Administration did not approve the drug, completing the research so quickly saved the pharmaceutical company three and a half years and $32 million in additional expenses that it was able to put toward the development of another drug.[17]

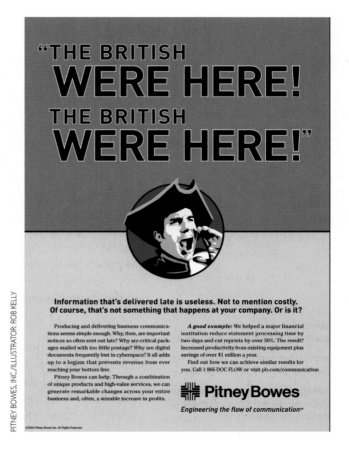

doing the **right** thing

Recycling and Disposing of Computer Equipment

With most companies replacing computers every four years, an estimated 250 million computers will be discarded over the next five years. Computers and computer monitors contain hazardous materials, however, so you can't just toss them in the trash. Doing that is not just wrong—it's against the law. Instead, contact your state's department of environmental protection for help in finding a recycling company. Or donate your old computers to deserving individuals or charitable organizations. Or sell the computers at a steep discount to your employees. And when you buy your new corporate computers, bargain with the vendor to make it responsible for recycling those computers the next time around.[19]

acquisition cost the cost of obtaining data that you don't have

processing cost the cost of turning raw data into usable information

storage cost the cost of physically or electronically archiving information for later use and retrieval

2.5 Acquisition Costs

Acquisition cost is the cost of obtaining data that you don't have. For example, among other things, AcXIOM, a billion-dollar company, gathers and processes data for direct-mail marketing companies. If you've received an unsolicited, "preapproved" credit card application recently (and who hasn't?), chances are Acxiom helped the credit card company gather information about you. Where does Acxiom get that information? The first place it turns is to companies that sell consumer credit reports at a wholesale cost of $1 each. Acxiom also obtains information from retailers. Each time you use your credit card, retailers' checkout scanners gather information about your spending habits and product preferences. Many retailers sell this information to companies like Acxiom that use it for market research. So why pay for this information? The reason is that acquiring it can help credit card companies do a better job of identifying who will mail back a signed credit card application and who will rip the credit card application in half and toss it in the trash.[18]

2.6 Processing Costs

Companies often have massive amounts of data, but not in the form or combination they need. Consequently, **processing cost** is the cost of turning raw data into usable information. For example, HEWLETT-PACKARD, which sells everything from handheld personal digital assistants to personal computers to large computer servers to high definition TVs, has 150,000 employees world wide. HP also has 85 different data centers in 29 countries, many of which can't "talk" to each other or share data. Why is this so? HP's chief information officer, Randy Mott explains, "Think about all of the steps involved from actually taking the order to having that order arrive on time, at all of the right locations, with all of the right components included and then promptly follow[ing]-up with accurate line-item billing, taxes, shipping costs, etc." Consequently, because of high processing costs, it's difficult for HP executives located throughout the world to obtain accurate, up-to-date information. It's Mott's job over the next three years to reduce HP's processing costs (that is, the cost of turning raw data into usable information) by consolidating those 85 data centers into just six data warehouses in the United States.[20]

2.7 Storage Costs

Storage cost is the cost of physically or electronically archiving information for later use and retrieval. For instance, Google and YAHOO! and Microsoft Live have incurred large storage costs to make it easy and fast for you to retrieve archived information. How costly can the storage for a simple web search be? Well, consider that each time you conduct a web search at Yahoo, 7,000 computers are activated to return the results of your search to you in less than 18/100 of a second.[21] And with the need for data storage doubling every 14 months, Yahoo, Google, Microsoft, and other *Fortune* 500 companies are building server farms, large collections of networked computer servers in 750,000-square-foot buildings (seven times the size of a Costco), to keep up with demand. Google's new server farm, located on 30 acres in Oregon where hydroelectric plants produce some of the cheapest electricity in the United States, will handle up to 2.7 billion online searches a month.

2.8 Retrieval Costs

Retrieval cost is the cost of accessing already-stored and processed information. One of the most common misunderstandings about information is that it is easy and cheap to retrieve once the company has it. Not so. First, you have to find the information. Then, you've got to convince whoever has it to share it with you. Then the information has to be processed into a form that is useful for you. By the time you get the information you need, it may not be timely anymore. Before the University of Illinois at Chicago Medical Center switched to the computer physician order entry (CPOE) system described in "What Would You Do?," doctors resisted the change, fearing that the new system would slow them down (that is, would have high retrieval costs). Dr. Patrick Tranmer says, "I have a maximum of 20 minutes to do everything when I see a patient. I have to find out what's wrong, get their history, do a physical exam, make a phone call, write a prescription, instruct the patient, make a follow-up appointment and then educate a student doctor about what I've just done."[22] The doctors were pleasantly surprised to find that the new system actually reduced retrieval costs. Before the new system, doctors and nurses used to waste time tracking down patient information. Now, when X-rays and lab reports are completed, they are immediately available for review at any computer in the hospital. When doctors noticed that it took nurses only one minute (rather than 10) to obtain these medical records, they started retrieving the X-rays and lab reports themselves, freeing nurses to spend more time attending to patients.[23] Overall, the new system saves physicians at the medical center 130,000 hours a year.

2.9 Communication Costs

Communication cost is the cost of transmitting information from one place to another. For example, the most important information that an electric utility company collects each month is the information from the electric meter attached to the side of your house. Traditionally, electric companies employed meter readers to walk from house to house to gather information that would then be entered into company computers. Now, however, meter readers are losing their jobs to water, gas, and electric meters built with radio frequency (RF) transmitters (see Section 3.1 for more on this technology). The transmitters turn on when a meter reader drives by the house in a utility company van that has a laptop computer specially equipped to receive the RF signals. Such a van, traveling at legal speeds, can read 12,000 to 13,000 meters in an eight-hour day. By contrast, a meter reader on foot would record data from 500 meters per day.[24] The Niagara Mohawk utility company in New York is spending $100 million over three years to install two million meters with RF transmitters, but expects to save $15 to $20 million a year in communication costs once they're installed.

retrieval cost the cost of accessing already-stored and processed information

communication cost the cost of transmitting information from one place to another

Review 2: *Characteristics and Costs of Useful Information*

Raw data are facts and figures. Raw data do not become information until they are in a form that can affect decisions and behavior. For information to be useful, it has to be reliable and valid (accurate), of sufficient quantity (complete), pertinent to the problems you're facing (relevant), and available when you need it (timely). Useful information does not come cheaply. The five costs of obtaining good information are the costs of acquiring, processing, storing, retrieving, and communicating information.

GETTING AND SHARING INFORMATION

In 1907, *METROPOLITAN LIFE INSURANCE* built a huge office building in New York City for its brand new, state-of-the-art information technology system. What was this great breakthrough in information management? Card files. That's right, the same card file system that every library in America used before computers. Metropolitan Life's information "technology" consisted of 20,000 separate file drawers that sat in hundreds of file cabinets more than 15 feet tall. This filing system held 20 million insurance applications, 700,000 accounting books, and 500,000 death certificates. Metropolitan Life employed 61 workers who did nothing but sort, file, and climb ladders to pull files as needed.[25]

A century later, the cost, inefficiency, and ineffectiveness of using this formerly state-of-the-art system would put an insurance company out of business within months. Today, if storms, fire, or accidents damage policyholders' property, insurance companies write checks on the spot to cover the losses. When policyholders buy a car, they call their insurance agent from the dealership to activate their insurance before driving off in their new car. And now, insurance companies are marketing their products and services to customers directly from the Internet.

> *From card files to Internet files in just under a century, the rate of change in information technology is spectacular. After reading the next two sections, you should be able to*
>
> 3 *explain the basics of capturing, processing, and protecting information.*
> 4 *describe how companies can access and share information and knowledge.*

3 Capturing, Processing, and Protecting Information

When you go to your local *RITE AID* pharmacy to pick up a prescription, the pharmacist reviews an electronic file that shows all of the medications you're taking. That same system automatically checks to make sure that your new prescription won't create adverse side effects by interacting with your other medications. When you pay for your prescription, Rite Aid's point-of-sale information system determines whether you've written any bad checks lately (to Rite Aid or other stores), records your payment, and then checks with the computer of the pharmaceutical company that makes your prescription drugs to see if it's time to reorder. Throughout the process, Rite Aid protects your information to make sure that your data are readily available only to you, your physician, and your pharmacist.

*In this section, you will learn about the information technologies that companies like Rite Aid use to **3.1 capture**, **3.2 process**, and **3.3 protect information**.*

3.1 Capturing Information

There are two basic methods of capturing information: manual and electronic. Manual capture of information is a labor-intensive process, which entails recording and entering data by hand into a data storage device. For example, when you applied for a driver's license, you probably recorded personal information about yourself by filling out a form. Then, after you passed your driver's test, someone typed your handwritten information into the department of motor vehicles' computer database so that local and state police could access it from their patrol cars when they pulled you over for speeding. (Isn't information great?) The problem with manual capture of information is that it is slow, expensive, and often inaccurate.

Consequently, companies are relying more on electronic capture, in which data are electronically recorded and entered into electronic storage devices. Bar codes, radio frequency identification tags, and document scanners are methods of electronically capturing data. **Bar codes** represent numerical data by varying the thickness and pattern of vertical bars. The primary advantage that bar codes offer is that the data they represent can be read and recorded in an instant with a handheld or pen-type scanner. One pass of the scanner (okay, sometimes several) and "beep!" The information has been captured. Bar codes cut checkout times in half, reduce data entry errors by 75 percent, and save stores money because stockers don't have to go through the labor-intensive process of putting a price tag on each item in the store.[26]

Radio frequency identification (RFID) tags contain minuscule microchips and antennas that transmit information via radio waves.[27] Unlike bar codes, which require direct line-of-sight scanning, RFID tags are read by turning on an RFID reader that, like a radio, tunes into a specific frequency to determine the number *and* location of products, parts, or anything else to which the RFID tags are attached. Turn on an RFID reader, and every RFID tag within the reader's range (from several hundred to several thousand feet) is accounted for. Each year, airlines mishandle or lose four million of the 700 million luggage bags checked by U.S. airline passengers. The annual cost to deliver late bags or to reimburse passengers for lost bags is approximately $400 million. Las Vegas's MᴄCᴀʀʀᴀɴ Iɴᴛᴇʀɴᴀᴛɪoɴᴀʟ Aɪʀᴘoʀᴛ is reducing those costs by attaching luggage tags with embedded RFID chips. RFID readers accurately read 99 percent of RFID-tagged bags, compared with 80 to 90 percent of bar-coded tags read by optical scanners. That means that of the 70,000 outbound bags that are handled each day at McCarran, only 700 (1%) have to be sorted by hand now that RFID chips are used, much fewer than the 7,000 to 14,000 (10%–20%) that would have to be hand-sorted if bar-coded tags were used.

bar code a visual pattern that represents numerical data by varying the thickness and pattern of vertical bars

radio frequency identification (RFID) tags tags containing minuscule microchips that transmit information via radio waves and can be used to track the number and location of the objects into which the tags have been inserted

RFID technology greatly increases the efficiency of getting the right luggage to the right person, something that baggage handlers and travelers can appreciate.

© STOCK CONNECTION/JUPITER IMAGES

Now that the price of RFID luggage tags has dropped dramatically from $5 just a few years ago to only 15 cents each, more airports will be using RFID tags to reduce their luggage handling costs.[28]

Because they are inexpensive and easy to use, **electronic scanners**, which convert printed text and pictures into digital images, have become an increasingly popular method of electronically capturing data. The first requirement for a good scanner is a *document feeder* that automatically feeds document pages into the scanner or turns the pages (often with a puff of air) when scanning books or bound documents.[29] Text that has been digitized cannot be searched or edited like the regular text in your word processing software, however, so the second requirement for a good scanner is **optical character recognition** software to scan and convert original or digitized documents into ASCII text (American Standard Code for Information Interchange) or Adobe PDF documents. ASCII text can be searched, read, and edited with standard word processing, e-mail, desktop publishing, database management, and spreadsheet software, and PDF documents can be searched and edited with Adobe's Acrobat software. Sloans Lake Managed Care, a Colorado health-care organization, uses scanners and optical character recognition software to read the medical claims forms submitted by the 450,000 people covered by its health plan. Sloans Lake can scan 450 to 500 characters per form with 98 percent accuracy. As a result, the company now automatically scans and processes over 5,000 claims forms per day and has lowered the time for processing claims by an average of 65 percent.[30]

3.2 Processing Information

Processing information means transforming raw data into meaningful information that can be applied to business decision making. Evaluating sales data to determine the best- and worst-selling products, examining repair records to determine product reliability, and monitoring the cost of long-distance phone calls are all examples of processing raw data into meaningful information. And with automated, electronic capture of data, increased processing power, and cheaper and more plentiful ways to store data, managers no longer worry about getting data. Instead, they scratch their heads about how to use the overwhelming amount of data that pours into their businesses every day. Furthermore, most managers know little about statistics and have neither the time nor the inclination to learn how to use them to analyze data.

One promising tool to help managers dig out from under the avalanche of data is data mining. **Data mining** is the process of discovering patterns and relationships in large amounts of data.[31] Data mining works by using complex algorithms such as neural networks, rule induction, and decision trees. If you don't know what those are, that's okay. With data mining, you don't have to. Most managers only need to know that data mining looks for patterns that are already in the data but are too complex for them to spot on their own. For example, when Yahoo decided to redesign its front page at Yahoo.com, it was faced with analyzing 10 terabytes (a terabyte is the same as 500 million pages of single-spaced text) of data per day generated by users clicks! Since there was no way to make sense of that much data, Yahoo bought DMX Group, a company that provides simple data mining tools to employees who pose simple questions such as "Are users more likely to click on an ad placed in the middle of the page or at the top of the page?" Bassel Ojjeh, vice president of DMX, which Yahoo has renamed the department of Strategic Data Solutions, says that Yahoo is now using data and not wild guesses to make changes to its websites. Says Ojjeh, "We say: Use data to make decisions. Don't make decisions based on a fad or what your competitors are doing."[32]

Data mining typically splits a data set in half, finds patterns in one half, and then tests the validity of those patterns by trying to find them again in the second

electronic scanner an electronic device that converts printed text and pictures into digital images

optical character recognition the ability of software to convert digitized documents into ASCII text (American Standard Code for Information Interchange) that can be searched, read, and edited by word processing and other kinds of software

processing information transforming raw data into meaningful information

data mining the process of discovering unknown patterns and relationships in large amounts of data half of the data set. The data typically come from a **data warehouse** that stores huge amounts of data that have been prepared for data mining analysis by being cleaned of errors and redundancy. The data in a data warehouse can then be analyzed using two kinds of data mining. **Supervised data mining** usually begins with the user telling the data mining software to look and test for specific patterns and relationships in a data set. Typically, this is done through a series of "what if?" questions or statements. For instance, a grocery store manager might instruct the data mining software to determine if coupons placed in the Sunday paper increase or decrease sales. By contrast, with **unsupervised data mining**, the user simply tells the data mining software to uncover whatever patterns and relationships it can find in a data set. For example, STATE FARM INSURANCE used to have three pricing categories for car insurance, depending on your driving record: preferred for the best drivers, standard for typical drivers, and nonstandard for the worst drivers. Now, however, it has moved to "tiered pricing" based on the 300 different kinds of driving records that its data mining software was able to discover. This allows State Farm to be much more precise in matching 300 different price levels to 300 different kinds of driving records.[33]

Unsupervised data mining is particularly good at identifying association or affinity patterns, sequence patterns, and predictive patterns. It can also identify what data mining "techies" call data clusters.[34] **Association or affinity patterns** occur when two or more database elements tend to occur together in a significant way. Surprisingly, OSCO DRUGS, based in Chicago, found that beer and diapers tended to be bought together between 5 and 7 PM. The question, of course, was "why?" The answer, on further review, was fairly straightforward: fathers, who were told by their wives to buy some diapers on their way home, decided to pick up a six-pack for themselves, too.[35] Likewise, because Wal-Mart's data mining indicated that people tend to buy bananas and cereal at the same time, Wal-Mart now places bananas near the cereal aisle, in addition to the fruits and vegetables aisle.[36]

Sequence patterns occur when two or more database elements occur together in a significant pattern, but with one of the elements preceding the other. StratBridge provides data mining capability to professional sports teams, like basketball's BOSTON CELTICS, to analyze their ticket sales in real time. One of its products is a "live" color-coded graphic of the Celtics stadium seating chart. Prior to a game, colors will change every few seconds to show whether a seat has been sold, at what price, and whether the seat was bought as part of a group purchase or an individual purchase. One season, after the Celtics had been eliminated from playoff eligibility, StratBridge's data mining software connected demographic data, sales data, seat location, and the timing of the seats to indicate that families typically bought tickets behind the basket just a few hours before tipoff. When the Celtics noticed that sales were lagging for those seats, they bundled those seats together in a family four-pack, dropped the prices, added food coupons, and then e-mailed a list of local families who had previously purchased tickets to the game. As a result, all of those unsold seats sold. Says Shawn Sullivan, a vice-president for the team, "If we'd done our usual newspaper ad [for those seats], there'd have been no return at all."[37]

Predictive patterns are just the opposite of association or affinity patterns. Whereas association or affinity patterns look for database elements that seem to go

data warehouse stores huge amounts of data that have been prepared for data mining analysis by being cleaned of errors and redundancy

supervised data mining the process when the user tells the data mining software to look and test for specific patterns and relationships in a data set

unsupervised data mining the process when the user simply tells the data mining software to uncover whatever patterns and relationships it can find in a data set

association or affinity patterns when two or more database elements tend to occur together in a significant way

sequence patterns when two or more database elements occur together in a significant pattern, but one of the elements precedes the other

Data mining can uncover some astounding patterns—like the fact that new dads tend to buy beer and diapers at the same time, at least at Osco.

together, **predictive patterns** help identify database elements that are different. On the day after Thanksgiving, typically the busiest shopping day of the year, Wal-Mart's data mining indicated that sales were unexpectedly slow for a boxed computer and printer combination that was offered at an extremely good price. Sales were slow everywhere, except one Wal-Mart store where sales greatly exceeded expectations. After noting the difference, headquarters called the store manager who said that the products were displayed in an open box that made it clear to customers that the low price was for the computer *and* the printer. Sales took off at all stores after headquarters relayed this simple message, "Open the box."[38]

Data clusters are the last kind of pattern found by data mining. **Data clusters** occur when three or more database elements occur together (that is, cluster) in a significant way. For example, after analyzing several years worth of repair and warranty claims, *FORD MOTOR COMPANY* might find that, compared with cars built in its Chicago plant, the cars it builds in Atlanta (first element) are more likely to have problems with overtightened fan belts (second element) that break (third element) and result in overheated engines (fourth element), ruined radiators (fifth element), and payments for tow trucks (sixth element), which are paid for by Ford's three-year, 36,000 mile warranty.

Traditionally, data mining has been very expensive and very complex. Today, however, data mining services and analysis are much more affordable and within reach of most companies' budgets. And, if it follows the path of most technologies, it will become even easier and cheaper to use in the future.

3.3 Protecting Information

Protecting information is the process of ensuring that data are reliably and consistently retrievable in a usable format for authorized users, but no one else. For instance, when customers purchase prescription medicine at *DRUGSTORE.COM*, an online drugstore and health-aid retailer, they want to be confident that their medical and credit card information is available only to them, the pharmacists at Drugstore.com, and their doctors. In fact, Drugstore.com has an extensive privacy policy (click "Privacy Policy" at **http://www.drugstore.com**) to make sure this is the case.

Companies like Drugstore.com find it necessary to protect information because of the numerous security threats to data and data security listed in Exhibit 17.3. People inside and outside companies can steal or destroy company data in various ways including denial-of-service web server attacks that can bring down some of the busiest and best-run sites on the Internet; viruses and spyware/adware that spread quickly and can result in data loss and business disruption; keystroke monitoring in which every mouse click and keystroke you make is monitored, stored, and sent to unauthorized users; password cracking software that steals supposedly secure passwords; and phishing, where fake but real-looking e-mails and websites trick users into sharing personal information (user names, passwords, account numbers) that leads to unauthorized account access. Indeed, on average, 19 percent of computers are infected with viruses, 80 percent have spyware, and only one-third are running behind a protected firewall (discussed shortly). Studies show that the threats listed in Exhibit 17.3 are so widespread that automatic attacks will begin on an unprotected computer just 15 seconds after it connects to the Internet.[39]

As shown in the right-hand column of Exhibit 17.3, numerous steps can be taken to secure data and data networks. Some of the most important are authentication and authorization, firewalls, antivirus software for PCs and e-mail servers, data encryption, and virtual private networks.[40] We will review those steps and then finish this section with a brief review of the dangers of wireless networks, which are exploding in popularity.

"If we'd done our usual newspaper ad [for those seats], there'd have been no return at all."

SHAWN SULLIVAN,
VICE-PRESIDENT, BOSTON CELTICS

---

predictive patterns patterns that help identify database elements that are different

data clusters when three or more database elements occur together (i.e., cluster) in a significant way

protecting information the process of ensuring that data are reliably and consistently retrievable in a usable format for authorized users, but no one else

Exhibit 17.3

Security Threats to Data and Data Networks

SECURITY PROBLEM	SOURCE	AFFECTS	SEVERITY	THE THREAT	THE SOLUTION
Denial of service, web server attacks, and corporate network attacks	Internet hackers	All servers	High	Loss of data, disruption of service, and theft of service.	Implement firewall, password control, serverside review, threat monitoring, and bug fixes, and turn PCs off when not in use.
Password cracking software and unauthorized access to PCs	Local area network, Internet	All users, especially digital subscriber line and cable Internet users	High	Hackers take over PCs. Privacy can be invaded. Corporate users' systems are exposed to other machines on the network.	Close ports and firewalls, disable file and print sharing, and use strong passwords.
Viruses, worms, Trojan horses, and rootkits	E-mail, downloaded and distributed software	All users	Moderate to high	Monitor activities and cause data loss and file deletion: compromise security by sometimes concealing their presence.	Use antivirus software and firewalls, and control Internet access.
Spyware, adware, malicious scripts, and applets	Rogue web pages	All users	Moderate to high	Invade privacy, intercept passwords, and damage files or file system.	Disable browser script support, and use security, blocking, and spyware/ adware software.
E-mail snooping	Hackers on your network and the Internet	All users	Moderate to high	People read your e-mail from intermediate servers or packets, or they physically access your machine.	Encrypt message, ensure strong password protection, and limit physical access to machines.
Keystroke monitoring	Trojan horses, people with direct access to PCs	All users	High	Records everything typed at the keyboard and intercepts keystrokes before password masking or encryption occurs.	Use antivirus software to catch Trojan horses, control Internet access to transmission, and implement system monitoring and physical access control.

(continued)

Exhibit 17.3 (Continued)

Security Threats to Data and Data Networks

SECURITY PROBLEM	SOURCE	AFFECTS	SEVERITY	THE THREAT	THE SOLUTION
Phishing	Hackers on your network and the Internet	All users, including customers	High	Fake but real-looking e-mails and websites that trick users into sharing personal information on what they wrongly thought was the company's website. This leads to unauthorized account access.	Educate and warn users and customers about the dangers. Encourage both not to click on potentially fake URLs, which might take them to phishing websites. Instead, have them type your company's URL into the web browser.
Spam	E-mail	All users and corporations	Mild to high	Clogs and overloads e-mail servers and inboxes with junk mail. HTML-based spam may be used for profiling and identifying users.	Filter known spam sources and senders on e-mail servers, and have users create further lists of approved and unapproved senders on their personal computers.
Cookies	Websites you visit	Individual users	Mild to moderate	Trace web usage and permit the creation of personalized web pages that track behavior and interest profiles.	Use cookie managers to control and edit cookies, and use ad blockers.

Sources: K. Bannan, "Look Out: Watching You, Watching Me," *PC Magazine*, July 2002, 99; A. Dragoon, "Fighting Phish, Fakes, and Frauds," CIO, 1 September 2004, 33; B. Glass, "Are You Being Watched?" *PC Magazine*, 23 April 2002, 54; K. Karagiannis, "DDoS: Are You Next?" *PC Magazine*, January 2003, 79; B. Machrone, "Protect & Defend," *PC Magazine*, 27 June 2000, 168–181.

authentication making sure potential users are who they claim to be

authorization granting authenticated users approved access to data, software, and systems

two-factor authentication authentication based on what users know, such as a password and what they have in their possession, such as a secure ID card or key

Two critical steps are required to make sure that data can be accessed by authorized users and no one else. One is **authentication**, that is, making sure users are who they claim to be.[41] The other is **authorization**, that is, granting authenticated users approved access to data, software, and systems.[42] For example, when an ATM prompts you to enter your personal identification number (PIN), the bank is authenticating that you are you. Once you've been authenticated, you are authorized to access your funds and no one else's. Of course, as anyone who has lost a PIN or password or had one stolen knows, user authentication systems are not foolproof. In particular, users create security risks by not changing their default account passwords (such as birth dates) or by using weak passwords such as names ("Larry") or complete words ("football") that are quickly guessed by password cracker software.[43] (See "Doing the Right Thing" on password do's and don'ts to learn how to prevent this.)

This is why many companies are now turning to **two-factor authentication**, which is based on what users know, such as a password, and what they have, such as a secure ID card. For example, to log onto their computer accounts, employees at BLOOMBERG, a global provider of business news, data, and analysis, must enter a password, such as a four-digit personal identification number, plus a secure number that changes every 60 seconds and is displayed on the tiny screen of the secure electronic ID (about the size of a pack of gum) they carry. For these same reasons, some companies are turning to biometrics for authentication. With **biometrics** such as fingerprint recognition or iris scanning, users are identified by unique, measurable body features.[44] Troy Appling, vice president of The Bankers Bank, says, "With fingerprint biometrics, we can reduce the risk of unauthorized people making millions of dollars off fraudulent transfers. And we don't have to spend up to 60 percent of our IT [information technology] time resolving lost or forgotten passwords."[45] Of course, since some fingerprint scanners can be fooled by fingerprint molds, some companies take security measures even further by requiring users to simultaneously scan their fingerprint *and* insert a secure, smart card containing a digital file of their fingerprint. This is another form of two-factor authentication.

> With fingerprint biometrics, we can reduce the risk of unauthorized people making millions of dollars off fraudulent transfers. And we don't have to spend up to 60 percent of our IT [information technology] time resolving lost or forgotten passwords.

TROY APPLING, VICE PRESIDENT, THE BANKERS BANK

Unfortunately, stolen or cracked passwords are not the only way for hackers and electronic thieves to gain access to an organization's computer resources. Unless special safeguards are put in place, every time corporate users are online there's literally nothing between their personal computers and the Internet (home users with high-speed DSL or cable Internet access face the same risks). Hackers can access files, run programs, and control key parts of computers if precautions aren't taken. To reduce these risks, companies use **firewalls**, hardware or software devices that sit between the computers in an internal organizational network and outside networks, such as the Internet. Firewalls filter and check incoming and outgoing data. They prevent company insiders from accessing unauthorized sites or from sending confidential company information to people outside the company. Firewalls also prevent outsiders from identifying and gaining access to company computers and data. Indeed, if a firewall is working properly, the computers behind the company firewall literally cannot be seen or accessed by outsiders.

A **virus** is a program or piece of code that, without your knowledge, attaches itself to other programs on your computer and can trigger anything from a harmless flashing message to the reformatting of your hard drive to a systemwide network shutdown. You used to have to do or run something to get a virus, such as double-clicking an infected e-mail attachment. Today's viruses are much more threatening. In fact, with some viruses, just being connected to a network can infect your computer. *Antivirus software for personal computers* scans e-mail, downloaded files, and computer hard drives, disk drives, and memory to detect and stop computer viruses from doing damage. However, this software is effective only to the extent that users of individual computers have and use up-to-date versions. With new viruses appearing all the time, users should update their antivirus software weekly or, even better, configure their virus software to automatically check for, download, and install updates. By contrast, *corporate antivirus software* automatically scans e-mail attachments, such as Microsoft Word documents,

biometrics identifying users by unique, measurable body features, such as fingerprint recognition or iris scanning

firewall a protective hardware or software device that sits between the computers in an internal organizational network and outside networks, such as the Internet

virus a program or piece of code that, without your knowledge, attaches itself to other programs on your computer and can trigger anything from a harmless flashing message to the reformatting of your hard drive to a systemwide network shutdown

doing the right thing

Password Do's and Don'ts

Anyone with access to sensitive personal (personnel or medical files), customer (credit cards), or corporate data (costs) has a clear responsibility to protect those data from unauthorized access. Use the following dos and don'ts to maintain a "strong" password system and protect your data.

- Don't use any public information such as part of your name, address, or birth date to create a password.
- Don't use complete words, English or foreign, that are easily guessed by password software using "dictionary attacks."
- Use eight or more characters and include some unique characters such as !@#$ to create passwords like "cow@#boy."
- The longer the password and the more unique characters, the more difficult it is to guess.
- Consider using "passphrases," such as "My European vacation starts July 8th," instead of shorter passwords. The longer password, including upper- and lowercase letters, spaces, and numbers, is easy to remember and much, much more difficult to guess using password cracking software.
- Remember your password and don't write it down on a sticky note attached to your computer.
- Change your password every six weeks. Better yet, specify that your computer system force all users to change their passwords this often.
- Don't reuse old passwords.

Together, these basic steps can make it much more difficult to gain unauthorized access to sensitive data.[47]

graphics, or text files, as they come across the company e-mail server. It also monitors and scans all file downloads across company databases and network servers. So, while antivirus software for personal computers prevents individual computers from being infected, corporate antivirus software for e-mail servers, databases, and network servers adds another layer of protection by preventing infected files from multiplying and being sent to others.

Another way of protecting information is to encrypt sensitive data. **Data encryption** transforms data into complex, scrambled digital codes that can be unencrypted only by authorized users who possess unique decryption keys. One method of data encryption is to use products by PGP (Pretty Good Privacy) (**http://www.pgp.com**) to encrypt the files stored on personal computers or network servers and databases. This is especially important with laptop computers, which are easily stolen. After a Boeing employee's laptop PC was stolen from his hotel room, the company implemented a training program that requires managers and employees to have data encryption software installed on their laptops and become certified in using it. Those not following the encryption procedures can be reprimanded and even fired.[46]

And, with people increasingly gaining unauthorized access to e-mail messages—e-mail snooping—it's also important to encrypt sensitive e-mail messages and file attachments. You can use a system called "public key encryption" to do so. First, give copies of your "public key" to anyone who sends you files or e-mail. Have the sender use the public key, which is actually a piece of software, to encrypt files before sending them to you. The only way to decrypt the files is with a companion "private key" that you keep to yourself.

Although firewalls can protect personal computers and network servers connected to the corporate network, people away from their offices (for example, salespeople, business travelers, telecommuters who work at home) who interact with their company networks via the Internet face a security risk. Because Internet data are not encrypted, packet sniffer software easily allows hackers to read everything sent or received, except files that have been encrypted before sending. Previously, the only practical solution was to have employees dial in to secure company phone lines for direct access to the company network. Of course, with international and long-distance phone calls, the costs quickly added up. Now, **virtual private networks (VPNs)** have solved this problem by using software to encrypt all Internet data at both ends of the transmission process. Instead of making long-distance calls, employees connect to the Internet. But, unlike typical Internet connections in which Internet data packets are unencrypted, the VPN encrypts the data sent by employees outside the company computer network, decrypts the data when they arrive within the company network, and does the same when data are sent back to the computer outside the network.

Alternatively, many companies are now adopting web-based **secure sockets layer (SSL) encryption** to provide secure off-site access to data and programs. If you've ever entered your credit card in a web browser to make an online purchase, you've used SSL technology to encrypt and protect that information. SSL encryption is being used if a gold lock (Internet Explorer) or a gold key (Netscape) appears along the bottom of your web browser. SSL encryption works the same way in the workplace. Managers and employees who aren't at the office simply connect to the Internet, open a web browser, and then enter a user name and password to gain access to SSL encrypted data and programs. For example, the Catholic Health System of Buffalo, New York, uses an SSL system to allow radiologists to access and review medical images like X-rays from their homes. Likewise, lawyers at Sonnenschein, Nath & Rosenthal, a Chicago law firm, use the Internet and their SSL encrypted system to securely access case records from anywhere in the world.[48] SSL encryption is cheaper than VPNs, but it typically provides only limited access to data and files. By contrast, VPN connections, though more expensive, provide complete, secure access to everything on a company's network.

Finally, many companies now have wireless networks, which make it possible for anybody with a laptop and a wireless card to access the company network from anywhere in the office. Though wireless networks come equipped with security and encryption capabilities that, in theory, permit only authorized users to access the wireless network, those capabilities are easily bypassed with the right tools. Furthermore, for ease of installation, many wireless networks are shipped with their security and encryption capabilities turned off.[49] Plus, although it's better to have it turned on than off, be wary of the WEP (Wired Equivalent Privacy) security protocol, which is easily compromised. See the Wi-Fi Alliance site at **http://www.wi-fi.org** for the latest information on wireless security and encryption protocols that provide much stronger protection for your company's wireless network.

Review 3: **Capturing, Processing, and Protecting Information**

Electronic data capture (bar codes, radio frequency identification [RFID] tags, scanners, and optical character recognition) is much faster, easier, and cheaper than manual data capture. Processing information means transforming raw data into meaningful information that can be applied to business decision making. Data mining helps managers with this transformation by discovering unknown patterns and relationships in data. Supervised data mining looks for patterns specified by managers, while unsupervised data mining looks for four general kinds of data patterns: association/affinity patterns, sequence patterns, predictive patterns, and data clusters. Protecting

data encryption the transformation of data into complex, scrambled digital codes that can be unencrypted only by authorized users who possess unique decryption keys

virtual private network (VPN) software that securely encrypts data sent by employees outside the company network, decrypts the data when they arrive within the company computer network, and does the same when data are sent back to employees outside the network

secure sockets layer (SSL) encryption Internet browser–based encryption that provides secure off-site web access to some data and programs

Seconds after connecting to the Internet, a computer starts being attacked by viruses and malicious scripts. This ad from Stay Safe Online underscores the importance of protecting information from outside threats.

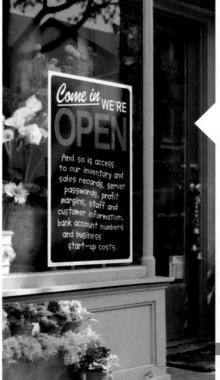

information ensures that data are reliably and consistently retrievable in a usable format by authorized users, but no one else. Authentication and authorization, firewalls, antivirus software for PCs and corporate e-mail and network servers, data encryption, virtual private networks, and web-based secure sockets layer (SSL) encryption are some of the best ways to protect information. Be careful with wireless networks, which are easily compromised even when security and encryption protocols are in place.

4 Accessing and Sharing Information and Knowledge

SIMPLEST-SHOP.COM sells a multitude of books, cameras, computers, DVDs, electronics, games, music, software, toys, and videos. Clicking on "DVD" brings up the 10 best-selling titles and the option of searching for 3,000 others. The page for each DVD (and every other product) lists customer advice, such as "recommended by 80 percent of our customers"; shares specific customer comments, such as "*Charlie and the Chocolate Factory* is a quirky but fun adaptation of Roald Dahl's classic children's tale"; and typically lists two or three different prices and places from which to order. Amazingly, with tens of thousands of products, this entire website and business is run by just one person, Calin Uioreanu, a software engineer from Munich, Germany. How can Uioreanu run this business by himself? He uses web services, a growing Internet technology that allows him to tie directly into Amazon.com's back-office resources. All of the product descriptions, pictures, and customer comments and feedback ratings on Simplest-Shop.com come straight from Amazon.com, which also verifies credit cards and arranges for shipping. Uioreanu uses web services software to connect his Simplest-Shop.com server to Amazon's servers for continuous information updates. The advantage for Amazon.com is that it has another website for selling its goods. The advantage for consumers is that they can buy many items directly from either Simplest-Shop.com or Amazon.com, whichever is cheaper. The advantage for Calin Uioreanu is that he can run a huge web business that sells over 50,000 products all by himself. According to Uioreanu, without web services and the ability to share information with Amazon.com, "it would have been 10 times more difficult to do."[50]

*Today, information technologies are letting companies communicate data, share data, and provide data access to workers, managers, suppliers, and customers in ways that were unthinkable just a few years ago. After reading this section, you should be able to explain how companies use information technology to improve **4.1 internal access and sharing of information, 4.2 external access and sharing of information, and 4.3 the sharing of knowledge and expertise**.*

4.1 Internal Access and Sharing

Executives, managers, and workers inside the company use three kinds of information technology to access and share information: executive information systems, intranets, and portals. An **executive information system (EIS)** uses internal and external sources of data to provide managers and executives the information they need to monitor and analyze organizational performance.[51] The goal of an EIS is to provide accurate, complete, relevant, and timely information to managers.

Managers at *LANDS' END*, the web/mail-order company, use their EIS, which they call their "dashboard," to see how well the company is running. With just a

executive information system (EIS)
a data processing system that uses internal and external data sources to provide the information needed to monitor and analyze organizational performance

few mouse clicks and basic commands such as *find, compare*, and *show*, the EIS displays costs, sales revenues, and other kinds of data in color-coded charts and graphs. Managers can drill down to view and compare data by region, state, time period, and product. Frank Giannantonio, Lands' End's CIO, says, "Our dashboards include an early alert system that utilizes key performance metrics to target items selling faster than expected and gives our managers the ability to adjust product levels far earlier than they were able to do in the past."[52] Exhibit 17.4 describes the capabilities of two of the best-selling products that companies use for EIS programs.

Intranets are private company networks that allow employees to easily access, share, and publish information using Internet software. Intranet websites are just like external websites, but the firewall separating the internal company network from the Internet permits only authorized internal access.[53] Companies typically use intranets to share information (for example, about benefits) and to replace paper forms with online forms. At *IBM*, however, the company intranet is used for electronic meetings, instant messaging, online libraries of policies and procedures, distance learning and training, online reimbursement of travel expenses, and travel schedules and

intranets private company networks that allow employees to easily access, share, and publish information using Internet software

Exhibit 17.4
Characteristics of Best-Selling Executive Information Systems

EASE OF USE	Few commands to learn.	Simply drag-and-drop or point-and-click to create charts and tables or get the information you need.
	Important views saved.	Need to see weekly sales by store every Monday? Save that "view" of the data, and it will automatically be updated with new data every week.
	3-D charts to display data.	Column, square, pie, ring, line, area, scatter, bar, cube, etc.
	Geographic dimensions.	Different geographic areas are automatically color-coded for easy understanding.
ANALYSIS OF INFORMATION	Sales tracking.	Track sales performance by product, region, account, and channel.
	Easy-to-understand displays.	Information is displayed in tabular and graphical charts.
	Time periods.	Data can be analyzed by current year, prior year, year to date, quarter to date, and month to date.
IDENTIFICATION OF PROBLEMS AND EXCEPTIONS	Compare with standards.	Compares actual company performance (actual expenses versus planned expenses, or actual sales by sales quotas).
	Trigger exceptions.	Allows users to set triggers (5 percent over budget, 3 percent under sales quota), which then highlight negative exceptions in red and positive exceptions in green.
	Drill down.	Once exceptions have been identified, users can drill down for more information to determine why the exception is occurring.
	Detect & alert newspaper.	When things go wrong, the EIS delivers a "newspaper" via e-mail to alert managers to problems. The newspaper offers an intuitive interface for easily navigating and further analyzing the alert content.
	Detect & alert robots.	Detect & alert robots keep an extra "eye" out for events and problems. Want to keep an eye out for news about one of your competitors? Use a news robot to track stories on Dow Jones News Retrieval. Robots can also be used to track stock quotes, internal databases, and e-mail messages.

Sources: "Business Intelligence: Overview: Enterprise Services from Pilot Software," Accrue Software, http://www.pilotsw.com, 9 February 2002; Comshare home page, http://www.comshare.com, February 2002.

- Intranets are inexpensive.
- Intranets increase efficiencies and reduce costs.
- Intranets are intuitive and easy to use and web-based.
- Intranets work across all computer systems and platforms (web-based).
- Intranets can be built on top of an existing computer network.
- Intranets work with software programs that easily convert electronic documents to HTML files for intranet use.
- Much of the software required to set up an intranet is either freeware (no cost) or shareware (try before you buy, usually less expensive than commercial software).

Exhibit 17.5

Why Companies Use Intranets

© SUSAN VAN ETTEN

reservations. As a result, 4,800 electronic meetings are held each month, one million instant message discussions are held each day, and 40 percent of company training is done online.[54] With 300,000 employees in 164 countries, the company's travel savings from online training have been huge. IBM's Jeanette Barlow says, "We saved between $4 million and $5 million a month not paying for travel."[55] Exhibit 17.5 further explains why companies use intranets.

Finally, corporate portals are a hybrid of executive information systems and intranets. While an EIS provides managers and executives with the information they need to monitor and analyze organizational performance, and intranets help companies distribute and publish information and forms within the company, **corporate portals** allow company managers and employees to access customized information *and* complete specialized transactions using a web browser. HILLMAN GROUP is the company that sells the nuts, bolts, fasteners, keys, and key cutting machines that you find in Home Depot, Lowes, Ace, and nearly every other hardware store. Hillman's 1,800 employees produce products for 25,000 customers. Two years ago, Hillman hired a new CIO, Jim Honerkamp, to improve the quality of information that Hillman's managers and employees used to make decisions. Says Honerkamp, "Our executives were trying to piecemeal information together to make business decisions on spreadsheets." So the first thing he did was to create a corporate portal that contained a real time revenue report for every product that updated sales and production numbers on a continuous basis. The portal and the report were so useful that CEO Mick Hillman began using them on a daily basis. Says Honerkamp, "The first thing he [Hillman] does when he arrives at 6:30 AM is to get on the portal and start looking at reports. He picks up the phone and starts calling my peers, the SVP of operations or the VP of distribution or the CFO and starts asking questions based on what he's seeing."[56] Today, Hillman's portal contains 75 specialized reports that are accessed by 800 managers and employees.

4.2 External Access and Sharing

Historically, companies have been unable or reluctant to let outside groups have access to corporate information. Now, however, a number of information technologies— electronic data interchange, extranets, web services, and the Internet—are making it easier to share company data with external groups like suppliers and customers. They're also reducing costs, increasing productivity by eliminating manual information processing (70 percent of the data output from one company, such as a purchase order, ends up as data input at another company, such as a sales invoice or shipping order), reducing data entry errors, improving customer service, and speeding communications. As a result, managers are scrambling to adopt these technologies.

corporate portal a hybrid of executive information systems and intranets that allows managers and employees to use a web browser to gain access to customized company information and to complete specialized transactions

> *Our executives were trying to piecemeal information together to make business decisions on spreadsheets.*
>
> **JIM HONERKAMP,** CIO, HILLMAN GROUP

With **electronic data interchange**, or **EDI**, two companies convert purchase and ordering information to a standardized format to enable direct electronic transmission of that information from one company's computer system to the other company's system. For example, when a Wal-Mart checkout clerk drags a CD across the checkout scanner, Wal-Mart's computerized inventory system automatically reorders another copy of that CD through the direct EDI connection that its computer has with the manufacturing and shipping computer at the company that publishes the CD, say, Atlantic Records. No one at Wal-Mart or Atlantic Records fills out paperwork. No one makes phone calls. There are no delays to wait to find out whether Atlantic has the CD in stock. The transaction takes place instantly and automatically because the data from both companies were translated into a standardized, shareable, compatible format.

Web services, as mentioned above in the Simplest Shop example, are another way for companies to directly and automatically transmit purchase and ordering information from one company's computer systems to another company's computer systems. **Web services** use standardized protocols to describe and transfer data from one company in such a way that those data can automatically be read, understood, transcribed, and processed by different computer systems in another company.[57] For instance, *ROUTE ONE*, which helps automobile processes auto loans for car buyers, was started by the financing companies of DaimlerChrysler, Ford, General Motors, and Toyota. Not surprisingly, each auto company had a different computer system with different operating systems, different programs, and different data structures. Route One relies on web services to connect these different computer systems to the wide variety of different databases and software used by various auto dealers, credit bureaus, banks, and other auto financing companies. Without web services, there's no way these different companies and systems could share information.[58]

Now, what's the difference between web services and EDI? For EDI to work, the data in different companies' computer, database, and network systems must adhere to a particular set of standards for data structure and processing. For example, company X, which has a 7-digit parts numbering system, and company Y, which has an 8-digit parts numbering system, would agree to convert their internal parts numbering systems to identical 10-digit parts numbers when their computer systems talk to each other. By contrast, the tools underlying web services, such as extensible markup language, or XML (don't worry if you don't how this works, just appreciate what it does), automatically do the describing and transcribing so that data with different structures can be shared across very different computer systems in different companies. As a result, web services allow organizations to communicate data without special knowledge of each other's computer information systems by automatically handling those differences.

In EDI and web services, the different purchasing and ordering applications in each company interact automatically without any human input. No one has to lift a finger to click a mouse, enter data, or hit the "return" key. An **extranet**, by contrast, allows companies to exchange information and conduct transactions by purposely providing outsiders with direct, web browser–based access to authorized parts of a company's intranet or information system. Typically, user names and passwords are required to access an extranet.[59] For example, to make sure that its distribution trucks don't waste money by running half empty (or make late deliveries to customers because it waited to ship until the trucks were full), *GENERAL MILLS* uses an extranet to provide web-based access to its

electronic data interchange (EDI) when two companies convert their purchase and ordering information to a standardized format to enable the direct electronic transmission of that information from one company's computer system to the other company's computer system

web services using standardized protocols to describe data from one company in such a way that those data can automatically be read, understood, transcribed, and processed by different computer systems in another company

extranets networks that allow companies to exchange information and conduct transactions with outsiders by providing them direct, web-based access to authorized parts of a company's intranet or information system trucking database to 20 other companies that ship their products over similar distribution routes. When other companies are ready to ship products, they log on to General Mills' trucking database, check the availability, and then enter the shipping load, place, and pickup time. Thus, by sharing shipping capacity on its trucks, General Mills can run its trucks fully loaded all the time. In several test areas, General Mills saved 7 percent on shipping costs, or nearly $2 million in the first year. Expanding the program company-wide is producing even larger cost savings.[60]

Finally, similar to the way in which extranets are used to handle transactions with suppliers and distributors, companies are reducing paperwork and manual information processing by using the Internet to electronically automate transactions with customers. For example, most airlines have automated the ticketing process by eliminating paper tickets altogether. Simply buy an e-ticket via the Internet, and then check yourself in online by printing your boarding pass from your personal computer or from a kiosk at the airport. Together, Internet purchases, ticketless travel, and automated check-ins have fully automated the purchase of airline tickets. Self-service kiosk uses are expanding, too. For example, ALAMO RENT-A-CAR has introduced kiosks that print rental agreements, permit upgrades to nicer cars, and allow customers to add additional drivers or buy rental insurance. Jerry Dow, Alamo's chief marketing officer, says, "Customers are already comfortable using the check-in kiosk for flights. Using a self-service kiosk for car rental is a natural progression."[61] Alamo has found that kiosks reduce check-in times by 50 percent.

"What's New"
Company

In the long run, the goal is to link customer Internet sites with company intranets (or EDI) and extranets so that everyone—all the employees and managers within a company, and the suppliers and distributors outside the company—who is involved in providing a service or making a product for a customer is automatically notified when a purchase is made. Companies that use EDI, web services, extranets, and the Internet to share data with customers and suppliers achieve increases in productivity 2.7 times larger than those that don't.[62]

4.3 Sharing Knowledge and Expertise

At the beginning of the chapter, we distinguished between raw data, which consist of facts and figures, and information, which consists of useful data that influence someone's choices and behavior. One more important distinction needs to be made, namely, that data and information are not the same as knowledge. **Knowledge** is the understanding that one gains from information. Importantly, knowledge does not reside in information. Knowledge resides in people. That's why companies hire consultants and why family doctors refer patients to specialists. Unfortunately, it can be quite expensive to employ consultants, specialists, and experts. So companies have begun using two information technologies, decision support systems and expert systems, to capture and share the knowledge of consultants, specialists, and experts with other managers and workers.

Whereas an executive information system speeds up and simplifies the acquisition of information, a **decision support system (DSS)** helps managers understand problems and potential solutions by acquiring and analyzing information with sophisticated models and tools.[63] Furthermore, whereas EIS programs are broad in scope and permit managers to retrieve all kinds of information about a company, DSS programs are usually narrow in scope and targeted toward helping managers solve specific kinds of problems. DSS programs have been developed to help managers pick the shortest and most efficient routes for delivery trucks, select the best combination of stocks for investors, and schedule the flow of inventory through complex manufacturing facilities.

It's important to understand that DSS programs don't replace managerial decision making; they improve it by furthering managers' and workers' understanding of the problems they face and the solutions that might work. Though used by just 2 percent

knowledge the understanding that one gains from information

decision support system (DSS) an information system that helps managers understand specific kinds of problems and potential solutions and analyze the impact of different decision options using "what if" scenarios of physicians, medical DSS programs hold the promise of helping doctors make more accurate patient diagnoses. A British study of 88 cases misdiagnosed or initially misdiagnosed (to be correctly diagnosed much later) found that a medical DSS made the right diagnosis 69 percent of the time.[64] With a medical DSS, doctors enter patient data, such as age, gender, weight, and medical symptoms. The medical DSS then produces a list of diseases and conditions, ranked by probability, low or high, or by medical specialty, such as cardiology or oncology. For instance, when emergency room physician Dr. Harold Cross treated a 10-year old boy who had been ill with nausea and dizziness for two weeks, he wasn't sure what was wrong, given that the boy had a healthy appetite, no abdominal pain, and just one brief headache. However, when the medical DSS that Dr. Cross used suggested a possible problem in the back of the boy's brain, he ordered an MRI scan that revealed a tumor, which was successfully removed two days later. Says Dr. Cross, "My personal knowledge of the literature and physical findings would not have prompted me to suspect a brain tumor."[65]

Expert systems are created by capturing the specialized knowledge and decision rules used by experts and experienced decision makers. They permit nonexpert employees to draw on this expert knowledge base to make decisions. Most expert systems work by using a collection of "if–then" rules to sort through information and recommend a course of action. For example, let's say that you're using your AMERICAN EXPRESS card to help your spouse celebrate a promotion. After dinner and a movie, the two of you stroll by a travel office with a Las Vegas poster in its window. Thirty minutes later, caught up in the moment, you find yourselves at the airport ticket counter trying to purchase last-minute tickets to Vegas. But there's just one problem. American Express didn't approve your purchase. In fact, the ticket counter agent is now on the phone with an American Express customer service agent.

So what put a temporary halt to your weekend escape to Vegas? An expert system that American Express calls "Authorizer's Assistant."[66] The first "if–then" rule that prevented your purchase was the rule "*if* a purchase is much larger than the cardholder's regular spending habits, *then* deny approval of the purchase." This if–then rule, just one of 3,000, is built into American Express's transaction-processing system that handles thousands of purchase requests per second. Now that the American Express customer service agent is on the line, he or she is prompted by the Authorizer's Assistant to ask the ticket counter agent to examine your identification. You hand over your driver's license and another credit card to prove you're you. Then the ticket agent asks for your address, phone number, Social Security number, and your mother's maiden name and relays the information to American Express. Finally, your ticket purchase is approved. Why? Because you met the last series of "if–then" rules. *If* the purchaser can provide proof of identity and *if* the purchaser can provide personal information that isn't common knowledge, *then* approve the purchase.

Review 4: **Accessing and Sharing Information and Knowledge**

Executive information systems, intranets, and corporate portals facilitate internal sharing and access to company information and transactions. Electronic data interchange, web services, and the Internet allow external groups, like suppliers and customers, to easily access company information. All three decrease costs by reducing or eliminating data entry, data errors, and paperwork, and by speeding up communication. Organizations use decision support systems and expert systems to capture and share specialized knowledge with nonexpert employees.

"WHAT'S NEW" COMPANY

expert system an information system that contains the specialized knowledge and decision rules used by experts and experienced decision makers so that nonexperts can draw on this knowledge base to make decisions

Expert systems like American Express's Authorizer's Assistant make available the knowledge of experienced decision makers to employees throughout the company—which is good if you're trying to buy tickets on the spur of the moment.

© TOPHAM/THE IMAGE WORKS

Computer Comfort

Computers are ubiquitous in modern society, but that does not mean that everyone embraces them. As with any innovation, some people are reluctant to adopt computer technology for whatever reason. How comfortable are you with computer technology?[67] Be candid as you complete the assessment by circling the appropriate responses.

	Strongly disagree				Strongly agree
1. I hesitate to use a computer for fear of making mistakes that I cannot correct.	1	2	3	4	5
2. The challenge of learning about computers is exciting.	1	2	3	4	5
3. I feel apprehensive about using computers.	1	2	3	4	5
4. I am confident that I can learn computer skills.	1	2	3	4	5
5. I feel insecure about my ability to interpret a computer printout.	1	2	3	4	5
6. I look forward to using a computer on my job.	1	2	3	4	5
7. I have avoided computers because they are unfamiliar and somewhat intimidating to me.	1	2	3	4	5
8. Learning to operate computers is like learning any new skill—the more you practice, the better you become.	1	2	3	4	5
9. It scares me to think that I could cause the computer to destroy a large amount of information by hitting the wrong key.	1	2	3	4	5
10. If given the opportunity, I would like to learn about and use computers.	1	2	3	4	5
11. I have difficulty in understanding the technical aspects of computers.	1	2	3	4	5
12. I am sure that with time and practice, I will be as comfortable working with computers as I am working with a typewriter.	1	2	3	4	5
13. You have to be a genius to understand all the special keys contained on most computer terminals.	1	2	3	4	5
14. Anyone can learn to use a computer if they are patient and motivated.	1	2	3	4	5
15. I do not think I would be able to learn a computer programming language.	1	2	3	4	5
16. I feel computers are necessary tools in both educational and work settings.	1	2	3	4	5
17. I dislike working with machines that are smarter than I am.	1	2	3	4	5

18. I feel that I will be able to keep up with the advances happening in the computer field.   1   2   3   4   5

19. I am afraid that if I begin using computers, I will become dependent upon them and lose some of my reasoning skills.   1   2   3   4   5

TOTAL = _____

Scoring

Reverse scores on even-numbered items. Reverse means, for instance, a 1 becomes a 5; a 4 becomes a 2, and so on. Using the reversed scores and the remaining scores, compute your score for the 19 items by adding up the scores.

You can find the interpretation for your score at: **academic.cengage.com/management/williams.**

MANAGEMENT DECISION

Can You See It Now?

After a long weekend working with your information technology team, you are confident that the company's server is thoroughly protected from outside attacks.[68] You and your team spent months planning and four days working around the clock to update the IT system, install, firewalls, and load SSL into the company's e-commerce tools, just to name a few of the security measures you upgraded. Now your company's information is protected with the latest and greatest.

When you stumble back to work on Wednesday, you follow your familiar route through the marketing department. Turning a corner, you overhear a junior marketing employee talking on her cell phone. She's saying, "I'm sooooooo far behind. No, really, I am. Check it out." Then she lifts her cell phone in the air and begins taking pictures of her desk.

Suddenly, you've lost your mission-accomplished swagger. Your team just spent thousands of labor hours protecting the company's digital assets, but anybody with a camera phone can take pictures of printouts, office layouts, client lists, accounting reports, marketing strategies, trade secrets—anything. A cell phone is the telecommunication version of a Swiss army knife: a versatile tool with potentially dangerous capabilities. Most cell phones have large memories for storing images, and what's more, they have GPRS technology, which enables them to connect them wirelessly to the Internet. Someone could take a picture of sensitive information, and in seconds, it could travel around the world and land on a competitor's computer (or cell phone, for that matter).

Camera-equipped cell phones are quickly becoming the norm. The market for the hybrid phones grew 200 percent in 2004, and researchers estimate that by 2008, 68 percent of all cell phones will be equipped with cameras and video capabilities—and the memory necessary to drive them.

Your pace quickens. You stop at your office to ditch your briefcase and then head straight to the CEO. Halfway there, however, you realize you need to be more composed before sounding alarm bells. Returning to your office, you fire up your computer and begin working on a memo.

Questions

1. What areas of a company are most likely to be compromised by the presence of camera phones?

2. Besides cell phones, can you think of other personal items that represent threats to a company's information, digital or otherwise? What are they? Should companies be able to restrict such items in the work place?

3. How could camera phones *improve* the collection and dissemination of information in a company?

4. Do you recommend banning camera phones in the workplace? Why or why not? Write a brief memo to the CEO explaining your position.

Brain Drain

The whistle blows signaling the end of the work day, and you automatically cringe. These days, that whistle seems like a warning bell for the mass exodus of employees you'll soon experience. You're a top manager at a nuclear power generator that employs thousands of engineers—for now, anyway. Very soon, though, you'll start loosing baby boomer workers to retirement. And you're not the only one. Within one decade, 43 percent of the workforce will be eligible to retire. United States businesses expect a 10 million worker shortage by 2010.

As you wait the arrival of your management team, you start to review the topic of your after-hours meeting. Your company will be hit hard by a double loss. Not only will you lose people (hard to replace), you'll lose their know-how (nearly impossible to replace). Skilled engineers have spent years acquiring the 'tricks-of-the-trade' and developing strategies for dealing with specific problems, so when they retire, a huge knowledge base will walk with them out the door.

A recent survey found that 63 percent of companies worry that the retirement of talented workers will create a "brain drain." Like many companies, yours has put off dealing with its aging workforce. Even though there's a plan for retaining some of your older workers on a part time basis, it's only a temporary measure. What you really need is a way to transmit knowledge from one group of employees to another—and to identify who has the knowledge you need to transmit.

Many companies in similar situations have developed knowledge management projects. Bruce Power—another nuclear power generator—uses a knowledge management system called Kana IQ that helps engineers document their solutions to certain problems so that future workers can search previous employees' notes using decision trees and other algorithms. Technology isn't the only way to stem the knowledge hemorrhage, however. Some companies are implementing mentoring programs to educate their next generation of skilled employees. At Tennessee Valley Authority power plants, younger engineers are assigned to shadow older engineers to facilitate the transfer of impossible-to-document skills.

So what will you do? Operating a nuclear power plant with less experienced workers is a dangerous proposition. Profitability and efficiency aren't the only concerns: safety is also paramount. You can't delay much longer or you'll be in a crisis when the retirements start in large number. When you open your door to see what on earth is keeping your management team you see them standing on your threshold mid-knock. It's time to get down to the hard business of creating a process for transmitting the wisdom of your older employees to your next generation of workers.

Questions

1. How can you find out which employees are about to retire? And how do you determine whose knowledge is most critical? Develop a strategy for identifying soon-to-retire workers and ranking the importance of their knowledge.

2. What are the pros and cons of developing a knowledge management database? What could you do to keep your engineers from becoming overly dependent upon a database? What steps might you take to ensure that your knowledge management project stays inclusive and accessible?

3. What if you developed a mentoring program? What would be the pros and cons of that?

4. Will you invest in a knowledge management project or a mentoring program? Explain your decision.

Information is the lifeblood of organizations and one of the keys to sustaining a competitive advantage. The tools for processing and sharing information have improved and proliferated rapidly over the past few decades. But growing sophistication has also meant growing challenges in maintaining quality and security across far flung corporate information systems. And managers increasingly feel deluged by the rising flow of e-mail, text messages, and near-instantaneous reports. To thrive in the information rich environment of modern business, managers must effectively utilize the various tools available. This exercise will give you an opportunity to consider which tools might work best for a given need.

Step 1: Get into groups and read the scenario. Your professor will organize you into pairs or groups of three.

Scenario: Suppose that you and your partner(s) are going into business together. Brainstorm about some new ventures that might interest you. Select one of these ideas that seem appealing, and then talk about how you might build a sustainable competitive advantage for your new business. (*Hint*: You may want to review the first few sections of the chapter.) With this initial sketch of your business plan in mind, discuss how you might use information systems and tools to accomplish the following tasks:

- Researching the likely competition that you will face

- Finding out what steps will be required to get the necessary permits, licenses, and/or regulatory approvals to open and maintain your business

- Determining what price you should charge for your product(s) or service(s)

- Deciding what computer and communication equipment you will need to buy to support your new venture

- Recruiting and hiring the best people for available jobs in your new company

Step 2: Discuss the issues. Discuss how you might develop the information system that your company needs to successfully launch and grow. Be sure to include security issues/concerns in your discussion.

Step 3: Debrief as a class. What are the major challenges in creating and maintaining a sustainable competitive advantage? What role does information and information technology play in successfully competing with other companies in a given market? Is it possible to secure sensitive information and at the same share information with employees and/or other key stakeholders (suppliers, customers)?

DEVELOP YOUR CAREER POTENTIAL

Learn to Talk Tech

Most people are intimidated by technology. But like many things, technology becomes easier if you familiarize yourself with the basics. One way to learn to "speak a geek" is to subscribe to *PC Magazine*, the premier magazine about personal computing. Depending on your budget, it may be more feasible (and possibly more productive) if you spend a set amount of time each week perusing the periodical section of the library and flipping through a selection of magazines dedicated to technology. The important thing is to be patient, however. After several issues, you should begin to understand what they're talking about. After that, it's easy to stay current. Subscribe at **http://pcmag.com**. You can also sign up for the "Term of the Day" e-mail newsletter at **http://webopedia.com**. Each day, Webopedia will e-mail you a new technology term and its definition. Either way, you'll soon be able to talk tech.

Why is talking tech so important? Information technology (IT) is an integral part of nearly every business, whether it's simple e-mail applications or more complex networking, e-commerce, and operations software. Very few companies are able to get by without

using IT regularly. This being the case, managers need to understand this critical component of their companies' operations. That's not to say that managers (other than IT managers, of course) need to know every last technical detail, but as a manager, you will need—and want—to know what your tech staff is talking about when they bring problems, concerns, or suggestions for improvement to your office.

Computers are becoming an integral part of all kinds of work, so you need to do more than just understand the terminology, however. You also need to be able to use technology effectively. The reason is that people with basic computer skills earn 15 to 30 percent higher lifetime incomes than those without them. What should you do to learn about computers? Subscribe to *PC Magazine, PC World*, or *Macworld*. Buy a book about Microsoft Office and then take tests to be Microsoft Office User certified (see the Microsoft website for more information) in Word, Excel, PowerPoint, or Access. Take more than the required computer classes for your degree. Unless you want less job security and earning power, start learning more about computers today.

Activities

1. If you are completely new to IT, you might be more comfortable reading about it in the context of your favorite business publication. Walter Mossberg has a regular technology column in the *Wall Street Journal*, and Peter Lewis has a column titled "Gadgets," which can always be found in the so-called First section of *Fortune* magazine. Articles in both publications are on the shorter side, so take an hour and read through a few weeks' worth of each.

2. The U.S. government operates a technology website at **http://www.technology.gov/reports.htm**. Go there to download a report, "Education and Training for the Information Technology Workforce," published in June 2003 on technology training opportunities (there may even be a more recent one). The table of contents alone will give you a wealth of ideas about where and what kind of IT training you may want to pursue in conjunction with your business degree.

REEL TO REAL

Lorenzo's Oil

This film tells the true story of young Lorenzo Odone, who suffers from adrenoleukodystrophy (ALD), an incurable degenerative brain disorder. (Six actors and actresses play Lorenzo throughout the film.) Physicians and medical scientists offer little help to Lorenzo's desperate parents, Michaela (Susan Sarandon) and Augusto (Nick Nolte). They use their resources to learn about ALD to try to save their son. Director George Miller cowrote the script, which benefited from his medical training as a physician.

Six months after Lorenzo's ALD diagnosis, his condition fails to improve with a restricted diet. Michaela and Augusto continue their research at the National Institutes of Health library in Bethesda, Maryland. Michaela finds a report of a critical Polish experiment that showed positive effects of fatty acid manipulation in rats. Convinced that a panel of experts could systematically focus on their problem, they help organize the First International ALD Symposium. This scene is an edited version of the symposium sequence that appears about midway through the film. The film continues with the Odones' efforts to save their son.

What to Watch for and Ask Yourself

1. Do the scientists present data or information during the symposium?
2. If it is information, who transformed the data into information? Speculate about how such data become information.
3. What do you predict will be the next course of action for the Odones?

Peapod—Data Management at Its Best

It's hard to imagine a time before e-commerce. The dot-com boom and bust seems to be ancient history, particularly because so many start-up firms didn't survive. But a few of them did, and one that not only survived but thrived is a company with the unlikely name of Peapod. Peapod was founded by brothers Andrew and Thomas Parkinson in 1989, several years before the dot-com boom began. Both brothers stayed with the firm after its sale to Royal Ahold.

Thomas Parkinson remains with the company today as its chief technology officer (CTO) and vice president. Peapod offers consumers a relatively simple service—online grocery shopping with delivery—but its success depends on a great deal more. Peapod wouldn't exist without Internet technology, the vehicle for e-commerce. Let's see how technology makes Peapod's management workplace so successful.

What to Watch for and Ask Yourself

1. Describe how Peapod uses data mining to process information.
2. How does Peapod share information both internally and externally?
3. In what ways might Peapod use a customer relationship management system to maintain its competitive advantage in the marketplace?

Managing Service and Manufacturing Operations

Learning Outcomes:

1 Discuss the kinds of productivity and their importance in managing operations.

2 Explain the role that quality plays in managing operations.

3 Explain the essentials of managing a service business.

4 Describe the different kinds of manufacturing operations.

5 Explain why and how companies should manage inventory levels.

In This Chapter:

WHAT WOULD YOU DO?

Louis Vuitton Manufacturing Plant, Asnières, France. Today as you walked out of the Louis Vuitton boutique on the Avenue Montaigne in downtown Paris, you found yourself at the center of Paris' high-end luxury fashion sector. With competition from less-expensive brands pushing into traditional upscale shopping districts, many high-end designers have relocated here. Similar movements have been occurring from New York to Tokyo and forced luxury fashion companies to regroup, a shift indicative of changing trends within the fashion world.

Louis Vuitton was founded in 1854 and opened its first workshop in 1860 in the Paris suburb of Asnières. Work at Asnières is still done by hand, and many current models are closely based on the original designs that made Vuitton a fashion icon. Workers specialize in making certain types of bags, and 20 to 30 craftsmen can take up to 8 days to complete one tote! That level of precision and care has been encouraged to maintain the traditional appeal of the brand.

As a fashion icon, Vuitton's reputation for high-quality handcrafted products is critical to its success. Over 150 years after its founding, Vuitton still considers make-to-order custom pieces as a central part of its production, and depending on their complexity, special requests can take as long as 8 months to complete. All work is done by craftsmen using hand tools (handsaws, hammers, pincers, cutters, brushes, punchers, sanders, and even stones).

Maintaining that caché involves creating high demand, frequent use of limited-edition products, and suppressing supply levels on their standard product lines. Vuitton sells its luggage at prices from roughly $2,000 to $4,000 per piece and has never put its products on sale. In the 1970s, the single factory in Asnières could not meet the increased demands of globalization, so Vuitton began adding new factories every other year. As a result of major pushes in marketing, store-opening, and expansion into the U.S. and Japan, Vuitton experienced annual sales increases from $760 million in 1990 to $3.7 billion in 2000.

That increase in volume is stressing your production system. Demand for new models is so high that at times people are on waiting lists for months. (You don't know how many sales you're losing because people are impatient.) As it is, manufacturing can't keep up with the new seasonal design schedule—it can take as long as a year for a new model to get from the design studio to the store shelves. What's worse, when an item becomes hot, your team is unable to quickly change its production to capitalize on the trend. If Vuitton wants to continue to grow, sales volume needs to increase, and the current limitations on your production process are preventing this.

So what is the best way to deal with the pressure toward increased revenue? Many competing brands are starting to make moves to increase sales and reduce customer waiting lists. That means increasing production volume and maybe even creating inventory. How do you accomplish this while maintaining your reputation for high-quality luxury? After all, that's what keeps customers loyal and made you successful in the first place! Finally, when items do become hot, how can you capitalize on the immediate demand? Not only do you need to make more, you need to make more and more quickly. **If you were the COO at Louis Vuitton, what would you do?**

Study Tip

Studying for comprehensive exams doesn't have to be a chore. Form a study group. Photocopy the glossary at the end of this text, and cut the copies into strips, one term per strip. Put all strips into a large bowl. Divide into two teams and have one team at a time draw out a strip. Quiz the opposing team and then read the correct answer. You can do the same with the chapter outlines at the beginning of each chapter. You can tabulate points, but you'll all win!

As you read in the opening vignette, Louis Vuitton Manufacturing Plant is trying to increase production volume without sacrificing quality. In this chapter, you will learn about **operations management**—managing the daily production of goods and services. You will begin by learning about the basics of operations management: productivity and quality. Next, you will read about managing operations, beginning with service operations, turning next to manufacturing operations, and finishing with an examination of the types, measures, costs, and methods for managing inventory.

MANAGING FOR PRODUCTIVITY AND QUALITY

"WHAT'S NEW" COMPANY

You're "crossing the pond" in September to visit your company's European offices and suppliers. Because business is down, your boss has given you a limited budget of $1,600 for airfare. Your round-trip ticket from Chicago to London costs $990 on American Airlines, but that leaves only $610 for airfare in Europe. The total cost of flying from London to Dublin (via British Airways), Dublin to Brussels (via Aer Lingus), Brussels to Venice (via Lufthansa), and Venice to London (via Alitalia) is $1,191—$581 more than your remaining budget and $201 more than your flight from the United States. At lunch, you're griping about the cost of European air travel when the company intern tells you to check out **RYANAIR**, which she flew when she backpacked in Europe last summer. So, after lunch, you surf to **http://www.ryanair.com** and find that the total cost to travel to the same cities on the same dates and times is an amazing $84, or just 7.5 percent of the cost of flying the other major European airlines!

Modeled after U.S.-based Southwest Airlines, Ryanair achieves dramatically lower prices through aggressive price cutting, much higher productivity, and quality customer service. Want a frequent-flier plan? You won't find one at Ryanair. It's too expensive. Want a meal on your flight? Pack a lunch. Ryanair doesn't even serve peanuts because it takes too much time (and thus expense) to get them out of the seat cushions. Passengers enter and exit the planes using old-fashioned rolling stairs because they're quicker and cheaper than extendable boarding gates. As a result of such cost-cutting moves, Ryanair does more with less and thus has higher productivity. For example, most airlines break even on their flights when they're 75 percent full, but even with its incredibly low prices, Ryanair's productivity allows it to break even when its planes are only half full. And with this low breakeven point, Ryanair attracts plenty of customers, who enable it to fill most of its seats (84 percent) and earn 20 percent net profit margins. Finally, because of its extremely low prices (and its competitors' extremely high prices), Ryanair has increased passenger traffic and profits for 17 straight years.[2]

After reading the next two sections, you should be able to

> 1 *discuss the kinds of productivity and their importance in managing operations.*
> 2 *explain the role that quality plays in managing operations.*

operations management
managing the daily production of goods and services

1 Productivity

At their core, organizations are production systems. Companies combine inputs, such as labor, raw materials, capital, and knowledge, to produce outputs in the form of finished products or services. **Productivity** is a measure of performance that indicates how many inputs it takes to produce or create an output.

$$\text{Productivity} = \frac{\text{Outputs}}{\text{Inputs}}$$

The fewer inputs it takes to create an output (or the greater the output from one input), the higher the productivity. For example, a car's gas mileage is a common measure of productivity. A car that gets 35 miles (output) per gallon (input) is more productive and fuel efficient than a car that gets 18 miles per gallon.

Let's examine **1.1 why productivity matters** *and* **1.2 the different kinds of productivity.**

1.1 Why Productivity Matters

Why does productivity matter? For companies, higher productivity, that is, doing more with less, results in lower costs. In turn, doing more with less can lead to lower prices, faster service, higher market share, and higher profits. For example, at fast-food restaurants, every second saved in the drive-through lane increases sales by 1 percent. Furthermore, increasing the efficiency of drive-through service by 10 percent adds nearly 10 percent to a fast-food restaurant's sales. And with 65 percent of all fast-food restaurant sales coming from the drive-through window, it's no wonder that Wendy's (average drive-through time of 124.7 seconds), MCDONALD'S (average time of 152.5 seconds), and Burger King (average time of 173.2 seconds) continue to look for ways to shorten the time it takes to process a drive-through order.[3] Productivity matters so much at the drive-through that McDonald's is experimenting with outsourcing its drive-through window operations to remote call centers. When you drive through at roughly 50 McDonald's franchises around the country, your order is taken by someone at a California call center. An operator takes orders from customers at restaurants in Honolulu one minute, and from Gulfport, Mississippi, the next. Although it seems counterintuitive, initial results show the system has improved order-taking accuracy and improved productivity. During the 10 seconds it takes for a car to pull away from the microphone at the drive through, a call center operator can take the order of a different customer who has pulled up to the microphone at another restaurant, even if it's thousands of miles away. According to Jon Anton, cofounder of Bronco Communications, which operates the call center for McDonald's, the goal is "saving seconds to make millions," because more efficient service can lead to more sales and lower labor costs.[4]

For countries, productivity matters because it results in a higher standard of living. One way productivity leads to a higher standard of living is through increased wages. When companies can do more with less, they can raise employee wages without increasing prices or sacrificing normal profits. For instance, when I wrote this chapter, recent government economic data indicated that companies were paying workers 3.5 percent more than in the previous year. But since workers were producing 5.1 percent more than they had the year before, real labor costs had actually decreased by 1.6 percent.[5] How much difference can productivity increases make to wages and standards of living? If productivity grows just 1 percent a year, it will

"WHAT'S NEW" COMPANY

productivity a measure of performance that indicates how many inputs it takes to produce or create an output

partial productivity a measure of performance that indicates how much of a particular kind of input it takes to produce an output

One of the largest drivers of manufacturing productivity has been the increased use of robotic technology. Using robotics, manufacturing facilities can keep producing through breaks, lunch, and the night to create a 24/7 manufacturing schedule.

take 70 years to double the standard of living. But if productivity grows 2 percent per year, the standard of living will double in just 35 years. One way to demonstrate this is to examine the effect that productivity has on wages. For example, the average American family earned approximately $56,914 in 2005. If productivity grows 1 percent a year, that family's income will increase to $71,351 in 2030. But if productivity grows 2 percent a year, their annual income in 2030 will be $90,384, more than $18,000 higher, and that's without working longer hours.[6] Thanks to long-term increases in business productivity, the average American family today earns 33 percent more than the average family in 1980 and 223 percent more than the average family in 1953—and that's after accounting for inflation.[7]

Rising income stemming from increased productivity creates numerous other benefits as well. For example, with productivity increases exceeding 3.8 percent per year from 1999 to 2005 the U.S. economy created three million new jobs.[8] In 2005 alone, the economy added two million jobs.[9] And when more people have jobs that pay more, they give more to charity. For example, in 2005 Americans donated over $260 billion to charities, 6.1 percent more than they gave in 2004.[10] Did Americans become more thoughtful, caring, conscientious, and giving? Probably not. Yet, because of strong increases in productivity during that time, the average American family saw its income increase by 15 percent. Because more people earned more money, they were able to share their good fortune with others by giving more to charity.[11]

Another benefit of productivity is that it makes products more affordable or better. For example, while inflation has pushed the average cost of a car to about $29,400 (after incentives and discounts), increases in productivity have actually made cars cheaper.[12] In 1960, the average family needed 26 weeks of income to pay for the average car. Today, the average family needs only 23.6 weeks of income—and today's car is loaded with accessories that weren't even available in 1960, including air bags, power steering and brakes, power windows, cruise control, stereo/CD/DVD players, seat warmers, air-conditioning, and satellite navigation.[13] So, in terms of real purchasing power, productivity gains have actually made today's $29,400 car of today cheaper than that $2,000 car in 1960.[14]

1.2 Kinds of Productivity

Two common measures of productivity are partial productivity and multifactor productivity. **Partial productivity** indicates how much of a particular kind of input it takes to produce an output.

$$\text{Partial Productivity} = \frac{\text{Outputs}}{\text{Single Kind of Input}}$$

Labor is one kind of input that is frequently used when determining partial productivity. *Labor productivity* typically indicates the cost or number of hours of labor it takes to produce an output. In other words, the lower the cost of the labor to produce a unit of output, or the less time it takes to produce a unit of output, the higher the labor productivity. For example, the automobile industry often measures labor productivity by determining the average number of hours of labor needed to completely assemble a car. The three most productive auto manufacturers can assemble a car with 32 or fewer hours of labor. TOYOTA assembles a car in only 27.9 hours of labor, Nissan does it in 29.4 hours, and Honda in 32 hours. These manufacturers have higher labor productivity than General Motors, which needs 34.3 hours of labor to assemble a car, DaimlerChrysler, which needs 35.8 hours, and Ford, which needs 36.9 hours.[15] These lower labor costs give Nissan, Honda, and Toyota an average cost advantage of $350 to $500 per car.[16]

Partial productivity assesses how efficiently companies use only one input, such as labor, when creating outputs. Multifactor productivity is an overall measure of productivity that assesses how efficiently companies use all the inputs it takes to make outputs. More specifically, **multifactor productivity** indicates how much labor, capital, materials, and energy it takes to produce an output.[17]

$$\text{Multifactor Productivity} = \frac{\text{Outputs}}{(\text{Labor} + \text{Capital} + \text{Materials} + \text{Energy})}$$

Exhibit 18.1 shows the trends in multifactor productivity across a number of U.S. industries since 1987. With a 78 percent increase between 1997 (scaled at 100) and 2001 (when it reached a level of 178) and nearly a sixfold increase since 1987, the growth in multifactor productivity in the computers and electronic products industry far exceeded the productivity growth in retail stores, auto manufacturing, mining, utilities, finance and insurance, and air transportation as well as most other industries tracked by the U.S. government.

Of course, the surge in productivity in the computer and electronics industry isn't a surprise. Each round of technology advances brings significantly smaller and cheaper, yet much more powerful electronic devices. Significantly less labor, capital, materials, and energy are needed to produce computers and electronic products (including cell phones, MP3 players, and computer game devices such as the PlayStation 3) today than in the past. An examination of some of the components of multifactor productivity shows how firms in the computer and electronics industry, such as DELL, have achieved such large increases in productivity.

First, with respect to labor, every time Dell opens a new factory, it increases productivity by producing more computers with fewer factory workers. John Egan, who directs manufacturing and distribution for one of Dell's most popular computer

multifactor productivity an overall measure of performance that indicates how much labor, capital, materials, and energy it takes to produce an output

Exhibit 18.1

Multifactor Productivity Growth across Industries

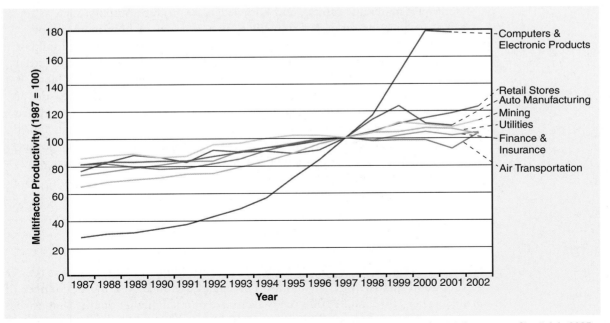

Source: "Productivity and Costs," Bureau of Labor Statistics, available at http://data.bls.gov/cgi-bin/surveymost?ip, 1 July 2005.

lines, says, "Every time [we open a new plant,] we get more and more efficient."[18] In fact, Dell's plant in Austin, Texas, is twice as productive as the plant it replaced. Likewise, Dell saves on labor costs because 95 percent of the orders processed by this plant are handled automatically when customers place their orders on the Internet.

Second, with respect to capital, multifactor productivity assesses how efficiently a company uses the money it spends on equipment, facilities (offices and operating plants), inventories, and land. Dell has greatly increased the productivity of its assembly plants by aggressively cutting costs and by building plants twice as fast as its competitors. For instance, Dell built its new assembly plant in Lebanon, Tennessee, in only 62 days. Dell cut two weeks out of the construction process by picking the architectural firm one morning and then working with the architects from noon until midnight on that same day to put together a construction schedule and budget.[19]

Finally, in terms of materials, that is, the components used to manufacture computers, Dell's new factories have almost no parts or finished product inventory. Computer parts are ordered when customers place their orders. And, according to Sharon Boyle, who manages Dell's Austin plant, "More than 95 percent of the orders received are shipped within eight hours." In fact, when the plant was designed, the company completely eliminated space that would normally hold parts and finished goods.[20]

Should managers use multiple or partial productivity measures? In general, they should use both. Multifactor productivity indicates a company's overall level of productivity relative to its competitors. In the end, that's what counts most. However, multifactor productivity measures don't indicate the specific contributions that labor, capital, materials, or energy make to overall productivity. To analyze the contributions of these individual components, managers need to use partial productivity measures.

Review 1: *Productivity*

At their core, companies are production systems that combine inputs, such as labor, raw materials, capital, and knowledge, to produce outputs, such as finished products or services. Productivity is a measure of how many inputs it takes to produce or create an output. The greater the output from one input, or the fewer inputs it takes to create an output, the higher the productivity. Partial productivity measures how much of a single kind of input, such as labor, is needed to produce an output. Multifactor productivity is an overall measure of productivity that indicates how much labor, capital, materials, and energy are needed to produce an output. Increased productivity helps companies lower costs, which can lead to lower prices, higher market share, and higher profits. Increased productivity helps countries by leading to higher wages, lower product prices, and a higher standard of living.

 2 Quality

With the average car costing $29,400, car buyers want to make sure that they're getting good quality for their money. Fortunately, as indicated by the number of problems per 100 cars (PP100), today's cars are of much higher quality than earlier models. In 1981, Japanese cars averaged 240 PP100. General Motors' cars averaged

670, Ford's averaged 740, and Chrysler's averaged 870 PP100! In other words, as measured by PP100, the quality of American cars was two to three times worse than Japanese cars. By 1992, however, U.S. carmakers had made great strides, significantly reducing the number of problems to an average of 155 PP100. Japanese vehicles had improved, too, averaging just 125 PP100. Exhibit 18.2 shows the results of the 2006 J. D. Power and Associates survey of initial car quality. Porsche, with just 91 PP100, had the best quality, followed by Lexus at 93 PP100 and Hyundai at 102 PP100; at the bottom of the list were Isuzu, with 191 PPM, and Land Rover, with 204 PP100, had the worst.[21]

The American Society for Quality gives two meanings for **quality**. It can mean a product or service free of deficiencies, such as the number of problems per 100 cars, or it can mean the characteristics of a product or service that satisfy customer needs.[22] In this sense, today's cars with their additional standard features (power brakes and steering, stereo/CD player, power windows and locks, air bags, cruise control) are of higher quality than those produced 20 years ago.

*In this part of the chapter, you will learn about **2.1 quality-related characteristics for products and services, 2.2 ISO 9000 and 14000, 2.3 the Baldrige National Quality Award**, and **2.4 total quality management**.*

2.1 Quality-Related Characteristics for Products and Services

As shown in Exhibit 18.3, quality products usually possess three characteristics: reliability, serviceability, and durability.[23] A breakdown occurs when a product

quality a product or service free of deficiencies, or the characteristics of a product or service that satisfy customer needs

Exhibit 18.2

J. D. Power and Associates Survey of Initial Car Quality

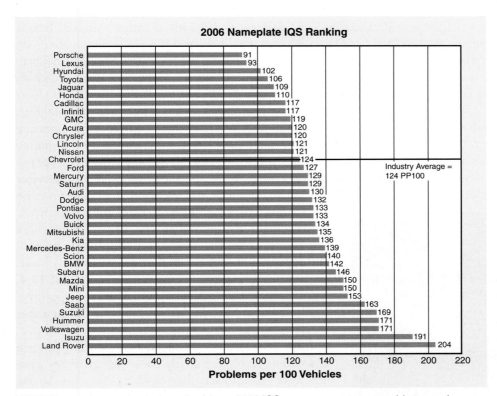

2006 Nameplate IQS Ranking

Nameplate	Problems per 100 Vehicles
Porsche	91
Lexus	93
Hyundai	102
Toyota	106
Jaguar	109
Honda	110
Cadillac	117
Infiniti	117
GMC	119
Acura	120
Chrysler	120
Lincoln	121
Nissan	121
Chevrolet	124
Ford	127
Mercury	129
Saturn	129
Audi	130
Dodge	132
Pontiac	133
Volvo	133
Buick	134
Mitsubishi	135
Kia	136
Mercedes-Benz	139
Scion	140
BMW	142
Subaru	146
Mazda	150
Mini	150
Jeep	153
Saab	163
Suzuki	169
Hummer	171
Volkswagen	171
Isuzu	191
Land Rover	204

Industry Average = 124 PP100

NOTE: Due to changes in study methodology, 2006 IQS scores are not comparable to previous years' scores. Scores are based on rounded figures for problems per 100 vehicles.

Source: "J. D. Power and Associates 2006 Initial Quality Study (IQS)," J. D. Power and Associates, http://www.jdpower.com/auots/quality-ratings, 10 March 2007.

Exhibit 18.3

Characteristics of Product Quality

An electric Reva automobile drives along a city street during Bangalore's celebration of World Environment Day. Reva uses a computer diagnostic system that can sync to the owner's cell phone and indicate the type of service the vehicle needs.

quits working or doesn't do what it was designed to do. The longer it takes for a product to break down, or the longer the time between breakdowns, the more reliable the product. Consequently, many companies define *product reliability* in terms of the average time between breakdowns. For example, QUANTUM CORPORATION sells the SDLT 600, a computer tape drive that customers can use to back up 600 gigabytes of data. The SDLT 600 is so reliable that the estimated mean time between breakdowns is 250,000 hours, or more than 28.5 years![24] Of course, this is just an average. Some SDLT 600 tape drives will break down much sooner, but others will last even longer than 28.5 years.

Serviceability refers to how easy or difficult it is to fix a product. The easier it is to maintain a working product or fix a broken product, the more serviceable that product is. The REVA is an electric two-seater car, built in India, for city use. It goes 50 miles on a single battery charge (a recharge takes just five hours), and its operating costs per mile are one-third that of a typical gasoline-powered car. The Reva has high serviceability by virtue of a computerized diagnostic system that plugs into a portable electronic tool (PET) about the size of a personal digital assistant that assesses how well the car is running. Because the PET can be linked to a phone, customers can easily transmit their Reva's operational history to instantly find out if their car needs work and, if so, what kind. In many instances, a simple computer change downloaded to the PET and then to the Reva will fix the problem.[25]

A product breakdown assumes that a product can be repaired. However, some products don't break down—they fail. *Product failure* means products can't be repaired. They can only be replaced. Thus, durability is a quality characteristic that applies to products that can't be repaired. *Durability* is defined as the mean time to failure. Durability is crucial for products such as the defibrillation equipment used by emergency medical technicians, doctors, and nurses to restart patients' hearts. Imagine the lost lives (and lawsuits) that would occur if this equipment were prone to frequent failure. The mean time between failures for PHYSIO-CONTROL's defibrillation units is 55.6 to 69.4 years.[26] If a Physio-Control Lifepak does break, however, the company replaces it within 24 hours.

While high-quality products are characterized by reliability, serviceability, and durability, services are different. With services, there's no point in assessing durability. Unlike products, services don't last. Services are consumed the minute they're performed. For example, once a lawn service has mowed your lawn, the job is done until the mowers come back next week to do it again. Likewise, services don't have serviceability. You can't maintain or fix a service. If a service wasn't performed correctly, all you can do is perform it again. Finally, the quality of service interactions often depends on how the service provider interacts with the customer. Was the service provider friendly, rude, or helpful? Consequently, as shown in Exhibit 18.4, five characteristics—reliability, tangibles, responsiveness, assurance, and empathy—typically distinguish a quality service.[27]

Service reliability is the ability to consistently perform a service well. Studies clearly show that reliability matters more to customers than anything else when buying services. Also, although services themselves are not tangible (you can't see or touch them), services are provided in tangible places. Thus, *tangibles* refer to the appearance of the offices, equipment, and personnel involved with the

AFP/ GETTY IMAGES

delivery of a service. *Responsiveness* is the promptness and willingness with which service providers give good service. *Assurance* is the confidence that service providers are knowledgeable, courteous, and trustworthy. *Empathy* is the extent to which service providers give individual attention and care to customers' concerns and problems.

EMC Corporation makes highly reliable computers that are used by some of the largest companies in the world (including banks, phone companies, and auto manufacturers). If EMC's equipment goes down for even a few minutes, its customers can lose millions from vanished sales. While its equipment is incredibly reliable, what distinguishes EMC from its competition is the level of service it provides when problems occur. In other words, EMC is a standout performer in *service reliability*, the ability to consistently perform a service well. Because of its excellent service, EMC retains an amazing 99 percent of its customers from year to year. When Carl Howe of Forrester Research, a marketing research firm, asked 50 *Fortune* 500 companies about the technology companies they worked with, "EMC came out looking like God." Howe says EMC "had the best customer-service reviews we have ever seen, in any industry."[28]

Exhibit 18.4

Characteristics of Service Quality

EMC also excels in *responsiveness*, the promptness and willingness with which service providers give good service. When a Wisconsin bank lost access to all its data (no account numbers, no deposits, no withdrawals, nada!), which were stored on an EMC machine, EMC service engineers were on the problem within minutes (EMC's computers "call home" automatically whenever a problem arises). In four hours EMC had created a setup identical to the bank's in a $1 billion facility designed for such purposes, where EMC engineers identified the problem and put together a software patch that had the bank up and running by the end of the day.[29]

EMC provides quality service by virtue of clear *assurance* that it can be trusted. Every customer knows that the company follows a disciplined procedure for addressing customer problems. First, every EMC system does a self-check every two hours to make sure it is running the way it's supposed to. If even the slightest thing is wrong, the system "phones home" to tell EMC's engineers what's happening. EMC gets 3,500 such "calls" from its machines and systems every day. Second, if a problem isn't fixed within four hours, Leo Colborne, the vice president of global technical support, is notified. After six hours, Colborne's boss, the senior vice president of global customer services, is contacted. After eight hours, the company's CEO and chairman are notified. In most cases, the CEO will leave immediately to visit the customer, apologize for the problem, reassure the customer that everything is being done to solve the problem, and begin working with the customer to implement procedures or solutions to prevent the problem from recurring in the future.[30]

Finally, EMC provides quality service because of the *empathy* it has for its customers' problems. Indeed, early in the company's history, its customers' businesses were suffering because EMC could not figure out why one of its best-selling systems had unexpectedly become unreliable. With key information systems frozen up, business ground to a halt for major customers. Rather than make excuses or empty promises, EMC gave its customers the choice between a brand new EMC computer system or a similar system, made by EMC's competitor, IBM. At the height of its problems, EMC installed more of IBM's machines than its own. But the company benefited in the long run as customers realized that EMC would do almost anything to solve their problems. And once EMC solved the problems with that machine, customers trusted the company enough to begin ordering again. EMC's then-CEO said, "What that proved to me, to all of us, was that when a customer believes in you, and you go to great lengths to preserve that relationship, they'll stick with you almost no matter what. It opened our eyes to the power of customer service."[31]

2.2 ISO 9000 and 14000

ISO, pronounced *ice-o*, comes from the Greek word *isos*, meaning *equal*, *similar*, *alike*, or *identical*. **ISO 9000** is a series of five international standards, from ISO 9000 to ISO 9004, for achieving consistency in quality management and quality assurance in companies throughout the world. **ISO 14000** is a series of international standards for managing, monitoring, and minimizing an organization's harmful effects on the environment.[32] (For more on environmental quality and issues, see Section 3.5 on controlling waste and pollution in Chapter 16.) The ISO 9000 and 14000 standards were created by the International Organization for Standardization, an international agency that helps set standards for 157 countries. The purpose of this agency is to develop and publish standards that facilitate the international exchange of goods and services.[33]

The ISO 9000 standards publications, which are available from the American National Standards Institute (see the end of this section), are general and can be used for manufacturing any kind of product or delivering any kind of service. Importantly, the ISO 9000 standards don't describe how to make a better-quality car, computer, or widget. Instead, they describe how companies can extensively document (and thus standardize) the steps they take to create and improve the quality of their products. Why should companies go to the trouble to achieve ISO 9000 certification? The reason is that, increasingly, their customers want them to. In fact, studies show that customers clearly prefer to buy from companies that are ISO 9000 certified. Companies, in turn, believe that being ISO 9000 certified helps them keep customers who might otherwise switch to an ISO 9000 certified competitor.[34]

Typically, "getting" ISO 9000 means having your company certified for ISO 9000 registration by an accredited third party. ISO 9000 certification is similar to having a certified public accountant indicate that a company's financial accounts are up-to-date and accurate. Like an accountant's audit, the certification process can take months. But in this case, the certification is for quality, not accounting procedures. To become certified, a company must show that it is following its own procedures for improving production, updating design plans and specifications, keeping machinery in top condition, educating and training workers, and satisfactorily dealing with customer complaints.[35]

Once a company has been certified as ISO 9000 compliant, the accredited third party will issue an ISO 9000 certificate that the company can use in its advertising and publications. This is the quality equivalent of the Good Housekeeping Seal of Approval. Continued ISO 9000 certification is not guaranteed, however. Accredited third parties typically conduct periodic audits to make sure the company is still following quality procedures. If it is not, its certification is suspended or canceled.

It's estimated that more than half of mid-sized U.S. manufacturers have achieved ISO 9000 certification. Two-thirds of the certified companies say they wanted certification because it increases customer satisfaction. Accordingly, most advertise their ISO certification in their promotional materials and mention or even post it on their website. For example, Midmark Medical Equipment, a maker of examination tables, sterilizers, electrocardiograms, and the like, has posted its certificate at **http://www.midmark.com/iso9000.asp** and states, "Midmark is proud to have the distinction of receiving the ISO 9001 certification for quality." See the American National Standards Institute (**http://www.ansi.org**; the ISO 9000 and ISO 14000 standards publications are available here for about $600 and $100, respectively), the American Society for Quality (**http://www.asq.org**), and the International Organization for Standardization (**http://www.iso.ch**) for additional information on ISO 9000 guidelines and procedures.

ISO 9000 a series of five international standards, from ISO 9000 to ISO 9004, for achieving consistency in quality management and quality assurance in companies throughout the world

ISO 14000 a series of international standards for managing, monitoring, and minimizing an organization's harmful effects on the environment

2.3 Baldrige National Quality Award

The Baldrige National Quality Award, which is administered by the U.S. government's National Institute for Standards and Technology, is given "to recognize U.S. companies for their achievements in quality and business performance and to raise awareness about the importance of quality and performance excellence as a competitive edge."[36] Each year, up to three awards may be given in these categories: manufacturing, service, small business, education, and healthcare (the latter two categories were added in 1999). Exhibit 18.5 lists the latest Baldrige Award winners.

The cost of applying for the Baldrige Award is $5,000 for manufacturing and service companies and $2,000 for small businesses.[37] At a minimum, each company that applies receives an extensive report based on 300 hours of assessment from at least eight business and quality experts. At $6.67 an hour for small businesses and about $16.67 an hour for manufacturing and service businesses, the *Journal for Quality and Participation* called the Baldrige feedback report "the best bargain in consulting in America."[38] Arnold Weimerskirch, former chair of the Baldrige Award panel of judges and vice president of quality at Honeywell, says, "The application and review process for the Baldrige Award is the best, most cost-effective and comprehensive business health audit you can get."[39]

The application and review process for the Baldrige Award is the best, most cost-effective and comprehensive business health audit you can get.

ARNOLD WEIMERSKIRCH, FORMER CHAIR, BALDRIGE AWARD PANEL OF JUDGES, AND VICE PRESIDENT OF QUALITY, HONEYWELL

The criteria for the Baldrige Award are different for business, education, and health-care organizations. As shown in Exhibit 18.6, businesses that apply for the Baldrige Award are judged on a 1,000-point scale based on seven criteria: leadership; strategic planning; customer and market focus; measurement, analysis, and knowledge management; workforce focus; process management; and results.[40] With 450 out of 1,000 points, "results" are clearly the most important. In other words, in addition to the six other criteria, companies must show that they have achieved superior quality when it comes to products and services, customers, financial performance and market share, treatment of employees, organizational effectiveness, and leadership and social responsibility. This emphasis on "results" is what differentiates the Baldrige Award from the ISO 9000 standards. The Baldrige Award indicates the

Exhibit 18.5

Latest Baldrige National Quality Award Recipients

Sector	2005	2006
Manufacturing	Sunny Fresh Foods, Inc.	——
Education	Jenks Public Schools	——
	Richland College	
Health care	Bronson Methodist Hospital	North Mississippi Medical Center
Service	DynMcDermott Petroleum Operations Co.	Premier, Inc.
Small business	Park Place Lexus	MESA Products, Inc.

Source: "1988–2006 Award Recipients' Contacts and Profiles," National Institute of Standards and Technology, http://www.quality.nist.gov/Contacts_Profiles.htm, 7 April 2007.

2007 Categories and Items	Point Values
1 **Leadership**	**120**
1.1 Senior Leadership	70
1.2 Governance and Social Responsibilities	50
2 **Strategic Planning**	**85**
2.1 Strategy Development	40
2.2 Strategy Deployment	45
3 **Customer and Market Focus**	**85**
3.1 Customer and Market Knowledge	40
3.2 Customer Relationships and Satisfaction	45
4 **Measurement, Analysis, and Knowledge Management**	**90**
4.1 Measurement, Analysis, and Improvement of Organizational Performance	45
4.2 Management of Information, Information Technology, and Knowledge	45
5 **Workforce Focus**	**85**
5.1 Workforce Engagement	45
5.2 Workforce Environment	40
6 **Process Management**	**85**
6.1 Work Systems Design	35
6.2 Work Process Management and Improvement	50
7 **Results**	**450**
7.1 Product and Service Outcomes	100
7.2 Customer-Focused Outcomes	70
7.3 Financial and Market Outcomes	70
7.4 Workforce-Focused Outcomes	70
7.5 Process Effectiveness Outcomes	70
7.6 Leadership Outcomes	70
TOTAL POINTS	**1,000**

Source: "Criteria for Performance Excellence," Baldrige National Quality Program 2007, available at http://www.quality.nist.gov/ PDF_files/2007_Business_Nonprofit_Criteria.pdf, 7 April 2007.

Exhibit 18.6

Criteria for the Baldrige National Quality Award

"WHAT'S NEW" COMPANY

extent to which companies have actually achieved world-class quality. The ISO 9000 standards simply indicate whether a company is following the management system it put in place to improve quality. In fact, ISO 9000 certification covers less than 10 percent of the requirements for the Baldrige Award.[41]

Why should companies go to the trouble of applying for the Baldrige Award? Earnest Deavenport, CEO of *EASTMAN CHEMICAL*, explains, "Eastman, like other Baldrige Award winners, didn't apply the concepts of total quality management to win an award. We did it to win customers. We did it to grow. We did it to prosper and to remain competitive in a world marketplace."[42] Furthermore, the companies that have won the Baldrige Award have achieved superior financial returns. Since 1988, an investment in Baldrige Award winners would have outperformed the Standard & Poor's 500 stock index 80 percent of the time.[43] For additional information about the Baldrige Award, see the National Institute of Standards and Technology website at **http://www.quality.nist.gov.**

2.4 Total Quality Management

Total quality management (TQM) is an integrated organization-wide strategy for improving product and service quality.[44] TQM is not a specific tool or technique. Rather, TQM is a philosophy or overall approach to management that is characterized by three principles: customer focus and satisfaction, continuous improvement, and teamwork.[45]

Contrary to most economists, accountants, and financiers who argue that companies exist to earn profits for shareholders, TQM suggests that customer focus and customer satisfaction should be a company's primary goals. **Customer focus** means that the entire organization, from top to bottom, should be focused on meeting customers' needs. The result of that customer focus should be **customer satisfaction**, which occurs when the company's products or services meet or exceed customers' expectations. At companies where TQM is taken seriously, such as ENTERPRISE RENT-A-CAR, paychecks and promotions depend on keeping customers satisfied.[46] For example, Enterprise Rent-a-Car measures customer satisfaction with a detailed survey called the Enterprise Service Quality index. Enterprise not only ranks each branch office by operating profits and customer satisfaction, but it also makes promotions to higher-paying jobs contingent on above-average customer satisfaction scores. According to Andy Taylor, Enterprise's CEO, "Once we showed we were serious—a couple of star performers who had achieved good growth and profit numbers but had generated below-average satisfaction scores were passed over for promotions—all doubt about the importance of the scores vanished."[47] Not surprisingly, this emphasis on quality increased the number of completely satisfied Enterprise Rent-a-Car customers from the high 60 percent range to the high 70 percent range in just five years. As a result, Enterprise customers are three times more likely to rent an Enterprise car again than are customers of other car rental companies.

Continuous improvement is an ongoing commitment to increase product and service quality by constantly assessing and improving the processes and procedures used to create those products and services. How do companies know whether they're achieving continuous improvement? Besides higher customer satisfaction, continuous improvement is usually associated with a reduction in variation. **Variation** is a deviation in the form, condition, or appearance of a product from the quality standard for that product. The less a product varies from the quality standard, or the more consistently a company's products meet a quality standard, the higher the quality. At FREUDENBERG-NOK, a manufacturer of seals and gaskets for the automotive industry, continuous improvement means shooting for a goal of "Six Sigma" quality, meaning just 3.4 defective or nonstandard parts per million (PPM). Achieving this goal would eliminate almost all product variation. In a recent year, Freudenberg-NOK made over 200 million seals and gaskets with a defect rate of 9 PPM.[48] As Exhibit 18.7 shows, this almost puts Freudenberg-NOK at Six Sigma, or 3.4 defective PPM. Furthermore, this represents a significant improvement from seven years ago when Freudenberg-NOK was averaging 650 defective PPM. General manager Gary VanWambeke says, "The whole goal is variation reduction," so Freudenberg-NOK expects the quality of its products to continue to improve.[49]

total quality management (TQM) an integrated, principle-based, organization-wide strategy for improving product and service quality

customer focus an organizational goal to concentrate on meeting customers' needs at all levels of the organization

customer satisfaction an organizational goal to provide products or services that meet or exceed customers' expectations

continuous improvement an organization's ongoing commitment to constantly assess and improve the processes and procedures used to create products and services

variation a deviation in the form, condition, or appearance of a product from the quality standard for that product

Exhibit 18.7
Number of Defects per Million with Six Sigma Quality

Defects per Million Parts

Reduction in variation is typically associated with even (and higher) quality. The pinnacle is achieving only 3.4 nonconforming parts per million which indicates attainment of Six Sigma.

© IMAGE100/JUPITER IMAGES

The third principle of TQM is teamwork. **Teamwork** means collaboration between managers and nonmanagers, across business functions, and between the company and its customers and suppliers. In short, quality improves when everyone in the company is given the incentive to work together and the responsibility and authority to make improvements and solve problems. At Valassis, a printing company long famous for its use of teams, management turned to employees for additional suggestions when business fell during a recession. Teams offered so many ideas to cut costs and raise quality that the company was able to avoid layoffs.[50]

Together, customer focus and satisfaction, continuous improvement, and teamwork mutually reinforce each other to improve quality throughout a company. Customer-focused continuous improvement is necessary to increase customer satisfaction. At the same time, continuous improvement depends on teamwork from different functional and hierarchical parts of the company.

Review 2: Quality

Quality can mean a product or service free of deficiencies or the characteristics of a product or service that satisfy customer needs. Quality products usually possess three characteristics: reliability, serviceability, and durability. Quality service means reliability, tangibles, responsiveness, assurance, and empathy. ISO 9000 is a series of five international standards for achieving consistency in quality management and quality assurance, while ISO 14000 is a set of standards for minimizing an organization's harmful effects on the environment. The ISO 9000 standards can be used for any product or service because they ensure that companies carefully document the steps they take to create and improve quality. ISO 9000 certification is awarded following a quality audit from an accredited third party. The Baldrige National Quality Award recognizes U.S. companies for their achievements in quality and business performance. Each year, up to three Baldrige Awards may be given for manufacturing, service, small business, education, and health care. Companies that apply for the Baldrige Award are judged on a 1,000-point scale based on leadership; strategic planning; customer and market focus; measurement, analysis, and knowledge management; workforce focus; process management; and results. Total quality management (TQM) is an integrated organization-wide strategy for improving product and service quality. TQM is based on three mutually reinforcing principles: customer focus and satisfaction, continuous improvement, and teamwork.

MANAGING OPERATIONS

At the start of this chapter, you learned that operations management means managing the daily production of goods and services. Then you learned that to manage production, you must oversee the factors that affect productivity and quality. In this half of the chapter, you will learn about managing operations in service and manufacturing businesses. The chapter ends with a discussion of inventory management, a key factor in a company's profitability.

teamwork collaboration between managers and nonmanagers, across business functions, and between companies, customers, and suppliers

After reading the next three sections, you should be able to

> 3 explain the essentials of managing a service business.

> 4 describe the different kinds of manufacturing operations.

> 5 explain why and how companies should manage inventory levels.

3 Service Operations

Imagine that your trusty VCR breaks down as you try to record your favorite TV show. (You're still saving your money for a TiVo.) You've got two choices. You can run to Wal-Mart and spend $45 to $75 to purchase a new VCR, or you can spend about the same amount (you hope) to have it fixed at a repair shop. Either way you end up with the same thing, a working VCR. However, the first choice, getting a new VCR, involves buying a physical product (a "good"), while the second, dealing with a repair shop, involves buying a service.

Services differ from goods in several ways. First, goods are produced or made, but services are performed. In other words, services are almost always labor-intensive: Someone typically has to perform the service for you. A repair shop could give you the parts needed to repair your old VCR, but without the technician to perform the repairs, you're still going to have a broken VCR. Second, goods are tangible, but services are intangible. You can touch and see that new VCR, but you can't touch or see the service provided by the technician who fixed your old VCR. All you can "see"

is that the VCR works. Third, services are perishable and unstorable. If you don't use them when they're available, they're wasted. For example, if your VCR repair shop is backlogged on repair jobs, then you'll just have to wait until next week to get your VCR repaired. You can't store an unused service and use it when you like. By contrast, you can purchase a good, such as motor oil, and store it until you're ready to use it. Finally, services account for 59.1 percent of gross national product whereas manufacturing accounts for only 30.9 percent. [51] So any review of operations management would be incomplete without an examination of how to manage service operations.

© IMAGE IDEAS/JUPITER IMAGES

Because services are different from goods, managing a service operation is different from managing a manufacturing or production operation. Let's look at **3.1 the service-profit chain** *and* **3.2 service recovery and empowerment**.

3.1 The Service-Profit Chain

One of the key assumptions in the service business is that success depends on how well employees, that is, service providers, deliver their services to customers. However, the concept of the service-profit chain, depicted in Exhibit 18.8, suggests that in service businesses, success begins with how well management treats service employees. [52]

The first step in the service-profit chain is *internal service quality*, meaning the quality of treatment that employees receive from a company's internal service providers, such as management, payroll and benefits, human resources, and so forth. For example, *SOUTHWEST AIRLINES*, which has the cheapest fares in the airline industry,

"WHAT'S NEW" COMPANY

Sources: R. Hallowell, L. A. Schlesinger, & J. Zornitsky, "Internal Service Quality, Customer and Job Satisfaction: Linkages and Implications for Management," *Human Resource Planning* 19 (1996): 20–31; J. L. Heskett, T. O. Jones, G. W. Loveman, W. E. Sasser, Jr., & L. A. Schlesinger, "Putting the Service-Profit Chain to Work," *Harvard Business Review*, March–April 1994, 164–174.

Exhibit 18.8

Service-Profit Chain

Exhibit 18.9

Components of Internal Service Quality

Policies and Procedures	Do policies and procedures facilitate serving customers?
Tools	Has the organization provided service employees the tools they need to serve customers?
Effective Training	Is effective, useful, job-specific training made available in a timely fashion?
Rewards and Recognition	Are individuals rewarded and/or recognized for good performance?
Communication	Does necessary communication occur both vertically and horizontally throughout the organization?
Management Support	Does management aid (versus hinder) employees' ability to serve customers?
Goal Alignment	Are the goals of senior management aligned with the goals of frontline service employees?
Teamwork	Do individuals and departments engage in teamwork when necessary?

Source: R. Hallowell, L. A. Schlesinger, & J. Zornitsky, "Internal Service Quality, Customer and Job Satisfaction: Linkages and Implications for Management," *Human Resource Planning* 19 (1996):20–31.

is legendary for its excellent treatment of employees and, to the surprise of many, its great customer service. Southwest's chairman Herb Kelleher says, "In the old days, my mother told me that in business school they'd say, 'This is a real conundrum: Who comes first, your employees, your shareholders, or your customers?' My mother taught me that your employees come first. If you treat them well, then they treat the customers well, and that means your customers come back and your shareholders are happy."[53]

Exhibit 18.9 defines the elements that constitute good internal service quality. For employees to do a good job serving customers, management must implement policies and procedures that support good customer service; provide workers the tools and training they need to do their jobs; reward, recognize, and support good customer service; facilitate communication; and encourage people and departments to work together as teams to accomplish company goals with respect to internal service quality and customer service. For example, at **CVS**, a large drugstore chain, the first step was to reward good customer service. CEO Tom Ryan says, "My bonus, the store manager's bonus, the assistant manager's bonus, the guys in information systems . . . a significant amount is based on customer service. We are 100 percent focused on it, and we are passionate about it." As the second step, CVS developed a special monthly scorecard to measure and reward internal service quality for 19 different areas in the company. Executive vice president Deborah Ellinger explains, "The [internal] service ethic is something that we think is important throughout the company. We can't expect our stores to be good at [customer] service if we don't provide them with good [internal] service."[54] Since CVS instituted the monthly scorecard, internal service quality ratings are up by 30 percent.[55]

As depicted in Exhibit 18.8, good internal service leads to employee satisfaction and service capability. *Employee satisfaction* occurs when companies treat employees in a way that meets or exceeds their expectations. In other words, the better employees are treated, the more satisfied they are, and the more likely they are to give high-value service that satisfies customers.

Service capability is an employee's perception of his or

her ability to serve customers well. When an organization serves its employees in ways that help them to do their jobs well, employees, in turn, are more likely to believe that they can and ought to provide high-value service to customers. Again, Southwest Airlines not only treats its employees well, but also takes a number of direct steps to strengthen their service capability. Chairman Herb Kelleher says, "I can't anticipate all of the situations that will arise at the stations [airport terminals] across our system. So what we tell our people is, 'Hey, we can't anticipate all of these things; *you* handle them the best way possible. *You* make a judgment and use *your* discretion; we trust you'll do the right thing. If we think you've done something erroneous, we'll let you know—without criticism, without backbiting.'"[56]

Finally, according to the service-profit chain shown in Exhibit 18.8, *high-value service* leads to *customer satisfaction* and *customer loyalty*, which, in turn, lead to *long-term profits and growth*. What's the link between customer satisfaction and loyalty and profits? To start, the average business keeps only 70 to 90 percent of its existing customers each year. No big deal, you say? Just replace leaving customers with new customers. Well, there's one significant problem with that solution. It costs 5 times as much to find a new customer as it does to keep an existing customer. Also, new customers typically buy only 20 percent as much as established customers. In fact, keeping existing customers is so cost-effective that most businesses could double their profits by simply keeping 5 percent more customers per year![57]

One service company that understands the relationship between high-value service, customer loyalty, and profits is **USAA**, a Texas-based finance/insurance company. USAA sends booklets on how to save for a college education to its customers who have young children. When its customers near the age of 50, the company contacts them about retirement and estate planning. And when USAA issues credit cards to college students, it takes the time to teach them how to manage their credit and avoid excessive credit card debt. Says USAA vice president Phyllis Stahle, "We build loyalty by convincing [customers] we're loyal to them."[58] Indeed, USAA has a 97 percent customer retention rate!

3.2 Service Recovery and Empowerment

When mistakes are made, when problems occur, and when customers become dissatisfied with the service they've received, service businesses must switch from the process of service delivery to the process of **service recovery**, that is, restoring customer satisfaction to strongly dissatisfied customers.[59] Sometimes, service recovery requires service employees to not only fix whatever mistake was made, but also perform heroic service acts that delight highly dissatisfied customers by far surpassing their expectations of fair treatment. When accountant Tom Taylor checked into his room at a **HAMPTON INN** in Greenville, South Carolina, he wasn't happy. The company website had given him incorrect directions. The lights in his room weren't plugged in. The shower controls were backwards—"hot" was cold and "cold" was hot. And the air-conditioning was malfunctioning, so his room was freezing cold. When he complained, the employee at the front desk immediately offered him two free nights of lodging. Taylor was delighted by the offer, but since he thought it was excessive, he took just one free night.[60]

Unfortunately, when mistakes occur, service employees often don't have the discretion to resolve customer complaints. Customers who want service employees to correct or make up for poor service are frequently told, "I'm not allowed to do that," "I'm just following company rules," or "I'm sorry, only managers are allowed to make changes of any kind." In other words, company rules prevent them from engaging in acts of service recovery meant to turn dissatisfied customers back into

service recovery restoring customer satisfaction to strongly dissatisfied customers

doing the right thing

Protect Your Frontline Staff: The Customer Isn't Always Right

In 1909, Harry Gordon Selfridge, an American who founded London's famous Selfridge's department store, coined the phrase "The customer is always right." Though managers and employees should do what they can to provide great service and make up for mistakes with great service recovery, the customer isn't always right. Companies should fire customers who use foul language, make threats against employees or other customers, lie, demand unethical or illegal service, try to bully frontline employees into granting special favors, or are just generally belligerent. Management consultant John Curtis says, "If you don't [fire these customers], you're telling your employees and your other customers that you care more about money than the safety of the people in the business." So, do the right thing. Protect your frontline staff by telling bad customers that you won't tolerate these kinds of behavior. Ask them to leave. Close their accounts. Inform them that they'll need to go elsewhere.[61]

satisfied customers. The result is frustration for customers and service employees and lost customers for the company.

Now, however, many companies are empowering their service employees.[62] In Chapter 9, you learned that *empowering workers* means permanently passing decision-making authority and responsibility from managers to workers. With respect to service recovery, empowering workers means giving service employees the authority and responsibility to make decisions that immediately solve customer problems.[63] At Hampton Inn, all employees are empowered to solve customer problems. Senior vice president Phil Cordell says, "You don't have to call an 800 number. Just mention it at the front desk or to any employee—a housekeeper, maintenance person or breakfast hostess—and, on the spot, your stay is free."[64]

In short, the purpose of empowering service employees is zero customer defections, that is, to turn dissatisfied customers back into satisfied customers who continue to do business with the company.

Empowering service workers does entail some costs, although they are usually less than the company's savings from retaining customers. For example, over a typical year, Hampton Inn will give back 0.5 percent of its room rental charges to dissatisfied customers. But according to Cordell, service recovery pays off because every dollar refunded to disgruntled customers results in a $7 payoff as those formerly dissatisfied customers return to Hampton Inn or recommend Hampton Inn to their friends.[65] Exhibit 18.10 describes some costs and benefits of empowering service workers to act in ways that they believe will accomplish service recovery.

Review 3: Service Operations

Services are different from goods. Goods are produced, tangible, and storable. Services are performed, intangible, and perishable. Likewise, managing service operations is different from managing production operations. The service-profit chain indicates that success begins with internal service quality, meaning how well management treats service employees. Internal service quality leads to employee satisfaction and service capability, which, in turn, lead to high-value service to customers, customer satisfaction, customer loyalty, and long-term profits and growth. Keeping existing customers is far more cost-effective than finding new ones. Consequently, to prevent disgruntled customers from leaving, some companies are empowering service employees to perform service recovery—restoring customer satisfaction to strongly dissatisfied customers—by giving them the authority and responsibility to immediately solve customer problems. The hope is that empowered service recovery will prevent customer defections.

4 Manufacturing Operations

*DaimlerChrysler makes cars; Dell makes computers. Shell produces gasoline; Sherwin-Williams makes paint. Boeing makes jet planes; Budweiser makes beer. Maxtor makes hard drives; Maytag makes appliances. The manufacturing operations of these companies all produce physical goods. But not all manufacturing operations, especially these, are the same. Let's learn how various manufacturing operations differ in terms of **4.1 the amount of processing that is done to produce and assemble a product** and **4.2 the flexibility to change the number, kind, and characteristics of products that are produced.***

4.1 Amount of Processing in Manufacturing Operations

As Exhibit 18.11 shows, manufacturing operations can be classified according to the amount of processing or assembly that occurs after a customer order is received. The highest degree of processing occurs in **make-to-order operations.** A make-to-order operation does not start processing or assembling products until it receives a customer order. In fact, some make-to-order operations may not even order parts until a customer order is received. Not surprisingly, make-to-order operations produce or assemble highly specialized or customized products for customers.

For example, Dell has one of the most advanced make-to-order operations in the computer business. Dell has no finished goods inventory—it does not build a computer until someone buys it. Because Dell doesn't order parts from suppliers until machines are purchased, its computers always have the latest, most advanced components. No one who buys a Dell computer gets stuck with old technology. Also, because prices of computer components tend to fall, Dell's make-to-order operation can pass on price cuts to customers. Plus, Dell can customize all of its orders, big and small. So whether you're ordering 5,000 personal computers for your company or just one personal computer for your home, Dell doesn't make the computers until you order them.

COSTS
1. Finding service workers who are capable of solving problems and dealing with upset customers increases selection costs.
2. Training service workers to solve different kinds of problems entails increased costs.
3. Higher wages are needed to attract and keep talented service workers.
4. A focus on service recovery may lead to less emphasis on service reliability, doing it right the first time. Ultimately, this could lead to slower delivery of services.
5. In their quest to please customers, empowered service workers may cost the company money by being too eager to provide "giveaways" to make up for poor or slow service.
6. Empowered service workers may unintentionally treat customers unfairly by occasionally being overly generous to make up for poor or slow service.

BENEFITS
1. Responses to customer complaints and problems are quicker.
2. Employees feel better about their jobs and themselves.
3. Employee interaction with customers will be warm and enthusiastic.
4. Employees are more likely to offer ideas for improving service or preventing problems.
5. Empowered employees who provide service recovery lead to great word-of-mouth advertising and customer retention.
6. Satisfied employees who take good care of customers are more likely to stay with the company.

Sources: D. E. Bowen & E. E. Lawler III, "The Empowerment of Service Workers: What, Why, How, and When," *Sloan Management Review* 33 (Spring 1992): 31–39; S. Kundu & J. Vora, "Creating a Talented Workforce for Delivering Service Quality," *Human Resource Planning* 27 (1 January 2004): 40.

Exhibit 18.10

Costs and Benefits of Empowering Service Workers for Service Recovery

make-to-order operation a manufacturing operation that does not start processing or assembling products until a customer order is received

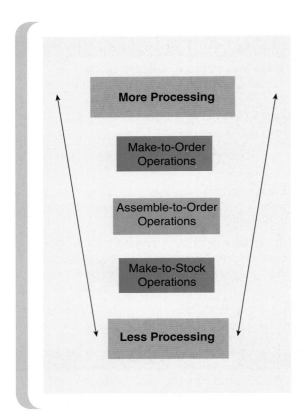

Exhibit 18.11

Processing in Manufacturing Operations

A moderate degree of processing occurs in **assemble-to-order operations**. A company using an assemble-to-order operation divides its manufacturing or assembly process into separate parts or modules. The company orders parts and assembles modules ahead of customer orders. Then, based on actual customer orders or on research forecasting what customers will want, those modules are combined to create semicustomized products. For example, when a customer orders a new car, General Motors may have already ordered the basic parts or modules it needs from suppliers. In other words, based on sales forecasts, GM may already have ordered enough tires, air-conditioning compressors, brake systems, and seats from suppliers to accommodate nearly all customer orders on a particular day. Special orders from customers and car dealers are then used to determine the final assembly checklist for particular cars as they move down the assembly line.

The lowest degree of processing occurs in **make-to-stock operations** (also called build-to-stock). Because the products are standardized, meaning each product is exactly the same as the next, a company using a make-to-stock operation starts ordering parts and assembling finished products before receiving customer orders. Customers then purchase these standardized products, such as Rubbermaid storage containers, microwave ovens, and vacuum cleaners, at retail stores or directly from the manufacturer. Because parts are ordered and products are assembled before customers order the products, make-to-stock operations are highly dependent on the accuracy of sales forecasts. If sales forecasts are incorrect, make-to-stock operations may end up building too many or too few products, or they may make products with the wrong features or without the features that customers want.

These disadvantages are leading many companies to move from make-to-stock to build-to-order systems. Mark Simons, a vice president at Toshiba, says, "Toshiba is expanding beyond make-to-stock systems and offering a quick and easy way to customize a notebook to fit the individual needs of our customers. We've listened to our customers' feedback and are answering their call to have direct access to Toshiba mobile technology on various levels and at all times."[66]

4.2 Flexibility of Manufacturing Operations

A second way to categorize manufacturing operations is by **manufacturing flexibility**, meaning the degree to which manufacturing operations can easily and quickly change the number, kind, and characteristics of products they produce. Flexibility allows companies to respond quickly to changes in the marketplace (that is, respond to competitors and customers) and to reduce the lead time between ordering and final delivery of products. There is often a tradeoff between flexibility and cost, however, with the most flexible manufacturing operations frequently having higher costs per unit and the least flexible operations having lower costs per unit.[67] Exhibit 18.12 shows different types of manufacturing operations arranged in order from the least flexible to the most flexible: continuous-flow production, line-flow production, batch production, job shops, and project manufacturing.

Most production processes generate finished products at a discrete rate. A product is completed, and then, perhaps a few seconds, minutes, or hours later, another is completed, and so on. For instance, if you stood at the end of an automobile assembly line, nothing much would seem to be happening for 55 seconds of every minute. In that last

assemble-to-order operation a manufacturing operation that divides manufacturing processes into separate parts or modules that are combined to create semicustomized products

make-to-stock operation a manufacturing operation that orders parts and assembles standardized products before receiving customer orders

manufacturing flexibility the degree to which manufacturing operations can easily and quickly change the number, kind, and characteristics of products they produce

5 seconds, however, a new car would be started and driven off the assembly line, ready for its new owner. By contrast, in **continuous-flow production**, products are produced continuously, rather than at a discrete rate. Like a water hose that is never turned off and just keeps on flowing, production of the final product never stops. Liquid chemicals and petroleum products are examples of continuous-flow production. If you're still struggling with this concept, think of Play-Doh. Continuous-flow production is similar to squeezing Play-Doh into a toy press and watching the various shapes ooze out of the Play-Doh "machine." With continuous-flow production, the Play-Doh machine would never stop oozing or producing rectangle- or triangle-shaped Play-Doh. Because of their complexity, continuous-flow production processes are the most standardized and least flexible manufacturing operations.

Line-flow production processes are preestablished, occur in a serial or linear manner, and are dedicated to making one type of product. In this way, the 10 different steps required to make product X can be completed in a separate manufacturing process (with separate machines, parts, treatments, locations, and workers) from the 12 different steps required to make product Y. Line-flow production processes are inflexible because they are typically dedicated to manufacturing one kind of product. For example, nearly every city has a local bottling plant for soft drinks or beer. The processes or steps in bottling plants are serial, meaning they must occur in a particular order. For example, after empty bottles are sterilized, they are filled with soft drinks or beer using a special dispenser that distributes the liquid down the inside walls of the bottle. This fills the bottle from the bottom up and displaces the air that was in the bottle. The bottles are then crowned or capped, checked for underfilling and missing caps, labeled, inspected a final time for fill levels and missing labels, and then placed in cases that are shrink-wrapped on pallets and put on trucks for delivery.[68]

The next most flexible manufacturing operation is **batch production**, which involves the manufacture of large batches of different products in standard lot sizes. Consequently, a worker in a batch production operation will perform the same manufacturing process on 100 copies of product X, followed by 200 copies of product Y, and then 50 copies of product Z. Furthermore, these "batches" move through each manufacturing department or process in identical order. So, if the paint department follows chemical treatment, and chemical treatment is now processing a batch of 50 copies of product Z, then the paint department's next task will be to paint 50 copies of product Z. Batch production is finding increasing use among restaurant chains. To ensure consistency in the taste and quality of their products, many restaurant chains have central kitchens, or commissaries, that produce batches of food, such as mashed potatoes, stuffing, macaroni and cheese, rice, quiche filling, and chili, in volumes ranging from 10 to 200 gallons. These batches are then delivered to the individual restaurant locations, which serve the food to customers.

Next in terms of flexibility is the job shop. **Job shops** are typically small manufacturing operations that handle special manufacturing processes or jobs. In contrast to batch production, which handles large batches of different products, job shops typically handle very small batches, some as small as one product or process per "batch." Basically, each "job" in a job shop is different, and once a job is done, the job shop moves on to a completely different job or manufacturing process for, most likely, a different customer. For example, *LEGGETT & PLATT MACHINE PRODUCTS* in Carthage, Missouri, is a job shop that makes coil springs, innerspring units, welded metal grids,

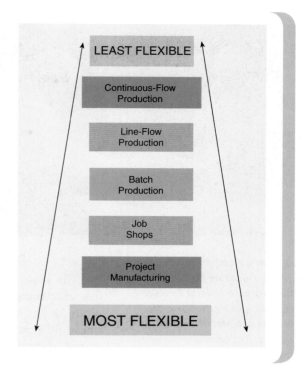

Exhibit 18.12
Flexibility of Manufacturing Operations

continuous-flow production a manufacturing operation that produces goods at a continuous, rather than a discrete, rate

line-flow production manufacturing processes that are preestablished, occur in a serial or linear manner, and are dedicated to making one type of product

batch production a manufacturing operation that produces goods in large batches in standard lot sizes

job shops manufacturing operations that handle custom orders or small batch jobs

MIKE MERGEN/ BLOOMBERG NEWS/ LANDOV

Just Born, maker of Marshmallow Peeps, uses a line-flow system that is also somewhat flexible. For example, by changing the mold in one part of the production line, the company can switch from making its hallmark Peep Chicks and Bunnies to making new shapes, like the pumpkins shown here.

"WHAT'S NEW" COMPANY

project manufacturing
manufacturing operations designed to produce large, expensive, specialized products

and various other parts for mattress manufacturers around the world. Since its inception, its 225 employees have made over 25,000 *different* parts; in other words, they have completed 25,000 different jobs for customers.[69] Another example of a job shop is **HEIL TRAILER INTERNATIONAL** in Athens, Tennessee. Heil specializes in the production of custom truck trailers that carry petroleum or dry bulk. Heil also makes intermodal trailers that can be pulled by trucks and transported by trains. Steve Slaughter, Heil's general manager, says, "Even when we get orders for multiple trailers, the trailers normally aren't the same. The shape of the tank itself doesn't really change that much. But with all the different weight laws and customer preferences, it's unusual to see two identical trailers going down the same assembly line."[70]

The most flexible manufacturing operation is project manufacturing. **Project manufacturing** is an operation designed to produce large, expensive, specialized products like custom homes; military systems such as aircraft carriers and submarines; and aerospace products such as passenger planes and the space shuttle. Project manufacturing is highly flexible because each project is usually significantly different from the one before it, even if the projects involve the same general type of product, such as a submarine. Because of each project's size, expense, and high degree of customization, project manufacturing can take an extremely long time to complete. For instance, General Dynamics uses project manufacturing when making new submarines. The U.S. Navy's Virginia class subs, which are its newest and most advanced attack submarines, are 377 feet long and able to attain speeds greater than 25 knots (28 miles per hour/46.3 kilometers per hour). Therefore, they will be significantly quieter and faster than the Los Angeles class submarines that they replace.[71] Project manufacturing is required for submarine construction because of the tremendous cost (budgeted cost of $1.6 billion each), the complexity of the subs, and the length of time it takes to complete a new submarine (six years). Because of these enormous challenges, only one new Virginia class submarine is being completed each year.

Review 4: **Manufacturing Operations**

Manufacturing operations produce physical goods. Manufacturing operations can be classified according to the amount of processing or assembly that occurs after receiving an order from customers. Make-to-order operations, in which assembly doesn't begin until products are ordered, involve the most processing. The next-highest degree of processing occurs in assemble-to-order operations, in which preassembled modules are combined after orders are received to produce semicustomized products. The least processing occurs in make-to-stock operations, in which standard parts are ordered, on the basis of sales forecasts, and assembled before orders are received.

Manufacturing operations can also be classified in terms of flexibility, the degree to which the number, kind, and characteristics of products can easily and quickly be changed. Flexibility allows companies to respond quickly to competitors and customers and to reduce order lead times, but it can also lead to higher unit costs. Manufacturing operations can be arranged in order from the least to the most flexible as follows: continuous-flow production, line-flow production, batch production, job shops, and project manufacturing.

5 Inventory

With SUVs and pickup trucks accounting for nearly 80 percent of its sales, CHRYSLER was reluctant to stop making them—even when consumer demand dried up. Unfortunately, though, the automaker built SUVs and pickups that people didn't want, and it ended up with nearly a three-month supply of inventory. In addition to what was already on dealer lots, the automaker had 50,000 vehicles sitting on random storage lots around the midwestern United States. Ultimately, Chrysler significantly reduced production for six months to sell off its unsold vehicles.[72]

Chrysler's SUV inventory was recently nearly three times that of Toyota. The costs for maintaining such a robust inventory can be quite high and, ultimately, crippling to the organization if the products being inventoried sit too long on the shelf (or the lot).

*Inventory is the amount and number of raw materials, parts, and finished products that a company has in its possession. Industry experts estimate Chrysler has more SUV inventory (82 days) than GM (77) and Ford (74) and almost three times as much as Toyota (28).[73] In this section, you will learn about **5.1 the different types of inventory**, **5.2 how to measure inventory levels, 5.3 the costs of maintaining an inventory**, and **5.4 the different systems for managing inventory**.*

5.1 Types of Inventory

Exhibit 18.13 shows the four kinds of inventory a manufacturer stores: raw materials, component parts, work-in-process, and finished goods. The flow of inventory through a manufacturing plant begins when the purchasing department buys raw materials from vendors. **Raw material inventories** are the basic inputs in the manufacturing process. For example, to begin making a car, automobile manufacturers purchase raw materials like steel, iron, aluminum, copper, rubber, and unprocessed plastic.

Next, raw materials are fabricated or processed into **component parts inventories**, meaning the basic parts used in manufacturing a product. For example, in an automobile plant, steel is fabricated or processed into a car's body panels, and steel and iron are melted and shaped into engine parts like pistons or engine blocks. Some component parts are purchased from vendors rather than fabricated in-house.

The component parts are then assembled to make unfinished **work-in-process inventories**, which are also known as partially finished goods. This process is also called *initial assembly*. For example, steel body panels are welded to each other and to the frame of the car to make a "unibody," which comprises the unpainted interior frame and exterior structure of the car. Likewise, pistons, camshafts, and other engine parts are inserted into the engine block to create a working engine.

Next, all the work-in-process inventories are assembled to create **finished goods inventories**, which are the final outputs of the manufacturing process. This process is also called *final assembly*. For a car, the engine, wheels, brake system, suspension, interior, and electrical system are assembled into a car's painted unibody to make the working automobile, which is the factory's finished product. In the last step in the process, the finished goods are sent to field warehouses, distribution centers, or wholesalers, and then to retailers for final sale to customers.

inventory the amount and number of raw materials, parts, and finished products that a company has in its possession

raw material inventories the basic inputs in a manufacturing process

component parts inventories the basic parts used in manufacturing that are fabricated from raw materials

work-in-process inventories partially finished goods consisting of assembled component parts

finished goods inventories the final outputs of manufacturing operations

5.2 Measuring Inventory

As you'll learn below, uncontrolled inventory can lead to huge costs for a manufacturing operation. Consequently, managers need good measures of inventory to prevent inventory costs from becoming too large. Three basic measures of inventory are average aggregate inventory, weeks of supply, and inventory turnover.

If you've ever worked in a retail store and had to "take inventory," you probably weren't too excited about the process of counting every item in the store and storeroom. It's an extensive task. Fortunately, "taking inventory" is somewhat easier today because of bar codes that mark items and computers that can count and track them. Nonetheless, inventories still differ from day to day. For example, an inventory count taken at the beginning of the month will likely be different from a count taken at the end of the month. Similarly, an inventory count taken on a Friday will differ from a count taken on a Monday. Because of such differences, companies often measure **average aggregate inventory**, which is the average overall inventory during a particular time period. Average aggregate inventory for a month can be determined by simply averaging the inventory counts at the end of each business day for that month. One way companies know whether they're carrying too much or too little inventory is to compare their average aggregate inventory with the industry average for aggregate inventory. For example, 72 days of inventory is the average for the automobile industry.

While the automobile industry records inventory in terms of days of supply, most other industries measure inventory in terms of *weeks of supply*, meaning the number of weeks it would take for a company to run out of its current supply of inventory. In general, there is an acceptable number of weeks of inventory for a particular kind of business. Too few weeks of inventory on hand, and a company risks a **stockout**—running out of inventory. During a recent holiday season, the busiest shopping time of the year, retail and online stores ran out of **APPLE COMPUTER**'s fast-selling iPods. Industry analyst Stephen Baker says, "Given how strong demand has been all year you would have thought [Apple] would have gotten every last one they could into stores."[74] Apple issued a statement saying, "To try to meet the high demand, we're making and shipping iPods as fast as we can. So, if one store has run out, you may find iPods in another authorized iPod reseller."[75] Nevertheless, iPods were in such short supply that the iPod mini was selling for $380 on eBay, $130 over the suggested retail price. On the other hand, a business that has too many weeks of

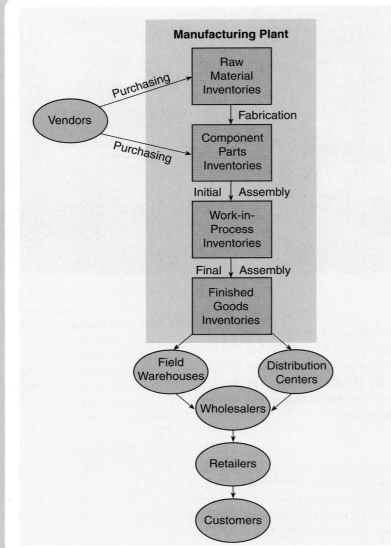

Manufacturing Plant

Exhibit 18.13

Types of Inventory

Source: R. E. Markland, S. K. Vickery, & R. A. Davis, *Operations Management*, 2nd ed. (Mason, OH: South-Western, 1998). Reprinted with permission.

average aggregate inventory average overall inventory during a particular time period

stockout the point when a company runs out of finished product inventory on hand incurs high costs (discussed below). For example, companies that make the linerboard used for corrugated cardboard boxes typically have too much inventory when they have more than six weeks' supply on hand; the right amount is about four weeks' supply.[76] Anything more than that results in excess inventory, which can be reduced only by cutting prices or temporarily stopping production.

Another common inventory measure, **inventory turnover**, is the number of times per year that a company sells or "turns over" its average inventory. For example, if a company keeps an average of 100 finished widgets in inventory each month, and it sold 1,000 widgets this year, then it "turned" its inventory 10 times this year.

In general, the higher the number of inventory "turns," the better. In practice, a high turnover means that a company can continue its daily operations with just a small amount of inventory on hand. For example, let's take two companies, A and B, which, over the course of a year, have identical inventory levels (520,000 widget parts and raw materials). If company A turns its inventories 26 times a year, it will completely replenish its inventory every two weeks and have an average inventory of 20,000 widget parts and raw materials. By contrast, if company B turns its inventories only two times a year, it will completely replenish its inventory every 26 weeks and have an average inventory of 260,000 widget parts and raw materials. So, by turning its inventory more often, company A has 92 percent less inventory on hand at any one time than company B.

Across all kinds of manufacturing plants, the average number of inventory turns is approximately eight per year, as shown in Exhibit 18.14, although the average can be higher or lower for different industries.[77] The exhibit also shows the inventory turn rates for some of the best companies in each industry (that is, the 75th percentile). For example, whereas the average auto company turns its entire inventory 13 times per year, some of the best auto companies more than double that rate, turning their inventory 27.8 times per year, or once every two weeks.[78] For an auto company, turning inventory more frequently than the industry average can cut costs by several hundred million dollars per year. Finally, it should be pointed out that even make-to-order companies like Dell turn their inventory. In theory, make-to-order companies have no inventory. In fact, they've got inventory, but you have to measure it in hours.

inventory turnover the number of times per year that a company sells or "turns over" its average inventory

Exhibit 18.14

Inventory Turn Rates across Industries

Source: D. Drickhamer, "Zeroing in on World-Class," *Industry Week*, November 2001, 36.

For example, in its factories, Dell turns its inventory 500 times a year, which means that on average it has 17 hours—that's hours and not days—of inventory on hand in its factories.[79]

5.3 Costs of Maintaining an Inventory

Maintaining an inventory incurs four kinds of costs: ordering, setup, holding, and stockout. **Ordering cost** is not the cost of the inventory itself, but the costs associated with ordering the inventory. It includes the costs of completing paperwork, manually entering data into a computer, making phone calls, getting competing bids, correcting mistakes, and simply determining when and how much new inventory should be reordered. For example, ordering costs are relatively high in the restaurant business because 80 percent of food service orders (in which restaurants reorder food supplies) are processed manually. It's estimated that the food industry could save $6.6 billion if all restaurants converted to electronic data interchange (see Chapter 17), in which purchase and ordering information from one company's computer system is automatically relayed to another company's computer system. In fact, a number of restaurants and food service trade groups have formed an interest group called Efficient Foodservice Response to encourage restaurants and food suppliers to use EDI and other methods of electronic commerce.[80]

Setup cost is the cost of changing or adjusting a machine so that it can produce a different kind of inventory.[81] For example, 3M uses the same production machinery to make several kinds of industrial tape, but it must adjust the machines whenever it switches from one kind of tape to another. There are two kinds of setup costs, downtime and lost efficiency. *Downtime* occurs whenever a machine is not being used to process inventory. So, if it takes five hours to switch a machine from processing one kind of inventory to another, then five hours of downtime have occurred. Downtime is costly because companies earn an economic return only when machines are actively turning raw materials into parts or parts into finished products. The second setup cost is *lost efficiency*. Typically, after a switchover, it takes some time to recalibrate a machine to its optimal settings. It may take several days of fine-tuning before a machine finally produces the number of high-quality parts that it is supposed to. Exhibit 18.15 illustrates the tradeoff between setup costs, meaning downtime and lost efficiency, and manufacturing flexibility, that is, the number of *different* products (or inventory) that can be processed or assembled on a particular machine. The data in Exhibit 18.15 assume that four hours of downtime and 3 percent lost efficiency occur each time a machine's setup has to be changed from one product to another. So, as shown in the exhibit, each time a machine has to be changed to handle a different kind of inventory, setup costs (downtime and lost efficiency) rise.

Holding cost, also known as *carrying* or *storage cost*, is the cost of keeping inventory until it is used or sold. Holding cost includes the cost of storage facilities, insurance to protect inventory from damage or theft, inventory taxes, the cost of obsolescence (holding inventory that is no longer useful to the company), and the opportunity cost of spending money on inventory that could have been spent elsewhere in the company. For example, it's estimated that at any one time, U.S. airlines have a total of $60 billion worth of airplane parts in stock for maintenance, repair, and overhauling their planes. The holding cost for managing, storing, and purchasing these parts is nearly $12.5 billion—or roughly one-fifth of the cost of the parts themselves.[82]

Stockout costs are the costs incurred when a company runs out of a product, as happened to Apple when it failed to have enough iPods during the holiday shopping season. There are two basic kinds of stockout costs. First, the company incurs the

ordering cost the costs associated with ordering inventory, including the cost of data entry, phone calls, obtaining bids, correcting mistakes, and determining when and how much inventory to order

setup cost the costs of downtime and lost efficiency that occur when a machine is changed or adjusted to produce a different kind of inventory

holding cost the cost of keeping inventory until it is used or sold, including storage, insurance, taxes, obsolescence, and opportunity costs

stockout costs the costs incurred when a company runs out of a product, including transaction costs to replace inventory and the loss of customers' goodwill transaction costs of over-time work, shipping, and the like in trying to quickly replace out-of-stock inventories with new inventories. The second and perhaps more damaging cost is the loss of customers' goodwill when a company cannot deliver the products that it promised. Stockouts occur more often than you might think. In the United States, the supermarket industry's average out-of-stock rate (the percentage of items that are unavailable at a given time) is 7.9 percent, according to research firm Market6. Highly promoted items have, as would be expected, a higher average

Exhibit 18.15

Tradeoff between Setup Costs and Manufacturing Flexibility

out-of-stock rate of 13.1 percent. How costly is it for stores to run out of stock? For a grocery store, research firm Market6 estimates that running out of stock on the 25 best-selling product categories reduces store revenue by an average of $200,000 per year, per store.[83] In general, retailers can increase sales 4 percent if they never run out of stock.

5.4 Managing Inventory

Inventory management has two basic goals. The first is to avoid running out of stock and thus angering and dissatisfying customers. Consequently, this goal seeks to increase inventory levels to a "safe" level that won't risk stockouts. The second is to efficiently reduce inventory levels and costs as much as possible without impairing daily operations. Thus, this goal seeks a minimum level of inventory. The following inventory management techniques—economic order quantity (EOQ), just-in-time inventory (JIT), and materials requirement planning (MRP)—are different ways of balancing these competing goals.

Economic order quantity (EOQ) is a system of formulas that helps determine how much and how often inventory should be ordered. EOQ takes into account the overall demand (D) for a product while trying to minimize ordering costs (O) and holding costs (H). The formula for EOQ is

$$EOQ = \sqrt{\frac{2DO}{4}}$$

For example, if a factory uses 40,000 gallons of paint a year (D), ordering costs (O) are $75 per order, and holding costs (H) are $4 per gallon, then the optimal quantity to order is 1,225 gallons:

$$EOQ = \sqrt{\frac{2(40,000)(75)}{4}} = 1,225$$

economic order quantity (EOQ) a system of formulas that minimizes ordering and holding costs and helps determine how much and how often inventory should be ordered

And, with 40,000 gallons of paint being used per year, the factory uses approximately 110 gallons per day:

$$\frac{40,000 \text{ gallons}}{365 \text{ days}} = 110$$

Consequently, the factory would order 1,225 new gallons of paint approximately every 11 days:

$$\frac{1,225 \text{ gallons}}{110 \text{ gallons per day}} = 11.1 \text{ days}$$

In general, EOQ formulas do a good job of letting managers know what size or amount of inventory they should reorder to minimize ordering and holding costs. However, EOQ formulas and models can become much more complex as adjustments are made for price changes, quantity discounts, setup costs, and many other factors.[84]

While EOQ formulas try to minimize holding and ordering costs, the just-in-time (JIT) approach to inventory management attempts to eliminate holding costs by reducing inventory levels to near zero. With a **just-in-time (JIT) inventory** system, component parts arrive from suppliers just as they are needed at each stage of production. By having parts arrive "just in time," the manufacturer has little inventory on hand and thus avoids the costs associated with holding inventory. For example, by combining a JIT inventory system with its make-to-order production system, Dell turns its inventory more than 500 times a year, as mentioned above. Regarding Dell's JIT inventory system, John Egan, who heads Dell's inventory fulfillment center in Austin, Texas, says "We used to measure our factory inventory in days; but now we manage it in hours. Our suppliers see demand changes every two hours. We try to achieve a perfect balance" between the parts that are needed and what's already in the factory.[85]

We used to measure our factory inventory in days; but now we manage it in hours.

JOHN EGAN, HEAD OF DELL'S INVENTORY FULFILLMENT CENTER

To have just the right amount of inventory arrive at just the right time requires a tremendous amount of coordination between manufacturing operations and suppliers. One way to promote tight coordination under JIT is close proximity. Most parts suppliers for Toyota's JIT system at its Georgetown, Kentucky, plant are located within 200 miles of the plant. Furthermore, parts are picked up from suppliers and delivered to Toyota as often as 16 times a day.[86]

A second way to promote close coordination under JIT is to have a shared information system that allows a manufacturer and its suppliers to know the quantity and kinds of parts inventory the other has in stock. Generally, factories and suppliers facilitate information sharing by using the same part numbers and names. Ford's seat supplier accomplishes this by sticking a bar code on each seat, which Ford then uses to route the seat through its factory.

Manufacturing operations and their parts suppliers can also facilitate close coordination by using the system of kanban. **Kanban**, which is Japanese for "sign," is a simple ticket-based system that indicates when it is time to reorder inventory. Suppliers attach kanban cards to batches of parts. Then, when an assembly-line worker uses the first part out of a batch, the kanban card is removed. The cards are then collected, sorted, and quickly returned to the supplier, who begins resupplying the factory with parts that match the order information on the kanban cards. Glenn

just-in-time (JIT) inventory system an inventory system in which component parts arrive from suppliers just as they are needed at each stage of production

kanban a ticket-based JIT system that indicates when to reorder inventory

Uminger, manager of production control and logistics at Toyota's Georgetown, Kentucky, plant, says, "We are placing orders for new parts as the first part is used out of a box." And, because prices and batch sizes are typically agreed to ahead of time, kanban tickets greatly reduce paperwork and ordering costs.[87]

A third method for managing inventory is **materials requirement planning (MRP)**. MRP is a production and inventory system that, from beginning to end, precisely determines the production schedule, production batch sizes, and inventories needed to complete final products. The three key parts of MRP systems are the master production schedule, the bill of materials, and inventory records. The *master production schedule* is a detailed schedule that indicates the quantity of each item to be produced, the planned delivery dates for those items, and the time by which each step of the production process must be completed in order to meet those delivery dates. Based on the quantity and kind of products set forth in the master production schedule, the *bill of materials* identifies all the necessary parts and inventory, the quantity or volume of inventory to be ordered, and the order in which the parts and inventory should be assembled. *Inventory records* indicate the kind, quantity, and location of inventory that is on hand or that has been ordered. When inventory records are combined with the bill of materials, the resulting report indicates what to buy, when to buy it, and what it will cost to order. Today, nearly all MRP systems are available in the form of powerful, flexible computer software.[88]

Which inventory management system should you use? Economic order quantity (EOQ) formulas are intended for use with **independent demand systems**, in which the level of one kind of inventory does not depend on another. For example, because inventory levels for automobile tires are unrelated to the inventory levels of women's dresses, Sears could use EOQ formulas to calculate separate optimal order quantities for dresses and tires. By contrast, JIT and MRP are used with **dependent demand systems**, in which the level of inventory depends on the number of finished units to be produced. For example, if Yamaha makes 1,000 motorcycles a day, then it will need 1,000 seats, 1,000 gas tanks, and 2,000 wheels and tires each day. So, when optimal inventory levels depend on the number of products to be produced, use a JIT or MRP management system.

Review 5: **Inventory**

There are four kinds of inventory: raw materials, component parts, work-in-process, and finished goods. Because companies incur ordering, setup, holding, and stockout costs when handling inventory, inventory costs can be enormous. To control those costs, companies measure and track inventory in three ways: average aggregate inventory, weeks of supply, and turnover. Companies meet the basic goals of inventory management (avoiding stockouts and reducing inventory without hurting daily operations) through economic order quantity (EOQ) formulas, just-in-time (JIT) inventory systems, and materials requirement planning (MRP). EOQ formulas minimize holding and ordering costs by determining how much and how often inventory should be ordered. By having parts arrive just when they are needed at each stage of production, JIT systems attempt to minimize inventory levels and holding costs. JIT systems often depend on proximity, shared information, and the system of kanban made popular by Japanese manufacturers. MRP precisely determines the production schedule, production batch sizes, and the ordering of inventories needed to complete final products. The three key parts of MRP systems are the master production schedule, the bill of materials, and inventory records. Use EOQ formulas when inventory levels are independent, and use JIT and MRP when inventory levels are dependent on the number of products to be produced.

materials requirement planning (MRP) a production and inventory system that determines the production schedule, production batch sizes, and inventory needed to complete final products

independent demand system an inventory system in which the level of one kind of inventory does not depend on another

dependent demand system an inventory system in which the level of inventory depends on the number of finished units to be produced

How to Handle Disgruntled Customers

How a company manages its customers is an important indicator of its future success. But managing customers can be as difficult as it is critical. For example, one customer may like to be greeted by an employee and immediately helped upon entering the store. Another might find this approach a bit aggressive. What is your style? If you were responsible for interacting with customers, which approach would you use? The following assessment will evaluate your perspectives on the relationship a company has with its customers. Be candid as you respond to the questions using a scale from 1 to 9 in which 1 means you strongly disagree, 5 means you are neutral, and 9 means you strongly agree (other numbers indicate varying degrees of agreement or disagreement).[89]

1. I try to bring a customer with a problem together with a product/service that helps solve that problem.
2. I keep alert for weaknesses in a customer's personality so I can use them to put pressure on them to agree with me.
3. I try to influence a customer by information rather than pressure.
4. It is necessary to stretch the truth in describing a product to a customer.
5. I decide what product/service to offer on the basis of what I can convince customers to accept, not on the basis of what will satisfy them in the long run.
6. I paint too rosy a picture of my product/service to make them sound as good as possible.
7. I try to find out what kind of products/services will be most helpful to a customer.
8. I try to sell a customer all I can convince them to buy, even if I think it is more than a wise customer would buy.
9. I begin talking about the product/service before exploring a customer's need with him or her.
10. I try to help a customer achieve their goals.
11. I try to figure out what a customer's needs are.
12. A good employee has to have the customer's best interest in mind.
13. I try to sell as much as I can rather than to satisfy a customer.
14. I try to give customers an accurate expectation of what our product/service will do for them.
15. I imply to a customer that something is beyond my control when it is not.
16. I try to achieve my goals by satisfying customers.
17. If I am not sure if our product/service is right for a customer, I will still apply pressure to get him or her to buy.
18. I answer a customer's question about product/services as correctly as I can.
19. I offer the product/service that is best suited to the customer's problem.
20. I treat a customer as a rival.
21. I spend more time trying to persuade a customer to buy than I do trying to discover his or her needs.
22. I am willing to disagree with a customer in order to help him or her make a better decision.
23. I try to get the customer to discuss their needs with me.
24. I pretend to agree with a customer to please them.

Scoring

Determine your score by entering your response to each survey item below, as follows. Total each column to derive two scores.

Customer Orientation

1. regular score _____
3. regular score _____
7. regular score _____
10. regular score _____
11. regular score _____
12. regular score _____
14. regular score _____
16. regular score _____
18. regular score _____
19. regular score _____
22. regular score _____
23. regular score _____
TOTAL = _____

Selling Orientation

2. regular score _____
4. regular score _____
5. regular score _____
6. regular score _____
8. regular score _____
9. regular score _____
13. regular score _____
15. regular score _____
17. regular score _____
20. regular score _____
21. regular score _____
24. regular score _____
TOTAL = _____

You can find the interpretation for your score at: **academic.cengage.com/management/williams**.

MANAGEMENT DECISION

Moving to a Make-to-Order Operation

You've never been so energized by a sales pitch in your entire career.[90] Consultants from a highly reputable software developer have just given a presentation to your management team on how to integrate your supply chain, which is no mean feat. Your company, Nike, sells multiple variations of 120,000 products in four sales cycles throughout the year. Anything that can help you get this process under control is welcome. The only problem with the consultants' presentation is their underlying assumption: Nike should move from a make-to-stock operation to a make-to-order operation. That is, the consultant wants Nike to begin making shoes only after a retailer sends in an order.

In the $16 billion U.S. running-shoe market, Nike commands a full 39 percent market share, much larger than that of any other athletic shoe company. Your closest competitor, Reebok, is at a significantly lower 14 percent. Nike grew to that stature by creating a supply chain for the fragmented running shoe market of the 1970s. Nike guaranteed delivery and an inflation-proof discount in return for getting orders six months in advance. Retailers went along happily because runners typically didn't care if the shoes were the latest fashion as long as they were technically advanced. Because Nike shoes functioned impeccably, they became the standard.

After over two decades of astronomical growth, however, Nike is suffering from its own fragmentation.

The company has 27 order management systems around the globe and uses tens of millions of product numbers (think number of models times available sizes). Even though the sales cycle is three months, the design and production cycle is nine months, so to meet sales deadlines, the company is building and holding a small fortune in inventory (think number of models times available sizes times cost per pair). Furthermore, today's customers want style, not just technically sophisticated shoes, and style changes a lot faster now than it did in the 1970s. Nike's extensive inventory, which was previously a strength, is becoming a weakness, as the risks of finished inventories becoming outdated are increasing sharply.

That's why you welcomed the consultants' initial recommendations to switch to make-to-order system. But you don't want to rush headlong into such a major change based only on the recommendation of outside consultants. After all, they're trying to sell you $400 million in software, and you have an $11 billion business on the line.

Questions

1. What issues do you need to consider as you make this decision? If you are overwhelmed thinking of a mammoth company like Nike, keep in mind that much smaller companies wrestle with this basic operations dilemma as well.

2. Do you invest in the $400 million software and commit to changing your manufacturing process from a make-to-stock to a make-to-order operation? (At this point, you are only considering make-to-order processing for retailers. That is, Nike wouldn't begin making shoes until a retailer, like FootLocker, actually ordered them.) Explain your rationale.

3. How would changing to make-to-order processing for retailers affect how Nike manages its inventory? Address all aspects of managing inventory.

4. The more you reflect on the sales proposal, the more you wonder why Nike would stop at make-to-order processing for retailers. Why not go all the way and do a make-to-order system for the consumer? Is that even feasible? Explain.

5. Think about the price of athletic shoes. If Nike began manufacturing customized products for consumers, how would you expect the changes in manufacturing operations, manufacturing flexibility, and inventory to affect the cost and final price of a pair of Nikes? Why?

MANAGEMENT TEAM DECISION

Recovery Plan

As you read in Chapter 5, crisis management planning is an important component of business planning and corporate communication.[91] Typically, when you hear "crisis management," you think of a company responding to catastrophic publicity, but companies also need to think about managing smaller negative encounters because those encounters play a large role in customer retention. The retention rate for customers whose complaints or problems are resolved satisfactorily is 70 percent; when complaints are resolved quickly as well—typically on the spot—the retention rate soars to 95 percent. But when complaints are not resolved to the customer's satisfaction, customer retention falls to 46 percent. And research shows that for major purchases (defined as being over $100), customers whose complaints are unresolved stay with the company only 19 percent of the time. So, companies should have a plan for responding to customers' complaints and problems. Putting service recovery plans in place enables companies to respond quickly, the biggest factor in reversing the damage from negative customer experiences.

In the spa industry, customer service and satisfaction are paramount. Not only do customers have high expectations for spa and salon services such as massage, skin treatments, nail treatments, and hair coloring and cutting, but spa service tabs can quickly surpass that $100 threshold defining major purchases. And what would upset a customer more than a horrendous haircut, botched fingernails, or losing half an eyebrow during a wax!

For this exercise, assemble four to five students to act as the management team for a local salon and day spa that is getting ready to expand into several new neighborhoods by adding four local salons. Your salon has always had a high reputation for service, but as you expand, your experienced staff will be spread thin. In the next month, your team plans to hire and train 25 new cosmetologists and estheticians (skin-care providers). To ensure that the new stores are successful, your team has decided to map out very clear service recovery procedures. After all, during the training periods and the first few months the new stores are open, mistakes are bound to happen. How you respond to them will mean the difference between a successful expansion and possible bankruptcy.

Questions

1. As a team, brainstorm a list of service failures that could occur in a salon and day spa. (The examples of a bad haircut, damaged nails, and losing half an eyebrow during a wax job were mentioned above, but there are many more possibilities.) Then identify ways that you can resolve each problem on the list quickly and to the customer's satisfaction.

2. There are bound to be situations that you haven't planned for. How will you instruct your employees to handle unanticipated problems?

3. How can a complaint-response system be considered part of delivering quality service?

4. What kind of metric(s) can you create to measure the quality of your service delivery? Manufacturing companies typically measure things like on-time delivery, defects per million, production rate (how many pieces per hour), and so forth. What can a spa measure to keep its service operation in control?

Success in service and manufacturing operations requires managers to maintain high levels of both productivity and quality. High productivity ensures that the company is cost competitive with rivals; and high quality helps the company to attract customers and grow revenues and profits. Because productivity and quality are basic drivers of company success, managers must be adept at measuring and improving both. This exercise will give you some practice in developing productivity and quality measures.

Step 1: Your professor will organize your class into small groups of three or four students.

Scenario: Your group is a management team working to improve productivity and quality in a pharmaceutical company. You have been assigned two units of this company as the focus of your improvement efforts. The first is a pill-packaging unit, and the second is a research and development (R&D) laboratory.

Workers in the packaging unit are responsible for checking to ensure that the pills in the box match the packaging and labeling; placing the appropriate labels and packaging information on each box; and then certifying with a stamp that the box of pills is ready for shipping to wholesale customers, for example, chains like Walgreens and Costco. Mistakes in packaging, if undetected by pharmacists, could have serious, even fatal, outcomes. These manufacturing workers are skilled and highly trained. If they detect a problem, they have the authority to halt production.

Workers in the R&D unit are responsible for developing new drugs and for testing their effectiveness and safety. The company relies for its success upon a steady pipeline of promising new products. At the same time, some basic research (for example, study of progression of a particular type of cancer) is necessary in order to develop new drugs. These workers are mostly Ph.D.s and highly skilled laboratory technicians.

Step 2: Develop metrics. Working as a team, develop some productivity and quality measures for (a) packaging unit workers and (b) R&D unit workers. Be sure to consider whether productivity and quality should be measured on an individual or unit basis, and why.

Step 3: Analyze the metrics. Critically examine your team's measures for each unit. What unintended consequences might develop as workers in each unit strive to improve on the measures you have designed? Are you more confident of your measures in one unit versus the other? Why or why not?

Step 4: Debrief as a class. What are some of the challenges of measuring productivity and quality? Are these challenges greater for particular types of work? Which level of measurement and accountability—individual or unit—is most likely to generate positive results? Why? What impact do productivity and quality systems of measurement and improvement have on workers? How can firms ensure productivity and quality without overloading workers and/or fostering unhealthy levels of stress?

Take a Factory Tour

Imagine that you arrive back at your dorm room one afternoon to find your roommate watching a *Mister Rogers* rerun. When asked why, your roommate replies, "Management homework." That may not be as crazy as it sounds. The late Fred Rogers, host of PBS's *Mr. Rogers' Neighborhood*, may well hold the record for factory tours. During his long career, he broadcast footage to millions of children showing how Cheerios,

plastic drinking straws, raincoats, pasta, blue jeans, spoons, and a host of other products are made. He was even at Crayola when the one-billionth crayon rolled off the production line. (He also broadcast footage of how Crayola crayons are made and packaged.)

Today, John Ratzenberger (known for his role as Cliff Clavin on *Cheers* and as a regular voice in Pixar animated feature movies (most recently Mustafa the waiter in *Ratatouille*), hosts a cable television program titled *Made in America* that features nothing but factory tours around the United States. The Food Network also broadcasts a program that describes how all kinds of food products are manufactured. Beyond the world of television, however, each year thousands of people visit corporate facilities like these:

- The Boeing Everett Tour Center outside Seattle introduces visitors to how Boeing makes its 747, 767, and 777 passenger jets.

- Steinway & Sons in Queens, New York, offers a two-and-a-half-hour tour that is like a master class. Each Steinway piano takes about a year to build, so you will be able to see pianos at every stage of the production process.

- Ben & Jerry's in Waterbury, Vermont, offers tours accompanied with a scoop of whatever flavor ice cream was made that day.

- Tabasco Factory on Avery Island, Louisiana, is part factory tour, part nature preserve. You can see how the pepper sauce is aged in oak barrels and then step outside to see Bird City, a special structure devised by E. A. McIlhenny to provide a sanctuary for snowy egrets.

- Mack Truck has an assembly plant in Macungie, Pennsylvania. The production line is a mile and a half long, so wear comfortable shoes!

- Yuengling Brewery (which you read about at the beginning of Chapter 5) in Pottsville, Pennsylvania, also offers tours, which include a trip to the cave where the nation's oldest brewery used to age its beer.

- Louisville Slugger in Louisville, Kentucky (where else?), offers a factory tour at the end of which you receive a miniature Slugger bat to take home.

- Harley-Davidson plants in Milwaukee, Kansas City, and York, Pennsylvania, offer factory tours for teens and adults.

- Carousel Magic in Mansfield, Ohio, is one of the few remaining carousel horse manufacturers and restorers.

Many companies no longer open their factories for tours. Kellogg's in Battle Creek, Michigan, ceased giving factory tours in 1986, but now the company operates a museum/activity center called Cereal City. Other companies say they offer factory tours, but in reality the tour is just a marketing device. Budweiser in St. Louis has an enormous visitor center for its tours, but you won't be able to see any of the actual production—just videos and the various outbuildings on the Anheuser-Busch campus. Still other companies offer virtual tours of their operations. Just Born, maker of Marshmallow Peeps, Mike & Ikes, and Hot Tamales, offers a static tour of the Peep production line at **http://www.marshmallowpeeps.com**. Hershey Foods also has an online tour at **http://www .hersheys.com/kidztown/factorytour.shtml**.[92]

Your assignment is to take a factory tour. Use the Internet or other resources to locate a factory tour near you. The site Factory Tours USA (**http://www.factorytoursusa.com**) organizes tours by state, so locating something interesting is easy.

Questions

1. What steps or procedures does the company take to ensure the quality of its products?

2. How does the company measure productivity, and how does its productivity compare with others in the industry?

3. Using the vocabulary from the chapter, describe the basic steps used to make the finished products in this factory.

4. What did you find most impressive about this company or its manufacturing processes? Based on what you read in the chapter, describe one thing the company could do differently to improve quality, increase productivity, or reduce inventory.

REEL TO REAL

Casino

Martin Scorsese's lengthy, complex, and beautifully filmed *Casino* offers a close look at the gambling casinos of Las Vegas and their organized crime connections in the 1970s. It completes his trilogy that began with *Mean Streets* (1973) and continued with *Goodfellas* (1990). In *Casino*, ambition, greed, drugs, and sex ultimately destroy the mob's gambling empire. The film includes strong performances by Robert De Niro, Joe Pesci, and Sharon Stone. The violence and expletive-filled dialogue give *Casino* an R rating.

This scene, which comes from the beginning of "The Truth about Las Vegas" sequence, opens the film and establishes important background about casino operations. Listen carefully to Sam Rothstein's (De Niro) voice-over. He quickly describes the casino's operation and explains how it tries to reach its goals.

What to Watch for and Ask Yourself

1. What type of operations management does this scene show—manufacturing operations management or service operations management?
2. Are the customers directly involved in this operation? If they are, in what way? What likely effects does their involvement have on the casino's operation and its management?
3. Does the casino have independent or interdependent demand systems?

Peapod—Blurring the Line between Product and Service

From the company's beginning, Peapod cofounder Thomas Parkinson insisted that his firm's website be inviting—packed with images of bright carrots, fresh-baked bread, deep red tomatoes, flavorful beef. But none of these images would have credibility if the food delivered to customers who shopped online at Peapod didn't live up to expectations. All it would take to turn a customer away from placing a second order would be one overripe banana, one slightly gray piece of meat, or a carton of ice cream with freezer burn. To get it right the first time and every time, Peapod relies on an operation that mixes elements of both manufacturing and service businesses. Watch the video to find out how managers at Peapod handle operations at this hybrid management workplace.

Questions

1. What systems and tools has Peapod implemented to insure the highest possible level of productivity?
2. Explain how quality affects the product and service aspects of Peapod's business.
3. Describe the inventory issues Peapod must manage.

ENDNOTES

Chapter 1

1. Factiva, "Q&A with Nortel's Mike Zafirovski," *BusinessWeek Online*, 8 November 2006; E. Gubbins, "Fired Nortel CEO Finds Work," *Prism Insight*, 8 January 2007; M. Heinzl, "Nortel's Plan for Recovery— CEO Is Cutting Costs, Adding Products; Analysts See Hurdles," *Wall Street Journal Asia*, 23 November 2006, 30; M. Heinzl, "Nortel's CEO Details Recovery Plan—Costs Will Be Cut to Save about $1.5 Billion a Year; New Products Part of Mix," *Wall Street Journal*, 24 November 2006, B2; B. Hill, "Nortel Inc. CEO Mike Zafirovski Has Initiated a Host of Changes to Try to Turn Canada's Telecom Giant around, But He Knows There's a Long Way to Go," *Ottawa Citizen*, 29 December 2006, E1; J. Lublin, "How a Rookie CEO Is Testing His Limits," *Wall Street Journal*, 2 January 2007, A1.

2. K. Voigt, "Top Dogs," *Wall Street Journal*, 15 March 2002, W1.

3. A. Horowitz, D. Jacobson, M. Lasswell & O. Thomas, "101 Dumbest Moments in Business," *Business 2.0*, 1 January 2006, 98.

4. M. Herper & R. Langreth, "Dangerous Devices," *Forbes*, 27 November 2006, 94.

5. N. Byrnes & J. Merritt, "Professional Services: The Help Needs Help," *Business Week*, 13 January 2003, 129.

6. T. Peters, "The Leadership Alliance" (Pat Carrigan excerpt), *In Search of Excellence* (Northbrook, IL: Video Arts distributor, 1985), videocassette.

7. K. Hickey, "Faster, Better, More," *Traffic World*, 6 October 2003, 24.

8. K. Jaher, "Wal-Mart Seeks New Flexibility in Worker Shifts," *Wall Street Journal*, 3 January 2007, A1.

9. D. A. Wren, A. G. Bedeian, & J. D. Breeze, "The Foundations of Henri Fayol's Administrative Theory," *Management Decision* 40 (2002): 906–918.

10. H. Fayol, *General and Industrial Management* (London: Pittman & Sons, 1949).

11. R. Stagner, "Corporate Decision Making," *Journal of Applied Psychology* 53 (1969): 1–13.

12. D. W. Bray, R. J. Campbell, & D. L. Grant, *Formative Years in Business: A Long-Term AT&T Study of Managerial Lives* (New York: Wiley, 1993).

13. N. Schwartzreporter & P. Neering, "The Biggest Company in America . . . Is Also a Big Target," *Fortune*, 17 April 2006, 77.

14. A. Lashinsky, "Search and Enjoy," *Fortune*, 22 January 2007, 70.

15. "Yahoo! Re-Aligns Organization to More Effectively Focus on Key Customer Segments and Capture Future Growth Opportunities," Yahoo!, http://yhoo.client .shareholder. com/ press/ReleaseDetail .cfm?ReleaseID = 220987, 5 December 2006.

16. R. J. Grisson, "Probability of the Superior Outcome of One Treatment over Another," *Journal of Applied Psychology* 79 (1994): 314–316; J. E. Hunter & F. L. Schmidt, *Methods of Meta-Analysis: Correcting Error and Bias in Research Findings* (Beverly Hills, CA: Sage, 1990).

17. B. Morris, "The Accidental CEO," *Fortune*, 28 June 2003, 58.

18. Ibid.

19. "Xerox's Chief Copies Good Practice, Not Past Mistakes," *Irish Times*, 21 March 2003, 62.

20. "Xerox's 3Q Profits Jump on Product Sales," *eWeek*, 21 October 2004.

21. A. Warren, "The Small Stuff: It's the Little Things That Add Up—and Often Annoy," *Wall Street Journal*, 10 May 2004, R9.

22. "Why Corporate Boardrooms Are in Turmoil," *Wall Street Journal*, 16 September 2006, A7.

23. "Why Corporate Boardrooms Are in Turmoil," *Wall Street Journal*, 16 September 2006, A7.

24. M. Arndt, "Creativity Overflowing," *BusinessWeek*, 8 May 2006, 50.

25. H. S. Jonas III, R. E. Fry, & S. Srivastva, "The Office of the CEO: Understanding the Executive Experience," *Academy of Management Executive* 4 (1990): 36–47.

26. M. Porter, J. Lorsch, & N. Nohria, "Seven Surprises for New CEOS," *Harvard Business Review*, October 2004, 62.

27. M. Murray, "As Huge Firms Keep Growing, CEOs Struggle to Keep Pace," *Wall Street Journal*, 8 February 2001, A1.

28. Ibid.

29. Q. Huy, "In Praise of Middle Managers," *Harvard Business Review*, September 2001, 72–79.

30. C. Hymowitz, "CEOs Work Hard to Maintain the Faith in the Corner Office," *Wall Street Journal*, 9 July 2002, B1; L. Mitchell, "How to Do the Right Thing," *Optimize*, February 2002, http://www.optimizemag .com, 1 February 2003.

31. C. Hymowitz, "Middle Managers Are Unsung Heroes on Corporate Stage," *Wall Street Journal*, 19 September 2005, B1.

32. "Management & Professional: Regional Manager," *Pharmacy Today*, 18 October 2006, 27.

33. T. Seideman, "Harnessing the Giant," *World Trade* 15 (2002): 28–29.

34. G. Will, "Waging War on Wal-Mart," *Newsweek*, 5 July 2004, 64.

35. S. Warren, "The Transient Workers," *Wall Street Journal*, 28 October 2002, R4.

36. J. Adamy, "A Menu of Options: Restaurants Have a Host of Ways to Motivate Employees to Provide Good Service," *Wall Street Journal*, 30 October 2006, R1, R6.

37. C. Hymowitz, "Today's Bosses Find Mentoring Isn't Worth the Time and Risks," *Wall Street Journal*, 13 March 2006, B1.

38. S. Tully, "What Team Leaders Need to Know," *Fortune*, 20 February 1995, 93.

39. B. Francella, "In a Day's Work," *Convenience Store News*, 25 September 2001, 7.

40. L. Liu & A. McMurray, "Frontline Leaders: The Entry Point for Leadership Development in the Manufacturing Industry," *Journal of European Industrial Training* 28, issue 2–4 (2004): 339–352.

41. Tully, "What Team Leaders Need to Know."

42. Ibid.

43. "What Makes Teams Work?" *Fast Company*, 1 November 2000, 109.

44. K. Hultman, "The 10 Commandments of Team Leadership," *Training & Development*, 1 February 1998, 12–13.

45. N. Steckler & N. Fondas, "Building Team Leader Effectiveness: A Diagnostic Tool," *Organizational Dynamics*, Winter 1995, 20–34.

46. L. Landro, "The Informed Patient: Bringing Surgeons Down to Earth—New Programs Aim to Curb Fear that Prevents Nurses from Flagging Problems," *Wall Street Journal*, 16 November 2005, D1.

47. Ibid.

48. H. Mintzberg, *The Nature of Managerial Work* (New York: Harper & Row, 1973).

49. C. P. Hales, "What Do Managers Do? A Critical Review of the Evidence," *Journal of Management Studies* 23, no. 1 (1986): 88–115.

50. "Grand Opening of Kikkoman Foods Europe," Kikkoman Corporation, http://www.kikkoman .com/news/news15.html, 26 January 2003.

51. "CDW Named One of the Best Companies to Work for in America for Fourth Consecutive Year," CDW Corporation, http://www .cdw.com, 26 January 2003.

52. J. Boorstin, "J. M. Smucker," *Fortune*, 12 January 2004, 58.

53. R. Levering & M. Moskowitz, "The 100 Best Companies to Work For," *Fortune*, 12 January 2004, 56.

54. B. Einhorn & M. Kripalani, "India 3.0: Bangalore Wants to Move Beyond Simple Code," *Business Week*, 26 February 2001, 16.

55. Francella, "In a Day's Work."

56. "Industry Specific: News Segmented by Major Industries," *Business Wire*, http://www.businesswire .com, 27 January 2003.

57. "Media Monitoring," *CyberAlert*, http://www .cyberalert.com, 27 January 2003.

58. "What Is FNS News Clips Online?" *FNS NewsClips*, http://www.news-clips .com, 27 January 2003.

59. "Cultural Practices of the Best Companies," *Great Place to Work Institute*, 4 January 2005, http://www .greatplacetoworkcom/ great/culture.php.

60. Murray, "As Huge Firms Keep Growing."

61. R. Guth, J. Delaney, & D. Clark, "Microsoft to Launch Challenge to Google, Yahoo," *Wall Street Journal*, 10 November 2004, A3.

62. C. Arnst, "The Best Medical Care in the U.S.: How Veterans Affairs Transformed Itself," *Business Week*, 17 July 2006, 50.

63. M. Langley, "Changing Gears," *Wall Street Journal*, 22 December 2006, A1.

64. M. Rieker, "E-Trade Raises Banking Sights for '07," *American Banker*, 8 January 2007, 1.

65. D. Welch & G. Khermouch, "Can GM Save an Icon?" *Business Week*, 8 April 2002, 60.

66. A. Sharma, "Poor Reception: After Sprint and Nextel Merge, Customers and Executives Leave," *Wall Street Journal*, 11 October 2006, A1.

67. L. A. Hill, *Becoming a Manager: Mastery of a New Identity* (Boston: Harvard Business School Press, 1992).

68. R. L. Katz, "Skills of an Effective Administrator," *Harvard Business Review*, September–October 1974, 90–102.

69. C. A. Bartlett & S. Ghoshal, "Changing the Role of Top Management: Beyond Systems to People," *Harvard Business Review*, May–June 1995, 132–142.

70. F. L. Schmidt & J. E. Hunter, "Development of a Causal Model of Process Determining Job Performance," *Current Directions in Psychological Science* 1 (1992): 89–92.

71. J. B. Miner, "Sentence Completion Measures in Personnel Research: The Development and Validation of the Miner Sentence Completion Scales," in *Personality Assessment in Organizations*, ed. H. J. Bernardin & D. A. Bownas (New York: Praeger, 1986), 147–146.

72. M. W. McCall, Jr. & M. M. Lombardo, "What Makes a Top Executive?" *Psychology Today*, February 1983, 26–31; E. van Velsor & J. Brittain, "Why Executives Derail: Perspectives across Time and Cultures," *Academy of Management Executive*, November 1995, 62–72.

73. McCall, Jr. & Lombardo, "What Makes a Top Executive?"

74. A. K. Naj, "Corporate Therapy: The Latest Addition to Executive Suite Is Psychologist's Couch," *Wall Street Journal*, 29 August 1994, A1.

75. Ibid.

76. P. Wallington, "Management2 Toxic!" *Financial Mail*, 28 July 2006, 48.

77. J. Sandberg, "Overcontrolling Bosses Aren't Just Annoying; They're Also Inefficient," *Wall Street Journal*, 30 March 2005, B1.

78. J. Pfeffer, *The Human Equation: Building Profits by Putting People First* (Boston: Harvard Business School Press, 1996); *Competitive Advantage through People: Unleashing the Power of the Work Force* (Boston: Harvard Business School Press, 1994).

79. D. McDonald & A. Smith, "A Proven Connection: Performance Management and Business Results," *Compensation & Benefits Review* 27, no. 6 (1 January 1995): 59.

80. I. Fulmer, B. Gerhart, & K. Scott, "Are the 100 Best Better? An Empirical Investigation of the Relationship between Being a 'Great Place to Work' and Firm Performance," *Personnel Psychology* (Winter 2003): 965–993.

81. B. Schneider & D. E. Bowen, "Employee and Customer Perceptions of Service in Banks: Replication and Extension," *Journal of Applied Psychology* 70 (1985): 423–433; B. Schneider, J. J. Parkington, & V. M. Buxton, "Employee and Customer Perceptions of Service in Banks," *Administrative Science Quarterly* 25 (1980): 252–267.

82. P. L. Hunsaker, *Management: A Skills Approach* (Upper Saddle River, New Jersey: Pearson Prentice Hall, 2005) 24–25.

83. N. Brodsky, "Pennies from Heaven," *Inc.*, 1 December 2004, 54.

84. S. McCartney, "A New Way to Prevent Lost Luggage," *Wall Street Journal*, 27 February 2007, D1; S. McCartney, "Why Airlines Keep Losing Your Luggage," *Wall Street Journal*, 16 January 2007, D1; S. McCartney, "Travelers Blast Airlines for Lost Bags," *Wall Street Journal*, 16 January 2007, online; J. Ogando, "It's the Luggage that Flies at Siemens' Mock Airport," *Design News*, 8 January 2007, 30; R. Grantham, "Heightened Security Leads to 40% Increase in Checked Baggage," *Atlanta Journal-Constitution*, 18 August 2006, online; K. Tagami, "Atlanta Airport's Finances Rated High," *Atlanta Journal-Constitution*, 16 July 2004, online; K. Tagami, "Airline Bankruptcies Blow Hole in Atlanta Airport Budget as Hangar Leases Flag," *Atlanta Journal-Constitution*, 26 January 2006, online; http://www.atlanta-airport.com/sublevels/airport_info/pdfs/Traffic/200701.pdf.

85. Hill, *Becoming a Manager*.

Chapter 2

1. J. Hough & M. White, "Using Stories to Create Change: The Object Lesson of Frederick Taylor's 'Pig-Tale,'" *Journal of Management* 27 (2001): 585–601; E. Locke, "The Ideas of Frederick W. Taylor: An Evaluation," *Academy of Management Review* 7 (1982): 14–24; F. W. Taylor, *The Principles of Scientific Management* (New York: Harper, 1911); C. Wrege & R. Hodgetts, "Frederick W. Taylor's 1899 Pig Iron Observations: Examining Fact, Fiction, and Lessons for the New Millennium," *Academy of Management Journal* 43 (2000): 1283–1291; D. Wren, *The History of Management Thought*, 5th ed. (New York: Wiley, 2005).

2. G. Glotz, *Ancient Greece at Work* (New York: Alfred A. Knopf, 1926).

3. C. S. George, Jr., *The History of Management Thought* (Englewood Cliffs, NJ: Prentice-Hall, 1972).

4. "Sumerian Language," *Britannica Online 2003*, http:// www.eb.com, 16 September 2003.

5. A. Erman, *Life in Ancient Egypt* (London: Macmillan & Co., 1984).

6. J. Burke, *The Day the Universe Changed* (Boston: Little, Brown, 1985).

7. "History of the Organization of Work: Organization of Work in Preindustrial Times: Medieval Industry," *Britannica Online*, http://www.eb.com, 15 January 1999.

8. "History of the Organization of Work: Organization of Work in Preindustrial Times: The Ancient World," *Britannica Online*, http://www.eb.com, 15 January 1999.

9. "History of the Organization of Work: Organization of Work in Preindustrial Times: From the 16th to the 18th Century," *Britannica Online*, http://www.eb.com, 15 January 1999.

10. J. B. White, "The Line Starts Here: Mass-Production Techniques Changed the Way People Work and Live throughout the World," *Wall Street Journal*, 11 January 1999, R25.

11. R. B. Reich, *The Next American Frontier* (New York: Times Books, 1983).

12. J. Mickelwait & A. Wooldridge, *The Company: A Short History of a Revolutionary Idea* (New York: Modern Library, 2003).

13. "How Business Schools Began," *Business Week*, 12 October 1963, 114–116.

14. *Industrial Management: The Engineering Magazine* 61 (1921): 232.

15. H. Kendall, "Unsystematized, Systematized, and Scientific Management," in *Scientific Management: A Collection of the More Significant Articles Describing the Taylor System of Management*, ed. C. Thompson (Easton, PA: Hive Publishing, 1972), 103–131.

16. United States Congress, House, Special Committee, *Hearings to Investigate the Taylor and Other Systems of Shop Management*, vol. 3. (Washington, D.C.: Government Printing Office, 1912).

17. Ibid.

18. Ibid.

19. Taylor, *The Principles of Scientific Management*.

20. A. Derickson, "Physiological Science and Scientific Management in the Progressive Era: Frederic S. Lee and the Committee on Industrial Fatigue," *Business History Review* 68 (1994): 483–514.

21. United States Congress, House, Special Committee, 1912.

22. Taylor, *The Principles of Scientific Management*.

23. Ibid.

24. Wrege & Hodgetts, "Frederick W. Taylor's 1899 Pig Iron Observations"; Hough & White, "Using Stories to Create Change."

25. Locke, "The Ideas of Frederick W. Taylor."

26. George, Jr., *The History of Management Thought*.

27. F. Gilbreth & L. Gilbreth, "Applied Motion Study," in *The Writings of the Gilbreths*, ed. W. R. Spriegel & C. E. Myers (1917; rpr. Homewood, IL: Irwin, 1953), 207–274.

28. D. Ferguson, "Don't Call It 'Time and Motion Study,'" *IIE Solutions* 29, no. 5 (1997): 22–23.

29. Ibid.

30. "Frank and Lillian Gilbreth: Motion Study Pioneers," *Thinkers*, December 2000.

31. J. Gotcher, "Assisting the Handicapped: The Pioneering Efforts of Frank and Lillian Gilbreth," *Journal of Management* 18 (1992): 5–14.

32. F. Gilbreth & L. Gilbreth, "Motion Study for the Crippled Soldier," *American Society of Mechanical Engineers Journal* 37 (1915): 669–673.

33. H. Gantt, "A Bonus System for Rewarding Labor," *Transactions of the American Society of Mechanical Engineers* 23 (1901): 373.

34. P. Peterson, "Training and Development: The View of Henry L. Gantt (1861–1919)," *SAM Advanced Management Journal*, Winter 1987, 20–23.

35. H. Gantt, "Industrial Efficiency," *National Civic Federation Report of the 11th Annual Meeting*, New York, 12 January 1991, 103.

36. Ibid.

37. M. Weber, *The Theory of Economic and Social Organization*, trans. by A. Henderson & T. Parsons (New York: Free Press, 1947).

38. M. Weber, *The Protestant Ethic and the Spirit of Capitalism* (New York: Scribner's, 1958).

39. George, Jr., *The History of Management Thought*.

40. D. Wren, "Henri Fayol As Strategist: A Nineteenth Century Corporate Turnaround," *Management Decision* 39 (2001): 475–487.

41. D. Reid, "Fayol: From Experience to Theory," *Journal of Management History* 3 (1995): 21–36.

42. H. Fayol, "Observations et expériences personnelles," *Archives Fayol*, no date, 4–11.

43. Wren, "Henri Fayol As Strategist"; Reid, "Fayol: From Experience to Theory."

44. Wren, "Henri Fayol As Strategist."

45. Ibid.

46. Ibid.

47. Ibid.

48. F. Blancpain, "Les cahiers inédits d'Henri Fayol," trans. D. Wren, *Extrait du bulletin de l'institut international d'administration publique* 28–9 (1974): 1–48.

49. H. Verney, "Un grand ingénieur: Henri Fayol," *La fondateur de la doctrine administrative: Henri Fayol* (Paris: Dunod, 1925), as cited in Wren, "Henri Fayol As Strategist."

50. D. A. Wren, A. G. Bedeian, & J. D. Breeze, "The Foundations of Henri Fayol's Administrative Theory," *Management Decision* 40 (2002): 906–918.

51. H. Fayol, *General and Industrial Management* (London: Pittman & Sons, 1949).

52. M. P. Follett, *Mary Parker Follett—Prophet of Management: A Celebration of Writings from the 1920s*, ed. P. Graham (Boston: Harvard Business School Press, 1995).

53. Ibid.

54. D. Linden, "The Mother of Them All," *Forbes*, 16 January 1995, 75.

55. E. O'Connor, "The Politics of Management Thought: A Case Study of the Harvard Business School and the Human Relations School," *Academy of Management Review* 24 (1999): 117–131.

56. M. Losey, "HR Comes of Age," *HRMagazine* 43, no. 3 (1998): 40–53.

57. J. H. Smith, "The Enduring Legacy of Elton Mayo," *Human Relations* 51, no. 3 (1998): 221–249.

58. E. Mayo, *The Human Problems of an Industrial Civilization* (New York: Macmillan, 1933).

59. Ibid.

60. "Hawthorne Revisited: The Legend and the Legacy," *Organizational Dynamics* (Winter 1975): 66–80.

61. E. Mayo, *The Social Problems of an Industrial Civilization* (Boston: Harvard Graduate School of Business Administration, 1945).

62. Mayo, *The Social Problems of an Industrial Civilization*, 65–67.

63. "Hawthorne Revisited: The Legend and the Legacy."

64. Mayo, *The Social Problems of an Industrial Civilization*, 45.

65. George, Jr., *The History of Management Thought*.

66. C. I. Barnard, *The Functions of the Executive* (Cambridge, MA: Harvard University Press, 1938), 4.

67. C. I. Barnard, *The Functions of the Executive: 30th Anniversary Edition* (Cambridge, MA: Harvard University Press, 1968), 5.

68. S. Parayitam, M. White, & J. Hough, "Juxtaposition of Chester I. Barnard and Frederick W. Taylor: Forerunners of Management," *Management Decision* 40 (2002): 1003–1012.

69. J. Dunkelberg & D. Jessup, "So Then Why Did You Do It?" *Journal of Business Ethics* 29 (2001): 422–426.

70. J. Fuller & A. Mansour, "Operations Management and Operations Research: A Historical and Relational Perspective," *Management Decision* 41 (2003): 422–426.

71. "Monge, Gaspard, comte de Péluse," *Britannica Online*, http://www.eb.com, 9 January 2005.

72. D. Ashmos & G. Huber, "The Systems Paradigm in Organization Theory: Correcting the Record and Suggesting the Future," *Academy of Management Review* 12 (1987): 607–621; F. Kast & J. Rosenzweig, "General Systems Theory: Applications for Organizations and Management," *Academy of Management Journal* 15 (1972): 447–465; D. Katz & R. Kahn, *The Social Psychology of Organizations* (New York: Wiley, 1966).

73. R. Mockler, "The Systems Approach to Business Organization and Decision Making," *California Management Review* 11, issue 2 (1968): 53–58.

74. F. Luthans & T. Stewart, "A General Contingency Theory of Management," *Academy of Management Review* 2, issue 2 (1977): 181–195.

75. C.K.W. de Dreu, A. Evers, B. Beersma, E.S. Kluwer, & A. Nauta, "A Theory-Based Measure of Conflict Management Strategies in the Workplace," *Journal of Organizational Behavior* 22 (2001) 645–668.

76. A. Scharf, "Scripted Talk: From 'Welcome to McDonald's' to 'Paper or Plastic?' Employers Control the Speech of Service Workers," *Dollars & Sense*, September–October 2003, 35; C. McCann, "Have a Nice Day and an Icy Stare," *Marketing Week*, 2 September 2004, 27; G. Garfinkel Weiss, "Improving Collections: To Collect at the Time of Service and Overcome Patient Excuses for Nonpayment, Tell Staffers to Stick to the Script," *Medical Economics*, 9 July 2004, 70.

Chapter 3

1. "Until Recently Full of Promise, Satellite Radio Runs Into Static," *Wall Street Journal*, 15 August 2006, A1.; S. Finlay, "XM Radio Ventures Beyond Audio Services," *Ward's Dealer Business*, July 2005, 39(7): 8; S. Finlay "XM Radio Looks Beyond Audio," *Ward's Auto World*, June 2005, 41(6): 18; N. Bussey, "Can Satellite Radio Become a Serious Medium?," *Campaign (UK)*, 27 January 2006, (4):17; T. Lowry & P. Lehman, "Grudge Match," *BusinessWeek*, 21–28 August 2006, 86–87; C. Edwards, "Taking XM Out for a Stroll," 14 August 2006, 18; "Record Companies Sue XM Radio for Copyright Infringement," *Computer & Internet Lawyer*, September 2006, 23(9): 38; S. Wildstrom, "Copyrights and Wrongs," *BusinessWeek*, 3 July 2006, 24; http://www.xmradio.com; http://www.sirius.com; "Two Upstarts Vie for Dominance in Satellite Radio," *Wall Street Journal*, 30, March 2005, A1–A9.

2. L. Heller, "Health Could Boost Declining US Cookie Sales: Report," www.foodnavigator.com, 18 August 2006. http://www.foodnavigator-usa.com/news/ng.asp?id=69965-cookies-whole-grains-healthy-eating.

3. "A Nation of Snackers Snubs Old Favorite," *Wall Street Journal*, 16 June 2004, A1.

4. D. Alexander, "Bread Makers Feel the Diet Pinch," *Chicago Tribune*, 30 December 2003, Business 1.

5. R. Guth, "Videogame Giant Links with Sony, Snubbing Microsoft," *Wall Street Journal*, 12 May 2003, A1; "Cost of Making Games Set to Soar," *BBC News*, 17, November 2005, http://news.bbc.co.uk/1/hi/technology/4442346.stm

6. E. Romanelli & M. L. Tushman, "Organizational Transformation as Punctuated Equilibrium: An Empirical Test," *Academy of Management Journal* 37 (1994): 1141–1166.

7. H. Banks, "A Sixties Industry in a Nineties Economy," *Forbes*, 9 May 1994, 107–112.

8. L. Cowan, "Cheap Fuel Should Carry Many Airlines to More Record Profits for 1st Quarter," *Wall Street Journal*, 4 April 1998, B17A.

9. "Annual Revenues and Earnings: U.S. Airlines—All Services," Air Transport Association, http://www.airlines.org, 15 January 2005; S. Carey, "Carrier Makes Deeper Cuts As It Seeks Federal

Backing Needed to Exit Chapter 11," *Wall Street Journal*, 27 November 2002, A3; S. Carey, "UAL Will Lay Off 1,500 Workers As Part of Cost-Cutting Strategy," *Wall Street Journal*, 6 January 2003, A3; D. Carty, "Oral Testimony of Mr. Donald J. Carty, Chairman and CEO, American Airlines: United States Senate, Committee on Commerce, Science, and Transportation," http://www.amrcorp .com 9 January 2003; S. McCartney, M. Trottman, & S. Carey, "Northwest, Continental, America West Post Losses As Delta Cuts Jobs," *Wall Street Journal*, 18 November 2002, B4.

10. "Airlines Still in Upheaval, 5 Years after 9/11," *CNNMoney .com*, 8 September 2006, http://money.cnn .com/2006/09/08/news/ companies/ airlines_ sept11/?postversion = 2006090812.

11. "New Product Review," *Dairy Foods*, http://www .dairyfoods.com, 15 January 2005; B. Jones, "The Changing Dairy Industry," Department of Agricultural & Applied Economics & Center for Dairy Profitability, http://www.aae.wisc .edu/jones/Presentations/ Wisc&TotalDairyTrends .pdf, 15 January 2003.

12. S. Ghosemajumder, "Digital Music Distribution," *MIT Sloan School of Management*, http://shumans.com/ digital-music/?p=1&p2=1 .html; "30 Products for 30 Years," *MacWorld*, June 2006, 15–16; T. Mennecke, "CD Sales, Shipments Down in 2005," *Slyck News*, 31 March 2006, http://www. slyck .com/news .php?story=1143; P. Burrows, "Microsoft Singing Its Own iTune," *Business Week Online*, 11 July 2006, 20; "Apple Presents iPod," 23 October 2001, http:// www.apple.com/pr/ library/2001/oct/23ipod

.html; http://www .wikipedia.com.

13. "Samsung Invests $2.1B in LCD Line," *Electronic News*, 7 March 2005; "L. G. Philips LCD Develops 100-Inch LCD Panel, the Largest in the World," L. G. Philips, www.lgphilips-lcd .com/homeContain/ jsp/eng/inv/inv101_j_ e.jsp?BOARD_IDX= 1054&languageSec=E; "Samsung, L. G. Philips start new LCD Production," *CyberMedia India Online*, www .ciol.com/content/ news/2006/106010202 .asp; "Samsung Develops World's Largest (82") Full HDTV TFT-LCD," Samsung, http://www .samsung.com/Products/ TFTLCD/News/category_ TFTLCD_20050307_ 0000101494.htm, "Samsung and L. G. Philips start new LCD Production," *Boston.com*, 1 January 2006, http://www .boston.com/business/ articles/2006/01/01/ samsung_and_lgphilips_ start_new_lcd_production; E. Ramstad, "I Want My Flat TV Now!" *Wall Street Journal*, 27 May 2004, B1.

14. "Consumer Products Brief—Kraft Foods Inc.: Price of Maxwell House Coffee to Rise 14% As Costs Increase," *Wall Street Journal*, 15 December 2004, A16.

15. R. Norton, "Where Is This Economy Really Heading?" *Fortune*, 7 August 1995, 54–56.

16. "First, by the Numbers, the CFO Poll," *Fortune*, 17 February 2003, 30.

17. A. Weintraub, "It's on the Tip of Your Tongue," *Business Week*, 31 July 2006, 32.

18. J. Fletcher, "Extreme Nesting," *Wall Street Journal*, 7 January 2000, W1.

19. "CDW Ranks on Best Places to Work List for Fifth Straight Year," *PR Newswire*, 7 January 2003.

20. M. Perotin, "Dallas-Based Baylor Health Care Offers Concierge Perk to

Employees," *Fort Worth Star-Telegram*, 8 December 2002.

21. R. Sharpe, "Nannies on Speed Dial: There Is Growing Army of Domestic Help Out There, and More and More Families Are Picking Up the Phone," *Business Week*, 18 September 2000, 108; N. Powell, "Going Above and Beyond," *The Hamilton Spectator*, 25 July 2006, http://www .circles.com/news/news_ Jul06_article_Above_and_ Beyond.htm.

22 C. R. Gentry & M. Wilson, "Living Made Easy: Service-Oriented Concepts Cater to Time-Starved Consumers," *Chain Store Age*, October 2006, 39–41.

23. The Civil Rights Act of 1991, available at U.S. Equal Employment Opportunity Commission, http://www.eeoc.gov/ policy/cra91.html, 16 January 2005.

24. Compliance Assistance— Family and Medical Leave Act (FMLA), U.S. Department of Labor: Employment Standards Administration Wage and Hour Division, http:// www.dol.gov/esa/whd/ fmla, 16 January 2005.

25. R. J. Bies & T. R. Tyler, "The Litigation Mentality in Organizations: A Test of Alternative Psychological Explanations," *Organization Science* 4 (1993): 352–366.

26. D. Jones, "Fired Workers Fight Back … and Win," *USA Today*, 2 April 1998, B1.

27. S. Gardner, G. Gomes, & J. Morgan, "Wrongful Termination and the Expanding Public Policy Exception: Implications and Advice," *SAM Advanced Management Journal* 65 (2000): 38.

28. Jones, "Fired Workers Fight Back."

29. T. Gerdel, "Liability Suits Have Lasting Effect on Transportation Companies," *Cleveland*

Plain Dealer, 13 August 2002, C5.

30. "Products Liability Law: An Overview," Legal Information Institute, http://www.law .cornell.edu/wex/index .php/Products_liability, 8 February 2003.

31. Gerdel, "Liability Suits."

32. R. Johnston & S. Mehra, "Best-Practice Complaint Management," *Academy of Management Experience* 16 (November 2002): 145–154.

33. D. Smart & C. Martin, "Manufacturer Responsiveness to Consumer Correspondence: An Empirical Investigation of Consumer Perceptions," *Journal of Consumer Affairs* 26 (1992): 104.

34. H. Appelman, "I Scream, You Scream: Consumers Vent over the Net," *New York Times*, 4 March 2001.

35. J. Pereira, "Trends (A Special Report)—It's a Whole New Game," *Wall Street Journal*, 22 November 2004, R9; http://www.kbtoys .com/help/giftcard.html; http://www4.toysrus.com/ corpgiftcard.

36. S. Gray, "Trends (A Special Report)—On the Menu: Speed and Variety," *Wall Street Journal*, 22 November 2004, R4.

37. S. A. Zahra & S. S. Chaples, "Blind Spots in Competitive Analysis," *Academy of Management Executive* 7 (1993): 7–28.

38. "The Cola Wars: Over a Century of Cola Slogans, Commercials, Blunders, and Coups," http:// www.geocities.com/ colacentury/.

39. M. Frazier, "You Suck: Dyson, Hoover and Oreck Trade Accusations in Court, on TV as Brit Upstart Leaves Rivals in Dust," *Advertising Age*, 25 July 2005, 1.

40. J. M. Moran, "Getting Closer Together— Videophones Don't Deliver TV Quality Sound, Visuals, but They're

Improving," *Seattle Times*, 15 March 1998.

41. P. Grant, "Comcast Plans Major Rollout of Phone Service over Cable," *Wall Street Journal*, 10 January 2005, B1.

42. R. Buckman, "Telecom Price Wars Get Brutal in Hong Kong," *Wall Street Journal*, 28 October 2004, B4.

43. A. Squeo, "FCC Is Poised to Clarify Future of Internet Phone Calls," *Wall Street Journal*, 22 January 2004, B1.

44. K. G. Provan, "Embeddedness, Interdependence, and Opportunism in Organizational Supplier-Buyer Networks," *Journal of Management* 19 (1993): 841–856.

45. C. Unninayar & N. P. Sindt, "Diamonds' an Industry in Transition: Sometimes the Speed of Change Is Alarming," *Couture International Jeweler*, August–Sept 2003, 68–75. N. Gaouette, "Israel's Diamond Dealers Tremble: Diamond Colossus De Beers Today Launches Fundamental Changes to $56 Billion Retail Market," *Christian Science Monitor*, 1 June 2001, online.

46. N. Shirouzu, "Chain Reaction—Big Three's Outsourcing Plan: Make Parts Suppliers Do It," *Wall Street Journal*, 10 June 2004, A1.

47. D. Birch, "Staying on Good Terms," *Supply Management*, 12 April 2001, 36.

48. S. Parker & C. Axtell, "Seeing Another Viewpoint: Antecedents and Outcomes of Employee Perspective Taking," *Academy of Management Journal* 44 (2001): 1085–1100; B. K. Pilling, L. A. Crosby, & D. W. Jackson, "Relational Bonds in Industrial Exchange: An Experimental Test of the Transaction Cost Economic Framework," *Journal of Business*

Research 30 (1994): 237–251.

49. "Carmakers Eye Economy with Unease," *USA Today*, 24 May 2004, B.06.

50. Title 25 Health Services Part 1: Texas Department of Health Chapter 229, Food and Drug Subchapter U, Permitting Retail Food Establishments," Texas Department of Health, http://www.tdh.state.tx.us/bfds/retail/permittingrules.html, 11 February 2003.

51. M. Horn, "Sinning in an SUV," *U.S. News & World Report*, 16 December 2002, 10; http://www.nhtsa.dot.gov/cars/rules/cafe/overview.htm

52. "Seafood HACCP," U.S. Food and Drug Administration Center for Food Safety & Applied Nutrition, http://www.cfsan.fda.gov/~comm/haccpsea.html, 11 February 2003.

53. S. Dudley, "The Coming Shift in Regulation," *Regulation*, 1 October 2002.

54. S. Dudley, "Regulation and Small Business Competitive," *Federal Document Clearing House*, Congressional Testimony, Prepared Remarks for the House Committee on Small Business Subcommittee on Regulatory Reform and Oversight, 20 May 2004.

55. H. Morley, "Bush Orders Cut in Regulations—Change Will Cut Red Tape for Small Businesses," *Knight-Ridder Tribune*, 17 August 2002.

56. "EU's Aggressive Anti-Smoking Campaign," *Creative Bits*, http://creativebits.org/eus_agressive_anti-smoking_campaign, 17 January 2005.

57. "Ethical Dangers Multiply," *Purchasing*, 17 October 1996; J. Dubinsky, "How to Foster Ethical Conduct: Companies Have a Clear Role in Preventing Conflicts of Interest," *Supplier Selection & Management*, 1 June 2001; "Amerinet

Joins Groups Issuing Compliance Documents Based on Code of Conduct," *Hospital Materials Management*, 1 January 2003, 6; M. Lawson, "The Ethical Dilemma of Corporate Generosity," *Australian Financial Review*, 5 December 2002, 16.

58. M. Hudson, "PETA Doll Ruffles KFC's Feathers," *Roanoke Times*, http://www.roanoke.com/extra%5C16581.html, 8 January 2005.

59. "Another Ford Trial: Steering around Activists," *Wall Street Journal*, 26 July 2006, A2.

60. N. E. Boudette & J. A. White, "At GM, Curbing Inventories Calls for Juggling Act," *Wall Street Journal*, 8 January 2007, A1.

61. J. Ball, "Detroit Fears Some Consumers May Be Souring on Big SUVs," *Wall Street Journal Online*, http://online.wsj.com/article/B1041979477724000464.html, 8 January 2003.

62. C. Hymowitz, "Top Marketing Officers Find Getting Together Helps Them Do the Job," *Wall Street Journal*, 11 January 2005, B1.

63. D. F. Jennings & J. R. Lumpkin, "Insights between Environmental Scanning Activities and Porter's Generic Strategies: An Empirical Analysis," *Journal of Management* 4 (1992): 791–803.

64. V. Vara, "Software Giants Seek Friends among Hackers," *Wall Street Journal*, 3 August 2006, B1.

65. S. E. Jackson & J. E. Dutton, "Discerning Threats and Opportunities," *Administrative Science Quarterly* 33 (1988): 370–387.

66. B. Thomas, S. M. Clark, & D. A. Gioia, "Strategic Sensemaking and Organizational Performance: Linkages among Scanning, Interpretation, Action, and

Outcomes," *Academy of Management Journal* 36 (1993): 239–270.

67. R. Daft, J. Sormunen, & D. Parks, "Chief Executive Scanning, Environmental Characteristics, and Company Performance: An Empirical Study," *Strategic Management Journal* 9 (1988): 123–139; V. Garg, B. Walters, & R. Priem, "Chief Executive Scanning Emphases, Environmental Dynamism, and Manufacturing Firm Performance," *Strategic Management Journal* 24 (2003): 725–744; D. Miller & P. H. Friesen, "Strategy-Making and Environment: The Third Link," *Strategic Management Journal* 4 (1983): 221–235.

68. P. Grant, "Comcast Plans Major Rollout of Phone Service over Cable."

69. L. Yuan & C. Bryan-Low, "iPhone Hinges On the Likes of Mr. Digate: In High-End Realm, Handset Must Court the Affluent Tech-Set," *Wall Street Journal*, 11 January 2007, B4.

70. K. Maney, "SAS Workers Won When Greed Lost," *USA Today*, 22 April 2004, B.01.

71. A. Harrington, N. Hira, & C. Tkaczyk, "Hall of Fame: If Making the 100 Best List Is an Enormous Accomplishment, Consider How Tough It Is to Repeat the Feat Every Single Year," *Fortune*, 24 January 2005, 94.

72. "SAS Makes the *Fortune* 'Hall of Fame,'" SAS, http://www.sas.com/news/feature/16jan05/fortune.html, 20 January 2005.

73. P. Elmer-DeWitt, "Mine, All Mine; Bill Gates Wants a Piece of Everybody's Action, but Can He Get It?" *Time*, 5 June 1995.

74. D. M. Boje, "The Storytelling Organization: A Study of Story Performance in an Office-Supply Firm," *Administrative Science Quarterly* 36 (1991): 106–126.

75. S. Walton & J. Huey, *Sam Walton: Made in America* (New York: Doubleday, 1992).

76. D. Rushe, "Wal-Martians," *Sunday Times–London*, 10 June 2001, 5.

77. M. Hayes, "Bowa Builders: NRS Excellence in Class, 50—Plus," *HousingZone.com*, http://www.housingzone.com/topics/pr/nrs/pr03ia009.asp, 19 January 2005.

78. D. R. Denison & A. K. Mishra, "Toward a Theory of Organizational Culture and Effectiveness," *Organization Science* 6 (1995): 204–223.

79. D. Jones, "When You're Smiling, Are You Seething Inside? Passive-Aggressive Culture Hurts Companies, Workers," *USA Today*, 12 April 2004, B.01.

80. F. Haley, "Mutual Benefit: How Does Genencor Maintain Its Incredibly Loyal Workforce? By Involving Its Employees in Almost Everything," *Fast Company*, October 2004, 98–100.

81. "Company Profile," F. H. Faulding & Company, http://www.faulding.com.au/home/comp_profile/mission/mission.html, 21 June 2001.

82. S. Yearout, G. Miles, & R. Koonce, "Multi-Level Visioning," *Training & Development*, 1 March 2001, 31.

83. T. Brown, "A Vision from Scratch," *Across the Board*, 1 May 2001, 77.

84. M. A. Salva-Ramirez, "McDonald's: A Prime Example of Corporate Culture," *Public Relations Quarterly*, Winter 1995, 30–32.

85. "Hamburger University," McDonald's Media Site, http://www.mcdonalds.com/corp/career/hamburger_university.html, 18 January 2005.

86. J. Sorenson, "The Strength of Corporate Culture and the Reliability of Firm Performance," *Administrative Science Quarterly* 47 (2002): 70–91.

87. A. Zuckerman, "Strong Corporate Cultures and Firm Performance: Are There Tradeoffs?" *Academy of Management Executive*, November 2002, 158–160.

88. *McDonald's Summary Annual Report 2005*, 2–4; D. Stires, "McDonald's Keeps Right on Cooking," *Fortune*, 17 May 2004, 102.

89. E. Schein, *Organizational Culture and Leadership*, 2d ed. (San Francisco: Jossey-Bass, 1992).

90. E. Byron, "'Call Me Mike!'—To Attract and Keep Talent, JCPenney CEO Loosens Up Once-Formal Workplace," *Wall Street Journal*, 27 March 2006, B1.

91. Ibid.

92. C. Daniels, "Does This Man Need a Shrink? Companies Are Using Psychological Testing to Screen Candidates for Top Jobs," *Fortune*, 5 February 2001, 205.

93. Ibid.

94. S. Chakravarty, "Hit 'Em Hardest with the Mostest (Southwest Airlines' Management)," *Forbes*, 16 September 1991, 48.

95. R. Suskind, "Humor Has Returned to Southwest Airlines after 9/11 Hiatus," *Wall Street Journal*, 13 January 2003, A1.

96. Ibid.

97. K. Godsey, "Slow Climb to New Heights; Combine Strict Discipline with Goofy Antics and Make Billions," *Success*, 1 October 1996, 20.

98. D.L. McCain, "The MSTAT-I: A New Measure of an Individual's Tolerance for Ambiguity," *Educational and Psychological Measurement*, 53 (1993): 183–190.

99. K. Maher, "For Some Co-Workers, Bringing Fido to Office Has Become Pet Peeve," *Wall Street Journal*, 12 January 2005, B1; "Making the Office Pet Friendly," *Plant Sites & Parks*, February 2001, 11; S. Linstedt, "Pets at Work Is Gnawing Subject for Many Buffalo, N.Y., Firms," *Buffalo News*, 30 September 2002; M. M. Perotin, "Some Fort Worth, Texas–Area Employers Allow Pets at Work," *Fort Worth Star-Telegram*, 12 August 2002; P. Lopes Harris, "Firms Begin to Ban Pets at Work," *San Jose Mercury News*, 2 January 2001; J. Saranow, "Anybody Want to Take a Nap? Fun Perks Didn't End with the Dot-Com Bust—They Just Changed," *Wall Street Journal*, 25 January 2005, R5.

100. "Yum Brands Temporarily Closes Restaurants after Rat Incident," *Wall Street Journal*, March 1, 2007, online; "Lettuce Most Likely Cause of Taco Bell E. coli," *Wall Street Journal*," December 14, 2006, B11; P. Flanagan, "Ten Public Relations Pitfalls," *Management Review*, October 1995, 45–48.

Chapter 4

1. "PETA Adopts Crude Tactics to Attack Milk Production," *Marketing Week*, 2 February 2006, 12; C. Roselli & J. Newman, "Responding to PETA," *The National Post* (Canada), 29 January 2007, A14; A. Enright, "PETA's PR Has Claws," *Marketing News*, 1 October 2005, 13–24; H. Harviliciz, "P&G Stops Most Animal Tests Victory Claimed by PETA," *Chemical Marker Reporter*, 5 July 1999, 25; G. Poste, "Animal Testing a Necessary Research Tool, for Now," *Arizona Republic*, 14 March 2007; A. Zuber, "BK Enacts Penalties, Surprise Inspection in Wake of PETA Boycott," *Nation's Restaurant News*, 9 July 2001, 6; A. Garber, "Fur Flies as PETA Sues KFC," *Nation's Restaurant News* 21 July 2003, 1; "Targeted Guinea Pig Farm Closes—A Farm that Has Been Breeding Guinea Pigs for Medical Research for More than 30 Years Is to Stop after Intimidation by Animal Rights Activist," available at http://findarticles.com/p/articles/mi_m3190/is_29_37/ai_106114301; D. Ward "'We Give Up,' Says Family Besieged by Activists," *The Guardian*, 24 August 2005; "Boycott Procter & Gamble," available at http://www.uncaged.co.uk/pg.htm; A. Kershaw, "Rise of World's Biggest Animal Rights Group," *The Press Association Newsfile*, 19 September 2006.

2. J. Schramm, "Perceptions on Ethics," *HR Magazine*, November 2004, available at http://www.shrm.org.

3. M. Jackson (Associated Press), "Workplace Cheating Rampant, Half of Employees Surveyed Admit They Take Unethical Actions," *Peoria Journal Star*, 5 April 1997.

4. M.A. Cohen, "Prosecutors of Corporate Scandals Share Insights," *The Legal Ledger* 16 November 2006; "Corporate Ethics," *Washington Post*, http://www.washingtonpost.com/wp-dyn/business/specials/corporateethics, 27 January 2005.

5. C. Smith, "The Ethical Workplace," *Association Management* 52 (2000): 70–73.

6. D. Jones, "More Workers Do Now Than Before Recent Big Scandals," *USA Today*, 12 February 2003, B7.

7. K. Tyler, "Do the Right Thing: Ethics Training Programs Help Employees Deal with Ethical Dilemmas," *HR Magazine*, February 2005, available at http://www.shrm.org/hrmagazine/articles/0205/0205tyler.asp.

8. F. Ahrens (*Washington Post*), "How Papers Faked Sales Figures," *Wall Street Journal Europe*, 1 December 2004, A5.

9. M. Bordwin, "Don't Ask Employees to Do Your

Dirty Work," *Management Review*, 1 October 1995.

10. C. Hymowitz, "Managers Must Respond to Employee Concerns about Honest Business," *Wall Street Journal*, 19 February 2002, B1.

11. M. Schweitzer, L. Ordonez, & B. Douma, "Goal Setting As a Motivator of Unethical Behavior," *Academy of Management Journal* 47 (2004): 422–432.

12. S. Power & C. Rauwald, "Daimler Audit Sparks Scrutiny as Executives Are Suspended: Disclosures about Bus Unit Prompt New Questions Tied to Internal Controls," *Wall Street Journal*, 14 November 2006, A17.

13. "2004 Report to the Nation on Occupational Fraud and Abuse," Association of Certified Fraud Examiners, http://www.acfe.com/documents/2004RttN.pdf; K. Gibson, "Excuses, Excuses: Moral Slippage in the Workplace," *Business Horizons* 43, no. 6 (2000): 65; S. L. Robinson & R. J. Bennett, "A Typology of Deviant Workplace Behaviors: A Multidimensional Scaling Study," *Academy of Management Journal* 38 (1995): 555–572.

14. Ibid.

15. J. Sandberg, "Office Sticky Fingers Can Turn the Rest of Us into Joe Fridays," *Wall Street Journal*, 19 November 2003, B1.

16. J. Norman, "Cultivating a Culture of Honesty," *The Orange County Register* (Santa Ana, CA), 23 October 2006.

17. S. Gaudin, "Computer Sabotage Case Back in Court," *Network World Fusion*, 19 April 2001, 12.

18. R. Hollinger & J. Davis, "2005 National Retail Security Final Report," Center for Studies in Criminology and Law, University of Florida, http://web.crim.ufl.edu/research/srp/srp.html, 15 June 2007.

19. M. Pressler, "Cost and Robbers; Shoplifting and Employee Thievery Add Dollars to Price Tag," *Washington Post*, 16 February 2003, H05.

20. G. Gatlin, "New, Improved! Way to Fight Theft Nears," *Boston Herald*, 17 June 2002, 21.

21. S. Miller, "Despite Workers' Comp Relief, Fraud Still Costly," available at http://www.shrm.org

22. M. France & M. Arndt, "After the Shooting Stops: When Employees Are Murdered on the Job, the Trauma Can Last for Years," *BusinessWeek*, 12 March 2001, 98.

23. D. Babwin, "Downtown Chicago Office Shooting Leaves 4 Dead, Including Gunman," *Associated Press State and Local Wire*, 9 December 2006, Saturday, 12:48 PM GMT.

24. Lehr Middlebrooks & Vreeland, P.C. (byline), "Many U.S. Employers Aren't Doing Enough to Address Workplace Violence," *Alabama Employment Law Letter*, December 2006.

25. J. Merchant & J. Lundell, "Workplace Violence: A Report to the Nation," University of Iowa Injury Prevention Center, http://www.public-health.uiowa.edu/iprc/nation.pdf, 15 June 2007.

26. M. P. Coco, Jr., "The New War Zone: The Workplace," *SAM Advanced Management Journal* 63, no. 1 (1998): 15; M. G. Harvey & R. A. Cosier, "Homicides in the Workplace: Crisis or False Alarm?" *Business Horizons* 38, no. 10 (1995): 11.

27. D. Palmer & A. Zakhem, "Bridging the Gap between Theory and Practice: Using the 1991 Federal Sentencing Guidelines as a Paradigm for Ethics Training," *Journal of Business Ethics* 29, no. 1/2 (2001): 77–84.

28. K. Tyler, "Do the Right Thing: Ethics Training Programs Help Employees Deal with Ethical Dilemmas."

29. D. R. Dalton, M. B. Metzger, & J. W. Hill, "The 'New' U.S. Sentencing Commission Guidelines: A Wake-Up Call for Corporate America," *Academy of Management Executive* 8 (1994): 7–16.

30. B. Ettore, "Crime and Punishment: A Hard Look at White-Collar Crime," *Management Review* 83 (1994): 10–16.

31. K. Tyler, "Do the Right Thing: Ethics Training Programs Help Employees Deal with Ethical Dilemmas."

32. F. Robinson & C. C. Pauze, "What Is a Board's Liability for Not Adopting a Compliance Program?" *Healthcare Financial Management* 51, no. 9 (1997): 64.

33. D. Murphy, "The Federal Sentencing Guidelines for Organizations: A Decade of Promoting Compliance and Ethics," *Iowa Law Review* 87 (2002): 697–719.

34. Robinson & Pauze, "What Is a Board's Liability?"

35. B. Schwartz, "The Nuts and Bolts of an Effective Compliance Program," *HR Focus* 74, no. 8 (1997): 13(2).

36. L. A. Hays, "A Matter of Time: Widow Sues IBM over Death Benefits," *Wall Street Journal*, 6 July 1995.

37. T. M. Jones, "Ethical Decision Making by Individuals in Organizations: An Issue-Contingent Model," *Academy of Management Review* 16 (1991): 366–395.

38. S. Morris & R. McDonald, "The Role of Moral Intensity in Moral Judgments: An Empirical Investigation," *Journal of Business Ethics* 14 (1995): 715–726; B. Flannery & D. May, "Environmental Ethical Decision Making in the U.S. Metal-Finishing Industry," *Academy of Management Journal* 43 (2000): 642–662.

39. S. Sparks, "Federal Agents Seize Computers in 27 Cities As Part of Crackdown on Software Piracy," *Wall Street Journal*, 12 December 2001, B4.

40. L. Kohlberg, "Stage and Sequence: The Cognitive-Developmental Approach to Socialization," in *Handbook of Socialization Theory and Research*, ed. D. A. Goslin (Chicago: Rand McNally, 1969); L. Trevino, "Moral Reasoning and Business Ethics: Implications for Research, Education, and Management," *Journal of Business Ethics* 11 (1992): 445–459.

41. L. Trevino & M. Brown, "Managing to be Ethical: Debunking Five Business Ethics Myths," *Academy of Management Executive* 18 (May 2004): 69–81.

42. L. T. Hosmer, "Trust: The Connecting Link between Organizational Theory and Philosophical Ethics," *Academy of Management Review* 20 (1995): 379–403.

43. R. K. Bennett, "How Honest Are We?" *Reader's Digest*, December 1995, 49–55; L. Callaway, "On the Wallet Watch— Honesty's Not Big Apple's Policy," *New York Post*, 31 July 2000, 41; A. Golab, "Results of Honesty Test: Mostly 'Finders, Keepers,'" *Chicago Sun-Times*, 12 March 1999, 3.

44. M. R. Cunningham, D. T. Wong, & A. P. Barbee, "Self-Presentation Dynamics on Overt Integrity Tests: Experimental Studies of the Reid Report," *Journal of Applied Psychology* 79 (1994): 643–658; J. Wanek, P. Sackett & D. Ones, "Toward an Understanding of Integrity Test Similarities and Differences: An Item-Level Analysis of Seven Tests," *Personnel Psychology* 56 (Winter 2003): 873–894.

45. H. J. Bernardin, "Validity of an Honesty Test in Predicting Theft among Convenience Store Employees," *Academy of Management Journal* 36 (1993): 1097–1108.

46. J. M. Collins & F. L. Schmidt, "Personality, Integrity, and White Collar Crime: A Construct Validity Study," *Personnel Psychology* (1993): 295–311.

47. W. C. Borman, M. A. Hanson, & J. W. Hedge, "Personnel Selection," *Annual Review of Psychology* 48 (1997).

48. S. Nonis & C. Swift, "An Examination of the Relationship between Academic Dishonesty and Workplace Dishonesty: A Multicampus Investigation," *Journal of Education for Business* (November 2001): 69–77.

49. L.W. Andrews, "The Nexus of Ethics," *HR Magazine*, August 2005, available at http://www.shrm.org.

50. P. E. Murphy, "Corporate Ethics Statements: Current Status and Future Prospects," *Journal of Business Ethics* 14 (1995): 727–740.

51. "More Corporate Boards Involved in Ethics Programs; Ethics Training Becoming Standard Practice," *PR Newswire*, 16 October 2006, http://www.prnewswire.com.

52. "Integrity Means . . ." Nortel Networks, http://www.nortel.com/corporate/community/ethics/collateral/code_of_conduct_nolinks.pdf, 15 June 2007.

53. Ibid.

54. S. J. Harrington, "What Corporate America Is Teaching about Ethics," *Academy of Management Executive* 5 (1991): 21–30.

55. G. Alliger & S. Dwight, "A Meta-Analytic Investigation of the Susceptibility of Integrity Tests to Faking and Coaching," *Educational and Psychological Measurement* 60 (2000): 59–72; D. S. Ones, C. Viswesvaran, & F. L. Schmidt, "Comprehensive Meta-Analysis of Integrity Test Validities: Findings and Implications for Personnel

Selection and Theories of Job Performance," *Journal of Applied Psychology* 78 (1993): 679–703; "2004 Report to the Nation on Occupational Fraud and Abuse."

56. L. A. Berger, "Train All Employees to Solve Ethical Dilemmas," *Best's Review—Life-Health Insurance Edition* 95 (1995): 70–80.

57. M. McCarthy, "How One Firm Tracks Ethics Electronically," *Wall Street Journal*, 21 October 1999, B1.

58. L. Trevino, G. Weaver, D. Gibson, & B. Toffler, "Managing Ethics and Legal Compliance: What Works and What Hurts," *California Management Review* 41, no. 2 (1999): 131–151.

59. "Business Ethics Training: Teaching Right from Wrong," *Salt Lake Tribune*, 11 June 2000, E5.

60. Trevino, Weaver, Gibson, & Toffler, "Managing Ethics."

61. A. Countryman, "Leadership Key Ingredient in Ethics Recipe, Experts Say," *Chicago Tribune*, 1 December 2002, Business 1.

62. "More Corporate Boards Involved in Ethics Programs; Ethics Training Becoming Standard Practice," *PR Newswire*, 16 October 2006, http://www.prnewswire.com.

63. Executive Summary, "2003 National Business Ethics Survey," Ethics Resource Center Research Department, http://www.ethics.org/research/2003-executive-summary.asp.

64. G. Weaver & L. Trevino, "Integrated and Decoupled Corporate Social Performance: Management Commitments, External Pressures, and Corporate Ethics Practices," *Academy of Management Journal* 42 (1999): 539–552; Weaver, Trevino, & Cochran, "Corporate Ethics Programs as Control Systems."

65. J. Salopek, "Do the Right Thing," *Training & Development* 55 (July 2001): 38–44.

66. M. Gundlach, S. Douglas, & M. Martinko, "The Decision to Blow the Whistle: A Social Information Processing Framework," *Academy of Management Executive* 17 (2003): 107–123.

67. M. Schwartz, "Business Ethics: Time to Blow the Whistle?" *Globe & Mail*, 5 March 1998, B2.

68. M. Jacobs, "The Legal Option: Employees Dreamed of Getting Rich from Stock Options; Now They're Heading to Court to Make Sure Those Dreams Come True," *Wall Street Journal*, 12 April 2001, R9.

69. "More Corporate Boards Involved in Ethics Programs; Ethics Training Becoming Standard Practice," *PR Newswire*, 16 October 2006, http://www.prnewswire.com.

70. M. P. Miceli & J. P. Near, "Whistleblowing: Reaping the Benefits," *Academy of Management Executive* 8 (1994): 65–72.

71. N. Weinberg, "Healing Thyself; Reformed Corporate Convict HCA Walks the Straight and Narrow—Very Slowly," *Forbes*, 17 March 2003, 64.

72. M. Master & E. Heresniak. "The Disconnect in Ethics Training," *Across the Board* 39 (September 2002): 51–52.

73. H. R. Bower, *Social Responsibilities of the Businessman* (New York: Harper & Row, 1953).

74. "Beyond the Green Corporation," *Business Week*, 29 January 2007.

75. Z. Zuno, "Americans Send the Message: Get Down to Business on Corporate Citizenship: Ben & Jerry's, Target, Patagonia, SC Johnson and Gerber Top the 4th GolinHarris Corporate Citizenship Index in Rating of

152 Brands by 5,000 Americans," *Business Wire*, 6 December 2006, http://www.businesswire.com.

76. J. Nocera, "The Paradoxes of Business as Do-Gooders," *New York Times*, C1.

77. J. Chipman, "U.S. Boy Scouts Pay Price for Anti-Gay Policy: High-Profile Corporations Cut Ties, Withdraw Donations," *National Post*, 29 December 2000, A16; Associated Press, "Justices Let Boy Scouts Ruling Stand: Move Upholds State's Right to Drop Group from Charity Program," *St. Louis Post-Dispatch*, 9 March 2004, A5.

78. S. L. Wartick & P. L. Cochran, "The Evolution of the Corporate Social Performance Model," *Academy of Management Review* 10 (1985): 758–769.

79. J. Nocera, "The Paradox of Businesses as Do-Gooders."

80. S. Waddock, C. Bodwell, & S. Graves. "Responsibility: The New Business Imperative," *Academy of Management Executive* 16 (2002): 132–148.

81. T. Donaldson & L. E. Preston, "The Stakeholder Theory of the Corporation: Concepts, Evidence, and Implications," *Academy of Management Review* 20 (1995): 65–91.

82. M. B. E. Clarkson, "A Stakeholder Framework for Analyzing and Evaluating Corporate Social Performance," *Academy of Management Review* 20 (1995): 92–117.

83. I. M. Jawahar & G. McLaughlin, "Toward a Descriptive Stakeholder Theory: An Organizational Life Cycle Approach," *Academy of Management Review* 26 (2001: 397–414).

84. B. Agle, R. Mitchell, & J. Sonnenfeld, "Who Matters to CEOs? An Investigation of Stakeholder Attributes and Salience, Corporate

Performance, and CEO Values," *Academy of Management Journal* 42 (1999): 507–525.

85. J. Bandler, "Losing Focus: As Kodak Eyes Digital Future, a Big Partner Starts to Fade," *Wall Street Journal*, 23 January 2004, A1.

86. L. Etter, "Smithfield to Phase Out Crates: Big Pork Producer Yields to Activists, Customers on Animal-Welfare Issue," *Wall Street Journal*, 25 January 2007, A14.

87. L. E. Preston, "Stakeholder Management and Corporate Performance," *Journal of Behavioral Economics* 19 (1990): 361–375.

88. E. W. Orts, "Beyond Shareholders: Interpreting Corporate Constituency Statutes," *George Washington Law Review* 61 (1992): 14–135.

89. A. B. Carroll, "A Three-Dimensional Conceptual Model of Corporate Performance," *Academy of Management Review* 4 (1979): 497–505.

90. Ibid.

91. R. Bates, "Zale Names New President and CEO," *JCK-Jewelers Circular Keystone*, 1 September 2006, 41.

92. C. Lawton & J. Lublin, "Dell's Founder Returns as CEO as Rollins Quits—Computer Firm Expects to Miss Earnings Mark: Stock Rises after Hours," *Wall Street Journal*, 1 February 2007, C1.

93. J. Lublin & M. Murrary, "CEOs Leave Faster Than Ever Before as Boards, Investors Lose Patience," *Wall Street Journal Interactive*, 27 October 2000.

94. D. Woodruff, "Europe Shows More CEOs the Door," *Wall Street Journal*, 1 July 2002.

95. C. Bowman, "Success of Capital Area's War on Smog Challenged," *Sacramento Bee*, 7 February 1998, A1.

96. "Air Guide 31: Implementation of Part 201 and Part 212 Permitting and Reasonably Available Control Technology Requirements for Bakeries," New York State Department of Environmental Conservation, http://www.dec.ny.gov/regulations/25211.html, 5 February 2005.

97. T. Howard, "Low-Carb Message Not Popular, but Sales Are Up," *USA Today*, 8 December 2003, 10B.

98. Ibid.

99. "Results: How You're Helping," The Hunger Site, http://www.thehungersite.com, 5 February 2005.

100. N. Aoki, "Retailer Discord Rings over Charity's Bells," *Boston Globe*, 17 November 2004, A1.

101. M. Tierney, "Target Incurs Wrath for Salvation Army Ban," *Atlanta Journal-Constitution*, 18 December 2004, 1F.

102. K. Scannell, "Witness Says Police-Vest Maker Ignored Safety Concerns," *Wall Street Journal*, 15 November 2004, C1.

103. S. Richardson, "No Time to Stop—Parsons Plant Gives Thanks," *The Pantagraph*, 14 July 2005, 1.

104. J. White, "Move by Honda Ups the Ante on Car Safety," *Wall Street Journal*, 30 October 2003, D1.

105. A. McWilliams & D. Siegel, "Corporate Social Responsibility: A Theory of the Firm Perspective," *Academy of Management Review* 26, no.1 (2001): 117–127.

106. H. Haines, "Noah Joins Ranks of Socially Responsible Funds," *Dow Jones News Service*, 13 October 1995. A meta-analysis of 41 different studies also found no relationship between corporate social responsibility and profitability. Though not reported in the meta-analysis, when confidence intervals are placed around its average sample-weighted correlation of .06, the lower confidence interval includes zero, leading to the conclusion that there is no relationship between corporate social responsibility and profitability. See M. Orlitzky, "Does Firm Size Confound the Relationship between Corporate Social Responsibility and Firm Performance?" *Journal of Business Ethics* 33 (2001): 167–180.

107. J. Pereira, "Doing Good and Doing Well at Timberland," *Wall Street Journal*, 9 September 2003, B1.

108. T. Singer, "Can Business Still Save the World?" *Inc.*, 1 April 2001, 58.

109. D. Kadlec & B. Van Voorst, "The New World of Giving: Companies Are Doing More Good, and Demanding More Back," *Time*, 5 May 1997, 62.

110. P. Carlin, "Will Rapid Growth Stunt Corporate Do-Gooders?" *Business & Society Review*, Spring 1995, 36–43.

111. K. Brown, "Chilling at Ben & Jerry's: Cleaner, Greener," *Wall Street Journal*, 15 April 2004, B1.

112. "Starbucks Timeline & History," Starbucks, http://www.starbucks.com/aboutus/timeline.asp.

113. M. Alexander, "Charity Begins at the Coffee Cup," *Sunday Star-Times*, 17 June 2001, E4.

114. J. E. Wanek, P. R. Sackett, & D. S. Ones, "Towards an Understanding of Integrity Test Similarities and Differences: An Item-Level Analysis of Seven Tests," *Personnel Psychology* 56 (2003): 873–894.

115. R. Anderson, "Sustainability Drives Innovation," *Environmental Design & Construction*, December 2004, 38; M. Conlin, "From Plunderer to Protector: In a New Documentary, Interface's Ray Anderson Discusses His Green Epiphany," *Business Week*, July 19, 2004, 60; L. Stevens, "It's Hip to Make Squares: Carpet Company Charts New Course," *Fort Worth Star-Telegram*, March 10, 2005; "Recyling Commercial Carpet Has Become Easier with INVISTA Carpet Reclamation Center's Announcement That It Will Accept Carpet," *Buildings*, March 2005, 7; K. Weeks, "A Walk in the Garden: Taking Carpet Sustainability to a New Level, Shaw and William McDonough Focus on a Cradle-to-Cradle Lifecycle to Develop a New Collection of Commercial Carpet Tile," *Contract*. April 2004, 36–38.

116. D. H. Dean, "Associating the Corporation with a Charitable Event through Sponsorship: Measuring the Effects on Corporate Community Relations," *Journal of Advertising*, Winter 2002, 77; D. Nelson, "Sponsorship or Selling Out?" *Fund Raising Management*, June 1998, 32; A. Taylor, "Poverty: Lack of Income Kills Off Low-Pay Unit," *Community Care*, February 20, 2003, 9.

Chapter 5

1. A. Ohnsman, "Ford Market Share Targets Suggest Toyota Soon No. 2," *Bloomberg.com*, http://www.bloomberg.com/apps/news?pid=20601101&sid=aAEsMChx_agU, 15 September 2006; C. Tierney, "Toyota Sets Big Goal for Tundra," *Detroit News*, http://www.detnews.com, 15 September 2006; J. McCracken & J. Stoll, "Ford Unveils Plan for Sweeping Cuts in '06

Production," *Wall Street Journal*, 18 August 2006, A1; A. Chozick, "Toyota Net Rises 39% as Auto Maker Deals with Growth Challenges," *Wall Street Journal*, 5 August 2006, A3.

2. L. A. Hill, *Becoming a Manager: Master a New Identity* (Boston: Harvard Business School Press, 1992).

3. N. Shirouzu, "Low-Key Chief of Toyota's U.S. Unit Discloses Bold Goals," *Wall Street Journal*, 17 March 2004.

4. A. Chozick, "Toyota Net Rises 39% As Auto Maker Deals with Growth Challenges," *Wall Street Journal*, 5 August 2006, A3.

5. E. A. Locke & G. P. Latham, *A Theory of Goal Setting & Task Performance* (Englewood Cliffs, NJ: Prentice Hall, 1990).

6. M. E. Tubbs, "Goal-Setting: A Meta-Analytic Examination of the Empirical Evidence," *Journal of Applied Psychology* 71 (1986): 474–483.

7. J. Bavelas & E. S. Lee, "Effect of Goal Level on Performance: A Trade-Off of Quantity and Quality," *Canadian Journal of Psychology* 32 (1978): 219–240.

8. D. Turner, "Ability, Aspirations Fine, but Persistence Is What Gets Results," *Seattle Times*, http://archives.seattletimes.nwsource.com/cgi-bin/texis.cgi/web/vortex/display?slug=dale15m&date=20030215, 13 February 2005.

9. Harvard Management Update, "Learn by 'Failing Forward,'" *Globe & Mail*, 31 October 2000, B17.

10. C. C. Miller, "Strategic Planning and Firm Performance: A Synthesis of More Than Two Decades of Research," *Academy of Management Performance* 37 (1994): 1649–1665.

11. H. Mintzberg, "Rethinking Strategic Planning: Part I: Pitfalls and Fallacies," *Long Range Planning* 27 (1994): 12–21, and "Part II: New Roles for Planners," 22–30; H. Mintzberg, "The Pitfalls of Strategic Planning," *California Management Review* 36 (1993): 32–47.

12. P. Dvorak, "Sony TVs Take Sibling Tips— Latest Machines Borrow from Videogame and Audio Technology," *Wall Street Journal*, 20 August 2004, B3.

13. Mintzberg, "The Pitfalls of Strategic Planning."

14. Locke & Latham, *A Theory of Goal Setting & Task Performance.*

15. A. King, B. Oliver, B. Sloop, & K. Vaverek, *Planning & Goal Setting for Improved Performance: Participant's Guide* (Cincinnati, OH: Thomson Executive Press, 1995).

16. C. Loomis, J. Schlosser, J. Sung, M. Boyle, & P. Neering, "The 15% Delusion: Brash Predictions about Earnings Growth Often Lead to Missed Targets, Battered Stock, and Creative Accounting—And That's When Times Are Good," *Fortune*, 5 February 2001, 102; H. Paster, "Manager's Journal: Be Prepared," *Wall Street Journal*, 24 September 2001, A24; P. Sellers, "The New Breed: The Latest Crop of CEOs Is Disciplined, Deferential, Even a Bit Dull," *Fortune*, 18 November 2002, 66. H. Klein & M. Wesson, "Goal and Commitment and the Goal-Setting Process: Conceptual Clarification and Empirical Synthesis," *Journal of Applied Psychology* 84 (1999): 885–896.

17. H. Klein & M. Wesson, "Goal and Commitment and the Goal-Setting Process: Conceptual Clarification and Empirical Synthesis," *Journal of Applied Psychology* 84 (1999): 885–886

18. Locke & Latham, *A Theory of Goal Setting & Task Performance.*

19. A. Pressman, "Ocean Spray's Creative Juices," *Business Week*, 15 May 2006, 88–90.

20. A. Bandura & D. H. Schunk, "Cultivating Competence, Self-Efficacy, and Intrinsic Interest through Proximal Self-Motivation," *Journal of Personality & Social Psycho-logy* 41 (1981): 586–598.

21. D. Ariely & K. Wertenboch, "Procrastination, Deadlines, and Performance: Self-Control by Precommitment," *Psychological Science* 13 (2002): 219–224.

22. N. Carr, "Curbing the Procrastination Instinct," *Harvard Business Review* (October 2001): 26.

23. Locke & Latham, *A Theory of Goal Setting & Task Performance.*

24. M. J. Neubert, "The Value of Feedback and Goal Setting over Goal Setting Alone and Potential Moderators of This Effect: A Meta-Analysis," *Human Performance* 11 (1998): 321–335.

25. E. H. Bowman & D. Hurry, "Strategy through the Option Lens: An Integrated View of Resource Investments and the Incremental-Choice Process," *Academy of Management Review* 18 (1993): 760–782.

26. M. Lawson, "In Praise of Slack: Time Is of the Essence," *Academy of Management Executive* 15 (2000): 125–135.

27. D. Lieberman, "Papers Take a Leap Forward, Opening Up to New Ideas," *USA Today*, 30 January 2006, http://www.usatoday.com/tech/news/techinnovations/2006–01–30-newspapers-change_x.htm.

28. N. A. Wishart, J. J. Elam, & D. Robey, "Redrawing the Portrait of a Learning Organization: Inside Knight-Ridder, Inc.," *Academy of Management Executive* 10 (1996): 7–20.

29. J. McGregor et al., "How Failure Breeds Success: Everyone Fears Failure. But Breakthroughs Depend on It. The Best Companies Embrace Their Mistakes and Learn from Them," *BusinessWeek*, 10 July 2006, 42.

30. J. C. Collins & J. I. Porras, "Organizational Vision and Visionary Organizations," *California Management Review* (Fall 1991): 30–52.

31. Ibid.

32. Ibid.

33. "President Bush Announces New Vision for Space Exploration Program," The White House, http://www.whitehouse.gov, 17 April 2005.

34. N. Gull, "Plan B (and C and D and …)," *Inc.*, March 2004, 40.

35. R. Rodgers & J. E. Hunter, "Impact of Management by Objectives on Organizational Productivity," *Journal of Applied Psychology* 76 (1991): 322–336.

36. E. Marlow & R. Schilhavy, "Expectation Issues in Management by Objectives Programs," *Industrial Management* 33, no. 4 (1991): 29.

37. "Web MBO Teams with Deloitte & Touche to Deliver Innovative Web-Based 'Management-by-Objectives and Performance Management' Solutions," *PR Newswire*, 19 June 2001.

38. L. Iacocca, with W. Novak, *Iacocca* (New York: Bantam, 1984).

39. J. Lyne, "Philip Morris Relocating NYC Headquarters to Native Virginia Area," *Site Selection*, http://www.conway.com/ssinsider/bbdeal/bd030324.htm, 17 February 2005.

40. R. Richmond, "It's 10 A.M. Do You Know Where Your Workers Are?" *Wall Street Journal*, 12 January 2004, R1.

41. Adapted from quality procedure at G & G Manufacturing, Cincinnati, Ohio.

42. N. Humphrey, "References a Tricky Issue for Both Sides," *Nashville Business Journal* 11 (8 May 1995): 1A.

43. K. R. MacCrimmon, R. N. Taylor, & E. A. Locke, "Decision Making and Problem Solving," in *Handbook of Industrial & Organizational Psychology*, ed. M. D. Dunnette (Chicago: Rand McNally, 1976), 1397–1453.

44. "Airbus's 'Big Baby,' the A380 Airliner, Fights a Weight Problem," *JEC Composites*, http://www.jeccomposites.com/composites-news/1095/Airbuss-%60big-baby.html, 19 February 2005.

45. D. Michaels, "Jumbo Bet: At Airbus, Picturing Huge Jet Was Easy; Building It Is Hard," *Wall Street Journal*, 27 May 2004, A1.

46. MacCrimmon, Taylor, & Locke, "Decision Making and Problem Solving."

47. G. Kress, "The Role of Interpretation in the Decision Process," *Industrial Management* 37 (1995): 10–14.

48. D. Milbrank, "We Feel Your Pain, Congress Is Saying, with Real Empathy," *Wall Street Journal*, 1 April 1996; S. Nelson, "Shays, Moran: Defend CAA," *Roll Call*, 30 September 2002.

49. Michaels, "Jumbo Bet: At Airbus, Picturing Huge Jet Was Easy."

50. *Consumer Reports Buying Guide 2006*, 129–131.

51. "New-Vehicle Ratings Comparison by Car Category," ConsumerReports.org, http://www.consumerreports.org/cro/cars/index.htm, 19 February 2005.

52. P. Djang, "Selecting Personal Computers," *Journal of Research on Computing in Education* 25 (1993): 327.

53. "European Cities Monitor," Cushman & Wakefield Healy & Baker, 2005. available at http://www.cushmanwakefield.com/cwglobal/docviewer/European%20Cities%20Monitor.pdf?id=ca1500006&repositoryKey=CoreRepository&itemDesc=document.

54. "The PLUS Decision Making Model," Ethics Resource Center, http://www.ethics.org/resources/decision-making-model.asp, 19 February 2005.

55. B. Dumaine, "The Trouble with Teams," *Fortune*, 5 September 1994, 86–92.

56. L. Pelled, K. Eisenhardt, & K. Xin, "Exploring the Black Box: An Analysis of Work Group Diversity, Conflict, and Performance," *Administrative Science Quarterly* 44, no. 1 (March 1, 1999): 1.

57. B. Scudamore, "Gather Round! For a Group Interview," *Inc.*, August 2006, 94.

58. I. L. Janis, *Groupthink* (Boston: Houghton Mifflin, 1983).

59. C. P. Neck & C. C. Manz, "From Groupthink to Teamthink: Toward the Creation of Constructive Thought Patterns in Self-Managing Work Teams," *Human Relations* 47 (1994): 929–952; J. Schwartz & M. L. Wald, "'Groupthink' Is 30 Years Old, and Still Going Strong," *New York Times*, 9 March 2003, 5.

60. M. Bazerman & D. Chugh, "Decisions without Blinders," *Harvard Business Review*, January 2006, 84(1): 88–97.

61. C. Gallo, "How to Run a Meeting Like Google," *Business Week Online*, 8 September 2006, 15.

62. A. Mason, W. A. Hochwarter, & K. R. Thompson, "Conflict: An Important Dimension in Successful Management Teams," *Organizational Dynamics* 24 (1995): 20.

63. C. Olofson, "So Many Decisions, So Little Time: What's Your Problem?" *Fast Company*, 1 October 1999, 62.

64. Ibid.

65. R. Cosier & C. R. Schwenk, "Agreement and Thinking Alike: Ingredients for Poor Decisions," *Academy of Management Executive* 4 (1990): 69–74.

66. Ibid.

67. B. Breen, "BMW: Driven by Design," *Fast Company*, 1 September 2002, 123.

68. K. Jenn & E. Mannix, "The Dynamic Nature of Conflict: A Longitudinal Study of Intragroup Conflict and Group Performance," *Academy of Management Journal* 44, no. 2 (2001): 238–251; R. L. Priem, D. A. Harrison, & N. K. Muir, "Structured Conflict and Consensus Outcomes in Group Decision Making," *Journal of Management* 21 (1995): 691–710.

69. A. Van De Ven & A. L. Delbecq, "Nominal versus Interacting Group Processes for Committee Decision Making Effectiveness," *Academy of Management Journal* 14 (1971): 203–212.

70. A. R. Dennis & J. S. Valicich, "Group, Sub-Group, and Nominal Group Idea Generation: New Rules for a New Media?" *Journal of Management* 20 (1994): 723–736.

71. C. R. Schwenk, "Effects of Devil's Advocacy and Dialectical Inquiry on Decision Making: A Meta-Analysis," *Organizational Behavior & Human Decision Performance* 47 (1990): 161–176; M. Orlitzky & R. Hirokawa, "To Err Is Human, to Correct for It Divine: A Meta-Analysis of Research Testing the Functional Theory of Group Decision-Making Effectiveness," *Small Group Research* 32, no. 3 (June 2001): 313–341.

72. S. G. Rogelberg, J. L. Barnes-Farrell, & C. A. Lowe, "The Stepladder Technique: An Alternative Group Structure Facilitating Effective Group Decision Making," *Journal of Applied Psychology* 77 (1992): 730–737; S. G. Rogelberg & M. S. O'Connor, "Extending the Stepladder Technique: An Examination of the Self-Paced Stepladder Groups," *Group Dynamics: Theory, Research, & Practice* 2 (1998): 82–91.

73. S. Rogelberg, M. O'Connor, & M. Sedergurg, "Using the Stepladder Technique to Facilitate the Performance of Audioconferencing Groups," *Journal of Applied Psychology* 87 (2002): 994–1000.

74. R. B. Gallupe, W. H. Cooper, M. L. Grise, & L. M. Bastianutti, "Blocking Electronic Brainstorms," *Journal of Applied Psychology* 79 (1994): 77–86.

75. R. B. Gallupe & W. H. Cooper, "Brainstorming Electronically," *Sloan Management Review*, Fall 1993, 27–36.

76. Ibid.

77. G. Kay, "Effective Meetings through Electronic Brainstorming," *Management Quarterly* 35 (1995): 15.

78. A. LaPlante, "90s Style Brainstorming," *Forbes ASAP*, 25 October 1993, 44.

79. R.J. Aldag & L. W. Kuzuhara, *Mastering Management Skills: A Manager's Toolkit* (Mason, OH: Thomson South-Western, 2005) 172–173.

80. N. Brodsky, "Just Say Yes: How a Policy That Sounds Tough Can Turn into a Lifeline for Some," *Inc.*, November 2004, 67; S. Smith, "What Every Employer Should Know

about Drug Testing in the Workplace: Think You Don't Have a Problem with Drugs in the Workplace? Think Again," *Occupational Hazards*, August 2004, 45; "Small Firms More Likely to See Drug Problems, Labor Department Study Reports," *Pueblo Chieftain*, 3 August 2004; D. Willoughby, "Drugs, Workplaces Don't Mix; Employers Take Steps to Prevent Substance Abuse," *Montgomery Advertiser*, 4 May 2004.

81. C. Fishman, "The Wal-Mart You Don't Know," *Fast Company*, December 2003, 68–80; M. Boyle, "Wal-Mart Keeps the Change," *Fortune*, 10 November 2003, 46; C. Y. Chen, "Wal-Mart Drives a New Tech Boom," *Fortune*, May 2004; "Is Wal-Mart Good for America?," *Frontline*, http://www.pbs.org/wgbh/pages/frontline/shows/walmart.

82. "20 Hot Job Tracks," *U.S. News & World Report*, 30 October 1995, 98–104; C. Boivie, "Planning for the Future … Your Future," *Journal of Systems Management* 44 (1993): 25–27; J. Connelly, "How to Choose Your Next Career," *Fortune*, 6 February 1995, 145–146; P. Sherrid, "A 12-Hour Test of My Personality," *U.S. News & World Report*, 31 October 1994, 109.

Chapter 6

1. S. Lacy, "The Hot Ticket Isn't Ticketmaster," *Business Week*, 4 September 2006, 36; S. Stecklow, "StubHub's Ticket to Ride," *Wall Street Journal*, 17 January 2006, B1-B2; "Jeff Fleur, 32," *Entrepreneur*, October 2006, 94.; "StubHub(A): January 2004," *Stanford Graduate School of Business Case*, 15 March 2005, Case SM-132A; V. Vara, D. Berman, & R. Adams, "EBay-StubHub Deal a Boon to Start-Ups," *Wall Street Journal*, 11 January 2007, B4; http://www.stubhub.com.

2. L. Kahney, "Inside Look at the Birth of the iPod," *Wired*, 21 July 2004, http://www.wired.com/news/culture/0,64286-0.html; http://www.apple-history.com/?page=gallery&model=ipod; K. Hall, "Sony's iPod Assault Is No Threat to Apple," *Business Week*, 13 March 2006, 53; N. Wingfield, "SanDisk Raises Music-Player Stakes," *Wall Street Journal*, 21 August 2006, B4; "Growing Louder: Microsoft Plods after iPod Like a Giant—Powerful, Determined, Untiring," *Winston-Salem Journal*, 15 November 2006, D1–D2; A. Athavaley & R. A. Guth, "How the Zune Is Faring So Far with Consumers," *Wall Street Journal*, 12 December 2006, D1, D7.

3. J. Barney, "Firm Resources and Sustained Competitive Advantage," *Journal of Management* 17 (1991): 99–120; J. Barney, "Looking Inside for Competitive Advantage," *Academy of Management Executive* 9 (1995): 49–61.

4. J. Snell, "Apple's Home Run," *Macworld*, November 2006, 7.

5. J. D'Arcy, & T. Davies, "The Walkman at 20," *Maclean's*, 30 August 1999, 10; K. Hall, "Sony's iPod Assault Is no Threat to Apple," *Business Week*, 13 March 2006, 53.

6. A. Athavaley & R.A. Guth, "How the Zune Is Faring So Far with Consumers," D7.

7. http://music.yahoo.com

8. J. Warren, "At New Web Store, Many Songs Sell for a Few Cents," *Wall Street Journal*, 14 October 2006, P2.

9. R. Levine, "Napster's Ghost Rises," *Fortune*, 6 March 2006, 30; "30 Products for 30 Years," *MacWorld*, June 2006, 15–16.

10. S. Hart & C. Banbury, "How Strategy-Making Processes Can Make a Difference," *Strategic Management Journal* 15 (1994): 251–269.

11. R. A. Burgelman, "Fading Memories: A Process Theory of Strategic Business Exit in Dynamic Environments," *Administrative Science Quarterly* 39 (1994): 24–56; R. A. Burgelman & A. S. Grove, "Strategic Dissonance," *California Management Review* 38 (1996): 8–28.

12. S. Ellison, "Kraft's Stale Strategy—Endless Extensions of Oreos, Chips Ahoy and Jell-O Brands Created a New-Product Void," *Wall Street Journal*, 18 December 2003, B1.

13. J. Barrett, "The 100-Calorie Snack Attack," *Newsweek*, 14 August 2006, 34; http://www.oreo.com.

14. S. Ellison, "Kraft's Stale Strategy."

15. Ibid.

16. R. Burgelman & A. Grove, "Strategic Dissonance," *California Management Review* (Winter 1996): 8–28.

17. E. Smith & M. Peers, "Cost Cutting Is an Uphill Fight at Warner Music," *Wall Street Journal*, 24 May 2004, B1.

18. A. Fiegenbaum, S. Hart, & D. Schendel, "Strategic Reference Point Theory," *Strategic Management Journal* 17 (1996): 219–235.

19. P. Buller & G. McEvoy, "Creating and Sustaining Ethical Capability in the Multi-National Corporation," *Journal of World Business* 34 (1999): 326–343.

20. Hart & Banbury, "How Strategy-Making Processes Can Make a Difference"; C. C. Miller & L. B. Cardinal, "Strategic Planning and Firm Performance: A Synthesis of More Than Two Decades of Research," *Academy of Management Journal* 37 (1994): 1649–1665; D. King, D. Dalton, C. Daily, & J. Covin, "Meta-Analyses of Post-Acquisition Performance: Indications of Unidentified Moderators," *Strategic Management Journal* 25 (2004): 187–200; C. R. Schwenk, "Effects of Formal Strategic Planning on Financial Performance in Small Firms: A Meta-Analysis," *Entrepreneurship Theory & Practice*, Spring 1993, 53–64.

21. D. Carpenter, "SWOT Team Solves Supply Chain Issues," *Materials Management in Health Care*, April 2006, 40–42.

22. "Reliability Histories: Detailed Histories for 1997 to 2004 Models," *Consumer Reports*, http://www.consumerreports.org, 5 March 2005.

23. C. Metz, "19th Annual Reader Satisfaction Survey," *PC Magazine*, 21 August 2006, http://www.pcmag.com/article2/0,1895,2006502,00.asp.

24. L. Margonelli, "How Ikea Designs Its Sexy Price Tags," *Business 2.0*, http://www.money.cnn.com, 1 October 2002.

25. A. Fiegenbaum & H. Thomas, "Strategic Groups as Reference Groups: Theory, Modeling and Empirical Examination of Industry and Competitive Strategy," *Strategic Management Journal* 16 (1995): 461–476.

26. R. K. Reger & A. S. Huff, "Strategic Groups: A Cognitive Perspective," *Strategic Management Journal* 14 (1993): 103–124.

27. http://homedepot.com; M. Hogan, "Big Box Battle: Home Depot vs. Lowe's," *Business Week Online*, 22 August 2006, 7; F. Miller, "Growing Pains," *Kitchen & Bath Business*, September 2006, 53.

28. http://ourcompany.acehardware.com/download/pdf_word/FACTFILE.PDF

29. http://www.hardwarestore.com/about-aubuchon-hardware.aspx

30. http://ourcompany.acehardware.com/

download/pdf_word/
FACTFILE.PDF.

31. http://84lumber.com/
About84/about.asp.

32. http://ourcompany
.acehardware.com/
download/pdf_word/
FACTFILE.PDF

33. http://www
.truevaluecompany.com/
overview/annualreport.asp

34. W. B. Werther, Jr. &
J. L. Kerr, "The Shifting
Sands of Competitive
Advantage," *Business
Horizons*, May–June
1995, 11–17.

35. Ibid.

36. "Menard, Inc.," *Hoover's
Company Profiles*, 8 May
2003.

37. J. Samuelson, "Tough Guy
Billionaire," *Forbes*, 24
February 1997, 64–66.

38. "Menards vs. Home
Depot," WCCO Channel
4000, http://www.
channel4000.com, 25
September 2001.

39. S. Bucksot, C. Jensen, &
D. Tratensek, "Where
Are We Headed?" *2005
Market Measure: The
Industry's Annual Report*,
http://www.nrha.org/
MM2004.pdf, 6 March
2005.

40. Ibid.

41. H. Murphy, "Menard's Tool
in Retail Battle: Gigantic
Stores," *Crain's Chicago
Business*, 12 August
2002, 3.

42. Ibid.

43. G. Bounds, "More than
Squeaking By," *Wall Street
Journal*, 23 May 2006, B1;
www.wd40.com;
www.wikipedia.com;
http://www.octanecreative
.com/WD40/; http://home
.howstuffworks.com/
question155.htm.

44. M. Lubatkin, "Value-
Creating Mergers: Fact or
Folklore?" *Academy of
Management Executive* 2
(1988): 295–302;
M. Lubatkin &
S. Chatterjee, "Extending
Modern Portfolio Theory
into the Domain of
Corporate Diversification:
Does It Apply?" *Academy
of Management Journal* 37
(1994): 109–136;

M. H. Lubatkin &
P. J. Lane, "Psst . . . The
Merger Mavens Still Have
It Wrong!" *Academy of
Management Executive*
10 (1996): 21–39.

45. "Who We Are," 3M,
http://www.3m.com, 6
March 2005.

46. "Our Company," Johnson
& Johnson, http://www
.jnj.com/our_company/
index.htm, 6 March 2005.

47. http://www.saralee.com.

48. "About Samsung,"
Samsung, http://
www.samsung.com/
AboutSAMSUNG/index
.htm, 6 March 2005.

49. http://www.bcg.com/
this_is_BCG/bcg_history/
bcg_history_2005.html;
http:www.wikipedia.org.

50. "Phonebook Company
Yellow Book Enters into
Lynchburg, Va.-Area
Market," *Lynchburg (VA)
News & Advance*, 16
January 2005; "Leading
Independents Project
Double-Digit Gains in
2004; Plan Aggressive
Expansion," *Yellow
Pages & Directory
Report*, 27 August 2004;
G. David, "The Good
Book/Unmellow Yellow:
A Battle among Business
Directories Could Cut
Your Ad Costs," *FSB*,
1 November 2003, 85.

51. K. Brooker, "Plugging
the Leaks at P&G: A
First-Year Report Card
for CEO Durk Jager,"
Fortune, 21 February
2000, 44; "R&D's
Formula for Success,"
Procter & Gamble, http://
www.pg.com/science/rd_
formula_success.jhtml, 14
May 2003.

52. P. Sellers, "P&G: Teaching
an Old Dog New Tricks,"
Fortune, 31 May 2004,
166.

53. J. A. Pearce II, "Selecting
among Alternative Grand
Strategies," *California
Management Review*
(Spring 1982): 23–31.

54. N. Deogun, C. Forelle,
D. Berman, & E. Nelson,
"Razor's Edge: P&G
to Buy Gillette for $54
Billion," *Wall Street
Journal*, 28 January 2005,
A1; A. Latour, "Closing

Bell: After a Year of
Frenzied Deals, Two
Telecom Giants Emerge,"
Wall Street Journal, 15
February 2005, A1;
G. Zuckerman, "What to
Do Amid All the Big Deals?"
Wall Street Journal Sunday,
6 February 2005, 1;
V. Tong, "Acquisitions
Made in 2006 Set
Records," 21 November,
2006, CBS News,
http://www.cbsnews
.com/stories/2006/11/21/ap/
business/mainD8LH4UM00
.shtml.

55. "Financial and Other
Numbers: Store Growth,"
Walgreens.com, http://
www.walgreens.com/
about/press/facts/fact1
.jhtml,8 May 2005;
A. Tsao, "Why CVS
May Be the Pick of the
Pack: While Walgreen Is
Considered the Drugstore
Sector's Blue Chip, CVS
Has a Much Cheaper
P-E and Plenty of Upside
Potential," *Business Week
Online*, http://www
.businessweek.com/
bwdaily/dnflash/may2003/
nf20030512_9097_db014
.htm, 13 May 2003.

56. S. Chandler, "Walgreens
Adding 500 Stores, Posts
Record Profit," *Chicago
Tribune*, 3 January
2001, 2.

57. "Subaru Archives
Homepage," Cars101
.com, http://www.cars101
.com/subaru_archives
.html, 8 March 2005.

58. J. A. Pearce II,
"Retrenchment Remains
the Foundation of Business
Turnaround," *Strategic
Management Journal* 15
(1994): 407–417.

59. J. Hyatt, J. Sloane,
E. Welles, & M. Overfelt,
"Beat the Beast,"
*Fortune Small
Business*, 1 September
2004, 42.

60. A. Lustgarden & R. Oliver,
"Seven Stocks to Bet On,"
Fortune, 6 September
2004, 137.

61. M. Maiello, "Prozac
Hangover," *Forbes*, 10
May 2004, 116.

62. E. Ramstad & P. Dvorak,
"Off-the-Shelf Parts
Create New Order in TVs,
Electronics," *Wall Street

Journal*, 16 December
2003, A1.

63. http://www.walmartfacts.
com/FactSheets/8252006_
Merchandising.pdf,
http://www.walmartfacts
.com/content/default
.aspx?id = 3.

64. P. Wonacott, "Wal-
Mart, Others Demand
Lowest Prices, Managers
Scramble to Slash Costs,"
Wall Street Journal, 13
November 2003, A1.

65. M. Veverka, "Bigger and
Better: Costco's Costly
Expansion Is About to Pay
Off—For Shoppers and
Shareholders," *Barron's*,
12 May 2003, 28.

66. L. Tischler, "The Price Is
Right," *Fast Company*,
1 November 2003, 83.

67. Ibid.

68. http://www.containerstore
.com

69. B. Breen, "What's Selling
in America: The Lamest
Question in Retails Is
'Can I Help You,'" *Fast
Company*, January 2003,
82.

70. R. E. Miles & C. C. Snow,
*Organizational Strategy,
Structure, & Process*
(New York: McGraw
Hill, 1978); S. Zahra &
J. A. Pearce, "Research
Evidence on the Miles-
Snow Typology," *Journal
of Management* 16 (1990):
751–768;
W. L. James & K. J.
Hatten, "Further Evidence
on the Validity of the
Self Typing Paragraph
Approach: Miles and
Snow Strategic
Archetypes in Banking,"
*Strategic Management
Journal* 16 (1995):
161–168.

71. E. Bellman & D. Ball,
"Unilever, P&G Wage
Price War for Edge in
India," *Wall Street Journal*,
11 August 2004, B1.

72. E. Bellman, "Hindustan
Lever Posts 27% Drop In
Quarterly Net—India's
Competitive Market for
Consumer Goods Forces
Company to Slash Prices,"
Wall Street Journal,
29 October 2004, A2.

73. "A Century of Innovation,"
3M. Available at http://

solutions.3m.com/wps/portal/_l/en_US/_s.155/123515, 10 March 2005.

74. G. Harris & J. Slater, "Bitter Pills: Drug Makers See 'Branded Generics' Eating into Profits," *Wall Street Journal*, 17 April 2003, A1.

75. B. Einhorn, M. Kripalani, & K. Capell, "The Little Drugmakers That Could: India's Scrappy Industry Is Making Big Western Outfits Sweat," *Business Week*, 3 March 2003, 20.

76. C. Emsden, "Fiat Set to Make Comeback Bid on Bumpy Road," *Wall Street Journal*, 27 October 2004, B2E.

77. G. Kahn & S. Power, "Fiat's CEO Grabs Wheel at Auto Unit—Surprise Firing of Demel by Marchionne May Augur Shifts in Turnaround Plan," *Wall Street Journal Europe*, 18 February 2005, A1; K. Maxwell, "Fiat Auto Unit Drives Sales Drive," *Wall Street Journal*, 27 October 2006, http://online.wsj.com/article/SB116187138996104636-search.html?KEYWORDS=fiat&COLLECTION=sjie/6month.

78. M. Chen, "Competitor Analysis and Interfirm Rivalry: Toward a Theoretical Integration," *Academy of Management Review* 21 (1996): 100–134; J. C. Baum & H. J. Korn, "Competitive Dynamics of Interfirm Rivalry," *Academy of Management Journal* 39 (1996): 255–291.

79. Ibid.

80. S. Leung, "Wendy's Sees Green in Salad Offerings— More Sophistication, Ethnic Flavors Appeal to Women, Crucial to Building Market Share," *Wall Street Journal*, 24 April 2003, B2.

81. M. Stopa, "Wendy's New-Fashioned Growth: Buy Hardee's," *Crain's Detroit Business*, 21 October 1996.

82. L. Lavelle, "The Chickens Come Home to Roost, and Boston Market Is Prepared to Expand," *The Record*, 6 October 1996.

83. "International Subway Locations," Subway, http://www.subway.com, 1 March 2007; "Investor Fact Sheet January 2004," McDonald's Corporation Annual Report 2005; N. Torres, "View from the Top: Subway Takes the Title of the #1 Franchise for the 13th Time," Entrepreneur.com, http://www.entrepreneur.com, 11 March 2005.

84. "Frequently Asked Questions," Subway Restaurants, http://www.subway.com/subwayroot/AboutSubway/subwayFaqs.aspx, 11 March 2005.

85. S. Leung, "Fast-Food Firms' Big Budgets Don't Buy Consumer Loyalty," *Wall Street Journal*, 24 July 2003, B4.

86. G. Marcial, "How Wendy's Stayed Out of the Fire," *Business Week*, 9 December 2002, 138.

87. S. Kilman, "Leading the News: Diageo Says Industry Price War Is Crimping Its Burger King Sale," *Wall Street Journal*, 8 November 2002, A3.

88. D. Ketchen, Jr., C. Snow, & V. Street, "Improving Firm Performance by Matching Strategic Decision-Making Processes to Competitive Dynamics," *Academy of Management Executive* 18 (2004): 29–43.

89. S. Matthews, "Financial: Salads Help McD Post First U.S. Sales Gain in 14 Months," *Chicago Sun-Times*, 14 May 2003, 69.

90. S. Ellison, "In Lean Times, Big Companies Make a Grab for Market Share," *Wall Street Journal*, 5 September 2003, A1.

91. J. C. Baum & H. J. Korn, "Competitive Dynamics of Interfirm Rivalry," *Academy of Management Journal* 39 (1996): 255–291.

92. S. Kirsner, "They May Not Be CNBC Regulars, but This Fab Four Represent What's Needed Today: CEOs with Vision Who Also Aren't Afraid to Get Their Hands Dirty," *Fast Company*, 1 February 2005, 68.

93. B. Antoncic & R. D. Hisrich, "Intrapreneurship: Construct Refinement and Cross-Cultural Validation," *Journal of Business Venturing* 16 (2001): 495–527.

94. D. Ball & S. Leung, "Latte versus Latte—Starbucks, Dunkin' Donuts Seek Growth by Capturing Each Other's Customers," *Wall Street Journal*, 10 February 2004, B1.

95. W. Symonds, D. Kiley, & S. Holmes, "A Java Jolt for Dunkin' Donuts," *Business Week*, 20 December 2004, 61.

96. Ball & Leung, "Latte versus Latte."

97. G. T. Lumpkin & G. G. Dess, "Clarifying the Entrepreneurial Orientation Construct and Linking It to Performance," *Academy of Management Review* 21 (1996): 135–172.

98. N. Venkatraman, "Strategic Orientation of Business Enterprises: The Construct, Dimensionality, and Measurement," *Management Science* 35 (1989): 942–962.

99. J. M. Houston & R. D. Smither, "The Nature of Competitiveness: The Development and Validation of the Competitiveness Index," *Educational and Psychological Measurement* 52 (1992): 407–418.

100. I. Brat, "GreenThumb's Profits Grow," *Wall Street Journal*, 17 April 2006, B5; http://www.scotts.com.

101. Y. I. Kane & N. Wingfield, "Out of the Box: Amid Videogame Arms Race, Nintendo Slows Things Down," *Wall Street Journal*, 2 November 2006, A1; J. Alabaster, "Nintendo's 9-Month Net Beats Full-Year Target," *Wall Street Journal*, 26 January 2007, B4; Y. Kim, "In War of Game Consoles, Chip Makers Are Winners," *Wall Street Journal*, 1 March 2007, online; R. Guth, "IPod Envy: Microsoft's Xbox Whiz Drives Strategic Shift," *Wall Street Journal*, 5 January 2007, A1.

102. P. Buhler, "Managing Your Career: No Longer Your Company's Responsibility," *Supervision*, May 1997.

Chapter 7

1. M. Arndt, "Creativity Overflowing," *Business Week*, 8 May 2006, 50–53; C. Salter, "Whirlpool Finds Its Cool," *Fast Company*, June 2005, 72–75; J. Rivkin, D. Leonard, & G. Hamel, "Change at Whirlpool Corporation (A)," *Harvard Business School*, 20 September 2005, Case 9, 705–762; http://www.whirlpoolcorp.com/about/corpfactsheet/default.asp.

2. T. M. Amabile, R. Conti, H. Coon, J. Lazenby, & M. Herron, "Assessing the Work Environment for Creativity," *Academy of Management Journal* 39 (1996): 1154–1184.

3. Ibid.

4. A. H. Van de Ven & M. S. Poole, "Explaining Development and Change in Organizations," *Academy of Management Review* 20 (1995): 510–540.

5. J. Adamy, "Pitching Tents That Go Up for Good: Chandeliers and Elevators," *Wall Street Journal*, 10 May 2004, A1.

6. Amabile, et al., "Assessing the Work Environment for Creativity."

7. P. Anderson & M. L. Tushman, "Managing through Cycles of Technological Change," *Research/Technology Management*, May–June 1991, 26–31.

8. R. N. Foster, *Innovation: The Attacker's Advantage* (New York: Summit, 1986).

9. "iComp Index 2.0," Intel, http://www.intel.com, 5 December 1997.

10. J. Burke, *The Day the Universe Changed* (Boston: Little, Brown, 1985).

11. http://www.kodak.com; "Industry Snapshot," *Time*, 5 December 2005, 110; W. Symonds, "Kodak: Is This the Darkest Hour?" *Business Week Online*, 8 August 2006, 3.

12. M. L. Tushman, P. C. Anderson, & C. O'Reilly, "Technology Cycles, Innovation Streams, and Ambidextrous Organizations: Organization Renewal through Innovation Streams and Strategic Change," in *Managing Strategic Innovation and Change*, ed. M. L. Tushman & P. Anderson (New York: Oxford Press, 1997), 3–23.

13. P. Landers, "Brain Surgery Made Simple—New Less-Invasive Procedures Reduce Pain, Recovery Time; Sending in the Tiny Robots," *Wall Street Journal*, 31 October 2002, D1.

14. "Pony Express," *Encyclopedia Britannica Online*, http://www.eb.com, 6 March 1999.

15. J. R. Aldern, "The Victorian Internet: The Remarkable Story of the Telegraph and the Nineteenth Century's On-Line Pioneers (Review)," *Smithsonian*, 1 January 1999.

16. E. Schlossberg, *Interactive Excellence: Defining and Developing New Standards for the Twenty-First Century* (New York: Ballantine, 1998).

17. W. Abernathy & J. Utterback, "Patterns of Industrial Innovation," *Technology Review* 2 (1978): 40–47.

18. "Glossary," MP3.com, http://www.mp3.com, 18 March 2005; B. Chaffin, "The Back Page: Music Format Wars," *Mac Observer*, http://www.macobserver.com/columns/thebackpage/2004/20040203.shtml, 18 March 2005; C. Goodwin,

"Technology Insights: Online Music Stores," *Ticker*, http://www.ticker.com, 18 March 2005.

19. J. Bosma, "Satellites Must Look to Earth for Success," *Satellite News*, 5 August 2002.

20. D. Young, "Foreign Mobile Telcos Look at Chinese 3G Standard," *Reuters News*, 15 March 2005.

21. Y. Utsumi, "Harmonizing Global Standards: The Future of 3G," International Telecommunication Union: 3G Mobile 2003, http://www.itu.int/osg/sg/speeches/2003/01143GMobile.html, 14 January 2003.

22. M. Schilling, "Technological Lockout: An Integrative Model of the Economic and Strategic Factors Driving Technology Success and Failure," *Academy of Management Review* 23 (1998): 267–284; M. Schilling, "Technology Success and Failure in Winner-Take-All Markets: The Impact of Learning Orientation, Timing, and Network Externalities," *Academy of Management Journal* 45 (2002): 387–398.

23. Amabile, et al., "Assessing the Work Environment for Creativity."

24. Ibid.

25. M. Csikszentmihalyi, *Flow: The Psychology of Optimal Experience* (New York: Harper & Row, 1990).

26. D. Garbato, "On the Beaten Track: Tractor Supply Co. Embraces Change but Stays Focused in All Areas of Its Business," *Retail Merchandiser*, January 2005, 30–31.

27. D. Murphy, "Ways That Managers Can Help Workers—Or Hinder Them," *San Francisco Chronicle*, 26 November 2000, J1; M. Schrage, "Your Idea Is Brilliant; Glad I Thought of It," *Fortune*, 16 October 2000, 412.

28. K. Capell, "Thinking Simple at Philips," 11 December 2006, 50.

29. M. Conlin, "Smashing the Clock," 11 December 2006, 60–68.

30. K. M. Eisenhardt, "Accelerating Adaptive Processes: Product Innovation in the Global Computer Industry," *Administrative Science Quarterly* 40 (1995): 84–110.

31. Ibid.

32. G. Bounds, "Sticky Fingers? How Avery Found an Office Problem to Solve," *Wall Street Journal*, 13 July 2004, B1.

33. R. Winslow, "Atomic Speed: Utility Cuts Red Tape, Builds Nuclear Plant Almost on Schedule," *Wall Street Journal Interactive*, 22 February 1984.

34. Jeff Howe, "The Rise of Crowdsourcing," *Wired*, June 2006, 176; http://www.innocentive.com.

35. C. Salter, "Ford's Escape Route," *Fast Company*, 1 October 2004, 106.

36. Ibid.

37. Ibid.

38. Ibid.

39. L. Kraar, "25 Who Help the U.S. Win: Innovators Everywhere Are Generating Ideas to Make America a Stronger Competitor. They Range from a Boss Who Demands the Impossible to a Mathematician with a Mop," *Fortune*, 22 March 1991.

40. M. W. Lawless & P. C. Anderson, "Generational Technological Change: Effects of Innovation and Local Rivalry on Performance," *Academy of Management Journal* 39 (1996): 1185–1217.

41. http://micro.gameboy.com.

42. "Sony Cuts Backward Compatibility for PlayStation 3 in Europe," *Wall Street Journal*, 27 February 2007, http://online.wsj.com.

43. P. Siekman, "The Snap-Together Business Jet," *Fortune*, 21 January 2002, 104[A].

44. J. Muller, "Chrysler Redesigns the Way It Designs: Karenann Terrell's High-Tech Quest for Change," *Business Week*, 2 September 2002, 26B.

45. http://movies.about.com/cs/upcomingreleases/a/harrypotter4dir.htm, http://www.wizardnews.com/, http://www.cinematical.com/2006/11/03/latest-harry-potter-director-michael-who/; K. Kelly, "Older Harry Rates a PG-13: The Awkward, Lovelorn Hero of 'Goblet of Fire' May Lose Kids, Gain Broader Audience," *Wall Street Journal*, 16 November 2005, B1.

46. B. Baumohl & W. Cole "The Perils of Having Way More than Enough," *Time*, 13 January 1997, 58; S. Forest, "Incredible Universe: Lost in Space," *Business Week*, 4 March 1996, http://www.businessweek.com/1996/10/b346580.htm.

47. P. Strebel, "Choosing the Right Change Path," *California Management Review*, Winter 1994, 29–51.

48. W. Weitzel & E. Jonsson, "Reversing the Downward Spiral: Lessons from W. T. Grant and Sears Roebuck," *Academy of Management Executive* 5 (1991): 7–22.

49. J. Peters, "Ford and GM Suffer as Buyers Shun SUVs," *New York Times*, 4 May 2005, C1.

50. T. Agins, L. Bird, & L. Jereski, "Overdoing It: A Thirst for Glitter and a Pliant Partner Got Barney's in a Bind," *Wall Street Journal Interactive*, 19 January 1996.

51. "The Rise and Fall of the House of Barneys: A Family Tale of Chutzpah, Glory, and Greed (Review)," *Publishers Weekly*, 22 February 1999, 73.

52. Ibid.

53. D. Moin, V. M. Young, & A. Friedman, "Dickson

Pool Sees Barney's IPO," *Women's Wear Daily*, 5 August 1997.

54. L. Bird, "Barney's to Close Original Store and Three Others," *Asian Wall Street Journal Interactive*, 19 June 1997.

55. D. Moin, "Barney's New Owners Plan to Retain Company, Grow Business: Strategy Calls for Boosting Sales, Increasing Cash Flow This Year," *Daily News Record*, 15 February 1999.

56. K. Lewin, *Field Theory in Social Science: Selected Theoretical Papers* (New York: Harper & Brothers, 1951).

57. A. Deutschman, "Making Change: Why Is It So Darn Hard to Change Our Ways?" *Fast Company*, May 2005, 52–62.

58. C. Taylor, "Changing Gears," *Sales & Marketing Management*, October 2005, 1.

59. K. Lewin, *Field Theory in Social Science*.

60. A. B. Fisher, "Making Change Stick," *Fortune*, 17 April 1995, 121.

61. J. P. Kotter & L. A. Schlesinger, "Choosing Strategies for Change," *Harvard Business Review*, March–April 1979, 106–114.

62. M. Johne, "The Human Factor: Integrating People and Cultures after a Merger," *CMA Management*, 1 April 2000, 30.

63. Ibid.

64. K. Booker & J. Schlosser, "The Un-CEO," *Fortune*, 16 September 2002, 88.

65. Ibid.

66. Ibid.

67. S. LaFee, "Professional Learning Communities: A Story of Five Superintendents Trying to Transform the Organizational Culture," *School Administrator*, 1 May 2003, 6.

68. B. Orwall, "Disney Decides It Must Draw Artists into Computer Age," *Wall Street Journal*, 23 October 2003, A1.

69. Ibid.

70. Ibid.

71. J. P. Kotter, "Leading Change: Why Transformation Efforts Fail," *Harvard Business Review* 73, no. 2 (March–April 1995): 59.

72. "The New Sears Holdings: Where America Speculates," *Chain Store Age*, 15 December 2004, 1; R. Berner, "At Sears, a Great Communicator," *BusinessWeek*, 31 October 2005, 50–52.

73. Booker & Schlosser, "The Un-CEO."

74. "Sears Results Mixed," *MMR*, 18 September 2006, 5.

75. "Sears Sees the Softer Side of Sales," *BusinessWeek Online*, 17 November 2006, 3.

76. R. Berner, "At Sears, a Great Communicator: New CEO Lewis Will Need His People Skills to Overhaul the Giant's Hidebound Culture," *BusinessWeek*, 31 October 2005, 50–52.

77. J. McCrackent & T. Kosdrosky, "Ford Plans to Offer Bonuses to Blue-Collar, Salaried Workers," *Wall Street Journal*, 9 March 2007, A10.

78. Berner, "At Sears, a Great Communicator."

79. "Sears Selects New Chief for Strategy: Former Best Buy Executive to Sharpen Focus on Customers," *Chicago Tribune*, 18 January 2007, online.

80. Ibid.

81. S. Cramm, "A Change of Hearts," *CIO*, 1 April 2003, http://www.cio.com/archive/040103/hs_leadership.html, 20 May 2003.

82. M. Ihlwan, L. Armstrong, & M. Eidam, "Hyundai: Kissing Clunkers Goodbye," *BusinessWeek*, 17 May 2004, 46.

83. Ibid.

84. Ibid.

85. R. N. Ashkenas & T. D. Jick, "From Dialogue to Action in GE WorkOut: Developmental Learning in a Change Process," in *Research in Organizational Change and Development*, vol. 6, ed. W. A. Pasmore & R. W. Woodman (Greenwich, CT: JAI Press, 1992), 267–287.

86. T. Stewart, "GE Keeps Those Ideas Coming," *Fortune*, 12 August 1991, 40.

87. J. D. Duck, "Managing Change: The Art of Balancing," *Harvard Business Review on Change* (Boston: Harvard Business School Press, 1998), 55–81.

88. C. Costanzo, "B of A's Six Sigma Teams Begin Work on Integration with Fleet," *American Banker*, 10 March 2004, 1.

89. W. J. Rothwell, R. Sullivan, & G. M. McLean, *Practicing Organizational Development: A Guide for Consultants* (San Diego, CA: Pfeiffer & Co., 1995).

90. N. Shirouzu, "Gadget Inspector: Why Toyota Wins Such High Marks on Quality Surveys—Hajime Oba Is a Key Coach as Japanese Auto Maker Steps Up U.S. Production—Striving to Reach Heijunka," *Wall Street Journal*, 15 March 2001, A1.

91. Ibid.

92. Rothwell, Sullivan, & McLean, *Practicing Organizational Development*.

93. P. J. Robertson, D. R. Roberts, & J. I. Porras, "Dynamics of Planned Organizational Change: Assessing Empirical Support for a Theoretical Model," *Academy of Management Journal* 36 (1993): 619–634.

94. J. E. Ettlie and R. D. O'Keefe, "Innovative Attitudes, Values, and Intentions in Organizations," *Journal of Management Studies* 19 (1982): 163–182.

95. "Can Colgate Brush Off the Competition?" *Marketing Week*, 27 January 2005, 23; Seth Mendelson, "The War of the Roses: Colgate and Crest Have Fought for Decades for Supremacy in the Toothpaste Category. Suddenly, One Has Gained an Edge and the Other Is Challenged to Change Its Strategy," *Grocery Headquarters*, January 2005, 64; David Kiley, "Reuben Mark: Profit and Floss," *BusinessWeek*, 20 December 2004, 46; Pallavi Gogoi, "Colgate's Big Bid to Freshen Up Profits," *BusinessWeek Online*, 8 December 2004; "Colgate: Brushing Mergers Aside," *BusinessWeek Online*, 4 February 2005; Eric Dash, "Colgate to Cut Jobs and Use Savings to Spur Sales," *New York Times*, 8 December 2004, C1; "Squeezed: Colgate-Palmolive Shuts Factories to Save $300 Million," *Sunday Business (London)*, 12 December 2004.

96. Julie Schlosser, "Inside-the-Box Thinking," *Fortune*, 1 November 2004, 54; http://www.mindwareonline.com; http://www.eurekaranch.com.

Chapter 8

1. "Business Brief—Tommy Hilfiger Corp. Revenue Drop of 6.4% Expected Amid Declines in U.S. Business," *Wall Street Journal*, 10 November 2005; T. Agins, "By A Thread: A Hot Designer Can Generate Buzz But Not Profits," *Wall Street Journal*, 16 September 2005, A1; T. Agins, "For U.S. Fashion Firms, A Global Makeover—Tommy Hilfiger Finds Assimilating in Europe Requires a New Look," *Wall Street Journal*, 2 February 2007; T. Agins & C. Rohwedder, "Hilfiger Tries on Lagerfeld Designs," *Wall Street Journal*, 14 December 2004, B6; D. Berman & T. Agins, "Apax Nears Deal To Buy Hilfiger For $1.5 Billion," *Wall Street Journal*, 23 December 2005, B2; A. Caroll, "Brand Barrage: When the Murjani Group, in a Joint Venture with Arvind . . . ," *Business Standard*, 13 February

2007, 11; S. Conti, "Hilfiger Signs French Soccer Star—Tommy to Design Capsule Line Inspired by Thierry Henry, Who will also Appear in Formal and Underwear Ads," *DNR*, 11 December 2006, 12; J. Greenberg, "Tommy Seeks to Revive Brand in U.S.," *Women's Wear Daily*, 12 July 2006, 6; P. Ho, "Li & Fung Surges on Hilfiger Buy," *The Standard*, 13 February 2007; R. Jana, "Bridging the Fashion Culture Gap; Apparel Company Murjani Group Is Leading the Charge, Bringing Western Labels such as Tommy Hilfiger and Calvin Klein to Indian Shoppers," *Business Week Online*, 5 February 2007.

2. T. Friedman, "It's a Flat World, After All," *New York Times*, 3 April 2005, 33.

3. World Investment Report, 2006," United Nations Conference on Trade & Development, http://www.unctad.org/en/docs/wir2006annexes_en.pdf, 30 January 2007.

4. G. Samor, "Steelmaker Girds for Growth—Gerdau of Brazil Looks to Bulk Up Further in United States Market," *Wall Street Journal*, 5 April 2005, B2.

5. C. Rong, "Chinese Assets Are Looking Pricey—How Much Is Too Much to Pay for Market Share? A Slew of Big-Profile Deals," *Wall Street Journal Europe*, 4 February 2005, M4.

6. C. Baughn & M. Buchanan, "Cultural Protectionism," *Business Horizons*, 1 November 2001, 5; "Senior US Trade Official Raises Limits on Hollywood Movies in Beijing," *AFX News Limited*, 27 May 2004.

7. J. Miller, "China's Low Fruit Prices Highlight EU's Vulnerabilities Over Trade," *Wall Street Journal*, 26 December 2006, A4.

8. L. Etter, "Can Ethanol Get a Ticket to Ride?" *Wall Street Journal*, 1 February 2007, B1.

9. G. Williams, III, "News on the Road Column," *San Antonio Express–News*, 3 March 2006.

10. "Determination of Total Amounts and Quota Period for Tariff-Rate Quotas for Raw Cane Sugar and Certain Imported Sugars, Syrups, and Molasses," *Federal Register*, 15 April 2002, 18162.

11. J. Sparshott, "U.S. Sugar Growers Fear Losses from Free-Trade Push," *Washington Times*, 24 March 2005, C07.

12. R. Geldenhuys, "China Import Quotas Illegal under WTO Law?" Floor, Inc. Attorneys, http://www.tradelaw.co.za/news/article.asp?newsID=101, 18 September 2006.

13. "The Agreements: Anti-Dumping, Subsidies, Safeguards, Contingencies, etc.," World Trade Organization, http://www.wto.org/english/thewto_e/whatis_e/tif_e/agrm8_e.htm, 22 April 2005.

14. C. Hale, "HortFACT—Why Fireblight Shouldn't Be a Market Access Problem," Hortnet, http://www.hortnet.co.nz/publications/hortfacts/hf205010.htm, 9 May 2003; "USTR Lists Barriers to U.S. Trade, Focusing on Agriculture—Annual Report Also Emphasizes Intellectual Property, Transparency," U.S. Department Press Releases & Documents, 7 February 2007.

15. J. Morgan, "Building Seeds of Case against OZ Apple Ban," *Dominion Post*, 18 January 2007, 7.

16. "USA Claims Airbus Drove out Rivals," *Flight International*, 23 January 2007.

17. "Rocky Receives Customs Clarification on Imported Boots," *FN*, 31 March 2003.

18. H. Blodget, "How to Solve China's Piracy Problem: A Dozen Ideas. Maybe One Will Work," *Slate*, 12 April 2005, http://www.slate.com/id/2116629.

19. G. Fowler, "Estimates of Copyright Piracy Losses Vary Widely," *Wall Street Journal*, 2 June 2006, A13.

20. Ibid.

21. "The History of the European Union," *Europa—The European Union Online*, 7 February 2007, http://europa.eu.int/abc/history/index_en.htm.

22. "The History of the European Union," *Europa—The European Union Online*, 22 April 2005, http://europa.eu.int/abc/history/index_en.htm.

23. D. Luhnow, "Crossover Success: How NAFTA Helped Wal-Mart Reshape the Mexican Market," *Wall Street Journal*, 31 August 2001, A1.

24. "Testimony of Under Secretary of Commerce for International Trade Grant D. Aldona: The Impact of NAFTA on the United States Economy," Senate Foreign Relations Committee, Subcommittee on International Economic Policy, Export & Trade Promotion, 7 February 2007.

25. Office of Industry Trade Policy, "NAFTA: 10 Years Later," U.S. Department of Commerce, International Trade Administration, http://ita.doc.gov/td/industry/otea/nafta/CoverPage.pdf, 7 February 2007.

26. Office of the United States Trade Representative, "The Case for CAFTA: Growth, Opportunity, and Democracy in our Neighborhood," United States Department of Agriculture: Foreign Agricultural Service, http://www.ustr.gov/assets/Trade_Agreements/Bilateral/CAFTA/Briefing_Book/asset_upload_file235_7178.pdf, 10 February 2007.

27. "South American Community of Nations," Andean Community, http://www.comunidadandina.org/ingles/sudamerican.htm, 10 February 2007.

28. "Selected Basic ASEAN Indicators, 2005," Association of Southeast Nations, http://www.aseansec.org/stat/Table1.pdf, 10 February 2007. "Top Ten ASEAN Trade Partner Countries/Regions, 2005," Association of Southeast Nations, http://www.aseansec.org/Stat/Table20.pdf, 10 February 2007.

29. "ASEAN Free Trade Area (Afta): An Update," Association of Southeast Nations, http://www.aseansec.org, 10 September 2001.

30. "Member Economies' Websites," Asia-Pacific Economic Cooperation, http://www.apecsec.org.sg/apec/member_economies/key_websites.html, 10 September 2001.

31. "Frequently Asked Questions (FAQs): How much of the world's trade takes place in the APEC Region?" *Asia-Pacific Economic Cooperation*, http://www.apecsec.org.sg/apec/tools/faqs.html, 10 February 2007.

32. "An Unofficial Price List of Everyday Items in Tokyo," *PriceCheckTokyo*, 10 February 2007, http://www.pricechecktokyo.com.

33. "The Big Mac Index," *Economist*, http://www.economist.com/markets/indicators/displaystory.cfm?story_id=8649005, 10 February 2007.

34. Ibid.

35. Ibid.

36. "Freer Trade Cuts the Cost of Living," World Trade Organization, http://www.wto.org/english/thewto_e/whatis_e/10ben_e/10b04_e.htm, 10 February 2007.

37. B. Thevenot, "Clawing for Survival, Louisiana's Crab Processors Are Being Pinched by Low Prices and Foreign Competition," *New Orleans Times-Picayune*, 6 October 1999, A1.

38. L. Grant, "More United States Diamond Buyers Turn to Canada: Gem Seekers Want to Avoid Stones at Center of

Conflicts," *USA Today*, 17 July 2001, B2.

39. Luhnow, "Crossover Success."

40. MTV Brasil, http://mtv.uol.com.br, 30 January 2007.

41. MTV China, http://mtvchina.com, 30 January 2007.

42. MTV India, http://www.mtvindia.com/sillypoint/sourav.php, 30 January 2007.

43. A. Sundaram & J. S. Black, "The Environment and Internal-Organization of Multinational Enterprises," *Academy of Management Review* 17 (1992): 729–757.

44. H. S. James, Jr., & M. Weidenbaum, *When Businesses Cross International Borders: Strategic Alliances & Their Alternatives* (Westport, CT: Praeger Publishers, 1993).

45. "Our Programmes: Idols," *Fremantle Media*, http://www.fremantlemedia.com/our-programmes/view/Global+Hit+Formats/viewprogramme/Idols, 10 February 2007.

46. "LNG Imports Needed to Meet Growing US Gas Supply Deficit," *Oil & Gas Journal*, 2 October 2001, 28.

47. "Workplace Code of Conduct," Fair Labor Association, http://www.fairlabor.org/all/code/index.html, 12 May 2003; A. Bernstein, M. Shari, & E. Malkin, "A World of Sweatshops," *Business Week*, 6 November 2000, 84.

48. "New Restaurants," McDonald's, http://www.mcdonalds.com/corp/franchise/purchasingYourFranchise/newRestaurants.html, 10 February 2007.

49. "McDonald's FAQ," McDonald's, 23 April 2005, http://www.mcdonalds.com/corp/about/mcd_faq.html.

50. M. Arndt, "McDonald's 24/7," *Business Week*, 5 February 2007, 64.

51. "Yum! Restaurants International," *Yum!*, http://www.yum.com/about/yri.asp, 10 February 2007.

52. K. Le Mesurier, "Overseas and Overwhelmed," *BRW*, 25 January 2007, 51.

53. C. Adler, "How China Eats a Sandwich: Opening Subway Franchises in the People's Republic," *Fortune*, 21 March 2005, F310 [B].

54. D. Hemlock, "World Wise: Strategies That Work around the Corner Don't Always Work in Locales Abroad, Office Depot's Chief Executive Says," *South Florida Sun*, 18 December 2000, 16.

55. Ibid.

56. "Company Profile," Fuji Xerox, http://www.fujixerox.co.jp/eng/company/profile.html, 12 February 2007;

57. P. Huber & M. Mills, "A Power Portfolio," *Forbes*, 11 April 2005, 76.

58. "Joint Venture Foundation of Giesecke & Devrient and Nokia Completed," Hugin Press Release, 20 December 2006.

59. B. R. Schlender, "How Toshiba Makes Alliances Work," *Fortune*, 4 October 1993, 116–120.

60. G. Fairclough, "GM's Partner in China Plans Competing Car," *Wall Street Journal*, 5 April 2006, B1.

61. G. Parker, "Going Global Can Hit Snags, Vodafone Finds," *Wall Street Journal*, 16 June 2004, B1.

62. M. W. Hordes, J. A. Clancy, & J. Baddaley, "A Primer for Global Start-Ups." *Academy of Management Executive*, May 1995, 7–11.

63. D. Pavlos, J. Johnson, J. Slow, & S. Young, "Micromultinationals: New Types of Firms for the Global Competitive Landscape," *European Management Journal* 21,

issue 2 (April 2003): 164; B. M. Oviatt & P. P. McDougall, "Toward a Theory of International New Ventures," *Journal of International Business Studies*, Spring 1994, 45–64; S. Zahra, "A Theory of International New Ventures: A Decade of Research," *Journal of International Business Studies*, January 2005, 20–28.

64. A. Grimes, "Venture Firms Seek Start-Ups That Outsource," *Wall Street Journal*, 2 April 2004, B1.

65. M. Copeland, "The Mighty Micro-Multinational," *Business 2.0*, 1 July 2006, 106.

66. "Operations Review: Selected Market Results: Estimated 2002 Volume by Operating Segment," The Coca-Cola Company 2002 Annual Report.

67. G. Smith, "Mexico: Piggybanks Full of Pesos," *Business Week*, 13 March 2006, 51.

68. D. Lynch, "Developing Nations Poised to Challenge USA as King of the Hill," *USA Today*, 8 February 2007, B.1. N. Srinivas, "Of Carats & Calories," *Economic Times*, 29 December 2006.

69. "Operations Review: Selected Market Results: Estimated 2002 Volume by Operating Segment," The Coca-Cola Company 2002 Annual Report.

70. F. Vogelstein, "How Intel Got Inside," *Fortune*, 4 October 2004, 127.

71. "Customer Care in the Netherlands," The Netherlands Foreign Investment Agency, available at http://www.nfia.com/solutions.php?pageid=11, 13 February 2007; "Customer Care Centers," Netherlands Foreign Investment Agency Information Manual, 13 February 2007, available at http://www.nfia.com/downloads/customercare.htm.

72. A. Snyder, "European Expansion: How to Shop Around," *Management*

Review, 1 November 1993, 16.

73. J. Oetzel, R. Bettis, & M. Zenner, "How Risky Are They?" *Journal of World Business* 36, no. 2 (Summer 2001): 128–145.

74. K. D. Miller, "A Framework for Integrated Risk Management in International Business," *Journal of International Business Studies*, 2nd Quarter 1992, 311.

75. J. Schuman, "The Morning Brief: Shell, Partners Give in to Kremlin Oil Game . . .," *Wall Street Journal*, 22 December 2006.

76. Chapter 1: Political Outlook," *UAE Business Forecast Report*, 2007 1st Quarter, 5–10.

77. "Foreign Corrupt Business Practices Act," U.S. Department of Justice, http://www.usdoj.gov/criminal/fraud/fcpa, 10 May 2003.

78. G. Fowler, "In China's Offices, Foreign Colleagues Might Get an Earful," *Wall Street Journal*, 13 February 2007, B1.

79. Ibid.

80. G. Hofstede, "The Cultural Relativity of the Quality of Life Concept," *Academy of Management Review* 9 (1984): 389–398; G. Hofstede, "The Cultural Relativity of Organizational Practices and Theories," *Journal of International Business Studies*, Fall 1983, 75–89; G. Hofstede, "The Interaction between National and Organizational Value Systems," *Journal of Management Studies*, July 1985, 347–357; M. Hoppe, "An Interview with Geert Hofstede," *Academy of Management Executive*, February 2004, 75–79.

81. R. Hodgetts, "A Conversation with Geert Hofstede," *Organizational Dynamics*, Spring 1993, 53–61.

82. T. Lenartowicz & K. Roth, "Does Subculture within a Country Matter?

A Cross-Cultural Study of Motivational Domains and Business Performance in Brazil," *Journal of International Business Studies* 32 (2001): 305–325.

83. M. Janssens, J. M. Brett, & F. J. Smith, "Confirmatory Cross-Cultural Research: Testing the Viability of a Corporation-Wide Safety Policy," *Academy of Management Journal* 38 (1995): 364–382.

84. R. G. Linowes, "The Japanese Manager's Traumatic Entry into the United States: Understanding the American-Japanese Cultural Divide," *Academy of Management Executive* 7 (1993): 21–40.

85. J. S. Black, M. Mendenhall, & G. Oddou, "Toward a Comprehensive Model of International Adjustment: An Integration of Multiple Theoretical Perspectives," *Academy of Management Review* 16 (1991): 291–317; R. L. Tung, "American Expatriates Abroad: From Neophytes to Cosmopolitans," *Columbia Journal of World Business*, 22 June 1998, 125; A. Harzing, "The Persistent Myth of High Expatriate Failure Rates," *International Journal of Human Resource Management* 6 (1995): 457–475; A. Harzing, "Are Our Referencing Errors Undermining Our Scholarship and Credibility? The Case of Expatriate Failure Rates," *Journal of Organizational Behavior* 23 (2002): 127–148; N. Forster, "The Persistent Myth of High Expatriate Failure Rates: A Reappraisal," *International Journal of Human Resource Management* 8 (1997): 414–433.

86. J. Black, "The Right Way to Manage Expats," *Harvard Business Review* 77 (March–April 1999): 52; C. Joinson, "No Returns," *HR Magazine*, 1 November 2002, 70.

87. C. Joinson, "No Returns," *HR Magazine*, November 2002, 70.

88. J. S. Black & M. Mendenhall, "Cross-Cultural Training Effectiveness: A Review and Theoretical Framework for Future Research," *Academy of Management Review* 15 (1990): 113–136.

89. K. Essick, "Executive Education: Transferees Prep for Life, Work in Far-Flung Lands," *Wall Street Journal*, 12 November 2004, A6.

90. Ibid.

91. P. W. Tam, "Culture Course—'Awareness Training' Helps U.S. Workers Better Know Their Counterparts in India," *Wall Street Journal*, 25 May 2004, B1.

92. J. Areddy, "Deep Inside China, American Family Struggles to Cope," *Wall Street Journal*, 2 August 2005, A1.

93. W. Arthur, Jr., & W. Bennett, Jr., "The International Assignee: The Relative Importance of Factors Perceived to Contribute to Success," *Personnel Psychology* 48 (1995): 99–114; B. Cheng, "Home Truths about Foreign Postings; To Make an Overseas Assignment Work, Employers Need More Than an Eager Exec with a Suitcase. They Must Also Motivate the Staffer's Spouse," *Business Week Online*, http://www .businessweek.com/ careers/content/jul2002/ ca20020715_9110.htm, 16 July 2002.

94. M. Netz, "It's Not Judging— It's Assessing: The Truth about Candidate Assessments," *NRRE Magazine*, March 2004, http://www.rismedia.com.

95. R. Donkin, "Recruitment: Overseas Gravy Train May Be Running Out of Steam—Preparing Expatriate Packages Is Challenging the Expertise of Human Resource Management," *Financial Times*, 30 November 1994, 10.

96. S. P. Deshpande & C. Viswesvaran, "Is Cross-Cultural Training of Expatriate Managers Effective? A Meta-Analysis," *International Journal of Intercultural Relations* 16, no. 3 (1992): 295–310.

97. J. Areddy, "Deep Inside China, American Family Struggles to Cope."

98. R. W. Boatler, "Study Abroad: Impact on Student Worldmindedness," *Journal of Teaching in International Business* 2, no. 2 (1990): 13–17; R. W. Boatler, "Worldminded Attitude Change in a Study Abroad Program: Contact and Content Issues," *Journal of Teaching in International Business* 3, no. 4 (1992): 59–68; H. Lancaster, "Learning to Manage in a Global Workplace (You're on Your Own)," The *Wall Street Journal*, 2 June 1998, B1; D. L. Sampson & H. P. Smith, "A Scale to Measure Worldminded Attitudes," *Journal of Social Psychology* 45 (1957): 99–106.

99. Starbucks Annual Report, 2006, Form 10-K / A; "Lattes in the Forbidden City," *Wall Street Journal*, 7 March 2007, online video in partnership with Reuters online at www .wsj.com; G. Fowler, "It's Called the Forbidden City for a Reason," *Wall Street Journal*, 19 January 2007, B1; "Question Authority: Starbucks—The Next Generation," *Fortune*, 4 April 2005, 30; C. Mee-young, "Starbucks Likely to Expand Asia Plan," *Reuters English News Service*, 23 August 2001, available online; "An American (Coffee) in Paris—and Rome," *United States News & World Report*, 19 February 2001, 47.

100. L. Stroh, "Why Are Women Left at Home? Are They Unwilling to Go on International Assignments?" *Journal of World Business*, Fall 2000.

101. A. Hanft, "Passport to America," *Inc.*, October 2004, 14.

Chapter 9

1. "About Alcan," Alcan, http://www.alcan .com /web/publishing .nsf/Content/About+ Alcan+-+Company+ Structure; R. Barker, "Novelis: All Set to Gain Speed," *Business Week*, 14 November 2005, 32.

2. B. Schlender, "Microsoft: The Beast Is Back," *Fortune*, 11 June 2001, 75.

3. Y. Noguchi, "Microsoft Remakes Corporate Structure," *Washington Post*, 21 September 2005, D5; "Microsoft Announces Plans for July 2008 Transition for Bill Gates," Microsoft, http://www.microsoft .com/presspass/ press/2006/jun06/ 06–15CorpNewsPR .mspx.

4. M. Hammer & J. Champy, *Reengineering the Corporation: A Manifesto for Business Revolution* (New York: Harper & Row, 1993).

5. "Sara Lee Announces Transformation Plan; Brenda C. Barnes Appointed the Company's CEO, Effective Immediately," *Retail Merchandiser*, 10 February 2005; "Our Timeline," Sara Lee Corporation, http://www.saralee .com/AboutSaraLee/ OurTimeline.aspx.

6. J. G. March & H. A. Simon, *Organizations* (New York: John Wiley & Sons, 1958).

7. "Bayer Group: Profile and Organization," Bayer AG, http://www.bayer .com/bayer-group/profile- and-organization/ page2351.htm.

8. "Outline of Principle Operations," Sony Corporation, http:// www.sony.com/SCA/ outline.shtml.

9. "Our Companies," United Technologies 2004 Annual Report, United Technologies, http:// www.utc.com/annual_ reports/2004/html/page5 .htm.

10. "Form 10-K, United Technologies Corporation: Segment Review," United States Securities and Exchange Commission, http://investors.utc.com.

11. "Company Info: Executive Team," Sprint Nextel, http://www2.sprint.com/mr/exListPrev.do?Span=20.

12. "Our Company: The Best Brands in the World," Coca-Cola Enterprises, http://www.cokecce.com/pages/allContent.asp?page_id=85.

13. "Corporate Info: Corporate Structure—Four Pillars," Procter & Gamble, http://www.pg.com/jobs/corporate_structure/four_pillars.jhtml; "P&G Management," Procter & Gamble, http://www.pg.com/news/management/bios_photos.jhtml.

14. L. R. Burns, "Adoption and Abandonment of Matrix Management Programs: Effects of Organizational Characteristics and Interorganizational Networks," *Academy of Management Journal* 36 (1993): 106–138.

15. D. Ball, "Unilever Shakes Up Its Management to Spur Growth," *Wall Street Journal*, 11 February 2005, A2.

16. "Unilever Streamlines Its Leadership Structure," Unilever, http://www.unilever.com/ourcompany/newsandmedia/pressreleases/2005/Unileverstreamlinesitsleadershipstructure.asp.

17. H. Fayol, *General and Industrial Management*, trans. Constance Storrs (London: Pitman Publishing, 1949).

18. M. Weber, *The Theory of Social and Economic Organization*, trans. and ed. A. M. Henderson & T. Parsons (New York: Free Press, 1947).

19. Fayol, *General and Industrial Management*.

20. J. Greene, S. Hamm, & J. Kerstetter, "How CEO Steve Ballmer Is Remaking the Company That Bill Gates Built," *Business Week*, 17 June 2002, 66.

21. S. Holmes, "Inside the Coup at Nike," *Business Week Online*, 26 January 2006, http://www.businessweek.com/bwdaily/dnflash/jan2006/nf20060126_9724_db016.htm?chan=search; S. Holmes, "Nike CEO Gets the Boot," *Business Week Online*, 24 January 2006, http://www.businessweek.com/bwdaily/dnflash/jan2006/nf20060124_6652_db016.htm?chan=search.

22. J. Whalen, "Bureaucracy Buster? Glaxo Lets Scientists Choose Its New Drugs," *Wall Street Journal*, 27 March 2006, B1.

23. J. Rutledge, "Management by Belly Button," *Forbes*, 4 November 1996, 64.

24. E. E. Lawler, S. A. Mohrman, & G. E. Ledford, *Creating High Performance Organizations: Practices and Results of Employee Involvement and Quality Management in Fortune 1000 Companies* (San Francisco: Jossey-Bass, 1995).

25. D. Welch, "Renault-Nissan: Say Hello to Bo," *Business Week*, 31 July 2006, 56–57.

26. S. Curry, "Retention Getters," *Incentive*, 1 April 2005.

27. R. W. Griffin, *Task Design* (Glenview, IL: Scott, Foresman, 1982).

28. F. Herzberg, *Work and the Nature of Man* (Cleveland, OH: World Press, 1966).

29. A. Markels, "Team Approach: A Power Producer Is Intent on Giving Power to Its People—Groups of AES Employees Do Complex Tasks Ranging from Hiring to Investing—Making Sure Work Is 'Fun,'" *Wall Street Journal*, 3 July 1995, A1.

30. Ibid.

31. J. R. Hackman & G. R. Oldham, *Work Redesign* (Reading, MA: Addison-Wesley, 1980).

32. T. Burns & G. M. Stalker, *The Management of Innovation* (London: Tavistock, 1961).

33. Y. Fried & G. R. Ferris, "The Validity of the Job Characteristics Model: A Review and Meta-Analysis," *Personnel Psychology* 40 (1987): 287–322; B. T. Loher, R. A. Noe, N. L. Moeller, & M. P. Fitzgerald, "A Meta-Analysis of the Relation of Job Characteristics to Job Satisfaction," *Journal of Applied Psychology* 70 (1985): 280–289.

34. M. Hammer & J. Champy, *Reengineering the Corporation*.

35. Ibid.

36. J. D. Thompson, *Organizations in Action* (New York: McGraw-Hill, 1967).

37. D. Pink, "Who Has the Next Big Idea?" *Fast Company*, 1 September 2001, 108.

38. J. B. White, "'Next Big Thing': Re-Engineering Gurus Take Steps to Remodel Their Stalling Vehicles," *Wall Street Journal Interactive*, 26 November 1996.

39. Ibid.

40. G. M. Spreitzer, "Individual Empowerment in the Workplace: Dimensions, Measurement, and Validation," *Academy of Management Journal* 38 (1995): 1442–1465.

41. M. Schrage, "I Know What You Mean. And I Can't Do Anything about It," *Fortune*, 2 April 2001, 186.

42. K. W. Thomas & B. A. Velthouse, "Cognitive Elements of Empowerment," *Academy of Management Review* 15 (1990): 666–681.

43. "Wegmans: History," Wegmans, http://www.wegmans.com/about/history/index.asp; M. Boyle & E. Kratz, "The Wegmans Way," *Fortune*, 24 January 2005, 62–68.

44. D. A. Morand, "The Role of Behavioral Formality and Informality in the Enactment of Bureaucratic versus Organic Organizations," *Academy of Management Review* 20 (1995): 831–872.

45. "Hot Tamale," *Wall Street Journal*, January 28–29, 2006, B3.

46. L. Munoz, "The Suit Is Back—Or Is It? As Dot-Coms Die, So Should Business Casual. But the Numbers Don't Lie," *Fortune*, 25 June 2001, 202; F. Swoboda, "Casual Dress Becomes the Rule," *Las Vegas Review-Journal*, 3 March 1996.

47. A. Merrick, "Tailors Spin a Yarn: Men's Suit Is Back! But Story Unravels—Stores Say 'Serious' Is In, Sales Keep Slacking Off; An Overstretched Theory," *Wall Street Journal*, 27 December 2002, A1; Munoz, "The Suit Is Back."

48. "Casual Office Attire Going, Going …" *USA Today*, 1 January 2005, 8; J. Fassnacht, "Pendulum Swings Away from Casual Attire in the Workplace," *Reading (PA) Eagle*, 18 October 2004.

49. "Suits Lose Appeal As Casual Dress Rules in London Offices," *Evening Standard* (London), 19 October 2004.

50. "SHRM Online Poll Results," Society for Human Resource Management, http://www.shrm.org/poll/results.asp?Question=89, 21 May 2003.

51. K. McCullough, "Analysis: More Companies Allowing Employees to Dress Down, Which Makes Productivity Go Up," *Money Club*, 26 March 1996.

52. W. Bounds, "Phone Calls Are Public Affairs for Open-Plan Office

Dwellers," *Wall Street Journal*, 10 July 2002, B1.

53. "Designing the Ever-Changing Workplace," *Architectural Record*, September 1995, 32–37.

54. H. Landy, "All Moved in at Radio Shack," *Fort Worth Star-Telegram*, 3 March 2005, 1C.

55. A. Frangos, "Property Report: See You on the Way Up! Office Stairs Get 'Aspirational,'" *Wall Street Journal*, 19 May 2004, B1.

56. J. Sandberg, "Cookies, Gossip, Cubes: It's a Wonder Any Work Gets Done at the Office," *Wall Street Journal*, 28 April 2004, B1.

57. Ibid.

58. Ibid.

59. L. Gallagher, "At Work: Get Out of My Face: Open Offices Were Hailed as the Answer to Hierarchical, Rigid Organizations. Employees Would Rather Have Privacy," *Forbes*, 18 October 1999, 105.

60. K. A. Edelman, "Take Down the Walls!" *Across the Board*, 1 March 1997.

61. S. Hwang, "Cubicle Culture: Office Vultures Circle Still-Warm Desks Left Empty by Layoffs," *Wall Street Journal*, 14 August 2002, B1.

62. M. Rich, "Shut Up So We Can Do Our Jobs!—Fed Up Workers Try to Muffle Chitchat, Conference Calls and Other Opens-Office Din," *Wall Street Journal*, 29 August 2001, B1.

63. J. Gannon, "GlaxoSmithKline, Alcoa, Marconi, PNC Open Up Office Environments," *Pittsburgh Post-Gazette*, 9 February 2003.

64. G. Kahn, "Making Labels for Less—Supply-Chain City Transforms Far-Flung Apparel Industry; Help for 'The Button Guy,'" *Wall Street Journal*, 13 August 2004, B1.

65. G. G. Dess, A. M. A. Rasheed, K. J. McLaughlin, &

66. R. L. Priem, "The New Corporate Architecture," *Academy of Management Executive* 9 (1995): 7–18.

66. W. Bulkeley, "New IBM Jobs Can Mean Fewer Jobs Elsewhere," *Wall Street Journal*, 8 March 2004, B1.

67. G. McWilliams, "Apple Uses Software, Outsourcing to Gain Share As Sony Struggles to Grow," *Wall Street Journal*, 10 March 2005, A1.

68. P. Cohen & J. Dalrymple, "Apple Updates iPod Line, Cuts Prices," *Computer World*, 23 February 2005, available at http://www .computerworld.com/ softwaretopics/os/macos/ story/0,10801,99956,00 .html.

69. "Overview: Collaborative Business Network Solutions," *G5 Technologies: Agile Web*, http://www .g5technologies.com/ agileweb/overview/index .html.

70. J. H. Sheridan, "The Agile Web: A Model for the Future?" *Industry Week*, 4 March 1996, 31.

71. Ibid.

72. C. C. Snow, R. E. Miles, & H. J. Coleman, Jr., "Managing 21st Century Network Organizations," *Organizational Dynamics*, Winter 1992, 5–20.

73. Sheridan, "The Agile Web: A Model for the Future?"

74. "Virtual Corporation Management System (VCMS) Solution," *G5 Technologies: Agile Web*, http://www .g5technologies.com/ VCMS.htm.

75. Bruner, James, Hensel, *Marketing Scales Handbook*, 931–934.

76. "Britain Mulls Life-Saving Garbage Men," *UPI News Track*, 13 January 2005; J. K. Borchardt, "Hey, It's a Dirty Job … But Garbage Collectors, Prison Guards, and Morticians Are Doing It—and Often Finding

Fulfillment," *Christian Science Monitor*, 9 August 2004, 14; T. Barry, "Ogden, Utah, Garbage Collector Takes Pride in Job," *Ogden (UT) Standard-Examiner*, 25 May 2001; P. Paul, F. M. Kuijer, et al., "Effect of Job Rotation on Work Demands, Workload, and Recovery of Refuse Truck Drivers and Collectors," *Human Factors*, Fall 2004, 437–449.

77. A. Cohen, "Lego Builds Self-Booking Tool," *Business Travel News*, 19 June 2006, 10; Q. Hardy, "Son of Lego," *Forbes*, 4 September 2006, 108; M. Defosse, "Toy Industry's Essential Block: Outsourcing. Few Markets Have Been More Speedily Outsourced to Low-Wage Lands than the Ones for Toys and Sporting Goods. Lego's Recent Announcement Is a Prime Example," *Modern Plastics Worldwide*, August 2006, 20–22; "Outsourcing Move by Lego," *New York Times*, 21 June 2006, C11; "What's NXT? Lego Embraces Third-Party Development," *PR Newswire*, 15 September 2006; J. Pisani, "The Making of a Lego. The Bricks Are so Versatile that Just Six of Them Can Be Arranged in 915,103,765 Ways. No Wonder Lego Has Been Named 'Toy of the Century'—Twice," *Business Week Online*, 29 November 2006; "Picking Up the Pieces: Lego's Turnaround," *Economist*, 28 October 2006, 76; "LEGO Group Outsources Logistics to DHL," *M2Presswire*, 27 October 2005; N. Schwartz, "One Brick at a Time," *Fortune*, 8 June 2006, 45.

78. K. Freiberg & J. Freiberg, *Nuts! Southwest Airlines' Crazy Recipe for Business and Personal Success* (Austin, TX: Bard, 1996).

Chapter 10

1. Catherine Larkin (16 October 2006), Gap grows

between best, worst care," *The Denver Post*, retrieved from http://www .denverpost.com/business/ ci_4500867 on 11 April 2007; Kaiser Permanente. *Wikipedia, the free encyclopedia*, retrieved from http:// en.wikipedia .org/wiki/kaiser_ Permanente 10 April 2007; "Building Rapid Response Teams," *Institute of Healthcare Improvement*, http://www.ihi.org/IHI/ Topics/ReducingMortality/ Reducing Mortality General/Improvement, 11 April 2007; "The Kaiser Papers," *California News Stories about Kaiser Permanente*, http://www .kaiserpapers.info/ californianews.html, on 11 April 2007; M. Marquez, "Trend: 'Dumping' Homeless on L.A.'s Skid Row," *ABC News, Good Morning America*, 24 March 2006, http://www .abcnews.go.com/GMA/ print?id=1761873; S. Hollander, L. Gunderson & J. Mechanic, "Process Improvements Boost Patient Satisfaction and Quality of Care at Stanford University Hospital," *Shaw Resources Online*, http://www .shawresource.com/ artstanford.htm; F. Vara-Orta, "State Lists Worst Hospitals for Care of Pneumonia: Five Kaiser Facilities Have among the Highest Mortality Rates," *Los Angeles Times Online*, 27 February 2007, http:// www.latimescom/news/ local/la-me-hospitals 27feb27,1, 3287281 .story?coll=laheadline.

2. B. Dumaine, "The Trouble with Teams," *Fortune*, 5 September 1994, 86–92.

3. J. Hoerr, "The Payoff from Teamwork—The Gains in Quality Are Substantial—So Why Isn't It Spreading Faster?" *Business Week*, 10 July 1989, 56.

4. J. R. Katzenbach & D. K. Smith, *The Wisdom of Teams* (Boston: Harvard Business School Press, 1993).

5. S. G. Cohen & D. E. Bailey, "What Makes Teams Work: Group Effectiveness Research

from the Shop Floor to the Executive Suite," *Journal of Management* 23, no. 3 (1997): 239–290.

6. S. E. Gross, *Compensation for Teams* (New York: American Management Association, 1995); B. L. Kirkman & B. Rosen, "Beyond Self-Management: Antecedents and Consequences of Team Empowerment," *Academy of Management Journal* 42 (1999): 58–74; G. Stalk & T. M. Hout, *Competing against Time: How Time-Based Competition Is Reshaping Global Markets* (New York: Free Press, 1990); S. C. Wheelwright & K. B. Clark, *Revolutionizing New Product Development* (New York: Free Press, 1992).

7. D. A. Harrison, S. Mohamed, J. E. McGrath, A. T. Florey & S. W. Vanderstoep, "Time Matters in Team Performance: Effects of Member Familiarity, Entrainment, and Task Discontinuity on Speed and Quality," *Personnel Psychology* 56(3) (2003, August): 633–669.

8. J. Marquez, "Hewitt-BP Split May Signal End of "Lift and Shift" Deals," *Workforce Management*, 29 December 2006: 3.

9. Anonymous, "Tailored Service Alters with Needs of Clients," *The Journal* (Newcastle, UK), 20 October 2006, 38.

10. D. Kiley, "Crafty Basket Makers Cut Downtime, Waste. So Far, Changes Saving $3 Million a Year," *USA Today*, 10 May 2001, B3.

11. R. D. Banker, J. M. Field, R. G. Schroeder, & K. K. Sinha, "Impact of Work Teams on Manufacturing Performance: A Longitudinal Field Study," *Academy of Management Journal* 39 (1996): 867–890.

12. C. Fishman, "The Anarchist's Cookbook: John Mackey's Approach to Management Is Equal Parts Star Trek and

1970s Flashback," *Fast Company*, 1 July 2004, 70.

13. "Beating the Joneses (Learning What the Competition Is Doing)," *Industry Week* 1 (7 December 1998): 27.

14. Stalk & Hout, *Competing against Time*.

15. H. K. Bowen, K. B. Clark, C. A. Holloway, & S. C. Wheelwright, *The Perpetual Enterprise Machine* (New York: Oxford Press, 1994).

16. C. Dahle, "Xtreme Teams," *Fast Company*, 1 November 1999, 310.

17. Ibid.

18. J. L. Cordery, W. S. Mueller, & L. M. Smith, "Attitudinal and Behavioral Effects of Autonomous Group Working: A Longitudinal Field Study," *Academy of Management Journal* 34 (1991): 464–476; T. D. Wall, N. J. Kemp, P. R. Jackson, & C. W. Clegg, "Outcomes of Autonomous Workgroups: A Long-Term Field Experiment," *Academy of Management Journal* 29 (1986): 280–304.

19. M. Vanac, "Working the Line: U.S. Businesses Retool Modes of Production and Ratchet Up Morale," *Cleveland Plain Dealer*, 2 September 2001, H1.

20. Ibid.

21. "Declaration of Interdependence," Whole Foods Market, http://www.wholefoodsmarket.com/company/declaration.html.

22. Fishman, "The Anarchist's Cookbook."

23. "Whole Foods Market Soars to Number 5 Spot on *Fortune*'s '100 Best Companies to Work For' List," Whole Foods, http://www.wholefoodsmarket.com/company/pr_01–09–07.html.

24. R. Lieber, "Leadership Ensemble: How Do the Musicians of Orpheus Get to Carnegie Hall? They Practice—Not Just Their Music, but a Radical Approach to Leadership

That Has Become a Compelling Metaphor for Business," *Fast Company*, 1 May 2000, 286.

25. A. Erez, J. Lepine, & H. Elms, "Effects of Rotated Leadership and Peer Evaluation on the Functioning and Effectiveness of Self-Managed Teams: A Quasi-Experiment," *Personnel Psychology* 55, issue 4 (2002): 929.

26. Hoerr, "The Payoff from Teamwork."

27. T. Aeppel, "Missing the Boss: Not All Workers Find Idea of Empowerment As Neat As It Sounds—Some Hate Fixing Machines, Apologizing for Errors, Disciplining Teammates—Rah-Rah Types Do the Best," *Wall Street Journal*, 8 September 1997, A1.

28. R. Liden, S. Wayne, R. Jaworski, & N. Bennett, "Social Loafing: A Field Investigation," *Journal of Management* 30 (2004): 285–304.

29. J. George, "Extrinsic and Intrinsic Origins of Perceived Social Loafing in Organizations," *Academy of Management Journal* 35 (1992): 191–202.

30. T. T. Baldwin, M. D. Bedell, & J. L. Johnson, "The Social Fabric of a Team-Based M.B.A. Program: Network Effects on Student Satisfaction and Performance," *Academy of Management Journal* 40 (1997): 1369–1397.

31. K. H. Price, D. A. Harrison & J. H. Gavin, "Withholding Inputs in Team Contexts: Member Composition, Interaction Processes, Evaluation Structure and Social Loafing," *Journal of Applied Psychology* 91(6) (2006): 1375–1384.

32. Hoerr, "The Payoff from Teamwork."

33. C. Joinson, "Teams at Work," *HR Magazine*, 1 May 1999, 30.

34. R. Wageman, "Critical Success Factors for Creating Superb Self-

Managing Teams," *Organizational Dynamics* 26, no. 1 (1997): 49–61.

35. A. Dragoon, "Small Teams, Big Returns," *CIO*, 1 December 2003, http://bpubs.tradepub.com/free/cio.

36. Ibid.

37. M. A. Cusumano, "How Microsoft Makes Large Teams Work Like Small Teams," *Sloan Management Review* 39, no 1 (Fall 1997): 9–20.

38. D. A. Harrison, S. Mohammed, J. E. McGrath, A. T. Florey & S. W. Vanderstoep, "Time Matters in Team Performance: Effects of Member Familiarity, Entrainment, and Task Discontinuity on Speed and Quality," *Personnel Psychology* 56(3) (2003, August): 633–669.

39. R. T. King, Jr., "Jeans Therapy: Levi's Factory Workers Are Assigned to Teams, and Morale Takes a Hit—Infighting Rises, Productivity Falls as Employees Miss the Piecework System," *Wall Street Journal*, 20 May 1998, A1.

40. Ibid.

41. M. Bolch, "Rewarding the Team: Make Sure Team-Oriented Compensation Plans Are Designed Carefully," *HR Magazine*, February 2007, 52(2).

42. K. Hammonds, "How Google Grows . . . and Grows . . . and Grows," *Fast Company*, 1 April 2003, 74.

43. G. Bylinsky, "Heroes of U.S. Manufacturing," *Fortune*, 19 March 2001, 177; D. Cadrain, "Put Success in Sight," *HR Magazine*, May 2003, 48(5).

44. Kirkman & Rosen, "Beyond Self-Management: Antecedents and Consequences of Team Empowerment."

45. K. Kelly, "Managing Workers Is Tough Enough in Theory. When Human Nature Enters the Picture, It's Worse," *BusinessWeek*, 21 October 1996, 32.

46. S. Easton & G. Porter, "Selecting the Right Team Structure to Work in Your Organization," in *Handbook of Best Practices for Teams*, vol. 1, ed. G. M. Parker (Amherst, MA: Irwin, 1996).

47. S. Metz & G. Walter, "From Skeptic to Believer: Involving Employees in Retirement and Benefits Planning," *Workspan*, 1 November 2004, 36.

48. R. M. Yandrick, "A Team Effort: The Promise of Teams Isn't Achieved without Attention to Skills and Training," *HR Magazine*, June 2001, 46(6).

49. Labor-Employee Participation Committees Receive NLRB's Approval," *Personnel Manager's Legal Letter*, 1 October 2001.

50. R. M. Yandrick, "A Team Effort: The Promise of Teams Isn't Achieved without Attention to Skills and Training."

51. A. Lashinsky, "RAZR's Edge: How a Team of Engineers and Designers Defied Motorola's Own Rules to Create the Cellphone that Revived Their Company," *Fortune*, 12 June 2006, 124–132.

52. R. J. Recardo, D. Wade, C. A. Mention, & J. Jolly, *Teams* (Houston: Gulf Publishing Co., 1996).

53. D. R. Denison, S. L. Hart, & J. A. Kahn, "From Chimneys to Cross-Functional Teams: Developing and Validating a Diagnostic Model," *Academy of Management Journal* 39, no. 4 (1996): 1005–1023.

54. J. Morgan, "Cessna Aims to Drive SCM to Its Very Core: Here Are 21 Steps and Tools It's Using to Make This Happen," *Purchasing*, 6 June 2002, 31.

55. A. M. Townsend, S. M. DeMarie, & A. R. Hendrickson, "Virtual Teams: Technology and the Workplace of the Future," *Academy of Management Executive* 13, no. 3 (1998): 17–29.

56. R. Karlgaard, "Flash Kid; Rich Karlgaard Meets a Teen Titan," *Forbes*, 17 March 2003, 39.

57. A. M. Townsend, S. M. DeMarie, & A. R. Hendrickson, "Are You Ready for Virtual Teams?" *HR Magazine* 41, no. 9 (1996): 122–126.

58. Wellins, Byham, & Dixon, *Inside Teams*.

59. Townsend, DeMarie, & Hendrickson, "Virtual Teams."

60. W. F. Cascio, "Managing a Virtual Workplace," *Academy of Management Executive* 14 (2000): 81–90.

61. S. Prashad, "Building Trust Tricky for 'Virtual' Teams," *Toronto Star*, 23 October 2003, K06.

62. R. Katz, "The Effects of Group Longevity on Project Communication and Performance," *Administrative Science Quarterly* 27 (1982): 245–282.

63. C. Kleiman, "Virtual Teams Make Loyalty More Realistic," *Chicago Tribune*, 23 January 2001, Business 1.

64. D. Mankin, S. G. Cohen, & T. K. Bikson, *Teams and Technology: Fulfilling the Promise of the New Organization* (Boston: Harvard Business School Press, 1996).

65. A. P. Ammeter & J. M. Dukerich, "Leadership, Team Building, and Team Member Characteristics in High Performance Project Teams," *Engineering Management* 14 (4) (2002, December): 3–11.

66. K. Lovelace, D. Shapiro, & L. Weingart, "Maximizing Cross-Functional New Product Teams' Innovativeness and Constraint Adherence: A Conflict Communications Perspective," *Academy of Management Journal* 44 (2001): 779–793.

67. G. Anthes, "Think Globally, Act Locally: Running Global IT Operations Effectively Often Means Creating Standard Systems and Processes That Have to Be Tweaked to Meet Local Requirements," *Computer World*, 28 May 2001, 36.

68. L. Holpp & H. P. Phillips, "When Is a Team Its Own Worst Enemy?" *Training*, 1 September 1995, 71.

69. S. Asche, "Opinions and Social Pressure," *Scientific American* 193 (1995): 31–35.

70. G. Smith, "How Nucor Steel Rewards Performance and Productivity," *Business Know How*, 26 May 2003, http://www.businessknowhow.com/manage/nucor.htm.

71. S. G. Cohen, G. E. Ledford, & G. M. Spreitzer, "A Predictive Model of Self-Managing Work Team Effectiveness," *Human Relations* 49, no. 5 (1996): 643–676.

72. M. Fischetti, "'Team Doctors, Report To ER': Is Your Team Headed for Intensive Care? Our Specialists Offer Prescriptions for the Five Illnesses That Can Afflict Even the Best Teams," *Fast Company*, 1 February 1998, 170.

73. K. Bettenhausen & J. K. Murnighan, "The Emergence of Norms in Competitive Decision-Making Groups," *Administrative Science Quarterly* 30 (1985): 350–372.

74. M. E. Shaw, *Group Dynamics* (New York: McGraw Hill, 1981).

75. Katzenback & Smith, *The Wisdom of Teams*.

76. E. Levenson, "The Power of an Idea," *Fortune*, 12 June 2006, 131.

77. S. M. Gully, D. S. Devine, & D. J. Whitney, "A Meta-Analysis of Cohesion and Performance: Effects of Level of Analysis and Task Interdependence," *Small Group Research* 26, no. 4 (1995): 497–520.

78. S. E. Jackson, "The Consequences of Diversity in Multidisciplinary Work Teams," in *Handbook of Work Group Psychology*, ed. M. A. West (Chichester, UK: Wiley, 1996).

79. A. M. Isen & R. A. Baron, "Positive Affect as a Factor in Organizational Behavior," in *Research in Organizational Behavior* 13, ed. L. L. Cummings & B. M. Staw (Greenwich, CT: JAI Press, 1991): 1–53.

80. C. R. Evans & K. L. Dion, "Group Cohesion and Performance: A Meta Analysis," *Small Group Research* 22, no. 2 (1991): 175–186.

81. R. Stankiewicsz, "The Effectiveness of Research Groups in Six Countries," in *Scientific Productivity*, ed. F. M. Andrews (Cambridge: Cambridge University Press, 1979), 191–221.

82. F. Rees, *Teamwork from Start to Finish* (San Francisco: Jossey-Bass, 1997).

83. Gully, Devine, & Whitney, "A Meta-Analysis of Cohesion and Performance."

84. E. Matson, "Four Rules for Fast Teams," *Fast Company*, August 1996, 87.

85. F. Tschan & M. V. Cranach, "Group Task Structure, Processes and Outcomes," in *Handbook of Work Group Psychology*, ed. M. A. West (Chichester, UK: Wiley, 1996).

86. D. E. Yeatts & C. Hyten, *High Performance Self Managed Teams* (Thousand Oaks, CA: Sage Publications, 1998); H. M. Guttman & R. S. Hawkes, "New Rules for Strategic Development," *Journal of Business Strategy* 25 (1) (2004): 34–39.

87. Ibid; J. Colquitt, R. Noe, & C. Jackson, "Justice in Teams: Antecedents and Consequences of Procedural Justice Climate," *Personnel Psychology*, 1 April 2002, 83.

88. D. S. Kezsbom, "Re-Opening Pandora's Box: Sources of Project Team Conflict in the '90s," *Industrial Engineering* 24, no. 5 (1992): 54–59.

89. A. C. Amason, W. A. Hochwarter, & K. R. Thompson, "Conflict: An Important Dimension in Successful Management Teams," *Organizational Dynamics* 24 (1995): 20.

90. A. C. Amason, "Distinguishing the Effects of Functional and Dysfunctional Conflict on Strategic Decision Making: Resolving a Paradox for Top Management Teams," *Academy of Management Journal* 39, no. 1 (1996): 123–148.

91. K. M. Eisenhardt, J. L. Kahwajy, & L. J. Bourgeois III, "How Management Teams Can Have a Good Fight," *Harvard Business Review* 75, no. 4 (July–August 1997): 77–85.

92. Ibid.

93. C. Nemeth & P. Owens, "Making Work Groups More Effective: The Value of Minority Dissent," in *Handbook of Work Group Psychology*, ed. M. A. West (Chichester, UK: Wiley, 1996).

94. J. M. Levin & R. L. Moreland, "Progress in Small Group Research," *Annual Review of Psychology* 9 (1990): 72–78; S. E. Jackson, "Team Composition in Organizational Settings: Issues in Managing a Diverse Work Force," in *Group Processes and Productivity*, ed. S. Worchel, W. Wood, & J. Simpson (Beverly Hills, CA: Sage, 1992).

95. Eisenhardt, Kahwajy, & Bourgeois, "How Management Teams Can Have a Good Fight."

96. Ibid.

97. B. W. Tuckman, "Development Sequence in Small Groups," *Psychological Bulletin* 63, no. 6 (1965): 384–399.

98. Gross, *Compensation for Teams.*

99. J. F. McGrew, J. G. Bilotta, & J. M. Deeney, "Software Team Formation and Decay: Extending the Standard Model for Small Groups," *Small Group Research* 30, no. 2 (1999): 209–234.

100. Ibid.

101 J. Case, "What the Experts Forgot to Mention: Management Teams Create New Difficulties, but Succeed for XEL Communication," *Inc.*, 1 September 1993, 66.

102. J. R. Hackman, "The Psychology of Self-Management in Organizations," in *Psychology and Work: Productivity, Change, and Employment*, ed. M. S. Pallak & R. Perloff (Washington, DC: American Psychological Association, 1986), 85–136.

103. A. O'Leary-Kelly, J. J. Martocchio, & D. D. Frink, "A Review of the Influence of Group Goals on Group Performance," *Academy of Management Journal* 37, no. 5 (1994): 1285–1301.

104. Smith, "How Nucor Steel Rewards Performance and Productivity."

105. A. Zander, "The Origins and Consequences of Group Goals," in *Retrospections on Social Psychology*, ed. L. Festinger (New York: Oxford University Press, 1980), 205–235.

106. M. Erez & A. Somech, "Is Group Productivity Loss the Rule or the Exception? Effects of Culture and Group-Based Motivation," *Academy of Management Journal* 39, no. 6 (1996): 1513–1537.

107. S. Sherman, "Stretch Goals: The Dark Side of Asking for Miracles," *Fortune*, 13 November 1995.

108. M. Gunther, "The Welshman, the Walkman, and the Salarymen."

109. S. Kerr & S. Landauer, "Using Stretch Goals to Promote Organizational Effectiveness and Personal Growth: General Electric and Goldman Sachs," *Academy of Management Executive* (November 2004): 134–138.

110. K. R. Thompson, W. A. Hochwarter, & N. J. Mathys, "Stretch Targets: What Makes Them Effective?" *Academy of Management Executive* 11, no. 3 (1997): 48–60.

111. S. Tully, "Why to Go for Stretch Targets," *Fortune*, 14 November 1994, 145.

112. Sherman, "Stretch Goals."

113. "Pfizer's Press Release," *Wall Street Journal.*

114. A. Lashinsky, "RAZR's Edge."

115. Dumaine, "The Trouble with Teams."

116. G. A. Neuman, S. H. Wagner, & N. D. Christiansen, "The Relationship between Work-Team Personality Composition and the Job Performance of Teams," *Group & Organization Management* 24, no. 1 (1999): 28–45.

117. M. A. Campion, G. J. Medsker, & A. C. Higgs, "Relations between Work Group Characteristics and Effectiveness: Implications for Designing Effective Work Groups," *Personnel Psychology* 46, no. 4 (1993): 823–850.

118. B. L. Kirkman & D. L. Shapiro, "The Impact of Cultural Values on Employee Resistance to Teams: Toward a Model of Globalized Self-Managing Work Team Effectiveness," *Academy of Management Review* 22, no. 3 (1997): 730–757.

119. P. Siekman, "Cessna Tackles Lean Manufacturing," *Fortune*, 1 May 2000, I222.

120. C. Fishman, "Engines of Democracy: The General Electric Plant in Durham, North Carolina Builds Some of the World's Most Powerful Jet Engines. But the Plant's Real Power Lies in the Lessons That It Teaches about the Future of Work and about Workplace Democracy," *Fast Company*, 1 October 1999, 174.

121. J. Bunderson & K. Sutcliffe, "Comparing Alternative Conceptualizations of Functional Diversity in Management Teams: Process and Performance Effects," *Academy of Management Journal* 45 (2002): 875–893.

122. J. Barbian, "Getting to Know You," *Training*, June 2001, 60–63.

123. Siekman, "Cessna Tackles Lean Manufacturing."

124. J. Hackman, "New Rules for Team Building—The Times Are Changing—And So Are the Guidelines for Maximizing Team Performance," *Optimize*, 1 July 2002, 50.

125. Joinson, "Teams at Work."

126. D. Zoia, "GM Manufacturing: Brand Spanking New," *Ward's Auto World*, March 2000, http://waw.wardsauto.com.

127. K. Mollica, "Stay Above the Fray: Protect Your Time—and Your Sanity—by Coaching Employees to Deal with Interpersonal Conflicts on Their Own," *HR Magazine*, April 2005, 111.

128. Wellins, Byham, & Dixon, *Inside Teams.*

129. S. Caudron, "Tie Individual Pay to Team Success," *Personnel Journal* 73, no. 10 (October 1994): 40.

130. Ibid.

131. Gross, *Compensation for Teams.*

132. G. Ledford, "Three Case Studies on Skill-Based Pay: An Overview," *Compensation & Benefits Review* 23, no.2 (1991): 11–24.

133. Wellins, Byham, & Dixon, *Inside Teams.*

134. J. R. Schuster & P. K. Zingheim, *The New Pay: Linking Employee and Organizational Performance* (New York: Lexington Books, 1992).

135. G. Shives & K. Scott, "Gainsharing and EVA: The U.S. Postal Service Experience," *Worldat Work Journal*, 1 January 2003, 21.

136. Cohen & Bailey, "What Makes Teams Work."

137. R. Allen & R. Kilmann, "Aligning Reward

Practices in Support of Total Quality Management," *Business Horizons* 44 (May 2001): 77–85.

138. J. H. Sheridan, "'Yes' to Team Incentives," *Industry Week*, 4 March 1996, 63.

139. J.A. Wagner, "Studies of Individualism-Collectivism: Effects on Cooperation in Groups," *Academy of Management Journal* 38, no. 1 (1995): 152–172.

140. G. Colvin, "Dream Teams Fail: It May Be Tempting to Recruit All-Stars and Let 'Em Rip. Don't Do It," *Fortune*, 12 June 2006, 87–92.

141. Alan Deutschman, "Building a Better Skunk Works," *Fast Company*, March 2005, 69–73.

142. M. A. West, ed., *Handbook of Work Group Psychology* (Chichester, UK: Wiley, 1996).

Chapter 11

1. R. Berner, "Weak Signals from RadioShack: The Electronics Retailer Can't Seem to Shake the Blues. It May Take Some Magic for New CEO Julian Day to Overcome Its Stalled Biz," *BusinessWeek Online*, 15 September 2006, http://web.lexis-nexis.com/universe/document?_m=4187417de)f92335dbeee2e110993a (accessed 9 February 2007); Greenebaum Doll & McDonald PLLC, "Employee's Race Claim against RadioShack Doesn't Compute," *Kentucky Employment Law Letter*, January 2007, http://web.lexis-nexis.com/universe/document?_m=1b6391082eb29c36ef09c6739830498b9 (accessed 9 February 2007); H. Landy, "Bad News Grows for RadioShack," *Fort Worth Star-Telegram*, 26 October 2006, http://web.lexis-nexis.com/universe/document?_m=e4ec5f178619a63122d825a4a9f3801d (accessed February 9 2007); "RadioShack," Wikipedia, http://www.en.wikipedia.org/wiki/RadioShack (accessed

9 February 2007); "RadioShack Uses E-mail to Fire Employees," *Associated Press Online*, 30 August 2006, http://web.lexis-nexis.com/universe/document?_m=705b09259308bc83c24a18520db60132 (accessed 9 February 2007); M. Schnurman, "Mitchell Shnurman Column," *Fort Worth Star-Telegram*, 13 September 2006, http://web.lexis-nexis.com/ universe/document?_m=db97b0109306ec21f9ac4adf9205b710 (accessed 9 February 2007); R. Strauss, "When the Resume Is Not to Be Believed," *New York Times*, 12 September 2006, G2.

2. "Facts on the Nursing Shortage in North America," Sigma Theta Tau International: Honor Society of Nursing, http://www.nursingsociety.org/media/facts_nursingshortage.html; C. Prystay, "U.S. Solution Is Philippine Dilemma—As Recruiters Snap Up More Nurses, Hospitals in Manila Are Scrambling," *Wall Street Journal*, 18 July 2002, A8; G. Zachary, "Shortage of Nurses Hits Hardest Where They Are Needed the Most," *Wall Street Journal*, 24 January 2001, A1.

3. B. Schneider & N. Schmitt, *Staffing Organizations*, 2d ed. (Glenview, IL: Scott, Foresman & Co., 1986).

4. D. M. Atwater, "Workforce Forecasting," *Human Resource Planning* 18, no. 4 (1995): 50.

5. "More Companies Turn to Workplace Planning to Boost Productivity and Efficiency, The Conference Board Reports in New Study," *PR Newswire*, 7 August 2006, http://web.lexis-nexis.com/universe/document?_m=2c3b0f8b6a240b2e39edabd16f4292c9 (accessed 9 February 2007); C. Donaldson, "Workforce Planning Comes of Age." *Human Resources*, 22 August 2006, available through http://www.lexis-nexis.com.

6. J. Eig, "Do Part-Time Workers Hold Key to When the Recession Breaks?" *Wall Street Journal*, 3 January 2002, A1.

7. Atwater, "Workforce Forecasting"; D. Ward, "Workforce Demand Forecasting Techniques," *Human Resource Planning* 19, no. 1 (1996): 54.

8. S. M. Director & J. Schramm, "Staffing Research: Estimating Future Staffing Levels: Implications for HR Strategy," Society for Human Resource Management, http://www.shrm.org / research/ staffresearch_published.

9. M. Brush & D. H. Ruse, "Driving Strategic Success through Human Capital Planning: How Corning Links Business and HR Strategy to Improve the Value and Impact of Its HR Function," *Human Resource Planning*, 2005, 49–60.

10. A. J. Walker, "The Analytical Element Is Important to an HRIS," *Personnel Administrator* 28 (1983): 33–35, 85.

11. L. Thornburg, "Case Study: HRIS Implementation: ER-One Chooses HROffice," Society for Human Resource Management, http://www.shrm.org.

12. C. Allen, "Enabling Faster HRIS Integration," Society for Human Resource Management, http://www.shrm.org.

13. T. Jolls, "Technology Continues to Redefine HR's Role," *Personnel Journal* 76, no. 7 (July 1997): 46.

14. S. Greengard, "Smarter Screening Takes Technology and HR Savvy," *Workforce*, 1 June 2002, 56–60.

15. S. Forster, "Technology (A Special Report)—The Best Way to Recruit New Workers," *Wall Street Journal*, 15 September 2003, R8.

16. S. Bing, "The Feds Make a Pass at Hooters," *Fortune*, 15 January 1996, 82.

17. J. Helyar, "Hooters: A Case Study," *Fortune*, 1 September 2003, 140.

18. A. Samuels, "Pushing Hot Buttons and Wings," *St. Petersburg (FL) Times*, 10 March 2003, 1A.

19. P. S. Greenlaw & J. P. Kohl, "Employer 'Business' and 'Job' Defenses in Civil Rights Actions," *Public Personnel Management* 23, no. 4 (1994): 573.

20. Associated Press, "Hooters Settles Suit, Won't Hire Waiters," *Denver Post*, 1 October 1997, A11.

21. D. Lewis, "EEOC: Damage Awards Reach $420m in 2004," *Boston Globe*, 20 February 2005, D2.

22. B. Morris, K. Bonamici, S. Kaufman, & P. Neering, "How Corporate America Is Betraying Women," *Fortune*, 10 January 2005, 64.

23. J. L. Ledvinka, *Federal Regulation of Personnel and Human Resource Management* (Boston: Kent Publishing Co., 1982), 137–198.

24. C. Cummins. "BP's Accident Put Its Celebrated CEO on the Hot Seat," *Wall Street Journal*, 16 June 2006, B1.

25. N. Adams, "Marketplace Report: BP Oil Fined for Lax Safety," National Pubic Radio, 23 September 2005, http://www.npr.org/templates/story/story.php?storyId=4860782.

26. A. Smith, "BP Faces Disaster Report from Baker Panel," CNNMoney.com, 17 January 2007, http://money.cnn.com/2007/01/15/news/companies/bp/index.htm.

27. Greenlaw & Kohl, "Employer 'Business' and 'Job' Defenses in Civil Rights Actions."

28. "Judge Approves Settlement of Coca-Cola Bias Lawsuit," *Wall Street Journal*, 30 May 2001, B7.

29. "Rent-A-Center Settles Gender-Bias Lawsuit, Will Pay $12.3 Million,"

Wall Street Journal, 2 November 2001, http://online.wsj.com.

30. W. Peirce, C. A. Smolinski, & B. Rosen, "Why Sexual Harassment Complaints Fall on Deaf Ears," *Academy of Management Executive* 12, no. 3 (1998): 41–54.

31. B. Mims, "Suit Claims Costco Forced Woman to Quit After She Complained of Harassment," *Salt Lake Tribune*, 24 February 2005, C14.

32. "The Baker & McKenzie Sexual Discrimination Case," Georgia Trial Lawyers Association, http://www.gtla.org?public/cases/baker.html; "Examples of Actual Judgments and Settlements," Employers Publications, http://www.sexualharassmentpolicy.com/judge.html.

33. "Facts about Sexual Harassment." U.S. Equal Employment Opportunity Commission, http://www.eeoc.gov/facts/fs-sex.html.

34. Peirce, Smolinski, & Rosen, "Why Sexual Harassment Complaints Fall on Deaf Ears."

35. Ibid.

36. E. Larson, "The Economic Costs of Sexual Harassment," http://www.hospitalitycampus.com/investors/facts.asp (accessed 16 July 2007).

37. K. Dunham & G. Ip, "Slow Economy Takes Unusually Heavy Toll on White-Collar Jobs," *Wall Street Journal*, 5 November 2001, A1.

38. Prystay, "U.S. Solution Is Philippine Dilemma."

39. G. Hyland-Savage, "General Management Perspective on Staffing: The Staffing Commandments," in N. C. Bukholder, P. J. Edwards, Jr., & L. Sartain (Eds.), *On Staffing* (Hoboken, NJ: Wiley, 2004), 280.

40. R. D. Gatewood & H. S. Field, *Human Resource Selection* (Fort Worth, TX: Dryden Press, 1998).

41. Ibid.

42. *Griggs v. Duke Power Co.*, 401 U.S. 424, 436 (1971); *Albemarle Paper Co. v. Moody*, 422 U.S. 405 (1975).

43. A. Embrey, "A Good Manager Is Hard to Find," *Convenience Store News*, 10 January 2005, http://www.csnews.com.

44. "Fujisawa Launches 'Jobs Challenge' Policy," *Market Letter*, 17 September 2001, http://www.marketletter.com/.

45. J. A. Breaugh, *Recruitment: Science and Practice* (Boston: PWS-Kent, 1992).

46. "Fujisawa Launches 'Jobs Challenge' Policy."

47. J. Badal, "Career Path Programs Help Retain Workers," *Wall Street Journal*, 24 July 2006, http://online.wsj.com.

48. A. Muoio, "Man with a (Talent) Plan," *Fast Company*, 1 January 2001, 83.

49. Ibid.

50. J. Breaugh & M. Starke, "Research on Employee Recruitment: So Many Studies, So Many Remaining Questions," *Journal of Management* 26 (2000): 405–434.

51. S. Gale, "Internet Recruiting: Better, Cheaper, Faster," *Personnel Journal*, 1 December 2000, 74.

52. K. Maher, "Corporations Cut Middlemen and Do Their Own Recruiting," *Wall Street Journal*, 14 January 2003, B10.

53. "Hire.com Customers Save Millions in Costs While Increasing Quality of Recruits," *Business Wire*, 9 March 2004, 08:00.

54. S. Forster, "Technology (A Special Report)—The Best Way To . . . Recruit New Workers," *Wall Street Journal*, 15 September 2003, R8.

55. "Job Opportunities," Subway Restaurants, http://www.subway.com/applications/InStoreJobs/index.aspx.

56. "Research Demonstrates the Success of Internet Recruiting," *HR Focus*, April 2003, 7.

57. "New Jobs Suffix Approved for Worldwide Recruiting/Hiring," *Human Resource Department Management Report*, May 2005, 9.

58. E. Agnvall, "Recruiting by Ones and Zeros," Society for Human Resource Management, http://www.shrm.org; D. Robb, "Career Portals Boost Online Recruiting," *HR Magazine*, April 2004, Society for Human Resource Management, http://www.shrm.org.

59. A. Milkovits, "Survey Shows Methods Vary for Selecting Police Recruits," *Providence Journal*, 19 May 2003, B-01.

60. C. Camden & B. Wallace, "Job Application Forms: A Hazardous Employment Practice," *Personnel Administrator* 28 (1983): 31–32.

61. K. Maher, "Career Journal: The Jungle," *Wall Street Journal*, 6 May 2003, B8.

62. J. Kennedy, "Europeans Expect Different Type of Résumé," *Chicago Sun-Times*, 3 June 1999, 73.

63. J. Tamen, "Job Applicants' Résumés Are Often Riddled with Misinformation," *South Florida Sun-Sentinel*, 24 February 2003, available at http://www.sun-sentinel.com/.

64. S. Adler, "Verifying a Job Candidate's Background: The State of Practice in a Vital Human Resources Activity," *Review of Business* 15, no. 2 (1993/1994): 3–8.

65. "More Than 70 Percent of HR Professionals Say Reference Checking Is Effective in Identifying Poor Performers," Society for Human Resource Management, http://www.shrm.org.

66. P. Babcock, "Spotting Lies: The High Cost of Careless Hiring," *HR Magazine*, October 2003, Society for Human Resource Management, http://www.shrm.org.

67. T. Thiesen, "Prisoners of the Past: Workers with Criminal Records Have Tough Time," *Orlando Sentinel*, 3 October 2001, G1.

68. M. Le, T. Nguyen, & B. Kleiner, "Legal Counsel: Don't Be Sued for Negligent Hiring," *Nonprofit World*, 1 May 2003, 14–15.

69. "Why It's Critical to Set a Policy on Background Checks for New Hires," *Managing Accounts Payable*, September 2004, 6; J. Schramm, "Future Focus: Background Checking," *HR Magazine*, January 2005, Society for Human Resource Management, http://www.shrm.org.

70. M. P. Cronin, "This Is a Test," *Inc.*, August 1993, 64–69.

71. C. Cohen, "Reference Checks," *CA Magazine*, November 2004, 41.

72. S. Marshall, "Spot Inflated Résumés with Simple Sleuthing," *Asian Wall Street Journal*, 7 April 2000, P3.

73. J. Hunter, "Cognitive Ability, Cognitive Aptitudes, Job Knowledge, and Job Performance," *Journal of Vocational Behavior* 29 (1986): 340–362.

74. F. L. Schmidt, "The Role of General Cognitive Ability and Job Performance: Why There Cannot be a Debate," *Human Performance* 15 (2002): 187–210.

75. K. Murphy, "Can Conflicting Perspectives on the Role of *g* in Personnel Selection Be Resolved?" *Human Performance* 15 (2002): 173–186.

76. E. E. Cureton, "Comment," in E. R. Henry, *Research Conference on the Use of Autobiographical Data as Psychological Predictors* (Greensboro, NC: The Richardson Foundation, 1965), 13.

77. G. Dean, "The Bottom Line: Effect Size," in *The Write Stuff: Evaluations of Graphology—The Study of Handwriting Analysis*,

ed. B. Beyerstein & D. Beyerstein (Buffalo, NY: Prometheus Books, 1992); K. Dunham, "Career Journal: The Jungle, Seeing the Future," *Wall Street Journal*, 15 May 2001, B12; J. Kurtz & W. Wells, "The Employee Polygraph Protection Act: The End of Lie Detector Use in Employment Decisions?" *Journal of Small Business Management* 27, no. 4 (1989): 76–80; B. Leonard, "Reading Employees," *HRMagazine*, April 1999, 67; S. Lilienfeld, J. Wood, & H. Garb, "The Scientific Status of Projective Techniques," *Psychological Science in the Public Interest* 1 (2000): 27–66; E. Neter & G. Ben-Shakhar, "The Predictive Validity of Graphological Inferences: A Meta-Analytic Approach," *Personality & Individual Differences* 10 (1989): 737–745.

78. J. R. Glennon, L. E. Albright, & W. A. Owens, *A Catalog of Life History Items* (Greensboro, NC: The Richardson Foundation, 1966).

79. Gatewood & Field, *Human Resource Selection.*

80. J. M. Digman, "Personality Structure: Emergence of the Five-Factor Model," *Annual Review of Psychology* 41 (1990): 417–440; M. R. Barrick & M. K. Mount, "The Big Five Personality Dimensions and Job Performance: A Meta-Analysis," *Personnel Psychology* 44 (1991): 1–26.

81. N. Schmitt, "Beyond the Big Five: Increases in Understanding and Practical Utility," *Human Performance* 17 (2004): 347–357.

82. I. Kotlyar & K. Ades, "HR Technology: Assessment Technology Can Help Match the Best Applicant to the Right Job," *HR Magazine*, 1 May 2002, 97.

83. K. Maher, "The Jungle: Focus on Recruitment, Pay and Getting Ahead,"

Wall Street Journal, 19 November 2002, B8.

85. M. S. Taylor & J. A. Sniezek, "The College Recruitment Interview: Topical Content and Applicant Reactions," *Journal of Occupational Psychology* 57 (1984): 157–168.

86. R. Burnett, C. Fan, S. J. Motowidlo, & T. DeGroot, "Interview Notes and Validity," *Personnel Psychology* 51, no. X (1998): 375–396; M. A. Campion, D. K. Palmer, & J. E. Campion, "A Review of Structure in the Selection Interview," *Personnel Psychology* 50, no. 3 (1997): 655–702.

86. Campion, et al., "A Review of Structure in the Selection Interview."

87. J. Cortina, N. Goldstein, S. Payne, K. Davison, & S. Gilliland, "The Incremental Validity of Interview Scores Over and Above Cognitive Ability and Conscientiousness Scores," *Personnel Psychology* 53, issue 2 (2000): 325–351; F. L. Schmidt & J. E. Hunter, "The Validity and Utility of Selection Methods in Personnel Psychology: Practical and Theoretical Implications of 85 Years of Research Findings," *Psychological Bulletin* 124, no. 2 (1998): 262–274.

88. T. Judge, "The Employment Interview: A Review of Recent Research and Recommendations for Future Research," *Human Resource Management Review* 10, issue 4 (2000): 383–406.

89. Cortina, Goldstein, Payne, Davison, & Gilliland, "The Incremental Validity of Interview Scores."

90. K. Tyler, "Training Revs Up," *HR Magazine*, April 2005, Society for Human Resource Management, http://www.shrm.org.

91. Ibid.

92. S. Livingston, T. W. Gerdel, M. Hill, B. Yerak, C. Melvin, & B. Lubinger, "Ohio's Strongest

Companies All Agree That Training Is Vital to Their Success," *Cleveland Plain Dealer*, 21 May 1997, 30S.

93. G. Kesler, "Why the Leadership Bench Never Gets Deeper: Ten Insights about Executive Talent Development," *Human Resource Planning*, 1 January 2002, 32.

94. "Frequently Asked Questions," WorkKeys, http://www.act.org/ workkeys/overview/faq .html#skills.

95. J. Borzo, "Almost Human: Using Avatars for Corporate Training, Advocates Say, Can Combine the Best Parts of Face-to-Face Interaction and Computer-Based Learning," *Wall Street Journal*, 24 May 2004, R4.

96. S. Overby, "The World's Biggest Classroom," *CIO*, 1 February 2002, www .cio.com/archive/020102/ dow.html.

97. M. Totty, "Better Training through Gaming," *Wall Street Journal*, 25 April 2005, R6.

98. Borzo, "Almost Human: Using Avatars for Corporate Training."

99. D. L. Kirkpatrick, "Four Steps to Measuring Training Effectiveness," *Personnel Administrator* 28 (1983): 19–25.

100. L. Bassi, J. Ludwig, D. McMurrer, & M. Van Buren, "Profiting from Learning: Do Firms' Investments in Education and Training Pay Off?" American Society for Training and Development, http://www .astd.org/NR/rdonlyres/ 15C0E2AB-B16D-4E3C-A081–4205B865DA3F/0/ PFLWhitePaper.pdf.

101. J. Stack, "The Curse of the Annual Performance Review," *Inc.*, 1 March 1997, 39.

102. D. Murphy, "Are Performance Appraisals Worse Than a Waste of Time? Book Derides Unintended Consequences," *San Francisco Chronicle*, 9 September 2001, W1.

103. K. R. Murphy & J. N. Cleveland, *Understanding Performance Appraisal: Social, Organizational and Goal-Based Perspectives*, (Thousand Oaks, CA: Sage, 1995).

104. T. D. Schellhardt, "Annual Agony: It's Time to Evaluate Your Work, and All Involved Are Groaning" *Wall Street Journal*, 19 November 1996, A1.

105. U. J. Wiersma & G. P. Latham, "The Practicality of Behavioral Observation Scales, Behavioral Expectation Scales, and Trait Scales," *Personnel Psychology* 39 (1986): 619–628; U. J. Wiersma, P. T. Van Den Berg, & G. P. Latham, "Dutch Reactions to Behavioral Observation, Behavioral Expectation, and Trait Scales," *Group & Organization Management* 20 (1995): 297–309.

106. D. J. Schleicher, D. V. Day, B. T. Mayes, R. E. Riggio, "A New Frame for Frame-of-Reference Training: Enhancing the Construct Validity of Assessment Centers," *Journal of Applied Psychology*, August 2002, 735–746.

107. Stack, "The Curse of the Annual Performance Review."

108. B. O'Reilly, "360-Degree Feedback Can Change Your Life," *Fortune*, 17 October 1994, 93.

109. C. Hymowitz, "Do '360' Job Reviews by Colleagues Promote Honesty or Insults?" *Wall Street Journal*, 12 December 2000, B1.

110. D. A. Waldman, L. E. Atwater, & D. Antonioni, "Has 360 Feedback Gone Amok?" *Academy of Management Executive* 12, no. 2 (1998): 86–94.

111. H. H. Meyer, "A Solution to the Performance Appraisal Feedback Enigma," *Academy of Management Executive* 5, no. 1 (1991): 68–76; G. C. Thornton, "Psychometric Properties of Self-Appraisals of Job Performance," *Personnel Psychology* 33 (1980): 263–271.

112. G. C. Thornton, "Psychometric Properties of Self-Appraisals of Job Performance," *Personnel Psychology* 33 (1980): 263–271.

113. J. Smither, M. London, R. Flautt, Y. Vargas, & I. Kucine, "Can Working with an Executive Coach Improve Multisource Feedback Ratings over Time? A Quasi-Experimental Field Study," *Personnel Psychology* (Spring 2003): 21–43.

114. A. Walker & J. Smither, "A Five-Year Study of Upward Feedback: What Managers Do with Their Results Matters," *Personnel Psychology* (Summer 1999): 393–422.

115. I. M. Jawahar, "Correlates of Satisfaction with Performance Appraisal Feedback," *Journal of Labor Research* 26 (2006): 213–236.

116. Ibid.

117. M. Fong, "Chinese Puzzle—Surprising Shortage of Workers Forces Factories to Add Perks; Pressure on Pay—and Prices," *Wall Street Journal*, 16 August 2004, B1.

118. K. Maher, "Coal Companies Are Slowed by Severe Shortage of Workers—Mines Can't Boost Output, So Utilities' Low Stockpiles May Lift Electricity Prices," *Wall Street Journal*, 5 May 2005, A2.

119. G. T. Milkovich & J. M. Newman, *Compensation*, 4th ed. (Homewood, IL: Irwin, 1993).

120. E. Rasmusson, "Ten Things Your Child Care Provider Won't Tell You," *SmartMoney*, 1 May 2003, 69.

121. S. Shellenbarger, "Tight Labor Market Is Putting Squeeze on Quality Day Care," *Wall Street Journal*, 21 October 1998, B1.

122. M. L. Williams & G. F. Dreher, "Compensation System Attributes and Applicant Pool Characteristics," *Academy of Management Journal* 35, no. 3 (1992): 571–595.

123. C. Windham, "Nursing Shortage Eases with Higher Pay and a Weak Labor Market," *Wall Street Journal*, 17 November 2004, D5.

124. "Renault SAS to Pay EUR174.2M in Profit Sharing for 2006," *Dow Jones Newswires*, 8 February 2007, http://online.wsj.com.

125. J. Kaufman, "Sharing the Wealth: At McKay Nursery, Migrant Workers Get a Chance to Own Part of the Company," *Wall Street Journal*, 9 April 1998, R10.

126. M. Bloom, "The Performance Effects of Pay Dispersion on Individuals and Organizations," *Academy of Management Journal* 42, no. 1 (1999): 25–40.

127. L. Lavelle, F. Jespersen, S. Ante, & J. Kerstetter, "Executive Pay: The Days of the Fantasyland CEO Pay Package Appear to Be in the Past. A 33% Decline in Compensation Has Returned America's Bosses to the Year 1996," *BusinessWeek*, 21 April 2003, 86; L. Lavelle, "A Payday for Performance; Compensation Is Less Outrageous This Year, Except for CEOs Who Delivered," *BusinessWeek*, 18 April 2005, 78.

128. W. Grossman & R. E. Hoskisson, "CEO Pay at the Crossroads of Wall Street and Main: Toward the Strategic Design of Executive Compensation," *Academy of Management Executive* 12, no. 1 (1998): 43–57.

129. Bloom, "The Performance Effects of Pay Dispersion on Individuals and Organizations."

130. M. Bloom & J. Michel, "The Relationships among Organizational Context, Pay Dispersion, and Managerial Turnover," *Academy of Management Journal* 45 (2002): 33–42.

131. J. S. Rosenbloom, "The Environment of Employee Benefit Plans," in *The Handbook of Employee Benefits*, ed. J. S. Rosenbloom (Chicago: Irwin, 1996), 3–13.

132. "Employer Costs for Employee Compensation Summary," Bureau of Labor Statistics, http://www.bls.gov/news.release/ecec.nr0.htm.

133. A. E. Barber, R. B. Dunham, & R. A. Formisano, "The Impact of Flexible Benefits on Employee Satisfaction: A Field Study," *Personnel Psychology* 45 (1992): 55–75; B. Heshizer, "The Impact of Flexible Benefits on Job Satisfaction and Turnover Intentions," *Benefits Quarterly* 4 (1994): 84–90; D. M. Cable & T. A. Judge, "Pay Preferences and Job Search Decisions: A Person-Organization Fit Perspective," *Personnel Psychology* 47 (1994): 317–348.

134. B. T. Beam & J. J. McFadden, *Employee Benefits* (Chicago: Dearborn Financial Publishing, 1996).

135. R. Lieber, "Employers Offer New Pretax Perk: Debit Cards Allow Instant Access to Accounts for Medical Fees and Commuting Expenses," *Wall Street Journal*, 2 September 2003, D1.

136. J. Lublin, "Left Out of a Meeting? Parking Space Taken? Worry about Your Job," *Wall Street Journal*, 3 April 2001, B1.

137. A. Rupe, "Horrors from the Bad-Firing File," *Workforce Management*, November 2003, 16.

138. "400 at RadioShack Are Told by E-Mail: You're Outta Here," Associated Press, 31 August 2006, available at http://seattletimes.nwsource.com/html/businesstechnology/2003236874_radioshack31.html.

139. P. Michal-Johnson, *Saying Good-Bye: A Manager's Guide to Employee Dismissal* (Glenview, IL: Scott, Foresman & Co., 1985).

140. M. Bordwin, "Employment Law: Beware of Time Bombs and Shark-Infested Waters," *HR Focus*, 1 April 1995, 19; D. Jones, "Fired Workers Fight Back . . . and Win; Laws, Juries Shift Protection to Terminated Employees," *USA Today*, 2 April 1998, 01B.

141. T. Bland, "Fire at Will, Repent at Leisure," *Security Management* 44 (May 2000), 64.

142. "Planned Layoffs May Top 1 Million for Fourth Year in a Row," U.S. Steel Workers of America, http://www.uswa.org.

143. J. Bandler, "Kodak to Cut Staff up to 21%, Amid Digital Push—As Film Business Shrinks, Company Retools for Future," *Wall Street Journal*, 22 January 2004, A1.

144. "Ford CEO Says It Must Change the Way It Does Business," *Wall Street Journal*, 3 September 2006, http://online.wsj.com.

145. J. R. Morris, W. F. Cascio, & C. E. Young, "Downsizing after All These Years: Questions and Answers about Who Did It, How Many Did It, and Who Benefited from It," *Organizational Dynamics* 27, no. 3 (1999): 78–87.

146. K. E. Mishra, G. M. Spreitzer, & A. K. Mishra, "Preserving Employee Morale during Downsizing," *Sloan Management Review* 39, no. 2 (1998): 83–95.

147. K. Frieswick, "Until We Meet Again?" *CFO*, 1 October 2001, 41.

148. J. Hilsenrath, "Adventures in Cost Cutting," *Wall Street Journal*, 10 May 2004, R1.

149. J. Ackerman, "Helping Layoff Survivors Cope: Companies Strive to Keep Morale High," *Boston Globe*, 30 December 2001, H1.

150. Ibid.

151. D. Ferrari, "Designing and Evaluating Early Retirement Programs: The State of Wyoming Experience," *Government Finance Review* 15, no. 1 (1999): 29–31.

152. Hilsenrath, "Adventures in Cost Cutting."

153. R. Mullins, "Early Retirement Programs Can End Up Being Costly," *Business Journal–Milwaukee*, 20 January 1996, Section 1, 25.

154. M. Willett, "Early Retirement and Phased Retirement Programs for the Public Sector," *Benefits & Compensation Digest*, April 2005, 31.

155. D. R. Dalton, W. D. Todor, & D. M. Krackhardt, "Turnover Overstated: The Functional Taxonomy," *Academy of Management Review* 7 (1982): 117–123.

156. J. R. Hollenbeck & C. R. Williams, "Turnover Functionality versus Turnover Frequency: A Note on Work Attitudes and Organizational Effectiveness," *Journal of Applied Psychology* 71 (1986): 606–611.

157. C. R. Williams, "Reward Contingency, Unemployment, and Functional Turnover," *Human Resource Management Review* 9 (1999): 549–576.

158. J. McCarthy & R. Goffin, "Measuring Job Interview Anxiety: Beyond Weak Knees and Sweaty Palms," *Personnel Psychology* 54, no. 3 (2004): 31.

159. S. Begley, "Behind 'Shortage' of Engineers, Employers Grow More Choosy," *Wall Street Journal*, 16 November 2005, A1, A12.

Chapter 12

1. C. Wittenauer, "Walgreens Is the Target of U.S. Racial-Bias Lawsuit," *Philadelphia Inquirer*, 8 March 2007, http://www.philly.com/inquirer; Walgreens press release, http://www.walgreensclass.com; M. Albright, "Walgreens Suit Cites Racial Bias," *St. Petersburg Times*, 21 June 2005, http://www.sptimes.ru; N. J. C. Pistor, "Federal Government Targets Walgreens in Discrimination Lawsuit," *St. Louis Post-Dispatch*, 8 March 2007, http://www.stltoday.com; "Walgreens Sued for Job Bias against Blacks," Equal Employment Opportunity Commission, http://www.eeoc.gov/press/3-7-07.html; "EEOC Files Class-Action Racial Bias Suit against Walgreens," *Financial Times*, 8 March 2007, https://www.financialtimes.net.

2. J. H. Boyett & J. T. Boyett, *Beyond Workforce 2000* (New York: Dutton, 1995).

3. Ibid.

4. "Preparing the Workforce of Tomorrow," Hewitt Associates, February 2004, http://www.hewitt.com.

5. R. Stodghill, "The Coming Job Bottleneck," *BusinessWeek*, 24 March 1997, 183–185.

6. "Preparing the Workforce of Tomorrow."

7. K. Wallsten, "Diversity Pays Off in Big Sales for Toyota Dealership," *Workforce*, September 1998, 91–92.

8. R. S. Johnson, "The 50 Best Companies for Asians, Blacks, & Hispanics: Talent Comes in All Colors," *Fortune*, 3 August 1999, 94.

9. D. D. Stanford, "Coke's Diversity Case Closed: Report Says Progress Made," *Atlanta Journal-Constitution*, 2 December 2006, 1C; "Racism Lawsuit against New York Manufacturer Settled for $1.25 Million," Associated Press Financial Wire, 28 December 2006, available at http://www.ap.org; "Payouts Delayed in Lawsuit Settlement with Los Alamos Lab," Associated Press State & Local Wire, 27 November 2006, available at http://www.ap.org; "Tyson Settles Discrimination Lawsuit for $871,000," *Financial Times*, 7 November 2006, http://www.financialtimes.net.

10. "Best Companies for Minorities: Diversity Leaders," *Fortune*, http://www.fortune.com.

11. D. D. Stanford, "Coke's Diversity Case Closed: Report Says Progress Made."

12. J. Hickman, "50 Best Companies for Minorities," *Fortune*, 28 June 2004, 136.

13. Affirmative action, available at http://www.dol.gov/dol/topic/hiring/affirmativeact.htm.

14. R. Rodriguez, "Diversity Finds Its Place: More Organizations Are Dedicating Senior-Level Executives to Drive Diversity Initiatives for Bottom-Line Effect," *HR Magazine*, August 2006, Society for Human Resource Management, http://www.shrm.org.

15. "Federal Laws Prohibiting Job Discrimination: Questions and Answers," Equal Employment Opportunity Commission, http://www.eeoc.gov/facts/qanda.html.

16. A. P. Carnevale & S. C. Stone, *The American Mosaic: An In-Depth Report on the Future of Diversity at Work* (New York: McGraw-Hill, 1995).

17. T. Roosevelt, "From Affirmative Action to Affirming Diversity," *Harvard Business Review* 68, no. 2 (1990): 107–117.

18. A. M. Konrad & F. Linnehan, "Formalized HRM Structures: Coordinating Equal Employment Opportunity or Concealing Organizational Practices?" *Academy of Management Journal* 38, no. 3 (1995): 787–820.

19. See, e.g., *Hopwood v. Texas*, 78 F.3d 932 (5th Cir., 18 March 1996). The U.S. Supreme Court has upheld the principle of affirmative action but has struck down some specific programs.

20. J. Madore, "Losing Historical Advantages: White Males Say They're Hurt, Too," *Newsday*, 9 April 2000, A45.

21. Ibid.

22. M. E. Heilman, C. J. Block, & P. Stathatos, "The Affirmative Action Stigma of Incompetence: Effects of Performance Information Ambiguity," *Academy of Management Journal* 40, no. 3 (1997): 603–625.

23. K. C. Cole, "Jury Out on Whether Affirmative Action Beneficiaries Face Stigma: Research Studies Arrive at Conflicting Conclusions," *Los Angeles Times*, 1 May 1995, 18.

24. E. Orenstein, "The Business Case for Diversity," *Financial Executive*, May 2005, 22–25; G. Robinson & K. Dechant, "Building a Business Case for Diversity," *Academy of Management Executive* 11, no. 3 (1997): 21–31.

25. E. Esen, "2005 Workplace Diversity Practices: Survey Report," Survey conducted by the Society for Human Resource Management. SHRM Research Department, Alexandria, Virginia (http://www.shrm.org/research), October 2005.

26. E. Orenstein, "The Business Case for Diversity."

27. E. Esen, "2005 Workplace Diversity Practices: Survey Report."

28. E. Orenstein, "The Business Case for Diversity."

29. "Judge Approves Settlement of Coca-Cola Bias Lawsuit," *Wall Street Journal*, 30 May 2001, B7; A. Reifenberg, "Texaco Settlement in Racial-Bias Case Endorsed by Judge," *Wall Street Journal*, 26 March 1997, B15.

30. B. Morris, K. Bonamici, S. Kaufman, & P. Neering, "How Corporate America Is Betraying Women,"

Fortune, 10 January 2005, 64.

31. S. Ellison & J. Lublin, "Dial to Pay $10 Million to Settle a Sexual-Harassment Lawsuit," *Wall Street Journal*, 30 April 2003, B4.

32. M. Selmi, "The Price of Discrimination: The Nature of Class Action Employment Discrimination Litigation and Its Effects," *Texas Law Review*, 1 April 2003, 1249.

33. D. Lewis, "EEOC: Damage Awards; Reach $420m in 2004," *Boston Globe*, 20 February 2005, D2.

34. P. Wright & S. P. Ferris, "Competitiveness through Management of Diversity: Effects on Stock Price Valuation," *Academy of Management Journal* 38 (1995): 272–285.

35. Ibid.

36. R. B. Lieber & L. Urresta, "Pacific Enterprises Keeping Talent: After Being Encouraged to Explore Jobs Elsewhere, Most Employees Stay Put," *Fortune*, 3 August 1998, 96.

37. R. Rodriguez, "Diversity Finds Its Place: More Organizations Are Dedicating Senior-Level Executives to Drive Diversity Initiatives for Bottom-Line Effect."

38. W. He & F. Hobbs, "Minority Purchasing Power: 2000 to 2045," Minority Business Development Agency, U.S. Department of Commerce, September 2000.

39. "The Emerging Minority Marketplace: Minority Purchasing Power 2000 to 2045," U.S. Department of Commerce, Minority Business Development Agency, http://www .mbda.gov/documents/ purchasing_power.pdf.

40. E. Esen, "2005 Workplace Diversity Practices: Survey Report."; L. E. Wynter, "Business & Race: Advocates Try to Tie Diversity to Profit," *Wall Street Journal*, 7 February 1996, B1.

41. W. W. Watson, K. Kumar, & L. K. Michaelsen, "Cultural Diversity's Impact on Interaction Process and Performance: Comparing Homogeneous and Diverse Task Groups," *Academy of Management Journal* 36 (1993): 590–602; K. A. Jehn, G. B. Northcraft, & M. A. Neale, "Why Differences Make a Difference: A Field Study of Diversity, Conflict, and Performance in Workgroups," *Administrative Science Quarterly* 44 (1999): 741–763.

42. F. Rice, "How to Make Diversity Pay," *Fortune*, 8 August 1994, 78.

43. R. Rodriguez, "Diversity Finds Its Place: More Organizations Are Dedicating Senior-Level Executives to Drive Diversity Initiatives for Bottom-Line Effect."

44. M. R. Carrell & E. E. Mann, "Defining Workplace Diversity Programs and Practices in Organizations," *Labor Law Journal* 44 (1993): 743–764.

45. D. A. Harrison, K. H. Price, & M. P. Bell, "Beyond Relational Demography: Time and the Effects of Surface- and Deep-Level Diversity on Work Group Cohesion," *Academy of Management Journal* 41 (1998): 96–107.

46. D. Harrison, K. Price, J. Gavin, & A. Florey, "Time, Teams, and Task Performance: Changing Effects of Surface-and Deep-Level Diversity on Group Functioning," *Academy of Management Journal* 45 (2002): 1029–1045.

47. Harrison, Price, & Bell, "Beyond Relational Demography."

48. Ibid.

49. N. Munk, "Finished at Forty: In the New Economy, the Skills That Come with Age Count for Less and Less," *Fortune*, 1 February 1999, 50.

50. K. Wrenn & T. Maurer, "Beliefs about Older Workers' Learning and Development Behavior in Relation to Beliefs about Malleability of Skills, Age-Related Decline, and Control," *Journal of Applied Social Psychology* 34 (February 2004): 223–242.

51. J. Helyar & B. Cherry, "50 and Fired," *Fortune*, 16 May 2005, 78.

52. Ibid.

53. S. E. Sullivan & E. A. Duplaga, "Recruiting and Retaining Older Workers for the Millennium," *Business Horizons* 40 (12 November 1997): 65.

54. Munk, "Finished at Forty."

55. J. Bravin, "Court Expands Age Bias Claims for Work Force," *Wall Street Journal*, 31 March 2005, B1.

56. J. Helyar & B. Cherry, "50 and Fired."

57. Hampshire & Isle of Wight. Useful websites for older workers, available at http://www.link2learn .co.uk/content/default .asp?PageId=372

58. S. R. Rhodes, "Age-Related Differences in Work Attitudes and Behavior," *Psychological Bulletin* 92 (1983): 328–367.

59. A. Fisher, "Wanted: Aging Baby-Boomers," *Fortune*, 30 September 1996, 204.

60. G. M. McEvoy & W. F. Cascio, "Cumulative Evidence of the Relationship between Employee Age and Job Performance," *Journal of Applied Psychology* 74 (1989): 11–17.

61. Sullivan & Duplaga, "Recruiting and Retaining Older Workers for the Millennium."

62. T. Maurer & N. Rafuse, "Learning, Not Litigating: Managing Employee Development and Avoiding Claims of Age Discrimination," *Academy of Management Executive* 15, issue 4 (2001): 110–121.

63. B. L. Hassell & P. L. Perrewe, "An Examination of Beliefs about Older Workers: Do Stereotypes Still Exist?" *Journal of Organizational Behavior* 16 (1995): 457–468.

64. "Women in the Labor Force: A Databook (Updated and Available on the Internet)," Bureau of Labor Statistics, http://www.bls.gov/bls/ databooknews2005.pdf.

65. "Top Facts about Women-Owned Businesses," Center for Women's Business Research, http:// www.cfwbr.org/facts/ index.php.

66. "Women Own 9 Million U.S. Businesses," U.S. Small Business Administration, http:// www.sba.gov/advo/ press/01–09.html.

67. "The 2005 *Fortune* 500: Women CEOs," *Fortune*, http://www.fortune.com.

68. "2003 Catalyst Census of Women Board Directors of the *Fortune* 1000," http:// www.catalystwomen.org.

69. M. Bertrand & K. Hallock, "The Gender Gap in Top Corporate Jobs," *Industrial & Labor Relations Review* 55 (2001): 3–21.

70. J. R. Hollenbeck, D. R. Ilgen, C. Ostroff, & J. B. Vancouver, "Sex Differences in Occupational Choice, Pay, and Worth: A Supply-Side Approach to Understanding the Male-Female Wage Gap," *Personnel Psychology* 40 (1987): 715–744.

71. A. Chaker & H. Stout, "Second Chances: After Years Off, Women Struggle to Revive Careers," *Wall Street Journal*, 6 May 2004, A1.

72. Korn-Ferry International, 1993.

73. Department of Industry, Labor and Human Relations, *Report of the Governor's Task Force on the Glass Ceiling Commission* (Madison, WI: State of Wisconsin, 1993).

74. M. Fix, G. C. Galster, & R. J. Struyk, "An Overview of Auditing for Discrimination," in *Clear and Convincing Evidence: Measurement of Discrimination in America*, ed. Michael Fix & Raymond Struyk (Washington, DC: Urban Institute Press, 1993), 1–68.

75. S. Hamm, "Why Are Women So Invisible?" *Business Week*, 25 August 1997, 136.

76. D. Chenevert, & M. Tremblay, "Managerial Career Success in Canadian Organizations: Is Gender a Determinant?" *International Journal of Human Resource Management* (2002: 13) 920–941; F. Neathey, S. Dench, & L. Thomas, "Monitoring Progress toward Pay Equality," Institute for Employment Studies report on behalf of the Equal Opportunities Commission 2003, available at http://www.eoc.org.uk; S. Wellington, M. B. Kropf, & P. R. Gerkovich, "What's Holding Women Back?" *Harvard Business Review* (2003: 81) 82–111.

77. S. Wellington et al., "What's Holding Women Back?"

78. B. R. Ragins, B. Townsend, & M. Mattis, "Gender Gap in the Executive Suite: CEOs and Female Executives Report on Breaking the Glass Ceiling," *Academy of Management Executive* 12 (1998): 28–42.

79. N. Lockwood, "The Glass Ceiling: Domestic and International Perspectives," *HRMagazine* (2004 Research Quarterly): 2–10.

80. T. B. Foley, "Discrimination Lawsuits Are a Small-Business Nightmare: A Guide to Minimizing the Potential Damage," *Wall Street Journal*, 28 September 1998, 15.

81. J. Johnson, "Black CEOs Gaining in Corporate America," *San Francisco Chronicle*, 10 February 2005, http://www.sfgate.com/cgi-bin/article.cgi?file=/chronicle/archive/2005/02/10/BUGDRB8K781.DTL&type=business.

82. "Household Data: Annual Averages, Table 11. Employed Persons by Detailed Occupation, Sex, Race, and Hispanic or Latino Ethnicity," Bureau of Labor Statistics, ftp://ftp.bls.gov/pub/special.requests/lf/aat11.txt.

83. D. A. Neal & W. R. Johnson, "The Role of Premarket Factors in Black-White Wage Differences," *Journal of Political Economy* 104, no. 5 (1996): 869–895.

84. Fix, Galster, & Struyk, "An Overview of Auditing for Discrimination."

85. M. Bendick, Jr., C. W. Jackson, & V. A. Reinoso, "Measuring Employment Discrimination through Controlled Experiments," in *African-Americans and Post-Industrial Labor Markets*, ed. James B. Stewart (New Brunswick, NJ: Transaction Publishers, 1997), 77–100.

86. P. B. Riach & J. Rich, "Measuring Discrimination by Direct Experimental Methods: Seeking Gunsmoke," *Journal of PostKeynesian Economics* 14, no. 2 (Winter 1991–1992): 143–50.

87. A. P. Brief, R. T. Buttram, R. M. Reizenstein, & S. D. Pugh, "Beyond Good Intentions: The Next Steps toward Racial Equality in the American Workplace," *Academy of Management Executive* 11 (1997): 59–72.

88. L. E. Wynter, "Business & Race: Federal Agencies, Spurred on by Nonprofit Groups, Are Increasingly Embracing the Use of Undercover Investigators to Identify Discrimination in the Marketplace," *Wall Street Journal*, 1 July 1998, B1.

89. S. J. Well, "When the Bias Is in the Hiring," *Journal Record* (Oklahoma City), 26 March 1998, 1.

90. D. Morris, "The Next Great Hiring Frontier," *Wall Street Journal*, 13 September 2005, B2.

91. "The Americans with Disabilities Act: Questions and Answers," U.S. Department of Justice, September 1992, http://www.usdoj.gov/crt/ada/ada.html.

92. "Frequently Asked Questions," *Disability Statistics: Online Resource for U.S. Disability Statistics*, Cornell University School of Industrial and Labor Relations, http://www.ilr.cornell.edu/edi/disabilitystatistics.

93. "Census Brief: Disabilities Affect One-Fifth of All Americans," U.S. Bureau of the Census, December 1997, http://www.census.gov/prod/3/97pubs/cenbr975.pdf.

94. F. Bowe, "Adults with Disabilities: A Portrait," *President's Committee on Employment of People with Disabilities* (Washington, DC: GPO, 1992); D. Braddock & L. Bachelder, *The Glass Ceiling and Persons with Disabilities*, Glass Ceiling Commission, U.S. Department of Labor (Washington, DC: GPO, 1994). "Disability Status 2000," *Census Brief 2000*, March 2003, 11, available at http://www.census.gov/prod/2003pubs/c2kbr-17.pdf.

95. Louis Harris & Associates, Inc., *Public Attitudes toward People with Disabilities* (Washington, DC: National Organization on Disability, 1991); Louis Harris & Associates, Inc., *The ICD Survey II: Employing Disabled Americans* (New York: 1987).

96. R. Greenwood & V. A. Johnson, "Employer Perspectives on Workers with Disabilities," *Journal of Rehabilitation* 53 (1987): 37–45.

97. "Low Cost Accommodation Solutions," Office of Disability Employment Policy, http://www.jan.wvu.edu/media/LowCostSolutions.html.

98. Ibid.

99. "Job Accommodation Network," Office of Disability Employment Policy, http://janweb.icdi.wvu.edu.

100. "Study on the Financing of Assistive Technology Devices and Services for Individuals with Disabilities: A Report to the President and the Congress of the United States," National Council on Disability, http://www.ncd.gov.

101. Ibid.

102. R. B. Cattell, "Personality Pinned Down," *Psychology Today* 7 (1973): 40–46; C. S. Carver & M. F. Scheier, *Perspectives on Personality* (Boston: Allyn & Bacon, 1992).

103. J. M. Digman, "Personality Structure: Emergence of the Five-Factor Model," *Annual Review of Psychology* 41 (1990): 417–440; M. R. Barrick & M. K. Mount, "The Big Five Personality Dimensions and Job Performance: A Meta-Analysis," *Personnel Psychology* 44 (1991): 1–26.

104. S. Bates, "Personality Counts: Psychological Tests Can Help Peg the Job Applicants Best Suited for Certain Job," *HR Magazine*, February 2002, http://www.shrm.org/hrmagazine/articles/0202/0202covstory.asp.

105. "NASA Fires Astronaut Nowak," CNN.com, 7 March 2007, http://www.cnn.com/2007/TECH/space/03/07/nasa.nowak/index.html.

106. R. Cook, "The Changing 'Face' of Your Business: Finding Good People . . . and Keeping Them Motivated," *PRO Magazine*, March 2005, 43.

107. O. Behling, "Employee Selection: Will Intelligence and Conscientiousness Do the Job?" *Academy of Management Executive* 12 (1998): 77–86.

108. Barrick & Mount, "The Big Five Personality

Dimensions and Job Performance."

109. Barrick & Mount, "The Big Five Personality Dimensions and Job Performance"; M. K. Mount & M. R. Barrick, "The Big Five Personality Dimensions: Implications for Research and Practice in Human Resource Management," *Research in Personnel & Human Resources Management* 13 (1995): 153–200; M. K. Mount & M. R. Barrick, "Five Reasons Why the 'Big Five' Article Has Been Frequently Cited," *Personnel Psychology* 51 (1998): 849–857; D. S. Ones, M. K. Mount, M. R. Barrick, & J. E. Hunter, "Personality and Job Performance: A Critique of the Tett, Jackson, and Rothstein (1991) Meta-Analysis," *Personnel Psychology* 47 (1994): 147–156.

110. Mount & Barrick, "Five Reasons Why the 'Big Five' Article Has Been Frequently Cited."

111. Ibid.

112. J. A. Lopez, "Talking Desks: Personality Types Revealed in State Workstations," *Arizona Republic*, 7 January 1996, Section D, 1.

113. T. W. Adorno, E. Frenkel-Brunswik, D. J. Levinson, & R. N. Stanford, *The Authoritarian Personality* (New York: Harper & Row, 1950).

114. C. Hymowitz, "In the Lead: Two Football Coaches Have a Lot to Teach Screaming Managers," *Wall Street Journal*, 29 January 2007, B1.

115. R. G. Vleeming, "Machiavellianism: A Preliminary Review," *Psychological Reports* 53 (1979): 295–310.

116. F. L. Geis & T. H. Moon, "Machiavellianism and Deception," *Journal of Personality & Social Psychology* 41 (1981): 766–775.

117. R. Christie & F. L. Geis, *Studies in Machiavellianism* (New York: Academic Press, 1970), 312.

118. J. Zaslow, "Why Jerks Get Ahead: Being Obnoxious Often Pays Off in the Workplace," *Wall Street Journal*, 29 March 2004, R6.

119. B. Kallestad, "Florida State Research Shows Bad Managers' Effect on Workers," Associated Press State & Local Wire, 1 January 2007, available at http://www.ap.org.

120. K. A. Matthews, "Psychological Perspectives on the Type A Behavior Pattern," *Psychological Bulletin* 91 (1982): 293–323.

121. M. Friedman & R. H. Rosenman, *Type A Behavior and Your Heart* (New York: Fawcett Crest, 1974).

122. M. Lee & R. Kanungo, *Management of Work and Personal Life* (New York: Praeger, 1984).

123. J. Schaubroeck, D. C. Ganster, & B. E. Kemmerer, "Job Complexity, 'Type A' Behavior, and Cardiovascular Disorders," *Academy of Management Journal* 37 (1994): 37.

124. "Cardiovascular Research: Type A Personality Is Not Linked to Heart Disease," *Science Letter*, 19 September 2006, 386.

125. R. Winslow, "Choose Your Neurosis: Some Type-A Traits Are Riskier Than Others," *Wall Street Journal*, 22 October 2003, D1.

126. J. E. Bishop, "Health: Hostility, Distrust May Put Type A's at Coronary Risk," *Wall Street Journal Interactive*, 17 January 1989.

127. P. E. Spector, "Behavior in Organizations as a Function of Employee's Locus of Control," *Psychological Bulletin* 91 (1982): 482–497.

128. J. B. Rotter, "Generalized Expectancies for Internal versus External Control of Reinforcement," *Psychological Monographs* 80 (1966): Whole No. 609; J. B. Rotter, "Some Problems and Misconceptions Related to the Construct of Internal versus External Control of Reinforcement," *Journal of Consulting & Clinical Psychology* 43 (1975): 56–67.

129. R. S. Lazarus, *Emotion and Adaptation* (New York: Oxford University Press, 1991).

130. "The Secrets of Happiness," *Psychology Today* 25 (July 1992): 38.

131. B. M. Staw, N. E. Bell, & J. A. Clausen, "The Dispositional Approach to Job Attitudes: A Lifetime Longitudinal Test," *Administrative Science Quarterly* 31 (1986): 56–77.

132. "Put Customer Service at the Heart of Marketing to Grow the Firm," Accounting Office Management & Administration Report, January 2007, http://www.ioma.com/issues/AOMAR/2007_1/1610735–1.html.

133. "Accenture Survey: Poor Customer Service Drives Nearly Half of U.S. Consumers to Take Their Business Elsewhere," *Wireless News*, 8 August 2006, available at M2 Communications, http://www.m2.com.

134. A. M. Isen & R. A. Baron, "Positive Affect and Organizational Behavior," in *Research in Organizational Behavior* 12, ed. B. M. Staw & L. L. Cummings (Greenwich, CT: JAI Press, 1990); J. M. George & A. P. Brief, "Feeling Good–Doing Good: A Conceptual Analysis of the Mood at Work—Organizational Spontaneity Relationships," *Psychological Bulletin* 112 (1992): 310–329; R. D. Iverson & P. J. Erwin, "Predicting Occupational Injury: The Role of Affectivity," *Journal of Occupational & Organizational Psychology* 70 (1997): 113–128; D. P. Skarlicki, R. Folger, & P. Tesluk, "Personality as a Moderator in the Relationship between Fairness and Retaliation," *Academy of Management Journal* 42 (1999): 100–108.

135. P. Totterdell, S. Kellett, K. Teuchmann, & R. B. Briner, "Evidence of Mood Linkage in Work Groups," *Journal of Personality & Social Psychology* 74 (1998): 1503–1515.

136. M. E. P. Seligman & S. Schulman, "Explanatory Style as a Predictor of Productivity and Quitting among Life Insurance Sales Agents," *Journal of Personality & Social Psychology* 50 (1986): 832–838.

137. Sonja, L., Laura, K., & E. Diener, "The Benefits of Frequent Positive Affect: Does Happiness Lead to Success?" *Psychological Bulletin*, November 2005, 803–855.

138. T. D. Schellhardt, "In a Tight Factory Schedule, Where Does Religion Fit In?" *Wall Street Journal Interactive*, 4 March 1999.

139. Staff, "The Diverse Work Force," *Inc.*, January 1993, 33.

140. D. A. Thomas & R. J. Ely, "Making Differences Matter: A New Paradigm for Managing Diversity," *Harvard Business Review* 74 (September–October 1996): 79–90.

141. E. Esen "2005 Workplace Diversity Practices: Survey Report."

142. D. A. Thomas & S. Wetlaufer, "A Question of Color: A Debate on Race in the U.S. Workplace," *Harvard Business Review* 75 (September–October 1997), 118–132.

143. Thomas & Ely, "Making Differences Matter."

144. A. Fisher, "How You Can Do Better on Diversity," *Fortune*, 15 November 2004, 60.

145. Aetna 2005 Diversity Annual Report (http://www.aetna.com), obtained from SHRM Research Department.

146. J. R. Norton & R. E. Fox, *The Change Equation: Capitalizing on Diversity for Effective Organizational Change* (Washington, DC: American Psychological Association, 1997).

147. Ibid.

148. Thomas & Ely, "Making Differences Matter."

149. R. R. Thomas, Jr., *Beyond Race and Gender: Unleashing the Power of Your Total Workforce by Managing Diversity* (New York: AMACOM, 1991).

150. Ibid.

151. T. Cox, Jr., "The Multicultural Organization," *Academy of Management Executive* 5 (1991): 34–47.

152. S. Lubove, "Damned If You Do, Damned If You Don't: Preference Programs Are on the Defensive in the Public Sector, but Plaintiffs' Attorneys and Bureaucrats Keep Diversity Inc. Thriving in Corporate America," *Forbes*, 15 December 1997, 122.

153. L. S. Gottfredson, "Dilemmas in Developing Diversity Programs," in *Diversity in the Workplace*, ed. S. E. Jackson & Associates (New York: Guildford Press, 1992).

154. Lieber & Urresta, "Pacific Enterprises Keeping Talent."

155. R. Rodriguez, "Diversity Finds Its Place."

156. "L'Oreal Receives Diversity Best Practices 2004 Global CEO Leadership Award," *PR Newswire*, 26 October 2004, 11:01.

157. A. Greenwald, B. Nosek, & M. Banaji, "Understanding and Using the Implicit Association Test: I. An Improved Scoring Algorithm," *Journal of Personality & Social Psychology* (August 2003): 197–206; S. Vedantam, "See No Bias; Many Americans Believe They Are Not Prejudiced," *Washington Post*, 23 January 2005, W12.

158. Carnevale & Stone, *The American Mosaic*.

159. D. Fenn, "Diversity: More Than Just Affirmative Action," *Inc.*, July 1995, 93.

160. J. R. Joplin & C. S. Daus, "Challenges of Leading a Diverse Workforce," *Academy of Management Executive* 11 (1997): 32–47.

161. A. Fisher, "Ask Annie: Should People Choose Their Own Mentors?" *Fortune*, 29 November 2004, 72.

162. Ibid.

163. Rice, "How to Make Diversity Pay."

164. T. Pepper, "Getting to Know You: Finding Out Which Job Candidate Would Make a Savvy Manager or a Level-Headed Cop Used to Be an Art, Now It's Cutting-Edge Science," *Newsweek International*, 17 January 2005, http://www.msnbc.msn.com/id/3037881/site/newsweek, 44; A. Overholt, "Personality Tests: Back with a Vengeance," *Fast Company*, November 2004, 115–117; A. Blantyre, "Testing, Testing: More Companies Are Giving Psychological Tests to Their Current Employees," *Inc.*, June 2004, 35–37; K. J. Sulkowicz, "The Corporate Shrink," *Fast Company*, October 2004, 48; A. Overholt, "Are You a Polyolefin Optimizer? Take This Quiz!" *Fast Company*, April 2004, 37; L. Gettler, "What You See Isn't Necessarily What You Get," *Australasian Business Intelligence*, November 23, 2004, available at http://www.highbeam.com/browse/Business-International-Australasian+Business+Intelligence; Douglas P. Shuit, "At 60, Myers-Briggs Is Still Sorting Out and Identifying People's Types," *Workforce Management*, December 2003, 72.

165. Donna Fenn, "Respect Your Elders," *Inc.*, September 2003, 29; Bureau of Labor Statistics, http://www.bls.gov.

166. M. Crowe, "UPS Managers Trained in the Real World to Deliver Results," *The Business Journal—San Jose*, 21 September 1998, 26; Rice, "How to Make Diversity Pay."

Chapter 13

1. Nucor 2006 Annual Report, http://www.nucor.com/indexinner.aspx?finpage=investorinfo; M. Polanco, "The Mill that Gives and Takes: Dedicated to the Job, Despite Heat, Dust and Danger," *Hartford Courant*, 29 January 2007, available at http://web.lexis-nexis.com; G. P. Smith, "How Nucor Steel Rewards Performance and Productivity," ManagerWise, available at http://www.managerwise.com; "The Nucor Story," http://www.nucor-fastener.com/nucor.html; C. Carpenter & M. Song, "Steel Is Beginning to Collect Rust in Stock Market," Bloomberg.com, 19 March 2007, http://www.bloomberg.com/apps/news?pid=20601109&refer=home&sid=avJsya9w6v84; L. Haoting, "China's Steel Sector Still Red Hot," China Daily, 9 May 2004, http://www.chinadaily.com. cn/english/doc/2004–05/ 09/content_329014. htm; D. Lague, "China's Demand for Steel Slows, but the Mills Keep Churning," *International Herald Tribune*, 20 July 2005, http://www.iht.com/articles/2005/07/19/business/steel.php.

2. T. Daniel & G. Metcalf, "The Science of Motivation," *SHRM White Paper*, Society for Human Resource Management, May 2005 http://www.shrm.org.

3. J. P. Campbell & R. D. Pritchard, "Motivation Theory in Industrial and Organizational Psychology," in *Handbook of Industrial and Organizational Psychology*, ed. M. D. Dunnette (Chicago: Rand McNally, 1976).

4. P. Thomas, "Waitress Makes the Difference in Bringing Deaf to Pittsburgh," *Wall Street Journal Interactive Edition*, 2 March 1999, available at http://online.wsj.com.

5. "Winter Olympics, Bobsled, Past Results," *ESPN*, 9 June 1999, http://espn.go.com.

6. "Jamaica Bobsleigh History," Team Jamaica.com, 9 June 1999, available at http://www.thereggaeboyz.com/bobsled.htm.

7. "Double-Drive-Thru Chain Awarded NRN's People and Performance Award for Excellence in Employee Recognition," Checkers press release, 14 October 2003, available at http://phx.corporate-ir.net/phoenix.zhtml?c=61892&p=irol-newsArticle_print&ID=458217.

8. S. Monson, "Feeling Perky," *Seattle Times*, 24 December 2006, G1.

9. Ibid.

10. Ibid.

11. E. A. Locke, "The Nature and Causes of Job Satisfaction," in *Handbook of Industrial and Organizational Psychology*, ed. M. D. Dunnette (Chicago: Rand McNally, 1976).

12. A. H. Maslow, "A Theory of Human Motivation," *Psychological Review* 50 (1943): 370–396.

13. C. P. Alderfer, *Existence, Relatedness, and Growth: Human Needs in Organizational Settings* (New York: Free Press, 1972).

14. D. C. McClelland, "Toward a Theory of Motive Acquisition," *American Psychologist* 20 (1965): 321–333; D. C. McClelland & D. H. Burnham, "Power Is the Great Motivator," *Harvard*

Business Review 54, no. 2 (1976): 100–110.

15. J. Spencer, "Shirk Ethic: How to Fake a Hard Day at the Office—White-Collar Slackers Get Help from New Gadgets: The Faux 4 A.M. E-Mail," *Wall Street Journal*, 15 May 2003, D1.

16. J. H. Turner, "Entrepreneurial Environments and the Emergence of Achievement Motivation in Adolescent Males," *Sociometry* 33 (1970): 147–165.

17. L. W. Porter, E. E. Lawler III, & J. R. Hackman, *Behavior in Organizations* (New York: McGraw-Hill, 1975).

18. C. Ajila, "Maslow's Hierarchy of Needs Theory: Applicability to the Nigerian Industrial Setting," *IFE Psychology* (1997): 162–174.

19. M. A. Wahba & L. B. Birdwell, "Maslow Reconsidered: A Review of Research on the Need Hierarchy Theory," *Organizational Behavior & Human Performance* 15 (1976): 212–240; J. Rauschenberger, N. Schmitt, & J. E. Hunter, "A Test of the Need Hierarchy Concept by a Markov Model of Change in Need Strength," *Administrative Science Quarterly* 25 (1980): 654–670.

20. E. E. Lawler III & L. W. Porter, "The Effect of Performance on Job Satisfaction," *Industrial Relations* 7 (1967): 20–28.

21. Porter, Lawler III, & Hackman, *Behavior in Organizations*.

22. E. White, "Employers Increasingly Favor Bonuses to Raises," *Wall Street Journal*, 28 August 2006, B3.

23. J. Wallace, "Many at Boeing Will Share Windfall 12 Days' Extra Pay for 45,000 in Area," *Seattle Post-Intelligencer*, 2 February 2007, C1.

24. K. Maher & K. Hudson, "Wal-Mart to Sweeten Bonus Plan for Staff," *Wall Street Journal*, 22 March 2007, A11.

25. S. Miller, "Countering the Employee Recognition Gap," SHRM Library, Society for Human Resource Management, February 2006, http://www.shrm.org.

26. Porter, Lawler III, & Hackman, *Behavior in Organizations*.

27. B. Coffee, "Motivating a Big Company in Small Ways," Forum for People Management and Measurement, 31 May 2005, http://www.performanceforum.org.

28. S. Miller, "Countering the Employee Recognition Gap."

29. D. Whitford, "A Human Place to Work," *Fortune*, 8 January 2001, 108.

30. C. Caggiano, "What Do Workers Want?" *Inc.*, November 1992, 101–104; "National Study of the Changing Workforce," Families & Work Institute, http://www.familiesandwork.org/summary/nscw.pdf.

31. L. Buchanan, "Managing One-to-One," *Inc.*, 1 October 2001, 82.

32. Ibid.

33. "America@Work: A Focus on Benefits and Compensation," Aon Consulting, http://www.aon.com/pdf/america/awork2.pdf.

34. J. Laabs, "Satisfy Them with More Than Money," *Personnel Journal* 77, no. 11 (1998): 40.

35. R. Kanfer & P. Ackerman, "Aging, Adult Development, and Work Motivation," *Academy of Management Review* (2004): 440–458.

36. "Staying Ahead of the Curve: The AARP Work and Career Study," AARP, http://assets.aarp.org/rgcenter/econ/d17772_multiwork.pdf.

37. S. J. O'Malley, "Motivate the Middle: How Mid-Level Performance Can Bring Top Growth to

the Bottom Line," *Bank Investment Consultant*, February 2007, 39.

38. S. Stecklow, "Fast Finns' Fines Fit Their Finances—Traffic Penalties Are Assessed According to Driver Income," *Wall Street Journal*, 2 January 2001, A1.

39. L. Lavelle, "A Payday for Performance; Compensation Is Less Outrageous This Year, except for CEO Who Delivered," *BusinessWeek*, 18 April 2005, 78.

40. S. DeCarlo, "Special Report: CEO Compensation," *Forbes Magazine*, 20 April 2006, http://www.forbes.com/2006/04/17/06ceo_ceo-compensation_land.html.

41. "Executive Paywatch," AFL-CIO, 16 March 2007, http://www.aflcio.org/corporatewatch/paywatch.

42. S. DeCarlo, "Special Report."

43. C. T. Kulik & M. L. Ambrose, "Personal and Situational Determinants of Referent Choice," *Academy of Management Review* 17 (1992): 212–237.

44. C. DeNavas-Walt, B. Proctor, & R. Mills, "Income, Poverty, and Health Insurance Coverage in the United States: 2003," U.S. Census Bureau, http://www.census.gov/prod/2004pubs/p60-226.pdf.

45. J. S. Adams, "Toward an Understanding of Inequity," *Journal of Abnormal Social Psychology* 67 (1963): 422–436.

46. J. Greenberg, "Employee Theft as a Reaction to Underpayment Inequity: The Hidden Costs of Pay Cuts," *Journal of Applied Psychology* 75 (1990): 561–568.

47. R. A. Cosier & D. R. Dalton, "Equity Theory and Time: A Reformulation," *Academy of Management Review* 8 (1983): 311–319; M. R. Carrell & J. E. Dittrich, "Equity Theory:

The Recent Literature, Methodological Considerations, and New Directions," *Academy of Management Review* 3 (1978): 202–209.

48. M. Patterson, "2,500 Staff Sacked by Text Message," *Daily Telegraph*, 31 May 2003, http://www.telegraph.co.uk/news/main.jhtml?xml=/news/2003/05/31/nsack31.xml.

49. "Iberia Pilots' Strike Causes Cancellation of 30% of Flights—Airline Plans to Ask Union to Pay for Earlier Slowdown," *Wall Street Journal Europe*, 20 June 2001, 5; C. Vitzthum, "Chairman Voices Optimism after Airline Weathers Difficult Year—Spanish Carrier Overcomes Labor Strife, Industry Woes to Post Small Profit," *Wall Street Journal Europe*, 28 January 2002, 5.

50. J. Bendich, "When Is a Temp Not a Temp?" *Trial Magazine*, 1 October 2001, 42.

51. "2002 Statistics Fact Sheet: Back Wages for Fair Labor Standards Act Violations Increased by 29%," U.S. Department of Labor, http://www.dol.gov/esa/whd/statistics/200212.htm; M. Orey, "Lawsuits Abound from Workers Seeking Overtime Pay," *Wall Street Journal*, 30 May 2002, B1.

52. A. Zimmerman, "Big Retailers Face Overtime Suits as Bosses Do More 'Hourly' Work," *Wall Street Journal*, 26 May 2004, A1.

53. J. Pollack, "Exemption under the Fair Labor Standards Act: The Cost of Misclassifying Employees," *Cornell Hotel & Restaurant Administration Quarterly* 42 (2001): 16.

54. C. Chen, J. Choi, & S. Chi, "Making Justice Sense of Local-Expatriate Compensation Disparity: Mitigation by Local Referents, Ideological Explanations, and Interpersonal Sensitivity in China-Foreign Joint Ventures," *Academy of*

Management Journal (2002): 807–817.

55. K. Aquino, R. W. Griffeth, D. G. Allen, & P. W. Hom, "Integrating Justice Constructs into the Turnover Process: A Test of a Referent Cognitions Model," *Academy of Management Journal* 40, no. 5 (1997): 1208–1227.

56. S. Barr, "While the SEC Watches the Markets, the Job Market Is Draining the SEC," *Washington Post*, 10 March 2002, C3.

57. D. Gullapalli, "Take This Job and . . . File It— Burdened by Extra Work Created by the Sarbanes-Oxley Act, CPAs Leave the Big Four for Better Life," *Wall Street Journal*, 4 May 2005, C1.

58. Ibid.

59. R. Folger & M. A. Konovsky, "Effects of Procedural and Distributive Justice on Reactions to Pay Raise Decisions," *Academy of Management Journal* 32 (1989): 115–130; M. A. Konovsky, "Understanding Procedural Justice and Its Impact on Business Organizations," *Journal of Management* 26 (2000): 489–512.

60. E. Barret-Howard & T. R. Tyler, "Procedural Justice as a Criterion in Allocation Decisions," *Journal of Personality & Social Psychology* 50 (1986): 296–305; Folger & Konovsky, "Effects of Procedural and Distributive Justice on Reactions to Pay Raise Decisions."

61. R. Folger & J. Greenberg, "Procedural Justice: An Interpretive Analysis of Personnel Systems," in *Research in Personnel and Human Resources Management*, Vol. 3, ed. K. Rowland & G. Ferris (Greenwich, CT: JAI, 1985); R. Folger, D. Rosenfield, J. Grove, & L. Corkran, "Effects of 'Voice' and Peer Opinions on Responses to Inequity," *Journal of Personality & Social Psychology* 37 (1979): 2253–2261; E. A. Lind & T. R. Tyler, *The Social Psychology of Procedural Justice* (New York: Plenum, 1988); Konovsky, "Understanding Procedural Justice and Its Impact on Business Organizations."

62. R. J. Bies & J. S. Moag, "Interactional Justice: Communication Criteria for Fairness," in R. J. Lewicki, B. H. Sheppard, & M. Bazerman (Eds.), *Research on Negotiation in Organizations* (Greenwich, CT: JAI, 1986), 43–55.

63. J. A. Colquitt, "On the Dimensionality of Organizational Justice: A Construct Validation of a Measure," *Journal of Applied Psychology* (2001: 86), 386–400; J. A. Colquitt, D. E. Conlon, M. J. Wesson, C. Porter & K. Yee Ng, "Justice at the Millennium: A Meta-Analytic Review of 25 Years of Organizational Justice Research," *Journal of Applied Psychology*, 86, 425–445.

64. K. A. Dolan, "When Money Isn't Enough," *Forbes*, 18 November 1996, 164–170.

65. V. H. Vroom, *Work and Motivation* (New York: John Wiley & Sons, 1964); L. W. Porter & E. E. Lawler III, *Managerial Attitudes and Performance* (Homewood, IL: Dorsey & Richard D. Irwin, 1968).

66. S. Miller, "Strategic HR Leadership Award," *HR Magazine*, November 2006, http://www.shrm.org.

67. S. Miller, "Countering the Employee Recognition Gap," SHRM Library, Society for Human Resource Management, February 2006, http://www.shrm.org.

68. P. V. LeBlanc & P. W. Mulvey, "How American Workers See the Rewards of Work," *Compensation & Benefits Review* 30 (February 1998): 24–28.

69. A. Fox, "Companies Can Benefit When They Disclose Pay Processes to Employees," *HR Magazine*, July 2002, 25.

70. S. Wellner, "Spoiled Brats—Your HR Policies May Be Contributing to a Sense of Employee Entitlement," *HR Magazine*, November 2004, http://www.shrm.org.

71. K. W. Thomas & B. A. Velthouse, "Cognitive Elements of Empowerment," *Academy of Management Review* 15 (1990): 666–681.

72. J. Sandberg, "Been Here 25 Years and All I Got Was This Lousy T-Shirt," *Wall Street Journal*, 28 January 2004, B1.

73. C. Hymowitz, "When Meeting Targets Becomes the Strategy, CEO Is on Wrong Path," *Wall Street Journal*, 8 March 2005, A8.

74. E. L. Thorndike, *Animal Intelligence* (New York: Macmillan, 1911).

75. D. Milbank, "Workplace: Companies Turn to Peer Pressure to Cut Injuries as Psychologists Join the Battle," *Wall Street Journal*, 29 March 1991, B1.

76. B. F. Skinner, *Science and Human Behavior* (New York: Macmillan, 1954); B. F. Skinner, *Beyond Freedom and Dignity* (New York: Bantam, 1971); B. F. Skinner, *A Matter of Consequences* (New York: New York University Press, 1984).

77. A. M. Dickinson & A. D. Poling, "Schedules of Monetary Reinforcement in Organizational Behavior Management: Latham and Huber Revisited," *Journal of Organizational Behavior Management* 16, no. 1 (1992): 71–91.

78. D. Harbrecht, "CEO Q&A: Baxter's Harry Kraemer: 'I Don't Golf,'" *BusinessWeek Online*, 28 March 2003, http://www.businessweek.com/bwdaily/dnflash/mar2002/nf20020328_0720.htm.

79. R. Ho, "Attending to Attendance," *Wall Street Journal Interactive*, 7 December 1998, available at http://online.wsj.com.

80. D. Grote, "Manager's Journal: Discipline without Punishment," *Wall Street Journal*, 23 May 1994, A14.

81. L. Lavelle, F. Jespersen, S. Ante, & J. Kerstetter, "Special Report: Executive Pay," *BusinessWeek*, 21 April 2003, 86.

82. L. Lavelle & F. Jespersen, "While the CEO Gravy Train May Be Slowing Down, It Hasn't Jumped the Rails," *BusinessWeek*, 16 April 2001, 76; B. Orwall, "Disney Awards Bonuses to Top Brass," *Wall Street Journal*, 29 January 2003, B5.

83. E. Pedalino & V. U. Gamboa, "Behavior Modification and Absenteeism: Intervention in One Industrial Setting," *Journal of Applied Psychology* 59 (1974): 694–698.

84. C. Cole, "Retooling Absentee Programs Bolsters Profits," *Workforce Management*, September 2002, http://www.workforce.com/section/09/feature/23/31/64.

85. J. B. Miner, *Theories of Organizational Behavior* (Hinsdale, IL: Dryden, 1980).

86. Dickinson & Poling, "Schedules of Monetary Reinforcement in Organizational Behavior Management."

87. F. Luthans & A. D. Stajkovic, "Reinforce for Performance: The Need to Go beyond Pay and Even Rewards," *Academy of Management Executive* 13, no. 2 (1999): 49–57.

88. D. Anderson, *Up Your Business! 7 Steps to Fix, Build or Stretch Your Organization* (New York: Wiley, 2003).

89. K. D. Butterfield, L. K. Trevino, & G. A. Ball, "Punishment from the Manager's Perspective: A Grounded Investigation and Inductive Model," *Academy of Management*

Journal 39 (1996): 1479–1512.

90. R. D. Arvey & J. M. Ivancevich, "Punishment in Organizations: A Review, Propositions, and Research Suggestions," *Academy of Management Review 5* (1980): 123–132.

91. R. D. Arvey, G. A. Davis, & S. M. Nelson, "Use of Discipline in an Organization: A Field Study," *Journal of Applied Psychology* 69 (1984): 448–460; M. E. Schnake, "Vicarious Punishment in a Work Setting," *Journal of Applied Psychology* 71 (1986): 343–345.

92. A. D. Stajkovic & F. Luthans, "A Meta-Analysis of the Effects of Organizational Behavior Modification on Task Performance, 1975–95," *Academy of Management Journal* 40, no. 5 (1997): 1122–1149; A. D. Stajkovic & F. Luthans, "Behavioral Management and Task Performance in Organizations: Conceptual Background, Meta-Analysis, and Test of Alternative Models," *Personnel Psychology* 56, issue 1 (2003): 155–194.

93. G. A. Yukl & G. P. Latham, "Consequences of Reinforcement Schedules and Incentive Magnitudes for Employee Performance: Problems Encountered in a Field Setting," *Journal of Applied Psychology* 60 (1975): 294–298.

94. C. Salter, "Can JetBlue Make the Leap from Popular (and Profitable) Niche Airline to Major Player—without Losing Its Soul?" *Fast Company*, 1 May 2004, 67.

95. E. A. Locke & G. P. Latham, *Goal Setting: A Motivational Technique That Works* (Englewood Cliffs, NJ: Prentice Hall, 1984); E. A. Locke & G. P. Latham, *A Theory of Goal Setting and Task Performance* (Englewood Cliffs, NJ: Prentice Hall, 1990).

96. P. Valade, "CDW's Formula for Success: Vernon Hills Company Says Happy Coworkers Can Create Culture for Even Happier Customers," *Chicago Daily Herald*, 5 June 2002, 1.

97. G. P. Latham & E. A. Locke, "Goal Setting—A Motivational Technique That Works," *Organizational Dynamics* 8, no. 2 (1979): 68.

98. Ibid.

99. Z. Zhiwei, J. A. Wallin, & R. A. Reber, "Safety Improvements: An Application of Behaviour Modification Techniques," *Journal of Applied Management Studies* 15 (2000): 135–140.

100. C. A. Arnolds & C. Boshoff, "Compensation, Esteem Valence, and Job Performance: An Empirical Assessment of Alderfer's ERG Theory," *International Journal of Human Resource Management* 13, no. 4 (2002): 697–719.

101. Maslow, "A Theory of Human Motivation," *Psychological Review*.

102. M. Conlin, "Compensation Is Getting Personal: Companies Are Mining Employee Data to Identify the Perks That Spur Productivity," *Business Week Online*, 6 December 2002, available at http://businessweek.com.

103. M. Boyle, "How to Cut Perks without Killing Morale," *Fortune* 19 February 2001; T. Pollock, " Managing for Better Morale, " *Automotive Manufacturing & Production*, February 2001, available at http://www.autofieldguide.com.

Chapter 14

1. G. Anders & A. Murray, "Behind H-P Chairman's fall, Clash with a Powerful Director," *Wall Street Journal*, 9 October 2006, A1; P. Burrows, "HP Says Goodbye to Drama," *Business Week*, 12 September 2005, 83; P. Burrows, "What Would Hewlett and Packard Say?" *Business Week*, 18 September 2006, 35; P. Burrows, L. Lee, R. Hof, & A. Carter, "Controlling the Damage at HP," *Business Week*, 9 October 2006, 36; G. Colvin, "A Growth Plan for HP's CEO," *Fortune*, 16 October 2006, 70; J. Hopkins & J. Swartz, "HP Chief Tackles Boardroom Scandal Head On," *USA Today*, 25 September 2006, A10; M. Kessler, "HP Restructuring Will Cut 14,500 Jobs," *USA Today*, 20 July 2005, B1; M. Kessler, "Strong PC Sales help Drive up HP's Earnings," *USA Today*, 21 February 2007, B2; M. Kessler & J. Swartz, "HP Leader Hurd Expected to Apologize at Hearing," *USA Today*, B1; M. Kessler, J. Swartz, & S. Kirchhoff, "HP Execs on Spying: It Wasn't Me," *USA Today*, 29 September 2006, B1; A. Lashinsky, "Coffee with Mark Hurd," *Fortune*, 16 October 2006, 44; A. Lashinsky, D. Burke, & S. Kaufman, "The Hurd Way: How a Sales-Obsessed CEO Rebooted HP," *Fortune*, 17 April 2006, 92; H. Maurer, "HP Settles," *Business Week*, 25 December 2006, 33; A. Murray, "H-P Board Clash over Leaks Triggers Angry Resignation," *Wall Street Journal*, 6 September 2006, A1; Staff, "'I Should Have Figured It Out," *Business Week*, 9 October 2006, 44.

2. S. Warren, "Remembrances: Lamar Muse (1920–2007) Steered Southwest Airlines' Take Off On Booze to Fliers and a Razor to Costs," *Wall Street Journal*, 10 February 2007, A4.

3. B. Gimbel, "Southwest's New Flight Plan," *Fortune*, 16 May 2005, 93.

4. J. Stancavage, "Southwest Has Fun, Profit," *Tulsa World*, 2 July 2006.

5. W. Bennis, "Why Leaders Can't Lead," *Training & Development Journal* 43, no. 4 (1989).

6. J. Adamy, "How Jim Skinner Flipped McDonald's," *Wall Street Journal*, 5 January 2007, B1.

7. M. Langley, C. Riley, & R. Sidel, "Tightening the Belt: In Citigroup Ouster, a Battle Over Expenses," *Wall Street Journal*, 24 January 2007, A1.

8. M. Langley, "Behind Citigroup Departures: A Culture Shift by CEO Prince," *Wall Street Journal*, 24 August 2005, A1.

9. A. Zaleznik, "Managers and Leaders: Are They Different?" *Harvard Business Review* 55 (1977): 76–78; A. Zaleznik, "The Leadership Gap," *Washington Quarterly* 6 (1983): 32–39.

10. Bennis, "Why Leaders Can't Lead."

11. K. Voigt, "Enron, Andersen Scandals—Offer Ethical Lessons—Businesspeople Can Strive to Avoid Common Pitfalls through the 'Three Ms,'" *Wall Street Journal Europe*, 3 September 2002, A12.

12. B. Grow, D. Foust, E. Thornton, R. Farzad, J. McGregor, S. Zegel, & E. Javers, "Out at Home Depot behind the Flameout of Controversial CEO Bob Nardelli," *Business Week*, 15 January 2007, http://www.businessweek.com/magazine/content/07_03/b4017001.htm.

13. J. P. Howell, D. E. Bowen, P. W. Dorfman, S. Kerr, & P. M. Podsakoff, "Substitutes for Leadership: Effective Alternatives to Ineffective Leadership," *Organizational Dynamics*, 22 June 1990, 20; S. Kerr & J. M. Jermier, "Substitutes for Leadership: Their Meaning and Measurement," *Organizational Behavior & Human Performance* 22 (1978): 375–403.

14. L. Black, "Telecommuting Offers Work Alternative for Some," *Rocky Mountain News*, 10 November 2003, 7B.

15. S. Berfield, "The Best of 2006: Leaders," *Business Week*, 18 December 2006, 58.

16. D. Jones, "Not all Successful CEOs are Extroverts," *USA Today*, 7 June 2006, B.1.

17. Ibid.

18. M. Gladwell, "Why Do We Love Tall Men?" Gladwell Dot Com, http://www.gladwell.com/blink/blink_excerpt2.html.

19. D. Sacks, "The Accidental Guru," *Fast Company*, 1 January 2005, 64.

20. R. J. House & R. M Aditya, "The Social Scientific Study of Leadership: Quo Vadis?" *Journal of Management* 23 (1997): 409–473; T. Judge, R. Illies, J. Bono, & M. Gerhardt, "Personality and Leadership: A Qualitative and Quantitative Review," *Journal of Applied Psychology* (August 2002): 765–782; S. A. Kirkpatrick & E. A. Locke, "Leadership: Do Traits Matter?" *Academy of Management Executive 5*, no. 2 (1991): 48–60.

21. House & Aditya, "The Social Scientific Study of Leadership"; Kirkpatrick & Locke, "Leadership: Do Traits Matter?"

22. J. J. Gabarro, *The Dynamics of Taking Charge* (Boston: Harvard Business School Press, 1987).

23. B. Morris, "The Accidental CEO," *Fortune*, 28 June 2003, 58.

24. J. B. Fuller, C. E. P. Patterson, K. Hester, & D. Stringer, "A Quantitative Review of Research on Charismatic Leadership," *Psychological Reports* 78 (1996): 271–287; R. G. Lord, C. L. De Vader, & G. M. Alliger, "A Meta-Analysis of the Relation between Personality Traits and Leadership Perceptions: An Application of Validity Generalization Procedures," *Journal of Applied Psychology* 71, no. 3 (1986): 402–410.

25. Ibid.

26. Kirkpatrick & Locke, "Leadership: Do Traits Matter?"

27. E. A. Fleishman, "The Description of Supervisory Behavior," *Journal of Applied Psychology* 37 (1953): 1–6; L. R. Katz, *New Patterns of Management* (New York: McGraw-Hill, 1961).

28. S. Tully & E. Levenson, "In This Corner! The Contender—Jamie Dimon—The New CEO of J.P. Morgan Chase," *Fortune*, 3 April 2006, 54.

29. L. Grant, "Retail Giant Wal-Mart Faces Challenges on Many Fronts; Protests, Allegations Are Price of Success, CEO Says," *USA Today*, 11 November 2003, B1.

30. Ibid.

31. P. Weissenberg & M. H. Kavanagh, "The Independence of Initiating Structure and Consideration: A Review of the Evidence," *Personnel Psychology* 25 (1972): 119–130.

32. R. J. House & T. R. Mitchell, "Path-Goal Theory of Leadership," *Journal of Contemporary Business* 3 (1974): 81–97; F. E. Fiedler, "A Contingency Model of Leadership Effectiveness," in *Advances in Experimental Social Psychology*, ed. L. Berkowitz (New York: Academic Press, 1964); V. H. Vroom & P. W. Yetton, *Leadership and Decision Making* (Pittsburgh: University of Pittsburgh Press, 1973); P. Hersey & K. H. Blanchard, The *Management of Organizational Behavior*, 4th ed. (Englewood Cliffs, NJ: Prentice Hall, 1984); Kerr & Jermier, "Substitutes for Leadership."

33. J. Pfeffer, "In Defense of the Boss from Hell," *Business 2.0*, 1 March 2007, 70.

34. F. E. Fiedler & M. M. Chemers, *Leadership and Effective Management* (Glenview, IL: Scott, Foresman, 1974); F. E. Fiedler & M. M. Chemers, *Improving Leadership Effectiveness: The Leader Match Concept*, 2d ed. (New York: Wiley, 1984).

35. Fiedler & Chemers, *Improving Leadership Effectiveness*.

36. F. E. Fiedler, "The Effects of Leadership Training and Experience: A Contingency Model Interpretation," *Administrative Science Quarterly* 17, no. 4 (1972): 455; F. E. Fiedler, *A Theory of Leadership Effectiveness* (New York: McGraw-Hill, 1967).

37. J. Helyar, "Why Is This Man Smiling?" *Fortune*, 18 October 2004, 130.

38. Ibid.

39. L. S. Csoka & F. E. Fiedler, "The Effect of Military Leadership Training: A Test of the Contingency Model," *Organizational Behavior & Human Performance* 8 (1972): 395–407.

40. House & Mitchell, "Path-Goal Theory of Leadership."

41. B. Andelman, "Keep 'em Happy," *Corporate Meetings & Incentives*, 1 May 2003, 24.

42. House & Mitchell, "Path-Goal Theory of Leadership."

43. G. Edmondson, K. Kerwin, & K. Anhalt, "Hot Audi: It's Finally Blasting into the Luxury-Car Pack. Can It Stay There?" *Business Week*, 14 March 2005, 24.

44. B. M. Fisher & J. E. Edwards, "Consideration and Initiating Structure and Their Relationships with Leader Effectiveness: A Meta-Analysis," *Proceedings of the Academy of Management*, August 1988, 201–205.

45. M. Gimein, "Wal-Mart's Founder Made a Pact with Employees: He Would Be Fair to Them, and They Would Work Hard for Him. It Was a Good Deal, but Can It Survive in the 24-Hour Service Economy?" *Fortune*, 18 March 2002, 120.

46. K. Edwards, "Utilizing Employee Innovation at Kwik-Fit Financial Services," *Strategic HR Review*, November–December 2004, 12–13.

47. M. Copeland, K. Crawford, J. Davis, S. Hamner, C. Hawn, R. Howe, P. Kaihla, M. Maier, O. Malik, D. McDonald, C. Null, E. Schonfeld, O. Thomas, & G. Zachary, "My Golden Rule," *Business 2.0*, 1 December 2005, 108.

48. J. C. Wofford & L. Z. Liska, "Path-Goal Theories of Leadership: A Meta-Analysis," *Journal of Management* 19 (1993): 857–876.

49. House & Aditya, "The Social Scientific Study of Leadership."

50. P. Hersey & K. Blanchard, *Management of Organizational Behavior: Leading Human Resources*, 8th ed. (Escondido, CA: Center for Leadership Studies, 2001).

51. W. Blank, J. R. Weitzel, & S. G. Green, "A Test of the Situational Leadership Theory," *Personnel Psychology* 43, no. 3 (1990): 579–597; W. R. Norris & R. P. Vecchio, "Situational Leadership Theory: A Replication," *Group & Organization Management* 17, no. 3 (1992): 331–342.

52. Ibid.

53. V. H. Vroom & A. G. Jago, *The New Leadership: Managing Participation in Organizations* (Englewood Cliffs, NJ: Prentice Hall, 1988).

54. C. Fishman, "How Teamwork Took Flight: This Team Built a Commercial Engine—and Self-Managing GE Plant—from Scratch," *Fast Company*, 1 October 1999, 188.

55. Ibid.

56. Ibid.

57. G. A. Yukl, *Leadership in Organizations,* 3d ed. (Englewood Cliffs, NJ: Prentice Hall, 1995).

58. B. M. Bass, *Bass & Stogdill's Handbook of Leadership: Theory, Research, and Managerial Applications* (New York: Free Press, 1990).

59. R. D. Ireland & M. A. Hitt, "Achieving and Maintaining Strategic Competitiveness in the 21st Century: The Role of Strategic Leadership," *Academy of Management Executive* 13, no. 1 (1999): 43–57.

60. K. Kranhold, "The Immelt Era, Five Years Old, Transforms GE," *Wall Street Journal,* 11 September 2006, B1.

61. G. Colvin, "Lafley and Immelt: Q & A," *Fortune,* 11 December 2006, 75.

62. P. Thoms & D. B. Greenberger, "Training Business Leaders to Create Positive Organizational Visions of the Future: Is It Successful?" *Academy of Management Journal* [Best Papers & Proceedings], 1995, 212–216.

63. M. Weber, *The Theory of Social and Economic Organizations,* trans. R. A. Henderson & T. Parsons (New York: Free Press, 1947).

64. C. Terhune, C. Mollenkamp, & A. Carrns, "Inside Alleged Fraud at HealthSouth, A 'Family' Plot—CEO Scrushy Cultivated Loyalties as Staffers Fixed Books, Played in His Band," *Wall Street Journal,* 3 April 2003, A1.

65. Ibid.

66. D. A. Waldman & F. J. Yammarino, "CEO Charismatic Leadership: Levels-of-Management and Levels-of-Analysis Effects," *Academy of Management Review* 24, no. 2 (1999): 266–285.

67. K. B. Lowe, K. G. Kroeck, & N. Sivasubramaniam, "Effectiveness Correlates of Transformational and Transactional Leadership: A Meta-Analytic Review

of the MLQ Literature," *Leadership Quarterly* 7 (1996): 385–425.

68. J. M. Howell & B. J. Avolio, "The Ethics of Charismatic Leadership: Submission or Liberation?" Academy of *Management Executive* 6, no. 2 (1992): 43–54.

69. G. Colvin, "Lafley and Immelt: Q & A."

70. A. Deutschman, "Is Your Boss a Psychopath?" *Fast Company,* July 2005, 44.

71. P. Sellers, "What Exactly Is Charisma?" *Fortune,* 15 January 1996, 68.

72. Deutschman, "Is Your Boss a Psychopath?"

73. Howell & Avolio, "The Ethics of Charismatic Leadership."

74. Ibid.

75. J. M. Burns, *Leadership* (New York: Harper & Row, 1978); B. M. Bass, "From Transactional to Transformational Leadership: Learning to Share the Vision," *Organizational Dynamics* 18 (1990): 19–36.

76. Bass, "From Transactional to Transformational Leadership."

77. B. M. Bass, *A New Paradigm of Leadership: An Inquiry into Transformational Leadership* (Alexandra, VA: U.S. Army Research Institute for the Behavioral and Social Sciences, 1996).

78. M. Adams, "Boeing Bounces Back against Odds," *USA Today,* 11 January 2007, B1.

79. "Read the Medtronic Mission Statement to Learn about the Company Goals at Medtronic.com," Medtronic, http://www .medtronic.com/corporate/ mission.html, 12 June 2003.

80. D. Whitford, "A Human Place to Work: A Company Can't Be Everything to All People, but It Can Try. Here's the Tale of Medtronic's Effort," *Fortune,* 8 January 2001, 108.

81. Sellers, "The New Breed."

82. Morris, "The Accidental CEO."

83. Byrne, "How to Lead Now."

84. Bass, "From Transactional to Transformational Leadership."

85. F. E. Fiedler and M. M. Chemers, *Improving Leadership Effectiveness: The Leader Match Concept* (New York: Wiley, 1984).

86. T. Rivas, "Atypical Workdays Becoming Routine," *Wall Street Journal,* 4 April 2006, A19; S. Shellenbarger, "When Working at Home Doesn't Work: How Companies Comfort Telecommuters," *Wall Street Journal,* 24 August 2006, B1; "Real Estate Exchange," U.S. Department of Transportation, Federal Highway Administration, http://knowledge.fhwa .dot. gov/cops/rex .nsf/discussion Display? Open&id=EF35 631CF1E86D918525709 200504C4E&Group= Relocation%20Forum& tab=DISCUSSION; M.-Y. Lee, "Don't Fall into the Trap of Paying Extra Moving Costs," BuyerZone.com, 15 May 2001, www.buyerzone .com/features/savvy_ shopper/ss051501.html.

87. J. Jewell, "New Times, New Leaders: Firing of Millard Fuller the Result of Longstanding Tensions," *Christianity Today,* April 2005, 24; L. D. Maloney, "No House of Cards: Leadership Changes Stirred a Cauldron of Emotions at Habitat for Humanity, but the Foundation of the World's Premier 'Sweat Equity' Housing Group Remains Strong," *Builder,* April 2005, 120; J. F. Krentz, "Davidson Man to Lead Habitat for Humanity," *Charlotte Observer,* 5 February 2005; "New CEO Takes Helm at Habitat for Humanity International; Millard Fuller to Continue as Founder President of House-

Building Ministry," *PR Newswire,* 11 October 2004, http://www .prnewswire.com; J. Pierce, "Habitat Founder and Board Disagree on His Retirement Date," *Christian Century,* 5 October 2004, 15.

88. J. Zaslow, "Mistakes Were Made: What to Take Away from the High-Profile Blunders of 2006," *Wall Street Journal,* 26 December 2006, D1; J. Brodkin, "Corporate Apologies Don't Mean Much: Data Breaches Force Company Executives to Apologize, But a Bad Apology Can Make Things Worse," *Network World,* 14 March 2007, 1; L. Smith, "How Your Corporate Clients Can and Sometimes Must Apologize for Their Mistakes," *Of Counsel,* October 2005, 11–13.

89. J. Zaslow, "Mistakes Were Made."

Chapter 15

1. K. Belson & M. Richtel, "Sony Shifts Duties of the Leader of the PlayStation Unit," *New York Times,* 1 December 2006, Section 3, 1; P. Dvorak, "Out of Tune: At Sony, Rivalries Were Encouraged," *Wall Street Journal,* 29 June 2005, A1; P. Dvorak, "Culture Clash Crimps Sony CEO," *Wall Street Journal,* 24 September 2005, A6; P. Dvorak, "Stringer Faces First Big Test as Sony's Chief," *Wall Street Journal,* 19 September 2005, B1; M. Gunther & P. Lewis, "The Welshman, the Walkman, and the Salary Men," *Fortune,* 12 June 2006, 70; K. Hall, "Sony Walkman Finally Gets the Picture," *Business Week Online,* 9 March 2007; Y. Kane & P. Dvorak, "Howard Stringer, Japanese CEO," *Wall Street Journal,* 3 March 2007, A1; Y. Kane & A. Morse, "Sony's Videogame Unit Names U.S. Marketing Star as President," *Wall Street Journal,* 1 December 2006, B7; L. Lewis,

"Sony Gains Ground on Margins," *Financial Times*, 30 January 2007, http://www.ft.com; W. Mossberg, "Boss Talk: Shaking up Sony," *Wall Street Journal*, 6 June 2006, B1; B. Schlender, "Inside the Shakeup at Sony," *Fortune*, 4 April 2005, 94; R. Siklos & M. Fackler, "Sony's Road Warrior," *New York Times*, 28 May 2006, Section 3, 1.

2. E. E. Lawler III, L. W. Porter, & A. Tannenbaum, "Manager's Attitudes toward Interaction Episodes," *Journal of Applied Psychology* 52 (1968): 423–439; H. Mintzberg, *The Nature of Managerial Work* (New York: Harper & Row, 1973).

3. J. D. Maes, T. G. Weldy, & M. L. Icenogle, "A Managerial Perspective: Oral Communication Competency Is Most Important for Business Students in the Workplace," *Journal of Business Communication* 34 (1997): 67–80.

4. R. Lepsinger & A. D. Lucia, *The Art and Science of 360 Degree Feedback* (San Francisco: Pfeiffer, 1997).

5. I. M. Botero, "Good Communication Skills Needed Today," *Business Journal: Serving Phoenix and the Valley of the Sun*, 21 October 1996.

6. J. Sandberg, "Bosses Often Sugarcoat Their Worst News, but Staffers Don't Bite," *Wall Street Journal*, 21 April 2004, B1.

7. E. E. Jones & K. E. Davis, "From Acts to Dispositions: The Attribution Process in Person Perception," in *Advances in Experimental and Social Psychology*, vol. 2, ed. L. Berkowitz (New York: Academic Press, 1965), 219–266; R. G. Lord & J. E. Smith, "Theoretical, Information-Processing, and Situational Factors Affecting Attribution Theory Models of Organizational Behavior," *Academy of*

Management Review 8 (1983): 50–60.

8. J. Zadney & H. B. Gerard, "Attributed Intentions and Informational Selectivity," *Journal of Experimental Social Psychology* 10 (1974): 34–52.

9. A. Taylor, "GM Gets Its Act Together. Finally," *Fortune*, 5 April 2004, 136.

10. M. Porter, J. Lorsch, & N. Nohria, "Seven Surprises for New CEOs," *Harvard Business Review* (October 2004): 62.

11. H. H. Kelly, *Attribution in Social Interaction* (Morristown, NJ: General Learning Press, 1971).

12. J. M. Burger, "Motivational Biases in the Attribution of Responsibility for an Accident: A Meta-Analysis of the Defensive-Attribution Hypothesis," *Psychological Bulletin* 90 (1981): 496–512.

13. D. A. Hofmann & A. Stetzer, "The Role of Safety Climate and Communication in Accident Interpretation: Implications for Learning from Negative Events," *Academy of Management Journal* 41, no. 6 (1998): 644–657.

14. C. Perrow, *Normal Accidents: Living with High-Risk Technologies* (New York: Basic Books, 1984).

15. A. G. Miller & T. Lawson, "The Effect of an Informational Opinion on the Fundamental Attribution Error," *Journal of Personality & Social Psychology* 47 (1989): 873–896; J. M. Burger, "Changes in Attribution Errors over Time: The Ephemeral Fundamental Attribution Error," *Social Cognition* 9 (1991): 182–193.

16. D. Sacks, "Scenes from the Culture Clash," *Fast Company*, 1 January 2006, 72.

17. F. Heider, *The Psychology of Interpersonal Relations* (New York: Wiley, 1958); D. T. Miller & M. Ross, "Self-Serving Biases in Attribution of Causality:

Fact or Fiction?" *Psychological Bulletin* 82 (1975): 213–225.

18. J. R. Larson, Jr., "The Dynamic Interplay between Employees' Feedback-Seeking Strategies and Supervisors' Delivery of Performance Feedback," *Academy of Management Review* 14, no. 3 (1989): 408–422.

19. Porter, Lorsch, & Nohria, "Seven Surprises for New CEOs."

20. Ibid.

21. Ibid.

22. C. Hymowitz, "Mind Your Language: To Do Business Today, Consider Delayering," *Wall Street Journal*, 27 March 2006, B1.

23. M. Reddy, "The Conduit Metaphor—A Case of Frame Conflict in Our Language about Our Language," in *Metaphor and Thought*, ed. A. Ortony (Cambridge: Cambridge University Press, 1979), 284–324.

24. G. L. Kreps, *Organizational Communication: Theory and Practice* (New York: Longman, 1990).

25. Ibid.

26. D. Roth, "How to Cut Pay, Lay Off 8,000 People, and Still Have Workers Who Love You," *Fortune*, 4 February 2002, 62.

27. K. Voight, "Office Intelligence," *Asian Wall Street Journal*, 21 January 2005, P1.

28. L. Landro, "The Informed Patient: Hospitals Combat Errors at the 'Hand-Off,'" *Wall Street Journal*, 28 June 2006, D1.

29. Kreps, *Organizational Communication: Theory and Practice.*

30. J. Sandberg, "Ruthless Rumors and the Managers Who Enable Them," *Wall Street Journal*, 29 October 2003, B1.

31. K. Moran, "Web Used to Answer Rumors: UT Medical Staff Gets Truth Quickly," *Houston*

Chronicle, 18 April 1999, 35.

32. W. Davis & J. R. O'Connor, "Serial Transmission of Information: A Study of the Grapevine," *Journal of Applied Communication Research* 5 (1977): 61–72.

33. Sandberg, "Ruthless Rumors and the Managers Who Enable Them."

34. K. Voight, "Office Intelligence," *Asian Wall Street Journal*, 21 January 2005, P1.

35. G. Hoover, "Maintaining Employee Engagement when Communicating Difficult Issues," *Communication World*, 1 November 2005, 25.

36. Davis & O'Connor, "Serial Transmission of Information: A Study of the Grapevine"; Hymowitz, "Managing: Spread the Word, Gossip Is Good."

37. D. Kirkpatrick & D. Roth, "Why There's No Escaping the Blog," *Fortune (Europe)*, 24 January 2005, 64.

38. W. C. Redding, *Communication within the Organization: An Interpretive View of Theory and Research* (New York: Industrial Communication Council, 1972).

39. D. T. Hall, K. L. Otazo, & G. P. Hollenbeck, "Behind Closed Doors: What Really Happens in Executive Coaching," *Organizational Dynamics* 27, no. 3 (1999): 39–53.

40. J. Kelly, "Blowing the Whistle on the Boss," *PR Newswire*, 15 November 2004, http://www.prnewswire.com.

41. R. McGarvey, "Lords of Discipline," *Entrepreneur Magazine*, 1 January 2000.

42. S. Needleman, "Career Journal: Tips for Managers on Handling Their Workers' Personal Problems," *Wall Street Journal*, 25 April 2006, B9.

43. C. Hirschman, "Firm Ground: EAP Training for HR and Managers Improves Supervisor-Employee Communication

and Helps Organizations Avoid Legal Quagmires," *Employee Benefit News*, 13 June 2005, http://www.benefitnews.com.

44. A. Mehrabian, "Communication without Words," *Psychology Today* 3 (1968): 53; A. Mehrabian, *Silent Messages* (Belmont, CA: Wadsworth, 1971); R. Harrison, *Beyond Words: An Introduction to Nonverbal Communication* (Upper Saddle River, NJ: Prentice Hall, 1974); A. Mehrabian, *Non-Verbal Communication* (Chicago: Aldine, 1972).

45. M. L. Knapp, *Nonverbal Communication in Human Interaction*, 2d ed. (New York: Holt, Rinehart & Winston, 1978).

46. H. M. Rosenfeld, "Instrumental Affiliative Functions of Facial and Gestural Expressions," *Journal of Personality & Social Psychology* 24 (1966): 65–72; P. Ekman, "Differential Communication of Affect by Head and Body Cues," *Journal of Personality & Social Psychology* 23 (1965): 726–735; A. Mehrabian, "Significance of Posture and Position in the Communication of Attitude and Status Relationships," *Psychological Bulletin* 71 (1969): 359–372.

47. J. Gottman & R. Levenson, "The Timing of Divorce: Predicting When a Couple Will Divorce over a 14-Year Period," *Journal of Marriage & the Family* 62 (August 2000): 737–745; J. Gottman, R. Levenson, & E. Woodin, "Facial Expressions during Marital Conflict," *Journal of Family Communication* 1, issue 1 (2001): 37–57.

48. T. Aeppel, "Career Journal: Nicknamed 'Nag,' She's Just Doing Her Job," *Wall Street Journal*, 14 May 2002, B1.

49. J. Saranow, "A Personal Trainer for Your Voice," *Wall Street Journal*, 3 February 2004, D1.

50. A. Joyce, "Confidentiality as a Valued Benefit; Loose Lips Can Defeat the Purpose of an Employee Assistance Program," *Washington Post*, 11 May 2003, F05.

51. C. A. Bartlett & S. Ghoshal, "Changing the Role of Top Management: Beyond Systems to People," *Harvard Business Review*, May–June 1995, 132–142.

52. E. Spragins, "Sending the Wrong Message," *Fortune Small Business*, 1 July 2003, 32.

53. J. Fry, "When Talk Isn't Cheap: Is Emailing Colleagues Who Sit Feet Away a Sign of Office Dysfunction, or a Wise Move?" *Wall Street Journal*, 28 November 2005, http://online.wsj.com.

54. T. Andrews, "E-Mail Empowers, Voice-Mail Enslaves," *PC Week*, 10 April 1995, E11.

55. "The Joys of Voice Mail," *Inc.*, November 1995, 102.

56. E. Wong, "A Stinging Office Memo Boomerangs; Chief Executive Is Criticized after Upbraiding Workers by E-Mail," *New York Times*, 5 April 2001, C1.

57. Ibid.

58. Ibid.

59. Ibid.

60. R. G. Nichols, "Do We Know How to Listen? Practical Helps in a Modern Age," in *Communication Concepts and Processes*, ed. J. DeVitor (Englewood Cliffs, NJ: Prentice Hall, 1971); P. V. Lewis, *Organizational Communication: The Essence of Effective Management* (Columbus, OH: Grid Publishing Company, 1975).

61. E. Atwater, *I Hear You*, rev. ed. (New York: Walker, 1992).

62. R. Adler & N. Towne, *Looking Out/Looking In* (San Francisco: Rinehart, 1975).

63. K. Brooker & J. Schlosser, "The Un-CEO; A. G. Lafley Doesn't Overpromise.

He Doesn't Believe in the Vision Thing. All He's Done Is Turn Around P&G in 27 Months," *Fortune*, 16 September 2002, 88.

64. P. LaBaree, "Feargal Quinn: Ireland's 'Pope of Customer Service' Dominates His Market—and Continues to Beat Bigger and Better-Financed Rivals—with a Leadership Philosophy That Is at Once Folksy and Radical," *Fast Company*, 1 November 2001, 88.

65. B. D. Seyber, R. N. Bostrom, & J. H. Seibert, "Listening, Communication Abilities, and Success at Work," *Journal of Business Communication* 26 (1989): 293–303.

66. Atwater, *I Hear You*.

67. C. Edwards, "Death of A Pushy Salesman," *BusinessWeek*, 3 July 2006, 108.

68. P. Sellers, A. Diba, & E. Florian, "Get over Yourself—Your Ego Is out of Control. You're Screwing up Your Career," *Fortune*, 30 April 2001, 76.

69. H. H. Meyer, "A Solution to the Performance Appraisal Feedback Enigma," *Academy of Management Executive* 5, no. 1 (1991): 68–76.

70. M. Heffernan, "The Wrong Stuff." *Fast Company*, 12 April 2004, http://www.fastcompany.com/resources/columnists/mh/041204.html.

71. T. D. Schellhardt, "Annual Agony: It's Time to Evaluate Your Work, and All Involved Are Groaning," *Wall Street Journal*, 19 November 1996, A1.

72. C. Hymowitz, "How to Tell Employees All the Things They Don't Want to Hear," *Wall Street Journal*, 22 August 2000, B1.

73. L. Anguish, N. Cossack, & A. Maingault, "Payroll Cuts, Personal Hygiene, Extra Leave," *HR Magazine*, 1 June 2003, 41.

74. G. Gitelson, J. Bing, & L. Laroche, "How the Cultural Trap Deepens in Cross-Border Deals," *Dealmakers*, 1 December 2001.

75. From N. J. Adler, *From Boston to Beijing: Managing with a World View* (Cincinnati, OH: South-Western, 2002), based on A. Laurent, "The Cultural Diversity of Western Conceptions of Management," in *International Studies of Management and Organization* 13, no. 1–2 (Spring–Summer 1983): 75–96.

76. J. S. Black & M. Mendenhall, "Cross-Cultural Training Effectiveness: A Review and Theoretical Framework for Future Research," *Academy of Management Review* 15 (1990): 113–136.

77. C. Timberlake, "The Ladder: Even Inside Europe, Cultures Can Collide in the Workplace," *Wall Street Journal Europe*, 16 October 2001, 25.

78. P. Garfinkel, "On Keeping Your Foot Safely out of Your Mouth," *New York Times*, 13 July 2004, 8.

79. F. Trompenaars, *Riding the Waves of Culture: Understanding Diversity in Global Business* (London: Economist Books, 1994).

80. N. Forster, "Expatriates and the Impact of Cross-Cultural Training," *Human Resource Management* 10 (2000): 63–78.

81. Adler, *From Boston to Beijing: Managing with a World View*.

82. Ibid.

83. Ibid.

84. Ibid.

85. Ibid.

86. R. Mead, *Cross-Cultural Management* (New York: Wiley, 1990).

87. Ibid.

88. Edward T. Hall, *The Dance of Life* (New York: Doubleday, 1983).

89. Trompenaars, *Riding the Waves of Culture*.

90. Adler, *From Boston to Beijing: Managing with a World View*.

91. E. T. Hall & M. R. Hall, *Understanding Cultural Differences* (Yarmouth, ME: Intercultural Press, 1990).

92. E. T. Hall & W. F. Whyte, "Intercultural Communication: A Guide to Men of Action," *Human Organization* 19, no. 1 (1961): 5–12.

93. N. Libman, "French Tip: Just Walk the Walk and Talk the Talk, but Not Too Loud," *Chicago Tribune Online*, 17 March 1996.

94. C. Tkaczyk & M. Boyle, "Follow These Leaders," *Fortune*, 12 December 2005, 125.

95. C. Hymowitz, "Diebold's New Chief Shows How to Lead after a Sudden Rise," *Wall Street Journal*, 8 May 2006, B1.

96. J. Lublin, "The 'Open Inbox'—Some CEOs Stay Up Late Reading Employee Emails; Replies Can Be Brief: 'Thanks,'" *Wall Street Journal*, 10 October 2005, B1.

97. Ernst & Young Online: "Collaborate," Ernst & Young, http://www.ey.com/global.

98. A. Lashinsky, "Lights! Camera! Cue the CEO!" *Fortune*, 21 August 2006, 27.

99. C. Olofson, Global Reach, "Virtual Leadership," *Fast Company*, August 1999, http://www.fastcompany.com/online/27/minm.html.

100. M. Campanelli & N. Friedman, "Welcome to Voice Mail Hell: The New Technology Has Become a Barrier between Salespeople and Customers," *Sales & Marketing Management* 147 (May 1995): 98–101.

101. D. Harbrecht, "CEO Q&A: Baxter's Harry Kraemer: 'I Don't Golf,'"

Business Week Online, 28 March 2003, http://www.businessweek.com/bwdaily/dnflash/mar2002/nf20020328_0720.htm.

102. E. Florian & W. Henderson, "Class of '01: Ellen Florian Spotlights Four Retirees—Their Legacies, Their Plans, and What They've Learned That Can Help You Work Better," *Fortune*, 13 August 2001, 185.

103. E. W. Morrison, "Organizational Silence: A Barrier to Change and Development in a Pluralistic World," *Academy of Management Review* 25 (2000): 706–725.

104. L. Landro, "The Informed Patient: Bringing Surgeons Down to Earth—New Programs Aim to Curb Fear That Prevents Nurses from Flagging Problems," *Wall Street Journal*, November 16, 2005, D1.

105. K. Maher, "Global Companies Face Reality of Instituting Ethics Programs," *Wall Street Journal*, 9 November 2004, B8.

106. Ibid.

107. HR, "Anytime, Anywhere," *Human Resources*, 16 May 2006, http://www.humanresourcesmagazine.com.au/articles/83/0C03FC83.asp?Type=60&Category=875.

108. C. Salter, "And Now the Hard Part: Can JetBlue Make the Leap from Popular (and profitable) Niche Airline to Major Player—without Losing Its Soul?" *Fast Company*, 1 May 2004, 67.

109. Ibid.

110. J. Bevan, "Leadership, Clarity, and a Very Thick Skin," *Spectator*, 14 October 2006, 32.

111. Kirkpatrick & Roth, "Why There's No Escaping the Blog."

112. S. Hargrave, "The Blog Busters," *Guardian*, 9 August 2004, http://www.guardian.co.uk.

113. W. Ross, Jr., "What Every Human Resource Manager Should Know about Web Logs," *SAM Advanced Management Journal*, 1 July 2005, 4.

114. J. Neff, "P&G Inks Deal with PlanetFeedback for Pampers and Tide," *Advertising Age*, 15 July 2002, 11.

115. C. G. Pearce, I. W. Johnson, & R. T. Barker, "Assessment of the Listening Styles Inventory: Progress in Establishing Reliability and Validity," *Journal of Business and Technical Communication* 17, no. 1 (2003): 84–113.

116. D. Kirkpatrick, "It's Hard to Manage if You Don't Blog," *Fortune*, 24 October, 2004, 46; L. Tiffany, "Easy Read: Build Business Relationships with a Company Blog," *Entrepreneur*, December 2003, 25.

Chapter 16

1. K. Dell, "Why the Gap Keeps Getting Crushed," *Time*, 5 February 2007, 50–51; A. Merrick, "Gap Will Fashion Its Future without Pressler," *Wall Street Journal*, 23 January 2007, B1; "Fashion Victim," *Economist*, 20 January 2007, 74; S. Ryst, "Sales Gap at the Gap," *Business Week Online*, 5 January 2007, 6; J. Boorstin, "Fashion Victim," *Fortune*, 17 April 2006, 160–166; A Merrick & J. Lublin, "Gap Needs a CEO and Many Qualify; Will Any Apply?" *Wall Street Journal*, 24 January 2007, B1; Gap home page, http://www.gap.com.

2. R. Leifer & P. K. Mills, "An Information Processing Approach for Deciding upon Control Strategies and Reducing Control Loss in Emerging Organizations," *Journal of Management* 22 (1996): 113–137.

3. D. Starkman, "Making 'Sick' Malls Better—Specialists Advise Landlords on Redesigns, Ejecting Stores;

Step One: Fix the Food," *Wall Street Journal*, 21 January 2004, B1.

4. R. Rundle & P. Davies, "Hospitals Start to Seek Payment Upfront," *Wall Street Journal*, 2 June 2004, D1.

5. W. Mossberg & K. Swisher, "Using a Computer to Clean Up Spilled Milk," *Wall Street Journal*, 24 May 2005, D5.

6. J. Welsh, "Drive Buys— Cadillac STS. Caddy Shock—U.S. Maker Matches Europeans with a Sharp, Sporty Sedan; Our Surprise Drive of the Year," *Wall Street Journal*, 31 December 2004, W1.

7. J. LaReau, "Absent New Cars, Cadillac Hopes for Modest Gain," *Automotive News*, 28 August 2006, 42; J. Henry, "Luxury Imports Roll Out Dec. Deals," *Automotive News*, 18 December 2006, 6,41.

8. B. Whitaker, "Yes, There Is a Job That Pays You to Shop," *New York Times*, 13 March 2005, 8.

9. J. Caplan, "Secret Travelers: That Fussy Tourist on Your Next Trip May Be Working for the Resort," *Time*, 6 June 2005, W14.

10. D. Bradbury, "Beta Test Numbers Skyrocket," *Computing Canada*, 3 March 2006, 1, 8.

11. M. Foley, "Blame Vista Delay on Quality?" *eWeek*, 3 April 2006, 33.

12. N. Wiener, *Cybernetics; Or Control and Communication in the Animal and the Machine* (New York: Wiley, 1948).

13. P. Sellers, J. Boorstin, J. Levinstein, "The Best Investor of His Generation (So What Is He Doing with Sears?)," *Fortune*, 20 February 2006, 90–104.

14. R. Berner, "Fashion Emergency at Wal-Mart," *Business Week*, 31 July 2006, 67.

15. J. Dalrymple & M. Honan, "Nike to Add iPod Integration," *MacWorld*, August 2006, 22–23.

16. R. Guth, "The To-Do List: Make Software More Reliable," *Wall Street Journal*, 17 November 2003, R4.

17. Leifer & Mills, "An Information Processing Approach for Deciding upon Control Strategies and Reducing Control Loss in Emerging Organizations."

18. B. Warner, "Deluged Telecoms Boss Bans Staff E-Mails," Yahoo News (Reuters), 19 September 2003, http://story.news.yahoo.com.

19. Ibid.

20. J. Welsh, "Why Your Car Has Lousy Gas Mileage," *Wall Street Journal*, 31 May 2007, D1; M. Spector, "Car Dealers to Lobby on Fuel Economy," *Wall Street Journal*, 12 July 2007, wsj.com; C. Conkey & M. Spector, "Behind the Wheel for Auto Makers," *Wall Street Journal*, 31 July 2007, A4.

21. R. Crockett & J. McGregor, "Six Sigma Still Pays Off at Motorola," *Business Week*, 4 December 2006, 50.

22. M. Higgins, "The Discounts You Aren't Meant to Have," *Wall Street Journal*, 3 December 2003, D1.

23. S. Greenhouse, "Workers Assail Night Lock-Ins by Wal-Mart," *New York Times*, 18 January 2004, 1.

24. Ibid.

25. Ibid.

26. Ibid.

27. S. Shellenbarger, "Is the Awful Behavior of Some Bad Bosses Rooted in Their Past?" *Wall Street Journal*, 17 May 2000, B1.

28. S. Shellenbarger, "Workers, Emboldened by Tight Job Market, Take on Their Bosses," *Wall Street Journal*, 17 May 2000, B1.

29. M. Weber, *The Protestant Ethic and the Spirit of Capitalism* (New York: Scribner's, 1958).

30. L. Criner, "Politicians Come and Go, Bureaucracies Stay and Grow," *Washington Times*, 11 March 1996, 33.

31. "Kwik Trip Fires Three over Online Postings," *Convenience Store News*, 15 January 2007, 10.

32. C. Forelle, "On the Road Again, but Now the Boss Is Sitting beside You," *Wall Street Journal*, 14 May 2004, A1.

33. P. Jonsson, "That a Spreadsheet on Your Screen, or Solitaire?" *Seattle Times*, 12 June 2005, F3.

34. M. Boyle, "Expensing It: Guilty As Charged—When Times Are Tough, Employees Become Even More Devoted to Mastering the Art of Self-Perking," *Fortune*, 9 July 2001, 179; R. Grugal, "Be Honest and Dependable: Integrity—The Must-Have," *Investor's Business Daily*, 11 April 2003, A03.

35. J. Lublin, "CEO Compensation Survey (A Special Report)—Goodbye to Pay for No Performance," *Wall Street Journal*, 11 April 2005, R1.

36. J. Lublin, "CEO Bonuses Rose 46.4% at 100 Big Firms in 2004," *Wall Street Journal*, 25 February 2005, A1.

37. S. Williford, "Nordstrom Sets the Standard for Customer Service," *Memphis Business Journal*, 1 July 1996, 21.

38. A. DeFelice, "A Century of Customer Love: Nordstrom Is the Gold Standard for Customer Service Excellence," *CRM Magazine*, 1 June 2005, 42.

39. R. T. Pascale, "Nordstrom: Respond to Unreasonable Customer Requests!" *Planning Review* 2 (May–June 1994): 17.

40. Ibid.

41. Ibid.

42. J. R. Barker, "Tightening the Iron Cage: Concertive Control in Self-Managing Teams," *Administrative Science Quarterly* 38 (1993): 408–437.

43. N, Byrnes, "The Art of Motivation," *BusinessWeek*, 1 May 2006, 56–62.

44. Ibid.

45. J. R. Barker, "Tightening the Iron Cage."

46. C. Manz & H. Sims, "Leading Workers to Lead Themselves: The External Leadership of Self-Managed Work Teams," *Administrative Science Quarterly* 32 (1987): 106–128.

47. J. Slocum & H. A. Sims, "Typology for Integrating Technology, Organization and Job Design," *Human Relations* 33 (1980): 193–212.

48. C. C. Manz & H. P. Sims, Jr., "Self-Management as a Substitute for Leadership: A Social Learning Perspective," *Academy of Management Review* 5 (1980): 361–367.

49. C. Manz & C. Neck, *Mastering Self-Leadership*, 3rd ed. (Upper Saddle River, NJ: Pearson, Prentice Hall, 2004).

50. J. Lublin, "More Big Companies End Perks; Critics Say Cutbacks Sap Morale," *Wall Street Journal*, 4 January 2001, B1.

51. R. S. Kaplan & D. P. Norton, "Using the Balanced Scorecard as a Strategic Management System," *Harvard Business Review*, January–February 1996, 75–85; R. S. Kaplan & D. P. Norton, "The Balanced Scorecard: Measures That Drive Performance," *Harvard Business Review*, January–February 1992, 71–79.

52. J. Meliones, "Saving Money, Saving Lives," *Harvard Business Review*, November–December 2000, 57–65.

53. S. L. Fawcett, "Fear of Accounts: Improving Managers' Competence and Confidence through Simulation Exercises," *Journal of European Industrial Training*, February 1996, 17.

54. J. Cole, "New Boeing CFO's Assignment: Signal a Turnaround Quickly," *Wall Street Journal*, 26 January 1999, B1.

55. M. H. Stocks & A. Harrell, "The Impact of an Increase in Accounting Information Level on the Judgment Quality of Individuals and Groups," *Accounting, Organizations & Society*, October–November 1995, 685–700.

56. B. Morris, "Roberto Goizueta and Jack Welch: The Wealth Builders," *Fortune*, 11 December 1995, 80–94.

57. G. Colvin, "America's Best & Worst Wealth Creators: The Real Champions Aren't Always Who You Think. Here's an Eye-Opening Look at Which Companies Produce and Destroy the Most Money for Investors—Plus a New Tool for Spotting Future Winners," *Fortune*, 18 December 2000, 207.

58. B. Birchard, "Metrics for the Masses," *CFO*, 1 May 1999, http://www.cfo.com/article.cfm/2989821?f=search.

59. E. Varon, "Implementation Is Not for the Meek," *CIO*, 15 November 2002, http://www.cio.com/article/31510.

60. "Welcome Complaints," Office of Consumer and Business Affairs, Government of South Australia, http://www.ocba.sa.gov.au/businessadvice/customers/complaints.html#Welcome_complaints.

61. C. Bielaszka-DuVernay, "How to Get the Bad News You Need," *Harvard Management Update*, January 2007, 3–5.

62. C. B. Furlong, "12 Rules for Customer Retention," *Bank Marketing* 5 (January 1993): 14.

63. M. Raphel, "Vanished Customers Are Valuable Customers," *Art Business News*, June 2002, 46.

64. F. F. Reichheld, "Lead for Loyalty," *Harvard Business Review* 79 (July–August 2001): 76.

65. C. A. Reeves & D. A. Bednar, "Defining Quality: Alternatives and Implications," *Academy of Management Review* 19 (1994): 419–445.

66. "The 2002 Readers' Choice Awards: Top Travel Services, Condé Nast Traveler," Concierge.com, http://www.concierge.com.

67. "Singapore Airlines Presents Our Awards & Accolades," Singapore Airlines, http://www.singaporeair.com/saa/en_UK/content/company_info/news/achievements.jsp

68. S. Holmes, "Creature Comforts at 30,000 Feet," *BusinessWeek*, 18 December 2006, 138.

69. "ATW Daily News," *ATW*, 8 March 2005, http://www.atwonline.com/news/story.html?storyID=186.

70. K. Nirmalya, " Strategies to Fight Low-Cost Rivals," *Harvard Business Review* 84 (December 2006): 104–112.

71. D. R. May & B. L. Flannery, "Cutting Waste with Employee Involvement Teams," *Business Horizons*, September–October 1995, 28–38.

72. F. Etherington, "Leak in City's Water Valve Angers Kitchener Man," *Kitchener-Waterloo (Ontario) Record*, 1 August 2002, B4.

73. "Pollution Prevention Pays (3P)," 3M, http://www.3m.com.

74. B. Burlingham, "The Coolest Little Start-up in America," *Inc.*, July 2006, 78–85.

75. M. Baer, A. Bluestein, M. Chafkin, J. Gill, B. Gossage, R. McCarthy, K. Mieszkowski, K. Wehrum, & A. Wellner, "The Recyclers," *Inc.*, November 2006, 100–103.

76. M. Conlin & P. Raeburn, "Industrial Evolution: Bill McDonough Has the Wild Idea He Can Eliminate Waste. Surprise! Business Is Listening," *BusinessWeek*, 8 April 2002, 70.

77. Ibid.

78. J. Sprovieri, "Environmental Management Affects Manufacturing Bottom Line," *Assembly*, 1 July 2001, 24.

79. B. Byrne, "EU Says Makers Must Destroy Their Own Brand End-of-Life Cars," *Irish Times*, 23 April 2003, 52.

80. S. Power, "Take It Back: Where Do Cars Go When They Die? In Europe, They Have Little Choice," *Wall Street Journal*, 17 April 2006, R6.

81. J. Szekely & G. Trapaga, "From Villain to Hero (Materials Industry's Waste Recovery Efforts)," *Technology Review*, 1 January 1995, 30.

83. "The End of the Road: Schools and Computer Recycling," Intel, http://www.intel.com/education/recycling_computers/recycling.htm.

84. B. Rose, "Where Old Computers Go: While Too Many Are Dumped Illegally, Sr. Center Salvages Thousands," *Santa Rosa (CA) Press Democrat*, 18 June 2001, D1.

85. "Hardware Recycling Services—US," Hewlett-Packard, https://warp1.external.hp.com/recycle.

85. Reeves & Bednar, "Defining Quality."

86. M. Tuckey, N. Brewer, P. Williamson, "The Influence of Motives and Goal Orientation on Feedback Seeking," *Journal of Occupational and Organizational Psychology* 75, no. 2 (2002): 195.

87. E. Shein, "Multifunction Junction," *CFO*, May 2007, 31.

88. G. Meyer, "H & R Block Sees Jump in Revenue," *Kansas City Star*, 18 March 2005; F. P. Gabriel, Jr., "Block Still Falling Short in Investment Services—Despite Aggressive Campaign, It Can't Retain Advisers," *Investment News*, 6 December 2004, 1; D. Stires, "Taxing Times at H & R Block," *Fortune*, 21 March 2005, 181–184; G. Meyer, "H & R Block to Add 1,000 Outlets to Bolster 2005 Tax Office Traffic," *Kansas City Star*, 19 September 2004.

89. S. Caulkin, "If You Want to Stay a Winner, Learn from Your Mistakes," *The Observer*, 3 March 1996, 7; J. Hyatt, "Failure 101," *Inc.*, January 1989, 18; B. McMenamin, "The Virtue of Making Mistakes," *Forbes*, 9 May 1994, 192–194; P. Sellers, "So You Fail," *Fortune*, 1 May 1995, 48–66; P. Sellers, "Where Failures Get Fixed," *Fortune*, 1 May 1995, 64; B. Weiner, I. Freize, A. Kukla, L. Reed, S. Rest, & R.M. Rosenbaum, "Perceiving the Causes of Success and Failure," in *Attribution: Perceiving the Causes of Behavior*, eds. E. Jones, D. Kanouse, H. Kelley, R. Nesbitt, S. Valins, and B. Weiner (Morristown, NJ: General Learning Press, 1971), 45–61.

Chapter 17

1. University of Pittsburgh Medical Center, http://www.upmc.com. "UPMC Reports Higher First-Half Revenue, Significant Investments for the Future," *Business Wire*, 14 February 2007; C. Becker, "Recent Health IT Security Breaches Are Unlikely to Improve the Public's Perception about the Safety of Personal Data," *Modern Healthcare*, 20 February 2006, 6; J. Ericson, "Trinity Health Harnesses Technology to Improve Care and Efficiency across 30 Hospitals," Business Intelligence Review, 1 December 2006, 20; J. Fahy, "1.5 Million Hurt by Med Errors," *Pittsburgh Post-Gazette*, 21 July 2006, A1; A. Gilbert, "High-Tech Hospitals Better at Keeping Patients Alive?" *CNet*, 12 July 2005, http://www.cnet.com; M. McGee, "Chief of the Year—Can Technology Transform Health Care?"; C. Shropshire, "Stat UPMC Throws out the Paper in Favor of Computerized System for Buying Medical Supplies," *Pittsburgh Post-Gazette*, 27 December 2006, E1; B. Schuerenberg, "Taking an Aggressive Approach to Technology Development," *Health Data Management*, 1 March 2007, 12.

2. R. Lenzner, "The Reluctant Entrepreneur," *Forbes*, 11 September 1995, 162–166.

3. S. Munoz, "How to Get a New Couch Delivered On Time," *Wall Street Journal*, 6 April 2006, D1.

4. M. Totty, "Who's Going to Win the Living-Room Wars? The Battle to Control Home Entertainment Is Heating Up," *Wall Street Journal*, 25 April 2005, R1.

5. P. Grant & A. Schatz, "For Cable Giants, AT&T Deal Is One More Reason to Worry," *Wall Street Journal*, 7 March 2006, A1.

6. J. Angwin & A Pasztor, "Satellite TV Growth Is Losing Altitude As Cable Takes Off," *Wall Street Journal*, 5 August 2006, A1.

7. P. Grant, "Cable Firms Woo Business in Fight for Telecom Turf," *Wall Street Journal*, 17 January 2007, A1.

8. R. D. Buzzell & B. T. Gale, *The PIMS Principles: Linking Strategy to Performance* (New York: Free Press, 1987); M. Lambkin, "Order of Entry and Performance in New Markets," *Strategic Management Journal* 9 (1988): 127–140.

9. G. L. Urban, T. Carter, S. Gaskin, & Z. Mucha, "Market Share Rewards to Pioneering Brands: An Empirical Analysis and Strategic Implications," *Management Science* 32 (1986): 645–659.

10. M. Garry & S. Mulholland, "Master of Its Supply Chain: To Keep Its Inventory Costs

Low and Its Shelves Fully Stocked, Wal-Mart Has Always Invested Extensively—and First—in Technology for the Supply Chain," *Supermarket News*, 2 December 2002, 55.

11. N. Buckley & S. Voyle, "Can Wal-Mart Conquer Markets outside the US?" *Financial Times*, 8 January 2003.

12. Garry & Mulholland, "Master of Its Supply Chain."

13. S. Rupley, "A Moveable Mesh," *PC Magazine*, 21 September 2004, 94.

14. L. Tischler, "Tech for Toques," *Fast Company*, 1 May 2006, 68.

15. R. Pastore, "Cruise Control," *CIO*, 1 February 2003, 60–66.

16. Ibid.

17. B. Worthen, "The Little Company That Could," *CIO*, 1 February 2003, 68–72.

18. C. Quintanilla & L. Claman, "Acxiom Corporation—Chmn. & Pres. Interview," *CNBC/Dow Jones Business Video*, 21 November 2002.

19. M. Santosus, "Technology Recycling: Rising Costs of High-Tech Garbage," *CIO*, 15 April 2003, 36.

20. P. Tam, "The Chief Information Officer's Job Isn't What It Used to Be; Just Ask Hewlett-Packard's Randy Mott," *Wall Street Journal*, 16 April 2007, R5.

21. S. Mehta, "Behold the Server Farm!" *Fortune*, 7 August 2006, 68.

22. C. Koch, "Off the Charts," *CIO*, 1 February 2003, 46.

23. Ibid.

24. T. Knauss, "Niagara Mohawk Meters to Send Readings by Radio; $100 Million Project Will Eventually Eliminate Need for Door-to-Door Readers," *Post-Standard Syracuse*, 17 September 2002, A1.

25. S. Lubar, *Infoculture: The Smithsonian Book of Information Age Inventions* (Boston: Houghton Mifflin, 1993).

26. Ibid.

27. B. Worthen, "Bar Codes on Steroids," *CIO*, 15 December 2002, 53.

28. S. McCartney, "A New Way to Prevent Lost Luggage," *Wall Street Journal*, 27 February 2007, D1.

29. M. Stone, "Scanning for Business," *PC Magazine*, 10 May 2005, 117.

30. "Check It Out: Efficient, Accurate Claims," *Health Management Technology*, 1 April 2003.

31. N. Rubenking, "Hidden Messages," *PC Magazine*, 22 May 2001, 86.

32. J. Hibbard, "How Yahoo! Gave Itself a Face-Lift," *BusinessWeek*, 9 October 2006, 74.

33. A. Carter & D. Beucke, "A Good Neighbor Gets Better," *BusinessWeek*, 20 June 2005, 16.

34. Rubenking, "Hidden Messages."

35. G. Saitz, "Naked Truth—Data Miners, Who Taught Retailers to Stock Beer Near Diapers, Find Hidden Sales Trends, a Science That's Becoming Big Business," *Newark (NJ) Star-Ledger*, 1 August 2002, 041.

36. E. Nelson, "Retailing: Why Wal-Mart Sings, 'Yes, We Have Bananas!'" *Wall Street Journal*, 6 October 1998, B1.

37. M. Overfelt, "A Better Way to Sell Tickets," *Fortune Small Business*, 1 December 2006, 76.

38. B. Saporita, W. Boston, N. Gough, & R. Healy, "Can Wal-Mart Get Any Bigger? (Yes, a Lot Bigger … Here's How)," *Time*, 19 January 2003, 38.

39. B. Gottesman & K. Karagiannis, "A False Sense of Security," *PC Magazine*, 22 February 2005, 72.

40. F. J. Derfler, Jr., "Secure Your Network," *PC Magazine*, 27 June 2000, 183–200.

41. "Authentication," Webopedia, http://www.webopedia.com/TERM/a/authentication.html.

42. "Authorization," Webopedia, http://www.webopedia.com/TERM/a/authorization.html.

43. L. Seltzer, "Password Crackers," *PC Magazine*, 12 February 2002, 68.

44. B. Grimes, "Biometric Security," *PC Magazine*, 22 April 2003, 74.

45. Ibid.

46. M. McQueen, "Laptop Lockdown," *Wall Street Journal*, 28 June 2006, D1.

47. K. Karagiannis, "Security Watch: Don't Make It Easy," *PC Magazine*, 8 April 2003, 72; M. Steinhart, "Password Dos and Don'ts," *PC Magazine*, 12 February 2002, 69; L. Seltzer, "Are Pa55.W0rd5 Dead?" *PC Magazine*, 28 December 2004, 86.

48. S. Patton, "Simply Secure Communications," *CIO*, 15 January 2003, 100.

49. C. Metz, "Total Security," *PC Magazine*, 1 October 2003, 83.

50. P. Loftus, "Web Services—Smooth Talk: New Software Allows Different Computer Systems to Communicate with Each Other Seamlessly," *Wall Street Journal*, 31 March 2003, R9.

51. J. van den Hoven, "Executive Support Systems & Decision Making," *Journal of Systems Management* 47, no. 8 (March–April 1996): 48.

52. "Business Objects Customers Take Off with Performance Management; Management Dashboards Help Organizations Gain Insight and Optimize Performance," *Business Wire*, 4 April 2005.

53. "Intranet," Webopedia, http://www.webopedia.com/TERM/i/intranet.html.

54. "IBM Dynamic Workplaces for Air," IBM, http://www.ibm.com.

55. V. Ganesan, "IBM Product Enables Firms to See Returns within One Year," *Business Times (Malaysia)*, 10 February 2003, 4.

56. J. Ericson, "The Hillman Group Leverages Consolidated Reporting, Geographic Analysis to Support its Hardware Manufacturing/distribution Leadership," *Business Intelligence Review*, 1 March 2007, 12.

57. "Web Services," Webopedia, http://www.webopedia.com/TERM/W/Web_Services.html.

58. S. Overby, "This Could Be the Start of Something Small," *CIO*, 15 February 2003, 54.

59. "Extranet," Webopedia, http://www.webopedia.com/TERM/E/extranet.html.

60. S. Hamm, D. Welch, W. Zellner, F. Keenan, & F. Engardio, "Down but Hardly Out: Downturn Be Damned, Companies Are Still Anxious to Expand Online," *BusinessWeek*, 26 March 2001, 126.

61. S. Nassauer, "Travel Watch: Eliminating the Human Element," *Wall Street Journal*, 14 November 2006, D7.

62. Hamm, Welch, Zellner, Keenan, & Engardio, "Down but Hardly Out."

63. K. C. Laudon & J. P. Laudon, *Management Information Systems: Organization and Technology* (Upper Saddle River, NJ: Prentice Hall, 1996).

64. J. Borzo, "Software for Symptoms," *Wall Street Journal*, 23 May 2005, R10.

65. Ibid.

66. R. Hernandez, "American Express Authorizer's Assistant," *Business Rules Journal*, August 2001,

http://bizrules.info/page/art_amexaa.htm.

67. Heinssen, Jr., R., Glass, C., & Knight, L. "Assessing Computer Anxiety: Development and Validation of the Computer Anxiety Rating Scale," *Computers in Human Behavior* (1987) 49–59.

68. A. Fisher, "Ask Annie: Can My Employer Really Ban Camera Phones?" *Fortune*, 9 August 2004, 54; C. Rhoads, "Cellphones Become 'Swiss Army Knives' as Technology Blurs," *Wall Street Journal*, 4 January 2005, B1; "In-STAT/MDR Reports 200% Growth in Shipments of Camera Phones," *AsiaPulse*, 15 December 2004; D. Takahashi, "Video Camera Phones Start to Pack Megapixel Punch," *San Jose Mercury News*, 25 October 2004; M. Thiruvengadam, "Popularity of Camera Phones Opens New Windows on Privacy Rights," *San Antonio Express-News*, 4 August 2004; K. Yatish Rajawat, "Camera Phones' Large Memories Pose Hidden Risk to India Business Security," *Economic Times*, 23 December 2004.

69. A. Fisher, "Retain Your Brains," *Fortune*, 24 July 2006, 49; A.Y.K. Chua, "The Curse of Success," *Wall Street Journal*, 28 April 2007, R8; S. Earley, "To Keep KM Current, Pay Attention to Context Changes," *Information Outlook*, April 2006, 31; E. Schwartz, "Reality Check: Filling the Void Left by Baby-Boomer Techies," *InfoWorld*, 6 March 2006, 22; "Putting It Off Until Tomorrow," *PR Newswire*, 26 January 2006.

Chapter 18

1. C. Passariello, "Louis Vuitton Tries Modern Methods on Factory Lines," *Wall Street Journal*, 9 October 2006, A1; "Blending New Technologies with Trustworthy Tradition and Creativity at Louis Vuitton," *i2 for Retail*, i2 Success Story #265, www.i2.com; C. Passariello, "A New Lease on Luxury," *Wall Street Journal*, 7 October 2006, wsj.com; R. Murphy, "LVMH, PPR Thriving and Bullish," *WWD*, 27 July 2007, 9; V. Vienne, "Luxe Luggage," *Town & Country*, January 2001, 140; C. Matlack, "The Vuitton Money Machine," *BusinessWeek*, 22 March 2004, businessweek.com; M. Socha, "Extras: Shoe-Licious," *WWD*, 7 August 2006, 38.

2. "Ryanair Celebrates 20 Years of Operations," Ryanair, http://www.ryanair.com/site/about/invest/docs/2005/q4_2005.pdf.

3. L. Tutor, "The Best Drive-Through in America, '04: Average Service Time Ranking," *Quick Service Restaurant*, http://www.qsrmagazine.com.

4. M. Richtel, "The Long-Distance Journey of a Fast-Food Order," *New York Times*, 11 April 2006, http://www.nytimes.com/2006/04/11/technology/11fast.html?ei=5090&en=fba08317788e24.

5. "Employment Cost Index News Release Text," Bureau of Labor Statistics, 1 July 2005, http://www.bls.gov/news.release/eci.nr0.htm; "Productivity and Costs, First Quarter 2005, Revised," Bureau of Labor Statistics, 1 July 2005, http://www.bls.gov/news.release/prod2.nr0.htm.

6. "HINC-03. People in Households—Households, by Total Money Income in 2003, Age, Race, and Hispanic Origin of Householder," U.S. Census Bureau, http://pubdb3.census.gov/macro/032004/hhinc/new03_001.htm.

7. "Historical Income Tables—Families," U.S. Census Bureau; "Table H-6. Regions—All Races by Median and Mean Income: 1975 to 2005," U.S. Census Bureau, http://www.census.gov/hhes/www/income/histinc/h06ar.html, 20 August 2007.

8. "Productivity and Costs, First Quarter 2005, Revised," Bureau of Labor Statistics, ftp://ftp.bls.gov/pub/news.release/History/prod2.06022005.news; "Employment, Hours, and Earnings from the Current Employment Statistics Survey (National)," Bureau of Labor Statistics, http://data.bls.gov/cgi-bin/surveymost?ce; "Productivity and Costs, First Quarter 200, Revised," Bureau of Labor Statistics, http://www.bls.gov/news.release/prod2.nr0.htm; "Employment, Hours, and Earnings from the Current Employment Statistics Survey (National)," Bureau of Labor Statistics, http://data.bls.gov/cgi-bin/surveymost?ce.

9. M. Ferguson, "It's the Right Time to Look for a New Job," *US News and World Report*, 9 April 2007, http://www.newsalerts.com/news/article/it-s-the-right-time-to-look-for-a-new-job.html:us2:926598.

10. Joanne Fritz, "Giving USA Releases Report on Charitable Giving for 2005," About.com, http://www.nonprofit.about.com/od/trendsissuesstatistics/a/givingusa.htm.

11. "Philanthropy in the American Economy," Council of Economic Advisers, 19 February 2002, http://clinton4.nara.gov/media/pdf/philanthropy.pdf.

12. "Cars' Affordability: Cheapest Since 1980," *CNN Money*, 13 November 2006, http://money.cnn.com/2006/11/13/autos/affordability/index.htm; "Auto Affordability Shows a Record Deterioration; Comerica Bank Chief Economist Reports," Auto Channel, 12 February 2007, http://www.theautochannel.com/news/2007/02/12/036903.html.

13. "Auto Affordability Slipped a Notch in Summer," Comerica, http://www.comerica.com.

14. "Cars' Affordability: Cheapest Since 1980."

15. B. Clanton, "Asians Outpace Big Three in Factory Efficiency," *Detroit News*, 3 June 2005, http://www.detnews.com/2005/autosinsider/0506/07/A01-202894.htm.

16. Ibid.

17. "Multifactor Productivity," Bureau of Labor Statistics, 31 January 2007, http://stats.bls.gov/bls/productivity.htm.

18. J. Dodge, "Dell's Internet-Based Plant Keeps Production Efficient," *Wall Street Journal Interactive Edition*, 26 September 2000, http://online.wsj.com.

19. J. Pletz, "Dell Computer's Basic Building Blocks: Famous Model for Computers Translates Well to Construction," *Austin American-Statesman*, 10 April 2000, D1.

20. J. Teresko, "The Value of Velocity," *Industry Week*, 1 October 2001, 43.

21. M. Rechtin "Porsche, Hyundai Score Big Gains in J. D. Power Quality Survey," *Auto Week*, 7 June 2006, http://www.autoweek.com/apps/pbcs.dll/article?AID=/20060608/FREE/60607007/1041&te.

22. "ASQ Glossary," American Society for Quality, http://www.asq.org/glossary/q.html.

23. R. E. Markland, S. K. Vickery, & R. A. Davis, "Managing Quality," ch. 7 in *Operations Management: Concepts in Manufacturing and Services* (Cincinnati, OH: South-Western College Publishing, 1998).

24. "SDLT 600 Tape Drive Product Specification," Quantum Corporation, http://www.quantum.com/ServiceandSupport/Softwareand Documentation Downloads/SDLT600/Index.aspx#Specifications.

25. G. Rao, "Computers to Be at the Heart of a Car," *Economic Times*, 12 February 2004, http://economictimes.indiatimes.com/.

26. "The 'R' Word: Product Reliability Is Measured at Physio-Control," *InSync*, http://www.medtronic-ers.com/insync/archives/istfal97.htm.

27. L. L. Berry & A. Parasuraman, *Marketing Services* (New York: Free Press, 1991).

28. P. Judge, "When a Customer Believes in You...They'll Stick with You Almost No Matter What," *Fast Company* 47 (June 2001): 138.

29. Ibid.

30. Ibid.

31. Ibid.

32. "ISO 9000 and ISO 14000 in Plain Language," International Organization for Standardization, http://www.iso.org/iso/en/iso9000–14000/understand/basics/general/basics_4.html.

33. "FAQs—General," International Organization for Standardization, http://www.iso.org/iso/en/faqs/faq-general.html.

34. J. Briscoe, S. Fawcett, & R. Todd, "The Implementation and Impact of ISO 9000 among Small Manufacturing Enterprises," *Journal of Small Business Management* 43 (1 July 2005): 309.

35. R. Henkoff, "The Hot New Seal of Quality (ISO 9000 Standard of Quality Management)," *Fortune*, 28 June 1993, 116.

36. "Frequently Asked Questions about the Malcolm Baldrige National Quality Award," National Institute of Standards & Technology, http://www.nist.gov/public_affairs/factsheet/baldfaqs.htm.

37. "Baldrige Award Application Forms," National Institute of Standards & Technology, http://www.baldrige.nist.gov/PDF_files/2005_Award_Application_Forms.pdf.

38. "Frequently Asked Questions and Answers about the Malcolm Baldrige National Quality Award."

39. Ibid.

40. "Criteria for Performance Excellence," Baldrige National Quality Program 2003, http://www.quality.nist.gov/PDF_files/2005_Business_Criteria.pdf.

41. Ibid.

42. Ibid.

43. "NIST Stock Studies Show Quality Pays (Baldrige National Quality Award)," National Institute of Standards & Technology, http://www.quality.nist.gov/Stock_Studies.htm.

44. J. W. Dean, Jr., & J. Evans, *Total Quality: Management, Organization, and Strategy* (St. Paul, MN: West, 1994).

45. J. W. Dean, Jr., & D. E. Bowen, "Management Theory and Total Quality: Improving Research and Practice through Theory Development," *Academy of Management Review* 19 (1994): 392–418.

46. R. Allen & R. Kilmann, "Aligning Reward Practices in Support of Total Quality Management," *Business Horizons*, 1 May 2001, 77.

47. A. Taylor, "Driving Customer Satisfaction," *Harvard Business Review*, July 2002, 24.

48. R. Carter, "Best Practices: Freudenberg-NOK/Cleveland, GA: Continuous Kaizens," *Industrial Maintenance & Plant Operations*, 1 June 2004, 10.

49. Ibid.

50. R. Levering, M. Moskowitz, L. Munoz, & P. Hjelt, "The 100 Best Companies to Work for," *Fortune*, 4 February 2002, 72.

51. "News Release: Gross Domestic Product and Corporate Profits," Bureau of Economic Analysis, U.S. Department of Commerce, http://www.bea.gov http://www.bea.gov/newsreleases/national/gdp/2007/gdp107a.htm.

52. R. Hallowell, L. A. Schlesinger, & J. Zornitsky, http://economictimes.indiatimes.com/ "Internal Service Quality, Customer and Job Satisfaction: Linkages and Implications for Management," *Human Resource Planning* 19 (1996): 20–31; J. L. Heskett, T. O. Jones, G. W. Loveman, W. E. Sasser, Jr., & L. A. Schlesinger, "Putting the Service-Profit Chain to Work," *Harvard Business Review*, March–April 1994, 164–174.

53. J. Huey, G. Bethune, & H. Kelleher, "Two Texas Mavericks Rant about the Wreckage of the U.S. Aviation Industry—And Reveal How They've Managed to Keep Their Companies above the Miserable Average," *Fortune*, 13 November 2000, 237.

54. R. Eder, "Customer-Easy Doesn't Come Easy," *Drug Store News*, 21 October 2002, 52.

55. "CVS Gears 'Service-Profit Chain' to the Customer" (Company Profile), *Chain Drug Review*, 11 December 2000, 44.

56. K. L. Freiberg & J. A. Freiberg, *NUTS! Southwest Airlines' Crazy Recipe for Business and Personal Success* (Austin, TX: Bard, 1996), 289.

57. G. Brewer, "The Ultimate Guide to Winning Customers: The Customer Stops Here," *Sales & Marketing Management* 150 (March 1998): 30; F. F. Reichheld, "The Loyalty Effect: The Hidden Force behind Growth, Profits, and Lasting Value," (Cambridge, MA: Harvard Business School Press, 2001).

58. Ibid.

59. L. L. Berry & A. Parasuraman, "Listening to the Customer—The Concept of a Service-Quality Information System," *Sloan Management Review* 38, no. 3 (Spring 1997): 65; C. W. L. Hart, J. L. Heskett, & W. E. Sasser, Jr., "The Profitable Art of Service Recovery," *Harvard Business Review*, July–August 1990, 148–156.

60. G. Stoller, "Companies Give Front-Line Employees More Power," *USA Today*, 27 June 2005, A.1.

61. S. Hale, "The Customer Is Always Right—Usually—Some Are Just Annoying, but Others Deserve the Boot," *Orlando Sentinel*, 15 April 2002, 54.

62. D. E. Bowen & E. E. Lawler III, "The Empowerment of Service Workers: What, Why, How, and When," *Sloan Management Review* 33 (Spring 1992): 31–39; D. E. Bowen & E. E. Lawler III, "Empowering Service Employees," *Sloan Management Review* 36 (Summer 1995): 73–84.

63. Bowen & Lawler III, "The Empowerment of Service Workers: What, Why, How, and When."

64. Stoller, "Companies Give Front-Line Employees More Power."

65. Ibid.

66. "Toshiba Offers Build-to-Order Option on Notebook Products for Customers Purchasing On-Line," EDP Weekly's IT Monitor, 7 April 2003 (available at http://findarticles.com/p/articles/mi_m0GZQ/is_14_44/ai_99824254).

67. G. V. Frazier & M. T. Spiggs, "Achieving Competitive Advantage through Group Technology," *Business Horizons* 39 (1996): 83–88.

68. "The Top 100 Beverage Companies: The List," *Beverage Industry*, July 2001, 30.

69. E. Gruber, "Cutting Time," *Modern Machine Shop*, March 2001, 102.

70. B. Sauer, "Heil 'Automated Job Shop' Produces Custom Trailers on Assembly Lines," Trailer/Body Builders, 1 December 1998, http://trailer-bodybuilders.com/mag/trucks_heil_automated_job.

71. "Attack Submarines—SSN," United States Navy Fact File, http://www.navy.mil/navydata/fact_display.asp?cid=4100&tid=100&ct=4.

72. S. Silke Carty, "Chrysler Wrestles with High Levels of Inventory as Unsold Vehicles Sit on Lots," *USA Today*, 2 November 2006, http://www.usatoday.com/money/autos/2006–11–02-chrysler-high-inventory_x.htm; J. D. Stoll, "Chrysler Maintains Plan to Cut Production as Inventory Rises," *Wall Street Journal*, 24 August 2006, http://www.wsj.com.

73. Ibid.

74. N. Wingfield, "Out of Tune: iPod Shortage Rocks Apple," *Wall Street Journal*, 16 December 2004, B1.

75. Ibid.

76. C. Marshall, "Linerboard: Market Recovery Will Continue; Price Hikes Predicted for 1998," *Pulp & Paper*, 1 January 1998, 13.

77. D. Drickhamer, "Reality Check," *Industry Week*, November 2001, 29.

78. D. Drickhamer, "Zeroing In on World-Class," *Industry Week*, November 2001, 36.

79. J. Zeiler, "The Need for Speed," *Operations & Fulfillment*, 1 April 2004, 38.

80. "About EFR," Efficient Foodservice Response, http://www.efr-central.com/aboutefr.html.

81. J. R. Henry, "Minimized Setup Will Make Your Packaging Line S.M.I.L.E.," *Packaging Technology & Engineering*, 1 February 1998, 24.

82. J. Donoghue, "The Future Is Now," *Air Transport World*, 1 April 2001, 78.

83. K. Clark, "An Eagle Eye for Inventory," *Chain Store Age*, May 2005, Supplement, 8A.

84. E. Powell, Jr., & F. Sahin, "Economic Production Lot Sizing with Periodic Costs and Overtime," *Decision Sciences* 32 (2001): 423–452.

85. J. Bonasia, "Just-in-Time Cuts Costs, but Has Risks," *Investor's Business Daily*, 3 October 2002, 4.

86. N. Shirouzu, "Why Toyota Wins Such High Marks on Quality Surveys," *Wall Street Journal*, 15 March 2001, A1.

87. Ibid.

88. G. Gruman, "Supply on Demand; Manufacturers Need to Know What's Selling before They Can Produce and Deliver Their Wares in the Right Quantities," *Info World*, 18 April 2005, http://www.infoworld.com/.

89. J. A. Perriat, S. LeMay, S. Chakrabarty, "The Selling Orientation—Customer Orientation (SOCO) Scale: Cross-Validation of the Revised Version," *Journal of Personal Selling & Sales Management* 24, no. 1 (2004): 49–54.

90. C. Koch, "Nike Rebounds," *CIO*, 15 June 2004, 57–62; J. Schlosser, "Just Do It," *Fortune*, 13 December 2004, 25; T. Wilson, "Nike Just Doesn't Do It," *Internet Week*, 28 December 2001, available at http://www.theopensourcecollective.com/press/InternetWeek/Internet_Week.htm; S. Holmes, "Nike," *BusinessWeek*, 24 November 2003, 98.

91. R. A. Donnelley, Jr., "Managing the Moment of Truth for a Service Organization," *Supervision*, December 2004, 3; M. De Paula, "Dispensing with the Data Dump to Achieve Customer Loyalty," *Banking Wire*, 11 February 2005, 24.

92. J. Craddock, ed., *VideoHound's Golden Movie Retriever* (Farmington Hills, MI: Gale Group, 2000); "John Ratzenberger," wikipedia.org, 6 September 2007; Grainger David, "Day Trippers," *Fortune*, 4 April 2005, 108–118; www.marshmallowpeeps.com; www.tabasco.com; www.factorytoursusa.com.

GLOSSARY

a-type conflict (affective conflict) disagreement that focuses on individuals or personal issues

absolute comparisons a process in which each decision criterion is compared to a standard or ranked on its own merits

accommodative strategy a social responsiveness strategy in which a company accepts responsibility for a problem and does all that society expects to solve that problem

achievement-oriented leadership a leadership style in which the leader sets challenging goals, has high expectations of employees, and displays confidence that employees will assume responsibility and put forth extraordinary effort

acquaintance time a cultural norm for how much time you must spend getting to know someone before the person is prepared to do business with you

acquisition the purchase of a company by another company

acquisition cost the cost of obtaining data that you don't have

action plan the specific steps, people, and resources needed to accomplish a goal

active listening assuming half the responsibility for successful communication by actively giving the speaker nonjudgmental feedback that shows you've accurately heard what he or she said

address terms cultural norms that establish whether you should address businesspeople by their first names, family names, or titles

adverse impact unintentional discrimination that occurs when members of a particular race, sex, or ethnic group are unintentionally harmed or disadvantaged because they are hired, promoted, or trained (or any other employment decision) at substantially lower rates than others

advocacy groups groups of concerned citizens who band together to try to influence the business practices of specific industries, businesses, and professions

affective cultures cultures in which people display emotions and feelings when communicating

affectivity the stable tendency to experience positive or negative moods and to react to things in a generally positive or negative way

affirmative action purposeful steps taken by an organization to create employment opportunities for minorities and women

age discrimination treating people differently (e.g., in hiring and firing, promotion, and compensation decisions) because of their age

agreeableness the degree to which someone is cooperative, polite, flexible, forgiving, good-natured, tolerant, and trusting

analyzers companies using an adaptive strategy that seeks to minimize risk and maximize profits by following or imitating the proven successes of prospectors

appointment time a cultural norm for how punctual you must be when showing up for scheduled appointments or meetings

Asia-Pacific Economic Cooperation (APEC) a regional trade agreement between Australia, Canada, Chile, the People's Republic of China, Hong Kong, Japan, Mexico, New Zealand, Papua New Guinea, Peru, Russia, South Korea, Taiwan, the United States, and all the members of ASEAN, except Cambodia, Laos, and Myanmar

assemble-to-order operation a manufacturing operation that divides manufacturing processes into separate parts or modules that are combined to create semicustomized products

assessment centers a series of managerial simulations, graded by trained observers, that are used to determine applicants' capability for managerial work

Association of Southeast Asian Nations (ASEAN) a regional trade agreement between Brunei Darussalam, Cambodia, Indonesia, Laos, Malaysia, Myanmar, the Philippines, Singapore, Thailand, and Vietnam

association or affinity patterns when two or more database elements tend to occur together in a significant way

attack a competitive move designed to reduce a rival's market share or profits

attribution theory the theory that we all have a basic need to understand and explain the causes of other people's behavior

authentication making sure potential users are who they claim to be

authoritarianism the extent to which an individual believes there should be power and status differences within organizations

authority the right to give commands, take action, and make decisions to achieve organizational objectives

authorization granting authenticated users approved access to data, software, and systems

autonomy the degree to which a job gives workers the discretion, freedom, and independence to decide how and when to accomplish the job

average aggregate inventory average overall inventory during a particular time period

awareness training training that is designed to raise employees' awareness of diversity issues and to challenge the underlying assumptions or stereotypes they may have about others

B

BCG matrix a portfolio strategy, developed by the Boston Consulting Group, that categorizes a corporation's businesses by growth rate and relative market share, and helps managers decide how to invest corporate funds

background checks procedures used to verify the truthfulness and accuracy of information that applicants provide about themselves and to uncover negative, job-related background information not provided by applicants

balance sheets accounting statements that provide a snapshot of a company's financial position at a particular time

balanced scorecard measurement of organizational performance in four equally important areas: finances, customers, internal operations, and innovation and learning

bar code a visual pattern that represents numerical data by varying the thickness and pattern of vertical bars

bargaining power of buyers a measure of the influence that customers have on a firm's prices

bargaining power of suppliers a measure of the influence that suppliers of parts, materials, and services to firms in an industry have on the prices of these inputs

batch production a manufacturing operation that produces goods in large batches in standard lot sizes

behavior control the regulation of the behaviors and actions that workers perform on the job

behavioral addition the process of having managers and employees perform new behaviors that are central to and symbolic of the new organizational culture that a company wants to create

behavioral formality a workplace atmosphere characterized by routine and regimen, specific rules about how to behave, and impersonal detachment

behavioral informality a workplace atmosphere characterized by spontaneity, casualness, and interpersonal familiarity

behavior observation scales (BOSs) rating scales that indicate the frequency with which workers perform specific behaviors that are representative of the job dimensions critical to successful job performance

behavioral substitution the process of having managers and employees perform new behaviors central to the "new" organizational culture in place of behaviors that were central to the "old" organizational culture

benchmarking the process of identifying outstanding practices, processes, and standards in other companies and adapting them to your company

biographical data (biodata) extensive surveys that ask applicants questions about their personal backgrounds and life experiences

biometrics identifying users by unique, measurable body features, such as fingerprint recognition or iris scanning

blog a personal website that provides personal opinions or recommendations, news summaries, and reader comments

bona fide occupational qualification (BFOQ) an exception in employment law that permits sex, age, religion, and the like to be used when making employment decisions, but only if they are "reasonably necessary to the normal operation of that particular business." BFOQs are strictly monitored by the Equal Employment Opportunity Commission.

bounded rationality a decision-making process restricted in the real world by limited resources, incomplete and imperfect information, and managers' limited decision-making capabilities

brainstorming a decision-making method in which group members build on each others' ideas to generate as many alternative solutions as possible

budgeting quantitative planning through which managers decide how to allocate available money to best accomplish company goals

budgets quantitative plans through which managers decide how to allocate available money to best accomplish company goals

bureaucracy the exercise of control on the basis of knowledge, expertise, or experience

bureaucratic control the use of hierarchical authority to influence employee behavior by rewarding or punishing employees for compliance or noncompliance with organizational policies, rules, and procedures

bureaucratic immunity the ability to make changes without first getting approval from managers or other parts of an organization

business confidence indices indices that show managers' level of confidence about future business growth

buyer dependence the degree to which a supplier relies on a buyer because of the importance of that buyer to the supplier and the difficulty of finding other buyers for its products

C

c-type conflict (cognitive conflict) disagreement that focuses on problem- and issue-related differences of opinion

cafeteria benefit plans (flexible benefit plans) plans that allow employees to choose which benefits they receive, up to a certain dollar value

cash cow a company with a large share of a slow-growing market

cash flow analysis a type of analysis that predicts how changes in a business will affect its ability to take in more cash than it pays out

Central America Free Trade Agreement (CAFTA-DR) a regional trade agreement between Costa Rica, the Dominican Republic, El Salvador, Guatemala, Honduras, Nicaragua, and the United States

centralization of authority the location of most authority at the upper levels of the organization

chain of command the vertical line of authority that clarifies who reports to whom throughout the organization

change agent the person formally in charge of guiding a change effort

change forces forces that produce differences in the form, quality, or condition of an organization over time

change intervention the process used to get workers and managers to change their behavior and work practices

character of the rivalry a measure of the intensity of competitive behavior between companies in an industry

charismatic leadership the behavioral tendencies and personal characteristics of leaders that create an exceptionally strong relationship between them and their followers

closed systems systems that can sustain themselves without interacting with their environments

closure the tendency to fill in gaps of missing information by assuming that what we don't know is consistent with what we already know

coaching communicating with someone for the direct purpose of improving the person's on-the-job performance or behavior

coercion the use of formal power and authority to force others to change

cognitive ability tests tests that measure the extent to which applicants have abilities in perceptual speed, verbal comprehension, numerical aptitude, general reasoning, and spatial aptitude

cognitive maps graphic depictions of how managers believe environmental factors relate to possible organizational actions

cohesiveness the extent to which team members are attracted to a team and motivated to remain in it

commission a compensation system in which employees earn a percentage of each sale they make

communication the process of transmitting information from one person or place to another

communication cost the cost of transmitting information from one place to another

communication medium the method used to deliver an oral or written message

company hotlines phone numbers that anyone in the company can call anonymously to leave information for upper management

company vision a company's purpose or reason for existing

compensation the financial and nonfinancial rewards that organizations give employees in exchange for their work

competitive advantage providing greater value for customers than competitors can

competitive analysis a process for monitoring the competition that involves identifying competition, anticipating their moves, and determining their strengths and weaknesses

competitive inertia a reluctance to change strategies or competitive practices that have been successful in the past

competitors companies in the same industry that sell similar products or services to customers

complex environment an environment with many environmental factors

complex matrix a form of matrix departmentalization in which managers in different parts of the matrix report to matrix managers, who help them sort out conflicts and problems

component parts inventories the basic parts used in manufacturing that are fabricated from raw materials

compression approach to innovation an approach to innovation that assumes that incremental innovation can be planned using a series of steps and that compressing those steps can speed innovation

compromise an approach to dealing with conflict in which both parties give up some of what they want in order to reach agreement on a plan to reduce or settle the conflict

concentration of effect the total harm or benefit that an act produces on the average person

conceptual skills the ability to see the organization as a whole, understand how the different parts affect each other, and recognize how the company fits into or is affected by its environment

concertive control the regulation of workers' behavior and decisions through work group values and beliefs

concurrent control a mechanism for gathering information about performance deficiencies as they occur, thereby eliminating or shortening the delay between performance and feedback

conduit metaphor the mistaken assumption that senders can pipe their intended messages directly into the heads of receivers with perfect clarity and without noise or perceptual filters interfering

with the receivers' understanding of the message

conscientiousness the degree to which someone is organized, hardworking, responsible, persevering, thorough, and achievement oriented

consideration the extent to which a leader is friendly, approachable, and supportive and shows concern for employees

consistent organizational culture a company culture in which the company actively defines and teaches organizational values, beliefs, and attitudes

constructive feedback feedback intended to be helpful, corrective, and/or encouraging

contingency approach holds that there are no universal management theories and that the most effective management theory or idea depends on the kinds of problems or situations that managers are facing at a particular time and place

contingency theory a leadership theory that states that in order to maximize work group performance, leaders must be matched to the situation that best fits their leadership style

continuous-flow production a manufacturing operation that produces goods at a continuous, rather than a discrete, rate

continuous improvement an organization's ongoing commitment to constantly assess and improve the processes and procedures used to create products and services

continuous reinforcement schedule a schedule that requires a consequence to be administered following every instance of a behavior

control a regulatory process of establishing standards to achieve organizational goals, comparing actual performance against the standards, and taking corrective action, when necessary

control loss the situation in which behavior and work procedures do not conform to standards

controlling monitoring progress toward goal achievement and taking corrective action when needed

conventional level of moral development the second level of moral development in which people make decisions that conform to societal expectations

cooperative contract an agreement in which a foreign business owner pays a company a fee for the right to conduct that business in his or her country

core capabilities the internal decision-making routines, problem-solving processes, and organizational cultures that determine how efficiently inputs can be turned into outputs

core firms the central companies in a strategic group

corporate portal a hybrid of executive information systems and intranets that allows managers and employees to use a web browser to gain access to customized company information and to complete specialized transactions

corporate talk shows televised company meetings that allow remote audiences (employees) to pose questions to the show's host and guests

corporate-level strategy the overall organizational strategy that addresses the question "What business or businesses are we in or should we be in?"

cost leadership the positioning strategy of producing a product or service of acceptable quality at consistently lower production costs than competitors can, so that the firm can offer the product or service at the lowest price in the industry

counseling communicating with someone about non-job-related issues that may be affecting or interfering with the person's performance

creative work environments workplace cultures in which workers perceive that new ideas are welcomed, valued, and encouraged

creativity the production of novel and useful ideas

cross-cultural communication transmitting information from a person in one country or culture to a person from another country or culture

cross-functional team a team composed of employees from different functional areas of the organization

cross-training training team members to do all or most of the jobs performed by the other team members

customer defections a performance assessment in which companies identify which customers are leaving and measure the rate at which they are leaving

customer departmentalization organizing work and workers into separate units responsible for particular kinds of customers

customer focus an organizational goal to concentrate on meeting customers' needs at all levels of the organization

customer satisfaction an organizational goal to provide products or services that meet or exceed customers' expectations

customs classification a classification assigned to imported products by government officials that affects the size of the tariff and imposition of import quotas

cybernetic the process of steering or keeping on course

cybernetic feasibility the extent to which it is possible to implement each step in the control process

D

data clusters when three or more database elements occur together (i.e., cluster) in a significant way

data encryption the transformation of data into complex, scrambled digital codes that can be unencrypted only by authorized users who possess unique decryption keys

data mining the process of discovering unknown patterns and relationships in large amounts of data

data warehouse stores huge amounts of data that have been prepared for data mining analysis by being cleaned of errors and redundancy

decentralization the location of a significant amount of authority in the lower levels of the organization

decision criteria the standards used to guide judgments and decisions

decision making the process of choosing a solution from available alternatives

decision support system (DSS) an information system that helps managers understand specific kinds of problems and potential solutions and analyze the impact of different decision options using "what if" scenarios

decoding the process by which the receiver translates the written, verbal, or symbolic form of a message into an understood message

deep-level diversity differences such as personality and attitudes that are communicated through verbal and nonverbal behaviors and are learned only through extended interaction with others

defenders companies using an adaptive strategy aimed at defending strategic positions by seeking moderate, steady growth and by offering a limited range of high-quality products and services to a well-defined set of customers

defensive bias the tendency for people to perceive themselves as personally and situationally similar to someone who is having difficulty or trouble

defensive strategy a social responsiveness strategy in which a company admits responsibility for a problem but does the least required to meet societal expectations

de-forming a reversal of the forming stage, in which team members position themselves to control pieces of the team, avoid each other, and isolate themselves from team leaders

delegation of authority the assignment of direct authority and responsibility to a subordinate to complete tasks for which the manager is normally responsible

Delphi technique a decision-making method in which members of a panel of experts respond to questions and to each other until reaching agreement on an issue

de-norming a reversal of the norming stage, in which team performance begins to decline as the size, scope, goal, or members of the team change

departmentalization subdividing work and workers into separate organizational units responsible for completing particular tasks

dependent demand system an inventory system in which the level of inventory depends on the number of finished units to be produced

design competition competition between old and new technologies to establish a new technological standard or dominant design

design iteration a cycle of repetition in which a company tests a prototype of a new product or service, improves on that design, and then builds and tests the improved prototype

de-storming a reversal of the storming phase, in which the team's comfort level decreases, team cohesion weakens, and angry emotions and conflict may flare

destructive feedback feedback that disapproves without any intention of being helpful and almost always causes a negative or defensive reaction in the recipient

devil's advocacy a decision-making method in which an individual or a subgroup is assigned the role of a critic

dialectical inquiry a decision-making method in which decision makers state the assumptions of a proposed solution (a thesis) and generate a solution that is the opposite (antithesis) of that solution

differentiation the positioning strategy of providing a product or service that is sufficiently different from competitors' offerings that customers are willing to pay a premium price for it

direct competition the rivalry between two companies that offer similar products and services, acknowledge each other as rivals, and act and react to each other's strategic actions

direct foreign investment a method of investment in which a company builds a new business or buys an existing business in a foreign country

directive leadership a leadership style in which the leader lets employees know precisely what is expected of them, gives them specific guidelines for performing tasks, schedules work, sets standards of performance, and makes sure that people follow standard rules and regulations

disability a mental or physical impairment that substantially limits one or more major life activities

disability discrimination treating people differently because of their disabilities

discontinuous change the phase of a technology cycle characterized by technological substitution and design competition

discretionary responsibilities the expectation that a company will voluntarily serve a social role beyond its economic, legal, and ethical responsibilities

discussion time a cultural norm for how much time should be spent in discussion with others

disparate treatment intentional discrimination that occurs when people are purposely not given the same hiring, promotion, or membership opportunities because of their race, color, sex, age, ethnic group, national origin, or religious beliefs

disposition the tendency to respond to situations and events in a predetermined manner

disseminator role the informational role managers play when they share information with others in their departments or companies

distal goals long-term or primary goals

distinctive competence what a company can make, do, or perform better than its competitors

distributive justice the perceived degree to which outcomes and rewards are fairly distributed or allocated

disturbance handler role the decisional role managers play when they respond to severe problems that demand immediate action

diversification a strategy for reducing risk by buying a variety of items (stocks or, in the case of a corporation, types of businesses) so that the failure of one stock or one business does not hurt the performance of the entire portfolio

diversity a variety of demographic, cultural, and personal differences among an organization's employees and customers

diversity audits formal assessments that measure employee and management attitudes, investigate the extent to which people are advantaged or disadvantaged with respect to hiring and promotions, and review companies' diversity-related policies and procedures

diversity pairing a mentoring program in which people of different cultural backgrounds, sexes, or races/ethnicities are paired together to get to know each other and change stereotypical beliefs and attitudes

dog a company with a small share of a slow-growing market

dominant design a new technological design or process that becomes the accepted market standard

domination an approach to dealing with conflict in which one party satisfies its desires and objectives at the expense of the other party's desires and objectives

downsizing the planned elimination of jobs in a company

downward communication communication that flows from higher to lower levels in an organization

dynamic environment an environment in which the rate of change is fast

dysfunctional turnover loss of high-performing employees who voluntarily choose to leave a company

E

early retirement incentive programs (ERIPs) programs that offer financial benefits to employees to encourage them to retire early

economic order quantity (EOQ) a system of formulas that minimizes ordering and holding costs and helps determine how much and how often inventory should be ordered

economic responsibility the expectation that a company will make a profit by producing a valued product or service

economic value added (EVA) the amount by which company profits (revenues, minus expenses, minus taxes) exceed the cost of capital in a given year

efficiency getting work done with a minimum of effort, expense, or waste

effectiveness accomplishing tasks that help fulfill organizational objectives

electronic brainstorming a decision-making method in which group members use computers to build on each others' ideas and generate many alternative solutions

electronic data interchange (EDI) when two companies convert their purchase and ordering information to a standardized format to enable the direct electronic transmission of that information from one company's computer system to the other company's computer system

electronic scanner an electronic device that converts printed text and pictures into digital images

emotional stability the degree to which someone is not angry, depressed, anxious, emotional, insecure, and excitable

empathetic listening understanding the speaker's perspective and personal frame of reference and giving feedback that conveys that understanding to the speaker

employee involvement team team that provides advice or makes suggestions to management concerning specific issues

employee separation the voluntary or involuntary loss of an employee

employee shrinkage employee theft of company merchandise

employee stock ownership plan (ESOP) a compensation system that awards employees shares of company stock in addition to their regular compensation

employee turnover loss of employees who voluntarily choose to leave the company

employment benefits a method of rewarding employees that includes virtually any kind of compensation other than wages or salaries

employment references sources such as previous employers or coworkers who can provide job-related information about job candidates

empowering workers permanently passing decision-making authority and responsibility from managers to workers by giving them the information and resources they need to make and carry out good decisions

empowerment feelings of intrinsic motivation, in which workers perceive their work to have impact and meaning and perceive themselves to be competent and capable of self-determination

encoding putting a message into a written, verbal, or symbolic form that can be recognized and understood by the receiver

entrepreneur role the decisional role managers play when they adapt themselves, their subordinates, and their units to change

entrepreneurial orientation the set of processes, practices, and decision-making activities that lead to new entry, characterized by five dimensions: risk taking, autonomy, innovativeness, proactiveness, and competitive aggressiveness

entrepreneurship the process of entering new or established markets with new goods or services

entropy the inevitable and steady deterioration of a system

environmental change the change in a company's general and specific environments

environmental complexity the number and the intensity of external factors in the environment that affect organizations

environmental scanning searching the environment for important events or issues that might affect an organization

equity theory a theory that states that people will be motivated when they perceive that they are being treated fairly

ethical behavior behavior that conforms to a society's accepted principles of right and wrong

ethical charismatics charismatic leaders who provide developmental opportunities for followers, are open to positive and negative feedback, recognize others' contributions, share information, and have moral standards that emphasize the larger interests of the group, organization, or society

ethical intensity the degree of concern people have about an ethical issue

ethical responsibility the expectation that a company will not violate accepted principles of right and wrong when conducting its business

ethics the set of moral principles or values that defines right and wrong for a person or group

evaluation apprehension fear of what others will think of your ideas

executive information system (EIS) a data processing system that uses internal and external data sources to provide the information needed to monitor and analyze organizational performance

expatriate someone who lives and works outside his or her native country

expectancy the perceived relationship between effort and performance

expectancy theory the theory that people will be motivated to the extent to which they believe that their efforts will lead to good performance, that good performance will be rewarded, and that they will be offered attractive rewards

experiential approach to innovation an approach to innovation that assumes a highly uncertain environment and uses intuition, flexible options, and hands-on experience to reduce uncertainty and accelerate learning and understanding

expert system an information system that contains the specialized knowledge and decision rules used by experts and experienced decision makers so that nonexperts can draw on this knowledge base to make decisions

exporting selling domestically produced products to customers in foreign countries

external environments all events outside a company that have the potential to influence or affect it

external locus of control the belief that what happens to you is largely the result of factors beyond your control

external recruiting the process of developing a pool of qualified job applicants from outside the company

extinction reinforcement in which a positive consequence is no longer allowed to follow a previously reinforced behavior, thus weakening the behavior

extranets networks that allow companies to exchange information and conduct transactions with outsiders by providing them direct, web-based access to authorized parts of a company's intranet or information system

extraversion the degree to which someone is active, assertive, gregarious, sociable, talkative, and energized by others

extrinsic reward a reward that is tangible, visible to others, and given to employees contingent on the performance of specific tasks or behaviors

F

feedback the amount of information the job provides to workers about their work performance

feedback control a mechanism for gathering information about performance deficiencies after they occur

feedback to sender in the communication process, a return message to the sender that indicates the receiver's understanding of the message

feedforward control a mechanism for monitoring performance inputs rather than outputs to prevent or minimize performance deficiencies before they occur

figurehead role the interpersonal role managers play when they perform ceremonial duties

financial ratios calculations typically used to track a business's liquidity (cash), efficiency, and profitability over time compared with other businesses in its industry

finished goods inventories the final outputs of manufacturing operations

firewall a protective hardware or software device that sits between the computers in an internal organizational network and outside networks, such as the Internet

firm-level strategy a corporate strategy that addresses the question "How should we compete against a particular firm?"

first-line managers managers who train and supervise the performance of non-managerial employees who are directly responsible for producing the company's products or services

first-mover advantage the strategic advantage that companies earn by being the first to use new information technology to substantially lower costs or to make a product or service different from that of competitors

fixed interval reinforcement schedule an intermittent schedule in which consequences follow a behavior only after a fixed time has elapsed

fixed ratio reinforcement schedule an intermittent schedule in which consequences are delivered following a specific number of behaviors

flow a psychological state of effortlessness, in which you become completely absorbed in what you're doing and time seems to pass quickly

focus strategy the positioning strategy of using cost leadership or differentiation to produce a specialized product or service for a limited, specially targeted group of customers in a particular geographic region or market segment

formal communication channel the system of official channels that carry organizationally approved messages and information

forming the first stage of team development, in which team members meet each other, form initial impressions, and begin to establish team norms

four-fifths (or 80 percent) rule a rule of thumb used by the courts and the EEOC to determine whether there is evidence of adverse impact. A violation of this rule occurs when the selection rate for a protected group is less than 80 percent or four-fifths of the selection rate for a nonprotected group.

franchise a collection of networked firms in which the manufacturer or marketer of a product or service, the franchisor, licenses the entire business to another person or organization, the franchisee

functional departmentalization organizing work and workers into separate units responsible for particular business functions or areas of expertise

functional turnover loss of poor-performing employees who voluntarily choose to leave a company

fundamental attribution error the tendency to ignore external causes of behavior and to attribute other people's actions to internal causes

G

gainsharing a compensation system in which companies share the financial value of performance gains, such as productivity, cost savings, or quality, with their workers

Gantt chart a graphical chart that shows which tasks must be completed at which times in order to complete a project or task

General Agreement on Tariffs and Trade (GATT) a worldwide trade agreement that reduced and eliminated tariffs, limited government subsidies, and established protections for intellectual property

General Electric workout a three-day meeting in which managers and employees from different levels and parts of an organization quickly generate and act on solutions to specific business problems

general environment the economic, technological, sociocultural, and political trends that indirectly affect all organizations

generational change change based on incremental improvements to a dominant technological design such that the improved technology is fully backward compatible with the older technology

geographic departmentalization organizing work and workers into separate units responsible for doing business in particular geographic areas

glass ceiling the invisible barrier that prevents women and minorities from advancing to the top jobs in organizations

global business the buying and selling of goods and services by people from different countries

global consistency for a multinational company, using the same rules, guidelines, policies, and procedures for offices, manufacturing plants, and distribution facilities in different countries

global new ventures new companies that are founded with an active global strategy and have sales, employees, and financing in different countries

goal a target, objective, or result that someone tries to accomplish

goal acceptance the extent to which people consciously understand and agree to goals

goal commitment the determination to achieve a goal

goal difficulty the extent to which a goal is hard or challenging to accomplish

goal-setting theory the theory that people will be motivated to the extent to which they accept specific, challenging goals and receive feedback that indicates their progress toward goal achievement

goal specificity the extent to which goals are detailed, exact, and unambiguous

government import standard a standard ostensibly established to protect the health and safety of citizens but, in reality, often used to restrict imports

grand strategy a broad corporate-level strategic plan used to achieve strategic goals and guide the strategic alternatives that managers of individual businesses or subunits may use

groupthink a barrier to good decision making caused by pressure within the group for members to agree with each other

growth strategy a strategy that focuses on increasing profits, revenues, market share, or the number of places in which the company does business

H

hearing the act or process of perceiving sounds

holding cost the cost of keeping inventory until it is used or sold, including storage, insurance, taxes, obsolescence, and opportunity costs

horizontal communication communication that flows among managers and workers who are at the same organizational level

hostile work environment a form of sexual harassment in which unwelcome and demeaning sexually related behavior creates an intimidating and offensive work environment

human resource information system (HRIS) a computerized system for gathering, analyzing, storing, and disseminating information related to the HRM process

human resource management (HRM) the process of finding, developing, and keeping the right people to form a qualified work force

human resource planning (HRP) using an organization's goals and strategy to forecast the organization's human resource needs in terms of attracting, developing, and keeping a qualified work force

human skills the ability to work well with others

I

ISO 9000 a series of five international standards, from ISO 9000 to ISO 9004, for achieving consistency in quality management and quality assurance in companies throughout the world

ISO 14000 a series of international standards for managing, monitoring, and minimizing an organization's harmful effects on the environment

imperfectly imitable resource a resource that is impossible or extremely costly or difficult for other firms to duplicate

income statements accounting statements, also called "profit and loss statements," that show what has happened to an organization's income, expenses, and net profit over a period of time

incremental change the phase of a technology cycle in which companies innovate by lowering costs and improving the functioning and performance of the dominant technological design

independent demand system an inventory system in which the level of one kind of inventory does not depend on another

individualism-collectivism the degree to which a person believes that people should be self-sufficient and that loyalty to one's self is more important than loyalty to team or company

industry regulation regulations and rules that govern the business practices and procedures of specific industries, businesses, and professions

industry-level strategy a corporate strategy that addresses the question "How should we compete in this industry?"

informal communication channel ("grapevine") the transmission of messages from employee to employee outside of formal communication channels

information useful data that can influence people's choices and behavior

initiating structure the degree to which a leader structures the roles of followers by setting goals, giving directions, setting deadlines, and assigning tasks

innovation streams patterns of innovation over time that can create sustainable competitive advantage

inputs in equity theory, the contributions employees make to the organization

instrumentality the perceived relationship between performance and rewards

integrative conflict resolution an approach to dealing with conflict in which both parties indicate their preferences and then work together to find an alternative the meets the needs of both

intermittent reinforcement schedule a schedule in which consequences are delivered after a specified or average time has elapsed or after a specified or average number of behaviors has occurred

internal environment the events and trends inside an organization that affect management, employees, and organizational culture

internal locus of control the belief that what happens to you is largely the result of your own actions

internal motivation motivation that comes from the job itself rather than from outside rewards

internal recruiting the process of developing a pool of qualified job applicants from people who already work in the company

interorganizational process a collection of activities that take place among companies to transform inputs into outputs that customers value

interpersonal skills skills, such as listening, communicating, questioning, and providing feedback, that enable people to have effective working relationships with others

interviews a selection tool in which company representatives ask job applicants job-related questions to determine whether they are qualified for the job

intranets private company networks that allow employees to easily access, share, and publish information using Internet software

intraorganizational process the collection of activities that take place within an organization to transform inputs into outputs that customers value

intrapreneurship entrepreneurship within an existing organization

intrinsic reward a natural reward associated with performing a task or activity for its own sake

inventory the amount and number of raw materials, parts, and finished products that a company has in its possession

inventory turnover the number of times per year that a company sells or "turns over" its average inventory

J

jargon vocabulary particular to a profession or group that interferes with communication in the workplace

job analysis a purposeful, systematic process for collecting information on the important work-related aspects of a job

job characteristics model (JCM) an approach to job redesign that seeks to formulate jobs in ways that motivate workers and lead to positive work outcomes

job description a written description of the basic tasks, duties, and responsibilities required of an employee holding a particular job

job design the number, kind, and variety of tasks that individual workers perform in doing their jobs

job enlargement increasing the number of different tasks that a worker performs within one particular job

job enrichment increasing the number of tasks in a particular job and giving workers the authority and control to make meaningful decisions about their work

job evaluation a process that determines the worth of each job in a company by evaluating the market value of the knowledge, skills, and requirements needed to perform it

job rotation periodically moving workers from one specialized job to another to give them more variety and the opportunity to use different skills

job shops manufacturing operations that handle custom orders or small batch jobs

job specialization a job composed of a small part of a larger task or process

job specifications a written summary of the qualifications needed to successfully perform a particular job

joint venture a strategic alliance in which two existing companies collaborate to form a third, independent company

just-in-time (JIT) inventory system an inventory system in which component parts arrive from suppliers just as they are needed at each stage of production

K

kanban a ticket-based JIT system that indicates when to reorder inventory

kinesics movements of the body and face

knowledge the understanding that one gains from information

L

leader role the interpersonal role managers play when they motivate and encourage workers to accomplish organizational objectives

leader-member relations the degree to which followers respect, trust, and like their leaders

leadership the process of influencing others to achieve group or organizational goals

leadership neutralizers subordinate, task, or organizational characteristics that can interfere with a leader's actions or make it impossible for a leader to influence followers' performance

leadership style the way a leader generally behaves toward followers

leadership substitutes subordinate, task, or organizational characteristics that make leaders redundant or unnecessary

leading inspiring and motivating workers to work hard to achieve organizational goals

learning-based planning learning better ways of achieving goals by continually testing, changing, and improving plans and strategies

legal responsibility the expectation that a company will obey society's laws and regulations

liaison role the interpersonal role managers play when they deal with people outside their units

licensing an agreement in which a domestic company, the licensor, receives royalty payments for allowing another company, the licensee, to produce the licensor's product, sell its service, or use

its brand name in a specified foreign market

line authority the right to command immediate subordinates in the chain of command

line function an activity that contributes directly to creating or selling the company's products

line-flow production manufacturing processes that are preestablished, occur in a serial or linear manner, and are dedicated to making one type of product

listening making a conscious effort to hear

local adaptation modifying rules, guidelines, policies, and procedures to adapt to differences in foreign customers, governments, and regulatory agencies

locus of control the degree to which individuals believe that their actions can influence what happens to them

M

Maastricht Treaty of Europe a regional trade agreement between most European countries

Machiavellian the extent to which individuals believe that virtually any type of behavior is acceptable in trying to satisfy their needs or meet their goals

magnitude of consequences the total harm or benefit derived from an ethical decision

make-to-order operation a manufacturing operation that does not start processing or assembling products until a customer order is received

make-to-stock operation a manufacturing operation that orders parts and assembles standardized products before receiving customer orders

management getting work done through others

management by objectives (MBO) a four-step process in which managers and employees discuss and select goals, develop tactical plans, and meet regularly to review progress toward goal accomplishment

manufacturing flexibility the degree to which manufacturing operations can easily and quickly change the number, kind, and characteristics of products they produce

market commonality the degree to which two companies have overlapping products, services, or customers in multiple markets

materials requirement planning (MRP) a production and inventory system that determines the production schedule, pro-

duction batch sizes, and inventory needed to complete final products

matrix departmentalization a hybrid organizational structure in which two or more forms of departmentalization, most often product and functional, are used together

maximizing choosing the best alternative

mechanistic organization an organization characterized by specialized jobs and responsibilities, precisely defined, unchanging roles, and a rigid chain of command based on centralized authority and vertical communication

media advocacy an advocacy group tactic that involves framing issues as public issues; exposing questionable, exploitative, or unethical practices; and forcing media coverage by buying media time or creating controversy that is likely to receive extensive news coverage

meta-analysis a study of studies, a statistical approach that provides one of the best scientific estimates of how well management theories and practices work

middle managers managers responsible for setting objectives consistent with top management's goals and for planning and implementing subunit strategies for achieving these objectives

milestones formal project review points used to assess progress and performance

mission a statement of a company's overall goal that unifies company-wide efforts toward its vision, stretches and challenges the organization, and possesses a finish line and a time frame

modular organization an organization that outsources noncore business activities to outside companies, suppliers, specialists, or consultants

monitor role the informational role managers play when they scan their environment for information

monochronic cultures cultures in which people tend to do one thing at a time and view time as linear

mood linkage a phenomenon in which one worker's negative affectivity and bad moods can spread to others

Moore's law the prediction that about every two years, computer-processing power would double and its cost would drop by 50 percent

motion study breaking each task or job into its separate motions and then eliminating those that are unnecessary or repetitive

motivation the set of forces that initiates, directs, and makes people persist in their efforts to accomplish a goal

motivation to manage an assessment of how enthusiastic employees are about managing the work of others

multifactor productivity an overall measure of performance that indicates how much labor, capital, materials, and energy it takes to produce an output

multifunctional teams work teams composed of people from different departments

multinational corporation a corporation that owns businesses in two or more countries

N

national culture the set of shared values and beliefs that affects the perceptions, decisions, and behavior of the people from a particular country

needs the physical or psychological requirements that must be met to ensure survival and well-being

needs assessment the process of identifying and prioritizing the learning needs of employees

negative affectivity a personality trait in which individuals tend to notice and focus on the negative aspects of themselves and their environments

negative reinforcement reinforcement that strengthens behavior by withholding an unpleasant consequence when employees perform a specific behavior

negotiator role the decisional role managers play when they negotiate schedules, projects, goals, outcomes, resources, and employee raises

neutral cultures cultures in which people do not display emotions and feelings when communicating

noise anything that interferes with the transmission of the intended message

nominal group technique a decision-making method that begins and ends by having group members quietly write down and evaluate ideas to be shared with the group

nonsubstitutable resource a resource that produces value or competitive advantage and has no equivalent substitutes or replacements

nontariff barriers nontax methods of increasing the cost or reducing the volume of imported goods

nonverbal communication any communication that doesn't involve words

normative control the regulation of workers' behavior and decisions through widely shared organizational values and beliefs

normative decision theory a theory that suggests how leaders can determine an appropriate amount of employee participation when making decisions

norming the third stage of team development, in which team members begin to settle into their roles, group cohesion grows, and positive team norms develop

norms informally agreed-on standards that regulate team behavior

North American Free Trade Agreement (NAFTA) a regional trade agreement between the United States, Canada, and Mexico

O

objective control the use of observable measures of worker behavior or outputs to assess performance and influence behavior

objective performance measures measures of job performance that are easily and directly counted or quantified

online discussion forums the in-house equivalent of Internet newsgroups. By using web- or software-based discussion tools that are available across the company, employees can easily ask questions and share knowledge with each other.

open office systems offices in which the physical barriers that separate workers have been removed in order to increase communication and interaction

open systems systems that can sustain themselves only by interacting with their environments, on which they depend for their survival

openness to experience the degree to which someone is curious, broad-minded, and open to new ideas, things, and experiences; is spontaneous; and has a high tolerance for ambiguity

operational plans day-to-day plans, developed and implemented by lower-level managers, for producing or delivering the organization's products and services over a 30-day to six-month period

operations management managing the daily production of goods and services

opportunistic behavior a transaction in which one party in the relationship benefits at the expense of the other

optical character recognition the ability of software to convert digitized documents into ASCII text (American Standard Code for Information Interchange) that can be searched, read, and edited by word processing and other kinds of software

options-based planning maintaining planning flexibility by making small, simultaneous investments in many alternative plans

ordering cost the costs associated with ordering inventory, including the cost of data entry, phone calls, obtaining bids, correcting mistakes, and determining when and how much inventory to order

organic organization an organization characterized by broadly defined jobs and responsibility, loosely defined, frequently changing roles, and decentralized authority and horizontal communication based on task knowledge

organization a system of consciously coordinated activities or forces created by two or more people

organizational change a difference in the form, quality, or condition of an organization over time

organizational culture the values, beliefs, and attitudes shared by organizational members

organizational decline a large decrease in organizational performance that occurs when companies don't anticipate, recognize, neutralize, or adapt to the internal or external pressures that threaten their survival

organizational development a philosophy and collection of planned change interventions designed to improve an organization's long-term health and performance

organizational heroes people celebrated for their qualities and achievements within an organization

organizational innovation the successful implementation of creative ideas in organizations

organizational plurality a work environment where (1) all members are empowered to contribute in a way that maximizes the benefits to the organization, customers, and themselves, and (2) the individuality of each member is respected by not segmenting or polarizing people on the basis of their membership in a particular group

organizational process the collection of activities that transform inputs into outputs that customers value

organizational silence when employees withhold information about organizational problems or issues

organizational stories stories told by organizational members to make sense of organizational events and changes and to emphasize culturally consistent assumptions, decisions, and actions

organizational structure the vertical and horizontal configuration of departments, authority, and jobs within a company

organizing deciding where decisions will be made, who will do what jobs and tasks, and who will work for whom

outcome/input (O/I) ratio in equity theory, an employee's perception of how the rewards received from an organization compare with the employee's contributions to that organization

outcomes in equity theory, the rewards employees receive for their contributions to the organization

outplacement services employment-counseling services offered to employees who are losing their jobs because of downsizing

output control the regulation of workers' results or outputs through rewards and incentives

overreward a form of inequity in which you are getting more outcomes relative to inputs than your referent

overt integrity test a written test that estimates job applicants' honesty by directly asking them what they think or feel about theft or about punishment of unethical behaviors

P

paralanguage the pitch, rate, tone, volume, and speaking pattern (i.e., use of silences, pauses, or hesitations) of one's voice

partial productivity a measure of performance that indicates how much of a particular kind of input it takes to produce an output

participative leadership a leadership style in which the leader consults employees for their suggestions and input before making decisions

path-goal theory a leadership theory that states that leaders can increase subordinate satisfaction and performance by clarifying and clearing the paths to goals and by increasing the number and kinds of rewards available for goal attainment

perception the process by which individuals attend to, organize, interpret, and retain information from their environments

perceptual filters the personality-, psychology-, or experience-based differences that influence people to ignore or pay attention to particular stimuli

performance appraisal the process of assessing how well employees are doing their jobs

performance feedback information about the quality or quantity of past performance that indicates whether progress is being made toward the accomplishment of a goal

performing the fourth and final stage of team development, in which performance improves because the team has matured into an effective, fully functioning team

personal aggression hostile or aggressive behavior toward others

personality the relatively stable set of behaviors, attitudes, and emotions displayed over time that makes people different from each other

personality-based integrity test a written test that indirectly estimates job applicants' honesty by measuring psychological traits, such as dependability and conscientiousness

personality tests tests that measure the extent to which applicants possess different kinds of job-related personality dimensions

phased retirement employees transition to retirement by working reduced hours over a period of time before completing retiring

piecework a compensation system in which employees are paid a set rate for each item they produce

planning (management functions) determining organizational goals and a means for achieving them

planning choosing a goal and developing a strategy to achieve that goal

policy a standing plan that indicates the general course of action that should be taken in response to a particular event or situation

policy uncertainty the risk associated with changes in laws and government policies that directly affect the way foreign companies conduct business

political deviance using one's influence to harm others in the company

political uncertainty the risk of major changes in political regimes that can result from war, revolution, death of political leaders, social unrest, or other influential events

polychronic cultures cultures in which people tend to do more than one thing at a time and view times as circular

pooled interdependence work completed by having each job or department independently contribute to the whole

portfolio strategy a corporate-level strategy that minimizes risk by diversifying investment among various businesses or product lines

position power the degree to which leaders are able to hire, fire, reward, and punish workers

positive affectivity a personality trait in which individuals tend to notice and focus on the positive aspects of themselves and their environments

positive reinforcement reinforcement that strengthens behavior by following behaviors with desirable consequences

postconventional level of moral development the third level of moral development in which people make decisions based on internalized principles

preconventional level of moral development the first level of moral development in which people make decisions based on selfish reasons

predictive patterns patterns that help identify database elements that are different

primary stakeholder any group on which an organization relies for its long-term survival

principle of distributive justice an ethical principle that holds that you should never take any action that harms the least among us: the poor, the uneducated, the unemployed

principle of government requirements an ethical principle that holds that you should never take any action that violates the law, for the law represents the minimal moral standard

principle of individual rights an ethical principle that holds that you should never take any action that infringes on others' agreed-upon rights

principle of long-term self-interest an ethical principle that holds that you should never take any action that is not in your or your organization's long-term self-interest

principle of personal virtue an ethical principle that holds that you should never do anything that is not honest, open, and truthful and that you would not be glad to see reported in the newspapers or on TV

principle of religious injunctions an ethical principle that holds that you should never take any action that is not kind and that does not build a sense of community

principle of utilitarian benefits an ethical principle that holds that you should never take any action that does not result in greater good for society

private spaces spaces used by and open to just one employee

proactive strategy a social responsiveness strategy in which a company anticipates responsibility for a problem before it occurs and does more than society expects to address the problem

probability of effect the chance that something will happen and then harm others

problem a gap between a desired state and an existing state

procedural justice the perceived fairness of the process used to make reward allocation decisions

procedure a standing plan that indicates the specific steps that should be taken in response to a particular event

processing cost the cost of turning raw data into usable information

processing information transforming raw data into meaningful information

product boycott an advocacy group tactic that involves protesting a company's actions by persuading consumers not to purchase its product or service

product departmentalization organizing work and workers into separate units responsible for producing particular products or services

product prototype a full-scale working model that is being tested for design, function, and reliability

production blocking a disadvantage of face-to-face brainstorming in which a group member must wait to share an idea because another member is presenting an idea

production deviance unethical behavior that hurts the quality and quantity of work produced

productivity a measure of performance that indicates how many inputs it takes to produce or create an output

profit sharing a compensation system in which a company pays a percentage of its profits to employees in addition to their regular compensation

project team a team created to complete specific, one-time projects or tasks within a limited time

project manufacturing manufacturing operations designed to produce large, expensive, specialized products

property deviance unethical behavior aimed at the organization's property or products

prospectors companies using an adaptive strategy that seeks fast growth by searching for new market opportunities, encouraging risk taking, and being the first to bring innovative new products to market

protecting information the process of ensuring that data are reliably and consistently retrievable in a usable format for authorized users, but no one else

protectionism a government's use of trade barriers to shield domestic companies and their workers from foreign competition

proximal goals short-term goals or subgoals

proximity of effect the social, psychological, cultural, or physical distance between a decision maker and those affected by his or her decisions

public communications an advocacy group tactic that relies on voluntary participation by the news media and the advertising industry to get the advocacy group's message out

punctuated equilibrium theory the theory that companies go through long periods of stability (equilibrium), followed by short periods of dynamic, fundamental change (revolution), and finishing with a return to stability (new equilibrium)

punishment reinforcement that weakens behavior by following behaviors with undesirable consequences

purchasing power the relative cost of a standard set of goods and services in different countries

quality a product or service free of deficiencies, or the characteristics of a product or service that satisfy customer needs

question mark a company with a small share of a fast-growing market

quid pro quo sexual harassment a form of sexual harassment in which employment outcomes, such as hiring, promotion, or simply keeping one's job, depend on whether an individual submits to sexual harassment

quota a limit on the number or volume of imported products

racial and ethnic discrimination treating people differently because of their race or ethnicity

radio frequency identification (RFID) tags tags containing minuscule microchips that transmit information via radio waves and can be used to track the number and location of the objects into which the tags have been inserted

rare resource a resource that is not controlled or possessed by many competing firms

rate buster a group member whose work pace is significantly faster than the normal pace in his or her group

rater training training performance appraisal raters in how to avoid rating errors and increase rating accuracy

rational decision making a systematic process of defining problems, evaluating alternatives, and choosing optimal solutions

raw data facts and figures

raw material inventories the basic inputs in a manufacturing process

reactive strategy a social responsiveness strategy in which a company does less than society expects

reactors companies using an adaptive strategy of not following a consistent strategy, but instead reacting to changes in the external environment after they occur

reciprocal interdependence work completed by different jobs or groups working together in a back-and-forth manner

recovery the strategic actions taken after retrenchment to return to a growth strategy

recruiting the process of developing a pool of qualified job applicants

reengineering fundamental rethinking and radical redesign of business processes to achieve dramatic improvements in critical measures of performance, such as cost, quality, service, and speed

referents in equity theory, others with whom people compare themselves to determine if they have been treated fairly

refreezing supporting and reinforcing new changes so that they "stick"

regional trading zones areas in which tariff and nontariff barriers on trade between countries are reduced or eliminated

regulation costs the costs associated with implementing or maintaining control

reinforcement the process of changing behavior by changing the consequences that follow behavior

reinforcement contingencies cause-and-effect relationships between the performance of specific behaviors and specific consequences

reinforcement theory the theory that behavior is a function of its consequences, that behaviors followed by positive consequences will occur more frequently, and that behaviors followed by negative consequences, or not followed by positive consequences, will occur less frequently

related diversification creating or acquiring companies that share similar products, manufacturing, marketing, technology, or cultures

relationship behavior the establishment of mutually beneficial, long-term exchanges between buyers and suppliers

relative comparisons a process in which each decision criterion is compared directly with every other criterion

resistance forces forces that support the existing state of conditions in organizations

resistance to change opposition to change resulting from self-interest, misunderstanding and distrust, or a general intolerance for change

resource allocator role the decisional role managers play when they decide who gets what resources

resource scarcity the abundance or shortage of critical organizational resources in an organization's external environment

resource similarity the extent to which a competitor has similar amounts and kinds of resources

resources the assets, capabilities, processes, employee time, information, and knowledge that an organization uses to improve its effectiveness and efficiency, create and sustain competitive advantage, and fulfill a need or solve a problem

response a competitive countermove, prompted by a rival's attack, to defend or improve a company's market share or profit

results-driven change change created quickly by focusing on the measurement and improvement of results

retrenchment strategy a strategy that focuses on turning around very poor company performance by shrinking the size or scope of the business

retrieval cost the cost of accessing already-stored and processed information

rules and regulations standing plans that describe how a particular action should be performed, or what must happen or not happen in response to a particular event

S

S.M.A.R.T. goals goals that are specific, measurable, attainable, realistic, and timely

satisficing choosing a "good enough" alternative

schedule of reinforcement rules that specify which behaviors will be reinforced, which consequences will follow those behaviors, and the schedule by which those consequences will be delivered

schedule time a cultural norm for the time by which scheduled projects or jobs should actually be completed

scientific management thoroughly studying and testing different work methods to identify the best, most efficient way to complete a job

S-curve pattern of innovation a pattern of technological innovation characterized by slow initial progress, then rapid progress, and then slow progress again as a technology matures and reaches its limits

secondary firms the firms in a strategic group that follow strategies related to but somewhat different from those of the core firms

secondary stakeholder any group that can influence or be influenced by a company

and can affect public perceptions about its socially responsible behavior

secure sockets layer (SSL) encryption Internet browser–based encryption that provides secure off-site web access to some data and programs

selection the process of gathering information about job applicants to decide who should be offered a job

selective perception the tendency to notice and accept objects and information consistent with our values, beliefs, and expectations, while ignoring or screening out or not accepting inconsistent information

self-control (self-management) a control system in which managers and workers control their own behavior by setting their own goals, monitoring their own progress, and rewarding themselves for goal achievement

self-designing team a team that has the characteristics of self-managing teams but also controls team design, work tasks, and team membership

self-managing team a team that manages and controls all of the major tasks of producing a product or service

self-serving bias the tendency to overestimate our value by attributing successes to ourselves (internal causes) and attributing failures to others or the environment (external causes)

semi-autonomous work group a group that has the authority to make decisions and solve problems related to the major tasks of producing a product or service

sequence patterns when two or more database elements occur together in a significant pattern, but one of the elements precedes the other

sequential interdependence work completed in succession, with one group's or job's outputs becoming the inputs for the next group or job

service recovery restoring customer satisfaction to strongly dissatisfied customers

setup cost the costs of downtime and lost efficiency that occur when a machine is changed or adjusted to produce a different kind of inventory

sex discrimination treating people differently because of their sex

sexual harassment a form of discrimination in which unwelcome sexual advances, requests for sexual favors, or other verbal or physical conduct of a sexual nature occurs while performing one's job

shadow-strategy task force a committee within a company that analyzes the company's own weaknesses to determine how competitors could exploit them for competitive advantage

shared spaces spaces used by and open to all employees

shareholder model a view of social responsibility that holds that an organization's overriding goal should be profit maximization for the benefit of shareholders

simple environment an environment with few environmental factors

simple matrix a form of matrix departmentalization in which managers in different parts of the matrix negotiate conflicts and resources

single-use plans plans that cover unique, one-time-only events

situational (SWOT) analysis an assessment of the strengths and weaknesses in an organization's internal environment and the opportunities and threats in its external environment

situational favorableness the degree to which a particular situation either permits or denies a leader the chance to influence the behavior of group members

situational theory a leadership theory that states that leaders need to adjust their leadership styles to match their followers' readiness

skill-based pay compensation system that pays employees for learning additional skills or knowledge

skills-based diversity training training that teaches employees the practical skills they need for managing a diverse work force, such as flexibility and adaptability, negotiation, problem solving, and conflict resolution

skill variety the number of different activities performed in a job

slack resources a cushion of extra resources that can be used with options-based planning to adapt to unanticipated change, problems, or opportunities

social consensus agreement on whether behavior is bad or good

social integration the degree to which group members are psychologically attracted to working with each other to accomplish a common objective

social loafing behavior in which team members withhold their efforts and fail to perform their share of the work

social responsibility a business's obligation to pursue policies, make decisions, and take actions that benefit society

social responsiveness the strategy chosen by a company to respond to stakeholders' economic, legal, ethical, or discretionary expectations concerning social responsibility

soldiering when workers deliberately slow their pace or restrict their work outputs

specific ability tests (aptitude tests) tests that measure the extent to which an applicant possesses the particular kind of ability needed to do a job well

specific environment the customers, competitors, suppliers, industry regulations, and advocacy groups that are unique to an industry and directly affect how a company does business

spokesperson role the informational role managers play when they share information with people outside their departments or companies

stability strategy a strategy that focuses on improving the way in which the company sells the same products or services to the same customers

stable environment an environment in which the rate of change is slow

staff authority the right to advise, but not command, others who are not subordinates in the chain of command

staff function an activity that does not contribute directly to creating or selling the company's products, but instead supports line activities

stakeholder model a theory of corporate responsibility that holds that management's most important responsibility, long-term survival, is achieved by satisfying the interests of multiple corporate stakeholders

stakeholders persons or groups with a "stake" or legitimate interest in a company's actions

standardization solving problems by consistently applying the same rules, procedures, and processes

standards a basis of comparison for measuring the extent to which various kinds of organizational performance are satisfactory or unsatisfactory

standing plans plans used repeatedly to handle frequently recurring events

star a company with a large share of a fast-growing market

stepladder technique a decision-making method in which group members are added to a group discussion one at a time (i.e., like a stepladder). The existing group members listen to each new member's thoughts, ideas, and recommendations; then the group shares the ideas and suggestions that it had already considered, discusses the new and old ideas, and makes a decision.

stock options a compensation system that gives employees the right to purchase shares of stock at a set price, even if the value of the stock increases above that price

stockout the point when a company runs out of finished product

stockout costs the costs incurred when a company runs out of a product, including transaction costs to replace inventory and the loss of customers' goodwill

storage cost the cost of physically or electronically archiving information for later use and retrieval

storming the second stage of development, characterized by conflict and disagreement, in which team members disagree over what the team should do and how it should do it

strategic alliance an agreement in which companies combine key resources, costs, risk, technology, and people

strategic dissonance a discrepancy between a company's intended strategy and the strategic actions managers take when implementing that strategy

strategic group a group of companies within an industry that top managers choose to compare, evaluate, and benchmark strategic threats and opportunities

strategic leadership the ability to anticipate, envision, maintain flexibility, think strategically, and work with others to initiate changes that will create a positive future for an organization

strategic plans overall company plans that clarify how the company will serve customers and position itself against competitors over the next two to five years

strategic reference points the strategic targets managers use to measure whether a firm has developed the core competencies it needs to achieve a sustainable competitive advantage

stretch goals extremely ambitious goals that employees initially don't know how to accomplish

structural accommodation the ability to change organizational structures, policies, and practices in order to meet stretch goals

structured interviews interviews in which all applicants are asked the same set of standardized questions, usually including situational, behavioral, background, and job-knowledge questions

subjective performance measures measures of job performance that require someone to judge or assess a worker's performance

suboptimization performance improvement in one part of an organization but only at the expense of decreased performance in another part

subsidies government loans, grants, and tax deferments given to domestic companies to protect them from foreign competition

subsystems smaller systems that operate within the context of a larger system

supervised data mining the process when the user tells the data mining software to look and test for specific patterns and relationships in a data set

supplier dependence the degree to which a company relies on a supplier because of the importance of the supplier's product to the company and the difficulty of finding other sources of that product

suppliers companies that provide material, human, financial, and informational resources to other companies

supportive leadership a leadership style in which the leader is friendly to and approachable, shows concern for employees and their welfare, treats them as equals, and creates a friendly climate

surface-level diversity differences such as age, sex, race/ethnicity, and physical disabilities that are observable, typically unchangeable, and easy to measure

survey feedback information that is collected by surveys from organizational members and then compiled, disseminated, and used to develop action plans for improvement

sustainable competitive advantage a competitive advantage that other companies have tried unsuccessfully to duplicate and have, for the moment, stopped trying to duplicate

synergy when two or more subsystems working together can produce more than they can working apart

system a set of interrelated elements or parts that function as a whole

T

tactical plans plans created and implemented by middle managers that specify how the company will use resources, budgets, and people over the next six months to two years to accomplish specific goals within its mission

tariff a direct tax on imported goods

task identity the degree to which a job, from beginning to end, requires the completion of a whole and identifiable piece of work

task interdependence the extent to which collective action is required to complete an entire piece of work

task significance the degree to which a job is perceived to have a substantial impact on others inside or outside the organization

task structure the degree to which the requirements of a subordinate's tasks are clearly specified

team diversity the variances or differences in ability, experience, personality, or any other factor on a team

team leaders managers responsible for facilitating team activities toward goal accomplishment

team level the average level of ability, experience, personality, or any other factor on a team

teamwork collaboration between managers and nonmanagers, across business functions, and between companies, customers, and suppliers

technical skills the ability to apply the specialized procedures, techniques, and knowledge required to get the job done

technological discontinuity the phase of an innovation stream in which a scientific advance or unique combination of existing technologies creates a significant breakthrough in performance or function

technological lockout the inability of a company to competitively sell its products because it relied on old technology or a nondominant design

technological substitution the purchase of new technologies to replace older ones

technology the knowledge, tools, and techniques used to transform input into output

technology cycle a cycle that begins with the "birth" of a new technology and ends when that technology reaches its limits and is replaced by a newer, substantially better technology

televised/videotaped speeches and meetings speeches and meetings originally made to a smaller audience that are either simultaneously broadcast to other locations in the company or videotaped for subsequent distribution and viewing

temporal immediacy the time between an act and the consequences the act produces

testing the systematic comparison of different product designs or design iterations

threat of new entrants a measure of the degree to which barriers to entry make it easy or difficult for new companies to get started in an industry

threat of substitute products or services a measure of the ease with which customers can find substitutes for an industry's products or services

360-degree feedback a performance appraisal process in which feedback is obtained from the boss, subordinates, peers and coworkers, and the employees themselves

time study timing how long it takes good workers to complete each part of their jobs

top managers executives responsible for the overall direction of the organization

total quality management (TQM) an integrated, principle-based, organization-wide strategy for improving product and service quality

trade barriers government-imposed regulations that increase the cost and restrict the number of imported goods

traditional work group a group composed of two or more people who work together to achieve a shared goal

training developing the skills, experience, and knowledge employees need to perform their jobs or improve their performance

trait theory a leadership theory that holds that effective leaders possess a similar set of traits or characteristics

traits relatively stable characteristics, such as abilities, psychological motives, or consistent patterns of behavior

transactional leadership leadership based on an exchange process, in which followers are rewarded for good performance and punished for poor performance

transformational leadership leadership that generates awareness and acceptance of a group's purpose and mission and gets employees to see beyond their own needs and self-interests for the good of the group

transient firms the firms in a strategic group whose strategies are changing from one strategic position to another

transition management team (TMT) a team of 8 to 12 people whose full-time job is to manage and coordinate a company's change process

two-factor authentication authentication based on what users know, such as a password and what they have in their possession, such as a secure ID card or key

Type A personality a person who tries to complete as many tasks as possible in the shortest possible time and is hard driving, competitive, impatient, perfectionistic, angry, and unable to relax

Type A/B personality dimension the extent to which people tend toward impatience, hurriedness, competitiveness, and hostility

Type B personality a person who is relaxed, easygoing, and able to engage in leisure activities without worrying about work

U

uncertainty extent to which managers can understand or predict which environmental changes and trends will affect their businesses

underreward a form of inequity in which you are getting fewer outcomes relative to inputs than your referent

unethical charismatics charismatic leaders who control and manipulate followers, do what is best for themselves instead of their organizations, want to hear only positive feedback, share only information that is beneficial to themselves, and have moral standards that put their interests before everyone else's

unfreezing getting the people affected by change to believe that change is needed

unity of command a management principle that workers should report to just one boss

unrelated diversification creating or acquiring companies in completely unrelated businesses

unstructured interviews interviews in which interviewers are free to ask the applicants anything they want

unsupervised data mining the process when the user simply tells the data mining software to uncover whatever patterns and relationships it can find in a data set

upward communication communication that flows from lower to higher levels in an organization

valence the attractiveness or desirability of a reward or outcome

validation the process of determining how well a selection test or procedure predicts future job performance. The better or more accurate the prediction of future job performance, the more valid a test is said to be.

valuable resource a resource that allows companies to improve efficiency and effectiveness

value customer perception that the product quality is excellent for the price offered

variable interval reinforcement schedule an intermittent schedule in which the time between a behavior and the following consequences varies around a specified average

variable ratio reinforcement schedule an intermittent schedule in which consequences are delivered following a different number of behaviors, sometimes more and sometimes less, that vary around a specified average number of behaviors

variation a deviation in the form, condition, or appearance of a product from the quality standard for that product

virtual organization an organization that is part of a network in which many companies share skills, costs, capabilities, markets, and customers to collectively solve customer problems or provide specific products or services

virtual private network (VPN) software that securely encrypts data sent by employees outside the company network, decrypts the data when they arrive within the company computer network, and does the same when data are sent back to employees outside the network

virtual team a team composed of geographically and/or organizationally dispersed coworkers who use telecommunication and information technologies to accomplish an organizational task

virus a program or piece of code that, without your knowledge, attaches itself to other programs on your computer and can trigger anything from a harmless flashing message to the reformatting of your hard drive to a systemwide network shutdown

visible artifacts visible signs of an organization's culture, such as the office design and layout, company dress code, and company benefits and perks, like stock options, personal parking spaces, or the private company dining room

vision an inspirational statement of an organization's enduring purpose

visionary leadership leadership that creates a positive image of the future that motivates organizational members and provides direction for future planning and goal setting

voluntary export restraints voluntarily imposed limits on the number or volume of products exported to a particular country

W

web services using standardized protocols to describe data from one company in such a way that those data can automatically be read, understood, transcribed, and processed by different computer systems in another company

whistleblowing reporting others' ethics violations to management or legal authorities

wholly owned affiliates foreign offices, facilities, and manufacturing plants that are 100 percent owned by the parent company

work force forecasting the process of predicting the number and kind of workers with specific skills and abilities that an organization will need in the future

work sample tests tests that require applicants to perform tasks that are actually done on the job

work team a small number of people with complementary skills who hold themselves mutually accountable for pursuing a common purpose, achieving performance goals, and improving interdependent work processes

worker readiness the ability and willingness to take responsibility for directing one's behavior at work

workplace deviance unethical behavior that violates organizational norms about right and wrong

work-in-process inventories partially finished goods consisting of assembled component parts

World Trade Organization (WTO) as the successor to GATT, the only international organization dealing with the global rules of trade between nations. Its main function is to ensure that trade flows as smoothly, predictably, and freely as possible.

wrongful discharge a legal doctrine that requires employers to have a job-related reason to terminate employees

NAME INDEX

A

AARP (American Association of Retired Persons), 442
ABC, 89
Abledata, 448
Academy of Management Journal, 10, 43
Academy of Management Perspectives, 43
Academy of Management Review, 10, 43
The Accident Group, 484–485
Accounting for Dummies (Tracy), 609
Accounting the Easy Way (Eisen), 609
Ace Hardware, 202–203, 212
Acura, 528
Acxiom, 636
Adams, Ed, 456
Addessi, Joan, 123, 124, 126–127
Addessi, Richard, 123
Addington, Gordon, 137
Adidas-Salomon, 281
Adler, Nancy J., 576
Administrative Science Quarterly, 10, 43
Aer Lingus, 662
AES, 324
Aetna, 456
Agilent, 495, 561
Agile Web, 338–339
Agnello, William, 335
Airbus, 170–171
Airline industry, 80
Alamo Rent-a-Car, 652
Albano, Monica, 397
Alcan, 309
Alcatel, 211
Aldi, 616
Alexander, Allison, 528
Alexander, Shane, 528
Alexander, Tom, 528
Alitalia, 662
Alteon WebSystems, 178
Amazon.com, 338
AMD, 288
American Airlines, 80
American College Testing, 409

American Council of the Blind, 448
American Express, 653
American Heart Association, 220
American International Group, 12
American National Standards Institute, 670
American Society for Quality, 667, 670
American Society for Training and Development, 412
American Society of Mechanical Engineers, 47
Ameritech Corporation, 424
AMP, 296
Anda, Luis de, 278
Anderson, Dave, 497
Angelini, Greg, 496
Angle, Colin, 595
Anheuser-Busch, 272
Anton, Jon, 663
Antonio's, 634
Apollo 13, 381
Apple Computer, 81, 96, 194–195, 196, 238, 366, 598, 684
Appling, Troy, 645
Aramark, 543
Argenti, Paul, 552
Arizona Public Service Company, 552
Armor Holdings, 615
Armstrong, Neil, 166
Arroyo, Raymond, 457
The Art of War (Sun Tzu), 39
Asian Wall Street Journal, 615
Associated Business Systems, 166
Associated Press, 19
Aston-Martin, 155
Asutek Computers, 337
Atkins diet, 79
Atlantic Records, 651
AT&T, 8, 24, 60
Audi, 528, 595
Automotive Resources Asia, 284–285
Avero LLC, 15, 634
Avery Dennison Corporation, 243
Avis, 222

Avon, 393
A&W Restaurants, 283
Axcellis Technologies, 295–296
Axis Performance Advisors, 358
Axtell, Roger E., 575

B

Babbage, Charles, 240
Bailey, Sheldon, 281
Baird, John, 240
Baker, Charlie, 143
Baker, Stephen, 684
Baker & McKenzie, 392
Bakke, Dennis, 324
Ball, Sharon, 405
Ballmer, Steve, 19, 310, 314
Banana Republic, 600
Banga, M. S., 217
The Bankers Bank, 645
Bank of America (BoA), 257–258
Baptist, Douglas, 237
Baratta, Sandy, 133
Bare, Mike, 596
Baretta, 63
Barger, Dave, 499
Barlow, Jeanette, 650
Barnard, Chester, 60–62
Barneys New York, 248–249
Barnholt, Ned, 495, 561
Barrett, Colleen, 512
Baseler, Randy, 170
Baxter International, 494, 581
Bayer, 312
BBDO, 182
Becoming a Manager: Mastery of a New Identity (Hill), 25, 34
Behlen Manufacturing, 385–386, 387
Bell, Alexander Graham, 240
Bell Atlantic, 435
Bello, Leslie, 223
Ben & Jerry's, 144
Bennis, Warren, 513–514, 515
Beretta, 63
Beretta, Barolomeo, 63
Berg, Paula, 512
Berkowitz, Amy, 354

Berman, Sara, 242
Bernard Suzanne, 295
Bernauer, Dave, 212
Best Buy, 242, 256
Bethune, Gordon, 526
Betts, Graem, 14
Bienaime, Jean-Jacques, 100
The Blog BuzzMachine (Jarvis), 564
Bloomberg, 645
Blunders in International Business (Ricks), 295
BMW, 179, 528, 595
Bock, Sam, 474
Boeing, 12, 20, 131, 170–171, 244, 348, 438, 477, 539, 542, 646
Bombardier Aerospace, 246, 295
Borat, 274
Borden, George, 575
Borg, Anita, 444
Borick, Steve, 91
Bosch, 238
Boston Celtics, 641, 642
Boston Consulting Group (BCG), 208–210
Boston Safe Deposit and Trust Company, 209
Bounty, 118, 216
The Bourne Identity, 191
Bowa Builders, 99, 100
Bowfinger, 431
Boyd, Jeff, 251
Boyl, Sharon, 666
Boy Scouts, 135
Brainard, Pat, 387
Brazil, 111, 627
BreakingPoint Systems, 95
Brennan, Jack, 615
Bridgestone Tire, 615
Brindley, Brigid, 477
Bristol-Myers Squibb, 103
British Airways, 164, 662
British Petroleum, 391
British Royal Navy, 633
British Telecom, 412
Britvic Corona, 282
Bronco Communications, 663
Bronfman, Edgar, Jr., 198–199
Brookson, Stephen, 169
Brown, Kathleen, 223
Brune, Michael, 94

Ethics Resource Center, 176, 603

European Cities Monitor, 173–174

European Union (EU), 272, 619

Evans, Ali, 216

E.W. Scripps, 163

Executiveplanet.com, 575

ExxonMobil Corporation, 9, 613

F

F. H. Faulding & Company, 100–101

Fandray, Dayton, 133

Fannie Mae, 12

Fanning, Shawn, 197

Farnsworth, Philo T., 240

Fassler, Matthew J., 514

FastCar, 246

Fast Company, 534, 540

Fastow, Andrew, 540

Fayol, Henri, 8, 12, 50, 52–55

Federal Aviation Administration (FAA), 608

Federal Communications Commission (FCC), 20

Federal Reserve System, 92

FedEx, 218, 582

Ferry, Jerry, 164

Fiat, 218

Fill, Cliff, 596

Finkel, James, 491

Fiorina, Carly, 512

First Command Financial Planning, 86

Fish, John, 163

Fisher, Donald, 593

Fisher, Doris, 593

Fisher, Phillip, 335

Fisher, Roger, 56

FleetBoston Financial, 257–258

Florida Power & Light, 244

Florist Network, 494

FNS NewsClips Online, 19

Follet, Mary Parker, 55–57, 60, 62

Forbes, 321

Ford, Henry, 155

Ford, Lynda, 606

Ford, William C., Jr., 134

Ford Motor Company, 20, 42, 91, 94, 134, 155, 156, 244–245, 255, 285, 296, 348, 350, 423, 583, 599, 642, 651, 667, 683, 688

Forecasting Budgets (Moore & Gardner), 609

For Love of the Game, 509

Forrester Research, 669

Forte, Mary, 139

Fortune, 13, 18, 29, 30, 84, 176, 290, 332, 358, 388, 398, 435, 438, 443, 444, 445, 471, 517, 518, 527, 542, 570, 571, 615, 630, 637, 669

Fowler, Geoffrey, 292

Fox channel, 89

Fox News, 289

Franklin, Hilary, 401

FreemantleMedia, 281

Free World Dialup, 90

French or Foe (Platt), 578

Freudenberg-NOK, 673

Friedman, Milton, 135–136

Friedman, Thomas, 271

Friedson, Art, 500

Frito-Lay, 439

Fritzsche, Peggy, 242

Fry, Jason, 568

Fuji, 138

Fujisawa Pharmaceuticals, 396

Fuji-Xerox, 283, 284

The Functions of the Executive (Barnard), 60

Funo, Yuki, 156

G

Gallo, Jennifer, 292

Gallup Organization, 452

Gantt, Henry, 48–49, 50

Gap, 593, 600

Gardner, Grover, 609

Gardner, Howard, 514

Gasaway, Roger, 352

Gates, Bill, 95, 98, 99, 310, 314

Gateway, 175

Gazprom, 290

GE Aircraft Engines, 534

Gee, Tom, 244

Genecor, 100

Genentech, 100, 565

General and Industrial Management (Fayol), 50

General Dynamics, 682

General Electric, 128, 138, 256, 257, 284, 348, 352, 371–372, 538, 565, 613, 614

General Mills, 651–652

General Motors, 7, 13, 20, 89, 91, 94–95, 248, 284, 322, 373, 555, 651, 664–665, 666–667, 680, 683

Genesco, 613

Gerdau SA, 271

Germano, Peter, 278

Germany Business Traveler, 615

Germany Seeks the Superstar, 281, 282

Giannantonio, Frank, 649

Giesecke & Devrient (G&D), 284

Gilbreth, Frank, 46–48, 49–50

Gilbreth Lillian, 46–48, 49–50

Gillette, 118, 211

Giuliano, Louis, 566

Gladwell, Malcolm, 517

GlaxoSmithKline Consumer Healthcare, 217, 320, 336

Goizueta, Roberto, 610

Goldberg, Ray, 603

Goldman Sachs, 370, 514

GolinHarris Change, 134

Good Housekeeping Seal of Approval, 670

Goodyear Tire Company, 87

Google, 9, 19, 29, 178, 356, 564, 583, 596, 636, 637

Goulding, Doug, 617

Graczyk, Bob, 396

Granakis, Huck, 350

Green, Darryl, 285

Greenberg, Glenn, 96

Greenfield, Jerry, 144

Greenstein, Martin, 392

Griffith, Scott, 222

GTE, 435

Gutenberg, Johannes, 65

H

Habitat International, 446

Haedicke, Ted, 633

Haines, Ray, 457

Hall, Edward, 577

Hall, Mildred, 577

Hamilton Sundstrand, 313

Hammer, Michael, 251, 330

Hampton Inn, 677–678

Hampton University, 461

Handy Andy, 203

Hapburg, Richard, 492

Haque, Promod, 285

Harbin Brewery Group, 272

Hardee's, 89

Harding, Ralph, 100

Harris, Ben, 613

Harry Potter series, 247, 350

Hartman, Stephen W., 609

Hartsfield-Jackson Atlanta International Airport, 32, 33

Hartz Moutanin Corp., 85

Harvard Business Review, 43

Harvard Business School, 25, 43, 252

Hatch, Jeff, 324

Hauser, Meghan De Goyler, 563

Haze, Paul, 562

Health Decisions, 635

HealthSouth, 114, 539

Heckert, Dick, 14

Heffernan, Margaret, 572

Heil Trailer International, 682

Henderson, Bruce, 209

Herman Miller, 335–336, 613

Hernandez, Joe, 419

Hershey, 282

Hertz, 222

Hewitt Associates, 349, 387, 434, 477

Hewlett-Packard, 16, 139, 175, 211, 408, 619, 636

Hilgert, Ray, 565

Hill, Linda, 25, 34

Hillman, Mick, 650

Hillman Group, 650, 651

Hindustan Lever, 217

Hinkle, Joe, 93

Hire.com, 397

Hitchcock, Steven, 358

Hoechst Celanese, 439, 440, 461

Hofstede, Geert, 292, 293

Hogan, Robert, 128

Holiday Inn, 99

Hollenbeck, John, 372

Holliday, Charles, Jr., 14

Holmes, Tim, 583

HomeBanc Mortgage Corp., 114, 133

Home Depot, 94, 128, 144, 202, 203, 204–205, 212, 446, 514, 601, 650

Honda Motors of America, 143–144, 285, 665

Honerkamp, Jim, 650, 651

Honeywell, 671

Hooters, 388–389, 390

Hoover, 89

Horgan, Sam, 442

Hosmer, Larue, 126

Hot Dogs & More, 595

HotJobs.com, 397

Howe, Carl, 669

How to Read a Financial Report (Tracy), 609

H&R Block, 388

HR Magazine, 572

Hukku, Rajesh, 18

The Human Equation (Pfeffer), 27

The Human Problems of an Industrial Civilization (Mayo), 57

The Hunger Site, 141

Hunt, Dan, 580

Hutchins, David, 605

Hymowitz, Carol, 557

Hyperspace Communications, 516

Hyundai, 256, 667

I

Iacocca, Lee, 166

Iberia, 485

IBM, 90, 98, 123, 124, 126–127, 649–650, 669

IBM Credit, 330–331

IComp Index, 233, 235

IKEA, 201

Immelt, Jeffrey, 538, 565

Impact Innovations Group, 614

Imperiale, John, 461

Implicit Association Test (IAT), 460

Incredible Universe, 248

Industrial Light & Magic (ILM), 350

Industry Week, 349

Infosys Technologies, 271

In Good Company, 75, 467

Inland Steel, 619

InnoCentive, 244

Insurance Institute for Highway Safety, 143

Intel Corporation, 233, 235–236, 239, 613

Interactive Excellence (Schlossberg), 238

International Harvester, 42

International Organization for Standardization, 670

International Steel Group, 271

Whitehead, Jay, 565
Whitman, Meg, 8
Whitney, Eli, 63–64
Whittle, Sir Frank, 240
Whitwan, David, 12
Whole Foods, 349, 350–351
William, Perez, 320
Williams, Mona, 600, 601
Williams, Tonie, 18
Wilson, Heather, 243
Winphoria Networks, 285
Winterkorn, Martin, 330, 528
The Wisdom of Teams (Katzenback), 354
Womble Carlyle Sandridge & Rice, 557
Wong, Mary, 336

WorldCom, 114
World Trade Center, 80
Worldwise, 144
Wright, Mary Ann, 245
Wuouma, Erkki, 482
Wyatt Company, 564

XEL Communications, 367, 374
Xerox, 11, 250–251, 283, 284, 362, 518, 542
XM Satellite Radio, 77
Xoceco, 215

Y

Yahoo!, 9, 19, 482, 636–637, 640
Yahoo, Inc., 565
Yahoo.com, 569
Yahoo! Music, 196, 197
Yale and Towne Manufacturing Company, 43
Yamaha, 689
Yellow Book Corporation, 210
Yellow Corporation, 579
Yeros, John, 517
Young, Mark, 385
Your Creative Power (Osborn), 182

Yuengling Brewery, 473
Yum! Brands, 283

Z

Zales, 139
Zantaz.com, 572
Zillow, 474
Zipcar, 222–223
Zollars, Bill, 579
Zune, 196

SUBJECT INDEX

A

Ability, 474
  perceived, 529
Above-market wages, 419
Absenteeism, 323, 328, 329
Absolute comparisons, 172
Access and legitimacy paradigms, 456, 457
Accommodative strategies, 142
Accountability, 320
Achievement-oriented leadership, 529, 530
Acquaintance time, 578
Acquisitions, 208
  acquisition costs, 636
  external growth through, 200
  portfolio strategy and, 208
Action plans, 161
Active listening, 570
Adaptability, 100
Adaptability screening, 296
Adaptive strategies, 216–218
Address terms, 576
Administrative management, 52–55
Adverse impact, 391
Advocacy groups, 92
Affective conflict, 179, 365
Affective cultures, 575
Affectivity, 453
Affirmative action
  defined, 436
  diversity vs., 436–437, 438
  purpose of, 437
African Americans
  discrimination lawsuits and, 391, 433, 435, 438
  in management, 445
  mentoring, 461
  purchasing power of, 439
  statistics, 434
  turnover rates for, 438
Age, and diversity, 441–443
Age discrimination, 441
Age Discrimination in Employment Act (1967), 390, 393
Aggression, personal, 118–119
Agreeableness, 403, 450
Airline industry, 79–80
Albermarle Paper Co. v. Moody, 395

American Sign Language, 473
Americans with Disabilities Act (ADA), 390, 446
Analyzers, 217
Application forms, 399–400
Appointment time, 577
Aptitude tests, 402
Asian Americans
  in management, 445
  purchasing power of, 439
  statistics, 434, 439
Asia-Pacific Economic Cooperation (APEC), 275, 277
Assemble-to-order operations, 680
Assessment centers, 403, 406
Assistive technology, 447
Association/affinity patterns, 641
Associational incentives, 61
Association of Southeast Asian Nations (ASEAN), 275, 277
Assurance, 669
Attack, 221
Attention, 553
Attribution error, fundamental, 556–557
Attribution theory, 555–557
A-type conflict, 179, 365
Authentication, 644
Authoritarian personality, 452
Authority. *See also* Organizational authority
  acceptance of managerial, 60–62
  centralization of, 321
  cooperation and, 60–62
  dangers of power, autonomy and, 61
  decentralization of, 321
  defined, 318
  delegation of, 320–321
  formal authority system, 530
  line vs. staff, 319
  in management positions, 115
Authority-compliance, 521
Authorization, 644
Autocratic decisions, 534
Automobile industry, 248, 667–668
Autonomy
  dangers of power, autonomy and, 61
  of entrepreneurial firms, 223

job, 326
  job satisfaction, 328
  work groups, 357–358
  work teams, 356–358
Average aggregate inventory, 684
Avoidance learning, 494
Avoidance strategies, 290
Awareness training, 460

B

Baby boomers, aging of, 434, 442
Background checks, 401–402
Balanced scorecard, 608
Balance sheets, 609
Baldrige National Quality Award, 671–672
  criteria for, 672
  recipients of, 671
Bar codes, 20, 639
Bargaining power, 215
Batch production, 681
BCG matrix, 208–210
Behavioral addition, 102
Behavioral formality, 333
Behavioral informality, 333
Behavioral substitution, 102
Behavior control, 602
  when to use, 607
Behavior observation scales (BOSs), 414, 415
Behaviors. *See also* Ethical behavior
  attribution theory and, 555–557
  consideration, 520–522
  counterproductive, 130
  of ethical/unethical charismatics, 541
  leadership, 520–522
  path-goal theory of leadership, 528–529
Benchmarking, 201, 595
Best guess forecasting, 386
Bias
  defensive, 555–556
  self-serving, 557
Big Five dimensions of personality, 449–451

Bilingualism, 294
Bill of materials, 689
Biographical data (biodata), 402
Biometrics, 645
Blake and Mouton leadership grid, 521
Blinded state of organizational decline, 248
Blogs, 583
Body language, 566
Bona fide occupational qualification (BFOQ), 390
Bottom managers. *See* First-line managers
Bounded rationality, 175
Boycott, product, 94
Brainstorming, 182, 183–184
Broadcast voice mail, 581
Brokers, 339
Budgeting, 168–169
Budgets, 168–169, 609
  kinds of, 612
Build-to-stock operations, 680
Bureaucracy
  characteristics of, 50–51
  defined, 50
Bureaucratic control, 601–602
  when to use, 607
Bureaucratic immunity, 370
Bureaucratic management, 50–52
Business confidence indices, 94
Buyer dependence, 91

C

Cafeteria benefit plans, 421
Career path, 396
Carrying costs, 686
Cash cows, 208–209
Cash flow analysis, 609
Casual dress policies, 334
Central American Free Trade Agreement (CAFTA; CAFTA-DR), 275, 277
Centralization, degree of, 321–322
Centralization of authority, 321
Central tendency error, 413
Chain of command, 319

D

Data. *See also* Information
  authentication, 644
  authorization, 644
  protecting, 642–647
  security threats to,
    643–644
  two-factor authentication,
    644–645
Data clusters, 642
Data encryption, 647
Data mining, 640
Data networks
  security threats to, 643
Data warehouse, 641
Decentralization, 321
Decisional role, 19–20
Decision criteria, 171–172
Decision making, 487. *See also*
    Ethical decision making;
    Group decision making;
    Normative Decision Theory;
    Rational decision making
  rational, 170
  work teams and, 373
Decision quality/acceptance, 535
Decision styles, 534
Decision support systems
    (DSSs), 387, 652
Decoding, 559
Deep-level diversity
  defined, 440–441, 448–449
  dimensions of personality and,
    449–451
  work-related personality
    dimensions and,
    451–454
Defenders, 217
Defensive bias, 555–556
Defensive strategies, 142
De-forming stage, 368
Degree of centralization,
    321–322
Delegating style, 533
Delegation of authority,
    320–321
Delphi technique, 180
Demographics, changing,
    85–86, 87
De-norming stage, 367
Departmentalization
  customer, 314–315
  defined, 312, 318
  functional, 312–313
  geographic, 315
  matrix, 315–318
  product, 313–314
Dependent demand sys-
    tems, 689
Design. *See also* Job design
  competition, 238
  computer-aided design
    (CAD), 246
  for disassembly, 618
  dominant design, 238
  iteration, 242
De-storming stage, 367–368
Destructive feedback, 572
Devil's advocacy, 179, 181
Dialectical inquiry, 179, 181
Differentiation, 216

Direct competition
  attack against, 221
  defined, 219
  strategies of, 220–221
Direct foreign investment,
    271, 272
Directive leadership, 528, 530
Direct managerial input, 386
Disability
  defined, 446
  workplace accommodations
    for worker's, 447
Disability discrimination, 446
Discontinuous change, 237
  innovation management
    during, 242–245
Discretionary responsibilities, 140
Discrimination
  age, 441
  disability, 446
  discrimination/fairness
    paradigms, 455–456
  employment, 391–392
  intentional, 391
  lawsuits, 391, 433, 435,
    437–438
  legislation, 390, 391–392,
    393, 459
  racial/ethnic, 391, 435,
    444–446
  sex, 443–444
Discussion time, 577–578
Disparate treatment, 391
Disposition, 449
Disseminator role, 19
Dissolution stage of organiza-
    tional innovation, 249
Distal goals, 161–162
Distinctive competence,
    201, 236
Distributive justice, 487
Disturbance handler role, 20
Diversification, 207
  related, 210
  unrelated, 208
Diversity. *See also* Deep-level
    diversity; Surface-level di-
    versity
  affirmative action vs.,
    436–437, 438
  age and, 441–443
  audits, 460
  defined, 435
  employment law and, 459
  as good business sense,
    437–440
  importance of, 435
  importance of differences, 459
  individual differences,
    440–441
  management of programs,
    458–460
  managing, 455, 462
  multinational corporations
    and, 292–294
  pairing, 461
  paradigms, 455–458
  principles, 458–460
  purpose of diversity programs,
    437
  realistic goals for, 460
  skills-based diversity train-
    ing, 460
  standards and, 459

  statistics, 434, 439
  team, 372
  training and practices,
    460–462
Documentary training, 295–296
Dogs, in portfolio strategies, 208
Dominance, 519
Dominant design, 238
Domination, 56, 364
Downsizing, 423–424
Downtime, 686
Downward communication,
    560, 562
Dress policies, 334
Drive, 517
Durability, 668
Dynamic environments, 79
Dysfunctional turnover, 425

E

Early retirement incentive pro-
    grams (ERIPs), 424–425
Economic order quantity
    (EOQ), 687
Economic performance, and so-
    cial responsibility, 143–145
Economic responsibilities, 139
Economic value added
    (EVA), 610
  calculating, 613
  MVA and, 613–614
Economy, and general environ-
    ment, 84
Effectiveness, 7
Efficiency, 7
  during product production/
    development, 349
Effort
  decreasing or withhold-
    ing, 485
  expectancy and, 488
  perceived relationship between
    performance and, 488
80 percent (four-fifths) rule,
    391–392
E-learning, 411
Electronic brainstorming,
    183–184
Electronic data interchange
    (EDI), 651
Electronic scanners, 640
Email
  defined, 579
  organizational process
    and, 311
  written communication and,
    569–570
Emotional stability, 403,
    449, 517
Empathetic listening, 571
Empathy, 669
Employee. *See also* Workers
  satisfaction, 676
  shrinkage, 118
  turnover, 425
Employee Assistance Program
    (EAP), 565, 566
Employee involvement teams,
    356–357

Employee Polygraph Protection
    Act, 403
Employee selection, 398–408.
    See also Recruitment
  interviews, 405–407
  references/background checks,
    401–402
  résumés/applications
    and, 399
  rule of three, 398–399
  tests for, 402–405
  topics employers should avoid
    during, 400
Employee separations
  defined, 422, 425
  downsizing, 423–424
  due to turnover, 425
  guidelines for conducting
    layoffs, 424
  termination, 422–423
  through retirement, 424–425
  voluntary/involuntary, 422
Employee stock ownership
    plans (ESOPs), 419, 420
Employment benefits, 421
Employment discrimination,
    391–392
Employment legislation,
    388–389, 393
  adverse impact and
    employment
    discrimination,
    391–392, 459
  discrimination and, 390,
    391–392, 393, 459
  fair/safe working conditions,
    281
  federal, 389–391
  résumés/applications, 399–400
  sexual harassment and,
    392–393
Employment references, 401
Empowering workers, 332, 678
Empowerment, 332
Encoding, 558
Encouragement, 241
Entrepreneurial orienta-
    tion, 223
Entrepreneur role, 19–20
Entrepreneurship, 222
Entropy, 67
Environmental change, 79
Environmental complexity,
    80–81
Environmental scanning,
    94–95, 97
  in situational analysis, 201
Environments. *See also* External
    environments; General envi-
    ronment; Specific environ-
    ment
  acting on threats/opportunities
    in, 96–97
  changing, 96–97
  factors in interpreting, 95–96
  hostile, 392
  internal, 98
  making sense of changing, 94
  simple, 80–81
  stable, 79
Equal Employment Opportunity
    Commission (EEOC), 92,
    391, 393, 436
Equal Pay Act (1963), 390

Job characteristics model
 (JCM), 324–327, 328
Job design, 327
Job enlargement, 324
Job enrichment, 324
Job evaluation, 418
Job performance. *See* Performance
Job performance appraisals. *See* Performance appraisals
Job posting, 130
Job rotation, 324
Job satisfaction, 323, 325, 328–329, 350
Job shops, 681
Job specialization, 323
Job specifications, 395
Joint ventures, 283
Just-in-time (JIT) inventory, 38, 688

K

Kanban, 688
Kinesics, 566
Knowledge
 of business, 517
 defined, 652
 external access, and sharing, 650–652
 internal access, and sharing, 648–650
 knowledge acquisition, 559–560
 of results, 325
 sharing expertise and, 652–653
Kohlberg's stages of moral development, 125–126

L

Labor productivity, 664
Language
 American Sign Language, 473
 cross-cultural training and, 295–296
 paralanguage or body, 566
Large system interventions, 259
Layoffs, 424
Leaderless group discussion, 403
Leader-member relations, 525
Leader role, 18
Leaders
 charismatic, 519, 539–541
 managers as team, 16–17
 managers vs., 513–514
 traits of, 517–519
Leadership. *See also* Fiedler's Contingency Theory; Normative Decision Theory; Path-goal theory; Strategic leadership; Visionary leadership
 achievement-oriented, 529, 530
 behaviors, 520–522
 Blake and Mouton leadership grid, 521

defined, 512–513
 directive, 528, 530
 executive turnover, 531
 Hersey and Blanchard's Situational Leadership Theory, 531–533
 mission, mentor, and mirror, 514
 neutralizers, 515–516
 participative, 529, 530
 path-goal theory of, 528–529
 situational approaches to, 522–523
 strategic, 538
 substitutes for, 515
 supportive, 528, 530
 transactional, 543
 transformational, 541
Leadership styles
 behaviors and, 521–522
 contingency theory of, 523–526
 least preferred coworker (LPC), 523–524
 matching situations to, 525–526
 path-goal theory, 528–529, 530
 situational leadership theory, 532–533
Leading, 11
Learned Needs Theory, McClelland's, 475, 476
Learning and effectiveness paradigms, 456, 457–458
Learning-based planning, 163–164
Least preferred coworker (LPC), 524
Legal responsibilities, 139–140
Leniency error, 413
Liaison role, 18
Licensing agreements, 282
Line authority, 319
Line-flow production, 681
Line function, 319
Listening, 570
 active, 570
 empathetic, 571
Litigation
 class-action, 389, 391, 433, 438, 446
 discrimination lawsuits, 391, 433, 435, 438
 negligent hiring suits, 401
 sexual harassment and, 392–393
 wrongful termination, 87, 423
Local adaptation policy, 280–281
Locus of control, 453, 529
Lost efficiency, 686
Lower-level managers. *See* First-line managers

M

Maastricht Treaty, 275, 276
Machiavellian personality, 452
Magnitude of consequence, 124

Make-to-order operation, 679
Make-to-stock operations, 680
Management, 6–7. *See also* Human relations management; Human resource management (HRM); Innovation management; Inventory management; Operations management; Paradigms for management
 administrative, 52–55
 bureaucratic, 50–52
 competitive advantage through people and, 27–29
 contingency, 67–68
 defined, 7
 of diversity programs, 458–460
 evolution of, 42
 Fayol's principles of, 52–55
 Follett's contributions of, 58
 Follett's principles of, 56–57
 functions of, 8–9, 11–12
 history of, 38–41
 human relations and, 55–62
 impression, 475
 information, 65–66
 minorities in, 445
 operations, 63–65
 origins of, 38
 scientific, 49–50
 self-management, 605
 systems, 66–67
 total quality, 673–674
 transition to, 25–27
 women in, 443–444
Management by objectives (MBO), 166–167
Managers, 12–17
 authority, autonomy, and power of, 61
 changing environments and, 94
 company's criteria for, 22–23
 decisional roles of, 19–20
 ethics and, 14
 first-level, 15, 168–169
 informational roles of, 18–19
 interpersonal roles of, 18
 leaders vs., 513–514
 meta-analysis used by, 8
 middle, 14–15, 166–167
 mistakes made by, 23–25
 need for, 41–42
 as team leaders, 16–17
 teamwork and, 674
 top, 12–14, 165–166
Manufacturing flexibility, 680
Manufacturing operations, 679–682. *See also* Inventory
 flexibility of, 680–682
 processing in, 679–680
Maritz Incentives poll, 477
Market commonality, 219
Market entries, 222
Market exits, 222
Market value added (MVA), 613–614
 EVA and, 613–614
Masculinity, 292
Maslow's Hierarchy of Needs, 475, 476
Master production schedule, 689
Material incentives, 61

Material/product substitution, 618
Materials requirement planning (MRP), 689
Matrix departmentalization, 315–318
 advantages/disadvantages of, 317–318
 distinguishing features of, 316
Maximizing decision, 175
McClelland's Learned Needs Theory, 475, 476
Mechanical Turk, 338, 344
Mechanistic organizations, 327, 329
Media advocacy, 92
Mental disabilities, and diversity, 446–448
Mentoring, 514
Mercosur trade agreement, 275
Meta-analysis, 10
Middle managers
 planning and, 166–167
 responsibilities/duties of, 14–15
Middle-of-the-road style, 522
Milestones, 244
Millennial generation, 480
Minority domination, 364
Mirror, 514
Mission, 165–166, 514
Modular organizations, 337–338
Monitor role, 19
Monochronic cultures
 defined, 576
 perception of time and, 574, 577–578
 polychronic vs., 577
Mood linkage, 454
Moore's law, 630, 631
Moral development, stages in, 125–126
Motion studies, 46–48
Motivation. *See also* Equity theory; Expectancy theory; Goal-setting theory; Needs; Reinforcement theory
 components of, 472
 defined, 472, 473
 effects of perceptions and expectations on, 481–482
 effects of rewards and goals on, 491–492
 effort and performance, 472, 473–474
 extrinsic/intrinsic rewards, 476–478
 guidelines for, 479–481, 503
 inspirational, 542
 integrated model for, 502–503
 internal, 325
 in JCM, 324–327, 328
 to manage, 23
 model, 474, 475
 need satisfaction, 474–477
 performance, and motivational effort, 449, 450, 472, 473–474
Multifactor productivity, 665
Multifunctional teams, 244
Multigenerational work force, 480

"What's New" Companies

A

Ace Hardware
Acxiom
AES
Aetna
Agile Web
Agilent
Airbus
Alamo Rent-a-Car
Alcan
Aldi
Alteon WebSystems
Amazon
American Express
Apple
Aramark
AT&T
Audi
Avero
Avery Dennison
Avon
Axcelis Technologies

B

Baker & McKenzie
Bank of America
Barneys New York
Baxter International
BBDO
Behlen Manufacturing
Ben & Jerry's
Beretta
Best Buy
Bloomberg
BMW
Boeing
Bombardier Aerospace
Boston Celtics
Boston Consulting Group
Bowa Builders
Bristol-Myers Squibb
British Petroleum
Burger King

C

Cadbury Schweppes
Cadillac
Canada Cordage
CareerBuilder.com
Caremark International
CBS
CDW
Cerner Corporation
Cessna
Chaparral Energy
Checkers Drive-In Restaurants
Chicago Harvester
Chicago Sun-Times
Chigo Air-Conditioning
Chipotle Mexican Grill
Chrysler
Chugach School District
Ciba-Geigy
CIGNA Behavioral Health
Cisco Systems
Citigroup
Coca-Cola
Coca-Cola Enterprises Three
    Counties
Comambault
Comcast
Container Store
Continental Airlines
Con-way
Corning Glass
Costco
Coventry Mall
Crate and Barrel
Crown Cork
CSX
CVS

D

DaimlerChrysler
De Beers Consolidated Mines
Dell
Deloitte Touche Tohmatsu
Denny's
Diebold
Dinner by Design
Dow Chemical
Drugstore.com

Duke Children's Hospital
Dunkin' Donuts
Dyson

E

E.W. Scripps
EA Sports
East Providence, Rhode Island
    Police Department
Eastman Chemical
Eastman Kodak
Eaton Corporation
EchoStar Communications
Edward Jones
84 Lumber
Electric Boat
Electronic Arts
Eli Lilly & Co.
EMC
Enron
Enterprise Rent-a-Car
Ernst & Young
EthicsPoint
ExxonMobil

F

FastCar
FedEx
Fiat
Ford Motor Company
FremantleMedia (American Idol)
Freudenberg-NOK
Frito-Lay
Fuji Xerox
Fujisawa Pharmaceuticals

G

Gallup Organization
GE Aircraft Engines Gap
Genencor
General Electric
General Mills
General Motors
Gillette
GlaxoSmithKline
Goodyear
Google

H

Habitat International
Hampton Inn
Health Decisions
Heil Trailer International
Hewlett-Packard
Hillman Group
Hoechst Celanese
Home Depot
Honda Motors of America
Hooters
Hoover
HotJobs.com
Hyperspace Communications
Hyundai

I

Iberia
IBM
IBM Credit
IKEA
Impact Innovations Group
Incredible Universe
Industrial Light & Magic
Infosys
InnoCentive
Intel
iRobot
ISG Steelton
ITT
iTunes

J

J. D. Power and Associates
J.M. Smucker
Jamaican Bobsled Team
JCPenney
JetBlue
JPMorgan Chase

K

Kaiser Permanente
KFC
Kikkoman
Kimberly-Clark
Kmart